Lecture Notes in Computer Science 4459

Commenced Publication in 1973
Founding and Former Series Editors:
Gerhard Goos, Juris Hartmanis, and Jan van

Christophe Cérin   Kuan-Ching Li (Eds.)

Advances in Grid and Pervasive Computing

Second International Conference, GPC 2007
Paris, France, May 2-4, 2007
Proceedings

Volume Editors

Christophe Cérin
Université de Paris Nord
LIPN, CNRS UMR 7030
99 avenue J.B. Clément, 93430 Villetaneuse, P.O. Box , France
E-mail: cerin@lipn.univ-paris13.fr

Kuan-Ching Li
Providence University
Department of Computer Science and Information and Engineering
200 Chung-Chi Road Shalu, Taichung 43301, Taiwan
E-mail: kuancli@pu.edu.tw

Library of Congress Control Number: 2007926259

CR Subject Classification (1998): F.1, F.2, D.1, D.2, D.4, C.2, C.4, H.4, K.6

LNCS Sublibrary: SL 1 – Theoretical Computer Science and General Issues

ISSN 0302-9743
ISBN-10 3-540-72359-5 Springer Berlin Heidelberg New York
ISBN-13 978-3-540-72359-2 Springer Berlin Heidelberg New York

Springer is a part of Springer Science+Business Media

springer.com

Printed in Germany

Typesetting: Camera-ready by author, data conversion by Scientific Publishing Services, Chennai, India
Printed on acid-free paper SPIN: 12060115 06/3180 5 4 3 2 1 0

Preface

GPC 2007 provided a high-profile, leading-edge forum for researchers and developers from industry and academia to report on the latest scientific and technical advances, discuss and debate the major issues, and showcase the latest systems in merging grid computing and the pervasive computing field.

This year, a total of 217 high-quality papers were submitted by researchers and practitioners from about 20 countries. All the submissions were rigorously reviewed by the Program Committee members. To ensure fairness and the quality of the papers, we put a number of measures in place. For example, each paper was assigned at least one reviewer from Australia, one reviewer from America, and one reviewer from Europe. Based on the originality, significance, correctness, relevance, and clarity of presentation, 56 submissions were selected as regular papers and 12 were selected as short papers. The acceptation rate is 32%. Also, the authors of accepted papers were required to submit a read-me file along with the camera-ready version of their paper explaining how the reviewers comments were taken into account in the final version of their paper.

The publication Co-chairs, Lucian Finta (Paris XIII, France) and Jemal H. Abawajy (Deakin University, Australia), painstakingly went through each read-me file and reviewers' comments to ensure that the comments were indeed incorporated into the final version of the papers. Only those papers that included reviewers' comments were finally accepted for inclusion in the proceedings. Undoubtedly, Lucian and Jemal had to work long hours to meet the tight deadline, which is greatly appreciated.

The overall outcome of the revision process is a selection of papers that showcase the very best of grid and pervasive computing technology today. After the conference, the proceedings editors selected and recommended some high-quality papers from the GPC 2007 conference to be published in special issues of international journals. Special thanks go to Jemal H. Abawajy for liasing with the chief editors of the journals.

The GPC 2007 program included presentations by accepted paper authors, keynote speeches, and a special round table on "Pervasive Grid." The special round table was organized by Lionel Brunie, Manish Parashar, and Jean-Marc Pierson. We thank them for this initiative.

We allocated a slot of 30 minutes for each paper presentation so that the participants had plenty of time for questions and answers. We were also delighted to be able to welcome three well-known international researchers, Thierry Priol (France) representing the European CoreGrid initiative, Minyi Guo, Professor at the School of Computer Science and Engineering, University of Aizu (Japan), and Laurence T. Yang representing St. Francis Xavier University (Canada), who delivered the keynote speeches.

We would like to take this opportunity to thank everyone involved with the organization of GPC 2007. First, we would like to thank all the authors for their submissions to the conference as well as for travelling some distance to participate in the conference. Second, we would like to thank the Program Committee members and external reviewers for their superb job in selecting a set of excellent papers that reflect the current research and development states of grid and pervasive computing.

Third, we would like to thank Franck Cappello (INRIA, France), Jean-Luc Gaudiot (University of California at Irvine), and Hai Jin (Huazhong University of Science and Technology, Wuhan) for their valuable comments during the year. Our appreciation also extends to Alfred Hofmann and Anna Kramer, both from Springer, for their helpful comments in strengthening the conferences. We will continue to improve further, in particular with the selection of the Program Committees and other scientific issues. We are also grateful to Christine Nora and Cyril Drocourt from IEEE France for the secure Web payment and for managing the finances. Jean-Christophe Dubacq (Paris XIII) was busy with the review system, the Web server, registration, and many other important issues regarding the technical program. Catherine Girard from the INRIA Office of the Colloqium did a superb job once again with the organization and the INRIA sponsorship. It is always a pleasure to work with Catherine Girard and her high level of professionalism is highly appreciated.

GPC2007 was sponsored by Hewlett Packard through the strong support of Franck Baetke, Philippe Devins, and Jean-Luc Assor, by INRIA and the University of Paris XIII through the 'Conseil Scientifique', and also through Laboratoire de Recherche en Informatique de Paris Nord (LIPN - UMR CNRS 7030).

Last but not least, we express our gratitude to François and Ludivine from Dakini Conseil for their help in organizing accommodation for conference attendees, finding a venue for the conference and also for its banquet. We would also like to thank Severine Bonnard from MGEN for allowing us to rent the beautiful MGEN building with all the services that a speaker dreams to find on a site (e.g., comfortable rooms, a restaurant for the gourmets, etc.) in the center of Paris.

Remember also that on August 8, 1900, the German mathematician David Hilbert during the International Congress of Mathematicians in Paris presented a list of 23 unsolved problems that he saw as being the greatest challenges for twentieth-century mathematics. One of them, the 10th problem, is about Diophantine equations. It has been relevant for many years and the basis of the work of many people including Church, Herbrand, Kleene, Godel, and Turing. The 10th problem is about how to find a method (what we now call an algorithm) for deciding whether a Diophantine equation has an (integral) solution. We hope readers will be inspired by these proceedings. We hope also that attendees will be inspired by the spirit of Paris and by the great history of our discipline to achieve new advance in the field of Grid and Pervasive computing.

March 2007

Christophe Cérin
Kuan-Ching Li

Organization

Steering Committee

Sajal K. Das	(The University of Texas at Arlington, USA)
Jean-Luc Gaudiot	(University of California - Irvine, USA)
Hai Jin	(Huazhong University of Science and Technology, PR China)
Chung-Ta King	(National Tsing Hua University, Taiwan)
Kuan-Ching Li	(Providence University, Taiwan)
Satoshi Sekiguchi	(AIST, Japan)
Cho-Li Wang	(The University of Hong Kong, PR China)
Chao-Tung Yang	(Tunghai University, Taiwan)
Albert Y. Zomaya	(The University of Sydney, Australia)
Michel Cosnard	(INRIA, France)

General Co-chairs

Franck Cappello	(INRIA Futurs, France)
Kai Hwang	(University of Southern California, USA)

Program Co-chairs

Christophe Cérin	(University of Paris XIII, France)
Kuan-Ching Li	(Providence University, Taiwan)

Program Committee

Ali Pinar	apinar@lbl.gov
Alvaro L.G.A. Coutinho	alvaro@nacad.ufrj.br
Andrew Wendelborn	andrew@cs.adelaide.edu.au
Celso L. Mendes	cmendes@cs.uiuc.edu
Chao-Tung Yang	ctyang@thu.edu.tw
Chien-Min Wang	cmwang@iis.sinica.edu.tw
Ching-Hsien Hsu	chh@chu.edu.tw
Cho-Li Wang	clwang@cs.hku.hk
Christina Pinotti	pinotti@unipg.it
Christophe Cérin	christophe.cerin@lipn.univ-paris13.fr
Cynthia A. Phillips	caphill@sandia.gov
Damon Shing-Min Liu	damon@computer.org
Dan Grigoras	d.grigoras@cs.ucc.ie
Dan Meng	md@ncic.ac.cn

Mohamed Ould-Khaoua	mohamed@dcs.gla.ac.uk
Nabil Abdennadher	nabil.abdennadher@hesge.ch
Nong Xiao	xiao-n@vip.sina.com
Noria Foukia	nfoukia@infoscience.otago.ac.nz
Omer F Rana	o.f.rana@cs.cardiff.ac.uk
Pangfeng Liu	pangfeng@csie.ntu.edu.tw
Pedro Medeiros	pm@di.fct.unl.pt
Philippe Navaux	navaux@inf.ufrgs.br
Ronald Perrott	r.perrott@qub.ac.uk
Rosa Badia	rosab@ac.upc.es
Ruay-Shiung Chang	rschang@mail.ndhu.edu.tw
Rudolf Eigenmann	eigenman@ecn.purdue.edu
Sanjay Ranka	ranka@cise.ufl.edu
Siang Wun Song	song@ime.usp.br
Song Wu	wusong@hust.edu.cn
Stephen Jenks	sjenks@uci.edu
Sbastien Tixeuil	tixeuil@lri.fr
Tien-Hsiung Weng	thweng@pu.edu.tw
Ting-Wei Hou	hou@nc.es.ncku.edu.tw
Tomas Margale	tomas.margalef@uab.es
Toni Cortes	toni@ac.upc.edu
Victor Malyshkin	malysh@ssd.sscc.ru
Wang-Chien Lee	wlee@cse.psu.edu
Weijia Jia	itjia@cityu.edu.hk
Wenbin Jiang	wenbinjiang@hust.edu.cn
Weng Fai Wong	wongwf@comp.nus.edu.sg
Wenguang Chen	cwg@tsinghua.edu.cn
Wolfgang Gentzsch	wgentzsch@mcnc.org
Won W. Ro	wro@csun.edu
Xiangjian He	sean@it.uts.edu.au
Xiaowu Chen	chen@buaa.edu.cn
Yeh-Ching Chung	ychung@cs.nthu.edu.tw
Yong-Kee Jun	jun@gnu.ac.kr
Yunhao Liu	liu@cse.ust.hk

Organization

Publication Co-chair	Jemal Abawajy (Deakin University, Australia)
Publication Co-chair	Lucian Finta (University of Paris XIII, France)
Publicity Co-chair	Philippe d'Anfray (Renater, France)
Publicity Co-chair	Ching-Hsien Hsu (Chung Hua University, Taiwan)
Finance Chair	Christine Nora (IEEE France Section)

Registration Co-chair Jean-Christophe Dubacq (University of Paris XIII, France)
Registration Co-chair Sébastien Tixeuil (University of Paris Sud, Orsay, France)
Local Arrangements Co-chair Catherine Girard (INRIA Futurs, France)
Local Arrangements Co-chair Sophie Toulouse (University of Paris XIII, France)

External Reviewers

Adel Essafi
Ahmed Elleuch
Ala Rezmerita
Alexandre Tabbal
Andrei Hutanu
Ayon Basumallik
Bin Chen
Bing-Rong Lin
Brett Estrade
Camille Coti
Cao Linchun
Chia-Yen Shih
Chuang-wen You
Chunming Hu
Congxing Cai
Connor Gray
Dan Meng
Daniel Wang
Derrick Kondo
Edson Midorikawa
Fabrizio Silvestri
Fathi Essalmi
Feng Liu
Francoise Andre
Gilles Fedak
Gisele Craveiro
Gongwei zhang
Guangwen Yang
Hailong Sun
Hansang Bae
Hao Ren
Heithem Abbes
Hsi-Min Chen
Hsi-Ya Chang
Hsiao-Hsi Wang
Huajing Li
Jairo Panetta
Jan-Jan Wu
Jiannong Cao
Jingling Xue
Joanne Ren
Jose Moreira
Joshua Abadie
Julian Winter
Ken C.K. Tsang
Krzysztof Rzadca
Laukik Chitnis
Leonardo Ferreira
Lin Chen
Manas Somaiya
Marcia Cera
Mark C. M. Tsang
Marta Mattoso
Matt Mutka
Mohamed Ould-Khaoua
Monica Py
Oleg Lodygensky
Olivier Delannoy
Pan Linfeng
Partha Sarathi
Paul Malecot
Pierre Lemarinier
Qiang Wang
Rafael Bohrer vila
Rahim Lakhoo
Rodrigo Rosa Righi
Ruay-Shiung Chang
Sebastien Varrette
Sevin Fide
Seyong Lee
Shantenu Ja
Srinivas Vadlamani
Tao Chen
Tien-Hsiung Weng
Troy Johnson
Vincent Roca
Vlady Ravelomanana
Weng-Fai Wong
Wolfgang Gentzsch
Xuanhua Shi
Yaakoub El Khamra
Yang Yanqin
Yong Wang
Yosr Slama
Yosra Hlaoui
Yu Yong
Zhang Da Qiang
Zhihang Yu
Zhou Lei

Table of Contents

A Grid Resource Broker with Network Bandwidth-Aware Job Scheduling for Computational Grids*

Chao-Tung Yang**, Sung-Yi Chen, and Tsui-Ting Chen

High-Performance Computing Laboratory
Department of Computer Science and Information Engineering
Tunghai University, Taichung, 40704, Taiwan, ROC
{ctyang, g942805, g95280003}@thu.edu.tw

Abstract. This work presents a workflow-based computational resource broker whose main functions are matching available resources with user requests and considering network information statuses during matchmaking. The resource broker provides an interface for accessing available and appropriate resources via user credentials. We use the Ganglia and NWS tools to monitor resource status and network-related information, respectively. We also report on using the Globus Toolkit to construct a grid platform called the TIGER project that integrates the distributed resources of five universities in Taichung, Taiwan, where the resource broker was developed. The proposed broker provides secure, updated information about available resources and serves as a link to the diverse systems available in the Grid.

1 Introduction

Grid computing can be defined as coordinated re source sharing and problem solving in dynamic, multi institutional collaborations [1, 2, 3, 4, 5, 6]. Grid computing involves sharing heterogeneous resources, based on different platforms, hardware/software, computer architecture, and computer languages, which located in different places belonging to different administrative domains over a network using open standards. The subject of this paper is the resource management for a grid system that is primarily intended to support computationally expensive tasks like simulations and optimizations on a grid [7, 8, 10, 11, 12, 13, 14, 17, 18, 19, 20]. Applications are represented as workflows that can be decomposed into single grid jobs. These jobs require resources from the grid that are described as accurately as necessary. The main task of the resource management is resource brokering to optimize a global schedule for all requesting grid jobs and all requested resources. Consequently, a global optimizing resource broker with network bandwidth-aware is proposed. It's embedding in the application and resource management system, and on important implementation decisions. The performance of the optimization method is demonstrated by an example.

---

* This work was partially supported by National Science Council of Republic of China under the number of NSC95-2221-E-029-004 and NSC95-2218-E-007-025.

** Corresponding Author.

C. Cérin and K.-C. Li (Eds.): GPC 2007, LNCS 4459, pp. 1 – 12, 2007.

In the grid environment, applications make use of shared grid resources to improve performance. The target function usually depends on many parameters, e.g., the scheduling strategies, the configurations of machines and links, the workloads in a grid, the degree of data replication, etc. In this paper, we examine how those parameters may affect performance. We choose an application's overall response time as an object function and focus on dynamically scheduling independent tasks. We define the job, scheduler, and performance model of a grid site and conduct experiments on TIGER grid platform [9]. We use the Ganglia [15] and NWS [16] tools to monitor resource status and network-related information, respectively. Understanding influence of each parameter is not only crucial for an application to achieve good performance, but would also help to develop effective schedule heuristics and design high quality grids.

The paper presents the design and the development of a Grid Network-Aware Resource Broker. It enhances the features of a Grid Resource Broker with the capabilities provided by a network information service form NWS tool [15]. Here, we will take a deeper look at what constitutes the scheduling discipline and its components. Scheduling is generally not well understood because scheduling products often integrate multiple functions into one package called a scheduler. So we are going to deconstruct scheduling into its constituent parts. The innovative contribution of the presented integration is the possibility to design and implement new mapping/scheduling mechanisms to take into account both network and computational resources.

The main contributions of this paper are listed in the following:

- The system design and implementation of computational grid resource broker is presented.
- A workflow model is presented to solve the dependency problem of jobs.
- A network bandwidth-award job scheduling algorithm is proposed for communication-intensive jobs.
- A model of monitoring and information service for grid resources is provided.
- A user friendly Grid Portal is conducted for general users to submit their jobs and monitor the detail status of resources.

2 Related Work

Among the research works focused on Grid Resource Broker (GRB) topics, in 2002 the authors in [17] described the Grid Resource Broker (GRB) portal, an advanced Web gateway for computational Grids in use at the University of Lecce. The portal allows trusted users seamless access to computational resources and Grid services, providing a friendly computing environment that takes advantage of the underlying Globus Toolkit middleware, enhancing its basic services and capabilities.

In [18, 20], the authors describe a resource management system which is the central component of a distributed network computing system. There have been many projects focused on network computing that have designed and implemented resource management systems with a variety of architectures and services. In this paper, an abstract model and a comprehensive taxonomy for describing resource management architectures is developed. The paper presents taxonomy for Grid RMSs. Requirements for RMSs are described and an abstract functional model has been developed. The requirements and model have been used to develop a taxonomy focused on types of Grid system, machine organization, resource model characterization, and scheduling characterization. Representative Grid systems are surveyed and placed into their various categories.

In [19], the authors present the design and implementation of an OGSI-compliant Grid resource broker compatible with both GT2 and GT3. It focuses on resource discovery and management, and dynamic policy management for job scheduling and resource selection. The presented resource broker is designed in an extensible and modular way using standard protocols and schemas to become compatible with new middleware versions. The author also gave experimental results to demonstrate the resource broker behavior.

3 Design and Implementation of Resource Broker

In the previous work [14], we implemented a computational grid resource broker which is used to discover and evaluate grid resources, and make informed job submission decisions by matching requirements of a job with an appropriate grid resource to meet user and deadline requirements. The system architecture of resource broker and the relation of each component are shown in Figure 1. Each rectangular represents a unique component of our system. Furthermore, this paper had implemented the boldface parts. Users could easily make use of our resource broker through a common Grid portal [6, 9, 10, 11, 12, 13, 14].

The primary task of Resource Broker is to compare requests of users and resource information provided by Information Service. After the most appropriate job assignment scheme is selected, machines of the Grid are assigned and the Scheduler is

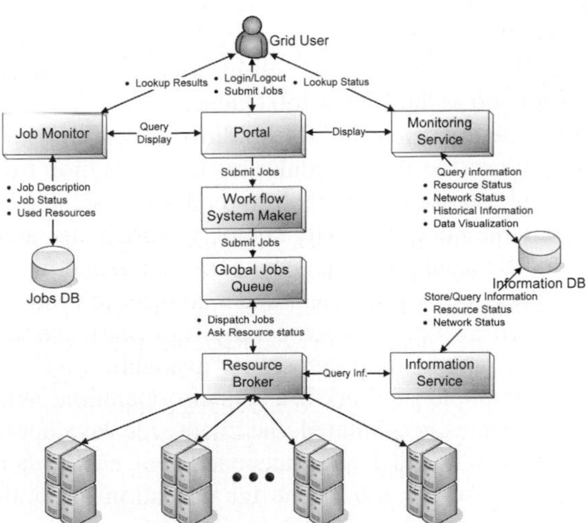

Fig. 1. System architecture

responsible to submit the job and execute the applications. The results are collected and returned to Resource Broker. Then, Resource Broker records results of execution in the database of Message Center through the Agent of Information Service. The user can catch the results from grid portal.

These Grids may span several domain administrations via internet. As a result of this, it may be difficult to monitor, control and manage those machines and resources. This paper aims at providing a multi-platform Grid monitoring service which can monitor resources such as CPU speed and utilization, memory usage, disk usage, and network bandwidth in a real-time manner. Monitoring data is extracted form Ganglia and NWS tools then stored and transmitted in XML form and then used for displaying. All the information is displayed using real-time graphs.

Most general resource brokers cannot handle jobs with dependencies, which means, for example, that Job B may have to be executed after Job A because Job B needs output from Job A as input data, as shown in Figure 2. The workflow-based resource broker presented in this paper copes with this in two phases: Client-side phase and Server-side phase.

Client-side phase is a GUI Java applet, called Workflow Maker, which is provided in the Grid Portal for users to create workflows in workflow description language (WDL), which allows job with dependency and sets the following attributes for each job:

- Job name
- Broker sorting algorithm
- Job type, parallel MPI or general sequential
- Job dependencies
- Working directory
- Program name
- Argument
- Number of processors

The Workflow Maker converts this workflow abstract into an actual XML file; and then delivers it to the Resource Broker by uploading this XML file. The Resource Broker parses the XML file, checking all job information and dependency relationships, and then adds the job to the Global Job Queue.

The Global Job Queue is responsible for holding all pending subjobs delivered to the Resource Broker. When the Job Scheduler retrieves a subjob from the Global Job Queue, it checks all node statuses, and sets busy nodes to "occupied" to prevent overloading, allocates available nodes to satisfy subjob requirements, and sets these nodes to "occupied". The Job Scheduler then gets the next subjob and repeats the procedure. If the Job Scheduler does not find sufficient nodes to meet job requirements, it pauses until sufficient nodes are available. When a subjob finishes, the scheduler frees the respective resources by changing their statuses to "available".

Figure 3 shows an example of Workflow System operation. When the job series A~F containing dependencies is submitted, the client-side Java applet applies a topological sort. Suppose Jobs A and E are independent of each other. The Workflow System simply adds them to the Job Queue for execution in parallel. When Job A finishes, it resolves its dependencies with Jobs B and C, and the Workflow System adds them to the Job Queue, removing Job A. When Jobs B and C finish, the Workflow System then adds Job D to the Job Queue for execution.

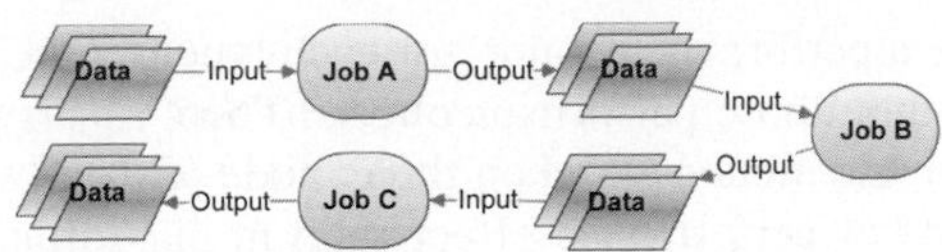

Fig. 2. A simple job dependency

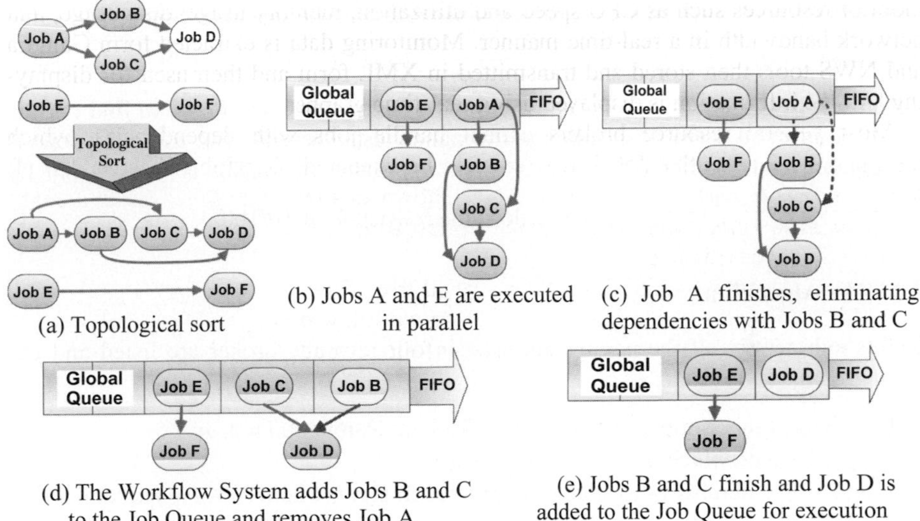

(a) Topological sort

(b) Jobs A and E are executed in parallel

(c) Job A finishes, eliminating dependencies with Jobs B and C

(d) The Workflow System adds Jobs B and C to the Job Queue and removes Job A

(e) Jobs B and C finish and Job D is added to the Job Queue for execution

Fig. 3. The detail steps of workflow operations

4 Design of Network Bandwidth-Award Job Scheduling

4.1 Mechanism of Performance Evaluation

Our grid environment is based on several clusters and the cluster nodes can directly accept the job which is submitted from the resource broker. We use *TP* to represent the total computing power of those machines in a single site which the resource broker can be allocated. The *TP* can be divided into three main parts (CPU, memory, and intra networking). User needs to input the number of CPU (*X*) which they want to use for job execution. Then, the information service of resource broker will check how many CPUs are available in each site (cluster) and the node's hardware information (CPU speed, CPU utilization, memory size, and network speed). Afterward the resource broker will calculate *TP* of each site and choose the enough processors based upon the value in this grid computing platform.

We use the statistics to analyze the execution results of HPL (High Performance Linpack) application. $Pval_{ij}$ and $Mval_{ij}$ mean the performance value of each machine based on the ith site and j^{th} node's CPU and memory, respectively. First, we fix the memory size and change the number of CPU to conduct the HPL performance test. Then, we fix the CPU number and changed the HPL problem size to conduct the performance test to find out the incidence of different memory size which was been used. Finally, we give a performance value for each type of CPU and memory size in our environment based on those performance tests. Then, Pu_{ij} is processor utility rate of each node over past one minute based on the jth node of the ith site.

There are two kinds of performance effect ratio in our formula: α_{PE} and α_{NE}. We use α_{PE} to represent performance effect ratio of processor, and $0 \leq \alpha_{PE} \leq 1$. The α_{PE} value is based on correlation coefficient value between CPU and HPL value. The $(1-\alpha_{PE})$ value represents the performance effect ratio of memory size and HPL value. The square bracket of our formula means the inner effect of the machine. So, the α_{PE} value is worked out by $\frac{Cov(CPU, HPL)}{Cov(CPU, HPL) + Cov(memory, HPL)}$. Then, we make the HPL performance test in one of the cluster and change the switch from gigabit to 10/100 to find out the effect of different network speed on performance test. There are two α_{NE} ratios, one is for gigabit, and another is for 10/100. The α_{NE} value of gigabit is worked out by $\frac{Cov(gigabit, HPL)}{Cov(gigabit, HPL) + Cov(10/100, HPL)}$, and so does the α_{NE} value of 10/100.

4.2 The Algorithm

In this subsection, all the parameters used in our resource broker are listed and explained in the following:

- S_i: The number of sites (domains) in Grid environment, $i = 1 \sim n$.
- S_{RB}: The site which resource broker is in.
- $P(S_i)$: The number of available processors in site i, where $N_i \leq P_i$, and total available processors for a job execution are summed as $Y = \sum_{i=1}^{n} P(S_i)$.
- X: The number of processors used for executing a job.
- $Pval_{ij}$: Processor performance value of each node based on the jth node of the ith site, $i = 1 \sim n, j = 1 \sim m$.
- $Mval_{ij}$: Memory performance value of each node based on the jth node of the ith site, $i = 1 \sim n, j = 1 \sim m$.
- Pu_{ij}: Processor utility rate of each node over past one minute based on the jth node of the ith site, $i = 1 \sim n, j = 1 \sim m$.
- α_{PE}: Performance effect ratio of processor, $0 \leq \alpha_{PE} \leq 1$.
- $1-\alpha_{PE}$: Performance effect ratio of memory.
- α_{NE}: Intra networking effect ratio in the site i, $0 \leq \alpha_{NE} \leq 1$.
- β: Internal networking effect ratio in the grid.
- E_{ij}: The graph constructed between sites i and j, the edge corresponding to the current available bandwidth forecasted by NWS tool.
- $ATP(S_i)$: The average total computing power of the site i, and

$$ATP(S_i) = \left(\frac{\sum_{j=1}^{n} Pval_{ij} \times (1 - Pu_{ij})}{P(S_i)} \times \alpha_{PE} + \frac{\sum_{j=1}^{n} Mval_{ij}}{P(S_i)} \times (1 - \alpha_{PE}) \right) \times \alpha_{NE}$$

We summarize the Network Bandwidth-Aware (NB-aware) job scheduling algorithm in Figure 4 and then illustrate an example below the algorithm.

```
//RB_Network Bandwidth-Aware Job Scheduler
{
  //Calculate the number of total available processors in all sites of the grid.
  Y = Σ_{i=1}^{n} P(S_i); for ∀S_i ∈ G, G is the grid.
  if (X≥Y) then break;
  // R is a set including the sites which will be allocated.
  R = ∅;
  Count = 0;
  // P(R) = ΣP(S_i) for ∀S_i ∈ R
  // n(R) is the amount of the elements in the set R
  while (P(R) < X)
  {
    Count = Count + 1;
    Find a set R which P(R) ≥ Y and n(R) = Count, such that
    β×ΣE_ij + (1−β)×ΣATP(S_i) is maximum for ∀S_i ∈ R;
  }
  Allocate processors ranked in top X speed of the R.
}
```

Fig. 4. The job scheduling algorithm in resource broker

Here is an example of this algorithm as shown in Figure 5. Suppose the Grid is constructed by five domains, and then resource broker is in Domain A. “A(8)” means there are eight working nodes (processors) in site A. The number “40” represents current communication bandwidth (Mbps) between sites A and B. At first, resource broker will query information service to get the current status of whole working nodes, there are three cases:

- Case 1: If the incoming current job needs 8 processors, resource broker will check the possible site in this contains more than 8 processors. If the number of available site is more than two, the resource broker will calculate the TP of each site and then allocate processors into the best site. In this example, resource broker could allocate directly into site A or site C based on TP value for running job.
- Case 2: If the incoming current job needs 12 processors, there does not exist in any single site that resource broker could immediately allocate processors. In this kind of situation, resource broker will sort all combination of the two sites in which the sum of total processors is more than 12 by the value of $\beta \times \sum E_{ij} + (1-\beta) \times \sum ATP(S_i)$. The resource broker will select the best combination to allocate processors ranking in top 12 speeds. In this example, resource broker will sort five kinds of combination of the two sites: (A, B), (A, C), (A, E), (C, B) and (C, E) then select the best one.

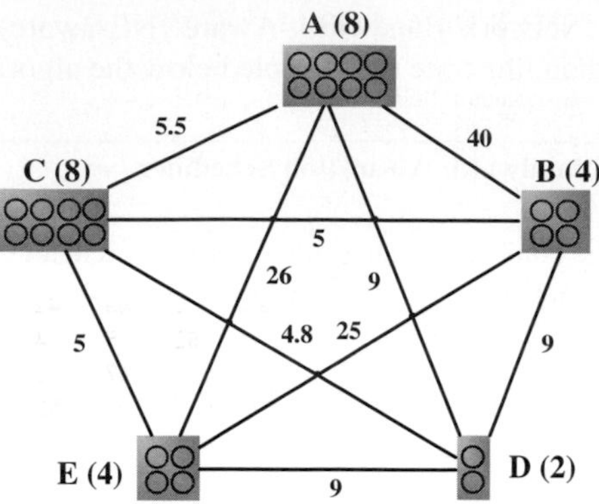

Fig. 5. An example of grid testbed

5 Experimental Environment and Results

A metropolitan-scale Grid computing platform named TIGER Grid (standing for Taichung Integrating Grid Environment and Resource) was used in this experiment. The TIGER grid interconnects 12 computing clusters which are scattered among seven educational institutes. The specifications, HPL performance value, and site ranking of TIGER testbed, are listed in Table 1. Their networking bandwidth information is listed in Table 2. The site topologies of THU and TIGER are shown in Figure 6, respectively.

Table 1. The specifications, HPL performance, and site ranking of TIGER testbed

Site	Number of Node/CPU	Total Speed (MHz)	Total Memory (MB)	HPL (G Flops)	Site Ranking
alpha	4/8	16,000	4,096	12.5683	10
beta	4/8	22,400	4,096	20.1322	11
gamma	4/4	11,200	4,096	5.8089	5
delta	4/4	12,000	4,096	10.6146	7
eta	2/4	12,800	2,048	11.2116	8
mu	2/4	8,000	4,096	11.8500	9
ncue	4/16	32,000	16,384	28.1887	12
ntcu	4/5	3,250	1,024	1.0285	2
hit	4/4	11,200	2,048	7.0615	6
dali	4/4	7,200	512	2.8229	3
lz	4/4	2,700	768	0.8562	1
lf	1/1	3,000	1,024	3.0389	4

In this experiment, a sequence of 100 jobs is randomly generated with "Template Job" and "np", which is used to simulate 100 running jobs submission and the number of processors used for each job. Dispatched by Network Bandwidth-Aware Job

Table 2. The network information of each site

	alpha	beta	gamma	delta	eta	mu	ncue	ntcu	hit	dali	lz	lf
alpha	578	47	423	47	44	47	6	48	57	8	23	9
beta		738	40	48	46	724	6	44	40	8	22	9
gamma			609	38	39	37	4	36	20	6	19	8
delta				763	49	22	3	29	37	4	14	6
eta					788	47	4	42	37	7	21	8
mu						793	6	49	42	23	8	9
ncue							82	5	4	11	19	3
ntcu								87	5	8	14	5
hit									52	9	25	3
dali										82	7	9
lz											83	9
lf												N/A

Scheduler, related information is logged, including queuing time, total execution time and resource utilization. Figure 7 shows the distribution of "Template Job". The X-axis represents the content of jobs, and the Y-axis represents the number of jobs.

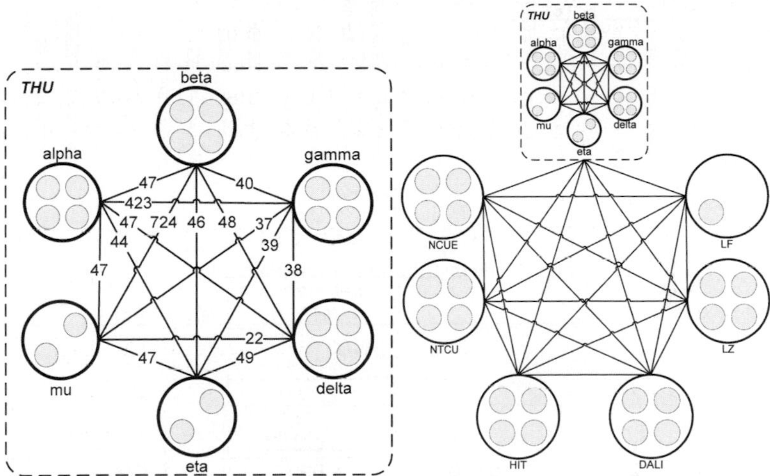

Fig. 6. The site topology of THU and TIGER, respectively

To show that RB_Network-Aware Job Scheduler has better performance, in this experiment, the same job sequence is submitted to another two scheduling schemes, Network-only and Speed-only, for execution and comparison.

- Network-only: considers network information only. If single cluster is enough to process the workload, then the fast cluster system in the intranet is chosen. If two cluster systems are needed, then the top-2 fast cluster systems in the intranet are chosen.

- Speed-only: considers CPU clock information only. If single cluster is enough to process the workload, then the cluster system with largest CPU clock summation in the intranet is chosen. If two cluster systems are needed, then the two cluster systems with the top-2 largest CPU clock summation in the intranet are chosen.

Experimental results are shown in Figures 8 and 9. The total execution time of one job is the average of queuing time and execution time. As shown in Figure 8, RB_Network-Aware Job Scheduler is better than the other two. Finally, Figure 9 shows the statistics of resource usage. We can see that RB_Network-Aware Job Scheduler can increase the utilization of powerful clustering systems, and decrease total completion time.

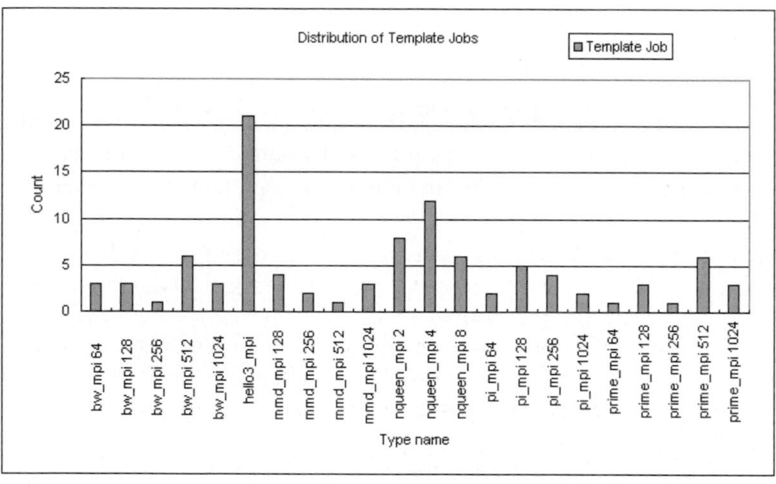

Fig. 7. The distribution of template jobs

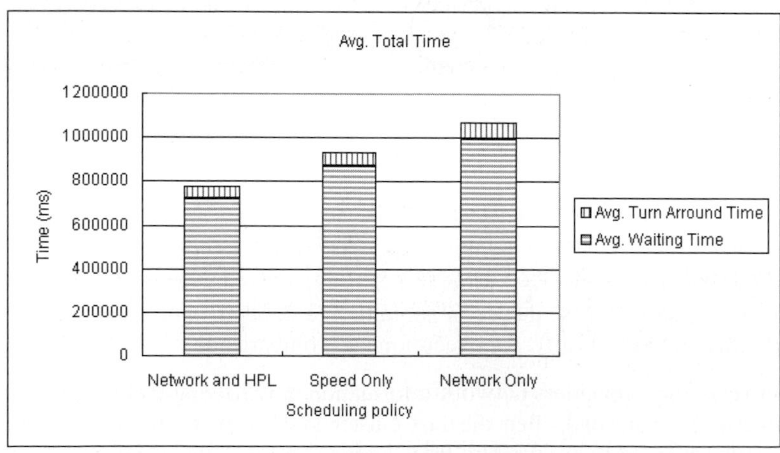

Fig. 8. The comparison of three policies for the average total time of jobs

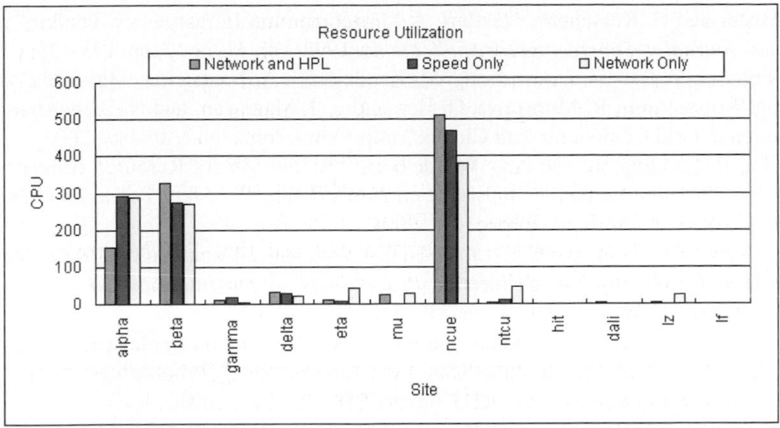

Fig. 9. The comparison of three policies for resource utilization

6 Conclusions

This paper is presented to help the user make better use of the grid resources available. This paper will look at the use of information services in a grid and discuss the monitoring use of the Ganglia toolkit to enhance the information services already present in the Globus environment. Our grid resource brokerage system discover and evaluate grid resources, and make informed job submission decisions by matching a job's requirements with an appropriate grid resource to meet budget and deadline requirements.

The paper presents the design and the development of a Grid Network-Aware Resource Broker. It enhances the features of a Grid Resource Broker with the capabilities that considers network bandwidth for job scheduling. Our grid resource broker provided a network information service by extract data form NWS tool. The innovative contribution of the presented integration is the possibility to design and implement new mapping/scheduling mechanisms to take into account both network and computational resources.

References

1. K. Czajkowski, S. Fitzgerald, I. Foster, and C. Kesselman, "Grid Information Services for Distributed Resource Sharing," *Proceedings of the Tenth IEEE International Symposium on High-Performance Distributed Computing*, IEEE press, 2001.
2. I. Foster and C. Kesselman, "The Grid 2: Blueprint for a New Computing Infrastructure," *Morgan Kaufmann*, 2nd edition, 2003.
3. I. Foster, "The Grid: A New Infrastructure for 21st Century Science," *Physics Today*, 2002, vol. 55, no. 2, pp. 42-47.
4. I. Foster and N. Karonis, "A Grid-Enabled MPI: Message Passing in Heterogeneous Distributed Computing Systems," *Proceedings of 1998 Supercomputing Conference*, 1998.

5. I. Foster and C. Kesselman, "Globus: A Metacomputing Infrastructure Toolkit," *International Journal of Supercomputer Applications*, 1997, vol. 11, no. 2, pp. 115-128.
6. L. Ferreira, V. Berstis, J. Armstrong, M. Kendzierski, A. Neukoetter, MasanobuTakagi, R. Bing-Wo, A. Amir, R. Murakawa, O. Hernandez, J. Magowan, and N. Bieberstein, "Introduction to Grid Computing with Globus," http://www.ibm.com/redbooks, 2003.
7. H. Le, P. Coddington, and A.L. Wendelborn, "A Data-Aware Resource Broker for Data Grids," *IFIP International Conference on Network and Parallel Computing (NPC'2004), LNCS*, vol. 3222, Springer-Verlag, Oct. 2004.
8. C.T. Yang, P.C. Shih, and K.C. Li, "A High-Performance Computational Resource Broker for Grid Computing Environments," *Proceedings of the International Conference on AINA'05*, vol. 2, pp. 333-336, Taipei, Taiwan, March 2005.
9. C.T. Yang, K.C. Li, W.C. Chiang, and P.C. Shih, "Design and Implementation of TIGER Grid: an Integrated Metropolitan-Scale Grid Environment," *Proceedings of the 6th IEEE International Conference on PDCAT'05*, pp. 518-520, Dec. 2005.
10. J. Nabrzyski, J.M. Schopf, and J. Weglarz, *Grid Rrsource Management*, Kluwer Academic Publishers, 2005.
11. S.M. Park and J.H. Kim, "Chameleon: A Resource Scheduler in a Data Grid Environment," *Proceedings of the 3rd IEEE/ACM International Symposium on Cluster Computing and the Grid*, pp. 258-265, May 2003.
12. C.T. Yang, C.L. Lai, P.C. Shih, and K.C. Li, "A Resource Broker for Computing Nodes Selection in Grid Environments," *Grid and Cooperative Computing - GCC 2004: 3rd International Conference,, Lecture Notes in Computer Science*, Springer-Verlag, vol. 3251, pp. 931-934, Oct. 2004.
13. C.T. Yang, P.C Shih, S.Y. Chen, and W.C. Shih, "An Efficient Network Information Modeling using NWS for Grid Computing Environments," *Grid and Cooperative Computing - GCC 2005: 4th International Conference, Lecture Notes in Computer Science*, vol. 3795, pp. 287-299, Springer-Verlag, Nov. 2005.
14. C.T. Yang, C.F. Lin, and S.Y. Chen, "A Workflow-based Computational Resource Broker with Information Monitoring in Grids," *Proceedings of the 5th International Conference on Grid and Cooperative Computing (GCC 2006)*, IEEE CS Press, pp. 199-206, China, Oct. 2006
15. Ganglia, http://ganglia.sourceforge.net/
16. Network Weather Service, http://nws.cs.ucsb.edu/ewiki/
17. Giovanni Aloisio and Massimo Cafaro, "Web-based access to the Grid using the Grid Resource Broker portal," *Concurrency Computation: Practice and Experience*, (14):1145-1160, 2002.
18. Klaus Krauter, Rajkumar Buyya, and Muthucumaru Maheswaran, "A taxonomy and survey of grid resource management systems for distributed computing," *Software Practice and Experience,* (32):135-164, 2002.
19. Ivan Rodero, Julita Corbalán, Rosa M. Badia, and Jesús Labarta, "eNANOS Grid Resource Broker", *LNCS*, vol. 3470, pp. 111-121, Springer, 2005.
20. Srikumar Venugopal, Rajkumar Buyya, and Lyle Winton, "A Grid service broker for scheduling e-Science applications on global data Grids," *Concurrency Computation: Practice and Experience*, (18):685-699, 2006.

Design of PeerSum: A Summary Service for P2P Applications

Rabab Hayek[1], Guillaume Raschia[1], Patrick Valduriez[2], and Noureddine Mouaddib[1]

Atlas team, INRIA and LINA, University of Nantes, France
[1]FirstName.LastName@univ-nantes.fr, [2]Patrick.Valduriez@inria.fr

Abstract. Sharing huge databases in distributed systems is inherently difficult. As the amount of stored data increases, data localization techniques become no longer sufficient. A more efficient approach is to rely on compact database summaries rather than raw database records, whose access is costly in large distributed systems. In this paper, we propose PeerSum, a new service for managing summaries over shared data in large P2P and Grid applications. Our summaries are synthetic, multidimensional views with two main virtues. First, they can be directly queried and used to approximately answer a query without exploring the original data. Second, as semantic indexes, they support locating relevant nodes based on data content. Our main contribution is to define a summary model for P2P systems, and the algorithms for summary management. Our performance evaluation shows that the cost of query routing is minimized, while incurring a low cost of summary maintenance.

1 Introduction

Research on distributed systems is focusing on supporting advanced applications which must deal with semantically rich data (e.g. XML documents, relational tables, etc.), using a high-level SQL-like query language. As a potential example of applications, consider the cooperation of scientists who are willing to share their private data for the duration of a given experiment. Such cooperation may be efficiently supported by improving the data localization and data description techniques.

Initially developed for moderate-sized scientific applications, Grid technology is now evolving to provide database sharing services, in large virtual organizations. In [9], a service-based architecture for database access (OGSA-DAI) has been defined over the Grid. OGSA-DAI extends the distributed database architecture [13] to provide distribution transparency using Web services. However, it relies on some centralized schema and directory management, which is not an adequate solution for supporting highly dynamic organizations, with a large number of autonomous members.

Peer-to-Peer (P2P) techniques that focus on scaling up, dynamicity, autonomy and decentralized control can be very useful to Grid data management. The complementary nature of the strengths and weaknesses of the two technologies suggests that the interests of the two communities are likely to grow closer over time [6]. For instance, P-Grid [1] and Organic Grid [3] develop self-organizing and scalable services on top of P2P systems.

C. Cérin and K.-C. Li (Eds.): GPC 2007, LNCS 4459, pp. 13–26, 2007.

In unstructured P2P systems, query routing relies on flooding mechanisms which suffer from high query execution cost and poor recall. To improve performance, several techniques have been proposed to locate data relevant to a user query. These techniques can be grouped in three classes: data indexing, mediation and content-based clustering. Data indexing maintains the location (e.g. [18], [15]) or the direction (e.g. [4]) to nodes storing relevant data. However, efficient data indexes must be small, distributed and refer to data based on their content, without compromising peer autonomy or mandating a specific network structure. Mediation consists in exploiting structural information on data schemas to guide query propagation. For instance, in Piazza [19], a query is propagated along pre-existing pairwise mappings between peer schemas. However, many limitations prevent these techniques from scaling up. Content-based clustering consists in organizing the network such that "similar" peers, e.g. peers answering similar queries, are grouped together ([12], [5]). Similarity between peers may be computed using techniques of the two preceding classes (e.g. similarity between indexes [11]).

With the ever increasing amount of information stored into databases, data localization techniques are no longer sufficient to support P2P data sharing. Today's Decision-Support and collaborative applications are typically exploratory. Thus, a user may prefer a fast, approximate answer to a long, exact answer. In other words, reasoning on compact data descriptions rather than raw database records, whose access is costly in large P2P systems, may be much more efficient. For instance, a doctor asking queries like "*young* and *fat* patients diagnosed with disease X" may prefer descriptions of result tuples to rapidly make a decision based on similar situations, treated by other doctors.

In this paper, we propose PeerSum, a new service for managing summaries over shared data in P2P systems. Our summaries are synthetic, multidimensional views with two main virtues. First, they provide an intelligible representation of the underlying data such that an approximate query can be processed entirely in their domain; that is, inputs and outputs are summaries. Second, as indexing structures, they support locating relevant nodes based on their data descriptions. PeerSum is done in the context of APPA, a network-independent P2P data management system [2].

This paper makes the following contributions. First, we define a summary model which deals with the distributed and autonomous nature of P2P systems. Second, we propose efficient algorithms for summary management. We validated our algorithmic solutions through simulation, using the BRITE topology generator and SimJava. The performance results show that the cost of query routing is minimized, while incurring a low cost of summary maintenance.

The rest of this paper is organized as follows. Section 2 describes PeerSum's summary model. Section 3 describes PeerSum's summary management with its algorithms. Section 4 discusses query processing with PeerSum. Section 5 gives a performance evaluation with a cost model and a simulation model. Section 6 compares our solution with related work. Section 7 concludes.

2 PeerSum Summary Model

In this section, we first present our summary model architecture and the principle of summary construction in P2P systems. Second, we discuss the scalability issues of the summarization process that is integrated to a peer DataBase Management System

(DBMS), to allow generating summaries of a relational database. Then, we formally define the notion of data summary in a P2P network.

2.1 Model Architecture

Our ultimate goal is to build a complete summary that describes the content of all shared data sources. However, such a summary is ideal in the context of P2P networks, because of their autonomous and dynamic nature. It is difficult to build and to keep this summary consistent relative to the current data instances it describes. In our approach, we

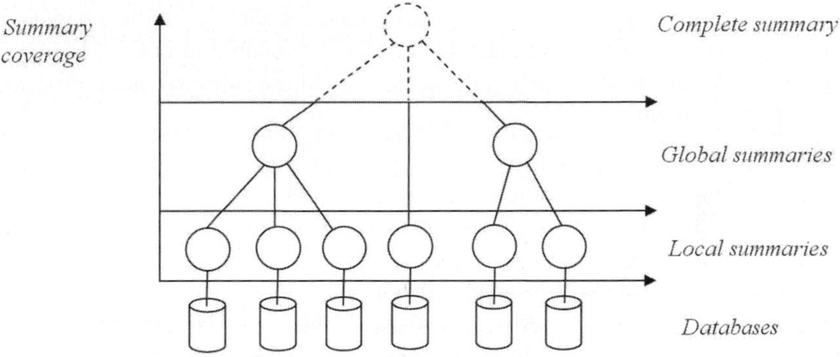

Fig. 1. Summary Model Architecture

adopt an incremental mechanism for summary construction, and define the notion of "*summary coverage*" as follows.

Definition 1. Summary coverage. *The* coverage *of a summary S in a network of size N is the fraction of the peers that own data described by the summary S.*

The coverage of a summary quantifies its convergence to the complete summary which is obviously characterized by a coverage = 1.

The architecture of our summary model is presented in Figure 1. Each peer generates the Local Summary (LS) of its database, which is characterized by the lowest-coverage level. Then, it cooperates with other peers through exchanging and merging summaries, in order to build a Global Summary (GS). The last one is characterized by a continuous evolution in term of coverage. In fact, the cooperation between two sets of peers, each having constructed a global summary, will result in a higher-coverage one. That is, in a large P2P system, one could see the global summary as an intermediate node in a global hierarchy where the virtual root is the ideal complete summary.

In this work, we propose fully distributed algorithms for global summary construction and maintenance. However, we will first give a brief description of the summarization process that generates summaries of relational databases with interesting features, making it scalable in a distributed environment.

2.2 Summarization Process: Scalability Issues

A summarization process is integrated to each peer's DBMS to allow constructing the local summary level of Figure 1. Our approach is based on SAINTETIQ [14], an on-line linguistic approach for summarizing databases. The system is organized into two separate web services. The *translation service* corresponds to the pre-processing step that prepares data for summarization while the *summarization service* produces a set of summaries arranged in a hierarchy. A unique feature of the summary system is its use of *Background Knowledge* (BK), a priori built on each attribute. It supports the translation of descriptions of database tuples into a user-defined vocabulary. Descriptors used for summary content representation are defined as linguistic variables [21] on the attribute domain. For example, Figure 2 shows a user-defined vocabulary on the attribute `age`. A detailed description of the SAINTETIQ process is available in [14] and [16]. Concerning our work, we are interested in the scalability of the summarization process in a distributed environment.

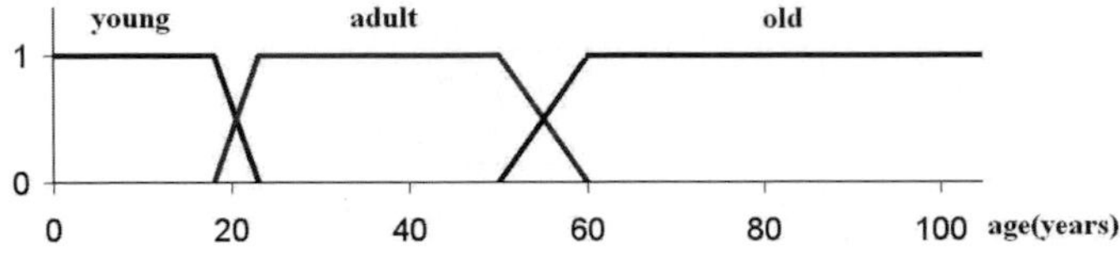

Fig. 2. Fuzzy Linguistic Partition on **age**

Memory consumption and time complexity are the two main factors that need to be taken care off in order to guaranty the capacity of the summary system to handle massive datasets. First, the process time complexity is in $O(n)$, where n is the number of tuples to incorporate into a hierarchy of summaries. Besides, an important feature is that in the summary algorithm raw data have to be parsed only once and it is performed with a low time cost. Second, the system requires low memory consumption for performing the summary construction algorithm as well as for storing the produced summaries. Moreover, a cache manager is in charge of summary caching in memory and it can be bounded to a given memory requirement. On the other hand, the parallelization of the summary system is a key feature to ensure a smooth scalability. The implementation of the system is based on the Message-Oriented Programming paradigm. Each sub-system is autonomous and collaborates with the others through disconnected asynchronous method invocations. It is among the least demanding approaches in terms of availability and centralization. The autonomy of summary components allows for a distributed computing of the process.

2.3 Summary Representation

A summary z is a pair (I_z, R_z) where I_z is the intentional content of the summary and R_z is its extent, that is the group of database tuples described by I_z. The intent I_z provides a short description of z in terms of linguistic labels defined in the Background Knowledge (BK) and used in the pre-processing step.

For our purpose, we consider a summary as an indexing structure over distributed data in a P2P system. Thus, we added a third dimension to the definition of a summary z: a *peer-extent* P_z, which provides the set of peers having data described by z.

Definition 2. Peer-extent. *Let z be a node in a given hierarchy of summaries S, and P the set of all peers who participated to the construction of S. The* peer-extent P_z *of the summary z is the subset of peers owning, at least, one record of its extent R_z:* $P_z = \{p \in P \mid R_z \cap R_p \neq \emptyset\}$ *, where R_p is the view over the database of node p, used to build summaries.*

Due to the above definition, we extend the notion of *data-oriented* summary in a given database, to a *source-oriented* summary in a given P2P network. In other words, our summary can be used as a database index (e.g. referring to relevant tuples), as well as a semantic index in a distributed database system (e.g. referring to relevant nodes).

A summary is an edge in the tree structure finally produced by the summarization service. The summary hierarchy S will be characterized by its *Coverage* in the P2P system; that is, the fraction of nodes (data sources) covered by S (see Definition1). Relative to the hierarchy S, we call *Partner Peer* a peer whose data is described by at least a summary node of S.

Definition 3. Partner peers. *The set of* Partner peers P_S *of a summary hierarchy S is the union of peer-extents of all the summary nodes:* $P_S = \{\cup_{z \in S} P_z\}$.

By now and for convenient purpose only, we designate by "summary" a hierarchy of summaries maintained in a P2P system, unless otherwise specified.

3 Summary Management in PeerSum

We present PeerSum, a summary management service for P2P systems. First, we study the integration of PeerSum in an existing P2P architecture. Here we work in the context of APPA (Atlas Peer to Peer Architecture) [2]. Then, we propose algorithms for PeerSum's summary management. APPA has a network-independent architecture so it can be implemented over different types of P2P networks. APPA provides three layers of services: P2P network, basic services and advanced services. PeerSum is integrated at the advanced layer and defined based on the underlying services. Due to space limitations, we will only mention the services required for PeerSum definition. According to Section 2.1, PeerSum must address the following requirements:

- Peers construct individually their local summaries,
- Peers cooperate for exchanging and merging summaries into a global summary,
- Peers share a common storage in which the global summary is maintained.

The first point is addressed by integrating the summarization process, previously defined, to each peer's DBMS. Second, the peer linking and peer communication services of the APPA's P2P network layer allow peers to communicate and exchange messages (through service calls), while cooperating for a global summary construction. However, two problems arise from the heterogeneous nature of peers in a P2P system. First, peers may have different processing and storage capabilities. Therefore, a main function of PeerSum is to ensure a distributed operation for summary merging. A partner peer that requires merging two summaries, calls the service which then delegates the right peers to perform merging calculations, using load balancing and distributed computing techniques. This function can be implemented since the summarization process, at each peer, can be distributed and parallelized, as discussed in Section 2.2.

Second, peers exchange summaries that are produced using local Background Knowledges (BKs). Thus, they may be represented in different vocabularies, making difficult their shared exploitation. In this work, we assume that the participants to a collaborative database application agree on a *Common Background Knowledge* (CBK) that will be used locally by each summarization process. An example of such a CBK is the Systematized Nomenclature of Medicine Clinical Terms (SNOMED CT) [10], which is a comprehensive clinical terminology covering diseases, clinical findings, and procedures.

On the other hand, several works have addressed the problem of semantic heterogeneity in advanced P2P applications (e.g. [19], [2]). Since our summaries are data structures that respect the original data schemas [16], we can assume that the techniques they proposed for a decentralized schema management can be also used to overcome the heterogeneity of summary representations, in the context of different BKs.

Finally, the P2P data management (P2PDM) service of the basic layer and the Key-based Storage and Retrieval (KSR) service of the P2P network layer, work together to provide a common storage in which a global summary is maintained. This common storage increases the probability that "*P2P data*" (e.g. metadata, indexes, summaries) produced and used by advanced services are available even if peers that have produced them are disconnected. P2PDM and KSR manage data based on keys. A key is a data identifier which determines which peer should store the data in the system, e.g. through hashing over all peers in DHT networks or using super-peers for storage and retrieval in super-peer networks. All data operations on the common storage are key-based, i.e. they require a key as parameter.

In the following, we will describe our algorithms for summary construction and maintenance. First, we work in a static context where all the participants remain connected. Then, we address the dynamicity of peers and propose appropriate solutions.

3.1 Summary Construction

Starting up with a local summary level (see Figure 1), we present the algorithm for peer cooperation that allows constructing a global summary GS. We assume that each global summary is associated with a *Cooperation List* (CL) that provides information about its partner peers. An element of the cooperation list is composed of two fields. A partner peer identifier *PeerID*, and a 2-bit freshness value v that provides information about the freshness of the descriptions as well as the availability of the corresponding database.

- value 0 (initial value): the descriptions are fresh relative to the original data,
- value 1: the descriptions need to be refreshed,
- value 2: the original data are not available. This value will be used while addressing peer volatility in Section 3.3.

Both the global summary and its cooperation list are considered as "summary data" and are maintained in the common storage, using the P2PDM and KSR services.

Cooperation Request. The algorithm starts at an *initiator peer* P_{init} who sends a cooperation request message to its neighbors, to participate to a global summary construction. This message contains P_{init}'s identifier and a given value of TTL (Time-To-Live). One may think that a large value of TTL allows to obtain directly a high-coverage summary. However, due to the autonomous nature of P2P systems, P_{init} may keep waiting for a very long time without having constructed that global summary. Therefore, we choose to limit the value to TTL and adopt an incremental construction mechanism, as discussed in Section 2.1.

Cooperation Response. A peer *p* who receives the message, performs the following steps. First, if the request has already been received, it discards the message. Else, it saves the address of the sender as its parent. Then, its decrements TTL by one. If the value of TTL remains positive, it sends the message to its neighbors (except the *parent*) with the new TTL value. After propagating the message, *p* must wait to receive the responses of its neighbors. However, since some of the neighbors may leave the system and never response, the waiting time must be limited. We compute *p*'s waiting time using a cost function based on TTL, and network dependent parameters.

A cooperation response of a peer p has the following structure: $Coop\_Resp$ =⟨CS, PeerIDs, GSKeys⟩. CS is the current summary obtained at p, $PeerIDs$ is the list of identifiers of peers that have responded to p, and $GSKeys$ is the list of keys of global summaries. If *p* is a partner peer, that is, *p* has already participated to an existing global summary, its $Coop\_Resp$ will include the key of the global summary it knows, as well as the peer identifiers contained in the corresponding *CL*, i.e. $Coop\_Resp$ =⟨∅, extractPeerIDs(CL), {GSKey}⟩. In that case, *p* locates at the boundary of two knowledge scopes of two different summaries. Hence, it allows merging them into a higher-coverage one (i.e. incremental construction). Otherwise, its response will include its local summary and its identifier, i.e. $Coop\_Resp$ =⟨p.LS, {p.ID}, ∅⟩.

Summary Data Storage. In the waiting phase, when a child's $Coop\_Resp$ arrives, a parent peer *p* merges it with its own response by making the union of $PeerIDs$ and $GSKeys$ lists, and merging the current summaries. Once the time expires, *p* sends the result to its parent. But, if *p* is the initiator peer P_{init}, it will store the new summary data, i.e. the new global summary GS and its cooperation list CL, using the KSR service: *GSKey := KSR_insert(CS, CL)*. CL contains each peer identifier obtained in the final $PeerIDs$ list, associated with a freshness value v equal to zero. At the end, P_{init} sends the new key (*GSKey*) to all participant peers, which become GS's *partner peers*.

3.2 Summary Maintenance

A crucial issue for any indexing structure is to maintain the index, relative to the current data instances, without incurring high costs. For a local summary, it has been demonstrated that the summarization process guarantees an incremental maintenance, using a *push* mode for exchanging data with the DBMS, while performing with a low complexity. In this section, we propose a strategy for maintaining a global summary based on both *push* and *pull* techniques, in order to minimize the number of messages exchanged in the system. The appropriate algorithm is divided into two phases: Data modification and summary reconciliation.

Push: Data Modification. Let GS be a global summary and P_{GS} the set of partner peers. Each partner is responsible for refreshing its own element in the GS's cooperation list. A partner peer p observes the modification rate issued on its local summary LS. When LS is considered as enough modified, p sets its freshness value v to 1, through a *push message*. This value indicates that the local summary version being merged while building GS does not correspond any more to the current instance of the database.

An important feature is that the frequency of push messages depends on modifications issued on local summaries, rather than on the underlying databases. It has been demonstrated in [16] that, after a given process time, a summary becomes very stable. As more tuples are processed, the need to adapt the hierarchy decreases. A summary modification can be determined by observing the appearance/disappearance of descriptors in summary intentions.

Pull: Service-Initiated Reconciliation. The summary service, in its turn, observes the fraction of old descriptions (i.e. number of ones) in the cooperation list. Whenever this fraction exceeds a threshold value, the global summary GS must be refreshed. In that case, the service pulls all the partner peers to merge their current local summaries into the new version of GS, which will be then under reconstruction. The algorithm is described as follows.

A reconciliation message that contains a new summary *NewGS* (initially empty), is propagated from a partner to another. When a partner *p* receives this message, it first merges NewGS with its local summary. Then, it sends the message to another partner (chosen from the cooperation list CL). If *p* is the last visited peer, it updates the GS's *summary data*, using the KSR service. All the freshness values in CL are reset to zero. This strategy guarantees a high availability of the summary data, since only one KSR_Update operation is performed by the last partner.

3.3 Peer Dynamicity

In large P2P systems, a peer connects mainly to download some data and may leave the system without any constraint. Therefore, the shared data can be submitted to a low modification rate, while the rate of node arrival/departure is very important. We propose now solutions for that peer dynamicity.

Peer Arrival. When a new peer *p* joins the system, it contacts some existing peers to determine the set of its neighbors. If one of those neighbors is a partner peer, *p* becomes a new partner: a new element is added to the cooperation list with a freshness value v equal to one. Recall that the value 1 indicates the need of pulling the peer to get new data descriptions. Furthermore, if *p* is a neighbor of two partners of two different summaries, it allows merging them in a higher-coverage one (Section 3.1).

Peer Departure. When a partner peer *p* decides to leave the system, it first sets its freshness value v to two in the cooperation list, through a push message. This value reminds the participation of the disconnected peer p to the corresponding global summary, but also indicates the unavailability of the original data. There are two alternatives to deal with such a freshness value. First, we can keep the data descriptions and use it, when a query is approximately answered using the global summary. A second alternative consists in considering the data descriptions as expired, since the original data are not accessible. Thus, a partner departure will accelerate the summary reconciliation initiating. In the rest of this paper, we adopt the second alternative and consider only a *1*-bit freshness value v: a value 0 to indicate the freshness of data descriptions, and a value 1 to indicate either their expiration or their unavailability. However, if p failed, it could not notify its partners by its departure. In that case, its data descriptions will remain in the global summary until we execute a new summary reconciliation. The reconciliation algorithm does not require the participation of a disconnected peer. The global summary GS is reconstructed, and descriptions of unavailable data will be then omitted.

4 Query Processing

Now we discuss how a query Q, posed at a peer p, is processed. Our approach consists in querying at first the available summary . This allows an efficient peer localization since we exploit data descriptions rather than structural information on data schemas, in order to propagate the query. Besides, when an exact answer is not required, summaries can directly provide approximate answers without accessing original database records. Query processing proceeds in two phases: 1) query extension and 2) query evaluation.

4.1 Query Extension

First, the query Q must be extended to a flexible query Q^* in order to be handled by a summary querying process. For instance, consider the following selection query Q[1]:

Select BMI From Patient Where age $\prec 30$ *And disease* = *"Malaria"*

This phase consists in replacing the original value of each selection predicate by the corresponding descriptors defined in the Background Knowledge (*BK*). According to the fuzzy partition of Figure 2, the above query is transformed to Q^*:

Select BMI From Patient Where age In $\{young, adult\}$ *And disease* = *"Malaria"*

Let QS (resp.QS^*) be the *Query Scope* of query Q (resp.Q^*), that is; the set of peers that should be visited to answer the query. Obviously, the query extension phase may induce false positives in query results. To illustrate, a patient having 35 years old will be returned as an answer to the query Q^*, while the selection predicate on the attribute age of the original query Q is not satisfied. However, false negatives can not occur which is expressed by the following inclusion: $QS \subseteq QS^*$.

In the rest of this paper, we suppose that a user query is directly formulated using descriptors defined in the BK (i.e. $Q = Q^*$). As we discussed in the introduction of this

[1] Body Mass Index (BMI) is the patient's body weight divided by the square of the height.

work, a doctor that participates to a given medical collaboration, may ask query Q like "the BMI of *young* and *adult* patients diagnosed with *malaria*".Thus, we eliminate eventual false positives that result from query extension.

4.2 Query Evaluation

This phase deals with matching a set of summaries organized in a hierarchy S, against the query Q. The query is transformed into a logical proposition P used to qualify the link between a summary node and the query. P is under a conjunctive form in which all descriptors appears as literals. In consequence, each set of descriptors yields on corresponding clause. For instance, the above query Q is transformed to $P =$ *(young OU adult) ET (malaria)*. A valuation function has been defined to valuate the proposition P in the context of a summary node z. Then, a selection algorithm performs a fast exploration of the hierarchy and returns the set Z_Q of most precise summaries that satisfy the query. For more details see [20]. Once Z_Q determined, the query evaluation process is able to achieve two distinct tasks depending on the user/application requirements: 1) Peer localization to return the original result records and 2) Summary answering to return approximate answers.

Peer Localization. Since the extended definition of a summary node z provides a peer-extent, i.e. the set of peers P_z having data described by its intent (see Definition 2), we can define the set P_Q of relevant peers for the query Q as follows: $P_Q = \{\cup_{z \in Z_Q} P_z\}$.

The query Q is directly propagated to these relevant peers. Thus, a distinctive feature of our approach is that the number of hops the queries makes to find the matching nodes is "ideally" reduced to one, and consequently, excessive delays are avoided. However, the efficiency of this query routing depends on the completeness and the freshness of summaries, since stale answers may occur in query results. We define a *False Positive* as the case in which a peer p belongs to P_Q and there is actually no data in the p source that satisfies Q (i.e. $p \notin QS$). A *False Negative* is the reverse case in which a p does not belong to P_Q, whereas there exists at least one tuple in the p data source that satisfies Q (i.e. $p \in QS$).

Summary Answering. Another distinctive feature is that a query can be processed entirely in the summary domain. An approximate answer can be provided from summary descriptions, without having to access original, distributed database records. The selected summaries Z_Q are aggregated according to their interpretation of proposition P: summaries that have the same required characteristics on all predicates (i.e. *age* and *disease*) form a class. The aggregation in a given class is a union of descriptors: for each attribute of the selection list (i.e. *BMI*), the querying process supplies a set of descriptors which characterize summaries that respond to the query through the same interpretation [20]. For example, for the class $\{$*young*, *malaria*$\}$, we can obtain an output set *BMI* = $\{$*underweight*, *normal*$\}$.

5 Performance Evaluation

In this section, we devise a simple model of the summary management cost in PeerSum. Then, we evaluate and analyze our model with a simulation.

5.1 Cost Model

A critical issue in summary management is to trade off the summary updating cost against the benefits obtained for queries.

Summary Update Cost. Here, our first undertaking is to optimize the update cost while taking into account *query accuracy*. In the next section, we discuss query accuracy which is measured in terms of the percentage of false positives and false negatives in query results. The cost of updating summaries is divided into: usage of peer resources, i.e. time cost and storage cost, and the traffic overhead generated in the network.

Time cost: A unique feature of SAINTETIQ is that the changes in the database are reflected through an incremental maintenance of the summary hierarchy. The time complexity of the summarization process is in $O(n)$ where n is the number of tuples to be incorporated in that hierarchy [16]. For a global summary, we are concerned with the complexity of merging summaries. Recently, a new MERGING method has been proposed, based on the SAINTETIQ engine. This method consists in incorporating the leaves of a given summary hierarchy S_1 into an another S_2, using the same algorithm described by the SAINTETIQ summarization service. It has been proved that the complexity C_{M12} of the MERGING(S_1, S_2) process is constant w.r.t the number of tuples.

Storage cost: We denote by k the average size of a summary node. In the average-case assumption, there are $\sum_{i=0}^{d} B^i = (B^{d+1} - 1)/(B - 1)$ nodes in a B-arity tree with d, the average depth of the hierarchy. Thus the average space requirement is given by: $C_m = k.(B^{d+1} - 1)/(B - 1)$. Based on real test, $k = 512$ bytes gives a rough estimation of the space required for each summary node. An important issue is that the size of the hierarchy is quite related to its stabilization (i.e. B and d). As more tuples are processed, the need to adapt the hierarchy decreases and incorporating a new tuple may consist only in sorting a tree. Hence, the structure of the hierarchy remains stable and no additional space is required.

According to the above discussion, the usage of peer resources is optimized by the summarization process itself. Thus, we restrict now our focus to the traffic overhead generated in the P2P network.

Network traffic: Recall that there are two types of exchanged messages: *push* and *reconciliation*. Let local summaries have an average lifetime of L seconds in a given global summary. Once L expired, the node sends a (push) message to update its freshness value v in the cooperation list CL. The reconciliation algorithm is then initiated whenever the following condition is satisfied: $\sum_{v \in CL} v/|CL| \geq \alpha$ where α is a threshold that represents the ratio of old descriptions tolerated in the global summary. During reconciliation, only one message is propagated among all partner peers until the new global summary version is inserted in the common storage. Let F_{rec} be the reconciliation frequency. The update cost is: $C_{up} = 1/L + F_{rec}$ messages per node per second. In this expression, $1/L$ represents the number of push messages which depends either on the modification rate issued on local summaries or the connection/disconnection rate of peers in the system. Higher is the rate, lower is the lifetime L, and thus a large number of push messages are entailed in the system. F_{rec} represents the number of reconciliation messages which depends on the value of α. This threshold is our system parameter that provides a trade-off between the cost of summary updating and query accuracy. If α is large, the update cost is low since a low frequency of reconciliation is required, but query results may be less accurate due both to false positives stemming from the descriptions of non existent data, and to false negatives due to the loss of relevant data descriptions whereas they are available in the system. If α is small, the update cost is high but there are few query results that refers to data no longer in the system, and nearly all available results are returned by the query.

Query Cost. We have seen that the use of summaries as data indexes may improve query processing. When a query Q is posed at a peer p, first it is matched against the global summary to determine the set of peers P_Q whose descriptions are considered as answers. Then, Q is directly propagated to those peers. As a consequence, the number of messages exchanged in the system is intended to be significantly reduced. Furthermore, the cooperation list associated with a global summary provides information about the relevance of each database description. Thus, it gives more flexibility in tuning the trade-off *recall* ρ / *precision* π of the query answers. Let V be the set of peers visited while processing a query. Then $\rho = |QS \cap V|/|QS|$ and $\pi = |QS \cap V|/|V|$, where QS is the set of all peers that really match the query (i.e. *Query Scope*).

The trade-off can be tuned by confronting the set P_Q with the cooperation list CL. The set of all partner peers P_H in CL can be divided into two subsets: $P_{old} = \{p \in P_H \mid p.v = 1\}$, the set of peers whose descriptions are considered old, and $P_{fresh} = \{p \in P_H \mid p.v = 0\}$ the set of peers whose descriptions are considered fresh according to their current data instances. Thus, if a query Q is propagated only to the set $V = P_Q \cap P_{fresh}$, then precision is maximum since all visited peers are certainly matching peers (no false positives), but recall depends on the fraction of false negatives in query results that could be returned by the set of excluded peers $P_Q \backslash P_{fresh}$. On the contrary, if the query Q is propagated to the extended set $V = P_Q \cup P_{old}$, recall value is maximum since all matching peers are visited (no false negatives), but precision depends on the fraction of false positives in query results that are returned by the set of peers P_{old}.

The above two situations are bounds of a range of strategies available to propagate the query. In our experiments, we assume $V = P_Q$, the initial peer set. Thus, the cost is computed as $C_Q = 2 \cdot |P_Q|$ number of messages.

5.2 Discussion

We evaluated the performance of PeerSum through simulation, using the SimJava package [7] and the BRITE [8] universal topology generator. We calibrated our simulator using real data gathered in [17].

In a first set of experiments we quantified the trade-off between query accuracy and the cost of updating a global summary. Interesting results showed that the fraction of stale answers in query results is limited to 3% for a network size lower than 2000 peers. For the update cost, we observed that the total number of messages increases with the number of peers, but not surprisingly, the number of messages per node remains almost the same. In the expression of the update cost C_{up}, the number of push messages for a given peer is independent of network size. On the other hand, the number of reconciliation messages decreases slowly with the number of peers, for a given value of the threshold α. More interestingly, when the threshold value decreases (from 0.8 to 0.3) we noticed a small cost increasing of 1.2 on average. However, a small value of the threshold α allows to significantly reduce the fraction of stale answers in query results. We concluded therefore that tuning our system parameter, i.e. the threshold α, do not incur additional traffic overhead in the system, while improving query accuracy.

In the second set of experiments, we compare our algorithm for query processing against non-index/flooding algorithms which are very used in real life, due to their simplicity and the lack of complex state information at each peer. Here, we limit the flooding by a value 3 of TTL (Time-To-Live). Our algorithm SI showed the best results that can be expected from any query processing algorithm, when no stale answers occur in query results (the ideal case). However, to give a real performance evaluation, we decided to study our algorithm in the worst case where the stale answers occur in query results. Even in that, SI showed a reduction of the number of messages, in comparison with flooding algorithms, that becomes more important with a large size of network. For instance, the query cost is reduced by a factor of 3 for a network of 2000 peers.

6 Conclusion

In this paper, we proposed PeerSum, a new service for managing data summaries in P2P and Grid systems. PeerSum supports scaling up in terms of two dimensions: number of participants and amount of data. As we discussed, our summaries are compact data descriptions that can approximately answer a query without retrieving original records from distributed databases. This is very interesting for Grid applications which tend to be more data intensive. On the other hand, as indexing structures, they support locating relevant data based on their content. Such semantic indexes are extremely efficient in large distributed systems, where accessing data becomes difficult and costly. Besides, we have addressed peer dynamicity which is critical in both P2P and Grid applications.

This paper made two main contributions. First, we defined a summary model for P2P systems, based on the SAINTETIQ process. SAINTETIQ generates database summaries with low complexity, and can be distributed and parallelized which makes it scalable in a distributed environment. Second, we proposed efficient algorithms for summary management in PeerSum. Our analysis and simulation results showed that the use of summaries as data indexes reduces the cost of query routing by an important factor compared to flooding approaches, without incurring high costs in terms of update messages exchanged in the network. Furthermore, our system guarantees a good query accuracy which is measured in terms of the fraction of stale answers in query results. Moreover, tuning our system parameter, i.e. the freshness threshold α, improves query accuracy while inducing a small increasing of summary update cost.

References

1. K. Aberer *et* al. P-grid: a self-organizing structured P2P system. *SIGMOD Rec.*, 32(3), 2003.
2. R. Akbarinia, V. Martins, E. Pacitti, and P. Valduriez. Replication and query processing in the APPA data management system. In *Workshop on Distributed Data and Structures (WDAS'2004)*, 2004.

3. A. Chakravarti, G. Baumgartner, and M. Lauria. The organic grid: self-organizing computation on a peer-to-peer network. *IEEE Transactions on Systems, Man, and Cybernetics, Part A*, 35(3):373–384, 2005.
4. A. Crespo and H. Garcia-Molina. Routing indices for peer-to-peer systems. In *Proc. of the 28 tn Conference on Distributed Computing Systems*, July 2002.
5. A. Crespo and H. Garcia-Molina. Semantic overlay networks for P2P systems. Technical report, Computer Science Department, Stanford University, 2002.
6. I. Foster and A. Iamnitchi. On death, taxes, and the convergence of peer-to-peer and grid computing. In *IPTPS*, pages 118–128, 2003.
7. F. Howell and R. McNab. Simjava: a discrete event simulation package for java with the applications in computer systems modeling. In *Int. Conf on Web-based Modelling and Simulation, San Diego CA, Society for Computer Simulation*, 1998.
8. http://www.cs.bu.edu/brite/.
9. http://www.ogsadai.org.uk. Open grid services architecture data access and integration.
10. http://www.snomed.org/snomedct.
11. G. Koloniari, Y. Petrakis, and E. Pitoura. Content–based overlay networks of xml peers based on multi-level bloom filters. In *Proc VLDB*, september 2003.
12. A. Oser, F. Naumann, W. Siberski, W. Nejdl, and U. Thaden. Semantic overlay clusters within super-peer networks. In *Proc of the International Workshop on Databases, Information Systems and Peer-to-Peer Computing in Conjunction with the VLDB 2003*, 2003.
13. T. Ozsu and P. Valduriez. *Principles of Distributed Database Systems*. Prentice Hall, 1999.
14. G. Raschia and N. Mouaddib. A fuzzy set-based approach to database summarization. *Fuzzy sets and systems 129(2)*, pages 137–162, 2002.
15. S. Ratnasamy, P. Francis, M. Handley, R. Karp, and S. Shenker. A scalable content–addressable network. In *Proc SIGCOMM*, 2001.
16. R. Saint-Paul, G. Raschia, and N. Mouaddib. General purpose database summarization. In *Proc VLDB*, pages 733–744, 2005.
17. S. Saroiu, P. Gummadi, and S. Gribble. A measurement study of peer-to-peer file sharing systems. In *Proc of Multimedia Computing and Networking (MMCN)*, 2002.
18. I. Stoica, R. Morris, D. Karger, M. Kaashoek, and H. Balakrishnan. Chord: A scalabale peer-to-peer lookup service for internet applications. In *Proc ACM SIGCOMM*, 2001.
19. I. Tartinov *et* al. The piazza peer data management project. In *SIGMOD Record, 32(3)*, 2003.
20. A. Voglozin, G. Raschia, L. Ughetto, and N. Mouaddib. Querying the SAINTETIQ summaries-a first attempt. In *Int Conf. On Flexible Query Answering Systems (FQAS)*, 2004.
21. L. Zadeh. Concept of a linguistic variable and its application to approximate reasoning. *Information and Systems*, 1:119–249, 1975.

A High-Performance Virtual Storage System for Taiwan UniGrid

Chien-Min Wang[1], Hsi-Min Chen[2], Chun-Chen Hsu[3], and Jan-Jan Wu[1]

[1] Institute of Information Science, Academia Sinica, Taipei, Taiwan
[2] Department of Computer Science and Information Engineering, National Central University, Taoyuan, Taiwan
[3] Department of Computer Science and Information Engineering, National Taiwan University, Taipei, Taiwan
{cmwang, seeme, tk, wuj}@iis.sinica.edu.tw

Abstract. In Taiwan, a community of educational and research organizations interested in Grid computing technologies founded a Grid computing platform, called Taiwan UniGrid. Taiwan UniGrid consists of three primary portions: Computational Grid, Data Grid, and Web Portal. In this paper, we present the development of a virtual data storage system for Taiwan UniGrid. In addition to developing basic data storage functions, we identify three main requirements of the current development: high-performance data transfer, data sharing and single sing-on. For these requirements, we come up with three corresponding features in our data storage system: Self-Adaptation for high-performance data transfer, forming user groups and specifying admission control for data sharing, and adopting GSI authentication to enable single sing-on. Besides, we also develop a Java-based graphic user interface of the storage system that allows Grid users to manage data transparently as using local file systems.

Keywords: Data Grid, data storage system, data transfer, web service, and single sign-on.

1 Introduction

With the rapid growth of computing power and storage capacity of computers, many researchers and scientists have been concentrated on the development of various Grid systems to efficiently utilize distributed computing and storage resources in recent years. In Taiwan, a community of educational and research organizations interested in Grid computing technologies founded a Grid computing platform, called Taiwan UniGrid [1]. These organizations contribute their resources of computer clusters for sharing and collaboration. The objective of Taiwan UniGrid is to provide educational and research organizations with a powerful computing platform where they can study Grid-related issues, practice parallel programming on Grid environments and execute computing/data-intensive applications.

As similar to other Grid systems, Taiwan UniGrid consists of three primary portions: Computational Grid, Data Grid and Web Portal. Computational Grid is responsible for managing scattered and heterogeneous computing resources and scheduling

C. Cérin and K.-C. Li (Eds.): GPC 2007, LNCS 4459, pp. 27 – 38, 2007.

the jobs submitted by users. Data Grid is a virtual storage infrastructure that integrates distributed, independently managed data resources and allows users to save and retrieve their data without understanding the configuration of underlying storage resources. Web Portal, developed by National Tsing Hua University, is a uniform user interface by which Grid users can design workflow, submit jobs, manage data, monitor job and resource status, etc. In this paper, we will present the development of the data management system for Taiwan UniGrid.

As the distribution of storage resources and the growth of data size, the needs for efficient Grid data management are continuously increasing. In these years, many research and scientific organizations have engaged in building data management and storage tools for Grids, such as SDSC SRB (Storage Resource Broker) [2], SciDAC Data Grid Middleware [3], GriPhyN Virtual Data System [4], etc. SRB is a general Data Grid middleware that integrates distributed and heterogeneous storage resources and provides virtualized access interface. It has been a production data management tool and adopted by several Grid projects. Thus, among these tools, we decide to build our virtual storage system for Taiwan UniGrid based on SRB, while developing additional features that are not well supported by SRB.

Before implementing the virtual storage system, we elicited requirements from the user and manager needs. Herein, in additional to the basic Data Grid functions provided by SRB, we identify three main requirements of the current development listed as follows.

- **High-performance data transfer:** Since the size of data generated by scientific instruments and Grid applications has grown into the range of Terabytes, large data transfer over the Internet usually leads to a long latency and becomes a bottleneck for job executions. Thus, the need for high-performance data transfer is an important issue in Taiwan UniGrid.
- **Data sharing:** Two important concepts of Grids are sharing and collaboration. Grid users, such as scientists and researchers, are accustomed to retrieve data collected by remote scientific instruments, analyze these retrieved data via various analysis tools, and share the analyzed results for further processing. Therefore, how to facilitate Grid users to contribute or get shared data with ease is a crucial requirement in the development of a data management system.
- **Single sign-on:** In essence, physical resources within a Grid system are distributed in different organizations and managed independently. Each organization has its own security policy. Without single sign-on mechanisms, Grid users have to keep a list of accounts for each machine by themselves. This becomes an obstacle for users to use Grid systems. Hence, we have to take the problem of single sign-on into account when we integrate our system with Computational Grid and UniGrid Portal.

Consequently, in our system, we come up with three features with respect to the corresponding requirements. For high-performance data transfer, we propose a multi-source data transfer algorithm, called Self Adaptation [5], which can speed up the data transfer rate in data replication, downloading, moving, and copying. For data sharing, our system allows Grid users to share their data in a manner of forming user groups and specifying admission control on each data object. For the issue of single sign-on, we choose GSI (Grid Security Infrastructure) [6] as our user certification mechanism by which Grid users only have to login once and utilize Grid resources through certificates, so that they have no need to keep all accounts for each machine. Besides these features, we also develop a Java-based graphic user interface of the storage system that allows Grid users to manipulate data transparently as using local file systems.

The remainder of the paper is organized as follows. In Section 2, we explain the system framework and deployment. Section 3 presents main features, including multi-source data transfer, data sharing, single sign-on, and the data management client. An operational scenario of Taiwan UniGrid is demonstrated in Section 4. Finally, we present some concluding remarks in the last section.

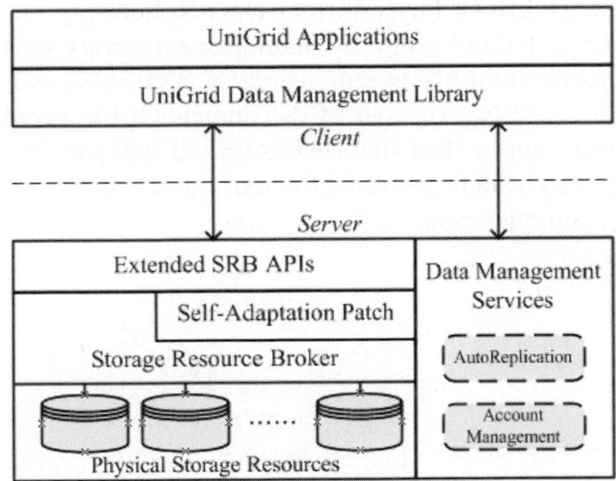

Fig. 1. The framework of the virtual storage system for Taiwan UniGrid

2 System Framework and Deployment

Figure 1 shows the framework of our virtual storage system. In the server side, the left bottom of the framework is a set of physical storage resources, including hard disks, tapes and databases, contributed by the members of Taiwan UniGrid. We adopt SRB as a data management middleware to integrate these scattered storage resources. SRB provides a list of data and storage management functions. Although SRB has furnished an efficient data transfer approach by using multiple TCP connections, we propose an alternative, called Self Adaptation, to get a higher data transfer rate in comparison with the original one. We will explain the detail of Self Adaptation in section 3. Therefore, we add the alternative (Self Adaptation Patch) into the original functions of SRB. A set of extended SRB APIs are built on top of SRB and the Self Adaptation Patch. The extended SRB APIs consist of primary APIs provided by SRB and the APIs for high-performance data transfer, such as `MSDTReplicate()` and `MSDTCopy()`.

The right of the server side of the framework is a number of Web services used for data management. Web service technologies are playing an increasingly important role in the new generation of Grids. Such technologies encapsulate heterogeneous software components, legacy systems and resources as services and simply describe their interfaces in a standard description language, i.e. WSDL [7]. Service providers can advertise their services in a registry, i.e. the UDDI [8] server, for clients to browse. If clients want to use the services advertised in a registry, the SOAP [9] technology helps them access the services through standard transport protocols, such as HTTP and SMTP. Therefore, we adopt Web services technologies in our system to integrate other software developed by third parties. There are two services implemented in the current system: the AutoReplication service, developed by Chung Hua University, and the Account Management service. The AutoReplication service help Grid users set various replication policies on data objects. The Account Management service is developed by wrapping up the functions of user authentication in UniGrid Portal for single sign-on.

In the client side, the bottom is the data management library for UniGrid which interacts with the corresponding server-side extended SRB APIs and data management services. We implemented two versions of the library. One is Java-based and another is C-based. The data management library provides a uniform interface of data and storage management by which programmers can build various Grid applications to access the underling storage resources.

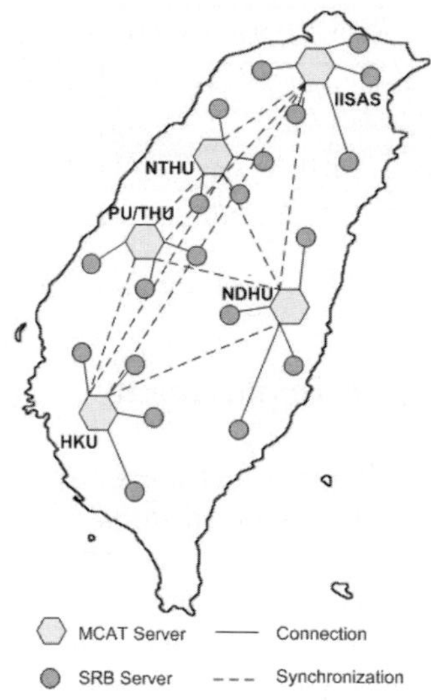

Fig. 2. The deployment of the virtual storage system for Taiwan UniGrid

Figure 2 presents the deployment of our virtual storage system. Since there is a huge amount of storage resources distributed in Taiwan UniGrid, using a single information server to maintain the metadata regarding users, data and storages may cause the problems of server overloading and single point of failure. To avoid these problems, we divided all storage resources in Taiwan UniGrid into five zones, i.e. Taipei_UniGrid, Hsinchu_UniGrid, Taichung_UniGrid, Tainan_UniGrid and Hualien_UniGrid. Each zone has a MCAT (SRB Metadata Catalog) server installed for maintaining the metadata of the users, data, and storage resources. To enable the flexibility of sharing, the administrators of a MCAT server can specify their won sharing policies, for instance, some resources can be shared with users registered in other zones, but some are utilized in private. In addition, each MCAT server periodically synchronizes its metadata with each other to keep the metadata consistency among zones. By synchronization, Grid users registered in one zone can access storage resources located in other zones and retrieve sharing data timely.

The members of Taiwan UniGrid contribute their storage resources by setting up SRB servers. Each SRB server consists of one or more physical storage resources and is registered to a MCAT server. Gird users can manipulate data objects in a specified storage resource of a SRB server, for example uploading data objects, creating replicas and modifying metadata of the data objects. Then the SRB server will automatically ask the MCAT server, which registers the SRB server, to update the metadata of the operated data object and synchronize with other MCAT servers. Thus, a Grid user who logins to one of close SRB servers can utilize storage resources in any zone of Taiwan UniGrid.

3 Main Features

In this section, we present the main features of our system, including multi-source data transfer, data sharing, single sign-on, for the requirements listed in Section 1. In addition, we also develop a friendly graphic user interface of the virtual storage system that helps Grid users manage their data as using local file systems.

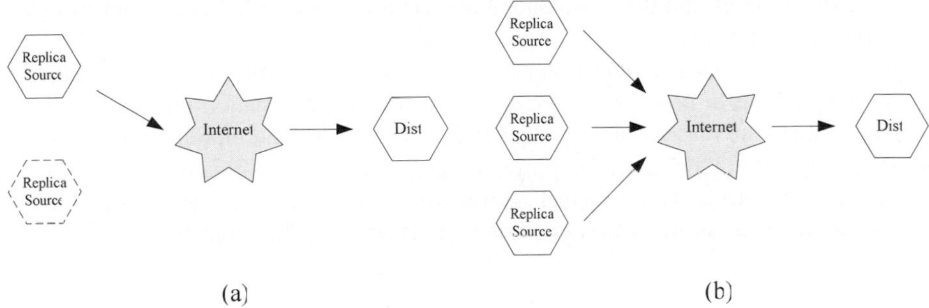

Fig. 3. (a) The replica selection approach. **(b)** The multi-source data transfer approach.

3.1 Multi-source Data Transfer

To achieve high-performance data transfer, data replication has been a widely used technique that facilitates a Grid user to select a best replica site closest to the specific destination and transfer the selected replica to it. Instead of transferring data from the source site, selecting the best replica can reduce the data transfer time on the Internet. A number of approaches have been proposed for selecting the best replica based on various criteria [10, 11]. However, as shown in Figure 3(a), since such an approach only allows users to specify one replica for transfer in each selection, they have two major shortcomings:

- When several replicas have almost the same network performance, choosing a slightly better replica and discarding all others does not fully utilize network resources.
- Selecting only one replica may degrade transfer reliability because, if the connection to the selected replica fails, it has to execute the selection algorithm again and reconnect to other replicas.

Some multi-source data transfer mechanisms have been presented recently to solve the above problems [12, 13], whereby a transferred data object can be assembled in parallel from multiple distributed replica sources as shown in Figure 3(b). To improve the data transfer rate, we propose an efficient data transfer algorithm, called Self-Adaptation. It not only enables the data transfer from multiple replica sites as other multi-source data transfer algorithms, but is also more adaptive to the network bandwidth fluctuations. Self-Adaptation assigns proper segments of transferred data to each replica site based on the overhead and bandwidth measured from the previous data transfer, so that it can achieve higher aggregate bandwidth. More information of Self-Adaptation and performance comparisons with other approaches can be found in [5].

Multi-source data transfer is the major contribution to the development of the data storage system. In the client-side library of the current system, we implement three alternative functions of data transfer based on Self-Adaptation to enable high-performance data transfer.

- *MSDTDownload()*: Grid users or programs can download data objects to their local file systems and the downloaded objects are reassembled in parallel from the source and replica sites.
- *MSDTReplicate()*: Grid users or programs, for example the AutoReplication service, can make new data replicas to the specified destination resources and the new replicas are reassembled in parallel from the source and replica sites.
- *MSDTCopy()*: Grid users or programs can make copies of data objects to the specified directories of the virtual storage system and the copies are reassembled in parallel from the source and replica sites of the original data objects.

3.2 Date Sharing

According to the literature survey, we found that Grid users usually need a platform where they can work collaboratively. Although most Data Grid middleware provides the sharing of storage resources, data sharing for collaborative work is not well supported. Therefore, in our system, we develop a collaborative platform through the combinations of forming user groups and specifying access permissions on each data object.

In our system, a group of users who need to work together can ask the administrators to form a user group. For instance, a user group can be built according to some research topics in which a group of users are interested. Each Grid user can take part in many user groups simultaneously as long as he/she gets the grants from the administrators. Once an administrator creates a user group, the system will create a group workspace, i.e. a group home directory, for sharing and collaboration. Each group workspace can assign one or more owners to manage the admission of the workspace.

In general, Grid users have their own personal workspace, i.e. a user home directory, where they can manage their private data objects. Data objects can be files, directories, replicas or links. Grid users can share their private data objects with others via specifying access permissions on data objects. Figure 4 shows a screenshot of admission control for data sharing, by which Grid users can specify read or write permission for each data object to other users or groups. It also supports the owner change of a specific data object. On the other hand, Grid users can share their data by uploading or copying private data objects directly to the group workspaces.

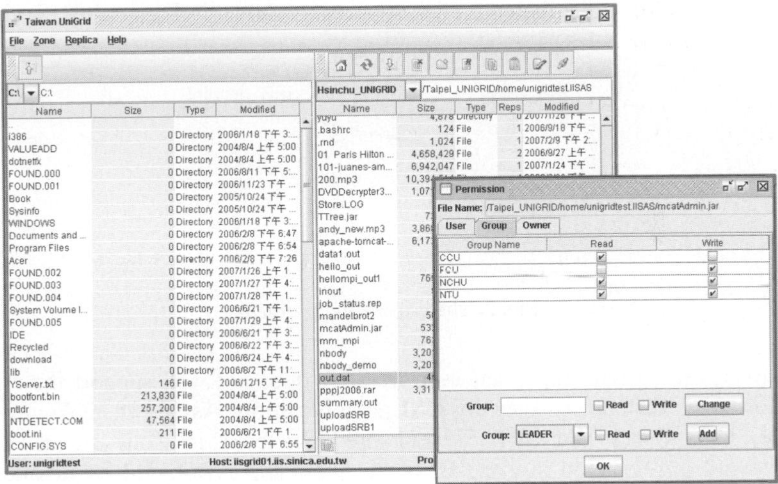

Fig. 4. A screenshot of the data management client and admission control for data sharing

3.3 Single Sign-On

Since software components and resources within a Grid system are distributed in different organizations and managed independently, using one account for a Grid user to utilize all these software components and resources becomes a crucial issue. GSI (Grid Security Infrastructure) [6] is a promising solution to the issue in Grids. GSI uses X.509 certificates to securely authenticate users across the network. Moreover, SRB supports two main methods of authentication, GSI and an SRB secure password system known as Encrypt1. GSI in SRB makes use of the same certificates and Public Key Infrastructure (PKI) [14] as do Globus Toolkit [15] such as GridFTP [16]. Since we adopt Globus Toolkit as the middleware for managing computing resources, in order to enable the single sign-on for utilizing Computational Grid and Data Grid, we choose GSI as the main user authentication mechanism in our system.

To use Taiwan UniGrid, Grid users have to register in UniGrid Portal first. The users will receive certificates issued from UniGrid CA after approved by system administrators. Meanwhile, the users' profiles are also registered to Computational Grid and

Data Grid, i.e. Globus and SRB. Once users want to use Taiwan UniGrid, they can login to UniGrid Portal through their certificates and the system will automatically generate corresponding secure proxy certificates which are good for a few hours to submit jobs and manage data in distributed resources.

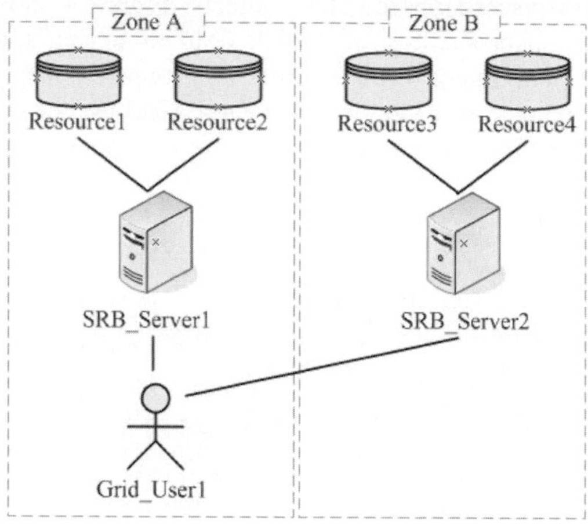

Fig. 5. The cross-zone problem

However, the current implementation of SRB does not well support the resource utilization cross difference zones by GSI authentication. As shown in Figure 5, for example, Grid_User1 and SRB_Server1 are registered in Zone A, as well as SRB_Server2 is registered in Zone B. If we adopt the Java-based client-side APIs, named Jargon, provided by SRB, Grid_User1 connecting to SRB_Server2 by GSI authentication will be failed to access the resources (Resouce3 and Resource4) in Zone B. We call this incident as the cross-zone problem. At present, SRB only supports the access to cross-zone resources through secure password authentication, Encrypt1. Since we deployed our system in five zones and developed Self-Adaptation approach to reassemble data objects in parallel from multiple replica sources, which may be located in different zones, it causes the cross-zone problem. We will address this problem from two perspectives, users and programs, in the following paragraphs.

From the perspective of users, we intent to make Grid users login once by certificates and launch the data management client to manipulate their data without concerning with the cross-zone problem. Thus, we propose an authentication process, as depicted in Figure 6(a), to enable single sing-on for UniGrid Portal and the data management client.

After a Grid user logins to Web Portal successfully, the portal asks the Account Management service to create a session and returns necessary information, including a generated session key and a profile for SRB to connect. The Grid user can launch the data management client to access data in storage resources after login to Web Portal. While launching the data management client, Web Portal passes the session key and SRB-related information to the client and then the client uses the session key to obtain the user's password through SSL from the Account Management service.

Finally, the client uses the password and SRB-related information to connect to a SRB server in Encrypt1. Once connecting successfully, the Account Management service removes the session. This prevents malicious users from using the cached session keys to retrieve passwords from the Account Management service.

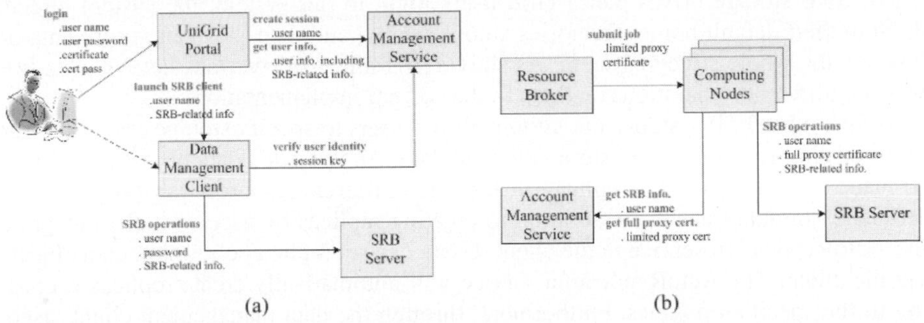

Fig. 6. **(a)** The proposed authentication process enabling single sing-on for UniGrid Portal and the data management client. **(b)** The proposed authentication process enabling single sing-on for computing nodes.

From the perspective of programs, Resource Broker delegates submitted jobs to computing nodes with limited proxy certificates, not full proxy certificate, for authentication. However, in the current implementation of SRB, the limited proxy certificates will be failed in accessing storage resources located in different zones. Only full proxy certificates are allowed to access the cross-zone resources in SRB. Hence, we propose an authentication process for computing nodes, as shown in Figure 6(b), to deal with this problem. After Resource Broker submits jobs to computing nodes with limited proxy certificates, the computing nodes use the limited proxy certificates to get full proxy certificates from the Account Management service. Finally, the nodes can connect to SRB servers located in different zones with full proxy certificates and access programs and data in the storage resources.

Table 1. The supported operations for data objects in the virtual storage system

Data object	Operations
File	download, upload, delete, copy, paste, rename
Directory	create, download, upload, delete, copy, paste, rename
Link	create, download, delete, copy, paste, rename
Replica	create, delete

3.4 The Data Management Client

We develop two kinds of clients of the virtual storage system. One is Java-based standalone version not integrated with UniGrid Portal and Computational Gird. It is suitable for users who just want to store their data without the need of computation support. Another one is Java Web Start version which is embedded in UniGrid Portal. Grid users can launch the client directly from UniGrid Portal after they login.

Figure 4 shows a screenshot of the data management client. The left of the client is the file and directory list of local storage drives and the right is the file and directory list of SRB storage drives. Once Grid users login to our system, the system directs them to their default home directories automatically, and then they can access data or traverse the whole storage system. As shown in Table 1, for various data objects, we provide difference operations on them in the current implementation.

Unlike other FTP systems, our system allows users to specify storage resources, for instance closest resources, to store uploaded data. An uploaded data object can further be made several copies, i.e. replicas, disturbed in different resources for reliability and efficiency of data transfer. In addition to creating replicas by users, we also integrate the AutoReplication service in the client. Users can set replica policies on data objects via the client. The AutoReplication service will automatically create replicas according to the specified policies. Furthermore, through the data management client, users can also specify access permissions on data objects, as shown in Figure 4, for sharing and collaboration.

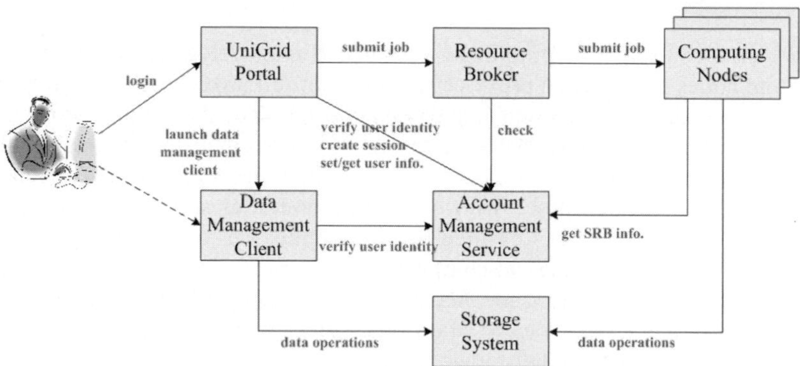

Fig. 7. The major components of Taiwan UniGrid and their interactions

4 Operation Scenario of Taiwan UniGrid

In this section, we will demonstrate an operation scenario of using Taiwan UniGrid. Figure 7 shows the major components of Taiwan UniGrid and their interactions. The high-level operation scenario is explained as follows.

- A Grid user logins to UniGrid Portal by entering his/her account and password and UniGrid Portal employs Account Management service to verify user's identity.
- If login successfully, UniGrid Portal directs the user to his/her working web page, as shown in Figure 8.
- He/she launches the data management client (Figure 4) and uploads programs and data needed for the jobs, which will be submitted later, to the data storage system.

- The user makes an execution plan for a job or designs a workflow of jobs on the working web page.
- Once the user has submitted a job, the portal asks Resource Broker to select computing resources based on the requirement of the submitted job.
- Resource Broker assigns the submitted job to the selected computing nodes. The selected computing nodes then retrieve programs and data from the storage system.
- The selected computing nodes start computing.
- Once all computing nodes finish their work, the computed results are merged and stored back to the storage system.
- For reliability, the newly stored data can be replicated to other storage resources by the user or the AutoReplocator service.

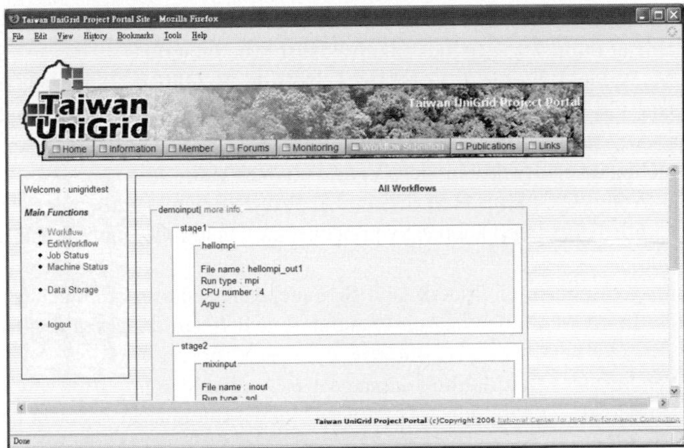

Fig. 8. The Taiwan UniGrid Portal

5 Conclusion

In this paper, we present the development of a high-performance virtual storage system for Taiwan UniGrid. We employ SRB (Storage Resource Broker) as a basis to implement the functions of the storage system. Besides, we identify three main requirements in the current implementation: high-performance data transfer, data sharing, and single sign-on. To meet these requirements, we propose the corresponding features: Self-Adaptation for high-performance data transfer, forming user groups and specifying admission control for data sharing, and adopting GSI authentication to enable single sing-on. We also develop a Java-based user interface of the storage system allowing Grid users to manage their data transparently without concerning the low-level deployment of storage resources. In the future, we will continue developing new features in our system to make it more useful. On the other hand, we will execute more data-intensive applications on our system to examine its reliability and scalability.

Acknowledgement

This work was supported in part by the National Center for High-performance Computing under the national project, “Taiwan Knowledge Innovation National Grid”, and in part by National Science Council under Contract No. NSC95-2221-E-001-002.

References

1. Taiwan UniGrid, http://www.unigrid.org.tw.
2. Chaitanya Baru, R. Moore, A. Rajasekar and M. Wan: The SDSC storage resource broker. CASCON '98: Proceedings of the 1998 conference of the Centre for Advanced Studies on Collaborative research, Canada (1998) also available at http://www.sdsc.edu/srb.
3. B. Allcock, A. Chervenak, I. Foster, C. Kesselman, and M. Livny: Data Grid tools: enabling science on big distributed data,” Journal of Physics: Conference Series 16 (2005) also available at http://www-fp.mcs.anl.gov/dsl/scidac/datagrid
4. Y. Zhao, M. Wilde, I. Foster, J. Voeckler, J. Dobson, E. Glibert, T. Jordan, and E. Quigg,: Virtual Data Grid Middleware Services for Data-Intensive Science. Concurrency and Computation: Practice & Experience, Vol. 18, Issue 6 (2004) also available at http://vds.uchicago.edu/twiki/bin/view/VDSWeb/WebMain
5. Chien-Min Wang, C.C. Hsu, H.M. Chen, J.J. Wu: Efficient multi-source data transfer in data grids,” 6th IEEE International Symposium on Cluster Computing and the Grid, Singapore (2006)
6. I. Foster, C. Kesselman, G. Tsudik, and S. Tuecke: A security architecture for computational grids. In ACM Conference on Computers and Security, pages 83–91, ACM Press (1998)
7. WSDL: Web Services Description Language 1.1. Available at http://www.w3.org/TR/wsdl
8. UDDI: Universal Description, Discovery and Integration (2001) Available at http://www.uddi.org
9. SOAP: Simple Object Access Protocol 1.1. Global Grid Forum, available at http://www.w3.org/TR/soap
10. Kavitha Ranganathan and I. Foster: Design and evaluation of dynamic replication strategies for a high performance data grid. In International Conference on Computing in High Energy and Nuclear Physics (2001)
11. S. Vazhkudai, S. Tuecke, and I. Foster: Replica selection in the globus data grid. In 1st International Symposium on Cluster Computing and the Grid, pages (2001) 106-113
12. Jun Feng and M. Humphrey, “Eliminating Replica Selection - Using Multiple Replicas to Accelerate Data Transfer on Grids,” In 10th International Conference on Parallel and Distributed Systems (2004). 359-366
13. C.T. Yang, S.Y. Wang, C.H. Lin, M.H. Lee, and T.Y Wu, “Cyber-Transformer: A Toolkit for Files Transfer with Replica Management in Data Grid Environments,” In the 2nd Workshop on Grid Technologies and Applications (WoGTA’05), Taiwan (2005)
14. Carlisle Adams and Steve Lloyd: Understanding Public-Key Infrastructure: Concepts, Standards, and Deployment Considerations. New Riders Publishing (1999)
15. Ian Foster and C. Kesselman: Globus: A Metacomputing Infrastructure Toolkit. The International Journal of Supercomputer Applications and High Performance Computing, vol. 11, No. 2, (1997) 115-128
16. B. Allcock, J. Bester, J. Bresnahan, A. L. Chervenak, I. Foster, C. Kesselman, S. Meder, V. Nefedova, D. Quesnel, and S. Tuecke: Data Management and Transfer in High-Performance Computational Grid Environments. Parallel Computing (2001)

Interoperable Grid PKIs Among Untrusted Domains: An Architectural Proposal

Valentina Casola[1], Jesus Luna[2], Oscar Manso[2], Nicola Mazzocca[1], Manel Medina[2], and Massimiliano Rak[3]

[1] University of Naples, Italy
Phone: +39-0817683907; Fax: +39-0817683916
{casolav,n.mazzocca}@unina.it
[2] Universitat Politècnica de Catalunya, Spain
Phone: +34-93 4016984; Fax: +34-9337947
{jluna, omanso, medina}@ac.upc.edu
[3] Second University of Naples, Italy
massimiliano.rak@unina2.it

Abstract. In the last years several Grid Virtual Organizations -VOs- have been proliferating, each one usually installing its own Certification Authority and thus giving birth to a large set of different and possibly untrusted security domains. Nevertheless, despite the fact that the adoption of Grid Certification Authorities (CAs) has partially solved the problem of identification and authentication between the involved parties, and that Public Key Infrastructure (PKI) technologies are mature enough, we cannot make the same assumptions when untrusted domains are involved. In this paper we propose an architecture to face the problem of secure interoperability among untrusted Grid-domains. Our approach is based on building a dynamic federation of CAs, formed thorough the quantitative and automatic evaluation of their Certificate Policies. In this paper we describe the proposed architecture and its integration into Globus Toolkit 4.

1 Introduction

Grid Resource owners can control access to their resources by means of well-established Authentication and Authorization processes for End-Entities. Nevertheless, despite the fact that the adoption of Certification Authorities (CAs) has partially solved the problem of identification and authentication between the involved parties, and that Public Key Infrastructure (PKI) technologies are mature enough, we cannot make the same assumptions when untrusted domains are involved. Let us take for example two different Grid-CAs which do not have a direct interoperability agreement (i.e. explicit cross-certifying procedure), but their researchers need to work together.

Furthermore, in the last years a lot of Grid Virtual Organizations (VOs) have been proliferating, each one usually installing its own Certification Authority and thus giving birth to a large set of different and possibly untrusted security domains. This represents one of the biggest interoperability problems that could arise among all Grid users and therefore one of the major security challenges to be faced before building a wide distributed infrastructure allowing the cooperation of existing Grid installations. In other words, this problem is related to the definition of a distributed infrastructure

C. Cérin and K.-C. Li (Eds.): GPC 2007, LNCS 4459, pp. 39–51, 2007.

able to guarantee a *secure degree of interoperability* among all the involved Grid-Certification Authorities.

In practice there are two commonly accepted approaches that provide interoperability between different security domains based on PKI technology:

1. Involved CAs *explicitly* build a trusted domain, defining a new CA hierarchy through cross certification techniques. In this case each CA explicitly trusts the others and therefore is able to accept their certificates.
2. Involved CAs do not build an explicit trusted domain, but interoperate through a "federation": any CA belonging to the federation *implicitly* trusts the others thanks to the definition of a well-established policy-based framework.

Even if the explicit trusted domain (first approach) is an attractive solution, it is not always possible to implement in Grid environments, because of the required agreements between the involved organizations, administrative overheads and technical problems that arise with current software (this is the case of the Globus Toolkit [1]).

For the computational Grid, the second of the aforementioned options (building a Federation of CAs) has been the most suitable solution for real-world projects so far. At this aim, the Policy Management Authorities (PMAs) have established a minimum set of requirements and best practices for Grid PKIs willing to join its federation. These minimum requirements comprise the *PMA's Authentication Profile*. It is important to note that the PMA itself does not provide identity assertions, but instead asserts that, within the scope of its charter, the certificates issued by their member-CAs meet or exceed its Authentication Profile. In summary, Grid's Policy Management Authorities represent "Federations of Grid PKIs" whose CA members accomplish minimum levels of security.

In the case of the existing Grid PMAs (TAGPMA [2], EUGridPMA [3], APGridPMA [4] and IGTF [5]) compliance with their respective authentication profile is given through a well-defined, but mostly manual, process involving a careful analysis of the applicant PKI's Certificate Policy (CP) [6], performed just once, when a new CA wishes to be part of an existing PMA. This is known as the PMA's *accreditation process*.

It is also interesting to note that even though all the Grid CA members of a PMA must fulfill with the established authentication profile, not all of them accomplish these minimum requirement on the same level. Despite the importance of such information for building comprehensive Grid PKI's trust relationships and for Authentication/Authorization purposes, to date there is no automatic way to quantitatively compute a CA's compliance level according to a particular PMA's Authentication Profile.

With independence of the interoperability mechanism chosen (explicit trust or CA-federation), any client (commonly called End-Entity) invoking a Grid Service's operation from the server, activates an authentication process to attest his identity. This process requires *validating* the end-entity's digital certificate according to the *path validation* procedure described in [7].

When involved CAs interoperate thanks to explicit trust agreements, only *basic* path validation is required: cryptographic verifications and status' checks over the involved certificates. State of the art Grid software, like the Globus Toolkit, provides static mechanisms for the basic path validation, i.e. the administrators manually declares the accepted CAs, and locally update respective CRLs.

However, if the involved CAs are part of a Grid-federation, then *extended path validation* is needed: basic validation path enhanced with a *policy mapping* process that compares the involved CAs' Certificate Policies to assert that they fulfil with a particular Accreditation Profile and therefore can interoperate among them.

In previous woerk towards achieving extended path validation, our research groups proposed a Grid-Validation Infrastructure based on the use of the Online Certificate Status Protocol (OCSP) [8], just as presented in [9] and [10]. On the trust-research topic, in previous works we have proposed a formal methodology to compare and evaluate Certificate Policies from different CAs as published in [11], [12] and [13]. This paper is the result of gathering both the experiences to propose an architecture for enabling extended path validation in Grid environments, using both the validation infrastructure and the evaluation methodology.

The remainder of the paper is structured as follows: next section outlines the state of the art on Grid validation and PKI's security evaluation. Section 3 details the problem of Grid security interoperability and its relationship with the need of implementing a Trusted Third Party (TTP), which we managed by using the extended path validation concept. Section 4 outlines the basis of our approach, by showing our proposal for an architectural model for Grid interoperability. Section 5 introduces "POIS", a real implementation of the proposed validation architecture for the Globus Toolkit 4, which enables interoperability between untrusted domains. Section 6 summarizes the conclusions and future work.

2 State of the Art

Next will be briefly reviewed two Grid security topics, milestones of the proposal introduced later in this paper: the Grid validation and the PKI's security evaluation.

2.1 Grid Validation

In a PKI, all entities (users and resourccs) are identified by a globally unique name known as Distinguished Name (DN). In order for entities to prove their identity, they possess a set of Grid credentials consisting of a X.509 version 3 digital certificates [7] and a private key. The certificate is digitally signed by a Certification Authority that guarantees for the binding of the entity's DN to its private key.

The authentication mechanism, by means of digital certificates, involves the presentation of the certificate and proving possession of the corresponding private key. So, with the certificate being public, the only critical point is the preservation of the private key; to limit the danger of an entity's private key being stolen, two strategies are commonly adopted: *i)* the key is protected with encryption or by storing it on a hardware token (e.g. a smart card); *ii)* the private key has limited lifetime after which it is no longer valid. The Globus Toolkit's security implementation known as the Grid Security Infrastructure (GSI) [14] follows the second strategy using Proxy Certificates [15]: short-term credentials that are created by a user, which can then be used in place of traditional long-term credentials to authenticate him. The proxy certificate has its own private key and certificate, and is signed using the user's long-term credential. A typical session with the GSI would involve the Grid user (End-Entity) using its passphrase and the GSI's command *grid-proxy-init* to create a proxy certificate from its long-term credential. The user could then use a GSI-enabled application to invoke a service's operation from a Globus Toolkit's Grid Services Container [16]. If Message Level Security is being used for authentication [17], then the user's application would use the GSI library and the corresponding proxy certificate to authenticate to the remote host by means of a digitally signed message containing the service invocation.

From the Grid resource point of view, to fully perform the authentication process, a certificate validation service interface should be defined that can be used within the Open Grid Services Architecture (OGSA) [18] implementation to:

1. Parse a certificate and return desired attribute values, as the validity period, the Distinguish Name -to map it to a resource's local user- and so on.
2. Perform path validation [7] on a certificate chain according to the local policy and with local PKI facilities, such as certificate revocation lists (CRLs) or through an Online Certificate Status Protocol [8].
3. Return attribute information for generic KeyInfo values, thus allowing the use of different certificate formats or single keys, or to pull attribute information from directory services instead of certificates.

A certificate path validation process (step 2 above) must comprise at least the following four phases:

1. Cryptographic verifications over the certificate path (i.e. verifying the digital signature of each certificate).
2. Verifying each certificate validity period.
3. Verify that the first certificate in the chain is a Trust Anchor.
4. Verify the certificate's status to ensure that is has not been revoked or suspended.

For the rest of this paper the process just described will be referenced as *basic path validation*. Modern Grid installations like the Globus Toolkit [1] provide static mechanisms to perform the last two phases of the basic path validation process described above:

- The first certificate in the chain is considered a Trust Anchor if it has been stored into the Grid node's */etc/grid-security/certificates/* directory.
- The certificate's status is retrieved from a locally stored Certificate Revocation List (CRL).

Both processes have an inherent static nature and because of this diverse security problems may arise into the Grid.

2.2 Evaluation of Grid PKIs

Next is described important related work on PKI's evaluation; in particular are summarized three techniques quite suitable for evaluating Grid PKIs policies, the core functionality of the validation infrastructure proposed later.

The first of these techniques is the Reference Evaluation Model (REM) presented in [11], and defined as a triplet *(Formalization, Technique, ReferenceLevels)* where a formalized certificate policy is evaluated with a novel evaluation technique. The proposed technique is based on the definition of a policy metric space and a distance criteria to numerically evaluate the CA's security level thus obtaining the so called Global Security Level.

In second place and closely related with REM is the work presented in [19] where the authors propose on-demand evaluation of Grid CA's policies and practices to achieve interoperability. A prototype for a trust evaluation system is presented in that paper, which is able to evaluate a CA based on its published policies and observed practices with respect to a set of rules based on the requirements from an Authentication Profile. In particular, its evaluation methodology encodes some features from the CP into a CA report file (involving key-value pairs coded in a Scheme-like language) so afterwards they can be evaluated relative to rulesets, assurance levels allow rulesets to be defined for each level specified by the GGF. A customized ruleset can be defined either based on a minimum requirements document from a PMA, or even on a set of rules created by the VO or the CA to override and extend the default ruleset. In this way the authors introduce the "ruleset inclusion principle" as the base for evaluating chained rulesets.

Finally in [20] is proposed an extension to the Grid Security Infrastructure that provides for dynamic establishment of trust between parties. This approach, called Trust Negotiation, seeks to implement authorization and authentication by establishing trust relationships in a bilateral and iterative way. This task is performed with the disclosure of certificates and by requests for certificates; those requests may be in the form of disclosures of access control policies that spell out exactly which certificates are incrementally required to gain access to a particular resource (an approach that differs from traditional identity-based access control systems that involves a trusted third party).

3 The Problem of Grid Security Interoperability

As Grid computing became more popular, VOs proliferated at the same rate, and this finally resulted in the breed of several Certification Authorities (as a common practice, each organization installing a Grid environment also defines its own Certification Authority). Soon this represented a big interoperability problem between the users and resources belonging to different institutions: the computing resources were in different domains, but the need of cooperation through a Grid environment required to share them all. A clear need arose for methodologies, techniques and tools able to build interoperable systems. According to [21] the interoperability problem in Grid environments can be subdivided into three levels:

- *Protocol Level*, i.e. the capability of Grid systems to communicate with known and accepted standard protocols.
- *Policy level*, i.e. the capability of each party of the Grid to be able to specify its security policy expressed in a way mutually comprehensible.
- *Identity level*, i.e. the capability of identifying users from one domain to another.

State of the art Grid solutions focus mainly on the first level, accepting the use of SOAP/HTTP protocols as the common platform for system interoperability. The proposal presented in this paper focuses on the Identity Level, adopting a policy-based approach to implement an extended path validation mechanism as introduced next.

The main idea behind the extended path validation mechanism is to define an approach that enables any Grid relying-party to validate in real-time a digital certificate issued by any other CA, even though they do not belong to the same trusted domain (i.e. Institution or project). To perform an extended validation path we need:

- A methodology to automatically perform the policy mapping (i.e. comparison of the Certificate Policies and their evaluation), to build a dynamic virtual CA federation;
- A mechanism to validate on-line and near-real time the certificate status.

As mentioned in section 1, most Grid PKIs working together are not completely unknown, but they have been previously accredited by a Policy Management Authority (PMA), which defines a minimum set of security requirements – in the form of an Authentication Profile as in [22]- that must be accomplished for interoperability reasons. Even though all Grid CAs from a PMA must pass the accreditation process, not all of them accomplish the respective Authentication Profile on the same level. Therefore it is very important to measure the degree of compliance of a Grid-PKI's Certificate Policy with respect to a PMA's Authentication Profile; with this information it is possible to build comprehensive trust relationships between those Grid PKIs.

At this aim we propose in this paper an architecture for building a Grid validation system, which guarantees secure interoperability among untrusted domains by both retrieving near real-time the status of any certificate issued by a CA, and evaluating the security level associated with this Authority.

4 The Architectural Model of an Interoperability System

As pointed in the previous sections, the goal of the proposed architecture is to enable extended path validation in untrusted Grid domains. Our approach is to build a dynamic federation of CAs by evaluating their certificate policies. In order to have grants about the CAs minimum security requirements (and that each CA respects its published Certificate Policy), we refer to a Trusted Third Party: the PMA.

At a coarse grain, the proposed Interoperability System (IS), see figure 1, acts as an intermediary between the certificate verifiers (relying parties) and the issuing CAs by managing (retrieving, elaborating and updating) the information needed to perform the extended path validation: the list of accredited CAs, the list of revocation sources and the Certificate Policies.

The IS may be collocated with the Trusted Third Party and must perform two main tasks:

1. Online validation of the certificates' status.
2. Evaluation of the issuing CA's security level.

For the first task we will use a Grid Validation System able to retrieve the status of a digital certificate through the OCSP protocol in a CA federation; further details of this system are available in [9] and [10]. About the second task, for evaluating a CA's security level we have adopted the Reference Evaluation Methodology, briefly summarized in 2.2 and which details are available in [11].

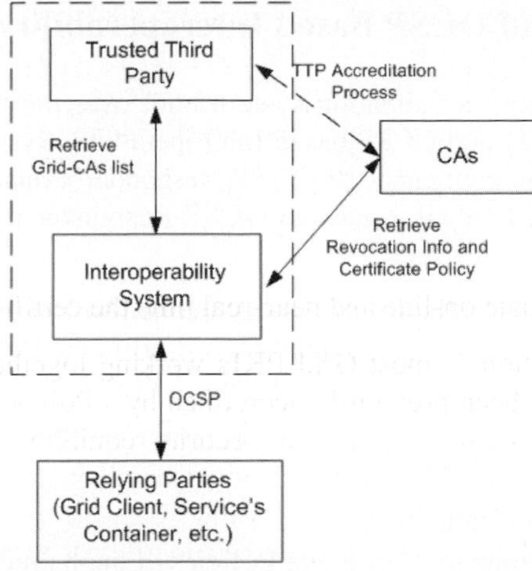

Fig. 1. Functional blocks of the proposed Interoperability System (IS)

REM's approach is based on the formalization of a Grid-CA's Certificate Policy to *i)* determine if this Authority is compliant with a PMA's Authentication Profile and *ii)* to quantitatively evaluate the Global Security Level of this CA. In figure 2 we show the results of the REM application to some of the Certification Authorities members of the EUGridPMA [3], in order to obtain their GSL; we have compared the EUGrid-PMA's minimum Authentication Profile [22] against Certificate Policies from IRIS Grid CA [23], US Department of Energy Grids CA [24], CERN CA [25] and INFN CA [26]. Further details about this results and the methodology are available in [27].

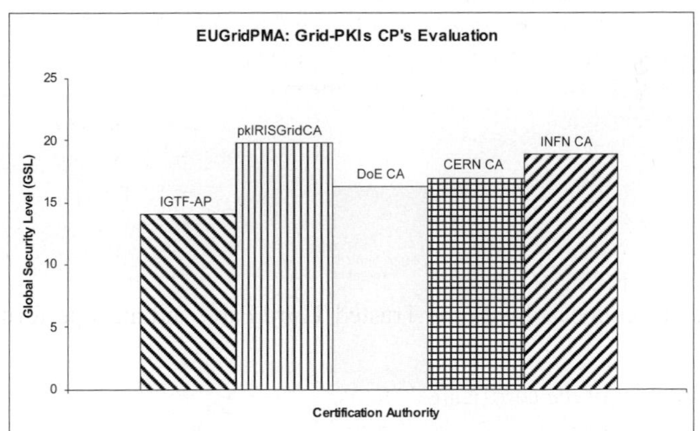

Fig. 2. GSLs obtained for a set of EUGridPMA's Certification Authorities

The GSL represents the CA security level that will be embedded as a Proxy Certificate extension using OGRO's prevalidation mechanism (please refer to [10] for more details about this feature), thus providing a final decision about a certificate validation and the Grid-PKIs interoperability issues.

5 POIS: Policy and OCSP Based Interoperability System

In this section we propose a validation system built over the basic blocks presented previously: POIS - Policy and OCSP based Interoperability System (figure 3). POIS is comprised of three basic elements: the OCSP Responder's database (tentatively CertiVeR [28]), the Policy Evaluator and the OCSP Responder itself. At a coarse view POIS offers the following features:

1. Manage (retrieve, update) the list of CAs accredited by PMA.
2. Manage (retrieve, update) the accredited CAs' Certificate Policies.
3. Manage (retrieve, update) the accredited CAs' CRLs.
4. Communicate validation information to relying parties over OCSP.
5. Perform Extended Path Validation:
   - Perform Basic Path Validation.
   - Evaluate and/or Compare Certificate Policies through precomputed GSLs.

In order to manage the list of accredited CAs and their policies (features 1 and 2) POIS, modern techniques assume an off-line communication with both PMA and CAs (the administrator manually downloads the list of accredited CAs and their Certificate Policies). The CRLs (feature 3) from each accredited CA are managed using CertiVeR's CRL Updater module (described in [28]), so they can be used later for the Extended Path Validation algorithm. POIS implements in its Policy Evaluator subsystem the REM technique explained in section 2.2, which allows offline evaluation of a member CA's Certificate Policy (after retrieving it) to obtain its respective Global Security Level. Afterwards into the OCSP Responder's database, the GSL data is linked to the existing Certification Authority information (i.e. its revocation data from the CRL).

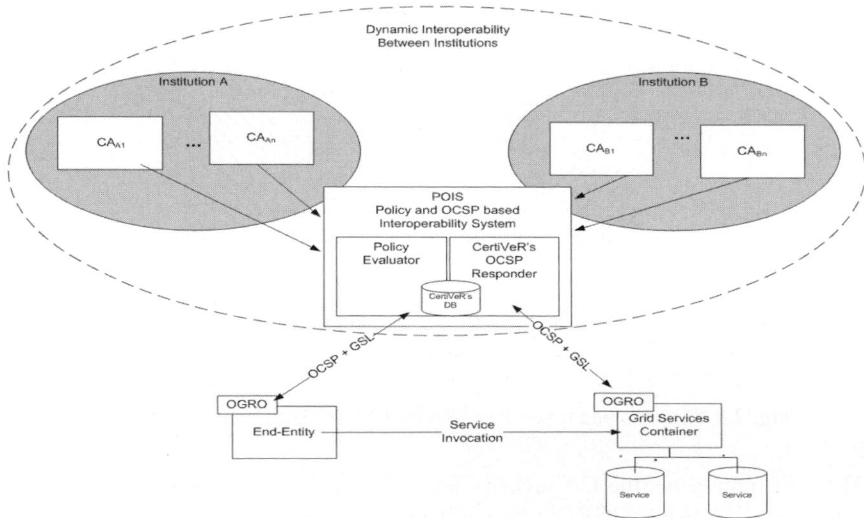

Fig. 3. POIS' Architecture

POIS is able to perform the Extended Path Validation thanks to the OGRO middleware [29], which builds over GT4's basic path validation algorithm the following two enhancements: *i)* certificates' statuses are extracted from the OCSP prevalidation data and *ii)* embedded GSL (from the End-Entity's CA) is compared against the GSL value required by the Relying Party.

Figure 3 shows a typical POIS' uses case, where interoperability is achieved between a Grid Client belonging to *Institution A* and a Grid Services Container from *Institution B*. Sections 5.1 and 5.2 will explain in greater detail this process from the point of view of both entities, the Grid Client and the Grid Services Container.

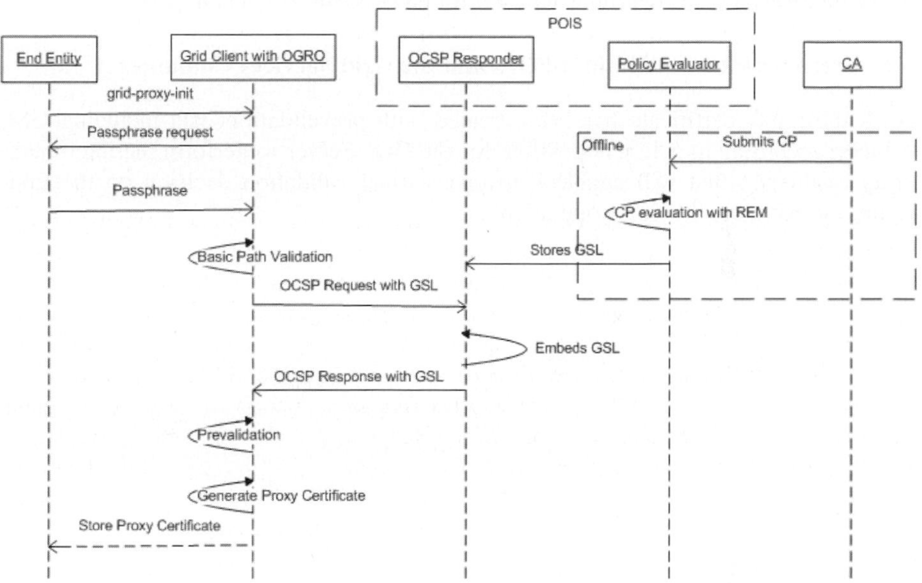

Fig. 4. End-Entity performing Extended Path Validation with POIS

5.1 Extended Path Validation: POIS and the End-Entity

When an End-Entity uses POIS to dynamically build Grid interoperability, the phases depicted in figure 4 take place. It is easy to note the addition of the GSL concept in the following steps:

- In an offline manner the CA submits its Certificate Policy (CP) to the POIS, and then the Policy Evaluator subsystem feeds it to its REM implementation to obtain a GSL. As mentioned in the previous section, this GSL is stored into OCSP Responder's DB along with the CA data already there. A further enhancement may provide a SOAP-based implementation for online CP's submission and evaluation (see section 6 for a discussion about our future works).
- The End-Entity builds an OCSP Request with a specific extension field (fully compliant with [7]), that our OCSP Responder will understand as a requirement to include its corresponding GSL, let us call it GSL_{EE}, along with the OCSP

Response. Note that each CA from the End-Entity's certificate chain may be associated with a different GSL.
- Finally, when the End-Entity receives the OCSP Response (with GSL_{EE} embedded also as an extension field), the prevalidation mechanism is executed to create a proxy certificate with this data embedded.

Our belief is that thanks to OGRO's prevalidation mechanism not only is the relying party able to improve validation process' performance, but also the Proxy Certificate is self-contained in the sense that includes all the data required by relying parties to perform the extended validation process without further contacting any authority. Performance measures related to the underlying Grid-OCSP process can be found in [28].

5.2 Extended Path Validation: POIS and the Grid Services Container

Once the proxy certificate has been created with prevalidation data including GSL value(s) according to 5.1, it is possible for the Grid Server to perform the interoperability evaluation that will enable it to take a final validation decision on the End-Entity invoking the Service's operation.

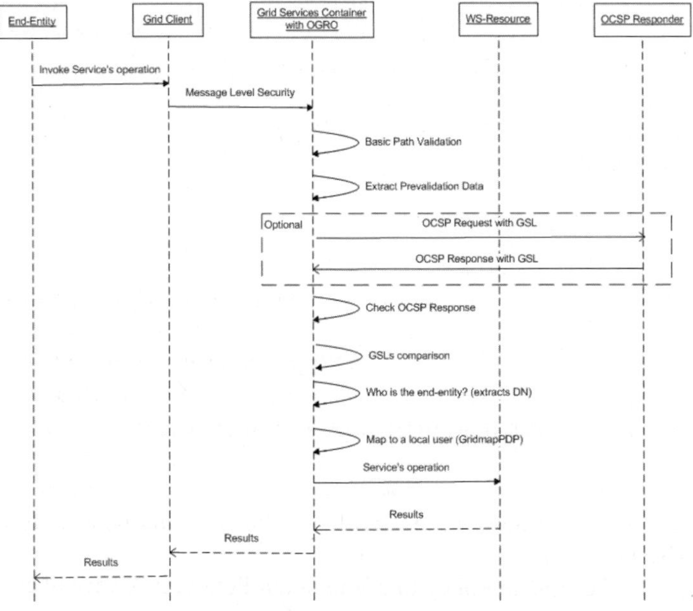

Fig. 5. Modified Server for Extended Path Validation with POIS

Figure 5 extends the validation process with the following enhancements:

1. If OGRO's prevalidation mechanism was used, then the End-Entity's GSL_{EE} is extracted from this data, Otherwise, this GSL value is requested directly from the OCSP Server.

2. The interoperability test is performed by comparing GSL_{EE} with the minimum required-GSL defined by the relying-party in OGRO's Grid Validation Policy, let us call it GSL_{SVR}. If $GSL_{EE} \geq GSL_{SVR}$ then both Grid-CAs may interoperate.

Notice that with POIS it is possible to dynamically test for an interoperability condition on the server-side, but the End-Entity could be also able to request a minimum expected GSL from a Grid-node. This *mutual-interoperability* will be a future enhancement in POIS just as explained in the section 6.

6 Conclusions and Future Work

The research collaboration undertaken between the "Università di Napoli, Federico II", the "Seconda Università di Napoli" and the "Universitat Politècnica de Catalunya" in the field of digital certificate path validation for the computational Grid has resulted in POIS, a promising alternative towards a practical solution to the dilemma of providing an interoperable and flexible trust environment between relying parties belonging to different and not cross-certified Grid-Certification Authorities. The proposal presented in this paper relies on a Grid-OCSP Validation System to convey the Global Security Level of any Certification Authority, which quantitatively represents the assurance level of its published Certificate Policy. Using this data any Grid-relying party may dynamically decide to interoperate or not with any other, without the need to perform cumbersome administrative processes.

For future extensions to the POIS implementation, we are working of the following topics:

- GSL for hierarchical PKI: even though most Grid-PKIs are only comprised of one Certification Authority (the Root CA itself), the entrance of Grid technology into new fields (i.e. enterprise applications) is likely to employ hierarchical PKIs in more than one case. GSL computation and OGRO's interoperability-checks should be extended to support these complex scenarios.
- Mutual interoperability: in this paper we have set up a scenario where the relying party is the Grid Server itself, which in turn defines its interoperability condition. But is it feasible to think that an end-entity can also define its own constraints? We believe that it is convenient from a security point of view to implement this functionality in the near future. This enhancement will allow us to differentiate among policies linked to institutions (i.e. Certificate Policies) and policies from individuals (i.e. Use Policies).
- Extending the Certificate Policy to a Validation Policy: it is very likely that all the entities participating in the computational Grid will require defining their own Validation Policies, containing their minimum interoperability requirements in a per-provision basis. These Validation Policies will be an instance of the Certificate Policy used in our proposal, so it is feasible to expect that POIS could be scaled easily to provide this requirement.

Finally with the development of the authentication and validation protocols around OGSA, it is possible that POIS would need to implement *protocol connectors* for specific functions: a SOAP-based protocol for CP conveying from CA to Policy

Evaluator, OCSP for Certificate status, etc. This may also enhance POIS performance and network bandwidth usage.

References

[1] "Globus Toolkit Version 4: Software for Service-Oriented Systems". I. Foster. IFIP International Conference on Network and Parallel Computing, Springer-Verlag LNCS 3779, pp 2-13, 2005.

[2] "The Americas Grid Policy Management Authority". Octuber, 2006. http://www.tagpma.org/

[3] "European Policy Management Authority for Grid Authentication". Octuber, 2006. http://www.eugridpma.org/

[4] "Asia-Pacific Grid Policy Management Authority". Octuber, 2006. http://www.apgridpma.org/

[5] "International Grid Trust Federation". Octuber, 2006. http://www.gridpma.org/

[6] "RFC 2527: Internet X.509 Public Key Infrastructure, Certificate Policy and Certification Practices Framework". Chokhani S. and Ford W. Internet Engineering Task Force. 1999. http://www.ietf.org/rfc/rfc2527.txt

[7] "RFC 3280: Internet X.509 Public Key Infrastructure Certificate and Certificate Revocation List (CRL) Profile". Housley R., et. al. Internet Engineering Task Force. 2002. http://www.ietf.org/rfc/rfc3280.txt

[8] "RFC 2560: X.509 Internet Public Key Infrastructure, Online Certificate Status Protocol". Myers M, et. al. Internet Engineering Task Force. 1999. http://www.ietf.org/rfc/rfc2560.txt

[9] "Using OGRO and CertiVeR to improve OCSP validation for Grids". Luna J., Manso O., Manel M. In 1st Grid and Pervasive Conference (GPC2006). Proceedings by Springer in Lecture Notes in Computer Science series. May 2006. http://hpc.csie.thu.edu.tw/gpc2006/

[10] "OCSP for Grids: Comparing Prevalidation versus Caching". Luna, Jesús. Manso, Oscar. Manel, Medina. In 7th IEEE/ACM International Conference on Grid Computing, Barcelona, September 2006. http://www.grid2006.org/

[11] "An innovative Policy-based Cross Certification methodology for Public Key Infrastructures". Casola V., Mazzeo A., Mazzocca N., Rak M. 2nd EuroPKI Workshop. Springer-Verlag LNCS 3545, pp 100-117, Editors: David Chadwick, Gansen Zhao. 2005. http://sec.cs.kent.ac.uk/europki2005/

[12] "A Reference Model for Security Level Evaluation: Policy and Fuzzy Techniques". Casola V., Preziosi R., Rak M., Troiano L. JUCS - Journal of Universal Computer Science. Editors: Ajith Abraham, L.C. January, 2005.

[13] "A SLA evaluation methodology in Service Oriented Architectures". Casola V., Mazzeo A., Mazzocca N., Rak M" in Proceedings of Quality of Protection Workshop 05, 15 September, 2005, Milan, in Advances in Information Security book series, Springer-Verlag

[14] "Globus Toolkit Version 4 Grid Security Infrastructure: A Standards Perspective". Welch, V. The Globus Security Team. 2005. http://www.globus.org/toolkit/docs/4.0/security/GT4-GSI-Overview.pdf

[15] "Internet X.509 Public Key Infrastructure proxy certificate profile". Tuecke S., et. al. Internet Engineering Task Force. 2004. http://www.ietf.org/rfc/rfc3820.txt

[16] "The WS-Resource Framework". 2006. http://www.globus.org/wsrf/

[17] "GT 4.0: Security: Message & Transport Level Security". 2006. http://www.globus.org/toolkit/docs/4.0/security/message/

[18] "The Physiology of the Grid: An Open Grid Services Architecture for Distributed Systems Integration". Foster, I., Kesselman, C., Nick, J. and Tuecke, S. Globus Project, 2002, http://www.globus.org/research/papers/ogsa.pdf
[19] "On-demand Trust Evaluation". O'Callaghan, David. Coghlan, Brian. Accepted for the 7th IEEE/ACM International Conference on Grid Computing, Barcelona, September 2006. http://www.grid2006.org/
[20] "Negotiating Trust on the Grid". Basney J., et. al.In 2nd Workshop on semantics in P2P and Grid Computing at the 13th International World Wide Web Conference. May, 2004. www.ncsa.uiuc.edu/~jbasney/sempgrid.pdf
[21] "The Security Architecture for Open Grid Services". Nagaratnam N., et. al. 2002. http://www.cs.virginia.edu/~humphrey/ogsa-sec-wg/OGSA-SecArch-v1-07192002.pdf
[22] "Classic AP Profile Version 4.03". Approved by the EUGridPMA. Edited by David Groep. 2005. http://www.eugridpma.org/igtf/IGTF-AP-classic-20050905-4-03.pdf
[23] "pkIRIS Grid Certification Authority: Certificate Policy". August 2006. http://www.irisgrid.es/pki/policy/
[24] "US Department of Energy Grids: Certificate Policy". August 2006. http://www.doegrids.org/Docs/CP-CPS.pdf
[25] "CERN Certification Authority: Certificate Policy". August 2006. http://service-grid-ca.web.cern.ch/service-grid-ca/cp_cps/cp_cps.html
[26] "INFN Certification Authority: Certificate Policy". August 2006. http://security.fi.infn.it/CA/CPS/
[27] "Static evaluation of Certificate Policies for GRID PKIs interoperability". Casola, V. et. al. Accepted in Second International Conference on Availability, Reliability and Security (ARES 2007). April 2007. http://www.ares-conference.eu
[28] "CertiVeR: Certificate Revocation and Validation Service". November 2006. http://www.certiver.com/
[29] "OGRO - The Open GRid Ocsp client API". November 2006. http://globus-grid.certiver.com/info/ogro

TCMM: Hybrid Overlay Strategy for P2P Live Streaming Services*

Hai Jin, Xuping Tu, Chao Zhang, Ke Liu, and Xiaofei Liao

Services Computing Technology and System Lab
Cluster and Grid Computing Lab
Huazhong University of Science and Technology, Wuhan, 430074 China
hjin@hust.edu.cn

Abstract. This paper proposes an application level multicast approach called *Tree-Control-Mesh-Media* (TCMM) to distribute live media streams to a large number of users efficiently. In TCMM, transmissions of media data are controlled by two independent relay protocols in a collaborative manner. One protocol here is used to help a peer to identify its neighbor peers using the location information while the other one is used to deliver of media stream among the peers. The two protocols organize all peers into two graphs with different topologies that the communications can benefit a lot from the hybrid control topology. We have studied the performance of TCMM approach using different simulation cases. The experimental results have shown that the broadcasting performance of TCMM can achieve that of a well constructed mesh network while it can adapt more dynamic and irregular network environment. We also see that the penalty of introducing two protocols is rarely low which implies the high scalability of TCMM.

1 Introduction

Recent research works reveal the brilliant future to provide media streaming services based on the P2P substrates. Many papers discuss the important roles that peer nodes have played in distributing streaming media. Till now, many P2P media streaming systems have been developed. They can be divided into three catalogues: tree-based (or hierarchical-based) system [20], DHT-based system [22] and mesh-based system [6]. In tree-based system, all peer nodes are organized as a spanning tree over the existing IP network, and the streaming data are distributed along that tree. As the parent nodes should provide streams to child nodes, the total bandwidth of a parent node having n child nodes would be $bw \times (n+1)$, where the bw is the minimum bandwidth needed by a peer. One disadvantage of the distribution topology is that a parent node will require more in bandwidth to feed its child nodes. Also, this kind of systems which only have one root node will become unstable when peers join and leave frequently [19].

* This paper is supported by National Science Foundation of China under grant 60433040, and CNGI projects under grant CNGI-04-12-2A and CNGI-04-12-1D.

C. Cérin and K.-C. Li (Eds.): GPC 2007, LNCS 4459, pp. 52–63, 2007.

The second distribution system is DHT-based. In this kind of systems, peers are organized as a circle. Due to the ring-alike topology, one peer node just has to bypass the stream to its neighbor peer. However, it also suffers for the instability and usually lacks methods to optimize the communication. The systems belong to the third catalog are mesh-based. In these structures, every peer node provides data to and gets data from several other nodes. Although this kind of structures have no stability problem, it is also very difficult to do traffic optimization [14][26].

In this paper, we propose a hybrid communication scheme, *Tree-Control-Mesh-Media* (TCMM). We organize all peers into two graphs, one is the spanning tree and the other one is a pure mesh. In the spanning tree, only control messages can be transmitted, therefore all the peers can quickly find its neighbor peers and establish data links using the control messages. Then all the media data can be transmitted in a constructed mesh network as traditional mesh-based systems. Extensive simulations demonstrate that this kind of hybrid structure gives a better solution for the locality optimization and stability. Usually, in a non mesh-based system, it is critical to avoid high quantity of messages transmitted from the parent node to each child node. However, in TCMM, nodes can receive control data from different peers simultaneously, which can reduce the risk of suffering from a high transmission rate.

The rest of the paper is organized as follows. Section 2 discusses related work. Section 3 presents TCMM scheme. Performance evaluation of the TCMM is presented in section 4. Finally, we conclude our work in section 5.

2 Related Works

Based on different network topology, application level multicast used in P2P media streaming systems can be divided into three categories: DHT-based, tree-based, and mesh-based.

The systems belonging to the first kind rely on those existing DHT network to optimize the paths according to certain metrics such as latency and bandwidth. For example, paper [18] is based on *content addressable network* (CAN) [17], and Bayeux [27] is based on Tapestry [4]. CoopNet [22] supports both live and on demand streaming. It employs *multi-description coding* (MDC) to construct multiple distribution trees (one tree for one strip). SplitStream [15] is based on Scribe [3] which is based on Pastry [2].

In tree-based systems (Yoid [9], ALMI [16], Nearcast [25], NICE [20], ZIGZAG [21], Anysee [11], and Chunkyspread [23]), peers are organized into a hierarchal structure. They just get streams from a single parent. The advantages of these systems include low overhead and can get optimal nearby nodes as data provider. However some peers usually have not enough bandwidth to support their children and it is difficult to resist the churn. Hence it limits the deployment of tree-based systems.

The mesh-based systems are named for the reason that each peer has multiple data senders and receivers, e.g., Narada [6], ScatterCast [5], PROMISE [13], DagStream [10], RandPeer [12]. They overcome the difficulties in tree but lead to redundant traffic of underlying physical networks.

CoolStreaming [24] is one of the most famous mesh-based application level multicast systems. By using DONet protocol, each node first exchanges data available information with all the partners periodically, and then retrieves the data from one or more partners. Actually, the data transferring mesh in our proposed approach is similar to CoolStreaming to inherit the efficiency of data exchanging.

BULLET [7] is the most similar structure to TCMM. It uses RanSub [8] to build an overlay tree, one peer, if not fed enough, can receive data from multiple ancestors in the tree. But the tree participating the data transferring is different from TCMM. Since in TCMM, the tree is to organize the peers in a locality-aware overlay. The mesh overlay is used to exchange media data.

Different from these systems, TCMM is proposed for the streaming system that each receiver should have multiple senders. Here the tree topology is just used to identify nearby senders.

3 Design of TCMM

The main focus of this paper is the design and implementation of TCMM which is based on our previous work Nearcast [25]. First we will give a brief introduction of TCMM, and then details of the TCMM approach will be introduced.

3.1 Overview of TCMM

All peers in TCMM are involved to distribute media data. They are organized into two overlays – one is used as control tree and the other is used as media mesh. The control tree structure is used to make all nodes in the tree close to each other physically, it means there must be few routers between each pair node, or the *Round Trip Time* (RTT) should be small. Also, the messages transmitted over the tree should be lightweighted messages such as ping/pong messages. Because the out-degree of each node in the tree graph can be very large while the tree height (log*N*) is relatively low. Further, when no media data transmitted, the tree can be loosely maintained, that is, even if some peers have left, other peers still can postpone to update the tree information without breaking transmitting media data in a long period.

The second overlay in TCMM is a data mesh which is similar to CoolStreaming. It is used to transmit media data. Each peer first registers to the network to get a *Global Unique Identity* (GUID). On the other hand, at the beginning, it is at the tree root, the scheduling algorithm then guides it to route to a peer which has a relatively similar GUID. In the routing path, this peer can collect information about the visited peers to build its own candidate partner list. After that, it selects a group of nodes to connect to for more partner information. Finally, it can start the media data exchanging. Fig.1 gives an overview of the two-layer structure of TCMM.

3.2 Tree Management

The tree management is based on Nearcast protocol [25]. In this protocol, leaf peers in the overlay multicast tree are self-organized to form the *H* layer hierarchical structures.

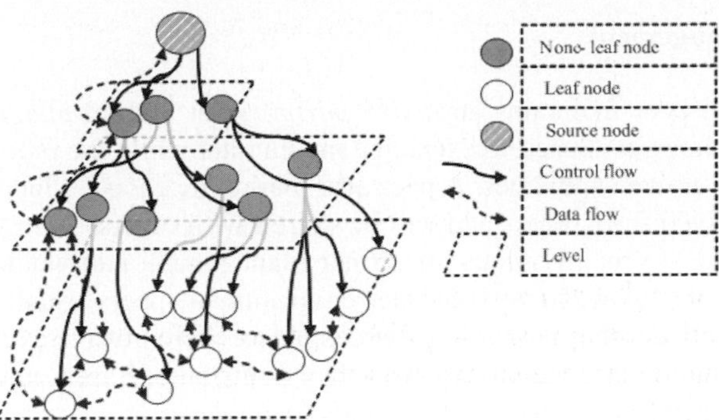

Fig. 1. Overview of TCMM, the dashed line stands for a data link, those of which construct a mesh, while thick line stands for control link for constructing a loosely maintained tree

Based on the network position coordinates of leaf peers, the intra-subtree structure is designed to be sensitive to the locality information. This strategy leads to that nearby leaf peers in the physical network are nearby with each other in the overlay. These two techniques help the overlay multicast tree to become a good represent of the underlying physical network, therefore the link stress and the total (or average) end-to-end delay can be effectively reduced.

The TCMM tree is constructed based on GUID, which consists of the peers' location information. It encodes the following information into 16-bytes of string: network type (firewall or NAT or else), ISP (internet service provider), city, postcode, public IP, and private IP, see Fig.2. Here we introduce briefly only the basic operation of the tree maintenance: Join Process and Leave Process. For more details of how to maintain the tree, readers can refer to Nearcast [25].

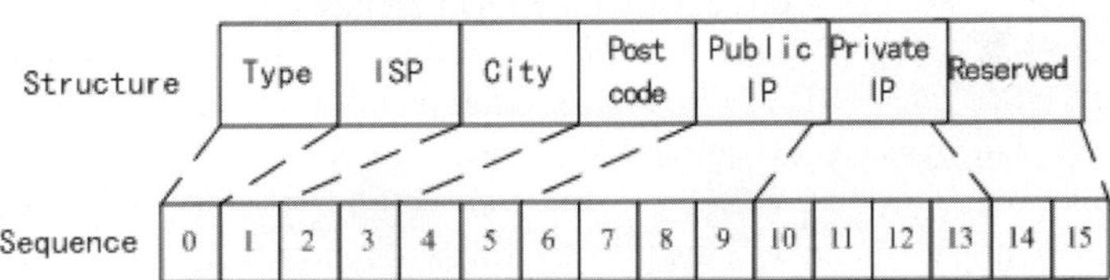

Fig. 2. The elements of GUID

Once an existing host *Y* receives the *"Join"* message from *X*, it uses the admission algorithm to compare the joiner's GUID with its own GUID, so as its children's GUIDs. Also, it tests the network bandwidth constraints to determine whether *Y* is the nearest host to *X*. If so, *X* should be admitted to be a child of *Y*. Otherwise, it is redirected to the nearest child of *Y*. This process will repeat until *X* finds its nearest parent. If a child receives the *"Leave"* message from a leaving peer, it should immediately response by sending a *"Join"* message to its original grandparent. The parent receives *"Join"* message, it will treat it as a new join process. Since in TCMM, the control tree only helps to find close peers without transmitting media data. It is unnecessary to absolutely maintain the tree structure.

3.3 Mesh Management

In TCMM, each peer maintains an *active partners* set and an *inactive partners* set. The *active partners* set is used to exchange media data while the *inactive partners* set is used to select active candidates. A peer also maintains a local window, which stores media data received from others and will be shared with others.

In this section, we mainly focus on partner management and window management techniques. As we know, in real internet environment, peers usually have different bandwidth as well as other network resources. Also, there always exist many partners which receive much more media data than they contribute. Based on this observation, we can classify active partners into two kinds, *provider partner* and *receiver partner*. Suppose node *A* has a partner *B*, whose sequence number of its window's first packet is bigger than that of *A* (usually close to the media source), Here, *B* is the provider partner of *A*, and *A* is the receiver partner of *B*. It is clear that each peer must maintain a minimum number of provider partners in order to maintain continuity. The classification of partners is illustrated in Fig.3. Fig.4 depicts the operations and algorithms applied between a peer and its partners, including a) how to produce inactive partners, b) how to select one from an inactive partners list to be an active partner, and c) how to schedule when more than one active partner possess the data to a peer.

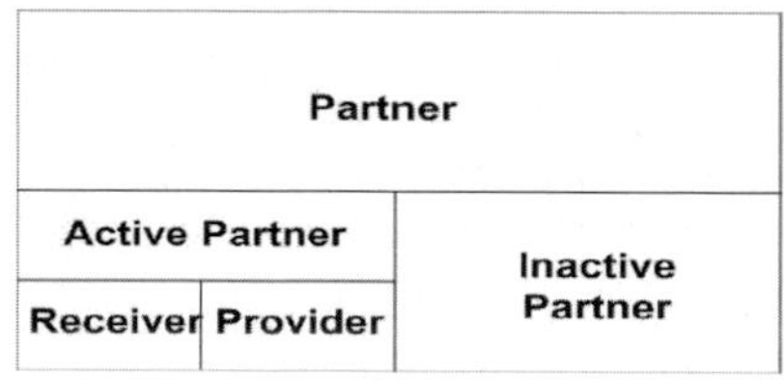

Fig. 3. Classification of partner

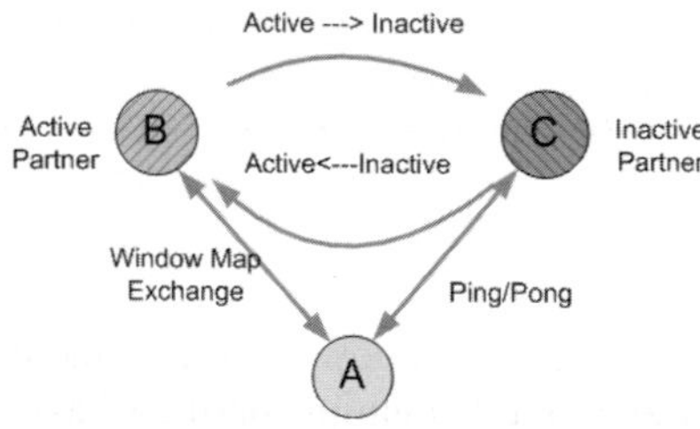

Fig. 4. Partner maintenance (origin node A), Ping/Pong with inactive partners and window map exchange with active partners

3.3.1 Inactive Partner Generation

There are three ways for a peer to get inactive partners to build up its inactive peer list: a) when a peer joins the overlay, it will receive a partner list as a piggyback message of "*OK Response*" message from its father node; b) send requests to its active partners when the peer's count of provider partner is less than a predefined minimum value. When a peer receives a "*Partner Request*" message, it responds by sending an active partner list to the requester. It is because a partner's active partners would proverbially to be active partners. On receiving the partners reply, if they do not exist in the inactive partners list, the peer will add them to the list to be candidates of active partners; c) a peer will periodically collect children and father information in the control tree to build local partners list. Because the tree is maintained by *"Alive"* message, the peers in the tree are very probable online and can perform data transmission well. Thus, each peer will periodically send ping message to those inactive partners to check whether they are still online. Suppose the number of members in inactive list is $N_{inactive}$, ping interval is $I_{inactive}$, packet size of Ping/Pong is $S_{inactive}$ the Ping/Pong overhead is $O_{inactive} = N_{inactive} \times I_{inactive} \times S_{inactive}$.

3.3.2 Active Partner Generation

All active partners are inactive partners before they change their state, therefore, a peer will prepare to select some inactive partners to become active partner candidates when the number of local provider partner is less than a given threshold. Several factors are considered, including: a) the difference of GUID is lower; b) the RTT between is lower; c) more data that it needs is in the window. After choosing several candidates, the peers send *"Identity Request"* message to them. On the other hand, once the peer receives an *"Identity Request"* message, it will check whether this partner can be accepted. If it is ok, then *"Identity Agree Response"* will be sent. Otherwise a reject message will appear as a response. After that they begin to exchange window map at a given interval. At the same time, another task will compare their window maps independently and periodically. Also, a *"Data Request"* request will be sent for the missing data. As the window sliding and the window map changing, the data producing and consuming process continue until the end of the live streaming program. If being rejected, a peer will try the second peer in the candidate list and if accepted, the remote peer will become its *active partner* and be added into the active partner set.

3.3.3 Active Partner Schedule

Before discussing partner selection algorithm, some concepts about windows should be introduced. Each peer maintains a sliding window to store data availability information, including the sequence number of the first segment it is sliding to and the segment states in bytes. In these bytes, each bit stands for a segment's state, 1 is for available, 0 for unavailable. Because each peer's local window is limited, it has to discard the old data and fill new data.

A peer will periodically check its window to request the missing segment by sending a *"Data Request"* message to it. If multiple partners have the unavailable segment, it will schedule which partner acts as the provider. Here, we give a principal to the scheduler scheme, 1) MAX_REQ, which limits the maximum segment one *"Data Request"* message can convey. 2) Every segment of data will have a transmitting pending time $T_{pending}$, if a partner's last transaction has not been completed and does not encounter a timeout error during the transaction time, it should be added to current task this time. 3) If two video segments are available simultaneously, the one with bigger sequence number should have higher priority. This means, we always request the video segment with higher sequence number than that with lower sequence number. The third principal can strengthen the "enlarge ability" of the system. Having the three principals in mind, we implement our own algorithm in Fig.5.

```
Input:
Band[k]: bandwidth from partner k;
wm[k]: window map of partner k;
task[k]: assigned task of k ;
pending[k]: not completed task of k;
num_partners: number of partners of the node;
local_window[i]: segment i of local window map is
available or not;
Scheduling:
for segment i =size(local_window) do
   i i-1;
   if local_window[i]=1 then
     continue;//if segment i is available,schedule next
   end if
   for j to num_partners do
      n n +wm[j,i];//get potential suppliers for i;
   end for j;
   if  n =1 then
   k arg_r{ wm[r,i]=1};// only one potential supplier;
     if task[k]+pending[k]>MAX_REQ then
        continue;
     end if
     supplier[i] k; task[k] task[k]+1;
     continue;
   end if;
   for j =2 to n
     if task[k]+pending[k]> MAX_REQ or
task[k]+pending[k]>band[k] then
        continue;
     end if
     supplier[i] j; task[k] task[k]+1;
   end for j;
end for i;
Output: supplier[i]: supplier for unavailable segment i
```

Fig. 5. Scheduling algorithm at a TCMM node

4 Performance Evaluation

4.1 Simulation Setup

To evaluate performance of TCMM, we first propose a GUID-based delay and bandwidth simulation method instead of using traditional physical topology generation tools to generate physical topology, such as GT-ITM [1]. Because the communication between each pair of nodes is affected by delay and bandwidth, thus, if we try to simulate the two characteristics in internet, we need not generate the physical topology. In our simulation platform, we just generate a peer sets.

We suppose that the delay and bandwidth between two peers can be determined by their GUIDs. In the sending queue, a packet can be sent when the previous sending operation has been finished. The communication delay between two logical neighbors is calculated according to formula 1. From formula 1, we can see that the delay will affect the bandwidth. Also, using GUID-based methods, we generate 5 physical peer sets each with 2000 nodes. The logical topologies are generated with a number of peers (nodes) ranging from 100 to 1,024. Suppose *N* is the number of the total peers, *N*/10 cities and *N*/5 postcodes are generated and randomly assign all the nodes to them. The expected number of inactive partner is 20, and the minimum number of each peer's provider partners is 3, the maximum number of active partner numbers is 15. We start the broadcaster and let 2 randomly selected peers join the system every second. The lifetime of each peer is set to 600 seconds. We collect the log to analyze the performance of our TCMM system.

$$\mathrm{Delay}(i,j)=\mathrm{ISP}_i\oplus\mathrm{ISP}_j\times W_{\mathrm{ISP}}+\mathrm{City}_i\oplus\mathrm{City}_j\times W_{\mathrm{city}}+\mathrm{postcode}_i\oplus\mathrm{postcode}_j\times W_{\mathrm{postcode}}+\mathrm{IP1}_i\oplus\mathrm{IP1}_j\times W_{\mathrm{IP1}}+\mathrm{IP2}_i\oplus\mathrm{IP2}_j\times W_{\mathrm{IP2}}+\mathrm{IP3}_i\oplus\mathrm{IP3}_j\times W_{\mathrm{IP3}}+\mathrm{IP4}_i\oplus\mathrm{IP4}_j\times W_{\mathrm{IP4}} \quad (1)$$

$$TotalDelay(i,j)= Delay(i,j)(1+L/2048) \quad (2)$$

In formula 1, $\oplus$ means exclusive OR operation. If ISP_i is equal to ISP_j, then $ISP_i\oplus ISP_j$ is 0, otherwise 1. W_{ISP} means the weight of *ISP* to the delay. It means that only nodes from different ISP can affect the delay in ISP item, so does other factors in this formula. Let the first byte of internet address of peer *i* is $IP1_i$, $IP1_i\oplus IP1_j$ compares the first byte of two addresses. Then *IP2, IP3* and *IP4* compare the second, third, fourth byte of the two peers' IP address, respectively. We set the weight of each factor as W_{ISP}=500, W_{city}=200, $W_{postcode}$=100, W_{IP1}=100, W_{IP2}=100, W_{IP3}=100, W_{IP4}=50. Because we send a message after its previous message has been sent, suppose we get a delay 50ms through formula 1, and formula 2 adds the effect of messages length to the delay, if the sending queue consists of 3 messages with the size 50, 10240, 10240 bytes, we get the total delay 50ms, 100ms, 100ms according to formula 2, then the completion sending time of the 3 messages are 50ms, 150ms and 250ms, respectively.

There are already some metrics to evaluate a peer to peer live streaming system, such as link stress method [6], and data path quality method [20]. Because in TCMM, there is no physical topology to evaluate the link stress, on the other hand, TCMM does not transmit media data through a multicast tree, thus avoids evaluating the data path quality either, therefore, in this paper, we use other metrics, such as starting delay, dynamic resistance, and overhead to evaluate the performance of TCMM. Each experiment result is got by averaging 5 tests cases.

4.2 Control Overhead

This index is categorized by tree overhead and mesh overhead. Tree overhead is defined as the ratio of the bytes that a peer received to maintain the tree structure over the total bytes a peer received. Mesh overhead is defined as the ratio of the bytes that a peer received to exchange window map over the total bytes the peer received. The tree overhead mainly includes alive messages cost happened in a peer periodically sends this message to its children and receives them from its parents. Fig.6 presents the average tree overhead of TCMM. The data are collected when sending an "*Alive*" message every 5 seconds. This figure implies that the tree overhead is nearly independent of the community size. That is because the alive messages are only sent to children by father, and children have no responsibility to answer them. So, when a peer can accept more children, its own overhead increases, but its children's overhead will decrease. This will cause the average overhead changes a little. Fig.6 also depicts that the tree maintain overhead is less than 0.5% of the total traffic.

Every peer also exchanges ping/pong messages with its inactive partners to declare its aliveness and exchanges their window map messages with active partners as well. Fig.7 shows that when the Ping/Pong interval is 9 seconds and window map exchange interval is 2 seconds, the total mesh overhead is less than 2% when number of minimum providers less than or equal to 6. Considering the mesh overhead increases with more partners, we believe that minimum provider partner equal to 4 is a good practical choice. So it is adopted in the following experiments, and this result also meets the point got from [24]. However, an important fact here is that number 4 is just for provider partner not for the total active partner.

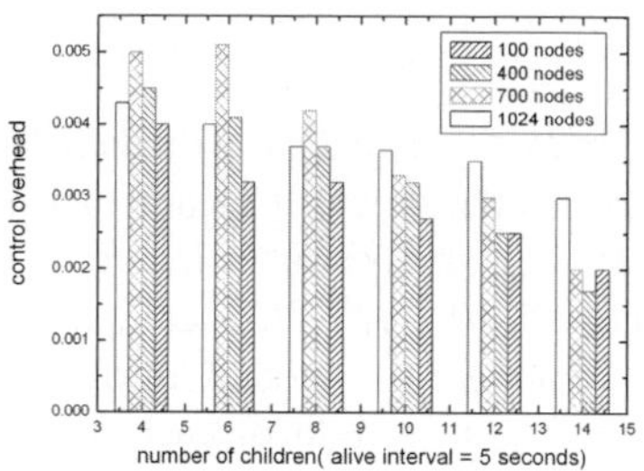

Fig. 6. Overhead of tree maintaining

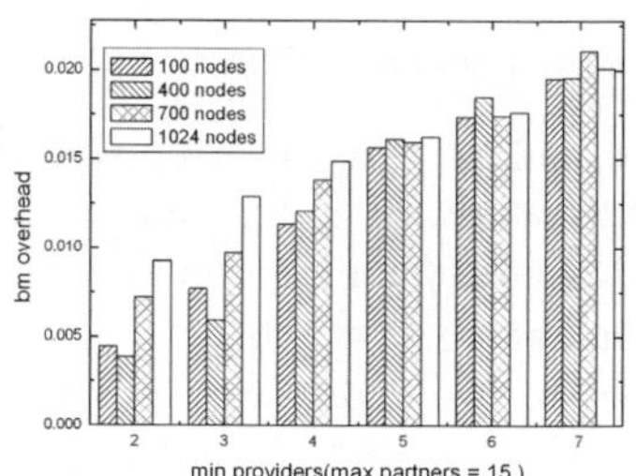

Fig. 7. Overhead of mesh maintaining

4.3 Starting Delay

This index is defined as the time period from a peer joins the multicast system to a peer starts to play back the media. This index describes how fast the system can provide service to a newcomer. Fig.8 presents the comparison of starting delay between TCMM and mesh-based scheme, this figure is for 1024 nodes. Actually the starting delay is almost independent of the system size.

We have ever thought that TCMM will have less starting delay than pure mesh-based structure, because peers in pure mesh-based overlay need much time to optimize their service providers, and this will increase the starting delay. However, data in Fig.8 proves it wrong. This data leads to a conclusion that although the TCMM provides a quick way to identify those nearby nodes, it has a little longer starting delay to build the control tree before starting to get media data, which causes about additional 4s-10s delay than pure mesh-based structure.

4.4 Dynamic Resistance

Because P2P environment is a dynamic environment, many peers' frequently joining and leaving will cause the source of each peer to become dynamic, therefore, a peer should have the ability to change at least part of its service providers at any time. We let the overlay with 1024 peers runs stably for 5 minutes, then we let a randomly produced 2 new peers join the overlay and another randomly selected 2 peers leave the overlay each second within 200 seconds.

In Fig.9, the y axis is sampling times of the window size of peers, x axis is the window size. We observe that the TCMM's window is fuller than the pure mesh-based method in most times. We set the dynamical peers ranging from 10 to 50, TCMM scheme produces a better average window size as shown in Fig.10. There are two reasons for this phenomenon. 1) Although the peers frequently join and leave, the peers in TCMM always fetch and transmit new segments before old segments. Definitely, this will accelerate the distribution of new segments (since most of peers are lacking new segments not old segments) and speeds up the data distribution dramatically. Also, this strategy strengthens the collaboration among peers. 2) The peers in TCMM can get provider partners efficiently from the control tree and reduce the effects of dynamics of peers.

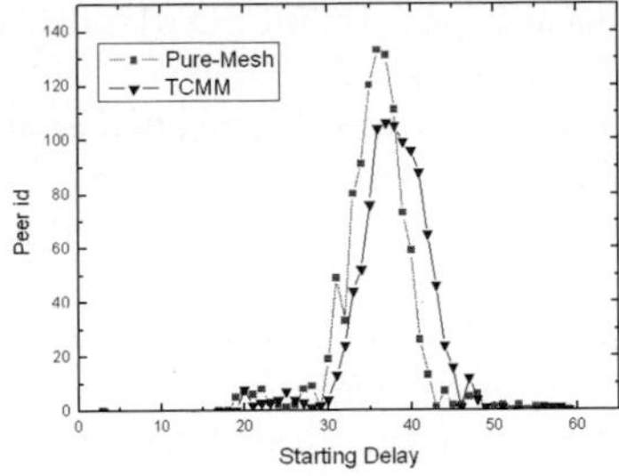

Fig. 8. Comparison of startup delay

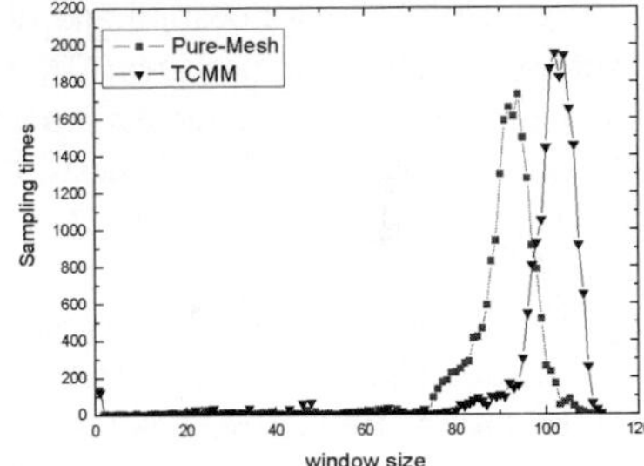

Fig. 9. Comparison of continuity

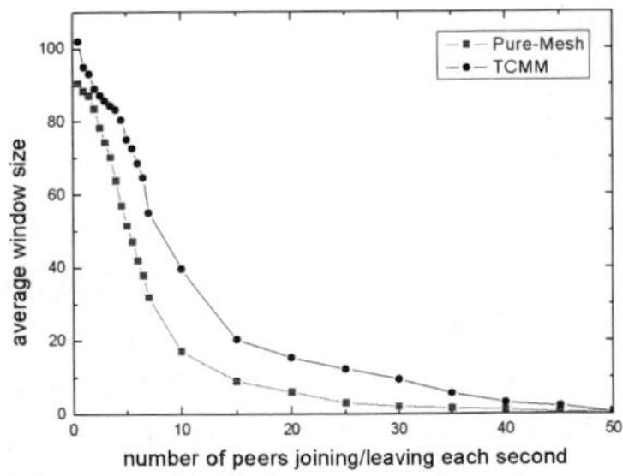

Fig. 10. Comparison of resistance to dynamics

5 Conclusions

In this paper, we have presented TCMM approach, which can support large scale live streaming service. TCMM just integrates two overlays, a tree based on GUID to overcome the mismatch problem between logical overlay and underlying physical networks, and a mesh to resist peer dynamics, instead of excluding any of them. The simulation results show that this approach not only benefits the overlay efficiently, decreases the time used to find close nodes, which is very important in reducing the redundancy of the P2P traffic, but also it strengthens the stability in a rigorous dynamic environment just by introducing additional slight starting delay.

References

[1] GT-ITM. http://www.cc.gatech.edu/projects/gtitm/.

[2] A. Rowstron and P. Druschel, "Pastry: Scalable, Distributed Object Location and Routing for Large Scale Peer-to-Peer Systems", In *Proc. of IFIP/ACM International Conference on Distributed Systems Platforms (Middleware)*, Nov. 2001.

[3] A. Rowstron, A. M. Kermarrec, M. Castro, and P. Druschel, "Scribe: The Design of a Large Scale Event Notification Infrastructure", In *Proc. of 3rd International Workshop on Networked Group Communication*, Nov. 2001.

[4] B. Y. Zhao, J. Kubiatowicz, and A. Joseph, "Tapestry: an Infrastructure for Fault-Tolerant Wide-Area Location and Routing", Technical Report, UCB/CSD-01-1141, University of California, Berkeley, CA. USA, Apr. 2001.

[5] Y. Chawathe, "Scattercast: An Architecture for Internet Broadcast Distribution as an Infrastructure Service", Ph.D. Thesis, University of California, Berkeley, Dec. 2000.

[6] Y. H. Chu, S. G. Rao, and H. Zhang, "A Case for End System Multicast", In *Proc. of ACM SIGMETRICS 2000.*

[7] D. Kostic, A. Rodriguez, J. Albrecht, and A. Vahdat, "Bullet: High Bandwidth Data Dissemination Using an Overlay Mesh", In *Proceedings of SOSP 2003.*

[8] D. Kostic, A. Rodriguez, J. Albrecht, A. Bhirud, and A. Vahdat, "Using Random Subsets to Build Scalable Network Services", In *Proc. of the USENIX Symposium on Internet Technologies and Systems*, March 2003.

[9] P. Francis, "Yoid: Extending the Multicast Internet Architecture", White paper, http://www.aciri.org/yoid/, 1999.

[10] J. Liang and K. Nahrstedt, "DagStream: Locality Aware and Failure Resilient Peer-to-Peer Streaming", In *Proc. of SPIE MMCN 2006.*

[11] X. Liao, H. Jin, Y. Liu, L. M. Ni, and D. Deng, "AnySee: Peer-to-Peer Live Streaming Service", In *Proc. of IEEE INFOCOM 2006.*

[12] J. Liang and K. Nahrstedt, "Randpeer: Membership Management for QoS Sensitive Peer to Peer Applications", In *Proceedings of IEEE INFOCOM 2006.*

[13] M. Hefeeda, A. Habib, B. Botev, D. Xu, and B. Bhargava, "PROMISE: Peer to Peer Media Streaming Using CollectCast", In *Proc. of ACM Multimedia 2003.*

[14] M. Ripeanu, A. Iamnitchi, and I. Foster, "Mapping the Gnutella Network", *IEEE Internet Computing*, 2002.

[15] M. Castro, P. Druschel, A M. Kermarrec, A. Nandi, A. Rowstron, and A. Singh, "SplitStream: High-bandwidth Multicast in a Cooperative Environment", In *Proc. of SOSP 2003.*

[16] D. Pendarakis, S. Shi, D. Verma, and M. Waldvogel, "ALMI: An Application Level Multicast Infrastructure", In *Proc. of 3rd Usenix Symposium on Internet Technologies & Systems*, March 2001.

[17] S. Ratnasamy, P. Francis, M. Handley, R. Karp, and S. Shenker, "A Scalable Content Addressable Network", In *Proc. of ACM SIGCOM 2001.*

[18] S. Ratnasamy, M. Handley, R. Karp, and S. Shenker, "Application-Level Multicast Using Content Addressable Networks", In *Proc. of 3rd International Workshop on Networked Group Communication*, Nov. 2001.

[19] S. Saroiu, P. Gummadi, and S. Gribble, "A Measurement Study of Peer-to-Peer File Sharing Systems", In *Proc. of MMCN 2002*.
[20] S. Banerjee, B. Bhattacharjee, and C. Kommareddy, "Scalable Application Layer Multicast", In *Proc. of ACM SIGCOMM*, 2002.
[21] D. A. Tran, K. A. Hua, and T. T. Do, "ZIGZAG: An Efficient Peer-to-Peer Scheme for Media Streaming", In *Proceedings of IEEE INFOCOM 2003*.
[22] V. N. Padamanabhan, H. J. Wang, P. A. Chou, and K. Scripanijkuichai, "Distributing Streaming Media Content Using Cooperative Networking", In *Proc. of ACM NOSSDAV 2002*.
[23] V. Venkataraman, P. Francis, and J. Calandrino, "Chunkyspread: Multi-tree Unstructured Peer-to-Peer Multicast", In *Proc. of IEEE IPTPS 2006*.
[24] X. Zhang, J. Liu, B. Li, and T.-S. P. Yum, "CoolStreaming/DONet: A Data-driven Overlay Network for Peer-to-Peer Live Media Streaming", In *Proc. of INFOCOM 2005*.
[25] X. Tu, H. Jin, X. Liao, and J. Cao, "Nearcast: A Locality-Aware Application Level Multicast for Peer-to-Peer Live Streaming Service", To appear in *ACM Transactions on Internet Technology*, 2007.
[26] Y. Liu, X. Liu, L. Xiao, L. M. Ni, and X. Zhang, "Location-aware Topology Matching in Unstructured P2P Systems", In *Proc. of INFOCOM 2004*.
[27] S. Q. Zhuang, B. Y. Zhao, A. D. Joseph, R. Katz, and J. Kubiatowicz, "Bayeux: An Architecture for Scalable and Fault Tolerant Wide-area Data Dissemination", In *Proc. of NOSSDAV 2001*.

Fault Management in P2P-MPI

Stéphane Genaud and Choopan Rattanapoka

ICPS-LSIIT - UMR 7005
Université Louis Pasteur, Strasbourg
{genaud,rattanapoka}@icps.u-strasbg.fr

Abstract. We present in this paper the recent developments done in P2P-MPI, a grid middleware, concerning the fault management, which covers fault-tolerance for applications and fault detection. P2P-MPI provides a transparent fault tolerance facility based on replication of computations. Applications are monitored by a distributed set of external modules called failure detectors. The contribution of this paper is the analysis of the advantages and drawbacks of such detectors for a real implementation, and its integration in P2P-MPI. We pay especially attention to the reliability of the failure detection service and to the failure detection speed. We propose a variant of the binary round-robin protocol, which is more reliable than the application execution in any case. Experiments on applications of up to 256 processes, carried out on Grid'5000 show that the real detection times closely match the predictions.

Keywords: Grid computing, middleware, Parallelism, Fault-tolerance.

1 Introduction

Many research works have been carried out these last years on the concept of *grid*. Though the definition of grid is not unique, there are some common key concepts shared by the various projects aiming at building grids. A grid is a distributed system potentially spreading over multiple administrative domains which provide its users with a transparent access to resources. The big picture may represent a user requesting some complex computation involving remotely stored data from its basic terminal. The grid middleware would then transparently query available and appropriate computers (that the user is granted access to), fetch data and eventually transfer results to the user.

Existing grids however, fall into different categories depending on needs and resources managed. At one end of the spectrum are what is often called "institutional grids", which gather well identified users and share resources that are generally costly but not necessarily numerous. At the other end of the spectrum are grids with numerous, low-cost resources with few or no central system administration. Users are often the administrators of their own resource that they accept to share. Numerous projects have recently emerged in that category [11, 5, 2] which have in common to target desktop computers or small clusters. P2P-MPI is a grid middleware that falls into the last category. It has been designed as a peer-to-peer system: each participant in the grid has an equal status

C. Cérin and K.-C. Li (Eds.): GPC 2007, LNCS 4459, pp. 64–77, 2007.

and may alternatively share its CPU or requests other CPU to take part to a computation. The proposed programming model is close to MPI. We give a brief overview of the system in Section 2 and a longer presentation can be found in [7]. P2P-MPI is particularly suited to federate networks of workstations or unused PCs on local networks.

In this context, a crucial point is fault management, which covers both failure detection and fault tolerance for applications. We describe in the paper several pitfalls arising when targeting such environments and what solutions have been put forward in P2P-MPI. The main issues to be addressed are (i) *scalability* since the fault detection system should work up to hundreds of processors, which implies to keep the number of messages exchanged small while having the time needed to detect a fault acceptable, and (ii) *accuracy* means the failure detection should detect all failures and failures detected should be real failures (no false positive).

This paper is organized as follows. Section 2 is a short overview of P2P-MPI which outline the principle of *robustness* of an application execution, through replication of its processes. Section 3 gives an expression of fault-tolerance as the failure probability of the application depending on the replication degree and on the failure events rate. To be effective, the failure detection must be far more reliable than the application execution. We first review in Section 4 the existing techniques to design a reliable fault detection service (FD hereafter). Then, Section 5 examines strengths and weaknesses of candidate solutions considering P2P-MPI requirements. We underline the trade off between reliability and detection speed and we propose a variant of an existing protocol to improve reliability. P2P-MPI implementation integrates the two best protocols, and we report in we report in Section 6 experimental results concerning detection speed for 256 processes.

2 P2P-MPI Overview

P2P-MPI overall objective is to provide a *grid* programming environment for parallel applications. P2P-MPI has two facets: it is a middleware and as such, it has the duty of offering appropriate system-level services to the user, such as finding requested resources, transferring files, launching remote jobs, etc. The other facet is the parallel programming API it provides to programmers.

API. Most of the other comparable projects cited in introduction (apart from P3 [11]) enable the computation of jobs made of independent tasks only, and the proposed programming model is a client-server (or RPC) model. The advantage of this model lies in its suitability to distributed computing environments but lacks expressivity for parallel constructs. P2P-MPI offers a more general programming model based on message passing, of which the client-server can be seen as a particular case.

Contained in the P2P-MPI distribution is a communication library which exposes an MPI-like API. Actually, our implementation of the MPI specification is in Java and we follow the MPJ recommendation [3]. Though Java is used for the sake of portability of codes, the primitives are quite close to the original C/C++/fortran specification [8].

Middleware. A user can simply make its computer join a P2P-MPI grid (it becomes a peer of a peer group) by typing `mpiboot` which runs a local *gatekeeper* process. The gatekeeper can play two roles: (i) it advertises the local computer as available to the peer group, and decides to accept or decline job requests from other peers as they arrive, and (ii) when the user issues a job request, it has the charge of finding the requested number of peers and to organize the job launch.

Launching a MPI job requires to assign an identifier to each task (implemented by a process) and then synchronize all processes at the MPI_Init barrier. By comparison, scheduling jobs made of independent tasks gives more flexibility since no coordination is needed and a task can be assigned to a resource as soon as the resource becomes available.

When a user (the submitter) issues a job request involving several processes, its local gatekeeper initiates a *discovery* to find the requested number of resources during a limited period of time. P2P-MPI uses the JXTA library [1] to handle all usual peer-to-peer operations such as discovery. Resources can be found because they advertised their presence together with their technical characteristics when they joined the peer group. Once enough resources have been selected, the gatekeeper first checks that advertised hosts are still available (by pinging them) and builds a table listing the numbers assigned to each participant process (called the *communicator* in MPI). Then, the gatekeeper instructs a specific service to send the program to execute along with the input data or URL to fetch data from, to each selected host. Each selected host acknowledges the transfer and starts running the received program. (If some hosts fail before sending the acknowledgement, a timeout expires on the submitter side and the job is canceled). The program starts by entering the MPI_Init barrier, waiting for the communicator. As soon as a process has received the communicator it continues executing its application process.

Before dwelling into details of the application startup process and the way it is monitored by the fault-detection service (described in section 5), let us motivate the need for a failure detector by introducing the capability of P2P-MPI to handle application execution robustly.

Robustness. Contrarily to parallel computers, MPI applications in our desktop grid context must face frequent failures. A major feature of P2P-MPI is its ability to manage replicated processes to increase the application robustness. In its run request, the user can simply specify a *replication degree* r which means that each MPI process will have r copies running simultaneously on different processors. In case of failures, the application can continue as long as at least one copy of each process survives. The communication library transparently handles all extra-communications needed so that the source code of the application does not need any modification.

3 Replication and Failure Probability

In this section, we quantify the failure probability of an application and how much replication improves an application's robustness.

Assume failures are independent events, occurring equiprobably at each host: we note f the probability that a host fails during a chosen time unit. Thus, the probability that a p process MPI application without replication crashes is

$$\begin{aligned} P_{app(p)} &= \text{probability that 1, or 2,} \ldots \text{, or } n \text{ processes crash} \\ &= 1 - (\text{probability that no process crashes}) \\ &= 1 - (1 - f)^p \end{aligned}$$

Now, when an application has its processes replicated with a replication degree r, a crash of the application occurs if and only if at least one MPI process has all its r copies failed. The probability that all of the r copies of an MPI process fail is f^r. Thus, like in the expression above, the probability that a p process MPI application with replication degree r crashes is

$$P_{app(p,r)} = 1 - (1 - f^r)^p$$

Figure 1 shows the failure probability curve depending on the replication degree chosen ($r = 1$ means no replication) where f has been arbitrary set to 5%. Remark that doubling the replication degree increases far more than twice

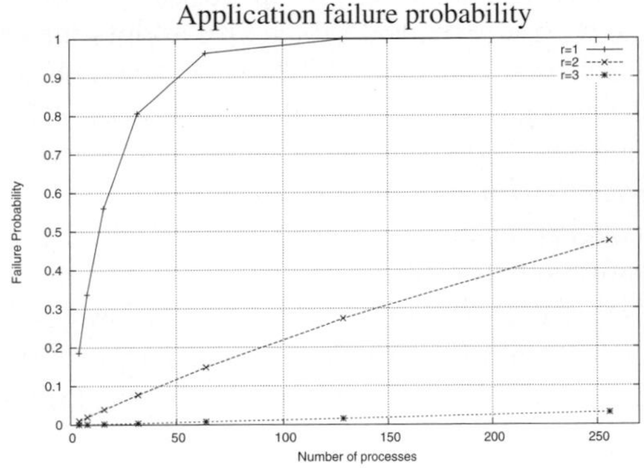

Fig. 1. Failure probability depending on replication degree r (f=0.05)

the robustness. For example, a 128 processes MPI application with a replication degree of only 2 reduces the failure probability from 99% to 27%.

But, for the replication to work properly, each process must reach in a definite period, a global knowledge of other processes states to prevent incoherence. For instance, running processes should stop sending messages to a failed process. This problem becomes challenging when large scale systems are in the scope. When an application starts, it registers with a local service called the *fault-detection service*. In each host, this service is responsible to notify the local application process of failures happening on co-allocated processes. Thus, the design of the failure detectors is of primary importance for fault-tolerance. For this discussion we first need to review state of the art proposals concerning fault detection since some of these concepts are the basis for our work.

4 Fault Detection: Background

Failure detection services have received much attention in the literature and since they are considered as first class services of distributed systems [4], many protocols for failure detection have been proposed and implemented. Two classic approaches are the *push* and *pull* models discussed in [6], which rely on a centralized node which regularly triggers push or pull actions. Though they have proved to be efficient on local area networks, they do not scale well and hence are not adapted to large distributed systems such as those targeted for P2P-MPI.

A much more scalable protocol is called *gossiping* after the gossip-style fault detection service presented in [10]. It is a distributed algorithm whose informative messages are evenly dispatched amongst the links of the system. In the following, we present this algorithm approach and its main variants.

A gossip failure detector is a set of distributed modules, with one module residing at each host to monitor. Each module maintains a local table with one entry per detector known to it. This entry includes a counter called *heartbeat*. In a running state, each module repeatedly chooses some other modules and sends them a gossip message consisting in its table with its heartbeat incremented. When a module receives one or more gossip messages from other modules, it merges its local table with all received tables and adopts for each host the maximum heartbeat found. If a heartbeat for a host A which is maintained by a failure detector at host B has not increased after a certain timeout, host B suspects that host A has crashed. In general, it follows a consensus phase about host A failure in order to keep the system's coherence.

Gossiping protocols are usually governed by three key parameters: the gossip time, cleanup time, and the consensus time. Gossip time, noted T_{gossip}, is the time interval between two consecutive gossip messages. Cleanup time, or $T_{cleanup}$, is the time interval after which a host is suspected to have failed. Finally, consensus time noted $T_{consensus}$, is the time interval after which consensus is reached about a failed node.

Notice that a major difficulty in gossiping implementations lies in the setting of $T_{cleanup}$: it is easy to compute a lower bound, referred to as $T_{cleanup}^{min}$, which is the time required for information to reach all other hosts, but this can serve as $T_{cleanup}$ only in synchronous systems. In asynchronous systems, the cleanup time is usually set to some multiple of the gossip time, and must neither be too long to avoid long detection times, nor too short to avoid frequent false failure detections.

Starting from this basis, several proposals have been made to improve or adapt this gossip-style failure detector to other contexts [9]. We briefly review advantages and disadvantages of the original and modified gossip based protocols and what is to be adapted to meet P2P-MPI requirements. Notably, we pay attention to the detection time ($T^{min}_{cleanup}$) and reliability of each protocol.

Random. In the gossip protocol originally proposed [10], each module randomly chooses at each step, the hosts it sends its table to. In practice, random gossip evens the communication load amongst the network links but has the disadvantage of being non-deterministic. It is possible that a node receives no gossip message for a period long enough to cause a false failure detection, i.e. a node is considered failed whereas it is still alive. To minimize this risk, the system implementor can increase $T_{cleanup}$ at the cost of a longer detection time.

Round-Robin (RR). This method aims to make gossip messages traffic more uniform by employing a deterministic approach. In this protocol, gossiping takes place in definite round every T_{gossip} seconds. In any one round, each node will receive and send a single gossip message. The destination node d of a message is determined from the source node s and the current round number r.

$$d = (s + r) \mod n, \quad 0 \leq s < n, 1 \leq r < n \tag{1}$$

where n is the number of nodes. After $r = n - 1$ rounds, all nodes have communicated with each other, which ends a *cycle* and r (generally implemented as a circular counter) is reset to 1. For a 6 nodes system, the set of communications taking place is represented in the table in Figure 2.

r	$s \rightarrow d$
1	$\boxed{0} \rightarrow \underline{1}$, $1 \rightarrow 2$, $2 \rightarrow 3$, $3 \rightarrow 4$, $4 \rightarrow 5$, $5 \rightarrow 0$
2	$0 \rightarrow \underline{2}$, $1 \rightarrow \underline{3}$, $2 \rightarrow 4$, $3 \rightarrow 5$, $4 \rightarrow 0$, $5 \rightarrow 1$
3	$0 \rightarrow \underline{3}$, $1 \rightarrow \underline{4}$, $2 \rightarrow \underline{5}$, $3 \rightarrow \underline{0}$, $4 \rightarrow 1$, $5 \rightarrow 2$
4	$0 \rightarrow 4$, $1 \rightarrow 5$, $2 \rightarrow 0$, $3 \rightarrow 1$, $4 \rightarrow 2$, $5 \rightarrow 3$
5	$0 \rightarrow 5$, $1 \rightarrow 0$, $2 \rightarrow 1$, $3 \rightarrow 2$, $4 \rightarrow 3$, $5 \rightarrow 4$

Fig. 2. Communication pattern in the round-robin protocol ($n = 6$)

This protocol guarantees that all nodes will receive a given node's updated heartbeat within a bounded time. The information about a state's node is transmitted to one other node in the first round, then to two other nodes in the second round (one node gets the information directly from the initial node, the other from the node previously informed), etc. At a given round r, there are $1+2+\cdots+r$ nodes informed. Hence, knowing n we can deduce the minimum cleanup time, depending on an integer number of rounds r such that:

$$T^{min}_{cleanup} = r \times T_{gossip} \quad \text{where} \quad r = \lceil \rho \rceil \quad , \quad \frac{\rho(\rho+1)}{2} = n$$

For instance in Figure 2, three rounds are required to inform the six nodes of the initial state of node 0 (boxed). We have underlined the nodes when they receive the information.

Binary Round-Robin (BRR). The binary round-robin protocol attempts to minimize bandwidth used for gossiping by eliminating all redundant gossiping messages. The inherent redundancy of the round-robin protocol is avoided by skipping the unnecessary steps. The algorithm determines sources and destination nodes from the following relation:

$$d = (s + 2^{r-1}) \mod n, \quad 1 \leq r \leq \lceil log_2(n) \rceil \tag{2}$$

The cycle length is $\lceil log_2(n) \rceil$ rounds, and we have $T^{min}_{cleanup} = \lceil log_2(n) \rceil \times T_{gossip}$.

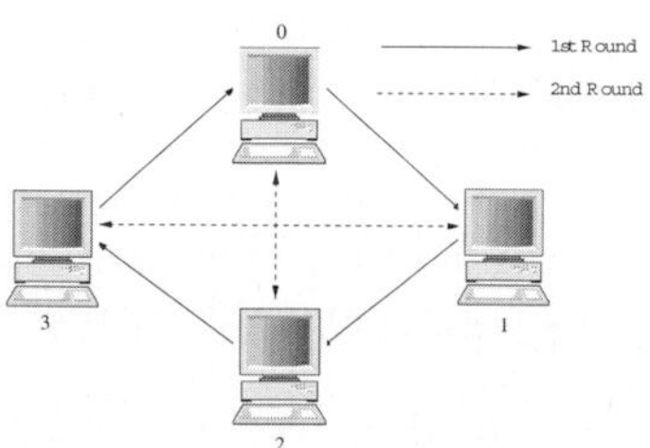

Fig. 3. Communication pattern in the binary round-robin protocol ($n = 4$)

From our experience (also observed in experiments of Section 6), in a asynchronous system, provided that we are able to make the distributed FD start nearly a the same time, i.e. within a time slot shorter (logical time) than a cycle, and that the time needed to send a heartbeat is less than T_{gossip}, a good choice for $T_{cleanup}$ is the smallest multiple of $T^{min}_{cleanup}$, i.e. $2 \times \lceil log_2(n) \rceil \times T_{gossip}$. This allows not to consider a fault, the frequent situation where the last messages sent within a cycle c on source nodes arrive at cycle $c+1$ on their corresponding receiver nodes.

Note however that the elimination of redundant gossip alleviates network load and accelerate heartbeat status dissemination at the cost of an increased risk of false detections. Figure 3 shows a 4 nodes system. From equation 2, we have that node 2 gets incoming messages from node 1 (in the 1st round) and from node 0 (2nd round) only. Therefore, if node 0 and 1 fail, node 2 will not receive any more gossip messages. After $T_{cleanup}$ units of time, node 2 will suspect node 3 to have failed even if it is not true. This point is thus to be considered in the protocol choice.

5 Fault Detection in P2P-MPI

From the previous description of state of the art proposals for failure detection, we retain BRR for its low bandwidth usage and quick detection time despite it relative fragility. With this protocol often comes a consensus phase, which follows a failure detection, to keep the coherence of the system (all nodes make the same decision about other nodes states). Consensus if often based on a voting procedure [9]: in that case all nodes transmit, in addition to their heartbeat table, an extra $(n \times n)$ matrix M. The value $M_{i,j}$ indicates what is the state of node i according to node j. Thus, a FD suspecting a node to have failed can decide the node is really failed if a majority of other nodes agree. However, the cost of transmitting such matrices would induce an unacceptable overhead in our case. For a 256 nodes system, each matrix represents at least a 64 Kib message (and 256 Kib for 512 nodes), transmitted every T_{gossip}. We replace the consensus by a lighter procedure, called *ping procedure* in which a node suspecting another node to have failed, directly ping this node to confirm the failure. If the node is alive, it answers to the ping by returning its current heartbeat.

This is an illustration of problems we came across when studying the behavior of P2P-MPI FD. We now describe the requirements we have set for the middleware, and which algorithms have been implemented to fulfill these requirements.

5.1 Assumptions and Requirements

In our context, we call a (non-byzantine) *fault* the lack of response during a given delay from a process enrolled for an application execution. A fault can have three origins: (i) the process itself crashes (e.g. the program aborts on a DivideByZero error), (ii) the host executing the process crashes (e.g. the computer is shut off), or (iii) the fault-detection monitoring the process crashes and hence no more notifications of aliveness are reported to other processes.

P2P-MPI is intended for grids and should be able to scale up to hundreds of nodes. Hence, we demand its fault detection service to be: a) scalable, i.e. the network traffic that it generates does not induce bottlenecks, b) efficient, i.e. the detection time is acceptable relatively to the application execution time, c) deterministic in the fault detection time, i.e. a fault is detected in a guaranteed delay, d) reliable, i.e. its failure probability is several orders of magnitudes less than the failure probability of the monitored application, since its failure would results in false failure detections.

We make several assumptions that we consider realistic accordingly to the above requirements and given current real systems. First, we assume an asynchronous system, with no global clock but we assume the local clock drifts remain constant. We also assume non-lossy channels: our implementation uses TCP to transport fault detection service traffic because TCP insures message delivery. TCP also has the advantage of being less often blocked than UDP between administrative domains. We also require a few available ports (3 for services plus 1 for each application) for TCP communications, i.e. not blocked by firewalls for any participating peer. Indeed, for sake of performances, we do not have relay mechanisms. During the startup phase, if we detect that the communication could not be establish back and forth between the submitter and all other peers, the application's launch stops. Last, we assume that the time required to transmit a message between any two hosts is generally less than T_{gossip}. Yet, we tolerate unusually long transmission times (due to network hangup for instance) thanks to a parameter T_{max_hangup} set by the user (actually $T_{cleanup}$ is increased by T_{max_hangup} in the implementation).

5.2 Design Issues

Until the present work, P2P-MPI's fault detection service was based on the random gossip algorithm. In practice however, we were not fully satisfied with it because of its non-deterministic detection time.

As stated above, the BRR protocol is optimal with respect to bandwidth usage and fault detection delay. The low bandwidth usage is due to the small number of nodes (we call them *sources*) in charge of informing a given node by sending to it gossiping messages: in a system of n nodes, each node has at most $log_2(n)$ sources. Hence, BRR is the most fragile system with respect to the simultaneous failures of all sources for a node, and the probability that this situation happens is not always negligible: In the example of the 4 nodes system with BRR, the probability of failure can be counted as follows. Let f be the failure probability of each individual node in a time unit T ($T < T_{cleanup}$), and let $P(i)$ the probability that i nodes simultaneously fail during T. In the case 2 nodes fail, if both of them are source nodes then there will be a node that can not get any gossip messages. Here, there are 4 such cases, which are the failures of {2,3},{0,3},{0,1} or {1,2}. In the case 3 nodes fail, there is no chance FD can resist. There are $\binom{4}{3}$ ways of choosing 3 failed nodes among 4, namely {1,2,3},{0,2,3},{0,1,3},{0,1,2}. And there is only 1 case 4 nodes fail. Finally, the FD failure has probability $P_{brr(4)} = P(4) + P(3) + P(2) = f^4 + \binom{4}{3} f^3(1-f) + 4f^2(1-f)^2$.

In this case, using the numerical values of section 3 (i.e. f=0.05), the comparison between the failure probability of the application (p=2, r=2) and the failure probability of the BRR for n=4, leads to $P_{app(2,2)} = 0.005$ and $P_{brr(4)} = 0.0095$ which means the application is more resistant than the fault detection system itself. Even if the FD failure probability decreases quickly with the number of nodes, the user may wish to increase FD robustness by not eliminating all redundancy in the gossip protocol.

5.3 P2P-MPI Implementation

Users have various needs, depending on the number of nodes they intend to use and on the network characteristics. In a reliable environment, BRR is a good choice for its optimal detection speed. For more reliability, we may wish some redundancy and we allow users to choose a variant of BRR described below. The chosen protocol appears in the configuration file and may change for each application (at startup, all FDs are instructed with which protocol they should monitor a given application).

The choice of an appropriate protocol is important but not sufficient to get an effective implementation. We also have to correctly initialize the heartbeating system so that the delayed starts of processes are not considered failures. Also, the application must occasionally make a decision against the FD prediction about a failure to detect firewalls.

Double Binary Round-Robin (DBRR). We introduce the double binary round-robin protocol which detects failures in a delay asymptotically equal to BRR ($O(log_2(n))$) and acceptably fast in practice, while re-inforcing robustness of BRR. The idea is simply to avoid to have one-way connections only between nodes. Thus, in the first half of a cycle, we use the BRR routing in a clock-wise direction while in the second half, we establish a connection back by applying BRR in a counterclock-wise direction. The destination node for each gossip message is determined by the following relation:

$$d = \begin{cases} (s + 2^{r-1}) \mod n & \text{if } 1 \leq r \leq \lceil log_2(n) \rceil \\ (s - 2^{r - \lceil log_2(n) \rceil - 1}) \mod n & \text{if } \lceil log_2(n) \rceil < r \leq 2\lceil log_2(n) \rceil \end{cases} \quad (3)$$

The cycle length is $2\lceil log_2(n) \rceil$ and hence we have $T_{cleanup}^{min} = 2\lceil log_2(n) \rceil \times T_{gossip}$. With the same assumptions as for BRR, we set $T_{cleanup} = 3\lceil log_2(n) \rceil \times T_{gossip}$ for DBRR.

To compare BRR and DBRR reliability, we can count following the principles of Section 5.2 but this quickly becomes difficult for a large number of nodes. Instead, we simulate a large number of scenarios, in which each node may fail with a probability f. Then, we verify if the graph representing the BRR or DBRR routing is connected: simultaneous nodes failures may cut all edges from sources nodes to a destination node, which implies a FD failure. In Figure 4, we repeat the simulation for 5.8×10^9 trials with f=0.05. Notice that in the DBRR protocol, we could not not find any FD failure when the number of nodes is more than 16, which means the number of our trials is not sufficient to estimate the DBRR failure probability for such n.

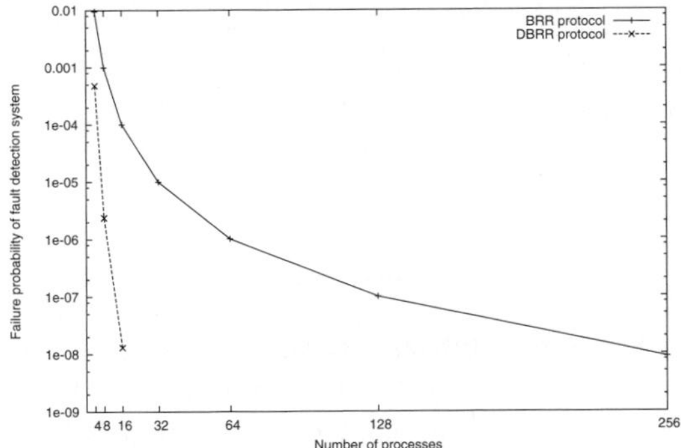

Fig. 4. Failure probabilities of the FD system using BRR and DBRR ($f = 0.05$)

Automatic Adjustment of Initial Heartbeat. In the startup phase of an application execution (contained in MPI_Init), the submitter process first queries advertised resources for their availability and their will to accept the job. The submitter construct a table numbering available resources called the communicator[1], which is sent in turn to participating peers. The remote peers acknowledge this numbering by returning TCP sockets where the submitter can contact their file transfer service. It follows the transfer of executable code and input data.

[1] The submitter always has number 0.

Once a remote node has completed the download, it starts the application which registers with its local FD instance.

This causes the FDs to start asynchronously and because the time of transferring files may well exceed $T_{cleanup}$, the FD should (i) not declared nodes that have not yet started their FD as failed, and (ii) should start with a heartbeat value similar to all others at the end of the MPI_Init barrier. The idea is thus to estimate on each node, how many heartbeats have been missed since the beginning of the startup phase, to set the local initial heartbeat accordingly. This is achieved by making the submitter send to each node, together with the communicator, the time spent sending information to previous nodes. Figure 5 illustrates the situation. We note ts_i, $1 \leq i < n$ the date when the submitter

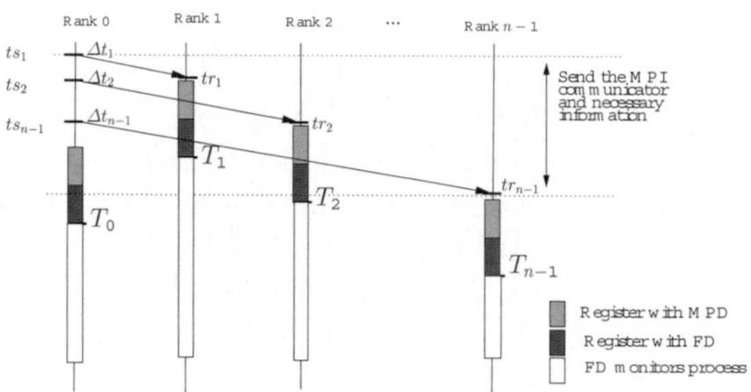

Fig. 5. Application startup

sends the communicator to peer i, and tr_i the date when peer i receives the communicator. Each peer also stores the date T_i at which it registers with its local FD. The submitter sends $\Delta t_i = ts_i - ts_1$ to any peer i ($1 \leq i < n$) which can then computes its initial heartbeat h_i as:

$$h_i = \lceil (T_i - tr_i + \Delta t_i)/T_{gossip} \rceil, \quad 1 \leq i < n \tag{4}$$

while the submitter adjusts its initial heartbeat to $h_0 = \lceil (T_0 - ts_1)/T_{gossip} \rceil$.

Note that we implement a flat tree broadcast to send the communicator instead of any hierarchical broadcast scheme (e.g. binary tree, binomial tree) because we could not guarantee in that case, that intermediate nodes always stay alive and pass the communicator information to others. If any would fail after receiving the communicator and before it passes that information to others, then the rest of that tree will not get any information about the communicator and the execution could not continue.

Application-Failure Detector Interaction. At first sight, the application could completely rely on its FD to decide whether a communication with a given node is possible or not. For instance, in our first implementation of *send* or related function calls (eg. Send, Bcast) the sender continuously tried to send a message to the destination (ignoring socket timeouts) until it either succeeded or received a notification that the destination node is down from its FD. This allows to control the detection of network communication interruptions through the FD configuration.

However, there exist firewall configurations that authorize connections from some addresses only, which makes possible that a host receive gossip messages (via other nodes) about the aliveness of a particular destination while the destination is blocked for direct communication. In that case, the send function will loop forever and the application can not terminate. Our new send implementation simply installs a timeout to tackle this problem, which we set to $2 \times T_{cleanup}$. Reaching this timeout on a send stops the local application process, and soon the rest of the nodes will detect the process death.

6 Experiments

The objective of the experiments is to evaluate the failure detection speed with both BRR and DBRR monitoring a P2P-MPI application running on a real grid testbed. We use the Grid'5000 platform, a federation of dedicated computers hosted across nine campus sites in France, and organized in a virtual private network over Renater, the national education and research network. Each site has currently about 100 to 700 processors arranged in one to several clusters at each site. In our experiment, we distribute the processes of our parallel test application across three sites (Nancy, Rennes and Nice).

The experiment consists in running a parallel application without replication and after 20 seconds, we kill all processes on a random node. We then log at what time each node is notified of the failure and compute the time interval between failure and detection. Figure 6 plots the average of these intervals on all nodes and for both protocols, with T_{gossip} set to 0.5 second. Also plotted for comparison is $T_{cleanup}$ as specified previously, termed "theoretical" detection time on the graph.

The detection speed observed is very similar to the theoretical predictions whatever the number of processes involved, up to 256. The difference with the

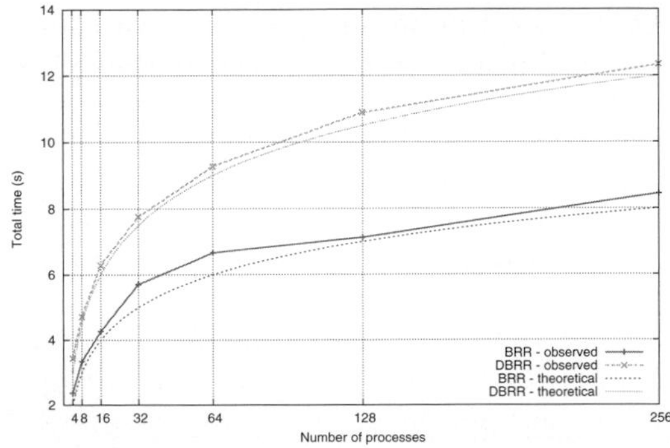

Fig. 6. Time to detect a fault for BRR and DBRR

predictions (about 0.5 s) comes from the ping procedure which adds an overhead, and from the rounding to an integer number of heartbeats in Equation 4. This difference is about the same as the T_{gossip} value used and hence we see that the ping procedure does not induce a bottleneck.

It is also important to notice that no false detection has been observed throughout our tests, hence the ping procedure has been triggered only for real failures. There are two reasons for a false detection: either all sources of information for a node fail, or $T_{cleanup}$ is too short with respect to the system characteristics (communication delays, local clocks drifts, etc). Here, given the briefness of execution, the former reason is out of the scope. Given the absence of false failures we can conclude that we have chosen a correct detection time $T_{cleanup}$, and our initial assumptions are correct, i.e. the initial hearbeat adjustment is effective and message delays are less than T_{gossip}.

This experiment shows the scalability of the system on Grid'5000, despite the presence of wide area network links between hosts. Further tests should experiment smaller values of T_{gossip} for a quicker detection time. We also plan to test the system at the scale of a thousand processes.

7 Conclusion

We have described in this paper the fault-detection service underlying P2P-MPI. The first part is an overview of the principles of P2P-MPI among which is replication, used as a means to increase robustness of applications executions, and external monitoring of application execution by a specific fault-detection module. In the second part, we first describe the background of our work, based on recent advances in the research field of fault detectors. We compare the main protocols recently proposed regarding their robustness, their speed and their deterministic behavior, and we analyze which is best suited for our middleware. We introduce an original protocol that increases the number of sources in the gossip procedure, and thus improves the fault-tolerance of the failure detection service, while the detection time remains low. Last, we present the experiments conducted on Grid'5000. The results show that the fault detection speeds observed in experiments for applications of up to 256 processes, are really close to the theoretical figures, and demonstrate the system scalability.

Acknowledgments. Experiments presented in this paper were carried out using the Grid'5000 experimental testbed, an initiative from the French Ministry of Research through the ACI GRID incentive action, INRIA, CNRS and RENATER and other contributing partners (see https://www.grid5000.fr)

References

[1] JXTA. `http://www.jxta.org`.

[2] N. Andrade, W. Cirne, F. Brasileiro, and P. Roisenberg. Our-grid: An approach to easily assemble grids with equitable resource sharing. In *9th Workshop on Job Scheduling Strategies for Parallel Processing*, June 2003.

[3] B. Carpenter, V. Getov, G. Judd, T. Skjellum, and G. Fox. Mpj: Mpi-like message passing for java. *Concurrency: Practice and Experience*, 12(11), Sept. 2000.
[4] T. D. Chandra and S. Toueg. Unreliable failure detectors for reliable distributed systems. *J. ACM*, 43(2):225–267, 1996.
[5] G. Fedak, C. Germain, V. Néri, and F. Cappello. XtremWeb: A generic global computing system. In *CCGRID*, pages 582–587. IEEE Computer Society, 2001.
[6] P. Felber, X. Defago, R. Guerraoui, and P. Oser. Failure detectors as first class objects. In *Proceeding of the 9th IEEE Intl. Symposium on Distributed Objects and Applications (DOA'99)*, pages 132–141, Sept. 1999.
[7] S. Genaud and C. Rattanapoka. A peer-to-peer framework for robust execution of message passing parallel programs. In *EuroPVM/MPI 2005*, volume 3666 of *LNCS*, pages 276–284. Springer-Verlag, September 2005.
[8] MPI Forum. MPI: A message passing interface standard. Technical report, University of Tennessee, Knoxville, TN, USA, June 1995.
[9] S. Ranganathan, A. D. George, R. W. Todd, and M. C. Chidester. Gossip-style failure detection and distributed consensus for scalable heterogeneous clusters. *Cluster Computing*, 4(3):197–209, 2001.
[10] R. V. Renesse, Y. Minsky, and M. Hayden. A gossip-style failure detection service. In *IFIP International Conference on Distributed Systems Platforms and Open Distributed Middleware*, pages 55–70, England, 1998.
[11] K. Shudo, Y. Tanaka, and S. Sekiguchi. P3: P2P-based middleware enabling transfer and aggregation of computational resource. In *5th Intl. Workshop on Global and Peer-to-Peer Computing*. IEEE, May 2005.

Heterogeneous Wireless Sensor Network Deployment and Topology Control Based on Irregular Sensor Model

Chun-Hsien Wu and Yeh-Ching Chung

Department of Computer Science, National Tsing Hua University,
Hsinchu 30013, Taiwan, R.O.C.
{chwu, ychung}@cs.nthu.edu.tw

Abstract. Heterogeneous wireless sensor network (heterogeneous WSN) consists of sensor nodes with different ability, such as different computing power and sensing range. Compared with homogeneous WSN, deployment and topology control are more complex in heterogeneous WSN. In this paper, a deployment and topology control method is presented for heterogeneous sensor nodes with different communication and sensing range. It is based on the irregular sensor model used to approximate the behavior of sensor nodes. Besides, a cost model is proposed to evaluate the deployment cost of heterogeneous WSN. According to experiment results, the proposed method can achieve higher coverage rate and lower deployment cost for the same deployable sensor nodes.

Keywords: Wireless sensor network, heterogeneous sensor deployment, topology control, sensor coverage, irregular sensor model.

1 Introduction

Wireless sensor network (WSN) is a key element of the pervasive/ubiquitous computing. With the advancement of manufacturing and wireless technologies, many feasible applications are proposed such as industrial sensor networks [4], volcano-monitoring networks [10], and habitat monitoring [11], etc. The heterogeneous WSN consists of sensor nodes with different abilities, such as various sensor types and communication/sensing range, thus provides more flexibility in deployment. For example, we can construct a WSN in which nodes are equipped with different kinds of sensors to provide various sensing services. Besides, if there are two types of senor nodes: the high-end ones have higher process throughput and longer communication/sensing range; the low-end ones are much cheaper and with limited computation and communication/sensing abilities. A mixed deployment of these nodes can achieve a balance of performance and cost of WSN. For example, some low-end sensor nodes can be used to replace high-end ones without degrading the network lifetime of WSN. Many research works have been proposed to address the deployment problem of heterogeneous WSN [3] [5].

To achieve a satisfying performance, the deployment of heterogeneous WSN is more complicated than homogeneous WSN. Deployment simulation is essential before actual installation of sensor nodes, since different deployment configurations can

C. Cérin and K.-C. Li (Eds.): GPC 2007, LNCS 4459, pp. 78–88, 2007.

be tested without considering the cost of real node deployment. However, to reflect the behavior of WSN correctly is a major challenge of sensor nodes deployment simulation. In many research works, disk model is commonly used [6] [7] [8]. However, a fixed communication or sensing range is not practical to a realistic senor node. Moreover, node deployment in heterogeneous WSN has to consider the topology control between different types of sensor nodes. For example, to maintain a symmetric communication, the distance between high-end and low-end sensor nodes cannot be larger than the maximum communication range of the low-end one. Besides, if the sensor nodes have different detection range, the sensor coverage area of low-end node cannot be fully covered by the high-end node.

In this paper, a heterogeneous sensor deployment and topology control method is presented. It aims to deal with the deployment problem of heterogeneous sensor nodes with different communication and sensing range. In addition, an irregular sensor model is proposed to approximate the behavior of sensor nodes. According to experiment results, the proposed method can achieve higher coverage rate under the same deployable sensor nodes. Besides, the deployment cost is much lower with different configurations of sensor nodes.

The rest of the paper is organized as follows. In Section 2, previous works related to heterogeneous sensor deployment and irregular sensor model are addressed. In Section 3, the irregular sensor model and some definitions of heterogeneous WSN used in this paper are given. In Section 4, we present the details of heterogeneous sensor node deployment. Section 5 evaluates the performance of the proposed method under various scenarios. Finally, we conclude the paper in Section 6.

2 Related Work

The benefit of heterogeneous wireless sensor networks has been studied in many research works. Lee et al. [5] analyze heterogeneous deployments both mathematically and through simulations in different deployment environments and network operation models considering both coverage degree and coverage area. Experiment results show that using an optimal mixture of many inexpensive low-capability devices and some expensive high-capability devices can significantly extend the duration of a network's sensing performance. In [3], Hu et al. investigate some fundamental questions for hybrid deployment of sensor network, and propose a cost model and integer linear programming problem formulation for minimizing energy usage and maximizing lifetime in a hybrid sensor network. Their studies show that network lifetime can be increased dramatically with the addition of extra micro-servers, and the locations of micro-servers can affect the lifetime of network significantly. In addition, the cost-effectiveness analysis shows that hybrid sensor network is financially cost efficient for a large case.

In many research works [6] [7] [8], unit disk graph (UDG) is a commonly used sensor model to reflect the correct behavior of sensor node. It assumes the effective communication and sensing region of sensor node is a circle with fixed radius. However, a constant communication and sensing range is not practical for a realistic senor node. In [2], He et al., propose a model with an upper and lower bound on signal propagation. If the distance between a pair of nodes is larger than the upper bound, they are out of communication range. If within the lower bound, they are guaranteed to be within communication range. The parameter DOI (degree of irregularity) is used to denote the irregularity of the radio pattern. It is the maximum radio range variation per unit degree change in the direction of radio propagation. When the DOI is set to zero, there is no range variation, resulting in a UDG model. Zhou et al. [12] extended the previous DOI model as radio irregularity model (RIM) based on the empirical data obtained from the MICA2 and MICAZ platforms.

3 Preliminaries

3.1 Irregular Sensor Model

In this paper, an irregular sensor model is proposed based on the radio propagation model inspired from Radio Irregularity Model (RIM) [12] and degree of irregularity (DOI) [2]. The irregular sensor model assumes that the sensor node use the same radio propagation model for communication and sensing. For each sensor node, a radio propagation range is pre-defined and denoted as R_{def}, and the effective radio propagation range ($R_{effective}$) is decided by the normal (Gaussian) distribution with a mean of R_{def} and a standard derivation of DOI, where DOI represents for the degree of irregularity of $R_{effective}$.

Figure 1 illustrates the radio propagation range under different DOI. According to the "68-95-99.7 rule", about 99.7% of the values are within three standard derivations away from the mean (R_{def}) [9]. Thus we define the $R_{effective}$ is ranged from R_{def} – 3*DOI (R_{min}) to R_{def} + 3*DOI (R_{max}), and the relationship between R_{def}, R_{min}, and R_{max} is illustrated in Figure 2.

After the effective radio propagation range is calculated, we can use it to derive the radio strength model based on the simple transmission formula for a radio circuit made up of an isotropic transmitting and a receiving antenna in free space [1]:

$$P_r / P_t = A_r A_t / d^2 \lambda^2 . \quad (1)$$

where P_t is the power fed into the transmitting antenna at its input terminals, P_r is the power available at the output terminals of the receiving antenna, A_r (or A_t) is the effective area of the receiving (or transmitting) antenna, d is the distance between antennas, and λ is the wavelength. Suppose that P_t, A_r, A_t, and λ are constants, then the received radio power (P_r) is proportional to $1/d^2$. Thus, we define the radio strength of senor node n at point p as follows:

$$R(n, p) = (R_{effective} / d(n, p))^2 . \quad (2)$$

where $d(n, p)$ is the Euclidean distance between node n and point p. If $R(n, p) \geqq 1$, then there exists radio connection between node n and point p.

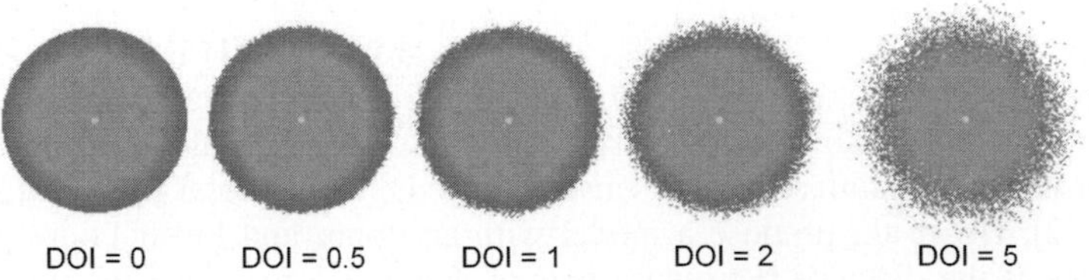

Fig. 1. The radio propagation range under different DOI

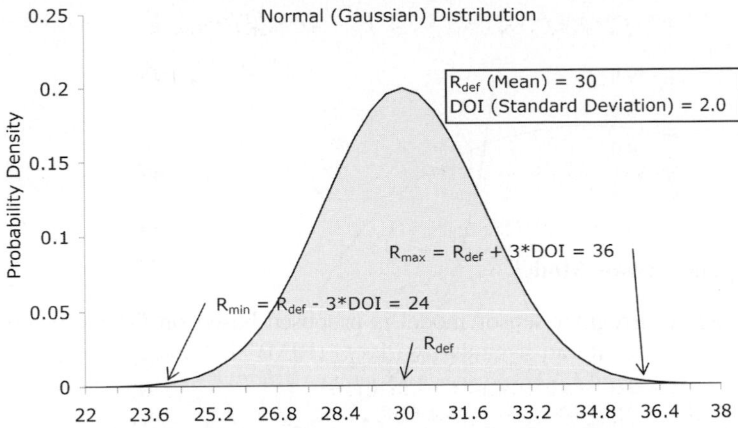

Fig. 2. The relationship between R_{def}, R_{min}, and R_{max}

According to the definition of $R_{effective}$, we have the following observations:

1. If $d(n, p) < R_{min}$, $R(n, p)$ must be larger than 1.
2. If $d(n, p) > R_{max}$, $R(n, p)$ must be less than 1.
3. If $d(n, p) > R_{effective}$, the radio connection between two nodes cannot be guaranteed. Here we define "out of range" as $R(n, p) = min\_strength$, where *min_strength* is the minimum threshold of radio strength that guarantees radio connection between node n and point p, thus the maximum connectable distance between node n and point p is R_{max}/sqrt(*min_strength*).
4. Similarly, we define "too closed" as $R(n, p) = max\_strength$, where *max_strength* is the maximum acceptable radio strength for node n, thus the minimal distance between node n and point p is R_{min}/sqrt(*max_strength*).

The relationship between $R(n, p)$ and $d(n, p)$ is illustrated in Figure 3. In the Section 4, the proposed irregular sensor model will be used to select a proper sensor node location and calculate coverage rate.

3.2 Some Definitions of Heterogeneous Wireless Sensor Network

In this paper, we define a heterogeneous WSN that consists of three types of nodes: sink node, high-end senor node (N_H), and low-end senor node (N_L). Each node has the same communication model and two types of sensor nodes have the same sensing model. The difference between N_H and N_L is that the pre-defined communication and sensing range are different. The default communication and sensing range of N_H are defined as R_{CH} and R_{SH}, respectively. Similarly, R_{CL} and R_{SL} are denoted as the default communication and sensing range of N_L, where $R_{CH} > R_{CL}$, and $R_{SH} > R_{SL}$.

To evaluate the results of sensor node deployment, we define a deployment cost model as:

$$deployment\_cost = (\text{Num}(N_H) * N_{H}\_cost + \text{Num}(N_L)) \,/\, total\_coverage\_rate \,. \quad (3)$$

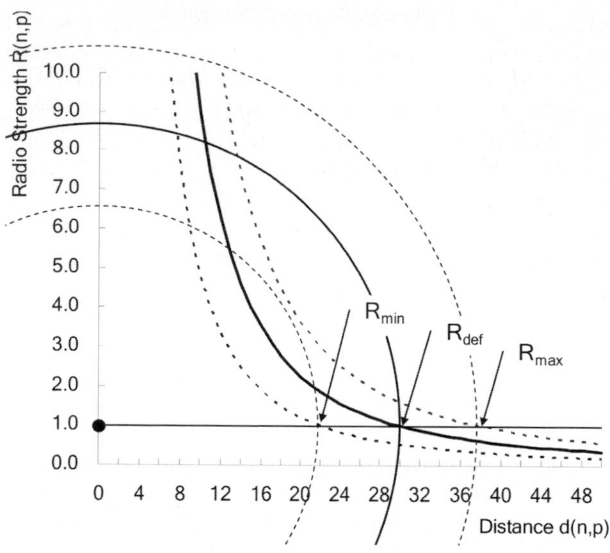

Fig. 3. The relationship between $R(n, p)$ and $d(n, p)$

$$N_H\_cost = (R_{CH} + R_{SH}^2) / (R_{CL} + R_{SL}^2)\,. \tag{4}$$

where *deployment_cost* is calculated as the total cost of deployed sensor nodes divided by the *total_coverage_rate* produced by these sensor nodes, and N_H_cost is the difference of sensor node cost between N_H and N_L. The sensor node cost is determined by two factors: communication distance and coverage area of sensor, represented by R_c and R_s^2 respectively. The calculation of *total_coverage_rate* is based on the irregular senor model described in Section 3.1. At first, the deployment area is filled with grid points. For a senor node *N*, its *coverage_rate* at grid point *p* is based on Equation (2) in Section 3.1:

$$coverage\_rate = (effective\_range\ /\ d(N, p))^2\,. \tag{5}$$

where *effective_range* is a random value with normal distribution between $\min(R_S)$ and $\max(R_S)$. After all sensor nodes are processed, each grid point will keep the highest coverage rate but not exceed one. The *total_coverage_rate* is equal to the sum of *coverage_rate* divided by the number of grid points.

4 Heterogeneous Sensor Deployment

In this section, a heterogeneous sensor deployment method is proposed. Given a deployment area and the upper bound of deployable high-end and low-end sensor nodes, the objective is to construct a communication-connected sensor network, in which high-end and low-end sensor nodes are deployed uniformly to achieve high coverage rate. In the initialization step, a deployment area is initialized base on the configuration file. In the neighbor-info collection step, starting from the sink node, the information of adjacent sensor nodes within the communication range is collected.

It can be used to decide the deployment ratio of high-end and low-end sensor nodes. In the candidate generation step, candidate positions are generated according to topology control policies, and a scoring mechanism based on the irregular sensor model is applied to each candidate. At least, a new sensor node with the most coverage gains is deployed while maintaining the communication connectivity. The number of deployable sensor nodes is limited by the pre-defined quota of sink/sensor node. If the quota is reached, then a deployed sensor node with available quota will be selected. The deployment process will be repeated until the upper bound of deployable sensor nodes is reached or no suitable place available to add a sensor node. In the following, we will describe each deployment step in details.

4.1 Initialization Step

In this step, a sensing area is generated from a given configuration file. This file includes the size of deployment area, the location of pre-deployed sink node and sensor nodes, the upper bound of deployable high-end and low-end sensor nodes, and default value of parameters defined in Section 3. These parameters include the default communication and sensing distance of high-end/low-end sensor node (R_{CH}, R_{SH}, R_{CL}, and R_{SL}), the degree of irregular (DOI), and the threshold of radio strength (*max_strength* and *min_strength*). Then the maximum/minimum value of the effective radio propagation range ($R_{effective}$) is calculated for each type of node according to the given DOI. For example, if the default R_{CH} = 30 and DOI = 2.0, then the maximum effective communication distance max(R_{CH}) = R_{CH} + 3*DOI = 36 and the minimum effective communication distance min(R_{CH}) = R_{CH} - 3*DOI = 24. Thus, the effective communication distance of high-end sensor node fits a normal distribution ranged from 24 to 36.

4.2 Neighbor-Info Collection Step

At first, a center node for deployment is selected. The selection of eligible center node is starting from sink node, and then expanding to all deployed sensor nodes. The criterion of eligible node is based on the available quota for node deployment, which is limited by the degree of node defined in the configuration file. The number of deployed high-end and low-end sensor nodes within minimum effective communication distance is denoted as Neighbor(N_H) and Neighbor(N_L). They will be used to decide the deploy ratio of high-end and low-end sensor nodes. Suppose the number of deployable high-end and low-end nodes is denoted as Remain(N_H) and Remain(N_L), respectively. Then the limit numbers of deployable high-end and low-end senor node are represented as Equation (6) and (7):

$$\text{Deploy}(N_H) = \text{limit degree of center node} * \text{Remain}(N_H) \,/\, (\text{Remain}(N_H) + \text{Remain}(N_L)) \,. \tag{6}$$

$$\text{Deploy}(N_L) = \text{limit degree of center node} - \text{Deploy}(N_H) \,. \tag{7}$$

If Deploy(N_H) $\leqq$ Neighbor(N_H), then Deploy(N_H) = 0, means that the number of high-end sensor nodes is sufficient. At last, if Deploy(N_H) + Deploy(N_L) > 0, then the following deployment step will be processed, otherwise, the deployment process for current center node will be terminated and restarted on the next eligible node.

4.3 Candidates Generation Step

In this step, the candidate positions for each type of the sensor node will be generated separately. In heterogeneous sensor node deployment, the symmetric connection must be maintained. It means that the distance between two sensor nodes cannot larger than the maximum communication distance of the low-end one. Besides, the overlap of sensor coverage area between two senor nodes has to be considered to prevent the sensor coverage area of low-end node to be fully covered by the high-end node, which means no coverage gains. In the following, we will discuss the requirement to produce coverage gains while maintaining symmetric connection under different conditions:

– Case I: $R_{CH} > R_{SH}$ and $R_{CL} > R_{SL}$

In this case, the communication distance is larger than sensing range. Figure 4(a) illustrates the condition when a low-end node N_L is added to a high-end sensor node N_H. For N_L, if $d(N_H, N_L) < R_{CL}$, then the symmetric connection is established, and we said that these two nodes are communication-connected. If $d(N_H, N_L) \leqq (R_{SH} - R_{SL})$, then the sensor coverage area of N_L is fully covered by N_H, which means no coverage gains. By combining these observations, if two nodes are communication-connected and have coverage gains, then the distance between two nodes is:

$$(R_{SH} - R_{SL}) < d(N_H, N_L) < R_{CL} . \tag{8}$$

Thus, if we want to produce coverage gains while maintaining symmetric connection when deploying a new sensor node, the following condition must be satisfied:

$$R_{CL} - (R_{SH} - R_{SL}) > 0 . \tag{9}$$

– Case II: $R_{CH} = R_{SH}$ and $R_{CL} = R_{SL}$

From Figure 4(b), the requirement of communication-connected deployment with coverage gains can be derived from Equation (9) by replacing R_{CL} with R_{SL}:

$$2\,R_{SL} > R_{SH} \text{ or } 2\,R_{CL} > R_{CH} . \tag{10}$$

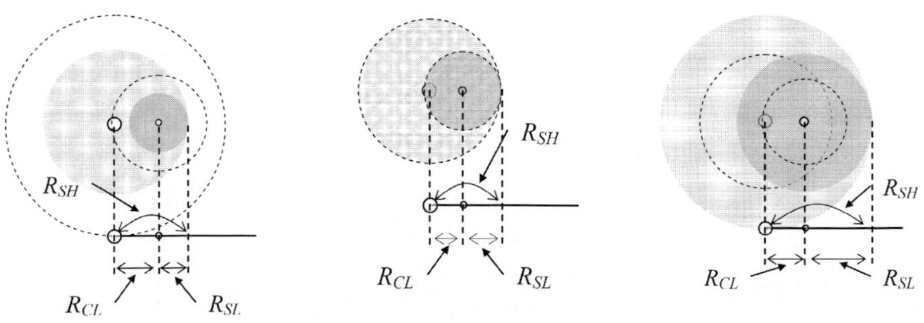

(a) $R_{CH} > R_{SH}$ and $R_{CL} > R_{SL}$ (b) $R_{CH} = R_{SH}$ and $R_{CL} = R_{SL}$ (c) $R_{CH} < R_{SH}$ and $R_{CL} < R_{SL}$

Fig. 4. Sensor node connection and coverage under different conditions

– Case III: $R_{CH} < R_{SH}$ and $R_{CL} < R_{SL}$

From Figure 4(c), we can find that the requirement of communication-connected deployment with coverage gains is identical to Case I.

Based on above results, candidate position is generated by the following topology control policies:

1. If a N_H is selected for node deployment, then the candidate positions of high-end/low-end senor nodes must be within the minimum effective communication distance of high-end/low-end senor node. That is, $d(N_H$, candidate position of high-end node) $\leqq$ min(R_{CH}), and $d(N_H$, candidate position of low-end node) $\leqq$ min(R_{CL}).
2. If a N_L is selected for node deployment, then the candidate positions of two types of sensor nodes must be within the minimum effective communication distance of low-end senor node. That is, $d(N_H$, candidate position of high-end/low-end node) $\leqq$ min(R_{CL}).
3. If $d(N_H$, candidate position of low-end node) $\leqq$ (R_{SH} - R_{SL}), then this candidate position is discard because the sensor coverage area will be fully covered by N_H.
4. The minimum distance between candidate position and deployed nodes is defined as R_{min}/sqrt(*max_strength*), where R_{min} = min(R_{CH}) or min(R_{CL}) is the minimum effective communication distance of sensor node. It can prevent the deployed sensor nodes are too closed.

4.4 Scoring Step

After candidate positions are generated for different types of sensor nodes, a scoring mechanism to each position is defined as follows: *total_score* = *connection_score* + *coverage_score*. The *connection_score* is the distance between candidate position and center node. The *coverage_score* of candidate position is defined as the coverage gains when a sensor node is deployed at the candidate position. The calculation of coverage gains is described as follows: At first, a square around center node with edge length = 2*max(R_S) is filled with grid points. Based on Equation (5) in Section 3.2, the total coverage rate produced by deployed sensor nodes is denoted as *base_coverage_rate*. Next, the total coverage rate with the contribution of candidate position is denoted as *target_coverage_rate*. Thus the *coverage_score* of candidate position = *target_coverage_rate* - *base_coverage_rate*.

4.5 Sensor Addition Step

After all candidate positions are scored, the candidate with the highest score is selected to deploy a new sensor, which has the most coverage gains while maintaining the communication connectivity to center node. If the deploy quota of current center node is reached, the next deployed sensor node with available quota will be selected. The deployment process will be repeated until the upper bound of deployable sensor nodes is reached or no suitable place available to add a sensor node.

5 Experiments

In this section, we evaluate the performance of the proposed sensor deployment method by comparing sensor coverage rate and deployment cost with several sensor node configurations. A simulation tool written in C++ language is running on an IBM eServer 326 (AMD Opteron 250 * 2 and 1GB memory). The deployment area is a 2-D square with 500 × 500 units. A sink node is deployed at (200, 200). The total number of deployable sensor nodes is ranged from 60 to 360. Other parameters are defined as follows: DOI = 2.0, *max_strength* = 1.2 and *min_strength* = 0.8.

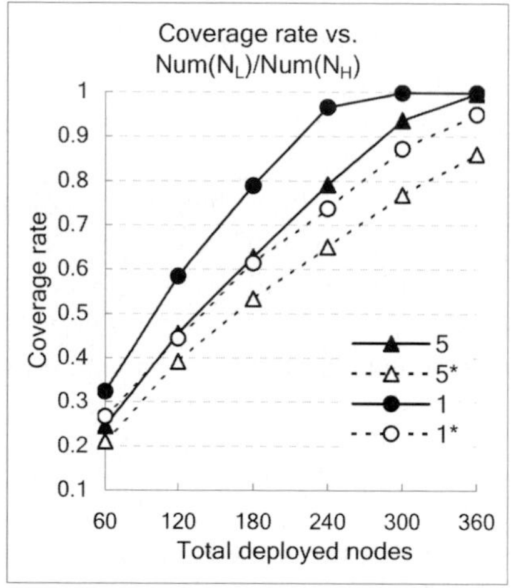

Fig. 5. Coverage rate of Test Case I

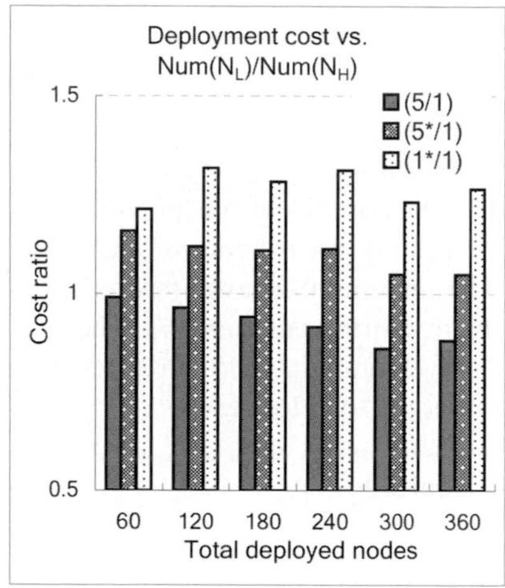

Fig. 6. Deployment cost of Test Case I

Test Case I is the coverage rate and deployment cost under different deployment ratio, where Num(N_L):Num(N_H) = 5:1 or 1:1. Besides, the ratio of communication/sensing range between N_H and N_L (R_H : R_L) is 1.5:1, and the ratio of communication and sensing range for N_H / N_L (R_C : R_S) is 1.5:1. We also compare the results with sensor deployment without topology control (case 2* and 5*). The deployment without topology control is based on the same deployment method, but it omits the topology control policies described in Section 4.3. The experiment results are illustrated in Figure 5 and Figure 6. In Figure 6, we compare the deployment cost of different cases (5, 5*, and 1*) with case 1 (denoted as 5/1, 5*/1, and 1*/1). With the help of topology control, the proposed method has higher coverage rate in comparison of the deployment method without topology control. It can be found lower deployment ratio can achieve higher coverage rate with the help of more high-end nodes. In addition, the reduction of deployment cost is significant for the deployment method with topology control. When deployment ratio is 5:1, it has higher coverage rate and lower deployment cost than the deployment method without topology control under the same deployment ratio.

Test Case II is the coverage rate and deployment cost under different ratio of the communication/sensing range between N_H and N_L ($R_H : R_L$), where $R_{CH} : R_{SH} = R_{CL} : R_{SL} = 1.5:1$, and deployment ratio of N_H and N_L is fixed to 5:1. Other configurations are identical to the Test Case I. Figure 7 and Figure 8 are experiment results. If $R_H / R_L = 1$, it can be regarded as homogeneous deployment since both N_H and N_L have the same communication and sensing range. With the help of high-end sensor nodes, the heterogeneous deployment can get higher coverage rate, but the homogeneous deployment has lower deployment cost. The deployment method without topology control still has higher deployment cost under the same ratio of R_H and R_L.

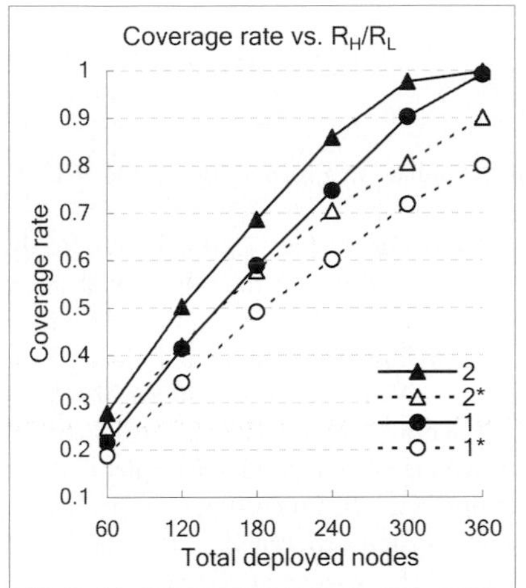

Fig. 7. Coverage rate of Test Case II

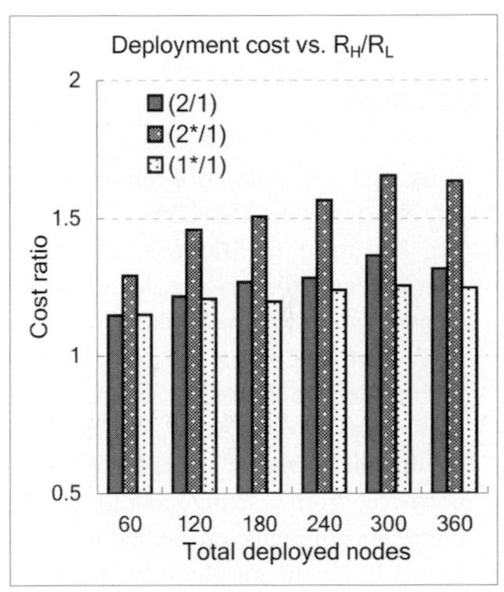

Fig. 8. Deployment cost of Test Case II

6 Conclusions

In this paper, we propose a heterogeneous WSN deployment method based on irregular sensor model. It aims to deal with the deployment problem of heterogeneous sensor nodes with different communication and sensing range. In addition, an irregular sensor model is proposed to approximate the behavior of sensor nodes. The deployment process is starting from sink node, and new nodes are deployed to the region centered with it. In neighbor-info collection step, the information of adjacent sensor nodes is used to decide the deployment ratio of different types of sensor nodes. In the scoring step, a scoring mechanism based on the irregular sensor model is applied to candidate positions. At least, a new sensor node is placed to the position with the most coverage gains while maintaining the communication connectivity to center node. Above process is running repeatedly until all eligible sensor nodes are processed.

According to experiment results, the proposed method can achieve higher coverage rate under the same deployable sensor nodes. Besides, the deployment cost is much lower with different configurations of sensor nodes. In the future work, a sensor node model considering environmental factors and individual behavior is needed. Besides, considering the interactions between different types of sensors is important. At least, the proposed method will be extended as the topology control protocol for heterogeneous WSN.

Acknowledgments. The work of this paper was partially supported by National Science Council and Ministry of Economic Affairs of the Republic of China under contract NSC 95-2221-E-007-018 and MOEA 95-EC-17-A-04-S1-044.

References

1. Friis, H.T.: A Note on a Simple Transmission Formula. In Proceedings of the IRE, Vol. 34, No. 5, (1946) 254- 256
2. He, T., Huang, C., Blum, B. M., Stankovic, J. A., and Abdelzaher, T.: Range-free localization schemes for large scale sensor networks. In Proceedings of the 9th Annual international Conference on Mobile Computing and Networking (MobiCom). (2003) 81-95
3. Hu, W., Chou, C.T., Jha, S., and Bulusu, N.: Deploying Long-Lived and Cost-effective Hybrid Sensor Networks. Elsevier Ad-Hoc Networks, Vol. 4, Issue 6. (2006) 749-767
4. Krishnamurthy, L., Adler, R., Buonadonna, P., Chhabra, J., Flanigan, M., Kushalnagar, N., Nachman, L., and Yarvis, M.: Design and deployment of industrial sensor networks: experiences from a semiconductor plant and the North Sea. In Proceedings of the 3rd international conference on Embedded networked sensor systems (SenSys). (2005) 64-75
5. Lee, J.J., Krishnamachari, B., Kuo, C.C.J.: Impact of Heterogeneous Deployment on Lifetime Sensing Coverage in Sensor Networks (IEEE SECON). (2004)
6. Li, L., Halpern, J. Y., Bahl, P., Wang, Y.-M., and Wattenhofer, R.: Analysis of cone-based distributed topology control algorithms for wireless multi-hop networks. In Proceedings of ACM Symposium on Principle of Distributed Computing (PODC). (2001)
7. Li, X.-Y., Wan, P.-J., Wang, Y., and Frieder, O.: Sparse power efficient topology for wireless networks. In Proceedings of IEEE Hawaii International Conference on System Sciences (HICSS). (2002)
8. Ramanathan, R. and Rosales-Hain, R.: Topology control of multihop wireless networks using transmit power adjustment. In Proceedings of the 20th Annual Joint Conference of the IEEE Computer and Communications Societies (INFOCOM). (2000)
9. Wikipedia contributors, "Normal distribution," Wikipedia, The Free Encyclopedia. (http://en.wikipedia.org/w/index.php?title=Normal_distribution&oldid=93201679)
10. Werner-Allen, G., Lorincz, K., Welsh, M., Marcillo, O., Johnson, J., Ruiz, M., and Lees, J.: Deploying a Wireless Sensor Network on an Active Volcano. IEEE Internet Computing 10(2) (2006) 18-25
11. Xu, N.: A Survey of Sensor Network Applications. University of Southern California. (http://enl.usc.edu/~ningxu/papers/survey.pdf)
12. Zhou, G., He, T., Krishnamurthy, S., and Stankovic, J.: A. Models and solutions for radio irregularity in wireless sensor networks. ACM Trans. Sen. Netw. 2(2) (2006) 221-262

Multiple Cluster Merging and Multihop Transmission in Wireless Sensor Networks

Siddeswara Mayura Guru[1], Matthias Steinbrecher[2], Saman Halgamuge[1], and Rudolf Kruse[2]

[1] Dynamic Systems and Control Group, Department of Mechanical and Manufacturing Engineering
University of Melbourne, Parkville Vic 3010, Australia
s.guru@pgrad.unimelb.edu.au, saman@unimelb.edu.au
[2] Department of Computer Engineering, University of Magdeburg, Magdeburg, Germany D-39106.
msteinbr@iws.cs.uni-magdeburg.de, kruse@iws.cs.uni-magdeburg.de

Abstract. Wireless sensor networks consist of sensor nodes that are deployed in a large area and collect information from a sensor field. Since the nodes have very limited energy resources, the energy consuming operations such as data collection, transmission and reception must be kept to a minimum. Low Energy Adaptive Clustering Hierarchy (LEACH) is a cluster based communication protocol where cluster-heads (CH) are used to collect data from the cluster nodes and transmit it to the remote base station. In this paper we propose two extensions to LEACH. Firstly, nodes are evenly distributed during the cluster formation process, this is accomplished by merging multiple overlapping clusters. Secondly, instead of each CH directly transmitting data to remote base station, it will do so via a CH closer to the base station. This reduces transmission energy of cluster heads. The combination of above extensions increases the data gathering at base station to 60% for the same amount of sensor nodes energy used in LEACH.

1 Introduction

Wireless sensor networks have become popular because of the advancement in the area of low power electronics, radio frequency communication and due to the desire to monitor the environment remotely with minimum human intervention. A large number of sensors can be deployed to form a self-organising network to sense the environment and gather information. A sensor can be data driven or event driven in nature and a network may be static or dynamic [1].

Sensor networks can be used in various applications ranging from military to domestic. Sensors can be deployed in an inhospitable condition for monitoring purposes, in a forest for monitoring the animal movement or as early fire detection systems. Sensor networks are used to improve the learning skill in kindergarten [2], environment and habitat monitoring and also to measure tension in a mechanical bolt [3].

C. Cérin and K.-C. Li (Eds.): GPC 2007, LNCS 4459, pp. 89–99, 2007.

Low Energy Adaptive Clustering Hierarchy (LEACH), which was first presented in [4], is an application specific communication protocol based on clustering of sensor nodes. The main idea behind LEACH is that sensor nodes located close to each other will have a high correlation in their measured data so that it is not necessary for each node to communicate with the base station. Nodes form clusters by grouping neighbouring nodes. Each cluster has a cluster-head whose tasks are to collect data from other cluster members, aggregate and send aggregated data to base station.

In LEACH, cluster-head will consume more energy than its member nodes. Therefore, the CHs are rotated after a fixed amount of time called rounds. Each round consists of two phases: the *setup phase* where the clusters are formed, and the *steady-state phase* where the actual sensing and communication takes place. The cluster-head election process takes place in a setup phase to determine K cluster-heads in a network but, it does not guarantee K cluster-heads. Furthermore, cluster-heads are selected randomly based on the probability given in Equation 1. where N is the number of sensor nodes in a network, k is the number of CHs required and r is the number of rounds passed. The Equation 1 increases the chance that cluster-heads are not distributed uniformly in a network. Due to above reasons there will be uneven cluster sizes and uneven distribution of cluster-heads in a network . All this leads to rapid energy dissipation. In this paper, the concept of merging of cluster-heads, which are in close proximity, is introduced. In LEACH, each cluster-head transmit the aggregated data to the base station. The base station is generally located far away from the network. This increases the energy dissipation in CHs. Instead of each CH directly transmitting to base station, a CH closest to the base station transmits aggregated data from all the CHs. Thus, reducing the energy dissipation of other cluster-heads. The combination of these two extensions improves the life span of the network. The first extension is named LEACHM (LEACH-Merging) and due to 2-hop communication to base station, the combination of first and second extension is called 2-Level LEACHM.

$$P_i(t) = \begin{cases} \frac{k}{N-k\cdot(r mod \frac{N}{k})} & : \quad C_i(t) = 1 \\ 0 & : \quad C_i(t) = 0 \end{cases} \tag{1}$$

There are few algorithms proposed and showed improvements to the LEACH protocol. PEGASIS (Power-Efficient Gathering in Sensor Information Systems) [5] is a chain based data gathering protocol, where only one node transmits to the base station. In this protocol the distance each node transmits is less than the distance a node transmits in LEACH. However, this is a greedy based algorithm with assumption that all nodes have global knowledge of the network. In [6], the same authors proposed two new protocols: chain-based binary scheme with CDMA (Code Division Multiple Access) nodes and a chain-based 3-level scheme with non-CDMA nodes other than PEGASIS to reduce energy $\times$ delay to gather data in sensor networks. Each protocol shows improvement over LEACH based on the percentage of nodes dying for different network sizes. However, none of the above protocols are cluster based and they may not give a consistent result for a randomly distributed varying population of the sensor network. This is due to greedy approach used to find the nearest neighbour to form a chain. The assumption that all the nodes have a global knowledge about the network is difficult to realise because of node capacity and density of a network. There are few centralised approaches to form clusters [7] based on [8]. The authors in [9] have successfully developed a centralised protocol superior to LEACH. However, we are not considering the centralised approach in our work. We want nodes to decide among themselves to form clusters and identify CHs.

The rest of the paper is organised as follows. Section 2 describes the motivation for the uniform cluster-head distribution and proposes a cluster merging technique as an extension to the setup phase. In section 3, 2-level LEACHM is proposed to transmit data by a single CH (master-cluster-head) to the base station. In section 4, we are providing experimental results comparing the LEACH protocol with LEACH-M and 2-level LEACHM. Finally, we conclude the paper in section 5.

2 Uniform Cluster-Head Distribution

Efficient communication protocols for sensor networks are important to keep the communication energy usage as low as possible to increase the system lifetime. Therefore, it is important to consider every aspect of the total energy usage. Since the cluster-head consumes more energy, it is reasonable to try to decrease the energy spent in these nodes. From the energy model that is used in LEACH [10], the energy dissipated in a cluster-head node during a single frame is:

$$E_{CH} = E_{RECV}(b, m) + E_{AGG}(b, m) + E_{BS}(d_{toBS}^4), \tag{2}$$

where b is the number of data bits sent by each cluster member, m is the average number of nodes per cluster ($\frac{N}{k}$), E_{RECV} is the energy used for reception of data from cluster members, E_{AGG} is the energy used for data aggregation, E_{BS} is the energy used for delivering results to base station and d_{toBS} is the distance to base station. The behaviour of these three components against the change of distance to the base station is shown in Figure 1.

In cases where the base station is in the range of 75m to 160m away from the network from (Figure 1), it can be concluded that most of the energy is dissipated while receiving data from the cluster members. The transmission energy increases as the base station is moved further away from the sensor field.

In order to optimise the consumption of reception energy E_{RECV}, its dependencies on the system parameters must be known. Reception energy is computed based on Equation 3.

$$E_{RECV} = bE_{elec}\frac{N}{k}. \tag{3}$$

where b, N and E_{elec} (radio amplifier energy) would have constant value. The k is the only value varies frequently because the number of cluster-members varies in each round. Thus, k has more influence on Equation 3.

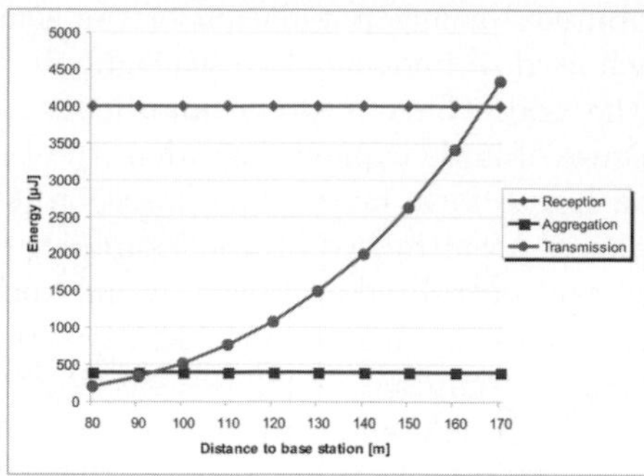

Fig. 1. Energy dissipated at cluster-head node during one LEACH round versus distance to base station

The assumption in [10] that a node can be a cluster-head at least once in its lifetime is valid only for an exact number of k cluster-head nodes. Since it is also possible that there are less than k cluster-head nodes in certain rounds, this leads to many nodes may have died before completing the first round of being a cluster-head. Thus, it is necessary to maintain balanced cluster sizes such that all nodes become cluster-head at least once in their lifetime.

2.1 Cluster Merging

A first approach in extending the cluster-head's lifetime was proposed in [11]. Even though these improvements guarantee the most powerful nodes to be elected as cluster-heads, the network may suffer from a malformed cluster in the initial stage. Since all nodes start at the same level of energy E_{Start}, no preference can be achieved because the term is very close to unity in the initial few rounds.

$$\frac{E_{n\_current}}{E_{n\_max}} \tag{4}$$

In order to increase the probability of the survival of the first round of a node being a cluster-head, it is necessary to avoid large clusters.Clusters being too large are resulted due to the following reasons:

1. Less than k nodes elected themselves to be cluster-heads thus resulting in large clusters covering the entire network.
2. The number of elected cluster-head nodes is at least k, but the cluster-heads are distributed in an uneven way as shown in Figure 2 (for example, the cluster-heads 3 and 4 are too close).

To avoid reason (2) the status of being a cluster-head is not declared until the end of the setup phase. In addition, another negotiation stage is introduced right after the cluster-head election. The nodes that have elected themselves to be cluster-heads in the initial election phase are now called cluster-head aspirants (*CHA*) because their status may change in the negotiation phase.

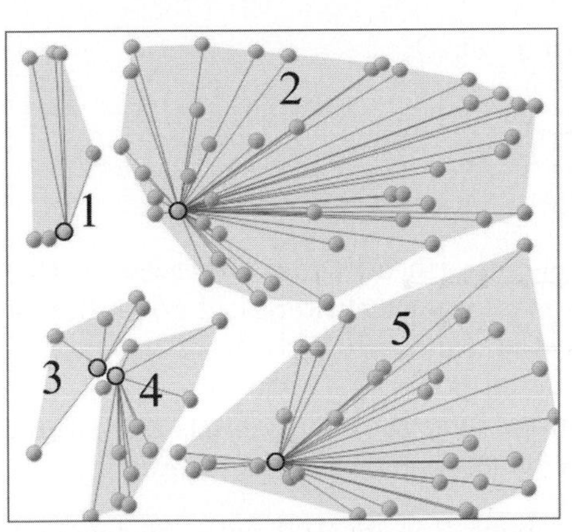

Fig. 2. Even if there are exactly k clusters ($k = 5$), there is no guarantee that the cluster sizes are balanced. (The framed nodes indicate the cluster-heads).

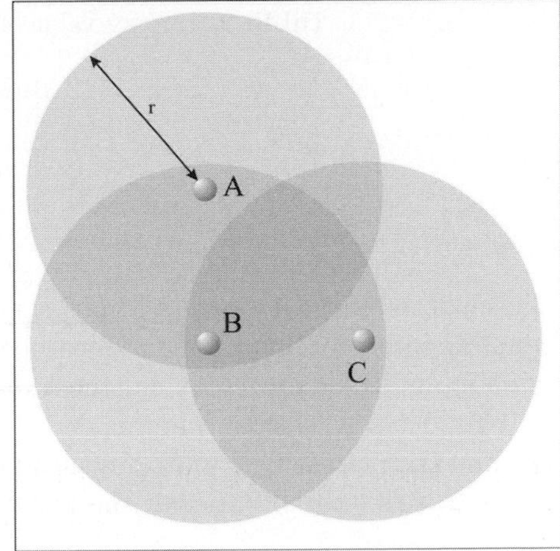

Fig. 3. Three cluster-head aspirants and their *AOI*s

In the new negotiation phase, a small *I-AM-HERE* message is broadcasted by each cluster-head aspirant to the others. Since a node can only be set to receive or transmit mode at a given time, this broadcast has to be accomplished within a TDMA frame, which has as many slots as number of nodes in the network. Each node is assigned a slot by means of its node ID. The TDMA frame length scales linearly by the network size. Each node transmit little amount of data (Table 1), which is not a burden. The *I-AM-HERE* message only contains the information depicted in Table 1.This message does not need to broadcast at maximum transmitting power. It is sufficient to reach all cluster-head aspirants in a special circumference with radius r. This area is called the *area of interest (AOI)* of the cluster-head aspirant and specifies its territory ideally not shared with another CHA, even though some overlap may be tolerated.

Table 1. Layout of *I-AM-HERE* message

Sender ID
Sender's energy level

As stated above it may occur that in case of cluster-head aspirants being located too close, these areas may overlap. In this case both clusters should be merged into one cluster. We illustrate this in Figure 3. Each cluster-head aspirant CHA_i (having E_i energy) determines the energy E_i^{max} of the most powerful cluster-head aspirant in its *AOI*. The future state of the cluster-head aspirant CHA_i is defined by the following policy: If $E_i^{max} > E_i$ then CHA_i abandons

Table 2. Energy values for CHA nodes, Example 1

CHA	Energy left
A	5
B	1
C	3

the cluster-head role and becomes a non-cluster-head node. Otherwise, CHA_i remains in its role and advances to become a proper cluster-head node. In case of a tie, a CHA chooses its cluster-head state randomly.

This decision is done independently by all potential cluster-head nodes. We assume the nodes A, B and C from Figure 3 have the energy levels as shown in Table 2. After the broadcast, the knowledge of each node is as follows:

- A with the energy of 5 units, knows about B in its AOI with the energy of 1 unit.
- B with the energy of 1 unit, knows about A and C having energy levels of 5 and 3 units, respectively.
- C with the energy of 3 units, knows about B in its AOI with the energy of 1 unit.

The following decisions are made:

- Node A changes its status from CHA to cluster-head, since the only other cluster-head aspirant known (B) has less than 5 units left.
- Node B becomes a non-cluster-head node since all other cluster-head aspirants known to it (A and C) have more energy left.
- Node C changes its status from CHA to cluster-head, since the only other cluster-head aspirant known (B) has less than 3 units left.

Thus, the number of cluster-head nodes located in AOI of each other can be reduced. If n cluster-head aspirants know each other then exactly one node will remain as a cluster-head, thus avoiding the overlap.

The proposed method will distribute nodes evenly among clusters. However, there should be enough cluster-heads to cover all nodes in a sensor field. This problem can be solved by increasing the value of 'k' in Equation 1. This also reduces the disadvantage of having less CH nodes.

3 2-Level LEACHM

The steady phase happens once the set-up phase finished in the LEACH protocol. In steady phase, data is transmitted to the base-station. If the base-station is located far away from the sensor field, it is more likely that the transmission distance from all the cluster-heads to base station is greater than $d_{crossover}$[10]. The $d_{crossover}$ ($d =$ transmission distance) is the critical distance between transmitter and receiver. The critical value is 86.2 m based on the channel propagation

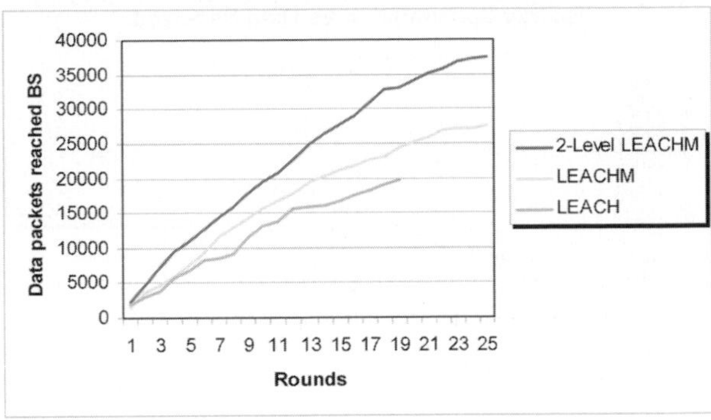

Fig. 4. The number of data packets reached to the base station located at (50,175) against the number of rounds

model used in [10]. If transmission distance is greater than $d_{crossover}$ the energy dissipation is proportional to d^4 else it is d^2. Therefore, it is important for transmission to be proportional to d^2. However, when base station is located remotely, which is the case for majority of applications, nodes will dissipate energy proportional to d^4. To improve the lifetime of a network, number of nodes dissipating energy proportional to d^4 should be minimum.

To minimise the transmission distance of cluster-heads, only master-cluster-head transmits data to remote base station. Here, the assumption is that each sensor knows the distance and direction of the base-station. It is a logical assumption where all sensors are static once they are deployed and the base station is also static. Once, the sensors are deployed, the base-station will broadcast a beacon to the sensor field thus, all sensors know the distance of the base station from them.

3.1 Master Cluster-Head Determination

After cluster-heads are elected, each of them will broadcast a message (MSG-MCH) using non-persistent carrier sense multiple Access (CSMA) protocol. The message consists of node's ID and its distance from the base-station (Table 3). This message will be broadcasted to reach all cluster-heads. Once each cluster-head receives all other cluster-heads information, they decide by themselves the master-cluster-head. The cluster-head closest to the base-station is determined as master-cluster-head. After CHs get a frame of data from its members they will transmit an aggregated data to the master-cluster-head using carrier sense multiple access (CSMA) approach. The master-cluster-head waits for data from all

Table 3. the format of the MSG-MCH message broadcast by each cluster-head

Node ID
BS distance from node

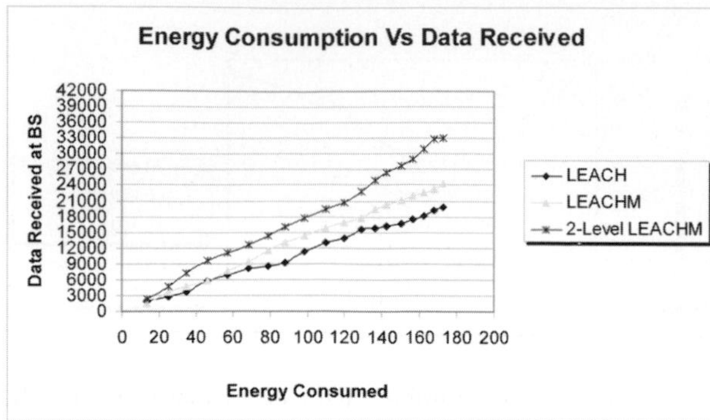

Fig. 5. The graph shows the energy consumption for number of data received. 2-Level LEACHM received more data spending lesser energy than LEACH and LEACHM. The BS is located at (50,175), outside the network.

cluster-heads before it transmits an aggregated data to the base-station. Therefore, except master-cluster-head all other CHs transmit short distance to save transmission energy. The main motivation is to reduce the energy dissipation of cluster-heads to the magnitude of d^2 instead of d^4 barring, master-cluster-head.

4 Simulation Results and Analysis

The simulation tool is developed in C++ to evaluate the LEACH protocol and new proposal presented in this paper. The simulation setup, electronics parameters and energy model used in the simulation is similar to [10]. The basic characteristics of the network setup is given in Table 4: In LEACH-M, during the cluster-head election process, nodes selected using Equation 1 are called potential-cluster-heads. Potential-cluster-heads decide among themselves as discussed in section 2 to become a cluster-head or non-cluster-head. The advantage of negotiation phase of potential-cluster-heads is that the cluster-heads will be distributed evenly in a network, which, LEACH fails. In the simulation, the overhead energy involved for the negotiation phase is also considered. Since the size of data broadcast is small (4 bytes) the energy spent to transmit 4 bytes of data with maximum power to reduce hidden terminal problem is $16.44\mu J$. This energy is spent once in every round. The proposed improvement to the LEACH protocol can be seen from the results in Figure 4. The 2-Level LEACHM gathers

Table 4. Network setup for simulation

No. of nodes	100
Area of the sensor field	$100m \times 100m$
Base station location	(50,175)
Data size	500 bytes
Initial energy of each node	2J

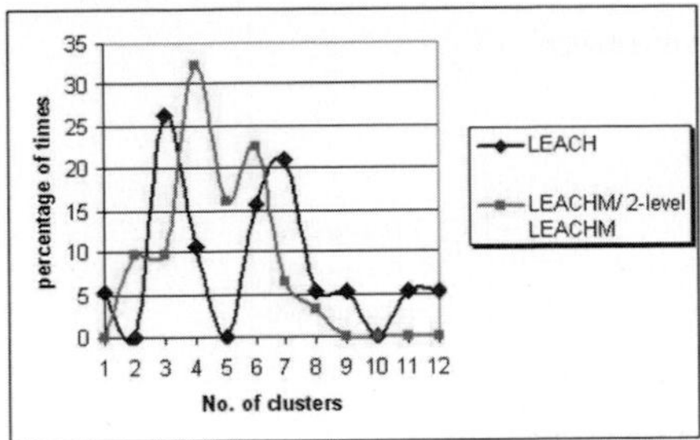

Fig. 6. The percentage of times number of clusters formed in one run of simulation. LEACHM formed majority of times clusters between 3 and 5. Thus making it energy efficient then LEACH.

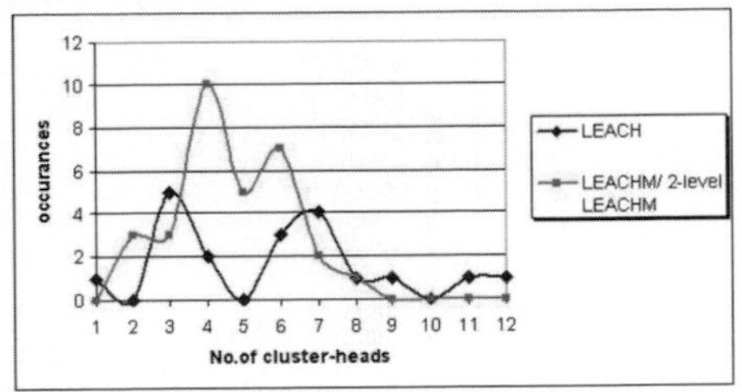

Fig. 7. Cluster-head distribution in LEACH and LEACHM

60% more data packets than LEACH and about 40% more than LEACHM. The improvement is mainly due to the even distribution of cluster-heads in a network and d^2 power dissipation for most CHs except master-cluster-head, which dissipate d^4 most of the times. Figure 5 shows the simulation results for the energy dissipation to number of data packet received. The 2-Level LEACHM transmits 60% more data packets than LEACH and 35% more data packets than LEACHM for the same amount of energy consumed.

Finally, we compare the cluster formation in LEACH and LEACHM in Figure 6 (the comparison is only between LEACH and LEACHM because 2-Level LEACHM has similar cluster formation as LEACHM). The results in Figure 4.4 of [10] shows that the LEACH is most energy-efficient when clusters are between 3 and 5. In Figure 6, LEACHM form clusters 60% of times between 3 and 5 when compare to 30% in LEACH. This proves that the clusters are more uniform and efficient in LEACHM. This is the main reason for LEACHM to perform better than LEACH. Figure 7 shows that LEACHM has more occurrences of clusters between 3 and 5 than LEACH. Overall results prove that LEACHM and 2-Level LEACHM perform better than LEACH.

4.1 Sensitivity Analysis of LEACHM

In this section we analyse the sensitivity of Area of Interest (AOI) in LEACHM. From Equation 4.22 of [10] the expected distance between nodes to a cluster-head is given by:

$$E[d^2_{toCH}] = \frac{1}{2\pi}\frac{M^2}{k} \quad (5)$$

In the above equation the distance between the cluster-head and nodes varies with the number of cluster-heads (k). From Figure 4.4 in [10], the energy is least dissipated when number of clusters are between 3 and 5. Therefore, we vary the number of clusters from 3 to 5 to find how LEACHM works. We conduct

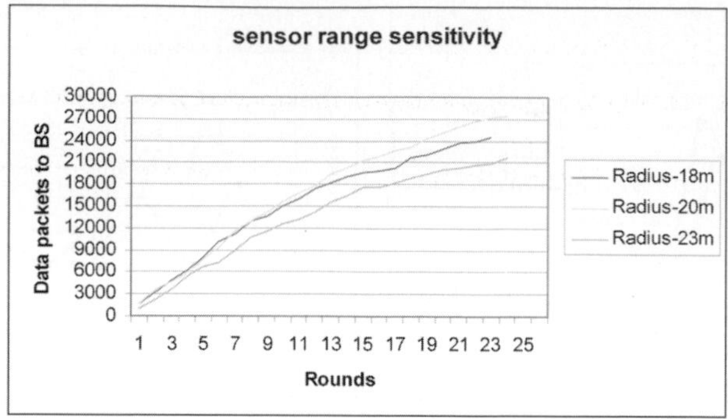

Fig. 8. Sensitivity of LEACHM for number of clusters

this experiments by simulating LEACHM with area of interest (AOI) of 18m for 5 clusters, 20m for 4 clusters and 23m for 3 clusters. All the AOIs can be calculated by substituting number of clusters to k in Equation 5. The result given in Figure 8 shows that network with clusterheads of 20m radius transmit more data to the base station.

5 Conclusion

The main focus of this paper was to improve the performance of LEACH. Based on the performance criteria considered the improvement is about 60%. The improvement was possible due to the even distribution of clusters in the setup phase and in the steady phase, instead of every cluster-heads transmitting data to base station, only master-cluster-head transmits aggregated data of all CHs. This reduces the transmission energy and further improves the performance of the protocol.

Acknowledgment

Authors would like to thank Australian Research Council for partly funding this project.

References

1. Tilak, S., Abu-Ghazaleh, N., Heinzelman, W.: A taxonomy of wireless micor-sensor network models. ACM SIGMOBILE Mobile Computing and Communications Review **6** (2002) 28–36
2. Park, S., Locher, I., Savvides, A., Srivastava, M., Chen, A., Muntz, R., Yuen, S.: Design of a wearable sensor badge for smart kindergarten. In: Wearable Computers, 2002. (ISWC 2002). Proceedings. Sixth International Symposium on. (2002) 231–238

3. Guru, S.M., Fernando, S., Halgamuge, S., Chan, K.: Intelligent fastening with a-bolt technology and sensor networks. Assembly Automation, The International Journal of assembly technology and management **24** (2004) 386–393
4. Heinzelman, W., Chandrakasan, A., Balakrishnan, H.: Energy-efficient communication protocol for wireless microsensor networks. In: System Sciences, 2000. Proceedings of the 33rd Annual Hawaii International Conference on. (2000) 3005–3014
5. Lindsey, S., Raghavendra, C., Sivalingam, K.: Data gathering algorithms in sensor networks using energy metrics. Parallel and Distributed Systems, IEEE Transactions on **13** (2002) 924–935
6. Lindsey, S., Raghavendra, C.: Pegasis: Power-efficient gathering in sensor information systems. In: Aerospace Conference Proceedings, 2002. IEEE. Volume 3. (2002) 3–1125–3–1130 vol.3
7. Guru, S.M., Hsu, A., Halgamuge, S., Fernando, S.: An extended growing self-organising map for selection of clusters in sensor networks. International Journal of Distributed Sensor Networks **1** (2005) 227–243
8. Hsu, A., Tang, S., Halgamuge, S.: An unsupervised hierarchical dynamic self-organising approach to class discovery and marker gene identification in microarray data. Bioinformatics **19** (2003) 2131–2140
9. Muruganathan, S., Ma, D., Bhasin, R., Fapojuwo, A.: A centralized energy-efficient routing protocol for wireless sensor networks. Communications Magazine, IEEE **43** (2005) S8–13
10. Heinzelman, W.: Application-Specific Protocol Architectures for Wireless Networks. PhD thesis, Massachusetts Institute of Technology (2000)
11. Handy, M., Haase, M., Timmermann, D.: Low energy adaptive clustering hierarchy with deterministic cluster-head selection. In: Mobile and Wireless Communications Network, 2002. 4th International Workshop on. (2002) 368–372

CFR: A Peer-to-Peer Collaborative File Repository System

Meng-Ru Lin, Ssu-Hsuan Lu, Tsung-Hsuan Ho, Peter Lin, and Yeh-Ching Chung*

Department of Computer Science, National Tsing Hua University
Hsin-Chu, Taiwan300, ROC
{mrlin, shlu, anson}@sslab.cs.nthu.edu.tw, peter@dr-lin.com, ychung@cs.nthu.edu.tw

Abstract. Due to the high availability of the Internet, many large cross-organization collaboration projects, such as SourceForge, grid systems etc., have emerged. One of the fundamental requirements of these collaboration efforts is a storage system to store and exchange data. This storage system must be highly scalable and can efficiently aggregate the storage resources contributed by the participating organizations to deliver good performance for users. In this paper, we propose a storage system, Collaborative File Repository (CFR), for large scale collaboration projects. CFR uses peer-to-peer techniques to achieve scalability, efficiency, and ease of management. In CFR, storage nodes contributed by the participating organizations are partitioned according to geographical regions. Files stored in CFR are automatically replicated to all regions. Furthermore, popular files are duplicated to other storage nodes of the same region. By doing so, data transfers between users and storage nodes are confined within their regions and transfer efficiency is enhanced. Experiments show that our replication can achieve high efficiency with a small number of duplicates.

Keywords: peer-to-peer, storage system, Coupon Collection Problem, CFR.

1 Introduction

The exploding growth of the Internet has enabled organizations across the globe to share resources and collaborate in large scale projects such as SourceForge [21], SEEK[20], and grid systems [1] [5] [11] [25], etc. One of the most fundamental needs of these types of projects is a platform to store and exchange data. A storage system is needed for keeping and distributing the large amounts of source codes, programs, and documentations. To construct such a storage system, machines contributed by volunteering organizations are used to store and mirror the generated data. How to build a scalable and efficient storage system to aggregate the resources contributed by the participating organizations has been an active research issue.

The peer-to-peer computing has received much attention in the past few years. Pioneering applications such as Napster [16] and KaZaA [9] offered platforms for users to easily exchange files without a centralized storage. The second generation of

* Corresponding author.

C. Cérin and K.-C. Li (Eds.): GPC 2007, LNCS 4459, pp. 100–111, 2007.

peer-to-peer storage systems [2] [10] [15] [18], mostly built on top of structured routing schemes [19][22], further provide mechanisms to guarantee on object location, and adopt more sophisticated replication and caching schemes.

The benefits of peer-to-peer techniques include scalability, fault tolerance, resource sharing, and load balancing among the participating machines. These appealing properties closely match the requirements of storage systems used in large scale collaboration projects mentioned above.

In this paper, we propose a scalable, loosely coupled, and efficient storage system, Cooperative File Repository (CFR), for large scale collaboration projects. The CFR consists of two modules, overlay management and file management modules. The overlay management module maintains connectivity between the participating nodes using a two-layer overlay network. The file management module provides an interface for users to access CFR and manages the files stored in CFR. Replicas are automatically created for all files stored in CFR. Caching is employed to further enhance performance. CFR achieves scalability by incorporating peer-to-peer techniques to aggregate the contributed storage nodes. Efficiency is achieved by exploiting the geographic locality of the storage nodes. Using the region overlay, CFR can replicate files to storage nodes in all geographic areas.

To evaluate the performance of CFR, both simulation analysis and experimental test are conducted. Simulation results verify that our proposed caching scheme can effectively reduce the average download time compared to the one without caching scheme. For the experimental test, we implement CFR on Taiwan UniGrid [25]. Different region configurations are implemented and the top 10 download files from the SourceForge site are used as the test data set. The experimental result shows that the downloading time of the 4-region configuration is almost 3 times faster than that of the 1-region configuration, that is, the region concept of CFR can enhance the performance of file downloading.

The remainder of this paper is organized as follows. In Section 2, we discuss various systems that are related to our system. In Section 3 we briefly describe the system overview of our CFR. In Sections 4 and 5, we introduce the overlay management and file management of CFR, respectively. The simulation results are presented in Section 6. In Section 7, we perform the experimental test on Taiwan UniGrid.

2 Related Work

Many peer-to-peer data storage systems have been proposed in the past, and there are quite a few papers on comparisons of various peer-to-peer file sharing/storage applications published [6] [7]. CFS [2] is a Unix-style read only file system layered on top of the Chord [22] [23] protocol. A DHash layer lies between the file system and Chord to handle block management. OceanStore [10] is a persistent wide-area transactional storage, layered on top of its own probabilistic routing protocol. OceanStore applies erasure coding to files, splitting them into multiple blocks, to achieve robustness. PAST [18] is a large scale persistent storage system layered on the Pastry [19] protocol. PAST can be layered on other routing protocols with some loss of locality and fault resilience properties. All of the storage systems mentioned above create replicas to the files or blocks stored in the system and employ caching. IVY [15] is a log-based file system that supports concurrent write operations. IVY, like CFS, uses Dhash to store the logs. Kelips [4] is a file system layered on its own routing scheme with $O(1)$ lookup time. The fast lookup, however, comes at the cost of larger memory usage and background communication overhead.

CFR shares many similarities with PAST. Like PAST, CFR stores and replicates whole files, and is not bounded to a specific routing scheme. Unlike PAST, we do not rely on the underlying routing protocol to take locality into consideration. Our system partitions the participating nodes into groups, like Kelips, but uses different partition scheme. Kelips uses hashing to determine the group of a node while ours is based on geographic locality.

Many past works have proposed different ideas of using hierarchical multiple ring topologies in overlay networks. HIERAS [26] and [14] are both routing schemes that adopt this topology. In [14], the participating peers are organized into multiple layers of rings with separate identifier spaces to reflect administrative domains and connectivity constraints. Boundary Chord [8] is a replica location mechanism used in grid environments. Boundary Chord adopts a two-layer multiple ring topology to group nodes according to logical domains. In comparison with these systems, CFR adopts a two-layer hierarchy of multiple rings.

3 System Overview

Figure 1 shows the system architecture of CFR and the functions offered by the system components. The CFR system consists of two modules: Overlay Management Module (OMM) and File Management Module (FMM).

CFR System Architecture
File Management Module (FMM)
User Interface Component (UIC)
put | del | get
File Duplication Component (FDC)
getPerms | getTrans | putReplica | putTransient | removeReplica
Overlay Management Module (OMM)
Region Overlay Management Component (ROMC)
getRegionTableEntry
Base Overlay Management Component (BOMC)
cwNeighbor | ccwNeighbor | locateStorageNode | stabilization

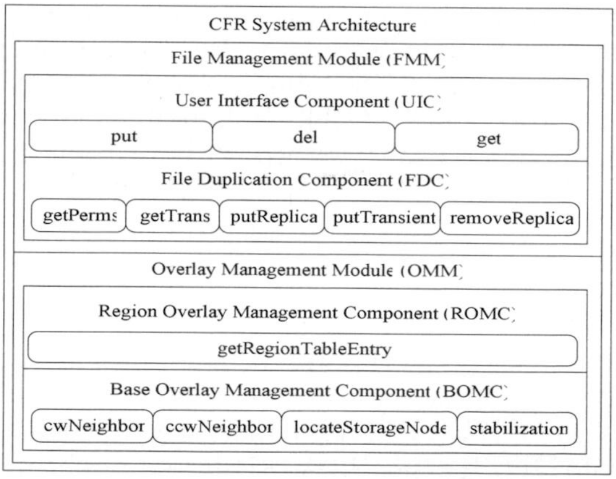

Fig. 1. The system architecture of CFR

OMM is responsible for maintaining connectivity between the participating storage nodes using a two-layer overlay network. The two-layer overlay network consists of two overlays, the base overlay and the region overlay. These two overlays are maintained by the Base Overlay Management Component (BOMC) and Region Overlay Management Component (ROMC), respectively. ROMC maintains the required routing information in a data structure called the region table.

FMM is used for providing functions that are related to files in CFR. FMM consists of two components: the User Interface Component (UIC) and the File Duplication Component (FDC). UIC provides an interface for users to access the files which are stored in CFR. Duplications of files in CFR are automatically created in order to enhance performance and increase availability. The File Duplication Component (FDC) is responsible for creating the duplications.

4 The Overlay Management of CFR

In this section, we will describe the overlay management of CFR. It can be divided into the base overlay and the region overlay.

4.1 The Base Overlay

The purpose of the base overlay is to route messages between any two storage nodes in the system. The base overlay is constructed and maintained by BOMC. In the base overlay, each participating storage node has a node ID that is obtained by hashing the IP address of the node using a consistent hash function, such as SHA-1 [3] or MD5 [17]. Using this method, participating storage nodes are organized as a ring, the *base* ring, according to their IDs.

4.2 The Region Overlay

4.2.1 Regions

The basic concept of region is inspired by mirroring scheme on the internet such as SourceForge. User usually can choose a server to download file according to their own geographic locality to achieve efficient downloading. Therefore, the geographic locality can be interpreted as network locality in two end hosts connected to the Internet. In [24], it is shown that topology of the Internet today obeys the Power Law and consists of several dense autonomous system clusters.

We adopt a model to capture the scenario that we mentioned above. We assume that the connection between two participants (storage nodes or users) of CFR is efficient if they are in the same geographic area. In our model, all storage nodes and users, both end hosts in the Internet, are partitioned into disjoint sets called *regions*. We assume that the partition reflects geographic locality.

4.2.2 Construct and Maintain the Region Overlay

Constructing the region overlay can allow the participating storage nodes to contact other storage nodes that are in different regions quickly. This ability aids the file duplication procedures to select target storage nodes to replicate desired files. Details of the file duplication procedures are described in Section 5.

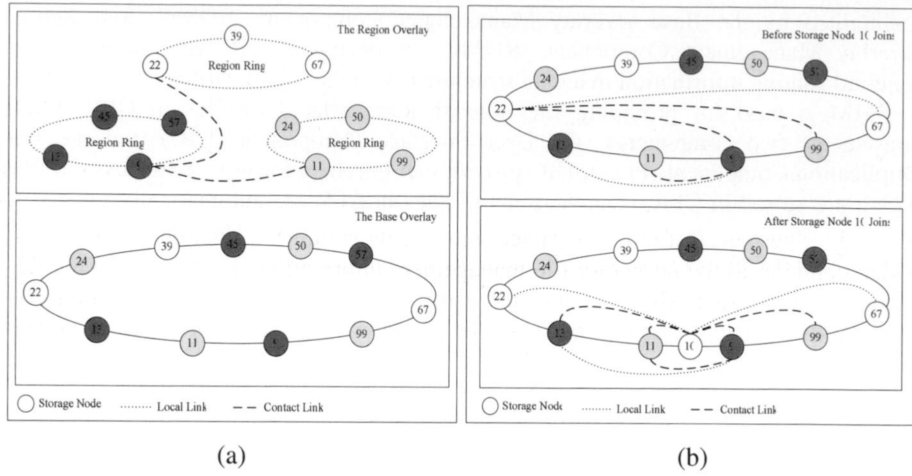

Fig. 2. (a). An example of region overlay with 3 regions. (b). An example of the join process.

We now describe the construction and maintenance procedures of ROMC. First we will introduce some terms and variables that will be used. *R* denotes the total number of regions in the system. Nodes that belong to the same region are called *locals* of each other. Nodes that belong to different regions are called *contacts* of each other. A *link* is an ID-to-address mapping, used to convert node ID to actual network address. Links that point to locals are called *local links*. Links that point to contacts are called *contact links*. Links that are required to form the region overlay which are stored in the *region table* of the participating nodes.

To form the region overlay, each node stores and maintains *R* links in their region tables. The local links in the region table of each node connect nodes from the same region into a ring, called the *region ring*. The region overlay is essentially made up of *R* interconnected region rings. Figure 2(a) shows a system with 3 regions. Storage node 9 stores and maintains 3 links in its region table. A local link points to the clockwise neighbor in its region ring, node 13. Two contact links point to the closest contacts from the remaining two regions in the base ring, nodes 11 and 22, respectively.

A node constructs its region table when it first joins the system, and maintains its region table throughout its lifetime in the system.

Figure 2(b) shows an example of the join process. In Figure 2(b), storage node 10 joins the system. As shown on top of Figure 2(b) all storage nodes between storage node 9 and storage node 67 have a link to storage node 22 before storage node 10 joins. The region table of storage node 9 contains links to storage nodes 11, 13, and 22. After storage node 10 joins, all nodes between storage node 9 and storage 67 are affected. As shown on the bottom of Figure 2(b), the region table of storage node 10 contains links to storage nodes 11, 13, and 22. These links are obtained from storage node 9. All the links that point to storage node 22 are modified to point to storage node 9.

5 The File Management of CFR

In this section, we give detailed descriptions of file management procedures in CFR. Files that are stored in CFR can be classified into two types: *permanent file*, and *transient file*. Permanent file will stay in the system until a remove operation is performed on it. Each transient file has a *lifetime* to determine how long it can stay in the system, and will be removed from the system when the system time exceeds its lifetime. A permanent file is associated with a data structure called *permanent table*, which contains all the necessary file management information about a permanent file. Likewise, a transient file is associated with a *transient table* which contains the necessary information about a transient file. The storage space of each storage node is divided into to two areas: *local* and *cache areas*. Permanent files are stored in the local areas of storage nodes, and transient files are stored in the cache areas.

Table 1. An example of a permanent table

filename	App.tgz		
fileID	8		
permNodes	8	11	22
caches	24	50	
hort	359		
long	50		
path	/opt/cfr/local		

Table 2. An example of a transient table

filename	App.tgz
fileID	8
lifetime	50000
path	/opt/cfr/cache

Table 1 shows a permanent table. The filename and the fileID field record the name of the file and the hash value of the filename. Each file will be replicated, and the permNodes field records the storage nodes in different regions that store the replicas when the caches field records the storage nodes in the same region that store the replicas. The long and short fields record the long term and short term access rates of that file, respectively. The path field stores the physical location of the file. Table 2 shows a transient table. The filename, fileID, and path fields are the same as the fields in the permanent table. The lifetime field stores the lifetime of that transient file.

5.1 Insert Files and Create Duplicates in CFR

The put function provides by UIC allows users to insert files into CFR. In CFR, a file will first be put to the node, n_i, whose id is closest to fileID. After the first stage of insertion is completed, node n_i will replicate files to nodes in other regions according to its contact link information.

Transient files are created for reducing the load of the storage nodes hosting popular files as proposed in [12]. In order to cope with this phenomenon, we record the long term download rate, in the scale of days, of each file in the long field of its permanent tables. The transient file will be created when one of the download rates of that file exceeds its threshold.

Figure 3(a) shows an example of file insertion and duplication process. The file App.tgz, which is the same file in Table 1, is inserted into a system with 3 regions. Since the fileID of App.tz is 8, its home is storage node 9. Storage node 9 uses its region table to create two replicas on storage nodes 11 and 22 according to the described creation procedure.

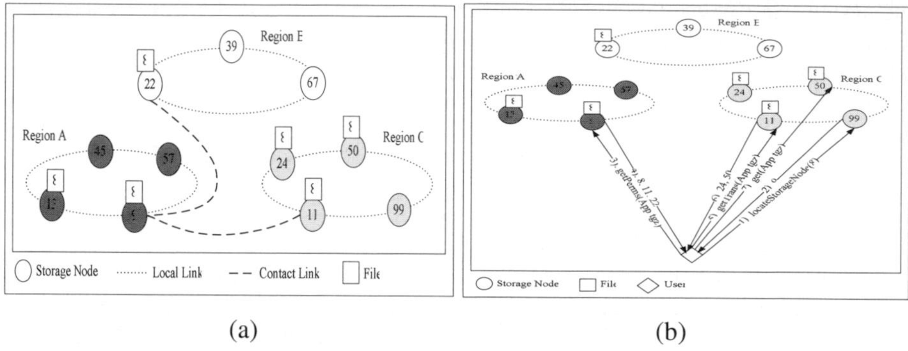

Fig. 3. (a). An example of file insertion and duplication. (b). An example of file retrieval.

5.2 Retrieve and Remove Files in CFR

The get function provided by UIC allows users to retrieve files from CFR. To retrieve a file f_j from CFR, a user u_i first finds the home of f_j, n_h. After n_h is found, u_i invokes the getPerms function on n_h to find the list of storage nodes that stores f_j as a permanent file, and selects the storage node that belongs to the same region as herself. Let this storage node be n_r. u_i invokes the getTrans function on n_r to obtain the list of caches of f_j. u_i then chooses a storage node from all the caches and n_r with equal probability. This will evenly distribute the requests among all the storage nodes that stores f_j or transient file of f_j in the same region.

The remove operation is similar to the get operation. A user first invokes the del function on the home of a file, n_h. n_h then finds all the storage nodes that store replicas and transient file of that file from the permanent tables, and issues requests to remove the files from their storage space. Figure 3(b) shows an example of the file retrieval process.

5.3 Dealing with Storage Node Dynamics

To ensure users can always locate their desired files, dynamic storage nodes must be considered. The addition of new storage nodes and the departure of existing storage nodes will cause files to migrate to different homes. If no corresponding actions are taken, future requests will be routed to their new homes and dropped because the new homes are unaware of their existence. However, migration of all files from one storage node to another will be very costly especially when the total size of files is large. We use redirection to deal with these problems. A storage node can store only the permanent table of a file and records a link to the storage node that store the actual file. This link is called a *reference*. References are created by storing links instead of local paths in the path field of permanent tables.

A joining or leaving storage node will affect its clockwise neighbor in the base ring. It will also affect the nodes between itself and the closest counter-clockwise storage node in its region. In the case of join and voluntary departure, the affected nodes will be notified. The affected nodes will first create references to deal with the change of topology, and schedule physical file migration to be done in the future.

6 Simulation Results

To evaluate CFR, we implemented a simulator and performed several experiments to further understand its behavior. All simulations were run on an IBM eServer, equipped with two Intel(R) Xeon(TM) 2.40GHz CPUs and 1GB of memory. The OS running on the eServer is Debian. The kernel version is 2.6.

6.1 Expected Number of Hops to Collect All Links

The objective of this experiment is to compare the average number of hops[13] to obtain a complete set of R links to the derived expected number of hops. We would also like to verify that the minimal average value appears when the population of storage nodes in all regions is equal. We only show the results with two and three regions. When the number of regions is larger than three, it is difficult to present the results using graphs. However, all results show similar characteristics.

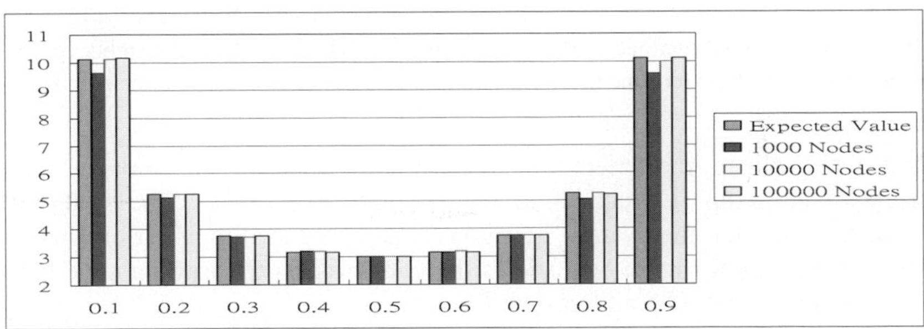

Fig. 4. Average number of hops and the expected number of hops to obtain all links in a system consisting of two regions and different number of storage nodes

Figure 4 shows the average number of hops in a system with two regions, with different node proportions and storage node populations. The x-axis is the proportion of the first region. We can see that all results are close to the expected value[13]. Note that the larger storage node population, the closer the average is to the derived value. This is because the distribution of nodes over the identifier space is more uniform as the number of nodes increase. Also note that the lowest expected value and average values occur at the point where the proportions of the nodes are equal (0.5), which concurs with our derived result.

6.2 Evaluation of File Management of CFR

The objective of next experiments is to evaluate the proposed replication strategy and to compare the proposed strategy to PAST. The reason PAST is chosen is because it shares most similarity with CFR. We use the download statistics from the "top 100 downloaded projects in 7 days" web page available from the SourceForge website.

Using this data, we simulated our replication strategy and compare it with the replication strategy of PAST. The system consists of five hundred nodes. The average download time of around 45000 downloads with varying number of replicas created for each file inserted in both CFR and PAST, are shown in Figure 5(a). As shown in the figure, download time decreases as the number of replicas created for both systems. We can see that CFR achieves lower average download time than PAST using the same number of replicas.

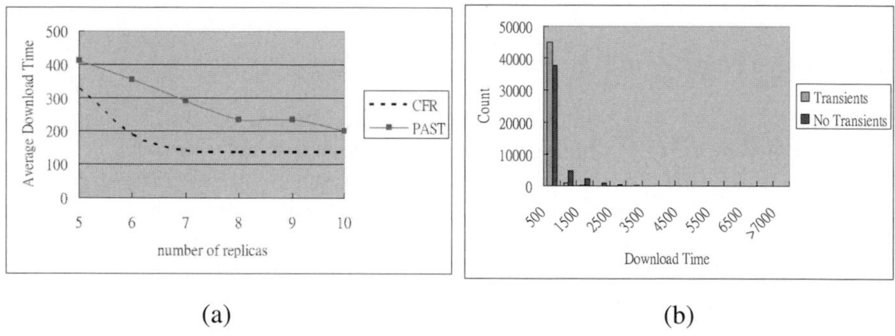

(a) (b)

Fig. 5. (a) The average download time of CFR versus PAST with different number of replicas. (b). Comparisons the transfer time between with transient files and without transient files.

Next we evaluate the effect of creating transients on performance. In this experiment, the setup is identical to the previous experiment. The result of the experiment shows that the average download time is reduced to about one half when transients are created. Figure 5(b) shows the comparisons the transfer time between with transient files and without transient files.

As shown in Figure 5(b), the use of transient files effectively reduces transfer time. With transient files, it has greatly reduced download time.

7 Experimental Results

To evaluate the real performance of CFR, we have implemented the CFR system on Taiwan UniGrid [25]. The Taiwan UniGrid is a Grid platform for researchers in Taiwan to do Grid related research. Currently, the platform contains about 30 sites. We execute the CFR program on 12 sites in 4 cities of Taiwan as shown in Figure 6(a). Each site has 3 storage nodes. We select the top 10 download files, as shown in Table 3, from the sourceforge.net [21] as our test data. To measure the performance of CFR, we have 4 region configurations, 1, 2, 3, and 4, for these 12 sites. For the

1-region configuration, all sites form a region. For the 2-region configuration, sites in {Taipei, Hsinchu} and {Tainan, Kaoshiung} form a region, respectively. For the 3-region configuration, sites in {Taipei}, {Hsinchu}, and {Tainan, Kaoshiung} form a region, respectively. For the 4-region configuration, sites in each city form a region. For each region configuration, a download program is executed in each site to randomly decide whether a client needs to download a particular program or not.

Table 3. Top 10 downloads from sourcesforge.net

Filename	Size (bytes)
7-Zip_Portable_4.42_R2.paf.exe	1193218
7z443.exe	862846
aresregular195_installer.exe	1253674
audacity-win-1.2.6.exe	2228534
Azureus_2.5.0.0_Win32.setup.exe	8799656
DCPlusPlus-0.698.exe	3836577
eMule0.47c-Installer.exe	3534076
eMulePlus-1.2a.Binary.zip	3047952
gimp-2.3.12-i586-setup.zip	14267302
Shareaza_2.2.3.0.exe	4366779

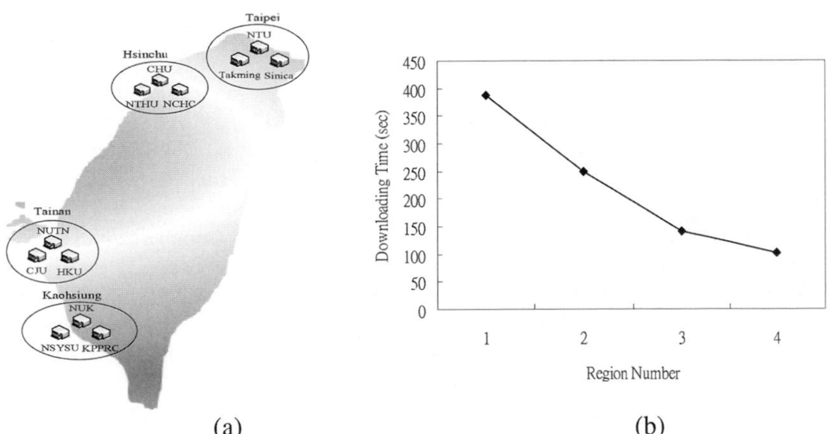

(a) (b)

Fig. 6. (a) Testbed map of CFR in TANET of Taiwan. (b) The average downloading time against region number.

Figure 6(b) shows the average downloading time against the region number. From Figure 6(b), we observe that the overall downloading time goes down while the number of regions increases. Since the region partitioning exploits the geographical relationships of sites, the experimental result also shows that the downloading time of the 4-region configuration is almost 3 times faster than that of the 1-region configuration.

8 Conclusions and Future Work

In this paper, we have proposed a scalable, loosely coupled, and efficient storage system, Cooperative File Repository (CFR), for large scale collaboration projects. The main concept of CFR is to use peer-to-peer techniques to achieve scalability, use a two-layer hierarchy managing participating organizations to eliminate centralized administration authority, and use the geographic locality of the storage nodes and caching mechanism to achieve the efficiency. The simulation and experimental results confirm that CFR can achieve those goals mentioned above.

From the simulation results, we observe that the CFR can produce the best performance when all regions have the same number of storage nodes. In real situation, the number of storage nodes of regions may not be equal. How to dynamically combine small regions to one larger region or split one larger region to small regions such that each region has approximate the same number of storages node to keep CFR remain efficient is an important issue for the future study.

Acknowledgement

The work of this paper is partially supported by National Science Council, National Center for High-Performance Computing of the Republic of China under contract NSC 95-2752-E-007-004-PAE, NSC 94-2218-E-007-057, and NCHC-KING_010200.

References

1. China Grid, http://www.chinagrid.net
2. F. Dabek, M. F. Kaashoek, D. Karger, R. Morris, and I. Stoica, "Wide-area Cooperative Storage with CFS," in the *Proceedings of 18th ACM Symposium on Operating Systems Principles*, Oct. 2001, pp. 202-215.
3. FIPS 180-1, Secure Hash Standard, U.S. Department of Commerce/NIST, National Technical Information Service, Springfield, VA, Apr. 1995.
4. I. Gupta, K. Birman, P. Linga, A. Derms, and R. van Renessie, "Kelips: Building and Efficient and Stable P2P DHT through Increased Memory and Background Overhead," in the *Proceedings of the 2nd International Workshop on Peer-to-Peer Systems (IPTPS '03).*
5. grid.org, http://www.grid.org/home.htm
6. R. Hasan, Z. Anwar, W. Yurcik, L. Brumbaugh, and R. Campbell, "A Survey of Peer-to-Peer Storage Techniques for Distributed File Systems," in the *Proceedings of International Conference on Information Technology: Coding and Computing*, Apr. 4-6, 2005, vol: 2, pp. 205-213.
7. H. C. Hsiao and C. T. King, "Modeling and Evaluating Peer-to-Peer Storage Architecture," in the *Proceedings of International Parallel and Distributed Processing Symposium*, Apr. 14-19, 2002, pp. 24-29.
8. H. Jin, C. H., and H. Chen," Boundary Chord: A Novel Peer-to-Peer Algorithm for Replica Location Mechanism in Grid Environment," in the *Proceedings of the 8th International Symposium on Parallel Architectures, Algorithms, and Networks (ISPAN 2005),* Dec. 2005, Las Vegas.
9. Kazaa. http://www.kazaa.com

10. J. Kubiatowicz, D. Bindel, Y. Chen, S. Czerwinski, P. Eaton, D. Geels, R. Gummadi, S. Rhea, H. Weatherspoon, W. Weimer, C. Wells, and B. Zhao, "Oceanstore: An Architecture for Global-Scale Persistent Storage," in the *Proceedings of 9th International Conference on Architectural Support for Programming Languages and Operating Systems*, Nov. 2000.
11. LCG, http://lcg.web.cern.ch/LCG/
12. N. Leibowitz, M. Ripeanu, and A. Wierzbicki, "Deconstructing the Kazaa Network," in the *Proceedings of 3rd IEEE Workshop on Internet Applications*, Jun. 2003.
13. M. R. Lin, "CFR: A Peer-to-Peer Collaborative File Repository System," National Tsing Hua University, Dept. of Computer Science, Master Thesis, Taiwan, 2006.
14. A. Mislove, and P. Druschel, "Providing Administrative Control and Autonomy in Structured Peer-to-Peer Overlays," in the *Proceedings of International Workshop on Peer-to-peer Systems*, Feb. 2004.
15. A. Muthitacharoen, R. Morris, T. M. Gil, and B. Chen, "Ivy: A Read/Write Peer-to-Peer File System," in the *Proceedings of International 5th USENIX Symposium on Operating Systems Design and Implementation (OSDI)*, Dec. 2002.
16. Napster, http://www.napster.com
17. R. Rivest, "Message Digest Algorithm MD5", RFC 1321, Apr. 1992.
18. A. Rowstron and P. Druschel, "Storage Management and Caching In PAST, a Large-Scale, Persistent Peer-to-Peer Storage Utility," in the *Proceedings of 18th Symposium On Operating Systems Principles (SOSP '01)*, Oct. 2001.
19. A. Rowstron and P. Druschel, "Pastry: Scalable, Distributed Object Location and Routing for Large-Scale Peer-to-Peer Systems," in the *Proceedings of 18th IFIP/ACM International Conference on Distributed Systems Platforms*, Nov. 2001, pp.329-350.
20. SEEK, http://seek.ecoinformatics.com
21. SourceForge.net, http://sourceforge.net
22. I. Stoica, R. Morris, D. Karger, M. F. Kaashoek, H. Balakrishnan, "Chord: A Scalable Peertopeer Lookup Service for Internet Applications," in the *Proceedings of conference on Applications, technologies, architectures, and protocols for computer communications SIGCOMM '01*, 2001, Volume 31, Issue 4, pp. 149-160.
23. I. Stoica, R. Morris, D. Liben-Nowell, D.R. Karger, M.F. Kaashoek, F. Dabek, H. Balakrishnan, "Chord: a scalable peer-to-peer lookup protocol for Internet applications," in the IEEE/ACM Transactions on Networking, Feb. 2003, Volume 11, Issue 1, pp. 17-32.
24. G. Sagie and A. Wool, "A clustering approach for exploring the Internet structure," in the *Proceedings of conference on 23rd IEEE Convention of Electrical & Electronics Engineers*, Sep. 2004.
25. Taiwan UniGrid, http://www.unigrid.org.tw/
26. Z. Xu, R. Min, and Y. Hu, "HIERAS: A DHT Based Hierarchical P2P Routing Algorithm," in the *Proceedings of International Conference on Parallel Processing*, Oct. 2003.

Optimal Deployment of Mobile Sensor Networks and Its Maintenance Strategy

Xiaoling Wu, Jinsung Cho, Brian J. d'Auriol, and Sungyoung Lee*

Department of Computer Engineering, Kyung Hee University, Korea
{xiaoling, brian, sylee}@oslab.khu.ac.kr
chojs@khu.ac.kr

Abstract. Sensor network deployment and its maintenance are very challenging due to hostile and unpredictable nature of environments. The field coverage of a wireless sensor network (WSN) can be enhanced and consequently network lifetime can be prolonged by optimizing the sensor deployment with a finite number of sensors. In this paper, we propose an energy-efficient fuzzy optimization algorithm (EFOA) for movement assisted self-deployment of sensor networks based on three descriptors – energy, concentration and distance to neighbors. The movement of each sensor node is assumed relatively limited to further reduce energy consumption. The existing next-step move direction formulas are improved to be more realistic. We also propose a network maintenance strategy in the post-deployment phase based on the sensor node importance level ranking. Simulation results show that our approach not only achieves fast and stable deployment but also greatly improves the network coverage and energy efficiency as well as prolongs the lifetime.

Keywords: Sensor networks, fuzzy logic, deployment, mobility, coverage.

1 Introduction

Sensor networks which are composed of tiny and resource constrained computing devices, have been widely deployed for monitoring and controlling applications in physical environments [1]. Due to the unfamiliar nature of such environments, deployment and maintenance of sensor networks has become a challenging problem and has received considerable attention recently.

Some of the work [2], [3], [4] assume that the environment is sufficiently known and under control. However, when the environment is unknown or inhospitable such as remote inaccessible areas, disaster fields and toxic urban regions, sensor deployment cannot be performed manually. To scatter sensors by aircraft is one of the possible solutions. However, using this scheme, the actual landing position cannot be predicted due to the existence of wind and obstacles such as trees and buildings. Consequently, the coverage may not be able to satisfy the application requirements. Some researchers suggest simply deploying large amount of static sensors to increase coverage; however it often ends up harming the performance of the network [5].Moreover, in many cases, such as during in-building toxic-leaks detection [6], chemical sensors

* Corresponding author.

C. Cérin and K.-C. Li (Eds.): GPC 2007, LNCS 4459, pp. 112 – 123, 2007.

must be placed inside a building from the entrance of the building. In such cases, it is necessary to take advantage of mobile sensors, which can move to the appropriate places to provide the required coverage.

To address this issue, a class of work has recently appeared where mobility of sensors is utilized to achieve desired deployment [7], [8], [9], [10], [11], [12]. Typically in such works, the sensors detect lack of desired deployment objectives such as coverage holes, estimate new locations, and move to the resulting locations. For example, in [9], the authors present the virtual force algorithm (VFA) as a new approach for sensor deployment to improve the sensor field coverage after an initial random placement of sensor nodes. The cluster head (CH) executes the VFA algorithm to find new locations for sensors to enhance the overall coverage. However none of the above work can well handle the random movement and unpredictable oscillation in deployment. In [13], fuzzy logic theory is applied to handle the uncertainty in sensor network deployment problem. Their approach achieve fast and relatively stable deployment and increase the field coverage as well as communication quality. However, their fuzzy inference system has only two antecedents, number of neighbors of each sensor and average Euclidean distance between sensor node and its neighbors, without energy consumption considered at all, which is one of the most critical issues in sensor networks.

In this paper, our contribution relies on the two propose strategies. The first is an energy-efficient fuzzy optimization algorithm (EFOA) for movement assisted self-deployment of sensor networks. It outperforms [13] in three aspects. The first is that we take the energy level of sensor node as one of the antecedents in fuzzy rules; the second is that the mobility of sensor nodes is set to be relatively limited, i.e., the movement distance is bounded by communication range, so that energy consumption can be further reduced; the last is represented by the more realistic next-step moving direction equations we derived. The second strategy we propose for network maintenance in the post-deployment phase is based on the derived sensor node importance level ranking.

The rest of the paper is organized as follows. Section 2 briefly introduces the overview of fuzzy logic system and preliminaries. In section 3 the Energy-efficient Fuzzy Optimization Algorithm (EFOA) is explained in detail for mobile nodes deployment design. In section 4 network maintenance strategy is proposed based on sensor node importance ranking. Simulation and performance evaluations of this work are presented in Section 5. We conclude with a summary and discuss future work in Section 6.

2 Technical Preliminaries

2.1 Fuzzy Logic Systems

The model of fuzzy logic system consists of a fuzzifier, fuzzy rules, fuzzy inference engine, and a defuzzifier. We have used the most commonly used fuzzy inference technique called Mamdani Method [14] due to its simplicity.

The process is performed in four steps:

1) Fuzzification of the input variables *energy, concentration and average distance to neighbors* - taking the crisp inputs from each of these and determining the degree to which these inputs belong to each of the appropriate fuzzy sets.
2) Rule evaluation - taking and applying the fuzzified inputs to the antecedents of the fuzzy rules. It is then applied to the consequent membership function.
3) Aggregation of the rule outputs - the process of unification of the outputs of all rules.
4) Defuzzification - the input for the defuzzification process is the aggregate output fuzzy set *moving* distance and the output is a single crisp number.

Information flows through the fuzzy inference diagram as shown in Figure 1.

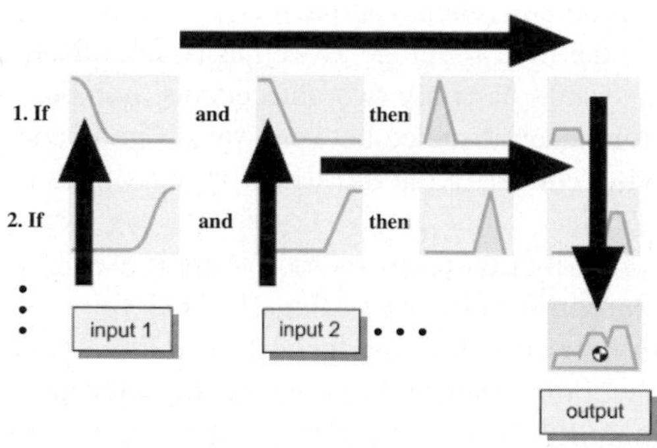

Fig. 1. Fuzzy inference diagram

2.2 Coverage

Generally, coverage can be considered as the measure of quality of service of a sensor network. In this paper, coverage [10] is defined as the ratio of the union of areas covered by each node and the area of the entire Region of Interest (ROI), as shown in Eq. (1), and binary sensing model [10] is adopted. Here, the covered area of each node is defined as the circular area within its sensing radius. Perfect detection of all interesting events in the covered area is assumed.

$$C = \frac{\bigcup_{i=1,\ldots,N} A_i}{A} \tag{1}$$

where

A_i is the area covered by the ith node;
N is the total number of nodes;
A stands for the area of the ROI.

In order to prevent recalculating the overlapped area, the coverage here is calculated using Monte Carlo method by creating a uniform grid in the ROI [11]. All the grid points being located in the sensing area are labeled 1 otherwise 0, depending on whether the Euclidean distance between each grid point and the sensor node is longer or shorter than sensing radius. Then the coverage can be approximated by the ratio of the summation of ones to the total number of the grid points.

If a node is located well inside the ROI, its complete coverage area will lie within the ROI. In this case, the full area of that circle is included in the covered region. If a node is located near the boundary of the ROI, then only the part of the ROI covered by that node is included in the computation.

3 Proposed Deployment Approach: EFOA

3.1 Assumptions and Model

Let *G(V, E)* be the graph defined on *V* with edges $uv \in E$ iff $uv \le R$. Here *uv* is the Euclidean distance between nodes *u* and *v*, *R* is the communication range. A sensor can detect any event within its sensing range *r*. Two sensors within *R* can communicate with each other. Neighbors of a sensor are nodes within its communication range. Detection and communication is modeled as a circle on the *2-D* sensor field.

According to the radio energy dissipation model, in order to achieve an acceptable Signal-to-Noise Ratio (SNR) in transmitting an *l* bit message over a distance *d,* the energy expended by the radio is given by [15]:

$$E_T(l,d) = \begin{cases} lE_{elec} + l\varepsilon_{fs}d^2 & \text{if } d \le d_0 \\ lE_{elec} + l\varepsilon_{mp}d^4 & \text{if } d > d_0 \end{cases} \tag{2}$$

where E_{elec} is the energy dissipated per bit to run the transmitter or the receiver circuit, ε_{fs} and ε_{mp} are amplifier constants, and *d* is the distance between the sender and the receiver. By equating the two expressions at $d=d_0$, we have $d_0 = \sqrt{\varepsilon_{fs} / \varepsilon_{mp}}$. Here we set electronics energy as $E_{elec}=50nJ/bit$, whereas the amplifier constant, is taken as $\varepsilon_{fs} = 10pJ/bit/m^2$, $\varepsilon_{mp} = 0.0013pJ/bit/m^2$, the same as in [15].

To receive *l* bit message, the radio expends:

$$E_R(l) = lE_{elec} \tag{3}$$

For simplicity, assume an area over which *n* nodes are uniformly distributed and the sink is located in the center of the field, so the distance of any node to the sink or its cluster head is $\le d_0$.

3.2 Energy-Efficient Fuzzy Optimization Algorithm

Expert knowledge is represented based on the following three descriptors:

- Node Energy - energy level available in each node, denoted by the fuzzy variable energy,

- Node Concentration - number of neighbors in the vicinity, denoted by the fuzzy variable concentration,
- Average distance to neighbors - average Euclidean distance between sensor node and its neighbors, denoted by the fuzzy variable d_n.

The linguistic variables used to represent the node energy and node concentration, are divided into three levels: *low, medium* and *high*, respectively, and there are three levels to represent the average distance to neighbors: *close, moderate* and *far*, respectively. The outcome to represent the moving distance d_m was divided into 5 levels: *very close, close, moderate, far* and *very far*. The fuzzy rule base includes rules like the following: IF the energy is *high* and the concentration is *high* and the distance to neighbor is *close* THEN the moving distance of sensor node *i* is *very far*.

Thus we used $3^3 = 27$ rules for the fuzzy rule base. We used triangle membership functions to represent the fuzzy sets *medium* and *moderate* and trapezoid membership functions to represent *low, high, close* and *far* fuzzy sets. The developed membership functions and their corresponding linguistic states are represented in Table 1 and Figures 2 through 5 respectively.

Table 1. Fuzzy rule base (d_n=average distance to neighbors, d_m=moving distance)

No.	energy	concentration	d_n	d_m
1	low	low	close	close
2	low	low	moderate	vclose
3	low	low	far	vclose
4	low	med	close	moderate
5	low	med	moderate	close
6	low	med	far	vclose
7	low	high	close	moderate
8	low	high	moderate	close
9	low	high	far	close
10	med	low	close	moderate
11	med	low	moderate	close
12	med	low	far	close
13	med	med	close	far
14	med	med	moderate	moderate
15	med	med	far	close
16	med	high	close	far
17	med	high	moderate	moderate
18	med	high	far	moderate
19	high	low	close	far
20	high	low	moderate	moderate
21	high	low	far	moderate
22	high	med	close	vfar
23	high	med	moderate	far
24	high	med	far	moderate
25	high	high	close	vfar
26	high	high	moderate	far
27	high	high	far	far

Legend: vclose=very close, vfar=very far, med=medium.

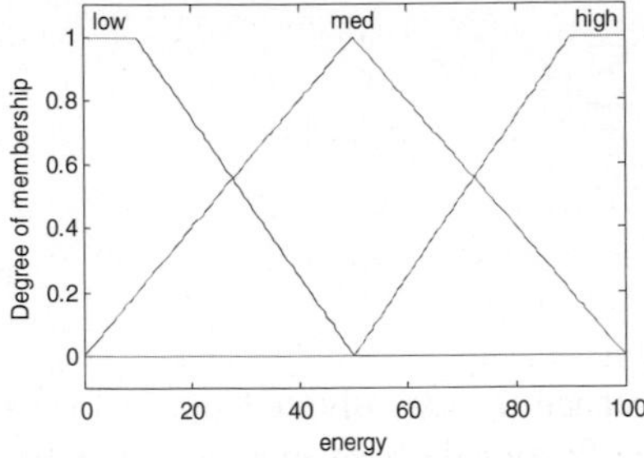

Fig. 2. Fuzzy set for fuzzy variable *energy*

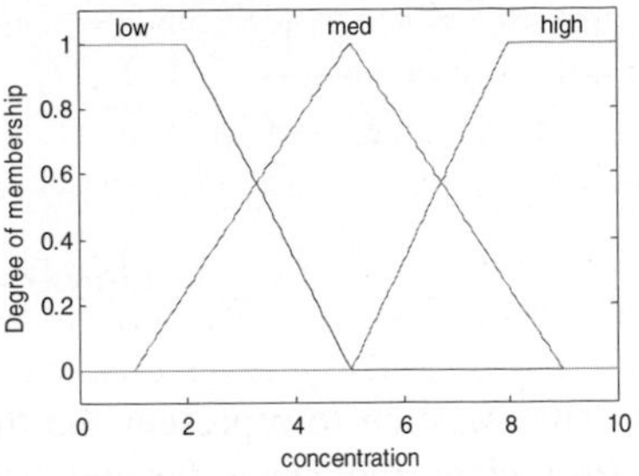

Fig. 3. Fuzzy set for fuzzy variable *concentration*

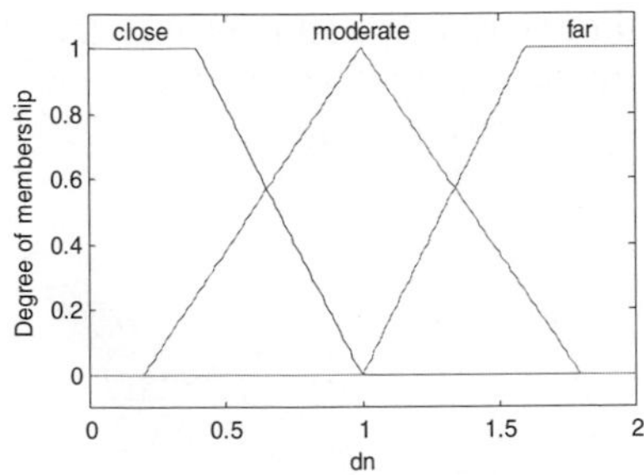

Fig. 4. Fuzzy set for fuzzy variable dn

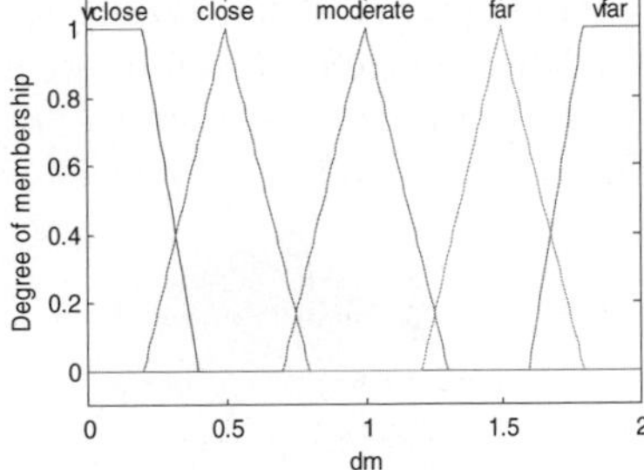

Fig. 5. Fuzzy set for fuzzy variable d_m

For the defuzzification, the Centroid is calculated and estimated over a sample of points on the aggregate output membership function, using the following formula:

$$Cen = \left(\sum \mu_A(x) * x\right) / \sum \mu_A(x) \tag{4}$$

where, $\mu_A(x)$ is the membership function of x in A. The membership function maps each element of X to a membership value between 0 and 1.

The control surface is central in fuzzy logic systems and describes the dynamics of the controller and is generally a time-varying nonlinear surface. From Fig. 6 and Fig. 7 obtained by computation in Matlab Fuzzy Logic Toolbox, we can see that although the concentration for a certain sensor is high, the moving distance can be smaller than some sensor with higher energy or sensor with fewer neighbors but more crowded. With the assistance of control surface, the next-step moving distance can be determined.

The next-step move direction is decided by virtual force. Assume sensor i has k neighbors, $k=k_1+k_2$, in which k_1 neighbors are within threshold distance d_{th} to sensor i, while k_2 neighbors are farther than d_{th} distance to sensor i. The coordinate of sensor i is denoted as $C_i = (X_i, Y_i)$, and that of neighbor sensor j is $C_j = (X_j, Y_j)$. The next-step move direction of sensor i is represented as Eq. (5) and (6), which are the improved version of moving direction equation in [13]. It is improved in the sense that threshold distance is set here so that attraction and repulsion forces can be represented in the equations. Thus after getting moving distance d_m and direction (angle α), sensor i clearly knows its next-step moving position.

$$\vec{v} = \frac{1}{\left|\vec{C}_i - \vec{C}_j\right|^2}\left(\sum_{j=1}^{k_1}(\vec{C}_i - \vec{C}_j) + \sum_{j=1}^{k_2}(\vec{C}_j - \vec{C}_i)\right) \tag{5}$$

$$\tan(\alpha) = \frac{Y(\vec{v})}{X(\vec{v})} \tag{6}$$

The threshold distance d_{th} here is set to a proper value $\sqrt{3}r$ which is proved as follows: We attempt to make distance between 2 sensor nodes moderate, i.e., not very close and not very far. This kind of stable structure is illustrated in Figure 8. Non-overlapped sensor coverage style is shown in Figure 8(a), however, an obvious drawback here is that a coverage hole exists which is not covered by any sensor. Note that an alternative way is to allow overlap, as shown in Figure 8(b) and it ensures that all grid points are covered. Therefore, we adopt the second strategy.

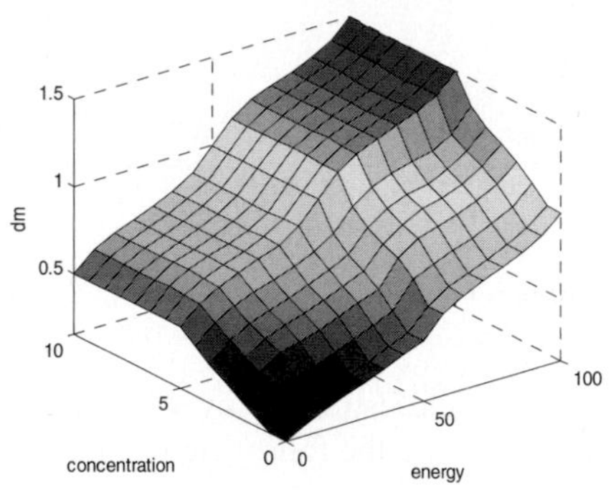

Fig. 6. Control surface (concentration, energy vs d_m)

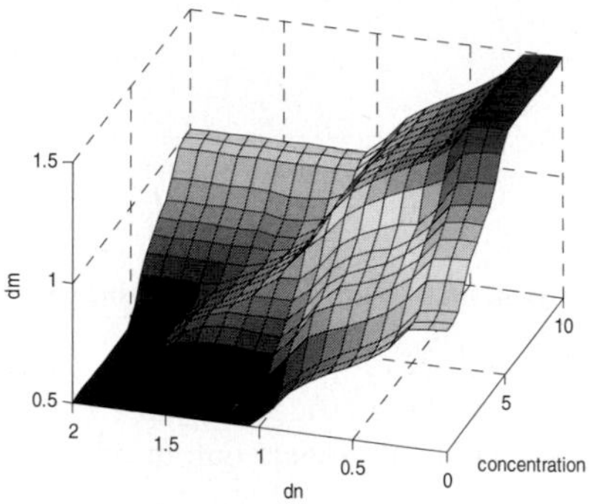

Fig. 7. Control surface (d_n, concentration vs d_m)

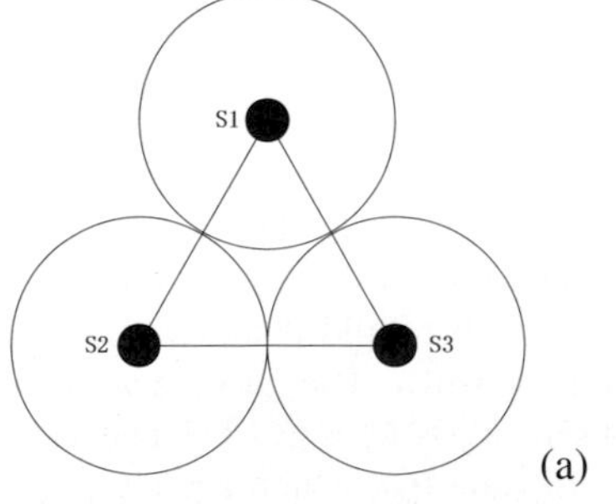

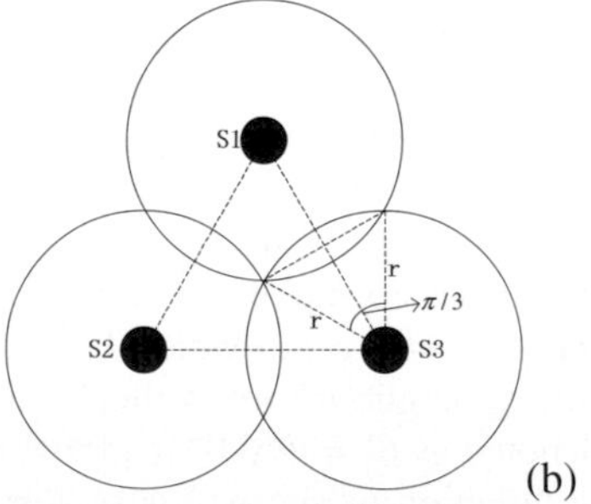

Fig. 8. Non-overlapped and overlapped sensor coverage cases

In Fig. 8(b), it is obvious that $\triangle S_1S_2S_3$ is equilateral triangle. Because the sensing radius is r, through some steps of simple geometry calculations, we can easily derive the distance between two sensor nodes in the latter case $S_1S_2 = S_2S_3 = S_1S_3 = 2\times\sqrt{3}r/2 = \sqrt{3}r$.

4 Proposed Network Maintenance Strategy

After the first stage deployment, the network maintenance is also necessary to be considered due to the uncertain environment. Thus, it is actually the post-deployment stage after the fuzzy optimization deployment stage and a certain period of network operation. The characteristic of the network in this situation is heterogeneous. The proposed network maintenance strategy is based on the sensor node importance level ranking. First, we take the importance level calculation of the node n as an example. Assume the total number of nodes in the network is N. Let the probability that node i can sense grid point j be denoted by $S_i(P_j)$, and then the probability $C(P_j)$ that grid point j is sensed by the whole network is derived as:

$$\begin{aligned} C(P_j) &= 1 - \prod_{i=1}^{N}(1 - S_i(P_j)) \\ &= 1 - (1 - S_n(P_j)) \times \prod_{i \neq n}^{N}(1 - S_i(P_j)) \end{aligned} \tag{7}$$

If delete node n, then the probability $C(P_j)$ becomes

$$C(P_j) = 1 - \prod_{i \neq n}^{N}(1 - S_i(P_j)) \tag{8}$$

For point j, the detection probability loss due to the deletion of node n becomes

$$\Delta C_n(P_j) = S_n(P_j) \times \prod_{i \neq n}^{N}(1 - S_i(P_j)) \tag{9}$$

Considering the importance difference of each node in the network, the detection ability loss of the whole network after deleting node n is:

$$\Delta C_n = \sum_j \Delta C_n(P_j) \times \nabla(P_j) \tag{10}$$

in which $\nabla(P_j)$ is the temporal gradient of sensing value at grid point j. The higher the gradient value the more often the interesting events occurrence. We assume that sensor measurement physically has a range ($0 \sim x_{max}$); if the sensing vale $v > x_{max}$, then let $v = x_{max}$.

According to importance level indicator ΔC_n, the importance level ranking of each node in the network can be sorted. Consequently we can either deploy several new sensor nodes close to the most important nodes or remove redundant nodes from "quiet" spot to the vicinity of those "busy" nodes as a backup.

5 Performance Evaluations

The proposed EFOA algorithm is evaluated first. For the convenience of comparison, we set the initial parameters the same as in [13]: various number of sensors deployed in a field of 10×10 square kilometers area are investigated; the r and R used in the experiment are *1km* and *2km* (*2km* and *4km*) respectively. So d_n should be ranged as 0~2 (0~4), not 0~10 as set by [13]. We assume each sensor is equipped with an omni-antenna to carry out the task of detection and communication. Evaluation of our EFOA algorithm follows three criteria: field coverage, energy consumption and convergence. Results are averaged over 100 Monte Carlo simulations.

Figure 9 shows that the coverage of the initial random deployment, fuzzy optimization algorithm (FOA) proposed in [13] and our proposed algorithm EFOA when *r=1km* and *R=2km*. The FOA and EFOA algorithm have similar results that both of them can improve the network coverage by 20% ~ 30% in average.

Figure 10 gives the results when *r=2km* and *R=4km*, the coverage comparison between random deployment, FOA and EFOA. In the case when 20 sensors are deployed, initially the coverage after random deployment is around 86%. After FOA and EFOA algorithm are executed, the coverage reaches 97%. The coverage is dramatically improved in the low density network. The above two figures indicate that instead of deploying large amount of sensors, the desired field coverage could also be achieved with fewer sensors.

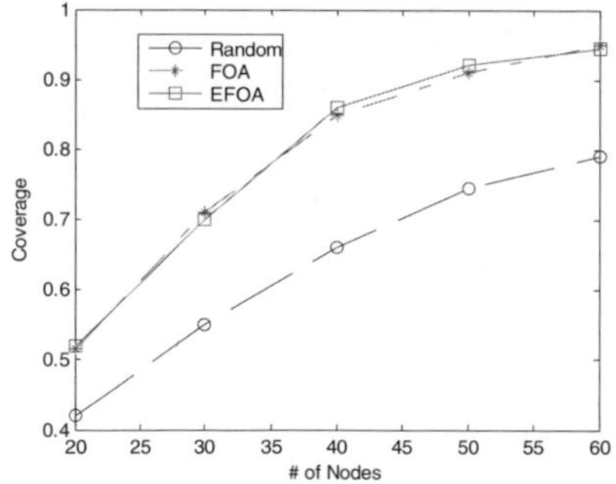

Fig. 9. Coverage vs. # of Nodes (*R=2, r=1*)

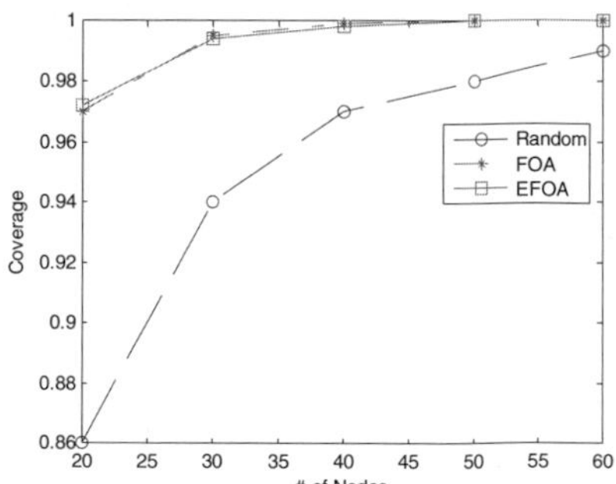

Fig. 10. Coverage vs. # of Nodes (*R=4, r=2*)

Figure 11 shows the total number of nodes that remain alive over time where each node begins with *2J* of energy and when *R=4km* and *r=2km*. The number of nodes in EFOA remains the same for a long time and they die out quickly almost at the same time while the first node dies early in FOA. The reason is that after some operation time, the network display heterogeneous characteristics, however, FOA doesn't consider the residual energy of nodes, so the energy difference among sensors becomes significant as time goes on. Network lifetime is the time span from the deployment to the instant when the network is considered nonfunctional. When a network should be considered nonfunctional, it is generally the instant when the first sensor dies or a percentage of sensors die and the loss of coverage occurs. Thus the lifetime is prolonged in EFOA compared with FOA.

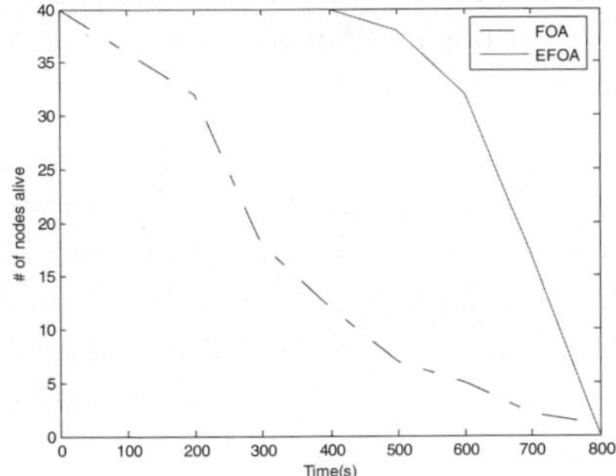

Fig. 11. # of nodes alive over time where each node begins with *2J* energy. (*R=4, r=2*)

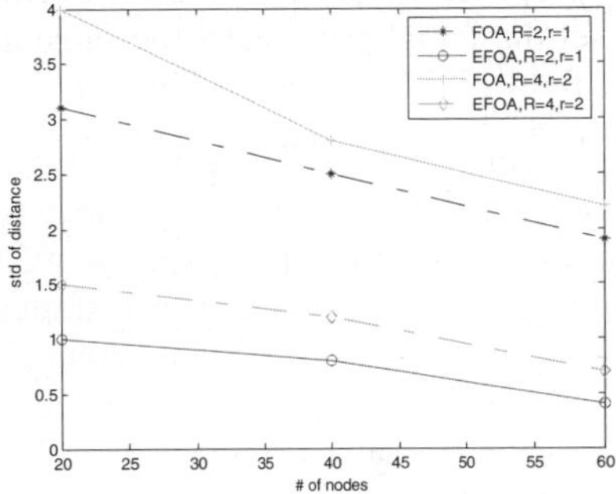

Fig. 12. Standard deviation of distance traveled verses number of nodes

Figure 12 shows EFOA has lower standard deviation of distance compared with FOA in both cases when *R=4km, r=2km* and *R=2km, r=1km* with various number of nodes. When the standard deviation of distance traveled is small, the variation in energy remaining at each node is not significant and thus a longer system lifetime with desired coverage can be achieved.

The network maintenance strategy is simulated thereafter as Figure 13 shows. The parameter x_{max} is set to be 50, sampling period is 5*s*.Total number of nodes in the network is 30, and two of the most importance nodes are the nodes labeled as 18 and 19 which have

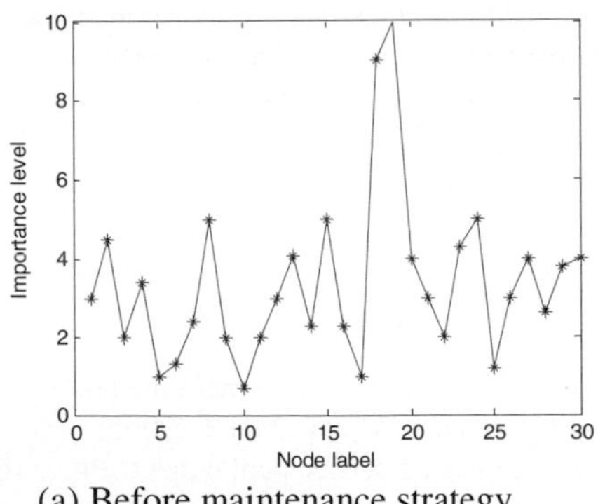

(a) Before maintenance strategy

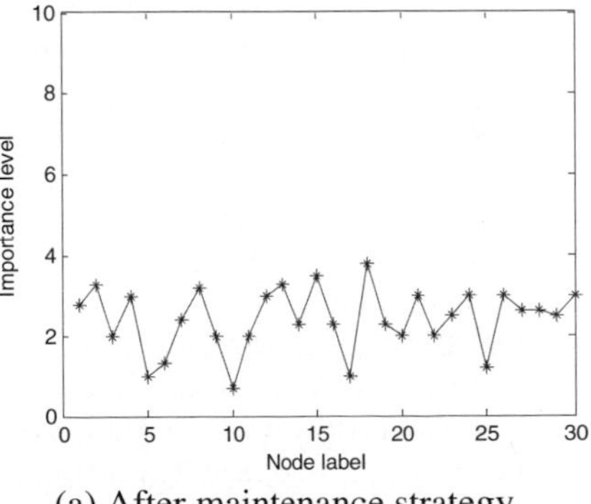

(a) After maintenance strategy

Fig. 13. Importance level verses node serial number

the highest importance level. After adding four new nodes close to node 18 and 19, the importance level distribution become nearly uniform compared with the case before executing network maintenance strategy. Thus the working load of the "busy" nodes can be shared by the backup nodes and the lifetime can be further prolonged.

6 Conclusions and Future Work

In this paper, an energy-efficient fuzzy optimization algorithm (EFOA) for self- deployment of mobile sensor networks was proposed. It was based on three descriptors – energy level of nodes, concentration and average distance to neighbors. The movement of each sensor node was assumed to be relatively limited for further reducing energy consumption. The existing next-step move direction formulas were also improved to be more realistic. Our approach has a great advantage to deal with the randomness in sensor deployment as well as minimize energy consumption. We also proposed a network maintenance strategy in the post-deployment phase based on the sensor node importance level ranking. Simulation results showed that our approach not only achieved fast and stable deployment but also greatly improved the network coverage and energy efficiency as well as extended the lifetime.

In the future work, the integration of environmental factors and realistic sensing model will be investigated.

Acknowledgments. This research was supported by the MIC (Ministry of Information and Communication), Korea, under the ITRC (Information Technology Research Center) support program supervised by the IITA (Institute of Information Technology Advancement) (IITA-2006-C1090-0602-0002).

References

1. Xiaoling Wu, Hoon Heo, et al.: Individual Contour Extraction for Robust Wide Area Target Tracking in Visual Sensor Networks. Proc of 9th ISORC (2006)
2. S. Meguerdichian, F. Koushanfar, G. Qu and M. Potkonjak: Exposure in Wireless Ad-Hoc Sensor Networks. Mobicom (2001)
3. S. Dhillon, K. Chakrabarty and S. Iyengar: Sensor placement for grid coverage under imprecise detections. Proc. International Conference on Information Fusion (2002)
4. T. Clouqueur, V. Phipatanasuphorn, P. Ramanathan and K. k. Saluja: Sensor Deployment Strategy for Target Detection. WSNA, (2003)
5. Sameer Tilak, Nael B. AbuGhazaleh, and Wendi Heinzelman: Infrastructure Tradeoffs for Sensor Networks.WSNA (2002)
6. A. Howard, M. J. Mataric and G. S. Sukhatme: An Incremental Self-Deployment Algorithm for Mobile Sensor Networks. Autonomous Robots, Special Issue on Intelligent Embedded Systems, September (2002)
7. J. Wu and S. Wang: Smart: A scan-based movement-assisted deployment method in wireless sensor networks. Proc. IEEE INFOCOM Conference, Miami, March (2005)
8. G. Wang, G. Cao, and T. La Porta: Movement-assisted sensor deployment. Proc. IEEE INFOCOM Conference, Hong Kong (2004)

9. Y. Zou and K. Chakrabarty: Sensor deployment and target localization based on virtual forces. Proc. IEEE INFOCOM Conference, Vol. 2 (2003) 1293-1303
10. Nojeong Heo and Pramod K. Varshney: Energy-Efficient Deployment of Intelligent Mobile Sensor Networks. IEEE Transactions on Systems, Man, and Cybernetics—Part A: Systems And Humans, Vol. 35, No. 1 (2005) 78 - 92
11. Xiaoling Wu, Shu Lei, Yang Jie, Xu Hui, Jinsung Cho and Sungyoung Lee: Swarm Based Sensor Deployment Optimization in Ad hoc Sensor Networks. Proc. of ICESS' 05 (LNCS), Xi'an, China, (2005) 533-541
12. Xiaoling Wu, Yu Niu, Lei Shu, Jinsung Cho, Young-Koo Lee, and Sungyoung Lee: Relay Shift Based Self-Deployment for Mobility Limited Sensor Networks. UIC-06 (LNCS), Wuhan, China (2006)
13. Haining Shu, Qilian Liang: Fuzzy Optimization for Distributed Sensor Deployment. IEEE Communications Society / Proc. of WCNC, New Orleans, USA (2005) 1903-1907
14. Indranil Gupta, Denis Riordan and Srinivas Sampalli: Cluster-head election using fuzzy logic for wireless sensor networks. Proc of the 3rd Annual Communication Networks and Services Research Conference (2005)
15. Wendi B. Heinzelman, Anantha P. Chandrakasan, and Hari Balakrishnan: An Application-Specific Protocol Architecture for Wireless Microsensor Networks. IEEE Transactions on Wireless Communications, Vol. 1, No. 4 (2002) 660 – 670

Server Placement in the Presence of Competition

Pangfeng Liu[1], Yi-Min Chung[1], Jan-Jan Wu[2], and Chien-Min Wang[2]

[1] Department of Computer Science and Information Engineering, National Taiwan University, Taipei, Taiwan, R.O.C.
[2] Institute of Information Science, Academia Sinica, Taipei, Taiwan, R.O.C.

Abstract. This paper addresses the optimization problems of placing servers in the presence of competition. We place a set of *extra servers* on a graph to compete with the set of *original servers*. Our objective is to find the placement that maximizes the benefit, which is defined as the profits from the requests made to the extra servers despite the competition, minus the cost of constructing those extra servers.

We propose an $O(|V|^3k)$ time dynamic programming algorithm to find the optimal placement of k extra servers that maximizes the benefit in a tree with $|V|$ nodes. We also propose an $O(|V|^3)$ time dynamic programming algorithm for finding the optimal placement of extra servers that maximizes the benefit, without any constraint on the number of extra servers. For general connected graphs, we prove that the optimization problems are NP-complete. As a result, we present a greedy heuristic for the problems. Experiment results indicate that the greedy heuristic achieves good results, even when compared with the upper bounds found by a linear programming algorithm. The greedy heuristic yields performances within 15% of the upper bound in the worst case, and within 2% of the same theoretical upper bound on average.

1 Introduction

This paper considers a strategy for setting up servers to compete with existing ones. For example, we assume that there are originally a number of McDonald's restaurants in a city, but no Kentucky Fried Chicken (KFC) restaurants. Now, if we decide to set up a number of KFC restaurants in the same city, where should we place them? We need to determine the locations for KFC so that they can compete with McDonald's and maximize their profits. Due to heavy competition among business of similar nature, it is important to choose locations of new servers in the area where the competitors have deployed their servers.

We define the servers we would like to set up as *extra* servers, and the existing (competitor) servers as *original* servers. Thus, in the above example, KFC restaurants are the extra servers and McDonald's restaurants are the original servers.

We use a graph to model the locations of the servers and users. A node in the graph represents a geographic location, and an edge represents a path between two locations. Building servers in these locations enables users at a node to

C. Cérin and K.-C. Li (Eds.): GPC 2007, LNCS 4459, pp. 124–135, 2007.

request services from the servers. Each edge has a communication cost. The distance between two nodes is the length of the shortest path that connects them.

For efficiency, We assume that requests from users always go to the nearest server. However, when the shortest distances from a user to the original and extra servers are the same, the user will go to the original server. That is, a user will NORMALLY go to the nearest restaurant, either McDonald's or KFC; however, if the distances to the two restaurants are the same, the user will go to McDonald's.

After extra servers have been established, users who previously went to McDonald's may now go to KFC. We define the benefit of an extra server placement to be the profit derived from user requests made to the server, minus the cost of constructing the server. The cost may vary, depending on the location of the extra server. This paper considers two placement problems related to extra servers, in the presence of competition from original servers.

1. Given the city configuration and a number k, locate k extra servers such that they will earn the most profit;
2. Given the city configuration, locate extra servers such that they earn the most profit, without any constraint on the number of extra servers.

We solve these two problems for a tree graph in $O(|V|^3k)$ and $O(|V|^3)$ time, respectively. For a general graph, we show that the two problems are intractable (NP-complete) and propose a heuristic to solve them. We also run experiments and compare our results for the heuristic with theoretical upper bounds.

Similar server placement problems, such as replica placement problems [4,3,6,10], p-Medians [5], and facility location problems [8], have been studied in the literature. For example, Kariv and Hakimi [5] formulate the p-median problem as locating p points such that the sum of each node's weight multiplied by its shortest distance to the p points is minimized. However, the p-median problem they considered does not take the building costs into account, and it minimizes the costs, instead of maximizing the profits. The facility location problem is similar to the p-median problem, with the additional consideration of the facility's costs.

Our extra server model differs from the model in [5] because it introduces the concept of competition. Extra servers must compete with original servers for user requests, in order to maximize their profits. The number of extra servers established is controlled by the building costs, which differ from location to location. Our dynamic programming model uses a similar technique to that in [4]. The presence of competition demands innovative proof techniques.

Tamir [9] described a dynamic programming model that solves p-median problems on a tree topology with building and access costs. The algorithm assumes that the cost for a client to request services is an increasing function of the distance between the client and the server. If the benefit function in our model is a decreasing function of the distance between the client and the server, our placement problem can be solved by transforming it into a p-median problem, and solving it by the dynamic programming described in [9]. However, the method proposed in this paper can deal with any arbitrary benefit functions, and still obtain the optimal solution for a tree topology.

The remainder of this paper is organized as follows. Section 2 formally describes our server placement models. In Section 3, we introduce the dynamic programming for finding the optimal extra server placement in a tree. Section 4 contains the proof that the problems are NP-complete for general graphs and presents a heuristic algorithm to solve them. Section 5 reports the experiment results, and Section 6 contains our conclusions.

2 Problem Formulation

We consider a connected graph $G = (V, E)$, where V is the set of nodes and E is the set of edges. Each edge $(u, v) \in E$ has a positive integer distance denoted by $d(u, v)$. For any two nodes $u, v \in V$, $d(u, v)$ also denotes the distance of the shortest path between them. For ease of representation, we also let $d(v, S) = \min_{u \in S} d(v, u)$ be the length of the shortest path from v to any node in $\mathcal{X}$, where $\mathcal{X} \subseteq \mathcal{V}$.

We consider *servers* that provide service to nodes in the graph. Every node v must go to the *nearest* server u for service. If a server is located at node v, then v will be serviced by that server. To simplify the concept of "the nearest server", we assuem that for every node v, its distances to all other nodes are different, i.e., $d(v, u) \neq d(v, w)$ for $u \neq w$. As a result the nearest server for every node is *uniquely* defined.

By serving a client v, a server node u earns a benefit of $b(v, u)$. Note that the function b can be arbitrary. For example, unlike [9], we do *not* assume that, for the same client node v, the function value must be monotonic with respect to the distance between v and the server node u.

We assume that there are a number of original servers $\mathcal{O} \subseteq V$ in G. In addition to the original server set $\mathcal{O}$, and we would like to add a number of extra servers to G to obtain the maximum benefit. Let $c(v)$ be the cost of building a server at node $v \in V$, and $\mathcal{X}$ be the set of new servers we would like to add into the system. A node $v \in V$ goes to either $\mathcal{O}$ or $\mathcal{X}$ for service - v goes to $\mathcal{X}$ for service when $d(v, \mathcal{X}) < d(v, \mathcal{O})$; otherwise $(d(v, \mathcal{X}) > d(v, \mathcal{O}))$, v goes to $\mathcal{O}$ for service. Let $V_{\mathcal{X}}$ denote the set of nodes that go to $\mathcal{X}$ for service, and $V_{\mathcal{O}} = V - V_{\mathcal{X}}$ be the set of nodes that go to $\mathcal{O}$ for service.

We define the *nearest servers* $NS(v)$ of v as the server v uses. Consequently $NS(v) \in \mathcal{O}$ if $v \in V_{\mathcal{O}}$, and $NS(v) \in \mathcal{X}$ if $v \in V_{\mathcal{X}}$. We can now define the *benefit function* of adding the servers $\mathcal{X}$ as follows.

$$B(\mathcal{X}) = \sum_{v \in V_{\mathcal{X}}} b(v, NS(v)) - \sum_{v \in \mathcal{X}} c(v). \tag{1}$$

We now define the problem as follows.

k-Extra-Server Problem. Given an integer k, $1 \leq k \leq |V - X|$, we want to find the optimal placement of k extra servers such that the benefit function is maximized (Equation (2)).

$$\max_{\mathcal{X} \subseteq (V - X), |\mathcal{X}| = k} B(\mathcal{X}) \tag{2}$$

Extra-Server Problem. We want to place extra servers to maximize the benefit function, without any constraint on the number of the extra servers. We call this optimization problem the **extra-server problem**.

3 Finding Extra Server Locations

We present algorithms that utilize global information to solve server placement problems. The use of global information facilitates the optimality of the algorithm and the assumption of global information is reasonable since we are dealing with a city or grid configuration and the location of servers are static and can be known completely in advance.

We focus on the case where the graph $G = (V, E)$ is a tree. Let T be the tree and r be the root of T. For each node $v \in V$, let T_v be the subtree of T rooted at v. If v is an internal node, then we use $child(v) = \{v_1, v_2, \dots, v_{|child(v)|}\}$ to denote the children of v. Following the notations in [4], let $T_v^{(i)}$ be the subtree of T that consists of v and the subtrees rooted at the first i children of v, i.e., $T_v^{(i)} = \{v\} \cup \cup_{j=1}^{i} T_{v_j}$.

Definition 1 (Benefit function, B). *For nodes $v, u \in V$, an integer k, and an integer i between 0 and $|child(v)|$, we define $B_{k,i}^{v,u}$ to be the maximum benefit derived by placing k extra servers in $T_v^{(i)}$, under the condition that $u = NS(v)$. Consequently u is either an original server or an extra server.*

We now consider the benefit function $B_{k,i}^{v,u}$ by placing $\mathcal{X}$ in $T_v^{(i)}$. We define $\mathcal{X}$ to be the set of k extra servers that maximize the following benefit function. Recall that $\mathcal{O}$ is the set of original servers.

$$B_{k,i}^{v,u} = \max_{\mathcal{X}}\{ \sum_{w \in T_v^{(i)}, NS(w) \in \mathcal{X} \cup u} b(w, NS(w)) - \sum_{s \in \mathcal{X}} c(s)\},\ u \notin \mathcal{O},$$

$$B_{k,i}^{v,u} = \max_{\mathcal{X}}\{ \sum_{w \in T_v^{(i)}, NS(w) \in \mathcal{X}} b(w, NS(w)) - \sum_{s \in \mathcal{X}} c(s)\},\ u \in \mathcal{O}.$$

The definition indicates that the benefit includes those nodes that will either go to the extra servers $\mathcal{X}$ or u (when $u \notin \mathcal{O}$) for service, minus the construction cost of the extra server set $\mathcal{X}$.

For the case where u is not in $\mathcal{O}$, by definition u is v's nearest server, so u has an extra server. However, u can be a node outside of $T_v^{(i)}$, – in which case it will not be in $\mathcal{X}$ because $\mathcal{X}$ is a subset of $T_v^{(i)}$. We still need to add the benefit from $T_v^{(i)}$ to u, since we assume that an extra server is placed in u.

Lemma 1. *For every node $v \in V$ and every child v_i of v, if $u \in T_{v_i}$ is the nearest server to v, then u is also the nearest server to v_i.*

Proof. We prove this lemma by contradictions and assume that the nearest server for v_i is u', not u. Since u' is the nearest server to v_i, the distance $d(v_i, u')$ must be *strictly* smaller than $d(v_i, u)$. The length of the shortest path between v and u' is $d(v, u') \leq d(v, v_i) + d(v_i, u') < d(v, v_i) + d(v_i, u) = d(v, u)$, which suggests that u' is closer to v than u; however, this contradicts the assumption that u is the nearest server of v. ■

For ease of discussion of the following lemma, we define a node set $V_{v,u,i}$. This set contains those nodes in T_{v_i} that could be the nearest server for v_i, under the condition that u is the nearest server for v, but not for v_i, i.e., $NS(v) = u$ and $NS(v_i) \neq u$. Intuitively, the set $V_{v,u,i}$ stands for those nodes in T_{v_i} that are far enough from v so that it will not be the nearest server for v (when compared with u), but close enough to v_i so that it is the nearest server of v_i.

Definition 2 ($\mathbf{V_{v,u,i}}$). *Let u be the nearest server of v and i be an integer between 1 and $|child(v)|$. $V_{v,u,i}$ is the subset of those u' in T_{v_i} such that u' is the nearest server to v_i, but it is* not *the nearest server to v. That is, $V_{v,u,i} = \{u' | u' \in T_{v_i}, d(v_i, u') < d(v_i, u),\ d(v, u)d(v, u')\}$*

Lemma 2. *For every node $v \in V$ and every child v_i of v, if $u \notin T_{v_i}$ is the nearest server of v, then either u is the nearest server of v_i or there exists a node $u' \in V_{v,u,i}$ that is the nearest server of v_i.*

Proof. If u *is* the nearest server of v_i, the lemma follows. Otherwise, we conclude that the nearest server of v_i must be within T_{v_i}, since the path from v_i to nodes not in T_{v_i} must pass through v, which already has u as its nearest server. The lemma then follows by the definition of $V_{v,u,i}$. ■

Theorem 1. *For every node $v \in V$ and an integer i between 0 and $|child(v)|$, if u is the nearest server of v, then for every node w in T_{v_i}, we can find the nearest server for w in $T_{v_i} \cup \{u\}$.*

Proof. The only way a shortest path from a node w in T_{v_i} to any node outside T_{v_i} is to go through the edge (v_i, v). However, any such shortest path must end at node u since u is the nearest server for v; otherwise we will be able to find a closer server for v other than u – a contradiction to the fact that $NS(v) = u$. ■

Terminal Conditions. We first derive two terminal conditions for the recursion of B, the benefit function.

k = 0. When k is 0, we do not place any extra servers in $T_v^{(i)}$. If u is an original server in $\mathcal{O}$, every node in $T_v^{(i)}$ will go to $\mathcal{O}$ for service, so the benefit is 0. If u is not in $\mathcal{O}$, we consider two cases. First if u is not in $T_v^{(i)}$, every node in $T_v^{(i)}$ will either go to an original server or to u for service; thus, the benefit can be determined by Equation (3).

$$B' = \sum_{w \in T_v^{(i)}, d(w,u) < d(w,\mathcal{O})} b(w, u) \tag{3}$$

In the second case, u is not an original server but u is in $T_v^{(i)}$, which means that there is at least one extra server in $T_v^{(i)}$. This contradicts the assumption that k is 0. For the purpose of dynamic programming, we define the benefit to be $-\infty$.

$\mathbf{k = 1, u \notin \mathcal{O}, u \in T_v^{(i)}}$. When k is 1, u is in $T_v^{(i)}$, so it is not an original server, but it is definitely the only extra server in $T_v^{(i)}$. Every node in $T_v^{(i)}$ will either go to $\mathcal{O}$ or u for service; thus, the benefit can be calculated in the same way as $B' - c(u)$. Note that, since u is now in the $\mathcal{X}$ that maximizes the benefit of $T_v^{(i)}$, $c(u)$ should be deducted from the benefit.

Recursion. Next, we derive the recursion function for $B_{k,i}^{v,u}$.

$$B_{k,i}^{v,u} = \begin{cases} 0, & \text{if } k = 0 \text{ and } u \in \mathcal{O} \\ B', & \text{if } k = 0,\ u \notin \mathcal{O}, \text{ and } u \notin T_v^{(i)} \\ B' - c(u), & \text{if } k = 1,\ u \notin \mathcal{O}, \text{ and } u \in T_v^{(i)} \\ B'', & \text{if } u \in T_{v_i} \\ \max\{B'', B'''\}, & \text{if } u \notin T_{v_i} \\ -\infty, & \text{otherwise,} \end{cases} \tag{4}$$

where

$$B'' = \max_{0 \le j \le k} \left\{ B_{k-j,i-1}^{v,u} + B_{j,|child(v_i)|}^{v_i,u} \right\}, \tag{5}$$

and

$$B''' = \max_{0 \le j \le k} \left\{ B_{k-j,i-1}^{v,u} + E_{j,i}^{v,u} \right\}. \tag{6}$$

The first three cases were discussed as the terminal conditions in Section 3, so we only need to consider the rest.

$\mathbf{u \in T_{v_i}}$

If $u \in T_{v_i}$, u will also be the nearest server to v_i by Lemma 1, since u is the nearest server of v. Then, by Theorem 1, every node in T_{v_i} goes to either T_{v_i} or u for service. In addition, u is the nearest server to v. By Theorem 1, all nodes in $T_v^{(i-1)}$ obtain service from u or $T_v^{(i-1)}$.

Assume that there are j extra servers in T_{v_i}, then there will be $k-j$ extra servers in $T_v^{(i-1)}$, where $0 \le j \le k$. To obtain the best $\mathcal{X}$ that maximizes the benefit, we need to consider all possible values of j, as formulated in Equation (5). The recursion follows.

$\mathbf{u \notin T_{v_i}}$

If u is not in T_{v_i}, we need to consider two sub-cases.

Case 1: If u is the nearest server of v_i, the value of $B_{k,i}^{v,u}$ is defined as in Equation (5), because we can isolate two subtrees, as we did in the previous case where $u \in T_{v_i}$.

Case 2: If the nearest server of v_i is *not* u, by Lemma 2, we can find the nearest server u' for v_i in T_{v_i}. We formulate the benefit as B''' in Equation (6).

Consider these two sub-cases, if $u \notin T_{v_i}$, $B_{k,i}^{v,u}$ is formulated as $\max\{B'', B'''\}$.

Now, in order to finish the recursion the only missing element is the new cost function $E_{k,i}^{v,u}$.

Definition 3 ($E_{k,i}^{v,u}$)**.** *For nodes $v, u \in V$, an integer k, and the i-th child of node v (denoted by v_i), we define $E_{k,i}^{v,u}$ to be the maximum benefit derived by placing k extra servers in the subtree T_{v_i}, where $u \notin T_{v_i}$ is the nearest server of v, but u is not the nearest server of v_i. Instead, the nearest server of v_i is a u' in T_{v_i}. The benefit is similarly defined in Equation (7):*

$$E_{k,i}^{v,u} = \max_{\mathcal{X}}\{ \sum_{w \in T_{v_i}, NS(w) \in \mathcal{X}} b(w, NS(w)) - \sum_{s \in \mathcal{X}} c(s)\}. \tag{7}$$

From the above discussion, the maximum benefit $E_{k,i}^{v,u}$ is derived by Equation (8). That is, we need to enumerate all the possible u' and use the one that maximizes $B_{k,|child(v_i)|}^{v_i,u'}$. The set $V_{v,u,i}$ is exactly the possible set to select u' from, since v_i will go to u' for service, but not to u. This is exactly the definition of $V_{v,u,i}$.

$$E_{k,i}^{v,u} = \max_{u' \in V_{v,u,i}} \left\{ B_{k,|child(v_i)|}^{v_i,u'} \right\}. \tag{8}$$

The Final Solution. Finally, the maximum benefit of locating k extra servers in the tree T can be calculated by Equation (9):

$$\max_{u \in T} \left\{ B_{k,|child(r)|}^{r,u} \right\}. \tag{9}$$

The possible candidates for u are subject to the following constraints: If u is an original server $d(r, u)$ must be $d(r, \mathcal{O})$, i.e., u is the nearest original server to the root. If u is not an original server, the distance $d(r, u)$ must be smaller than $d(r, \mathcal{O})$ to ensure that u is the nearest extra server to the root.

Theorem 2. *Given a tree $T = (V, E)$ and a set $\mathcal{O} \subseteq V$ as the original servers, the k-extra-server problem for T can be solved in $O(|V|^3 k)$ time, where $0 \leq k \leq |V - \mathcal{O}|$ is an integer.*

Proof. The problem can be solved by Equations (3) to (9). The time of the dynamic programming is derived by calculating all the entries of $B_{k,i}^{v,u}$ and $E_{k,i}^{v,u}$. Consider each pair of v and i, so that there are totally $\sum_{v \in V} |child(v)| = |V| - 1$ pairs. Thus, the number of entries of $B_{k,i}^{v,u}$ is $(k+1) \cdot |V| \cdot (|V| - 1) = O(|V|^2 k)$, and it takes $O(|V|)$ time to calculate each entry; hence, the time required to calculate all the entries of $B_{k,i}^{v,u}$ is bounded by $O(|V|^3 k)$. Similarly, there are $O(|V|^2 k)$ entries of $E_{k,i}^{v,u}$, and it takes $O(|V|)$ time to calculate each entry; therefore, the time required to calculate all the entries of $E_{k,i}^{v,u}$ is $O(|V|^3 k)$. The total time required is therefore $O(|V|^3 k)$. ∎

Using similar techniques we derive the following theorem. The proof is removed due to space limitation.

Theorem 3. *Given a tree graph $T = (V, E)$ and $\mathcal{O} \subseteq V$ are the original servers of T, the extra-server problem for T can be solved in $O(|V|^3)$ time.*

Proof. The proof is similar to that of Theorem 2. There are $O(|V|^2)$ entries of $B_i^{v,u}$ and $O(|V|^2)$ entries of $E_i^{v,u}$, and the calculation of each entry requires at most $O(|V|)$ computing time. Hence, the problem can be solved in $O(|V|^3)$ time. ∎

4 NP-Completeness

The NP-complete proof is derived from the *dominating set* problem [2], and is removed due to space limitation. A subset $V' \subseteq V$ is a dominating set if for all $u \in V - V'$, there is a $v \in V'$ such that the edge (u, v) is in E. The decision problem of the *dominating set* can be formulated as follows: Given a graph $G = (V, E)$ and a positive integer $K \leq |V|$, is there a dominating set of size K or less?

k-EXTRA-SERVER. We now consider the k-extra-server problem and define the corresponding decision problem as follows: In a k-extra-server problem instance, is there a placement of k extra servers such that the benefit is at least B?

EXTRA-SERVER. Similarly, we define the decision problem of EXTRA-SERVER as follows: In a extra-server problem instance, is there a placement of extra servers such that the benefit is at least B?

Theorem 4. *The k-EXTRA-SERVER problem is NP-complete.*

Theorem 5. *The EXTRA-SERVER problem is NP-complete.*

Since the k-extra-server problem and the extra-server problem are both NP-complete, we propose a greedy heuristic (denoted as **Greedy**) for these problems. Here, we only describe **Greedy** for the k-extra server problem because the method for the extra-server problem is very similar.

The greedy method works in rounds. In each round, we locate an extra server that maximizes its benefit. We add the benefit produced by the selected extra server to the total benefit, which was set to 0 initially, and then mark the selected server as an *original* server. We repeat the process until k extra servers are selected.

5 Experiment Results

We conduct simulations to compare performance of **Greedy** with the linear programming optimal solutions acquired using GLPK (*GNU Linear Programming Kit*) [7] for the *k-extra-server* problem. GLPK is a set of routines designed to solve large-scale linear programming (LP), mixed integer programming (MIP), and other related problems. It is written in ANSI C and organized in the form of a library [7]. Let the 0-1 variable X_u and $u \in V$ denote whether there is an extra server on u, and let the 0-1 variable Z_{uv}, $u \in V$, $v \in V$ denote whether v is a client of u. The integer programming for the k-extra-server problem is formulated as follows:

$$\text{maximize} \quad \sum_{u \in (V-X)} \sum_{v \in V} Z_{uv} b(v,u) - \sum_{u \in V} X_u c(u), \tag{10}$$

subject to

$$\begin{aligned}
X_u &\in \{0,1\}, && \text{for each } u \in V, && \text{(11a)}\\
Z_{uv} &\in \{0,1\}, && \text{for each } u \in V,\ v \in V, && \text{(11b)}\\
X_u &= 0, && \text{for each } u \in \mathcal{O}, && \text{(11c)}\\
\sum_{u \in V} X_u &= k, && && \text{(11d)}\\
\sum_{u \in V} Z_{uv} &= 1, && \text{for each } v \in V, && \text{(11e)}\\
X_u - Z_{uv} &\geq 0, && \text{for each } u \in (V - \mathcal{O}), \text{ each } v \in V, && \text{(11f)}\\
Z_{uv} &= 0, && \text{for each } u \in V, \text{ each } v \in V, \text{ and } d(v,u) > d(v,\mathcal{O}). && \text{(11g)}
\end{aligned}$$

Consider the 0-1 variables X_u and Z_{uv} in constraints (11a) and (11b) respectively. We replace them with constraints (12a) and (12b) respectively, so that we have a linear programming formulation.

$$\begin{aligned}
0 \leq X_u &\leq 1, && \text{for each } u \in V, && \text{(12a)}\\
0 \leq Z_{uv} &\leq 1, && \text{for each } u \in V,\ v \in V. && \text{(12b)}
\end{aligned}$$

The optimal benefit gained from linear programming only serves as a upper bound, since it allows a fraction number of an extra server to be placed on a node. However, in our experiments, we find that, in most cases, linear programming produces integer solutions, i.e., X_u and Z_{uv} are in the range $\{0, 1\}$.

5.1 Experiment Setting

In our experiments, we use GT-ITM [1] to generate random graphs according to Waxman model [11]. Each of the graphs is connected, and nodes are added randomly in a $s \times s$ square. The probability of an edge between u and v is given by

$$p(u,v) = \alpha e^{-d/\beta L},$$

where $0 < \alpha, \beta \leq 1$, d is the Euclidean distance between u and v, and $L = \sqrt{2}s$ is the largest possible distance between any two nodes. In our experiments, we set s to 20, α to 0.2 and β to 1.

For each v, we set a value $r(v)$ to be a random integer between 20 and 40, and set the building cost $c(v)$ to be $r(v)$ plus a random integer between 1 and 10. The benefit function $b(v,u)$ is defined as $r(v)$ divided by the distance from v to u. Finally, we place original servers randomly in the graph. We simulate up to 150 nodes since this is a reasonable size for city or grid configuration.

5.2 Effect of α

We evaluate the performance of **Greedy** compared with the upper bounds found by linear programming under different values of α. In these experiments, for each α we set $|V|$ from 50 to 150, and for each $|V|$ we set $|\mathcal{O}|$ from 0 to $0.1|V|$. As a result, we have 1066 graphs to simulate, and for each graph we set k from 1 to $0.1|V|$. Figure 1 shows that when α increases the average degree of each node also increases. Figure 1 shows that **Greedy** performs very well; on average, its performance differs from the theoretical upper bounds by only 1% and in the worst case the difference is no more than 15% of the upper bound.

Figure 1 also shows that as α increases, the average difference between **Greedy** and the upper bound derived by linear programming also increases. Since the average degree of each node increases as α increases, there is a higher probability that the extra servers will affect each other. However, to maximize the benefit, **Greedy** only considers the current configuration when it selects the next location to place an extra server; thus, it can not predict the "long range" effects and the interaction among the extra servers. Hence, as α increases, the average difference (as a percentage) between **Greedy** and the upper bound also increases.

$\|V\|$	$\alpha = 0.2$	$\alpha = 0.3$	$\alpha = 0.4$	$\alpha = 0.5$
50	3.56	5.37	7.11	8.78
150	10.45	15.59	20.87	26.12
Average	8.11	12.01	16.03	20.03

α	Avg. difference	Max. difference
0.2	0.43%	9.54%
0.3	0.49%	14.35%
0.4	0.52%	13.20%
0.5	0.58%	11.95%

Fig. 1. The average degree of a node under different values of α and the average difference (as a percentage) between **Greedy** and the upper bound under different values of α

5.3 Effect of the Number of Original Servers

We now consider the effect of the number of original servers on the average difference as a percentage of the upper bounds. In these experiments we set $|V|$ to 100, $|\mathcal{O}|$ from 1 to 50, and k to 10.

Figure 2 (a) shows the error-bar between **Greedy** and the upper bounds derived by the linear programming. The upper markers are the average upper bounds and the lower markers are the average benefits of **Greedy**. In the figure, the average benefits produced by **Greedy** are so close to the upper bounds that they coincide. Furthermore, the figure suggests that as $|\mathcal{O}|$ increases the benefit will decrease. This is reasonable since a large number of competitors only have a negative impacts on the extra servers.

5.4 Effect of k

Next, we consider the effects of k on the average difference as a percentage between **Greedy** and the theoretical upper bound. In these experiments we set

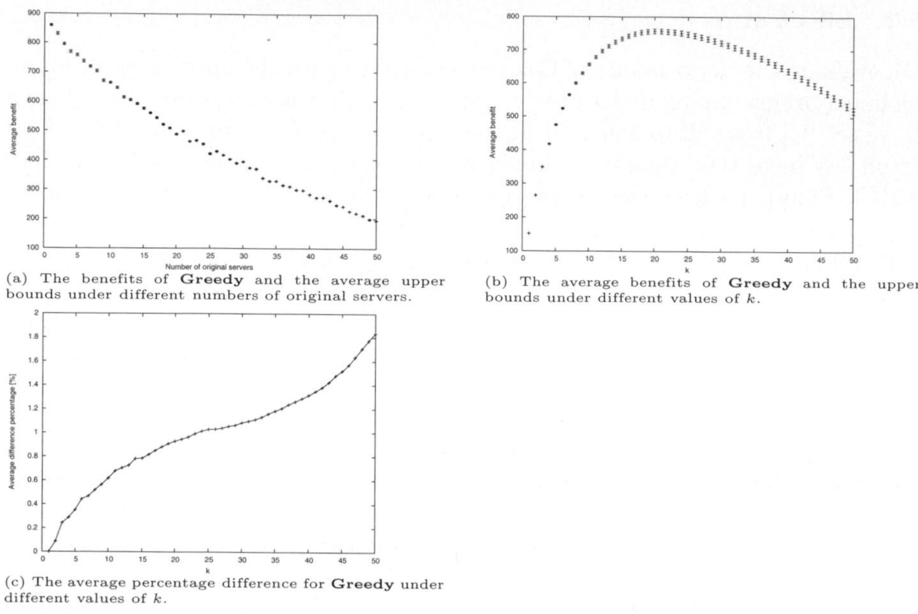

(a) The benefits of **Greedy** and the average upper bounds under different numbers of original servers.

(b) The average benefits of **Greedy** and the upper bounds under different values of k.

(c) The average percentage difference for **Greedy** under different values of k.

Fig. 2. Average benefits under different number of original and extra servers ((a) and (b)), and derivation percentage from the theoretical bounds (c)

$|V|$ to 100 and $|\mathcal{O}|$ to 10, so we generate 100 graphs in total. For each graph we set k from 1 to 50, which gives us 5000 simulation results.

Figure 2 (b) shows the error-bars in our simulations. We observe that the benefit of **Greedy** is extremely close to the theoretical upper bounds. The figure also shows that, initially, as k increases, the benefit increases because we can make more profit. As the number of extra servers increases substantially, the benefit decreases due to the cost of constructing the extra servers.

Figure 2(c) shows that as k increases the average difference between **Greedy** and the theoretical upper bound also increases. This is because **Greedy** places an extra server to maximize the benefit at each step because it can not consider the overall situation; thus, the difference accumulates at each step – more servers means a larger difference between **Greedy** and the upper bound.

In summary, we conclude that the **Greedy** algorithm performs extremely well. Considering all the simulation parameter setting, the greedy algorithm yields average benefits that are within 2% of the average theoretical upper bounds. It is also extremely efficient and easy to implement.

6 Conclusion

We have formulated two optimization problems, the k-extra-server problem and the extra-server problem. We consider the profit and construction costs at each location, and place extra servers to maximize the benefit in the presence of competition from original servers. For trees, we formulate dynamic programming algorithms to solve the k-extra-server problem and the extra-server problem in $O(|V|^3k)$ time and $O(|V|^3)$ time, respectively. For general graphs, we prove that the problems are NP-complete and propose a greedy heuristic to solve them. The experiment results demonstrate that the greedy heuristic yields performances within 15% of the theoretical upper bound in the worst case, and within 2% of the same theoretical upper bound on average.

In the future we will investigate the possibility of designing efficient and effective algorithms for graphs other than trees. For example, our greedy algorithms perform well on general graphs, so we should be able to show that the greedy algorithm performance is guaranteed to be within a constant factor of the optimum. We would also like to generalize dynamic programming to other graphs, such as planar graphs.

References

1. K. Calvert and E. Zegura. Gt-itm: Georgia tech internetwork topology models. http://www-static.cc.gatech.edu/projects/gtitm/.
2. M. R. Garey and D. S. Johnson. *Computers and Intractability: A Guide to the Theory of NP-Completeness*. W. H. Freeman & Co., New York, NY, USA, 1979.
3. X. Jia, D. Li, X. Hu, W. Wu, and D. Du. Placement of web-server proxies with consideration of read and update operations on the internet. *The Computer Journal*, 46(4):378–390, 2003.
4. K. Kalpakis, K. Dasgupta, and O. Wolfson. Optimal placement of replicas in trees with read, write, and storage costs. *IEEE Transactions on Parallel and Distributed Systems*, 12(6):628–637, June 2001.
5. O. Kariv and S. L. Hakimi. An algorithmic approach to network location problems. ii: The p-medians. *SIAM J. Appl. Math.*, 37(3):539–560, 1979.
6. B.-J. Ko and D. Rubenstein. A greedy approach to replicated content placement using graph coloring. In *SPIE ITCom Conference on Scalability and Traffic Control in IP Networks II*, Boston, MA, July 2002.
7. A. Makhorin. http://www.gnu.org/software/glpk/glpk.html.
8. D. B. Shmoys, E. Tardos, and K. Aardal. Approximation algorithms for facility location problems (extended abstract). In *Proc. 29th ACM STOC.*, pages 265–274, 1997.
9. A. Tamir. An $o(pn^2)$ algorithm for the p-median and related problems on tree graphs. *Operations Research Letters*, 19(2):59–64, 1996.
10. O. Unger and I. Cidon. Optimal content location in multicast based overlay networks with content updates. *World Wide Web*, 7(3):315–336, 2004.
11. B. M. Waxman. Routing of multipoint connections. pages 347–352, 1991.

A Scalable Mechanism for Semantic Service Discovery in Multi-ontology Environment

Zhizhong Liu, Huaimin Wang, and Bin Zhou

College of Computer Science, National University of Defense Technology, Changsha China
liuzane@gmail.com, whm_w@163.net, Bin.Zhou.cn@gmail.com

Abstract. Semantic service discovery improves the performance of service matching, due to using ontology and logical reasoning. However, in open distributed computing environment available mechanisms for semantic service discovery face new challenges: increasing scale of systems, multiple coexistent ontologies and so on. Aiming to these problems, a semantic service discovery mechanism based on ontology community, SSD_OC, is proposed in this paper. Multiple coexistent ontologies are supported by SSD_OC and bridging axioms between different ontologies enable users to match services across ontologies. Experiment results show that SSD_OC is scalable and outperform other systems in term of F-Measure.

1 Introduction

Semantic service discovery (SSD), the infrastructure of semantic web service, matches services on the basis of their capability by using ontology and logical reasoning[1]. Semantics is both a blessing and a curse. It can improve the precision and recall of service matching. On the negative side, logic reasoning results in greater responding time of service discovery and worse scalability. In addition, most available SSDs assume that all services refer to identical ontology. In practice, there are mostly multiple coexistent ontologies, especially in open distributed computing environment where providers provide services with similar functions, but refer to different ontologies. For example, Google, Amazon.Com etc. provided some services with similar functions according to their own class hierarchy. Ideal SSD should support multiple coexistent ontologies and enable service discovery across ontologies. But most available service discovery mechanisms can't cover those requirements.

The aim of this paper is to study a novel SSD mechanism which supports multiple coexistent ontologies and SSD across ontologies. In addition, it must be scalable. For these aims, a SSD mechanism based on ontology community, SSD_OC, is proposed. SSD_OC partitions advertised services into different ontology communities according to their referred ontologies. It also establishes relations among communities as bridging axioms, and implements service discovery across ontologies through ontology translation based on these axioms. Within community, SSD builds upon previous works done by Paolucci on semantic matching of web service capabilities [2] and importing semantics into UDDI [3].

This paper is organized as follows. Section 2 reviews related works. Then in section 3, the architecture of SSD_OC is described. The corresponding algorithms of service matching are presented in section 4. To evaluate our approach, a set of experiments are conducted in section 5. Finally, we conclude this article.

C. Cérin and K.-C. Li (Eds.): GPC 2007, LNCS 4459, pp. 136 – 145, 2007.

2 Related Works

Ontology interoperability is the essential precondition for SSD across ontologies. Ontology mapping is one of mature approaches[4] to achieve that interoperability. It establishes relations between ontology entities by calculating semantic similarity between them. There are many methods for ontology mapping, such as GLUE, FCA-Merge, IF-MAP, QOM, Anchor-PROMPT/PROMPT, OLA and so on. Dejiang Dou[5] claimed ontology translation can be thought of in terms of inference. Therefore they represented mapping rules as first order axioms, and implemented OntoEngine, an ontology translation engine basing on first order reasoning.

LARKS[6] is the first system implementing semantic service matching. LARKS identified a set of filters that progressively restrict the number of candidate services. LARKS identified four degrees of match: Exact, Plug-in, Subsumes, Fail. To enable UDDI support semantic discovery, Paolucci added a DAML-S/UDDI engine on UDDI[3]. Further, they proposed a matching algorithm on the basis of DAML ontology[2]. Klusch[7] complemented logic based reasoning with approximate matching based on syntactic IR, and proposed OWLS-MX, which applies this approach to match services and requests specified in OWL-S. Furthermore, they provided a collection of OWL-S service, OWLS-TC[1] to test matching algorithms.

Meteor-S provided a federate of registry to enable service partition[8]. It supported multiple ontologies and described the data partitioning criteria as Extended Registries Ontology (XTRO) in MWSDI. And, they developed a Web service discovery algorithm for a multi-ontology environment[9]. The matching process is based on a service template related to WSDL-S. Based on Paolucci's works, Akkiraju[10] added ontology selection process during service discovery. But how to implement that is not mentioned. WSMO matched service across ontologies by OO-Mediator[11]. It provided a conceptual model for the semantic-based location of services. Jyotishman Pathak[12] described a framework for ontology-based flexible discovery of Semantic Web services. The proposed approach relied on user-supplied, context-specific mappings from user ontology to relevant domain ontologies. YIN Nan[13] proposed a general framework of ontology-based service discovery sub-system, where context-based domain matching algorithms located service domains; ontology-based service matching algorithms matched services in specific domain. Most approaches mentioned above supported multiple ontologies. But they considered domains separately, that's to say, they didn't not support service discovery across ontologies.

3 Architecture of SSD_OC

To support multiple coexistent ontologies, we design the architecture of SSD_OC as figure 1. The architecture consists of three components: Ontology Community, Ontology Bridging and Translation, Request Parser and Community Selection.

Ontology community (OC) includes services referring to the identical consistent ontology set. OC takes charge of service registration and management, and service matchmaking within OC. OC adapts Paolucci's UDDI + DAML-S framework[3] for

---

1 http://projects.semwebcentral.org/projects/owls-tc/

OWL-S. It is composed of UDDI Register, UDDI/OWL-S Translator, OWL-S Matching Engine, OWL Ontology and Communication Module. UDDI/OWL-S Translator maps OWL-S description into UDDI specification (e.g. tModel). The OWL-S Matching Engine performs the capability matching on basis of OWL-Lite ontology. The process of service advertisement and discovery is similar to that in Paolucci's study.

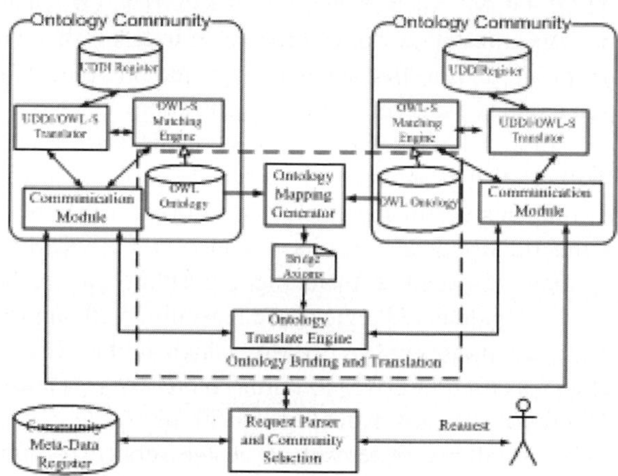

Fig. 1. Architecture for SSD_OC

Ontology Bridging and Translate module consists of an Ontology Mapping Generator, a set of Bridging Axioms and an Ontology Translation Engine. The Generator establishes the relations, namely Bridging Axioms, between entities. In this paper, how to establish these mappings is not the focus. And we assume that bridging axioms are available. Translator Engine translates the request for one community to another using Bridge Axioms, which enables service discovery across communities. Our work is inspired by the Bridge Axiom proposed by Dejiang Dou[5]. The aim of his work was to translate dataset or queries for one ontology to another. And they implemented it in OntoEngine.

Request Parser and Community Selection parses user requests, and forwards the request to corresponding communities after community selection. SSD_OC provides a central register which manages the metadata of ontology community to support community selection. The metadata includes the URL of community register; the ontologies which some ontology community refers to. Therefore this register can answer following questions: 1) where is the register of some community? 2) which community refers to some ontologies? 3) which ontology is referred by a community?

4 Semantic Service Matching in SSD_OC

4.1 Related Definitions

From different viewpoints, ontology can be defined in different ways. In this paper, ontology is defined formally as follows:

Definition 1 Ontology. Ontology can be described as a 4-tuple $O := (C, R, H_C, A)$, where C represents the set of concepts in ontology; $R_C \subseteq C \times C$ is the set of relations over concepts; $H_C \subseteq R_C$ is a subset of R_C, represents hierarchical relation set between concepts; and axioms A characterize the relations.

In this paper, we focus on two special relations, i.e. **equal semantically** and **subsume semantically**. Given two concepts α, β in an ontology, if they are equivalent concept, α is equal semantically to β, denoted as "$\alpha \simeq \beta$"; if they have relation H_C, β subsume semantically α, denoted as "$\alpha \sim\prec \beta$". Within an ontology, the relations between them are following:

(1) If $\alpha \simeq \beta, \beta \sim\prec \gamma, \alpha \sim\prec \gamma$;

(2) If $\alpha \sim\prec \beta, \beta \simeq \gamma, \alpha \sim\prec \gamma$;

(3) If $\alpha \sim\prec \beta, \beta \sim\prec \gamma$, $\alpha \sim\prec \gamma$;

(4) If $\alpha \simeq \beta, \beta \simeq \gamma$, $\alpha \simeq \gamma$.

An ontology snapshot about book is shown as figure 2. In Sell_Book (shown as Fig.2 (a)), the ontology defines concepts: "Book" "Price", "Amount" as well as "Date", "Title", "Author"; and the relations between them: "hasPrice", "hasTitle", "by" and so on. However, Lib_Book defines concepts "Item" ,"RetDate" as well as "Date", "Title", "Author", and the relations between them: "Return", "hasName", "hasAuthor", "Available" etc. (shown as Fig.2 (b)).

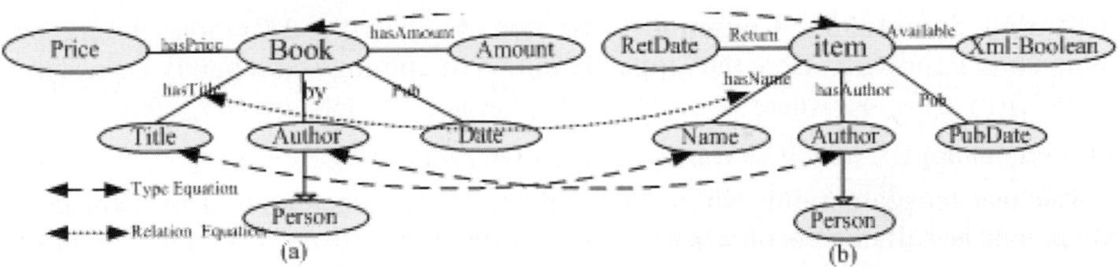

Fig. 2. An Example of Ontology

As shown in the above figure, there are multiple ontologies for the same concepts. Ontology mapping establishes relations between different ontology entities by calculating the semantic similarity between them. It can be defined formally as follows:

Definition 2 Ontology Mapping. Given source ontology O_s and target ontology O_t, the mappings between them are described as:

$$Mapping : O_s \rightarrow O_t$$
$$Mapping(e_s) = e_t \;\; if \;\; Sim(e_s, e_t) > t$$

where e_s, e_t are entities of source and target ontologies respectively; $Sim(x, y)$ is the function calculating semantic similarity between x, y; t is the threshold. In this paper, we assume mappings were stored as Bridging Axioms in first logic knowledge base. Fig.2 describes some mappings, including type equation and relation equation.

Definition 3 Ontology Translation. Ontology translation applies above bridging axioms to translate user requests from one ontology to another. Given source ontology O_s , target ontology O_t , and bridging axioms KB , ontology translation can be represented by " $\sim\!\rightarrow$ ":

$$(KB;\alpha_s) \sim\!\rightarrow \beta_t$$

where α_s is a expression referring to O_s and β_t referring to O_t .

Definition 4 Service Template. Service Template (ST) depicts service advertisement or service request. It specifies IOPEs of service using a specific domain ontology. Formally, Service Template is describes as:

$$ST := (N_{ST}, D_{ST}, I_{ST}, O_{ST}, P_{ST}, E_{ST}, Ont_{ST})$$

where N_{ST} is the name of service; D_{ST} is the textual description of service; I_{ST} denotes the Inputs set of service; O_{ST} denotes the Outputs set of service; P_{ST} is the Preconditions set of service; E_{ST} is the Effects set of service; in addition, Ont_{ST} describes the referred ontologies.

Many semantic service description languages, for instance OWL-S, WSDL-S, can be mapped to ST easily. Therefore, our work doesn't limit to specific language.

Definition 5 Ontology Community. Section 3 gave the definition of ontology community informally. Here the formal definition of ontology community is presented as $OC := (S, Ont_{OC})$, where S is the set of Service Templates, Ont_{OC} is the set of referred ontologies, and $\forall ST \in S, ST.Ont_{ST} = OC.Ont_{OC}$.

The matching algorithm within OC builds upon which proposed by Paolucci[2], which matches all outputs of request against those of advertisements; and all inputs of request against those of advertisements. Given candidate service Template $CS = (N_{CS}, D_{CS}, I_{CS}, O_{CS}, P_{CS}, E_{CS}, Ont_{CS})$ and request service template $SR = (N_{SR}, D_{SR}, I_{SR}, O_{SR}, P_{SR}, E_{SR}, Ont_{SR})$, the match degree between CS and SR is computed as following Table 1.

Table 1. Match Degree between CS and SR

	$I_{CS} = I_{SR}$ (Exact)	$I_{SR} \prec I_{CS}$ (Subsume)	Others(Fail)
$O_{SR} \prec O_{CS}$ (Plug-in)	Subsume	Subsume	Fail
$O_{CS} = O_{SR}$ (Exact)	Exact	Subsume	
$O_{CS} \prec O_{SR}$ (Subsume)	Plug_in	Plug_in	
Others(fail)	Fail		

Where "$\prec$" is a partial order relation between two sets; "$=$"is the equal relation between two sets. Given two sets A, B, $A \prec B$ if and only if, for every elements e_A in A, there exists one elements e_B in B such that $e_B \sim\prec e_A$; and $A = B$ if and only if, for every elements e_A in A, there exists one elements e_B in B such that $e_B \sim= e_A$. In this paper, only candidate services with match degree "Exact" or "Subsume" are considered as matched services. Racer[14] is adapted the semantic equality and subsumption.

Definition 6 Service Request Translation. While SR, CS refer to different ontologies, SSD_OC implements ontology translation for SR. Based on ontology bridging axioms, service request translation translates request ST from one ontology to another by first logic reasoning. Given service template $SR = (N_{SR}, D_{SR}, I_{SR}, O_{SR}, P_{SR}, E_{SR}, Ont_{SR})$ and bridging axioms KB between $Ont_{SR}, Ont_{SR}^{'}$, service request translation can be denoted as:

$$(KB; SR) \sim\longrightarrow SR^{'},$$

Where: $SR^{'} = (N_{SR'}, D_{SR'}, I_{SR'}, O_{SR'}, P_{SR'}, E_{SR'}, Ont_{SR'})$ and

$$(KB; SR) \sim\longrightarrow SR^{'} \Leftrightarrow (KB; I_{ST}) \sim\longrightarrow I_{SR'} \wedge (KB; O_{SR}) \sim\longrightarrow O_{SR'} \wedge$$
$$(KB; P_{SR}) \sim\longrightarrow P_{SR'} \wedge (KB; E_{SR}) \sim\longrightarrow E_{SR'}$$

4.2 Semantic Service Matching in SSD_OC

Semantic service matching in SSD_OC consists of three steps (shown as algorithm 1): SelectCommunity, MatchinOC and Ontology Translation. **MatchinOC** which based on Paolocci's study matches Service Template ST in OC.

Algorithm 1. Match(ServiceTemplate SR) : MatchedServiceList L_m

```
1: OC ← SelectCommunity(SR)
2:Foreach Strict Match Community S_Com do
3:    L_m ← L_m + MatchinOC(OC,SR)
4:Endfor
3: For Relaxed Match Community R_Com do
4:    T_ST ← OntoTranslate(SR)
5:    L_m ← L_m + MatchinOC(ROC,T_SR)
6:end for
7:return L_m
```

SelectCommunity returns communities supporting ontologies referred by SR. According to the relations between Ont_{SR}, Ont_{OC}, those communities are classified into two classes: S_Com whose ontologies subsume SR's ontologies, and R_Com whose ontologies overlap with SR's ontologies. The details are shown as algorithm 2.

Algorithm 2. SelectCommunity(ServiceTemplate S_R): Communities L_{Com}

Foreach Community C in Meta-Data Register do
  If $S_R.Ont_{S_R} \subseteq C.Ont_C$ then
    LCom.S_Match.Append(C)
  else if $S_R.Ont_{S_R} \cap C.Ont_C \neq \phi$ then
    LCom.R_Match.Append(C)
  endif
endfor
Return LCom

OntoTranslate translates service template of request from an ontology to another by using the bridging axioms between them. It implements ontology translation for each factor of service template. OntEngine[4] developed by Dou Dejiang fufills the reasoning based on first order logical. Figure 4 demonstrates the OntoTranslate and the OutputTrans. First logical reasoning is based on Modus-Ponens.

Algorithm 3. OntologyTranslate(ServiceTemplate SR, OntologyCommunit S_OC, OntologyCommity T_OC): ServiceTempalte T_SR

```
if OutputTrans(ST.Outputs, S_OC, T_OC) is NULL then return NULL
T_ST.Outputs ← OutputTrans(ST.Outputs, S_OC, T_OC)
if OutputTrans(ST.Inputs, S_OC, T_OC) is NULL then return NULL
T_ST.Inputs ← OutputTrans(ST.Inputs, S_OC, T_OC)
Return T_ST
```

Algorithm 4. OutputTrans(Ouputs ST_Outputs, OntologyCommunit S_OC, OntologyCommity T_OC): Outputs T_ST_Outputs

```
KB is the bridging Axioms between S_OC and T_OC
for each elements Output in ST_Outputs
    T_Output ← Modus-Ponens(Output,KB)
    if T_Output is NULL then return NULL
    T_ST_Outputs.Append(T_Output)
end for
return T_ST_OutPuts
```

4.3 Put Them Together-A Service Discovery Example

Table 2 shows a whole example of service discovery in SSD_OC. In this example, the service discovery request described by Service Template requires services that have capability of finding books with specific author and topic. And advertised services are published in three ontology communities: Sell_Book, Lib_Book and Sell_Good. With respect to referred ontologies, Sell_Book and Lib_Book are related. And Trans_Request is the translated request.

Table 2. The Requests and Advertised Services

	OC	Name	Inputs	Outputs	Degree of Match
Request	Sell_Book		#_Author #_Topic	#_Book	
Trans_Request	Lib_Book		#_Author #_Topic	#_Item	
Advertised Service	Sell_Book	**QueryBook Service**	#_Author #_Topic	#_Book	Exact
		BrowseBook Service	#_Name	#_Book	Fail
	Lib_Book	**QueryItem Service**	#_Person	#_Item	Subsume
	Sell_Good	SellGood Service	#_ID	#_Good	

In this example, SellGoodService is in a community irrelative to service request, therefore the matching algorithm does not take it as candidate services. QueryBookService is discovered firstly in Sell_Book for it has same inputs and outputs as request, and QueryItemService semantically matched with the translated request Trans_Request, for its inputs subsume that of request and its outputs equal to that of request. And BrowseBookService's inputs are not matched, so it is not matched service.

5 Experiments

The performance of service discovery is usually evaluated by Responding Time of service discovery, scalability of system, recall and precision of service matching or their harmonic mean F-measure (F-Measure=2*Recall*Precision/(Recall+ Precision)). To evaluate our mechanism, we conduct experiments in Java 1.4.2, using OWL-S 1.0, and the tableaux OWL-DL reasoner Racer developed at Concordia University. The service sample is a subset of OWLS-TC v2.1 provided by DFKI, includes 3 communities (Education, Communication and Economy) and 220 services in these community. And 20 requests are proposed to those services. Further, we compare the results with that of JAXR Register[2] and augment UDDI Register with DAML-S[6].

Fig.3 shows the preliminary statistical results of those requests. Analysis of these results provide, in particular, evidence in favor of the following conclusions:

1) SSD_OC and augment UDDI is outperformed by JAXR in term of responding time for they match service using logical reasoning (cf. Fig. 3 (a)). For SSD_OC spare time in ontology translation, it is outperformed by augment UDDI, when the system scale is small. However, with the increasing of system scale, SSD_OC should outperform augment UDDI.

[2] http://www.sun.com/xml/jaxr

2) Both augment UDDI and SSD_OC increase responding time with the increasing scale of system, while JAXR holds the line. Further, because SSD_OC limits the communities where semantic matching occurs, the increasing rate of SSD_OC is lower than that of augment UDDI, that's to say, the scalability of SSD_OC is better than that of augment UDDI. And the scalability of system will be improved by the number increasing of community (cf. Fig. 3 (a)).

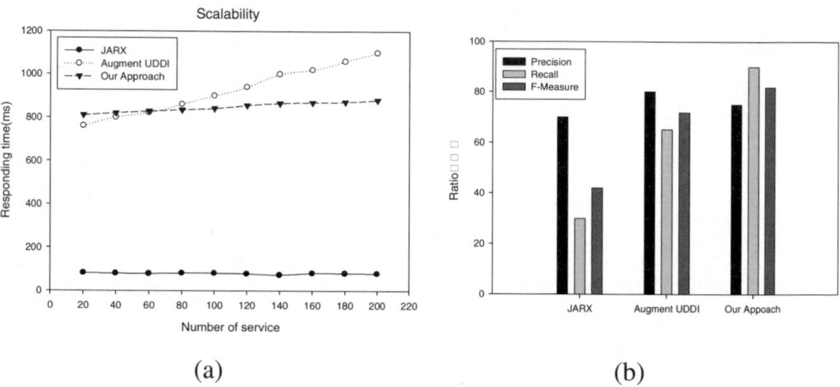

Fig. 3. The Responding time, Precision, Recall and F-Measure of Different Mechanisms

3) With logical reasoning, SSD_OC and augment UDDI have higher recall, precision and F-measure than JAXR. SSD_OC has higher Recall and F-measure for its capability of service discovery across communities. However, due to loss of information during ontology translation, SSD_OC is outperformed by augment UDDI in term of precision (cf. Fig. 3 (b)).

6 Conclusions and Future Works

Aiming to support semantic service discovery in multi-ontology environment and improve the scalability of SSD system, we proposed a mechanism based on ontology community, SSD_OC. It uses the divide-and-conquer approach with respect to the ontology used by services, to provide scalable data integration. Within community, traditional semantic matchmaking is employed. And to enable service matching across ontologies, the mechanism implements ontology translation by using bridging axioms. The mechanism improves scalability of system and efficiency of service discovery due to limiting service matchmaking in a relative small scope. Further service matching across communities improves the recall of service matching. In addition, the coexistent ontologies enable users describe their requirements with respect to their context, that's to say, users have more flexibility.

In the next step, we will improve the algorithms for service matchmaking, and mend the service template with some personal information (e.g. across ontology or not, the accepted degree of service match, etc.). Then service matching will be taken according to those preferences. Furthermore, we will take the QoS of service into account to ranking and selecting services with similar functionality. And the loss of information during ontology translation will be considered in our future work.

Acknowledgement. Research reported in this paper has been partially financed by National Basic Research Program of China under Grant, No.2005CB321800, National Natural Science Foundation of China under Grant, No.90412011

References

1. Sheila A, T.C.S., Honglei Zeng. , *Semantic web service.* IEEE Intelligent systems, 2001. **16**(3): p. 46-53.
2. Massimo Paolucci, T.K., Terry R. Payne, Katia Sycara. *Semantic Matching of Web Services Capabilities.* in *Proceeding of 1st Int. Semantic Web Conference (ISWC).* 2002. Sardinia, Italy: Springer.
3. Massimo Paolucci, T.K., Terry R. Payne, and Katia Sycara. *Importing the Semantic Web in UDDI.* in *In Web Services, E-Business and Semantic Web Workshop*. 2002.
4. Sure., M.E.a.Y. *Ontology mapping - an integrated approach.* in *In Proceedings of the First European Semantic Web Symposium.* 2004. Heraklion, Greece: Lecture Notes in Computer Science.
5. Dou, D., *Ontology Translation by Ontology merging and Automated Reasoning*. 2004, Yale.
6. K. Sycara, S.W., M. Klusch, J. Lu, *LARKS: Dynamic Matchmaking Among Heterogeneous Software Agents in Cyberspace.* Autonomous Agents and Multi-Agent Systems, 2002. **Vol.5**: p. 173-203.
7. Matthias Klusch, B.F., Mahboob Khalid Katia Sycara. *OWLS-MX: Hybrid OWL-S Service Matchmaking*. in *AAAI 2005 symposium on agents agent and semantic web*. 2005.
8. Kaarthik Sivashanmugam, K.V., Amit Sheth *Discovery of Web Services in a Federated Registry Environment.* in *In the proceeding of ICWS'04*. 2004. San Diago: IEEE Computer Society.
9. Oundhakar, S., *Semantic Web Service Discovery in a Multi-ontology Environment.* 2004, Georgia University.
10. Akkiraju R, G.R.D.P., et al. . *A method for semantically enhancing the service discovery capabilities of uddi.* in *in the proceeding the Workshop on Information Integration on the Web*. 2003. Acapulco,Mexico.
11. U. Keller, R.L., H. Lausen, A. Polleres, and D. Fensel. *Automatic Location of Services.* in *the 2nd European Semantic Web Conference (ESWC 2005).* 2005. Crete Greece.
12. Jyotishman Pathak, N.K. *A Framework for Semantic Web Service Discovery.* in *In Proceedings of the 7th annual ACM international workshop on Web information and data management.* 2005. Bremen Germany: ACM Press.
13. Yin Nan, S.D.R., Yu Ge,Kou Yue ,Nie Tiezheng, CAO yu, *A ontology-based service matching strategy in Grid Enviroment* Wuhan Univeristy journal of Natural science 2004. **9**(5): p. 781-786.
14. M¨oller, V.H.R., *Racer: A Core Inference Engine for the Semantic Web*. 2004.

A Collaborative-Aware Task Balancing Delivery Model for Clusters

José Luis Bosque[1], Pilar Herrero[2], Manuel Salvadores[2], and María S. Pérez[2]

[1] Dpto. de Electrónica y Computadores. Universidad de Cantabria.
AV. de los Castros S/N, 39.005 Santander, Spain
joseluis.bosque@unican.es
[2] Facultad de Informática. Universidad Politécnica de Madrid
Campus de Montegancedo S/N. 28.660 Boadilla del Monte. Madrid. Spain
{pherrero, mperez}@fi.upm.es

Abstract. In this paper, we present a new extension and reinterpretation of one of the most successful models of awareness in Computer Supported Cooperative Work (CSCW), called the Spatial Model of Interaction (SMI), which manages awareness of interaction through a set of key concepts, to provide task delivery in collaborative distributed systems. This model also applies some theoretical principles and theories of multi-agents systems to create a collaborative and cooperative environment that can be able to provide an autonomous, efficient and independent management of the amount of resources available in a cluster. This model has been implemented in a cluster based on a multi-agent architecture. Some results are presented with the aim of emphasizing the performance speedup of the system using the Collaborative Awareness Model for Task-Balancing-Delivery (CAMT).

1 Introduction

Clusters of workstations provide a good price/performance ratio, which makes these systems appropriate alternatives to supercomputers and dedicated mainframes. With the aim of providing better capabilities on clusters, it is essential to use a resource manager, which will take the suitable, and complex, decision about the allocation of processes to the resources in the system.

Even though load balancing has received a considerable amount of interest, it is still not definitely solved [11]. Nevertheless, this problem is central for minimizing the applications' response time and optimizing the exploitation of resources. Clusters require from load distributions that take into consideration each node's computational features [5]. The resources utilization can be improved by assigning each processor a workload proportional to its processing capabilities.

Multi-agent systems offer promising features to resource managers. The reactivity, proactivity and autonomy, as essential properties of agents, can help in the complex task of managing resources in dynamic and changing environments. Additionally, the cooperation among agents, which interchange information and resources status, allows load balancing mechanisms to be performed and efficiently deployed on clusters. In this sense, these mechanisms have common goals with current collaborative systems, and several synergies between both disciplines can be arisen.

C. Cérin and K.-C. Li (Eds.): GPC 2007, LNCS 4459, pp. 146 – 157, 2007.

In this paper, we present a new extension and reinterpretation of the Spatial Model of Interaction (SMI), an abstract awareness model designed to manage awareness of interaction, in cooperative applications. Thus, this paper presents a new reinterpretation of this model, and its key concepts, called CAMT (Collaborative Awareness Model for Task-Balancing-Delivery), in the context of an asynchronous collaboration in clusters. This reinterpretation has been designed, form the beginning to be a parametrical, generic, open, scalable, free of bottleneck and extensible be adapted easily to new ideas and purposes. CAMT takes advantage of the aggregated power of all the cluster nodes.

The CAMT model manages not just resources and information but also interaction and awareness. It allows: i) controlling the user interaction (through the aura concept); ii) guiding the awareness towards specific users and resources; iii) scaling interaction through the awareness concept. This model has also been designed to apply successful agent-based theories, techniques and principles to deal with resources sharing as well as resources assignment inside the cluster environment.

This paper is organized as follows: section 2 discusses the related work in the area; section 3 provides an overview of the Spatial Model of Interaction (SMI) and presents CAMT as an extension of the SMI; section 4 describes the load balancing algorithm in CAMT; section 5 provides readers with more specific details about the architecture of the model; section 6 describes the empirical evaluation and then section 7 concludes this paper with a summary of the research carried out and points out some future research lines.

2 Related Work

A taxonomy of load balancing methods has been defined in [3], taking into account different aspects. Three important criteria for this classification are: time in which workload distribution is performed (static [5] or dynamic [11]); Control, which can be centralized or distributed [6]; and finally the system state view that is can be global [6] or local [4]. Other solution is presented in[15], which defines a generic and scalable architecture for the efficient use of resources in a cluster based on CORBA. However, CORBA has as main disadvantage its complexity, which has made difficult to extend its use. DASH (Dynamic Agent System for Heterogeneous) [14] is an agent-based architecture for load balancing in heterogeneous clusters. The most noticeable characteristic of this proposal is the definition of a collaborative awareness model, used for providing global information that helps establish a suitable load balance. Unlike this work, our proposal (CAMT) extends and reinterprets one of the most successful models of awareness, the Spatial Model of Interaction (SMI), which manages awareness of interaction through a set of key concepts. Most of the agent-based load balancing systems use mobile agents, which makes easier the migration of tasks [7]. Nevertheless, the study published in [13] concludes that the task migration only obtains moderate benefits for long duration tasks.

3 CAMT: Reinterpreting the Key Awareness Concepts

The Spatial Model of Interaction was defined for application to any Computer Supported Cooperative Work (CSCW) system where a spatial metric can be identified

[2]. The model itself defines some key concepts: *Aura* is the sub-space which effectively bounds the presence of an object within a given medium and which acts as an enabler of potential interaction [8]. *Focus,* which delimits the observing object's interest; *Nimbus*, that represents the observed object's projection; and *Awareness,* which quantifies the degree, nature or quality of interaction between two objects. For a simple discrete model of focus and nimbus, there are three possible classifications of awareness values when two objects are negotiating [9].

Let's consider a system containing a set of nodes $\{n_i\}$ and a task T that requires a set of processes to be solved in the system. Each of these processes need some specifics requirements, being r_i the set of requirements associated to the process p_i, and therefore each of the processes will be identified by the tuple (p_i, r_i). The CAMT model intends to increase the collaboration capabilities of the system to start by a simple, abstract and preliminary interpretation of the SMI key concepts in the context of an asynchronous collaboration. Thus the CAMT model proposes an awareness infrastructure based on these concepts capable of managing the load management of clusters. This model reinterprets the SMI key concepts as follow:

Focus: It is interpreted as the subset of the space on which the user has focused his attention with the aim of interacting with. The focus will be delimited by the Aura of the node in the system.

Nimbus: It is defined as a tuple (Nimbus=(NimbusState, NimbusSpace)) containing information about: (a) the load of the system in a given time (NimbusState); (b) the subset of the space in which a given node projects its presence (NimbusSpace). As for the NimbusState, this concept will depend on the processor characteristics as well as on the load of the system in a given time. In this way, the NimbusState could have three possible values: Null, Medium or Maximum, as we will see in section 4. The NimbusSpace will determine those machines that could be taking into account in the tasks assignment process and it is delimited by the Aura of the node in the system.

Awareness of Interaction (AwareInt): This concept will quantify the degree, nature or quality of asynchronous interaction between distributed resources. Following the awareness classification introduced by Greenhalgh in [9], this awareness could be *Full, Peripheral or Null.*

$$AwareInt(n_i, n_j) = Full \quad \text{if } n_j \in Focus(\{n_i\}) \;\wedge\; n_i \in Nimbus(n_j)$$

Peripheral aware of interaction if

$$AwareInt(n_i, n_j) = Peripheral \quad \text{if} \begin{array}{l} n_j \in Focus(\{n_i\}) \;\wedge\; n_i \notin Nimbus(n_j) \\ or \\ n_j \notin Focus(\{n_i\}) \;\wedge\; n_i \in Nimbus(n_j) \end{array}$$

The CAMT model is more than a reinterpretation of the SMI, it extends the SMI to introduce some new concepts such us:

Interactive Pool: This function returns the set of nodes $\{n_j\}$ interacting with the n_i node in a given moment. Given a System and a task T to be executed in the node n_i:

$$\text{if } AwareInt(n_i, n_j) = Full \text{ then } n_j \in InteractivePool(n_i)$$

Task Resolution: This function determines if there is a service in the node n_i, being NimbusState(n_i)/=Null, such that could be useful to execute the task T (or at least one of its processes).

$$n_i = \sum_i \{s_i\} \quad Task\ \mathrm{Re}\ solution: \quad Node \times Task \rightarrow Task$$
$$n_i \times T \rightarrow \{(p_i, s)\}$$

Where "s" is the "score" to execute p_i in n_i node, being its value within the range [0, ∞): 0 if the node n_i fulfils the all the minimum requirements to execute the process p_i; the higher is the surplus over these requirements.

This concept would also complement the Nimbus concept, because the NimbusSpace will determine those machines that could be taking into account in the tasks assignment process because they are not overload yet. This only means that they could receive more working load, but the task T or at least one of its processes p_i will be executed in n_i if, an only if, there is a service s_i in the node n_i that could be useful to execute any of these p_i processes

Collaborative Organization: This function will take into account the set of nodes determined by the InteractivePool function and will return those nodes of the System in which it is more suitable to execute the task T (or at least one of its processes p_i). This selection will be made by means of the TaskResolution function.

4 Load Balancing Algorithm in CAMT

In this section we will introduce the load balancing algorithm as it has been introduced in the CAMT awareness model. The main characteristics of this algorithm are that it is dynamic, distributed and global, and it takes into account the system heterogeneity. The load balancing process can be performed by means of different stages or phases [12], which are explained in this section.

4.1 State Measurement Rule

This rule will be in charge of getting information about the computational capabilities of the node in the system. This information, quantified by a load index, provides aware of the NimbusState of the node. Several authors have proposed different load index and they have studied their effects on the system performance [10]. In this paper the concept of *CPU assignment* is used to determine the load index. The CPU assignment is defined as the CPU percentage that can be assigned to a new task to be executed in a node. The calculation of this assignment is based on two dynamic parameters: the number of tasks N, in the CPU queue and the percentage of occupation of the CPU, U, and it would be calculated as:

$$If(U \geq \frac{1}{N}) => A_{CPU} = \frac{1}{N+1}$$
$$If(U < \frac{1}{N}) \Rightarrow A_{CPU} = 1 - Usage$$

As the system is heterogeneous, a normalization with the computational power of the more powerful node of the cluster, P_{max}, is needed in order to compare load index of different nodes:

$$I = \frac{P_i \cdot A_{CPU}}{P_{MAX}}$$

The NimbusState of the node will be determined by the load index and it will depend on the node capacity at a given time. This state determines if the node could execute more (local or remotes) tasks. Its possible values would be:

- *Maximum*: The load index is low and therefore this infrautilized node will execute all the local tasks, accepting all new remote execution requests.
- *Medium*: The node will execute all the local tasks, but they will not accept requests to execute tasks from other nodes in the system.
- *Null:* The load index has a high value and therefore the node is overload. In this situation, it will reject any request of new remote execution.

4.2 Information Exchange Rule

The knowledge of the global state of the system will be determined by a policy on the information exchange. This policy should keep the information coherence without overloading the network with an excessive number of unnecessary messages. An optimum information exchange rule for the CAMT model should be based on events [1]. This rule only collects information when a change in the Nimbus of the nodes is made. If later, the node that has modified its nimbus will be in charge of notifying this modification to all of the nodes in the system (global algorithm), avoiding thus synchronization points. Each of the nodes has information about the rest of the nodes of the cluster. This information is stored in a list containing the node's NimbusState and its NimbusSpace.

4.3 Initiation Rule

As the model implements a non user interruption algorithm, the selection of the node must be made just before sending the task execution. Once the execution of the process starts in a specific node it would have to finish in the same node. The decision of starting a new load balancing operation is completely local. If an overloaded node receives a new task T to be executed, and it can not execute it (NimbusState =*Null*), the load balancing operation will be automatically thrown. Then the initialization rule which the node has to evaluate is the following:

- If (NimbusState = *Maximum*) or (NimbusState = *Medium*), the task is accepted to be executed locally.
- If (NimbusState = Null), a new load balancing operation is started.

4.4 Load Balancing Operation

Now the node has made the decision of starting a load balancing operation, which will be divided in another three different rules: localization, distribution and selection.

Localization Rule: Given a task T to be executed in the node n_i, the localization rule has to determine which nodes are involved in the CollaborativeOrganization of the node n_i. In order to make it possible, firstly, the CAMT model will need to determine the awareness of interaction of this node with those nodes inside its focus. To optimize the implementation, the previous awareness values are dynamically updated based on the information exchange rule. Those nodes whose awareness of interaction with n_i was *Full* will be part of the Interactive Pool of n_i to solve the task T, and from that pre-selection the TaskResolution method will determine those nodes that are suitable to solve efficiently the task in the environment.

Selection and Distribution Rule: This algorithm joins selection and distribution rules because the proposed algorithm takes into account the NimbusState of each of the nodes as well as the TaskResolution to solve any of the T's processes. The goal of this algorithm is to find the more equilibrate assignment of processes to computational nodes based on a set of heuristics. This spread is made in an iterative way. The sequence of steps that implements the assignment heuristic is:

1. The nodes belonging to the CollaborativeOrganization will be arranged by the number of processes (associated to the T task) that could execute.
2. The first node of the arranged list is selected.
3. The process having the maximum score is assigned to the selected node and both process assigned and node are removed from the list.
4. The following process of the ordered list is selected and the steps 2 and 3 of this algorithm are repeated again.
5. This loop continues until the process had finalized with all the nodes of the CollaborativeOrganization.
6. This algorithm doesn't guarantee that all the processes could be assigned in a first round. So, if any of the processes is out of the assignment, a new task with all the pending processes is created, and the whole process starts again.

5 The CAMT Architecture

The load balancing multi-agent architecture, is composed of four agents replicated for each of the nodes of the cluster (see figure 1): a) the Load Agent (LA), which in charge of the state measurement rule; b) the Global State Agent (GSA), in charge of the information rule; c) the Initiation Agent (IA), which decide if the task is executed locally or if a new load balancing operation needs to be carried out; d) the Load Balancer Agent (LBA) which implements the load balancing operation, strictly speaking, including the localization, selection and distribution rules.

5.1 The Load Agent

The Load Agent calculates, periodically, the load index of the local node and evaluates the changes on its NimbusState. When it detects a change on the state, this modification is notified to the local GSA and IA. The load index is evaluated, following the expressions introduced in section 4.1. The first step of the LA is to obtain the node computational power, P_i. Then this information is communicated to

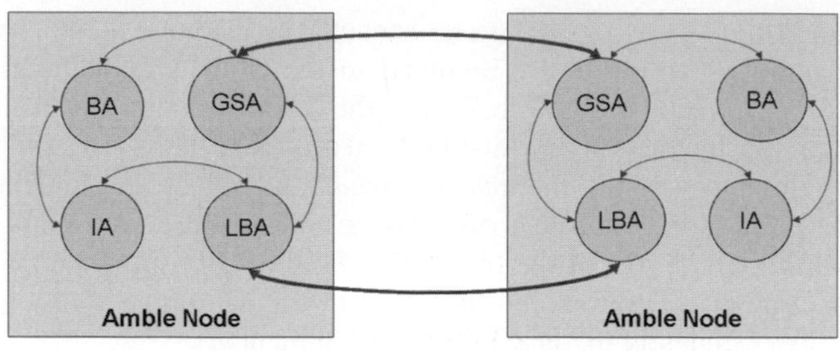

Fig. 1. CAMT Architecture

the rest of the nodes through the *MPI_Reduce* function, which is in charge of calculating the maximum of the computational power of all the nodes, P_{MAX}. Next, the agent starts an infinite loop until the application is ended. In this loop the first step is, to get dynamic node load information: the number of running task and the CPU usage. Then the new state of the node is calculated and the agent determines if a node state change has occurred. If the later, the agent communicates it to the local GSA and IA. Finally, the agent sleep a time span, defined as a parameter by the user.

5.2 The Global State Agent

The main functionality of this agent is to manage the flux information exchanged among the nodes of the system and provide LBA with this information as soon as it requires it. Firstly, the agent gets information about its focus, its NimbusSpace and its NimbusState. Once this information is communicated to the rest of the nodes, it determines the current InteractivePool. Next, the agent enters in an infinite loop in which it is waiting for receiving messages from other agents, which could be:

- LOCAL_STATE_CHANGE: This message comes from the Load Agent local and it has to be notified to all the GSAs of all of the cluster nodes.
- REMOTE_STATE_CHANGE: In this case, only the local state list should be modified to update the new state of the remote node.
- INTERACTIVE_POOL_REQUEST: The local LBA requests the InteractivePool to the GSA.
- STATE_LIST_REQUEST: the local LBA requests the state list that the GSA agent keeps updated with the state of all the nodes composing the cluster.

5.3 The Initiation Agent

When a user intends to execute a task in a node of the cluster, this request is sent to the IA of that node. Then, this agent evaluates the initialisation rule to determine if it can be executed locally or if a new load balancing operation has be carried out. Its main structure contains an infinite loop and, for each of these iterations, the pending tasks in the execution queue are checked. There are two types of messages:

- LOCAL_STATE_CHANGE: It receives a message from the local LA to notify a change on the local state.
- EXECUTE_TASK_REQUEST: It requests execution of a new task. For each process of the task, the NimbusState is checked to corroborate if its value is equal to *Full or Medium*. If later, the process is executed locally. This loop will finish when all the processes had been executed or when NimbusState of the local node changed its value. In that moment a message would be sent to the local LBA to start a new load balancing operation.

5.4 The Load Balancer Agent

This agent contains an infinite loop that is waiting to receive messages from other agents. Its functionality depends on the messages received:

- BALANCER_EXECUTION: This message comes from the local IA and it indicates that a new load balancing operation needs to start. For the localization rule, the LBA will follow the following sequence of steps:
    1. Request the InteractivePool and the states list to the local GSA
    2. Determine the TaskResolution, analyzing which nodes of the InteractivePool have their NimbusState different to *Null*.
    3. Request the scores, to the nodes included in the TaskResolution
    4. Determine the CollaborativeOrganization by analyzing those nodes that, belonging to the TaskResolution, can execute at least one of the processes of the task.

  As for the selection and distribution rule, the algorithm presented in section 4.4 has been implemented. Once all the processes had been assigned, they would be sent to the designated nodes. If the process is accepted by the node, the assignment of the process would have finalized otherwise the process would be pending of assignment and it would add to the new task.
- REMOTE_EXECUTION: This message comes from the remote LBA, asking for the remote execution of a process. Once the LBA has checked its own state, it replies to the remote LBA with an acceptance or rejection message. If the process is accepted, the LBA would execute the process locally. The rejection could be due to a change on its NimbusState (to Null).
- SCORE_REQUEST: This message is a request to the LBA to send the scores of a specific task. The LBA evaluates the scores for each of the processes belonging to that task.

6 Experimental Results

These tests were performed over a 32 node PC cluster connected through a Myrinet Network. The CAMT model has been developed using GNU tools and LAM/MPI 7.1.1 Library. In order to generate a set of CPU-bound task the NAS Parallel Benchmark NPB 2.3 has been used. Besides the multi-agent architecture presented in previous sections of this paper, an additional agent, named Task_Executor_Agent, has been implemented to simulate the throwing of tasks to any node of the cluster. In all the experiments presented the focus and the nimbus of each of the nodes include the rest of the nodes, and therefore the algorithm has been processed as global. All the tasks have been launched with a 3 seconds interval.

First Experiment: This experiment intends to get a measure of the overhead introduced by the CAMT model in the execution of a set of tasks while the size of the cluster increases. With this purpose, the algorithm has been executed in different clusters configurations: 4, 8, 16 and 32 nodes. In all these cases, 50 tasks with 10 processes per task were run. The experimental results obtained from the execution of this experiment are presented in the table 1 and in the figure 2.

Table 1. Speedup, maximal overhead, average overhead, number of load balancing operations and number of attempts to assign a process with respect to the cluster size

Cluster Size	Speedup	Max. Overhead per Process	Average Overhead /process	Balancing Operations	N. attempts
4	2.85	59.4	17.12	41	30816
8	7,24	2.33	0.41	48	1338
16	15,87	1.59	0.28	44	0
32	31,65	1.92	0.29	48	1

These results show that cluster size has a benefit impact on the algorithm performance when the number of tasks remains constant. From figure 2 we can point out that when there are many more processes in the system that the cluster can manage, all the nodes are overloaded and the overhead as well as the number of attempts to assign a new process increases dramatically. On the other hand when the cluster size is increased up to 32 nodes, the overhead remains almost constant. Therefore this algorithm has very good scalability features.

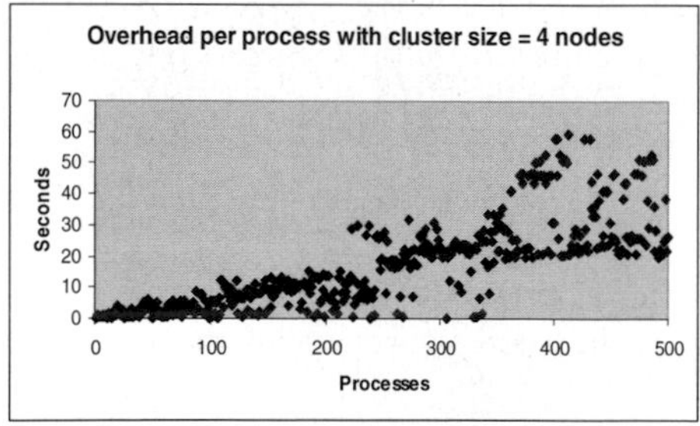

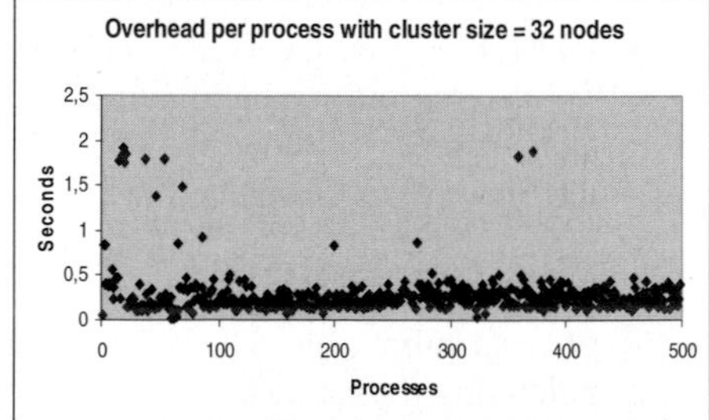

Fig. 2. Overhead per process with 4 and 32 nodes in the cluster

Second Experiment: This second test has only been achieved for the biggest cluster, 32 nodes. In all these cases, 50 tasks have been thrown. The objective was to get a measure of how the number of processes of the T task affects the algorithm performance. The experimental results obtained from the execution of this experiment are presented in the table 2 and in the figure 3.

Table 2. Speedup, maximal overhead, average overhead, number of load balancing operations and number of attempts to assign a process with respect to the number of processes per task

Processes/task	N processes	Speedup	Max overhead	Average Overhead	Balancing operations	N. attempts
10	259	31.76	1.73	0.24	45	0
20	458	31.69	2,89	0.30	47	3
30	854	30.98	12.47	2.81	45	1401
40	1028	28.48	41.93	5.62	43	10299

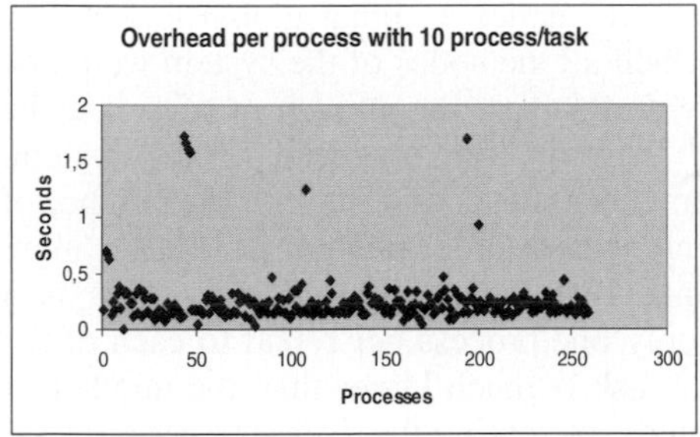

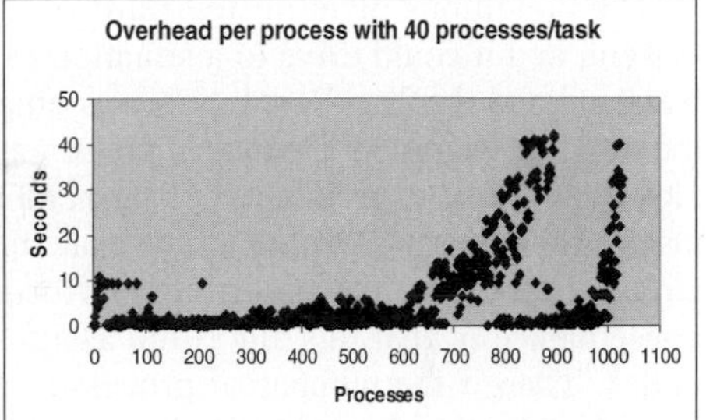

Fig. 3. Overhead per process with 10 and 40 processes per task

It can be to highlight that increasing the number of processes of the task, even over the number of the nodes, we get the situation in which all the processes can not be assigned in the first round of the selection rule. Additionally, increasing the total number of processes that the system has to manage causes an increment in the global load of the system that could lead to a TaskResolution empty. These two factors provoke an increase on the overhead introduced by the algorithm. Moreover, the number of tries to assign each of the processes needs to be taken into account. This can be seen in figure 3 when the number of processes is around 600 and the overhead value is dramatically increased. On the other hand when the number of processes is not so high the overhead remains almost constant for all of the processes and tasks. In table 2 we can see that in these cases the number of attempts to assign the processes is drastically increased too.

Third Experiment: The last test has been carried out on a cluster of 32 nodes. The size of the task is between 1 and 16 processes. The aim of this experiment is to measure the impact that the number of consecutive tasks executed over the overhead of the system. In order to make this evaluation, this experiment has been accomplished with a number of tasks between 25 and 100. The experimental results obtained from the execution of his first experiment are presented in the table 3 and in the figure 4.

Table 3. Speedup, maximal overhead, average overhead, number of load balancing operations and number of attempts to assign a process with respect to the number of consecutive tasks.

N Tasks	N. Processes	Speedup	Max. overhead/ Process	Average overhead/ process	Balancing Operations	N. attempts
25	227	29.11	2.42	0.38	23	0
50	443	30,24	2.54	0.35	47	0
75	708	31.85	2.63	0.28	72	2
100	919	32.03	3.1	0.32	96	7

The conditions given in the third experiment implies a higher global load of the system, and it could drive to a situation in which all the nodes of the system would be overload and the TaskResolution was empty. In this case the number of tries to make the tasks assignment should increase and therefore the overhead of the system. However in this experiment the overhead remains almost constant with the number of tasks. Therefore we can conclude that the number of processes per task has a more strong impact on the algorithm performance that the number of task. This is a consequence of that this algorithm assigns only one process per round to each of the nodes. Then if the number of processes in a task is much larger than the number of cluster nodes the algorithm needs several rounds, increasing the overhead per process.

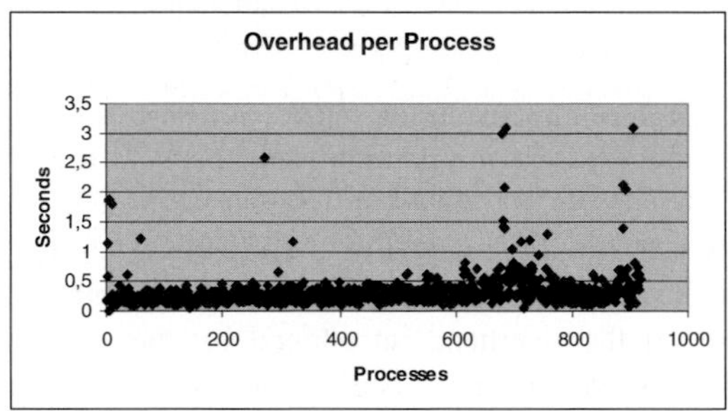

Fig. 4. Overhead per process with 100 consecutive tasks

7 Conclusions

This paper presents an awareness model for balancing the load in collaborative cluster environments, CAMT (Collaborative Awareness Model for Task-Balancing-Delivery), in a collaborative multi-agent system. CAMT is a new reinterpretation of the SMI model in the context of an asynchronous collaboration in clusters. The CAMT model allows managing not just resources and information but also interaction and awareness; guiding the awareness towards specific users and resources; and scaling interaction through the awareness concept. This model has also been designed to apply successful agent-based theories, techniques and principles to deal with resources sharing as well as resources assignment inside the cluster environment. CAMT manages the interaction in the environment allowing the autonomous, efficient and independent task allocation in the environment.

This model has been evaluated in a real cluster infrastructure. Different scenarios were designed for this purpose. The most important conclusions that could be extracted from the experimental results presented in this paper are: Firstly, the introduction of the load balancing algorithm based on the CAMT model on a cluster achieves very important improvements with respect to the response time and speedup. These results are reflected on the speedup figures and therefore on the scalability degree of the algorithm. Secondly, we have to point out that the overhead incurred by the algorithm to assign a process to a node is mainly determined by the number of processes per tasks. Finally, the algorithm performs a number of load balancing operations close to the maximum achievable value.

Acknowledgments. This work has been partially funded by the Government of the Community of Madrid (grant S-0505/DPI/0235).

References

1. M. Beltrán, J. L. Bosque, A. Guzmán. Resource Disseminatioin policies on Grids. Lectures Notes in Computer Science. Springer-Verlag 135 – 144. October 25-29, 2004
2. Benford S.D. and Fahlén L.E. A Spatial Model of Interaction in Large Virtual Environments. Proceedings of the Third European Conference on Computer Supported Cooperative Work. Milano. Italy. Kluwer Academic Publishers, 109-124, 1993.
3. T. L. Casavant and J. G. Kuhl. "A taxonomy of scheduling in general-purpose distributed computing systems", Readings and Distributed Computing Systems, pp. 31-51, 1994.
4. Corradi, L. Leonardi, and F. Zambonelli. "Diffusive load-balancing policies for dynamic applications", IEEE Concurrency 7(1), pp. 22-31, 1999.
5. Bajaj, R. and Agrawal, D. P. Improving Scheduling of Tasks in a Heterogeneous Environment. IEEE Trans. Parallel Distrib. Syst. Vol 15, N. 2, 2004. 107-118.
6. S. K. Das, D. J. Harvey, and R. Biswas. Parallel processing of adaptive meshes with load balancing. IEEE Trans. on Parallel and Distributed Systems, (12):1269–1280, 2001.
7. S. Desic and D. Huljenic. Agents based load balancing with component distribution capability. Proc. of the 2nd Int. Symposium on Cluster Computing and the Grid 2002.
8. Fahlén, L. E. and Brown, C.G., The Use of a 3D Aura Metaphor for Compter Based Conferencing and Teleworking. Proc. of the 4th Multi-G Workshop, 69-74, 1992.
9. Greenhalgh, C., Large Scale Collaborative Virtual Environments, Doctoral Thesis. University of Nottingham. October 1997.
10. T. Kunz, "The influence of different workload descriptions on a heuristic load balancing scheme," IEEE Trans. on Software Engineering, vol. 17, no. 7, pp. 725–730, July 1991.
11. L. Xiao, S. Chen, and X. Zhang. Dynamic cluster resource allocations for jobs with known and unknown memory demands. IEEE Trans. on Parallel and Distributed Systems, 13(3):223–240, March 2002.
12. C. Xu and F. Lau, Load balancing in parallel computers: theory and practice. Kluwer Academic Publishers, 1997.
13. W. Leland and T. Ott. "Load-balancing heuristics and process behavior", ACM SIGMETRICS, pp. 54-69, 1986.
14. Rajagopalan and S. Hariri, An Agent Based Dynamic Load Balancing System, Proc. of the International Workshop on Autonomous Decentralized Systems, 2000, pp. 164-171.
15. S. Vanhastel, et al. Design of a generic platform for efficient and scalable cluster computing based on middleware technology. Proc. of the CCGRID 2001, 40-47.

An Improved Model for Predicting HPL Performance

Chau-Yi Chou, Hsi-Ya Chang, Shuen-Tai Wang, Kuo-Chan Huang*, and Cherng-Yeu Shen

National Center for High-Performance Computing
* Department of Electronic Commerce, Hsing Kuo University, Taiwan

Abstract. In this paper, we propose an improved model for predicting HPL (High performance Linpack) performance. In order to accurately predict the maximal LINPACK performance we first divide the performance model into two parts: computational cost and message passing overhead. In the message passing overhead, we adopt Xu and Hwang's broadcast model instead of the point-to-point message passing model. HPL performance prediction is a multi-variables problem. In this proposed model we improved the existing model by introducing a weighting function to account for many effects such that the proposed model could more accurately predict the maximal LINPACK performance R_{max}. This improvement in prediction accuracy has been verified on a variety of architectures, including IA64 and IA32 CPUs in a Myrinet-based environment, as well as in Quadrics, Gigabits Ethernet and other network environments. Our improved model can help cluster users in estimating the maximal HPL performance of their systems.

1 Introduction

The continuous improvement in commodity hardware and software has made cluster systems the most popular alternative [1-5] for high performance computing for both academic institutions and industries.

In 1998, Pfister [5] estimated over 100,000 cluster systems were in use worldwide. In November 2006, more than 70% of machines on the 26th Top500 List were labeled as clusters [6]. Most of these clusters used HPL (High performance Linpack) to benchmark their system performance, in accordance with the requirement of the Top500 List.

HPL utilizes LU factorization with row partial pivoting to solve a dense linear system while using a two-dimensional block-cyclic data distribution for load balance and scalability. A number of analysis models [7, 8] have been developed for HPL performance prediction for different architectures. However, these models did not consider the effect of hardware overhead, such as cache misses, pipeline startups, memory load or store and floating point arithmetic. Most models adhere to Hockney's message passing model [9] in dealing with the message interchange overhead.

C. Cérin and K.-C. Li (Eds.): GPC 2007, LNCS 4459, pp. 158 – 168, 2007.

In this paper we propose an improved HPL performance prediction model where we use a weighting function to account for the hardware overhead on the computation side. On the communication side we adopt Xu and Hwang's broadcast model [10]. This improved model comes up with a closer prediction of the actual performance than the other models in the literature, after a series of experiments on the Myrinet-based, Gigabits Ethernet based, IA64- and IA32-based architectures.

2 HPL Algorithm and Performance Score Model

We first introduce the HPL algorithm in Section 2.1 and then the existing HPL performance prediction model from [7] in Sections 2.2.1-2.2.5. The improved model is discussed in Section 2.2.6. Here we list the definitions of the pertinent variables in Table 1.

Table 1. Definition of the variables

Variable	Definition
B	Block size
$N \times N$	Dimension of linear system
$P \times Q$	Two dimensional map of computational processors
α	Latency of Hockney's mode (point to point), constant
β	The reciprocal of throughput of Hockney's model (point to point), constant
α'	Latency of Xu and Hwang's model (MPI broadcast), function of (PQ)
β'	The reciprocal of throughput of Xu and Hwang's model (MPI broadcast), function of (PQ)
g_3	Floating-point operation rate of matrix-matrix operations
g_2	Floating-point operation rate of matrix-vector operations
γ_3	the approximate floating-point operations per second when the processor is performing matrix-matrix operations
$\gamma = w \times \gamma_3$	The real computational performance of HPL, not including message passing overhead. w is the weighting function in our proposed performance model

2.1 HPL Algorithm

The HPL algorithm is designed to solve a linear system by LU factorization with row partial pivoting. The data are first logically partitioned into $B \times B$ blocks, and then distributed onto a two-dimensional $P \times Q$ grid, according to the block-cyclic scheme to ensure load balance as well as scalability. The block size B is for the data distribution as well as for the computational granularity. The best B value is a function of the computation-to-communication performance ratio in a system. A smaller B performs better load balance from a data distribution point of view; but when it becomes too small, it may limit the computational performance because no data reuse occurs at the higher level of the memory hierarchy from a computational point of view. The recommended B value is between 32 and 256.

At a given iteration of the main loop, each panel factorization occurs in one column of processes because of the Cartesian property of the distribution scheme. Once the panel factorization has been computed, this panel of columns is broadcast to the other process columns. The update of the trailing sub-matrix by the last panel in the look-ahead pipe is made in two phases. First, the pivots must be applied to form the current row panel U. U should then be solved by the upper triangle of the column panel. Finally U needs to be broadcast to each process row so that the local rank-B update can take place.

2.2 Performance Score Model

2.2.1 Assumption and Definition

Let the communication time to transfer L length of double precision messages be $T_c = \alpha+\beta L$, where$\alpha$and$\beta$are latency and the reciprocal of maximum bandwidth, respectively. Both $\alpha$and$\beta$are constants. Also, g_1, g_2 and g_3 are defined as the times needed for performing one floating point of the vector-vector, matrix-vector and matrix-matrix operations, respectively. With the definitions behind us, we may proceed to solve an $N\times N$ linear system.

2.2.2 Panel Factorization and Broadcast

Let us consider an $I\times J$ panel distributed over a P-process column. The execution time for panel factorization and broadcast can be approximated by:

$$T_{pfact}(I, J) = (I/P - J/3)\, J^2\, g_3 + J \ln(P)(\alpha + 2\beta J) + \alpha + \beta I\, J\, /\, P \tag{1}$$

2.2.3 Trailing Sub-matrix Update

Let's consider the update phase of an $I\times I$ trailing sub-matrix distributed on a $P\times Q$ process grid. From a computational point of view, one has to (triangular) solve I right-hand sides and to perform a local rank-J update of this trailing sub-matrix. Thus, the execution time for the update operation can be approximated by:

$$T_{update}(I, J) = g_3\, (I\, J^2/Q + 2\, I^2\, J\, /P/Q) + \alpha(\ln(P)+P-1) + 3\beta I\, J\, /Q. \tag{2}$$

2.2.4 Backward Substitution

The number of floating point operations performed during the backward substitution is given by $N^2/P/Q$. Then, the execution time of the backward substitution can be approximated by:

$$T_{backs}(N, B) = g_2\, N^2/(PQ) + N\, (\alpha/\, B + 2\beta). \tag{3}$$

2.2.5 The Original HPL Performance Model

The total execution time T is given by:

$$\begin{aligned}
T = & \sum_{k=0,\ B,\ 2B,\cdots}^{N} \left[T_{pfact}(N-k,B)+T_{update}(N-k-B,B)\right]+T_{backs}(N,B) \\
= & g_3\left\{\frac{2}{3PQ}N^3+\left(\frac{1}{2P}+\frac{1}{2Q}-\frac{1}{PQ}\right)BN^2+\left(\frac{2}{PQ}-\frac{1}{Q}-\frac{1}{3}\right)B^3\right\}+g_2\left\{\frac{N^2}{PQ}\right\} \\
& +\alpha\left\{N\left[\frac{(B+1)ln(P)+P+1}{B}\right]+B\,ln(P)+log(P)+P\right\} \\
& +\beta\left\{\left(\frac{3P+Q}{2PQ}\right)N^2+\left(\frac{1}{2P}+2ln(P)-\frac{3}{2Q}+2\right)BN+\left(2ln(P)-\frac{3}{Q}\right)B^2\right\}
\end{aligned} \tag{4}$$

The algorithm totally perform $2N^3/3 + 3\,N^2/2$ of floating point operations, Then, the performance score, hereinafter called $R_{est\_original}$, becomes:

$$\begin{aligned}
R_{est_original} = & \frac{2N^3/3+2N^2/2}{T} \\
= & \left\langle\frac{2N^3}{3}+\frac{3N^2}{2}\right\rangle \Bigg/ \left\langle \begin{aligned} & g_3\left\{\frac{2}{3PQ}N^3+\left(\frac{1}{2P}+\frac{1}{2Q}-\frac{1}{PQ}\right)BN^2+\left(\frac{2}{PQ}-\frac{1}{Q}-\frac{1}{3}\right)B^3\right\}+g_2\left\{\frac{N^2}{PQ}\right\} \\ & +\alpha\left\{N\left[\frac{(B+1)log(P)+P+1}{B}\right]+B\,ln(P)+ln(P)+P\right\} \\ & +\beta\left\{\left(\frac{3P+Q}{2PQ}\right)N^2+\left(\frac{1}{2P}+2ln(P)-\frac{3}{2Q}+2\right)BN+\left(2ln(P)-\frac{3}{Q}\right)B^2\right\}\end{aligned}\right\rangle
\end{aligned} \tag{5}$$

For a very large N, we need only to consider the dominant term in g_3, α, and β. Then, Eq.(5) becomes:

$$R_{est\_original} = \frac{1}{\dfrac{g_3}{PQ}+\dfrac{3\alpha[(B+1)ln(P)+P]}{2\,B\,N^2}+\dfrac{3\beta(3P+Q)}{4\,N\,P\,Q}} \tag{6}$$

2.2.6 Our HPL Performance Model

Wang and co-workers [8] defined a new variationγ_3 as the approximate floating point operations per second when the processor is performing matrix-matrix operations. Then, $\gamma_3 = \dfrac{1}{g_3}$.

Now, we propose a weighting function w to include overheads such as cache misses, pipeline startups, and memory load or store. This weighting function w will be taken as the ratio of the time for matrix multiplication to the total HPL execution time on a single processor; and $0 \leq w \leq 1$. Next, we define a new variable $\gamma = w \times \gamma_3$ to represent the approximate floating point operations per second for the total HPL solution.

The parameters representing the communication overhead, α and β in Eq.(5) and Eq.(6), are based on Hockey's model; that is, they are constants. However, in our proposed model, we will adopt Xu and Hwang's model to account for the communication overhead. The communication time to transfer L length of double precision messages is then $T_c = \alpha' + \beta' L$, where α' and β' are latency and the reciprocal of maximum bandwidth, respectively. Now, both α' and β' are functions of the total number of processors (PQ). Therefore, the performance score of our modified HPL performance model, hereinafter call $R_{est\_modified}$, becomes:

For small size cluster, $R_{est\_modified} =$

$$\left(\frac{2N^3}{3}+\frac{3N^2}{2}\right) \Bigg/ \left(\begin{array}{l} \frac{1}{\gamma}\left\{\frac{2}{3PQ}N^3+\left(\frac{1}{2P}+\frac{1}{2Q}-\frac{1}{PQ}\right)BN^2+\left(\frac{2}{PQ}-\frac{1}{Q}-\frac{1}{3}\right)B^3\right\}+g_2\left\{\frac{N^2}{PQ}\right\} \\ +\alpha'\left\{N\left[\frac{(B+1)log(P)+P+1}{B}\right]+B\,log(P)+log(P)+P\right\} \\ +\beta'\left\{\left(\frac{3P+Q}{2PQ}\right)N^2+\left(\frac{1}{2P}+2\,log(P)-\frac{3}{2Q}+2\right)BN+\left(2\,log(P)-\frac{3}{Q}\right)B^2\right\} \end{array} \right) \tag{7}$$

For large cluster,

$$R_{est\_modified} = \frac{1}{\frac{1}{PQ\gamma}+\frac{3\alpha'[(B+1)log(P)+P]}{2N^2B}+\frac{3\beta'(3P+Q)}{4NPQ}} \tag{8}$$

The denominator of Eq. (8) consists of three terms. The first term dominates the performance of the system if communication overhead is not considered, with the best score being $PQ\gamma$. The second and the third terms account for the communication overhead resulting from discrete computing, while α' and β' depend on the latency and bandwidth of the network for MPI collective message, respectively. In general, when the size of a cluster system increases, so do the influences of α' and β'.

3 Comparative Analysis of Different Models on Various Clusters

We now proceed to analyze the HPL performance on three different cluster systems, i.e., the Formosa Cluster [11], the Triton Cluster [12], and Dawning 4000A [13]. The Formosa cluster is equipped with IA32 CPUs and in a Gigabit Ethernet environment. The Triton Cluster uses the IA64 CPUs with Quadrics interconnection network [14]. The Dawning 4000A is a cluster of IA64 CPUs with Myrinet [15] network environment. Details of the systems are described in Sections 3.1, 3.2, and 3.3.

3.1 NCHC Formosa PC Cluster

This PC Cluster was built by the National Center for High-Performance Computing (NCHC) in September 2003. Our team had diligently optimized the system, specifically the network drive, the MTU, two network interface cards with two different private subnets, and with unused services turned off. It was the 135th on the 22th Top500 List in November 2003, and it was then the fastest computer system in Taiwan [11].

The system utilizes IBM X335 servers with Intel Xeon 2.8GHz dual processors. There are 300 CPUs connected together by a Gigabit Ethernet network. We adopted Debain 3.0 (kernel 2.6.0) operating system (OS), Intel compile 8.0 compiler, LAM/MPI 7.0.6 [16], and GOTO BLAS [17].

To compare Eq.(7) with Eq.(5), we need to first decide the parameters in these two equations. We apply the *DGEMM* function in HPL; that is, matrix multiplication of double precision random numbers of HPL, to compute the floating-point operations per second of matrix multiplication, shown in figure 1. From figure 1, we obtain $\gamma_3 = 4.6$ *GFLOPS*. Similarly, $1/g_2 = 633$ *MFLOPS*.

Next, we determine the value of the weighting function, w, by adding a timing merit of matrix multiplication in HPL software and enabling the option: `-DHPL_DETAILED_TIMING`. The output is shown as figure 2, and then $w = 516.42 / 586.77 = 0.88$.

In our previous research [18], we obtain $\alpha = 51.8\mu s$, $\beta = 0.011\mu s$, $\alpha' = 81.3154\,ln(PQ) - 63.81$, and $\beta' = 0.0193\,ln(PQ) - 0.0085$. Both α' and β' are in μs.

Table 2 lists the performance scores in *GFLOPS* of the measured R_{max} value and the $R_{est\text{-}original}$ using Eq. (5), and $R_{est\text{-}modified}$ using Eq. (7) on 4, 6, and 8 processors. It demonstrates that $R_{est\text{-}modified}$ is indeed closer to R_{max} than $R_{est\text{-}original}$.

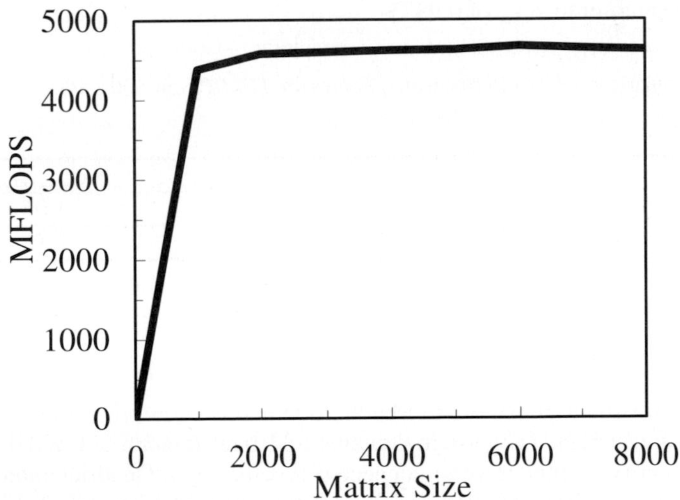

Fig. 1. MFLOPS vs. Matrix size on the Formosa Cluster

```
T/V                N    NB   P    Q          Time        Gflops
W00L2L88  15840 88  1  1     586.77  4.516e+00
--VVV--VVV--VVV--VVV--VVV--VVV--VVV--VVV--VVV-
Max aggregated wall time HPL_DGEMM. . :[516.42]
Max aggregated wall time rfact. . . : 17.06
+ Max aggregated wall time pfact . . : 17.06
+ Max aggregated wall time mxswp . . : 0.27
Max aggregated wall time update  . . : 569.30
+ Max aggregated wall time laswp . . : 9.71
Max aggregated wall time up tr sv  . : 0.41
```

Fig. 2. The output of HPL

Table 2. Comparison of two Performance Scores in *GFLOPS* on 4-, 6-, and 8- CPUs on the Formosa Cluster

No. of Procs		R_{max}	$R_{est\text{-}original}$	$R_{est\text{-}modified}$
4	Score	16.06	17.00	15.79
	error	--	6 %	2 %
6	Score	23.47	26.98	23.47
	error	--	15%	0%
8	Score	31.51	35.96	31.02
	error	--	14%	2%

Note: R_{max} is the maximal LINPACK performance achieved.

We reported a measured R_{max} = 0.9975 *TFLOPS* to the Top500 List in October 2003. R_{max}, as defined in the Top500 List, represents the maximal LINPACK performance achieved where B = 88, N = 188000, P = 12, and Q = 25.

Table 3 lists the performance scores in *TFLOPS* of the measured R_{max} value and the $R_{est\text{-}original}$ using Eq. (6), and $R_{est\text{-}modified}$ using Eq. (8). It demonstrates that $R_{est\text{-}modified}$ of 1.05 is indeed closer to R_{max} of 0.9975.

Table 3. Comparison of two Performance Scores in *TFLOPS* on 300 CPUs on the Formosa Cluster

	R_{max}	$R_{est\text{-}original}$	$R_{est\text{-}modified}$
Score	0.9975	1.35	1.05
error	--	35 %	5 %

Note: R_{max} is the maximal LINPACK performance achieved.

3.2 NCHC Triton Cluster

This Cluster was built by NCHC in March 2005 and is currently the fastest computer system in Taiwan [12]. The system contains 384 Intel Itanium 2 1.5GHz processors (192 HP Integrity rx2600 servers) connected together by a Quadrics interconnection network, with a RedHat AS3.0 operating system and Intel compile 8.1, HP MLIB v.19B, and HP MPI v2.01 software.

As in Section 3.1, we must first determine the parameters in Eqs. (6) and (8). With a sequential static analysis and curve fitting, we obtain α= 2.48μs, α' = 20.55μs, β= 0.0040μs and β' = 0.010665μs.

R_{max} = 2.03 was measured and reported to the Top500 List with the following parameters B = 72, N = 25500, P = 12, and Q = 32.

By the *DGEMM* function in HPL, we plot figure 3 and obtain γ_3 of 5.88 *GFLOPS*.

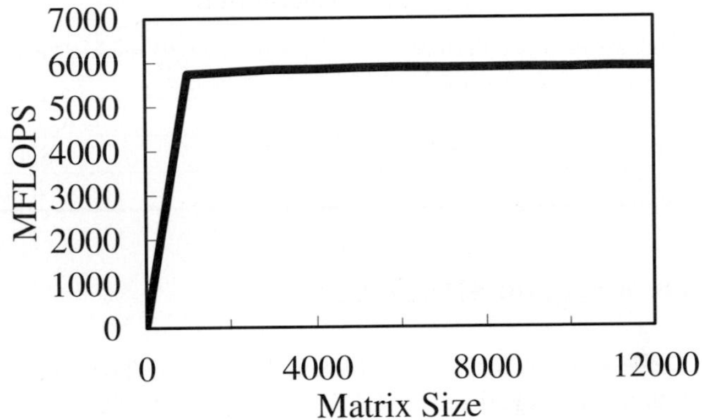

Fig. 3. MFLOPS vs. Matrix size multiplication on the Triton Cluster

Following the similar procedure in Section 3.1 gives the weighting factor w of 0.93. Table 4 lists the performance scores of the measured R_{max} value and the scores using Eq. (6) and Eq. (8) for the Triton Cluster. It is clear that $R_{est\text{-}modified}$ yields a score of 2.07, a much better prediction than $R_{est\text{-}original}$ of 2.25 using the original model.

Table 4. Comparison of two Performance Scores in *TFLOPS* on Triton Cluster

	R_{max}	$R_{est\text{-}original}$	$R_{est\text{-}modified}$
Score	2.03	2.25	2.07
error	-	11 %	2 %

3.3 Dawning 4000A

This cluster system was ranked 10th in the 23rd Top500 List in November 2003. It contains 2560 AMD Opterons running at 2.2 *GHz* connected together by a Myrinet network. Parameters used on Eqs. (6) and (8) are: R_{max} = 8.061 *TFLOPS* and N = 728400 from the Top500 List. P = 40 and Q = 64 are assumed.

We choose an B *of* 240 from reference [19], assuming identical behavior to the AMD Opterons running at 1.6 *GHz* found in the literature (AMD 2.2 *GHz* Opteron were used in the Dawning 4000A) and γ_3 = 4.4 × 0.918 = 4.0392 *GFLOPS* [17].

The message passing overhead is assumed to be similar to the Gunawan and Cai's results [20] with a Linux platform with 64bit 66 MHz PCI; then $\alpha = 14.08\mu s$, $\alpha' = 259.79\mu s$, $\beta = 0.009\mu s$ and $\beta' = 0.11\mu s$.

Assuming that the behavior of HPL on the Dawning 4000 was similar to that of reference [19], we then calculate the weighting function w to be 0.9. The prediction results $R_{est\text{-}original}$ and $R_{est\text{-}modified}$ are listed in Table 6. Again, our improved model gives an error of 4 % versus 27 % if we use the original model.

Table 6. Comparison of two Performance Scores in *TFLOPS* on the Dawning 4000A

	R_{max}	$R_{est\text{-}original}$	$R_{est\text{-}modified}$
Score	8.061	10.28	8.417
error	-	27 %	4 %

4 Prediction of R_{max} on SIRAYA

The maximal LINPACK performance achieved R_{max} in the Top500 List depends on network communication overhead, BLAS, motherboard, PCI system, size and bandwidth of main memory, compiler, MPI-middleware. In Sections 3.1-3.3, our improved model of Eq. (8) has resulted in a better correlation with R_{max} in all three clusters: the Formosa, the Triton, and the Dawning 4000A clusters. It should be noted on the first two clusters we use the actually measured parameters, and in the cases of the last, only "estimated" parameters are used. We believe once the parameters for the last become available, the prediction results should be even more accurate.

The authors of HPL suggest that the problem size N should be about 80% of the total amount of memory in reference[7]; that is $N = 0.8 \times N_{max}$, where $N_{max} = \mathrm{SQRT}(TM/8)$ is the allowable maximum problem size, TM is total memory size, reserving 20% of the total memory for system kernel overhead. In our experience, the problem sizes of the IA32-based cluster, Formosa, is quite near N_{max}, and may be larger than the suggested values. On the other hand, the problem sizes for the two IA64-based platforms--both Triton and Dawning--are smaller than the suggested, where $N = 0.58 \times N_{max}$ for the Triton and $N = 0.46 \times N_{max}$ for the Dawning 4000A, because the IA64 based clusters need to save large memory for system kernel overhead [6].

SIRAYA is a high-performance Beowulf cluster located within the Southern Business Unit of NCHC. The cluster was designed and constructed by the 'HPC Cluster Group' at NCHC for computational science applications.

The computing nodes in SIRAYA are 80 IBM eSeries e326 in 1U cases mounted in three racks. Each IBM eSeries e326 has two AMD Opteron 275 DualCore processors running at 2.2 *GHz* with 1 *MB* of L2 cache, 4 *GB* of DDR400 registered ECC SDRAM. This means SIRAYA has 320 cores. All computers are connected together in a star topology to six stackable Nortel BayStack 5510-48T 10/100/1000 *Mbps* switches.

Based on above elaboration, we use the following parameters to predict the maximal performance score on SIRAYA. $N = 0.5 \times N_{max} = 10^5$, $B = 240$, $w = 0.9$, $\gamma_3 = 4.0392$

GFLOPS from section 3.4, $\alpha' = 405.24\mu s$, and $\beta' = 0.10283\mu s$ from section 3.1. Then, $R_{est\text{-}modified}$ of 835.6 *GFLOPS* using Eq. (8) is very close to R_{max} of 848.2 *GFLOPS*.

Next phase, we will upgrade the system to 8 *GB* RAM for each node and fat-tree high performance network. Moreover, the system will be increased sixteen nodes. Then, the parameters become $N = 1.5 \times 10^5$. Therefore, we predict the maximal performance score on SIRAYA will be 1.37 *TFLOPS* after upgrade at the second phase.

5 Conclusion

Building on Wang's HPL performance model, we propose an improved HPL performance prediction models. Four existing clusters are used for comparing the prediction results. One of them is IA32 system and the other three are IA64 systems. The intercommunication media used in these four clusters are Myrinet, Quadrics, and Gigabit Ethernet network. In all cases, our improved model shows consistently better predictions than those using the existing model.

Our improved HPL performance prediction model would be a great help for those who wish to better understand their systems. It helps reduce the time for trial-and-error runs; it provides a user in scientific computing with useful information in predicting the performance and scalability of his own program as well.

References

1. Sterling, T., Becker, D., Savarese, D., et al.: BEOWULF: A Parallel Workstation for Scientific Computation. Proc. Of the 1995 International Conf. On Parallel Processing (1995)
2. Sterling, T., Savarese,D., Becker, D., et al.: Communication Overhead for Space Science Applications on the Beowulf Parallel Workstation. Proc. of 4th IEEE Symposium on High Performance Distributed Computing (1995)
3. Reschke, C., Sterling T. and Ridge, D.: A Design Study of Alternative Network Topologies for the Beowulf Parallel Workstation. Proceedings of the 5th IEEE Symposium on High Performance and Distributed Computing (1996)
4. Ridge, D., Becker, D. and Merkey, P.: Beowulf: Harnessing the Power of Parallelism in a Pile-of-PCs. Proceedings of IEEE Aerospace (1997)
5. Pfister, G. F.: In Search of Clusters. Prentice-Hall, Inc. (1998)
6. Top 500 List, http://www.top500.org
7. HPL Web site, http://www.netlib.org/benchmark/hpl/
8. Wang, P., Turner, G., Lauer, D., Allen, M., Simms, S., Hart, D., Papakhian, M. and Stewart, C.: LINPACK Performance on a Geographically Distributed Linux Cluster. 18th International Parallel and Distributed Processing Symposium (IPDPS'04), Santa Fe, New Mexico (2004)
9. Hockney, R. W.: The Communication Challenge for MPP: Intel Paragon and Meiko CS-2. Parallel Computing 20 (1994) 389-398
10. Xu, Z. and Hwang, K.: Modeling Communication Overhead: MPI and MPL Performance on the IBM SP2. IEEE Parallel & Distributed Technology 4(1) (1996) 9-23

11. NCHC Formosa PC Cluster Home Page, http://formosa.nchc.org.tw
12. NCHC Triton Cluster Home Page, http://www/english/pcCluster.php
13. Zhang, W., Chen, M. and Fan, J. : HPL Performance Prevision to Intending System Improvement. Second International Symposium on Parallel and Distributed Processing and Applications (2004)
14. Boden, N. J., et al.: Myrinet: A Giga-bit-per-second Local-area Network. IEEE micro (1995)
15. Burns, G.., Daoud, R. and Vaigl, J.: LAM:An Open Cluster Environment for MPI. Proceedings of Supercomputing Symposium'94 (1994) 379-386
16. Petrini, F., et al. : Performance Evaluation of the Quadrics Interconnection Network. Cluster Computing (2003)
17. GOTO library, http://www.cs.utexas.edu/users/kgoto
18. Chou, Chau-Yi, Chang, His-Ya, Wang, Shuen-Tai, Tcheng, Shou-Cheng: Modeling Message-Passing overhead on NCHC Formosa PC Cluster. GPC 2006, LNCS 3947 (2006) 299 – 307
19. Zhang, W., Fan, J. and Chen, M. : Efficient Determination of Block Size NB for Parallel Linpack Test. The 16th IASTED International Conference on Parallel and Distributed Computing and Systems (2004)
20. Gunawan, T. and Cai, W.: Performance Analysis of a Myrinet-Based Cluster. Cluster Computing 6 (2003) 229-313

An Ad Hoc Approach to Achieve Collaborative Computing with Pervasive Devices

Ren-Song Ko[1] and Matt W. Mutka[2]

[1] National Chung Cheng University, Department of Computer Science and Information Engineering,
Chia-Yi 621, Taiwan
korenson@cs.ccu.edu.tw

[2] Michigan State University, Department of Computer Science and Engineering,
East Lansing MI 48824-1226, USA
mutka@cse.msu.edu

Abstract. Limited computing resources may often cause poor performance and quality. To overcome these limitations, we introduce the idea of ad hoc systems, which may break the resource limitation and give mobile devices more potential usage. That is, several resource-limited devices may be combined as an ad hoc system to complete a complex computing task. We illustrate how the adaptive software framework, FRAME, may realize ad hoc systems by automatically distribute software to appropriate devices via the assembly process. We discuss the problem that ad hoc systems may be unstable under mobile computing environments since the participating devices may leave the ad hoc systems at their will. We also propose the reassembly process for this instability problem; i.e., assembly process will be re-invoked upon environmental changes. To further reduce the performance impact of reassembly, two approaches, partial reassembly and caching, are described. Our experimental results show that the caching improves performance by a factor of $7 \sim 40$.

1 Introduction

As technology improves, small devices and task-specific hardware begin to emerge. These devices usually have limited resources or specialized interfaces to address the desired goal of mobility and friendly usage. Thus, it will be a challenge to execute complex applications on these devices with reasonable performance and quality. However, the ubiquitous existence of computers may bring many possible solutions for this challenge. For instance, it is possible for computers to move and interact with their environment to seek the available resources to accomplish resource-intensive tasks more efficiently.

That is, instead of running software on a single device, one may look for available devices nearby and connect them together to form a temporarily organized system for short-term usage. Once the software is launched, the appropriate part of the code will be automatically distributed to each participating device. After that, these devices will execute the assigned code to accomplish the task collaboratively. Such a system without prior planning is called *ad hoc* [5].

C. Cérin and K.-C. Li (Eds.): GPC 2007, LNCS 4459, pp. 169–180, 2007.

Image the scenario that a person may watch a movie with his mobile phone. Because of limited computing capability, the video and audio quality may be unacceptable, and the viewing experience may not be pleasant. On the other hand, he may look for available intelligent devices nearby. For example, he may find an ATM machine for its larger screen and a MP3 player for its stereo sound quality. Thus, he may connect them together to form an ad hoc system as shown in Fig. 1. After the video playback software is launched, the appropriate part of the code will be distributed to each device, such as the code for audio processing to the MP3 player and the code for video processing to the ATM. As a consequence, instead of watching the movie on the mobile phone, he may enjoy the movie on the ad hoc system with larger image on the screen of the ATM and better sound on the MP3 player.

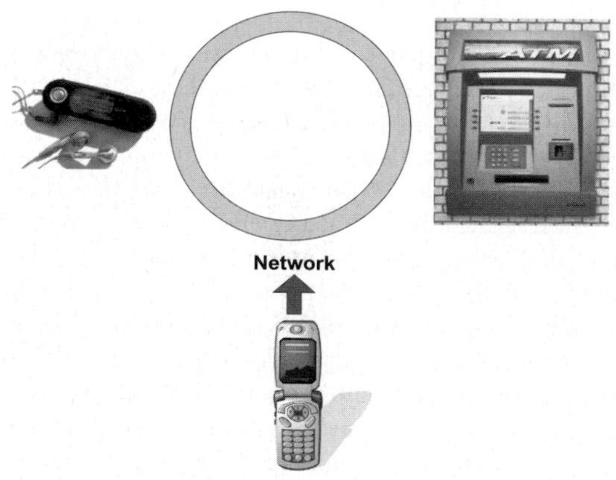

Fig. 1. A video playback application running on an ad hoc system

Such ad hoc systems may be realized by an adaptive Java software framework, `FRAME` [6, 7]. `FRAME` may automatically distribute software components to each participating devices and provide the functionalities of a middleware to allow these components to execute cooperatively. However, mobile computing environments are not likely static and, hence, ad hoc systems may be unstable. For example, some participating devices may leave the ad hoc system during the execution of the application. Therefore, the code on these leaving devices have to migrate to other devices in the system for proper execution of the application. In this paper, we shall illustrate the approach to improve `FRAME` for this challenge. We also discuss the issue of the performance impact on the application execution, and introduce two possible performance improvement.

We shall briefly describe the architecture of `FRAME` in the next section. Section 3 illustrates an approach for solving instability problem of ad hoc systems, discusses the performance issue, and describes how we improve it. We applied the improved `FRAME` to a robot application and measured the performance impact. The results are illustrated in Sect. 4. Finally, the last two sections will give a summary, survey of related work, and then discuss potential future investigations.

2 Adaptive Software Framework: `FRAME`

The central themes of `FRAME` are component, constraint, and assembly. The architecture of `FRAME` [6, 7] may be summarized as follows.

Component: An application is composed of components. Each component provides services to cooperate with other components. The services define the dependency of the components and form a software hierarchy tree, i.e., a parent component requires services from its child components and vice versa.

Implementation: A component may have more than one implementation. Each implementation provides the same functionality of the component but with different performance, quality, and resource requirements. Only one implementation of each component is needed to execute a program. For example, the audio component of the video playback application may have two implementations. Each is able to process the audio of the movie but with different sound quality and computation resources. The implementation with better sound quality may require more computation resources than the mobile phone has. Of course, such an implementation should not be executed on the mobile phone. The question for which implementation is feasible on the given device will be answered with help from constraints. Finally, the software hierarchy information, such as what components the application has and what implementations of the component has, will be registered to a database server called the *component registry*.

Constraint: Each implementation may have a set of constraints embedded. A constraint is a predicate and used to specify whether the given computing environment has resources that the implementation requires. It may also specify the execution performance and quality of the implementation. The constraints of the implementation are used by the assembly process to determine whether the implementation is feasible on the given device.

Assembly: A process called *assembly* will resolve, on the fly by querying the component registry, what components and their implementations an application has. For each component, the assembly process will load each implementation and check its constraints on a given device. If all constraints are satisfied, the implementation is feasible on the device. Hence, the component with the feasible implementation will be distributed to the device. As shown in Fig. 2, there may be an implementation for audio component with better sound quality and all its constraints are satisfied on the MP3 player but not the mobile phone and the ATM. Thus the audio component will be distributed to the MP3 player.

Execution: After all the components are distributed, the application begin to execute.

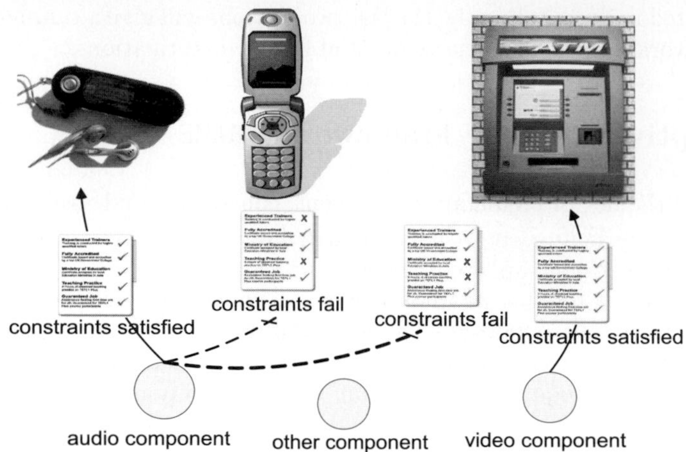

Fig. 2. Components will be distributed to appropriate devices based on their constraints

Table 1. `if-else` statement structure

```
if (constraints of component 1 with implementation 1)
{   // select component 1 with implementation 1

    if (constraints of component 2 with implementation 1)
    {   // select component 2 with implementation 1

        // check each implementation of component 3, 4,...
    }
    else if (constraints of component 2 with implementation 2)
    {   // select component 2 with implementation 2

        // check each implementation of component 3, 4,...
    }
    ... // more else if blocks for other implementations of component 2
}
else if (constraints of component 1 with implementation 2)
{   // select component 1 with implementation 2

    // similar as the code in the if block of
    // component 1 with implementation 1
}
... // more else if blocks for other implementations of component 1
```

The traditional approach to distribute components to appropriate devices based on constraints is to use condition statements such as if-else statements. For example, suppose there is an application that may have components $1, 2, \ldots, N$, where component i has M_i implementations. Thus, there may be nested if-else statements similar to Table 1. First, it checks if the constraints of component 1 with implementation 1 are true. If yes, it will has code in its `if` block to check appropriate implementation of component 2, then 3, and so on. If not, it will jump to `else if` block to check the component 1 with implementation 2. The code in its `else if` block of implementation 2 are same as implementation 1. Thus, if constraints of implementation 2 are true, it will check appropriate implementation of component 2, then 3, and so on. The process will find an appropriate implementation for component 1 first, then 2, 3, and so on.

The condition statements approach is primitive from the software engineering perspective. As the number of components and their implementations increase, the code tends toward so called "spaghetti code" that has a complex and tangled control structure and the software will become more difficult to maintain or modify.

The most important limitation of the condition statements approach is that condition statements are hard-coded. Thus, the availability of all implementations need to be known during the development stage. It is not flexible enough to integrate newly developed implementations without rewriting and recompiling the code, and, of course, the down-time.

To avoid the above limitations, the assembly process uses the following two-step approach:

1. **Components distribution:** In this step, the assembly process will distribute components to participating devices. Note that there will be n^c different component distributions with n participating devices and c components. By using the information stored in the component registry, the assembly process may be able to identify all the component implementation of an application. Since the assembly process queries this information during run-time, the above limitations of the condition statements approach are avoided as long as newly developed implementations register their information to the component registry. When all components of a distribution are distributed, all the constraints will be collected and the assembly process will proceed to next step for solving these constraints.
2. **Constraints solving:** For each component, the assembly process will find out if all the constraints are satisfied. If all the constraints of the distribution are satisfied, the distribution is feasible and the application may execute on this distribution. `FRAME` uses a backtracking algorithm [8] for solving constraint satisfaction problems. If one of the constraints within this distribution is not satisfied, the assembly process will return to the first step for next distribution.

3 Reassembly

A straightforward idea for solving the instability problem of ad hoc systems is to monitor the computing environment changes. If some of constraints fail due to environmental changes, the application execution will be temporarily suspended, the component assembly process will be re-invoked, and then the application execution will resume with appropriate implementations of the components. However, one challenge for this reassembly approach is performance, since the assembly process involves I/O activities, such as communication between devices, and intense computation, such as constraints solving to find the feasible distribution. In our experiments, the assembly process of the robot application is about 650 times slower than the similar application hard coded by if-else condition statements. It will be not feasible to simply re-invoke the assembly process for the reassembly, especially on a small temporal scale of environment change. Therefore, we propose two schemes, partial reassembly and caching, to improve the performance.

First, we observe that not all components need to be changed for the reassembly process and it is unnecessary to examine the constraints of these components. Thus, developers may only specify the subset of the components to be examined to reduce the run-time monitoring performance impact and the constraints solving time. For the video playback application example, the person may always carry the mobile phone and MP3 player, but not the ATM. As the person walks around, the connections between the ATM and other devices may drop, and then the ATM will leave the ad hoc system. Therefore, as shown in Fig. 3, it is only necessary to monitor the ATM and perform the video component migration when the ATM leaves.

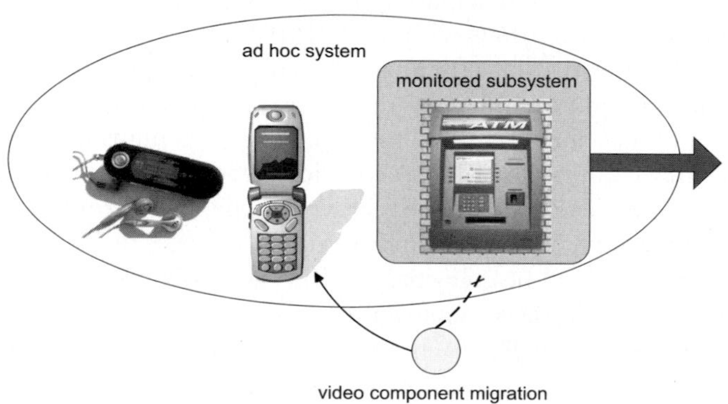

Fig. 3. Example of partial reassembly

The other performance improvement is to use cache, which may be done in two different levels. The first level is to cache the component distribution results, i.e., the first step of the assembly process. The purpose of the first step is to find possible distributions and collect all the constraints of each distribution for constraints solving. If no component implementation is added or removed, the constraints of each distribution will remain the same and the first step may be avoided.

The second level is to cache the computing environment, a more aggressive scheme based on the assumption that the computing environments will repeat.

A computing environment will be used as a key, and its assembly results are cached in a hash table with the key as shown in Fig. 4. That is, a computing environment may contain information that an application requires for execution, such as number of participating devices, network bandwidth, hardware, etc. Thus the information may be converted to a key for caching via a hash function. If the computing environment repeats, its assembly results may be obtained from the cache with the key.

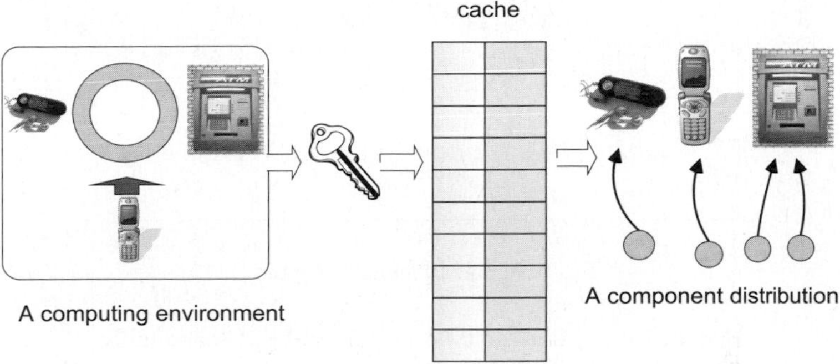

Fig. 4. Flow of reassembly cache

4 Performance Evaluation

We use a robot, XR4000 [12], to evaluate the performance of the component reassembly process. We compare the performance of different implementation selection schemes, including component reassembly with and without caching, and also evaluate the performance of the similar application using hard coded if-else condition statements. The performance is measured versus different number of the component implementations registered in the component registry.

To highlight the relationship between the performance and these different implementation selection schemes, we simplify the software hierarchy so the measured application has only one component with multiple implementations to be assembled. As a consequence, what the reassembly process actually does is to select an appropriate implementation of the component. Note that performance is application dependent, and, therefore, the performance comparison may not be same for different applications.

Figure 5 shows that the time required for the constraints solving step, which is about 50% $\sim$ 60% of the total time for assembly or non-cached reassembly. If the application hierarchy does not change and no new implementation is added, the first level caching may be used. The non-cached reassembly may be approximately reduced to the constraint solving step, which is a 40% $\sim$ 50% time saving.

Figure 6 compares the time required to search for the appropriate implementation of the component by the different schemes, i.e., non-cached reassembly, cached reassembly, and hard coded if-else statement. The if-else scheme requires about 0.003 $\sim$ 0.018 ms that depends on the number of implementations. The

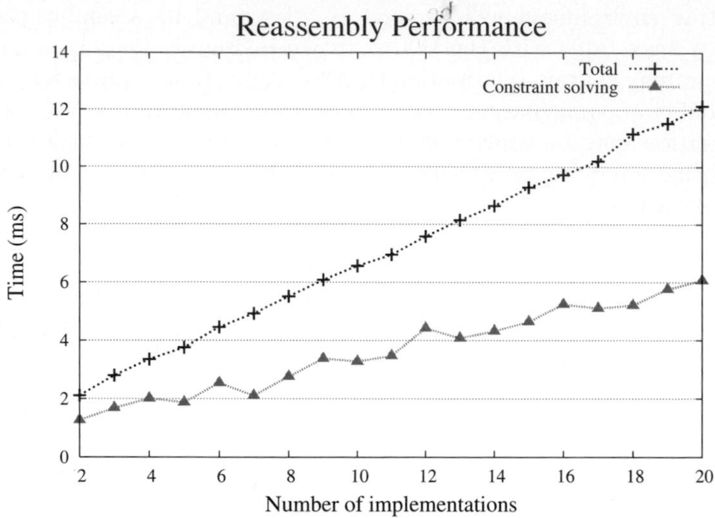

Fig. 5. Constraints solving performance of reassembly

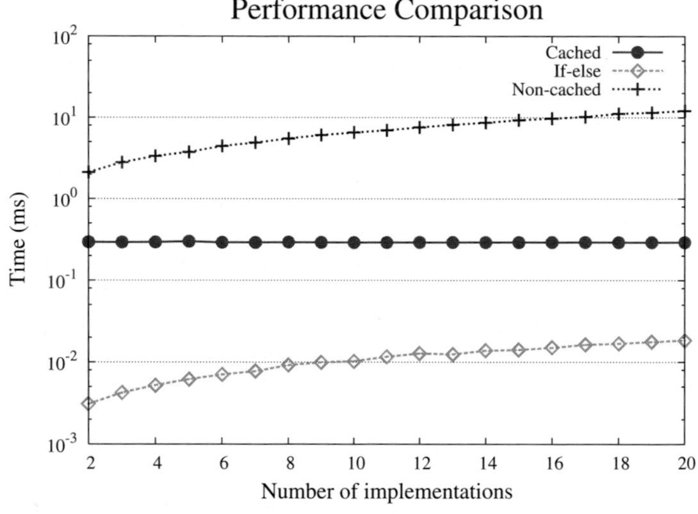

Fig. 6. Performance comparison for different component selection scheme

non-cached reassembly requires about 2.1 $\sim$ 12.1 ms that also depends on the number of implementations, and it is about 650 times slower than the if-else scheme.

The result also shows that the cached reassembly requires about 0.29 ms and improves the reassembly speed by a factor of 7 $\sim$ 40, and may be only about 15 times slower than if-else scheme. Unlike if-else and non-cached schemes, the cache access time is constant and independent on the number of implementations. Thus, the performance improvement becomes more significant while the number of implementations increases. Also, the constant assembly time of cache makes the execution time of the application more predictable, which is an important issue for real-time applications.

Reassembly will load and unload the implementations of component whenever necessary, which will free some unnecessary memory, a scarce resource in embedded systems. Depending on how the application is developed, reassembly may save the memory usage. For example, the robot application using hard coded if-else statements has all implementations preloaded for better performance. However, this is a trade-off with memory usage. Fig. 7 shows that preloaded components require about 50% more memory than the reassembly scheme.

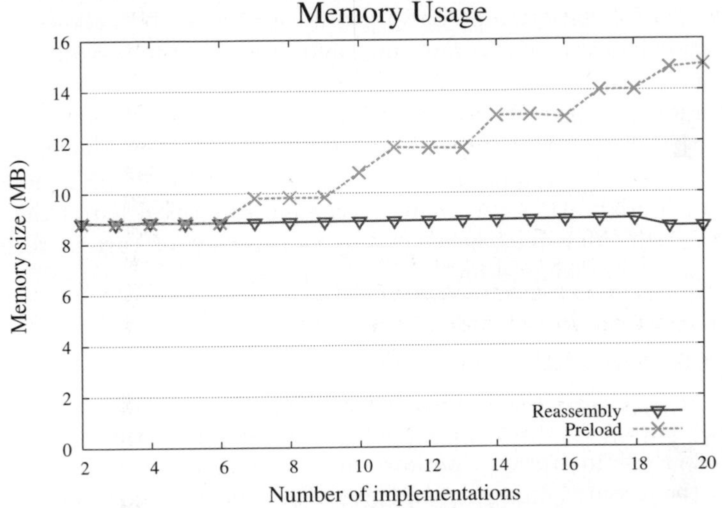

Fig. 7. Memory usage comparison for ASAP and component-preloaded

5 Related Work

The original idea of ad hoc systems is introduced in [5]. Lai, et al. [9] use infrared communication, which allows users to easily connect several devices as an ad hoc system via infrared communication. They also propose an approach to improve the performance of the assembly process by grouping the participating devices into "virtual subsystems" based on the hardware characteristics of the devices. With properly specifying the constraints, a component will only be distributed to the devices of the specified virtual subsystem and the time for the assembly process will be reduced.

There are several other related projects that may deliver applications on resource-limited devices and perform adaptation when necessary. The Spectra project [2] monitors both application resource usage and the availability of resources in the environment, and dynamically determines how and where to execute application components. In making this determination, Spectra can generate a distributed execution plan to balance the competing goals of performance, energy conservation, and application quality.

Puppeteer [1] is a system for adapting component-based applications in mobile environments, which takes advantage of the exported interfaces of these applications and the structured nature of the documents they manipulate to perform adaptation without modifying the applications. The system is structured in a modular fashion, allowing easy addition of new applications and adaptation policies.

Gu, et al. [3] propose an adaptive offloading system that includes two key parts, a distributed offloading platform [11] and an offloading inference [4]. The system will dynamically partition the application and offload part of the application execution data to a powerful nearby surrogate. This allows delivery of the application in a pervasive computing environment without significant fidelity degradation.

Compositional adaptation exchanges algorithmic or structural system components with others that improve a program's fit to its current environment. With this approach, an application can add new behaviors after deployment. Compositional adaptation also enables dynamic recomposition of the software during execution. McKinley, et al. [10] gives a review of current technologies about compositional adaptation.

6 Conclusion and Future Work

Limited computing resources may often cause poor performance and quality. To overcome these limitations, we introduce the idea of ad hoc systems, which may break the resource limitation and give mobile devices more potential usage. That is, several resource-limited devices may be combined as an ad hoc system to complete a complex computing task. We also illustrate how the adaptive software framework, `FRAME`, may realize ad hoc systems. `FRAME` provides the functionalities of a middleware to allow software components to execute cooperatively. Most importantly, with constraints embedded in the component implementations, the assembly process of `FRAME` is able to automatically distribute these components to appropriate devices.

However, mobile computing environments are dynamic and ad hoc systems may be unstable since the participating devices may leave the ad hoc systems at their will. Thus, the code on some devices may need to migrate to another devices. We propose the reassembly process for this instability problem; i.e., if some constraints fail due to environmental changes, the application execution will be temporarily suspended, the component assembly process will be re-invoked, and then the application execution will resume with appropriate implementations of the components. Furthermore, the reassembly performance is an important issue for seemlessly execution of applications. To further reduce the performance impact of the reassembly process, two approaches, partial reassembly and caching, are proposed. Our experimental results show that the caching improves the reassembly speed by a factor of $7 \sim 40$ and the time for reassembly is constant and hence predictable.

There is room for performance improvement. For instance, the constraints solving performance depends on the number of distributions and the number of constraints in each distribution. To improve the backtracking algorithm, if more information may be extracted from the relationship between constraints, some redundancy may be found between the constraints. Thus, truth checking for some constraints may be avoided. Moreover, more performance evaluation and measurement will be conducted in the future, including power consumption of large-scale ad hoc systems.

One important aspect of ubiquitous computing is the existence of disappearing hardware [13] that are mobile, have small form factor and usually limited computation resources. Since the constraints solving may require a lot of computation, these disappearing hardware may not have enough resources. One solution is to use a dedicated server for the off-site assembly process. Therefore, the participating devices may send the environment information to the server for assembly, and retrieve assembly results and the appropriate implementations of the components.

References

[1] E. de Lara, D. S. Wallach, and W. Zwaenepoel. Puppeteer: Component-based Adaptation for Mobile Computing. In *Proceedings of the 3rd USENIX Symposium on Internet Technologies and Systems*, San Francisco, California, Mar. 2001.

[2] J. Flinn, S. Park, and M. Satyanarayanan. Balancing Performance, Energy, and Quality in Pervasive Computing. In *Proceedings of the 22nd International Conference on Distributed Computing Systems*, Vienna, Austria, July 2002.

[3] X. Gu, A. Messer, I. Greenberg, D. Milojicic, and K. Nahrstedt. Adaptive offloading for pervasive computing. *IEEE Pervasive Computing*, 3(3):66–73, July-September 2004.

[4] X. Gu, K. Nahrstedt, A. Messer, I. Greenberg, and D. Milojicic. Adaptive Offloading Inference for Delivering Applications in Pervasive Computing Environments. In *Proceedings of IEEE International Conference on Pervasive Computing and Communications*, pages 107–114, 2003.

[5] R.-S. Ko. `ASAP` *for Developing Adaptive Software within Dynamic Heterogeneous Environments.* PhD thesis, Michigan State University, May 2003.

[6] R.-S. Ko and M. W. Mutka. Adaptive Soft Real-Time Java within Heterogeneous Environments. In *Proceedings of Tenth International Workshop on Parallel and Distributed Real-Time Systems*, Fort Lauderdale, Florida, Apr. 2002.

[7] R.-S. Ko and M. W. Mutka. `FRAME` for Achieving Performance Portability within Heterogeneous Environments. In *Proceedings of the 9th IEEE Conference on Engineering Computer Based Systems (ECBS)*, Lund University, Lund, SWEDEN, Apr. 2002.

[8] V. Kumar. Algorithms for Constraints Satisfaction problems: A Survey. *The AI Magazine, by the AAAI*, 13(1):32–44, 1992.

[9] C.-C. Lai, R.-S. Ko, and C.-K. Yen. Ad Hoc System : a Software Architecture for Ubiquitous Environment. In *Proceedings of the 12th ASIA-PACIFIC Software Engineering Conference*, Taipei, Taiwan, Dec. 2005.

[10] P. K. Mckinley, S. M. Sadjadi, E. P. Kasten, and B. H. Cheng. Composing Adaptive Software. *IEEE Computer*, 37(7), July 2004.

[11] A. Messer, I. Greenberg, P. Bernadat, D. S. Milojicic, D. Chen, T. J. Giuli, and X. Gu. Towards a Distributed Platform for Resource-Constrained Devices. In *Proceedings of the IEEE 22nd International Conference on Distributed Computing Systems*, pages 43–51, Vienna, Austria, 2002.

[12] Nomadic Technologies, Inc., Mountain View, CA. *Nomad XRDEV Software Manual*, Mar. 1999. Information available at *http://nomadic.sourceforge.net/production/manuals/xrdev-1.0.pdf.gz.*

[13] M. Weiser. The Computer for the 21st Century. *Scientific American*, 265(3):66–75, Sept. 1991. Reprinted in IEEE Pervasive Computing, Jan-Mar 2002, pp. 19-25.

Optimizing Server Placement for QoS Requirements in Hierarchical Grid Environments

Chien-Min Wang[1], Chun-Chen Hsu[2], Pangfeng Liu[2],
Hsi-Min Chen[3], and Jan-Jan Wu[1]

[1] Institute of Information Science, Academia Sinica, Taipei, Taiwan, R.O.C.
{cmwang,wuj}@iis.sinica.edu.tw
[2] Department of Computer Science and Information Engineering, National Taiwan University, Taipei, Taiwan, R.O.C.
{d95006,pangfeng}@csie.ntu.edu.tw
[3] Department of Computer Science and Information Engineering, National Central University, Taoyuan, Taiwan, R.O.C.
seeme@selab.csie.ncu.edu.tw

Abstract. This paper focuses on two problems related to QoS-aware I/O server placement in hierarchical Grid environments. Given a hierarchical network with requests from clients, the network latencies of links, constraints on servers' capabilities and the service quality requirement, the solution to the *minimum server placement problem* attempts to place the minimum number of servers that meet both the constrains on servers' capabilities and the service quality requirement. As our model considers both the different capabilities of servers and the network latencies, it is more general than similar works in the literatures. Instead of using a heuristic approach, we propose an optimal algorithm based on dynamic programming to solve the problem. We also consider the *optimal service quality problem*, which tries to place a given number of servers appropriately so that the maximum expected response time is minimized. We prove that an optimal server placement can be achieved by combining the dynamic programming algorithm with a binary search on the service quality requirement. The simulation results clearly show the improvement in the number of servers and the maximum expected response time.

1 Introduction

Grid technologies enable scientific applications to utilize a wide variety of distributed computing and data resources [1]. A Data Grid is a distributed storage infrastructure that integrates distributed, independently managed data resources. It addresses the problems of storage and data management, data transfers and data access optimization, while maintaining high reliability and availability of the data. In recent years, a number of Data Grid projects [2,3] have emerged in various disciplines.

One of the research issues in Data Grid is the efficiency of data access. One way of efficient data access is to distribute multiple copies of a file across different

C. Cérin and K.-C. Li (Eds.): GPC 2007, LNCS 4459, pp. 181–192, 2007.

server sites in the grid system. Researches [4,5,6,7,8,9] have shown that file replication can improve the performance of the applications.

The existing works focus on how to distribute the file replicas in Data Grid in order to optimize different criteria such as I/O operation costs [5], mean access latencies [8] and bandwidth consumption [9]. However, few works use the quality of services as an performance metric of Data Grid. We believe the service quality is also an important performance metric in Data Grid due to the dynamic nature in the grid environment. In [10,11], quality of service is considered. Those works, however, fail to take the heterogeneity of servers' capabilities into consideration. That is, in those works, servers are assumed to be able to serve all I/O requests it received. This assumption omits one of the characteristics in grid computing infrastructure: the heterogeneity of its nature. In an early work by Wang [12], they considered the servers' capabilities when minimizing the number of servers.

In this paper, we focus on two QoS-aware I/O server placement problems in hierarchical Grid environments which consider the service quality requirement, the capabilities of servers and the network latencies. As our model consider both the different capabilities of servers and the network latencies, it is more general than similar works in the literatures. The *minimum server placement problem* asks how to place the minimum number of servers to meet both the constrains on servers' capabilities and the service quality requirement. We propose an optimal algorithm based on dynamic programming to solve this problem. We also consider the *optimal service quality problem*, which tries to place a given number of servers appropriately so that the maximum expected response time is minimized. We prove that such a server placement can be achieved by combining the dynamic programming algorithm with a binary search on the maximum expected response time of servers. The experimental results clearly show the improvement in the number of servers and the maximum expected response time.

2 The System Model

In this paper we use a hierarchical Grid model, one of the most common architectures in current use [7,9,10,11,12,13]. Consider Fig. 1 as an example. Given a tree $T = (V, E)$, V is the set of sites and $E \in V \times V$ represents network links between sites. A distance d_{uv} associated with each edge $(u, v) \in E$ represents the latency of the network link between sites u and v. We may further extend the definition of d_{uv} as the latency of a shortest path between any two sites u and v.

Leaf nodes represent client sites that send out I/O requests. The root node is assumed to be the I/O server that stores the master copies of all files. Without loss of generality, we assume that the root node is the site 0. Intermediate nodes can be either routers for network communications or I/O servers that store file replicas. We assume that, initially, only one copy (i.e., the master copy) of a file exists at the root site, as in [9,10,11,12,13]. Let T_i be the sub-tree rooted at node i.

Associated with each client site i, there is a parameter r_i that represents the arrival rate of read requests for client site i. A data request travels upward from

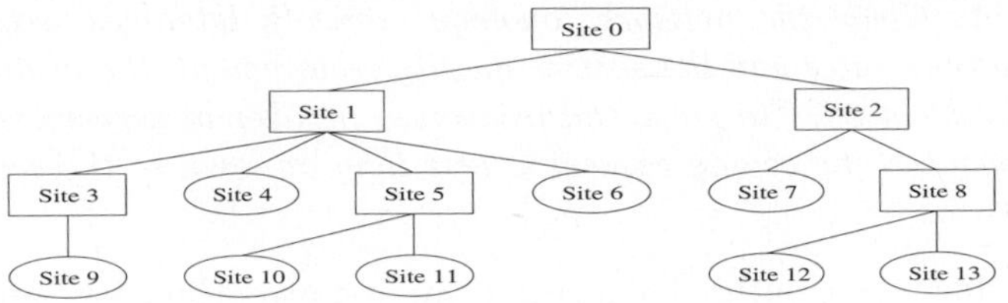

Fig. 1. The hierarchical Grid model

a client site and passes through routers until it reaches an I/O server on the path. Upon receiving the request, the I/O server sends the requested file back to the client site if it owns a copy of the requested file. Otherwise, it forwards the request to its parent server. This process continues up the hierarchy recursively until a node that has the requested file is encountered or the root node is reached. The network latency of a I/O request from a client site to a server site can be computed as the sum of the network latencies of all intermediate links between both sites. The root server might update the contents of a file. For each update, corresponding update requests are sent to the other I/O servers to maintain file consistency. Let u be the arrival rate of update requests from the root server.

For each server site j, μ'_j and λ'_j are represented as the service rate and the arrival rate of I/O requests of server site j respectively. λ'_j can be computed as: $\lambda'_j = \sum_{i \in C_j} r_i + u$, where C_j is the set of clients served by server site j. We assume each server in the grid system is a M/M/1 queueing system. Thus, the expected waiting time at server j will be $1/(\mu'_j - \lambda'_j) = 1/(\mu'_j - u - \sum_{i \in C_j} r_i)$. To simplify the notations, we will use $\mu_j = \mu'_j - u$ and $\lambda_j = \sum_{i \in C_j} r_i$ as the service rate and the arrival rate of server site j throughout this paper.

μ_j and λ_j will be used to decide the expected response times of requests it served. Suppose the I/O requests from site i are served by server j. The expected response time of a request from site i can be defined as the sum of the network latencies in the path and the server j's expected waiting time, i.e., $d_{ij} + \frac{1}{\mu_j - \lambda_j}$.

Given the service quality requirement t, a server site j must satisfy the following conditions: (1) the arrival rate of all requests it served is less than its service rate, i.e., $\lambda_j < \mu_j$ and (2) the expected response times of all requests it served are less than or equal to t, i.e., $max_{i \in C_j}\{d_{ij} + \frac{1}{\mu_j - \lambda_j}\} \leq t$, where C_j is the set of clients served by server site j. Let the expected response time of server$j$ be the maximum expected response time of requests it served.

3 The Minimum Server Placement Problem

In this section, we formally define the minimum server placement problem and introduce our optimal algorithm to this problem. Our first problem is to place the minimum number of I/O servers that will satisfy capability constrains of servers as well as the service quality requirement from clients.

Definition 1. *Given the network topology, network latencies, request arrival rates, I/O service rates and the service quality requirement, the minimum server placement problem tries to place the minimum number of servers such that the expected response time of any request is less than or equal to the service quality requirement.*

Before introducing the optimal algorithm, we first give definitions on three basic functions as follows:

Definition 2. *Let $\lambda(i, m, d, t)$ be the minimum arrival rate of requests that reach node i among all the server placements that meet the following three conditions.*

1. *At most m servers are placed in $T_i - \{i\}$*
2. *The expected response time of any request served by these servers must be less than or equal to t.*
3. *If requests that reach node i exist, the maximum latency of these requests to node i must be less than or equal to d.*

Definition 3. *Let $\omega(i, m, d, t)$ be the minimum arrival rate of leakage requests that pass through node i among all the server placements that meet the following three conditions.*

1. *At most m servers are placed in T_i.*
2. *The expected response time of any request served by these servers must be less than or equal to t.*
3. *If leakage requests that pass through node i exist, the maximum latency of these leakage requests to node i must be less than or equal to d.*

Definition 4. *$\Omega(i, m, d, t)$ is an optimal server placement that meets all the requirements for $\omega(i, m, d, t)$.*

Leakage requests that pass through node i are those requests generated by leaf nodes in the sub-tree rooted at node i, but not served by servers in that sub-tree. Such requests must be served by a server above node i in the hierarchy. Hence, it is desirable to minimize the arrival rate of these leakage requests. Depending on the server placement, the arrival rate of leakage requests may changes. $\omega(i, m, d, t)$ represents the minimum arrival rate of leakage requests among all possible server placements that satisfy the above three conditions while $\Omega(i, m, d, t)$ represents an optimal server placement. If no server placement satisfy the above three conditions, $\omega(i, m, d, t)$ simply returns null. Let n be the number of nodes in the grid system. By definition, we can derive the following lemmas.

Lemma 1. *$\omega(i, m_1, d, t) \leq \omega(i, m_2, d, t)$ for any node i, $m_1 \geq m_2 \geq 0, d \geq 0$ and $t \geq 0$.*

Lemma 2. *$\omega(i, m, d, t_1) \leq \omega(i, m, d, t_2)$ for any node i, $m \geq 0, d \geq 0$ and $t_1 \geq t_2 \geq 0$.*

Lemma 3. *$\omega(i, m, d_1, t) \leq \omega(i, m, d_2, t)$ for any node i, $m \geq 0, d_1 \geq d_2 \geq 0$ and $t \geq 0$.*

Lemma 4. *If* $\omega(i, m, d_1, t) = 0$ *for some* d_1*, then* $\omega(i, m, d, t) = 0$ *for any* $d \geq 0$.

Based on the above lemmas, theorems for computing the minimum arrival rate of leakage requests can be derived. We show that it can be computed in a recursive manner.

Theorem 1. *If node* i *is a leaf node, then* $\omega(i, m, d, t) = \lambda_i$ *and* $\Omega(i, m, d, t)$ *is an empty set for* $0 \leq m \leq n$, $d \geq 0$ *and* $t \geq 0$.

Proof. Since a leaf node cannot be a server, all requests generated by a client site will travel up the tree toward the leaf node's parent. In addition, the latency to node i must be 0. By definition, $\omega(i, m, d, t) = \lambda_i$ and $\Omega(i, m, d, t)$ is an empty set for $0 \leq m \leq n$, $d \geq 0$ and $t \geq 0$. ∎

Theorem 2. *For an intermediate node* i *with two child nodes,* j *and* k*, we can derive:*

$$\begin{aligned}
&\lambda(i, m, d, t) = min_{0 \leq r \leq m}\{\omega(j, r, d - d_{ji}, t) + \omega(k, m - r, d - d_{ki}, t)\} \\
&\omega(i, m, d, t) = 0 \textit{ if there exists } 0 \leq d' \leq t \textit{ such that} \\
&\qquad\qquad\qquad \lambda(i, m - 1, d', t) + 1/(t - d') \leq \mu_i. \\
&\omega(i, m, d, t) = \lambda(i, m, d, t), \textit{ otherwise.}
\end{aligned}$$

Proof. For node i, there are two possibilities for an optimal placement of at most m servers:

Case 1: A server is placed on node i. At most $m - 1$ servers can be placed on T_j and T_k. Suppose that, in an optimal server placement, there are p servers on T_j and q servers on T_k, as shown in Fig. 2(a). Obviously, we have $0 \leq p, q \leq m - 1$

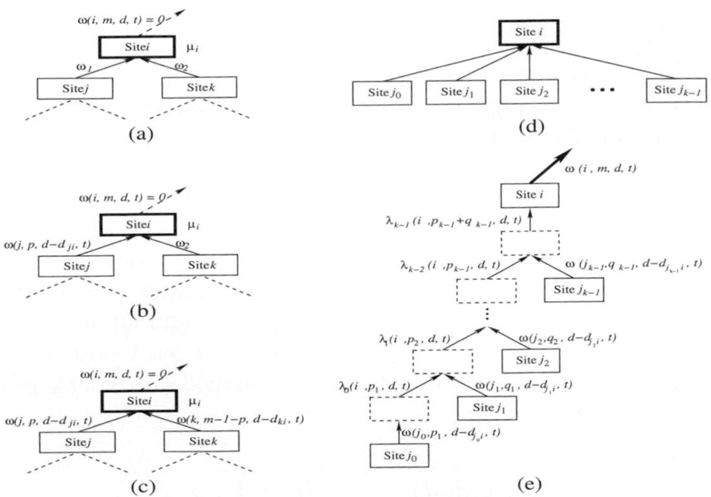

Fig. 2. (a), (b) and (c) illustrate the concept of Theorem 2. (d) and (e) illustrate the basic concept of Theorem 3.

and $p + q \leq m - 1$. Without loss of generality, we may assume the arrival rates of leakage requests from node j and node k are ω_1 and ω_2 and the maximum latencies of their leakage requests are d_1 and d_2, respectively. The maximum latency of requests that reach node i is assumed to be d'.

Next, we show that another optimal server placement can be generated by substituting the placement of p servers on T_j with $\Omega(j, p, d' - d_{ji}, t)$ as shown in Fig. 2(b). If $\omega_1 \neq 0$, then $d' \geq d_1 + d_{ji}$. We can derive

$$\omega_1 \geq \omega(j, p, d_1, t) \geq \omega(j, p, d' - d_{ji}, t)$$

After the substitution, the arrival rate of requests that reach node i can be reduced while the maximum latency of requests remains unchanged. Thus, it is also an optimal server placement. On the other hand, if $\omega_1 = 0$, we can derive

$$0 = \omega_1 = \omega(j, p, d_1, t) = \omega(j, p, d' - d_{ji}, t)$$

In this case, it is also an optimal server placement. Therefore, another optimal server placement can be generated by substituting the placement of p servers on T_j with $\Omega(j, p, d' - d_{ji}, t)$. Similarly, we can show that another optimal server placement can be generated by replacing the placement of q servers on T_k with $\Omega(k, m - 1 - p, d' - d_{ki}, t)$ as shown in Fig. 2(c).

$$\omega_2 \geq \omega(k, q, d_2, t) \geq \omega(k, q, d' - d_{ki}, t) \geq \omega(k, m - 1 - p, d' - d_{ki}, t) \text{ if } \omega_2 \neq 0$$

$$0 = \omega_2 = \omega(k, q, d_2, t) = \omega(k, q, d' - d_{ki}, t) = \omega(k, m - 1 - p, d' - d_{ki}, t) \text{ if } \omega_2 = 0$$

By assumption, the maximum expected response time of leakage requests that reach node i is less than or equal to t. In other words, $d' + 1/(\mu_i - \omega_1 - \omega_2) \leq t$. Accordingly, we an derive

$$\begin{aligned}\mu_i &\geq \omega_1 + \omega_2 + 1/(t - d') \\ &\geq \omega(j, p, d' - d_{ji}, t) + \omega(k, m - 1 - p, d' - d_{ki}, t) + 1/(t - d') \\ &\geq \lambda(i, m - 1, d', t) + 1/(t - d')\end{aligned}$$

Therefore, there exists $0 \leq d' \leq t$ such that $\lambda(i, m - 1, d', t) + 1/(t - d') \leq \mu_i$. In this case, Fig. 2(c) is an optimal server placement and $\omega(i, m, d, t) = 0$. This completes the proof of Case 1.

Case 2: No server is placed on node i. Consequently, at most m servers are placed on T_j and T_k. Obviously, we have $0 \leq p, q \leq m$ and $p + q \leq m$. Suppose that, in an optimal server placement, there are p servers on T_j and q servers on T_k. Without loss of generality, we may assume the arrival rates of leakage requests from node j and node k are ω_1 and ω_2 and their maximum latencies are d_1 and d_2, respectively. The maximum latency of requests that reach node i is assumed to be d. Similar to the proof of Case 1, the optimal arrival rate of leakage requests can be computed as

$$\begin{aligned}\omega(i, m, d, t) &= \omega_1 && +\omega_2 \\ &\geq \omega(j, p, d_1, t) && +\omega(k, q, d2, t) \\ &\geq \omega(j, p, d - d_{ji}, t) && +\omega(k, q, d - d_{ki}, t) \\ &\geq \omega(j, p, d - d_{ji}, t) && +\omega(k, m - 1 - p, d - d_{ki}, t) \\ &\geq \lambda(i, m, d, t)\end{aligned}$$

Since it is an optimal server placement, all the equalities must hold. Therefore, this theorem holds for Case 2. Since an optimal server placement must be one of the two cases, this completes the proof of this theorem. ■

Theorem 3. *For an intermediate node i with k child nodes $j_0, \ldots, j_{k-1}$, the minimum arrival rate of leakage requests that pass through node i can be computed iteratively as follows:*

$$\begin{aligned} \lambda_0(i,m,d,t) &= \omega(j_0, m, d - d_{j_0 i}, t) \\ \lambda_q(i,m,d,t) &= min_{0 \le r \le m}\{\lambda_{q-1}(i,r,d,t) + \omega(j_q, m-r, d - d_{j_q i}, t)\}, \\ &\quad 1 \le q \le k-1, \\ \omega(i,m,d,t) &= 0 \text{ if there exists } 0 \le d' \le t \text{ such that} \\ &\quad \lambda_{k-1}(i, m-1, d', t) + 1/(t-d') \le \mu_i \\ \omega(i,m,d,t) &= \lambda_{k-1}(i,m,d,t), otherwise \end{aligned}$$

Proof. Fig. 2(d) and 2(e) illustrate the basic concept of this theorem. To find an optimal server placement, we can view an intermediate node with k child nodes in Fig. 2(d) as the sub-tree in Fig. 2(e). Then, the minimum arrival rate of leakage requests can be computed recursively along the sub-tree. As the detailed proof of this theorem is similar to that of Theorem 3, it is omitted here. ■

Theorem 4. *The minimum number of I/O servers that meet their constraints can be obtained by finding the minimum m such that $\omega(0, m, 0, t) = 0$.*

Corollary 1. *Let m' be the minimum number of servers found by the dynamic programming algorithm. m' grows nondecreasingly when the service quality requirement t decreases.*

Based on Theorems 1 to 3, we can compute the minimum arrival rates of leakage requests that start from leaf nodes and work toward the root node. After the minimum arrival rate of leakage requests that reach the root node has been computed, the minimum number of I/O servers that meet their constraints can be computed according to Theorem 4. The proposed algorithm is presented in Fig. 3.

In the first line of the algorithm, we sort all nodes according to their distances to the root node in decreasing order. This ensures that child nodes will be computed before their parents so that Theorems 1 to 3 can be correctly applied. The execution time of this step is $O(n \log n)$. The loop in line 2 iterates over every node in the system. Note that there are at most n values on the maximum latency to some node i. Thus, for each leaf node, it takes $O(n^2)$ execution time in line 4. For an intermediate node that has k child nodes, it takes $O(n^3)$ execution time in line 9, and iterates $k-1$ times in line 8. This results in $O(kn^3)$ execution time for lines 8 to 10. Lines 11 to 16 also take $O(n^2)$ execution time. Consequently, the complexity of lines 3 to 16 is $O(kn^3)$ and the complexity of the whole algorithm is $O(n^4)$, where n is the number of nodes in the Grid system. The complexity can be further reduced to $O(p^2n^2)$, where p is the minimum number of servers, by computing $\omega(i, m, d, t)$ incrementally from $m = 0$ to $m = p$.

Algorithm Minimum_Leakage

Input: 1. the arrival rate λ_i for all leaf nodes.
2. the service rate μ_i for all intermediate nodes.
3. the network latency d_{ji}
4. the service quality requirement t.

Output: the minimum arrival rate $\omega(i, m, d, t)$ for $0 \leq i, m \leq n$.

Procedure:

sort all nodes according to their distance to the root node in decreasing order.
for each node i do
  if node i is a leaf node then
    compute $\omega(i, m, d, t) = \lambda_i$ for $0 \leq m \leq n$
  else
    let the child nodes of node i be nodes $j_0, \ldots, j_{k-1}$
    compute $\lambda_0(i, m, d, t) = \omega(j_0, m, d - d_{j_0 i}, t)$, $0 \leq m \leq n$
    for q from 1 to $k - 1$ do
      $\lambda_q(i, m, d, t) = min_{0 \leq r \leq m}\{\lambda_{q-1}(i, r, d, t) + \omega(j_q, m - r, d - d_{j_q i}, t)\}$, $0 \leq m \leq n$
    endfor
    for m from 0 to n do
      if exists d', $0 \leq d' \leq t$, such that $\lambda_{k-1}(i, m - 1, d', t) + 1/(t - d') \leq \mu_i$
        $\omega(i, m, d, t) = 0$
      else
        $\omega(i, m, d, t) = \lambda_{k-1}(i, m, d, t)$
    endfor
  endif
endfor

Fig. 3. An optimal algorithm for the minimum server placement problem.

4 The Optimal Service Quality Problem

In this section, we try to place a given number of servers appropriately so that the maximum expected response time of servers is minimized. We call this the *optimal service quality problem.*

Definition 5. *Given the network topology, request arrival rates, service rates and network latencies of links, the optimal service quality problem aims at placing a given number of I/O servers so that the maximum expected response time of the Grid system is minimized.*

Let m be the number of servers to be placed. We aim to place m servers such that the maximum expected response time is minimized. To achieve this goal, we can perform a binary search on the service quality requirement t. Given a service quality requirement t, we can use the dynamic programming algorithm described in Section 3 to find an optimal server placement such that the maximum expected response time of servers is less or eqaul to t. Let the minimum number of servers be m'. If $m' > m$, according to Corollary 1, we cannot find a placement of m servers whose maximum expected response time is less than or equal to t. Therefore, when $m' > m$, we need to increase t to find a server placement with m servers and, when $m' < m$, we may decrease t to find if a better server placement exists.

Before applying a binary search, we have to determine an upper bound and a lower bound. It is rather easy to get an upper bound and a lower bound on the maximum expected response time. We can use $1/(\mu_{max} - \lambda_{min})$ as a proper lower bound, where μ_{max} is the maximum server capability of servers and λ_{min} is the minimum requests of clients. A upper bound can be computed by the following steps. First, we set t to a sufficient large value and find a server placement. According to Corollary 1, the number of used servers must be smaller than or equal to m. Then we can use the maximum expected response time of servers as a proper upper bound. Next, we can combine a binary search of the maximum expected response time and the dynamic programming algorithm for the minimum server placement problem to find the optimal value of the maximum expected response time. Because the lower bound and the upper bound of the binary search are both functions of the input parameters, the algorithm is strongly polynomial.

5 Experimental Results

In this section we conduct several experiments to evaluate the proposed algorithms. Test cases are generated based on the proposed Grid model. The height of each case is at most 8. Each node has at most 4 children. The number of nodes in each test case is between 1250 and 1500. The request arrival rates for the leaf nodes and the service rates for intermediate nodes are generated from a uniform distribution. There are four testing groups. Each group has a different range of network latencies: 0.00005∼0.00015, 0.0005∼0.0015, 0.005∼0.015, and 0.05∼0.15. We will refer them as group 1, 2, 3 and 4, respectively. There are 1000 test cases in each group. Table 1 shows the summary of these parameters.

Table 1. Parameters of experiments

Parameter	Description
Height of tree	≤ 8
Number of child nodes	≤ 4
Number of nodes in each case	≈ 1300
Range of arrival rates	1∼4
Range of service rates	50∼350
Range of network latencies	0.00005∼0.00015, 0.0005∼0.0015, 0.005∼0.015 and 0.05∼0.15

First, the experiments for the minimum server placement problem are conducted. We use a greedy heuristic algorithm as a performance comparison with our dynamic programming algorithm since, to the best of our knowledge, there are no similar studies on QoS server placement problems that both consider the server's capacity and the network latency. The Greedy algorithm works as follows: in each iteration, it first selects all candidate servers that can satisfy the service quality requirement t, i.e., the expected response time of requests it served will less than t. Then it selects a site who has the maximum arrival rate of I/O requests. The process is repeated until all requests are served.

As the experiments with the four testing groups show similar results , we will present only the result with group 4. The performance metric is the difference in the number of servers used by Greedy and DP, i.e., the extra number of servers used by Greedy. The experimental results for the minimum server placement problem is shown in Fig. 4. The vertical axis shows the number of test cases, while the horizontal axis shows the difference in the number of servers used by these two algorithms.

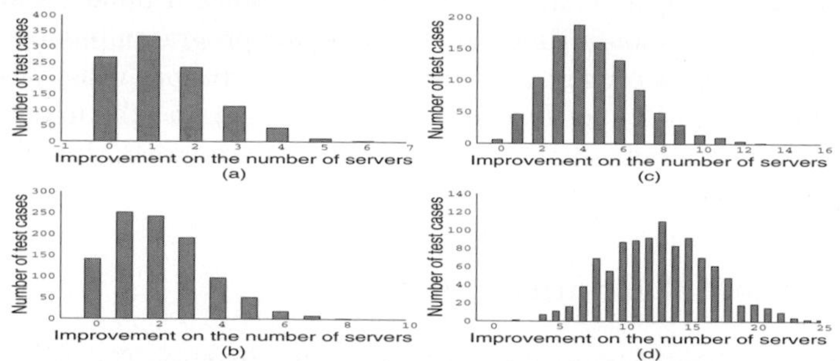

Fig. 4. Performance comparison for the minimum server problem. (a), (b), (c) and (d) are experimental results when t is set to 1, 0.75, 0.6 and 0.45 respectively.

In Fig. 4, it is clear that the difference in the number of servers used becomes significant as t decreases, i.e., as the service quality requirement becomes crucial. In Fig. 4(a), Greedy generates optimal solutions in 23.9% of the test cases and, in 84.4% of the test cases, the differences are between 0 and 2. However, in Fig. 4(d), Greedy generates no optimal solution and over 80% of test cases, the differences are between 10 and 28 when t is set to 0.45. Although Greedy is rather fast and easy to implement, the results show that it cannot generate acceptable solutions when the service quality requirement becomes crucial.

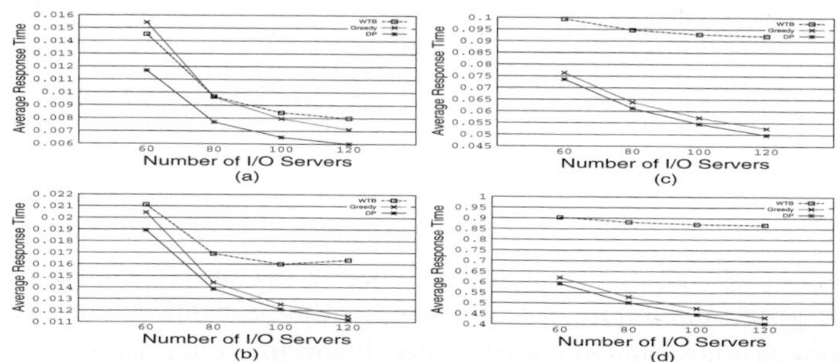

Fig. 5. Performance comparison for the optimal service quality problem. (a), (b), (c) and (d) are experimental results for group 1, 2, 3, and 4 respectively.

We next conduct the following experiments for the optimal service quality problem. We compare three algorithms: (1) the DP algorithm combined a binary search as described in Section 4, (2) the Greedy algorithm combined a binary search and (3) a waiting-time based(WTB) server placement algorithm described in [12]. Note that there is no guarantee of performance for the Greedy algorithm combined a binary search since the Greedy algorithm does not have the property of Corollary 1. A binary search is only used to adjust t such that Greedy can generate a placement with m servers. The WTB algotithm is similar to the algorithm described in Section 4 except it only tries to minimize the maximum waiting time of servers.

In the experiments, for each group of test cases, we use 4 different values of server numbers m: 60, 80, 100 and 120. The performance metric is the average of maximum expected response times of test cases. For each test case, there will be a maximum expected response time among those m servers. We use the average of maximum expected response times in 1000 test cases as our performance metric. The experimental results are shown in Fig. 5. The vertical axis shows the average expected response time, while the horizontal axis shows the number of servers m.

In Fig. 5, it is clear that the difference in performance between DP and WTB becomes larger as the network latency increases. When the network latency is small with respect to the server's waiting time, the difference of the average expected response time is less significant. However, as the network latency increases, the difference becomes larger because the expected response time is dominated by the network latency and WTB does not take network latencies into consideration. This result explains the advantage of DP algorithm: it takes both the server's waiting time and the network latency into consideration. Thus, DP can always get the best performance no matter the expected response time is dominated by either server's waiting time as the result shown in Fig. 5(a) or the network latency as the result shown in Fig. 5(d).

In Fig. 5(c) and 5(d), Greedy has a good performance when the number of I/O servers increases and the network latency dominates the expected response time. This is mainly due to the power of the binary search. However, as the expected waiting time dominates the expected response time, Greedy performs worse than WTB as shown in Fig. 5(a). Therefore, Greedy does not perform well in all kind of situations like DP does.

6 Conclusions

In this paper, we focus on two QoS I/O server placement problems in Data Grid environments. We consider the minimum server placement problem which asks how to place the minimum number of servers that meet both the constrains on servers' capabilities and the service quality requirement. Instead of using a heuristic approach, we propose an optimal algorithm based on dynamic programming as a solution to this problem.

The optimal service quality problem is also considered, which tries to place a given number of servers appropriately so that the maximum expected response time of servers can be minimized. By combining the dynamic programming algorithm with a binary search on the service quality requirement, we can find an optimal server placement. Several experiments are also conducted, whose results clearly show the improvement on the number of servers and the maximum expected response time compared with other algorithms.

Acknowledgments

The authors acknowledge the National Center for High-performance Computing in providing resources under the national project, "Taiwan Knowledge Innovation National Grid". This research is supported in part by the National Science Council, Taiwan, under Grant NSC NSC95-2221-E-001-002.

References

1. Johnston, W.E.: Computational and data Grids in large-scale science and engineering. Future Generation Computer Systems. **18**(8) (2002) 1085–1100
2. Grid Physics Network (GriphyN). (http://www.griphyn.org)
3. TeraGrid. (http://www.teragrid.org)
4. Wang, C.M., Hsu, C.C., Chen, H.M., Wu, J.J.: Efficient multi-source data transfer in data grids. In: CCGRID '06. (2006) 421–424
5. Lamehamedi, H., Shentu, Z., Szymanski, B.K., Deelman, E.: Simulation of Dynamic Data Replication Strategies in Data Grids. In: IPDPS 2003. (2003) 100
6. Deris, M.M., Abawajy, J.H., Suzuri, H.M.: An efficient replicated data access approach for large-scale distributed systems. In: CCGRID. (2004) 588–594
7. Hoschek, W., Jaén-Martínez, F.J., Samar, A., Stockinger, H., Stockinger, K.: Data Management in an International Data Grid Project. In: GRID 2000. (2000) 77–90
8. Krishnan, P., Raz, D., Shavitt, Y.: The cache location problem. IEEE/ACM Transactions on Networking **8**(5) (2000) 568–582
9. Ranganathan, K., Foster, I.T.: Identifying Dynamic Replication Strategies for a High-Performance Data Grid. In: GRID 2001. (2001) 75–86
10. Tang, M.X., Xu, M.J.: QoS-aware replica placement for content distribution. IEEE Trans. Parallel Distrib. Syst. **16**(10) (2005) 921–932
11. Wang, H., Liu, P., Wu, J.J.: A QoS-aware heuristic algorithm for replica placement. In: International Conference on Grid Computing. (2006) 96–103
12. Wang, C.M., Hsu, C.C., Liu, P., Chen, H.M., Wu, J.J.: Optimizing server placement in hierarchical grid environments. In: GPC. (2006) 1–11
13. Abawajy, J.H.: Placement of File Replicas in Data Grid Environments. In: International Conference on Computational Science. (2004) 66–73

AHSEN – Autonomic Healing-Based Self Management Engine for Network Management in Hybrid Networks

Junaid Ahsenali Chaudhry and Seungkyu Park

Graduate School of Information and Communication, Ajou University, Woncheon-dong, Paldal-gu, Suwon, 443-749, Korea
{junaid, sparky}@ajou.ac.kr

Abstract. In this paper, we present a novel self-healing engine for autonomic network management. A light weight Self Management Frame (SMF) performs monitoring and optimization functions autonomously and the other self management functions, driven by context, are invoked on demand from the server. The policies are maintained to calculate the trust factor for network entities and those trust factors will be used at the later stages of our project to enforce resource utilization policies. The plug-ins, residing at the server, are used to perform the on-demand management functions not performed by SMF at client side. A Simple Network Management Protocol (SNMP) based monitoring agent is applied that also triggers the local management entities and passes the exceptions to the server which determines the appropriate plug-in. Considering the amount of resources being put into current day management functions and contemporary autonomic management architectures our findings show improvement in certain areas that can go a long way to improve the network performance and resilience.

1 Introduction

As the complexity and size of networks increase so does the costs of network management [1]. The preemptive measures have done little to cut down on network management cost. Hybrid networks cater with high levels of QoS, scalability, and dynamic service delivery requirements. The amplified utilization of hybrid networks i.e. ubiquitous-Zone based (u-Zone) networks has raised the importance of human resources, down-time, and user training costs. The u-Zone networks [3] are the fusion of the cluster of hybrid Mobile Ad-hoc NETworks (MANETs) and high speed mesh network backbones. They provide robust wireless connectivity to heterogeneous wireless devices and take less setup time. The clusters of hybrid networks feature heterogeneity, mobility, dynamic topologies, limited physical security, and limited survivability [2] and the mesh networks provide the high speed feedback to the connected clusters. The applications of MANETs vary in a great range from disaster and emergency response, to entertainment and internet connectivity to mobile users. Ubiquitous networks are metropolitan area networks which cover great distances and provide service to heterogeneous users. In this situation, the network availability is critical for applications running on these networks. This distributed utilization and network coverage requires some effective management framework that could bring

C. Cérin and K.-C. Li (Eds.): GPC 2007, LNCS 4459, pp. 193–203, 2007.

robustness and resilience to the functionality of these networks. A sample u-Zone network scenario is shown in figure 1. There are various clusters of devices that are attached with their gateways and are physically parted but connected with a high speed backbone. The devices can have variable mobility levels and hence can roam among various clusters.

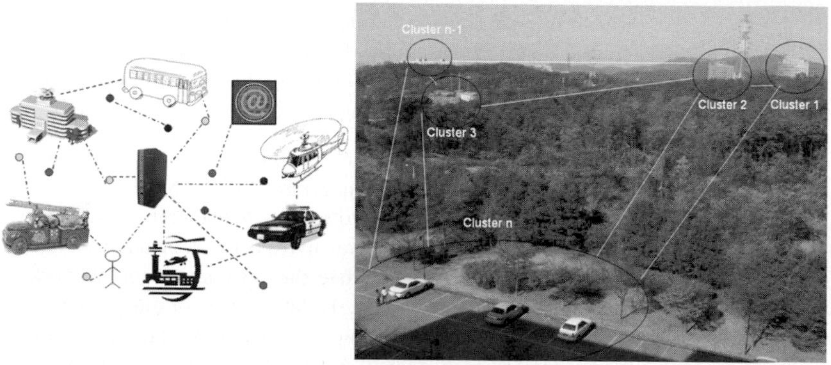

Fig. 1. A Ubiquitous-Zone Based Network

Several network management solutions have been proposed in [3], [4], [5], [6], [7] for wireless sensor networks. The schemes proposed in [4], [5], [6] are confined strictly to their domains i.e. either mesh network or MANETs. The self management architecture proposed in [8] might not be appropriate for thin clients. The following questions rise while considering the self management architecture proposed in [8] for MANETs.

1. If self healing is one of the FCAPS functions[1] (Fault, Configuration, Accounting, Performance, Security) then what is the physical location of self healing functions?
2. How does the control, information etc flow from one function to another?
3. If self healing is a fault removing function, then what does the Fault Management function do?
4. Are these sub-functions functionally independent? If so, then there is evidence of significant redundancy and if not then how can self healing be thought of, as an independent entity? In other words, what is the true functionality definition of self healing?

There has not been a considerable amount of work published on self management of u-Zone networks. In [3] the authors present unique management architecture for u-Zone networks. The questions posted above motivates us to propose a flexible self healing architecture [9] that can not only define the individual functionality of the participating management functions but can also be lightweight for different nodes. In

[1] FCAPS is the ISO Telecommunications Management Network model and framework for network management.

this paper, we propose flexible autonomic self management architecture for u-Zone networks. We propose that the Context Awareness and Self Optimization should be '*always-on*' management functions and the rest should be 'on-demand' functions e.g. Self Configuration, Fault Management etc. This way we split the information flow between nodes and servers into two categories 1) service flow: containing service information and its contents 2) Management plug-in flow: the plug-in(s) delivered to remote user on request. We implement our scheme and compare it with the contemporary architectures.

The proposed scheme follows in section 2. The implementation details are furnished in section 3. In section 4 we compare our scheme with some of the contemporary solutions proposed. This paper ends with a conclusion and discussion of future work.

2 Related Work

A considerable amount of research has been done in the area of network management and thus it is a mature research area. With the advent of Autonomic Computing (AC), network management has acquired a new dimension. Since then there has not been a lot of work done for ubiquitous autonomic network management. Although network management has existed for some time, not much literature has been published on the subject of autonomic self management in hybrid networks especially on ubiquitous zone based networks. In this section we compare our research with the related work. The Robust Self-configuring Embedded Systems (RoSES) project [13] aims to target the management faults using self configuration. It uses graceful degradation as means to achieve dependable systems.

In [14] the authors propose that there are certain faults that can not be removed through configuration of the system, which means that RoSES does not fulfill the definition of self management proposed in [18]. The AMUN is an autonomic middleware that deals with intra-cluster communication issues better than RoSES with higher support for multi-application environments. Both architectures rely mainly on regressive configuration and do not address the issues such as higher traffic load leading to management framework failure, link level management, and framework synchronization.

The AMUSE [15] is an autonomic management architecture proposed in the domain of e-health. The peer-to-peer communication starts once the node enters into a self-managed cluster. But publish-subscribe services can create serious issues like service consistency, synchronization and coordination as discussed in [16]. An Agent-based Middleware for Context-aware Ubiquitous Services proposed in [16] gives a more distinct hierarchy for the management framework to define the boundaries and performance optics but the payload attached with agents may not work for weaker nodes this can be a big drawback in a heterogeneous environment.

The HYWINMARC [3] is novel autonomic network management architecture that targets ubiquitous zone based networks. It aims at managing the hybrid clusters supported by a high speed mesh backbone. The HYWINMARC uses cluster heads to manage the clusters at local level but does not explain the criteria of their selection. Moreover the Mobile Code Execution Environment (MCEE) and use of intelligent agents can give similar results as discussed above in the case of [16] and [17]. To enforce management at local level, the participating nodes should have some management liberty. However HYWINMARC fails to answer the questions raised in the previous section. We compare the architectures discussed in this section in a table to observe their efficacy.

In table 1 we compare AHSEN with other architectures. The comparison reveals that the entity profiling, functional classification of self management entities at implementation level, and assurance of the functional compliance is not provided in the schemes proposed. In very dynamic hybrid networks these functionalities go a long way in improving the effectiveness of the self management system implemented.

Table 1. The comparison table

	RoSES	AMUN	AMUSE	HYWINMARC	AHSEN
Fault Detection	State variable staleness	Traffic monitoring	Notification to event bus	-	Detected through SNMP interrupt messages.
Fault Response	Reconfigure software, based on data & control flow graphs	Event dispatcher notifies to the Autonomic Manager	Policy-based	Agent search and execution	Two stepped: the target management service is decided either locally or globally
Recovery	Reconfigure and reboot	Configuration-based recovery	Policy-based	Agent initiate policy upgrade	Fault-based recovery
Assurance	Future work	Transport layer level assurance	-	Future work	Trust-based (components assigned trust factors)
System Self-Knowledge	System knows the potential point of failures	Node-based local knowledge management	Component-based	Partial	Device profiling creates high level of self knowledge
Management Functions Classification	No	No	Initiated by Self Managed Cell (SMC), policy-based	Independent	Interdependent, hierarchical, can be applied concurrently
Mobile Code Management	No	n/a, JXTA based p2p reconfiguration service	No	Agent-based but no terminal tracking of agent's TTL	End to End TTL for management functions and services
Service Repository	No	Yes, managed by service provider	Group-based service delivery	Yes, managed by service provider	Yes, managed by service provider
Monitoring and Profiling	Constant monitoring but no profiling	Constant monitoring but no profiling	Optional, fault-based	Optional, fault-based, no profiling	Constant

3 Proposed Architecture

3.1 Software Architecture

In hybrid wireless networks, there are many different kinds of devices attached with the network. They vary from each other in the bases of their power, performance etc.

One of the characteristics not present in the related literature is the separate classification of the client and the gateway architectures. Figure 2 shows the client and gateway self-management software architectures.

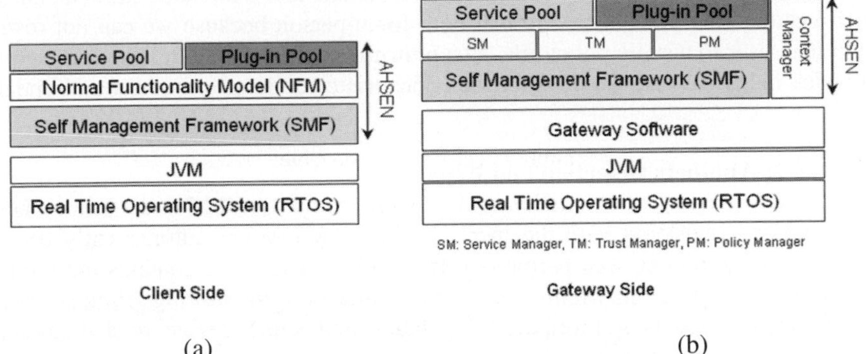

Fig. 2. The AHSEN architectures for client (a) and gateway (b)

The Normal Functionality Model (NFM) is a device dependent ontology that is downloaded on the device at network configuration level. It provides a mobile user with an initial default profile at gateway level and device level functionality control at user level. It contains the normal range of functional parameters of the device, services environment and network which allows the prompt anomaly detection.

There are two kinds of Self Management Frameworks (SMFs) one for clients and one for gateways. The SMF at client end constantly *traps* the user activities and sends them to the SMF at the gateway. The SMF at the gateway directs the *trap* requests to the context manager who updates the related profile of the user. The changes in service pool, Trust Manager (TM), and Policy Manger (PM) are reported to the context manager. The context manager consists of the Lightweight Directory Access Protocol (LDAP) directory that saves sessions after regular intervals in the gateway directory. LDAP directory servers store their information hierarchically. The hierarchy provides a method for logically grouping (and sub grouping) certain items together. It provides scalability, security and resolves many data integrity issues.

The Policy Manager (PM) and Service Manager (SM) follow the same registry based approach to enlist their resources. The presence of NFM provides the decision based reporting unlike ever-present SNMP. The Trust Manager uses the reputation-based trust management scheme in public key certificates [10]. The trust is typically decided on trustee's reputation. The trust based access relies on "dynamic values", assigned to each client, to mitigate risks involved in interacting and collaborating with unknown and potentially malicious users.

3.2 Operational Details

In this section we describe the operational details of the architecture proposed in this paper through simple scenarios.

Scenario 1: Initial Mobile Node Configuration
When a mobile user enters into the area under the influence of a gateway, it sends a *join* request to the gateway. The *join* message contains node specification, connection type, previous session reference etc. After the *join* request is processed by the gateway, the SMF and NFM is downloaded to the client and the node starts its normal functionality. The NFM is an optional item for u-person because we can not restrict the human user to a static policy file. The returning node presents its previous *session ID* which helps the gateway to offer the appropriate services to the user and updated NFM.

Scenario 2: Anomaly Detection and Reporting
We use the role based functionality model by enforcing the NFM at the joining node. The processes registered with the local operating system are automatically trusted. The network operations seek permission from NFM. The NFM contains the security certificate generating algorithms, network connection monitoring entities (in/out bound), trust based peer level access policies and some device related anomaly solutions i.e. related plug-ins.

Scenario 3: Normal State Restoration
The SMF at gateway predicts the relevant plug-in needed at the requesting node and notifies the plug-in manager along with the certificates to communicate with the faulty node. The plug-in manager *talks* with node and provides the plug-ins mentioned by the SMF. Once a plug-in finishes its operation, the node context is provided to the SMF at the gateway which analyzes the context and specifies another plug-in (if needed). This feed back loop continues until the normal status of the node is restored.

3.3 Self Management Framework

Although there is not much published work on self management in hybrid networks, Shafique et. al. [3] proposes an autonomic self management framework for hybrid networks. Our approach is different from their work in basic understanding of the functionality of self management functions. We argue that the self management functions do not stem from one main set rather they are categorized in such a way that they form on-demand functions and some functions are always-on/pervasive functions [11]. Figure 3 gives a clearer description.

As shown in figure 3, we place self awareness and self optimization in the always-on category and the others as on-demand functions. This approach is very useful in hybrid environments where there are clients of various battery and computing powers. The NFM regulates the usage of self management functions according to computing ability of the client. This gives the client local self management. The management services come in the form of plug-ins registered in the plug-in manager present on the gateway. A SOAP request carries Simple Object Access Protocol-Remote Procedure Call (SOAP-RPC) and the latest node context to the SMF located on the gateway which decides the anomaly type and suggests the appropriate plug-in. The SOAP-RPC requests are considered when the SMF at gateways polls for the nodes. The frequency of the poll depends upon the network availability and traffic flux.

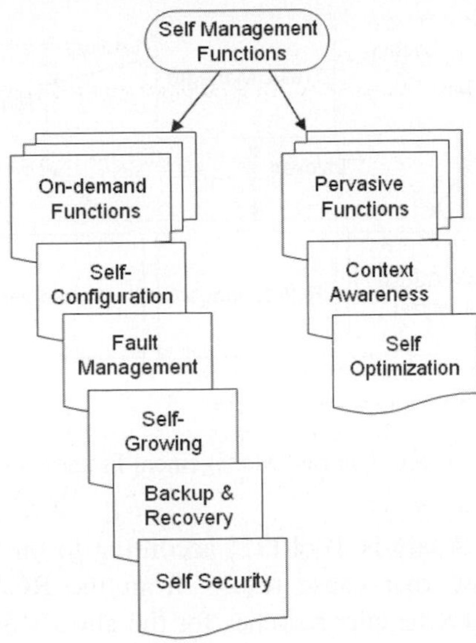

Fig. 3. The proposed Classification of Self Management Functions

The Self Management Framework (SMF) consists of a Traffic Manager that redirects the traffic to all parts of SMF. As proposed in [18] the faults can be single root-cause based or multiple root-causes based. We consider this scenario and classify a Root Cause Analyzer (RCA) that checks the root cause of failure through the algorithms proposed in [19]. After identifying the root causes, the Root Cause Fragmentation Manager (RCF manager) looks up for the candidate plug-ins as solution. The RCF manager also delegates the candidate plug-ins as possible replacement of the most appropriate. The scheduler schedules the service delivery mechanism as proposed in [20]. The processed fault signatures are stored in signature repository for future utilization. The plug-in manager is a directory service for maintaining the latest plug-in context. This directory service is not present at the client level.

In [3] the authors classify self management into individual functions and react to the anomaly detected through SNMP messages. The clear demarcation of *self-** functions is absent in modern day systems as there is no taxonomy done for various fault types. This is one of the main reasons why we prefer component integration over conventional high granularity modules for self management [12]. A detailed architecture of the Self Management Framework (SMF) is shown in figure 4.

The Root Cause Analyzer plays the central part in problem detection phase of self healing. The State Transition Analysis based approaches [21] might not be appropriate as Hidden Markov Models (HMMs) take long training time along with their 'exhaustive' system resources utilization. The profile based Root Cause Detection might not be appropriate mainly because the domain of errors expected is very wide [22], [23], [24]. We use the meta-data obtained from NFM to trigger Finite State Automata (FSA) series present at root cause analyzer. In future we plan to

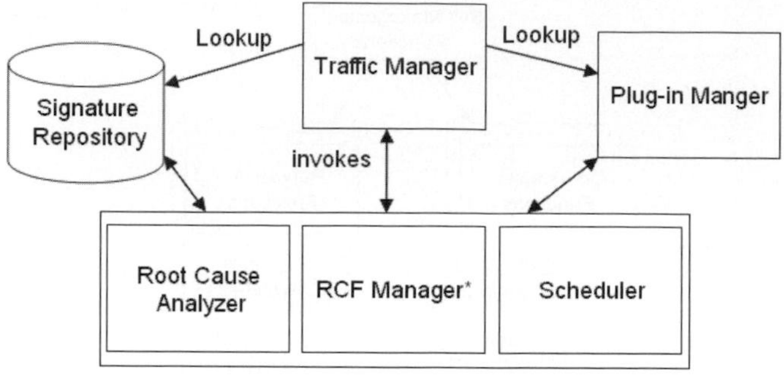

Fig. 4. Architecture of Self Management Framework (SMF)

modify State Transition Analysis Tool [21] according to on fault analysis domains [25]. After analyzing the root cause results from the RCA, the RCF manager, Signature Repository and Scheduler searches for the already developed solutions, for a particular fault if not, it arranges a time slot based scheduler as proposed in [26] for plug-ins. The traffic manager directs the traffic towards different parts of AHSEN.

4 Implementation Details

In order to verify our scheme, we have implemented the design using Java Enterprise Edition (Java EE) technologies. We used the template mechanism, nested classes and parameter based system call and inheritance in our software prototype. We define the properties of types of entities involved into various classes i.e. the mobile nodes differ from each other on many bases power, mobility rates, speed, energy levels, and hierarchical position in the cluster. We categorize the cluster headers into a separate class derived from the base class *mobnd*. Due to their unique functionality, the backbone servers are defined into a different class. The devices can be connected to the wireless gateway through Wireless LAN interface and sensor nodes are connected through miscellaneous interfaces i.e. blue tooth, 802.1.5 etc. The link type is also defined into a separate class names *lnktyp*. The SMF is defined as a separate base class with various entities i.e. RCF Manager, root cause analyzer, etc as independent classes. A log service is used to keep track of instances and fault flow. The Java Naming and Directory Interface (JNDI) provides unified interface to multiple naming and directory services. We use JNDI as a directory service in our architecture.

The scenario mentioned above was developed for a past project but we consider that it can provide good evaluation apparatus for testing the healing engine proposed in this paper. The current prototype can handle very limited number of clusters and mobile nodes. We plan to improve the system in future work. We defined two clusters with 8 mobile nodes. Each cluster contains two cluster headers and 6 child nodes. At first, we run our system without faulty nodes. After that in order to test the performance of our system, we introduce a malicious node in each cluster. The activities of that malicious node result into identifiable fault signatures that are detected and removed by the SMF present at the gateway. As shown in figure 5 and figure 6, the Transactions Per Second (TPS) decreases with increase in time as the malicious node is introduced. We observe that a considerable decrease in transactions is because every time a request times out, the SMF reacts and provides the healing policies to cover the interruption in service delivery.

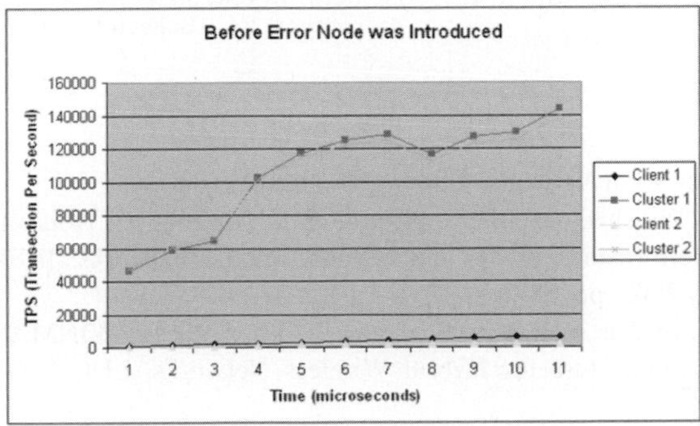

Fig. 5. Simulation Results of the scenario before the error node was introduced

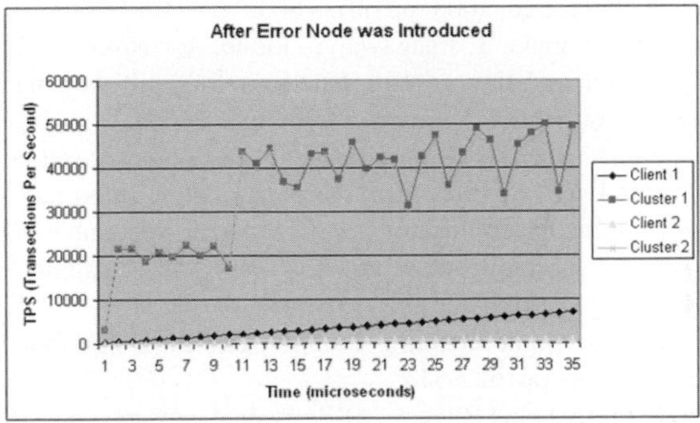

Fig. 6. Simulation Results of the scenario after the error node was introduced

5 Concluding Remarks

In this paper we present a trust based autonomic network management framework using self healing techniques. We re-categorize the self management functions and dissolve the mapping created between errors and self management functions in [3]. We offer the healing solutions in the form of atomic plug-ins that can either work independently and atomically or they can be meshed into a composed file. The individual self management at the node level is done by NFM which sends the exceptions to the SMF at gateway. The SMF at gateway is the entity that decides the plug-in selection for an anomaly detected at the client level. The entity profiling enables the trust calculation against every node which allows a user to use certain privileged services. Some scenarios are described for better understanding. We share our implementation experience and compare our work with cotemporary work.

In the scheme proposed in this research article we have put an effort to contour the trust in device profiles but we have not studied effect on the trust of a migrating node. Although, in our previous research, we studied the context migration from one cluster to another we will try to study the relationship between the two research approaches. Moreover we plan to study the signature independent anomaly identification at NFM level. We also plan to implement the post-healing test strategy.

References

1. Firetide: Instant Mesh Networks: http://www.firetide.com.
2. Doufexi A., Tameh E., Nix A., Armour S., Molina, A.: Hotspot wireless LANs to enhance the performance of 3G and beyond cellular networks. IEEE Communications Magazine, July 2003, pp. 58- 65.
3. Chaudhry S.A., Akbar A.H., Kim K., Hong S., Yoon W.: HYWINMARC: An Autonomic Management Architecture for Hybrid Wireless Networks. EUC Workshops 2006: 193-202.
4. Burke J. R.: Network Management. Concepts and Practice: A Hands-on Approach. Pearson Education, Inc., 2004.
5. Minseok O.: Network management agent allocation scheme in mesh networks. IEEE Communications Letters, Dec. 2003, pp.601 – 603.
6. Kishi, Y. Tabata, K. Kitahara, T. Imagawa, Y. Idoue, A. Nomoto, S.: Implementation of the integrated network and link control functions for multi-hop mesh networks. IEEE Radio and Wireless Conference, September 2004, pp. 43- 46.
7. Shi Y., Gao D., Pan J., Shen P.: A mobile agent- and policy-based network management architecture. Proceedings of the Fifth International Conference on Computational Intelligence and Multimedia Applications (ICCIMA’03), September 2003, pp. 177-181.
8. IBM white paper, Autonomic Computing: Enabling Self-Managing Solutions, SOA and Autonomic Computing December 2005.
9. Chaudhry J. A., Park S.: Some Enabling Technologies for Ubiquitous Systems, Journal of Computer Science, 2006, pp. 627-633.
10. Garfinkel S.: PGP: Pretty Good Privacy. O’Reily & Associates Inc., 1995.
11. Chaudhry J. A., and Park S.: Using Artificial Immune Systems for Self Healing in Hybrid Networks", To appear in Encyclopedia of Multimedia Technology and Networking, Idea Group Inc., 2006.
12. Ma J., Zhao Q., Chaudhary V., Cheng J., Yang L. T., Huang H., and Jin Q.: Ubisafe Computing: Vision and Challenges (I). Springer LNCS Vol.4158, Proc. of ATC-06, 2006, pp. 386-397.
13. Shelton, C. & Koopman, P.: Improving System Dependability with Alternative Functionality. Proceedings of the 2004 International Conference on Dependable Systems and Networks (DSN'04), June 2004, pp. 295.
14. Morikawa, H.: The design and implementation of context-aware services. International Symposium on Applications and the Internet Workshops (SAINT-W'04), 2004, pp. 293 – 298.
15. Strowes S., Badr N., Dulay N., Heeps S., Lupu E., Sloman M., Sventek J.: An Event Service Supporting Autonomic Management of Ubiquitous Systems for e-Health. 26th IEEE International Conference on Distributed Computing Systems Workshops 2006. (ICDCS-w'06), pp. 22-22.

16. Chaudhry J. A., Park S.: A Novel Autonomic Rapid Application Composition Scheme for Ubiquitous Systems. The 3rd International Conference on Autonomic and Trusted Computing (ATC-06), September 2006, pp. 48-56.
17. Trumler W., Petzold J., Bagci J., Ungerer T.: AMUN – Autonomic Middleware for Ubiquitious eNvironments Applied to the Smart Doorplate Project. International Conference on Autonomic Computing (ICAC-04), May 2004, pp. 274-275.
18. Gao, J., Kar, G., Kermani, P.,: Approaches to building self healing systems using dependency analysis. IEEE/IFIP Network Operations and Management Symposium 2004 (NOMS'04), April 2004, pp. 119-132.
19. Chaudhry J. A., Park S.: On Seamless Service Delivery", The 2nd International Conference on Natural Computation (ICNC'06) and the 3rd International Conference on Fuzzy Systems and Knowledge Discovery (FSKD'06) , September 2006, pp. 253-261.
20. Ilgun, K., Kemmerer R.A., Porras P.A.,: State transition analysis: a rule-based intrusion detection approach, IEEE Transactions on Software Engineering, March 1989, pp.181-199.
21. Lunt T. F.: Real-time intrusion detection. Thirty-Fourth IEEE Computer Society International Conference: Intellectual Leverage, Digest of Papers (COMPCON Spring '89.), March 1989, pp. 348-353.
22. Lunt T.F., Jagannathan R.: A prototype real-time intrusion-detection expert system. Proceedings of IEEE Symposium on Security and Privacy 1988, Apr 1988, pp. 59-66.
23. Lunt T.F., Tamaru A., Gilham F., Jagannathan R., Neumann P.G., Jalali C.: IDES: a progress report [Intrusion-Detection Expert System]. Proceedings of the Sixth Annual Computer Security Applications Conference 1990, Dec 1990, pp.273-285.
24. Radosavac, S., Seamon, K., Baras, J.S.: Short Paper: bufSTAT - a tool for early detection and classification of buffer overflow attacks. First International Conference on Security and Privacy for Emerging Areas in Communications Networks 2005 (SecureComm 2005), Sept. 2005, pp. 231- 233.

Development of a GT4-Based Resource Broker Service: An Application to On-Demand Weather and Marine Forecasting

R. Montella

Dept. of Applied Science, University of Naples "Parthenope" – Italy

Abstract. The discovery and selection of needed resources, taking into account optimization criteria, local policies, computing and storage availability, resource reservations, and grid dynamics, is a technological challenge in the emerging technology of grid computing.

The Condor Project's ClassAd language is commonly adopted as a "*lingua franca*" for describing grid resources, but Condor itself does not make extensive use of Web Services. In contrast, the strongly service-oriented Globus Toolkit is implemented using the web services resource framework, and offers basic services for job submission, data replica and location, reliable file transfers and resource indexing, but does not provide a resource broker and matchmaking service.

In this paper we describe the development of a Resource Broker Service based on the Web Services technology offered by the Globus Toolkit version 4 (GT4). We implement a fully configurable and customizable matchmaking algorithm within a framework that allows users to direct complex queries to the GT4 index service and thus discover any published resource. The matchmaking algorithm supports both the native simple query form and the Condor ClassAd notation. We achieve this flexibility via a matchmaking API java class framework implemented on the extensible GT4 index service, which maps queries over ClassAds in a customizable fashion.

We show an example of the proposed grid application, namely an on demand weather and marine forecasting system. This system implements a Job Flow Scheduler and a Job Flow Description Language in order to access and exploit shared and distributed observations, model software, and 2D/3D graphical rendering resources. The system combines GT4 components and our Job Flow Scheduler and Resource Broker services to provide a fully grid-aware system.

1 Introduction

Our proposed grid infrastructure is based on the Globus Toolkit [1] version 4.x (GT4) middleware, developed within the Globus Alliance, a consortium of institutions from academia, government, and industry. We choose GT4 because it exposes its features, including service persistence, state and stateless behavior, event notification, data element management and index services, via the web services resource framework (WSRF).

The brokering service that we have developed is responsible for interpreting requests and enforcing virtual organization policies on resource access, hiding many

C. Cérin and K.-C. Li (Eds.): GPC 2007, LNCS 4459, pp. 204–217, 2007.

details involved in locating suitable resources. Resources register themselves to the resource broker, by performing an availability advertisement inside the virtual organization index [4]. These entities are classified as resource producers using many advertisement techniques, languages and interfaces. Resource are often discovered and collected by means of a performance monitor system and are mapped in a standard and well known description language [5] such as the Condor [8] ClassAd [9]. Ideally, the entire resource broking process can be divided into two parts. First, a matchmaking algorithm finds a set of matching resources using specific criteria such as "all submission services available on computing elements with at least 16 nodes using the PBS local scheduler and where the MM5 [3] weather forecast model is installed." Then, an optimization algorithm is used to select the best available resource among the elements [6]. Usually, the broker returns a match by pointing the consumer directly to the selected resource, after which the consumer contacts the resource producer. Alternatively, the client may still use the resource broker as an intermediary. When the resource broker selects a resource, the resource is tagged as claimed in order to prevent the selection of the same resource by another query with the same request. The resource will be unclaimed automatically when the resource broker catalogue is refreshed reflecting the resource state change [10].

In this scenario, the resource broker service is a key element of grid-aware applications development. Thus, users can totally ignore where their data are processed and stored, because the application workflow reacts to the dynamic nature of the grid, adapting automatically to the resource request and allocation according to grid health and status.

The allocation and scheduling of applications on a set of heterogeneous, dynamically changing resources is a complex problem without an efficient solution for every grid computing system. Actually, the application scenario and the involved resources influence the implemented scheduler and resource broker system while both the implicit complexity and the dynamic nature of the grid do not permit an efficient and effective static resource allocation.

Our demo applications are based on the use of software for the numerical simulation in environmental science, and are built and developed using a grid computing based virtual laboratory [11]. Weather and marine forecasts models need high performance parallel computing platforms, to ensure an effective solution and grid computing is a key technology, allowing the use of inhomogeneous and geographically-spread computational resources, shared across virtual organization. The resource broker service is the critical component to transform the grid computing environment in a naturally used operational reality. The buildup of grid-aware environmental science applications is a "grand challenge" for both computer and environmental scientists, hence on-demand weather forecast is used by domain experts, common people, amateur and enthusiasts sailing racers.

In this paper we describe the implementation of a GT4-based Resource Broker Service and the application of this component to a grid-aware dynamic application, developed using our grid based virtual laboratory tools. The resource broker architecture and design is described in the section 2, while in sections 3 and 4 we give a short description of the native matchmaking algorithm and of the interface to the Condor ClassAd querying features. In section 5, we show how all these components work together in an on-demand weather and marine forecasting application. The final section contains concluding remarks and information about plans for future work.

2 The Resource Broker Architecture and Design

Our resource brokering system, leveraging on a 2-phase commit approach, enables users to query a specified virtual organization index service for a specific resource, and then mediates between the resource consumer and the resource producer(s) that manage the resources of interest. Resources are represented by web services that provide access to grid features such as job submission, implemented by the Grid Resource Allocation Manager (GRAM) service and the file transfer feature, implemented by the Reliable File Transfer (RFT) service [2].

The sequence begins when the Resource Broker service is loaded into the GT4 Web Services container to create an instance of a Resource Home component. The Resource Home invokes the Resource initialization, triggering the creation of the matchmaking environment and collecting the grid-distributed published resources using the index service. The collector is a software component living inside the matchmaker environment managing the lifetime of the local resource index. The collector processes query results in order to evaluate and aggregate properties, map one or more properties to new ones, and store the result(s) in a local data structure ready to be interrogated by the requesting resource consumer.

The collector is a key component of the resource broker. Thus, we provide a fully documented API to extend and customize its behavior. In the implementation, a generic collector performs a query to the GT4 Monitor Discovery Service (MDS) [7] to identify all returned elements where the local name is "Entry." Element properties are parsed and stored in a format suitable for the resource brokering algorithm. The end point reference of each entry is retrieved to obtain the host name from which the resource is available. This step is needed because the collected properties are stored in a hostname-oriented form, more convenient for the matchmaking instead of the resource-oriented form published by the index service. In this way, each grid element is characterized by a collection of typed name/value properties.

Each entry has an aggregator content used to access the aggregator data. In the case of the ManagedJobFactorySystem, the aggregator data contains a reference to a GLUECE Useful Resource Property data type, where information about the grid element is stored by the MDS data provider interfaced to a monitor system such as Ganglia [13]. The collector navigates through the hierarchically organized properties performing aggregation in the case of clusters where master/nodes relationships are solved. A property builder helper component is used to perform this task, analyzing the stored data and producing numeric properties concerning hosts, clusters and nodes. In the collecting process new properties may be added to provide a better representation of resources available on grid elements.

A configurable property mapping component is used by the collector to perform some properties processing such as lookup: the value of a resource is extracted from a lookup table using another resource value as key; ranging: the resource value is evaluated using a step function defined using intervals; addition: a resource value is retrieved using and external component and added to the resource set; averaging: the value of a resource is calculated using the mean value of other resources.

The use of the property mapping component is needed in order to aggregate or better define resources from the semantic point of view: in the resource broker native representation, the available memory on a host is "MainMemory.RAMAvailable.Host," while usually the ClassAd uses the simple "Memory" notation, hence a copy operation between two properties is needed. A less trivial use of the property mapping tool is done by evaluating the Status property: there is no Status property definition in the GLUECE Useful Resource Property, while ProcessorLoad information are available. The property mapping algorithm averages the ProcessorLoad values storing this value in the LoadAvg property, then the LoadAvg property is range evaluated to assign the value to the Status property (Idle, Working) [14].

A principal resource broker service activity is to wait for index service values changing notification in order to perform an index service entity query and to collect data about the grid health represented by the availability of each VO resource. The resource brokering initialization phase ends when the collector's data structure is filled by the local resource index and the Resource component registers itself to the virtual organization main Index Services as a notification sink, and waits for index resource property data renewal events. In our resource broker, many users have to interact with the same stateful service querying resources that are tracked in order to be in coherence with the grid health status. Due to these requirements, we create the service using the singleton design pattern with the stateless web service side is interfaced with the stateful one via resource properties [12]. Due to the dynamic nature of grid resources, the resource property is not persistent and it is automatically renewed each time the index service notifies to the resource broker service that its entity status is changed. In this way the resource lifetime is automatically controlled by the effective update availability and not scheduled in a time dependent fashion [15]. Registered entity status changes are transferred upstream to the Index Service and then propagated to the Resource notification sink. Due to our application behavior, this approach could be inefficient because many events may be triggered with high frequency, degrading performance. We choose a threshold time interval value to trigger the data structure update.

From the resource consumer point of the view, the sequence starts when the user runs the resource broker client using one of the query notations that our system accepts.

Native notation: each selection criteria expression is separated by a space with the meaning of the logical and. Properties reflects the GLUECE Useful Resource Properties nomenclature with the dot symbol as property and sub property separator. The criteria are the same of the majority of query languages, plus special ones such as "max" and "min" to maximize or minimize a property and "dontcare" to ignore a pre-set condition.

```
Globus.Services.GRAM!="" Processor.InstructionSet.Host=="x86"
Cluster.WorkingNodes>=16 MainMemory.RAMAvailable.Average>=512
ComputingElement.PBS.WaitingJobs=min
```

This query looks for a PC cluster with at least 16 working nodes and 512 megabytes of available RAM using the PBS as local queue manager and where the GRAM Globus web service is up and running. Computing elements with the minimum number of waiting jobs are preferred.

ClassAd notation: the selection constraints are expressed as requirements using the well-known Condor classified advertisement notation for non structured data definition queries. In this notation, the query is enclosed in a brackets envelope and each couple of property name/value is separated by a semicolon. Special mandatory fields are Rank and Requirements. The Requirements field contains the constraints criteria expressed using the standard C language notation.

```
[ Type="Job"; ImageSize=512; Rank=1/other.ComputingElement_PBS_WaitingJobs;
Requirements= other.Type=="Machine" && other.NumNodes>=16 && other.Arch=="x86" &&
other.Globus_Services_GRAM!="" ]
```

The shown classad performs the same query previously shown with the native notation. The NumNodes property is equivalent to the Cluster.WorkingNodes. The underscore substitutes the dot for the property/sub property access notation to avoid ambiguity with the dot meaning in ClassAd language. The ranking is mathematically computed using a simple expression involving the number of PBS waiting jobs [16].

The implementation of the matchmaking algorithm differs in relation to the chosen strategy, but can be formerly divided in two phases: the search and the selection.

In the search phase, some constraints are strictly satisfied, such as the number of nodes equal to or greater than a particular value, and the available memory being not less than a specified amount. If none suitable resource is available, the fail result is notified to the client applying the right strategy in order to prevent deadlock and starvation issues. After this step, resources satisfying the specified constraints are passed to the second phase, where the best matching resource is found using an optimization algorithm based on a ranking schema. The selected resource is tagged as claimed to prevent another resource broker query selecting the same resource causing a potential overload. At the end of the query process the resource broker client receives the End Point Reference (EPR) of the best matching resource and is ready to use it. The resource remains claimed until a new threshold filtered update is performed and the resource status reflects their actual behavior.

3 The Native Latent Semantic Indexing Based Matchmaking Algorithm

We implemented a matchmaking algorithm from scratch; it is based on an effective and efficient application of Latent Semantic Indexing (LSI) [17].

In the case of search engines, a singular-value decomposition (SVD) of the terms by document association matrix is computed producing a reduced dimensionality matrix to approximate the original as the model of "semantic" space for the collection. This simplification reflects the most important associative patterns in the data, while ignoring some smaller variations that may be due to idiosyncrasies in the word usage of individual documents [18]. The underlying "latent" semantic structure of the information is carried out by the LSI algorithm. In common LSI document search engine applications, this approach overcomes some of the problems of keyword matching based on the higher level semantic structure rather than just the surface level word choice [19].

In order to apply LSI to resource matchmaking, we have to map some concepts from the document classification and indexing to the grid resource discovery and selection field. As documents, in the web identified by URLs, are characterized by some keywords, resources, identified by EPRs in the grid, have name properties typed as string, integer, double and boolean values. A document may or may not contain a particular word, so the matrix of occurrence document/words is large and sparse; in the same way each grid resource is not characterized by a value for each defined property, because not all properties are relevant to a specific grid resource description. Documents and grid resources share the same unstructured characterization, but while words and aggregated relations between words could have a special meaning because of the intrinsic semantic of the aggregation itself, grid resource properties are self descriptive, self contained and loosely coupled in the aggregation pattern. Under this condition, we have no need to apply the dimension reduction in grid resource properties indexing, while the application of the SVD is mandatory if dealing with documents. The grid resource description property values can be numeric, alphanumeric and boolean, but alphanumeric values have not hidden semantic mean build by aggregation, while a query can be performed specifying the exact value of one or more properties. Due to the deterministic behavior needed by the resource matchmaking process, a criteria based selection process is done before grid resources are threaded by our LSI based matchmaker algorithm. This kind of selection is performed in order to extract from all available resources the set of close matching requirements.

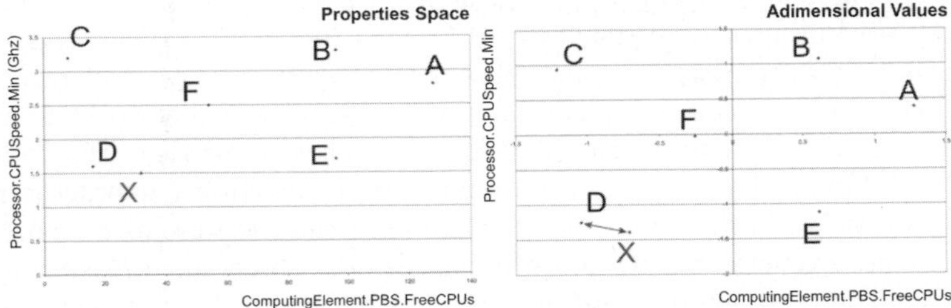

Fig. 1. The A ... F grid elements properties and the X query property. On the left in the dimensional space, on the right in the adimensional space.

Our LSI approach to matchmaking is based on the assumption that all boolean and alphanumeric query criteria are strictly satisfied in the selection phase, so the set of available grid resources comprises all suitable resources, from which we must extract the best one characterized by only numerical property values. After selection, the grid resources have a specific position in a hyperspace with a number of dimensions equal to those of the query: for example, after the ComputingElement.PBS.FreeCPUs>=25 Processor.ClockSpeed.Min==1500 Globus.Service.GRAM!="" query, the hyperspace is reduced to a Cartesian plane with the ComputingElement.PBS.FreeCPUs on the x axis and the Processor.ClockSpeed.Min on the y axis (Figure 2, left side). We assume, if the user asks for 25 CPUs or more, the best resource is the machine with 25 CPUs, while more CPUs are acceptable but something of better as in the case of ComputingElement.PBS.FreeCPUs=max. The best fitting resource could be considered to be the one that minimize the distance between the position of the requested resource and the offered one. This kind of ranking approach could be correct if all property values are in the same unit. If Processor.ClockSpeed.Min is expressed as GHz or MHz, and ComputingElement.PBS.FreeCPUs as an integer pure number the computed distance is biased, because of the anisotropic space. An adimensionalization process is needed in order to map all offered and asked grid resources in an isotropic unitless n-dimensional space, with the goal of making distances comparable.

The goal of our adimensionalization process is to re-normalize property values so that they have a mean of zero and standard deviation equal to one. In order to achieve this result, we calculate the mean and standard deviation for each involved property. Then, using a lookup data structure, both the asked and offered grid resource, identified by their characteristics, are adimensionalized and projected in a isotropic space in which distance units on each axis are the same. Finally, a ranking table, ordered in ascending order of distance, is computed using the Euclidean distance; then the resource in the first position represents the best one fitting the querying criteria (Figure 2, right side).

4 The Condor ClassAd Based Matchmaking Algorithm

The world wide Condor open source ClassAds framework [20] is robust, scalable, flexible and evolvable as demonstrated by the production-quality distributed high throughput computing system developed at the University of Wisconsin-Madison. Classified Advertisements are stated as the "*lingua franca*" of Condor and are used for describing jobs, workstations, and other resources. In order to implement a GT4 resource oriented matchmaker algorithm using ClassAds framework, a mapping between Index Service entries and ClassAds component is needed. The component have to be flexible, full configurable, customizable and extensible in order to manage any kind of entries. In the GT4 Index Service each entry represents a resource of a specified type characterized by property values for which the ClassAd mapping process is trivial or straightforward. Resource properties, such as the GLUECE, are complex and data rich and the mapping process could be more tricky because some aggregation, synthesis and evaluation work is needed (as in the case of clusters computing elements).

Once the ClassAd representation of unclaimed GT4 grid element resources is available thanks to the developed mapping component, our matchmaker algorithm compares each ClassAd with the ClassAd form of the submitted query. The grid element vector is filled and each element each is characterized by the self and other Rank property (formerly the ClassAd Rank attribute computed from the query point of view, self, and the resource one, other). The Rank ClassAd parameter is used to perform a sort criteria in order to choose the best fitting resource represented by the one that maximize both self.Rank and other.Rank properties. Thanks to the native matchmaker algorithm, we have all tools needed to perform the best fitting resource selection, using a native query in the form "self.Rank=max other.Rank=max", that selects the grid element that maximize both properties.

5 An Application to on Demand Weather and Marine Forecasting

In our grid computing based virtual laboratory we grid enabled several atmospheric, marine and air/water quality models such as MM5 (Mesoscale Model 5) [3], POM (Princeton Ocean Model) [21], the STdEM (Spatio-temporal distribution Emission

Model) [22], the PNAM (Parallel Naples Airsheld Model) [23], WRF (Weather and Research Forecasting model), sea-wave propagation models WW3 (WaveWatch III) and the CAMx (Comprehensive Air quality Model with eXtension) air quality model [26]. We made this models grid enabled using the black-box approach implementing a modular coupling system with the goal to perform several experiments and environmental science simulations without the need of a deep knowledge about grid computing. We are still working about the grid enabling of other environmental models developing other virtual laboratory components in order to deliver a comfortable environment for earth observation grid aware application deployment.

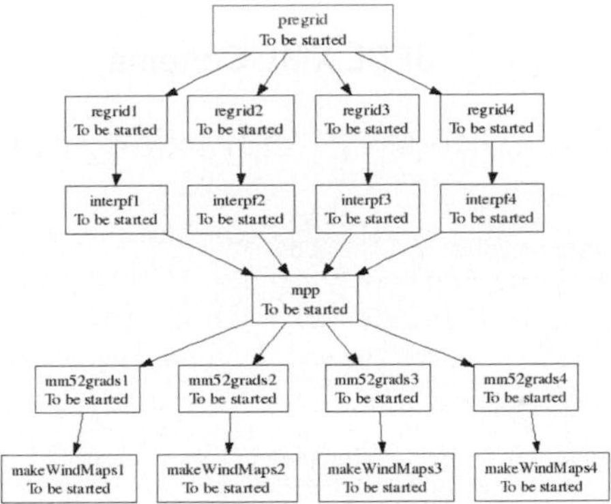

Fig. 3. The application workflow as represented by the JFDL file

We developed an on-demand weather and marine forecast, which is a full grid-aware application running in an effective ad efficient fashion on our department grid as test-bed for our resource broking service. The application environment in which the application runs is based on our virtual laboratory runtime grid software integrating our Job Flow Scheduler and the ResourceBroker Service. Using this tool, we develop the application using the Job Flow Description Language (JFDL), based on XML, with the needed extension for resource broking interfacing and late binding reference management [24].

The user need only specify the starting date and the number of hours for the simulation or the forecast. Then, all needed resources are requested from the resource broker and allocated at runtime. In the job elements of the JFDL application file, queries are coded to select resources using both the native and the ClassAd notation, while some design optimizations are made using the dynamic reference management syntax of the JFDL to run application components minimizing the data transfer time.

From the data point of view, the grid-aware application computes weather forecast and wind driven sea wave propagation on four nested domains ranging from the Mediterranean Europe (81 Km cell size) to the Bay of Naples (3 Km cell size), produces both thematic maps and GRIB data files ready for other processes and uses via standard, commercial or free software. This application is a smart and simplified version of the one we run operationally for regional weather and marine forecasts used by different local institutions.

The application workflow (Figure 3) begins with the starting event produced by the on-demand request coming, for example, from a multi access, mobile device enabled web portal. Then, the weather forecast model is initialized and the output data is rendered by a presentation software and concurrently consumed by the sea wave propagation model. Then each application branch proceeds on a separate thread.

The workflow could be represented as an acyclic direct graph into a JFDL file where each job to be submitted is described by an inner coded RSL [25] file while the launching scripts are stored in a separate repository (Figure 4). Our JFS component permits the grid application implementation using a single XML self describing file, while the RB service makes the application grid-aware.

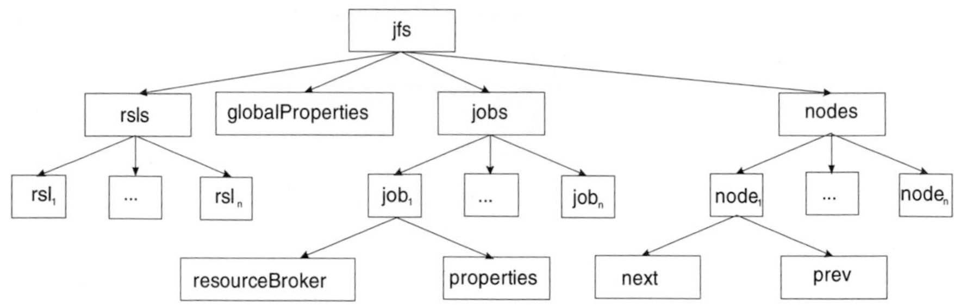

Fig. 4. The JFDL developed schema

In the element jfdl:globalProperties the developer can specify the values read in each job definition and substituted at runtime. The jfdl:rsls element contains a collection of jfdl:rsl named elements used to describe jobs with the Globus GRAM RSL file. In this files the use of environment variables place holding for scratch directory path and provided utility macros.

The file describing the grid aware application can be divided into two parts: inside the element <jfdl:jobs> each job belonging to the application is described specifying its symbolic name, the computing node where it will be submitted, and the name of the RSL file specifying all needed resources.

The statically assigned grid element unique identifying name, specified in the job element host attribute, could be omitted, in which case a resource broker jfdl:resourceBroker element would have to be used. In this element could be specified the classAlgorithm attribute to select the matchmaker implementation class identifying the matchmaking algorithm using the native one if this parameter is omitted as shown in the following example:

```
<jfdl:resourceBroker
  classAlgorithm="it.uniparthenope.dsa.grid.ClassAdMatchmakingAlgorithm">
  [Type="Job"; ImageSize=512;
  Rank=1/other.ComputingElement.PBS.WaitingJobs;
  Requirements= other.Type=="Machine" &&
  other.Software_MM5_Regrid==true &&
  other.Disk>=64 && other.NumNodes==0 ]
</jfdl:resourceBroker>
```

Where the application is looking for a non cluster machine, such as a workstation or a dedicated server, on which the Regrid component is installed. Moreover, the job needs at least 64 MB of available space on disk, and the best fitting resource is the one that minimizes the number of waiting jobs in the PBS queue manager (implicitly the PBS local queue manager is needed as requirement).

In each job definition the user can specify local properties using the jfdl:propeties element. Properties are runtime accessible using the conventional name $propertyname; global properties referred to a particular job are referred by $jobname.propertyname. This is really useful if a sort of optimization is needed using an integrated grid-enabled/aware approach. In our application we want to assign grid elements dynamically but some components have data strictly related as the case of Regrid/Interpf pairs or mm52grads/makeWindMaps pairs, so it is better to execute Regrid and Interpf, as well mm52grads and makeWindMaps, on the same computing element to achieve best performances avoiding heavy data transfers.

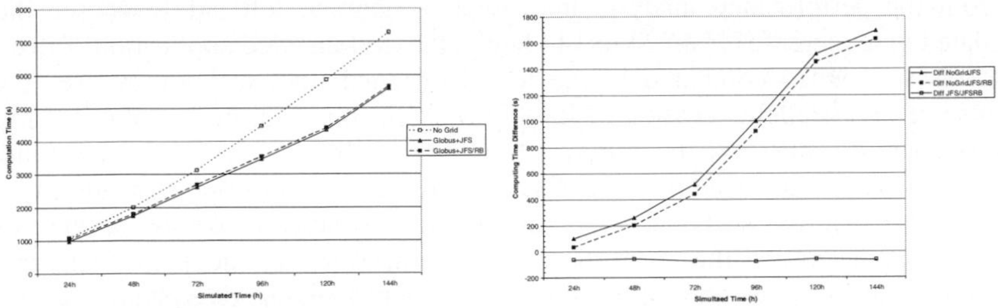

Fig. 5. Simulated Time versus Computing Time under several configurations. On the left absolute times, on the right relative times.

In order to evaluate the grid-aware application performance, we repeated the experiment 10 times and then averaged total computing time for 24, 48, 72, 96, 120, and 144 simulated hours.

We evaluated three different grid behavior configuration scenarios:

No grid technology use: The application runs as a common Bash shell script on the master node (Pentium IV at 2.8 GHz Hyper Threading equipped with 4 GByte of RAM and 2 160 GB hard disk and running Fedora Core 3 Linux) of the computing element named dgbeodi.uniparthenope.it formed by a cluster of 25 workstation powered by a hyper heading PentiumIV at 2.8 GHz, each with 1GByte of RAM and 80 GB hard disk, running Fedora Core 3 Linux. The local network is a copper gigabit using a high performance switch. This workstations are used also for student learning activities running concurrently Windows XP Professional operating system hosted by virtual environment. In this case no kind of explicit parallelism is performed and there is no need to use an external network for data transfer.

Grid-enabled mode: Globus+JFS, the application is developed using JFDL and runs under our virtual laboratory tools. Computational loads are distributed statically over available grid elements, with a design optimization performed regarding computing power and data file transfer needs. In this approach the Job Flow Scheduler component is used, but the Resource Broker Service is switched off. The application takes advantage of the explicit parallelism carried out by parallel execution of regrid/intepf and mm52grads/makeWindMaps software modules pairs. As in the previous case of not us of grid technology, MM5 and WW3 models run on the same 25 CPUs computing element dgbeodi.uniparthenope.it.

Grid-aware mode: Globus+JFS/RB, the application is developed using JFDL and runs under our tools as in the previous case, but resources are assigned dynamically using our resource broker service performing queries each time it is needed. To achieve better performance and to avoid unnecessary data file transfers, Regrid and Interpf jobs and mm52grads/makeWindMaps are submitted to the same computing element using the Job Flow Scheduler late binding capabilities: the resource broker is invoked to choose the computing element for the Regrid job and then the same CE is used for the Interpf job. The query for parallel computing intensive load characterized jobs MM5 and WW3 is performed, but dgbeodi.uniparthenope.it is always used because the constraints.

From the performance analysis line graph (Figure 5, left side), we see that as simulated time increases from 24 to 144 hours, the grid-enabled application (filled line) performs well when compared to the no-grid (dotted line) technology use. This is because of the parallel execution of loosely coupled jobs and the optimized data high performance transfer. When resource broking capabilities are activated (outlined graph), the grid-aware system still performs better than the no-grid application version, but is slower than the grid-enabled version without resource brokering because of the latency introduced by the Web Services interactions, the adopted matchmaking technique related issues and the deadlock/starvation avoiding subsystem interactions. In the other graph (Figure 5, right side) are drown computing time differences between the no grid setup and the grid-enabled (filled line) and the grid-aware one (outlined graph). The dotted line represents the difference in computing time between the two approaches. The time consumed by the resource broker in all tests is quite constant because our grid was used in a exclusive manner (without other users). On the other hand, in production conditions (not exclusive grid use), the overall computing load of the department grid is better distributed using the grid-aware behavior, allowing for efficient and effective resource allocation optimization.

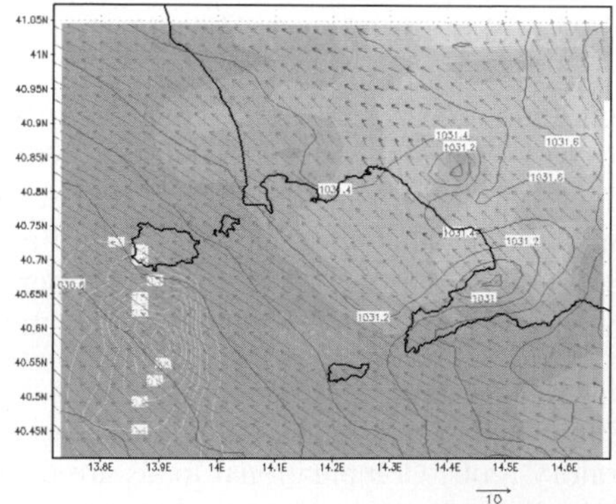

Fig. 6. Demo grid aware application results

6 Conclusions and Future Works

We have described some results in the field of grid computing research, with particular regard to the challenging issue of resource discovery and selection with matchmaking algorithms.

We developed a resource broker service, fully integrated with Globus Toolkit version 4, that is both modular and easy to expand. The plug-in architecture for both collector and matchmaking algorithm implementations we developed makes this tool an excellent environment for resource handling algorithms experiments and productions in the Globus Toolkit grid approach world. Our next goal develop an accurate testing suite, based on both real and simulated grid environment, in order to evaluate and compare native and ClassAd algorithm performances and effectiveness. In this scenario is our interest in developing a matchmaking algorithm based on the minimization of cost functions evaluated using resource characterization benchmarks in order to implement dynamic performance contracts. A better self registering approach to grid available application have to be followed to make the real use of our tools in a straightforward fashion.

In order to achieve a better, and more standard, application workflow environment, a Job Flow Scheduler refactoring is planned with the aim to be BPEL [27] compliant leveraging on open source workflow engines [28].

Our virtual laboratory for earth observation and computational environmental sciences based on the grid computing technology is enriched by the features provided by the Resource Broker Service, making possible the design and the implementation of truly grid-aware applications. The integration between the Job Flow Scheduler service and the Resource Broker service is a powerful tool that can be used both for research and application-oriented uses for running any kind of complex grid application (Figure 6).

Acknowledgments. I would like to thank Ian Foster for his suggestions and support in the revision of this paper.

References

1. I. Foster, "Globus Toolkit Version 4: Software for Service-Oriented Systems," I. Foster, Journal of Computational Science and Technology, 21(4):523-530, 2006.
2. W. Allcock, J. Bresnahan, R. Kettimuthu, M. Link, C. Dumitrescu, I. Raicu, I. Foster. *"The Globus Striped GridFTP Framework and Server,"* .SC05, November 2005
3. The PSU/NCAR mesoscale model (MM5), Pennsylvania State University / National Center for Atmospheric Research, www.mmm.ucar.edu/mm5/mm5-home.html
4. I. Foster, C. Kesselman, *The Grid 2: Blueprint for a new Computing Infrastructure.* Morgan Kaufman, 2003
5. C. Liu, I. Foster. *A Constraint Language Approach to Matchmaking*. Proceedings of the 14th International Workshop on Research Issues on Data Engineering (RIDE 2004), Boston, 2004
6. I. Foster, C. Kesselman, S. Tuecke. *The Anatomy of the Grid: Enabling Scalable Virtual Organizations.* Intl. J. High Performance Computing Applications, 15(3):200-222, 2001.

7. J. M. Schopf, M. D'Arcy, N. Miller, L. Pearlman, I. Foster, and C. Kesselman. Monitoring and Discovery in a Web Services Framework: Functionality and Performance of the Globus Toolkit's MDS4. Argonne National Laboratory Tech Report ANL/MCS-P1248-0405, April 2005.
8. D. Thain, T. Tannenbaum, M. Livny. *Distributed Computing in Practice: The Condor Experience.* Concurrency and Computation: Practice and Experience, Vol. 17, No. 2-4, pages 323-356, February-April, 2005.
9. R. Raman. *Matchmaking Frameworks for Distributed Resource Management.* Ph.D. Dissertation, October 2000
10. R.Raman, M. Livny, M. Solomon. *Matchmaking: Distributed Resource Management for High Throughput Computing*. Proceedings of the Seventh IEEE International Symposium on High Performance Distributed Computing, July 28-31, 1998, Chicago, IL
11. I. Ascione, G. Giunta, R. Montella, P. Mariani, A. Riccio. *A Grid Computing Based Virtual Laboratory for Environmental Simulations*. Proceedings of 12th International Euro-Par 2006, Dresden, Germany, August/September 2006. LNCS 4128, Springer 2006
12. B. Sotomayor, L. Childers. *Globus Toolkit 4: Programming Java Services*. Morgan Kaufman, 2005
13. M. L. Massie, B. N. Chunm D. E. Culler. *The Ganglia Distributed Monitoring System: Design, Implementation, and Experience*. Parallel Computing, Elsevier 2004
14. S. Andreozzi, S. Burke, L. Field, S. Fisher, B. K´onya, M. Mambelli, J. M. Schopf, M. Viljoen, and A. Wilson. Glue schema specification version 1.3 draft 1, INFN, 2006
15. R. Raman, M. Livny, M. Solomon. *Policy Driven Heterogeneous Resource Co-Allocation with Gangmatching*. Proceedings of the Twelfth IEEE International Symposium on High-Performance Distributed Computing, June, 2003, Seattle, WA.
16. S. Andreozzi, G. Garzoglio, S. Reddy, M Mambelli, A. Roy, S. Wang, T. Wenaus. *GLUE Schema v1.2 Mapping to Old ClassAd Format*, INFN, July 2006
17. S.Deerwester, S. T. Dumais, T. K. Landauer, G. W. Furnas and R. A. Harshman. *Indexing by latent semantic analysis.* Journal of the Society for Information Science, 41(6), 391-407, 1990
18. P. Drineas, A Frieze, R. Kannan, S. Vempala, V. Vinay.Clustering Large Graphs via the Singular Value Decomposition.Machine Learning, 56, 9–33, 2004
19. S. T. Dumais. Using LSI for Information Retrieval, Information Filtering, and Other Things". Cognitive Technology Workshop, April 4-5, 1997.
20. Condor High Throughput Computing. Classified Advertisements. Univeristy of Wisconsin, http://www.cs.wisc.edu/condor/classad
21. G. Giunta, P. Mariani, R. Montella, A. Riccio. *pPOM: A nested, scalable, parallel and Fortran 90 implementation of the Princeton Ocean Model.* Envirnonmental Modelling & Software 22 (2007) pp 117-122.
22. G. Barone, P. D'Ambra, D. di Serafino, G. Giunta, R. Montella, A. Murli, A. Riccio, *An Operational Mesoscale Air Quality Model for the Campania Region* – Proc. 3th GLOREAM Workshop, Annali Istituto Universitario Navale (special issue), 179-189, giugno 2000
23. G. Barone, P. D'Ambra, D. di Serafino, G. Giunta, A. Murli, A. Riccio, *Parallel software for air quality simulation in Naples area,* J. Eviron. Manag. and Health, 2000(10), pp. 209-215
24. G. Giunta, R. Montella, A. Riccio. *Globus GT4 based Job Flow Scheduler and Resource Broker development for a grid computing based environmental simulations laboratory.* Technical Report 2006/07 Dept. of Applied Sciences, University of Naples "Parthenope"

25. Resource Specification Language (RSL), Globus Alliance, www-unix.globus.org/developer/rsl-schema.html
26. G. Giunta, R. Montella, P. Mariani, A. Riccio. *Modeling and computational issues for air/water quality problems. A grid computing approach.* Il Nuovo Cimento, vol 28C, N.2, March-April 2005
27. T. Andrews, F. Curbera, H. Dholakia, Y. Goland, J. Klein, F. Leymann, K. Liu, D. Roller, D. Smith, S. Thatte, I. Trickovic, S. Weerawarana, IBM, *Business Process Execution Language for Web Services Version 1.1*, http://www.oasis-open.org, 2003
28. Active BPEL Engine Site. http://www.activebpel.org

Small-World Network Inspired Trustworthy Web Service Evaluation and Management Model

Qinghua Meng[1,2] and Yongsheng Ding[1]

[1] College of Information Sciences and Technology
Donghua University, Shanghai 201620, P.R. China
[2] Department of Computer Sciences and Technology
Weifang University, Weifang, Shandong 261401, P.R. China
ysding@dhu.edu.cn

Abstract. The trustworthiness between anonymous web service client and provider influences service stability and collaboration. Trustworthiness includes some aspects such as service's security, controllability and survivability. So, a definition of trustworthiness for web service is given in the paper, and then a web service trustworthiness evaluation and management model is brought forth inspired by human small-world network. The model consists of three web service federations: WSRRC, APAEAS and AWSORT. WSRRC is a Web Service Resource Register Center, which is established by UDDI protocol. APAEAS is an Area Proxy Authentication Evaluating Autonomy System, which collects some authentication information of web service clients, accepts clients' special requirement and feedbacks service's trustworthiness values to AWSORT. AWSORT is an Area WS Resource Organizing Tree, which organizes and manages web service resources; records web service trustworthiness values, keeps web service state, assigning web service. The model establishes a trustworthy environment for anonymous web service clients and providers. Furthermore, some detailed evaluating parameters about service trustworthiness and quality is discussed and some service management algorithms are proposed in the paper. The simulation results show that model is feasible for semantic grid integration and establishment for virtual organization.

Keywords: web service federation, trustworthy web service, small-world network, loading-balance, quality of service.

1 Introduction

Web service (WS) are quickly maturing as a technology that allows for the integration of applications belonging to different administrative domains, enabling much faster and more efficient business-to-business arrangements [1]. For the integration to be effective, the provider and the consumer of a service must negotiate some parameters, such as quality of service, security auditing and communication speed [2-4]. However, security auditing can be very challenging when the parties do not blindly trust each other, which is expected to be the common case for large WS deployments [5, 6].

By now some WS-security specifications and trust auditing framework are available [7, 8]. Microsoft and IBM propose a set of WS security specifications includes a message security layer, a policy security layer, a federated security layer

C. Cérin and K.-C. Li (Eds.): GPC 2007, LNCS 4459, pp. 218–228, 2007.

[9-11]. However, the specifications demand all of the provider and customer be authenticated by a trustworthy verification center [11]. Especially for anonymous WS providers, the WS customer needs to pre-evaluate their trustworthiness, and then it will choose a provider which trustworthiness is the highest.

Thus, we propose a trustworthiness evaluation and management model inspired by human small-world network. The model establishes an integrated loosed-trustworthy WS environment for the anonymous users and resources. Whether web clients and services are authenticated or not, the model will ensure some initial effective trustworthiness. Furthermore, it can optimize WS and manage effectively service traffic.

This paper is organized as follows: Section 2 introduces characters of trustworthiness in human small word and gives the definition of trustworthiness. Section 3 puts forward WS trustworthiness evaluating and managing model. Section 4 presents web service federation organization protocols, data structures and instructions. Section 5 presents WS trustworthiness evaluating & managing algorithm. Section 6 discusses the simulation of WS loading-balance in the web service federation. Section 7 concludes the paper by discussing the research trends of the trustworthiness model.

2 Small-World Network and WS Trustworthiness

2.1 Trustworthiness in the Human Small-World Network

M. Stanley proposed the assumption of 'six degrees' in human society as early as 1967. Watts and Strogatz built the small-world networks theory according to the assumption in 1998. The small world model widely exists in the human society and bio-network. It describes ubiquitous resource searching characteristics such as self-like, self-organizing and self-adjusting. WS network presents some characteristics like small world, and users would like to obtain service in the nearer 'small world' from internet. So, we expect to establish a service evaluation framework to organize and manage WS based on small world model.

Small world is a relation network centralized on a person in the human society, in which he decides how to choose friends and what resource to select for use. From another point of view, the small world is a trustworthiness evaluating and dynamically selecting network, which structure and nodes' trustworthiness values will change with the environment and time. People add or delete the partial node to the small world according to their needs. They constantly do some trustworthiness-evaluating work about surrounding 'node', and at the same time they change their trustworthiness value and adjust their behaviors. Thus, it is clear that the small world network is a trustworthiness and benefit driven network. People choose these required resources or services and give up those disabled nodes in order to get the largest benefits in minimum costs.

2.2 WS Trustworthiness

Along with SOA (service-oriented-architecture) is more and more popular, it is necessary that the SOA applications should provide trustworthy services. Trustworthy network should have three essential properties: security, controllability and survivability [8]. From the view of trustworthiness, we attempt to give the definition of the trustworthiness of WS. WS trustworthiness also should include three properties: security, controllable and survivable. The following is the detailed definition. Namely

$$T_{WS} = \Gamma(Seu, Ctrl, Sur)$$

Define 1: Security
WS security includes a series of attributes: service entity being security, service context being security, WS structure being security. That is service entity must be legal and authenticated; WS content must be effective and security, no error and no virus. As WS is stateless, WS structure security is that WS can keep its service state and its state is stable in a certain period. Namely

$$\Gamma(Seu) = \Psi_{se}(En, Con, Stru)$$

Define 2: Controllability
WS controllability is that WS role can be managed, its behavior can be controlled, and its services quality can be ensured. WS client or provider should have right role in the SOA system, and these roles should be managed in the security policy. WS behavior being controlled means that WS' access policy should have been integrated managed. WS quality being controlled means that WS should satisfy different business needs. Therefore, WS can provide different quality and security grade service for different requirement. Namely

$$\Gamma(Ctrl) = \Omega(Role, Act, Qua)$$

Define 3: Survivability
WS survivability is that WS have the ability of withstanding intrusions or attacks. That is that WS can still provide service in case of being damaged. WS survivability includes fault-toleration, intrusion-toleration, and self-recovery.

$$\Gamma(Sur) = \Phi(Fault\_tol, Intru\_tol, Rcov)$$

WS Trustworthiness should include all of the three factors. So, the trustworthiness value should be expressed as following:

$$\begin{aligned} T_{WS} &= \Gamma(Seu, Ctrl, Sur) = \alpha * \Gamma(Seu) + \beta * \Gamma(Ctrl) + \gamma * \Gamma(Sur) \\ &= \alpha * \Psi_{se}(En, Con, Stru) + \beta * \Omega(Role, Act, Qua) + \gamma * \Phi(Fault\_tol, Intru\_tol, Rcov) \end{aligned}$$

Here, α, β, γ are the weights of the three factors. No matter what the detailed parameters are changed, its value should be in a scope. Namely

$$T_{WS} \in [0,1]$$

3 WS Trustworthiness Evaluating and Managing Model

3.1 WS Trustworthy Management Model

Fig 1(a) describes normal WS structure. WS provider publishes its services into WSRRC (WS Resources Register Center). Web client submits service querying to

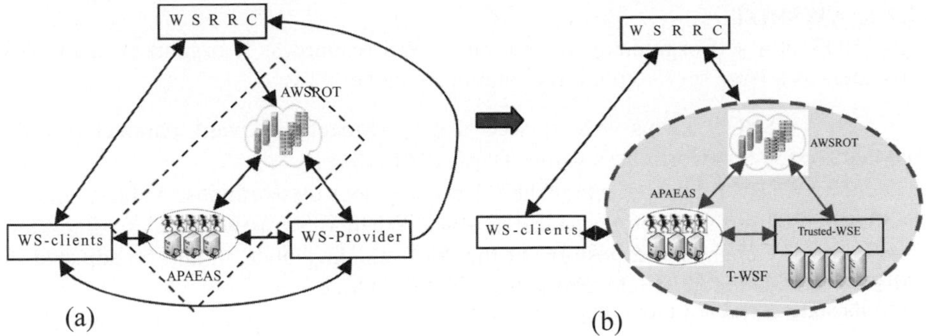

Fig. 1. WS Trustworthiness Evaluation & Management model

WSRRC, and after getting resource identification, then bind each other to deal with corresponding transaction.

Inspired by human small-world network, we put forward a WS trustworthiness evaluation and management model (fig.1 (a)). We add two modules: APAEAS (area proxy authentication evaluating autonomy system) and AWSORT (area WS resource organizing tree). APAEAS consists of a great many of authenticated or anonymous WS-clients, and it will supervise and evaluate their trustworthiness. AWSORT is in charge of recording WS quality, keeping its service state, and implementing loading-balance. Thus, the two web service federations establish a trustworthy environment for WS-clients and WS-providers, a normal WS-Provider become a trusted WS entity (Trusted-WSE), shown in fig.1 (b).

APAEAS and AWSORT don't change working patterns of WS-clients and WS-providers. Furthermore they make simple and stateless service to become Trusted-WS. Thus, APAEAS AWSORT and Trusted–WSE form a trusted WS federation (T-WSF).

3.2 APAEAS and AWSORT

3.2.1 APAEAS

APAEAS is a small-world web service federation for evaluating WS-client's trustworthiness and submitting service requirement instead of WS-client. Its functions include:

① It collects security information of users, such as authentication information, security grade and their personnel service demands. According to the information, APAEAS will communicate with AWSORT to satisfy users' needs.

② As to high-security grade WS, APAEES must authenticate users, and verify whether the user is able to require a high-security grade services. Since only authenticated user have the qualification to apply security transaction. If the requirement is permitted, APAEES will record these events, and make logs about users' working states and results.

③ On the other hand, APAEES can automatically distribute these requirements to different area AWSORT to prevent DOS (deny of service).

3.2.2 AWSROT

AWSROT is a self-organizing federation of WS resources. It organizes many WS providers as a large service pool. Its functions include:

① AWSROT keeps WS service states, registers relevant parameters, and records service trustworthiness values from APAEAS.

② AWSROT can be established according to trustworthiness values, service quality of WS and maximum service capacity. When WS trustworthiness values and service quality change, the position of the corresponding node should be adjusted in order to provide the most effective service in minimum costs.

③ AWSROT can automatically design a the best WS-provider to a WS-client with a set of service optimization policy.

④ AWSROT can implement WS loading-balance. When a WS-client roams in different APAEAS, AWSROT will design a local optimized WS-provider instead of previous WS-provider.

After the WS normal structure is changed by adding the two models, WSRRC not only takes charge of registering and querying services, but also assign different tasks to corresponding AWSROT. Therefore, WSRRC, APAEAS and AWSROT together provide a trustworthy WS environment.

4 Web Service Federation Organization Protocols, Data Structures and Instructions

4.1 AWSROT Protocol

Fig. 2. is the structure of AWSROT. AWSROT is the core of trustworthy web service environment. Its functions include states keeping, service recommending, loading balance, trustworthiness evaluating. Its organization structures are a hybrid structure. It consists of a four-rank B-tree and some circulating double-linked-list.

The four-rank B-tree is used to locate and organizes different category service, and the double circulating linked-list is used to organize the same category service. Because for users, querying services is hoped to get a quick answer, B-tree can high-effectively search for a resource; get a service is hoped the service provider is the best, the circulating linked-list always place the best service in the header point. Furthermore, the double circulating linked-list can dynamically adjust the location of service provider by its trustworthiness value, QOS, capacity and responding speed. So, the hybrid structure can high-effectively and quickly provide an optimized service.

4.2 APAEAS Protocol

APAEAS has a layered structure, shown in fig.3. It is a small world for WS-Clients. It will register in WSRRC; some little APAEAS will form a large APAEAS. So, the whole ARAEAS has a tree structure in logic. Each APAEAS is a management unit to anonymous or authenticated users. Its main functions are collecting users' information, accepting users' service request, feed-backing trustworthiness value to AWSROT and satisfying users' special demand.

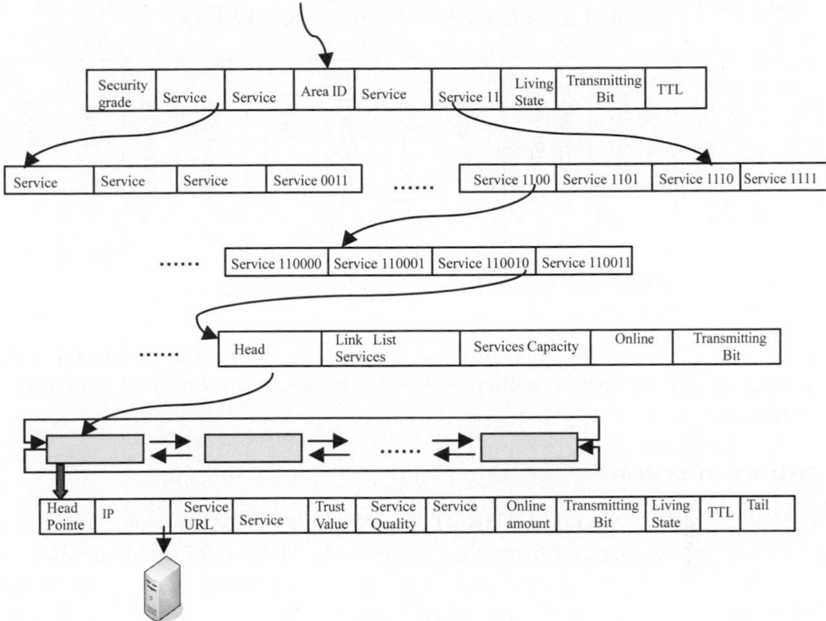

Fig. 2. The Structure AWSROT

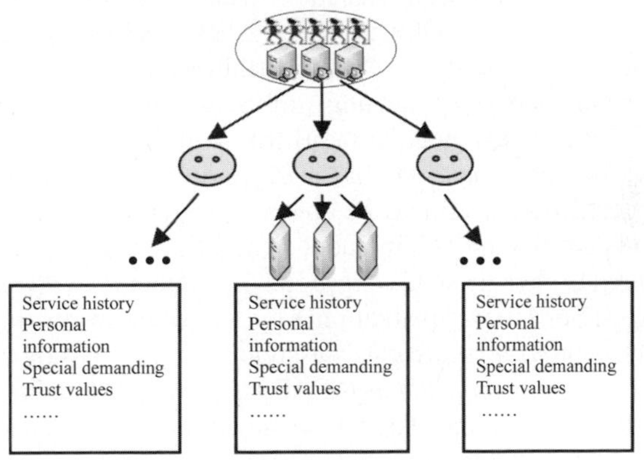

Fig. 3. The Structure of APAEAS

APAEAS keeps a great number of users' information. The information has been stored in database, and each user has a recorder in the database. The recorder includes some information of WS-Clients, such as service access history, security grade, personal information, particular service demands etc. So, actually an APAEAS is a user authenticating server.

Table 1 is the record format of customer; in which APAEAS record recent used resources. Service histories keep such items as service's using frequency, service ID, trust values and service's quality etc. According to the information, APAEAS can

Table 1. User Recorder's Format in the APAEAS

IP address	User.ID	Security Grade	Individual Feature	Last-used Resource ID	Frequency	Resource.ID	Trust Value	QOS	Frequency	Resource.ID	Trust Value	QOS	

learn about WS-Client's needs and provide appropriate services to satisfy its demand. APAEAS also collect user's authentication parameters in order to monitor web service process.

4.3 Instruction System

The WSRRC, APAEAS and AWSROT together cooperate to make up a loosed trustworthiness evaluating and managing framework. The model divide a whole large work into some small procedures, and each finish a part work. So, all of WSRRC, APAEAS and AWSROT is an integrated loosed security system for web service. Although WSRRC, APAEAS and AWSROT have own attributes and instructions, most of them are the same. So, we give a summary to the all attributes and instructions.

All attributes of these protocols include: *.state, *.TTL(), *.living(), *.warning, *.security_grade, *.IP_address, *.fellow, *.SID, *.URL, *.service_type, *.federation_ID, *.QOS, *.header, *.tail, *.trustworthiness_value, *.service_capacity, *.online_connectting_amount, *.Connecting _online etc. Here, * denotes a certain object, such as APAEAS, AWSROT, a node in the B-tree, a WS-Client, a service resource etc. The attributes describe some characters of the object in the framework. The information are collected and recorded to determine the object how to respond a special event.

The instructions of the model include: *.invite(), *.register(), *.authenticate(), *.TTL(), *.roaming(), *.request(), *.respond(), *.Query(), *.cost(), *.connect(), *.close(), *.trustworthiness_evaluating(), *.QOS_evaluating(), *.sort(), *.adjust_position(), *.provide_service(), *.assign(); *.relay_assign() etc. As the same way, * denotes a certain object, such as APAEAS, AWSROT, a node in the B-tree, a WS-Client, a service resource etc. The whole function of these instructions cooperate each other to drive the model to provide the best service in the lowest cost. Here, the interpretation of how to use the each instruction is omitted.

5 WS Evaluating and Managing Algorithm

5.1 WS Assigning Algorithm

In order to provide high-quality and low-cost WS, we design two-layer assigning structure. Firstly, by querying APAEAS or WSRRC, user can get the nearest AWSROT; secondly, AWSROT will recommend proper WS-Provider according to trustworthiness, QOS, responding speed and Maximum connecting capacity.

WSRRC divides the whole service area into some parts, each part has an AWSROT, and all WS-Providers in a part will register itself into the local AWSROT. So, in WSRRC, all the registered resources are organized according to geography feature. Every AWSROT is a small word of resource. When a WS-Client queries a WS-Provider, it will be relocated to the local AWSROT. Thus, communication between the client and the provider is confined to a small word. Therefore, it will reduce the main traffic of bone network.

In the AWSROT, all resources will be organized by services category and sorted by trustworthiness, QOS, maximum connecting capacity and responding speed etc. So, according to these parameters, AWSROT will recommend the most popular WS-Provider to WS-Client. In order to fairly evaluate a service, we introduce an evaluating concept: believed zone.

Believed zone is an evaluating range, when two or more values of an item are in a range of $[\mathrm{m}, \mathrm{m}+\varepsilon]$, we consider that they have the same value. So, believed zone is a range of probability. We evaluate trustworthiness and QOS using the method of believed zone. But for maximum connecting capacity and online connecting amount, we use precise values to evaluate them.

WS assigning algorithm is shown as the following:

```
While (Double_cir_link.live and Double_cir_link.state) {
if (Double_cir_link.ttl())
{Double_cir_link.live=false; Double_cir_link.closed;} // if no TTL returns, then close closed link-list.
link.sort (Trust_eva()); // Firstly , nodes will be sorted by trust value.
If Trust_eva()∈ [Θ', Θ]
   link.sort (Qua_eva ()); //Secondly, nodes will be sorted by service quality.
If Qua_eva()∈ [Θ', Θ]
link.sort (connect_max); //Finally, nodes will be sorted by maximum connecting amount.
When WS_Client.request ();
AWSROT.Query ();
Double_cir_link.head_pointer.provide_service(); //Firstly, head-node provides WS
Double_cir_link.head_pointer.connect_onle ++; //adding one to head nodes' online connecting amount
link.connect_onle ++ ; // adding one to link-list's online connecting amount
If head_pointer.connect_only ≥0.8* head_pointer.connect_max
P↑.Head_pointer=Head_pointer.next;
P↑.Tail_pointer=Head_pointer; //if head nodes' online connecting amount is 80 percents of the whole service capacity, then insert it into the tail node.
If link.connect_onle ≥0.8* link.connect_max
Double_cir_link.state=false; // if link-list' online connecting amount is 80 percents of the whole service capacity of the link-list, then its state bit become false.
Link_content_warning (federation_ID) or warning.sending to WSRRC; // sending a warning of full-loading to its sedation fellow or WSRRC. }}
```

5.2 WS Loading-Balance Algorithm

All of the WS-Providers, AWSORT, APAEAS and WSRRC compose a large virtual organization. The whole virtual organization will deal with loading-balance from three steps in the whole process.

(1) Firstly, WSRRC will distribute the network traffics in the whole virtual organization. For web service request from the local APAEAS, WSRRC will transmit the requests to the local AWSROT. Thus WSRRC confine local service traffic in certain range, so decrease chances of traffic blocks.

(2) Secondly, when AWSROT receive the service request, according to the trustworthiness value, QOS, service capacity and responding speed, it will select the best WS-Provider to WS-Client from its resource tree. Thus, AWSROT always remain the lowest communicating cost for the web service.

(3) Finally, if the user is roaming out of its local APAEAS, it will send a message to WSRRC, and then WSRRC will give the several nearer AWSROT. The user will calculate the communicating cost according the roaming relaying algorithm. The step aims at connecting the best WS-Providers in the lowest cost. So in different conditions, coefficients in the roaming relaying algorithm will be adjusted according to the actual circumstance. For example, if the network is busy, the coefficient of TTL () should be added, namely its rate in the cost should be the more than others. If the network is very free, the rates of trustworthy and QOS should be added.

Here, the detailed loading-balance algorithm is shown as the following.

While (WS. Request ())
{If (WS-client. Roaming !==0)) then WS.connect=min(cost$_1$*.connect| cost*$_2$*.connect|......| cost*$_n$*.connect) //If the user is in the roaming state, it will calculate the lowest cost to connect the nearest AWSORT according to roaming relaying algorithm.*
Else
WS.connect=WSRRC.assign (); // Normal user connects the local AWSROT
If (AWSROT.state==0) then
WS.connect= AWSROT.provide_service () //If the capacity of local AWSROT is enough; it will accept the service request.
Else
WS.connect=WSRRC.relay_assign ();//if the local AWSROT already has be up to the maximum connecting amount, it will transmit the request to the fellow AWSROT or send a warning message to the WSRRC.
AWSROT.assign (); //the best resource is normally assigned in the AWSROT. }

6 Simulations of Trustworthy WS Assigning

In order to verify the WS trustworthiness management middleware, we simulate in a local area network environment. We design four APAEAS and AWSROT, one WSRRC, 200 WS-Clients and 50 WS-Providers. They consist of a trusted WS environment; all the four AWSROT are an AWSROT-federation.

The loading-balance algorithm is simulated only on invariable loading. In the beginning all the WS-Clients are in roaming state, so received requires amounts of different AWSROT are different. Along with the rule of lowest connect-cost, WS assigning algorithm begin to work, finally the four AWSROT get the average and stable connecting amount, shown in the Fig.4. The Simulation results imply that the structure of APAEAS and AWSROT is available in implementing loading-balance and connecting the nearest AWSROT in the lowest cost.

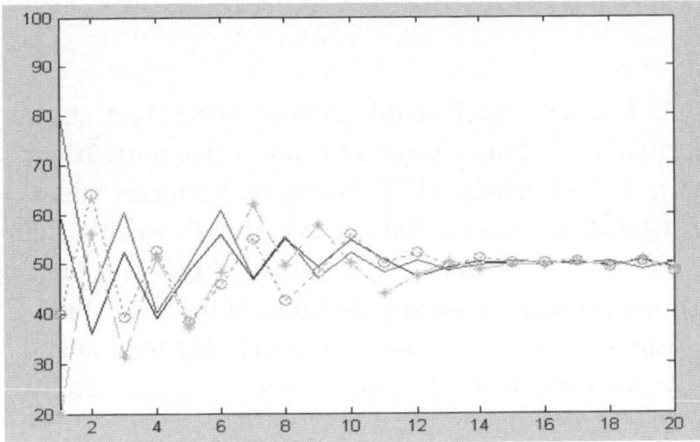

Fig. 4. WS assigning process in the case of keeping invariable loading

7 Conclusions

The paper establishes a trustworthiness appreciable and manageable model for WS. The model provides a trustworthy WS environment for anonymous WS-Clients and WS-Providers. It can record service' state, optimize service quality, carry out loading-balance.

The model has three web service federations: WSRRC, APAEAS and AWSROT. They are small-worlds of user or resource. These federations provide a trustworthy, controllable and reliable WS environment. The model has the ability of automatically assigning services and trustworthiness evaluating.

By increasing AWSROT and APAEAS, some disadvantages of WS are also eliminated. Stateless WS becomes trustable and stable service, and the process of WS be supervised, managed. But the model still remains WS original working pattern, only adding some management procedure, such as registering, trustworthiness feed-backing and evaluating, resource optimizing. At the other hand, all of WS-Clients and WS-Providers still remain independent and free. The model also provides a scaleable and trustworthy service resolution for anonymous service applications of SOA, Grid, and P2P.

Acknowledgments

This work was supported in part by the Key Project of the National Nature Science Foundation of China (No. 60534020), the National Nature Science Foundation of China (No. 60474037), and Program for New Century Excellent Talents in University from Ministry of Education of China (No. NCET-04-415), the Cultivation Fund of the Key Scientific and Technical Innovation Project from Ministry of Education of China, International Science Cooperation Foundation of Shanghai (061307041), and Specialized Research Fund for the Doctoral Program of Higher Education from Ministry of Education of China (No. 20060255006).

References

[1] A. A. Pirzada, A. Datta, C. McDonald. Incorporating trust and reputation in the DSR protocol for dependable routing. *Computer Communications*, 2006, 29(15):2806-2821.

[2] M. E. Schweitzer, J. C. Hershey, E. T. Bradlow. Promises and lies: Restoring violated trust. *Organizational Behavior and Human Decision Processes,* 2006, 101(1):1-19.

[3] B. Blobel, R. Nordberg, J. M. Davis, P. Pharow. Modeling privilege management and access control. *International Journal of Medical Informatics,* 2006, 75(8):597-623.

[4] A. Antoci, M. Galeotti, P.Russu, L. Zarri. Generalized trust and sustainable coexistence between socially responsible firms and nonprofit organizations. *Chaos, Solitons & Fractals,* 2006, 293(3):783-802.

[5] L. Mekouar, Y. Iraqi, R.Boutaba. Peer-to-peer's most wanted: Malicious peers. *Computer Networks,* 2006, 50(4): 545-562.

[6] C. Busco, A. Riccaboni, W. Scapens. Trust for accounting and accounting for trust. Management Accounting Research, 2006, 17(1):11-41.

[7] C. Selin. Trust and the illusive force of scenarios, *Futures,* 2006, 38(2):1-14.

[8] P. Ratnasingam. Trust in inter-organizational exchanges: a case study in business to business electronic commerce. *Decision Support Systems*, 2005, 39(3):525-544.

[9] J. Riegelsberger, M. Angela Sasse, J. D. McCarthy. The mechanics of trust: A framework for research and design. *International Journal of Human-Computer Studies,* 2005, 62(3):381-422.

[10] Y-F Chang, C-Cn Chang, H. Huang. Digital signature with message recovery using self-certified public keys without trustworthy system authority. *Applied Mathematics and Computation,* 2005, 161(4):211-227.

[11] A. R. Sadeghi, C. Stüble. Towards multilaterally secure computing platforms—with open source and trusted computing. *Information Security Technical Report,* 2005, 10(2):83-95.

Towards Feasible and Effective Load Sharing in a Heterogeneous Computational Grid

Kuo-Chan Huang[1], Po-Chi Shih[2], and Yeh-Ching Chung[2]

[1] Department of Electronic Commercce
Hsing Kuo College of Management
No. 89, Yuying Street, Tainan, Taiwan
kchuang@mail.hku.edu.tw
[2] Department of Computer Science
National Tsing Hua University
101, Section 2, Kuang-Fu Road, Hsinchu, Taiwan
shedoh@sslab.cs.nthu.edu.tw, ychung@cs.nthu.edu.tw

Abstract. A grid has to provide strong incentive for participating sites to join and stay in it. Participating sites are concerned with the performance improvement brought by the gird for the jobs of their own local user communities. Feasible and effective load sharing is key to fulfilling such a concern. This paper explores the load-sharing policies concerning feasibility and heterogeneity on computational grids. Several job scheduling and processor allocation policies are proposed and evaluated through a series of simulations using workloads derived from publicly available trace data. The simulation results indicate that the proposed job scheduling and processor allocation policies are feasible and effective in achieving performance improvement on a heterogeneous computational grid.

Keywords: feasibility, load sharing, simulation, heterogeneous grid.

1 Introduction

This paper deals with scheduling and allocating independent parallel jobs in a heterogeneous computational grid. Without grid computing local users can only run jobs on the local site. The owners or administrators of different sites are interested in the consequences of participating in a computational grid, whether such participation will result in better service for their local users by improving the job response time. Therefore, we say a computational grid is feasible if it can bring performance improvement and the improvement is achieved in the sense that all participating sites benefit from the collaboration. In this paper that means no participating sites' average response time for their jobs get worse after joining the computational grid.

In addition to feasibility, heterogeneity is another important issue in a computational grid. Many previous works have shown significant performance improvement for multi-site homogeneous grid environment. However, in the real world a grid usually consists of heterogeneous sites which differ at least in the computing speed. Heterogeneity puts a challenge on designing effective load sharing methods. Methods developed for homogeneous grids have to be improved or even redesigned to make them effective in a heterogeneous environment. This paper

C. Cérin and K.-C. Li (Eds.): GPC 2007, LNCS 4459, pp. 229–240, 2007.

addresses the potential benefit of sharing jobs between independent sites in a heterogeneous computational grid environment. To construct a feasible and effective computational grid, appropriate load sharing policies are important. The load sharing policies have to take into account several job scheduling and processor allocation issues. These issues are discussed in this paper, including job scheduling for feasible load sharing benefiting all sites, site selection for processor allocation, multi-site parallel execution. Several job scheduling and processor allocation policies are proposed and evaluated through a series of simulations using workloads derived from publicly available trace data. The simulation results indicate that a significant performance improvement in terms of shorter job response time is achievable.

2 Related Work

Job scheduling for parallel computers has been subject to research for a long time. As for grid computing, previous works discussed several strategies for a grid scheduler. One approach is the modification of traditional list scheduling strategies for usage on grid [1, 2, 3, 4]. Some economic based methods are also being discussed [5, 6, 7, 8]. In this paper we explore non economic scheduling and allocation policies with support for a heterogeneous grid environment.

England and Weissman in [9] analyzed the costs and benefits of load sharing of parallel jobs in the computational grid. Experiments were performed for both homogeneous and heterogeneous grids. However, in their works simulations of a heterogeneous grid only captured the differences in capacities and workload characteristics. The computing speeds of nodes on different sites are assumed to be identical. In this paper we deal with load sharing issues regarding heterogeneous grids in which nodes on different sites may have different computing speeds.

For load sharing there are several methods possible for selecting which site to allocate a job. Earlier simulation studies in our previous work [10] and in the literature [1] showed the best results for a selection policy called *best-fit*. In this policy a particular site is chosen on which a job will leave the least number of free processors if it is allocated to that site. However, these simulation studies are performed based on a computational grid model in which nodes on different sites all run at the same speed. In this paper we explore possible site selection policies for a heterogeneous computational grid. In such a heterogeneous environment nodes on different sites may run at different speeds.

In [11] the authors addressed the scheduling of parallel jobs in a heterogeneous multi-site environment. They also evaluated a scheduling strategy that uses multiple simultaneous requests. However, although dealing with a multi-site environment, the parallel jobs in their studies were not allowed for multi-site parallel execution. Each job was allocated to run within a single site.

The support of multi-site parallel execution [12, 13, 14, 15, 16] on a computational grid has been examined in previous works, concerning the execution of a job in parallel at different sites. Under the condition of a limited communication overhead, the results from our previous work [10] and from [1, 3, 4] all showed that multi-site parallel execution can improve the overall average response time. The overhead for multi-site parallel execution mainly results from the slower communication between different sites compared to the intra-site communication. This overhead has been modeled by extending the execution time of a job by a certain percentage [2, 3, 10].

In [2] the authors further examined the multi-site scheduling behavior by applying constraints for the job fragmentation during the multi-site scheduling. Two parameters were introduced for the scheduling process. The first parameter *lower bound* restricted the jobs that can be fragmented during the multi-site scheduling by a minimal number of necessary requested processors. The second parameter was implemented as a vector describing the maximal number of job fragments for certain intervals of processor numbers.

However, the simulation studies in the previous works are performed based on a homogeneous computational grid model in which nodes on different sites all run at the same speed. In this paper we explore possible multi-site selection policies for a heterogeneous computational grid. In [17] the authors proposed job scheduling algorithms which allow multi-site parallel execution, and are adaptive and scalable in a heterogeneous computational grid. However, the introduced algorithms require predicted execution time for the submitted jobs. In this paper, we deal with the site selection problem for multi-site parallel execution, requiring no knowledge of predicted job execution time.

3 Computational Grid Model and Experimental Setting

In this section, the computational grid model is introduced on which the evaluations of the proposed policies in this paper are based. In the model, there are several independent computing sites with their own local workload and management system. This paper examines the impact on performance results if the computing sites participate in a computational grid with appropriate job scheduling and processor allocation policies. The computational grid integrates the sites and shares their incoming jobs. Each participating site is a homogeneous parallel computer system. The nodes on each site run at the same speed and are linked with a fast interconnection network that does not favor any specific communication pattern [18]. This means a parallel job can be allocated on any subset of nodes in a site. The parallel computer system uses space-sharing and run the jobs in an exclusive fashion.

The system deals with an on-line scheduling problem without any knowledge of future job submissions. The jobs under consideration are restricted to batch jobs because this job type is dominant on most parallel computer systems running scientific and engineering applications. For the sake of simplicity, in this paper we assume a global grid scheduler which handles all job scheduling and resource allocation activities. The local schedulers are only responsible for starting the jobs after their allocation by the global scheduler. Theoretically a single central scheduler could be a critical limitation concerning efficiency and reliability. However, practical distributed implementations are possible, in which site-autonomy is still maintained but the resulting schedule would be the same as created by a central scheduler [19].

For simplification and efficient load sharing all computing nodes in the computational grid are assumed to be binary compatible. The grid is heterogeneous in the sense that nodes on different sites may differ in computing speed and different sites may have different numbers of nodes. When load sharing activities occur a job may have to migrate to a remote site for execution. In this case the input data for that job have to be transferred to the target site before the job execution while the output data of the job is transferred back afterwards. This network communication is neglected in our simulation studies as this latency can usually be hidden in pre- and post-fetching phases without regards to the actual job execution phase [19].

In this paper we focus on the area of high throughput computing, improving system's overall throughput with appropriate load sharing policies. Therefore, in our studies the requested number of processors for each job is bound by the total number of processors on the local site from which the job is submitted. The local site which a job is submitted from will be called the *home site* of the job henceforward in this paper. We assume the ability of jobs to run in multi-site mode. That means a job can run in parallel on a node set distributed over different sites when no single site can provide enough free processors for it due to a portion of resources are occupied by some running jobs.

Our simulation studies were based on publicly downloadable workload traces [20]. We used the SDSC's SP2 workload logs [1] on [20] as the input workload in the simulations. The workload log on SDSC's SP2 contains 73496 records collected on a 128-node IBM SP2 machine at San Diego Supercomputer Center (SDSC) from May 1998 to April 2000. After excluding some problematic records based on the *completed* field [20] in the log, the simulations in this paper use 56490 job records as the input workload. The detailed workload characteristics are shown in Table 1.

Table 1. Characteristics of the workload log on SDSC's SP2

	Number of jobs	Maximum execution time (sec.)	Average execution time (sec.)	Maximum number of processors per job	Average number of processors per job
Queue 1	4053	21922	267.13	8	3
Queue 2	6795	64411	6746.27	128	16
Queue 3	26067	118561	5657.81	128	12
Queue 4	19398	64817	5935.92	128	6
Queue 5	177	42262	462.46	50	4
Total	56490				

In the SDSC's SP2 system the jobs in this log are put into five different queues and all these queues share the same 128 processors on the system. In the following simulations this workload log will be used to model the workload on a computational grid consisting of five different sites whose workloads correspond to the jobs submitted to the five queues respectively. Table 2 shows the configuration of the computational grid under study. The number of processors on each site is determined according to the maximum number of required processors of the jobs belonged to the corresponding queue for that site.

Table 2. Configuration of the computational grid

	total	site 1	site 2	site 3	site 4	site 5
Number of processors	442	8	128	128	128	50

To simulate the speed difference among participating sites we define a speed vector, speed=(sp1,sp2,sp3,sp4,sp5), to describe the relative computing speeds of all the five sites in the grid, in which the value 1 represents the computing speed resulting in the job execution time in the original workload log. We also define a load vector, load=(ld1,ld2,ld3,ld4,ld5), which is used to derive different loading levels from the original workload data by multiplying the load value ld*i* to the execution times of all jobs at site *i*.

4 Site Selection Policies for Load Sharing in a Heterogeneous Grid

This section explores the potential of a computational grid in improving the performance of user jobs. The following describes the scheduling structures of two system architectures with/without grid computing respectively.

- **Independent clusters.** This architecture corresponds to the situation where no grid computing technologies are involved. The computing resources at different sites are independent and have their own job queues without any load sharing activities among them. Each site's users can only submit jobs to their local site and those jobs would be executed only on that site. This architecture is used as a comparison basis to see what performance gain grid computing can bring.
- **Load-sharing computational grid.** Different sites connected with an interconnection network form a computational grid. In the computational grid, there is a global job scheduler as well as a globally shared job queue. Jobs submitted by users at different sites are automatically redirected to the global queue and the jobs retain the identities of their home sites. In this section, different sites in the computational grid are viewed as different processor pools and each job must be allocated to exactly one site. No jobs can simultaneously use processors on different sites. Support for multi-site parallel execution will be discussed in later sections.

Two kinds of policies are important regarding load sharing in a computational grid: *job scheduling* and *site selection*. Job scheduling determines the sequence of starting execution for the jobs waiting in the queue. It is required in both the *independent clusters* and *computational grid* architectures. On the other hand, site selection policies are necessary in a computational grid, which choose an appropriate site among a set of candidate sites for allocating a job according to some specified criteria.

The *best-fit* site selection policy has been demonstrated to be the best choice on a homogeneous grid in previous works [1, 10]. In the *best-fit* policy a particular site is chosen for a job on which the job will leave the least number of free processors if it is allocated to that site. As for job scheduling policy, we compared both the FCFS (First-Come-First-Serve) policy and the NJF (Narrowest-Job-First) policy. The NJF policy was shown to outperform other non-FCFS policies, including *conservative backfilling*, *first-available*, *widest-first*, in our previous work [10]. Here, the word "narrowest" means requiring the least number of processors. In this paper we use the average response time of all jobs as the comparison criterion in all simulations, which is defined as:

$$AverageResponseTime = \frac{\sum_{j \in AllJobs} (endTime_j - submitTime_j)}{TotalNumberofJobs}$$

However, in the real world a computational grid is usually heterogeneous, at least, in the aspect of computing speeds at different sites. The *best-fit* site selection policy without considering the speed difference among participating sites may not achieve good performance in a heterogeneous grid, sometimes resulting in even worse performance than the original *independent-site* architecture.

To deal with the site selection issue in a heterogeneous grid, we first propose a two-phase procedure. At the first phase the grid scheduler determines a set of candidate sites among all the sites with enough free processors for a specific job under consideration by filtering out some sites according to a predefined threshold ratio of computing speed. In the filtering process, a lower bound for computing speed is first determined through multiplying the predefined threshold ratio by the computing speed of a single processor on the job's home site, and then any sites with single-processor speed slower than the lower bound are filtered out. Therefore, adjusting the threshold ratio is an effective way in controlling the outcomes of site selection. When setting the threshold ratio to 1 the grid scheduler will only allocate jobs to sites with single-processor speed equal to or faster than their home sites. On the other hand, with the threshold ratio set to zero, all sites with enough free processors are qualified candidates for a job's allocation. Raising the threshold ratio would prevent allocating a job to a site that is much slower than its home site. This could ensure a job's execution time would not be increased too much due to being allocated to a slow site. However, for the same reason a job may consequently need to wait in the queue for a longer time period. On the other hand, lowering the threshold ratio would make it more probable for a job to get allocation quickly at the cost of extended execution time. The combined effects of shortened waiting time and extended execution time are complicated for analysis. At the second phase the grid scheduler adopts a site selection policy to choose an appropriate site from the candidate sites for allocating the job.

Figure 1 compares the performances of two different values, 0 and 1, for the threshold ratio. The results indicate that when the speed difference among sites is large, speed=(0.6, 0.7, 2.4, 9.5, 4.3), setting the threshold ratio to 1 can enable the *best-fit* policy to make performance improvement in a heterogeneous computational grid compared to the *independent-site* architecture.

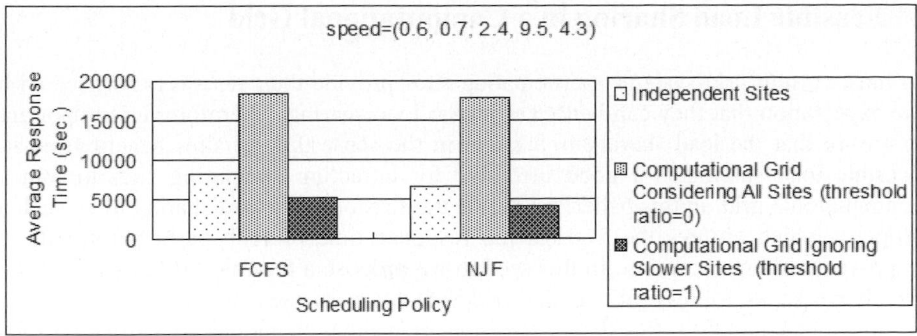

Fig. 1. Performance of *best-fit* policy with large speed difference among participating sites

Another possible policy for the second phase of the site selection process is called the *fastest one*. The *fastest-one* policy chooses the site with the fastest computing speed among all the sites with enough free processors for a job without consideration of the difference between the number of required processors and a site's free capacity. To deal with the difficulty in determination of an appropriate site selection policy, in this section we propose an *adaptive* policy, which dynamically changes between the *best-fit* and the *fastest-one* policies, trying to make a better choice at each site selection activity. The decision is made based on a calculation of which policy can further accommodate more jobs for immediate execution. Figure 2 shows that the *adaptive* policy has potential for outperforming the *best-fit* and the *fastest-one* policies in some cases.

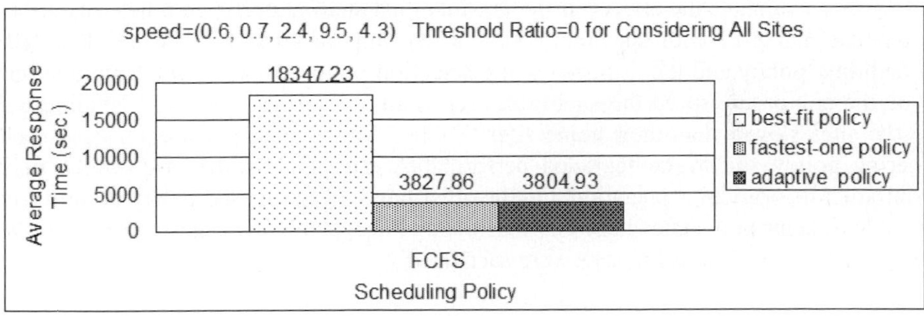

Fig. 2. Performance of the adaptive policy

We also performed a series of 120 simulations representing all kinds of relative speed sequences for the 5 sites, permutations of speed=(1, 3, 5, 7, 9), in the computational grids. In the 120 simulations, among the three policies the *adaptive* policy is the most stable one. It is never the last one and always quite close to the best one in performance for all the 120 cases, while the other two policies would lead to poor performance in some cases, being distant from the best and the second policies. Therefore, while it is not clear whether the *best-fit* or the *fastest-one* policy could achieve better performance under current grid configuration and workload, it may be a way for playing safe adopting the proposed *adaptive* policy.

5 Feasible Load Sharing in a Computational Grid

In most current grid systems, participating sites provide their resources for free with the expectation that they can benefit from the load sharing. Therefore, it is important to ensure that the load sharing is feasible in the sense that all sites benefit from it. Feasible load sharing is a good incentive for attracting computing sites to join a computational grid. In this paper, we define the feasibility of load sharing to be such a property which ensures the average job response time of each participating site is improved without exception. In this section we propose a feasible load sharing policy which works as follows. When the grid scheduler chooses the next job from the waiting queue and finds that there exists no single site with enough free processors for this job's immediate execution, instead of simply keeping the job waiting in the queue the grid scheduler inspects the status of the job's home site to see if it is possible to make enough free processors by reclaiming a necessary amount of occupied processors from some of the running remote jobs. If so, it stops the necessary amount of these running remote jobs to produce enough free processors and put the stopped remote jobs back to the front of the waiting queue for being re-scheduled to other sites for execution. This feasible load sharing policy tries to benefit all sites by giving local jobs a higher priority than remote jobs.

For performing the feasible load sharing policy, the grid scheduler maintains a separate waiting queue for each site. Each time it tries to schedule the jobs in one queue as more as it can until no more jobs can be allocated. At this time the grid scheduler moves on to the next queue for another site. Multi-queue is an effective mechanism to ensure that local jobs have higher priority than remote jobs during the processor reclaiming process.

Table 3 evaluates the effects of the feasible load sharing policy in a heterogeneous computational grid with speed=(1, 3, 4, 4, 8) and load=(5, 4, 5, 4, 1). The NJF scheduling policy and the *fastest-one* site selection policy are used in the simulations with the computing speed threshold ratio set to one, ensuring jobs won't be allocated to the sites slower than their home sites. Table 3 shows that with the ordinary load sharing policy site 5 got degraded performance after joining the grid, which may contradict its original expectation. On the other hand, our proposed policy is shown to be able to achieve a somewhat more feasible and acceptable load sharing result in the sense that no sites' performances were sacrificed.

Table 3. Average job response times (sec.) for different load sharing policies

	Entire grid	Site 1	Site 2	Site 3	Site 4	Site 5
Independent sites	9260	14216	10964	10199	6448	57
Ordinary load sharing policy	4135	191	4758	4799	3881	559
Feasible load sharing policy	4152	193	4750	4798	3939	57

6 Multi-site Parallel Execution in a Heterogeneous Grid

In the load sharing policies described in the previous sections, different sites in the computational grid are viewed as independent processor pools. Each job can only be allocated to exactly one of these sites. However, one drawback of this multi-pool processor allocation is the very likely internal fragmentation [4] where no pools individually can provide enough resources for a certain job but the job could get enough resources to run if it can simultaneously use more than one pool's resources.

Multi-site parallel execution is traditionally regarded as a mechanism to enable the execution of such jobs requiring large parallelisms that exceed the capacity of any single site. This is a major application area in grid computing called distributed supercomputing [21]. However, multi-site parallel execution could be also beneficial for another application area in grid computing: high throughput computing [21]. In our high throughput computing model in this paper, each job's parallelism is bound by the total capacity of its home site. That means multi-site parallel execution is not inherently necessary for these jobs. However, for high throughput computing a computational grid is used in the space-sharing manner. It is therefore not unusual that upon a job's submission its requested number of processors is not available from any single site due to the occupation of a portion of system resources by some concurrently running jobs. In such a situation, splitting the job up into multi-site parallel execution is promising in shortening the response time of the job through reducing its waiting time. However, in multi-site parallel execution the impact of bandwidth and latency has to be considered as wide area networks are involved. In this paper we summarize the overhead caused by communication and data migration as an increase of the job's runtime [2, 10]. The magnitude of this overhead greatly influences the achievable response time reduction for a job which is allowed to perform multi-site parallel execution.

If a job is performing multi-site parallel execution, the runtime of the job is extended by the overhead which is specified by a parameter p [2]. Therefore the new runtime r^* is:

$$r^* = (1 + p) \times r$$

where r is the runtime for the job running on a single site. As for the site selection issue in multi-site parallel execution, previous works in [1, 10] suggested the *larger-first* policy for a homogeneous grid environment, which repeatedly picks up a site with the largest number of free processors until all the selected sites together can fulfill the requirement of the job to be allocated. As a heterogeneous grid being considered, the speed difference among participating sites should be taken into account. An intuitive heuristic is called the *faster-first* policy, which each time picks up the site with the fastest computing speed instead of the site having the most amount of free processors. This section develops an *adaptive* site selection policy which dynamically changes between the *larger-first* and the *faster-first* policies based on a calculation of which policy can further accommodate more jobs for immediate single-site execution.

Figure 3 shows that supporting multi-site parallel execution can further improve the performance of a heterogeneous load sharing computational grid when the multi-site overhead p=2. Moreover, our proposed *adaptive* site selection policy outperforms the *larger-first* and the *faster-first* policies significantly. Actually in all the 120 simulations we performed for different speed configurations the *adaptive* policy performs better than the other two policies for each case.

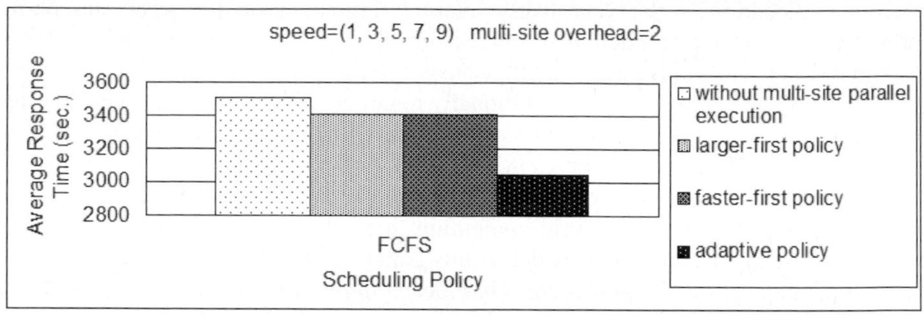

Fig. 3. Performance evaluation of adaptive site selection in multi-site parallel execution

7 Conclusion

Most current grid environments are established through the collaboration among a group of participating sites which volunteer to provide free computing resources. Each participating site usually has its own local user community and computing jobs to take care of. Therefore, feasible load sharing policies that benefit all sites are an important incentive for attracting computing sites to join and stay in a grid environment. Moreover, a grid environment is usually heterogeneous in nature in the real world at least for the different computing speeds at different participating sites. The heterogeneity presents a challenge for effectively arranging load sharing activities in a computational grid. This paper explores the feasibility and effectiveness of load sharing activities in a heterogeneous computational grid. Several issues are discussed including site selection policies for single-site and multi-site parallel execution as well as feasible load sharing mechanisms. For each issue a promising policy is proposed and evaluated in a series of simulations. The quality of scheduling and allocation policies largely depends on the actual grid configuration and workload. The improvements presented in this paper were achieved using example configurations and workloads derived from real traces. The outcome may vary in other configurations and workloads. However, the results show that the proposed policies are capable of significantly improving the overall system performance in terms of average response time for user jobs.

Acknowledgement

The work of this paper is partially supported by National Science Council and National Center for High-Performance Computing under NSC 94-2218-E-007-057, NSC 94-2213-E-432-001 and NCHC-KING_010200 respectively.

References

[1] V. Hamscher, U. Schwiegelshohn, A. Streit, and R. Yahyapour, "Evaluation of Job-Scheduling Strategies for Grid Computing", *Proceedings of the 7th International Conference on High Performance Computing, HiPC-2000*, pp. 191-202, Bangalore, India, 2000.

[2] C. Ernemann, V. Hamscher, R. Yahyapour, and A. Streit, "Enhanced Algorithms for Multi-Site Scheduling", *Proceedings of 3rd International Workshop Grid 2002, in conjunction with Supercomputing 2002*, pp. 219-231, Baltimore, MD, USA, November 2002.

[3] C. Ernemann, V. Hamscher, U. Schwiegelshohn, A. Streit, R. Yahyapour, "On Advantages of Grid Computing for Parallel Job Scheduling", *Proceedings of 2nd IEEE International Symposium on Cluster Computing and the Grid (CC-GRID 2002)*, pp. 39-46, Berlin, Germany, 2002.

[4] C. Ernemann, V. Hamscher, A. Streit, R. Yahyapour, ""On Effects of Machine Configurations on Parallel Job Scheduling in Computational Grids", *Proceedings of International Conference on Architecture of Computing Systems, ARCS 2002*, pp. 169-179, 2002.

[5] R. Buyya, D. Abramson, J. Giddy, H. Stockinger, "Economic Models for Resource Management and Scheduling in Grid Computing", Special Issue on Grid Computing Environments, *The Journal of Concurrency and Computation: Practice and Experience(CCPE)*, May 2002.

[6] R. Buyya, J. Giddy, D. Abramson, "An Evaluation of Economy-Based Resource Trading and Scheduling on Computational Power Grids for Parameter Sweep Applications", *Proceedings of the Second Workshop on Active Middleware Services (AMS2000), In conjunction with the Ninth IEEE International Symposium on High Performance Distributed Computing (HPDC 2000)*, Pittsburgh, USA, August 2000.

[7] Y. Zhu, J. Han, Y. Liu, L. M. Ni, C. Hu, J. Huai, "TruGrid: A Self-sustaining Trustworthy Grid", *Proceedings of the First International Workshop on Mobility in Peer-to-Peer Systems (MPPS) (ICDCSW'05)*, pp. 815-821, June 2005.

[8] C. Ernemann, V. Hamscher, R. Yahyapour, "Economic Scheduling in Grid Computing", *the 8th International Workshop on Job Scheduling Strategies for Parallel Processing, Lecture Notes In Computer Science*; Vol. 2537, pp. 128-152, 2002.

[9] D. England and J. B. Weissman, "Costs and Benefits of Load Sharing in Computational Grid", *10th Workshop on Job Scheduling Strategies for Parallel Processing, Lecture Notes In Computer Science*, Vol. 3277, June 2004.

[10] K. C. Huang and H. Y. Chang, "An Integrated Processor Allocation and Job Scheduling Approach to Workload Management on Computing Grid", *Proceedings of the 2006 International Conference on Parallel and Distributed Processing Techniques and Applications (PDPTA'06)*, pp. 703-709, Las Vegas, USA, June 26-29, 2006.

[11] G. Sabin, R. Kettimuthu, A. Rajan and P. Sadayappan, "Scheduling of Parallel Jobs in a Heterogeneous Multi-Site Environment", *Proceedings of 9th Workshop on Job Scheduling Strategies for Parallel Processing*, June 2003.

[12] M. Brune, J. Gehring, A. Keller, A. Reinefeld, "Managing Clusters of Geographically Distributed High-Performance Computers", *Concurrency – Practice and Experience*, 11(15): 887-911, 1999.

[13] A. I. D. Bucur and D. H. J. Epema, "The Performance of Processor Co-Allocation in Multicluster Systems", *Proceedings of the Third IEEE International Symposium on Cluster Computing and the Grid (CCGrid'03)*, pp. 302-, May 2003.

[14] A. I. D. Bucur and D. H. J. Epema, "The Influence of Communication on the Performance of Co-Allocation", *the 7th International Workshop on Job Scheduling Strategies for Parallel Processing, Lecture Notes in Computer Science*; Vol. 2221, pp. 66-86, 2001.

[15] A. I. D. Bucur and D. H. J. Epema, "Local versus Global Schedulers with Processor Co-Allocation in Multicluster Systems", *the 8th International Workshop on Job Scheduling Strategies for Parallel Processing, Lecture Notes In Computer Science*, pp. 184-204, 2002.

[16] S. Banen, A. I. D. Bucur and D. H. J. Epema, "A Measurement-Based Simulation Study of Processor Co-Allocation in Multicluster Systems", *the 9th Workshop on Job Scheduling Strategies for Parallel Processing, Lecture Notes In Computer Science*; Vol. 2862, pp. 105-128, 2003.

[17] W. Zhang, A. M. K. Cheng, M. Hu, "Multisite Co-allocation Algorithms for Computational Grid", *Proceedings of the 20th International Parallel and Distributed Processing Symposium*, pp. 8-, April 2006.

[18] D. Feitelson and L. Rudolph, "Parallel Job Scheduling: Issues and Approaches", *Proceedings of IPPS'95 Workshop: Job Scheduling Strategies for Parallel Processing*, pp. 1-18, 1995.

[19] C. Ernemann, V. Hamscher, R. Yahyapour, "Benefits of Global Grid Computing for Job Scheduling," *Proceedings of the Fifth IEEE/ACM International Workshop on Grid Computing*(GRID'04), pp. 374-379, November 2004.

[20] Parallel Workloads Archive, http://www.cs.huji.ac.il/labs/parallel/workload/

[21] I. Foster, C. Kesselman, *The Grid: Blueprint for a New Computing Infrastructure*, Morgan Kaufmann Publishers, Inc., 1999.

Meeting QoS Requirements of Mobile Computing by Dual-Level Congestion Control

Yi-Ming Chen and Chih-Lun Su

Department of Information Management, national Central University
300, Jhongda Rd., Jhongli, Taiwan, 32054, R.O.C.
{cym, 90423216}@cc.ncu.edu.tw

Abstract. As the resources in a wireless network are limited and freely shared by all network users, Call Admission Control (CAC) plays a significant role in providing the Quality of Service (QoS) in wireless networks. However, when the network is congested with too many users, traditional CAC that mainly focuses on the tradeoff between new call blocking probability and handoff call dropping probability cannot guarantee QoS requirements to users. To address this issue, this paper proposes a dual level congestion control scheme which considers not only the call level admission control but also the user's decision to enter the network or not during the network traffic burst interval (we call it as user-level burst control). We adopt the economical terms of externality and introduce a total user utility function to formally model the user's perceived QoS metric. Our simulation shows that the weighted blocking probability (Pb) of our scheme can decreases 70~80% than traditional CAC systems and increase the total user utility to 2~3 times.

Keywords: Call admission control, congestion control, utility function, quality of service, wireless network.

1 Introduction

As 802.11 wireless LANs becomes more and more popular, the demand for mobile communication services, such as Internet phone, is increasing. Since such communication services require high quality of transmission, how to provide desired *Quality of Service (QoS)* to users becomes an important research issue. Generally, *call admission control (CAC)* plays a significant role in providing desired QoS in wireless networks [1]. Traditional CAC usually limits the number of call connections into the networks to reduce the network congestion and call blocking. In mobile networks, there are two classes of call connections: new calls and handoff calls. Both of them may be blocked or dropped due to the limited resources in a wireless cell. Therefore, *call blocking probability (CBP)* and *call dropping probability (CDP)* are two important connection level QoS parameters [2]. Many CAC schemes, such as guard channel scheme and queueing priority scheme, have been proposed to balance the tradeoffs between new call blocking and handoff call droppings [3][4].

However, above schemes only concentrate on the tradeoff between CBP and CDP, that is, decreasing the CDP at the cost of increasing the CBP. It's noticeably that when the traffic load is heavy, for example in peak hours, no matter how CAC adjusts

C. Cérin and K.-C. Li (Eds.): GPC 2007, LNCS 4459, pp. 241 – 251, 2007.

to allocate the resources, CBP and CDP are still high [5]. The reason for QoS degradation in such case can be explained by an economical term- *externality*, which means that some wireless users bear the costs of QoS degradation stemmed from other users being admitted freely into the network (we assume wireless resources are public good and can be freely shared by all network users). As the causes of QoS degradation is from too many users entering into the networks in a burst mode, a rational solution is to regulate the users. A problem arises naturally: how to do the user regulation?

To address the user regulation problem mentioned above, in this paper, we first define a *total user utility* to model the total users' perceived QoS metric, then define a congestion threshold which represents the balance point where the number of satisfied users is maximized and channel resources are most efficiently used. With these two definitions, we propose a scheme, named *UBC-CAC*, to integrate *User-level Burst Control (UBC)* with CAC. UBC-CAC comprises three components: congestion detection, user traffic shapes and user notification. We have developed a method to decide whether the network enters the congestion state or not, a leaky-bucket algorithm to perform user traffic shaping, and a SIP-based protocol to implement the user notification. Our simulation shows that the weighted blocking probability (P_b) of our scheme can decreases 70~80% than traditional CAC only systems and increase the total user utility to 2~3 times.

The remaining of this paper is organized as follows: Section 2 introduces some congestion control schemes. Section 3 introduces our system model. Section 4 describes the three components of our system. In Section 5, we describe the simulation which compares the performance between UBC-CAC system and conventional CAC system under various user behavior modes. Finally, we give short conclusion and explore future research direction in Section 6.

2 Research Background

In general, there are three types of congestion control schemes: call-level control, packet-level control, and user-level control.

Packet-level control is also called input rate control, which aims controlling the input rate of traffic sources to prevent, reduce, or control the level of congestion. Some well-known packet-level control schemes, such as traffic shaping [6], develops the algorithms of leaky (token) bucket and random early detection (RED)[7].

Call-level control is defined as a set of actions, performed at call set-up phase, to determine whether or not the call requesting the resources can be accepted. CAC is one representation. The major design concern of CAC is to prioritize handoff calls, because mobile users tend to be much more sensitive to call dropping than to call blocking. Various handoff priority-based CAC schemes have been proposed [4], which can be classified into two broad categories of guard channel scheme [8][9] and queueing priority scheme[10][11].

User-level control aims to control user traffic to prevent, reduce, or control the congestion caused by the burst of user traffic. A well-known scheme is Pricing-based scheme[5], which integrates CAC and pricing where the price is adjusted dynamically based on the current network conditions.

3 UBC-CAC System Model

3.1 Utility Function

In terms of economics, *utility* describes how users satisfy with their consumptions. Here, we use utility to describe network users' satisfaction with the perceived QoS and *utility function* to measure how sensitive users are due to the changes of congestion state in a network. In this paper, we assume the utility function is a function of CBP and CDP[5].

First of all, we let the average number of admitted users (N) as a function of the new call arrival rate λ_n, i.e., $N = f(\lambda_n)$ and define the function of the QoS metric P_b as a weighted sum of new call blocking probability (P_{nb}) and handoff call dropping probability (P_{hb}). In other words, $P_b = \alpha \times P_{nb} + \beta \times P_{hb}$, where α and β are constants that denote the penalty associated with rejecting new calls and handoff calls, respectively. The case of $\beta > \alpha$ means that dropping a handoff call has higher cost than blocking a new call.

It is noted that both P_{nb} and P_{hb} are monotonically increasing function of λ_n, therefore $P_b = g(\lambda_n)$ holds. In addition, the increase of function P_b implies the users will face higher call blocking probability and lower level of user satisfaction. Therefore, we can reasonably make the assumption that the utility function of a single user (U_s) is a function of the QoS metric P_b, i.e., $U_s = h\ (P_b)$. Note that U_s achieves maximum value at $P_b = 0$. It means that if the blocking probability is zero percent, i.e., every user could acquire the wireless resource, the user has the highest level of satisfaction with the QoS.

Definition [total user utility]
Given the average number of admitted users (N) and the utility function of a single user (U_s), a *total user utility* U can be defined as follows:

$$U = N \times U_s = f(\lambda_n) \times h\ (P_b) = f(\lambda_n) \times h\ [\ g(\lambda_n)\ ] \tag{1}$$

The above equation shows that the total user utility in wireless networks depends on the new call arrival rate (λ_n). Based on the proof in [5], we learn that there exists an optimal new call arrival rate where the total utility is maximized. We denote this optimal value as λ_n^*.

Definition [congestion threshold]
The *congestion threshold* is defined as λ_n^*. When the condition of $\lambda_n = \lambda_n^*$ holds, the user arrival rate has reached a point where the number of satisfied users is maximized and the channel resources are most efficiently used. However, when $\lambda_n > \lambda_n^*$ holds, the network enters congestion states, where both the total user utility and the QoS decrease.

3.2 System Model

The system is made up of two parts: User-level Burst Control (UBC), and CAC, which is shown in Figure 1.

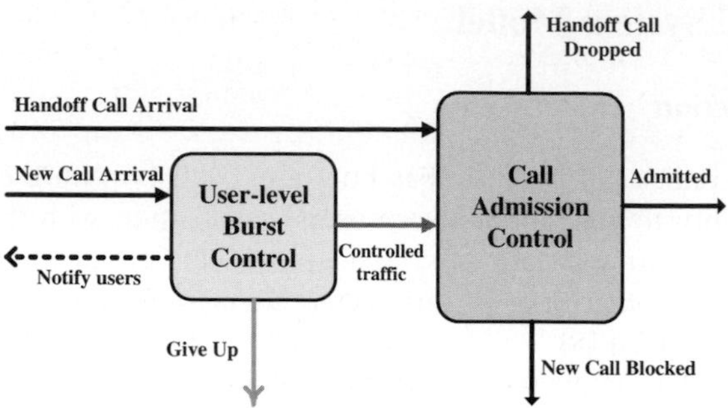

Fig. 1. UBC-CAC scheme

In our design, we will take the following steps to alleviate the problem of congestion and get maximum total user utility.

1. Handoff users do not need to go through UBC because they are a continuation of previously admitted users. They are controlled by traditional CAC scheme.
2. While the network is not congested, new users just go through UBC and proceed to CAC.
3. The UBC scheme begins to control the user traffic when the network becomes congested.
4. The UBC scheme will notify users when the network becomes congesting, so that users could make informed decisions to wait or leave. We assume the users do not leave after joining the waiting queue.

4 Design of UBC Module

The UBC module is composed of three modules: congestion detection, user traffic shaper and SIP-based user notification.

Congestion detection module periodically checks whether the traffic load exceeds the congestion threshold. User traffic shaper module uses leaky bucket algorithm to control the user traffic when the network becomes congesting. The function of notification module is to inform users of important information, such as expected waiting time.

4.1 Congestion Detection

The core of UBC is to determine whether the network has entered into a congested state or not. In other words, we have to determine whether the network exceeds the congestion threshold by estimating the current user traffic.

At any given access point (AP) of an 802.11 WLAN, the user traffic load, i.e., how many new users arrive in a period, is observable. Therefore, our congestion detection make use of so-called exponential smoothing technique in RED[7] to compute the assessed value of user traffic in an AP from the observed real user traffic. This technique is briefly described as follows:

First of all, we divide the time into many assessed period. We denote $\lambda_n^{(r)}(i)$ as the real user traffic (new call arrival rate) and $\lambda_n^{(a)}(i)$ as the assess traffic load in the i th assessed period. We could obtain $\lambda_n^{(r)}(i)$ at the beginning of the $i+1$ th assessed period (i.e. the end of i th assessed period) and also estimate $\lambda_n^{(a)}(i)$ at the beginning of the i th assessed period. By exponential smooth technique, we assess the user traffic of the next period ($i+1$ th) by the following equation:

$$\lambda_n^{(a)}(i+1) = (1\text{-}w)\times \lambda_n^{(a)}(i) + w\times\lambda_n^{(r)}(i) \tag{2}$$

By this assessed user traffic of the next period, we can determine whether the oncoming user traffic is beyond λ_n^* (congestion threshold) or not. In Equation (2), w is a "weight" ($0 < w < 1$) that should be related to the change curve of $\lambda_n^{(r)}(i)$. If we rearrange this equation and gather all the terms multiplied by w, we could make the equation more meaningful and calculation faster, and we get:

$$\lambda_n^{(a)}(i+1) = \lambda_n^{(a)}(i) + w\times[\lambda_n^{(r)}(i) - \lambda_n^{(a)}(i)] \tag{3}$$

Now $\lambda_n^{(a)}(i+1)$ is the prediction of the user traffic of the next period, $\lambda_n^{(r)}(i)-\lambda_n^{(a)}(i)$, and is considered the error of the prediction. The above equation indicates that we predict the traffic load of next period (new forecast) on the basis of previous prediction plus a percentage of the difference between that previous prediction and the actual value of the traffic load at that point (forecast error).

4.2 User Traffic Shaper

User traffic shaper is based on the well known token bucket algorithm. The basic idea is that each incoming user can pass through the UBC only after obtaining a token. Tokens 'leak' at a constant rate r out of a leaky bucket. The size of bucket imposes an upper bound on the burst length and determines the number of users that can pass.

It is noted that token leaking rate r is set to the optimal new call arrival rate of λ_n^*, for from Section 3.2, we know that maximum total user utility can be achieved at this point. When the network is congested, there's no token available for users and they are queued in the waiting queue, not discarded. We let users make their own decision.

4.3 User Notification

Since our UBC scheme puts the users in a queue, we have to inform users of the congestion information and the expected waiting time. We adopt the Session Initiation Protocol (SIP) [12] to achieve this goal and use it to implement the call set-up and tear-down.

We use one of SIP response messages- *Provisional 182 (Queue)*, which would contain the network states and queue information, e.g., "the network is in congested state; 2 calls queued; expected waiting time is 5 minutes ", to users. Here we adopt a simple method to calculate the expected waiting time. First, we assume a user a arriving at time t when the network is detected to be congested. Let the waiting queue length be L_t, the number of tokens at time t be TK_t, and the optimal new call arrival rate be λ_n^*, then the expected waiting time, eWT_a, is the time that user a must wait to obtain a token subtracting the time that the users who are in front of user a and can pass through the waiting queue without delay (for they could obtain the token immediately). Weobtain the following equation:

$$eWT_a = ([^{(Lt+1)} / _{\lambda n*}]+1) - [^{TK}t/_{\lambda n*}] \tag{4}$$

where [ ] is Gauss' symbol. Since L_t and TK_t are known at time t, so eWT_a could be computed easily.

Figure 2 shows an example of SIP messages flows. It is noticeable that PRACK is used here for reliable delivery of provisional responses, because this information is important to users.

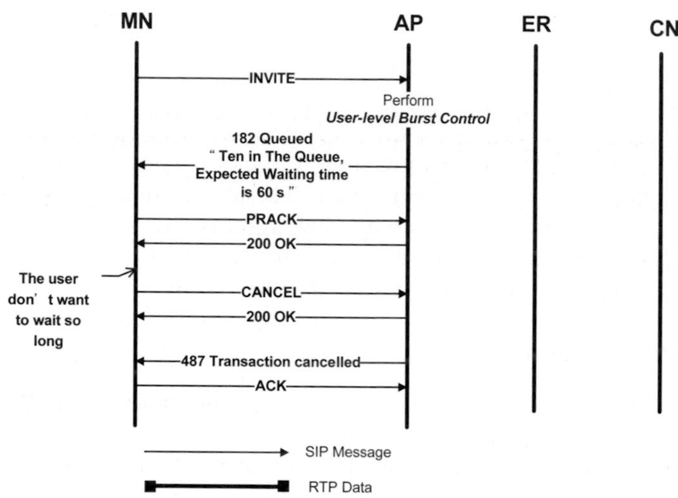

Fig. 2. SIP message flows to indicate the user want to leave in long queue

5 User Behavior Modes and Performance Evaluation

In this section, we first describe the various user behavior modes when a user waits in a waiting queue, then we use simulations to compare our UBC-CAC scheme with traditional CAC scheme.

5.1 User Behavior Modes

When a user waits in a waiting queue, what will he/she do if the queue length is very long? In [13], W. Feng *et al.*, think that there are two cases for such situation: (1) users have no information about the system; (2) users are informed of the queue length upon arrival. In the first case, users may balk (leave upon arrival) or renege (leave after joining the waiting line). In the second case, users are hopefully able to make a better decision with respect to balking. We believe the latter is more user friendly, so we adopt the scheme that the users are informed of expected waiting time upon arrivals. There are four possible user behavior modes when they are entering a congested network:

1. Retry**:** Give-up or blocked users retry to request the resources after waiting some time.
2. Leave**:** Give-up or blocked users just leave the system and not requests the resources.
3. Leave/Retry**:** The probabilities of the give-up or blocked user retry or leave is fixed, e.g., users leave with probability of one third and retry with probability of two thirds [5].
4. State-dependant Leave/Retry**:** In [13], the authors propose that the customer decides to join the queue based simply on the number of customers in front of them, i.e., if the number of customers in the queue is large, the probability that the incoming customer will balk should also be large. In this paper, the probability for the users to leave or retry is based on the expected waiting time. Thus, if the expected waiting time is large, the probability for them to leave is also large. The user knows that the network is seriously congested and cannot obtain the resources at that time even after a long time, so he would like to leave.

A. Conventional CAC systems

In conventional systems where no UBC scheme is used, we don't need to take into consideration of the state-dependant leave/retry because users need not to wait in UBC queue. The following notations are used in our simulation:

1. CSwL: All blocked users just leave the system and not retry to request the resources.
2. CSwR: All blocked users retry to request the resources after waiting some time.
3. CswLR: Blocked users leave with probability of one third and retry with probability two thirds. In other words, one third of the blocked users leave the system and the rest wait and retry.

B. UBC-CAC system

The user may behave differently in UBC-CAC scheme (refer to Figure 3). We use the following notations in our simulations:

1. User-level Burst Control System with Leave (UBCSwL): All blocked Users leave as in CCwL. All give-up users retry to request the resources after waiting some time, i.e., α=0 and β=1.
2. User-level Burst Control System with Retry (UBCSwR): Both all blocked users and give-up users retry after waiting some time, i.e., α=β=0.
3. User-level Burst Control System with Leave/Retry (UBCSwLR): Both give-up users and blocked users leave and retry with probability one third and two thirds, i.e., α=β=⅓.
4. User-level Burst Control System with State-dependant Leave/Retry (UBCSwSLR): The probability for users to leave and retry depends on the expected waiting time. Thus, as the expected waiting time increases, the probability for users to leave the system also increases.

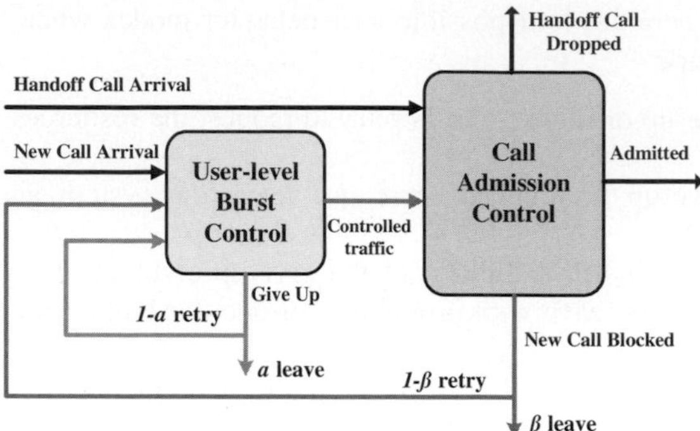

Fig. 3. User behavior modes inUBC-CAC scheme

5.2 Simulation

We use C language to write a simulation program to analyze the performance of CAC and UBC-CAC schemes.

A. Simulation parameters

We use guard channel scheme as CAC scheme, and assuming that each wireless cell is assigned capacity $C = 40$ channels and two of them are reserved for guard channels. Each call uses only one channel for service. We assume both new call arrival and handoff call arrival follow Poisson process with mean rates λ_n and λ_h respectively. λ_n increases little by little (with values range from 0 to 1 user per second), it means that the network is more and more congested. And like the models in [14][15], we assume that λ_h is proportional to λ_n, i.e., $\lambda_h = 1/5 * \lambda_n$.

For both new calls and handoff calls, the call duration times are exponentially distributed with mean $1/\mu$. (240 seconds) and the cell resident times are also exponentially distributed with mean $1/\eta$ (120 seconds). Parameters α and β in P_b are set to be ⅓ and ⅔, respectively. Assessed period (T) is set to be 50 seconds. We also assume that user patience time, and waiting time for blocked users and dropped users to retry are exponential distributed with mean values of 60 , 240, 60 seconds respectively.

B. Simulations Results

Figure 4 shows the comparisons of P_b between conventional systems (CSwL, CSwR, and CSwLR). We observe that CSwL has lowest P_b and CSwR is the worst one among them. It is reasonable, because in CSwL, all blocked users leaves and they don't compete with original users for the resources. However, in CSwR, all blocked users retry to compete with original users, so that more users are blocked and the total user utility decreases.

Figure 5 compares the achievable total user utility between conventional systems and UBC-CAC. The total user utility of UBCSwL increases around 3.3 times than that of CSwL; the total user utility of UBCSwR increases around 4.3 times than that of CSwR; the total user utility of UBCSwLR and UBCSwSLR increases around 3.8 times more than that of CSwLR.

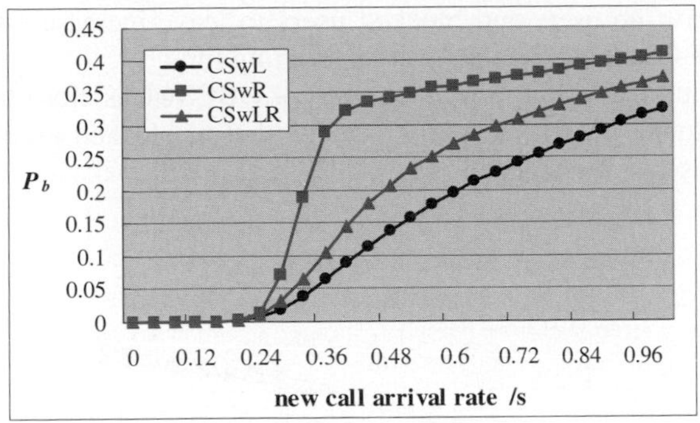

Fig. 4. P_b for conventional systems

We can conclude that no matter how users behave, the performance (P_b and total user utility) improves quite much after taking UBC into consideration.

Figure 5 also compares the achievable total user utility between UBCSwL, UBCSwR, UBCSwLR, and UBCSwSLR. We can easily find that CCSwLR achieves larger total user utility than UBCSwSLR. Besides, UBCSwR has the largest total user utility, and UBCSwL has the lowest one. It's because in UBCSwR all give-up users and blocked users choose to retry, so that more users can be served. On the contrary, UBCSwL can only serve the minimum number of users, because all blocked users leave the system. In UBCSwLR, two thirds of give-up users and blocked users choose to retry, but in UBCSwSLR the probability for give-up users and blocked users to retry decreases with the states of network, so that more and more give-up users and blocked users leave the system. Therefore, UBCSwLR can serve more users than UBCSwSLR. But remember that UBCSwSLR is more realistic than UBCSwLR.

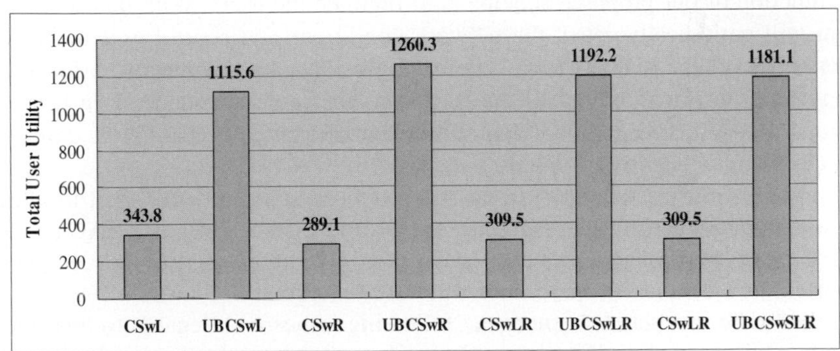

Fig. 5. Comparisons of total utility

Figure 6 shows the comparison of average waiting time. The average waiting time is the average time from users' entering of the queue to their leaving. We can easily find that UBCSwR has largest average waiting time. That is because all give-up users and blocked users choose to retry. Compared with UBCSwLR and UBCSwSLR, the probability for give-up users and blocked users to leave increases with the network conditions, so UBCSwSLR has less average waiting time.

Besides, we find that average waiting time of UBCSwL is close to UBCSwR. We think that the number of give-up users exceeds that of blocked users quite many, so that all give-up users who choose to retry (UBCSwL) will make average waiting time increase fast.

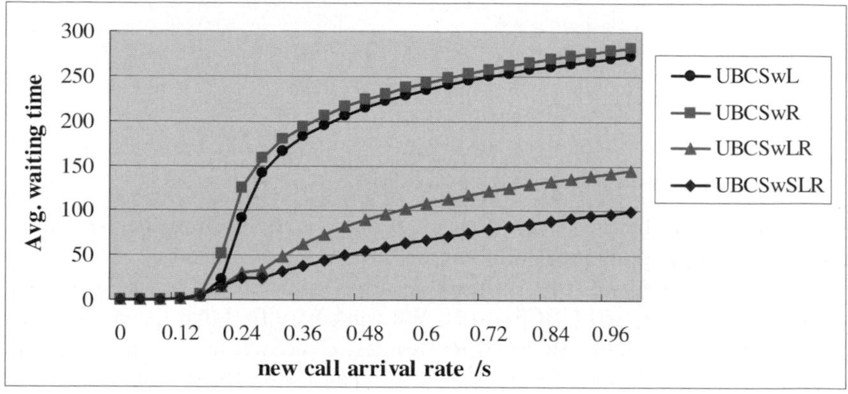

Fig. 6. Average waiting time for UBC systems

5 Conclusions

In this paper we propose a dual-level control scheme which combines user-level burst control (UBC) with CAC to meet the QoS requirements of wireless networks. The basic function of our proposed scheme is to regulate the users. With this scheme, the system will periodically detect the network conditions and control user traffic when the network is congested with too many users. Besides, our scheme also informs users of congestion information via SIP messages, so that users can depend on it to make decisions. UBC-CAC can not only control user traffic but also restrain the demand for resources when the network is congested.

The simulation results showed that our proposed scheme works well to alleviate the problem of congestion and guarantee the QoS to users. P_b of UBC-CAC decreases 70~80% than conventional systems and achievable total user utility, which is a measure of how efficiently the resources are used increases 2~3 times.

In the future, we plan to explore the following issues with regards to this scheme: (1)Mathematical proving: Since we only verify our proposed scheme via simulation, it is worth proving it by the concepts of mathematics. For example, our UBC scheme can be analyzed as queueing models with user's patience, since it queues users in the waiting queue; (2)Message overhead evaluation: Since we use SIP to deal with call set-up and tear-down and inform users of the information, we should also take SIP message overhead into consideration. The evaluation is needed in the future.

References

1. Hou, J. and Fang, Y., "Mobility-based call admission control schemes for wireless mobile networks," *Wireless Communication and Mobile Computing*, (2001)
2. Islam, M.M., Murshed, M. and Dooley, L.S., "New mobility based call admission control with on-demand borrowing scheme for QOS provisioning," *Proceedings of the International Conference on Information Technology: Computers and Communications (ITCC 03)*, (2003) 263 – 267
3. Kulavaratharasah, M.D. and Aghvami, A.H., "Teletraffic Performance Evaluation of Microcellular Personal Communication Networks (PCN's) with Prioritized Handoff Procedures," *IEEE Trans. Vehicular Technology*, Vol. 48, Jan. (1999)
4. Katzela, I. and Naghshineh, M., "Channel assignment schemes for cellular mobile telecommunication system: a comprehensive survey," *IEEE Personal Communications*, Vol. 3, No. 3, (1996)
5. Hou, J., Yang, J. and Papavassiliou, S., "Integration of Pricing with Call Admission Control to Meeto QoS Requirements in Cellular Networks," *IEEE Trans. On Parallel and Distributed Systems*, Vol. 13, No. 9, (2002)
6. ATM Forum, "ATM Traffic Management Specification Version 4.0," April (1996)
7. Floyd, S. and Jacobson, V., "Random Early Detection Gateways for Congestion Avoidance," *IEEE/ACM Transactions on Networking*, August (1993)
8. Kuo, J., "Dynamic QoS Management for Wired and Wireless IP Networks," *IMSC's 2001 NSF Report*, Access from http://imsc.usc.edu/demos/research/dynQoS.html, (2001)
9. Lee, J.H., Jung, T.H. and Yoon, S.U., et al., "An adaptive resource allocation mechanism including fast and reliable handoff in IP-based 3G wireless networks," *IEEE Personal Communications*, Vol. 7, No. 6, (2000) 42-47
10. Guerin, R. A., "Queueing-blocking system with two arrival streams and guard channels," *IEEE Trans. Communication*, Vol. 36, No. 2, (1988) 153–163
11. Re, E. D., Fantacci, R. and Giambene, G., "Handover queueing strategies with dynamic and fixed channel allocation techniques in low earth orbit mobile satellite systems," *IEEE Trans. Communication*, Vol. 47, No. 1, (1999) 89–102
12. Rosenberg, J., Schulzrinne, H. and Camarillo, G., et al., "SIP: Session Initiation Protocol," *IETF RFC 3261*, June (2002)
13. Feng, W. and Hurley, R., "Performance Comparison for Service Systems With or Without Anticipated Delay Information by Analysis and Simulation," *International Journal of Computers and their Applications*, (2004)
14. Choi, J., Kwon, T.g, Choi, Y. and Naghshineh, M., "Call admission control for multimedia services in mobile cellular networks: a Markov decision approach," *Computers and Communications*, July (2000) 594 – 599
15. Kim, Sooyeon, Kwon, Taekyoung and Choi, Yanghee, "Call admission control for prioritized adaptive multimedia services in wireless/mobile networks," *Vehicular Technology Conference Proceedings*, Vol. 2 , May (2000) 1536 – 1540

A Transaction Model for Context-Aware Applications*

Shaxun Chen, Jidong Ge, Xianping Tao, and Jian Lu

State Key Laboratory for Novel Software Technology, Nanjing University
Nanjing City, P.R. China, 210093
csx@ics.nju.edu.cn

Abstract. Pervasive computing is widely researched and a large number of context-aware applications have been built in the recent years. However, correctness of contexts and fault handling of these applications have always been ignored. This paper proposes a transaction model for context-aware applications. In this model, context-aware applications are organized as a number of logic units and each unit may have a compensation module, which will be executed when errors or exceptions occur in context-aware applications in order to minimize the bad infection. This model supports nested scopes and the number of levels of subtransactions is unlimited. We also present an implementation of this transaction model, which is specialized for context-aware use.

1 Introduction

Pervasive computing was introduced by Mark Weiser in 1991 [1] and has attracted a lot of attention from both academic researchers and industrial practitioners in the recent years. The long-term goal of pervasive computing is to build large-scale smart environments that provide adequate services for users, and making computation invisible to us. Context-aware computing plays a key role to achieve this goal.

Context-aware applications are driven by contexts which are collected from environments by sensors or other devices automatically. In this way, it decreases users' attention of computation and users' intended input sometimes becomes unnecessary.

However, when wrong contexts are provided or some exceptions occur, the situation will be disgusting. The system may provide users with wrong services, and even worse, it may cause waste or damage of users' belongings, since context-aware applications have the ability to control electrical appliances and other devices. We take the following scenario for example.

When Tom leaves his office and drives home at 6:00 pm, the GPS on his car reports his location and the smart environment knows that Tom is on his way home and predicts he will have his supper at home. The system opens the air conditioner at home and turns on the coffee maker, so that when Tom gets home, he can enjoy hot coffee and comfortable temperature. However, Tom suddenly receives a call from a friend, who invites him for dinner, and he swerves his car towards his friend's home.

In this case, some compensating work should be done. The air conditioner should be turned off to save energy and the coffee maker may be turned to heat-preservation state.

* Funded by 973 Program of China (2002CB312002) and 863 Program of China (2006AA01Z159), NSFC (60233010, 60403014, 60603034).

C. Cérin and K.-C. Li (Eds.): GPC 2007, LNCS 4459, pp. 252–262, 2007.

In this paper, we propose a transaction model for context-aware applications. It provides a uniform framework for these applications to handle errors, exceptions and other abnormal cases. In this model, context-aware applications are formalized, and compensations are fulfilled in a uniform way. In addition, our transaction model supports nested scopes and the number of levels of subtractions is unlimited, where flexibility and description ability are the concern.

We also present an implementation of this model, in which internal logic of context-aware applications are described with a XML based declarative language. In this implementation, RDF is supported and RDQL [2] sentences can be used for transition conditions between functional modules of applications. This property makes the implementation more suitable for context-awareness.

The rest of the paper is organized as follows. Section 2 reviews related works. Section 3 discusses why transaction properties are necessary in pervasive computing contexts and presents some further analyses. Section 4 describes our transaction model for context-aware applications and section 5 presents an implementation of this model. In section 6, we discuss the rationality of our model. Finally, section 7 concludes the paper.

2 Related Work

Transaction models were deeply researched in the past two decades. Some classic models have been proposed, such as Linear Sagas [3], flexible transactions [4], etc. Linear Sagas is suitable for solving the problems related to long lived transactions and flexible transactions work in the context of heterogeneous multidatabase environments. Years later, several transaction models have been proposed to address non-traditional applications: [5] [6] [7] to name a few. However, most of these models are developed from a database point of view, where preserving the data consistency of the shared database by transactional method is the main concern. They are usually good at theoretical properties but have difficulties when applied in the real word applications. These models are not suitable for context-awareness because context-aware applications are far different from traditional ones simply based on databases. We will discuss it in section 3.

Some researchers have noticed that wrong contexts may lead to unpleasant results in context-aware applications. Ranganathan tried to resolve semantic contradictious contexts using fuzzy logic in the first order predicate calculus [8]. Dey gave a novel solution for ambiguity resolution by user mediation [9]. These attempts try to improve the quality of contexts. However, errors in contexts can be reduced but cannot be eliminated. Accordingly, a compensational mechanism is desired by context-aware applications, yet we find little work focus on this domain.

This paper is part of work of FollowMe project, which is a pluggable infrastructure for building context-aware applications. [10] gives an overview of FollowMe system. The first version prototype of FollowMe did not include a transactional mechanism and in this paper, we propose a transaction model providing the compensation ability for context-aware applications.

3 Motivation and Further Analyses

In this section, we first discuss what leads to anomalies in context-aware service providing, and then present the motivations why we introduce a transaction model to solve this problem. Finally, we point out the requirements of a transaction model specially serving for context-aware applications.

3.1 Cause for Anomalies in Context-Aware Service Providing

In context-aware service providing, we refer to anomalies as providing wrong or inappropriate services to users and abnormal termination of the service. These anomalies stem from the facts listed as follows.

a) Inaccurate contexts. When wrong or inaccurate contexts are input to the system, an application may offer wrong services to users or meet other exceptions. An application, for example, is responsible for opening the door when the host comes home and closing the door when he/she leaves. If the context describes the host's action in error, the result will be awful.

b) Deficiencies in policies and algorithms of context-aware applications. Recall the scenario in section 1. The system uses the route Tom has finished to predict his whole route, in order to prepare coffee in advance. This kind of prediction, actually all predictions, are risk bearing. Another example, an application detects users' gesture to recognize his activity and then provides appropriate services. However, even best algorithms cannot recognize peoples' activities and minds accurately. Prediction is a kind of policy, and recognizing is a sort of algorithm. Deficiencies in these policies and algorithms may cause anomalies in service providing. This case is a character of context-aware computing.

c) Hardware errors and unexpected software runtime errors or exceptions. This is much the same as other applications. In this case, service providing may terminate amorally.

3.2 Necessity and Benefits of Applying Transaction Models

Anomalies in context-aware applications may cause users' displeasure and even more serious effects, such as waste of energy, loss of users' assets, etc. In this section, we will list the methods solving this problem and expound the necessity of the transaction model according to the three cases mentioned in section 3.1.

a) To address the problem caused by inaccurate contexts, there are mainly two categories of methods, *ex-ante* and *ex-post*. The *ex-ante* method is to improve the quality of contexts to prevent the abnormity beforehand, while the *ex-post* compensating after error occurs. However, we will show that the ex-ante method has some inherent limitation.

Apparently, there is a gap between real world contexts and contexts input to computing systems. This gap is mainly caused by two facts. The first is that sensors, which collect the contexts, may fall into errors and their accuracy is limited. The second is that real world contexts are continuous but sensors always send data to the sink periodically. Computing systems cannot know what exactly happens during the time interval between two senor signals. It's conceivable that this gap can be reduced but cannot be erased, because physical errors of sensors are inevitable, and von Neumann computing model is inherently discrete other than continuous. Therefore, we can make efforts to improve context quality (ex-ante method) to reduce the gap, but compensating ability (ex-post method) should also be included since the gap always exists.

b) For the anomalies caused by imperfect policies and algorithms in context-aware applications, situation is similar to the case above. Of course, we can develop more powerful and clever algorithms (ex-ante method), however, only the person himself knows really what he wants to do and what he needs. Computers are not human beings. Even best rules or artificial intelligent algorithms can only try to get close to facts or people's minds, but cannot replace them. When context-aware applications do recognition or judgments inaccurately and anomalies occur, we have to resort to ex-post methods.

c) Let's move on to the last case. Evidently, software and hardware exceptions and errors are inevitable in any computer systems. We can try to produce more reliable software and hardware, but can never promise that no errors will occur. To deal with anomalics of services caused by such matters, ex post facto handling is indispensable.

From the above discussion, we can conclude that ex post facto measurements are necessary for anomalies handling in context-aware services. Then, why is the transaction model a proper solution for such needs?

Firstly, transaction models are naturally used for error handling and consistency maintenance. These models, especially ones proposed to address non-traditional applications, as mentioned in section 2, provide inspiration and show common points with our problem.

Secondly, a transaction model can provide an infrastructure upon which all context-aware applications can perform ex post facto handling in a uniform way. If many applications in a smart environment do the compensating work autonomically, the software structure will become complicated and confused. Moreover, applications in one smart environment may share contexts each other, therefore, handling anomalies autonomically will make data dependence among these applications very hard to maintain. By employing a uniform framework, it is possible to maintain data dependence by the system other than application developers.

Thirdly, a transaction model is able to treat all anomalies caused by three kinds of factors mentioned in section 3.1. It provides a convenient way and a succinct style for application development.

Hence, a transaction model is a good choice. Also it is feasible. We define *context* as a kind of natural *input*, that is, input with little artificial processing. This definition conforms to our experience, because contexts are usually collected by sensors and input to the system automatically. In this way, context-aware computing follows Mark Weiser's idea that people can pay more attention to their task itself instead of computational devices [1]. Since *context* is a kind of *input*, classic computing models can be applied in the context-aware domain as well.

3.3 Requirements of Transaction Model for Context-Awareness

First, let's consider when the compensations should be fulfilled. We discuss this issue still according to the three cases mentioned above. In case c), apparently, the compensating work, if any, should be executed as soon as errors or exceptions occur. This is simply the same as traditional transaction models. In case a) and b), as time elapses, the system will get more contexts and will be possibly able to detect whether its original judgment was right or wrong. In the example mentioned in section 1, when Tom changes his way and drives towards his friend's home, the smart environment can find out the change of his route and trigger the compensating work. On the other hand, sometimes, users may notice that the environment provides a service in error, and then abort it by sending a command to the system. This kind of manual abortions may also require compensations. To sum up, there are three points when compensations will start to execute: an error or an exception occurs; the context-aware application itself notices it has provided an inappropriate service; the user aborts the service. The second and third cases are different from traditional transaction models. It requires our transaction model for context-aware applications offer an external entrance to abort the abnormal service and trigger the compensating modules.

Then we pay attention to the differences between operations on databases and operations in context-aware environments. Traditional transaction models are developed mostly from a database point of view and operations on databases are the changes of soft states, so that all such operations can be redone and undone. When system rollback is performed, all the states recover to that of a certain moment before. However, many operations in context-aware environment are performed on the objects beyond software systems and cannot be revoked. For example, cooked beef will not turn back to raw beef in any case. Therefore, the concept of *transaction* in pervasive computing context is different from that in the traditional fields. In context-aware applications, the abortion of a *transaction* does not mean all the operations in this transaction should be revoked and the whole state will be turned back to the state before the execution of this transaction. Instead, it just means some compensating work should be done, in order to decrease the waste or damage, mitigate users' displeasure, and set the system to a proper state.

According to the above analysis, we conclude that a transaction model for context-aware applications needs an external entrance to abort a transaction. In addition, the semantics of abortion in context-aware computing is not performing overall revoking but doing proper compensations.

4 A Transaction Model: TMfm

In this section, we first formalize the context-aware applications and then build a transaction model for such applications.

4.1 Formalizing of Context-Aware Applications

We divide context-aware applications into logic units, each of which stands for an atomic operation, such as turn on the air conditioner, make coffee, show a map on users' PDA, etc. We refer such a logic unit as an *activity*. Therefore, a context-aware application or a group of applications related closely in a smart environment can be represented as a set of activities and the data (context) flows and control flows between these activities. Here "related closely" refers to data sharing or dependency among applications. The rationality of this formalization will be discussed in section 6.

More formally, let *T* be a context-aware application (or a group of closely related applications) and let a_1, a_2, …, a_n be activities in *T*. Each of a_i ($1 \leq i \leq n$) can have a compensating facility ct_i, and if a_i has ct_i, we use t_i to represent (a_i, ct_i) pair. We may call t_i transactional activities. Each of t_i can own a monitoring activity mt_i. The compensating facility performs compensations for corresponding activity, which is straightforward to understand, while a monitoring activity is a software module that serves to validate the service provided by the corresponding transactional activity. Recall the scenario in section 1, system predicates that Tom is driving home and an activity prepares coffee for him in advance. A monitoring activity may be activated at the same time, which monitors whether Tom follows the route to home all along his way. If not, the monitoring activity throws an exception and the corresponding compensating facility may be triggered.

Pay attention, ct_i is not an activity, but an accessional facility attached to a_i. For example, *T'* has five activities and among them, only a_2, a_4 have compensating facilities and only a_2 has monitoring activity. In this case, activity set *A'* of *T'* is $\{a_1, t_2, a_3, t_4, a_5, mt_2\}$.

Definition 1. (Activity Set). Let *A* be *activity set* of an application. *A* is the smallest set satisfying:

1) If a_i is an activity in this application and ct_i does not exist, then $a_i \in A$;
2) If a_i and ct_i both exist, then $t_i \in A$;
3) If mt_i is in this application, then $mt_i \in A$.

Definition 2. (Application). Let *T* be an *application* (or a group of closely related applications). *T* is a partial order set $< A, \prec >$, where *A* is *activity set* of this application (these applications), and $\prec$ is a partial order relation on *A*.

In definition 2, $\prec$ indicates data dependencies between activities and implies execution order. For example, if t_2, $a_1 \in A$, and t_2 dependents on a_1, then ordered pair $<a_1, t_2> \in \prec$.

4.2 Scopes

Definition 3. (Scope). Let *s* be a *scope* of an *application T*, and $T=< A, \prec >$. *s* is a non-empty subset of *A*.

Definition 4. (Scope Set). Let *S* be *scope set* of an *application T*. *S* is the smallest set satisfying the condition: if *s* is a *scope* of *T*, then $s \in S$.

Stipulative Definition. For convenience, we use $< A, \prec, S >$ to denote an application *T* with defined *scope set S*.

We have defined the scope and scope set, then we will give five rules that scopes must follow.

Scope Rule 1 (SR1): $T = < A, \prec, S >$, if $s \in S$, $a_i \in s$, $a_j \in s$, then $\exists a' \in s$, such that $<a', a_i> \in \prec$ and $<a', a_j> \in \prec$.

This rule indicates that if s is a scope, and activities a_i, a_j are both elements of s, then s must have an activity a', on which both a_i and a_j directly or indirectly depend. Of course, the partial order relation is a reflexive relation, so that a' may equal to a_i or a_j.

Scope Rule 2 (SR2): $T = < A, \prec, S >$, if $s \in S$, $a_i \in s$, $a_j \in s$, $<a_i, a'> \in \prec$, $<a', a_j> \in \prec$, then $a' \in s$.

Intuitively speaking, this rule indicates that if two activities, one of which indirectly depends on another, are both in a scope, then the activities on the dependency path of these two activities must be also in the same scope.

Scope Rule 3 (SR3): $T = < A, \prec, S >$, if $s_1 \in S$, $s_2 \in S$, then $s_1 \cap s_2 = \phi$ or $s_1 \cap s_2 = s_1$ or $s_1 \cap s_2 = s_2$.

This rule indicates that if s_1 and s_2 are both scopes and not the subset of one another, then they do not have intersection. However, nested scopes are legal.

Scope Rule 4 (SR4): $T = < A, \prec, S >$, if $s \in S$, $a_i \in s$, $a_j \in s$, $a_k \in A$, $<a_i, a_j> \in \prec$, $<a_i, a_k> \in \prec$, $a_i \neq a_j$, then $a_k \in s$ or $<a_j, a_k> \in \prec$.

This rule is a little hard to describe intuitively. We will explain it according to an example later.

Scope Rule 5 (SR5): $T = < A, \prec, S >$, if $t_i \in A$, $mt_i \in A$, then $\exists s \in S$, such that $t_i \in s$, $mt_i \in s$.

This rule is tightly bounded to the semantics of mt_i.

Definition 5. (Legal Scope and Legal Scope Set). If s follows SR1-SR5, then s is a *legal scope*. If for any $s \in S$, s is legal, then S is legal.

Since $\prec$ is a partial order relation, T can be described by an acyclic directed graph. Figure 1 shows a fragment of directed graph of T'. $s=\{a_3, a_5\}$ is not a legal scope, because it does not follow SR1. $s_1=\{t_2, a_3\}$ is not a legal scope either, for violating SR4 ($t_2 \in s_1$, $a_3 \in s_1$, $<t_2, a_3> \in \prec$, $<t_2, a_5> \in \prec$, but $a_5 \notin s_1$ and $<a_3, a_5> \notin \prec$). However, $\{a_3, t_4\}$ complies with all of the rules and so dose s_2.

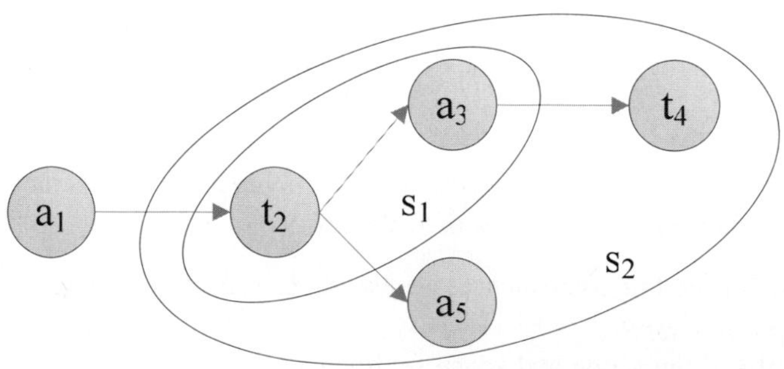

Fig. 1. A fragment of directed graph of T'

Now we move on to the semantics of *scope*. While t_i is an atomic transaction of a context-aware application *T*, a *scope* is an upper-tier transaction. A scope could be view as an activity in the upper layer. In this model, scopes can be nested, so we have a multi-layer transaction structure. However, a complete context-aware application *T* is not necessarily a transaction in our model, which is determined by characters of the context-aware domain and differs significantly from most traditional transaction models. This property will be further discussed in section 6.

4.3 TMfm Model

Definition 6. (Compensation Handler). A *compensation handler* is a trigger, which invokes compensating facilities in proper order. A compensation handler should be bounded to a transactional activity t_i (referred as CHt_i) or a scope s_i (CHs_i).

For an activity can be viewed as a trivial scope, we will not distinguish CHt_i and CHs_i hereinafter.

Compensating Rule 1 (CR1): If CHs_i ($s_i \in S$) captures an exception thrown from an activity a_k (both normal and transactional) where $a_k \in s_i$, all elements of the set $\{ct_j | t_j \in s_i\}$ should be executed in the reverse order of t_j ($t_j \in s_i$).

In figure 1, assuming the original execution sequence of *T'* is a_1, t_2, a_3, t_4, a_5. If t_4 throws an exception, and s_2 is a scope owning a compensation handler, then according to CR1, the compensated sequence should be a_1, t_2, a_3, t_4, ct_4, ct_2.

Compensating Rule 2 (CR2): s_i ($s_i \in S$) throws an exception if and only if a_k throws an exception and $a_k \in s_i$ and CHs_i do not exist.

Consider s_i as an upper-tier activity, CR2 defines recursive handling process of compensating.

Definition 7. (TMfm Model). *TMfm model* $M =< T, R_1, R_2 >$, where $T =< A, \prec, S >$, R_1={CR1, CR2}, and R_2={SR1, SR2, SR3, SR4, SR5}.

Such defined *M* is our transaction model for context-aware applications. In the next section, we will give an implementation of this model.

5 An Implementation of TMfm

In this section, we will define an xml-based declarative language to implement the transaction model and describe the internal logic of context-aware applications.

In our system, one file defines one context-aware application or a group of closely related applications. *<ApplicationGroup>* is the root element of a file and the element *<Application>* stands for a specific context-aware application. *<Scope>* element defines scopes and *<Activity>* refers to an atomic functional unit in an application. The element of *<Compensation>* describes the compensating facility of a transactional activity, while *<CompensationHandler>* serves to captures exceptions and triggers compensating facilities in proper order. *<Source>* and *<Destination>* are used to portray control flows of the application. For reasons of space, detailed schema of this language cannot be provided. A segment of the description file of the "guests reception" application is shown as follows.

```
<ApplicationGroup>
<Link id = "from_s001_to_s002"/>
......
<Container id = "input_of_show_welinfo">
......
</Container>
<Application id = "http://moon.nju.edu.cn/followme#010" name =
"guests_reception">
    <Scope id = "s001">
        <Source linkId = "from_s001_to_s002" transitionCondition =
    "select ?x where (?x prefix:locateIn prefix:Room311) using prefix for
    &lt;http://moon.nju.edu.cn/followme#&gt; GENERATED">
        <CompensationHandler>
            <Catch faultName = "unknown_exception">
                <Compensate excuteAuto = "True"/>
            </Catch>
        </CompensationHandler>
        <Activity id = "a001" name = "welcome">
            <ProcessUnit id = "show_welcomeinfo" isAuto = "True">
                <Assign>
                    ......
                </Assign>
                <Input containerId = "input_of_show_welinfo"/>
            </ProcessUnit>
            <Compensation>
                <ProcessUnit id = "compen_of_a001" isAuto =
    "True">
                    <Input containerId = "errorInfo_001"/>
                </ProcessUnit>
            </Compensation>
        </Activity>
        ......
```

The transitions between activities reflect control flows and data dependencies of the application. The transition condition returns a boolean value, directing the application whether goes through that path or not. In our implementation, transition conditions can be expressed using RDQL sentences, which is powerful and convenient for context description and queries.

We add a special user interface to the system. This UI enables users to abort the services by inputting a command to his/her PDA or handset, when users find that the system provides wrong services or services he/she does not need. Receiving this command, the running activity will throw an exception. By this way, all the three cases mentioned in section 3 (1. software or hardware errors; 2. system finds itself inappropriate services are provided; 3. user aborts) can be performed uniformly. They all trigger the compensation handler by throw exceptions (Exceptions are thrown by mt_i in case 2).

In this implementation of the model, a context-aware application is consist of a definition file and a number of process units, which actually performs atomic operations such as open the light, cook coffee, etc. When deploying the file and process units on FollowMe infrastructure, the system will parse and execute the definition file and invoke proper process units. With this infrastructure, workload on development and deployment of context-aware applications is reduced. [11] presents the first version of this infrastructure and we add transactional properties in this version.

6 Discussion

In section 4, we formalize a context-aware application (or a group of closely related applications) and divide it into a number of atomic functional units. For simple applications, this method seems not very valuable, because they may only have one or two atomic functional units, and the control flows and dependencies between units are very simple. An application responsible for opening and closing the door automatically is an example of this category. Formalizing such simple applications may be regard as a waste of time. However, the long-term goal of pervasive computing is to build smart environments everywhere and provide adequate services to meet users' needs. In such an environment, most services could not be very simple and they may have complex internal logic, such as a patients' guide system in smart hospitals. Even if some simple applications exist, they are closely tied to other applications. For example, an application for opening and closing the door automatically uses people's location contexts, which could also be used for many other applications. In addition, the state of the door itself may used as contexts for other applications, such as safe guard system and applications controlling the light and temperature conditions in the room. Therefore, simple applications are not that simple in a smart environment view. Moreover, generally speaking, models should be built on general cases. Simple applications with only one or two activities can be regard as the trivial-case of general applications. However, that's not the case by contrary.

We have mentioned that in our transaction model, a context-aware application is not necessarily a transaction, and some components may be "transactions", such as transactional activities and scopes. It is far different from traditional transaction models, such as [3] [4]. They are researched on the premise that all subtransactions compose an upper-tier transaction. This difference is caused by the idiosyncrasy of context-aware computing. In most cases, work having been done needn't and cannot be revoked when exceptions occur in the context-aware environment, because the range that context-aware applications effect is far beyond software systems and soft states. Even the transactional components of context-aware applications are not classic transactions. They can only recover part of the states and do some compensations when an exception occurs. There is another difference between traditional models and ours. For the former, if an exception occurs, the abortion of lower-tier transactions will definitely spread to the upper-tier transactions. However, in our model, if compensation handler works, exceptions will not spread to the upper-tier. This difference is caused by transactional semantics in the context-aware domain. Actually, after compensations are performed, the state of the activity is close to "*committed*" in the traditional sense instead of "*aborted*".

In section 5, we implement the model by a declarative language. Readers may notice that it shares some common points with workflow definition language. In our model, context-aware applications consist of logic units and dependencies between these units, which originally is a workflow-like structure. Moreover, as [12] has pointed out, workflow has a more powerful description ability than transaction models. So it is possible and rational to describe a transaction model by a workflow-like declarative language.

7 Conclusion

In this paper, we analyze the necessity of a transaction model in context-aware computing domain, and present such a model called TMfm. In addition, a declarative language has been proposed to implement our model. With this model, context-aware applications are able to perform compensations when inaccurate contexts appear or exceptions occur. Besides, compensating tasks of various applications are fulfilled in a uniform way, which benefits software architecture, especially for complicated smart environments.

References

1. Weiser M.: The Computer for the 21st Century. In: Scientific American, September 1991. (1991)94–100
2. RDQL, http://www.w3.org/Submission/2004/SUBM-RDQL-20040109/
3. H. Garcia-Molina, and K. Salem.: Sagas. In: Proc. 1987 SIGMOD International Conference on Management of Data. (1987)249–259
4. A.K. Elmagarmid, Y. Leu, W. Litwin, and M.E. Rusinkiewicz.: A Multidatabase Transaction Model for Interbase. In: Proc. of the 16th VLDB Conference. (1990)23–34
5. U. Dayal, M. Hsu, and R. Ladin.: A Transaction Model for Long-running Activities. In: Proc. of the 17th International Conference on Very Large Databases. (1991)113–122
6. H. Waechter and A. Reuter.: The ConTract Model. In: A.K. Elmagarmid, editor, Database Transaction Models for Advanced Applications, chapter 7. Morgan Kaufmann Publishers, San Mateo (1992)219–263
7. A. Biliris, S. Dar, N. Gehani, H.V. Jagadish, and K. Ramamritham.: ASSET: A System for Supporting Extended Transactions. In: Proc. of 1994 SIGMOD International Conference on Management of Data. (1994)44–54
8. A. Ranganathan, J. Al-Muhtadi, and R. H. Campbell.: Reasoning about Uncertain Contexts in Pervasive Computing Environments. In: IEEE Pervasive Computing, 03(2). (2004)62–70
9. A. K. Dey and J.Mankoff.: Designing Mediation for Contextaware Applications. In: ACMTransactions on Computer-Human Interaction(TOCHI), 12(1). (2005)53–80
10. Jun Li, Yingyi Bu, Shaxun Chen, Xianping Tao, Jian Lu.: FollowMe: A Pluggable Infrastructure for Context-Awareness. In: Ubicomp2005. Tokyo, Japan (2005)
11. Shaxun Chen, Yingyi Bu, Jun Li, Xianping Tao, and Jian Lu.: Toward Context-Awareness: A Workflow Embedded Middleware. In: Proc. of IFIP 2006 International Conference on Ubiquitous and Intelligent Computing (UIC2006). Volume 4159 of LNCS. (2006)766–775
12. G. Alonso, D. Agrawal, A.E. Abbadi, M. Kamath, R. Günthör, C. Mohan.: Advanced Transaction Models in Workflow Contexts. In: Proc. of the 12th International Conference on Data Engineering. (1996)574–581

A Grid-Based Remote Experiment Environment in Civil Engineering

Jang Ho Lee[1], Taikyeong Jeong[2], and Song-Yi Yi[3]

[1] Dept. of Computer Engineering, Hongik University, Korea
janghol@cs.hongik.ac.kr
[2] Dept. of Communication Engineering, Myongji University, Korea
ttjeong@mju.ac.kr
[3] School of Computer Science and Engineering, Seoul National University, Korea
yis@snu.ac.kr

Abstract. Recently, there is an increasing need for researchers in engineering to share the result of the experiment without having to visit the experiment facilities. Especially in the civil engineering, researchers feel the need for participating in a number of experiments conducted at distant places. In addition, it has been suggested that high-cost facilities should be used by remote researchers for the high utilization rate. This paper proposes a remote experiment environment in civil engineering that are being developed in a project called Korea Construction Engineering Development(KOCED), which connects major civil engineering experiment facilities using grid technology. This environment enables researchers to participate in a remote experiment, and allows the experiment results shared by remote researchers automatically. Then, based on the suggested environment, we designed a hybrid test facility that involves two physical experiment facility sites and one numerical simulation site that are geographically apart. Then, we implemented its prototype and ran some tests, which showed a possibility of grid-based civil engineering experiment.

1 Introduction

The flow of information brings a tremendous change in the area of civil engineering research as well as the economy, politics and culture of a society. This trend induces the combination of information technology with construction technology and provides web services for remote users.

In order to bring the efficient design of grid-based collaboratory research to a large-scale civil engineering technologies, such as experimentation, simulation, and design, we produce a grid computing software system and tools for the research facilities across the nation [16]. The purpose of this large-scale grid design is to share the facilities and maximize the effectiveness of their use, through information technology innovation. By connecting all the research facilities across the nation with grid computing infrastructure, we expect to have a balanced development of all the regions nation-wide as well as the combination of research and education [10] [15].

C. Cérin and K.-C. Li (Eds.): GPC 2007, LNCS 4459, pp. 263–273, 2007.

These computing technologies and the development of extreme technology become an essential part of a nation's competitive construction strategy. However, related huge experiment facilities are too expensive for an organization, which makes the building and application of them difficult.

This paper is organized as follows: In Section 3 we will present an overview of the KOCEDgrid system architecture including the grid-computing architecture, the communication networks connecting each research facilities, and the control network for system initialization under the control of grid software. In Section 4, we describe an outline of the remote system software and the experimental results of Hybrid Test model. In Section 5, we briefly discuss related work. Conclusions are presented in Section 6.

2 Related Works

In recent decade, grid-based telescience project was started in US and some European countries. Some of the well-known grid-based telescience projects in US are Network for Earthquake Engineering Simulation(NEES) [20] [12], Biomedical Informatics Research Network(BIRN) [1], and National Virtual Observatory(NVO) [11] while EUROGRID [2] [17] and G-Civil [3] are some of the leading grid projects in Europe. Among them, NEES and G-Civil are similar to our KOCED in the sense that they applied grid technology to the research in the area of civil engineering.

NEES is a network that connects seismological experiment facilities of US with grid techonology that provides a collaboratory. It is managed by a consortium and consists of 16 interconnected nation-wide next-generation seismological research facilities that supports teleobservation, teleoperation, sharing of experiment data, numerical simulation and collaboration tools. NEESgrid is a software system that consists of a NEESpop server for a experimental facilities, Telepresence Mode software, data acquisition software, and data repository software.

G-Civil is a project in UK that supports remote monitoring of experimental facilities and collaboration tool using grid technology. It provides real-time monitoring of civil engineerig experiment site through portal on the Internet and allows teams geographically apart to share data and collaborate. Besides civil engineering, grid projects in other area are in progress around the world, which include BIRN in medical and NVO in astronomy. BIRN is a geographically distributed virtual community of shared resources funded by National Institute of Health(NIH) in US since 2001. It hosts a collaborative environment for biomedical scientists and clinical researchers and facilitates the understanding of the diseases and the discovery of treatment methods by collecting and sharing biological data that are distributed. BIRN consists of four test beds and a coordinating center that supports networking, distributed storage, software development, etc. BIRN exploits the grid technology in security, resource management and data management for the effective sharing of the research results about the diagnosis and treatment of disease. NVO is a US NSF-funded project to build a collaboration framework for the national virtual oberservatory that can provide the world's leading astronomical information services and data collections to astronomers, educators, and students at a distance. NVO takes advantage of grid techonology in creating prototypes for access, publishing and discovery of terabytes of astronomical data generated by new telescope, detector, etc. Finally, EUROGRID granted by European Commission established a European GRID network of leading High Performance Computing centers from different European countries and demonstrated distributed simulation codes from different application areas such as biomolecular simulations, weather prediction, coupled CAE simulations, structural analysis and real-time data processing. For this purpose, EUROGRID supports software infastructure for building grid system, standardizes major grid software components and provides stable and secure connection to the grid network.

As the need to build grid system increases worldwide, it became necessary to standardize the grid service and it resulted in the proposal of the Open Grid Services Architecture(OGSA) [15] [13]. OGSA describes a grid middleware standard for sharing and managing of resources and a Web service standard for application sharing. It is independent of operating systems or system environment. It supports Web service as an interface to service facilitating the access to the resources or services, which has an advantage over other standards for distributed computing. As more grid systems follow the OGSA standard, toolkits based on OGSA emerged. One of most well known toolkits among them is Globus Toolkit(GT) [14] [19]. Globus Toolkit provides services for each service component described by OGSA, respectively. Through the reconfiguration of those supported services, a target grid system can be built. The prototype of the hybrid test system presented in this paper has been built with Globus Toolkit 3 and is being upgraded to Globus Toolkit 4.

3 KOCEDgrid

Based on our previous experiment of grid computing, we performed a grid-based collaboratory for construction project. The KOCEDgrid system is nation-wide distributions of computing systems associated with each research facility connected by a wired communication information network and integrated to a grid system, which makes the facilities become one facility.

This grid system is aimed to integrate the computing facilities and share the resources such as simulation data and experiments for remote users. We demonstrate the KOCEDgrid software system so that we can use some of the functions and will extend the role of the system. We identified the major functions that the KOCEDgrid system should provide roles e.g., resource management and data management functions.

Resource management provides authorization to confirm the identity of users as well as the delegation of rights. It also allows users to locate the required resources when they need to use the experiment facilities and related data from remote sites. The resource management enables users to monitor the status of the resources for the effective usage and management of resources including experimental facilities. Consequently, it includes not only facilities for experiments but also high-end computers with which researches perform large-scale scientific calculation and simulations. It allows researchers to allocate jobs to high-end computers regardless of their physical location and to see the results.

Another aspect of the KOCEDgrid system function is data management. Data generated in experiments and simulations are transferred to the database in a secure way. Reliable File Transfer(RFT) Service [8] transfers data from local repository to central respository using GridFTP service [5] based on Grid Security Infrastructure(GSI) [4] on each repositories. Users are allowed to look up data effectively in a pre-specified meta data. Access to the data from remote places is performed in a trusted way using standard secure protocol.

The system model for building a large-scale grid system enables the abovementioned main functions as well remote experimentations such as *teleobservation*, *teleoperation*, which discuss in section 4. Each university locates a selected huge experiment facility. Using this facility, each university can perform research within the region, as well as remotely perform experiments. The remote access of facilities is restricted to the grid portal. This grid portal plays the role of connecting fragmented universities' facilities, sharing research data as a web service, and monitoring the process of research.

Our results have been verified with this implementation of grid computing system. Through camera and video connected to research facilities, it is possible to look into and modify the process of research, and prove services for a collaboration. The grid portal also performs the role of connecting users and facilities by the data acquisition system (DAQ), which receives data from research and sends them to users, local data servers, or servers. Consequently, this makes possible a remote control of facilities by means of a controlling system that receives the order from users and sends it to facilities.

Simulated data from research forms meta-data and is stored in local data storage facilities, and completed data are managed in a huge database system. This database provides an efficient searching mechanism for these data, manages meta-data, and informs storage place when data are managed redundantly. This construction of the database can be possible by development of application programs accompanied by existing data management systems, and by file transfer services through grid middle-ware.

Current effort of KOCEDgrid consists of 6 different research facilities, which can be described as follows: real-time hybrid testing facility for multi-DOF structural systems, dynamic geo-centrifuge facility, multi-support excitation facility for earthquake simulations, wind-tunnel facility for large-scale long structures, ocean environment simulation facility and large-scale testing facility for new advanced construction materials.

Fig 1 illustrates a connection of each research facilities of grid-based commodataries. It should be noted that we will extend to double size of research facilities in the second phase of project by 2009.

Fig. 1. KOCEDgrid interconnecting 6 different research facilities

4 Collaborative Research Environment

4.1 Remote Experiment

We describe main concept of remote experiment in KOCEDgrid which can be shown as follows: teleobservation, teleoperation, and controlling the experimental devices.

Teleobservation is one of the main feature of KOCEDgrid software system. This function should obviously make possible into the grid portal. Users from a remote site should be able to see the experiment data. Also, the video and audio from where the experiment is being performed should be accessible from a distance in real time. In this case, experiment data can be seen in a remote place with a visualization program based on real-time streaming. A synchronization mechanism is needed for synchronizing the experiment data and video in real time as well.

Consequently, *teleoperation* is another key feature of this collaborative research. This unique feature also provided a control experiment facilities from a distance, but the capability of control of experiment facilities is different depending on the research facilities. Moreover, a control layer is independent from the experiment devices that are separated from the control layer that is dependent on the experiment devices. In particular, separation of those two layers is made in order to reduce the cost in extending the KOCEDgrid system to include the new experiment equipment.

The experiment device-independent control layer is implemented as control commands and protocols that are general to experiment devices. In addition, the experiment device-dependent control layer converts commands from the device-independent layer to device-specific commands to control the experiment device, which can be extensible.

Since the experiment facilities are shared by researchers, users can look up the usage schedule of experiment facilities by others as well as apply for using the experiment facilities on line.

Although we can control and schedule of users access, some function should be done by on site, both manually and remotely, such as installation of sensors, change of video camera location for observation, and displacement of experiment prototype. In this case, we required some services to perform the above actions, people who can assist in the experiment, a video communication system that connects people in the experiment facility and researchers in a remote site, and a wireless communication system.

4.2 Collaborative Environment

We address the following aspects regarding collaborative research environment while we develop a grid software infrastructure.

- Integrated Research Environment: With a single sign on to a grid portal that is a gateway to experiment facility grid and collaborative research environment, they should be able to use the services and resources in the grid with their access rights in an integrated research environment. The grid software system should allow researchers to perform the experiment in an integrated research environment.
- Chat: Researchers from remote sites should be able to discuss the experiment situation through chat as they observe the ongoing remote experiment. Therefore, collaborative researchers should be able communicate multi-party discussion in real-time basis.
- Scheduling of community: It is required to schedule to look up and modify the schedule of his community among collaborative researchers. This scheduling function provides to collaborative researchers so that they can form the community for collaboration. The scheduling is maintained for each collaborative research community.
- e-Notebook: The grid architecture allows researchers to collect and organize data for collaborative research. The data includes not only text but also pictures, CAD, voice, video and application-generated data such as Word and PowerPoint. E-notebook enables collaborators to organize and look up the data.

5 Supporting Remote Experiment

Among the overall architecture of collaborative research environment, we focus on the remote experiment environment using grid architecture in this section.

The remote experiment model is based on the hybrid experiment where the experiment includes not only physical model but also mathematical simulation.

5.1 Hybrid Test Model

In hybrid test, the entire test structure consists of independent substructures that are modelled computationally or physically. These substructures can be located at different facilities, tested separately, and integrated via a computational simulations. A hybrid test consists of parts of two types: one part of a structure is modelled computationally and run on a simulation computer numerically, and another part is constructed and instrumented physically. Fig. 2 shows our design of the hybrid test model.

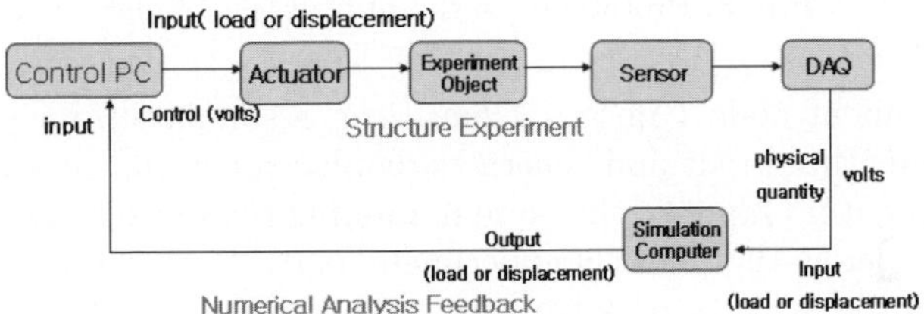

Fig. 2. A hybrid test model

The control system of the physical experiment node communicates with the simulation computer sending feedback during the experiment. The physical experimental results acquired by DAQ are fed to the simulation computer for numerical analysis. The simulation computer, in turn, provides input to an actuator of the physical substructure by simulating the interactions between the physical and the virtual model. A hybrid test is performed by repeating each simulation step which sends a feedback of the simulation to the physical equipment.

5.2 Building a Prototype for Hybrid Test Model

Fig. 3 shows a prototype of a simple hybrid experiment model with seismic wave input. Our prototype is a modified version of Mini-MOST experiment [6] of NEES. Mini-MOST experiment is a miniature version of the MOST(Multi-site Online Simulation Test) that aims to examine the dynamics of a structure in response to the seismic wave. The Mini-MOST model consists one physical experiment node and two simulation nodes. These nodes are geographically apart and conduct physical experiments or perform numerical simulations using tools such as Matlab.

We modified the Mini-MOST model by decreasing the number of simulation nodes to one and by increasing the number of physical experiment nodes to two, which resulted in modifying the part of the Mini-MOST code and building another physical experimental body as in Fig. 4. In Mini-MOST experiment the

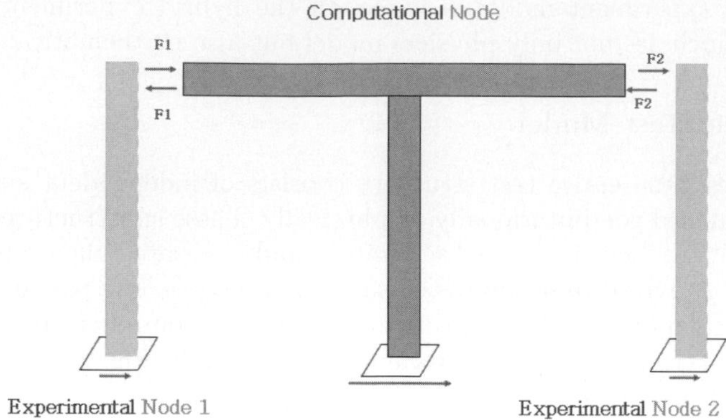

Fig. 3. Prototype for the hybrid test model

physical experiment node 1 in Fig. 4 had been a simulation node that accepts force and momentum input and generates displacement and rotation. We eliminated the momentum input of the node in making the physical experiment node 1 the same model as the physical experiment node 2. As shown in Fig. 4, software consists of three parts: a control part, an experiment part, and a monitoring part. The detailed explanation for each part are as follows.

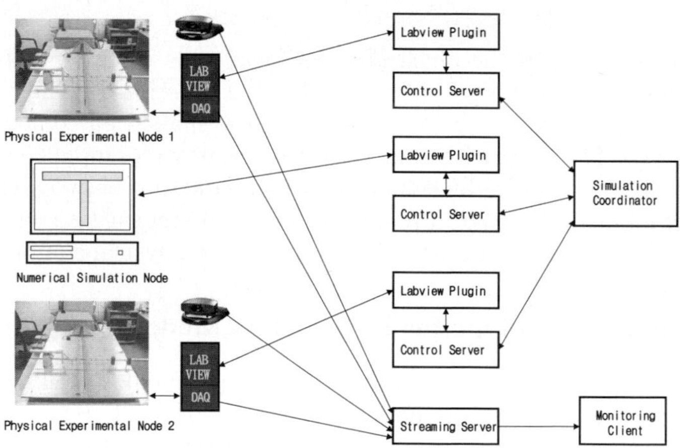

Fig. 4. A software architecture of the prototype for hybrid test model

The control part consists of Simulation Coordinator, a control server for each node, and plugin that provides interface between a node and a control server. Simulation Coordinator manages the hybrid test during the entire period of experiment by sending control command to control servers for each node. When a hybrid test starts, Simulation Coordinator notifies the beginning of the experiment and receives commands to be delivered to the control server for a physical

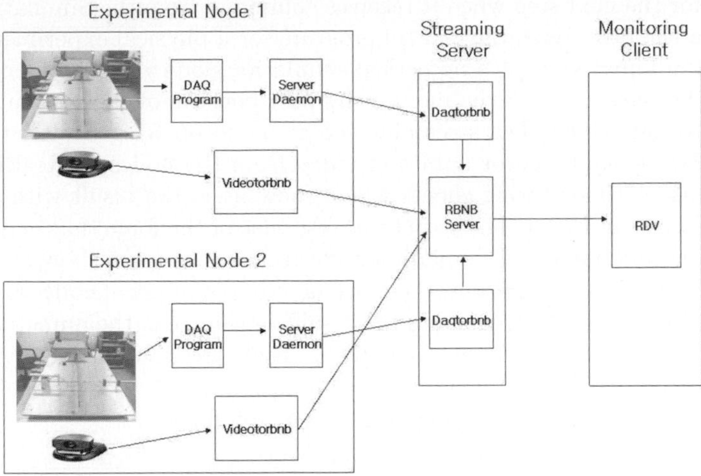

Fig. 5. An architecture for monitoring in hybrid test model

Fig. 6. Screenshot of remote monitoring client in the hybrid prototype test

experiment node. Based on the commands received, the control server controls the physical experiment node through plugin which communicates with a control program running on a DAQ computer. In our experiment, Simulation Coordinator is coded in Matlab and the control server uses NTCP(NEESgrid Teleoperations Control Protocol) [18]. There are two types of plugins: Labview plugin for a physical experiment node and Matlab plugin for a numerical simulation node.

An experiment part can be either physical experiment part or numerical simulation part. In a physical experiment part, a DAQ program acquires sensor values and sends them to the streaming server. A numerical simulation part calculates the value for the next step when it receives command from the Simulation Coordinator. In the prototype, the control program for a physical experimental node was coded in Labview while a numerical simulation node was written in Matlab.

As can be seen in Fig. 5 the monitoring part consists of the streaming server and monitoring clients. The streaming server based on Ring Buffered Network Bus(RBNB) [9] sends sensor data and video from the nodes to Realtime Data Viewer(RDV) [7] monitoring clients which show users the result with graphical user interface as in Fig. 6. The structural response of the force that acts between Seismic wave and numerical simulation node are measured and shown in the form of graph. During the experiment, the movement of the physical nodes are visually represented in the video stream and the resulting change of the numeric data are shown in the form of two-dimensional graph. Eight windows in the Fig. 6 shows the video from two physical experimental nodes and sensor data(displacement, load, resistance) from those two node in the graph form.

6 Conclusions

In this paper, we presented a grid-based remote experiment environment in KOCED project that connects large civil engineering facilities distributed across the nation. We discussed the design and implementation of the model that provides remote experiment to researchers geographically apart and allows the experiment results to be shared among them. Remote researchers are allowed to observe the experiment in real time. If the characteristics of the experiment permits, a researcher can conduct an experiment from a distance. After the experiment, the result of the experiment including video and sensor data are shared among researchers. The functions described above provide basic environment for collaboration among researchers at a distance. We designed and implemented a hybrid test prototype connecting two physical experiment sites and one numerical simulation site, which shows a possibility of conducting remote experiment in grid-based collaborative research environment.

We are modifying the client from a executable file on a local PC to a Web-based client based on Globus Toolkit 4 so that researchers can access the grid system with a Web browser without having to preinstall the client system. The presented prototype system is currently being used by researchers in civil engineering who can give us feedback that can be used for building the final version of the experimental facility. Furthermore, we plan to expand the current grid network to include more experimental facilities so that more experiment results can be shared by researchers. We expect this presented remote experiment environment to be applied to other engineering area.

References

1. Biomedical informatics research network. http://www.nbirn.net.
2. Eurogrid. http://www.eurogrid.org.
3. G-civil project. http://www.soton.ac.uk/ gcivil/.

4. Grid security infrastructure. http://www.globus.org/toolkit/docs/4.0/security/GT4-GSI-Overview.pdf.
5. Gridftp. http://www.globus.org/toolkit/docs/4.0/data/gridftp/.
6. Mini-most. http://cive.seas.wustl.edu/wusceel/minimost/.
7. Real-time data viewer. http://it.nees.org/software/rdv.
8. Reliable file transfer service. http://www.globus.org/toolkit/docs/4.0/data/rft/.
9. Ring buffered network bus. http://outlet.creare.com/rbnb.
10. System Architecture v1.1. http://www.neesgrid.org.
11. Us national virtual observatory. http://www.us-vo.org.
12. I. Foster J. Futrelle D. Marcusiu S. Gulipalli L. Pearlman C. Kesselman, R. Butler and C. Severance. NEESgrid System Architecture Version 1.1. http://it.nees.org/documentation/pdf/NEESgrid_SystemArch_v1.1.pdf
13. J. M. Nick I. Foster, C. Kesselman and S. Tuecke. The Physiology of the Grid: An Open Grid Services Architecture for Distributed Systems Integration. http://www.globus.org/research/papers/ogsa.pdf, 2002.
14. I. Foster and C. Kesselman. Globus: A Metacomputing Infrastructure Toolkit. *International Journal of Supercomputer Application*, 11(2):115–129, 1998.
15. I. Foster, C. Kesselman, J. Nick, and S. Tuecke. Grid Services for Distributed System Integration. *IEEE Computer*, 35(6):37–46, 2002.
16. I. Foster K. Czajkowski, S. Fitzgerald and C. Kesselman. Grid Informaion Services for Distributed Resource Sharing. In *HPDC-10*, pages 344–353, Boston, Massachusetts, August 2001.
17. M. Niezgodka K. Nowinski, B. Lesyng and P. Bala. Project EUROGRID. In *Proceedings of PIONIER 2001 Conference*, pages 187–191, 2001.
18. E. Johnson C. Kesselman L. Pearlman, M. D'Arcy and P. Plaszczak. NEESgrid Teleoperation Control Protocol(NTCP): NEESgrid-2004-23. http://it.nees.org/documentation/pdf/TR-2004-23.pdf, September 2004.
19. S. Fitzgerald I. Foster A. Johnson C. Kesselman J. Leigh S. Brunett, K. Czajkowski and S. Tuecke. Application Experiences with the Globus Toolkit.
20. The NEESgrid System Integration Team. Introduction to NEESgrid: NEESgrid-2004-13. http://it.nees.org/documentation/pdf/TR_2004_13.pdf, August 2004.

Mobile Ad Hoc Grid Using Trace Based Mobility Model

V. Vetri Selvi, Shakir Sharfraz, and Ranjani Parthasarathi

Dept. of Computer Science and Engineering,
College of Engineering Guindy
Anna University,
Chennai, Tamil Nadu, India
vetri@annauniv.edu, rp@annauniv.edu

Abstract. Ad hoc network is an infra structure less network, which is formed by mobile devices like laptops, PDAs, cell phones etc. Each device has different computational capability, power, hardware and software, which forms a heterogeneous network. These devices can be integrated to form an infrastructure known as grid. A grid integrates and coordinates resources and users that are within the same network with different capabilities. Hence we can visualize a grid over an ad hoc network that effectively utilizes the heterogeneity in the mobile devices. The major challenge in forming a grid over an ad hoc network is the mobility of the nodes. In this paper, we address the challenges due to mobility by considering a trace model for the movement of the nodes. Next, we demonstrate the feasibility of forming a grid over a mobile ad hoc network by proposing lightweight algorithms for grid formation, resource discovery, negotiation, job scheduling, and resource sharing. We have analyzed the performance of mobile ad hoc grid both by using a theoretical model and by simulation. The results point to a promising approach to form a mobile ad hoc grid.

1 Introduction

A mobile ad hoc network is a collection of wireless mobile nodes that are capable of communicating with each other without the use of network infrastructure or any centralized administration. Each node in an ad hoc network acts as a router, and is in charge of maintaining routes and connectivity in the network. Thus, there is an element of cooperation among the nodes to perform the routing process or the network layer function itself. Taking this cooperation one-step further, one can envisage a scenario where in the devices can coordinate and support each other in terms of higher layer services, (i.e) we can envision the concept of mobile ad hoc grid. We can see that such a grid would be desirable in an ad hoc network due to the heterogeneity of the mobile devices. Since the mobile devices like laptops, PDAs, mobile phones, etc., have different computation capabilities, power, hardware and software functions, the nodes with higher computation capabilities and power can share the resources with devices of lesser capabilities. Thus a mobile ad hoc grid can facilitate the interconnection of heterogeneous mobile devices to enable the delivery of a new class of services.

A grid by definition is a system that coordinates resources that are not subject to centralized control. The fundamental functions in a grid are resource discovery, negotiation, resource access, job scheduling and authentication. A grid allows its

C. Cérin and K.-C. Li (Eds.): GPC 2007, LNCS 4459, pp. 274–285, 2007.

resources to be used in a coordinated way to deliver various qualities of service in terms of response time, throughput, etc [1]. The definition and function of a grid will also be applicable to the mobile ad hoc grid.

In the Internet scenario, the grid uses architectures like Globus Toolkit 3.0 [2] and SETI@Home which is now an application running on top of the BONIC platform [3]. However, the APIs for these architectures need high computational power and require a lot of disk space for their installation. Thus, it may not be possible to use such architectures on every mobile device [4], since these devices have limitations on hardware and software capabilities and may not provide an ideal computing environment for complex and data intensive functions. Hence it is necessary to device lightweight grid enabling mechanisms that can be adopted for the mobile ad hoc grid.

There are several challenges involved while forming a mobile ad hoc grid. This paper discusses various such issues and proposes an architecture for the mobile ad hoc grid. The stability of the grid is one of the major issues to be considered in an ad hoc scenario due to the movement of the nodes. This has been dealt with by exploiting the regularity in the movement of nodes. Su et al [5] have shown that exploitable regularity of user mobility patterns exist in common day-to-day environments. Capturing this regularity in movement as a movement pattern is done using a Trace Based Mobility Model (TBMM) [6]. This model collects a number of movement patterns, and generates a final trace pattern. From the final trace, the probable position and stability time of a node are obtained. Using this mobility model, trace based source routing protocol for QoS (TBSR-Q) was proposed for an ad hoc network [6]. The TBSR-Q protocol uses the stability and position information obtained from the trace file for obtaining a stable route. In our mobile ad hoc grid, we use this trace based mobility model to obtain the probable position and stability time of a node in order to build a stable grid, or in other words, to take care of the instability of the nodes.

This paper is organized as follows. Section 2 discusses the background and related work. Section 3 deals with the proposed architecture of a mobile ad hoc grid. Section 4 evaluates the mobile ad hoc grid using a theoretical model and by simulation. Section 5 concludes the paper.

2 Related Work

Grid computing enables the sharing and coordination of resources across a shared network. Integrating grid computing with ad hoc network is a very recent concept, and introduces lot of new challenges. The following are some of the solutions that have been proposed by various researchers.

Ihsan et al [7] have proposed a mobile ad hoc service grid that maps the concepts of grid on to ad hoc networks. This mobile ad hoc service grid uses the under-lying connectivity and routing protocols that exist in ad hoc networks. The availability of the service in a node is broadcast to all one-hop neighbors. Since the grid is formed within one-hop neighbors, there is a chance for resource discovery to fail when there is no service provider within one hop. In this grid, each node is responsible for maintaining the resource look up table, which can be a burden to devices with less storage capabilities.

Wang et al [8] have proposed a mobile agent based approach for building computational grids over mobile ad hoc networks (MANET). Here, the mobile agent has been used to distribute computations and aggregate resources. The mobile agent searches for resources and executes the computations on the node that is willing to accept it and is responsible for negotiation of resource provision for running the computation job.

Anda et al [9] have proposed a computing grid over a vehicular ad hoc network (VANET) by leveraging inter-vehicle and vehicle to-roadside wireless communications. This grid has been used for solving traffic related problems by exchanging data between vehicles. Forming a grid is not a problem in VANETs, because the vehicles have ample power and energy and can be equipped with computing resources.

Roy et al [10] have investigated the use of the grid as a candidate for provisioning computational services to applications in ubiquitous computing environments. The competitions among grid service providers bring in an option for the ubiquitous users to switch their service providers, due to unsatisfactory price and QoS guarantees.

Our approach differs from these in that it provides a mechanism to capture the mobility patterns of the nodes and use that information to effectively form a grid over an ad hoc network.

3 Proposed Architecture for Mobile Ad Hoc Grid

One of the major challenges in forming a grid over ad hoc network is the mobility of the nodes and an infrastructure-less network. Resource identification and sharing become difficult tasks in a mobile environment. To overcome this, we propose a model to identify the stability of the nodes which in turn helps to predict the stability of the grid. The stability of the node is predicted using the TBM model [6].

The TBM model

Mobility models are application dependent. Hence application scenarios are important in choosing a model. Although typical application domains of ad hoc networks are military networks, conferences and search/rescue operations, for the kind of grid based sharing of resources, we consider offices and institutions where people meet regularly, with a myriad of heterogeneous mobile devices, as the application domain. In these domains, there exist fair amounts of regularity in the movement of the mobile nodes. Hence as opposed to the former group of applications where the mobility models try to model the randomness in the movement, in our application domain, we are more concerned with capturing the regularity of the movement. Hence we use a mobility model that records regular movements to efficiently manage mobility.

TBMM identifies regularity in movement of the nodes and captures them as a movement pattern. Each node is assumed to be location aware, and the network is assumed to be mapped on to a virtual grid structure, depending upon the transmission region and the area of the network. A light-weight algorithm [6] is used to arrive at the trace representing the regular movement of the nodes over a period of time. The information in the trace consists of a series of stable positions and associated time duration.

Architecture of proposed grid
We propose a trace-based approach to form a grid over an ad hoc network using the above-mentioned trace. Further, the mobile ad hoc grid uses a lightweight algorithm for grid formation, resource discovery, negotiation, job scheduling, and resource sharing, in keeping with the limited resource characteristic of the mobile nodes. Load balancing is a challenge unique to the dynamic nature of ad hoc network, and it is not considered for the initial study of formation of grid over an ad hoc network. The architecture of the grid is shown in Fig. 3.1.

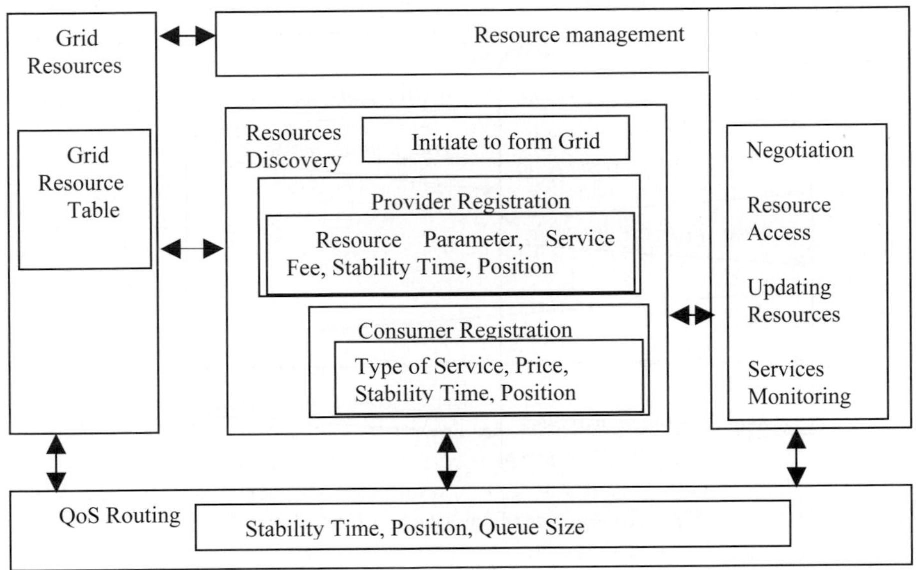

Fig. 3.1. Architecture of a mobile ad hoc grid

The grid layer is built on top of a QoS guaranteeing network layer that provides stable routes. The grid layer consists of a grid resources module, resource discovery module, and resource management module. The resource discovery module initiates grid formation, and allows the service providers and consumer nodes to register. Grid resources module maintains and keeps track of the registered resources. Resource management module is responsible for negotiation, resource access, updating of resources and service monitoring. All these modules are built on the QoS routing of network layer, which could in turn make use of the same stability information obtained from the TBMM.

3.1 Grid Formation

A node willing to provide service with higher computational capability and power is called as a service provider node (SPN) and the node which requests for the service is called as a consumer node (CN). The SPNs and CNs are the members of the grid. The nodes that are willing to share their resources specify a cost for their resources. The consumer node accepts a service based on the cost, service time, etc. This leads to some negotiation between the consumer node (CN) and the service provider node (SPN). Since ad hoc network is an infrastructure-less network, there is no centralized authority to keep track of the negotiation between a CN and a SPN. In order to form a grid and to keep track of the negotiation between a CN and a SPN, we have an SPN that volunteers to act as a grid head node (GHN). The GHN takes care of the negotiation between the CN and SPN. The GHN of a grid acts as a central point and is responsible for resource discovery and resource access. Figure 3.2 shows the messages that are exchanged between the nodes that are willing to form a grid.

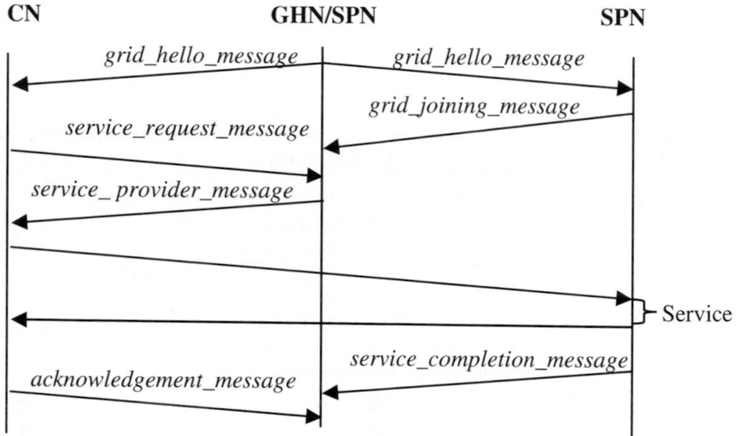

Fig. 3.2. Sequence of messages for Grid formation

Resource Discovery

A node that is willing to provide service will initiate the action of forming the grid by sending a *grid_hello_message*. The nodes that are willing to be a member of a grid respond to the *grid_hello_message*. The format of *grid_hello_message* is as shown in figure 3.3a. It consists of node ID, stability time, position and hop count. The node ID is the identification of the node that sends the *message*; and stability time and position which are obtained from its trace file denote the current position and the associated stability time. When two nodes send a *grid_hello_message* at the same time, the grid head elected is the one that has a larger stability time. Hop count restricts the propagation of the *grid_hello_message* to a limited number of hops. This helps to avoid the formation of one large centralized grid, and instead facilitates multiple decentralized grid structures.

A node, after receiving a *grid_hello_message*, sends a response message depending on whether it wants to become a member of the grid or wants to request for a service. The node joining a grid sends a *grid_joining_message*. The format of the *grid_joining_message* is shown in Figure 3.3b. It consists of SPN ID, GHN ID, Resource parameter, service fee, Position and Stability. The SPN ID is the ID of the node that is willing to join the grid and GHN ID is the head ID under which it wants to become a member. Resource parameter indicates the resource parameter that is available with a SPN like the computational capability, power, storage etc. The service fee indicates at what cost it will service a request. Similarly a node requesting for service sends a *service_request_message* whose format is shown in figure 3.3c. *Service_request_message* consists of the requesting node ID, GHN ID, ToS, Price, Position and Stability. The GHN is the grid head ID to which it is requesting service. ToS is the type of service requested by a CN. The price field indicates at what price it is willing to accept a service. A node can also become a member of two grids based on the resources available with it or the services it desires.

Grid Resources

The GHN after receiving responses from the member nodes forms a grid table. The format of the grid table is shown in Table 3.1

Table 3.1. Grid Table

Node ID	SPN /CN	RP/ ToS	Service Fee	Price	Position	Stability	Job ID	Busy/ Free

Abbreviations: SPN/CN – Service Provider Node/ Consumer Node, RP/ToS – Resource Parameters/Type of Service

This table maintains the details about the member nodes. The node ID column lists the identification of the member nodes. The SPN/CN indicates whether it is a SPN or CN. The resource parameters specify the resources available with that node like computational capability, power, storage etc. Type of service indicates what type of service is needed by a CN. Service fee of a SPN specifies at what cost it will service a CN. Price of a CN specifies at what price it needs a service. Position is the physical location of a node and stability is how much time a node is going to be present at that location. Job ID is a unique ID assigned to the communication of a SPN and a CN. Busy indicates whether a node is being serviced in the case of a CN or is providing service in the case of an SPN. Free indicates that an SPN is free to provide service. The head maintains all the details about its members.

Resource Management

The head node is responsible for the negotiation between a SPN and a CN. When a node requests for a service it sends the details of what type of service it needs and at what cost. So the head node looks at the table to find out a SPN that offers the service at that cost. Re-negotiation also can be done by a GHN and it is in the pipeline. The job scheduling is done based on the stability time and the location of the SPN. A GHN first verifies, whether the service time of a CN is greater than the stability time of a SPN. If many SPNs have greater stability time, then an SPN that is nearer to the CN requesting for a service is assigned. Then the GHN sends a *service_provider_message* to CN. The format of the *service_provider_message* is given in Figure 3.3d. It consists of CN ID, GHN ID, SPN ID, Job ID, cost, position and stability. The CN ID is the ID of the node requesting service, GHN ID is the ID of the node sending the message and SPN ID is the ID of the node that has been assigned to provide service. The job ID is a unique ID assigned by GHN to identify the communication between the CN and SPN. Position indicates the physical position of the SPN that has been assigned to the CN.

On receiving this message the CN starts communicating with the SPN for its service. The position of the SPN is available in the message, hence the CN can easily communicate with the SPN using the routing protocol in the network layer.

After getting the service, the CN sends an acknowledgement about its completion of the service to the GHN. Service completion field indicates that the service is completed. The Job ID is sent so that the GHN can understand which service was completed. The format of the *acknowledgement_message* is given in figure 3.3e.

Node ID	Stability Time	Position	Hop count

Fig. 3.3a. grid_hello_message

SPN ID	GHN ID	RP	Service Fee	Position	Stability

Fig. 3.3b. *grid_joining_message* sent by SPN

CN ID	GHN ID	ToS	Price	Position	Stability

Fig. 3.3c. service_request_message sent by CN

CN ID	GHN ID	SPN ID	Job ID	Cost	Position	Stability

Fig. 3.3d. *service_provider_message* sent by GHN

CN ID	GHN ID	Job ID	Service Completion

Fig. 3.3e. *acknowledgement_message* sent by CN

SPN ID	GHN ID	Job ID	WtoC	URP	Service Fee

Fig. 3.3f. service_completion_message sent by SPN

CN/SPN ID	GHN ID	LG

Fig. 3.3g. *bye_message*

GHN ID	New GHN ID	Stability Time	Position	Hop Count

Fig 3.3h. New GHN message

Abbreviations: GHN ID – Grid Head Node ID, SPN/CN – Service Provider Node/ Consumer Node, RP/ToS – Resource Parameter/Type of Service WtoC – Willing to Continue, URP – Updated Resource Parameters, LG – Leaving Grid

Similarly the SPN sends a *service_completion_message* to the GHN after completing the service for a CN. The format of the *service_completion_message* is given in Figure 3.3f. It consists of SPN ID, GHN ID, job ID, WtoC, URP and service fee. The job ID to identify the job that has been completed and if the SPN is willing to continue (WtoC) in a grid it sends the willingness as well as the updated resources parameters (URP) to the GHN. Using this information the GHN will know that the service has been successfully completed and updates the resource parameters of the SPN in its table.

The GHN has to periodically send a *grid_hello_message* to its member nodes, so that the members will know that the GHN is alive, and a new member will also know about the GHN. Since, it is an ad hoc network there might be situations where the members have to leave the grid even before the stability time expires. During this case, the members have to inform the GHN by sending a *bye_message* that consists of its ID and leaving grid information. The format of *bye_message* is shown in Figure 3.3g.

Similarly when a GHN leaves the grid, it has to select a new head from its grid table, the new head will be a SPN which has the largest stability time (after ascertaining its willingness to be the new GHN). The GHN informs the members of the grid about the selection of a new head by sending a new GHN message. This message consists of old grid head ID (GHN), new grid head ID (New GHN) as well as the stability time and position of the new grid head. The format is as shown in Figure 3.3h. The node selected as a new head sends a *grid_hello_message* to its members. The previous GHN hands over the table it maintained to the new GHN. Even when a GHN fails, it is identified by the non-receipt of the *grid_hello_message* and any SPN can initiate the formation of the grid by sending the *grid_hello_message.* But this will involve grid formation overhead. Similarly, situations like network splits or networks merge can also be handled. When a network split occur the members leaving the grid will inform the GHN by sending a *bye_message* and the grid will still exists with the available resources. When network merge happens it will not affect the existing grid, instead new members will join the grid. But this situation will not happen frequently in a low mobile scenario. The evaluation of mobile ad hoc grid is presented below.

4 Mobile Ad Hoc Grid Evaluation

The Mobile ad hoc grid is modeled as an M/M/m queuing system [12] in order to estimate the performance theoretically. The service requests from the CNs form the arrival process, and the SPNs are the m servers servicing these requests. In keeping with the M/M/m model, the arrival process (with arrival rate λ) is Poisson and the service times (with mean – $1/\mu$ sec) are independent and exponentially distributed. The successive interarrival times and service times are assumed to be statistically independent of each other.

In a mobile ad hoc grid, the CN request for a service to the GHN and the GHN is responsible for assigning a SPN to the requesting CN. Hence, the probability that an arriving request in a GHN will find all servers busy and will be forced to wait in queue is an important measure of performance. If a GHN does not have sufficient number of SPNs to assign for the services requested, then there is a probability of queuing (or waiting). A service request from a CN can be considered as a customer in the M/M/m parlance.

The probability of queuing is given in equation (1).

$$P\{\text{Queuing}\}=p_0(m\,\rho)^m/m!(1-\rho) \tag{1}$$

Where ρ is given by $\rho=\lambda/m\,\mu<1$ and $p_0=[\,\sum(m\,\rho)^n/n!+(m\,\rho)^m/m!(1-\rho)\,]^{-1}$ where $n = 1\text{-}(m\text{-}1)$

A request in a waiting state is serviced when a new SPN registers with the GHN or a SPN has completed its service and it is willing to continue in the grid. Duration of time a request has to wait in a queue is known as the waiting time of the customer.

Equation (2) gives, the average waiting time (W), that a service request has to wait in queue.

$$W = N_Q/\lambda = \rho P_Q/\lambda(1-\rho) \tag{2}$$

Delay per customer includes the time taken by a SPN to service the request as well as the waiting time of a request in the queue of the GHN. Equation (3) gives the average delay per customer (which includes service time and waiting time).

$$T = 1/\mu+W = 1/\mu + \rho P_Q/(\lambda(1-\rho)) \tag{3}$$

The number of customers in the system is the total number of requests received by a GHN. Equation (4) gives the average number of customers in the system.

$$N=\lambda\,T=(\lambda/\mu)+\lambda P_Q/(m\,\mu-\lambda) \tag{4}$$

The values obtained for these parameters by varying the number of consumers are tabulated in table 4.2. We choose the λ value to be 50 and μ to be 20.

Simulation studies have also been carried out to evaluate the mobile ad hoc grid. The simulation tool used is Glomosim [11]. The parameters used for the simulation are given in Table 4.1.

Table 4.1. Parameters for the simulation

Number of Nodes	50
Simulation Time	1000 Seconds
Terrain Dimension	(1000,1000) meters
Mobility	Mobility Trace, Mobility-Trace-File
Radio-Tx-Power	8 dBm (with a reach of 250 meters)
MAC-Protocol	802.11
Routing-Protocols	TBSR-Q

Mobile ad hoc grid has been simulated using 4 GHNs and 12 SPNs. The performance is analyzed by increasing the number of consumer nodes (from 4 to 20 in steps of 4) that in turn will increase the number of service requests. Here the SPN and GHN are considered to be static whereas CN and all the other nodes are mobile. To analyze the performance of grid, the parameters of interest are average number of customers in the system, probability of queuing, average time a customer has to wait in queue and average delay per customer.

Fig 4.1a and b show the average time a customer has to wait in queue and average delay per customer. It can be seen that there is minimal variation between the theoretical and simulation results. This is due to the fact that during simulation, a CN sends a service request to the GHN only when it finds a stable position based on its trace file, which in turn reduces the number of customers in the system. This factor in turn affects the probability of queuing. We can observe that up to case III (i.e no of CNs = 12), there is a sufficient number of SPNs available with the GHN to provide service. Hence the waiting time is low. In case IV and V, number of SPNs to service the request is not enough which in turn, increases the waiting time in queue.

Overhead in forming a grid

The overhead in forming a grid is the additional grid-forming messages that are communicated among the nodes to form the grid and the average routing delay. Figure 4.2a and b shows the control message overhead and the average routing delay. Average routing delay considers the delay in routing the control packets at the network layer. Since we consider the stability of a node to find out the stable routes in the routing protocol, the routing delay is considerably less than the service time considered. However, the average routing delay increases as the number of CNs increases; this is due to the increase in the number of service requests.

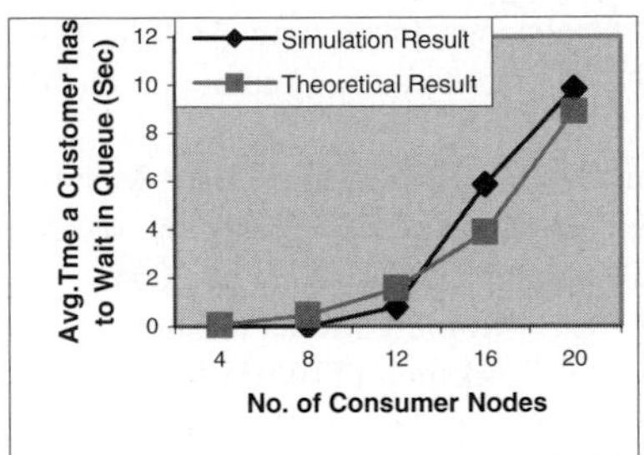

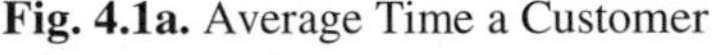
Fig. 4.1a. Average Time a Customer

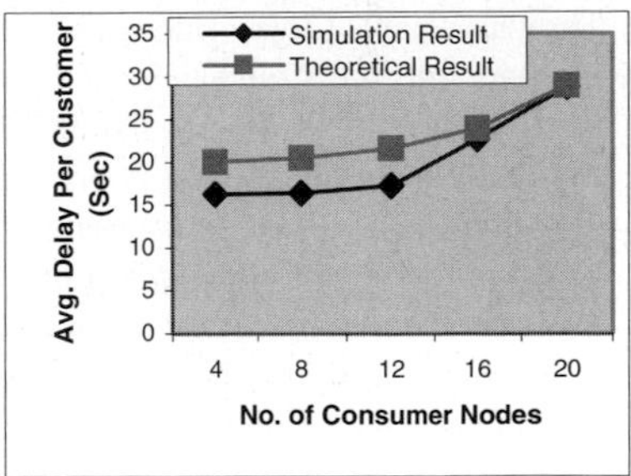

Fig. 4.1b. Average Delay per Customer has to Wait in Queue

The performance of the mobile ad hoc grid shows the feasibility of forming a grid in a mobile environment.

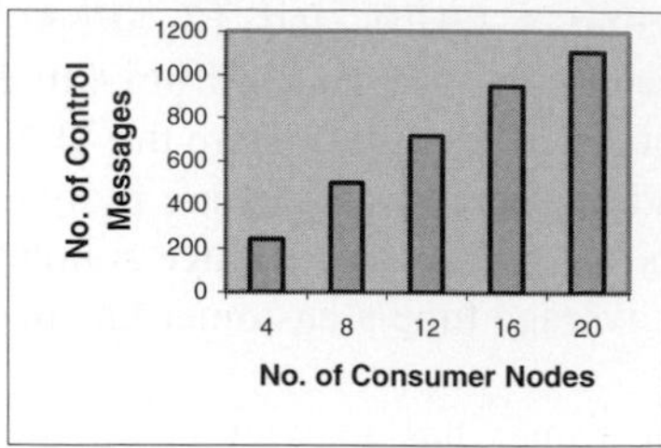

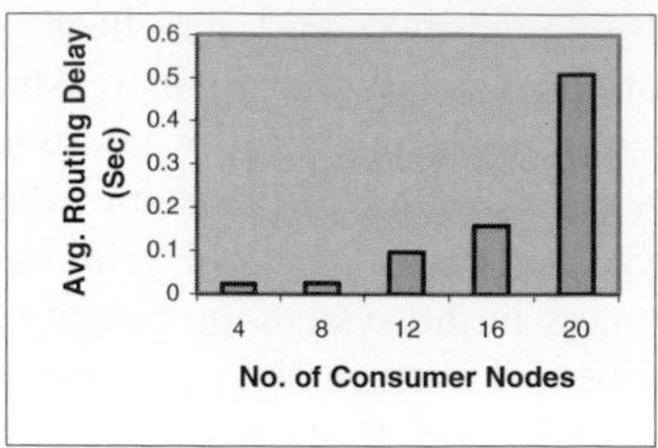

Fig. 4.2a. Control Message Overhead

Fig. 4.2b. Average Routing Delay

5 Conclusion and Future Work

This paper has proposed an architecture to form a grid over a mobile ad hoc network by using trace files that capture the regularity in the movement or rather the stability of the nodes. It has also shown the feasibility of sharing the resources using such a grid using both a theoretical model and simulation. The overhead present due to mobile environment is also very less. This paper has opened a number of possibilities for further studies in this area. Some of the future work that are to be explored are building trust over the mobile ad hoc grid based on the resource sharing and mechanisms for the nodes to cooperate to share their resources.

References

1. I.Foster, "What is the Grid? A Three Point Checklist", GRID Today, July 20, 2002
2. Open Grid Services Architecture http://www.globus.org/ogsa/
3. David P. Anderson, "BONIC: A system for Public-Resource Computing and storage", 5th IEEE/ACM International Workshop on Grid Computing, Nov2004.
4. Thomas Phan, Lloyd Huang, Chris Dulan, "Challenge: Integrating Mobile Wireless Devices into the Computational Grid", IEEE/ACM International Conference on Mobile Computing and Networking (MOBICOM) 2002.
5. Jing Su, Alvin Chin, Anna Popivanova, Ashvin Geol, Eyal De Lara, "User Mobility for Opportunistic Ad-hoc Networking", Proceedings of Sixth IEEE Workshop on Mobile Computing Systems and Applications(WMCSA'04)-Volume 00, 41-50, Dec 2004.
6. V.Vetri Selvi and Ranjani Parthasarathi, "Trace Based Mobility Model to Support Quality of Service in Ad Hoc Networks ", Trusted Internet Workshop (TIW05) held along with 12th International Conference on High Performance Computing (HiPC2005), 18-21 Dec. 2005.
7. Imran Ihsan, Muhammed Abdul Qadir, Nadeem Iftikhar, " Mobile Ad- Hoc Service Grid-MASGRID", Third World Enformatika Conference, WEC'05, pp 124-127,April 2005.
8. Zhi Wang, Bo Yu, Qi Chen, Chuanshan Gao, "Wireless Grid Computing over Mobile Ad-Hoc Networks with Mobile Agent", First International Conference on Semantics, Knowledge and Grid, Nov 2005.
9. J. Anda, J. LeBrun, D. Ghosal, C-N. Chuah, and H. M. Zhang, "VGrid: Vehicular Ad Hoc Networking and Computing Grid for Intelligent Traffic Control," IEEE Vehicular Technology Conference, Spring 2005.

10. Roy, N. Das, S.K.Basu, K.Kumar M, "Enhancing Availability of Grid Computational Services to Ubiquitous Computing Applications", 19th IEEE International Symposium on Parallel and Distributed Processing, April 2005.
11. http://pcl.cs.ucla.edu/projects/glomosim, 2000.
12. Dimitri Bertsekas, Robert Gallager, "Data Networks", 2nd Edition, Prentice-Hall India pp 174-176, 1999.

Self Managing Middleware for Dynamic Grids

Sachin Wasnik, Terence Harmer, Paul Donachy, Andrew Carson, Peter Wright, John Hawkins, Christina Cunningham, and Ron Perrott

Belfast e-Science Centre, The Queen's University of Belfast, Belfast, BT7 1NN, UK
{s.wasnik, t.harmer, p.donachy, a.carson, pwright04, j.hawkins, christina.cunningham, r.perrott}@qub.ac.uk

Abstract. As grid infrastructures become more dynamic in order to cope with the uncertainty of demand, they are becoming extremely difficult to manage. At the Belfast e-Science Centre, we are attempting to address this issue by developing Self Managing Grid Middleware. This paper gives an overview of the middleware and focuses on the design, implementation and evaluation of a Resource Manager. Also in this paper we will see how our approach, which is based on federated UDDI registries, has enabled us to implement some of the desired features of next generation grid software.

Keywords: Grid Computing, UDDI Registries, Grid Resource Manager, SLA.

1 Introduction

Most production Grids [1], irrespective of whether they are being deployed in commercial or academic environments, must cope with variation in demand. A goal for next generation Grid research and development is to produce a "...fully distributed, dynamically reconfigurable, scalable and autonomous infrastructure to provide location independent, pervasive, reliable, secure and efficient access to a coordinated set of services encapsulating and virtualizing resources (computing power, store, instruments, data etc) in order to generate knowledge", according to the CoreGrid European Network of Excellence [2]. There has been a significant improvement in focus of the vision of Grid Computing [3] since the term was introduced. A vital improvement still to be implemented satisfactorily is to make Grid Computing more dynamic so that it is able to cope with uncertainty of demand. Some recent work including HAND [4] and Dynamic Deployments [5] has focused on dynamically deploying and scaling Grids in production as and when needed.

The term "autonomic computing" is representative of a vast and somewhat tangled hierarchy of natural self governing systems, which consist of many interacting, self governing components that are often compromised of a large number of interacting, autonomous self governing components at the next level down. According to the vision of Autonomic Computing [6], the self-managing systems feature automatic mechanisms for operator free maintenance of stand alone and distributed resources, including self-configuration, self optimization, self-healing, self-protection and

C. Cérin and K.-C. Li (Eds.): GPC 2007, LNCS 4459, pp. 286 – 297, 2007.

others. This vision overlaps in its' goals with the pursuits of adaptability and dependability as described above in the recent definition of Grid Computing.

In particular, the adaptability of Grids can be interpreted as self-management on a different scale (and environment), thus making it worthwhile to exploit the discovered approaches in both domains. On the other hand, dependability mechanisms share a lot of scenario problems and approaches with self-management mechanisms (e.g. automatic fault recovery and preventive management actions such as software rejuvenation), thus calling for a convergence of research in these areas.

Trends in automating Service Level Agreement (SLA) management [7], from SLA creation to the performance monitoring of SLA's, can help the Resource Manager to sense the exact needs of users. With the help of an SLA Manager, middleware can act as a biological system which can sense and respond to the needs of the user. This should enable the effective utilization of resources by dynamically deploying, un-deploying and reconfiguring resources as and when needed. In such an infrastructure, Resource Managers are not only responsible for managing the resources, but also for selecting the resources on which the applications are to be deployed on. Thus the Resource Manager can act as the backbone of the self managing grid middleware.

Although a centralized Resource Manager can be very useful for a small number of resources, it may not be able to scale as the number of resources increases. A centralized Resource Manager acts as single point of failure and is vulnerable to security attacks. A decentralized Resource Manager can provide fault tolerance for the middleware by devolving responsibilities to a number of Resource Managers interacting with each other. A decentralized Resource Manager provides us with the necessary backbone of the next generation grid middleware but it is also difficult to maintain. This is where the self managing approach can assist in enabling the development of middleware which is self configuring, self healing, self optimizing and self protect.

The rest of the paper is organized as follows. Section 2 describes the architecture of the Self Managing Middleware. Section 3 describes the design and implementation of the federated Registries. Section 4 describes a use case for the middleware followed by the conclusion in section 5.

2 Self Managed Grid Middleware

According to our view of an infrastructure, infrastructure components are organised or grouped into *domains*. The name "domain" attempts to indicate that it is an area of responsibility and also serves to separate this infrastructural component view from other users and organizations ideas such as virtual organizations—a virtual organization might, for example, be built upon a collection of domains as shown in Figure 1.

A domain is a group of computing resources that it is natural to manage collectively; for example, it could be all of the resources in a small organization or it could be the resources in a particular computing rack that share a network

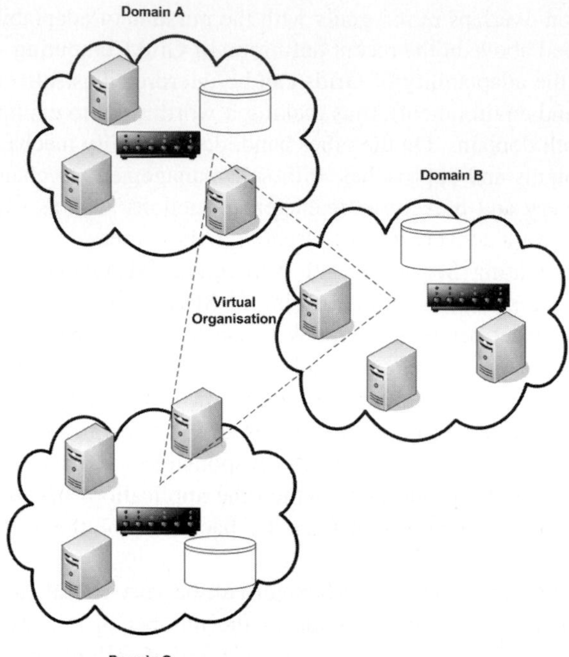

Fig. 1. Different organizations A, B and C forming a virtual organization

connection via a shared network connection or switch. The identification and selection of domains is performed as part of infrastructure design with the intention of identifying natural organizational units. A domain is our mechanism for providing a simple and distributed collection of managed infrastructure components.

The (self) management of grid resources is performed at the domain level. A domain provides a mechanism by which a group of related resources (i.e. services or applications) can be deployed and managed.

A domain may have sub domains. This hierarchical view enables requests to be directed to high-level management components and split between the organization units that are available within a domain—these high level components may enforce local management rules or act as brokers by selecting the best available local domains for deployment.

As shown in figure 2, each domain is managed using the core components of a Software Manager, a Security Manager, a Software Repository and a Resource Manager. A Resource Manger at the domain level is based on a single Registry but at the Grid level, Resource Manager is based on Registry Federation. Resource Manager at the grid level appears as a single logical Resource Manager of all the domains, to which a software manager can issue a single request against multiple Resource Manager and get a single response that contains results based on all the data contained in all the registries.

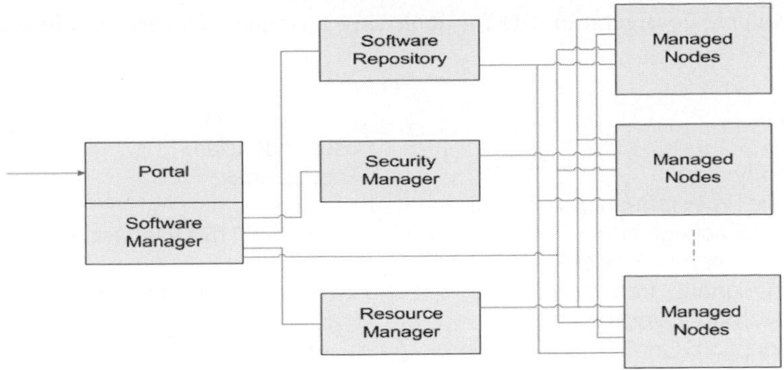

Fig. 2. Managed nodes being directed by the Managers

2.1 Software Manager

The Software Manager component takes a deployment request and performs the specified deployment. A deployment request consists of the deployment action and a configuration definition that enables management of the deployment action. A deployment action can be the installation of software, the execution of a particular application, the deployment of a web/grid service, the un-deployment of an application or web/grid service, thc storage of a data source such as a database, the un-deployment of a data source, the recovery of the data held in a data source, or the deployment of a security definition, for example the modification of firewall rules.

The Software Manager may require several deployment actions to fulfil a particular user deployment action; for example, the deployment of a web service may require the deployment of a specific Java environment, a web service container application, applications or web services to support the user web service.

A portal provides a user interface where a user can upload a package by supplying its configuration file—a web service provides the same functionality for an application.

A deployment request may be in one of the following formats:

- A war file
- An RPM
- A resource bundle for Globus container
- A resource bundle for OMII container
- A security configuration schema instance
- A data source bundle
- A meta tar file containing a combination of the above resources

The configuration definition specifies the required environment for the deployment. The action of the Software Manager is to select a suitable host, deploy software to that host that is required, deploy a security and the resources deployed.

An example configuration file for deploying a simple web service might look like this:

```
<config>
 <bundle>
  <summary>
   <bundleType>rpm</bundleType>
   <systemPackageInfo>
    <vendor>none</vendor>
    <name>gridftp_transfer</name>
    <version>2.1</version>
    <description>GridFTP</description>
   </systemPackageInfo>
   <validFrom>12/02/07</validFrom>
   <validTo>12/03/08</validTo>
  </summary>
  <firewall/>
  <callback><url/></callback>
...
...
   <dependencies>
   <hardware>
    <cpu>
     <speed>1500</speed>
    </cpu>
    <memory>512</memory>
    <storage>
     <freeSpace>15</freeSpace>
     <raid>5</raid>
    </storage>
   </hardware>
   <software/>
  </dependencies>
 </bundle>
</config>
```

2.2 Security Manager

The Security Manager is responsible for configuring and maintaining security on infrastructure components—currently this involves the deployment of digital certificates to enable user and host authentication, updating certificate revocation lists and defining firewall rules.

The Security Manager keeps track of the status of the firewall on each of the managed nodes with the help of an agent installed on them. When a service or application being deployed has a particular security requirement, the Software Manager sends a request to the infrastructure component of the Security Manager which performs the necessary security modifications. A security modification that conflicts with the basic security rules defined for an infrastructure component will cause a deployment request to be rejected; a modification that conflicts with rules deployed to support other applications will result in a different infrastructure component being selected as the deployment target. When a service or application is un-deployed, the security modifications are also un-deployed.

2.3 Software Repository

A Software Repository is maintained to hold different versions of applications and services that can be specified as software dependencies in the configuration file as shown above. When a user submits a configuration file for deployment to the software manager, the Software Repository provides the software to carry out the deployment action. For example, a deployment of war file needs java and a web service container. In this case war file will be provided by the user and the software repository will provide dependent packages of java and web service container.

3 Resource Manager

The convergence of grid computing and service oriented computing has enabled the service registries to take on the role of a Resource Manager [8]. Job scheduling in grid environments has taken a new form relating to the interaction between the service provider and the service consumer, which is shown here in Figure 3.

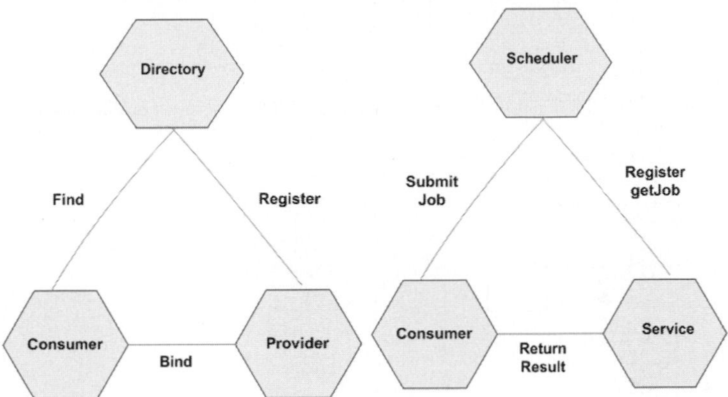

Fig. 3. Interaction diagram showing the interactions between the Service Provider and the Service Consumer

As the user demand on Grids becomes more agile and dynamic, service discovery using static information is not enough and a need emerges for storing Quality of Service (QoS) information inside service registries as well as a complete abstract mapping of compute resources. The compute resources should be mapped in such a way so as to allow a consistent view and management of the resources and this mapping may vary across different infrastructures.

3.1 Resource Mapping

The GLUE Schema [9] is an abstract modelling for Grid resources and mapping to concrete schemas that is being used by most of the production Grids. Glue Schema is widely used in most of the production grids. It has been integrated in number of Grid middleware such as EGEE [10], LCG [11], OSG [12], Globus [13] and NorduGrid [14]. We have represented the GLUE Schema as shown in Figure 4, inside the service registry. A number of specifications for service registries such as UDDI [15], ebXml [16] are available and their implementations are being used for web/grid service discovery. For our middleware we chose the Universal Description, Discovery and Integration (UDDI) registry.

A web/grid ***service*** is represented inside the UDDI registry as a Business Service. A service runs within a compute resource. These compute resources are mapped as Business Entity inside the UDDI registry in a similar way as if they own the service.

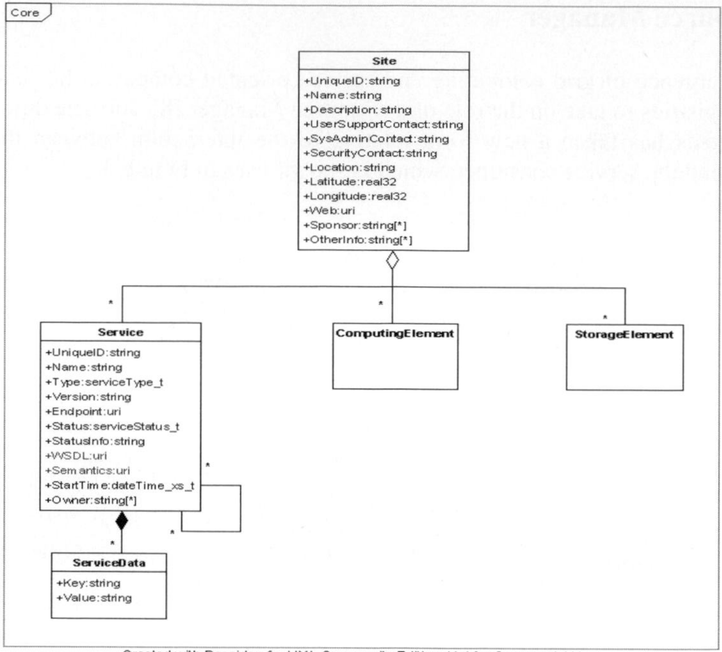

Fig. 4. GLUE Schema

As described in section 2, a site which consists of compute and storage resource is considered as domain which is represented as a business entity. This site business entity can have one or more compute resources and storage resources. The relationship between the machine business entity and the service container business entity is represented as a parent-child relation by using publisher assertions.

3.2 Architecture

An analysis of the individual and collective state of the compute resources can determine the performance of a Grid and enable (self) management activities to respond in an efficient and directed manner; for example, if the Grid is performing poorly then the Resource Manager should identify the compute resources which are contributing to the poor performance and enable the activation of a reactive procedure. The Resource Manager is named as Open Grid Manager (OGM). To achieve the above objective, the OGM for each domain is composed number of components, namely

1) GridManagerAgents (GMA)
2) GridManagerServer (GMS)
3) Web based User Interface (GMUI)
4) UDDI Registry

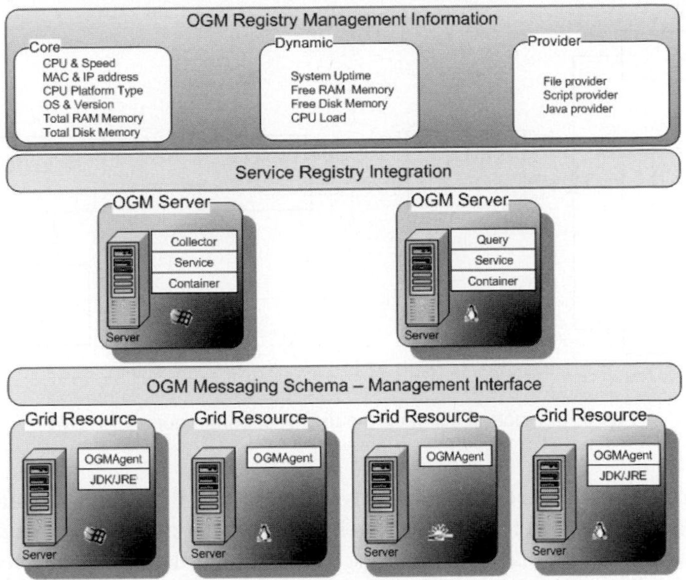

Fig. 5. Architecture of Open Grid Manager (OGM)

The GridManagerServer consists of two services – a Collector Service and a Query Service. The GridManagerAgents are responsible for deducing a machine's state and reporting this to a Collector Service. The Collector Service collects state data from nodes in a distributed environment and forwards this to the UDDI registry.

Each Managed Node registers itself by sending core information to the Collector Service with the help of installed GridManagerAgent. The process of registration is carried out by following steps as shown in the Interaction diagram Figure 6.

1) GridManagerAgent sends the core information to the Collector Service.
2) Collector Service of the GridManagerServer, upon receiving the core information address, makes a create Business Entity call to the UDDI registry.
3) UDDI registry creates a Business Entity and sends back the business key to the Collector Service.
4) Collector Service sends the Business Key back to the GridManagerAgent.

The GridManagerAgent uses the same Business key to continuously update the Business Entity with dynamic information and Provider information. The process of update follows the same steps. The frequency of update is configured via the GridManagerAgent's configuration file.

Apart from the resource information, a collector service also stores information about deployments and un-deployments sent by the Software Manager which is considered as static data, as it doesn't change frequently. Whenever a deployment request is made to the Software Manager, the manager sends the information about the deployment request to the Collector Service. Upon receiving the deployment request and the IP address of the machine on which it is to be deployed, the Collector Service creates a business entity with the resource name, which is a child of the Business Entity representing the machine on which it is deployed.

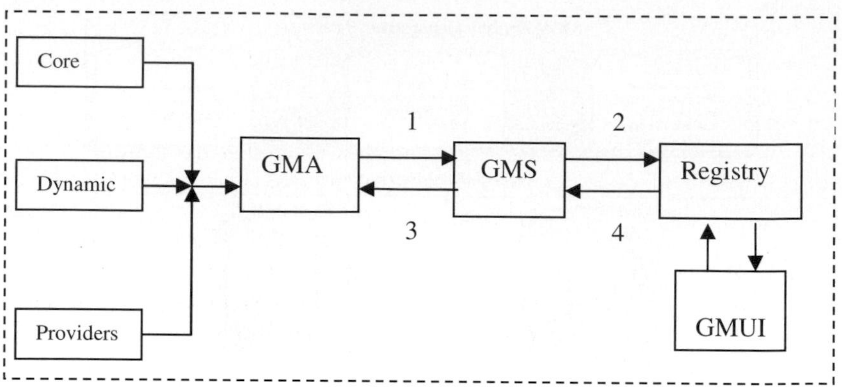

Fig. 6. Interaction between the different components of OGM

For example, while deploying packages such as Grid-FTP, the Software Manager sends information such as the port on which the deployed packages will be running, a username and their associated credentials. When the Collector Service receives this information, it is stored inside the UDDI registry as a Business Entity. These Business Entities have descriptions of transport packages and are children of the Machine Entity on which they are installed.

The Query Service is responsible for answering the queries sent by the software manager. The Software Manager can send queries:

1) To check which machines satisfy certain hardware requirements.
2) To ascertain what packages are already deployed on a given machine. This can help the software manager to discover which machines satisfy the software dependency requirements of a given package to be installed.

To make the domain fault tolerant, the domain operator can keep a backup of their domain registries using database mirroring. In case of a failure of the Resource Manager in a particular domain, a Collector Service and a Query Service is installed and configured to use the stored backup data. Thus the domain manager can roll back to its state just before the failure.

3.3 Federation of Registry

In large distributed grid environments, a single registry can degrade the performance of the whole system as number of clients becomes too large. Also, it becomes a single point of failure, as the whole system depends on the single registry. To make the system more scalable, multiple registries should be utilized.

The latest UDDI version 3 [17] specifications promotes a replication model of data for multiple registries to enable a single view of multiple registries; such a replication model is not suited to the grid environment.

It is preferable that each domain in the federation would have complete autonomy of the data related to the domain. Each domain operator should be able to configure what data to share and with whom it is to be shared. Thus replication between registries owned by multiple independent operators is more complex but more relevant in a

Grid environment which is targeted at cooperating yet independent stake holders. Such a setup requires communication between individual registries to synchronise registration data.

Replication adds communication traffic between the registries for keeping registration data in sync. There is a trade-off between the amount of traffic and the timeliness of the replicated data. If changes to the registration data are propagated to all registries immediately, all registries will have a more or less consistent and current view of the service setup, resulting in a large amount of traffic between the registries. If the registration updates are propagated less frequently and in batches the traffic size decreases (as communication set-up costs are averaged over all changes), but registries will be out of sync for some time. Depending on the application domain, inconsistencies may or may not be tolerable.

Although replication enables scalability, the load is not distributed automatically. Registration is performed at the domain registry but queries can arrive at any of the participating registries. Which registry is to be used is decided by the Query Peer. Load distribution is taken care by the cluster of Query Peers, each of which maintains a list of possible registries. After initial setup, the list could be maintained by automatically updating it with the information from the registry to use.

Each replicated registry keeps a copy of the complete registration data of the whole system. The advantage is that every registry can answer a query by just looking at its database. However a disadvantage of this approach is the large amount of data which may be kept at every site. In our approach, each registry keeps only a subset of the registration data and can only answer query relating to that subset. The data distribution is based on locality.

As the registration data is distributed across registries, multiple registries are involved in answering a query. Orchestrating the devolved registries is performed by the Query Peer which knows all the registries that have answers to their query.

4 Use Case

As part of its core business, a Financial Company analyses Stock Market data from each of the world's main Stock Exchanges. This depends heavily on process and data intensive computations for Risk Management purposes. Feeds are received from each of the exchanges which are fed into a high performance financial database. A number of databases are also maintained containing historical financial data. A number of financial calculations are performed, such as Implied Volatility calculations, on each portfolio managed by the company using the data held in each of the databases.

This system works well for the company on a day-to-day basis. However, to allow them to react more quickly to changes in stock prices as a result of unforeseen major world events, the company would like the option to bring in additional computation power and resources as required. This would enable the Financial Company to react more quickly than their competitors, performing all the additional calculations required to obtain results in near real time, thus gaining a market advantage for their clients.

A system such as the one provided by the Self Managing Middleware described in this paper would clearly benefit this company when they need to react quickly to unpredictable events. Once the increased activity within the stock exchanges has been identified, the company could increase their computational power by quickly deploying additional services to a 3rd party hardware provider and running some calculations from there. This would require transport services to be deployed both at the company's home location and the 3rd party hardware provider's location so that the high performance financial databases could be deployed onto the additional machines. Three databases are required to perform the calculations. One database is required for capturing the data from the live feeds, one database for the intra-day data and another database where historical data is stored. Services which undertake the calculations could then be deployed and initiated, the various calculations performed and the results transported back to the Financial Company for dissemination or use by another application. When the additional capacity was no longer required, the services and databases deployed to the 3rd party hardware provider would be un-deployed.

The Financial Company would be able to impose certain conditions on where their data and services were deployed to. Certain financial regulations imposed upon the Financial Company dictate that the data cannot leave the United Kingdom. The Financial Company may also impose certain restrictions such as 'Don't deploy services or data onto machines owned or managed by one of our competitors'. Information such as this can be included in the configuration file sent with the bundle to be deployed. The Self Managing Middleware enables the Company to have immediate access to additional computational power when required without having to maintain this hardware on a day to day basis.

Secure on-demand provisioning of Risk Management capabilities represents a real and valuable next step for the financial services industry to increase competitiveness and reduce costs. It is also relevant to service provision and consultancy companies currently competing in the international market.

5 Conclusion

In this paper we have discussed the use of Self Managing Software and a Resource Manager to enable the management and control of large-scale grid infrastructures. In the Belfast e-Science centre we have deployed this software in the field for approximately a year and it is an integral part of the testing development of grid of our large-scale commercial projects.

References

1. Foster, I., Gieraltowski, J., Gose, S., et al, : The Grid2003 Production Grid: Principles and Practice. Proc. 13th IEEE Intl. Symposium on High Performance Distributed Computing (2004) 236–245.
2. http://www.coregrid.net
3. Foster, I., Kesselman, C., Nick, J., Tuecke, S., : The Physiology of the Grid: An Open Grid Services Architecture for Distributed Systems Integration. Open Grid Service Infrastructure WG, Global Grid Forum (2002).
4. Qi, Li., Foster, I., Gawor, J.,: HAND: Highly Available Dynamic Deployment Infrastructure for Globus Toolkit 4. Submitted for publication (2006)

5. Watson, P., Fowler, C., Kubicek, C., et al, : Dynamically Deploying Web Services on a Grid using Dynasoar. Proc. 13th IEEE Intl. Symposium on Object And Component-Oriented Real-Time Distributed Computing. ISORC 2006, April (2006)
6. Kephert, J., Chess., D. : The Vision of Autonomic Computing. Computer. Vol. 36 Issue 1. (2003)
7. Sahai, A., Durante, A., Machiraju, V. : Towards automated SLA management for web services. Research Report HPL-2001-310(R.1) Hewlett-Packard laboratories Palo Alto. (2002)
8. Joseph, J., Ernest, M., Fellenstein, C.: Evolution of Grid Computing architecture and Grid adoption models. IBM Syst. J. 43, 624-625 (2004)
9. Andreozzi, S., Burke S., et al: GLUE Schema Specification version 1.2 (2005)
10. Enabling Grids for E-sciencE Project http://www.eu-egee.org/
11. LHC Computing Grid Project http://lcg.web.cern.ch/LCG/
12. Open Science Grid http://www.opensciencegrid.org/
13. http://www.globus.org/
14. http://www.nordugrid.org/
15. Bellwood, T., UDDI Version 2.04 API Specification
16. http://www.ebxml.org
17. Bellwood, T., UDDI Version 3.0 Spec Technical Committee Specification July (2002)

Adaptive Workflow Scheduling Strategy in Service-Based Grids*

JongHyuk Lee[1], SungHo Chin[1], HwaMin Lee[2], TaeMyoung Yoon[1], KwangSik Chung[3], and HeonChang Yu[1,**]

[1] Dept. of Computer Science Education, Korea University
{spurt, wingtop, tmyoon, yuhc}@comedu.korea.ac.kr
[2] The Korean Intellectual Property Office
hwamin@kipo.go.kr
[3] Dept. of Computer Science, Korea National Open University
kchung0825@knou.ac.kr

Abstract. During the past several years, the grid application executed same jobs on one or more hosts in parallel, but the recent grid application is requested to execute different jobs linearly. That is, the grid application takes the form of workflow application. In general, efficient scheduling of workflow applications is based on heuristic scheduling method. The heuristic considering relation between hosts would improve execution time in workflow applications. But because of the heterogeneity and dynamic nature of grid resources, it is hard to predict the performance of grid application. In addition, it is necessary to deal with user's QoS as like performance guarantee. In this paper, we propose a service model for predicting performance and an adaptive workflow scheduling strategy, which uses maximum flow algorithms for the relation of services and user's QoS. Experimental results show that the performance of our proposed scheduling strategy is better than common-used greedy strategies.

Keywords: adaptive grid scheduling, workflow, maximum flow.

1 Introduction

In the mid 1990s, Grid computing has emerged as an important new field, distinguished from conventional distributed computing by its focus on large-scale resource sharing, innovative applications, and high-performance orientation [1]. Grid computing system [2] consists of large sets of diverse, geographically distributed resources that are grouped into virtual computers for executing specific applications. In common Grid computing, resource components could be processes, processors within a computer, network interfaces, network connections, entire sites, database, file system and specific computers. Today, Grid computing offers the strongest low cost and high throughput solutions [1, 2] and is spotlighted as the key technology of the next generation Internet. Grid computing is used in fields as diverse as astronomy, biology, drug discovery, engineering, weather forecasting, and high-energy physics.

* This work was supported by the Korea Research Foundation Grant funded by the Korean Government(MOEHRD) (KRF-2006-D00173).

** Corresponding author.

C. Cérin and K.-C. Li (Eds.): GPC 2007, LNCS 4459, pp. 298 – 309, 2007.

Recently, the Grid and Web Service are converging as WSRF (Web Service-Resource Framework)[3] that defines a system for creating stateful resources between Web services in terms of an implied resource pattern. The current methodology in Grid computing is service oriented architecture.

In service-based Grids, Grid resources are virtualized as services(e.g., database, data transfer). So the Grid not only provides computational resource and data resource, but also supports logic application that cooperates with services integration with the composition of the Grid service. Instead of application executing a single job, Grid application consists of a collection of several dependency services. Therefore, many grid applications belong to the category of workflow application. Most of science and business grid applications take the form of linear workflow structure. That is, the science grid application is a parameter sweep application processed using same code for different data, and the business grid application is a transaction application that queries at databases, processes data, and stores in database. Because of processing data in parallel with extensive parameter bounds, workflow application is of benefit to performance. In service-based Grids, it is necessary to consider a relation of services for execution performance because a linear workflow application executed parallel jobs via several services on one or more hosts.

It is easy for workflow structure not only to compose services but also to visualize, verify, schedule, execute, and monitor services. Many kinds of workflow management systems are developed for grid workflow applications. There are two steps for producing workflow. The first step is a service composition to use workflow language and the second step is a scheduling to map sub-task to service. In general, an efficient scheduling of workflow applications is based on heuristic scheduling method. The heuristic considering relation between hosts would improve execution time in workflow applications. But due to the heterogeneity and dynamic nature of grid resources, it is hard to predict the performance of grid application. In addition, it is necessary to deal with user's QoS like performance guarantee.

In this paper, we propose service model for predicting performance and adaptive workflow scheduling strategy, which uses maximum flow algorithms for considering the relation of services and user's QoS.

The rest of the paper is as follows. In section 2, we state a scheduling problem and propose a service model for predicting performance. Section 3 describes the novel strategy to execute the workflows adaptively. In section 4, we present an experimental evaluation of our scheduling by comparing it with existing scheduling strategies. Section 5 presents related works. In section 6, we conclude the paper and discuss some future works.

2 Problem Statement

Workflow scheduling system is to translate application task graph into service graph in computing environment.

2.1 Task Graph

A task graph is an abstract workflow that represents an application as a general model of directed acyclic graph. It is represented as follows;

$G^T = (V^T, E^T)$
V^T : the set of tasks
E^T : the set of edges between tasks that represent a partial order among them

The fact that an edge $e_{i,j}$ is a partial order between task v_i and v_j means that a task v_j is executed after completing a task v_i. In case a task v_i and v_j are a same parent, two task can be executed parallelly. Representing G^T as matrix M of size $v \times v$, $d_{i,i}$ is a computation cost of v_i, and $d_{i,j}$ is a communication cost between v_i and v_j. In this paper, we assume that a task graph implies a start task and a end task.

2.2 Service Graph

A service graph is an directed weighted graph of services in grid computing environments. It is represented as follows.

$G^S = (V^S, E^S)$
V^S : $\{s_1, s_2, \ldots, s_n\}$ the set of services that can be executed at available node
E^S : the set of edges between services

A service graph is a complete connected graph. V^S denotes a computation performance and E^S denotes a communication performance between services. A k-th service node that executes service s_j is $s_{j,k}$. The computation cost of task v_i at service $s_{i,k}$ is $w_{i,j,k}$. If service $s_{i,k}$ can't execute task v_i, then $w_{i,j,k} = \infty$. The communication cost between service node $s_{m,k}$ for task v_i and $s_{n,k}$ for v_j is $c_{i,m,k|j,n,k}$.

2.3 Performance Criteria

Application completion time is consist of computation time and communication time. We assume that grid application executes task t_1 and t_2 sequentially. A task graph is composed with two nodes and one edge between them. That is, $G^T = (\{t_1, t_2\}, E^T)$. For mapping this task graph to service graph, we have to search service s_1 and s_2 that can process task t_1 and t_2. That is $G^S = (\{s_1, s_2\}, E^S)$. If service s_1 completes before communicating with s_2, completion time of this application is defined as follows.

$$\textit{completion time} = \textit{communication time}(A, s_1) + \textit{computation time}(s_1) + \textit{communication time}(s_1, s_2) + \textit{computation time}(s_2) + \textit{communication time}(s_2, A) + \textit{computation time}(A) \quad (1)$$

Grid application A invokes service s_1 and the result of service s_1 is sent to service s_2. Service s_2 processes a task and the result of service s_2 is sent to grid application A. In practice, completion time is determined according to a node that a service is executed in. Therefore, completion time of a node about some service should be predicted and be applied for mapping task graph to service graph.

For predicting completion time of grid service, it is necessary to select optimized service according to performance model described the characteristics of service and to compose workflow. In addition, we need to consider not only scheduling using information of physical resource, but also supporting user's QoS. Hence, in this paper, the performance model is considered as follows.

- service static model : considering a static information of resources like CPU, memory, disk space, and network bandwidth.
- service dynamic model : Owing to influencing service performance by resource capability directly, considering a dynamic information of resources like available CPU, available memory, available disk space, available network bandwidth, and network latency. We also consider the predicted resource status using service patterns like service reservation, frequency of service use, and service throughput.

Since Grid is free of participation and withdrawal of a node, it is necessary that grid service scheduler predicts the performance of a service and applies it dynamically. In this paper, we use a statistical method to predict the performance of a service. Regression is a statistical method that supports relationships between variables and is an appropriate method for predicting an effect about a cause. In regression, the dependent variable(y) that is an effect and the independent variable(x) that is a cause denote as $x \rightarrow y$. That is, the relation between x and y is represented as follows;

$$y = \beta_0 + \beta_1 x + \varepsilon \tag{2}$$

where β_0 is a constant; β_1 is a coefficient of regression; ε is an error rate.

After regression analysis, we can determine a relationship between a dependent variable and an independent variable. If we applied this regression technique with performance as a dependent variable and each resource status as an independent variable, we can predict the performance of a service that participates newly in Grids using existing regression coefficient. In our work, we use a multiple linear regression that allows the modeling of multiple independent variables, which are information of resources defined by service model in Grids.

We consider static and dynamic physical elements x_i such as CPU, memory, disk space, network bandwidth, service reservation, frequency of service use in a service model. The service throughput (y_s), the equation applied these elements to multiple regression, is as follows.

$$y_s = \beta_0 + \sum_{i=1}^{n} \beta_i x_i + \varepsilon \tag{3}$$

where β_0 is a constant; β_i is a coefficient of regression; n is a count of elements; ε is an error rate.

Table 1 is an example data for performance model using multiple linear regression that is executed in same service. The Independent variables are CPU, CPU available, memory available, disk available, and network bandwidth. The dependent variable is throughput. Table 2 is a model summary that multiple linear regression is done. As shown in Table 2, this model can be explained well because coefficient of determination(R Square) is 0.971. That is, the strength of the linear association between independent variables and dependent variable of this model is high. As shown in Table 3, F-test is 93.634 and significant probability is 0.000. Therefore, the one of regression coefficients in the population is not 0 at least. Table 4 is regression coefficients about each independent variable. We can predict a throughput of new entrance node using these coefficients.

Table 1. Example data for performance model

CPU	CPU available	Memory available	Disk available	Network bandwidth	Throughput
1600	.80	234	3320	25	40
1800	.40	346	4592	35	28
2000	.60	78	9295	29	33
2400	.40	321	2934	90	34
1600	.50	398	2039	34	45
...	...	...	...	...	...
3000	.30	455	3945	10	36

Table 2. Model summary

R	R Square	Adjusted R Square	Std. Error of the Estimate
.985(a)	.971	.961	3.678

Table 3. ANOVA(Analysis Of Variance between groups)

	Sum of Squares	df	Mean Square	F	Sig.
Regression	6333.602	5	1266.720	93.634	.000
Residual	189.398	14	13.528		
Total	6523.000	19			

Table 4. Coefficients

	Unstandardized Coefficients		Standardized Coefficients	t	Sig.
	B	Std. Error	Beta		
(Constant)	-41.266	5.793		-7.124	.000
CPU	.016	.002	.510	8.863	.000
CPU_available	64.981	5.261	.724	12.350	.000
memory_available	.026	.004	.339	5.826	.000
disk_available	.000	.000	.037	.704	.493
network_bandwidth	.015	.037	.022	.417	.683

3 Adaptive Scheduling Using Dynamic Maximum Flow Algorithm

It is important to select a computation node and a data node for minimizing overall job completion time. It is necessary to minimize completion time for processing data and communication time between computation node and data node. Moreover, it is essential to optimize use of resource through scheduling algorithm. Our objective is to minimize overall job completion time and to optimize use of resource. For our objective, we present an adaptive scheduling using dynamic maximum flow algorithm that finds a flow of maximum value in flow network G with source *s* and sink *t*.

The adaptive workflow scheduling algorithm presented in Algorithm 1 works as follows. The input of WorkflowScheduling in Algorithms 1 is task graph G^T and service level agreement SLA which involve user's QoS. G^T is mapped to service graph G^S by SLA and resource performance criteria. Then Algorithm 2 is invoked with G^S. MaximumFlow in Algorithm 2 is based on Ford-Fulkerson method[9] which finds some augmenting path *p* and increases the flow *f* on each edge of *p* by the residual capacity $c_f(p)$. Algorithm 3 based on breadth-first search is to find augmenting path in residual network of G^S. FindAugmentingPath in Algorithm 3 assumes that the input graph G^S is represented by adjacency lists in descending order by sufferage heuristic value. Migration in Algorithm 1 is a function that migrates the tasks through comparison of flow before rescheduling with flow after rescheduling if a performance guarantee is violated. After all tasks executed, scheduler updates service's makespan(e.g. throughput) for performance criteria.

```
WorkflowScheduling(G^T, SLA)
    G^S ← Find available services satisfied SLA about G^T
    MaximumFlow(G^S)
    while all tasks not executed
        do Fetch task
           if a performance guarantee is violated
              then do update V^S[G^S]
                      MaximumFlow(G^S)          // rescheduling
                      Migration(G^S, G^S_prev)
    update service's makespan
```

Algorithm 1. Workflow Scheduling

```
MaximumFlow(G^S) // find maximum flow about workflow G^S
    for each edge (s_i, s_j) j E^S[G^S]
        do f[s_i, s_j]   0
           f[s_j, s_i]   0
    while (there exists a path p from start service to end
           service in the residual network G^S)
        // min{c_f(s_i, s_j) : (s_i, s_j) is in p}
        do c_f(p)   FindAugmentingPath(G^S, source, sink)
           for each edge (s_i, s_j) in p
               do f[s_i, s_j]   f[s_i, s_j] + c_f(p)
                  f[s_j, s_i]   -f[s_i, s_j]
```

Algorithm 2. Maximum Flow

```
FindAugmentingPath(GS, source, sink)
    for each vertex u j V[GS] - {source}
         do color[u]    WHITE
    color[source]    GRAY
    Enqueue(Q, source)
    cf[source]    -1
    while Q ≠ 0
         u = Dequeue(Q)
        // Adj[u] is sorted by sufferage value
         for each v j Adj[u]
        do if (color[v] == WHITE &&
               capacity[u][v] - flow[u][v] > 0)
         then color[v]    GRAY
               Enqueue(Q, v)
               cf[v] = u
         color[u]    BLACK
return cf;
```

Algorithm 3. Find Augmenting Path

For example, assume that Grid application A is composed of task T_B, T_C, and T_D. The number of service nodes for tasks T_B, T_C, and T_D is 2, 3, and 1 respectively. The linear workflow and the workflow mapped service are represented in Fig. 1. The edge capacity of workflow is calculated by performance criteria.

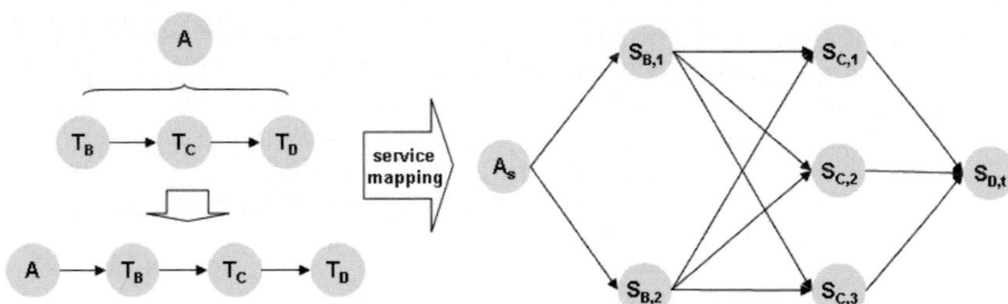

Fig. 1. Linear workflow and workflow mapped service

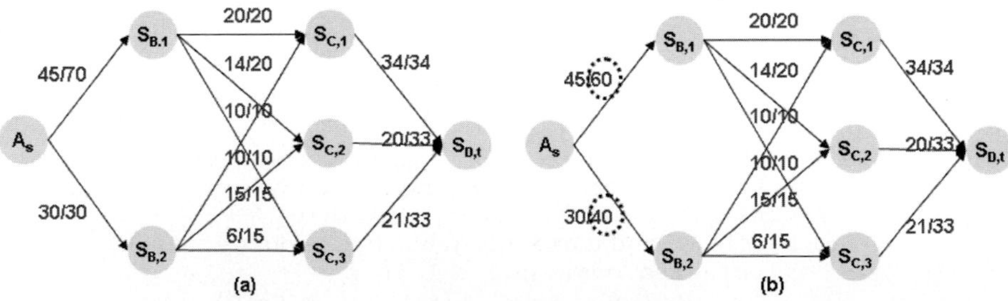

Fig. 2. Result through performance modeling and maximum flow

Fig. 2(a) is a result through performance modeling and MaximumFlow in Algorithm 2. The edge of workflow denotes 'flow/capacity'. The capacity of 70 between A_s and $S_{B,1}$ means that $S_{B,1}$ can process requested job of A_s at the throughput rate of 70. If a performance guarantee is violated, the workflow scheduler reschedules after updating current capacity of workflow. Fig. 2(b) is the result of rescheduling. As shown in Table 5, the maximum flow increases. If the maximum flow decreases, it means that a new service node should be added.

Table 5. Service order and comparison of flow before rescheduling and flow after rescheduling

Service order	Flow before rescheduling	Flow after rescheduling
$A_SB_1C_2D_t$	10	10
$A_SB_1C_1D_t$	20	20
$A_SB_1C_3D_t$	15	15
$A_SB_2C_1D_t$	14	14
$A_SB_2C_2D_t$	10	10
$A_SB_2C_3D_t$	6	15

4 Experiment

Although experiments and performance evaluations need to be performed in a practical large-scale grid platform, it is difficult to build a large-scale grid platform and to experiment repeatedly. Therefore, we simulate our scheduling algorithm using SimGrid toolkit and experiment performance of real grid application implemented a service based virtual screening system in practical small-scale grid environments.

Simulation scenario is classified into two categories: adding service and adding task. In this paper, we compare our scheduling with greedy heuristic scheduling that allocates more tasks to node with better performance. Performance prediction scheduling is greedy heuristic scheduling with performance model described in this paper. Experiment workflow is a generic science workflow that searches, downloads, processes data, and stores result in Fig. 1.

4.1 Performance Evaluation According to the Number of Nodes for Services

In Grid workflow, the number of nodes for service A requesting workflow is 1, the number of nodes for service D collecting results is 1, the number of nodes for service B is 3, and the number of nodes for service C is 5, 10, 15 in each experiments. The number of tasks is 5,000. Fig. 3 shows the result of evaluation. As shown in Fig. 3, our scheduling is better than other algorithms by 15% ~ 20%. The difference of execution time between case that the number of nodes for service C is 10 and case that the number of nodes for service C is 15 is small. It is because the collection of service C could process mostly data from the collection of service B in the former. Therefore, although the number of nodes for service increases in some collection of service, the efficiency of performance doesn't increase. Through our scheduling, we predict a sudden change of efficiency in that the number of nodes for service C is 10.

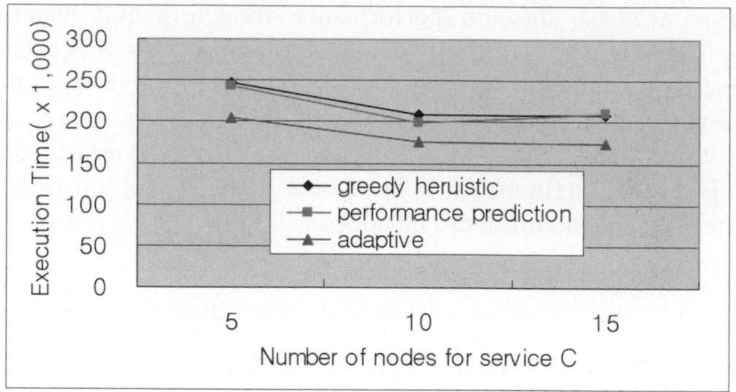

Fig. 3. Result of performance evaluation according to the number of nodes for service C

4.2 Performance Evaluation According to the Number of Tasks

In Grid workflow, the number of nodes for service A requesting workflow is 1, the number of nodes for service D collecting results is 1, the number of nodes for service B is 3, and the number of nodes for service C is 10. The number of tasks is from 1,000 to 11,000 at intervals of 2,000. Fig. 4 shows the result of evaluation. As shown in Fig. 4, our scheduling is better than other algorithms by 10% ~ 15%.

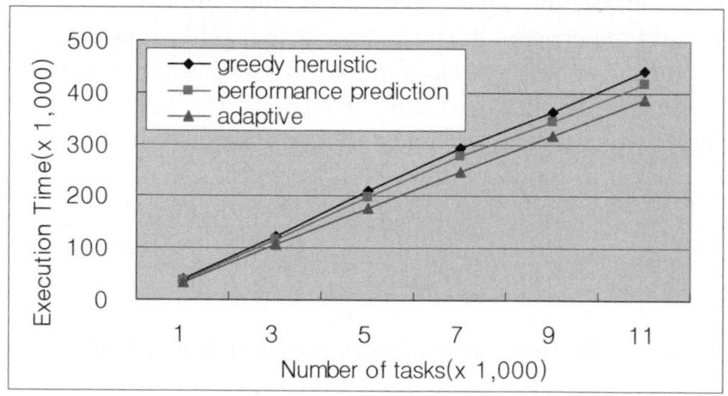

Fig. 4. Result of performance evaluation according to the count of tasks

4.3 Performance Evaluation in Real Grid Application

We implemented a service-based virtual screening system which is one of large-scale scientific applications that require large computing power and data storage capability. A virtual screening is the process of reducing an unmanageable number of compounds to a limited number of compounds for the target of interest by means of computational techniques such as docking [10, 11]. Thus this application suits with Grid computing technology which supports a large data intensive operation.

We experimented our virtual screening system in a testbed that consists of 15 computation nodes and 5 data nodes. We performed docking jobs with 30,000 ligand molecules on a target receptor. Fig. 5 shows the comparison of execution times as the number of docking jobs increases. We compared three different approaches to execute docking jobs. The first approach is to execute docking jobs on only single node which has the best computing performance. The second approach is to execute docking jobs on selected 5 computation nodes. We selected 5 computation nodes according to high computing performance. The third approach is to execute docking jobs using our Grid service-based virtual screening system applied our scheduling. Fig. 5 shows that the performance of our virtual screening system is better than other approaches. When 30,000 docking jobs were executed, the execution time of first approach was 587,541 seconds, the execution time of second approach was 221,516 seconds, and third approach was 162,964 seconds.

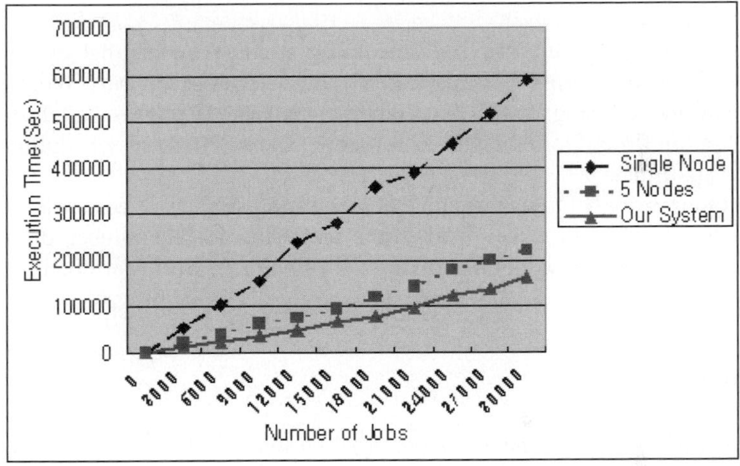

Fig. 5. Comparison of execution time for three cases

5 Related Works

Grid Scheduling is a superscheduling[4] or metascheduling that is the process of scheduling resource where that decision involves using multiple administrative domains. Scheduling is classified into a static scheduling and a dynamic scheduling according to a point of scheduling time. The static scheduling resolves the order of all jobs before executing jobs. The dynamic scheduling can modify the order of jobs in runtime.

In [5], Muthucumaru et al gives an overview of two types of mapping heuristics: on-line and batch mode heuristic. These heuristics are dynamic mapping heuristics for a class of independent tasks in heterogeneous distributed computing. In online mode, mapper allocates tasks to resources as soon as it arrives at the mapper. In batch mode, mapper collects tasks until calling mapping events and allocates tasks to resources after calling mapping events. In particular, sufferage heuristic is newly proposed, which is different with min-min, max-min heuristic[6]. Sufferage value is defined as difference between minimum earliest completion time and second earliest completion time. In [7], Casanova et al extends sufferage heuristic as Xsufferage. In XSufferage, the sufferage vaule is computed not with minimum earliest completion time, but with cluster-level minimum earliest completion time, which is important in Grid environment. In [8], Eduardo et al proposed the GridWay framework which executes and schedules efficiently parameter sweep application in Grid environment. This framework applied adaptive scheduling to reflect the dynamic Grid characteristic, adaptive execution to migrate running jobs to better resource, and reuse of common file to reduce file transfer overhead. [5] and [7] are a static scheduling and [8] is a dynamic scheduling. But [5], [7], and [8] can't support the form of workflow. In this paper, we support the dynamic scheduling of dependent task using sufferage value.

6 Conclusion

In this paper, we proposed adaptive scheduling strategy for parallel execution of a linear workflow considering dynamic resource in service-based Grids. We presented a performance model using regression technique and an adaptive scheduling strategy using maximum flow algorithm. Our experiments showed that our scheduling is better than other algorithms.

In the future, we plan to investigate our scheduling strategy at commercial point of view as shown in performance evaluation according to the number of nodes for services. We also plan to work on applying not only linear workflow but also complex workflow.

References

1. I. Foster, C. Kesselman and S. Tuecke, The Anatomy of the Grid : Enabling Scalable Virtual Organizations, International Supercomputer Applications, Vol. 15, No. 3 (2001)
2. Ian Foster, and Carl Kesselman, The Grid : Blueprint for a New Computing Infrastructure, Morgan Kaufmann Publishers (1998)
3. K. Czajkowski, D. Ferguson, I. Foster, J. Frey, S. Graham, T. Maguire, D. Snelling, S. Tuecke, From Open Grid Services Infrastructure to WS-Resource Framework: Refactoring & Evolution,
4. http://www.ibm.com/developerworks/library/ws-resource/ogsi_to_wsrf_1.0.pdf, (2004)
5. J.M. Schopf, Ten Actions when SuperScheduling, Global Grid Forum Document GFD.04, July (2001)
6. Muthucumaru Maheswaran, Shoukat Ali, Howard Jay Siegel, Debra Hensgen, and Richard F. Freund, Dynamic Matching and Scheduling of a Class of Independent Tasks onto Heterogeneous Computing Systems, Proceedings of the 8th Workshop on Heterogeneous Computing Systems (HCW '99), San Juan, Puerto Rico, Apr. (1999)
7. O. Ibarra and C. Kim, Heuristic Algorithms for Scheduling Independent Tasks on Nonidentical Processors. Journal of the ACM, 24(2):280-289, (1977)
8. Casanova, H., Legrand, A., Zagorodnov, D., and Berman, F., Heuristics for Scheduling Parameter Sweep Applications in Grid Environments, Proceedings of the 9th Heterogeneous Computing Workshop (HCW'00), pp. 349-363, (2000)

9. Eduardo Heudo, Ruben S. Montero, Ignacio M. Lorente, Experiences on Adaptive Grid Scheduling of Parameter Sweep Applications, Proceedings of the 12th Euromicro Conference on Parallel Distributed and Network-Based Processing(EUROMICRO-PDP'04), (2004)
10. Lestor R. Ford, Jr. and D. R. Fulkerson, Flows in Networks, Princeton University Press, (1962)
11. Jordi Mestres and Ronald Knegtel, Similarity versus docking in 3D virtual screening, Journal of Perspectives in Drug Discovery and Design, Vol. 20, (2000)
12. Shoichet, Bodian, and Kuntz, Molecular docking using shape descriptors, Journal of Computational Chemistry, Vol. 13, No. 3, pp. 380-397, (1992)

Scalable Thread Visualization for Debugging Data Races in OpenMP Programs

Young-Joo Kim, Jae-Seon Lim, and Yong-Kee Jun*

Gyeongsang National University
Jinju, 660-701 South Korea
{yjkim,dember99,jun}@gnu.ac.kr

Abstract. It is important to debug unintended data races in OpenMP programs efficiently, because such programs are often complex and long-running. Previous tools for detecting the races does not provide any effective facility for understanding the complexity of threads involved in the reported races. This paper presents a thread visualization tool to present a partial order of threads executed in the traced programs with a scalable graph of abstract threads upon a three-dimensional cone. The scalable thread visualization is proved to be effective in debugging races using a set of synthetic programs.

Keywords: OpenMP programs, data race debugging, scalable thread visualization, three-dimensional visualization.

1 Introduction

OpenMP program model [14] is an industry standard of parallel programming model which supports Fortran and C language. However, it is still more difficult to debug OpenMP programs than sequential programs, because unexpected non-deterministic executions may be incurred from unintended data races [12] and such programs are often complex and long-running with a huge number of threads and accesses to shared variables. Thus these problems make users still difficult to debug races efficiently.

Thread Checker [4,5,16] of Intel Corporation is a unique tool to detect threading errors including data races in the relaxed sequential program which is a kind of programs parallelized only with OpenMP directives. During a sequentially monitored execution, Thread Checker projects the parallel memory traces of logical threads derived from the annotated sequential memory trace, and detects threading errors including races while every instruction in the program is executed. But this tool does not provide any effective facility for understanding the complexity of threads involved in the reported races.

This paper presents a thread visualization tool to represent the partial order of threads in the traced OpenMP programs with a scalable graph of abstract

* *Corresponding author*: In Gyeongsang National University, he is also involved in the Research Institute of Computer and Information Communication (RICIC).

C. Cérin and K.-C. Li (Eds.): GPC 2007, LNCS 4459, pp. 310–321, 2007.

threads upon a three-dimensional cone. We consider OpenMP programs which may include critical sections and nested parallelism. The visualization on three-dimensional cone makes it overcome the limitation of visual space on one plane and use an execution graph [1,11] to represent effectively a partial order over threads. This tool solves the visual complexity using the abstract visualization which replaces a set of events with an abstract symbol and provides the thread information which is traced by RaceStand [9], an on-the-fly race detection tool. The abstraction concept reduces the space complexity of thread visualization and helps programmers to understand the complex structure of threads effectively. We experimented this visualization tool on a Windows-XP computer based on Pentium-4 using Visual C++ and OpenGL libraries.

Section 2 illustrates data races that occur in OpenMP programs, indicates the problems of the previous tool for debugging races. Section 3 presents the design concepts of our scalable thread-visualization tool. Section 4 shows the screen-shots of the implemented tool using a set of synthetic programs to demonstrate that scalable thread visualization is effective to debugging races efficiently. The last section includes conclusions and future work.

2 Background

This section illustrates data races which occur in OpenMP programs and introduces the problem of the previous tools, Thread Checker and RaceStand, that detect data races.

2.1 OpenMP Program

OpenMP [14] is an industry standard model of shared memory with a set of directives and libraries that extend standard C/C++ and Fortran 77/90. OpenMP can easily convert sequential programs into parallel programs using OpenMP directives, and can provide scalable parallel programs using the orphan directive to make coarse-grain parallelism. The OpenMP directives include parallelism directives and synchronization directives. The parallelism directives include "#pragma omp parallel for" for parallel loops and "#pragma omp section" for parallel sections. We consider the parallel loop as an example of parallelism. If there is no other loop contained in a loop body, the loop is called an *innermost* loop. Otherwise, it is called an *outer* loop. In a nested loop, an individual loop can be enclosed by many outer loops. The *nesting level* of an individual loop is equal to one plus the number of the enclosing outer loops. The nesting depth of a loop is the maximum nesting level of loops in the loop. The synchronization directives include "#pragma omp atomic," "#pragma omp barrier," and "#pragma omp critical" that control an execution order among threads. OpenMP also provides library functions and environment variables that can control run-time execution of programs. For example, two logical threads are created by "#pragma omp parellel" through line 11 and line 13 of Figure 1. Due to "#pragma omp for private(i, y, z)" of line 12, the created thread takes the specified job in the loop

```
10:  ...
11:  #pragma omp parallel
12:  #pragma omp for private (i,y,z)
13:  for (i=1 ; i < 3 ; i++) {
14:    if (i==1) { y = x + 2;
15:  #pragma omp critical(L1)
16:      z = x + 2; x = y + z;
17:    } else {
18:  #pragma omp critical(L1)
19:      x = 100; y = x + 1;
20:    }}
21:  printf("x value = %d ", x);
22:  ...
```

Fig. 1. An OpenMP Parallel Program and its POEG

body from line 14 to the brace of line 20, in which, the index variable i is a private variable used in each thread, and the integer variable x is a shared variable shared by the two threads.

Data races may occur in the program of Figure 1 during its program executions. First, we assume that the variable x has zero as an initial value. The statements of line 14, 15, and 16 are executed by the first thread of the two created threads and the statement of line 18 and 19 are executed by the second thread. Unintended races do not exist toward the variable x between line 16 and line 19, because these two blocks are protected as critical sections by "#pragma omp critical($L1$)." However, regarding the read access in the statement of line 14 and the write access to the shared variable x in the statement of line 19, the random speed of two threads may make the value of variable x in the statement of line 21 become 100 or 104 nondeterministically. It is because these two accesses are involved in a race which include at least one write access without proper inter-thread coordination for the accesses to the shared variable x.

The right of Figure 1 shows an execution instance of the program in Figure 1 by means of a directed acyclic graph called Partial Order Execution Graph (POEG) [1]. A vertex of POEG means a fork or join operation for parallel threads, and an arc started from a vertex represents a thread started from the vertex. The access r and w drawn with small disks upon the arcs represent a read and a write access which access a same shared variable. A number attached to each access indicates an observed order, and an arc segment delimited by the symbols $\{\sqcap, \sqcup\}$ means a critical section protected by the lock variable $L1$. With POEG, we can easily understand the partial order or happened-before relationship [10] of accesses occurred in an execution instance of programs. POEG of Figure 1 makes it easy to understand that $r1$ and $w4$ are involved in a race, because it shows that $r1$ in thread $T1$ and $w4$ in thread $T2$ are concurrent with each other, and $r1$ is not protected by any lock variable.

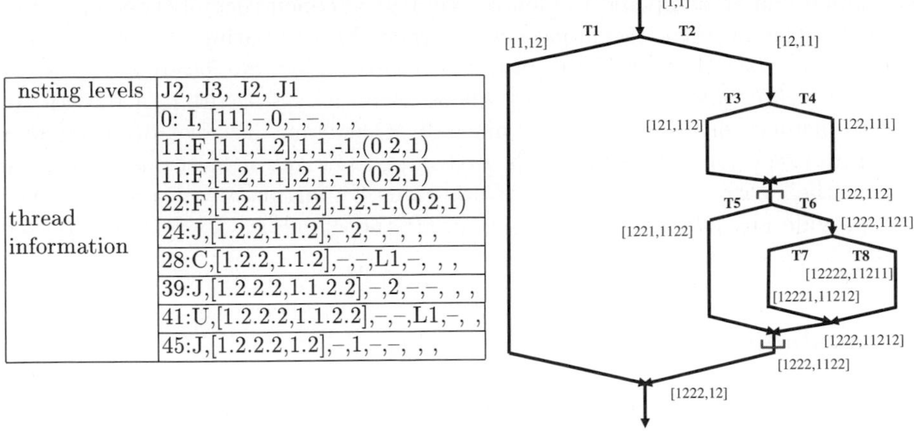

nsting levels	J2, J3, J2, J1
thread information	0: I, [11],–,0,–,–, , ,
	11:F,[1.1,1.2],1,1,-1,(0,2,1)
	11:F,[1.2,1.1],2,1,-1,(0,2,1)
	22:F,[1.2.1,1.1.2],1,2,-1,(0,2,1)
	24:J,[1.2.2,1.1.2],–,2,–,–, , ,
	28:C,[1.2.2,1.1.2],–,–,L1,–, , ,
	39:J,[1.2.2.2,1.1.2.2],–,2,–,–, , ,
	41:U,[1.2.2.2,1.1.2.2],–,–,L1,–, ,
	45:J,[1.2.2.2,1.2],–,1,–,–, , ,

Fig. 2. An Example of RaceStand Traces and Labeling Information in POEG

2.2 Race Detection Tools

The projection technique of Thread Checker [4,5,16] for OpenMP programs collects execution information obtained during the compilation of program and checks data dependency detected during the sequential run-time of program. This technique is applied only to the relaxed sequential OpenMP programs [16] which provides only OpenMP directives for parallelism. Thread Checker detects races as follows. First, when the programs written in OpenMP directives are compiled by Intel C/C++ Compiler [3], a part of this tool integrated in the compiler modifies the programs to trace the information related to OpenMP directives and shared variables into an exclusive database. Second, when the complied program is executed sequentially, the tool uses the traced information in the database to check data dependency of accesses to shared variables whenever an OpenMP directive is located. Last, the tool reports the accesses as races if it satisfies an anti, flow, or output data dependency except an input data dependency.

Unfortunately, Thread Checker has some problems. First, although $r1$ and $w4$ are involved in a race in the POEG of Figure 1, this tool can not report the race because it ignores access $r1$ involved in the race. Second, this tool does not provide any effective information about the dynamic view of the detected races. This kind of reporting is difficult for users to understand the detected races and debug effectively OpenMP programs, because it does not provide any facility for understanding the complexity of threads involved in the reported races.

RaceStand [9] can verify the existence of races in OpenMP programs using a set of scalable thread-labeling techniques [2,13] and protocol techniques [2,11] for detecting races. The labeling techniques generate information called label for logical concurrency among the created threads during a program execution. A label is a unique identifier of thread, and is used to detect races because any two labels can be compared to identify the logical concurrency between any two threads. The protocol techniques detect races by comparing the label of the current access with that of the previous accesses that are saved in a shared-data structure called *access history* whenever an access occurs in a thread. An access history consists of a set of mutually-concurrent accesses occurred in a program execution. These protocols guarantee to detect at least one race [12] if any in their corresponding model of programs. Unfortunately, RaceStand does not provide any effective information about the dynamic view of the reported races.

3 Scalable Thread Visualization

For a visual environment which can help users to debug races effectively using the additional information traced by RaceStand, this section presents two function modules for thread visualization and two abstraction concepts for scalable visualization.

3.1 Thread Visualization

Our tool visualizes a partial order of threads executed in the traced programs through a scalable graph of abstract threads upon a three-dimensional cone to help programmers to debug races intuitively. This tool requires the levels of nested parallelism and the thread information generated by RaceStand. The nesting levels can be traced whenever a join operation occurs in an execution. The thread information includes the thread labels generated whenever a parallel or synchronization directive is executed. The table of Figure 2 shows the information traced in an execution of OpenMP program captured with POEG in Figure 2. In the figure, the nesting depth is three since the nesting levels of $T1$ and $T2$ are one, the nesting levels of $T3$, $T4$, $T5$, and $T6$ are two, and the nesting levels of $T7$ and $T8$ are three. Each thread label in the right POEG of Figure 2 is a English-Hebrew (EH) label [13].

Our tool consists of two function modules: The *Cone Visualizer* and The *Thread Visualizer*. The Cone Visualizer parses the trace of nesting levels and then draws a three-dimensional cone by calculating the nesting depth and the number of multi-way loops which are defined as executed serially in a thread at each nesting level. The number of multi-way loops executed in a thread at a nesting level i is the number of 'J_i's generated by the thread, where J means a join operation and an integer i means a nesting level less than i. The maximum value of i is the nesting depth. The table of Figure 2 shows a trace of four nesting levels, by which the nesting depth is three because the maximum level is three. In the initial thread or $T6$, the number of multi-way loops is one, and the thread $T2$ executed two multi-way loops.

The Thread Visualizer parses the thread information and then draws the threads on the three-dimensional cone. The thread information consists of seven elements: source line number, event type, EH-label, loop index, nesting level, lock

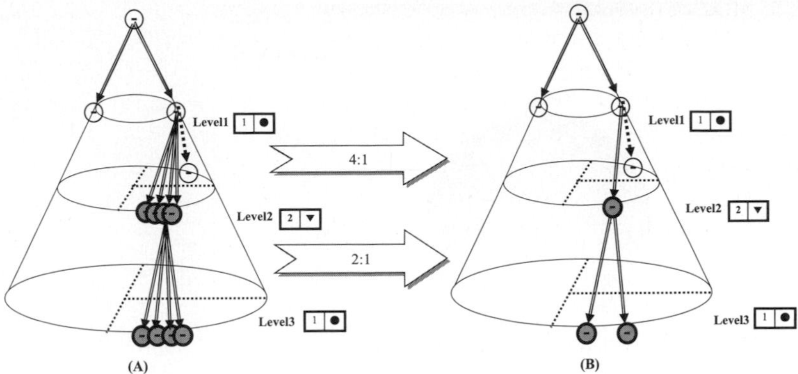

Fig. 3. The Abstract Visualization

variables, and for-statement information. The source line number identifies the source code location at which the threads occurred. The event type expresses a type of operations occurred in the execution: I-type for the initial thread, F-type for a fork operation, J-type for a join operation, C-type for a lock operation, and U-type for an unlock operation. An EH label is a thread label created by English-Hebrew Labeling scheme [13]. The table of Figure 2 shows an example trace of thread information.

3.2 Scalable Visualization

This section presents the concepts of *space abstraction* and *thread abstraction* for scalable three-dimensional visualization using the traced information. To illustrate an abstract visualization, we use the visualization information shown in POEG and the table of Figure 2.

The space of thread visualization is represented with a three-dimensional cone which is divided vertically as many layers as the nesting depth. Each nesting level is associated with a combo box which represents the number of loops executed by the thread in the upper nesting level. Figure 3(A) shows an example of the space abstraction. The first or third nesting level has only one loop and the second nesting level has two loops. The combo box for the second level allows to select one of the two loops as shown in Figure 3(A). the user can set the nesting depth at will. For example, if the user set the value of the nesting depth to five in the case of nesting levels ($J4$, $J3$, $J3$, $J2$, $J1$), the cone becomes divided into five layers. In this case, each combo box for the nesting level but the third has one loop. The combo box for the third nesting level has two loops, because $J3$ appears twice. The combo box for the fifth nesting level can not be created, because the information corresponding to the nesting level does not exist.

The threads at the same nesting level are visualized as circles on the same circumference of the corresponding cone layer with the optional vertical and horizontal abstraction. The vertical abstraction represents a thread which created

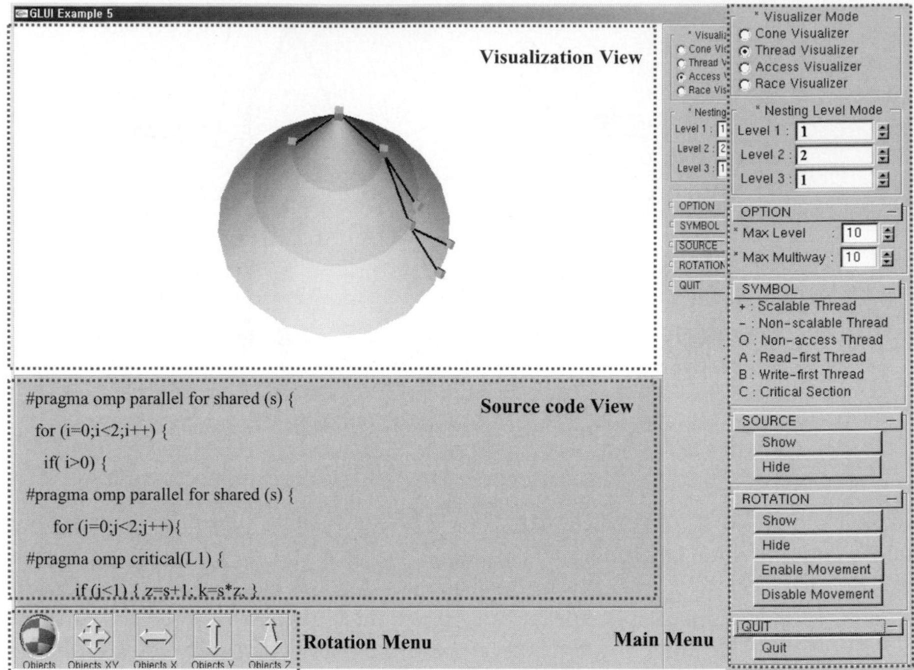

Fig. 4. The Overall Interface for Scalable Thread Visualization

child thread in the lower nesting levels with a special circle symbol. A parent thread can be represented with a symbol "+" or "-" inside a circle. The symbol "+" means that the parent thread has child threads which are not shown and the symbol "-" means that the parent thread has child threads which are drawn on the cone. A circle symbol which is colored and rounded by a thick line is an abstract thread which includes a critical section. Figure 3(A) shows an expanded example of the vertical abstraction. Although threads can be visualized with vertical abstraction, the space complexity for visualization may be still big. The horizontal abstraction reduces the number of threads visualized on the same circumference, by representing a set of threads with one abstract thread. Figure 3(B) shows an example of horizontal abstraction. The second nesting level in the figure shows horizontal abstraction by the rate of four and the third nesting level by the rate of two.

The thread abstraction allows us to understand intuitively whether a pair of threads is concurrent or ordered with each other, because we can see easily an explicit path between any two threads on the cone. For example, in the Figure 3(B), the left thread in the first nesting level is concurrent with the right thread in the third nesting level, because the explicit path from the upside to the downside does not exist on the visualized cone. Users can check easily whether a pair of threads at the different nesting levels are concurrent or ordered with each other through the thread abstraction.

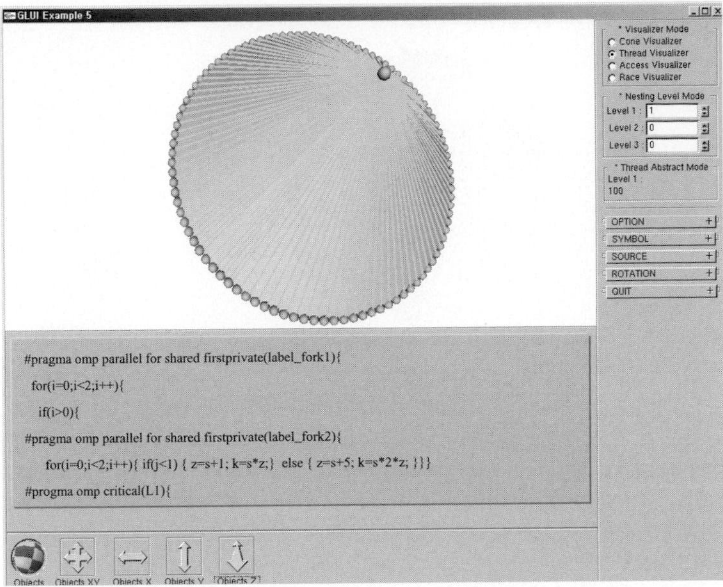

Fig. 5. No Critical Sections and No Nested Parallelisms

4 Experimentation

We implemented scalable thread visualization and experimented its functionality using a set of synthetic programs. This section presents the interface of implemented tool and the principles in which the tool draws the symbols using an execution trace of the synthetic programs.

4.1 Visualization Engines

Figure 4 shows the interface of our thread visualization tool which is composed two views and two menus: *Visualization View*, *Source code View*, *Main Menu*, and *Rotation Menu*. In the Main Menu, *Visualizer Mode* has four modes in which two modes are currently implemented: *Cone Visualizer* and *Thread Visualizer*. *Nesting Level Mode* provides the possible values of each nesting level and then users can select a numeral in each nesting level. The *OPTION* menu make it possible to set the maximum value of nesting levels and multi-way loops. The *SYMBOL* menu shows the legend of symbols to be used for scalable visualization. The *SOURCE* and *ROTATION* menus allow users to control the activation of Source code View and Rotation Menu. The *QUIT* menu quits the interface. The Rotation Menu located at the lower left part of the interface allows users to rotate on the three-dimensional space or move up, down, left, and right using one button labelled *Objects* or the other four buttons labelled *Objects XY*, *Objects X*, *Objects Y*, and *Object Z*. When the visualized cone is rotated, its position and size are fixed. The Visualization View shown at the top of the figure visualizes

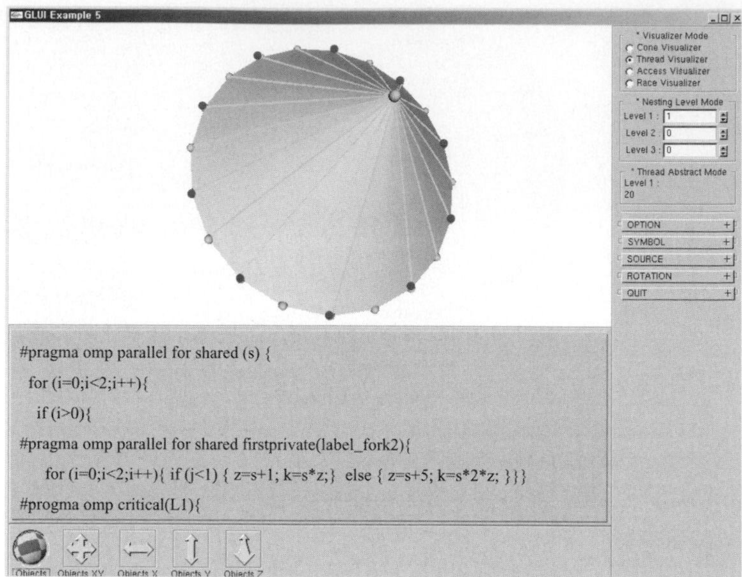

Fig. 6. Critical Sections and No Nested Parallelisms

the cone and abstract threads. The Source code View shows the corresponding program codes.

For visualization, a cone is divided horizontally by the nesting depth acquired from trace as shown in the figure. A thread is drawn on the cone based on the calculated height, angle, and symbol's position and can be abstracted for a thread set, critical sections, and nested parallel loop which are created during a program execution. The user understands races intuitively by visualizing a partial order of threads involved in races selectively. For example, in Figure 4, left symbol at the first nesting level is concurrent with the right symbol at the second nesting level, because these is no path between the left symbol and the right symbol.

4.2 Visualization Cases

The visualization tool has been implemented using Visual C++ and OpenGL library under Windows XP on Pentium 4 computer. We verified the cone and thread visualization with four kinds of synthetic programs with respect to the existence of critical sections and nested parallelisms: (1) *no nested parallelisms and no critical sections*, (2) *nested parallelisms and no critical sections*, (3) *no nested parallelisms and some critical sections*, (4) *nested parallelisms and critical sections*. Any critical section uses one lock variable. The nesting depth is three, and each nesting level has 20, 100, 300 threads.

For example, Figure 5 visualizes an execution of synthetic program with no nested parallelism and no critical section, which creates one hundred threads.

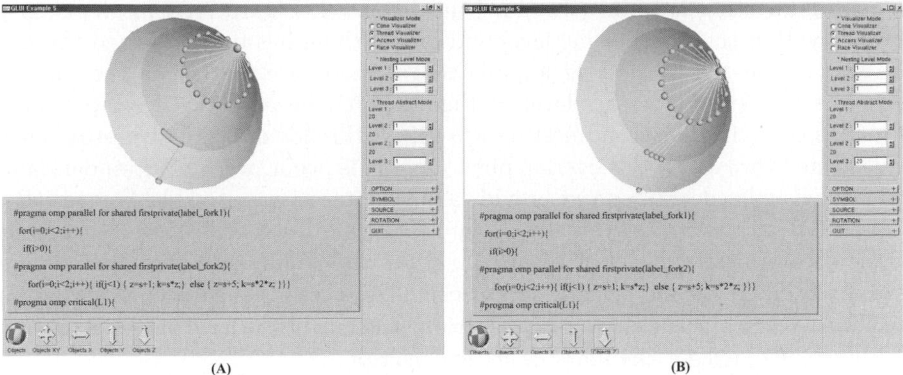

Fig. 7. Nested Parallelisms and No Critical Sections

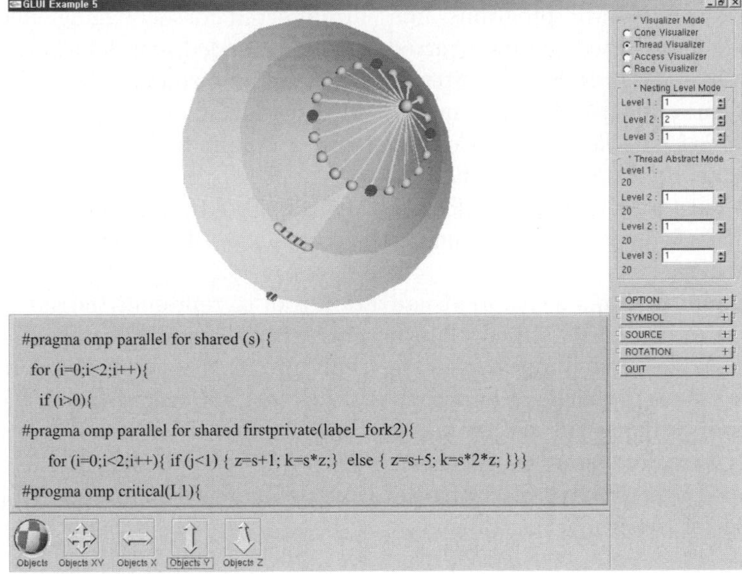

Fig. 8. Critical Sections and Nested Parallelisms

The cone in the figure is not divided, because the execution does not include nested parallelism. Figure 6 visualizes an execution of synthetic program with critical sections and no nested parallelisms, which has twenty threads and contains critical sections in every other thread. The figure shows every thread with critical section has a unique color according to its lock variable. Figure 7 visualizes an execution of synthetic program with nested parallelisms and no critical sections. Each nesting level has twenty threads; the nesting depth is three; a one-way loop within the second nesting level is two, the second one-way loop of the second nesting level has the third nesting level. Figure 7(A) marks twenty threads within the first nesting level and one of them has twenty nested threads to exist in the second nesting level. These threads are marked in the limited area like the second nesting level of Figure 7(A), because the overlap among threads occurs in the second nesting level if all threads of the first nesting level have nested threads. If this overlap phenomenon is occur, we can not understand duly the visualized results so we provide a horizontal abstraction like Figure 7(B). Figure 7(B) abstracts the threads at the rate of a quarter about twenty threads of the second nesting level of Figure 7(A). As the result, only four threads are visualized in the second level. Figure 8 visualizes threads the synthetic program with nested parallelism and critical section. It is identical with the explanation of Figure 7(A) except the mark of critical section.

5 Conclusion

Data race in OpenMP programs must be detected for debugging, because it may cause unexpected results incurred from unintended non-deterministic executions. OpenMP programs are often complex and long-running, because parallel programs may consist of a large number of threads and accesses to shared variables. Thread Checker of Intel Corporation is a unique tool to detect threading errors including data races in the relaxed sequential program which is defined as parallelized only with OpenMP directives. The tool however does not provide any effective facility for understanding the complexity of threads involved in the reported races.

This paper presents a thread visualization tool to represent the partial order of threads in the traced OpenMP programs with a scalable graph of abstract threads upon a three-dimensional cone. This tool solves the visual complexity using the abstract visualization which replaces a set of events with an abstract symbol and provides the thread information which is traced by RaceStand, an on-the-fly race detection tool. We have been trying to apply this tool using a set of published benchmark programs in addition to our synthetic programs specially developed for experimenting this tool.

References

1. Dinning, A., and E. Schonberg, "An Empirical Comparison of Monitoring Algorithms for Access Anomaly Detection," *2nd Symp. on Principles and Practice of Parallel Programming*, pp. 1-10, ACM, March 1990.
2. Dinning, A., and E. Schonberg, "Detecting Access Anomalies in Programs with Critical Sections," *2nd Workshop on Parallel and Distributed Debugging*, pp. 85-96, ACM, May 1991.
3. Intel Corp., *Getting Started with the Intel C++ Compiler 9.0 for Windows.*, 2200 Mission College Blvd., Santa Clara, CA 95052-8119, USA, 2004.
4. Intel Corp., *Getting Started with the Intel Thread Checker*, 2200 Mission College Blvd., Santa Clara, CA 95052-8119, USA, 2004.

5. Intel Corp., *Intel Thread Checker for Windows 3.0 Release Notes*, 2200 Mission College Blvd., Santa Clara, CA 95052-8119, USA, 2005.
6. Intel Corp., *VTune(TM) Performance Analyzer 8.0 Release Notes*, 2200 Mission College Blvd., Santa Clara, CA 95052-8119, USA, 2006.
7. Jun, Y. and K. Koh, "On-the-fly Detection of Access Anomalies in Nested Parallel Loops," *3rd ACM/ONR Workshop on Parallel and Distributed Debugging*, pp.107-117, ACM, May 1993.
8. Kim, Y., M. Park, S. Park, and Y. Jun, "A Practical Tool for Detecting Races in OpenMP Programs," Proc. of 8th Int'l Conf. on Parallel Computing Technologies (PaCT), Krasnoyarsk, Russia, Lecture Notes in Computer Science, 3606: 321-330, Springer-Verlag, Sept. 2005.
9. Kim, Y., and Y. Jun, "An Optimal Tool for Verifying Races in OpenMP Programs," *06 Int'l Conference on Hybrid Information Technology*, SERC, Cheju Island, Korea, Nov., 2006
10. Lamport, L., "Time, Clocks, and the Ordering of Events in a Distributed System," *Comm. of ACM*, 21(7): 558-565, ACM, July 1978.
11. Mellor-Crummey, J. M., "On-the-fly Detection of Data Races for Programs with Nested Fork-Join Parallelism," *Supercomputing*, pp. 24-33, ACM/IEEE, Nov. 1991.
12. Netzer, R. H. B., and B. P. Miller, "What Are Race Conditions? Some Issues and Formalizations," *Letters on Programming Lang. and Systems*, 1(1): 74-88, ACM, March 1992.
13. Nudler, I., and L. Rudolph, "Tools for the Efficient Development of Efficient Parallel Programs," *In 1st Israeli Conference on Computer System Engineering*, 1986.
14. OpenMP Architecture Review Board, *OpenMP Application Programs Interface*, Version 2.5, May 2005.
15. Park, S., M. Park, and Y. Jun, "A Comparision of Scalable Labeling Schemes for Detecting Races in OpenMP Programs," *Int'l Workshop on OpenMP Applications and Tools* (Wompat), pp. 66-80, West lafayette, Indiana, July 2001.
16. Petersen, P., and S. Shah, "OpenMP Support in the Intel Thread Checker," *Proc. of the Int'l Workshop on OpenMP Application and Tools* (WOMPAT), Berlin Heidelberg, Lecture Notes in Computer Science, 2716: 1-12, Springer-Verlag, 2003.

MPIRace-Check: Detection of Message Races in MPI Programs*

Mi-Young Park[1], Su Jeong Shim[1], Yong-Kee Jun[2,**], and Hyuk-Ro Park[3]

[1] Chonnam National University, Gwanju
openmp@korea.com, sjsim@chonnam.ac.kr
[2] Gyeongsang National University, Jinju
jun@gsnu.ac.kr
[3] Chonnam National University, Gwanju
South Korea
hyukro@chonnam.ac.kr

Abstract. Message races, which can cause nondeterministic executions of a parallel program, should be detected for debugging because nondeterminism makes debugging parallel programs a difficult task. Even though there are some tools to detect message races in MPI programs, they do not provide practical information to locate and debug message races in MPI programs. In this paper, we present an on-the-fly detection tool, which is MPIRace-Check, for debugging MPI programs written in C language. MPIRace-Check detects and reports all race conditions in all processes by checking the concurrency of the communication between processes. Also it reports the message races with some practical information such as the line number of a source code, the processes number, and the channel information which are involved in the races. By providing those information, it lets programmers distinguish of unintended races among the reported races, and lets the programmers know directly where the races occur in a huge source code. In the experiment we will show that MPIRace-Check detects the races using some testing programs as well as the tool is efficient.

Keywords: message-passing programs, debugging, message races, MPIRace-Check.

1 Introduction

In a distributed parallel program [1,4,9,14], processes communicate with each other through message-passing and those messages may arrive at a process in a nondeterministic order by variations in process scheduling and network latencies.

* This work was supported in part by Research Intern Program of the Korea Science and Engineering Foundation and in part by the 2th BK21.

** Corresponding author. Also involved in Research Institute of Computer and Information Communication (RICIC) as a research professor in Gyeongsang National University.

C. Cérin and K.-C. Li (Eds.): GPC 2007, LNCS 4459, pp. 322–333, 2007.

Nondeterministic arrival of messages causes nondeterministic executions of a parallel program [7,10,11]. If two or more messages are sent over communication channels on which a receive listens, and they are simultaneously in transit without guaranteeing the order of their arrivals, a message race [2,3,5,6,8,12,13] occurs in the receive event and causes nondeterministic executions of the program.

Message races, which can cause nondeterministic executions of a parallel program, should be detected for debugging because nondeterminism, intended or otherwise, makes debugging message-passing parallel programs a difficult task [7,10,11]. Even though some parallel programs are designed to have message races in order to improve their performance, detecting message races is critical in debugging parallel programs for two reasons. First, message races complicate debugging because their nondeterministic nature can prohibit equivalent re-execution of a program from being repeated [7]. Second, message races can prevent a program from being tested in all the possible executions of a program [7]. Therefore message races should be detected for debugging message-passing programs.

There are several tools for detecting message races such as MAD [8], MARMOT [5,6], and MPVisualizer [2,3]. However those tools are not practical for debugging message-passing programs because they do not provide practical information to locate and debug message races. Also some of them can not exactly detect race conditions because they detect message races just by identifying the use of wild card receives as sources of race conditions. Therefore, due to lack of information and wrong detection, programmers can be easily overwhelmed by the incorrect information or be incapable of finding where the races occurred in a huge source code.

In this paper, we present an on-the-fly detection tool, which is MPIRace-Check, for debugging MPI [14,15] programs written in C language. MPIRace-Check detects and reports all race conditions in all processes during an execution by checking the concurrency of the communications between processes. Also it reports message races with some practical information such as the line number of a source code, the processes number, and the channel information which are involved in the races. By providing those information, it lets programmers distinguish of unintended races among the reported races, and lets the programmers know directly where the races occur in a huge source code. In the experiment we will show that MPIRace-Check detects and reports the races using MPI_RTED [15] testing programs as well as this tool is efficient using a kernel benchmark program.

In the following section 2, we describe the notion of message races and explain the problem of the previous tools. In section 3 we explain the methods used in developing MPIRace-Check and then we show that the accuracy and the efficiency of MPIRace-Check using MPI_RTED testing programs and a kernel benchmark program in the experiment of section 4. In the last section we conclude this paper and discuss future work.

2 Background

In this section, we describe our model of parallel programs, and the notion of message races. Also we introduce the previous tools to detect the races and explain the problem of the previous tools.

2.1 Message Races

An execution of a message-passing program [1,10,11,13] can be represented as a finite set of events and the *happened-before* relations [4,9] defined over those events. If an event a always occurs before another event b in all executions of the program, it satisfies that a happens before b, denoted $a \rightarrow b$. For example, if there exist two events $\{a, b\}$ executed in the same process, $a \rightarrow b \vee b \rightarrow a$ is satisfied. If there exist a send event s and the corresponding receive event r between a pair of processes, then $s \rightarrow r$ is satisfied. We denote a message, sent by a send event s, as $msg(s)$. The binary relation $\rightarrow$ is defined over its irreflexive transitive closure; if there are three events $\{a, b, c\}$ that satisfy $a \rightarrow b \wedge b \rightarrow c$, it also satisfies $a \rightarrow c$. When an event a does not happen before an event b, we denote the relation between them as $a \nrightarrow b$.

A *message race* [2,3,5,6,8,13] occurs in a receive event, if two or more messages are sent over communication channels on which the receive listens and they are simultaneously in transit without guaranteeing the order of their arrivals. A message race is represented as $\langle r, M \rangle$: r is the first receive event and M is a set of racing messages toward r. Any send event s included in M, but not the one received by r, satisfies $s \nrightarrow r$ or $r \nrightarrow s$.

Even though some parallel programs are designed to have message races in order to improve their performance, detecting message races is critical in debugging parallel programs for two reasons. First, message races complicate debugging because their nondeterministic nature can prohibit equivalent re-execution of a program from being repeated [7]. Second, message races can prevent a program from being tested in all the possible executions of a program [7]. Therefore message races should be detected for debugging message-passing programs.

Figure 1 shows a partial order of events that occurred during an execution of a message-passing program. In the figure two processes P_3 and P_4 send two messages $msg(i)$ and $msg(k)$ to P_2. At this time two messages $msg(i)$ and $msg(k)$ are racing toward the receive event j of P_2 because the send event k satisfies $k \nrightarrow j$. Also the message $msg(m)$, which is sent by process P_5, is also racing toward j. Therefore the race, which occurs at the receive event j, can be denoted as $\langle j, J \rangle$: the first receive event j, $J = \{msg(i), msg(k), msg(m)\}$.

2.2 Related Work

There are several tools for detecting message races such as MAD [8], MARMOT [5,6], and MPVisualizer [2,3]. MAD offers a variety of debugging features such as placement of breakpoints on multiple processes, inspection of variables, an event manipulation feature, and a record&replay mechanism. MARMOT is to verify the standard conformance of an MPI [14,15] program automatically during runtime and help to debug the program in case of problems such as deadlocks, and race conditions. MPVisualizer includes a trace/reply mechanism, a graphical interface, and the engine of the tool which detects and notifies the occurrence of race conditions.

In case of MAD and MARMOT, those tools detect message races just by identifying the use of wild card receives, mpi_any_source, as sources of race conditions.

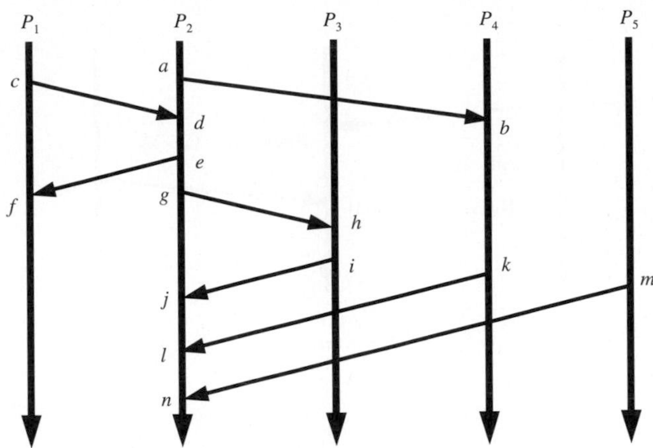

Fig. 1. An Example

In this case the detection result is not correct and also programmers will be overwhelmed by the vast and incorrect information.

Figure 2 shows the cases that there are no race conditions even though receive events are called with mpi_any_source. In Figure 2.(a), process P_1 sends a message to process P_2 with a tag (1). Also process P_3 sends a message to process P_2 with a tag (2). At this time, two receive events in process P_2 are called with mpi_any_source, but with different tags. In this example, even though two send events are concurrent, two messages being sent by processes P_1 and P_3 will be always received deterministically because of the different tags.

In Figure 2.(b), the second receive event in process P_2 is called with mpi_any_source and mpi_any_tag. In this example, however, two messages will be received deterministically because the first message being sent by process P_1 will be always received at the first receive event in process P_2.

In Figure 2.(c), two messages are sent from the same process P_1 and they are received in the process P_2. In process P_2, two receive events receive the messages respectively using mpi_any_source and mpi_any_tag. In this case, there are no race conditions if successive messages sent by a process to another process are ordered in a sequence and if receive events posted by the process are also ordered in a sequence.

As shown in Figure 2, there are no race conditions even though mpi_any_source or mpi_any_tag are used in the receive events. Therefore, if we detect race conditions just by identifying the use of mpi_any_source, that will include wrong detections of race conditions and then mislead programmers.

One the other hand, the method suggested by Nezer [12] can detect more exactly race conditions. This technique focuses on detecting unaffected races [12,13] so that it detects the first race in each process. For this, it requires two executions of a program. In the first execution it checks if a race occurs and

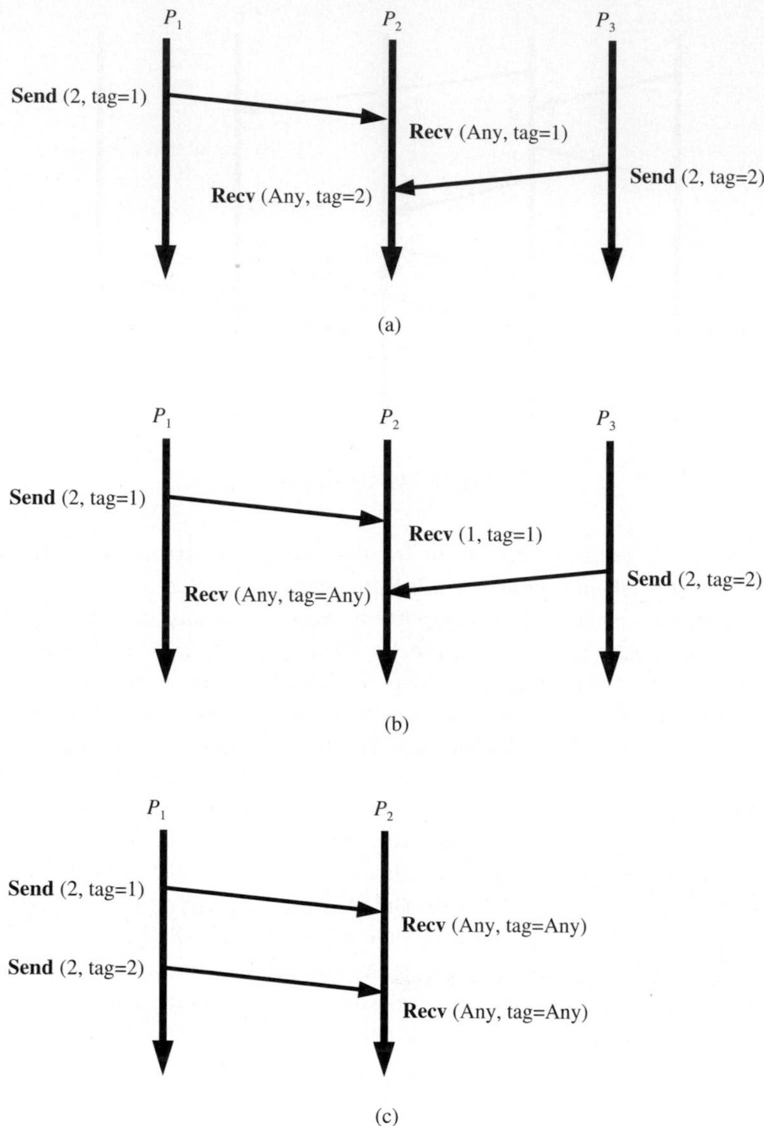

Fig. 2. No Race Conditions with MPI_ANY_SOURCE

identifies the location where the race occurs. In the second execution it halts the execution at the location where the race occurred and then detects racing messages. Even though this technique can detect race conditions more accurately, it is not efficient because it requires two executions of a program.

```
TimestampInit()
localclock := 0
for i from 0 to size do
    timstamp[i] := 0
    prevrecv[i] := 0
    sender[i] := 0
end for
```

(a)

```
CheckConcurrency()
if prevrecv[pid] > sender[pid]
    report this race
end if
```

(b)

```
TimestampInSend()
localclock := localclock + 1
timestamp[pid] := localclock
```

(c)

```
TimestampInRecv()
call CheckConcurrency()
for i from 1 to size do
    timestamp[i] := max(timestamp[i],
        sender[i])
end for
localclock := localclock + 1
timestamp[pid] := localclock
prevrecv := timestamp
```

(d)

Fig. 3. Algorithms for Timestamp

3 Race Detection

In this section, we explain the methods used in developing MPIRace-Check. First we explain several algorithms to maintain vector timestamps during an execution in order to detect race conditions. Also we show how the algorithms can be called inside of MPI profiling interface.

3.1 Concurrency Check

Vector timestamps [4,9] have been used to determine the "happened before" relations between two events during an execution. Each vector timestamp consists of n values, where n is the number of processes involved in an execution. In this paper, we use vector timestamps to check concurrency between send/receive events in MPI parallel programs. Figure 3 shows the algorithms for maintaining vector timestamps during an execution.

In Figure 3.(a), all variables are initialized with zero: *localclock, timestamp, prerecv,* and *sender*. In the algorithm, *size* is an integer variable and indicates the number of processes involved in an execution. *localclock* is an integer variable for counting the number of events which occurred in each process. This will be incremented by one whenever a send or a receive event occurs.

The variables *timestamp, prerecv,* and *sender* for maintaining the vector timestamps are an array which consists of n elements, where n is the number of processes. Whenever a send or a receive event occurs in a process, *timestamp* will be updated by the current *localclock* during an execution. Only one element of *timestamp*, corresponding to the process itself, will be updated. *sender* will be used for keeping a vector timestamp of a sender which sends a message to the current receive event. *prevrecv* will be used for keeping a vector timestamp of the previous receive event.

Figure 3.(c) shows the algorithm, **TimestampInSend()**, which will be called in each send event. The variable *pid* indicates the current process which sends a message. In each send event, it increments *localclock* by one and sets the element of *timestamp*, corresponding to the current process *pid*, equal to *localclock*. This *timestamp* will be attached to the outgoing message.

Figure 3.(d) shows the algorithm, **TimestampInRecv()**, which will be called in each receive event. In each receive event, first of all, it checks if a race occurs by calling **CheckConcurrency()**. In **CheckConcurrency()**, it checks if the element of *prevrecv*, corresponding to the current process *pid*, is greater than that of *sender*. If then, it means that the message, which was received in the current receive event, can be received in the previous receive event. In this case it reports that a message race occurs.

After calling **CheckConcurrency()**, it updates its *timestamp* using *sender*, which was attached to this incoming message, by the operation **max**(). And it increments *localclock* by one and sets the element of *timestamp*, corresponding to the current process *pid*, equal to *localclock*. For the next receive event, it copies *timestamp* into *prevrecv* because this receive event will become the previous receive event in the next receive event.

Figure 4 shows the vector timestamps in each event when we applied the algorithms to Figure 1. In the figure, *lc* means *localclock* in each event and each *timestamp* in each event is represented with "[]".

In the send event a in P_2, **TimestampInSend()** will be called and *localclock* will be incremented by one. And *localclock* will be set into the element of *timestamp* corresponding to the current process P_2. So *localclock* becomes 1 and *timestamp* becomes [01000]. In the receive event b in P_4, **TimestampInRecv()** will be called and *localclock* will be incremented by one. And *localclock* will be set into the element of *timestamp* corresponding to the current process P_4. Also it updates its *timestamp* using *sender* by the operation **max()**. So *localclock* becomes 1 and *timestamp* becomes [01010]. In this way *timestamp* will be updated and maintained in each event during an execution.

Let us show you how to detect race conditions using *timestamp* in each receive event. For example, in the receive event j of process P_2, **TimestampInRecv()** calls **CheckConcurrency()**. **CheckConcurrency()** compares *prevrecv*, which is the vector timestamp at d of P_2, with *sender* which is the vector timestamp of the send event i of P_3. In this case, *prevrecv*[*pid*], which is "2" from [12000] (*pid* is P_2), is not greater than *sender*[*pid*] which is "4" from [14200]. This means that the message, which was received by the current receive event j of P_2, is not racing toward the previous receive event d of P_2.

On the other hand, in the receive event l of process P_2, *prevrecv* is greater than *sender*. In case of the receive event l, *prevrecv* is at j which is [15200], and *sender* is at k of P_4 which is [01020]. Therefore, *prevrecv*[*pid*], which is "5", is greater than *sender*[*pid*] which is "1" (*pid* is P_2). This means that the message, which was received by the current receive event l of P_2, is racing toward the previous receive event j of P_2. So there is a message race. In this way we can detect message races.

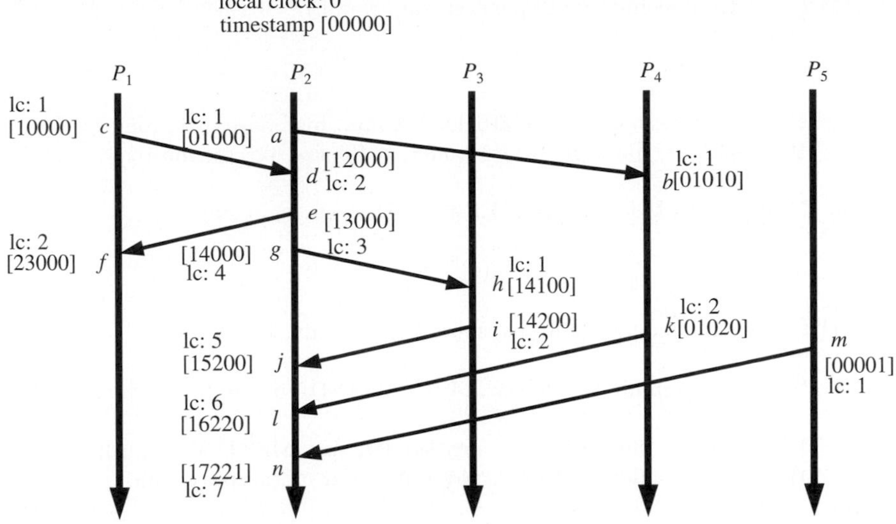

Fig. 4. An Example of Vector Timestamp

3.2 MPI Profiling Interface

MPI Profiling Interface included in MPI specification allows anyone to intercept every call to the MPI library and perform an additional action. For this, the MPI specification states that every MPI routine is callable by an alternative name; every routine of the form MPI_xxx is also callable by the name of the form PMPI_xxx, allowing users to implement and experiment their own MPI_xxx.

For implementing MPIRace-Check, we used MPI profiling interface and we wrapped all point-to-point functions. In each wrapped function, we used MPI-_PACK in order to attach a vector timestamp to the outgoing message and we used MPI_UNPACK in order to detach a vector timestamp from the incoming message.

Figure 5 is an example of how we wrapped each function with the algorithms explained before. Figure 5.(a) shows the wrapped MPI_Send function. First it calls **TimestampInSend()** in line 2 and packs the user message(*buf*) and *timestamp* together using MPI_PACK in order to attach *timestamp* to the outgoing message in line from 4 to 5. After that, it calls PMPI_Send.

Figure 5.(b) shows the wrapped MPI_Recv function. First it received a message by calling PMPI_Recv and unpack the message into *sender* and *buf* in line from 4 to 5. After that, it calls **TimestampInRecv()** in order to update its *timestamp* and check if a race occurs.

In this way, we wrapped all point-to-point functions so that users can apply our tool to their programs without modifying their code.

```
MPI_Send(buf, count, datatype, dest, tag, comm)
{
    TimestampInSend();

    MPI_Pack(timestamp, size, MPI_INT, buffer, buffersize, pos, comm);
    MPI_Pack(buf, count, datatype, buffer, buffersize, pos, comm);

    PMPI_Send(buffer, pos, MPI_PACKED, dest, tag, comm);
}
```

(a)

```
MPI_Recv(buf, count, datatype, source, tag, comm, status)
{
    PMPI_Recv(buffer, buffersize, MPI_PACKED, source, tag, comm, status);

    MPI_Unpack(buffer, buffersize, pos, sender, size, MPI_INT, comm);
    MPI_Unpack(buffer, buffersize, pos, buf, count, datatype, comm);

    TimestampInRecv();
}
```

(b)

Fig. 5. Examples of Wrapped MPI Functions: MPI_Send and MPI_Recv

4 Experimentation

We implemented MPIRace-Check as a library using C language and MPI Profiling Interface so that users can apply our tool to their programs without modifying their source code. Also we used *gdb* to provide detail information for debugging race conditions. When a race is detected, *gdb* will be called within MPI Profiling Interface. To enable this, users have to use the compiler option '-g' when they compile their programs.

In this experiment we evaluated the accuracy and the efficiency of MPIRce-Check. For evaluating the accuracy of race detection, we used MPI_RTED [15] testing programs written in C language. MPI_RTED was developed to evaluate MPI debugging tools. So some of them were designed to have message races to evaluate the ability of detection of race conditions.

Table 1 shows all test programs and the detection results when we applied our tool to MPI_RTED programs. In the table, we can see each name of tested programs, and MPI functions which are used in the testing programs. In those programs, MPIRace_Check detected all races as shown in the table.

Figure 6 shows an error message of our tool when it detects a race in a test program. In the first line, it shows the *localclock*s of the events, and the process number which are involved in the race: P_1 (1) and P_2 (1). In the second line, it shows the channel information, the program name, and its line number: $-2-1$, 'c_B_1_1_a_M1.c' and 76. In the third line, it shows the source code

Table 1. The Result in MPI_RTED

Name	MPI Functions	Detection
c_B_1_1_a_M1.c	MPI_RECV	Yes
c_B_1_2_a_M1.c	MPI_RECV	Yes
c_B_1_1_b_M1.c	MPI_SENDRECV	Yes
c_B_1_2_b_M1.c	MPI_SENDRECV	Yes
c_B_1_1_c_M1.c	MPI_SENDRECV_REPLACE	Yes
c_B_1_2_c_M1.c	MPI_SENDRECV_REPLACE	Yes
c_B_1_1_d_M1.c	MPI_IRECV	Yes
c_B_1_2_d_M1.c	MPI_IRECV	Yes
c_B_1_1_e_M1.c	MPI_RECV	Yes
c_B_1_2_e_M1.c	MPI_SENDRECV	Yes
c_B_1_1_f_M1.c	MPI_RECV	Yes
c_B_1_2_f_M1.c	MPI_SENDRECV_REPLACE	Yes
c_B_1_1_g_M1.c	MPI_RECV	Yes
c_B_1_2_g_M1.c	MPI_IRECV	Yes

```
WARNING(RaceCondition):
The message which was sent at '1' from 'P_2' is racing toward '1' receive event in 'P_1'
(the current channel is -2-1)  at c_B_1_1_a_M1.c:76
>>        MPI_Recv(&recvbuf_2, 1, MPI_INT, MPI_ANY_SOURCE, MPI_ANY_TAG, MPI_COMM_WORLD, &status);
```

Fig. 6. An Example of Error Messages

Table 2. Overhead in MPIRace-Check

The number of Send/Recv	Original Run Time (s)	Monitored Run Time (s)	Slowdown
10000	0.168	0.212	26%
100000	1.673	2.234	34%
1000000	16.399	22.034	34%
10000000	164.471	221.736	35%

which is involved in the race: 'MPI_Recv(&recvbuf_2, ..., &status)'. Using those information, programmers can easily notice whether the race was intended or not, and they can directly modify the bug because they know where it occurs in their source code.

For estimating the efficiency of our tool, we wrote a simple kernel benchmark program. This benchmark program consists of MPI_Send() and MPI_Recv() operations and users can change the number of those operations in the command line. In this program, only a process with the rank 0 receives any messages with mpi_any_source and the other processes send a message to the process with rank 0. To measure the slowdown of MPIRace-Check, we used MPI_Wtime() in the benchmark program.

Table 2 shows the slowdown of MPIRace-Check. For example, when we set the number of send/recv operations 10000, it took 0.168 seconds without our tool. However, the monitored execution by our tool took 0.212 seconds so that the slowdown is 26%. As we increase the number of send/recv operations, the slowdown does not change proportionally. The worst case in the table shows only 35% slowdown when the number of send/recv operations is 10,000,000. Therefore our tool is efficient as an on-the-fly detection tool.

5 Conclusion

In this paper, we have presented an on-the-fly detection tool, which is MPIRace-Check, for debugging MPI programs written in C language. MPIRace-Check detects and reports all race conditions in all processes during an execution by checking the concurrency of the communications between processes. In our experiment, we showed that MPIRace-Check detects and reports message races using MPI_RTED testing programs as well as our tool is efficient using a kernel benchmark program.

Also our tool provides useful information for debugging such as the line number of a source code, the processes number, and the channel information which are involved in the races. By providing those information, it lets programmers distinguish of unintended races among the reported races, and lets the programmers know directly where the races occurred in a huge source code. Therefore this tool will be useful to develop and debug MPI C parallel programs. In the future we will expand MPIRace-Check to cover all collective routines of MPI-1.

References

1. Cypher, R., and E. Leu, "The Semantics of Blocking and Nonblocking Send and Receive Primitives," *8th Intl. Parallel Processing Symp.*, pp. 729-735, IEEE, April 1994.
2. Cláudio, A.P., J.D. Cunha, and M.B. Carmo, "MPVisualizer: A General Tool to Debug Message Passing Parallel Applications," *7th High Performace Computing and Networking Europe*, Lecture Notes in Computer Science, 1593:1199-1202, Springer-Verlag, April 1999.
3. Cláudio, A.P., J.D. Cunha, and M.B. Carmo, "Monitoring and Debugging Message Passing Applications with MPVisualizer," *8th Euromicro Workshop on Parallel and Distributed Processing*, pp.376-382, IEEE, Jan. 2000.
4. Fidge, C. J., "Partial Orders for Parallel Debugging," *SIGPLAN/SIGOPS Workshop on Parallel and Distributed Debugging*, pp. 183-194, ACM, May 1988.
5. Krammer, B., K. Bidmon, M.S. Müller, and M.M. Resch, "MARMOT: An MPI Analysis and Checking Tool," *In proceedings of PARCO'03*, 13:493-500, Elsevier, Sept. 2003.
6. Krammer, B., M.S. Müller, and M.M. Resch, "MPI Application Development Using the Analysis Tool MARMOT," *4th International Conference on Computational Science*, Lecture Notes in Computer Science, 3038:464-471, Springer-Verlag, june 2004.
7. Kranzlmüller, D., and M. Schulz, "Notes on Nondeterminism in Message Passing Programs," *9th European PVM/MPI Users' Group Conf.*, Lecture Notes in Computer Science, 2474:357-367, Springer-Verlag, Sept. 2002.

8. Kranzlmüller D., C. Schaubschläger, and J. Volkert, "A Brief Overview of the MAD Debugging Activities," *4th International Workshop on Automated Debugging* (AADEBUG 2000), Aug. 2000.
9. Lamport, L., "Time, Clocks, and the Ordering of Events in a Distributed System," *Communications of the ACM*, 21(7):558-565, ACM, July 1978.
10. Lei, Y., and K. Tai, "Efficient Reachability Testing of Asynchronous Message-Passing Programs," *8th Int'l Conf. on Engineering of Complex Computer Systems* pp. 35-44, IEEE, Dec. 2002.
11. Mittal, N., and V. K. Garg, "Debugging Distributed Programs using Controlled Re-execution," *19th Annual Symp. on Principles of Distributed Computing*, pp. 239-248, ACM, Portland, Oregon, 2000.
12. Netzer, R. H. B., T. W. Brennan, and S. K. Damodaran-Kamal, "Debugging Race Conditions in Message-Passing Programs," *SIGMETRICS Symp. on Parallel and Distributed Tools*, pp. 31-40, ACM, May 1996.
13. Park, M., and Y. Jun, "Detecting Unaffected Race Conditions in Message-Passing Programs," *11th European PVM/MPI User's Group Meeting*, Lecture Notes in Computer Science, 3241:268-276, Springer-Verlag, Sept. 2004.
14. Snir, M., S. Otto, S. Huss-Lederman, D. Walker, and J. Dongarra, *MPI: The Complete Reference*, MIT Press, 1996.
15. HPC Group, MPI Run Time Error Detection Test Suites: http://rted.public.iastate.edu/MPI/, Iowa State University, USA, 2006

The Modified Grid Location Service for Mobile Ad-Hoc Networks

Hau-Han Wang and Sheng-De Wang

Department of Eletrical Engineering
National Taiwan University, Taipei, Taiwan
sdwang@ntu.edu.tw

Abstract. Position-based routing has been proven to be a scalable and efficient solution for packet routing in mobile ad hoc networks (MANETs) by utilizing location information of mobile nodes. The location service provides geographic locations for all nodes and is therefore critical to position-based routing. In general, the control overhead in a position-based routing protocol is mainly dominated by location updates. In this paper, we propose a location service called Modified Grid Location Service (MGLS), which employs a binary grid partitioning scheme to reduce the control overhead associated with the location management and supports large scale ad hoc networks. We then use a theoretical model to analyze both MGLS and GLS. Both theoretical analysis and simulation results show that MGLS can reduce the location update overhead in location services.

1 Introduction

Routing protocols in MANETs are commonly categorized into two different types: *topology-based* and *position-based routing*. M. Mauve et al. [1] has presented such an overview of ad hoc routing protocols. The routing performance can be significantly improved by utilizing location information of nodes. That is, if each node is aware of the location of the destination and all its one-hop neighbors in the network, it can geographically forward a packet toward its destination. Position-based routing algorithms uses such additional location information to eliminate the limitations of topology-based routing. Commonly, each node determines its own position through the use of GPS (Global Positioning System). Before sending a packet to the destination, senders always include the location of destination which is provided by the so-called location service in the header of outgoing packets. The routing decision at each node is then based on the destination's position contained in the packet and the position of the forwarding node's neighbors. Position-based routing thus does not require the establishment or maintenance of routes; furthermore, it scales well even if the network is highly dynamic.

Location services provide the positions of the destination nodes to senders all around the geographic region. Existing location services can be classified according to the number of nodes that host the service and the range of nodes

C. Cérin and K.-C. Li (Eds.): GPC 2007, LNCS 4459, pp. 334–347, 2007.

that is maintained by one location server. This can be either some specific nodes or all nodes of the network. Thus there are the four possible combinations as some-for-some, some-for-all, all-for-some, and all-for-all in the of location services. Recent algorithms [2]-[5] present some possible ways of finding destination and distributing location updates.

The Grid Location Service (GLS[2]), which provides a location service by mapping from node_id to current location. GLS divides the area that contains the ad hoc network into a hierarchy of squares. Each node maintains its current location at a small subset of network nodes, called the node's location servers. Location Servers for a node are relatively dense near the node and sparse farther away from the node. The route discovery for a destination is then equivalent to recursively querying the location servers until the query packet arrives at the one having the destination's location. Quorum systems[3][4], which route most packets through arbitrary participants. This reduces the danger that the special participants may become a bottleneck. The role of the special participants is limited to storing location tables and computing routes through the general network. DREAM[5] forces nodes to proactively flood their current location information over the entire network, enabling each node to build a complete location database. However, DREAM does not scale well to large networks due to its use of global flooding.

Forwarding strategies help nodes make routing decisions based on the destination's position included in the packet and the position of their neighbors. The Location Aided Routing (LAR[6]) uses geographic location to determine the search space for a destination, hence reducing the number of route-discover y packets of reactive ad hoc routing approaches. Besides, LAR restricts the search for a route to a so-called request zone which is determined based on the expected location of the destination node at the time of route discover. However, LAR uses flooding as a means of route discovery. This is done in a fashion similar to that of the DREAM approach. [7] had presented a complete comparison between these two schemes, because of the similarity of DREAM and LAR.

The Greedy Perimeter Stateless Routing (GPSR[8]) is such an instance of greedy packet forwarding, which uses a planer subgraph of the wireless network graph to route around dead-end. In GPSR, senders first include the approximate destination positions obtained from a location service into packets. Nodes then use the positions of routers and packets' destinations to make packet forwarding decisions; forward the received packet to a neighbor lying in the direction of the destination until the destination has been reached.

In geographic forwarding, a node announces its current position and velocity to its neighbors by broadcasting periodic HELLO packets. Each node maintains a table of its current neighbors' identities and geographic positions. Therefore, nodes may learn about two hop neighbors: nodes that cannot be reached directly, but can be reached in two hops via the neighbor that sent the HELLO message, it's called 2-hop distance vector. 2-hop distance vector helps alleviate holes in the topology and ensures that each node knows the location of all nodes in its own smallest grid. The header of a packet destined for a particular node contains the destination' s identity as well as its geographic position. When node needs to forward a packet to location D, the node consults its neighbor table and chooses the neighbor closest to D. It then forwards the packet to that neighbor, which itself applies the same forwarding algorithm. The packet stops when it reaches the destination. GLS adopts geographic forwarding as its forwarding strategy. Actually, both geographic forwarding and GLS belong to the GRID project[9].

Another survey of position-based routing in ad hoc networks was presented by I. Stojmenovic[10]. T. Park et al. proposed a hybrid routing protocol[11] constructed by combining well-known location-update schemes, which minimizes the overall routing overhead in terms of location-update thresholds. Some location services with fixed static hierarchy such as DLM[12], SLURP[13], SLALoM[14] and HIGH-GRADE[15] are compared systematically in [16].

In this paper, we proposed a distributed location service scheme for positionba sed routing in mobile ad hoc networks, called Modified Grid Location Service (MGLS) which is an improvement to GLS. Similar to GLS, in our scheme, the entire network is partitioned into hierarchi cal grids. Each node is randomly assigned an integer as its node ID and is placed at uniformly random location over the network. These nodes act as end systems and routers at the same time. In order to maintain the location information in a decentralized way, each node has several location servers in the network. As nodes move, this location information is constantly updated. Before sending a packet to a node, the sender first queries the destination's location and then uses the geographic routing protocol to forward the packet to the destination. Since the cost of location management usually dominates the overall protocol overheads. MGLS was designed to reduce the amount of location updates with a delicate grid hierarchy. We also use a theoretical model for studying the location service scalability, based on which we analyze our scheme as well as GLS. The analytical results are then validated by simulation in medium to large size networks.

2 Overview of MGLS Scheme

MGLS exploits geographic forwarding as its forwarding strategy. First, all nodes know the same global partitioning of the ad hoc network into a hierarchy of grids, as we will describe in the following section. Next, since every node in the network acts as an end system and a location server of other nodes at the same time, the mechanism of location server selection has to be defined clearly. Nodes will periodically update their location servers with their current location obtained by GPS. Finally, if one node A wants to transmit a packet to another node B, A queries the location servers of node B for B's current location before using geographic forwarding. Actually, every node in the network has a predefined unique ID in integer, as well as our wireless card has an unique MAC address in a wireless network.

2.1 Grid Hierarchy

The whole network is partitioned into grids as shown in Figure 1. The grids in the figure are unit grids in the network referred to as *level-0* grids with the ratio $1 : \sqrt{2}$ in width and length. Two *level-0* grids adjoined on the larger side make up a *level-1* grid, two *level-1* grids adjoined on the larger side make up a *level-2* grid, and so on. Obviously, our grid hierarchy has a characteristic of recurrence. Grids of all levels keep the same ratio of $1 : \sqrt{2}$, and the area of *level-(n+1)* is twice as large as level-n.

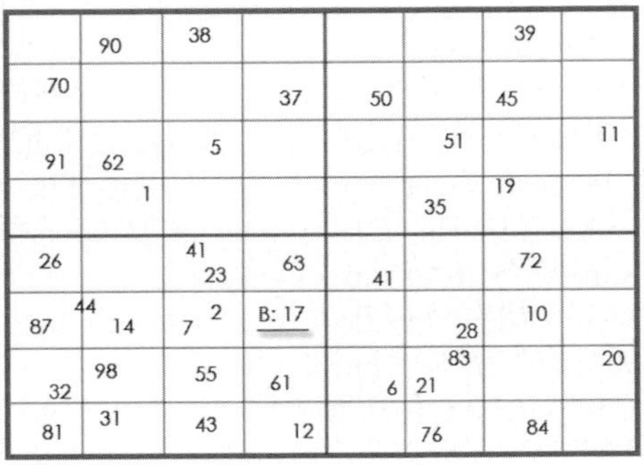

Fig. 1. Formatting an ad hoc network

2.2 Location Servers

We believe that using centralized location servers is not a good idea. Due to the limitation of radio transmission range, the only one location sever may be out of reach of most mobile nodes. Besides, a single server is too weak to provide reliability of location service, it is unlikely to scale a large number of mobile nodes. In order to offer a fault-tolerant scheme, we have to make our location service distributed. That is, one mobile node has multiple location servers located in the whole network. So that MGLS can provide distributed lookup service by replicating the information of nodes' current locations.

Selecting Location Servers and Updating Location Information. Every node uses its ID and the predefined grid hierarchy to determine which nodes are its location servers. In the Figure 2, node B has an ID of 17 and wants to update its location servers after moving a certain distance. The strategy is that one node picks one other node with ID "least greater" than its own ID to be its location server for each level of the grid hierarchy. Note that the ID space is ordered in a circular fashion. We defined 2 is closer to 17 than 7 is to 17.

Here is an example. Let's start from the Figure 2(a). B is located in its own *level-0* grid. Then in Figure 2(b), the *level-0* grid of node B "grows" to be a *level-1* grid containing another node 63. Since 63 is the "least greater" node in ID space than B, so 63 is selected as a location sever of B in its *level-1* grid. In

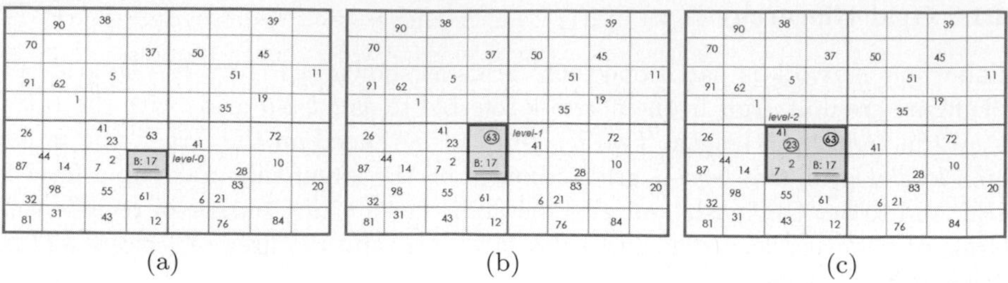

(a) (b) (c)

Fig. 2. A flow diagram illustrates how does a node B seek its location servers. The nodes which become B's location servers are circled.

Figure 2(c), 23 is the least greater node than B again, following a rational line, 23 is B's location server in its *level-2* grid, and so on. The same location server selection process repeats until the *level-i* grid of B covers the whole network, where i is supposed here to be 6 in our example.

Grid Location Service (GLS) divides an a network into a hierarchy grid of squares, too. The *level-i*square is recursively divided into 4 *level-(i-1)* squares until *level-0* squares are reached, forming a so-called quad-tree. In each *level-i* square, node B selects 3 location servers, one in each *level-(i-1)* square that B isn't in. However, in both schemes, the number of location servers that a node must recruit is equal to the number of neighbors per level in the geographic hierarchy multiplied by the number of levels in the hierarchy. For GLS, this means that a node must maintain $3 \log_4 n$ location servers in a network. While MGLS, which splits the network in half at each level, rather than in fourths, by using rectangles with an aspect ratio of $1 : \sqrt{2}$. This leads to a network in which nodes recruit only $\log_2 n$ location servers, that is, 2/3 the number of location servers needed in GLS. Figure 3 gives a contrast to GLS.

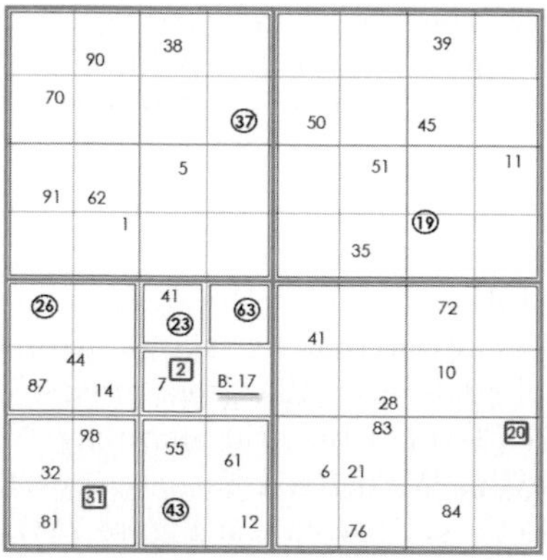

Fig. 3. The same case of GLS, location server 2, 20, 31 are demanded in addition for node B

As a node moves, it must update its location servers. Nodes avoid generating excessive amounts of update packets by bounding their location update rates to their traveled distance. A node updates its *level-1* location servers every time after moving a particular threshold distance δ since sending the last update. The node updates its *level- 2* servers after each movement of $\sqrt{2}\delta$. In general, a node updates its *level-i* servers after each movement of $\sqrt{2}^{i-1}\delta$. As a result, a node sends out updates at a rate proportional to its speed and that updates are sent to distant location servers less often than to local servers.

Location Query. In Figure 4, each node is shown with the list of nodes for which it has up-to-date location information. To perform a location query, node A sends a request by using geographic forwarding to the least greater node than B for which A has location information. That node forwards the query in the same way. In the end, the query will reach a location server of B which will forward the query to B. Since the query contains the location of A, B thus can respond to A directly using geographic forwarding.

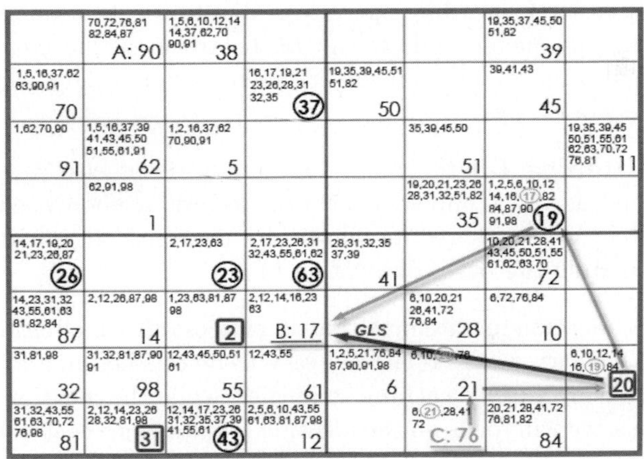

Fig. 4. An example of location querying operations in MGLS

2.3 Design Tradeoffs

As we have seen, MGLS changed the grid organization from quad- to binary-partitioning. As a result, the number of location servers kept by each node is reduced and thus the cost of location maintenance for MGLS may be redueced. However, MGLS may come with an increased query path length due to the decrement of the number of location servers, as shown in Figure 4, where a location query packet was sent from node C (with ID: 76) to 21. It was then forwarded to node 20, a location server of B in GLS, so that this query packet could be forwarded directly to the query destination in one hop earlier than the query packet in MGLS.

3 Comparisons Based on a Theoretical Model

In this section, we exploit a developed theoretical model [16] to analyze the scalibility of MGLS and GLS. The focus of this analytical work is to demonstrate how design choices affect the protocol costs of the two schemes.

3.1 Metrics

We first define three metrics to be the criteria of evaluating the scalability of each scheme.

Definition - ***Location Maintenance Cost:*** The location maintenance cost C_m is defined as the number of forwarding operations each node needs to perform in one second to deal with the location update packets. It can be regarded as the cost of maintaining up-to-date location information on location servers in the network.

Definition - ***Location Query Cost:*** The location query cost C_q is defined as the number of packet forwarding operations due to location queries each node needs to perform in one second. It can be regarded as the cost of acquiring location information from location servers before sending data packets to other nodes in the network.

Definition - ***Storage Cost:*** The storage requirement cost C_s of a location service is defined as the number of location records a node needs to store as a location server. We measure this metric by counting the number of entries instead of calculating the bytes of location tables.

We separate the location maintenance and query costs for one reason. We believe that the location query cost is relatively easy to be reduced in a location service scheme by employing various caching strategies, while the location maintenance cost is not. Thus, we will focus on the location maintenance cost in the following.

3.2 Model Assumptions

The rest of this section derives the expected values of the first and the third metrics as functions of N and v. The node density γ is supposed to be a constant. We also assume that γ is high enough that geographic forwarding is operational. (According to GLS, geographic forwarding works fine only if $\gamma \geq 50\ nodes/km^2$. Actually, the variable γ approaches $100\ nodes/km^2$ in our experiments.) We assume that nodes are moving according to a simplified random way-point mobility model. Each node picks a random point in the network and moves toward it with a random velocity v chosen uniformly between $[0,\ v_{max}]$. After the point is reached, node selects a new random point with zero pause time. Let $P_i, \forall i = 0, \cdots, H$ denote the probability that node B (the querying node) and A (the node being queried) are co-located in the same $level - i$ grid. Based on the size of the $level - i$ grids, P_i can be easily estimated as:

Lemma 1: *(Grid Coexistence Probability).* The probability of the querying node and the queried node are located in the same $level-i$ grid is

$$P_i = \begin{cases} \frac{1}{2^{H-i}} \text{ if MGLS} \\ \frac{1}{4^{H-i}} \text{ if GLS} \end{cases} \quad \forall i = 0 \cdots H$$

3.3 MGLS

Location Maintenance Cost. As we described in Section 2.1, MGLS uses binary grid-partitioned algorithm instead of quad grid-partitioned. A node A selects one location server in each $level-i$ grid $(i = 1 \cdots H)$. Since all location servers of A have to store the current location positions of A, they are expected to be updated periodically to ensure freshness of location information and to reduce the query failure rate. In MGLS, A updates its $level-i$ server after each movement of $(\sqrt{2}^{i-1} \cdot \delta)$, where δ represents the update threshold which can probably be a few hundreds of meters. The updating period is set as the expected time a node moves a distance of $(\sqrt{2}^{i-1} \cdot \delta)$, namely $(\sqrt{2}^{i-1} \cdot \delta)/v$.

Theorem 1. *For MGLS,* $E(C_m) = \dfrac{c_1 \cdot \sqrt{2} \cdot R}{\delta \cdot z} \cdot v \log N$*;* $E(C_s) = \log N$*.*

Proof: To compute the location maintenance cost C_m, we first consider the expected distance that an updating packet has to travel in the $level-i$ grid, denoted as $E(d_i^u)$, and the average number of hops a updating packet takes from node A to $A's$ location server in the $level-i$ grid, denoted as $E(n_i^u)$. Since one node may be randomly located anywhere in a $level-i$ grid, we can view d_i^u as the distance between two random points in two $level-i$ grid adjoined on a side. Therefore,

$$\begin{aligned} E(d_i^u) &= \sqrt{2}^i R \int_0^{\sqrt{2}} \int_0^1 \int_0^{\sqrt{2}} \int_0^1 \sqrt{(x_1 - x_2)^2 + (y_1 - y_2)^2} dx_1 dy_1 dx_2 dy_2 \\ &= c_1 \cdot \sqrt{2}^i R \end{aligned}$$

where R is a constant representing the shorter side length of a $level-0$ grid. Since the size lengths of $level-i$ grid are in the ratio of $1 : \sqrt{2}$, the term $\sqrt{2}^i R$ thus corrects the computation of integral in any $level-i$ of grid. And c_1 is a constant factor representing the average random distance between two neighboring grids, as shown in Fig. 5(a), $c_1 \leq \sqrt{6}$.

The expected number of hops in forwarding the packet is the expected distance divided by z, the average progress of each hop, which can be viewed as a function of the radio transmission range and the node density. Since we assume both as constants in our model, so is z. Thus,

$$E(n_i^u) = \frac{E(d_i^u)}{z} = \frac{c_1 \cdot \sqrt{2}^i R}{z}$$

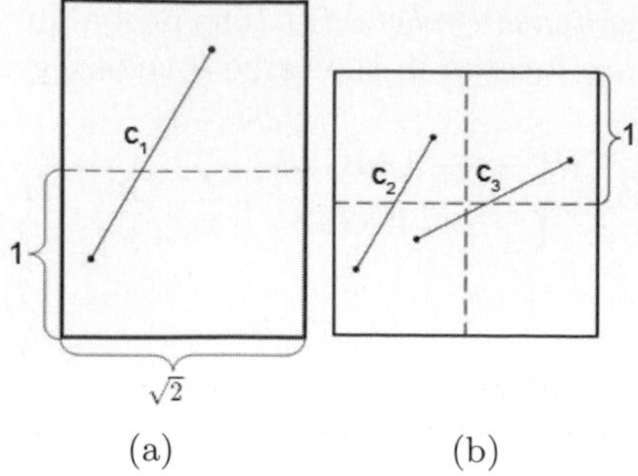

Fig. 5. (a) Constant c_1- random distance between a pair of nodes in two MGLS unit squares adjoined on a side. (b) c_2- random distance between a pair of nodes in two GLS unit squares adjoined on a side; c_3- random distance between a pair of nodes in two unit squares adjoined on a corner.

Since updates are sent out at a rate of $v/(\sqrt{2}^{i-1}\cdot\delta)$($\delta$ represents the update threshold), we have

$$\begin{aligned}
E(C_m) &= \sum_{i=1}^{H} \frac{v}{\sqrt{2}^{i-1}\cdot\delta}\cdot E(n_i^u) \\
&= \sum_{i=1}^{H} \frac{v}{\sqrt{2}^{i-1}\cdot\delta}\cdot\frac{c_1\cdot\sqrt{2}^{i}R}{z} \\
&= \frac{c_1\cdot\sqrt{2}\cdot R}{\delta\cdot z}\cdot\sum_{i=1}^{H} v \\
&= \frac{c_1\cdot\sqrt{2}\cdot R}{\delta\cdot z}\cdot vH \\
&= \frac{c_1\cdot\sqrt{2}\cdot R}{\delta\cdot z}\cdot v\log N
\end{aligned}$$

where H=log N.

As for the Storage Requirement Cost: C_s, remember that the storage requirement is defined as the number of location records a node needs to store as a location server. The average number of records a node stores is the total number of records stored in the network divided by the total number of nodes. Since every node has one location server in each level, we have

$$E(C_s) = \frac{N\cdot H}{N} = \log N. \qquad \blacksquare$$

3.4 GLS

The GLS scheme uses a similar multilevel structure of the grid hierarchy as MGLS. A node A selects three location servers in each $level-i$ square, one in each $level-(i-1)$ squares quadrants that A is not in, as shown in Figure 3. An important difference between GLS and MGLS is the distinct hierarchies of the grid structure. The same as MGLS, all the location servers need to be updated periodically in order to ensure freshness of location information and to reduce the query failure rate. We now prove the following theorem for GLS.

Theorem 2. *For GLS,* $E(C_m) = \frac{(2c_2+c_3)\cdot R}{z\cdot\delta}\cdot v\log\sqrt{N}$; $E(C_s) = \frac{3}{2}\log N$;

Proof: We first consider the location maintenance cost C_m. According to the GLS algorithm, all moving nodes update their location servers after the distance of $(2^{i-1}\cdot\delta)$; at a period of $(2^{i-1}\cdot\delta)/v$. Consider the expected distances the three update packets traveled to update the three locations servers in the $level-i$ square, denoted $E(d_i)$. We have

$$E(d_i^u) = (2c_2+c_3)\cdot 2^i R, \text{and}$$
$$E(n_i^u) = \frac{E(d_i^u)}{z} = \frac{(2c_2+c_3)\cdot 2^i R}{z},$$

where $2^i R$ is the side length of a $level-i$ square, c_2 and c_3 are two constant factors representing the average random distance between two points in two neighboring squares, as shown in Figure 5(b). Simply, we have $c_2 \le \sqrt{5}$, and $c_3 \le 2\sqrt{2}$. Since updates are sent out at a rate of $v/(2^{i-1}\cdot\delta)$, we have

$$\begin{aligned} E(C_m) &= \frac{v}{(2^{i-1}\cdot\delta)}\cdot\sum_{i=1}^{H}\frac{(2c_2+c_3)\cdot 2^i R}{z} \\ &= \frac{(2c_2+c_3)\cdot R}{\delta\cdot z}\cdot\sum_{i=1}^{H}\frac{v\cdot 2^i}{2^{i-1}} \\ &= \frac{(2c_2+c_3)\cdot R}{\delta\cdot z}\cdot 2vH \\ &= \frac{(2c_2+c_3)\cdot R}{z\cdot\delta}\cdot v\log\sqrt{N} \end{aligned}$$

where $H = (1/2)\log\sqrt{N}$, since GLS use a quad-grid partitioning. Finally, since every node in GLS has three location servers in each level, the expected value of the storage cost for GLS is,

$$E(C_s) = \frac{N\cdot 3H}{N} = \frac{3}{2}\log N. \qquad \blacksquare$$

3.5 Summary of Theoretical Analyses

The analytical results of MGLS and GLS share the same asymptotic costs, as their designs exhibit the same philosophy. However, the constant factors in the cost are different. It is obviously that the storage cost of MGLS is smaller than that of GLS. As for the location update cost, which is usually the dominating overhead in location services, MGLS are also smaller than GLS since $c_1\cdot\sqrt{2}$ is smaller than $2c_2+c_3$ in the worst case, where $c_1 \le \sqrt{6}$, $c_2 \le \sqrt{5}$, and $c_3 \le 2\sqrt{2}$.

4 Performance Evaluation Using Simulation

This section presents simulation results for both MGLS and GLS. The GLS implementation we used for simulation is that of [17, NS-2 simulation for Grid]. An outstanding study of GLS's simulator was presented by M. Kasemann et al.[18]. Our MGLS simulation was implemented by making some necessary modifications to the GLS simulator.

Simulation Settings. The simulations use CMU's wireless extensions for the NS-2 simulator. The radio transmission range for each node is generally acknowledged $250m$. The simulations use 2 Megabits per second radios. Each simulation runs for 300 seconds, during which time, each node generates on average 4 data packets to other nodes per second. Nodes move according to the random waypoint model. Each time a random target is chosen, a moving speed is selected between zero and a maximum moving speed, where the maximum moving speed of the simulation is $30m/s$ by default. When the node reaches the destination, it chooses a new destination and begins moving toward it immediately, with no pause time.

Protocol Constants. All nodes are initially randomly placed across the entire network area. For all the simulation runs, the initial node density is about $100nodes/km^2$. One reason for this choice is that we intend the system to be used over relatively large areas such as a campus or municipality, rather than in concentrated locations such as a conference hall. Therefore, the size of network area increases linearly with the number of nodes. For a network of 500 nodes in MGLS, which is the biggest simulation we have done, the grid hierarchy goes up to $level - 7$ in a universe of $2800m \times 2000m$. For both MGLS and GLS, the side length of a $level - 0$ grid is set to be $250m$ (in MGLS, it would be $354m \times 250m$). The location updating threshold is $150m$ in both schemes.

Performance Metrics. We considered the performance metrics, includeing average update cost and the qurery success rate [2][15]. In order to have precise experimental results, we created three levels of traffic loadings in our simulation: *100%, 50%, 10%* of N. We make this by giving three distinct bounds (which can be set in the CBR scenario files) to the number of connections between mobile nodes. For the case of high loading in the simulation, the number of maximum connectio ns between nodes is set to be equal to the total number of nodes. The number of maximum connections equals half the total number of nodes in the case of medium loading. In the low loading network, the number of maximum connections is only one-tenth the number of nodes. Each data point in each of the three levels of traffic loading networks is an average of five simulation runs. In the results presented below, each data point is an average of the three scales traffic loadings. The simulations will demonstrate that MGLS fulfills an impressive balance between designing choice against N and v.

We are interested in the effects of mobility in nodes. High mobility will result in a significant protocol overhead. Dealing with mobility needs a tradeoff between the quality of location maintenance and the bandwidth available for data packets. Aggressive updating can increase query success rate but will occupy the bandwidth shared with data packets, while loosely location updates may have an opposite effect.

Protocol Overhead. Figure 6 shows the average location update cost as a function of (a) the total number of nodes N and (b) maximum moving speeds of nodes v. The location update cost of MGLS is smaller than that of GLS as expected in our analysis.

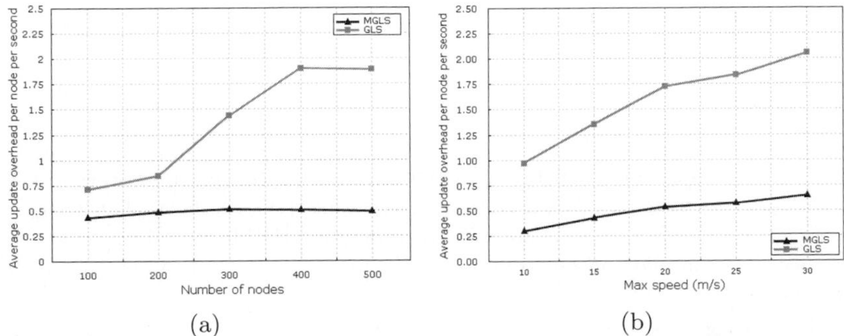

Fig. 6. Average location update cost as a function of total number of nodes and the nodes moving speeds

Protocol Performance. Figure 7 shows the query success rate for both two schemes, as a function of (a) the total number of nodes N and (b) maximum moving speeds of nodes v. Most query failures are due to stale location information stored on the servers. Both schemes maintain quite satisfactory query success rate, around *90%* or above, where the MGLS has a little bit better query success rate than GLS. This result may be due to the lower overhead associated with the MGLS.

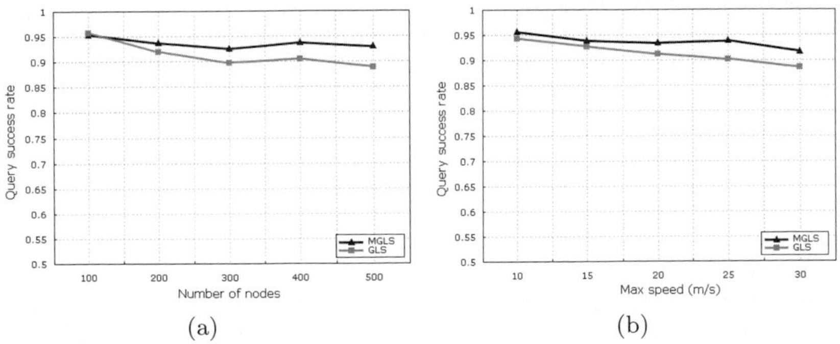

Fig. 7. Query success rate as a function of total number of nodes and the nodes moving speeds

5 Conclusions

In this paper, we presented the design and performance of an efficient location service for mobile ad hoc networks. We also used a theoretical model to analyze the behaviors of both MGLS and GLS. With an enhanced grid partitioning scheme and reasonable tradeoffs, MGLS reduces the protocol overheads in comparison with GLS. Mathematical analysis and simulation results confirmed the performance advantages of our scheme. Future work may be aimed at supporting energy-efficient or quality-of-service (QoS) for discovering routes, where single-path routing used in both MGLS and GLS.

References

1. M. Mauve, J. Widmer, and H. Hartenstein. *A survey on position-based routing in mobile ad hoc networks.* IEEE Network Magazine, p30-39, November 2001.
2. J. Li, J. Jannotti, D. De Couto, D. Karger, and R. Morris. *A scalable location service for geographic ad-hoc routing.* In Proceedings of ACM MobiCom, p120-130, August 2000.
3. Z. J. Haas and B. Liang. *Ad Hoc Mobility Management with Uniform Quorum Systems.* IEEE/ACM Trans. Net., vol. 7, no. 2, p228-240, Apr. 1999.
4. I. Stojmenovic et al.. *A routing strategy and quorum based location update scheme for ad hoc wireless networks.* SITE, University of Ottawa, Tech. Rep. TR-99-09, September 1999.
5. S. Basagni, I. Chlamtac, V.R. Syrotiuk, and B.A. Woodward. *A distance routing effect algorithm for mobility (DREAM).* In Proceedings of the ACM/IEEE International Conference on Mobile Computing and Networking (Mobicom), p76-84, 1998.
6. Y.Ko and N.H.V aidya. *Location-aided routing (LAR) in mobile ad hoc networks.* In Proceedings of the ACM/IEEE International Conference on Mobile Computing and Networking (Mobicom), p66-75, 1998.
7. T. Camp, J. Boleng, B. Williams, L. Wilcox, and W. Navidi. *Performance comparison of two location based routing protocols for Ad Hoc networks.* In Proceedings of the IEEE INFOCOM, 2002.
8. B. Karp and H. T. Kung. *GPSR: greedy perimeter stateless routing for wireless networks.* In International Conference on Mobile Computing and Networking (MobiCom 2000).
9. The grid project homepage, http://www.pdos.lcs.mit.edu/grid
10. I. Stojmenovic. *Position based routing in ad hoc networks.* IEEE Commmunications Magazine, Vol. 40, No. 7, p128-134, July 2002.
11. Taejoon Park , Kang G. Shin. *Optimal tradeoffs for location-based routing in large-scale ad hoc networks.* IEEE/ACM Transactions on Networking (TON), v.13 n.2, p.398-410, April 2005.
12. Y. Xue, B. Li, and K. Nahrstedt. *A scalable location management scheme (DLM) in mobile ad-hoc networks.* In Proceedings of the IEEE Conference on Local Computer Networks (LCN '01), 2001.
13. Seung-Chul M. Woo and Suresh Singh. *Scalable routing protocol (SLURP) for ad hoc networks.* Wireless Networks, 7(5):513-529, 2001.

14. Christine T. Cheng, H. L. Lemberg, Sumesh J. Philip, E. van den Berg, and T. Zhang. *SLALoM: A scalable location management scheme for large mobile ad-hoc networks.* In Proceedings of IEEE WCNC, March 2002.
15. Yinzhe Yu, Guor-Huar Lu, and Zhi-Li Zhang. *Enhancing Location Service Scalability with HIGH-GRADE.* Dept. of Comp. Sci. & Eng., U of Minnesota, Technical Report TR-04-002, 2004.
16. Y Yu, GH Lu, ZL Zhang. *Location Service in Ad-Hoc Networks: Modeling and Analysis.* In Proceeding of NSF Workshop on Theoretical and Algorithm Aspect of Ad Hoc Wireless Networks, Chicago, June 2004.
17. NS-2 simulation for Grid, http://pdos.csail.mit.edu/grid/sim/index.html
18. H. Hartenstein, M. Kasemann, H. Fubler, and M. Mauve. *A simulation study of a location service for position-based routing in mobile ad hoc networks.* Technical report, Department of Science, University of Mannheim, TR-02-007, July 2002.

Authentication and Access Control Using Trust Collaboration in Pervasive Grid Environments

Rachid Saadi[1], Jean Marc Pierson[2], and Lionel Brunie[1]

[1] LIRIS lab, INSA de Lyon, France
{rachid.saadi,lionel.brunie}@liris.cnrs.fr
[2] IRIT lab, University Paul Sabatier Toulouse, France
jean-marc.pierson@irit.fr

Abstract. Pervasive Grids emerge as a new paradigm for providing nomadic users with ubiquitous access to digital information and computing resources. However, pervasive grids arise a number of crucial issues related to privacy and security, especially authentication and access control, which constitute the security front-end.

In this paper, we propose a trust based model of authentication and access control that allows nomadic users to roam from site to site and to gain access to surrounding/remote resources wrt her status in her home site and to the local policy of the site where she is standing. This model is supported by a software architecture called Chameleon.

The Chameleon permits users to access grid resources and to implement adhoc interactions with the local grid site.

1 Introduction

In the last decade, Grid Computing and Pervasive computing have emerged as two new visions of computing system. Both systems focus on the user accessibility, offering her a large access to resources, services, and data. The deployment of these technologies arises new security challenges to perform a nomadic user authentication and a distributed access control policy [18].

The Grid [1] provides the ability, using a set of open standards and protocols, to gain access to applications and data, processing power, storage capacity and a vast array of other computing resources over the Internet or distributed system. A Grid enables the sharing, selection, and aggregation of distributed resources across multiple administrative domains or organizations based on the resources availability, capacity, performance, cost and users' quality-of-service requirements.

Pervasive computing [2] is the next generation of computing environments involving information and communication technology. The main purpose of that technology is to prompt the personal computer to "everyday" devices where embedded technology and connectivity, as computing devices, become progressively smaller and more powerful. Also called ubiquitous computing [3], the challenge of pervasive computing, which combines current network technologies with wireless

C. Cérin and K.-C. Li (Eds.): GPC 2007, LNCS 4459, pp. 348–361, 2007.

computing, Internet capability and artificial intelligence, is to create an environment where the connectivity of devices is embedded in such a way that the connectivity is unobtrusive and always available.

Either the pervasive computing or the grid computing aims to extend the access scope of the user. Thus, according to our conviction, the pervasive security architecture cannot be deployed without an existing grid and distributed infrastructure. Respectively, the grid cannot evolve without a pervasive architecture entourage. Thus, organizations operate as a grid and constitute the core of the environment. The Grid is considered as a meta administrator which controls accessibility and sharing of the set of included resources or services.

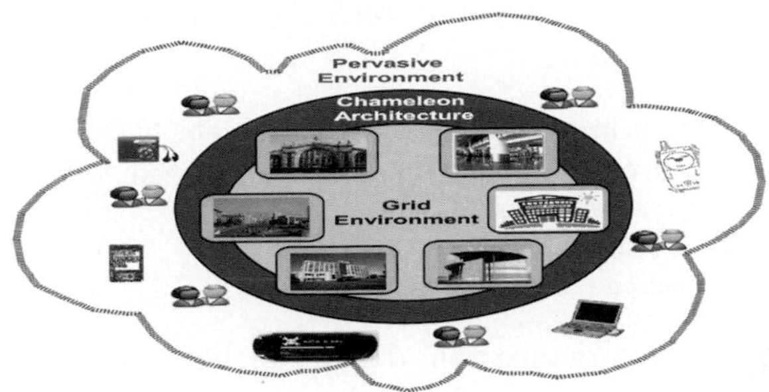

Fig. 1. Pervasive Grid

In order to tackle security issues inside a pervasive grid we aim at defining a generic security architecture, which we called "The Chameleon Architecture".

The Chameleon Architecture is grafted around the grid among organizations as well as between users and organizations. Our architecture considers each nomadic user as a Chameleon, which has the capacity to become a local user anywhere anytime with any device. Unlike existing approaches that enabling broad user access using certification chain and delegation [4] [16], our proposal perform a distrust mathematical function to compute the user trustworthiness before giving her a corresponding access.

This paper is organized as follows. Section 2 presents a Pervasive Grid scenario. Next, in section 3 we introduce our proposal the Chameleon architecture, and show its implementation in the pervasive grid environment. Then we describe how a foreign user accesses unknown sites in section 4. Finally, we discuss benefits and conclude this paper along with future directions.

2 Pervasive Grid Scenario

The challenge is to allow each nomadic user to roam and access inside this environment easily and transparently, by exceeding certain barriers like the heterogeneity of the different access policies. Let's consider the following use case. Pr Bob is a member of University A. This Professor goes to a conference in

University B and then to a meeting in University C. He communicates with the different surrounding "objects" including students, professors and resources e.g. printer, video projector etc. In fact, Bob owns a professional card or conference badge that defines his status and includes a picture or a fingerprint to identify his identity. This card or badge allows Bob an access inside these universities according to a convention or shared collaboration (the same working group). These Universities do not know the owner of the card, but trust his card.

If we map this scenario in the pervasive grid environment, universities correspond to sites (grid). A certificate simulates the professional card; the fingerprint or the picture is seen as an authentication system embedded in the certificate. In this manner, if Bob has the right to attend a conference, according to his certificate, he obtains a new temporary certificate (like a badge in a conference). This certificate allows Bob:

- to access authorized resources inside this new site like all other members,
- to share his resources with surrounding authorized local users e.g. make presentation only to registered lecturer.

In this paper we use the following terms:

- **Site:** Represents an organization, domain or host that implements a local independent security policy and is limited geographically,
- **Target site "T":** Represents the site which user likes to access.
- **Home site:**: Represents the site where user is member.
- **Trusted site of "T":** Represents a site on which "T" trusts.
- **Trust set of "T":** Gathers all "T" trusted sites.
- **Environment:** Is composed by sites like universities, restaurants, posts office, airports etc.
- **Profile:** Each user has a profile, depending on the access policies, it can represent a role (student, doctor) or an access level (trust, distrust, confidential) etc.
- **Certificate:** It represents a digital passport of the users. One user owns some certificates (like professional cards) that prove her membership to each site.

3 The Chameleon Architecture

The Chameleon architecture represents the backbone to set a security layer inside a pervasive grid environment. It provides sites and users the ability to perform authentication and access control policy.

Our architecture identifies two actors: User and Site.

The user has as main characteristics the mobility and the dynamism; she roams in the environment and uses surrounding or remote resources or services.

The site dubbed as domain or organization represents the entity providing to the user some services or resources. These pertain to the organization, which applies inside an access control policy.

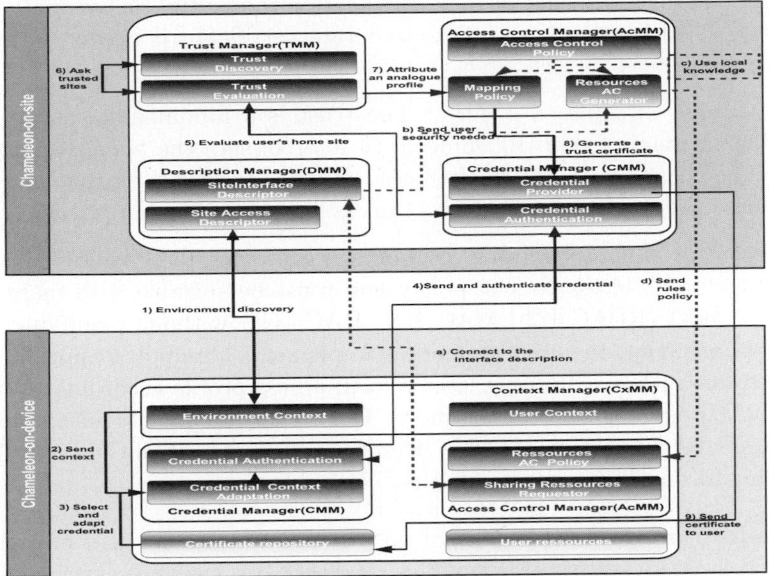

Fig. 2. Chameleon architecture

According to each site the user could have one of these two facets: Local and Foreign user. The former is recognized as a member of the organization, whereas the latter is considered as foreigner. With existing security models, she can't have any access to any local organization resources.

Our architecture is divided into two parts:

– *Chameleon-on-site*: Is implemented on each site.
– *Chameleon-on-device*: Is implemented on the user device.

3.1 The Architecture Description

Chameleon-on-site. It is implemented on the site performing all the interaction and the inter-connection between sites policy. It is composed of four modules. (S designates Site)

Description Manager Module (S-DMM) : This module represents the environment by describing its identity (Site Access Descriptor SAD) and its policy (Site Interface Descriptor SID). The role of S-DMM is crucial, because it represents the front-end of the site. Thus, according to its description the user can manage and adapt her device policy.

Certificate Manager Module (S-CrMM) : Like all distributed system [5] [6] [7], the Chameleon architecture performs a certification mechanism to enhance the flexibility of the security policy. Indeed the certification model (X509 [8], SPKI [9]) allows to prove the user rights without home site interference. S-CrMM manages and maintains a system of certification to identify the credential owner (Credential Authentication) and to generate certificate if needed (Credential Provider).

Trust Manager Module (S-TMM) : The trust is a fundamental aspect for an inter-domain relationship [10]. Indeed, to interconnect the pervasive grid community the "trust paradigm" is often used. It offers to each site a dynamic system to evaluate the surrounding trustworthiness environment even further.

Access control Manager Module (S-AcMM): This module is generic, it doesn't modify the local access control policy and must be suitable with many access security model (RBAC [13], MAC [12], DAC [11]) without modifying the local policy behavior. Indeed, this module implements a mapping approach which grants to an authorized foreign user a local access profile according to her certificate (Mapping Policy). Furthermore, The S-AcMM can help authorized users to manage their own devices policy (Resources Access control Generator RAcG) according to target site characteristics.

Chameleon-on-device. A part of our architecture is installed into the user device; it is composed of three modules (D designates Device): *Context Manager*

Module D-CxMM: In the pervasive environment, the context paradigm is critical. The user device policy must be convenient to context such as: device type, user practice, environment etc. This module describes the context of the user (User Context) and undertakes discovering the surrounding environment (Environment Context).

Credential Manager Module D-CrMM: According to the context manager, this module takes charge of selecting and adapting a corresponding credential from the certificate repository (Credential Context Adaptation) according to the specific connection with a target site or a user.

Access control Manager Module D-AcMM: Once the user is connected and identified by the environment, if she wants to share her resources, this module provides the means to control (Resources Access Control Policy), parameterize and customize (Sharing Resources Requestor) her own device policy.

In order to build a security architecture, which connects the mobile user to the pervasive grid community, thus providing authentication and access control, we identify this challenges.

Each user wants to interact with some resources of surrounding sites. The challenge is how each target site can recognize, evaluate the trustworthiness and give then an access to this unknown foreign user?

4 How Foreign User Accesses Unknown Site?

Our Architecture allows user to authenticate on a remote site and to assign access inside the environment without being locally recognized. Our proposal is based on a "Trust Model" using a new certification mechanism "X316" [14].

4.1 Requirements

Trust Relation: Once Bob is authenticated, the site A attempts to assign him a profile according to the certificate issuer. So, a trust model must be defined to enable all organizations (Grid) to communicate and share some information about their members. We define a trust relation to interconnect the grid community, offering to each site a means to evaluate its surroundings. Let S denote a set of sites. Let A and B two sites, $A \in S, B \in S$. If A trusts B then we say that the relation Trust is verified between A and B and we note "*A Trust B*". This relation is reflexive, symmetric and transitive.

Trust Evaluation: This property is fundamental for the effectiveness of our proposition. It allows defining "trust chains" between sites that do not know each other (see below).

Based on the *Trust* relation, we introduce ***the distrust function*** t^0 [**17**], to estimate the level of (dis)trust between two sites.

Distrust function. We call distrust function and we note t^0, the function defined as:

$$\begin{array}{ll} t^0 : S * S \rightarrow \mathbb{N} & \text{S: Set of sites} \\ \quad (A, B) \rightarrow d & \mathbb{N}\text{: Set of natural numbers} \end{array}$$

$$t^0(A, B) = \begin{cases} -1 & if \neg (A\ Trust\ B) \\ 0 \leq d \leq T_A^0 & otherwise \end{cases}$$

where d represents ***the distrust degree*** and T_A^0 denotes the distrust threshold of the site A.

This function quantifies the degree of distrust that the site A shows wrt the site B. When $t^0(A, B)$ increases, the distrust increases (i.e. the trust decreases). As consequences :

- $t^0(A, B) = 0$: Any site has a complete trust in itself.
- $t^0(A, B) < t^0(A, C)$: Means that the site A has a higher trust in B than in C.

The distrust threshold represents the maximum level of distrust beyond which A does not trust B (i.e. the relation A Trust B is not verified).

A feature of the distrust function is the use of the value -1 to denote the fact that a site does not trust another site. Indeed, as the distrust degree can range a priori from 0 to any positive number, there is not a priori superior limit value. Consequently it is necessary to introduce and use a symbolic value to state that a site does not trust another one. We could have chosen ∞ or $\perp$ but for easiness of computing reasons, -1 is more convenient.

The distrust function shows properties related to the properties of the Trust relation.

Properties of distrust degree:

- *Self trust:* $\forall A \in S, t^0(A,A) = 0$
- *Non-commutativity:* $\exists A, B \in S / t^0(A,B) = d_1 \wedge t^0(B,A) = d_2 \wedge d_1 \neq d_2$
- *Composition:* Let A, B, C 3 sites. The *composition* of the distrust degrees $t^0(A,B)$ and $t^0(B,C)$, noted $t^0(A,B) \oplus t^0(B,C)$ is defined as:

$$\begin{array}{c} t^0(A,B) \\ \oplus \\ t^0(B,C) \end{array} = \begin{cases} -1 & if(t^0(A,B) \vee t^0(B,C)) = -1 \\ \begin{array}{c} t^0(A,B) \\ + \\ t^0(B,C) \end{array} & otherwise \end{cases}$$

Generalization: Trust chains

The composition of distrust degrees is generalized to n sites by composing two by two the distrust degrees:

$t^0(A1, ..., An) = t^0(A_1, A_2) \oplus ... \oplus t^0(A_{n-1}, A_n)$
$(A_1, ..., A_n)$ is called a trust chain.

Notation: Distrust propagation function:

Let A and C 2 sites of S; let $B_1 ... B_n$ n sites of S.
Let us note T = $(B_1, ..., B_n)$
We note $P^0_T(A,C)$ and we call distrust propagation degree between A and C based on T the value:

$P^0_T(A,C) = t^0(A, B_1, ..., B_n, C)$.

Property: $P^0_\phi(A,C) = t^0(A,C)$

Theorem: $P^0_\phi(A,C) = -1 \Leftrightarrow \exists F, G \in (A, B_1, ..., B_n, C) / t^0(F,G) = -1$.

Proof : trivial by application of the definition of t^0 : The composition of distrust degrees equals -1 if and only if one at least of the distrust degrees equals -1. Indeed, this distributed system can be seen as a Trust graph noted $T_g(S,E)$ a valued and directed graph such that:

- The nodes of the graph represent the sites of S.
- Each Trust relation between two sites is represented by a directed edge e. The set of edges is consequently identified with the set of relations, E.
- Each edge is valued by the distrust degree between the sites represented by the source and destination nodes of this edge (use of the t^0 function).

A Certification Model: Actually, all distributed systems use a certification mechanism to enhance the system flexibility and dynamism. Indeed, the user become more autonomous and can authenticate and proves her rights. In the Chameleon architecture we define a new format for certificate called X316:

Morph Access Pass Certificate. This format facilitates creating any sort of certificates or credentials e.g. Attribute certificate, Role certificate etc. This "X316" works as a pass, allowing its owner to roam and gain access in the environment.

This certificate mainly testifies the user profile (status or access level) and rights in a Home/Trusted site. If the user wants to access a particular target site, her device selects one of her certificates, which is recognized by this one.

Our contribution has an objective to define a very flexible model of certification. It is inspirited by the W3C standards: "XML Digital signature"(XMLDSig) [19] and "XML Encryption" (XMLEnc) [20]. The X316 is designed for nomadic user. Indeed, unlike all certification system, the same X316 certificate can be used and authenticate from various devices with different capacity and characteristics, and can be generated dynamically along to user trip. In fact, by defining specific tags to delimit the dynamic parts, this certificate acquires the capability to transform and to morph easily its content according to context, situation, and environment.

Therefore, the X316 fulfills three constraints:

- Format Flexibility.
- Multi authentication.
- Contextual adaptation.

X316 could be obtained by two different ways:

- Each site gives a Home Certificate or H316, to all its members.
- Each site gives a Trust certificate or T316, to a guest, when it trusts her Home Site.

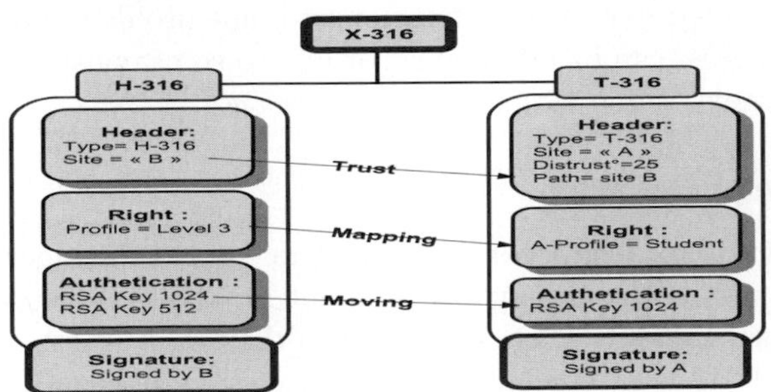

Fig. 3. X316 Type

As illustrated in the figure 3, the X316 is composed by:

- *The header:* It identifies the certificate.
- *The right:* It is a variable part of a certificate, depending on the site policy. This part contains information about user rights, such as status or access level in a Home/Trusted Site (certifying site). The use of this profile is original. Indeed, unlike other systems of certification that certify an access to particular resources, this one certifies the profile that represents all authorized access to site resources.

– *Authentication:* This part permits one to identify the owner of the X316. Authentications are numerous, and related to the variety of devices used in the pervasive environment (PDA, mobile phone, terminals). Facilitating certificates authentication could be fulfilled by embedding some identifications (picture, fingerprint etc.) according to device capabilities and the site security policy.

A Context Description: All standards e.g X509, PGP use a hash algorithm to obtain a residual value from the certificate data. This value is signed by the private key of the certification authority. Consequently if the content of the certificate is modified, the residual result will be erroneous. In this case, the users can't adapt her certificate by masking any information inside.

In our approach, we use a single certificate that mainly contains the user profile, all user access rights and some authentication systems. Yet we define in this model a specific signature method (X316 signature), using specific tags. In fact, using dictionary ontology and a learning mechanism, the certificate structure can morph according to user and environment context (X316 context). Thus, the certificate owner can freely mask some information. In this manner the user device extracts a sort of sub-certificate (credential) from the original one, which only contains the essential information for each specific transaction or context.

Mapping Policy: The main feature of our approach is to append an additional security component without modifying the local policy behavior. So, each site defines some local profiles, which can be attributed (externalized) to trusted foreign users. In the aim to assign to foreign users the adequate profile, a mapping policy is implemented to correspond each user home profile to an analogous one. The mapping process can be adapted according to some constraints such as user profile, user context, home user trustworthiness, etc.

4.2 Chameleon Behavior

Selecting and morphing a certificate. The context manager (D-CxMM) of Bob device scan the surrounding environment and collects needed information to inform the user context. Then, according to the target site A, the "Credential Manager" selects a valid credential according to "A" identity (Hospital, university, airport etc.) and the user context (device, type of connexion...). Thus, the "Credential Authentication" Component uses the generated credential to identify its owner by selecting one authentication process from the credential authentication part (challenge response, biometric etc.)

Evaluating the user trustworthiness. The core of the system works as a trust graph. In fact, when the user Bob comes to a target site, this one explores the graph (by asking its trusted site) to evaluate and recognize Bob home site "H". Once H is recognized, a trust chain is created between the target site "T" and the trusted site "D". This chain can be evaluated in two directions.

As illustrated in the figure 4, the first path which starts from the target site "T" to the trusted site "D" (trusted site of the Bob's home site) allows D to

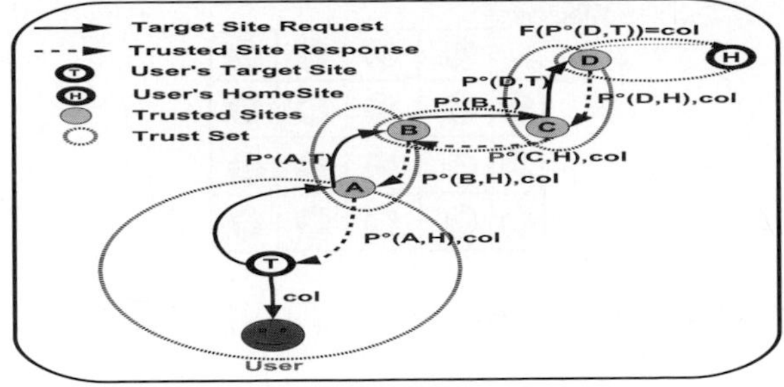

Fig. 4. Trust propagation

return to Bob its evaluation about "T" ; the second path which is the inverse of the first one gives to the target site a trust evaluation about the foreign user's home site.

– *First path evaluation (Target Site Request):* Since the trust chain is built, a trust evaluation is performed while the chain is propagated. Consequently, when the last trust site "D" is retrieved, it evaluates and computes the target site trustworthiness $P^0_{C,B,A}(D,T)$.

  However, the main challenge of pervasive environment is the fluency of the interaction between the environment and the user. Indeed, when the last trusted site computes the final trust propagation value, it returns its assessment (e.g. $P^0_{C,B,A}(D,T) = 23$) of path. The problem is: How the user can interpret this value '23'?

  To help user, we define a classification based on human living, by using the Highway Code. These colors have an intuitive signification to the user, as following:

  • Green : Very safe site
  • Orange : Safe site (warning)
  • Red : Less safe site (not recommended)
  • Black : Unsafe site

  Thus, before sending the $P^0_{C,B,A}(D,T)$ to concerned user, the trusted site D implements a function "F" to compute the corresponding color "col" form the trust value. For confidentiality and no repudiation, the "col" value is ciphered, signed with the private key of the site C, and sent back with the response to "D". Consequently, only the user can read "col" and verify its authenticity.

  Once the user receives the 'col' Value, she could recognize the D trustworthiness about the target site. Furthermore, as illustrated in the figure 5, by combining the "col" value and the user home site trust evaluation for each trusted site (TScol), the user computes a more precise Trust Path Evaluation TP(col, TScol). In fact, each site classifies its trusted sites into three

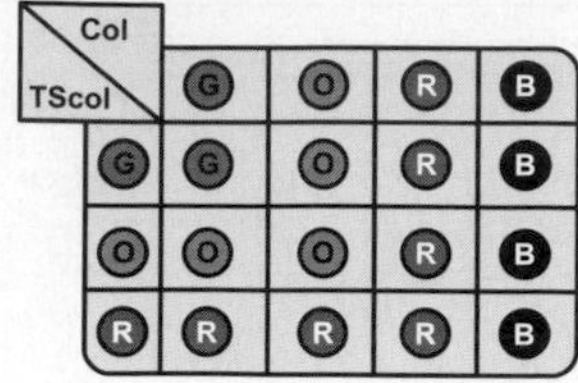

Fig. 5. User Trust Path evaluation "TP"

groups: Red, Orange and Green, and defines for each group a specific pair of keys(Public and Private). Therefore, each trusted site signs the computed trust value with the group private key before replying to target site.

Consequently, according to the used key:

- the user is sure that the given access is initiated by a trusted site since only a trusted site can use one of home site group key.
- the user can identify the corresponding "TScol" of the trusted site, since each color corresponds to a group key.

– *Second path evaluation (Trusted Site Response):* The evaluation of this path ($P^0_{B,C,D}(A, H)$) permits the target site to decide if a "foreign" user can be allowed to access target site resources (e.g. to decide if a user having no account within the system can get log in). Thus, we consider two kinds of access: Direct access and Transitive access.

  - ***A direct access*** is provided by a target site to all users registered by its trusted sites e.g. site A. This direct access is assessed by the trust value. In fact, as illustrated in the figure 4, the target site endeavors to recognize this foreign user. A direct access is given if this foreign user is member of the target site trust set. Otherwise the target site investigates the closest trusted site about the user's home site.
  - ***A Transitive access*** can be provided by a target site (Site T) to a user who does not belong to its trusted sites (e.g. Site B,C or D) on condition that it exists a (positive) trust chain between one of the user's home sites and "T". This transitive access is valued by a computed trust value between these two sites (as before, in case of the existence of several possible chains, the target site is responsible for choosing the reference chain).

Therefore, this model, using the community collaboration, enables the target site to evaluate the user according to her home site. Moreover the context (user device, communication protocol...) can be used to increase or decrease the new user rights.

Attributing an access profile. Once a user is allowed to access the site T, the latter attributes her an analogous profile using the mapping policy. Consequently, this new profile defines all user access rights inside the target site. Indeed, a mapping policy must be defined in order to give each foreign user an analogous profile (A-Profile). Each site creates a mapping table that enables matching between the different profiles of trusted sites and its local ones. For example: User Bob, having an access profile as level 5 in his home site, wants to access the site T, which provides Bob a new access level for instance, level 3 (it is T responsibility to map the original level accordingly with its local policy). Further works in this mapping policy is not part of the presented work.

5 Implementation and Discussion

A demonstrator has been implemented to illustrate the Chameleon architecture behavior. This demonstrator allows the user to roam inside three universities, her home university (using Username and Password), and two other universities (using M316 and T316).

The user enters her home university U0 and claims an M316. She uses this M316 and accesses university U1, who trusts U0. When the user is allowed to access U1, she can claim another T316. Finally, this one provides a user an access to U2, thanks to the trust that is given by U2 to U1.

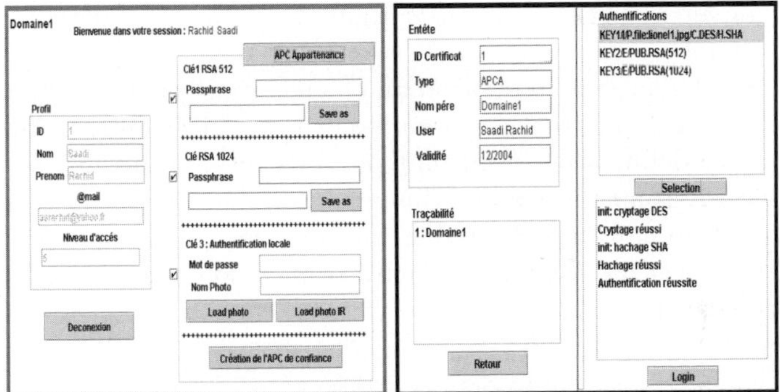

Fig. 6. The demonstrator

The generated X316 embeds three authentications: Two remote (Public keys 512 and 1024) and one local (using an Infrared connection with a mobile phone).

The authentication system uses the challenge response mechanism for remote authentication. Each user is authenticated by signing the challenge with corresponding private key to one of public keys in the X316. However the local authentication is fulfilled in the following process: The user captures a picture with her mobile phone, then sends it trough infrared connexion. Afterward, she attached a password to this picture. Finally, the site embeds the hash function generated by this authentication as an authenticator. In the same way, when the user wants to authenticate her certificate in the trusted site, she sends, by infrared connection, the photo and introduces an associated password to authenticate it.

The main constraint of our architecture is illustrated mainly by difficulties arisen while managing relationship among organizations (sites) and applying the mapping policies. In fact, an organization, having a trust relationship with other organizations, must validate and value relations manually (semi-manually) by the administrator. However, each organization has a trust relationship with only a few other organizations, and it builds this relationship only once. When the relationship is validated and the Mapping DB created, the system becomes standalone. The mapping policy is applied in the site set which generally uses a similar policy e.g., RBAC, MAC, DAC. For example: In a medical community, it is probable that roles such as "Doctor", "Nurse" or "Patient" exist in all organizations, allowing for an easy mapping through the community.

6 Conclusion

The Chameleon architecture allows the user to roam transparently in an environment simply by using her certificates. The Chameleon using the X316 presents a number of advantages. Indeed, it consists in a decentralized architecture since each site, knowing only its neighbors, can perform a large but controlled access to user communities. Chameleon reduces the human interaction where many security management functions can be processed dynamically. In addition, Chameleon increases the user rights along her trip without modifying the local site policy.

However the challenge is to perform an efficient and generic HMI providing to user a very usual interface to express her security requirements. As future works, we investigate to define a platform that provides integrating specific services to define any site environment. And for fluency, we will integrate our team works on context description [15] to X316 giving the user device the capacity to manage and adapt the certificate dynamically with respect to context without soliciting any user intervention.

References

1. I. Foster and C. Kesselman. *The Grid: Blueprint for a New Computing Infrastructure.* Morgan Kaufmann, 1999.
2. M. Satyanarayanan . *Pervasive Computing: Vision and Challenges.* IEEE Personal Communications journal, pages 10-17. Aug 2001.
3. N. Shankar, W. Arbaugh. *On Trust for Ubiquitous Computing.* Workshop on Security in Ubiquitous Computing, Sep 2004.
4. L. Seitz, J.M. Pierson and L. Brunie. *Semantic Access Control for Medical Applications in Grid Environments.* A International Conference on Parallel and Distributed Computing, pp374-383, Aug 2003
5. G. Aloisio, M. Cafaro, P. Falabella, K Kesselman and R. Wiiliams, *Grid Computing in the Web Using the Globus Toolkits.* Editor HPCN Europe, pp 32-40, 2000.
6. D. Chadwick and A. Otenko. *The PERMIS X.509 Role Based Privilege Management Infrastructure.* In Proceedings of the 7th ACM Symposium on Access Control Models and Technologies, pages 135140, Jun 2002.

7. M. Lorch, D. Adams, D. Kafura, and al. *The PRIMA System for Privilege Management, Authorization and Enforcement.* In Proceedings of the 4th International Workshop on Grid Computing, Nov 2003.
8. *ITU-T Rec. X.509 (2000).* ISO/IEC 9594-8 The Directory: Authentication Framework
9. *ITU-T Simple public key infrastructure* (SPKI) charter, http://www.ietf.org/html.charters/OLD/spki-charter.html.
10. A. Abdul-Rahman and S. Hailes. *A Distributed Trust Model.* In proceedings of the ACM Workshop on New Security Paradigms, pp48-60, sep 1997.
11. M. H. Harrison, W. L. Ruzzo, and J. D. Ullman. *Protection in Operating Systems.* Communications of the ACM, 19(8):461-471, 1976.
12. D. E. Bell. *A Refinement of the Mathematical Model.* Technical Report ESD-TR-278 vol. 3, The Mitre Corp., Bedford, MA, 1973.
13. R. Sandhu, E. J. Coyne, H. L. Feinstein, and al. *Role-Based Access Control Models.* IEEE Computer, 29(2):38-47, 1996.
14. R.Saadi, J. M. Pierson and L. Brunie.*X316: Morph Access Pass certificate.* Technical Report, INSA de Lyon France. 2006.
15. T. Chaari, D. Ejigu, F. Laforest , M. Scuturici.*Modeling and Using Context in Adapting Applications to Pervasive Environments*, In the Proceedings of the IEEE International Conference on Pervasive Services (ICPS'06), Pages 111-120, Lyon, France, Jun 2006
16. J. Basney, W. Nejdl, D. Olmedilla, V. Welch, and M. Winslett. *Negotiating trust on the grid.* In 2nd WWW Workshop on Semantics in P2P and Grid Computing. may 2004.
17. R. Saadi, J. Pierson, L. Brunie. *(Dis)trust Certification Model for Large Access in Pervasive Environment.* JPCC International Journal of Pervasive Computing and Communications. Volume 1, Issue 4. pp 289-299. oct 2005.
18. N. Sklavos and O. Koufopavlou. *Mobile Communications World: Security Implementations Aspects - A State of the Art.* CSJM Journal, Institute of Mathematics and Computer Science, Vol. 11, Number 2 (32), pp. 168-187, 2003.
19. T. Imamura, B. Dillaway and E. Simon. *XML-signature syntax and processing.* In W3C Recommendation. Dec 2002. http://www.w3.org/TR/2002/REC-xmlenc-core-20021210/
20. M. Bartel, J. Boyer, B. Fox, B. LaMacchia, and E. Simon. *XML-encryption syntax and processing.* In W3C Recommendation. Feb 2002. http://www.w3.org/TR/2002/REC-xmldsig-core-20020212/

Architecture-Based Autonomic Deployment of J2EE Systems in Grids

Didier Hoareau[1], Takoua Abdellatif[2], and Yves Mahéo[1]

[1] Valoria, University of South Brittany, France
{didier.hoareau,yves.maheo}@univ-ubs.fr
[2] ENISO, University of Sousse, Tunisia
takoua_abdellatif@yahoo.fr

Abstract. The deployment of J2EE systems in Grid environments remains a difficult task: the architecture of these applications are complex and the target environment is heterogeneous, open and dynamic. In this paper, we show how the component-based approach simplifies the design, the deployment and the reconfiguration of a J2EE system. We propose an extended architecture description language that allows specifying the deployment of enterprise systems in enterprise Grids, driven by resources and location constraints. With respect to these constraints we present a deployment process that instantiates propagatively the application, taking into account resources and hosts availability. Finally, we present an autonomic solution for recovery from failures.

1 Introduction

Grid environments have moved from the mere aggregation of computational resources dedicated to parallel and scientific applications to more general sharing of networked resources. The kind of Grids we consider in this paper can be seen as a set of heterogeneous machines interconnected by links of various capacities. Moreover a number of factors impacting the dynamism of the system (machine crashes, user disconnections, system failures etc.) cannot be neglected. Such Grids become attractive to multi-tier Internet service providers who want to improve the quality of service they offer. For this reason, many recent research works aim at finding the best models and techniques to exploit the Grids for better performance and high availability (e.g. [1,2]). However, these works concentrate more on finding models and proving their effectiveness and do not propose efficient solutions automating the deployment and the recovery from failures of enterprise middleware and applications. Such features are very important and are still challenging in the context of interactive applications. Indeed, unlike scientific parallel applications whose parts can be independently deployed and executed, multi-tier middleware and applications are composed of interdependent pieces of software that have to coexist at execution time. Furthermore, the failure of one part of the enterprise system may involve service discontinuity or performance degradation. Recovering the system architecture, as initially defined at deployment time, is very important to preserve the agreed quality of service.

In this paper, we propose a solution for deploying enterprise systems in Grids and automating the recovery from failure of parts of the system. To achieve this goal, we

C. Cérin and K.-C. Li (Eds.): GPC 2007, LNCS 4459, pp. 362–373, 2007.

consider a J2EE system that we call a *virtual cluster*, similar to a classical J2EE cluster in that EJB and Web containers are replicated for backup fault-tolerance considerations. We believe that our solution is applicable to other models and other configurations of multi-tier Internet applications on wide-area networks, and it can be of interest to researchers in this field to easily experiment their different models on Grids and for service providers to easily handle an important number of clients. Our approach consists in applying an architecture-based deployment [3] and in automating the management of distributed systems. The idea is to abstract the managed system into an assembly of explicitly bound components and to use these components as units of configuration, deployment and reconfiguration. We adopted this approach for J2EE systems in a previous work—in classical cluster environments—by re-engineering an open source application server [4]. The re-engineering work consists in transforming the server parts into explicitly connected components. With the same component model, Fractal [5] in our case, we also represent the underlying resources like the nodes of the Grid. An ADL (Architecture Description Language) permits the description of the different parts of the distributed system, their configuration and their relations in terms of bindings and encapsulation. Finally, a deployment engine allows automating the deployment of the J2EE system using its description on the cluster targets. Compared to J2EE clusters, Grids are highly distributed, heterogeneous and dynamic. For this reason, our deployment system needs to be extended to manage virtual clusters within the Grid constraints. In this paper, we demonstrate the extension of the Fractal ADL to describe the component resources, a resource allocation mechanism and a solution for an automatic recovery from failures.

The layout of this paper is the following. In Section 2, we present more in details the context of our work and the main underlying assumptions. In Section 3, we describe our deployment process and its resource allocation service. We detail the current state of our implementation and some first results in Section 4. Section 5 discusses related work. Finally, Section 6 concludes the paper and identifies future work.

2 Context and Main Assumptions

2.1 J2EE System Configuration and Deployment

J2EE application servers are complex service-oriented architectures. In a previous work, we demonstrated that solving the deployment of J2EE applications requires that the internal software architecture of the J2EE server, in terms of the services that compose it and their various interaction and containment dependencies, be made explicit and modifiable at run time [4]. Indeed, the configuration of the system and its deployment parameters have to be described using the elements of the system's architecture. This description can then be used as a basis to implement and automate different deployment and reconfiguration policies. This is what is generally called *architecture-based management* [3]. For this purpose, we created JonasALaCarte, obtained by re-engineering the JOnAS (Java Open Application Server[1]) open source application server using the Fractal component model [5].

[1] http://jonas.objectweb.org

Thanks to a componentization of the server itself, where all the services are encapsulated into Fractal components, the architecture of the server is explicit. Both the hardware and the software entities are represented by components.

2.2 Deployment in a J2EE Cluster

Building a J2EE cluster consists in replicating the Web and EJB tiers for load balancing and fault tolerance. A front-end load balancer (generally a HTTP server like Apache) dispatches the HTTP requests to the containers. A group communication system allows the consistency between stateful data hosted in the containers to be maintained. In order to deploy a clustered JonasALaCarte, the administrator has to produce an architecture descriptor (written with an ADL) together with a deployment descriptor. The first one defines the architecture of JonasALaCarte as a set of interconnected components and the second one exhibits the resource requirements of each component. The instantiation of this description allows the application server components to be configured and deployed on the target machines in an automated manner. Unlike in current JOnAS clusters, the unit of replication in JonasALaCarte is the service component and not the whole server. This selective replication is important since the EJB containers and the Web containers are generally execution bottlenecks and we need more replicas for these services than for other ones (Registry service, Transaction service, etc).

Figure 1 presents an example of an architecture for a J2EE clustered application server. Notice that we abstract the deployment and the configuration of an application server cluster into the uniform handling of Fractal components. Besides, a cluster configuration is just a particular configuration of the application server where components are distributed and replicated (represented in greyed boxes) on different JVMs. The same management tools are used to manage a stand-alone server in a single JVM and to manage a cluster of servers.

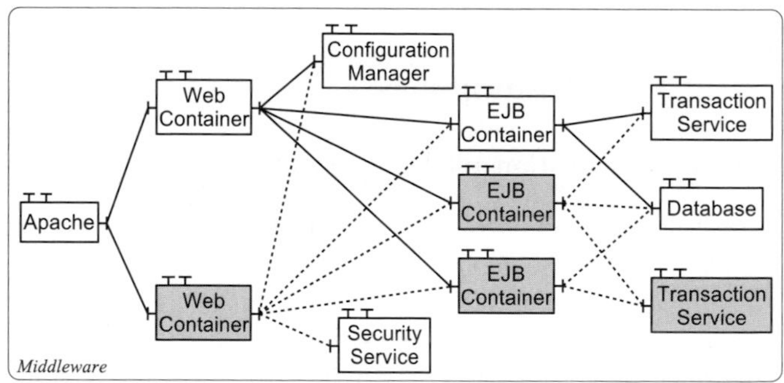

Fig. 1. Component-based view of JonasALaCarte in a cluster environment

2.3 From J2EE Clusters Management to *Virtual Clusters* Management

We call a *virtual cluster* a J2EE system having the same configuration as a classical cluster (a front-end load balancer, a set of replicated containers and a group communication system for stateful data replication) but deployed in a Grid. By defining the number of replicas and the configuration of the services, the virtual cluster can represent different deployment models in wide-area networks. In this paper, we consider that our Grid system is composed of different zones; each zone groups a set of machines geographically close. Moreover, for each zone, some particular machines are well identified and are made public (on a Web site for example). We call *zone managers* these machines because they contribute in the deployment process.

Unlike a J2EE cluster, a Grid environment is highly distributed and are heterogeneous in terms of software and hardware configurations. Resource allocation is consequently a complex task. Grid machines are more dynamic either because they belong to end-users that frequently join and leave the Grid or because they are shared with other dynamic applications. However, if a machine involved in the execution of a multi-tier application leaves the system, a service discontinuity or a performance degradation may be induced leading to disastrous economic consequences. In front of these limitations, we identify the following requirements:

- Resource allocation should be automated. Each component has to explicitly define its required resources and the deployment system has to automatically find the appropriate target machine offering necessary resources for each component.
- Each variation in the Grid machines involved in an application execution has to be systematically detected and recovered. Indeed, in order to maintain the agreed quality of service, the configuration of the J2EE system has to be preserved. If the unavailable component is not replicated, its recovery allows ensuring the service continuity. In some cases, the service continuity is ensured thanks to the replication of the leaving component, like for containers. If the replica is a simple backup, this component needs to be replaced in order to preserve the fault-tolerance degree of the system and if the replica is involved in the load balancing, it also needs to be replaced to preserve the same level of performance.

3 Virtual Cluster Deployment System

In order to deploy a J2EE server system in a network such as the one described in Section 2.3, we cannot rely on a total knowledge of the different machines: this is hardly feasible as the size of a zone is important and as they are heterogeneous. Moreover, some machines—that were disconnected when the deployment was launched—can enter the network. Thus, traditional approaches, consisting in defining a target machine for each component of the application to be deployed, are not feasible in our context. We propose an extension to existing ADLs (xAcme[2], [6]) that allows the description of the resource properties that must be satisfied by a machine for hosting a specific component. In our approach, it is no more mandatory to give an explicit name or address of a target machine: the placement of components is mainly driven by constraints on the resources the target host(s) should satisfy. Then, we use the description of the architecture and the deployment specification to define a deployment of a J2EE system in a zone: installation and redeployment of the component are made in an automatic way.

[2] http://www-2.cs.cmu.edu/ acme/pub/xAcme

In the following we present the general deployment algorithm in two steps. First, we describe the deployment process that allows the parts of the application to be deployed in a propagative way. Then, we present the mechanisms we have implemented to handle failures of the machines and of the different parts of the system.

3.1 Deployment Specification

In order to specify the deployment of a J2EE system, we define two descriptor files written with FractalADL. The *architecture descriptor* contains the architecture of the system in terms of component definitions (their name, their client and server interfaces, their implementation) and component interactions (the bindings between components). The other descriptor, named *deployment descriptor*, contains, for each component, the description of the resources that the target platform must satisfy and references to component instances (defined in the architecture descriptor).

In the deployment descriptor a *deployment context* is defined for each component. Such a context lists all the constraints that a hosting machine has to verify. There are two types of constraints that can be defined in a deployment context: resource constraints and location constraints. Resource constraints allow hardware and software needs to be represented. Each of these constraints defines a domain value for a resource type that the target host(s) should satisfy. With location constraints some control on the placement of a component can be defined when more than one host applies for its hosting.

Figure 2 shows the deployment descriptor associated with the J2EE system represented in Figure 1 (Some repeated parts have been omitted). This descriptor contains the resource constraints associated with every component (e.g. lines 10–17: EJB container ejb1 has to be installed on a host that have at least 512 MB of free memory) and location constraints, that indicate the co-location of some components (e.g. lines 45–47: transaction service component transac1 must reside on the same host as the configuration manager, for example because they share local resources). We can also control the location of a component according to the bandwidth of the network: lines 51–53 specify that the bandwidth between the machines hosting component web1 and the others machines must be greater than 150 Mb/s).

For both performance scalability and high availability, each tier can be replicated. However, we should not require that all replicas be started at the same time. What is usually desired is to activate as soon as possible the Internet application when an EJB container is deployed and a Transaction Service is available. The other replicas, mainly used for performance, can be deployed later as soon as necessary resources become available. For this purpose, we have added a *cardinality* attribute to the description of a component's interface. This attribute takes the form of a couple of values that specify the minimum and the maximum number of bindings allowed through the interface.

3.2 Deployment Process

As stated in section 2.3, dedicated machines—the zone managers—are defined for each zone. A given zone manager has two roles: (1) Maintaining a list of the machines in a zone and (2) orchestrating the deployment process in the zone.

We consider in this section a single manager per zone. The address of this manager is maintained on an already known site. A machine joining a zone gets the zone manager

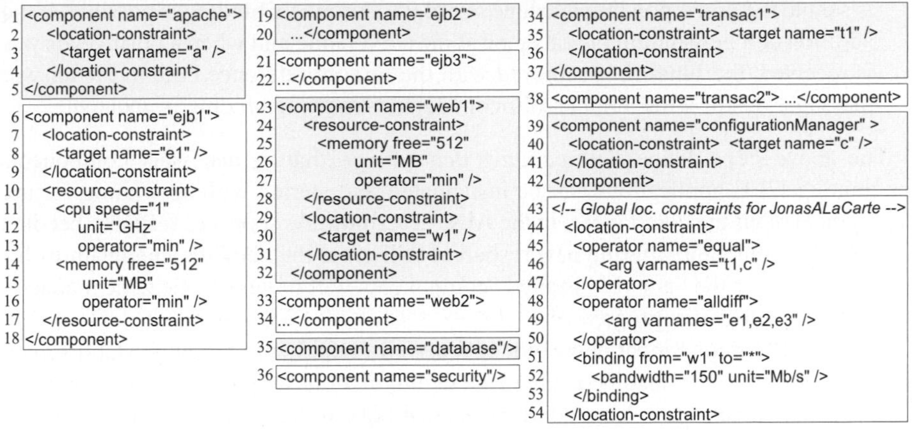

```
<component name="apache">
    <location-constraint>
        <target varname="a" />
    </location-constraint>
</component>

<component name="ejb1">
    <location-constraint>
        <target name="e1" />
    </location-constraint>
    <resource-constraint>
        <cpu speed="1"
            unit="GHz"
            operator="min" />
        <memory free="512"
            unit="MB"
            operator="min" />
    </resource-constraint>
</component>

<component name="ejb2">
    ...</component>

<component name="ejb3">
...</component>

<component name="web1">
    <resource-constraint>
        <memory free="512"
            unit="MB"
            operator="min" />
    </resource-constraint>
    <location-constraint>
        <target name="w1" />
    </location-constraint>
</component>

<component name="web2">
...</component>

<component name="database"/>

<component name="security"/>

<component name="transac1">
    <location-constraint> <target name="t1" />
    </location-constraint>
</component>

<component name="transac2"> ...</component>

<component name="configurationManager" >
    <location-constraint> <target name="c" />
    </location-constraint>
</component>

<!-- Global loc. constraints for JonasALaCarte -->
  <location-constraint>
    <operator name="equal">
        <arg varnames="t1,c" />
    </operator>
    <operator name="alldiff">
        <arg varnames="e1,e2,e3" />
    </operator>
    <binding from="w1" to="*">
        <bandwidth="150" unit="Mb/s" />
    </binding>
  </location-constraint>
```

Fig. 2. Deployment descriptor of JonasALaCarte

address and sends a presence notification message. The zone manager adds the newly connected machine in a list. The case of multiple zone managers, necessary for fault-tolerance, will be detailed in section 3.3.

The first step of the deployment process consists in sending the ADL files of the J2EE system to deploy to the zone manager (whose identity has been obtained beforehand by the administrator, from a given web site for example). As soon as the deployment descriptor is received by the manager, the deployment tasks are performed as follows:

1. The manager multicasts the deployment and architecture descriptors to all the zone nodes that are connected. The deployment descriptor contains resource and location constraints, and the identity of the manager.
2. Having received the deployment and architecture descriptors, each node checks the compatibility of its local resources with the resources required for each component. If it satisfies all the resource constraints associated with a component, it sends to the manager its candidature for the instantiation of this component.
3. The manager receives several candidatures and tries to compute a placement solution in function of the location constraints and the candidatures. In the case there is no location constraint associated with a component, the first candidate is chosen.
4. Once a solution has been found (or if a candidate has been chosen in the previous step), the manager updates the deployment descriptor with the new placement information and broadcasts it to all the zone nodes.
5. Each node that receives the new deployment descriptor updates its own one and is thus informed of which component it is authorized to instantiate and of the new location of the other components.
6. The final step consists in downloading necessary packages from well defined package repositories. The location of these repositories is defined in the deployment descriptor (not shown in the example for sake of clarity). For the components that are instantiated locally, their client interfaces (if any) must be bound to remote components. When the remote component possesses a constrained cardinality, a request

is sent to the corresponding machine in order to know if a binding is possible. If the addition of a new binding is accepted at the server side and when a positive answer is received, the binding is achieved with the remote reference hold in the answer message. Besides, the number of incoming and outgoing binding is updated.

The above steps define a *propagative deployment*, that is, necessary components for running J2EE applications can be instantiated and started without waiting for the deployment of all the components in the ADL descriptor. As soon as a resource become available or a machine offering new resources will enter the network, candidatures for the installation of the "not yet installed" components will be sent to the zone manager, making the deployment progress.

When a new deployment descriptor is received (step 5) the binding establishment described at step 6 can also be made if the deployment descriptor contains new information on the location of some components that have to be bound with some already (locally) deployed components.

Let's consider an example of resource constraint. The constraint alldiff in the deployment descriptor (lines 48–49) indicates that the three EJBContainer must reside on three distinct hosts. In order to resolve this constraint, a machine must at least have the information of three machines that can hosts each one an EJBContainer. Thus, by collecting candidatures (step 3), the zone manager may decide on the placement of component provided there exists a combination of candidatures that solves the location constraints.

We can notice that in this deployment process: (1) the host selection of a component is made by the zone manager; (2) the instantiation of a component is achieved by the host selected by the zone manager; (3) the bindings needed by a component are initiated by the machine hosting it; (4) the activation of a component can be made as soon as its client interfaces are bound. Note that in our case, the activation of the container components (i.e. EJB and Web containers) involves the activation of the J2EE application running inside.

3.3 Automatic Recovery from Failures

In the environment we target, resources can also become unavailable (e.g. the amount of free memory demanded may decrease and become not sufficient), some parts of the J2EE system can be faulty, some machine may fail etc. In this paper, a failure can be due to a hardware crash of a machine, a disconnection from the network or a software bottleneck. This last case constitutes a failure of a component.

Failure of a component. The recovery of a component and thus its redeployment consists in sending to the zone manager a message holding the identity of the component to redeploy. This is done by the machine hosting the faulty component (The failure, i.e. the non-responsiveness of the component, is detected through a probe associated with a control interface of the component.). Then, the zone manager updates the deployment descriptor by removing the location of the component and broadcasts the new descriptor to all the machines connected in the zone, automating the redeployment of the faulty component. Indeed, for all the machines, a component remains undeployed (i.e. it has no location), thus, they find themselves back in the propagative deployment.

The phases of local evaluation of the resource constraints and the announcement of candidatures will go along.

When a component fails, it is important to consider its state. If the component is replicated, like the EJB container and the Web container services, the stateful data are automatically sent to any replica added to the group. This ensured by the group communication systems embedded within these components. Regarding the database, we consider that a regular copy is done on a data-center allowing to obtain stateful data when the database fails. This solution is frequently used in Internet applications deployed in wide-area networks, like in the edge-computing models.

When Apache fails, all the incoming requests are lost during the reconfiguration time. One solution consists in deploying a lightweight component storing the incoming requests in a list during the time the Apache component is recovering.

Resource violation. When a resource constraint associated with a component is no longer verified on a specific host (for example the amount of free memory required is not sufficient), the corresponding component must be redeployed. This redeployment is performed the same way, except that the state of the component can be saved properly.

Failure of a machine other than a zone manager. In a zone, a machine hosting one or several components may definitively crash. A crash is detected by the zone manager which maintains the list of the machine connected in the zone. When the manager detects a crash, as in the case of the failure of a component, it updates its deployment descriptor by removing the location of the component(s) that was running on the faulty machine. Then, the deployment descriptor is broadcast to other machines so that the missing components can eventually be re-instantiated.

Failure of a zone manager. The crash of the zone manager is critical as it is responsible for choosing a host for each component. In order to deal with the failure of such a manager, we define several managers within a zone. Every manager has the same role as defined previously: it maintains the list of the machines that are connected in the zone; it collects the candidatures for the instantiation of components; and it resolves the location constraints depending on the received candidatures. To ensure the fault-tolerance of the zone manager, we consider a number of replicas. At a given time, a *leader* is in charge of establishing the deployment process. The address of the zone manager is mentioned in the deployment descriptor sent to the machines of the zone. Each information received by the leader is multicast to the backup managers using a group communication system offering the FIFO order and reliability. The failure of the leader is detected by the backup machines and a new leader is elected. The zone manager identity is updated in the deployment descriptor and like any descriptor change, this piece of information is sent to the machines of the zone that will then deal with the new leader.

4 Implementation Status and Evaluation

4.1 Implementation Status

The ADL presented in section 3.1 allows the specification of the placement of the components according to some conditions on resource and location constraints. We have chosen FractalADL to support the definition of deployment descriptors in an XML format. The main aspect with resource and location constraints are their manipulation at run time in order to observe and detect changes in the environment, to react on these changes and to find a placement solution at a given time according to some machine candidatures. We use Cream[3], a Java library for writing and solving constraint satisfaction problems or optimization problems, to represent interface cardinality, possible bindings and resource and location constraints.

Specific probes are used in order to introspect the resources needed by the components. We use DRAJE (Distributed Resource-Aware Java Environment) [7], an extensible Java-based middleware to model hardware resources (processor, memory, network interface...) or software resources (process, socket, thread...). For every resource constraint of the deployment descriptor, a resource in DRAJE is created and a periodic observation is launched. The value returned by a probe allows a host to check the consistency of a resource constraint according to the local resource state. If all the resource constraints associated with a component are verified by a machine, it applies for its instantiation. When the value returned by a probe does not respect a resource constraint, our run-time support is notified in order to redeploy the components that requires this resource as described in section 3.3. The current implementation of our system does not support the computation of bandwidths between machines but relies on a predefined file describing the properties of network links within a zone.

Component instantiation are made by a host when this host has been chosen by the zone manager. When an updated deployment descriptor is received, the location of the newly instantiated components is discovered, resulting in binding requests. When a binding is accepted, a stub component and a skeleton component are dynamically created thanks to the ASM library[4] and are deployed with FractalRMI. The server interfaces of the stub component are of the same type as the one of the local client interface that has to be bound. When the location of the EJBContainer is known, a new pair stub/skeleton is created and deployed if the number of outgoing bindings allowed (i.e. the interface cardinality) has not been reached.

4.2 Evaluation

A complete evaluation of the deployment and redeployment in the kind of environment we target implies to precisely control the dynamism of the different resources and hosts. We have indeed to take into account the announcement of machines' candidatures—which implies the availability of resources—in order to compute a placement solution. However the feasibility and the performance of the deployment process and recovery mechanisms can be measured accurately when all the resources are available. In this case we can evaluate the time needed by a zone manager to compute a placement solution for the components of a virtual cluster.

Figure 3 shows the time for a zone manager to compute a placement solution when the number of received candidatures is sufficient, in function of the number of components to instantiate. We have considered a zone composed of a thousand of simulated

[3] http://kurt.scitec.kobe-u.ac.jp/~shuji/cream/

[4] http://asm.objectweb.org

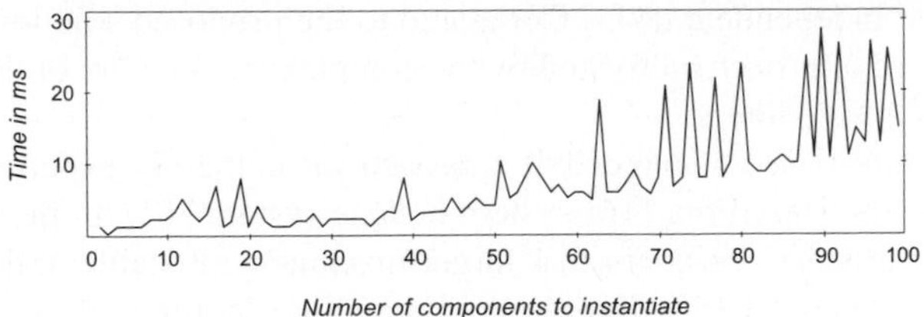

Fig. 3. Time required for a zone manager to decide on the placement of a set of components in function of the number of candidatures

machines on which the number of components to instantiate varies from one to one hundred. The experiment corresponds to the deployment of the architecture of Figure 1 according to the constraint "each component must reside on a distinct host" (alldiff constraint). Somewhat contrived, this constraint encompasses the complexity of other constraints involved in our deployment specification (resource constraints resolution has a negligible impact on the computation time). The evaluation has been conducted on a laptop (1,7 GHz Pentium Centrino). This experiment allowed us to verify that the time to compute—with the Cream library—a placement solution (when all conditions are met) remains acceptable regarding communication cost between machines. This computation time is likely not to be the prevalent factor in number of Grids configurations. We are currently conducting the evaluation of the deployment of a virtual cluster and the automatic management of failures on a Grid. The main difficult aspect remains the control of hosts and resources availability.

5 Related Work

Our work is related to several different open-source and research domains. We single out the following ones: component-based deployment in Grid environments, multi-tier deployment in wide-area networks, resource allocation for distributed systems and architecture-based systems.

We share with GridCCM [8], GridKit [9] and Proactive [10] the same approach consisting in abstracting the system to deploy on the grids to an assembly of components. Proactive work is closer to ours since it considers Fractal component model to represent hierarchical and parallel systems. However, our work covers both the resource management issues and the automatization of recovery from failures.

Exploiting the Grid resources to increase multi-tier application performance and fault-tolerance become recently the aim of many research teams [2,1,11]. However, focus is more on defining the best configuration and models to increase performance rather than on the management aspects.

Many works deal with resource allocation in distributed systems [12,13,14,15]. In our work, we propose a simple solution for resource allocation and we believe that, thanks to our modular component-model, we can easily adopt different policies and algorithms for an optimal resource usage. Furthermore, to our knowledge, most of the works on the Grids like PlanetLab and Globus, focus on parallel applications that are composed of independent tasks. Compared to the proposed solutions, we adopt an architecture-based approach motivated by the complex architecture of the multi-tier Internet application we address.

The architecture-based management approach [3] is mainly experimented in close environment like in SmartFrog [16] system or Jade system [17]. In these two systems, the deployment process considers that target machines are stable and homogeneous, which is not the case in Grids. Furthermore, handling failures relies on a centralized management unit, which hardly applies to the highly distributed Grid machines. In our solution, the machines collaborate in finding appropriate resources and for handling failures.

6 Conclusion

This paper proposes a solution for the deployment of enterprise systems in Grids and an automatic recovery management in face of failures. Deployment in such environment is quite challenging as the platforms we target are highly distributed, heterogeneous and dynamic. We offer a resource-aware deployment feature for J2EE systems, which is essential in Grid heterogeneous environments. We also demonstrate that the constraint-resolution is performed in a reasonable time. The role of the administrator is reduced to the writing of the deployment descriptor. All the deployment process and the recovery from failures are automated. Furthermore, the administrator does not need to be expert of the heterogeneous and complex J2EE systems. All the parts of the system are abstracted into Fractal components and the configuration is therefore unified. In our work, we aimed at maintaining the structure described in the ADL descriptor by replacing each time a faulty component by another. This allows ensuring the continuity of Internet services and maintaining their quality of service.

In this paper we adopted a special architecture of the J2EE system, the virtual clusters. We believe that our solution and mechanisms are applicable to other architectures. It is only necessary to write appropriate deployment descriptors and constraints. We are currently investigating a more complete evaluation of our approach on a Grid by taking into account resources and hosts availability. Moreover, some optimization can be defined when dealing with the placement decision of replicas by considering the symmetry of such components.

References

1. Rabinovich, M., Spatscheck, O.: Web Caching and Replication. Addison Wesley, Reading, Massachusetts, USA (2002)
2. Pierre, G., van Steen, M.: Globule: a Collaborative Content Delivery Network. IEEE Communications Magazine **44** (2006)
3. Dashofy, E., van der Hoek, A., Taylor, R.: Towards Architecture-Based Self-Healing Systems. In: Workshop on Self-Healing Systems, Charleston, South Carolina, USA (2002)
4. Abdellatif, T., Kornaś, J., Stefani, J.B.: J2EE Packaging, Deployment and Reconfiguration Using a General Component Model. In: Int. Working Conference on Component Deployment, Grenoble, France (2005)

5. Bruneton, E., Coupaye, T., Leclercq, M., Quéma, V., Stefani, J.B.: An Open Component Model and its Support in Java. In: Int. Symposium on Component-based Software Engineering, Edinburgh, Scotland (2004)
6. Dashofy, E., van der Hoek, A., Taylor, R.: An Infrastructure for the Rapid Development of xml-based Architecture Description Languages. In: Int. Conference on Software Engineering, Orlando, Florida, USA (2002)
7. Mahéo, Y., Guidec, F., Courtrai, L.: A Java Middleware Platform for Resource-Aware Distributed Applications. In: Int. Symposium on Parallel and Distributed Computing, Ljubljana, Slovenia (2003)
8. Denis, A., Pérez, C., Priol, T., Ribes, A.: Padico: A Component-Based Software Infrastructure for Grid Computing. In: Int. Parallel and Distributed Processing Symposium, Nice, France (2003)
9. Cai, W., Coulson, G., Grace, P., Blair, G.A., Mathy, L., Yeung, W.K.: The Gridkit Distributed Resource Management Framework. In: European Grid Conference, Amsterdam, The Netherlands (2005)
10. Baude, F., Caromel, D., Morel, M.: From Distributed Objects to Hierarchical Grid Components. In: Int. Symposium on Distributed Objects and Applications, Catania, Italy (2003)
11. Sivasubamanian, S., Alonso, G., Pierre, G., van Steen, M.: GlobeDB: Autonomic Data Replication for Web Applications. In: Int. World-Wide Web Conference, Chiba, Japan (2005)
12. Aron, M., Druschel, P., Zwaenepoel, W.: Cluster reserves: a mechanism for resource management in cluster-based network servers. In: Conference on Measurement and Modeling of Computer Systems, Santa Clara, California, USA (2000)
13. Appleby, K., Fakhouri, S., Fong, L., Goldszmidt, G., Kalantar, M., Krishnakumar, S., Pazel, D., Pershing, J., Rochwerger, B.: Oceano - SLA based management of a computing utility. In: Int. Symposium on Integrated Network Management, Seattle, Washington, USA (2001)
14. Fu, Y., Chase, J., Chun, B., Schwab, S., Vahdat, A.: SHARP: an architecture for secure resource peering. In: Symposium on Operating Systems Principles, Bolton Landing, New York, USA (2003)
15. Chase, J., Irwin, D., Grit, L., Moore, J., Sprenkle, S.: Dynamic Virtual Clusters in a Grid Site Manager. In: Int. Symposium on High Performance Distributed Computing, Seattle, Washington, USA (2003)
16. Goldsack, P., Guijarro, J., Lain, A., Mecheneau, G., Murray, P., Toft, P.: SmartFrog: Configuration and Automatic Ignition of Distributed Applications. In: Plenary Workshop of the HP OpenView University Association, Geneva, Switzerland (2003)
17. Bouchenak, S., Boyer, F., Hagimont, D., Krakowiak, S., Mos, A., de Palma, N., Quéma, V., Stefani, J.B.: Architecture-Based Autonomous Repair Management: An Application to J2EE Clusters. In: Symposium on Reliable Distributed Systems, Orlando, Florida, USA (2005)

Dynamic Workload Balancing for Collaboration Strategy in Hybrid P2P System

[1]Suhong Min, [2]Byong Lee, and [1]Dongsub Cho

[1] Department of Computer Science and Engineering,
Ewha Womans University, Seoul, Korea
[2] Department of Computer Science,
Seoul Women's University, Seoul, Korea
shmin@ewhain.net, byongl@swu.ac.kr, dscho@ewha.ac.kr

Abstract. The peer-to-peer (P2P) systems have grown significantly over the last few years due to their high potential of sharing various resources. Analyzing the workload of P2P system, however, is very challenging as it involves with the cooperation of many peers. Researches have shown that P2P systems become very effective when dividing the peers into two layers, SP (Super-Peer) and OP (Ordinary-Peer). In this configuration, SP based P2P systems have to deal with a large volume of queries from OPs. Therefore, it is important for SPs to keep their workload stable to provide quality service to the OPs. In this study, we present a collaboration strategy for workload balancing based on SP's workload characteristics and status. Through the SP's load balancing mechanism, the message response time is decreased and the workload of P2P system becomes more stable.

Keywords: Peer-to-Peer (P2P), Super-Peer, workload balancing, collaboration strategy.

1 Introduction

For the last few years, there has been a large volume of research on Peer-to-Peer (P2P) system, resulting in many hybrid P2P models. Many researches have shown that P2P systems become very effective, especially in query processing, when dividing the peers into two layers, SP (Super-Peer) and OP (Ordinary-Peer). With this layer separation, SP deals with all the queries from OPs so that OPs can be waived from the burden of query processing [1, 2]. Compared with the pure P2P systems, SP based P2P systems have to deal with a large volume of queries from OPs. In this case, it is important for SPs to keep their workload stable to provide quality service to the OPs. Workload analysis, however, is very challenging as it involves many cooperative peers. Current SP based P2P systems have paid little attention to balancing the SP's workload. The existing research only focuses on sharing the resources or objects among peers to minimize the workload. For example, they can replicate an object based on the access probability to the neighbor peers or can migrate the object between peers for load balancing. In this scheme, load balancing is aimed at reducing the workload of OP. SP then checks the peer's load information in

C. Cérin and K.-C. Li (Eds.): GPC 2007, LNCS 4459, pp. 374–384, 2007.

their group to determine whether it is overload or not. If it is overloaded, SP helps them to minimize their workload by means of replication or migration [10].

In this paper, we investigate the problem of SP's workload balancing and propose an enhanced mechanism to distribute SP's workload by its characteristics and status. Workload balancing is performed only through the peer collaboration based on this information. We suggest the three approaches: First, we analyze SP's workload characteristic categorizing it into a private workload and a public workload. The private workload is defined as the traffic overhead incurred by the use of application objects such as word process, on-line game, or Internet usage. The public workload is defined as the traffic overhead in maintaining P2P system. Second, we evaluate SP's workload status by different load levels. Each load level is determined by pre-specified threshold. Third, we propose the collaboration policy between SPs in accordance with load characteristics and load status. An overloaded SP can give some of its work to a neighbor SP or even remove himself from the P2P system by refusing to be an SP. By considering the private and the public workload separately, workload balancing becomes more accurate and efficient. Also SP's message response time is improved by applying collaboration policy according to each different workload level.

The rest of the paper is organized as follows: Section 2 reviews some related works briefly. Section 3 states the workload management which evaluates the workload status based on the predefined definition. It also proposes the collaboration policy; Section 4 shows the simulation results of the proposed mechanism; finally, the conclusion and the future work are added in Section 5.

2 Related Works

In this section, we describe existing techniques for load balancing in P2P system. Load balancing can be achieved by transferring popular objects from heavily loaded peers to lightly loaded peers via data replication and data migration [10].

A number of replication approaches are discussed in [12]. In [12], data objects are replicated along the search path that is traversed as part of the search in path replication. Data objects are replicated a pre-defined number of times to control the spread of replica. This method, however, does not adapt to the changes of system environment and variable resource availability. Edith Cohen [11] shows that replicating objects proportionally to their popularity achieves optimal load balance, while replicating them proportionally to the square root of their popularity minimizes the average search latency. Pure P2P systems use the replication strategies to reduce the search latency and find objects in a short distance between peers.

For the replication strategies, Gopalakrishnan [14] proposes each SP distributes load by its capacity and queue length. To achieve this, the author assumes that each SP defines a high-load and low-load threshold. So if a SP is overloaded, it attempts to create new replicas on its neighboring SP. We consider more detailed factors in capacity and have several collaboration options not just replication of files. On the other hand, Rajasekhar [13] replicates the most frequently accessed data files based on the access probabilities and uses restricted gossip algorithm to propagate the file location to its neighboring SPs within its scope. In this approach, the author uses two techniques such as, periodic push-based replication and on demand replication when they update their replication information.

The object migration can occur when a popular object is transferred from its original peer to a destination peer. Mondal [10], however, indicates that migration makes data availability decrease as the peers which have accepted the object may leave the system.

In this paper, we propose a collaboration strategy which can provide the load status information of SP based on the characteristics of workload. Proposed collaboration policy is further adapted into the workload balancing through the proposed dynamic workload analysis.

3 Dynamic Workload Management

In this section, we manage SP's workload dynamically by its load status for workload balance. We first discuss the importance of maintaining an appropriate workload of SP. We then propose a SP workload status evaluation and workload status classification by SP's workload character. Finally, in order to provide a stable SP workload and efficient message handling, we consider the collaboration strategy to distribute workload between SPs.

3.1 Importance of SP Workload

In a super peer based P2P system, searches are mainly performed by SPs, which actually forms the "backbone" of the P2P network [8]. SP based P2P systems take advantage of peer's heterogeneity by dividing peers into two layers: SP and OP, thereby scaling better by reducing the number of query paths. This model, both SP and OP can submit queries, but only SP can relay queries and response. After receiving a query, a SP first checks to see if it is stored locally or in its OPs. If some results are found in SP's group, it sends them to the requested OP.

Comparing with pure P2P models, SP based P2P models such as KaZaA and Gnutella [3, 4] have higher search efficiency because, instead of all the OPs, only SPs are involved in search processes. Therefore, SP's capacity has considerable influence on message handling of OPs and the performance of the entire network. Consequently, it is a very important factor for SP to control adequate workload according to its dynamic workload status. The question is: How does the SP keep its own workload stable to improve the performance of P2P network? How does the SPs increase QueryHit rate so that they help OPs by processing the query messages in a shorter response time?

The problems with SPs providing their stable capacity and fast response time are as follows: First, SP is probably not the server for client OPs in a traditional client/server architectures. Most of SPs participating in a P2P system are general computer systems with general operating systems such as Window XP or Mac OS. Comparing with the server, users classified as SP have difficulty supplying an accurate stable workload because they should work as SP in P2P system while they are doing their own private jobs like word processor, e-mail, and Internet surfing, etc, at the same time. Therefore, SP's workload should consider both user's private workload and public workload. As a result, we should be able to analyze workload characteristics by each workload status. Second, we should provide an adequate collaboration policy to distribute SP's workload by each load level.

3.2 Workload Value Evaluation

In this section, we evaluate system's workload characteristics. The conventional load balancing strategies in P2P systems focus on sharing objects between peers. They replicate popular peer's objects based on their access probability to neighbor peers. Our workload value evaluation is different from the existing schemes in that we analyze SP's workload characteristics to perform workload balancing. We assume that SP's system environment is not a server and it just operates on user's operating system. Thus, a user could work as a SP in the P2P system while doing his own private jobs at the same time. We assume that SP's workload is affected by both its public workload due to P2P system and its private workload.

To evaluate total workload of SP in P2P system, we calculate the private workload and the public workload using formula (1). We obtained this formula through experiments on incurred load by each workload characteristic in section 4. First, in case of public workload by P2P system, SP's workloads are caused by requested message processing time from SP's group peers and cooperating neighbor SPs. In public workload, CPU load value is not crucially affected by the entire P2P system performance. The reason is that when a large number of messages for the SP arrive, some are dropped because the queue length in the network channel is limited. Thus, they are never received by the CPU and the CPU load is increased just a little bit or decreased. Hence, we consider public workload as network load by P2P system usage using formula (2).

On the other hand, private workload is calculated by the number of tasks in the CPU queue length and network queue length in formula (3).

$$SP_{tw} = C_{pri\_w} + C_{pub\_w} \tag{1}$$

$$C_{pub\_w} = NWP \tag{2}$$

$$C_{pri\_w} = CWP + NWP \tag{3}$$

CWP (CPU workload Processing time) is defined as the average time needed to perform a task in CPU queue length in formula (4). TP is the number of total processes. NWP (Network Workload Processing time) is defined by public workload and private workload in formula (5). In case of public workload, NWP is the average message processing time needed to search peer's requested files and connection request to SP to join in formula. In case of private workload, it is defined as the average task processing time needed to perform user's Internet tasks. Therefore, we should classify the net workload into private load and public load. To distinguish between the two workloads, we set identifier to 0 or 1 using a binary digit. If network traffic is incurred by the private workload, pi=0, otherwise pi=1.

$$CWP = \frac{1}{TP}\sum_{k \in x}(Task \times t) \tag{4}$$

$$NWP = \frac{1}{TM}\sum_{i \in x}(Mc_i * t) \tag{5}$$

$$(where,\ x = \{i|pi = 0\ or\ 1,\ for\ 0<i \leq n\})$$

3.3 Workload Status Classification

SP estimates its workload status by a number of tasks in the CPU queue length and Network channel. We classify each workload into two kinds of type such as a stable and an unstable type by given threshold [7]. Finally, we use a 4-level scheme to represent the each load type on its CPU and Network of queue length.

First of all, we show a stable type that includes an "underload" and a "normal level". Underload, level-1, is a lower bound of threshold and it is possible to process message without delay at CPU and Network when OPs request query processing to SPs. In normal status, level-2, is working harder but still able to process messages normally. Second, we show an unstable type that it classifies the load status into "potential overload" status and "overload" status. Potential overload status, level-3, is current normal status but it is expected to increase the workload of system by user's private workload or public workload. Hence, user's system status is possible to be overloaded status in the near future. In this paper the potential overload status will be a standard to decide a performance type is either stable or unstable. To measure this value, we apply EMA (Exponential Moving Average) algorithm. EMA is a time series which gives more weight to more recent measurements than to other historical data. Potential Overload status is calculated using the previous queue length value and current queue length value [5, 6]. Through this process, we can expect the status of system and we can control the workload of P2P system using proposed collaboration policy before it becomes overloaded status. Finally, the overload status, level-4, is defined when the measured workload exceeds the threshold of upper-bound. A SP stops OP's message processing and connection requests of new OPs. In this state, the SP temporarily seems to leave the P2P system.

Table 1. Load level classification by load status

Type	Status	Level	Criteria
Stable	Underload	Level-1	$SP_{low} \leq QL$
	Normal	Level-2	$SP_{low} \leq QL < SP_{ema}$
Unstable	Potential Overload	Level-3	$SP_{ema} \leq QL < SP_{high}$
	Overload	Level-4	$SP_{high} \leq QL$

3.4 Collaboration Policy

In this section, we propose the collaboration policy to distribute workload of SP. The aim of collaboration is that we select appropriate SP by considering load status and its resulting workload characteristics. In this approach, each SP periodically checks its workload status. When SPs detect a load imbalance we perform the collaboration policy which is shown in table 2. First, we analyze SP's workload status of the private workload and the public workload, and decide on its load level. According to each load level, we divide it into 4 different cases. Second, we evaluate each workload status to determine whether SP's workload is stable or unstable. If workload status is unstable, we distribute load using the collaboration policy for load balancing. In this paper, collaboration policy is initiated when SP detects that its workload is level-3 shown in table 2.

In case 1, a SP detects its private workload is level-3 and public workload is stable type. We define that SP's workload could be potentially increased by its private workload such as CWP and NWP. In this case, the SP initiates the collaboration policy. SP replicates the most frequently accessed objects based on the access probabilities to SP's neighbor SPs. To create new replicas, first, the SP should check the load status of neighbors whether they have good capacity and stable workload status such as level 1 or level 2. If possible, the SP asks them to create replicas of the most highly loaded files on SP. If neighbor SPs admit replicas, the SP sends replicas to them. In this case, the SP can still deal with OP's query processing but the SP rejects new OP's connection request to prevent increase of current workload.

In case 2, a SP detects that its private workload is level-4 and public workload is stable type. We define SP's private workload is overloaded. A user is working the large number of private jobs though the user works as a SP in P2P system. So the SP can not deal well with message processing for OPs in group. In this case, the SP stops peer's message processing and new OP's connection request. First, the SP should select neighbor SP to handle queries from own OPs instead of himself or herself. To select new SP for OPs, the SP checks the load status of own neighbors, and selects a SP who has the lowest load. Second, as soon as choosing a neighbor, the SP sends OP's information such as peer's name, type, its object lists to selected SP. Lastly, the SP advertises OPs to be selected new SP and then OPs request query processing to a new SP instead of original SP. This means the existing SP temporarily secedes from P2P system.

In case 3, a SP identifies that its public workload is level-3 and private workload is stable. We define SP's public workload could be potentially increased by its public workload such as the increase of group size, the number of message and QueryHit rate etc. Through the experiment (Fig.2), we found the performance of public workload is largely affected by QueryHit rate. If SP's QueryHit rate is low, SP should broadcast the large number of messages to neighbor SPs to search requested objects from OPs, which, in result, SP's message response time is increased. Hence, a SP requests its neighbor SPs to share popular object's lists. The SP request neighbor SP's object list with the most frequently access rate or query hit rate. In this case, instead of receiving objects, the SP obtains neighbor object lists which contain object's owner, owner's physical address, object name, size, and type. Through this procedure, SP will able to respond OP's queries fast and efficiently through preempting object lists with high query hit rate although the SP does not include object lists in own group OPs. Also the SP still admits the connection request from new OP and adds it to SP's object list and continually performs query processing of the existing OPs.

In case 4, a SP perceives that its public workload is level-4, overload and private workload is stable. In this case, it is defined when a SP has a big group size of OPs that request queries very frequent to the SP. Thus, this case is defined that the ratio of the number of Ops to the number of SPs, is not appropriate so that more SPs are needed in the network. First, the SP selects the most eligible OP to encourage new SP that has good capacity and good load status at the same time. Second, the SP divides

Table 2. Collaboration Policy by four different Cases

Case	Cpri_w	Cpub_w	Collaboration Criteria
Case 1	Level-3	stable	Replication
Case 2	Level-4	stable	Re-selection
Case 3	Stable	Level-3	Pre-emption
Case 4	Stable	Level-4	Re-distribution

own OP lists with new selected SP. The SP processes remained OP's queries but rejects new connection request until its load status is stable. However it is not easy to meet Case 2 and Case 4. Proposed scheme predicts the potential workload status at Level-3 and perform SP'S workload balancing before we meet the worst case. In case both private and public workloads are unstable, we won't consider it here because we've already seen in Case 2 that the user will potentially stop P2P system.

4 Experimental Evaluations

In this section, we present the simulation model used to evaluate the characteristics of workload and proposed collaboration policy and discuss the simulation results. The simulation model is implemented in C++ using CSIM [9]. It consists of a number of OPs and SPs. Every SP is assigned with different capacity to be sufficiently heterogeneous when a SP is created. During simulation, OPs join and leave the network following a Poisson process with an arrival rate of λ and departure rate of μ . Table 3 summarizes the parameters used for the simulation and their default values.

Table 3. Default Parameter Settings

Parameters	Default Values
SIMTIME	5000
The number of OP	10 ~ 300
The number of SP	10 ~ 50
CPU power factor	{1.0,1.5,2.0,2.5,3.0}
The number of query frequency	10
The number of objects	20
The delay per hop	100ms
The range of QueryHit rate	10~100%

In our simulation, we tried to verify that our proposed SP's workload balancing strategy can improve SP's message response time by evaluating its workload characteristics. First, we experiment with P2P system performance as SP's group size increases. To do this, we assume the performance of system as follows. A user does

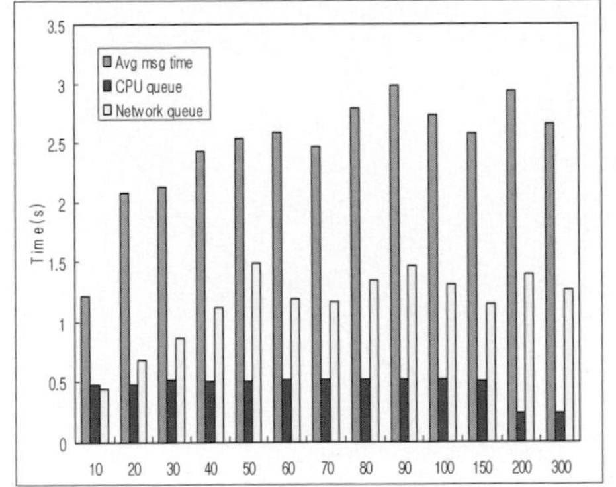

Fig. 1. Response Time vs. The number of Peers

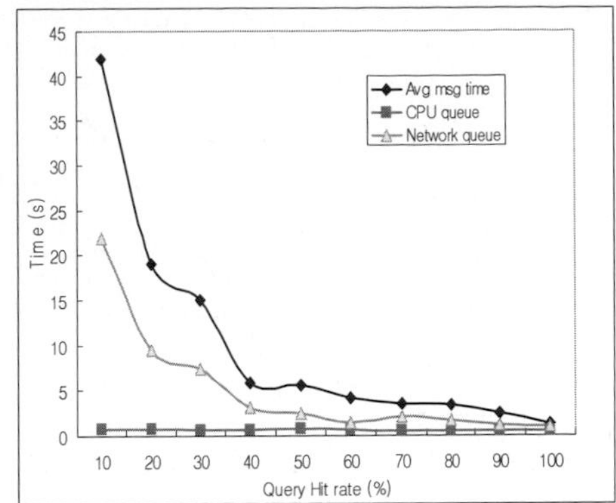

Fig. 2. QueryHit rate vs. Response time

not work its private job and just operates SP on P2P system. OPs send messages at the same frequency to SPs to connect to a SP and request queries. Then SP's QueryHit rate is 100%. At this status, we estimate 1) the average message response time, 2) message processing time in network queue length, and 3) CPU processing time in CPU queue length as SP's group size varies. In Fig. 1, we found that all of them are not largely affected as the number of message is increased.

Second, we experiment with the public workload performance as SP's QueryHit rate changes. We set the group size of SP to 10 and each OP requests queries at the same frequency. Fig. 2 shows the message response time is largely decreased as QueryHit rate increases. When QueryHit rate is low, message response time and message processing time in network queue length varies significantly. But, the CPU processing time barely changes. The reason is that the large number of message in network queue is dropped before it arrives at CPU queue length. Therefore, we consider the network queue length and QueryHit rate as threshold except the CPU processing time when we evaluate the public workload.

Third, based on private workload, we examine the change of message response time influenced by CPU queue length and network queue length. Fig. 3 shows the average message response time as CPU queue length varies. To do this experiment, we set the group size of SP to 10 to minimize the effect due to the public workload. User dose not perform private network jobs, instead, just operates off-line tasks. In Fig. 3, we compare the performance of average message response time as CPU queue length changes through increasing SP's private works, the number of tasks. In this experiment, we show that message response time is highly increased by CPU queue length. Fig. 4 examines message response time as private network queue length changes. We don't operate the private CPU jobs and set the group size of SP to 10. In Fig. 4, it shows user's network jobs affected message processing time. Thus, we found that SP's private workload changes the performance of message handling capacity in P2P system.

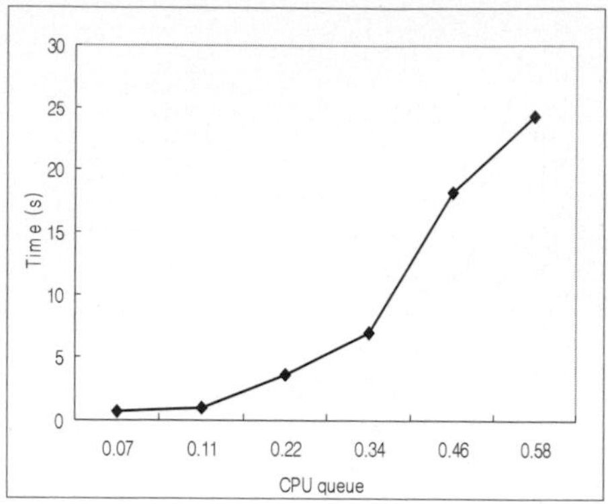

Fig. 3. Response time vs. CPU queue length

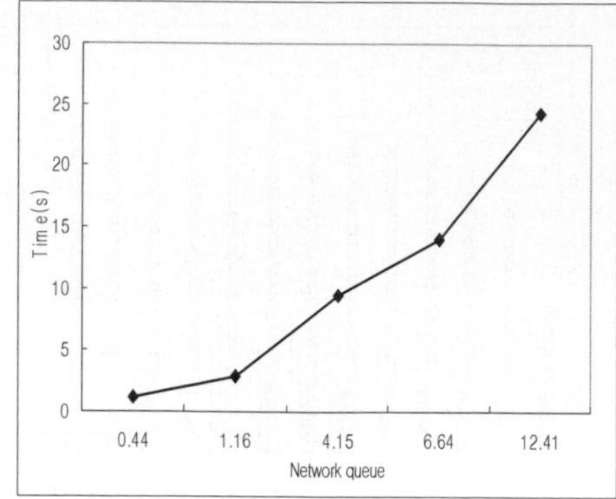

Fig. 4. Response time vs. Network queue length

Fourth, based on level of load status, we estimate the range of threshold and message response time by each four different level. In Fig. 5, we approximately evaluated the threshold of CWP and NWP values of the private workload and NWP of public workload at each different level. Fig. 5 shows the different threshold values for each workload characteristic at four different levels. Fig. 6 shows each private workload and public workload has similar message response time when they are included in the same level. Thus, we found that they can handle messages with similar capacity at same level though each workload characteristic has different threshold.

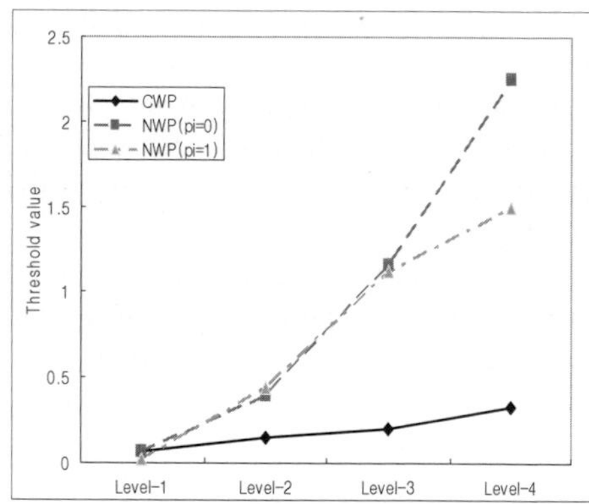

Fig. 5. Threshold values at each level

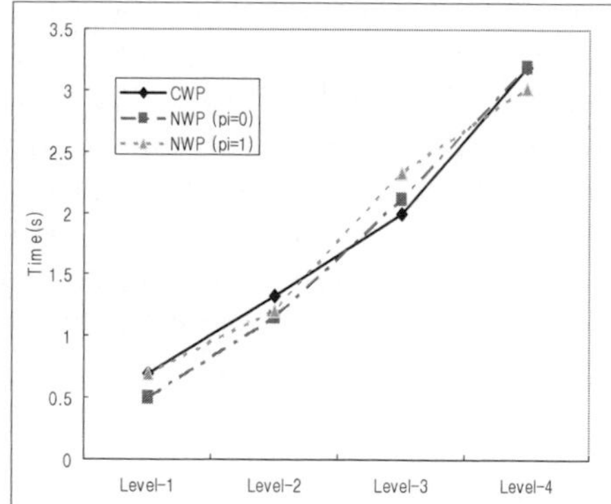

Fig. 6. Response times at each level

Finally, we experiment if SP can stably keep workload balance and improve message response time. In Fig. 7, we compare the performance of proposed collaboration policy with no-load-balancing scheme. This experiment environment is shown in Table 4.

Table 4. Parameter Settings

Parameters	Default Values
SIMTIME	5000
# of OP	10 ~ 100
# of SP	10
CPU power	{1.0,1.5,2.0,2.5,3.0}
# of query frequency	10
# of objects	30
QueryHit rate	60%
CWP value	15%
NWP value (pi=0)	15%
NWP value (pi=1)	70%

Fig 7 shows the message response time as SP's group size increases. Comparing with no load balancing scheme, it is clear that proposed collaboration policy significantly improve message response time and keep SP's workload status stable. We demonstrate the effectiveness of proposed scheme which can show good performance with considering public workload and private workload at the same time and adequate collaboration policy for each workload status.

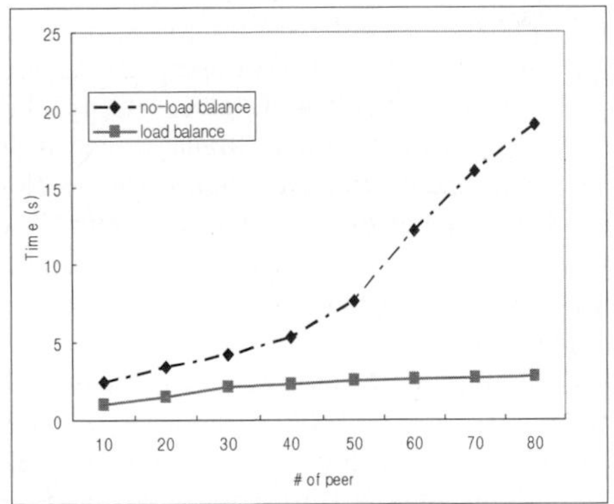

Fig. 7. Response time vs. SP's group size

5 Conclusion

We presented the collaboration policy for analyzing SP's workload characteristics and evaluating each workload status to perform workload balancing. In the Super-Peer based P2P systems, SPs should handle all queries received from OPs. As a result, the control of SP's workload has considerably influenced on the performance of P2P network. The existing systems performed the workload balancing with replication strategies to distribute popular objects between peers. They, however, have paid little attention to the SP's workload balancing from the view point of the workload status characteristics. Proposed paper presents a collaboration strategy based on SP's workload characteristics. We demonstrated the performance of the proposed scheme using a number of simulations. In our experiments, we show that each workload characteristics and status can have a big effect on message handling capacity of SP. Also through the proposed collaboration policy, we can not only improve the performance of message response time, but also keep the status of SP system stable. We plan to implement additional collaboration policies features in the future work.

References

1. B. Yang, H. Garcia-Molina, "Designing a super-peer network", IEEE International Conference on Data Engineering, Bangalore, India, March 2003.
2. Y. Chawathe, S. Ratnasamy, L. Breslau, N. Lanham and S. Shenker, "Making Gnutella-like P2P systems scalable", Proceedings of the 2003 conference on Applications, technologies, architectures, and protocols for computer communications, Karlsruhe, Germany, August 25-29, 2003.
3. J. Liang, R. Kumar, K Ross, "The KaZaA Overlay: A Measurement Study", Proceedings of the Fifth New York Metro Area Networking Workshop, 2005.
4. Gnutella protocol spec. v.0.6 - http://rfc-gnutella.sourceforge.net/src/rfc-0_6-draft.html
5. Box, G.E., Jenkins, G.M, "Time Series Analysis Forecasting and Control, Holden day, 1976.
6. V. Kalogeraki, D. Gnuopulos and D. Zeinalipour-Yazti, "A Local Search Mechanism for Peer-to-Peer Networks", Proceedings of CIKM'02, McLean VA, USA, 2002.
7. 7 T. knuz, "The influence of Different Workload Descriptors on a Heuristic Load Balancing Scheme", IEEE Trans on Software Engineering, vol. 17, No. 7, July 1991.
8. Li Xiao, Z. Zhuang, Y. Liu, "Dynamic Layer Management in Superpeer Architectures", IEEE Transactions on parallel and distributed systems, 16(11), Nov. 2005.
9. CSIM Development toolkit for simulation and modeling. http://www.mesquite.com.
10. A. Mondal, K. Goda and M. Kitsuregawa "Effective Load-Balancing via Migration and Replication in Spatial GRIDs", Proceedings of the International Conference on Database and Expert Systems Applications. 2003.
11. E. Cohen, S. Shenker, "Repliaction Strategies in Unstructured Peer-to-Peer Networks", SIGCOMM '02: Proceedings of the 2002 conference on Applications, technologies, architectures, and protocols for computer communications, Vol. 32, No. 4. Oct. 2002.
12. Q. L. et. Al. "Search and Replicaton in Unstructured Peer-to-Peer Networks", In Proc. of International conference on Supercomputing, 2002.
13. S. Rajasekhar, B. Rong, K. Y. Lai, I. Khali and Z. Tari, "Load Sharing in Peer-to-Peer Networks using Dynamic Replication", Advanced Information Networking and Applications (AINA), 2006.
14. V. Gopalakrishnan, B. Silaghi, B. Bhattacharjee, and P. Keleher, "Adaptive Replication in Peer-to-Peer Systems", The 24th International Conference on Distributed Computing Systems (ICDCS'04), Mar. 2003.

Performance-Based Workload Distribution on Grid Environments*

Wen-Chung Shih[1], Chao-Tung Yang[2,**], Tsui-Ting Chen[2], and Shian-Shyong Tseng[1,3]

[1] Department of Computer Science
National Chiao Tung University, Hsinchu, 30010, Taiwan (R.O.C.)
{gis90805, sstseng}@cis.nctu.edu.tw

[2] High-Performance Computing Laboratory
Department of Computer Science and Information Engineering
Tunghai University, Taichung, 40704, Taiwan (R.O.C.)
{ctyang, g95280003}@thu.edu.tw

[3] Department of Information Science and Applications
Asia University, Taichung, 41354, Taiwan (R.O.C.)
sstseng@asia.edu.tw

Abstract. Imbalanced workload-distribution can significantly degrade performance of grid computing environments. In the past, the theory of divisible load has been widely investigated in static heterogeneous systems. However, it has not been widely applied to grid environments, which are characterized by heterogeneous resources and dynamic environments. In this paper, we propose a performance-based approach to workload distribution for master-slave types of applications on grids. Furthermore, applications with irregular workloads are addressed. We implemented three kinds of applications and conducted experimentations on our grid test-beds. Experimental results show that this approach performs more efficiently than conventional schemes. Consequently, we claim that dynamic workload distribution can benefit applications on grid environments.

1 Introduction

Grid platforms, which consist of various computational and storage resources, have become promising alternatives to traditional multiprocessors and computing clusters [3, 4, 7-9, 14, 25-28, 40]. The goal of grid computing is to share resources through the internet. Therefore, users can access more computing resources through grid technologies. On the other hand, inappropriate management of grid environments might result in using grid resources in an inefficient way. Moreover, the characteristic of dynamic changing makes it different from conventional parallel and distributed computing systems, such as multiprocessors and computing clusters. Consequently, it is challenging to use the grid efficiently.

---

* This work was partially supported by National Science Council of Republic of China under the number of NSC95-2752-E-009-015-PAE.

** Corresponding author.

C. Cérin and K.-C. Li (Eds.): GPC 2007, LNCS 4459, pp. 385–396, 2007.

In the past, the master-slave paradigm is a common model for task dispatching in parallel and distributed computing environments [16]. In this model, the master node holds a pool of tasks to be dispatched to other slave nodes. A well-known application of this model is Divisible Load Theory (DLT) [1, 17-19, 32, 36], which deals with the case where the total workload can be partitioned into any number of independent subjobs. In [23], a data distribution method was proposed for host-client type of applications. Their method was an analytic technique, and only verified on homogeneous and heterogeneous cluster computing platforms. In [24], an exact method for divisible load was proposed, which was not from a dynamic and pragmatic viewpoint as ours.

This paper aims to address the problem of dynamic distribution of workload for master-slave applications on grids. Since grid environments are dynamically changing and heterogeneous, the problem is more challenging than the traditional DLT problem. We propose a performance-based approach, which is implemented in three types of applications, Matrix Multiplication, Association Rule Mining and Mandelbrot Set Computation, and is executed a grid test-bed. Experimental results show that effective workload partitioning can significantly reduce the total completion time.

Our major contributions can be summarized as follows. First, this paper proposes a new performance function to estimate the performance of grid nodes. Second, we apply this approach to programs with irregular workload distribution. Consequently, experimental results show the obvious effectiveness of our approach. Our previous work [37-39] presents different heuristics to the parallel loop self-scheduling problem. This paper generalizes their main idea and proposes to solve the dynamic workload distribution problem. This approach is applied to both the parallel loop self-scheduling application and the association rule mining application. There have been a lot of researches of parallel and distributed data mining [12, 13, 29, 47]. However, this paper focuses on workload distribution, instead of proposing a new data mining algorithm.

The remainder of this paper is organized as follows. In Section 2, background on parallel loop scheduling and association rule mining is reviewed. In Section 3, we describe the proposed approach to solve the dynamic workload distribution problem. Next, the configuration of our grid testbed is specified and experimental results on three types of applications are also presented in Section 4. Finally, the concluding remarks are given in the last section.

2 Background Review

In this section, parallel loop scheduling and association rule mining are briefly reviewed.

2.1 Dynamic Loop Scheduling Schemes

Dynamic loop scheduling schemes make a scheduling decision at runtime. Its disadvantage is more overhead at runtime, while the advantage is load balance. The schemes we focus in this paper are self-scheduling, which a large class of dynamic loop scheduling schemes. Several self-scheduling schemes have been reviewed in [15, 21, 22, 30, 33, 41, 42, 46], and they are restated here as follows.

- **Pure Self-scheduling (PSS).** This is a straightforward dynamic loop scheduling algorithm [32]. Whenever a processor becomes idle, a loop iteration is assigned to it. This algorithm achieves good load balance but also induces excessive overhead.

- **Chunk Self-scheduling (CSS).** Instead of assigning one iteration to an idle processor at one time, CSS assigns k iterations each time, where k, called the chunk size, is a constant.
- **Guided Self-scheduling (GSS).** This scheme can dynamically change the number of iterations assigned to each processor [35]. More specifically, the next chunk size is determined by dividing the number of remaining iterations of a parallel loop by the number of available processors.
- **Factoring Self-scheduling (FSS).** The Factoring algorithm addresses this problem [31]. The assignment of loop iterations to working processors proceeds in phases. During each phase, only a subset of the remaining loop iterations (usually half) is divided equally among the available processors.
- **Trapezoid Self-scheduling (TSS).** This approach tries to reduce the need for synchronization while still maintaining a reasonable load balance [43]. This algorithm allocates large chunks of iterations to the first few processors and successively smaller chunks to the last few processors.

In [44], the authors enhanced well-known loop self-scheduling schemes to fit an extremely heterogeneous PC cluster environment. A two-phased approach was proposed to partition loop iterations and it achieved good performance in heterogeneous test-beds. In [20, 45, 46], NGSS was further enhanced by dynamically adjusting the parameter α according to system heterogeneity. A performance benchmark was used to determine whether target systems are relatively homogeneous or relatively heterogeneous. In addition, the types of loop iterations were classified into four classes, and were analyzed respectively. The scheme enhanced from GSS is called ANGSS in this paper.

2.2 Association Rule Mining

The objective of association rule mining is to discover correlation relationships among a set of items [29]. The well-known application of association rule mining is market basket analysis. This technique can extract customer buying behaviors by discover what items they buy together. The managers of shops can place the associated items at the neighboring shelf to raise their probability of purchasing. For example, milk and bread are frequently bought together.

The formulation of association rule mining problem is described as follows [12-13]. Let $I=\{I_1, I_2, I_3, \ldots, I_m\}$ be a set of items, and D a database of transactions. Each transaction in D is a subset of I. An association rule is a rule of the form $A \Rightarrow B$, where $A \subset I$, $B \subset I$, and $A \cap B=\{\}$. The well-known algorithm for finding association rules in large transaction databases is Apriori. It utilizes the Apriori property to reduce the search space.

As the rising of parallel processing, parallel data mining have been well investigated in the past decade. Especially, much attention has been directed to parallel association rule mining. A good survey can be found in [47].

3 Approach: Performance-Based Workload Distribution (PWD)

In this section, the system and programming model is introduces first. Then, the parameters of performance ratio and static-workload ratio are described. Finally, we present the skeleton algorithm for the performance-based workload distribution.

3.1 The System Model

The system in this work is modeled by a master-slave paradigm, which is represented by a star graph, G = (N, E). In this graph, N means the set of all nodes on the grid, and E is the set of all edges between the master and the slaves. In this model, there are two kinds of attributes associated with nodes, constants and variables. The values of the constant attributes do not vary during the lifetime of the node. For example, CPU clock speed, memory size, etc. are all constant attributes. On the other hand, the values of the variable attributes may fluctuate during the lifetime of the node. For example, CPU loading, available memory size, etc. are all constant attributes. In the following sections, the two kinds of attributes are utilized to model the heterogeneity of the dynamic grid.

3.2 Performance Ratio

The concept of performance ratio was previously defined in [37-39] in different forms and parameters, according to the requirements of applications. In this work, a different formulation is proposed to model the heterogeneity of the dynamic grid nodes. The purpose of calculating performance ratio is to estimate the current capability of processing for each node. With this metric, we can distribute appropriate workloads to each node, and load balancing can be achieved. The more accurate the estimation is, the better the load balance is.

To estimate the performance of each slave node, we define a performance function (PF) for a slave node j as

$$PF_j(V_1, V_2, \ldots, V_m) \tag{1}$$

where V_i, $1< i <m$, is a variable of the performance function. In more detail, the variables could include CPU speed, networking bandwidth, memory size, etc. We propose to utilize a Grid Resource Monitoring Tool [11] to acquire the values of variable attributes for all slaves, and to acquire the values of constant attributes by MDS. In this paper, the PF for node j is defined as

$$PF_j = w_1 \times \frac{CS_j / CL_j}{\sum\limits_{\forall node_i \in \mathrm{N}} CS_i / CL_i} + w_2 \times \frac{B_j}{\sum\limits_{\forall node_i \in S} B_i} \tag{2}$$

where

- N is the set of all grid nodes.
- CS_i is the CPU clock speed of node i, and it is a constant attribute. The value of this parameter is acquired by the MDS service.
- CL_i is the CPU loading of node i, and it is a variable attribute. The value of this parameter is acquired by the Ganglia tool, as shown in Figure 1.
- B_i is the bandwidth (Mbps) between node i and the master node.
- w_1 is the weight of the first term.
- w_2 is the weight of the second term.

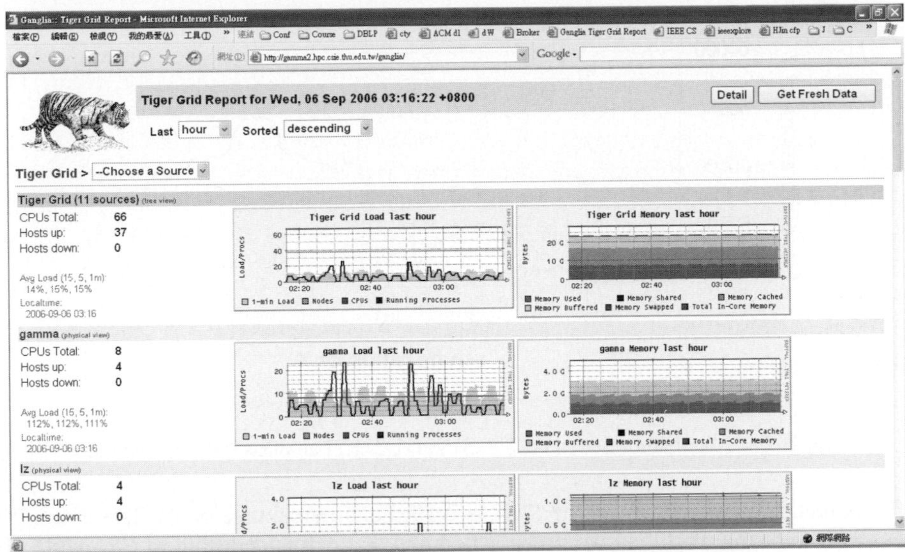

Fig. 1. The snapshot of the monitoring tool on the TIGER Grid

3.3 Determination of Static-Workload Ratio (*SWR*)

Another important factor to be estimated is the proportion of the workload which can be statically scheduled. For example, Mandelbrot Set Computation is a problem involving irregular workloads. In each iteration, the workload is different and varies significantly, as shown in Figure 2. Obviously, a distribution scheme which does not consider the effect of irregular workload could not estimate PR accurately.

We propose to use a parameter, *SWR* (Static-Workload Ratio), to alleviate the effect of irregular workload. In order to take advantage of static scheduling, *SWR* percentage of the total workload is dispatched according to Performance Ratio. If the workload of the target application is regular, *SWR* can be set to be 100. However, if the application has irregular workload, such as Mandelbrot Set Computation, it is reasonable to reserve some amount of workload for load balancing. We propose to randomly take five sampling iterations, and compute their execution time. Then, the *SWR* of the target application *i* is determined by the following formula.

$$SWR_i = \frac{min_i}{MAX_i} \tag{3}$$

where

- min_i is the minimum execution time of all sampled iterations for application *i*.
- MAX_i is the maximum execution time of all sampled iterations for application *i*.

For example, for a regular application with uniform workload distribution, the five sampled iterations are the same. Therefore, the *SWR* is 100%, and the whole workload can be dispatched according to Performance Ratio, with good load balance. However, for another application, the five sampling execution time might be 7, 7.5, 8, 8.5 and

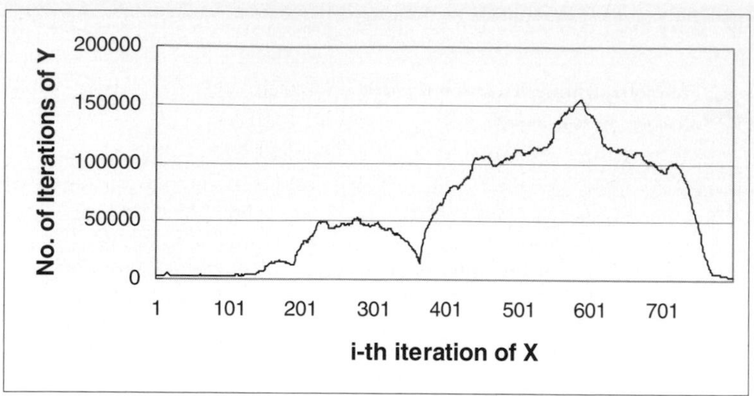

Fig. 2. The Mandelbrot Set on [-1.8, 0.5] to [-1.2, 1.2] an 800×800 pixel window

10 seconds, respectively. Then the *SWR* is 7/10, i.e. a percentage of 70. Therefore, 70 percentages of the workload would be scheduled statically according to *PR*, while 30 percentages of the workload would be scheduled dynamically by *GSS*.

3.4 Algorithm

Our algorithm is composed of four stages. In stage one, the related information are acquired. Then, stage two calculates the Static-workload Ratio and Performance Ratio. Next, *SWR* percentage of the total workload is statically scheduled according to the performance ratio among all slave nodes in stage three. Finally, the remainder of the workload is dynamically scheduled by Guided Self-Scheduling for load balancing. The algorithm of our approach is described as follows.

Module MASTER

```
Stage 1: Gathering the following information
       - CPU_Loading
       - CPU_Clock_Speed
       - the sample execution time
Stage 2: Calculate two scheduling parameters
Stage 3: Static Scheduling for SWR% of workload
Stage 4: dynamic Scheduling for the remaining
END MASTER
```

Module SLAVE

```
While (a chunk of workload arrives) {
   Receive the chunk of workload
   Compute on this chunk
   Send the result to the Master
}
END SLAVE
```

4 Experimental Results

To verify our approach, a grid test-bed is built based on the TIGER grid [11], and three types of application programs are implemented with MPI (Message Passing Interface) to be executed on this test-bed. This grid test-bed consists of one master and four domains, totally 33 nodes. The master node is at Tunghai University (THU), and the 32 slave nodes are located at Tunghai University (THU), Providence University (PU), Li-Zen High School (LZ), and Hsiuping Institute of Technology School (HIT). We have built this grid test-bed by the following middleware:

- Globus Toolkit 4.0.1 [2, 10]
- Mpich library 1.2.6 [5, 6]

In this study, we have implemented applications in C language, with message passing interface (MPI) directives for parallelizing code segments to be processed by multiple CPUs. For readability of experimental results, the brief description of all implemented programs is listed in Table 1.

Table 1. Description of all implemented programs

Scheduling Scheme	Description	Reference
static	Weighted static scheduling	
gss	Dynamic scheduling (GSS)	[35]
fss	Dynamic scheduling (FSS)	[31]
tss	Dynamic scheduling (TSS)	[43]
ngss	Fixed α scheduling + GSS	[44]
angss	Adaptive α scheduling + GSS	[46]
pwd	Performance-based Workload Distribution	

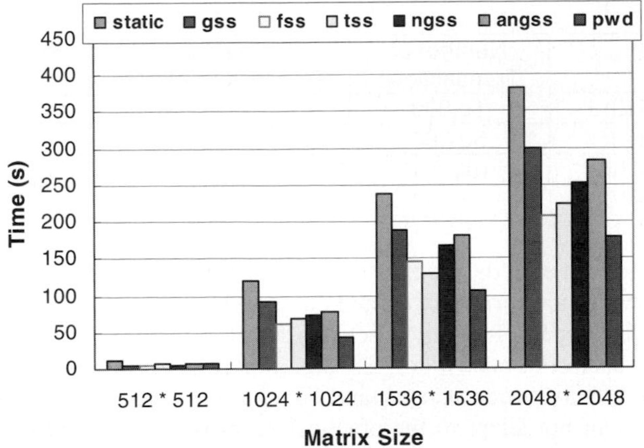

Fig. 3. Execution time for Matrix multiplication with different input sizes

4.1 Application 1: Matrix Multiplication

Matrix Multiplication is a fundamental operation in many numerical linear algebra applications. In this application, the workload is loop iterations. First, we want to compare the proposed PWD scheme with previous schemes with respect to the execution time. Figure 3 illustrates the execution time for input matrix size 512×512, 1024×1024, 1536×1536 and 2048×2048 respectively. The results are shown as follows.

- Among these schemes, PWD performs better than other schemes. The reason is that PWD accurately estimates the PR, and takes the advantage of static scheduling, thus reducing the runtime overhead.
- The weighted static scheme obviously performs worse than other dynamic schemes. It is reasonable to say that the static scheme is not suitable for a dynamic environment, with respect to performance.
- It is interesting that traditional self-scheduling schemes (FSS and TSS) perform slightly better than NGSS and ANGSS. However, this result is inconsistent with that of previous research. The reason might be that the parameter α is set too high, 75. If the parameter α is set appropriately, it is possible for NGSS and ANGSS to perform better, as previous work has shown.

4.2 Application 2: Association Rule Mining

In this application, the workload is the dataset to be mined on. We implemented the Apriori algorithm, and applied our approach to conduct data distribution. Specifically, the parallelized version of Apriori we adopt is Count Distribution (CD) [12, 13]. In this experiment, "cd_eq" means to distribute the workload to slaves equally, and "cd_cpu" means to distribute the workload to slaves according to the ratio of CPU speed values of slaves. And, cd_pwd is the proposed scheme. Our datasets are generated by the tool as in [13]. The parameters of the synthetic datasets are described in Table 2.

Table 2. Description of our dataset

Dataset	Number of Transactions	Average Transaction Length	Number of Items
D10KT5I10	10,000	5	10
D50KT5I10	50,000	5	10
D100KT5I10	100,000	5	10
D200KT5I10	200,000	5	10

First, execution time on the grid for the three schemes is investigated. As shown in Figure 4, cd_pwd outperforms cd_eq and cd_cpu. From this experiment, we can see the significant influence of partition schemes on the total completion time. In grid environments, network bandwidth is an important criterion to evaluate the performance of a slave node. Cd_eq and cd_cpu are static data partition schemes. Therefore, they can not adapt to the practical network status. When communication cost becomes a major factor, the proposed scheme would be well adaptive to the dynamic network environment.

Moreover, the reason why cd_cpu got the worst performance can be contributed to the inappropriate estimation of node performance. In grid computing environments, CPU speed is not the only factor to determine the node performance. A node with the fastest CPU is not necessary the node with optimal performance.

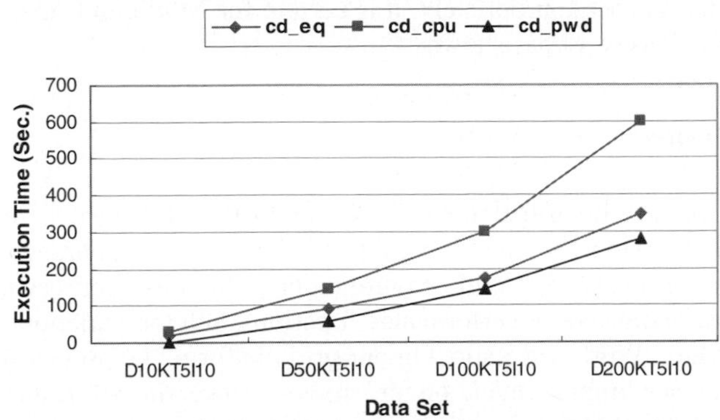

Fig. 4. Performance of data partition schemes for different datasets

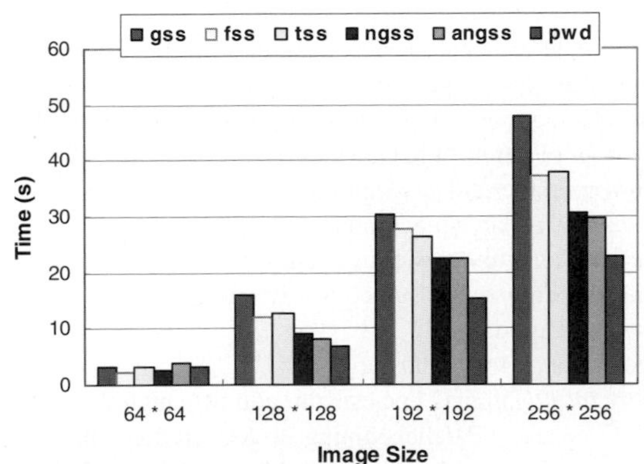

Fig. 5. Execution time for Mandelbrot Set Computation with different input sizes

4.3 Application 3: Mandelbrot Set Computation

The Mandelbrot set computation is a problem involving the same computation on different data points which have different convergence rates [34]. In the following experiment, we want to compare the execution time of previous schemes with the proposed approach. Figure 5 illustrates the results for input image size 64×64, 128×128, 192×192 and 256×256 respectively. The execution time of weighted static scheduling is omitted due to its bad performance. According to the experience in Matrix Multiplication example, the parameter α is set to 30. The results are discussed as follows.

- Among these schemes, the PWD still performs better than other schemes. The reason is also that PWD accurately estimates the PR, and takes the advantage of static scheduling, thus reducing the runtime overhead.
- Traditional self-scheduling schemes (GSS, FSS and TSS) perform worse than NGSS and ANGSS. The reason is that irregular workload is difficult to schedule. If the parameter α is set appropriately, it is certain for NGSS and ANGSS to perform better, as previous work has shown.

5 Conclusions

In this paper, we have investigated the workload distribution problem on dynamic and heterogeneous grid environments. First, a performance-based approach was proposed to schedule workloads on grid environments. In this approach, the system heterogeneity is estimated by performance functions, and the variation of workload is estimated by Static-Workload Ratio. On our grid platform, the proposed approach can obtain performance improvement on previous schemes. In our future work, we will implement more types of application programs to verify our approach.

References

[1] Divisible Load Theory, http://www.ee.sunysb.edu/~tom/MATBE/index.html

[2] Global Grid Forum, http://www.ggf.org/

[3] Introduction to Grid Computing with Globus, http://www.ibm.com/redbooks

[4] KISTI Grid Testbed, http://Gridtest.hpcnet.ne.kr/

[5] MPICH, http://www-unix.mcs.anl.gov/mpi/mpich/

[6] MPICH-G2, http://www.hpclab.niu.edu/mpi/

[7] Network Weather Service, http://nws.cs.ucsb.edu/

[8] Sun ONE Grid Engine, http://wwws.sun.com/software/Gridware/

[9] TeraGrid, http://www.teragrid.org/

[10] The Globus Project, http://www.globus.org/

[11] TIGER Grid Report, http://gamma2.hpc.csie.thu.edu.tw/ganglia/

[12] R. Agrawal and J. C. Shafer, "Parallel Mining of Association Rules," *IEEE Transactions on Knowledge and Data Engineering*, vol. 8, no. 6, pp. 962-969, Dec. 1996.

[13] R. Agrawal and R. Srikant, "Fast algorithms for Mining Association Rules," *Proc. 20th Very Large Data Bases Conf.*, pp. 487-499, 1994.

[14] M. A. Baker and G. C. Fox. "Metacomputing: Harnessing Informal Supercomputers." *High Performance Cluster Computing*. Prentice-Hall, May 1999. ISBN 0-13-013784-7.

[15] I. Banicescu, R. L. Carino, J. P. Pabico, and M. Balasubramaniam, "Overhead Analysis of a Dynamic Load Balancing Library for Cluster Computing," *Proceedings of the 19th IEEE International Parallel and Distributed Processing Symposium,* 2005.

[16] C. Banino, O. Beaumont, L. Carter, J. Ferrante, A. Legrand, Y. Robert, "Scheduling strategies for master-slave tasking on heterogeneous processor platforms," *IEEE Transactions on Parallel and Distributed Systems*, Vol. 15, No. 4, pp. 319-330, Apr. 2004.

[17] O. Beaumont, H. Casanova, A. Legrand, Y. Robert and Y. Yang, "Scheduling Divisible Loads on Star and Tree Networks: Results and Open Problems," IEEE Transactions on Parallel and Distributed Systems, Vol. 16, No. 3, pp. 207-218, Mar. 2005.

[18] V. Bharadwaj, D. Ghose, V. Mani, and T.G. Robertazzi, *Scheduling Divisible Loads in Parallel and Distributed Systems*, IEEE Press, 1996.

[19] V. Bharadwaj, D. Ghose and T.G. Robertazzi, "Divisible Load Theory: A New Paradigm for Load Scheduling in Distributed Systems," *Cluster Computing*, vol. 6, no. 1, pp. 7-18, Jan. 2003.

[20] K. W. Cheng, C. T. Yang, C. L. Lai, and S. C. Chang, "A Parallel Loop Self-Scheduling on Grid Computing Environments," *Proceedings of the 2004 IEEE International Symposium on Parallel Architectures, Algorithms and Networks*, pp. 409-414, KH, China, May 2004.

[21] A. T. Chronopoulos, R. Andonie, M. Benche and D.Grosu, "A Class of Loop Self-Scheduling for Heterogeneous Clusters," *Proceedings of the 2001 IEEE International Conference on Cluster Computing*, pp. 282-291, 2001.

[22] A. T. Chronopoulos, S. Penmatsa, J. Xu and S.Ali, "Distributed Loop-Self-Scheduling Schemes for Heterogeneous Computer Systems," *Concurrency and Computation: Practice and Experience*, vol. 18, pp. 771-785, 2006.

[23] N. Comino and V. L. Narasimhan, "A Novel Data Distribution Technique for Host-Client Type Parallel Applications," *IEEE Transactions on Parallel and Distributed Systems*, Vol. 13, No. 2, pp. 97-110, Feb. 2002.

[24] M. Drozdowski and M. Lawenda, "On Optimum Multi-installment Divisible Load Processing in Heterogeneous Distributed Systems," *Euro-Par 2005 Parallel Processing: 11th International Euro-Par Conference, Lecture Notes in Computer Science*, vol. 3648, pp. 231-240, Springer-Verlag, August 2005.

[25] I. Foster, N. Karonis, "A Grid-Enabled MPI: Message Passing in Heterogeneous Distributed Computing Systems." *Proc. 1998 SC Conference*, November, 1998.

[26] I. Foster, C. Kesselman., "Globus: A Metacomputing Infrastructure Toolkit," *International J. Supercomputer Applications*, 11(2):115-128, 1997.

[27] I. Foster, C. Kesselman, S. Tuecke, "The Anatomy of the Grid: Enabling Scalable Virtual Organizations," *International J. Supercomputer Applications*, 15(3), 2001.

[28] I. Foster, "The Grid: A New Infrastructure for 21st Century Science." *Physics Today*, 55(2):42-47, 2002.

[29] J. Han and M. Kamber, *Data Mining: Concepts and Techniques*, Morgan Kaufmann Publishers, 2001.

[30] J. Herrera, E. Huedo, R. S. Montero, and I. M. Llorente, "Loosely-coupled loop scheduling in computational grids," *Proceedings of the 20th IEEE International Parallel and Distributed Processing Symposium*, 2006.

[31] S. F. Hummel, E. Schonberg, and L. E. Flynn, "Factoring: a method scheme for scheduling parallel loops," *Communications of the ACM*, Vol. 35, 1992, pp. 90-101.

[32] `C. Kruskal and A. Weiss, "Allocating independent subtaskson parallel processors," *IEEE Transactions on Software Engineering*, vol. 11, pp 1001–1016, 1984.

[33] H. Li, S. Tandri, M. Stumm and K. C. Sevcik, "Locality and Loop Scheduling on NUMA Multiprocessors," *Proceedings of the 1993 International Conference on Parallel Processing*, vol. II, pp. 140-147, 1993.

[34] B. B. Mandelbrot, *Fractal Geometry of Nature*, W. H. Freeman: New york, 1988.

[35] C. D. Polychronopoulos and D. Kuck, "Guided Self-Scheduling: a Practical Scheduling Scheme for Parallel Supercomputers," *IEEE Trans. on Computers*, vol. 36, no. 12, pp 1425-1439, 1987.

[36] T.G. Robertazzi, "Ten Reasons to Use Divisible Load Theory," *Computer*, vol. 36, no. 5, pp. 63-68, May 2003.

[37] W. C. Shih, C. T. Yang, and S. S. Tseng, "A Performance-Based Parallel Loop Self-Scheduling on Grid Environments," *Network and Parallel Computing: IFIP International Conference, NPC 2005, Lecture Notes in Computer Science*, vol. 3779, pp. 48-55, Springer-Verlag, December 2005.

[38] W. C. Shih, C. T. Yang, and S. S. Tseng, "A Hybrid Parallel Loop Scheduling Scheme on Grid Environments," *Grid and Cooperative Computing: 4th International Conference, GCC 2005, Lecture Notes in Computer Science*, vol. 3795, pp. 370-381, Springer-Verlag, December 2005.

[39] W. C. Shih, C. T. Yang, and S. S. Tseng, "A Performance-based Approach to Dynamic Workload Distribution for Master-Slave Applications on Grid Environments," *GPC 2006, Lecture Notes in Computer Science*, vol. 3947, pp. 73-82, Springer-Verlag, 2006.

[40] L. Smarr, C. Catlett, "Metacomputing," *Communications of the ACM*, vol. 35, no. 6, pp. 44-52, 1992.

[41] S. Tabirca, T. Tabirca and L. T. Yang, "A convergence study of the discrete FGDLS algorithm," *IEICE Transactions on Information and Systems*, vol. E89-D, no. 2, pp. 673-678, 2006.

[42] P. Tang and P. C. Yew, "Processor self-scheduling for multiple-nested parallel loops," Proceedings of the 1986 International Conference on Parallel Processing, pp. 528-535, 1986.

[43] T. H. Tzen and L. M. Ni, "Trapezoid self-scheduling: a practical scheduling scheme for parallel compilers," *IEEE Transactions on Parallel and Distributed Systems*, Vol. 4, 1993, pp. 87-98.

[44] C. T. Yang and S. C. Chang, "A Parallel Loop Self-Scheduling on Extremely Heterogeneous PC Clusters," *Journal of Information Science and Engineering*, vol. 20, no. 2, pp. 263-273, March 2004.

[45] C. T. Yang, K. W. Cheng, and K. C. Li, "An Efficient Parallel Loop Self-Scheduling on Grid Environments," *NPC'2004 IFIP International Conference on Network and Parallel Computing, Lecture Notes in Computer Science*, Springer-Verlag Heidelberg, Hai Jin, Guangrong Gao, Zhiwei Xu (Eds.), Oct. 2004.

[46] C. T. Yang, K. W. Cheng, and K. C. Li, "An Efficient Parallel Loop Self-Scheduling Scheme for Cluster Environments," *The Journal of Supercomputing*, vol. 34, pp. 315-335, 2005.

[47] M. J. Zaki, "Parallel and Distributed Association Mining: A Survey," *IEEE Concurrency*, vol. 7, no. 4, pp. 14-25, 1999.

A Visual Framework for Deploying and Managing Context-Aware Services

Ichiro Satoh*

National Institute of Informatics
2-1-2 Hitotsubashi, Chiyoda-ku, Tokyo 101-8430, Japan

Abstract. A framework for managing pervasive computing is presented. It enables end-users to easily and naturally build visual interfaces for monitoring and customizing context-aware services. It is built on an exiting a symbolic location model to represent the containment relationships between physical entities, computing devices, and places. It supports a compound document framework for visualizing and customizing the model. It provides physical entities, places, computing devices, and services in smart spaces with visual components to annotate and control them and to dynamically assemble visual components into a visual interface for managing the spaces. It can visualize and configure the spatial structure of physical entities and places and the status and attributes of computing devices and services, e.g., the location in which context-aware services are available. By using the framework, end-users can monitor and customize pervasive computing environments by viewing and editing documents.

1 Introduction

Pervasive computing tends to consist of many computing devices like grid computing. However, the former often lacks management systems, unlike the latter. In fact, the focus of current research on pervasive computing is on the design and implementation of application-specific context-aware services. As a result, the task of management in pervasive computing has attracted scant attention so far. This is a serious obstacle in the growth of pervasive computing. The purpose of pervasive computing is to bridge the gap between computing systems and the real world. In fact, one of the most typical and popular applications of pervasive computing is in context-aware services. To support such services, pervasive computing systems must be able to know the context and process this in the real world, e.g., people, location, and time. Such information tends to depend on the offices/houses, businesses and lifestyles of users. Therefore, they must customize many pervasive computing devices to their individual requirements and applications. Pervasive computing systems often lack professional administrators unlike grid computing systems.

This paper presents a user-friendly management framework to solve these problems. It was inspired by our experiences with practical applications of pervasive computing in the real world, e.g., home appliance controls and location/user-aware user-assistance

* e-mail: ichiro@nii.ac.jp

C. Cérin and K.-C. Li (Eds.): GPC 2007, LNCS 4459, pp. 397–411, 2007.

systems. The framework provides visual interfaces for deploying, customizing, and controlling computing devices and context-aware services. Since pervasive computing environments are changed dynamically, such a management framework, including visual interfaces, for these environments, must be able to autonomously adapt itself to the changes. For example, when devices and services are added to a smart space, a visual interface for managing the devices or services should be added to the interface for the space. The framework is constructed as a combination of a location model, called M-Spaces [11], and an active document framework, called MobiDoc [12,13], developed by the author. The former is a symbolic-location model to maintain the locations of computing devices and software for defining context-aware services as well as the locations of physical spaces and entities in the real world. The latter is constructed as a Java-based compound document framework. It enables one document to be composed of various visible parts, such as text, image, and video created by different applications, like other compound document frameworks, e.g., COM/OLE [3], OpenDoc [1], CommonPoint [10], and Bonobo [7]. The framework presented in this paper provides visual interfaces for a location model as a management tool for end-users to deploy, customize, and monitor context-aware services. Since the framework itself is designed independently of the location model as much as possible, it can be used for other location models for pervasive computing.

2 Background

The framework presented in this paper has two bases, i.e., symbolic-location model and compound document framework. The former is useful for providing context-aware services in smart spaces, because such a model is useful for context-aware services as discussed in the previous section. The latter enables end-users to build a visual management interface from components for compound documents and customize context-aware services through GUI-manipulations. This paper addresses location-aware communication between humans-machines or between machines-machines indoors, e.g., in buildings and houses, rather than in outdoor settings.

2.1 Symbolic Location Model

The current implementation is constructed with a symbolic-location model, called *M-Spaces* [11]. The framework can be used with other existing symbolic location models. It enables us to monitor contextual information in the models, but we cannot manage context-aware services, because the models themselves do not support services and computing devices. The M-spaces model can spatially bind the positions of entities and spaces with the locations of their virtual counterparts by using location sensing systems, and when they move in the physical world, it can automatically deploy their counterparts at proper locations within it. Physical spaces and entities are often organized in a containment relationship, where each space is often composed of more than one sub-space. For example, each floor is contained within at most one building, each room is contained within at most one floor, and a person or object may be contained in at most one room. Unlike other existing location models, it can maintain the location and deployment of software to define context-aware services and information about the computational resources of computing devices that can execute the services, as well as represent contextual information in the real world like other existing location models.

2.2 Compound Document-Based Management Interface

The framework presented in this paper uses a compound document component framework, called MobiDoc [12,13], as a visual user interface to monitor changes in the real world and deploy and customize context-aware services. It enables an enriched document to be dynamically and nestedly composed of software components corresponding to various types of content, e.g., text, images and windows. Unlike other existing compound document frameworks, it permits the content of all components and program codes to access the content that is inseparable within the components so that the components can be viewed or modified without the need for any applications. It provides an editing environment to enable the visual components to be manipulated. It also provides in-place editing services similar to those provided by OpenDoc and OLE. It offers several value-added mechanisms to allow the visual estate of a container to efficiently be shared among embedded components and to coordinate their use of shared resources, such as keyboards, mice, and windows.

2.3 Basic Approach

The framework presented in this paper provides more than one visual component for a virtual counterpart object corresponding to a physical entity, space, computing device, and service to bridge the gap between the location model and the compound document framework. Visual components are organized according to the structure of their target virtual counterpart objects and they enable the spatial relationships between the objects's targets to be visualized, e.g., physical entities, objects, and computing devices in the model (Fig. 1).

The framework supports bidirectional communications between runtime systems for virtual components and the model and communications between each visual component and virtual counterpart objects that the component represents. The framework reflects the structure of virtual counterpart objects in the structure of visual components and it permits the runtime systems to request the model to change the structure of virtual counterpart objects. We can customize the locations that the services should be available at and the users that the services should be provided for, by deploying visual components for context-aware services at other visual components corresponding to entities and places through GUI manipulations. Furthermore, since each virtual component is a programmable entity, it can directly communicate with its target counterpart object to visualize and customize the status and attributes of the object's target, e.g., physical entity, and place, computing device, and service via the object, through its built-in protocols or the object's favorite protocols.

Since compound document technology supports the dynamic composition of components, compound document-based management interfaces for pervasive computing environments can adapt themselves to changes in the physical world. For example, when computing devices and services are added, their visual components are dynamically

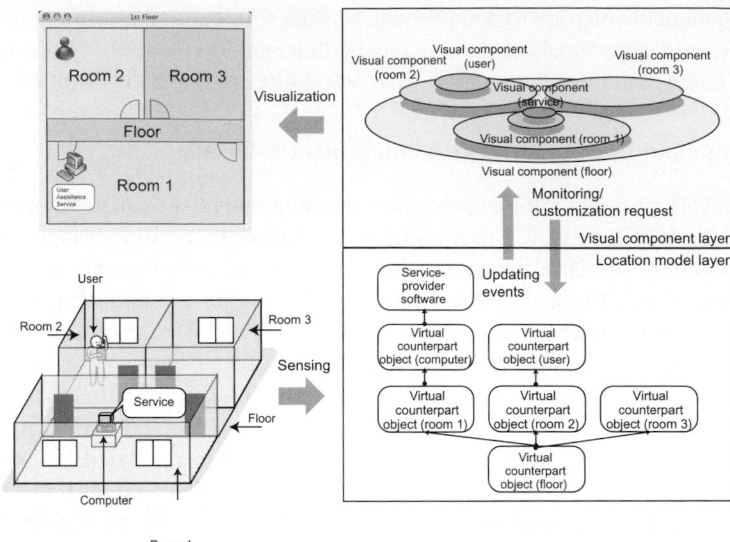

Fig. 1. Rooms on floor in physical world and virtual counterpart objects in location model

downloaded from specified servers or devices and then automatically displayed within the scope of the components corresponding to the spaces that contain them.

2.4 Remarks

We should explain the reason why our framework supports two layers. This is because the upper layer, i.e., visual interfaces, should be general so that is can be used for other models and other computing, including grid computing. In fact, it is designed independently of the lower layer, i.e., the M-Spaces model and can support non tree-based models. We should also note that the framework itself can be easily used for other locations models to monitor them but it does not support the deployment and customization of context-aware services, because they cannot maintain any services and computing devices unlike the M-Spaces model.

3 M-Space: Location Model for Smart Spaces

Existing location models can be classified into two: physical world and symbolic world. The former represents the position of people and objects as geometric information, which can be measured by GPS and ultra-sonic location sensing systems. The former is not suitable in indoor settings, because although the geometric locations of two objects may be neighboring, the objects themselves may be in different rooms. In fact, most emerging applications in indoor settings require a more symbolic notion. We use a symbolic location model, called *M-Spaces* model. This section outlines the model before explaining the framework.[1]

[1] Detail of the model was presented in our previous paper[11].

3.1 Containment Relationship Model

This model is unique to other existing location models, because it not only consists of data elements but also programmable entities, called agents, as virtual counterpart objects of physical entities or places. Agents have the following notions: (1) Each agent is a virtual counterpart of a physical entity or place, including the coverage area of the sensor, computing device, or service-provider software. (2) Each agent can be contained within at most one agent according to containment relationships in the physical world and cyberspace. It can move between agents as a whole with all its inner agents. Agents When an agent contains other agents, we call the former a *parent* and the latter *children*. The model permit agents to interact with each others. The model represents facts about entities or places in terms of the semantic or spatial-containment relationships between agents that are associated with these entities or places. When physical entities, spaces, and computing devices move from location to location in the physical world, the model detects their movements through location-sensing systems and changes the containment relationships between agents corresponding to moving entities, their sources, and destinations. The below figures of Fig. 1 shows the correlation between spaces and entities in the physical world and their counterpart agents. Each agent is a virtual counterpart object of its target in the world model and maintains the target's attributes.

3.2 Agent

The model cannot only maintains the location of physical entities, such as people and objects, but also the locations of computing devices and services in a unified manner.

- **The virtual counterpart agent (VCA)** is a digital representation of a physical entity, such as a person or object, except for the computing device itself, or physical surroundings such as a building or room,
- **The proxy agent (PA)** bridges the model and computing device, and maintains a subtree of the model or executes services located in a VCA.
- **The service agent (SA)** is software that defines application-specific services dependent on physical entities or places.

For example, a car carries two people and moves from location to location with its occupants. The car is mapped into a VCA on the model and this contains two VCAs that correspond to the two people. The movement of the car is mapped into the VCA migration corresponding to the car, from the VCA corresponding to the source to the VCA corresponding to the destination. Also, when a person has a computer for executing services, his or her VCA has a PA, which represents the computer and runs SAs to define the services.

Virtual counterpart agent. A person, physical object, or place can have more than one VCA, and each VCA can contain other VCAs and PAs according to spatial containment relationships in the physical world. However, unlike other existing location models, ours does not distinguish between entities and places in the physical world; some entities can be viewed as spaces, e.g., cars and desks, in the sense that they can contain other entities inside them.

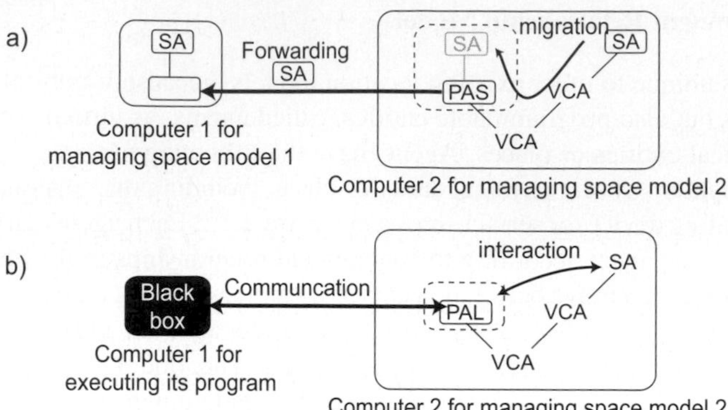

Fig. 2. Two types of proxy agents

Proxy agent. VCAs can have software to define the context-dependent services inside them. However, they may not be able to be executed in the software, because none of the computing devices that maintain these have unlimited computational resources. Instead, there are two facilities through which services can be provided. The first is to forward such services to computing devices embedded in or visiting a space and execute them on the devices. The second is to directly use services provided by computing devices within a space. We introduced proxy agents to maintain the location of computing devices and used the devices as service providers.[2] Our model also allows PAs to be classified into two sub-types that handle computing devices according to their functions.

- The first agent, i.e., PAS (PA for Service provider), is a proxy of a computing device that can execute services (Fig. 2(a)). If such a device is in a place, its proxy is contained in the VCA corresponding to the space. When a PAS receives software for defining services, it forwards this to the device to which the software refers. After the PAS forwards the software, it enables other agents to fetch the software as if this were in it.
- The second agent, called PAL (PAC for Legacy device), is a proxy of a computing device that cannot execute SAs (Fig. 2(b)). If such a device is in a space, its proxy is contained in the VCA corresponding to the space and it communicates with the device through the device's favorite protocols.

Service agent. We should reuse existing location-based and personalized services as much as possible. The model introduces several typical software agents, e.g., Java Beans and Java Applets as service-provider programs. However, such existing agents may not be suitable for our model. Each SA is a wrapper for software modules to define application-specific services and each specifies the attributes of its services, e.g., the requirements that a device must satisfy to execute these services. The model maintains the locations of services by using SAs.

[2] Proxy agents are unique to other existing location models and are useful for maintaining and using computing devices.

4 Compound Document Framework for Managing Pervasive Computing

This section presents a compound document framework for building and operating visual interfaces for context-aware services. The framework inherits many features of our compound document framework, `MobiDoc`, but is extended to manage pervasive computing. The framework provides each agent in the model with more than one visual component to view and customize the status and attributes of the agent by using the program code defined in the agent. It organizes these components in a tree structure according to their target agents. It consists of two parts: component runtime systems and visual components. The former can communicate with the model and organize visual components. The latter maintains its visual content and program code to enable content inside it be viewed or edited.

4.1 Visual Component

Each visual component is a collection of Java objects wrapped in a component and it has its own unique identifier and image data displayed as its icon. All the objects that each component consists of need to implement the `java.io.Serializable` interface, because they must be marshaled using Java's serialization mechanism. Each visual component needs to be defined as a subclass of either the `java.awt.Component` or `java.awt.Container` from which most of Java's visual or GUI objects are derived. To reuse existing software, we implemented an adapter to use typical Java components, e.g., Java Applets and JavaBeans, that are defined as subclasses of the `java.awt.Component` or `java.awt.Container` class within our components. This is not compatible with all kinds of Applets and JavaBeans, because some of those existing components manage their threads and input and output devices depreciatively. Nevertheless, the framework provide adapters for several canonical Applets and JavaBeans to be used as visual components.

4.2 Component Runtime System

Each runtime system governs all the components within it and provides them with APIs for components in addition to Java's classes. It assigns one or more threads to each component and interrupts them before the component migrates, terminates, or is saved. Each component can request its current runtime system to terminate, save, and migrate itself and its inner components to the destination that it wants to migrate to. This framework provides each component with a wrapper, called a *component tree node*. Each node contains its target component, its attributes, and its containment relationship and provides interfaces between its component and the runtime system. When a component is created in a runtime system, it creates a component tree node for the newly created component. When a component migrates to another location or duplicates itself, the runtime system migrates its node with the component and makes a replica of the whole node.

Each VCA, PA, and SA, has more than one visual component and the structure of VCAs, PAs, and SAs in the model is reflected in the hierarchical structure of visual components. Each hierarchy is maintained in the form of a tree structure of component tree

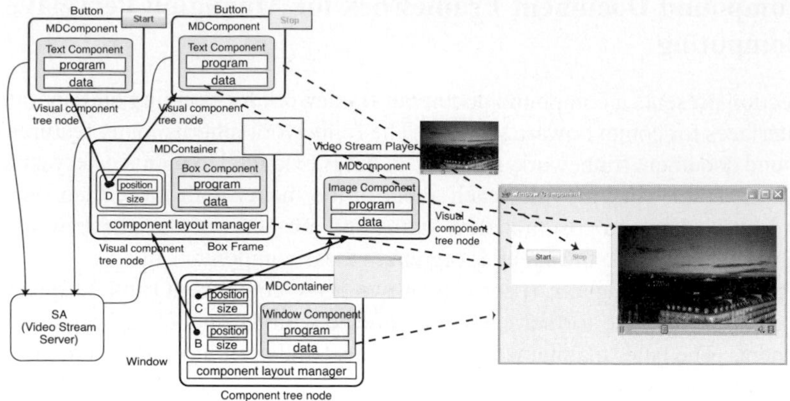

Fig. 3. Visual component hierarchy

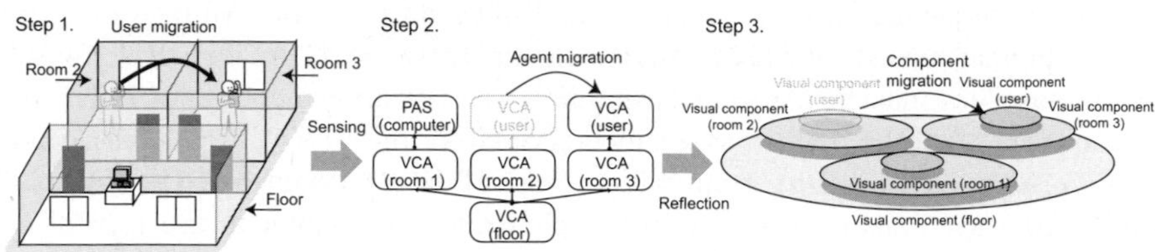

Fig. 4. The movement of agents and components when changes in the real world

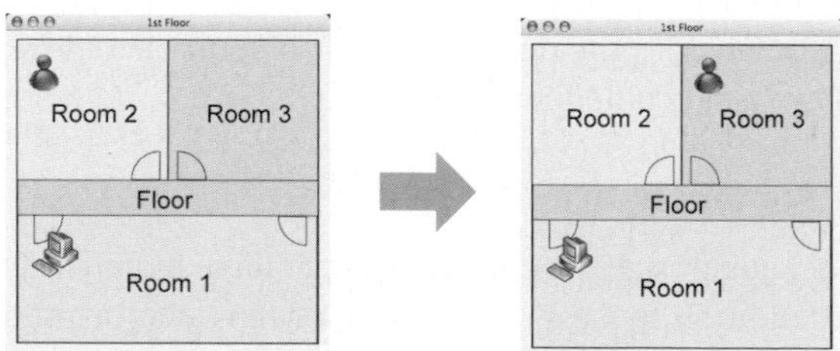

Fig. 5. Relocation of visual components

nodes of components (Fig. 3). Each node is defined as a subclass of `MDContainer` or `MDComponent`, where the first supports components, which can contain more than one component inside them while the second supports components, which cannot contain any components. For example, when a component has two other components inside it, the nodes that contain these two inner components are attached to the node that wraps the container component. Component migration is only performed as a transformation of the subtree structure of the hierarchy. The framework does not support direct-interactions between visual components. Instead, it permit each VCA, PA, or SA, to have more than one visual component.

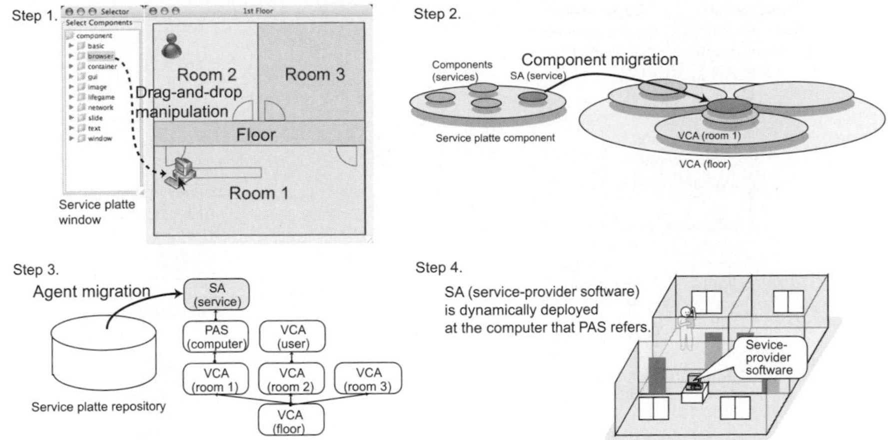

Fig. 6. Dynamic service-deployment according to migration of visual component

5 Binding Between Visual Components and Virtual Counterparts

The framework permits each agent to have more than one visual component. When it detects changes in the attributes of an agent, it sends events to the visual components that refer the agent.

5.1 Updating the Structure and Attributes of Visual Components

Component runtime systems support WebDAV servers. When the framework detects changes in the structure of agents in the model (Fig. 4), it transforms the structure of visual components that refer the agents by sending WebDAV-based commands to the runtime systems (Fig. 5). When new physical entities and people arrive at spaces, visual components that refer the counterpart objects for the visiting entities or people may not be available in these runtime systems. When entities or people leave from spaces, visual components for the missing entities or people may be unnecessary. To solve these problems, the framework provides a mechanism for fetching/dispatching components from/to specified servers, called repository servers. When a component is fetched from or dispatched to servers, the runtime system marshals the node of the component, including its state and codes, and the nodes of its descendants, into a bit-stream by using Java's object serialization mechanism and then transmits the bit-stream to/from the servers. Therefore, the attributes and structure of visual components become persistent, even while they are stored in these servers.

5.2 Updating the Structure and Attributes of Agents

Each component can display its content within the rectangular estate maintained by its container component. The node of the component, which is defined as a subclass of the `MDContainer` or `MDComponent` class, specifies attributes, e.g., its minimum size and preferable size, and the maximum size of the visible estate of its component

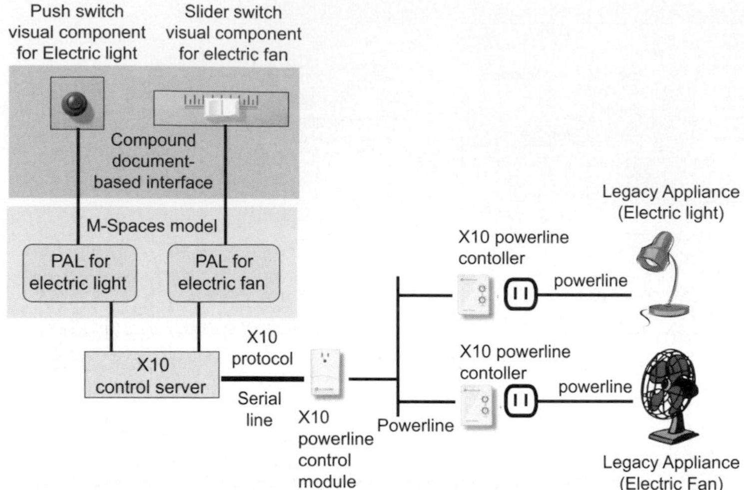

Fig. 7. X10-based power-outlet controlling system

in the estate is controlled by the node of its container component. These classes can define their new layout manager as subclasses of the `java.awt.LayoutManager` class. When a component is dynamically added to a container, the layout manager of the container's MDContainer manage the position and size of the new component. For example, if a container has an instance of Java's `java.awt.FlowLayout` as its layout manager, components that visit it automatically stand in rows in its estate.

This framework provides an editing environment for manipulating the components for network processing, as well as for visual components. It offers several value-added mechanisms for effectively sharing the visual estate of a container among embedded components and for coordinating their use of shared resources, such as keyboards, mice, and windows. Each component tree node can dispatch certain events to its components to notify them when certain actions occur within their surroundings. `MDContainer` and `MDComponent` classes support built-in GUIs for manipulating components. For example, when we want to place a component on another component, including a document, we move the former to the latter through GUI manipulations, e.g., drag-and-drop or cut-and-paste.

When users change the structure or attributes of visual components, the framework sends events to the model to update the structure or attributes of corresponding agents (Fig. 6). When the underlying sensing system detects the arrival of people and physical objects, the model fetch and load agents corresponding to these people and objects from such storage and then issue specified events to runtime systems. To duplicate agents or components, the system marshals them into a bit-stream and then duplicates the marshaled agent or component, because Java has no deep-copy mechanisms that can make replicas of all objects embedded in and referred to from these components.[3]

[3] Since the framework treats a component and its clones as independent, it does not support any consistency control mechanisms between them.

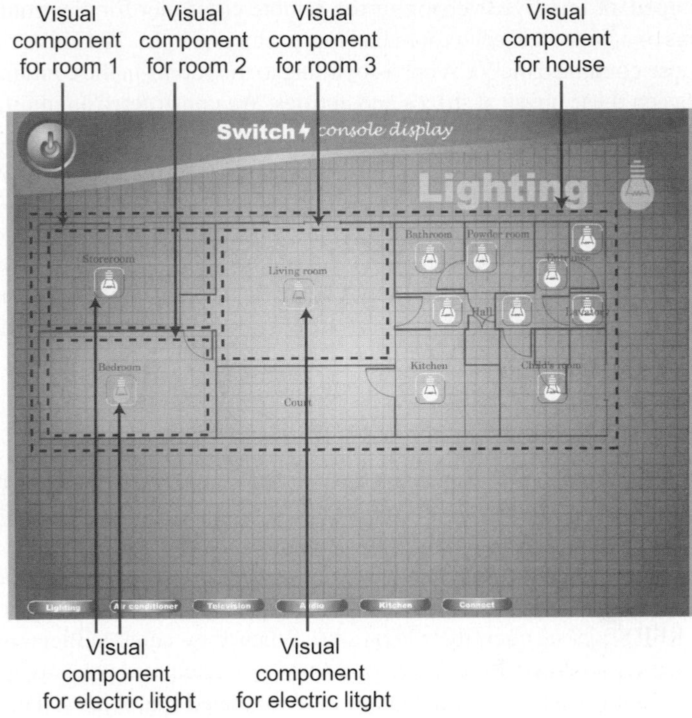

Fig. 8. Screenshot of remote control interface

6 Early Experience

We developed various components for managing VCAs, PASs, PALs, and SAs as well as basic visual components, e.g., text viewer/editor component , JPEG or GIF viewer components, and stream-video player components.[4] Most java Swing and AWT GUI Widgets can be used as our components in the framework without modifications, because they have been derived from the `java.awt.Component` class. The performance of visual components is reasonable as management interfaces.

We describe a remote controller for power-outlets of lights through a commercial protocol called X10 with this framework. The lights are controlled by switching their power sources on or off according to the X10-protocol. We provide all lights with their PALs to switch them on or off. Each PAL communicates with an X10-base server, which controls an X10-module connected to the power-outlet to switch the outlet on or off, and it has its own visual component to display the GUI of its target (Fig. 7). The current implementation of the component sends commands to its PAL through an HTTP-based protocol. When a new PAL is added to the model, it sends a specified event to the component runtime system, which downloads a visual component for the PAL.

[4] Visual components corresponding to visual components, e.g., documents, image viewers, and text editors, were presented in our previous papers [12,13].

We developed an improved version of the remote controller for electronic lights in several rooms of a house and each room had more than one light. The VCA corresponding to the house contained the VCA corresponding to the rooms in the containment relationship between these physical spaces and entities, We constructed an interface for the controller with the framework (Fig. 8). The visual component for the VCA corresponding to the house had several visual components displayed for the VCAs corresponding to the rooms in its area. The visual component for the house drew a map of arrangement of the rooms in the house. It contained VCAs corresponding to the rooms in spaces corresponding to the rooms on the map. A VCA corresponding to a room could contain PALs and PASs, e.g., PALs for controlling X10 modules connected to power outlets in the room through the X10 protocol. The interface was used to control home appliances, including lights.

6.1 Management System for Context-Aware Services

The second application is a management system for context-aware assistant services. The system was constructed with the framework and actually used at an exhibition in a public museum. This was in the Museum of Nature and Human Activities at Hyogo, Japan, which mainly has information and objects that concerned the natural environment. The exhibition space had RFID-tag readers installed and visitors were provided with active RFID-tags to track their locations. When they came sufficiently close to some objects, e.g., zoological specimens and fossils, located at several spots in the exhibition, they could listen to sound content that annotated the objects. The RFID-tag readers identified all the visitors within their coverage range, i.e., a 2-meters diameter and selected sound content according to their knowledge and interests. Fig. 9 shows

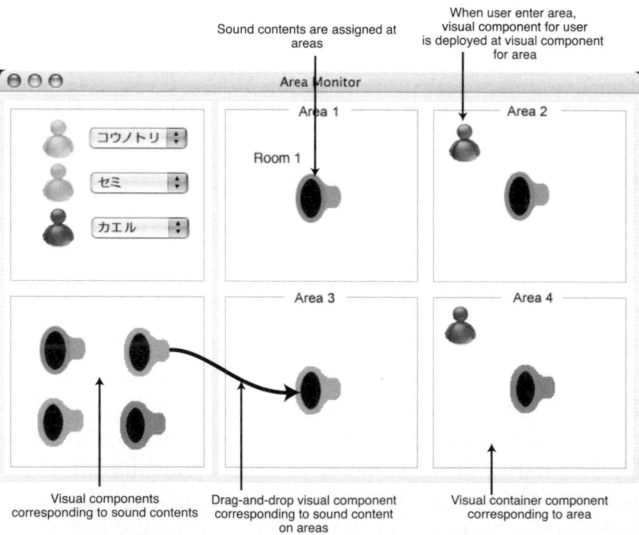

Fig. 9. Screenshot of monitor system windows for location/user-aware audio guiding system

a screenshot of the visual interface for the management system. The interface enables users to deploy services at areas by using drag-and-drop manipulation. Each day the exhibition has more than 200 visitors and the system continued to monitor and manage RFID-tag readers and location-aware services for one week without any experiencing problems.

The interface consisted of four visual components that monitored four RFID-tag readers located at spots throughout the exhibition. When a visitor with an RFID-tag entered a spot, the VCA corresponding to him or her is deployed at the VCA corresponding to the spot. We could dynamically add/remove location-aware services to/from spots. To add a service to a spot, we deployed SA to define the service at the VCA corresponding to the spot by a drag-and-drop operation of the visual component of the SA on the visual component of the VCA. Curators who have no knowledge about pervasive computing systems, can easily and naturally change audio-based assistance services at the exhibition.

7 Related Work

This paper addresses a user-friendly management system of context-aware services in indoors settings, e.g., in buildings and houses, rather than in outdoor settings.

7.1 Location Models

Perceptual technologies have made it possible to sense contextual information in the real world. For example, indoor location systems, such as Radio Frequency IDentification (RFID) tag systems, measure and track the locations of physical entities attached to RFID tags. Existing context-aware services tend to be selected and operated in an ad-hoc manner. For example, most existing services explicitly and implicitly depend on the underlying sensing systems. They are not available with other sensing systems that they have not initially assumed. To solve these problems, some research projects on context-aware services have attempted to offer general-purpose world models to cancel the differences between sensing systems. Since location is one of the most typical and useful kinds of contextual information, location models will be discussed [2]. Existing location models, unfortunately, lack any user-friendly interfaces to enable end-users to easily manage and customize them.

7.2 Management Systems for Pervasive Computing

As mentioned in the previous section, there have been a few attempt to construct management systems or tools that monitor and customize context-aware services in pervasive computing environments. The EasyLiving project [4] provides context-aware spaces, with a particular focus on homes and offices. It uses mounted sensors such as stereo cameras on a room's walls and tracks the locations and identities of people in the room. The system can dynamically aggregate networked-enabled input/output devices, such as keyboards and mice, even when they belong to different computers in the space. It provides monitoring tools for visualizing the positions of users in rooms. However, the project, including its monitoring tools, seemed only to be designed for its target rooms in an ad-hoc manner. Cambridge University's Sentient Computing project [5] provides a platform for location-aware applications using an ultrasonic-based locating system in a building. It can track the movement of tagged entities, such as individuals and objects, so that the graphical user interfaces of the users' applications follow them while they move around. It provides a visual editor to enable the ranges of location-aware services to be configured, but cannot deploy services at locations.

There have been several mechanisms for automatically generate graphical user interfaces for pervasive computing services and devices [6,9,8]. Most existing approaches can provide GUIs for individual devices and can support the dynamic generation of GUIs for devices, which may be added. However, they assume the use of specified protocols to communicate with their target devices. They do not support the deployment and configuration of context-aware services.

8 Conclusion

We presented a visual framework for monitoring and managing context-aware services in smart spaces. It supports a symbolic location model to represent the containment relationships between physical entities, spaces, computing devices, and software for defining services as virtual counterpart objects that correspond to them. It enables physical entities, places, computing devices, and services in smart spaces to have visual components to annotate and control them and to dynamically and seamlessly assemble multiple visual components into a visual interface for managing the spaces. It can monitor the spatial structure of physical entities and places and customize the status and attributes of computing devices, and services, e.g., the location in which context-aware services are available. It provides document-based interfaces to monitor and customize pervasive computing environments as viewing and editing documents by using a GUI to manipulate the compound document technology. For example, end-users can add and customize location-aware services at specified locations by deploying the visual component corresponding to the services at the visual component corresponding to the location. The framework presented in this paper can be used for the management of grid computing. Our visual components themselves are independent of the model. Since they are also programmable entities, they can communicate with computers in grid computing environments and displays various information of the computers.

References

1. Apple Computer Inc., OpenDoc: White Paper, 1995.
2. M. Beigl, T. Zimmer, C. Decker, A Location Model for Communicating and Processing of Context, Personal and Ubiquitous Computing, vol. 6 Issue 5-6, pp. 341-357, Springer, 2002.
3. K. Brockschmidt, Inside OLE 2, Microsoft Press, 1995.
4. B. L. Brumitt, B. Meyers, J. Krumm, A. Kern, S. Shafer, EasyLiving: Technologies for Intelligent Environments, Proceedings of International Symposium on Handheld and Ubiquitous Computing, pp. 12-27, 2000.

5. A. Harter, A. Hopper, P. Steggeles, A. Ward, and P. Webster, The Anatomy of a Context-Aware Application, Proceedings of Conference on Mobile Computing and Networking (MOBICOM'99), pp. 59-68, ACM Press, 1999.
6. K. Gajos and D. S. Weld, SUPPLE: automatically generating user interfaces, Proceedings of the 9th International Conference on Intelligent User Interface (IUI'04) pp.93-100, ACM Press, 2004.
7. The GNOME Project, Bonobo, http://developer.gnome.org/ arch/component/ bonobo.html, 2002.
8. T. D. Hodes, R. H. Katz, E. Servan-Schreiber, L. Rowe, Composable ad-hoc mobile services for universal interaction, Proceedings of International Conference on Mobile Computing and Networking (MobiCom'97), pp.1-12, 1997.
9. J. Nichols, B. A. Myers, M. Higgins, J. Hughes, T. K. Harris, R. Rosenfeld, and M. Pignol, Generating remote control interfaces for complex appliances, Proceedings of Symposium on User Interface Software and Technology (UIST'02), pp.161-170, ACM Press, 2002.
10. M. Potel and S. Cotter Inside Taligent Technology, Addison-Wesley, 1995.
11. I. Satoh, A Location Model for Pervasive Computing Environments, Proceedings of IEEE 3rd International Conference on Pervasive Computing and Communications (PerCom'05), pp,215-224, IEEE Computer Society, March 2005.
12. I. Satoh, Network Processing of Documents, for Documents, by Documents, Proceedings of ACM/IFIP/USENIX 6th International Middleware Conference (Middleware'2005), Lecture Notes in Computer Science (LNCS), vol. 3790, pp.421-430, December 2005.
13. I. Satoh, A Document-centric Component Framework for Document Distributions, Proceedings of 8th International Symposium on Distributed Objects and Applications (DOA'2006), Lecture Notes in Computer Science (LNCS), vol.4276, pp.1555-1575, Springer, October 2006.

Towards a Peer-To-Peer Platform for High Performance Computing

Nabil Abdennadher and Régis Boesch

University of Applied Sciences, Geneva, Switzerland
{nabil.abdennadher, regis.boesch}@hesge.ch

Abstract. *XtremWeb-CH (XWCH)* is a software system that makes it easy for scientists and industrials to deploy and execute their parallel and distributed applications on a public-resource computing infrastructure. The objective of *XWCH* is to develop a real High Performance Peer-To-Peer platform with a distributed scheduling and communication system. The main idea is to build a completely symmetric model where nodes can be providers and consumers at the same time.

This paper describes the different "components" of an *XWCH* infrastructure and the new features proposed by this platform compared to other similar Global Computing projects. It also describes the porting, the deployment and the execution of a phylogenetic CPU time consuming application on an experimental *XWCH* platform.

Keywords: Grid, Peer-To-Peer, Scheduling algorithm, High Performance Computing.

1 Introduction

Since the early 90s, computing power consumers are adopting a new approach which takes advantage of the Internet development. The idea consists of deploying High Performance applications on Distributed platforms instead of supercomputer centres. This concept, known as Grid Computing, provides the ability to perform higher throughput computing by taking advantage of many networked computers. The Grid platforms use the resources of many separate computers connected by a network (usually the Internet) to solve large-scale computation problems. These "platforms", equipped with appropriate middlewares, involve organizationally-owned resources: supercomputers, clusters, and PCs owned by universities, research labs, and private companies.

Simultaneously with Grid Computing, a second alternative emerged. It consists of executing High Performance applications on anonymous connected computers by using their available resources. This concept is called Global Computing (GC). Consumers are typically small academic research groups and/or private companies with limited computer expertise and manpower. Most providers are individuals who own PCs and Macintosh, connected to the Internet by cable modems or DSL. Providers are not computer experts, and participate in a project only if they are interested, or receive "incentives". In the context of GC, consumers have no control over providers.

C. Cérin and K.-C. Li (Eds.): GPC 2007, LNCS 4459, pp. 412–423, 2007.

The majority of GC projects adopted a centralized structure based on a Master/Slave Architecture: BOINC [1], Entropia [2], United Devices [3], Parabon [4], XtremWeb [5], etc. A natural extension of the GC consists on distributing the "decisional degree" of the master in order to avoid any form of centralization. Thus, architectures such as Clients/Servers and Master/Slaves would be withdrawn. This concept, known as Peer-To-Peer, was successfully used to share and exchange files between computers connected to Internet and broadcast micro-news among internet users. The most known projects are BitTorrent [6], eDonkey [7], Kazaa [8], Gnutella [9], Freenet [10] and FeedTree [11].

The requirements of GC and P2P computing are different from those of Grid computing. In fact, most of the features described in the remainder of this paper apply to GC and P2P computing.

The *XtremWeb-CH* (www.xtremwebch.net) project aims to build an effective Peer-To-Peer System for CPU time consuming applications. Initially, *XWCH* is an upgraded version of a Global Computing environment called *XtremWeb (XW)*. Major improvements have been brought in order to obtain a reliable and efficient system. The software's architecture was completely re-designed. The communication routines based initially on Remote Procedure Calls (Java RMI) were replaced by socket communications.

This document is organized in 5 sections. After the introductory section 1, section 2 presents the different components of the *XWCH* package. Section 3 details the new features *XWCH* introduces, compared to other GC and P2P projects. Section 4 presents the experiments carried out in order to evaluate *XWCH*. Finally, section 5 gives some perspectives of this research.

2 *XtremWeb-CH* Ingredients

XtremWeb-CH (XWCH) is composed of four modules: coordinator, worker, warehouse and broker. Several modules can be installed on the same node. A typical *XWCH* platform is composed of one coordinator and a set of workers, warehouses and brokers (Fig. 1).

The coordinator module is the main component of *XWCH*. It is considered as the master of the *XWCH* system; it has the responsibility of managing communication between the clients (users) and the workers (resource providers).

The worker module is installed on each provider node. It manages execution of tasks and the transfer of data from/to the worker. Workers are considered as the slaves of the *XWCH* system.

When two communicating tasks are executed by two workers that can not reach each other (firewalls, NAT addresses, etc.), a warehouse node is used as a depository: the producer worker stores the result of its execution while the consumer worker fetches for the input data it needs to launch its execution.

A broker module is a "compiler" which transforms the user request (application submission) into a set of tasks compliant to the "format" recognized by *XWCH*. Every family of applications has its own broker. The *XWCH* broker module can be compared to the Globus broker which is responsible of transforming a high level RSL (Request Specification Language) request into a low level RSL request [12].

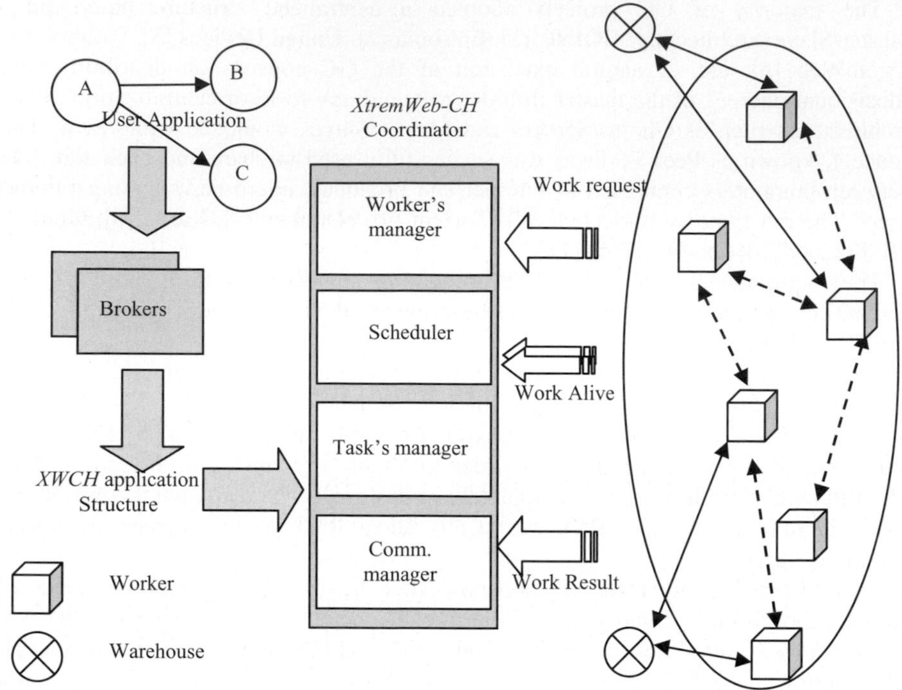

Fig. 1. *XWCH* architecture

2.1 The Coordinator

It is a three-tier architecture which adds a middle tier between client and workers. There is no direct submission/result transfer between clients and workers. The coordinator accepts execution requests coming from clients, assigns the tasks to the workers according to a scheduling policy and the availability of data, transfers binary codes to workers (if necessary), supervises task execution on workers, detects worker crash/disconnection, re-launches tasks on any other available worker, and controls the transfer traffic on the network to ensure the balancing of bandwidth load. The coordinator is composed of four services: the workers' manager, the tasks' manager, the scheduler and the communication manager.

2.1.1 The Workers' Manager

The workers' manager maintains a list of connected workers. It receives four types of common requests/signals from the workers: Register Request (RR), Work Request (WR), Life Signal (LS) and Work Result Signal (WRS). In order to minimize the response time of these requests/signals, every "type" is received on a dedicated port. The Register Request allows a worker to subscribe nearby the coordinator. When the Workers' Manager receives a Work Request, it searches for the most appropriate task (see detail in section 3.3) to be assigned to the concerned worker. During the execution of the task, workers send LS to the coordinator to inform about their status. Life Signals are considered, by the coordinator, as the "proof" that the workers are still "alive" (connected). When a worker finishes its execution, it sends a Work Result Signal to inform the coordinator about the location of the data it has produced.

2.1.2 The Tasks' Manager

A parallel and distributed application is composed of a set of communicating tasks whose structure is described in section 3.1. A task is considered to be "ready" for execution if its input data are available (given by the user or produced by a previous task). A task is in "blocked" status if its input data are not yet available. Two lists are maintained by the Tasks' Manager: blocked tasks and ready tasks. When receiving a Work Result Signal, the Tasks' Manager checks whether the new available data correspond to input data awaited by one or several blocked tasks; it updates the lists of blocked and ready tasks accordingly.

2.1.3 The Scheduler

A Work Request transmits, as input parameter, the performance that can be delivered by the concerned worker. When receiving this request, the coordinator launches a scheduler module which selects the "most appropriate" ready task to be allocated to that worker. The concept of "most appropriate" is detailed in section 3.3.

2.1.4 The Communication Manager

XWCH is supposed to be a Public Large Scale Distributed Platform. It is assumed to be deployed on a "public" network. In this context, the system should insure that the bandwidth provided by the network is not completely consumed by the traffic generated by *XWCH*: common requests, data transfers, etc. The data transmitted between two *XWCH* nodes (coordinators, workers, warehouses) are split into fixed size packets. A sleep time separates the transmission of two successive packets. This time depends on the load of the network as sensed by the coordinator: the higher the load the bigger the sleep time.

Similarly, the number of competing *Work Requests* and *Life Signals* processed by the coordinator is fixed by the communication manager according to the workload of the network as sensed by the coordinator.

2.2 The Workers

The worker module includes three components: the activity monitor, the execution thread and the communication manager.

The activity monitor controls whether some computations are taking place in the hosting machine regarding parameters such as CPU idle time and mouse/keyboard activity. According to this monitoring, it processes the effective performance that can be provided by the worker and sends it to the coordinator via the *Work Request*.

The execution thread extracts the assigned task, recreates its environment as provided by the coordinator (binary code, input data, directories structure, etc.), starts computation and waits for the task to complete.

The communication manager of the worker is similar to the communication manager of the coordinator. It "spies" the workload of the network and splits output files into fixed size packets. A sleep time separates the transmission of two successive packets. This time depends on the load of the network load: the higher the load the bigger the sleep time.

Each worker could be in one of the four states: *ready* to execute a task, *receiving* input data of the allocated task, *running* a task or *sending* output data to the warehouse.

When it is in a *ready* state, a worker sends periodically *Work Requests* to the coordinator to inform it about its availability. The worker passes to a *receiving* state if a task is assigned to it: the input data needed by the task is downloaded by the communication manager.

The third state (*running*) indicates that the worker is executing its allocated task. A worker passes from *running* to *sending* state when the task finishes its execution; the result file is then uploaded to the warehouse.

2.3 The Warehouses

XWCH supports direct communication between workers executing two communicating tasks. Direct communication can only take place when the workers can "see" each other. Otherwise (one of the two workers is protected by a firewall or by a NAT address), this kind of communication is impossible. In this case, it is necessary to pass by an intermediary (*XWCH* coordinator for example). However, to avoid overloading the coordinator, one possible solution consists of installing "warehouse" nodes which acts as an intermediary. These nodes are used by workers to download input data needed to execute their allocated task and/or upload output data produced by the task. A warehouse node acts as a repository or file server. It must be reachable by all workers contributing to the execution of a given application. The protocol is the following:

1. The list of available warehouses is received by a worker when it registers nearby a coordinator (Register Request)
2. When a worker finishes the execution of a task it uploads its result in a one of the known warehouses (selected randomly). Thus, the result is stored in the worker and in the warehouse,
3. The worker sends a work result to the coordinator with the two locations (IP address and path) of the result produced by the given task,
4. When a worker sends a Work Request to execute a new task, it receives as a reply, the binary code of the allocated task and the two locations of its input data.

2.4 The Brokers

XWCH optimizes the granularity of the application according to the "state" of the platform. The broker splits the user application into a set of tasks according to the state of the platform. The broker module depends on the application itself. In other words, the broker module "compiles" the user request (application submission) and generates the optimal number of tasks and the best workload (quantity of data to be processed) of each task according to the number of the available workers and their performance. The broker module can be installed in the client node (computer from which the user launches its application).

During execution, a broker node does not interfere with the *XWCH* platform. An API has been developed to allow programmers develop their own brokers specific to their own applications.

3 *XWCH* Characteristics

XWCH supports three new features which, from our knowledge, do not exist in similar "prototypes"

1. support of communicating tasks,
2. direct communication between workers,
3. granularity and load balancing management.

3.1 Support of Communicating Tasks

In the majority of GC environments, jobs submitted to the system are standalone. In case of parallel/distributed applications, communicating modules are executed as separate tasks. It's the user responsibility to link manually output and input data of two communicating tasks. Contrary to this approach, *XWCH* supports the execution of parallel/distributed applications containing communicating tasks. These application as often modelled by a data flow graph where nodes are tasks and edges are communications inter-tasks. The data flow graph is represented by an XML file.

In addition to the four states (detailed in section 2.2) a task can have: *ready*, *running*, *sending* and *receiving*, *XWCH* adds a fifth state: *blocked*. Tasks of a given application are initially *blocked* and cannot be assigned to any worker, since their input data are not available. Only tasks whose input data are given by the user are in *ready* state and can be allocated to workers. When a task is assigned to a worker, it moves from *ready* to *running* state. Input data needed by *blocked* tasks are progressively provided by *running* tasks which finish their processing. *XWCH* detects the *blocked* tasks which can pass to ready state and can, thus, be assigned to a worker.

3.2 Direct Communication Between Workers

Two versions of *XWCH* were developed. The first, called *XWCH-sMs*, manages inter-tasks communications in a centralized way. The second version, called *XWCH-p2p*, allows a direct communication between workers without passing by the coordinator [13]. In the *XWCH-sMs* (slave-Master-slave) version, workers cannot directly communicate, they cannot "see" each other. Any communications between tasks take place through the coordinator. This architecture overloads the coordinator and could affect the application performances.

In order to cure the gaps of the *XWCH-sMs* version, it is necessary to have direct worker-to-worker communications. Every worker receives the binary code of the task it will execute and the necessary information relating to its input file (IP address, path and name of the input file). Data transfer between the two concerned workers can thus take place on the initiative of the receiver. This *XWCH-p2p* version has two main advantages: it discharges the coordinator from data routing and avoids the duplication of communications (whenever it's possible). In this context, the coordinator keeps only the responsibility of tasks scheduling. *XWCH-p2p* tends towards the Peer-To-Peer concept which one of its principles is to avoid any centralized control.

Direct communication can only take place when the workers can "see" each other. Otherwise (one of the two workers is protected by a firewall or by a NAT address), direct communication is impossible. In this case, a warehouse node is used as a depository (see details in section 2.3).

3.3 Granularity and Scheduling

In parallel computing, the grain's size (granularity) depends on the application and the number of processors in the target parallel machine. This number is generally known and fixed before the execution. In this case, the granularity is fixed during the development of the application. In our context, the computer is the network, workers are free to join and/or leave the *XWCH* platform whenever they want. The exact number of available workers is known just before the execution and could be varied later. As a consequence, the best granularity can not be fixed before execution time. This section describes how *XWCH* optimizes the granularity of tasks and how these tasks are scheduled during execution.

The data flow graph which represents an application comprises a set of stages $\{S_i\}$. A stage S_i is a set of tasks having the same source code. They can be executed in parallel on different workers. The precedence rules between two stages S_i and S_{i+1} depends on the application. Tasks belonging to the same stage have no precedence rules. They are fed with different data and are executed according to the Single Program Multiple Data (SPMD) model. Thus, every stage is responsible of processing a "quantity" of data noted Q_i. The number of tasks belonging to stage S_i depends also on application but could be fixed according to the number of workers. To deploy an application on *XWCH*, three steps are required:

3.3.1 Discovery Step

This step consists of searching for a set of available workers W to execute the application (or one stage of the application). The output of this step is a set of workers W = {(wj, pj)} where pj is the effective performance of wj. pj can be expressed in term of CPU performance, main memory size, network bandwidth, etc.

3.3.2 Configuration Step

Assuming that $|W| = n$, this step dispatches the quantity of data to process by a stage S_i (Q) among the n tasks that will compose the given stage. A task t_k, supposed to be executed by worker w_j (with performance p_j), is assigned a quantity of data q_k function of p_j. q_k is called the workload of t_k. The more the worker is powerful, the bigger is q_k. At this point, the system behaves as if the n workers are fully monitored by the coordinator. In other words, granularity of the parallelization and load balancing are fixed according to the number and performance of available workers.

The output of the configuration step for a given stage S of a given application is a set of couples $\{(q_k, p_j)\}$ where p_j is the performance of the worker that will process the task having the workload q_k.

The XML file, describing the application, is automatically generated at the end of this step.

3.3.3 Execution Step

Configuration step assumes that available workers W are fixed and controlled by the coordinator. However, during execution, tasks allocation is not totally controlled by the coordinator. Indeed, tasks are allocated to workers when the coordinator receives work requests from workers. At this point, it is worth going into some details:

1. A work request is sent by the workers and received by the coordinator.
2. The arrivals of work requests are unpredictable.
3. A work request, sent by a worker, indicates its current performance p.
4. One or several workers selected during discovery step can disappear during execution step.

One or several new workers can register and start to send work requests after discovery step.

During execution, the coordinator manages a set of tasks $T = \{t_k\}$ belonging to different applications. Every task t_k has its workload q_k.

Ideally, tasks belonging to a given stage of a given task are executed in parallel on workers selected during configuration step (or new workers with higher performance). Since workers are volatiles, a Work Request received by the coordinator is not necessarily sent by one of the workers selected during the configuration step. For that reasons, the scheduling policy of *XWCH* is the following: when receiving a work request from a worker w having performance p, the task t allocated to w is the one which workload q is closer to p. Thus, the scheduler of *XWCH* allocates task t of T to w if: $|q - p| = \min (|q_k - p|)$ for all t_k belonging to T (I)

The scheduling algorithm is executed when a work request is received by the coordinator. According to this algorithm, a given task is not executed unless an appropriate worker sends a work request. This means that a task could stay indefinitely in a *ready* state and never assigned to a worker. In order to avoid this situation, a deadline is affected to each stage of the application: if a task spends in a ready state a time higher than its deadline, it is automatically allocated to the first free worker. A small value of the deadline, means that the user prefers allocate tasks to workers as soon as possible. In this case, tasks could be assigned to a non appropriate worker. A high value of the deadline means that the user prefers wait and allocate tasks to the best appropriate worker. In this case, the task could be blocked indefinitely.

4 Experiments

This section presents some performance analysis of *XWCH*. Our results demonstrate the performance characteristics of the system and highlight promising areas for further research.

The objective of these experiments is to validate our approach. They are not carried out to prove that the system delivers a maximum power for a given application: the project's challenge is to extract, at low cost, a reasonable computing power from a widely distributed platform rather than extracting the maximum power from a local supercomputer or a dedicated GRID platform.

XWCH was evaluated in the case of a phylogenetic application: *PHYLIP* (the *PHYL*ogeny *I*nference *P*ackage) package [14]. The parallelized version of *PHYLIP* is used to generate evolutionary tree related to HIV viruses. No optimization was brought to the parallel version of *PHYLIP*. However, several improvements could be carried out in order to adapt the algorithm to the targeted platform.

Executions were carried out on a platform with one coordinator (Linux OS), 250 heterogeneous windows workers ranging from Pentium II to Pentium IV, and 2 warehouses. The workers are geographically located in two different places (Engineering Schools of Geneva and Yverdon). During execution, the 250 workers are used by students; they are often switched off or disconnected.

4.1 The Application

Phylogenetic is the science which deals with the relationships that could exist between living organisms. It reconstructs the pattern of events that have led to "the distribution and diversity of life". These relationships are extracted from comparing Desoxyribo Nucleic Acid (DNA) sequences of species. An evolutionary tree, termed life tree, is then built to show relationship among species.

A multitude of applications aiming at building evolutionary trees are used by the scientific community [15] [16] [17] [18]. These applications are known to be CPU time consuming, their complexity is exponential (*NP-difficult* problem). Approximate and heuristic methods do not solve the problem since their complexity remains polynomial with an order greater than 5: $O(n^m)$ with $m > 5$. Parallelization of these methods could be useful in order to reduce the response time of these applications.

PHYLIP is a package of programs for inferring phylogenies (evolutionary trees). It is the most widely-distributed phylogeny package. *PHYLIP* has been used to build the largest number of published trees. It has been in distribution since 1980, and has over 15,000 registered users. *PHYLIP* was ported on *XWCH* platform.

An evolutionary tree is composed of several branches. Each branch is composed of sub-branches and/or leaf nodes (sequences). Two sequences belonging to the same branch are supposed to have the same ancestors. To construct the tree, the application defines a "distance" between all pairs of sequences. Evolutionary tree is then gradually built by sticking to the same branch, the pairs of sequences having the smallest distance between them. Even if the concept is simple, the algorithm is a CPU time consuming. Moreover, the application constructs not only one tree from the origin data set, but a set of trees generated from a large number of bootstrapped data sets (somewhere between 100 and 1000 is usually adequate). This parameter is called ***r***. The final (or consensus) tree is obtained by retaining groups that occur as often as possible. If a group occurs in more than a fraction *f* of all the input trees it will definitely appear in the consensus tree.

The application, as adapted to *XWCH*, is composed of 5 programs: *Seqboot, Dnadist, Fitch-Margoliash, Neighbor-Joining* and *Consensus*.

The structure of the obtained parallel/distributed application is shown in Fig. 2.

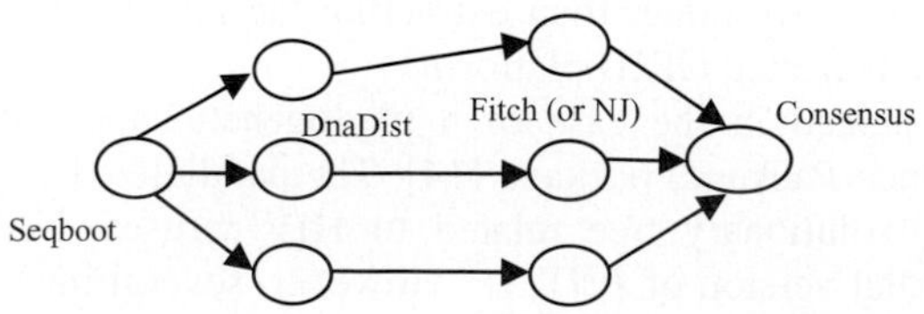

Fig. 2. Data flow graph of the *PHYLIP* package

4.2 Evaluation of the Scheduling Algorithm

This paragraph evaluates the performance of the scheduling algorithm proposed in section 3.3. Two versions of *PHYLIP* were deployed on *XWCH*:

1. The first version (*Version 1* in Fig.3) is composed of a given number of *Fitch* tasks. Each task processes a fixed number of trees.
2. In the second version (*Version 2* in Fig.7), the number of tasks and their workload are processed as explained in section 3.3. This means that that the number of trees generated by a given *Fitch* task depends on the performance of the worker.

Execution times consumed by the two versions are shown in Fig. 3.

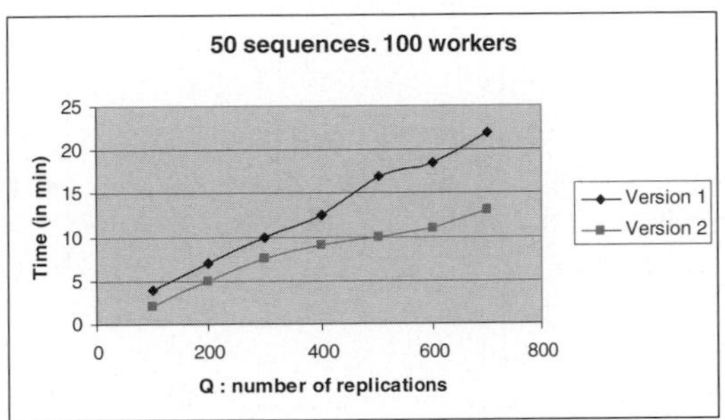

Fig. 3. Execution times of PHYLIP

For both versions, *XWCH* insures that executing codes are transferred from coordinator to workers only at the start of the execution: if the same task is re-executed on the same worker, its code is not downloaded again. The difference of execution times in Fig. 3 is due to the synchronization between the coordinator and workers: When a worker ends its execution it stores the results locally and on the warehouse, generates a work request to ask for a new task, and finally generates a data request to receive input data it needs.

The goal of the scheduling algorithm (described in section 3.3) is to load balance tasks belonging to the same stage *S*. Fig. 4 shows the variation of the total number of tasks during the execution of the application (Phylip).

Fig. 4 shows the total number of executed tasks during the execution of the *PHYLIP* application. Since the "Fitchs" are the most consuming time tasks, this study will focus on the number of these tasks.

Steps I correspond to the execution of the *Fitch* tasks. These curves show that these tasks finish, in general, at the same time. Thus, the scheduling algorithm ensures a good load balancing. However, some *Fitch* tasks finish their execution lately (step II in Fig. 4). This is due to one or many of the following factors:

1. The workers collected during the discovery step disappear during the execution,
2. Workers not selected during the discovery step appear during the execution,
3. As it is implemented today, workers' performance is only represented by the CPU power (CPU frequency). This model is not realistic; the system should take into account other criteria such as main memory, processes, applications and services installed locally on the workers, etc.

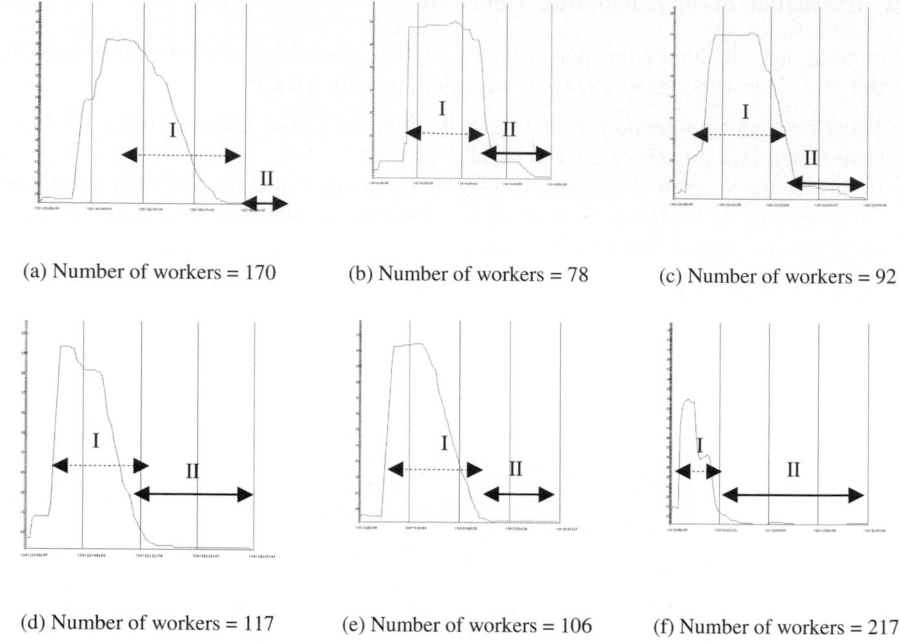

(a) Number of workers = 170 (b) Number of workers = 78 (c) Number of workers = 92

(d) Number of workers = 117 (e) Number of workers = 106 (f) Number of workers = 217

Fig. 4. Total number of executing tasks. x : time, y : number of parallel executing tasks

5 Conclusion

This paper presents a new GC environment (*XtremWeb-CH*), used for the execution of high performance applications on a highly heterogeneous distributed environment. *XWCH* can support direct communications between workers, without passing by the coordinator. A scheduling policy is proposed in order to minimize synchronization between coordinator and workers and optimize load balancing of workers. The porting of PHYLIP on *XWCH* has demonstrated the feasibility of our solution. Other experiments are in progress to evaluate *XWCH* in other High Performance applications cases.

The current version of *XWCH* allows the decentralization of communications between workers. The next step consists of designing a distributed scheduler. This scheduler shall avoid allocating communicating tasks to workers that can not reach each other and/or not belonging to the same domain (Local Area Network). This approach offers a strong basis for the development of distributed and dynamic scheduler and could confirm and reinforce the tendency detailed in the introduction.

References

1. BOINC: A System for Public-Resource Computing and Storage. David P. Anderson. 5th IEEE/ACM International Workshop on Grid Computing. November 8, 2004, Pittsburgh, USA.
2. http://www.entropia.com/

3. http://www.ud.com/home.htm
4. Parabon Computation, Inc: The Frontier Application. Programming Interface, Version 1.5.2. 2004
5. Gilles Fedak et al. XtremWeb : A Generic Global Computing System. CCGRID2001, workshop on Global Computing on Personal Devices. Brisbane, Australia. May 2001.
6. Incentives Build Robustness in BitTorrent, Bram Cohen, May 2003. http://www.bittorrent.org/bittorrentecon.pdf
7. http://www.edonkey2000.com/
8. http://www.kazaa.com/us/index.htm
9. KAN G., Peer-to-Peer: harnessing the power of disruptive technologies, Chapter Gnutella, O'Reilly, Mars 2001.
10. Ian Clarke. A Distributed Decentralised Information Storage and Retrieval System. Division of Informatics. Univ. of Edinburgh. 1999.
11. http://feedtree.net/
12. http://www.globus.org/
13. N. Abdennadher, R. Boesch, A Large Scale Distributed System for High Performance needs. HP-ASIA 2005. December 2005, Biejing, China
14. http://www.phylip.com/
15. http://biowulf.nih.gov/apps/puzzle/tree-puzzle-doc.html
16. http://www.tree-puzzle.de/
17. http://www.dkfz.de/tbi/tree-puzzle/
18. Heiko A. Schmidt, Phylogenetic Trees from Large Datasets, 'Ph.D.' in Computer Science, Düsseldorf, Germany, 2003.

Assessing Contention Effects on MPI_Alltoall Communications

Luiz Angelo Steffenel[1], Maxime Martinasso[2], and Denis Trystram[2]

[1] Université Nancy-2, LORIA, AlGorille Team, Nancy, France
Luiz-Angelo.Steffenel@univ-nancy2.fr
[2] LIG - Laboratoire d'Informatique de Grenoble, Grenoble, France
{Maxime.Martinasso,Denis.Trystram}@imag.fr

Abstract. One of the most important collective communication patterns used in scientific applications is the *complete exchange*, also called *All-to-All*. Although efficient algorithms have been studied for specific networks, general solutions like those available in well-known MPI distributions (e.g. the MPI_Alltoall operation) are strongly influenced by the congestion of network resources. In this paper we present an integrated approach to model the performance of the All-to-All collective operation, which consists in identifying a contention signature that characterizes a given network environment, using it to augment a contention-free communication model. This approach, assessed by experimental results, allows an accurate prediction of the performance of the All-to-All operation over different network architectures with a small overhead.

Keywords: Network Contention, MPI, Collective Communications, Performance Modeling.

1 Introduction

One of the most important collective communication patterns for scientific applications is the *total exchange* [1] (also called *All-to-All*), in which each process holds n different data items that should be distributed among the n processes, including itself. An important example of this communication pattern is the All-to-All operation, where all messages have the same size m.

Although efficient All-to-All algorithms have been studied for specific networks structures like meshes, hypercubes, tori and circuit-switched butterflies, general solutions like those found in well-known MPI distributions rely on direct point-to-point communications among the processes. Because all communications are started simultaneously, architecture independent algorithms are strongly influenced by the saturation of network resources and subsequent loss of packets - the network contention.

In this paper we present a new approach to model the performance of the All-to-All collective operation. Our strategy consists in identifying a *contention signature* that characterizes a given network environment. Using such *contention signature*, we are able to accurately predict the performance of the All-to-All operation, with an arbitrary number of processes and message sizes. To demonstrate

C. Cérin and K.-C. Li (Eds.): GPC 2007, LNCS 4459, pp. 424–435, 2007.

our approach, we present experimental results obtained with different network architectures (Fast Ethernet, Gigabit Ethernet and Myrinet). We believe that this model can be extremely helpful on the development of application performance prediction frameworks such as PEMPIs [2], but also in the optimization of grid-aware collective communications (e.g.: LaPIe [3] and MagPIe [4]).

This paper is organized as follows: Section 2 presents a survey of performance modeling under communication contention. Section 3 presents the network models used in this paper, and in section 4 we formalize the *total exchange* problem, as well as some performance lower bounds. In Section 5 we propose a strategy to characterize the *contention signature* of a given network and for instance, to predict the performance of the All-to-All operation. Section 6 validates our model against experimental data obtained on different network architectures (Fast Ethernet, Gigabit Ethernet and Myrinet). In Section 7 we provide a study case for predicting the performance of a grid-aware All-to-All algorithm. Finally, Section 8 presents some conclusions and the future directions of our work.

2 Related Works

In the *All-to-All* operation, every process holds $m \times n$ data items that should be equally distributed among the n processes, including itself. Because general implementations of the All-to-All collective communication rely on direct point-to-point communications among the processes the network can easily become saturated, and by consequence, degrade the communication performance. Indeed, Chun and Wang [5][6] demonstrated that the overall execution time of intensive exchange collective communications are strongly dominated by the network contention and congestive packet loss, two aspects that are not easy to quantify. As a result, a major challenge on modeling the communication performance of the All-to-All operation is to represent the impact of network contention.

Unfortunately, most communication models like those presented by Christara *et al.* [1] and Pjesivac-Grbovic *et al.* [7] do not take into account the potential impacts of network contention. Indeed, these works usually represent the All-to-All operation as parallel executions of the *personalized one-to-many* pattern [8], as presented by the linear point-to-point model below, where where α is the start-up time (the latency between the processes), $\frac{1}{\beta}$ is the bandwidth of the link, m represents the message size in bytes and n corresponds to the number of processes involved in the operation:

$$T = (n-1) \times (\alpha + \beta m) \tag{1}$$

The development of contention-aware communication models is relatively recent, as shown by Grove [9]. For instance, Adve [10] presented one of the first models to take into account the effects of resource contention. This model considers that the total execution time of parallel programs is the sum of four components, namely:

$$T = t_{computation} + t_{communication} + t_{resource-contention} + t_{synchronization} \tag{2}$$

While conceptually simple, this model was non-trivial in practice because of the non-deterministic nature of resource contention, and because of the difficulty to estimate average synchronization delays.

While the non-deterministic behavior of the network contention is a major obstacle to modeling communication performance, some authors suggested a few techniques to adapt the existing models. As consequence, Bruck [11] suggested the use of a *slowdown factor* to correct the performance predictions. Similarly, Clement *et al.* [12] introduced a technique that suggested a way to account contention in shared networks such as non-switched Ethernet, consisting in a contention factor γ that extends the linear communication model T:

$$T = \alpha + \beta \times m \times \gamma \tag{3}$$

where γ is equal to the number of processes. A restriction on this model is that it assumes that all processes communicate simultaneously, which is only true for a few collective communication patterns. Anyway, in the cases where this assumption holds, they found that this simple contention model enhanced the accuracy of their predictions for essentially zero extra effort.

The use of a contention factor was supported by the work of Labarta et *al.* [13], that intent to approximate the behavior of the network contention by considering that if there are m messages ready to be transmitted, and only b available buses, then the messages are serialized in $\lceil \frac{m}{b} \rceil$ communication waves. Also, König *et al.* [14] have shown indeed that some All-to-All algorithms that are optimal with unlimited buffers become less efficient when communications depend on restricted buffers size.

A similar approach was followed by Jeannot *et al.* [15], who designed scheduling algorithms for data redistribution through a backbone. In their work, they suppose that at most k communications can be performed at the same time without causing network contention (the value of k depending on the characteristics of the platform). Using the knowledge of the application transfer pattern, they proposed two algorithms to schedule the messages transfer, performing an application-level congestion control that in most cases outperforms the TCP contention control mechanism.

Most recently, some works aimed to design contention-aware performance models. For instance, LoGPC [16] presents an extension of the LogP model that tries to determine the impact of network contention through the analysis of k-ary n-cubes. Unfortunately, the complexity of this analysis makes too hard the application of such model in practical situations.

Another approach to include contention-specific parameters in the performance models was introduced by Chun [6]. In his work, the contention is considered as a component of the communication latency, and by consequence, the model uses different latency values depending on the message size. Although easier to use than LoGPC, this model does not take into account the number of messages passing in the network nor the link capacity, which are clearly related to the occurrence of network contention.

3 Network Models Definition

In this work we assume that the network is fully connected, which corresponds to most current parallel machines with distributed memory.

Communication Model: The links between pairs of processes are bidirectional, and each process can transmit data on at most one link and receive data on at most one link at any given time.

Transmission Model: We use Hockney's notation [17] to describe our transmission model. Therefore, the time to send a message of size $w_{i,j}$ from a process p_i to another process p_j, is $\alpha + w_{i,j}\beta$, where α is the start-up time (the communication latency between the processes) and $\frac{1}{\beta}$ is the bandwidth of the link. As in this paper we assume that all links have the same latency and bandwidth, and because we only investigate the regular version of the MPI_Alltoall operation where all messages have the same size m, $\forall i, \forall j, w_{i,j} = m$, and therefore the time to send a message from a process p_i to a process p_j is $\alpha + m\beta$.

Synchronization Model: We assume an asynchronous communication model, where transmissions from different processes do not have to start at the same time. However, all processes start the algorithm simultaneously. This synchronization model corresponds to the execution of the MPI_Alltoall operation, used as reference in this work.

4 Problem Definition

In the *total exchange* problem, n different processes hold each one n data items that should be evenly distributed among the n processes, including itself. Because each data item has potentially different contents and sizes according to their destinations, all processes engage a total exchange communication pattern. Therefore, a total exchange operation will be complete only after all processes have sent their messages to their counterparts, and received their respective messages.

Formally, the *total exchange problem* can be described using a weighted digraph $dG(V, E)$ of order n with $V = \{p_0, ..., p_{n-1}\}$. This digraph is called a message exchange digraph or MED for short. In a MED, the vertices represent the process nodes, and the arcs represent the messages to be transmitted. An integer $w(e)$ is associated with each arc $e = (p_i, p_j)$, representing the size of the message to be sent from process p_i to process p_j. Note that there is not necessarily any relationship between a MED and the topology of the interconnection network.

The port capacity of a process for transmission is the number of other processes to which it can transmit simultaneously. Similarly, the port capacity for reception is the number of other processes from which it can receive simultaneously. We will concentrate on the performance modeling problem with all port capacities restricted to one for both transmitting and receiving. This restriction is well-known in the literature as *1-port full-duplex*.

4.1 Notation and Lower Bounds

In this section, we present theoretical bounds on the minimum number of communications and on the bandwidth for the general message exchange problem. The number of communications determines the number of start-ups, and the bandwidth depends on the message weights.

Given a MED $dG(V;E)$, we denote the in-degree of each vertex $p_i \in V$ by $\Delta_r(p_i)$, and the out-degree by $\Delta_s(p_i)$. Let $\Delta_r = \max_{p_i \in V}\{\Delta_r(p_i)\}$ and $\Delta_s = \max_{p_i \in V}\{\Delta_s(p_i)\}$. Therefore, we obtain the following straightforward bound on the number of start-ups.

Claim 1. *The number of start-ups needed to solve a message exchange problem on a digraph $dG(V;E)$ without message forwarding is at least* $\max(\Delta_s, \Delta_r)$.

Given a MED $dG(V,E)$, the bandwidth bounds are determined by two obvious bottlenecks for each vertex - the time for it to send its messages and the time for it to receive its messages. Each vertex p_i has to send messages with sizes $\{w_{i,j} \mid j = 0 \ldots n-1\}$. The time for all vertices to send their messages is at least $t_s = \max_i \sum_{j=0}^{n-1} w_{i,j}\beta$. Similarly, the time for all vertices to receive their messages is at least $t_r = \max_j \sum_{i=0}^{n-1} w_{i,j}\beta$.

Claim 2. *The time to complete a personalized exchange is at least* $\max\{t_s, t_r\}$.

We can combine the claims about the number of start-ups and the bandwidth when message forwarding is not allowed.

Claim 3. *If message forwarding is not allowed, and either the model is synchronous or both maxima are due to the same process, the time to complete a personalized exchange is at least* $\max(\Delta_s, \Delta_r) \times \alpha + \max\{t_s, t_r\}$.

Because in this paper we do not assume messages forwarding, the fan-in and fan-out of a process must be $(n-1)$. Further, as we consider messages to be the same size and the network to be homogeneous, we can simplify Claim 3 so that the following bound holds.

Proposition 1. *If message forwarding is not allowed, and all messages have size* m, *and both bandwidth and latency are identical to any connection between two different processes p_i and p_j, the time to complete a total exchange is at least $(n-1) \times \alpha + (n-1) \times \beta m$.*

Proof. The proof is trivial, as the time to complete a total exchange is at least the time a single process needs to send one message to each other process. ■

5 Contention Signature Approach

To cope with this problem and to model the contention impact on the performance of the All-to-All operation, we adopt an approach similar to Clement *et al.* [12], which considers the contention sufficiently linear to be modeled. Our approach, however, tries to identify the behavior of the All-to-All operation with regard to the theoretical lower bound (Proposition 1) on the *1-port* communication model. In our hypothesis, the network contention depends mostly on the physical characteristics of the network (network cards, links, switches), and consequently, the ratio between the theoretical lower bound and the real performance represents a "*contention signature*" of the network. Once identified the *signature* of a network, it can be used in further experiments to predict the communication performance, provided that the network infrastructure does not change.

Initially, we consider communication in a contention-free environment. In this case, a process that sends messages of size m to $n-1$ processes needs at least $(n-1) \times \alpha + (n-1) \times m\beta$ time units. Further, by the properties of the *1-port* communication model, the total communication time of the All-to-All operation must be at least $(n-1) \times \alpha + (n-1) \times m\beta$ time units if all processes start communicating simultaneously, as stated by Proposition 1.

In the case of the All-to-All operation, however, the intensive communication pattern tends to saturate the network, causing message delays and packet loss that strongly impact on the communication performance of this collective communication. In this network congestion situation, traditional models such as those presented by Christara [1] do not hold anymore, even if the communication pattern has not changed.

Therefore, our approach to model the performance of the MPI_Alltoall operation despite network contention consists on determining a *contention ratio* γ that express the relationship between the theoretical performance (lower bound) and the real completion time. For simplicity, we consider that this *contention ratio* γ is constant and depends exclusively on the network characteristics. Therefore, the simplest way to integrate this *contention ratio* γ in our performance model would be as follows:

$$T = (n-1) \times (\alpha + m\beta \times \gamma) \tag{4}$$

5.1 Non-linear Aspects

Although the performance model augmented by use of the *contention ratio* γ improves the accuracy of the predictions, we observe nonetheless that some network architectures are still subject to performance variations according to the message size. To illustrate this problem, we present in Fig. 1, a detailed mapping of the communication time of the MPI_Alltoall operation in a Gigabit Ethernet network. We observe that the communication time does not increase linearly with the message size, but instead, present a non-linear behavior that prevents our model to accurately predict the performance when dealing with small messages.

To cope with this non-linearity, we propose an extension of the *contention ratio* model to better represent this phenomenon when messages are sufficiently large. Hence, we augment the model with a new parameter δ, which depends on the number of processes but also on a given message size M. As a consequence, the association of different equations helps to define a more realistic performance model for the MPI_Alltoall operation, as follows:

$$T = \begin{cases} (n-1) \times (\alpha + m\beta \times \gamma) & if\, m < M \\ (n-1) \times (\alpha + m\beta \times \gamma + \delta) & if\, m \geq M \end{cases} \tag{5}$$

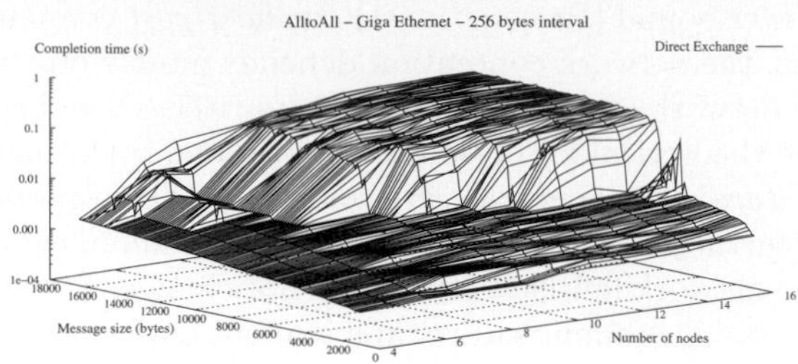

Fig. 1. Non-linearity of communication cost with small messages

6 Validation

To validate the approach proposed in this paper, this section presents our experiments to model the performance of MPI_Alltoall operation using three network architectures, Fast Ethernet, Gigabit Ethernet and Myrinet. As previously explained, our approach consists on comparing the expected and real performance of the MPI_Alltoall operation using a sample experiment with n' nodes; the relationship between these two measures allows us to define the γ and δ parameters that characterize the "network contention signature".

To obtain these parameters, we compare the sample data obtained from both theoretical lower bound and experimental measure, when varying the message size. Indeed, the lower bound comes from Proposition 1, with parameters α and β obtained from a simple point-to-point measure. The parameters γ and δ are obtained through a linear regression with the Generalized Least Squares method, comparing at least four measurement points in order to better fit the performance curve.

The different experiments presented in this paper represent the average of 100 measures for each set of parameters (message size, number of processes), and were conducted over two clusters of the Grid'5000[1]:

The *icluster2* cluster, located at INRIA-Rhone-Alpes, composed of 104 dual Itanium2 nodes at 900 MHz, used for the experiments with the Fast Ethernet network (5 Fast Ethernet switches - 20 nodes per switch - interconnected by 1 Gigabit Ethernet switch) and the Myrinet 2000 network (one 128 ports M3-E128 Myrinet switch). All machines run Red Hat Enterprise Linux AS release 3, with kernel version 2.4.21.

The *GdX* (GriD'eXplorer) cluster, operated by INRIA-Futurs. This cluster includes 216 nodes with dual AMD Opteron processors at 2 GHz running Debian Linux kernel 2.6.8 and a Broadcom Gigabit Ethernet network.

6.1 Fast Ethernet

Taking as basis the measured performance for a 24 machines network, we were able to approximate the performance of the Fast Ethernet network with a

[1] *http://www.grid5000.org/*

contention ratio $\gamma = 1.0195$. Indeed, this relatively small difference must be considered in the light of the retransmission policy: although the communication latency (and therefore the timeouts) is relatively small (around 60 μs), the reduced bandwidth of the links minimizes the impact of the retransmission of a lost packet. More important, we observe that the experimental measure behave like an affine equation, showing a start-up cost usually not considered by the traditional performance model which corresponds to the δ parameter proposed in our model. Therefore, we determined $\delta = 8.23\,ms$ for messages larger than $M = 2\,kB$, which means that each simultaneous communication induces an overload of $8.23\,ms$ to the completion time of the All-to-All operation. Applying both γ and δ parameters we were able to approximate our predictions from the performance of the MPI_Alltoall operation with an arbitrary number of processes, as demonstrate in Fig. 2a. We observe indeed that our error rate is usually smaller than 10% when there are enough processes to saturate the network, as presented in Fig. 2b.

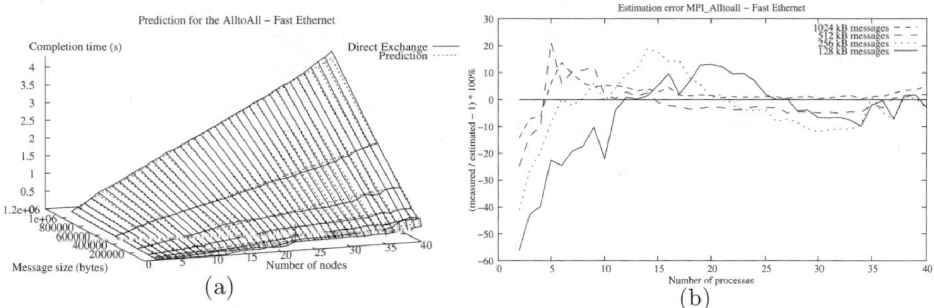

Fig. 2. Performance prediction on a Fast Ethernet network

6.2 Gigabit Ethernet

To compute the *contention ratio* γ and a *start-up cost* δ, we use sample data for an arbitrary number of processes. Indeed, we chose in this example the results for an execution of the All-to-All operation with 40 processes (one by machine). Using linear regression on these data we obtain $\gamma = 4.3628$ and $\delta = 4.93\,ms$ (to be used only for messages larger than $M = 8\,kB$). As a result, the performance predictions from our model correspond to the curve presented on Fig. 3a. As in the case of the Fast Ethernet network, the error rate is quite small when the network becomes saturate, even when we consider different message sizes (Fig. 3b).

6.3 Myrinet

Although the two previous experiments give important proofs on the validity of our modeling method, they share many similarities on both network architecture and transport protocol (TCP/IP). To ensure that our method is not bounded to a specific infrastructure, we chose to validate our performance model also in a Myrinet

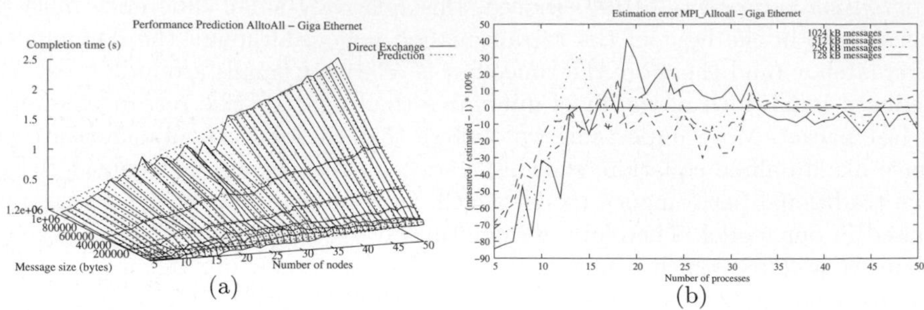

Fig. 3. Performance prediction on a Gigabit Ethernet network

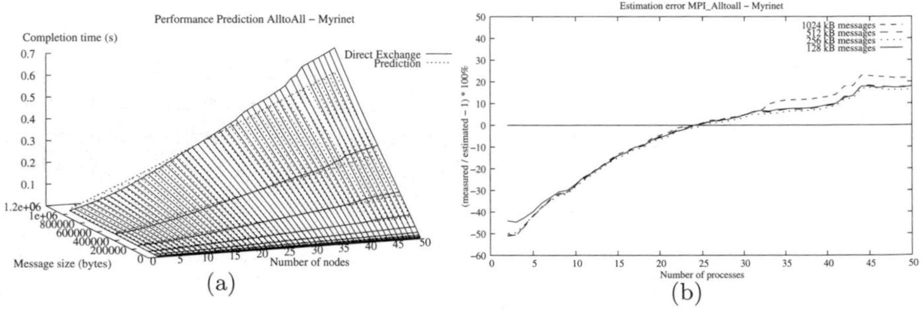

Fig. 4. Performance prediction on a Myrinet network

network, using the *gm* transport protocol. Because of the *Myrinet+gm* stack differs considerably from the Ethernet+TCP/IP stack, any systematic behavior introduced into our sampling data by these architectures should be exposed.

Indeed, the Myrinet network differs from Ethernet-based architectures due to an *start-up* cost almost inexistent (one of the main characteristics of the *Myrinet+gm* stack). Indeed, we were able to fit the performance of a 24-processes All-to-All operation using only the *contention ratio* $\gamma = 2,49754$ (as the linear regression pointed a *start-up cost* δ smaller than 1 microsecond).

Nevertheless, when applying this factor to an arbitrary number of machines, as presented in Fig. 4a, we observe that our predictions do not follow the experimental data as observed before with Fast Ethernet and Gigabit Ethernet. Actually, a close look at the error rate (Fig. 4b) indicates that network saturation occurs only when there are more then 40 communicating processes (evidenced by the constant error rate from that point). These results demonstrate the limitations of our approach: while a *contention ratio* may provide precise performance predictions, it depends on the data used to define the network signature. By using reference data from a partially saturated network we are subjected to inaccurate approximations (even if they are better than the contention unaware predictions).

7 Applications to Grid-Aware Communications

Actually, most of the complexity of the All-to-All problem in grid environments resides on the need to exchange different messages through different networks (local and distant). The traditional implementation of the MPI_Alltoall operation cannot differentiate these networks, leading to poor performances. However, if we assume that communications between clusters are slower than intra-clusters ones, it might be useful to collect data in the local level before sending it through the backbone, in a single transmission. Indeed, in [18] we propose a grid-aware solution which performs on two phases. In the first phase only local communications are performed. During this phase the total exchange is performed on local nodes on both cluster and extra buffers are prepared for the second (inter-cluster) phase. During the second phase data are exchanged between the clusters. Buffers that have been prepared during the first phase are sent directly to the corresponding nodes in order to complete the total exchange.

More precisely, our algorithm works as follow. Without loss of generality, let us assume that cluster $\mathcal{C}_1$ has less nodes than $\mathcal{C}_2$ ($n_1 \leq n_2$). Nodes are numbered from 0 to $n_1 + n_2 - 1$, with nodes from 0 to $n_1 - 1$ being on $\mathcal{C}_1$ and nodes from n_1 to $n_1 + n_2 - 1$ being on cluster $\mathcal{C}_2$. We call $\mathcal{M}_{i,j}$ the message (data) that has to be send form node i to node j. For instance, the algorithm proceeds in two phases:

First phase. During the first phase, we perform the local exchange: Process i sends $\mathcal{M}_{i,j}$ to process j, if i and j are on the same cluster. Then it prepares the buffers for the remote communications. On $\mathcal{C}_1$ data that have to be send to node j on $\mathcal{C}_2$ is first stored to node $j \ mod \ n_1$. Data to be sent from node i on $\mathcal{C}_2$ to node j on $\mathcal{C}_1$ is stored on node $\lfloor i/n_1 \rfloor \times n_1 + j$.

Second phase. During the second phase only n_2 inter-cluster communications occurs. This phase is decomposed in $\lceil n_2/n_1 \rceil$ steps with at most n_1 communications each. Steps are numbered from 1 to $\lceil n_2/n_1 \rceil$ During step s node i of $\mathcal{C}_1$ exchange data stored in its local buffer with node $j = i + n_1 \times s$ on $\mathcal{C}_2$ (if $j < n_1 + n_2$). More precisely i sends $\mathcal{M}_{k,j}$ to j where $k \in [0, n_1]$ and j sends $\mathcal{M}_{k,i}$ to i where $k \in [n_1 \times s, n_1 \times s + n_1 - 1]$.

As our algorithm minimizes the number of inter-cluster communications between the clusters, we need only $2 \times \max(n_1, n_2)$ messages in both directions (against $2 \times n_1 \times n_2$ messages in the traditional algorithm). For instance, the exchange of data between two clusters with the same number of process will proceed in one single communication step of the second phase. Our algorithm is also wide-area optimal since it ensures that a data segment is transferred only once between two clusters separate by a wide-area link.

7.1 Performance Prediction in a Grid Environment

As shown above, the algorithm we propose to optimize All-to-All communications in a grid environment rely on the relative performances of both local and remote networks. Indeed, we extend the total exchange among nodes in the same cluster in order to reduce transmissions through the backbone.

This approach has therefore two consequences for performance prediction: First, it prevents contention in the wide-area links, which are hard to model. Second, transmission of messages packed together is easy to be predicted in a wide-area network (large messages are less subjected to network interferences). For instance, we can design a wide-area performance model by composing local-area predictions obtained with our performance model and wide-area predictions that can be easily obtained from traditional methods. Hence, an approximate model for the communication between two clusters would be similar to:

$$T = max(T_{\mathcal{C}_1}, T_{\mathcal{C}_2}) + \lceil n_2/n_1 \rceil \times (\alpha_w + \beta_w \times m \times n) \qquad (6)$$

Although not in the scope of this work, preliminary experiments indicate that this model holds. We expect to develop this subject in a future work.

8 Conclusions and Future Works

In this paper we address the problem of modeling the performance of *Total Exchange* communication operations, usually subject to important variations caused by network contention. Because traditional performance models are unable to predict the real completion time of an All-to-All operation, we try to cope with this problem by identifying the *contention signature* of a given network. In our approach, two parameters γ and δ are used to augment a linear performance model in order to fit the performance of the MPI_Alltoall operation. Because these parameters characterize the network contention and are independent of the number of communicating processes, they can be used to accurately predict the communication performance when communications tend to saturate the network. Indeed, we demonstrate our approach through experiments conducted on popular network architectures, Fast Ethernet, Gigabit Ethernet and Myrinet.

We intend to pursue this research by validating our model under other network architectures like Infiniband. Indeed, we expect to extend our models to other collective communication operations, which are especially affected by contention when scaling up to a grid level. We are also investigating different strategies to model collective communications in grid environments.

Acknowledgments

We are grateful to the anonymous referees for many comments and helpful suggestions which helped us improve the focus of the paper.

References

1. Christara, C., Ding, X., Jackson, K.: An efficient transposition algorithm for distributed memory computers. In: Proceedings of the High Performance Computing Systems and Applications. (1999) 349–368

2. Midorikawa, E.T., Oliveira, H.M., Laine, J.M.: PEMPIs: A new metodology for modeling and prediction of MPI programs performance. In: Proceedings of the SBAC-PAD 2004, IEEE Computer Society/Brazilian Computer Society (2004) 254–261
3. Barchet-Steffenel, L.A., Mounie, G.: Scheduling heuristics for efficient broadcast operations on grid environments. In: Proceedings of the Performance Modeling, Evaluation and Optimization of Parallel and Distributed Systems Workshop - PMEO'06 (associated to IPDPS'06), Rhodes Island, Greece, IEEE Computer Society (2006)
4. Kielmann, T., Bal, H., Gorlatch, S., Verstoep, K., Hofman, R.: Network performance-aware collective communication for clustered wide area systems. Parallel Computing **27** (2001) 1431–1456
5. Chun, A.T.T., Wang, C.L.: Realistic communication model for parallel computing on cluster. In: Proceedings of the International Workshop on Cluster Computing. (1999) 92–101
6. Chun, A.T.T.: Performance Studies of High-Speed Communication on Commodity Cluster. PhD thesis, University of Hong Kong (2001)
7. Pjesivac-Grbovic, J., Angskun, T., Bosilca, G., Fagg, G.E., Gabriel, E., Dongarra, J.J.: Performance analysis of MPI collective operations. In: Proceedings of the Wokshop on Performance Modeling, Evaluation and Optimisation for Parallel and Distributed Systems (PMEO), in IPDPS 2005. (2005)
8. Johnssonn, S.L., Ho, C.T.: Optimum broadcasting and personalized communication in hypercubes. IEEE Transactions on Computers **38** (1989) 1249–1268
9. Grove, D.: Performance Modelling of Message-Passing Parallel Programs. PhD thesis, University of Adelaide (2003)
10. Adve, V.: Analysing the Behavior and Performance of Parallel Programs. PhD thesis, University of Wisconsin, Computer Sciences Department (1993)
11. Bruck, J., Ho, C.T., Kipnis, S., Upfal, E., Weathersby, D.: Efficient algorithms for all-to-all communications in multiport message-passing systems. IEEE Transactions on Parallel and Distributed Systems **8** (1997) 1143–1156
12. Clement, M., Steed, M., Crandall, P.: Network performance modelling for PM clusters. In: Proceedings of Supercomputing. (1996)
13. Labarta, J., Girona, S., Pillet, V., Cortes, T., Gregoris, L.: DiP: A parallel program development environment. In: Proceedings of the 2nd Euro-Par Conference. Volume 2. (1996) 665–674
14. König, J.C., Rao, P.S., Trystram, D.: Analysis of gossiping algorithms with restricted buffers. Parallel Algorithms and Applications **13** (1998) 117–133
15. Jeannot, E., Wagner, F.: Two fast and efficient message scheduling algorithms for data redistribution through a backbone. In: Proceedings of the IPDPS. (2004)
16. Moritz, C.A., Frank, M.I.: LoGPC: Modeling network contention in message-passing programs. IEEE Transactions on Parallel and Distributed Systems **12** (2001) 404–415
17. Hockney, R.: The communication challenge for MPP: Intel paragon and meiko cs-2. Parallel Computing **20** (1994) 389–398
18. Jeannot, E., Steffenel, L.A.: Fast and efficient total exchange on two clusters. (Submitted to EuroPar'07 - 13th International Euro-Par Conference European Conference on Parallel and Distributed Computing)

An Energy-Efficient Clustering Algorithm for Large-Scale Wireless Sensor Networks*

Si-Ho Cha[1] and Minho Jo[2]

[1] Dept. of Information and Communication Engineering, Sejong University
sihoc@sejong.ac.kr
[2] School of Information and Communication, SungKyunKwan University
minhojo@gmail.com

Abstract. Clustering allows hierarchical structures to be built on the nodes and enables more efficient use of scarce resources, such as frequency spectrum, bandwidth, and energy in wireless sensor networks (WSNs). This paper proposes an energy efficient clustering algorithm for self-organizing and self-managing high-density large-scale WSNs, called SNOWCLUSTER. It introduces region node selection as well as cluster head election based on the residual battery capacity of nodes to reduce the costs of managing sensor nodes and of the communication among them. Each sensor node autonomously selects cluster heads based on a probability that depends on its residual energy level. The role of cluster heads or region nodes is rotated among nodes to achieve load balancing and extend the lifetime of every individual sensor node. To do this, SNOWCLUSTER clusters periodically to select cluster heads that are richer in residual energy level, compared to the other nodes, according to clustering policies from administrators. To prove the performance improvement of SNOWCLUSTER, the ns-2 simulator was used. The results show that it can reduce the energy and bandwidth consumption for clustering and managing WSNs.

1 Introduction

A large-scale wirelss sensor network (WSN) consists of a large number of sensor nodes, which are tiny, low-cost, low-power radio devices dedicated to performing certain functions such as collecting various environmental data and sending them to sink nodes (or base stations). In this WSN, a large number of sensor nodes are deployed over a large area and long distances and multi-hop communication is required between nodes and sensor nodes have the physical restrictions in particular energy and bandwidth restrictions. So managing numerous wireless sensor nodes directly is very complex and is not efficient [1]. Self-organization of WSNs, witch involves network decomposition into connected clusters, is a challenging task because of the limited bandwidth and energy resources available

* This research was funded by Dual Use Technology Program and ADD Korea and has been conducted by the Research Grant of Kwangwoon University in 2007.

C. Cérin and K.-C. Li (Eds.): GPC 2007, LNCS 4459, pp. 436–446, 2007.

in these networks. Sensor nodes therefore should be organized and managed automatically in a energy efficient method.

In [2], we proposed a self-management framework for WSNs called SNOWMAN (SeNsOr netWork MANagement), which is based on policy-based management (PBM) paradigm. SNOWMAN framework includes a policy manager (PM), one or more policy agent (PAs) and a large number of policy enforcers (PEs) as shown in Fig. 1. The PM is used by an administrator to input different policies. A policy in this context is a set of rules that assigns management actions to sensor node states. The PA is responsible for interpreting the policies and sending them to the PE. The enforcement of rules on sensor nodes is handled by the PE. It is the job of the PA to maintain this global view, allowing it to react to larger scale changes in the network and install new policies to reallocate policies (rules). If node states are changed or the current state matches any rule, the PE performs the corresponding local decisions based on local rules rather than sends information to base station repeatedly. Such policy execution can be done efficiently with limited computing resources of the sensor node. It is well known that communicating 1 bit over the wireless medium at short ranges consumes far more energy than processing that bit [4].

This paper present an energy-efficient clustering algorithm, SNOWCLUSTER, which is designed using a clustering algorithm for SNOWMAN [2]. SNOWCLUSTER can reduce the costs of organizing and managing sensor nodes

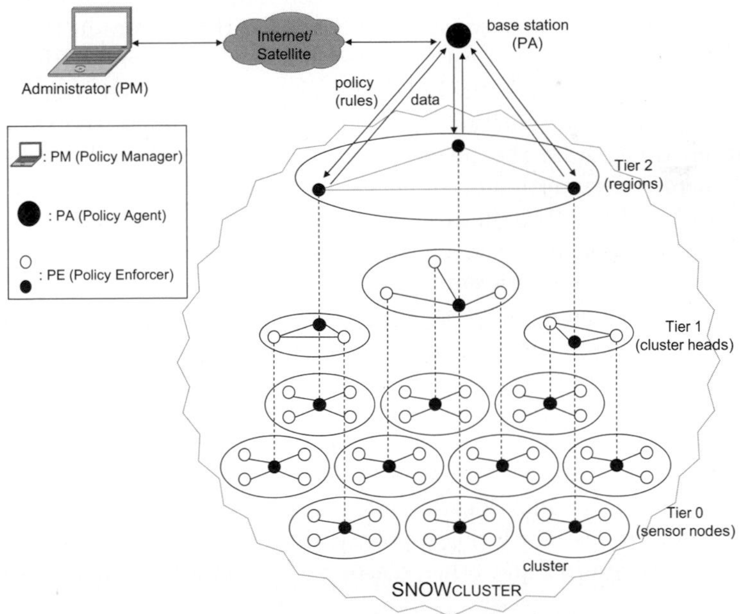

Fig. 1. SNOWMAN Framework

and of the communication among them. It introduces region node selection as well as cluster head selection based on the residual battery capacity of nodes. To prove the performance improvement of SNOWCLUSTER, the ns-2 [3] was used. SNOWCLUSTER shows better results than low-energy adaptive clustering hierarchy (LEACH) and low energy adaptive clustering hierarchy with deterministic cluster (LEACH-C) in performance evaluation of clustering and managing WSNs.

In this paper, section 2 investigates related researches. The SNOWCLUSTER algorithm is discussed in section 3. Section 4 presents the simulation results. Finally in section 5 we conclude the paper.

2 Related Works

When a sensor network is first activated, nodes near one another may wish to organize themselves into clusters, so that sensing redundancy can be avoided and scarce resources, such as radio frequency, may be reused across non-overlapping clusters [4]. Clustering also allows the health of the network to be monitored and misbehaving nodes to be identified, as some nodes in a cluster can play watchdog roles over other nodes [5]. In the clustered environment, the data gathered by the sensor nodes is communicated to the data processing center through a hierarchy of cluster heads.

To improve the clustering, several clustering algorithms have been proposed. Noted two schemes are LEACH and LEACH-C.

LEACH [6] is a self-organizing, adaptive clustering protocol that uses randomization to distribute the energy load evenly among the sensors in the network. In LEACH, the nodes organize themselves into local clusters, with one node acting as the local cluster-head. LEACH includes randomized rotation of the high-energy cluster-head position such that it rotates among the various sensors in order to not drain the battery of a single sensor. These features leads a balanced energy consumption of all nodes and hence to a longer lifetime of the network. Because LEACH didn't evaluate their energy storages and the requirements of the network, however, in the environment that nodes have different battery capacity, it is not efficient.

An improved version of LEACH, called LEACH-C [7] does cluster formation at the beginning of each round using a centralized algorithm by the base station. Using a central control algorithm to form the clusters may produce better clusters by dispersing the cluster head nodes throughout the network. This is the basis for LEACH-C, a protocol that uses a centralized clustering algorithm and the same steady-state protocol as LEACH. Therefore the base station determines cluster heads based on nodes' location information and energy level. This feature leads to organize robust clustering topology. However, frequent communications between the base station and other sensor nodes increase communication cost and energy usage.

From this background, The SNOWCLUSTER clustering algorithm is designed in this research to increase energy efficiency for self-organizing and managing large-scale WSNs.

3 SNOWCLUSTER Algorithm

SNOWMAN [2] constructs an hierarchical cluster-based senor network using SNOWCLUSTER clustering algorithm as shown in Table 1. Each sensor node autonomously elects cluster heads based on a probability that depends on its residual energy level. The SNOWCLUSTER allows neighboring nodes exchange their current energy level information. This strategy lets neighboring nodes by themselves determine the cluster heads. The role of cluster heads or region nodes is rotated among nodes to achieve load balancing and extend the lifetime of every individual sensor node. To do this, SNOWCLUSTER clusters periodically to select cluster heads that are richer in residual energy level, compared to the other nodes, according to clustering policies from administrators.

We assumed that all sensor nodes are stationary, and have knowledge of their locations. Even though nodes are stationary, the topology may be dynamic

Table 1. SNOWCLUSTER Algorithm

```
// CLUSTER HEAD SELECTION
For All node(x), where x is # of nodes
    let node(x).role ← cluster_head
    let node(x).cluster_id ← node(x).node_id
    do node(x).broadcast(discovery_msg)
    if node(i).hears_from(node(j))
        if node(i).energy_level < node(j).energy_level
            do node(i).request_join(node(j))
    if node(j).role ≠ cluster_head
        do node(j).reject_join(node(i))
    else
        do node(j).confirm_join(node(j))
    if node(i).receive_confirm(node(j))
        let node(i).role ← cluster_member
        let node(i).cluster_id ← node(j).node_id

// REGION NODE SELECTION
For All node(x), where is # of nodes
    if node(x).role = cluster_head
        do node(x).broadcast(cluster_info_msg)
    if PA.receive(cluster_info_msg)
        do PA.assign(region_nodes) & PA.broadcast(region_decision_msg)
    if node(k).receive(region_decision_msg)
        if node(k).role = cluster_head
            if node(k).node_id = region_decision_msg.region_id
                let node(k).role ← region_node
                let node(k).region_id ← node(k).node_id
            else if node(k).node_id ∈ region_decision_msg.region_list
                let node(k).region_id ← region_decision_msg.region_id
        do node(k).broadcast(region_conf_msg)
```

because new nodes can be added to the network or existing nodes can become unavailable with faults and battery exhaustion.

SNOWCLUSTER takes a couple of steps to accomplish the hierarchical clustering: 1) cluster head selection and 2) region node selection. In order to select cluster heads, each node periodically broadcasts a discovery message that contains its node ID, its cluster ID, and its remaining energy level.

A node declares itself as a cluster head if it has the biggest residual energy level of all its neighbor nodes, breaking ties by node ID. Each node can independently make this decision based on exchanged discovery messages. Each node sets its cluster ID (*cluster_id*) to be the node ID (*node_id*) of its cluster head (*cluster_head*). If a node i hears from another node j with a bigger residual energy level (*energy_level*) than itself, node i sends a message to node j requesting to join the cluster of node j. If node j already has resigned as a cluster bead itself, node j returns a rejection, otherwise node j returns a confirmation. When node i receives the confirmation, node i resigns as a cluster head and sets its cluster ID to node j's node ID. This After forming clusters, region nodes are elected from the cluster heads.

When the cluster head selection is completed, the entire network is divided into a number of clusters. A cluster is defined as a subset of nodes that are mutually reachable within 2 hops at most. A cluster can be viewed as a circle around the cluster head with the radius equal to the radio transmission range of the cluster head. Each cluster is identified by one cluster head, a node that can reach all nodes in the cluster within 1 hop.

After the cluster heads are selected, the PA should select the region nodes in the cluster heads. The PA receives cluster information messages (*cluster_info_msgs*) that contain cluster ID, the list of nodes in the cluster, residual energy level, and location data from all cluster heads. The PA suitably selects region nodes according to residual energy level and location data of cluster heads. If a cluster head k receives region decision messages (*region_decision_msgs*) from the PA, the node k compares its node ID with region ID (*region_id*) from the messages. If the previous comparison is true, node k declares itself as a region node (*region_node*) and sets its region ID to its node ID. Otherwise, if node k's node ID is included in a special region list (*region_list*) from the message, node k sets its region ID to a corresponding region ID of the message. The region node selection is completed with region confirmation messages (*region_conf_msgs*) broadcasted from all of cluster heads.

4 Performance Evaluation

This section describes experimental environments and results of a comparison of the proposed SNOWCLUSTER algorithm and legacy clustering algorithms.

4.1 Simulation Environments

In the experiment, the ns-2 [3] network simulation tool with Red Hat Linux 9.0 was used. The elements for establishing a virtual experimental environment are as follows:

- Sensor network topology formed with each of 50, 100, 150, 200 nodes.
- Sensor field with dimension of 100 x 100
- Transmission speed of 1Mbps
- Wireless transmission delay of 1ps
- Radio speed of 3 x 108m/s
- Omni-directional Antenna
- Lucent WaveLAN DSSS (Direct-Sequence Spread-Spectrum) wireless network interface of 914MHz
- Use of DSDV (Destination Sequenced Distance Vector) for routing protocol

Each experiment was conducted on LEACH, LEACH-C, and SNOWCLUSTER. In addition, management messages were applied for all cases and the processing power of sensor nodes was eliminated because it was insignificant compared to the amount of energy consumed in communications.

For the network topology used in the experiment, distribution of 50, 100, 150, and 200 nodes on each dimension as shown in Fig. 2 was assumed.

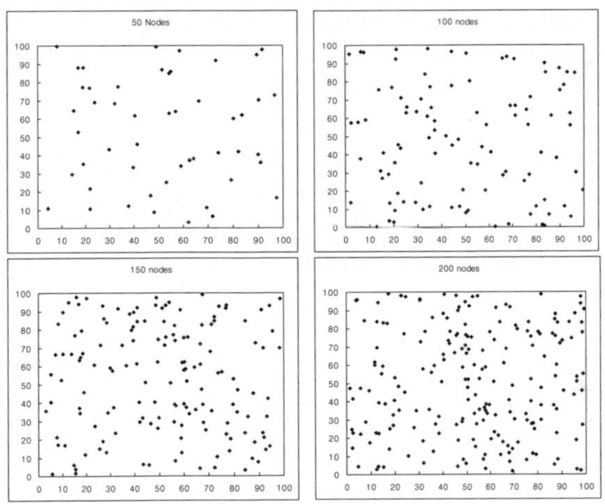

Fig. 2. Network topology (50, 100, 150, and 200 nodes)

4.2 Energy Consumption

Fig. 3 is a graph that shows the generation of 1 to 10 clusters in a network topology formed with 100 sensor nodes for each clustering algorithm. The graph also illustrates the results of energy consumption measurement during 10 rounds based on the number of each cluster generated.

In case of LEACH, until the number of clusters generated is 2, it shows significantly higher energy consumption compared to the other clustering algorithms, but after generations of more than 3, the energy consumption was stabilized with a gradual increase. LEACH-C showed progressive increase in energy consumption

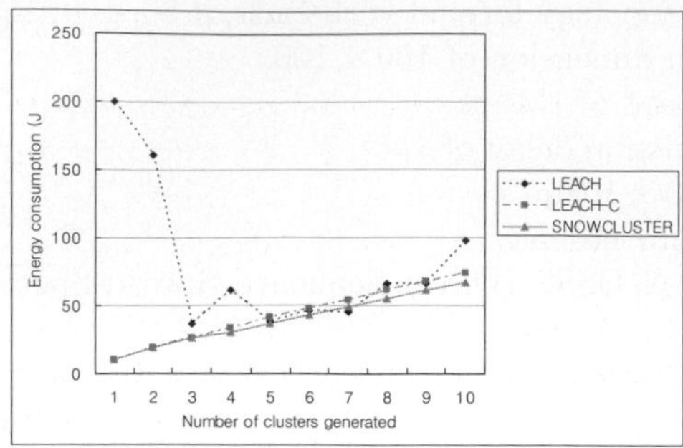

Fig. 3. The amount of energy consumed during 10 rounds with the number of clusters

from round 1 to round 10. Similar to LEACH-C, SNOWCLUSTER also showed a gradual increase in energy consumption, but its consumption rate was slightly less than that of LEACH-C. However, in both of LEACH-C and SNOWCLUSTER, due to a unexpected increase in the number of cluster formations the energy consumption increased. The most efficient number of clustering formation in the both methods must be 1 from the perspective of energy consumption. It has not been taken account of the amount of data transmission. The optimized number of clusters therefore cannot be determined merely based on this data.

Fig. 4 is a graph that depicts energy consumption during a single round of cluster formation for each clustering method. In the graph, LEACH showed the highest level of energy consumption, and LEACH-C and SNOWCLUSTER resulted in a slight difference each other. SNOWCLUSTER showed the least amount of energy consumption.

The LEACH is simple in principle but because it does not have location information of the sensor nodes, an inefficient routing is made which in turn resulted in a relatively high energy consumption. Unlike the LEACH-C requires

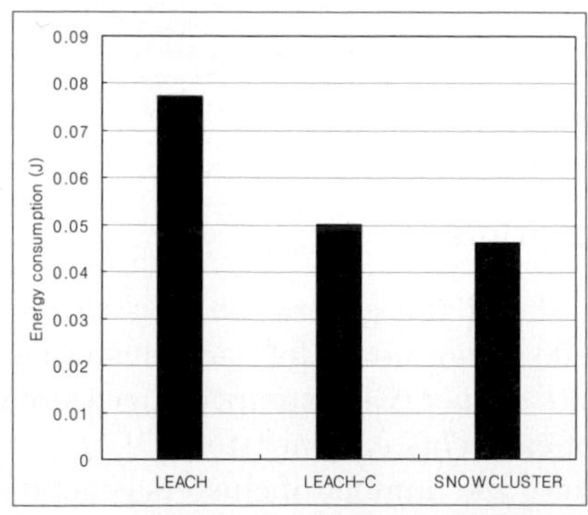

Fig. 4. The amount of energy consumed during a single round of cluster organization

all of nodes to send their current energy level information to the base station which determines the cluster heads, the SNOWCLUSTER allows neighboring nodes exchange their current energy level information. Thus even though the SNOWCLUSTER needs an additional time to select the region node, the SNOWCLUSTER gives less energy consumption than the LEACH-C.

Fig. 5 is a graph that shows experimental results of amount of energy consumed for an entire sensing data to reach the base station for each clustering algorithm.

As expected, it was found that LEACH has a higher level of energy consumption than the other two clustering algorithms. The SNOWCLUSTER has a lower rate of energy consumption than LEACH-C. The reason is that while each cluster head directly transmits sensing data to the base station in the LEACH-C, SNOWCLUSTER allows only region node to communicate with the base station so that the number of communications is decreased in the entire network.

Fig. 6 is the results showing the amount of energy consumed during transmission of management message from the base station to the sensor node after organization of three clusters in the network topology of 200 nodes.

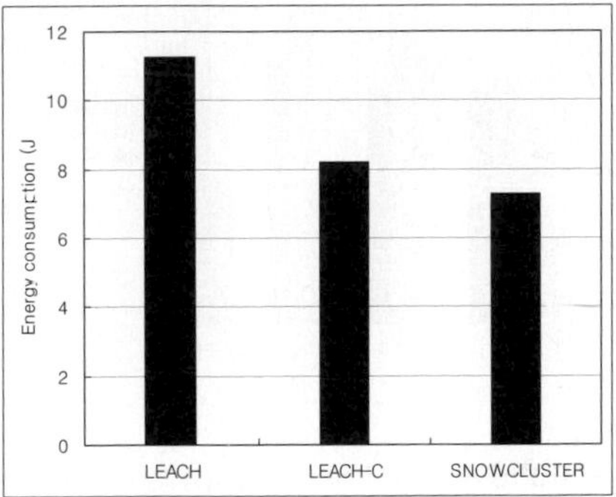

Fig. 5. The amount of energy consumed for an entire sensing data to reach the base station

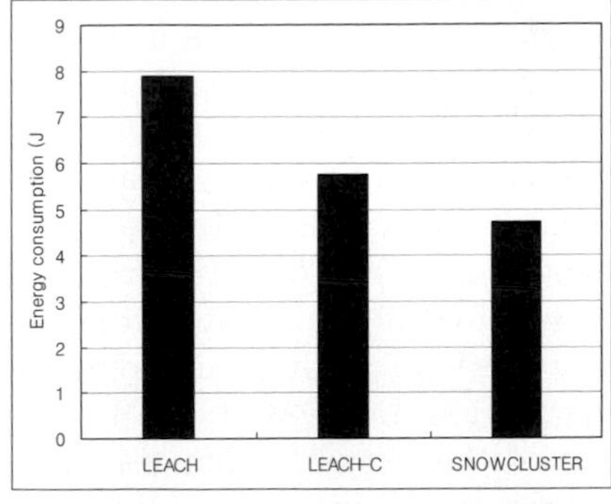

Fig. 6. The amount of energy consumed during transmission of management message

In LEACH, because it does not have the location information of the nodes, an inefficient routing is made. As a result, significantly greater amount of energy is consumed in transmitting management messages. SNOWCLUSTER showed a result of decrease in the amount of energy consumed in the transmission of message compared to LEACH-C. In SNOWCLUSTER, a region node plays the role of primary message transmission through addition of region node selection process, different from LEACH-C. And the SNOWCLUSTER transmits messages using the remaining two cluster heads, with a decrease of the total number of saving communications energy.

4.3 The Amount of Data

Fig. 7 displays the amount of sensing data that reaches the base station in a single round in each network topology with the different numbers of nodes.

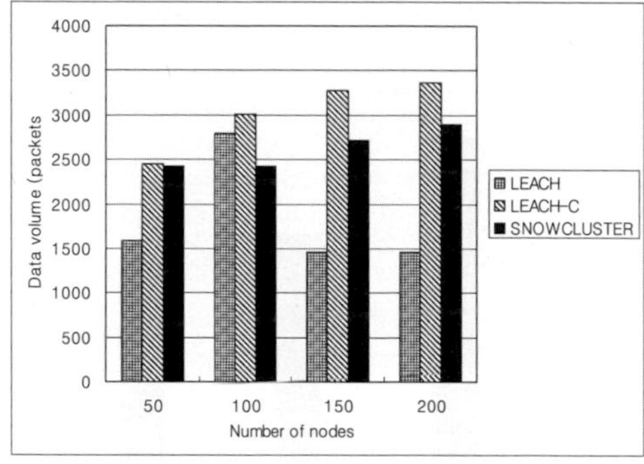

Fig. 7. The amount of data reached the base station in single round after cluster organization

The LEACH shows abnormally low amount of sensing data. This is a result of accumulated untransmitted data due to frequent occurrences of collision in an irregular pattern between the nodes in the transmission process. In SNOWCLUSTER, the amount of sensing data to reach the based station was found to be less than that of LEACH-C. The SNOWCLUSTER allows sensing data to be sent to the base station after an additional local data fusion in the region node, which decreases the amount of data transmitted to the base station.

Fig. 8 displays the amount of sensing data that reached the base station with the number of cluster generations in the network topology of 200 nodes.

Decrease in the communication rate of sensing data gives diminish in energy consumed during communication. In LEACH, the transmission volume of data is very irregular because of the irregular changes in the number of collision occurrences during cluster organization. Both LEACH-C and SNOWCLUSTER showed increase in the amount of data with the increased number of clusters. However in SNOWCLUSTER because sensing data is transmitted to the base

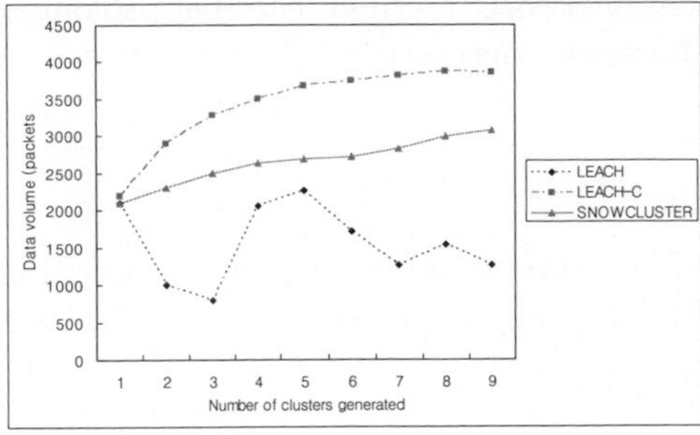

Fig. 8. The amount of sensing data reached the base station with the number of clusters

station in a region node for every three clusters, the number of sensing data received by the base station was significantly reduced compared to LEACH-C. As a result, the SNOWCLUSTER saves energy through use of region nodes.

4.4 Network Lifetime

Fig. 9 shows results of changes in the network lifetime when 6 clusters are formed in network topologies within the different numbers of sensor nodes, 50, 100, 150, and 200. In LEACH, almost the same length of lifetime was made in topologies of 50 and 100 sensors, and the network lifetime was the longest with 150 nodes.

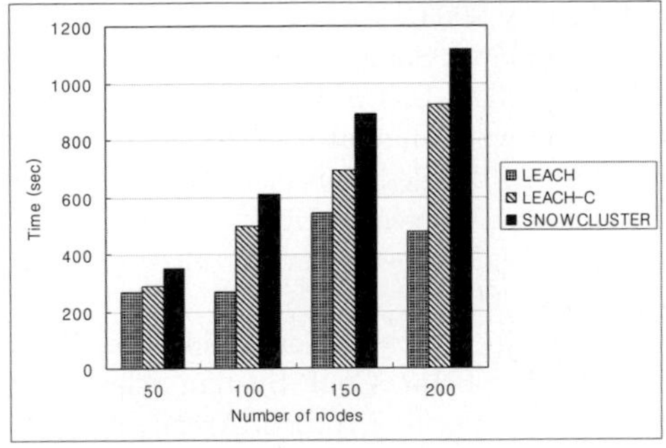

Fig. 9. Network lifetime

However, the total network lifetime in a network formed by 200 nodes was shorter than that of 150 nodes. The location of the nodes is not at all taken into account in the selection method of cluster heads in the LEACH. Because of the lack of location information, the energy consumed in forming the routing path between nodes is greater than those of other clustering methods. The SNOWCLUSTER showed a network lifetime that is 18 $\sim$ 20% greater than that of LEACH-C due to additional energy reduction effect through the region node selection process. The network lifetime can be prolonged by applying the SNOWCLUSTER in the sensor network.

5 Conclusion

This paper presented an energy efficient clustering algorithm for self-organizing and self-managing WSNs, called SNOWCLUSTER. The SNOWCLUSTER introduces region node selection as well as cluster head selection based on the residual battery capacity of nodes. The region node selection and cluster head selection policy is able to save energy by reducing the transmission amount from nodes to the base station, i.e., only selected cluster heads sent to the base station. The SNOWCLUSTER is also able to extend the network life time by rotating the role of cluster heads and region nodes with all other sensor nodes periodically. In the experiments conducted in this research, the better energy efficiency of the SNOWCLUSTER than LEACH and LEACH-C in the clustering and managing WNS was proven. The SNOWCLUSTER therefore is an efficient clustering algorithm to implement a self-management framework for large-scale WSNs. We are currently at the stage of implementation of the SNOWCLUSTER algorithm on our WSN testbed using Nano-24 [8] sensor nodes.

References

1. Linnyer B. Ruiz, José M. Nogueira, Antonio A. F. Loureiro, MANNA: A Management Architecture for Wireless Sensor Networks, IEEE Communications Magazine, Volume 41, Issue 2, February 2003.
2. Si-Ho Cha, Jongoh Choi, JooSeok Song, A Self-Management Framework for Wireless Sensor Networks, APWEB 2006, LNCS 3842, January 2006.
3. The VINT Project, The network simulator - ns-2, http://www.isi.edu/nsnam/ns/.
4. Feng Zhao, Leonidas Guibas, Wireless Sensor Networks: An Information Processing Approach, Morgan Kaufman Publishers, Elsevier, 2004.
5. Holger Karl, Andreas Willing, Protocols and Architectures for Wireless Sensor Networks, John Wiley & Sons, 2005.
6. W. Heinzelman, et al., Energy-Efficient Communication Protocol for Wireless Microsensor Networks, Proc. IEEE Int. Conf. System Sciences, vol. 8, January 2000.
7. W. Heinzelman, Application-Specific Protocol Architectures for Wireless Networks, PhD thesis, Massachusetts Inst. of Technology, June 2000.
8. Nano-24: Sensor Network, Octacomm, Inc., http://www.octacomm.net/.

An Algorithm Testbed for the Biometrics Grid*

Anlong Ming and Huadong Ma

Beijing Key Laboratory of Intelligent Telecommunications Software and Multimedia, School of Computer Sci. and Tech., Beijing Univ. of Posts and Telecommunications, Beijing 100876, China
anthonyming@gmail.com, mhd@bupt.edu.cn
http://bklab.cs.bupt.cn/

Abstract. In this paper, we propose a novel application on grid, the biometrics grid, to promote the development of both biometrics technology and grid computing. The biometrics grid aims to overcome/resolve some main problems of existing biometric technology using grid computing. The most important service provided by the biometrics grid is an algorithm testbed for biometrics researchers on single biometric or multi-modal biometrics. We give a case of two respective biometrics recognition processes in voiceprint and face on grid to show that it is feasible in deploying different biometrics applications on a testbed for performance evaluation.

Keywords: Grid computing, Biometrics, Face, Voiceprint.

1 Introduction

Biometrics usually refers to identifying an individual based on his or her distinguishing characteristics. The premise is that a biometrica measurable physical characteristic or behavioral traitis a more reliable indicator of identity than legacy systems such as passwords and PINs. Physiological biometrics is based on data derived from direct measurement of a body part (i.e., fingerprints, face, retina, iris), while behavioral biometrics is based on measurements and data derived from a human action [1] (i.e., gait and signature). Recent global terrorism is pushing the need for secure, fast, and non-intrusive identification of people as a primary goal for homeland security. As commonly accepted, biometrics seems to be the first candidate to efficiently satisfy these requirements. For example, from October 2004, the United States have controlled the accesses to/from country borders by biometric passports [2, 3].

Biometrics technology not only need advanced biometric technology interfaces but also the ability to deal with security and privacy issues. The integration of

* The work is supported by the National Natural Science Foundation of China (90612013), the National High Technology Research and Development Program of China under Grant No.2006AA01Z304, the Specialized Research Fund for the Doctoral Program of Higher Education (20050013010) and the NCET Program of MOE, China.

C. Cérin and K.-C. Li (Eds.): GPC 2007, LNCS 4459, pp. 447–458, 2007.

biometrics with access control mechanisms and information security is another area of growing interest. The challenge to the research community is to develop integrated solutions that address the entire problems from sensors and data acquisition, to biometric data analysis and systems design. Biometrics technology suffers problems in its way of research and applications:

Multimodal biomsetrics and information fusion. The performance of a biometric system is not reliable. This problem can be alleviated by installing multiple sensors that capture different biometric traits. Such systems, known as multimodal biometric systems, are expected to be more reliable due to the presence of multiple pieces of evidence. Use of multiple biometric indicators for identifying individuals has been shown to increase the accuracy and population coverage, while decreasing vulnerability to spoofing [4].Multimodal biometric systems are able to meet the stringent performance requirements imposed by various applications. Moreover, it will be extremely difficult for an intruder to violate the integrity of a system requiring multiple biometric indicators. However, an integration scheme is required to fuse the information churned out by the individual modalities. The key to multimodal biometrics is the fusion of various biometric modality data at the feature extraction, matching score, or decision levels [5].

Duplicated works and cooperation in diverse fields. Currently, most biometrics technology researches in offered production are either actually intra-organizational or operated by application domains, such as FaceVACS-SDK produced by Cognitec. It is wasteful with duplicated efforts in building test databases as well as difficulty in providing uniform performance standards. For example, face recognition researchers have spent great efforts in building face databases(i.e., FERET, PIE, BANCA, CAS-PEAL, AR) while these databases are not easily accessed by others. Furthermore, from a technical viewpoint, biometrics spans various technologies, such as fingerprint and face recognition, mathematics and statistics, performance evaluation, integration and system design, integrity, and last but not least, privacy and security. Therefore, there is a need for scientists and practitioners from the diverse fields of computing, sensor technologies, law enforcement and social sciences to exchange ideas research challenges and results.

Large scale biometric database. The population in a database can significantly affect performance [6]. In a system with a large scale database, the ordinary recognition processes perform poorly: with the increase of the database scale, the identification rates of most algorithms may decline rapidly; meanwhile, querying in a large scale database may be quite time-consuming. So how to deal with a large scale database has been a difficult problem faced by researchers on biometrics technology in recent years. Su Guangda et al presented a face recognition system framework constructed on the client-server architecture [7]. A distributed and parallel architecture is introduced to this system (see Fig. 1 (a)). The clients and servers are connected by $1000MB$ networking switch. Although this system has gained good performance: querying one face image in 2,560,000 faces costs only 1.094s and the identification rate is above 85% in most cases, it is limited in accessing and extending due to its C/S framework.

A grid [8, 9] is a high-performance hardware and software infrastructure providing scalable, dependable and secure access to the distributed resources. Grid systems are the gathering of distributed and heterogeneous resources (CPU, disk, network, etc.). Unlike distributed computing and cluster computing, the individual resources in grid computing maintain administrative autonomy and allow system heterogeneity; this aspect of grid computing guarantees scalability and vigor. Therefore, the grids resources must adhere to agreed-upon standards to remain open and scalable. They are promising infrastructures for executing large scale applications and to provide computational power to everyone. In order to promote both biometrics technology and grid computing, we combine biometrics applications with grid computing to give a novel grid application - the biometrics grid (BMG).

The remainder of this paper is organized as follows: related work is presented in Section 2, design issues of system are described in Section 3. The BMG-specific testbed is discussed in Section 4. Finally, we give a case study in Section 5. We conclude our work in Section 6.

2 Related Work

Biometric systems have been defined by the U.S. National Institute of Standards and Technology (NIST) [10, 11] as systems exploiting "automated methods of recognizing a person based on physiological or behavioral characteristics" (biometric identifiers, also called features). Biometric systems are being used to verify identities and restrict access to buildings, computer networks, and other secure sites [12]. A biometric system is essentially a pattern-recognition system. Such a system involves three aspects: data acquisition and preprocessing, data representation, and decision-making. Biometric systems are traditionally used for three different applications [13]: *physical access control* for the protection against unauthorized person to access to places or rooms, *logical access control* for the protection of networks and computers, and *time and attendance control*. Due to have been designed for only traditional biometrics applications, biometric systems can't used to solve the problems mentioned in Section 1.

However, the proposed BMG is more than a biometrics system. Considering *multimodal biometrics*, *duplicated works*, *cooperation in diverse fields*, *information fusion* and *Large scale biometric database*, BMG provides an algorithm testbed for the research on single biometric or multimodal biometrics. The testbed enables researchers mainly focus their energy on algorithm design and programming.

Also, BMG can conquer disadvantages of C/S framework because in the heterogeneous grid environments, we can hide the heterogeneity of computational resources and networks by providing Globus Toolkit Services and can implement the distributed parallel computing of a large scale problem by taking full advantage of Internet resources. According to the applied demand, grid MPI parallel program is offered for specialized applications.

3 Design Issues of System

3.1 Concepts

BMG is designed to develop integrated solutions that address the entire problems from sensors and data acquisition, to biometric data analysis and system design. BMG aims to

1. Provide a testbed for the research on biometrics algorithms. The testbed enables researchers mostly or only pay their attention on algorithm design and programming. BMG would test modules designed by researchers on uniform databases.

   In biometrics algorithms test, such efforts are wasteful, with duplicated work in building test databases as well as difficulty in providing uniform performance standards. A basic requirement is for tools that allow data managers to make licensed and uniform "person" data available to the BMG community. These tools include the means to create searchable databases of persons, provide catalogs of the data that locate a given piece of data on an archival system or online storage, and make catalogs and data accessible via the Web. Prior to the advent of the grid, these capabilities did not exist, so potential users of the model data had to contact the data managers personally and begin the laborious process of retrieving the data they wanted.
2. Create a virtual collaborative environment linking distributed centers, users, models, and data to simplify both the resource management task, by making it easier for resource managers to make resource available to others, and the resource access task, by making biometrics data as easy to access.
3. Support mature biometric applications with different QoS demands including applications with large scale databases or applications of multi-modal biometrics can be solved by grid computing. However, BMG does not guarantee that biometrics applications are meeting with the QoS goals, when defining QoS more broadly than the bandwidth and capacity.
4. Develop a specialized grid workflow for multimedia computing and data mining in biometrics applications on BMG.

In this paper, we only discuss one of the BMG issues, the algorithm testbed.

3.2 A Framework of the Biometrics Grid

We present a description of the BMG framework in Fig. 1 (b). BMG is divided into four layers:

Resources. These are the basic resources on which BMG is constructed including computational resources and data resources.

Platform. This provides remote, authenticated access to shared BMG resources. All these components are based on the Globus Toolkit and the WS-Resource

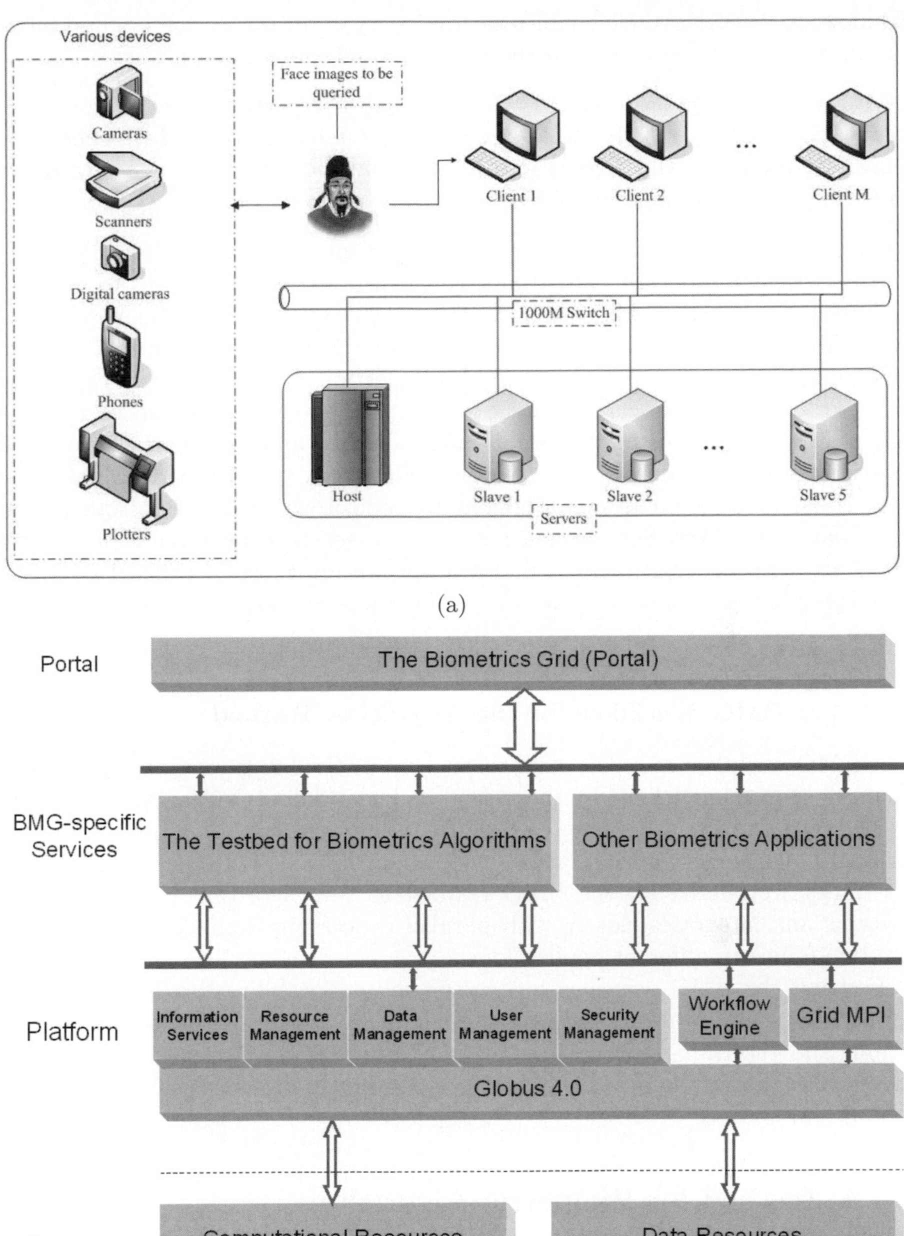

Fig. 1. a) An example of C/S framework to support large scale database. (b) The BMG framework schematic showing four layers.

Framework (WSRF) which enables the discovery of, introspection on, and interaction with stateful resources in the standard and interoperable ways.

BMG-specific services. The testbed is the most important of these biometrics applications. The testbed enables researchers intend to focus their energy on algorithm designing and programming. All biometrics applications are wrapped to Web Services specified by WSRF and deployed into Web Services container.

Portal. Web portal control and render the user interface-interaction. BMG creates a virtual collaborative environment which provides advantages to urge cooperations in diverse fields. Generally, portal let you take multiple Web pages, automatically produce controls to link between them, and let subsets of them be displayed on a single Web page. All biometric applications are wrapped to Web Services (each with user-facing ports) are aggregated for the user into a single client environment. We assume that all data and information presented to users originates from a Web Service, called a content provider. This content could come from a simulation, data repository, or stream from an instrument. Each Web Service has resource- or service-facing ports that communicate with other services [14]. However, we are more concerned with the user-facing ports, which produce content for users and accept input from client devices.

3.3 The BMG Workflow for the Algorithm Testbed

The BMG workflow is simply defined as a set of Grid resources and services, a quality expectation defined by the user(s) and a workflow model acting on them.

The BMG workflow pays more attention to multimedia computation and data mining in biometrics applications on BMG, the BMG-MPI parallel programming interfaces are offered for the BMG testbed to run algorithm jobs. Its design sustains and integrates closely with parallel processing from the bottom, so it can be applied in different applications.

Further, the BMG workflow has strong self-adaptability to effectively overcome the dynamic variation during the operating process of a biometrics algorithm, and the BMG workflow engine can also perform dynamic resource discovery and allocation, dynamically collects the status of nodes of BMG by MDS modules in Globus.

4 A Testbed for Biometric Algorithms

To solve the problems of *duplicated works*, *multimodal biometrics*, and *information fusion*, BMG provides the testbed for the research on single biometric or multimodal biometrics to enable researchers intend to only focus their energy on algorithm designing and programming. For example, researchers' works are limited to design the modules of feature extracting, feature matching, information fusion, etc. Researchers code these modules according to the testbed interface description and then submit their works to BMG.

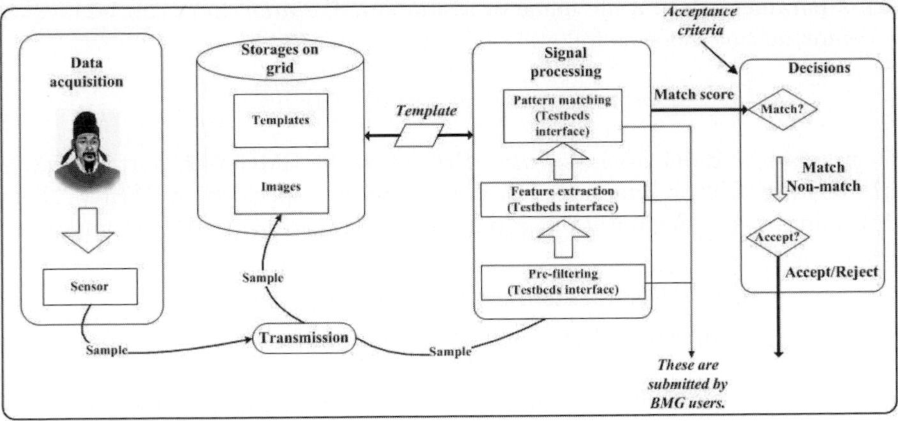

Fig. 2. Structure of a general single biometric system

4.1 Single Biometric Test

A biometric system has a general structure [15]. First of all, a sensor acquires a sample of the user presented to the biometric system (i.e., fingerprint, face, iris images). As defined in [15], a sample is a biometric measure presented by the user and captured by the data collection subsystem as an image or signal. The sample can be transmitted, eventually exploiting compression/decompression techniques. BMG stores the complete sample data in the storage unit. BMG uses and stores only a mathematical representation of the information extracted from the presented sample by the signal processing module that will be used to construct or compare against enrolment templates: the biometric feature. If the extracted feature is stored (enrolled) into BMG, a template for future identification or verification (matching) is added. BMG has a measure of the similarity between features derived from a presented sample and a stored template. The measure produces a typical index called matching score. Hence, a match/nonmatch decision may be made according to whether this score exceeds a decision threshold or not. The term transaction refers to an attempt by a user to validate a claim of identity or nonidentity by consecutively submitting one or more samples, as allowed by the system decision policy [16]. Lastly, a transmission process is implemented to transmit the collected data to the signal processing section. The signal-processing module represents the core of the system and is generally composed by sub-modules implementing preprocessing functions (i.e., image filtering and enhancement), the feature extraction, and the matching between two features.

BMG deploys this general single biometric system on the testbed. Of course, some definitions should be firstly done such as feature extracting interface, feature matching interface, pre-filtering interface. All these definitions together are defined as part of the testbed interface description. For example, a simple feature extracting interface can be defined as c executable file (e.g. *FeatureExt.exe*) with a parameter (e.g. a file name of a sample), *FeatureExt.exe* can be invoked by command line mode as follows:

$$FeatureExt.exe \quad a\_sample\_file\_name$$

When a user of BMG submits *featureExt.exe* to the BMG Web portal, *featureExt.exe* itself will be wrapped into a Web Service specified by WSRF. Then BMG can provide this service as a part of the testbed using BMG components (e.g. GRAM).

4.2 Multimodal Biometrics Test

Multimodal biometrics fusion that is possible when combining multiple biometric systems:

① Fusion at the feature extraction level, where features extracted using multiple sensors are concatenated.
② Fusion at the confidence level, where matching scores reported by multiple matchers are combined [15,16].
③ Fusion at the abstract level, where the accept/reject decisions of multiple systems are consolidated [17].

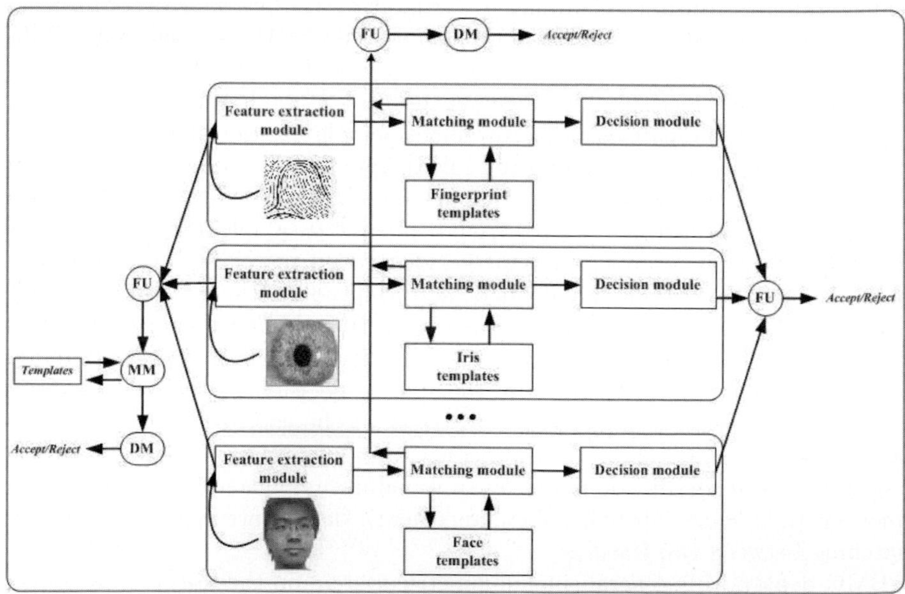

Fig. 3. Structure of a general multimodal biometrics system showing the three levels of fusion; FU: Fusion Module, MM: Matching Module, DM: Decision Module. FU, MM, DM are programed and submitted by BMG users.

Fusion in the context of biometrics can take the following forms: ① Single biometric multiple classifier fusion, where multiple classifier on a single biometric indicator are combined [18]. ② Single biometric multiple matcher fusion, where scores generated by multiple matching strategies (on the same representation) are combined [19]. ③ Multiple biometric fusion, where multiple biometrics are utilized [20, 21, 22]. An important aspect that has to be dealt with is the normalization of the scores obtained from the different domain experts [23]. Normalization typically involves mapping the scores obtained from multiple domains into a common framework before combining them. This could be viewed as a two-step process in which the distributions of scores for each domain is first estimated using robust statistical techniques and these distributions are then scaled or translated into a common domain.

Also, BMG deploys this general multimodal biometric system on the testbed just like that mentioned in single biometric.

5 A Case Study

5.1 The Environment

In the case, we carry out two respective biometrics recognition processes for voiceprint and face on grid. The voiceprint recognition approach we used is described in [24]. The face recognition approaches we used are listed as: the line based face recognition algorithm [25], the improved linc based face recognition algorithm [26], PCA and PCA+LDA [27]. Our development OS is Linux Fedora Core 4, and the development toolkit is Globus Tookit 4.0, Web server platform is Apache Tomcat 5.0, DBMS is MySQL 5.0, the development languages are HTML, JSP, Servlet, Java Bean, Java class and XML.

In voiceprint recognition, 24 samples from 44 persons are collected. The first 20 samples are put in the training set, and 4 samples left are made as the test set.

In face recognition, we use a face database established by ourselves to evaluate the performance of our algorithm. Pictures of 35 persons are taken by a standard camera (6 pictures per person) under different illumination intensity (weak, medium and strong). We select 3 views of each person for training, and the other 3 views (in weak, medium, and strong illumination intensity respectively) is used to test.

5.2 Two Biometrics Recognition Processes

We define 3 simple interfaces, which are executable files of *c* language in Linux platform, to run two respective biometrics recognition processes in speech and face.

- Interface 1 *Training.exe*, an executable file for biometrics data training, can be invoked as follows:

$$Training.exe \quad samples$$

– Interface 2 *FeatureExt.exe*, an executable file for extracting feature vectors using training results, can be invoked as follows:

$$FeatureExt.exe \quad a\_samples$$

– Interface 3 *FeatureMat.exe*, an executable file for matching feature vectors between two samples, can be invoked as follows:

$$FeatureMat.exe \quad sample\_1 \quad sample\_2$$

We program each recognition method and build 3×2 exe files respectively, then these files would be submitted to grid by GRAM Server and RSL (XML file) for recognition.

In voiceprint recognition, one is selected among 44 persons and tagged as *imposter*, and 43 persons left are seen as *client*. Every person can enter at his own status, *imposter* tries to enter at other 43 persons' status and repeats 20 times. Then we get $44 \times 43 \times 20$ verification results. In our voiceprint recognition job, the FAR (False Accept Rate) is 0.092%, FRR (False Reject Rate) is 2.27%.

In face recognition, we have tested four face recognition methods on the same, but individually processed, face database. The performance of different algorithms in face recognition is shown in Fig. 4 (a). Moreover, as illustrated in Fig. 4 (b), the average execution times of the improved line based face recognition algorithm can be shorten by increasing the number of grid computation nodes.

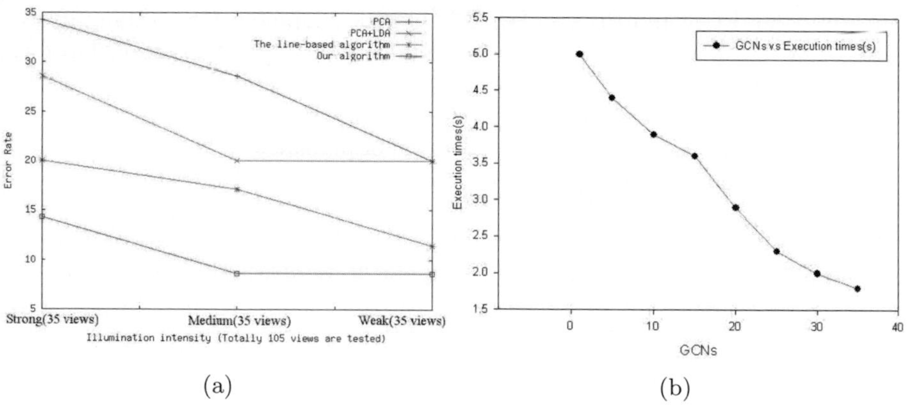

Fig. 4. (a) The performance of different algorithms on error rate (Totally 105 pictures are tested). (b) The relation between the execution times and the numbers of grid computation nodes (GCNs) of the improved line based face recognition algorithm.

5.3 Analysis

According to results of the case study above, we can conclude that:

– It's feasible to deploy biometrics applications on BMG.
– The algorithm testbed of BMG can provide uniform interfaces to different algorithms belonged to different types of biometrics.

- The algorithm testbed of BMG can provide uniform interfaces to different algorithms belonged to a same type of biometrics.
- BMG can meet with some QoS demand (i.e. execution times) by using methods such as increasing computation nodes.

6 Conclusions

We propose a concept of BMG to simplify both the resource management task, by making it easier for resource managers to make resource available to others, and the resource access task, by making biometrics data as easy to access as Web pages via a Web browser. BMG would test modules designed by users based on uniform database, modules would be wrapped to Web Services based on WSRF and deployed into Web Services container. We give a case study about two respective biometrics recognition processes in voiceprint and face deployed to grid. The results show that it is feasible in deploying not only algorithms belonged to different types of biometrics (i.e., face recognition, voiceprint recognition) but also different algorithms belonged to a same type of biometrics (such as face recognition) on grid to provide services using grid computing. Also, the time-consuming algorithms can be shortened by grid computing.

However, there exist great difficulties in building BMG nowadays. For example, it is not an easy case to build an uniform biometrics database because there are fears of an invasion of privacy. The advent of BMG should be under the legal guidelines of governments. With the development of grid computing, the technical scheme of BMG will also be improved.

References

1. R. Bolle, S. Pankanti, and A. K. Jain: Guest editorial, IEEE Computer (Special Issue on Biometrics), vol. 33, No. 2, (2000) 46-49
2. S. Waterman: Biometric borders coming, Times, Washington (2003)
3. General Accounting Office (GAO).: Technology assessment: Using biometrics for border security, GAO-03-174, Washington, (2002)
4. A.K. Jain, R. Bolle, et al.: Biometrics: Personal Identification in Networked Society, Kluwer Academic (1999)
5. D. Maltoni, D. Maio, A.K. Jain, and S. Prabhakar: Handbook of Fingerprint Recognition, Springer (2003)
6. PJouathou Phillips, Patrick Grother, et al.: Face recognitiou vendor test 2002: Evaluatiou report, Audio- and Video-Based Person Authentication (AVBPA) (2003)
7. Kai Meng, Guangda Su, et al.: A High Performence Face Recognition System Based on A Huge Face Database, Proceedings of the Fourth International Conference on Machine Learning and Cybernetics, Guangzhou (2005)
8. Satoshi Matsuoka, et al.: Japanese computational grid research project: NAREGI, Digital Object Identifier , Vol. 93, Issue 3, (2005) 522–533
9. David Bernholdt, et al.: The Earth System Grid: Supporting the Next Generation of Climate Modeling Research, Digital Object Identifier, Vol. 93, Issue 3 (2005) 485–495

10. M. Gamassi, Massimo Lazzaroni, et al.: Quality Assessment of Biometric Systems: A Comprehensive Perspective Based on Accuracy and Performance Measurement, IEEE Transactions on Instrumentation Measurement, Vol. 54, No. 4, (2005)
11. R. Bolle, S. Pankanti, and A. K. Jain: Guest editorial, IEEE Computer (Special Issue on Biometrics), vol. 33, No. 2, (2000) 46-49
12. J. D. M. Ashbourn: Biometrics: Advanced Identify VerificationThe Complete Guide, Springer-Verlag, Berlin (2000)
13. R. Norton, The evolving biometric marketplace to 2006, Biometric Technology Today, vol. 10, No. 9, (2002) 7C8
14. Geoffrey Fox: Grid computing environments, Digital Object Identifier, Vol.5(2) (2003): 68-72
15. A. J. Mansfield, J. L. Wayman: Best practices in testing and reporting performance of biometric devices, National Physical Lab., Center for Mathematics and Scientific Computing (2002)
16. Arun Ross, Anil Jain, Jian-Zhong Qian: Information Fusion in Biometrics, 3rd International Conference on Audio- and Video-Based Person Authentication (AVBPA), Sweden (2001) 354-359
17. Y. Zuev and S. Ivanon: The voting as a way to increase the decision reliability, in Foundations of Information/Decision Fusion with Applications to Engineering Problems, Washington (1996) 206–210
18. R. Cappelli, D. Maio, and D. Maltoni, Combining fingerprint classifiers, in First International Workshop on Multiple Classifier Systems, (2000) 351-361
19. A. K. Jain, S. Prabhakar, and S. Chen: Combining multiple matchers for a high security fingerprint verification system, Pattern Recognition Letters, vol. 20 (1999) 1371 - 1379
20. J. Kittler, M. Hatef, R. P. Duin, and J. G. Matas: On combining classifiers, IEEE Transactions on PAMI (1998) 226-239
21. E. Bigun, J. Bigun, B. Duc, and S. Fischer: Expert conciliation for multi-modal person authentication systems using bayesian statistics, in First International Conference on AVBPA, Crans-Montana (1997) 291-300
22. S. Ben-Yacoub, Y. Abdeljaoued, and E. Mayoraz: Fusion of face and speech data for person identity verification, Research Paper IDIAP-RR 99-03, Switzerland (1999)
23. R. Brunelli and D. Falavigna: Person identification using multiple cues, IEEE Transactions on PAMI, vol. 12, (1995) 955-966
24. Liu Y: Research on identity verification system based Institute of Automation, Chinese Academy of Sciences on voiceprint and semanteme[Mnater dissertation], Beijing, china, (2002)
25. O.de Vel and S.Aeberhard.: Line-based face recognition under varying pose, IEEE Trans. Pattern Analysis and Machine Intelligence, vol. 21 (1999) 1081-1088
26. Anlong Ming, Huadong Ma: An improved Approach to the line-based face recognition.pdf, Proceedings of the 2006 IEEE International Conference on Multimedia and Exposition (ICME), Toronto, 2006
27. Zhao WY, Chellappa R, Phillips PJ, Rosenfeld A: Face recognition: A literature survey, ACM Computing Surveys, Vol. 35 (2003) 399-458

Task Migration in a Pervasive Multimodal Multimedia Computing System for Visually-Impaired Users*

Ali Awde[1], Manolo Dulva Hina[1,2], Yacine Bellik[3], Amar Ramdane-Cherif[2], and Chakib Tadj[1]

[1] LATIS Laboratory, Université du Québec, École de technologie supérieure
1100, rue Notre-Dame Ouest, Montréal, Québec H3C 1K3 Canada
{ali.awde.1@ens,manolo-dulva.hina.1@ens,ctadj@ele}.etsmtl.ca
[2] PRISM Laboratory CRNS, Université de Versailles-Saint-Quentin-en-Yvelines
45, avenue des Etats-Unis, 78035 Versailles Cedex, France
rca@prism.uvsq.fr
[3] LIMSI-CRNS, Université de Paris-Sud
B.P. 133, 91043 Orsay, France
yacine.bellik@limsi.fr

Abstract. In a pervasive multimodal multimedia computing system, the user can continue working on a computing task anytime and anywhere using forms of modality that suit his context. Similarly, the media supporting the chosen modality are selected based on their availability and user's context. In this paper, we present the infrastructure supporting the migration of a visually-impaired user's task in a pervasive multimodal multimedia computing environment. Using user's preferences which quantify user's satisfaction, we derive the user's task feasible configuration. The heart of this work is the machine learning-derived training to acquire knowledge leading to configuration optimization. Data validation is presented through scenario simulations and design specification. This work is our continuing contribution to advance research on making informatics more accessible to handicapped users.

1 Introduction

As the consequence of computing being present in many facets of our lives, a computing system needs to evolve to become adaptive to the environment and user's needs. For a pervasive computing [1], its infrastructure must allow users to continue working on their task when and where they wish to. This requirement should serve all types of users, including those with disability, such as the visually-impaired ones.

As the user moves from one *multimodal multimedia* (MM) system to another, computing resources and user context change. In our work, *media* refers to a set of physical interaction devices (and software supporting physical devices) while *modality* refers to the logical interaction structure. For a visually-impaired user to continue working on a task, the system takes account of user's profile, data and current

* This work has been made possible the funding awarded by the Natural Sciences and Engineering Research Council (NSERC) of Canada, and the scholarship grants from *Décanat à la formation* of École de technologie supérieure and of the National Bank of Canada.

C. Cérin and K.-C. Li (Eds.): GPC 2007, LNCS 4459, pp. 459–471, 2007.

environment conditions. This means determining the form of modality the user could work on a computing task. Available resources and their constraints determine the media supporting the chosen modality to use. A basic requirement of a MM infrastructure is that it must have sufficient media devices that support various forms of modality.

This paper is a continuation of our previous work [2] which presented the architectural model of a pervasive MM computing system for users with visual disability. In that work, we defined the relationships among data format, environment conditions, user's preferences and modalities and media selections. In this paper, we visualize a mobile visually-impaired user and the migration of his data and task as he moves across computing environments. We set the foundation for feasible configuration to realize the user's task. Our objective is to realize a self-adaptive system taking into account the user's needs and the changes in his environment. This work is our contribution to improving visually-impaired users' access to information and computing.

The rest of this paper is structured as follows. Related work is presented in Section 2. The building of a machine learning knowledge for feasible configuration is discussed in Section 3. The system's specification and scenario simulations are presented in Section 4. The paper is concluded in Section 5.

2 Related Work

There are various tools for people with visual disabilities to access electronic information, such as screen reader, transcription data for Braille, access to mathematics [3, 4] and speech synthesis. For instance, for screen data access, JAWS [5] identifies and interprets what is displayed on the screen. It is then presented to blind users as speech (through text-to-speech software) or as translated data meant for Braille terminal. This is integrated into our work as one data conversion tool. HOMERE [6] allows blind users to use haptic/touch and audio modalities to explore virtual environments. Although functional, the system's effectiveness is limited as the modalities for user interaction are already pre-defined. In contrast, a computing system becomes more flexible if no pre-defined input-output modalities are set. In fact, the output presentation of information should be based on the user's application and interaction context (user, system, and environment) which could possibly be in constant evolution. The framework for intelligent multimodal presentation of information [7] is an example. The system's user interface also should be adaptive to these context variations while preserving its usability. Demeure's work [8] exhibits plasticity in context adaptation. Indeed, the forms of modality should be chosen only based on their merits to a user's interaction context. This is the approach adopted in our work.

Our focus has always been pervasive multimodality for the blind. This work was initially inspired by [9]. As our work evolves, however, the knowledge representation that we have derived becomes different as we affirm that our optimization model is best reflective for our intended user. The methodology is different as this paper uses *machine learning* (ML) to acquire knowledge. Such knowledge is stored onto the knowledge database (KD) accessible from a member of server group so that it can be made omnipresent, accessible anytime and anywhere via wired or wireless networks.

A major challenge in designing systems for the blind is how to deliver autonomy onto the user. To this end, several tools and gadgets have emerged in recent years, among them are the GPS (global positioning system), walking stick that detects user context [10] and the talking Braille [11]. Our work aims the same goal. Our system is adaptive to user's condition and environment. Through pervasive computing networks, the ML knowledge, and user's profile and task all become omnipresent; our system's user task configuration is generated without any human intervention.

3 Building a ML Knowledge for Configuration Optimization

3.1 Machine Learning Training to Build User Preferences

A *task* is a computing work the user needs to do. To accomplish the task, the user runs one or more computing applications. For example, a user wishing to shop for a second-hand car may access a web browser, a text editor and a video player.

Given a filename (*filename*.extension), the first function to be learned, $\mathbf{f_1}$, is a mapping of a data type to an application (**$\mathbf{f_1}$: data format → Application**). A diagram showing the learning process is shown in Fig. 1. Each mapping is given a score of *H* (high), *L* (low) or *I* (inappropriate). For example, the mapping (.doc, Text Editor) gets H, (.doc, Web Browser) has an L, and (.doc, Video Player) gets an I. The knowledge obtained from this mapping contains a set of data format and application mappings whose scores are H. The following is a sample set of mappings of $\mathbf{f_1}$:

f_1 = {(.txt, Text Editor), (.doc, Text Editor), (.rtf, Text Editor), (.html, Web Browser), (.xml, Web Browser), (.wav, Audio/Video Player), (.mp3, Audio/Video Player), (.mpg, Audio/Video Player), etc.}

An application may have several suppliers. Another function to be learned, $\mathbf{f_2}$, maps an application to the user's preferred supplier (**$\mathbf{f_2}$: Application → Preferred supplier, Priority**). For simplicity purposes, we assume that the user chooses his 3 preferred suppliers and ranks them by priority. The learned function is saved onto KD and is called user supplier preference. The following is a sample content of $\mathbf{f_2}$:

f_2 = {(Text Editor, (MSWord, 1)), (Text Editor, (WordPad, 2)), (Text Editor, (NotePad, 3)), (Web Browser, (Internet Explorer, 1)), (Web Browser, (Netscape, 2)), (Web Browser, (BrailleSurf, 3)), (Audio/Video Player, (Windows Media Player, 1)), (Audio/Video Player, (Real One Player, 2)), etc.}

An application has its *quality of service* (QoS) dimensions that consumes computing resources. Here, the only important QoS dimensions are those that are valuable to blind users. A function $\mathbf{f_3}$ maps an application and its QoS dimensions that the user prefers (**$\mathbf{f_3}$: Application *i* → QoS dimension *j*, Priority**) where $1 \leq i \leq$ app_max (max. no. of applications) and Application $i \in$ user task. Also, $1 \leq j \leq$ qos_max (max. no. of QoS dimensions) and QoS dimension $j \in$ Application i. Priority is of type $\mathbb{N}_1$. Since there are many possible values for each QoS dimension, the user arranges these values by their priority ranking. A sample $\mathbf{f_3}$ is given below:

f_3 = {(Text Editor, (40 characters per line, 1)), (Text Editor, (60 characters per line, 2)), (Text Editor, (80 characters per line, 3)), (Web Browser, (medium page loading, 1)), (Web Browser, (high page loading, 2)), (Web Browser, (low page loading, 3)), (Audio/Video Player, (medium volume, 1)), etc.}

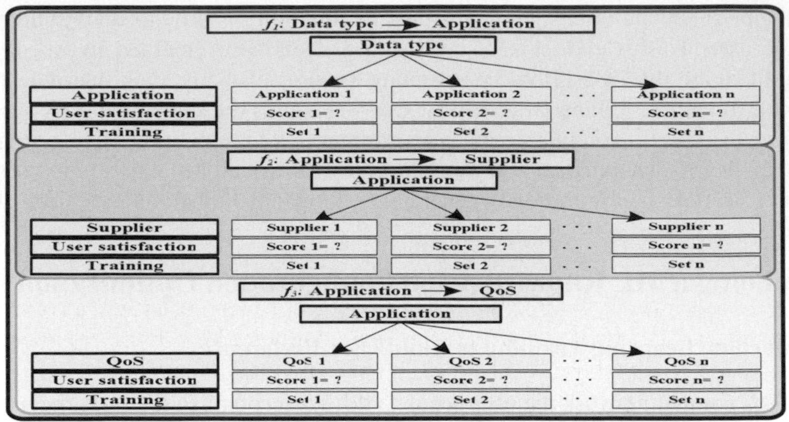

Fig. 1. The training process: (Top) the mapping of data type to an application, (Middle) building a user's preferred supplier list, and (Bottom) building a user's preferred QoS dimensions

3.2 Alternative Configuration Spaces

Given a user task, one or more applications are instantiated. For an application, however, there are some suppliers and QoS dimensions selections that can be invoked. Respecting the user's preferences is the way to instantiate an application, but if it is not possible, the dynamic reconfiguration mechanism must look upon the various configuration spaces and determine the one that is feasible to the user's needs. Fig. 2 shows typical invoked applications for a computing task of a blind user. Note the data type, the suppliers and the QoS dimensions that are mapped with an application. Also shown are the modalities and media that are invoked. The modalities abbreviations are as follows: SP_{in}=Speech input, SP_{out}=Speech output, T_{in}= Tactile input and T_{out} = Tactile output. For media devices, MIC=microphone, KB=keyboard, OKB= overlay keyboard, SPK=speaker, HST=headset, BRT = Braille terminal, TPR = tactile printer.

Application	*Data Type*	*Supplier*	*Selected QoS Dimensions*	*Modality*	*Media*
Text Editor	<filename> txt		40 Characters per line	SP_{In}, T_{In}	MIC KB OKB
	<filename> doc		60 Characters per line		
	<filename> rtf		80 Characters per line	SP_{Out}, T_{Out}	SPK HST BRT TPR
Web Browser	<filename> htm		Medium page loading	SP_{In}, T_{In}	MIC KB OKB
	<filename> html		High page loading		
	<filename> xml		Low page loading	SP_{Out}, T_{Out}	SPK HST BRT TPR
Audio/ Video Player	<filename> wav		Medium volume	SP_{In}, T_{In}	MIC KB OKB
	<filename> mp3		High volume		
	<filename> wmv		Low volume	SP_{Out}	SPK HST BRT TPR

Fig. 2. The user task as a collection of applications; instantiation of application is based on supplier and QoS dimension preferences. Needed modalities and media are also shown.

In the next sections, the following logic symbols appear: $\otimes$ = Cartesian product yielding a set composed of tuples, the basic logical connectives $\wedge$ (AND) and $\vee$ (OR), and $(a, b]$ denotes that a valid data is higher than a and up to a maximum of b.

A *QoS dimension* is an application's parameter that consumes *computing resources* (battery, CPU, memory, bandwidth). As an application's QoS dimension improves, then the application's quality of presentation (e.g. sound, crispiness of images, etc.) also improves but at the expense of larger resources' consumption. Given a task that is implemented by various applications, the task's QoS dimension space is given by:

$$\text{QoS Dimension space} = \bigotimes_{i=1}^{qos\_max} D_i \tag{1}$$

In this work, the QoS dimensions that matter are those that are valuable to the blind, namely: *the character per line* (for Text editor and Web browser), the *volume* (for Video and Audio player), and *page loading latency* (for Web browser). Given two applications *s* and *t*, their dimension space is $D_i(s) \otimes D_i(t)$.

The supplier's space, given below, denotes all possible applications' suppliers combinations for user's task, given that every application *i* has its own set of suppliers.

$$\text{Supplier space} = \bigotimes_{i=1}^{app\_max} Supp_i \tag{2}$$

3.3 Optimizing Configuration of User's Applications

A *feasible configuration* is a set-up that tries to satisfy the user's preferences given the user's context, and the resources' constraints. When the configuration is feasible, it is said that the user's satisfaction is achieved. Let the *user's satisfaction* to an outcome be within the *Satisfaction space*. It is in the interval of [0, 1] in which 0 means the outcome is totally unacceptable while a 1 corresponds to a user's satisfaction. Whenever possible, the system strives to achieve an outcome that is closer to 1.

Given an application, the user's satisfaction is enhanced if his preferences are enforced. The supplier preferences in instantiating an application are given by:

$$\text{Supplier preferences} = h_s{}^{x_s} \bullet f_s\, c_s \tag{3}$$

where $s \in$ Supplier space is an application supplier and the term $c_s \in [0, 1]$ reflects how the user cares about supplier *s*. Given an application, if it has *n* suppliers which are arranged in order of user's preference, then $c_{supplier1} = 1$, $c_{supplier2} = 1 - 1/n$, $c_{supplier3} = 1 - 1/n - 1/n$, and so on. The last supplier therefore has c_s close to zero which means that the user cares not to have it if given a choice. In general, in each application, the c_s assigned to supplier i, $1 \leq i \leq n$, is given by:

$$c_{supplier\,i} = 1 - \sum_{1}^{i-1} (1/n) \tag{4}$$

The term f_s: dom(s)→[0,1] denotes the expected features present in supplier *s*. The supplier *features* are those that are important to the user, other than the QoS dimensions. For example, in a text editor application, the user might prefer a supplier that provides *spelling and grammar checking*, or *equation editor* or feature to *build a table*, etc. For example, if the user listed $n= 3$ preferred features for an application, and the selected supplier supports them, then $f_s= 1$. If, however, one of these features is missing (either because the feature is not installed or the supplier does not have such feature), then the number of *missing* feature $m = 1$ and $f_s = 1 - m/(n + 1) = 1 - ¼ = 0.75$. In general, the user satisfaction with respect to application features is given by:

$$f_{supplier} = 1 - \frac{m}{n+1} \tag{5}$$

The term $h_s^{\ Xs}$ expresses the user's satisfaction with respect to the change of the supplier, and is specified as follows: $h_s \in (0, 1]$ is the user's tolerance for a change in the supplier. If this value is close to 1, then the user is fine with the change while a value close to 0 means the user is not happy with the change. The optimized value of h_s is:

$$h_s = \arg\max\,(c_s + c_{rep})/2 * c_s \tag{6}$$

where c_{rep} is a value obtained from equation (4) for replacement supplier. x_s indicates if change penalty must be considered. $x_s = 1$ if the supplier exchange is due to the dynamic change of environment, while $x_s = 0$ if the exchange is instigated by the user.

Similarly, a user's preferences for QoS dimensions of his applications as given by:

$$\text{QoS preferences} = h_q^{\,X_q} \bullet c_q \tag{7}$$

where and $q \in$ QoS dimension space is a QoS dimension of an application. Note that equations (3) and (7) are almost identical except for the differences in the subscripts and the absence of feature in QoS dimensions. The algorithms for finding the optimized QoS and supplier configuration of any application are given in Fig. 3. In each algorithm, the default configuration is compared with other possible configurations until the one yielding the maximum value of user's satisfaction is found and is returned as result of each algorithm. A feasible configuration is achieved if the user's

```
Optimize_QoS
Input
        1 Application a current QoS q_curren
        2 All QoS q 1 ≤ i ≤ n for an application a
Output Best_QoS for application a
Procedure
        get c_curren of q_curren
        Preference = c_curren
        Max = Preference
        Best_QoS = q_curren
        for each QoS q do
          if q_curren is replaced with q by dynamic configuration
            then X=1
          else X=0
          endif
        get c of QoS replacement q
        h =(c_curren + c)/(2*c_curren)
        User_Satisfaction = Preference * h * X
        if User_Statisfaction > Max then
          Max= User_Statisfaction
          Best_QoS = q
        endif
endfor
return Best_QoS
Endprocedure
```

```
Optimize_Supplier
Input
        1 Application a current Supplier S_curren
        2 All suppliers S 1 ≤ i ≤ n for an application a
Output Best_Supplier for application a
Procedure
        calculate f_curren and c_curren of supplier S_curren
        Preference = f_curren * c_curren
        Max = Preference
        Best_Supplier = S_curren
        for each supplier S do
          if S_curren is replaced with S by dynamic configuration
            then X=1
          else X=0
          endif
        get c of replacement supplier S
        h =(c_curren + c)/(2*c_curren)
        User_Satisfaction = Preference * h * X
        if User_Statisfaction > Max then
          Max = User_Statisfaction
          Best_Supplier= S
        endif
endfor
return Best_Supplier
Endprocedure
```

Fig. 3. Algorithms for optimized QoS and supplier configuration of an application task can be realized by appropriate applications that are instantiated using the user's preferred suppliers and QoS dimensions. The feasible configuration is given by:

$$\underset{\substack{app(a)\in task \\ s\in supplier(app(a)) \\ q\in QoS\dim(s)}}{\arg\max} = \prod_{a=1}^{app\_max} \text{Supplier preferences}(a) \bullet \text{QoS preferences}(a) \quad (8)$$

The algorithm for finding the feasible configuration of applications within the user's task is shown in Fig. 4. It finds the feasible configuration in every application.

As earlier said, [9] has positively influenced our work. Equations (1), (2), and (8) were taken from such work. Although previously defined in the same reference, Equations (3) and (7) have since evolved that their final forms in this paper have become ours. The rest of the other equations are all ours.

```
Optimize_task
Input
        1  Application ε  1 ≤ i ≤ max_app
        2  Current Supplier for each application a
        3  Current QoS for each application a
Output  Appropriate suppliers and QoS for the task
Procedure
for i = 1 to max_app
 optimize_supplier()
 optimize_QoS()
 configuration_a = Best_QoS * Best_Supplier
endfor
Endprocedure
```

Fig. 4. The algorithm for optimizing user's task configuration

3.4 Realizing User Task Through Appropriate Modalities and Media

Having known the user's task and context, then a feasible modality needs to be found for the computing to proceed. The modalities available to the user are *speech input* (SP_{in}), *speech output* (SP_{out}), *tactile input* (T_{in}) and *tactile output* (T_{out}). At any time, each of these modalities is either active or inactive (on or off). The truth table for all possible combinations of various modalities for the blind is shown in Fig. 5 (Left). A value of *T* (true) means a modality is possible. Hence, successful modality is given by:

$$\text{Modality} = (SP_{in} \vee T_{in}) \wedge (SP_{out} \vee T_{out}) \quad (9)$$

Therefore, a successful modality can be implemented if there is at least one input modality and at least one output modality.

Given the user's task and the applications to realize it, we then determine when a modality is possible or not which, for a blind user, is a function of the user's computing device and the noise level in his workplace. Given that:

Application = {Web Browser, Text Editor, Audio/Video Player}, Modality = {SP_{in}, T_{in}, SP_{out}, T_{out}}
Computing Device = {PC, MAC, Laptop, PDA, Cell phone}, Noise Level = {Quiet/Acceptable, Noisy}

then modality is possible under various parameters' combinations. There exists, however, a system and environment condition where modality is not possible as given by:

$$\text{Modality Failure} = (\text{Computing Device} = (\text{PDA} \vee \text{Cellphone})) \wedge (\text{Noise Level} = \text{Noisy}) \quad (10)$$

In this condition, tactile input and output, and speech input are not possible leaving only speech output as the remaining possible modality. As stated in (9), a modality requires at least one mode for data input and at least one mode for data output. Such restriction is violated in the preceding condition which renders multimodality to fail.

Let there be a function $\mathbf{f_4}$ that maps a specific modality to its appropriate media device(s) as given by **$\mathbf{f_4}$: Modality → Media**. See Fig. 5 (Right). The presence of the necessary media is important if a modality is to be implemented. The function $\mathbf{f_4}$ for visually-impaired users would be similar to the one given below:

f_4 = {(SP_{in}, Microphone), (SP_{in}, Speech Recognition), (SP_{out}, Speaker), (SP_{out}, Headset), (SP_{out}, Text-to-Speech), (T_{in}, Keyboard), (T_{in}, Overlay Keyboard), (T_{out}, Braille Terminal), (T_{out}, Tactile Printer)}

Note that although media technically refers to hardware components, a few software elements, however, are included in the list as speech input modality would not be possible without a speech recognition software and the speech output modality cannot be realized without the presence of a text-to-speech translation software. From $\mathbf{f_4}$, we can obtain the relationship in implementing multimodality:

$f_4(SP_{in})$ = Microphone $\wedge$ Speech Recognition, $f_4(SP_{out})$ = (Speaker $\vee$ Headset) $\wedge$ Text-to-Speech
$f_4(T_{in})$ = Keyboard $\vee$ Overlay Keyboard, $f_4(T_{out})$ = Braille Terminal $\vee$ Tactile Printer

Modality	*SP_{in} SP_{out}*			
T_{in} T_{out}	*00*	*01*	*11*	*10*
00	*F*	*F*	*T*	*F*
01	*F*	*F*	*T*	*T*
11	*T*	*T*	*T*	*T*
10	*F*	*T*	*T*	*F*
Modality = $(SP_{in} \vee T_{in}) \wedge (SP_{out} \vee T_{out})$				

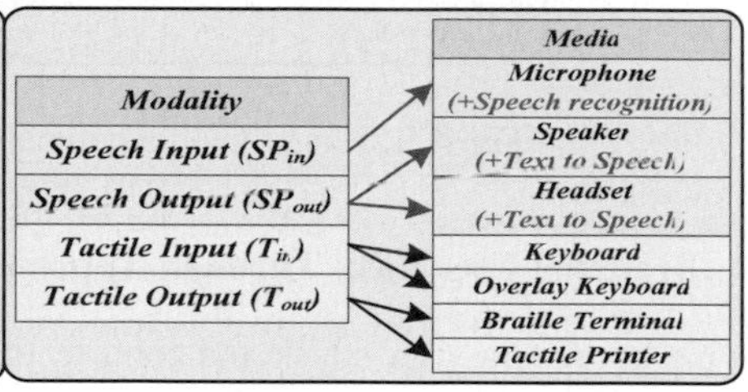

Fig. 5. (Left): The truth table to realize an effective implementation of modality, (Right): Media selections to realize a modality operation

Therefore, the assertion of modality, as expressed in equation (9), with respect to the presence of media devices becomes:

$$\begin{aligned}\text{Modality} = &((\text{Microphone} \wedge \text{Speech Recognition}) \vee (\text{Keyboard} \vee \text{Overlay Keyboard}))\\ &\wedge (((\text{Speaker} \vee \text{Headset}) \wedge \text{Text-to-Speech}) \vee (\text{Braille Terminal} \vee \text{Tactile Printer}))\end{aligned} \tag{11}$$

Therefore, in order to realize a pervasive multimodal multimedia computing, given the constraints that we have considered, it is imperative that equation (10) *should not exist* and equation (11) *should be satisfied*.

The presence of needed media devices does not automatically mean the success of a modality. Why? First, an available media device may not be working at all. Some methods for detecting device failure is available in [12]. Second, it is possible that even if a media device is present and functional, it still cannot be used due to the restriction imposed on the environment (e.g. in a library where "silence is required", a functional microphone serves no use at all). Hence, a failure in modality as a function of the media devices failure and environment restriction is given by:

$$\begin{aligned}&\text{Modality Failure} = (T_{in} = \text{Failed}) \wedge [(SP_{in} = \text{Failed}) \vee (\text{Environment Restriction} = \text{SilenceRequired}] \vee \\ &\{(T_{out} = \text{Failed}) \wedge [(SP_{out} = \text{Failed}) \vee (\text{HST} = \text{Failed}) \wedge (\text{Environment Restriction} = \text{SilenceRequired}]\}\end{aligned} \quad (12)$$

4 Design Specification and Scenario Simulations

Having formulated various ML knowledge to optimize the configuration setting of user's task, this knowledge is then put to test via sample scenarios. The design specification comes along as these scenarios are further explained.

4.1 Specification for User's Task

Consider a student user who wishes to do his homework which compares the works of two great composers, *Beethoven* and *Mozart*. To do so, our user needs access to a web browser, a text editor and a video player. Our user would work on his homework at home using his personal computer. The following day, he may continue working on his task in the school's library. In this case,

f_1 = {(assignment1.doc, Text Editor), (www.classicalmusic.com/Beethoven.html, Web Browser), (www.classicalmusic.com/Mozart.html, Web Browser), (beethoven1.wav, Audio/Video Player), (beethoven2.wav, Audio/Video Player), (mozart1.wav, Audio/Video Player), etc.}.

Formally, $\forall$ x: data format, $\exists$ y: Application | x→y $\in$ $\mathbf{f_1}$. Consider our user being in the school library working on his task using a laptop. After logging in, our system determines the applications that are suitable to the data format of the latest files in his task folder. This is done with reference to function $\mathbf{f_1}$. Using $\mathbf{f_2}$, the system determines the supplier for each application. Since a supplier priority is involved in $\mathbf{f_2}$ then the most-preferred supplier is sought. Fig. 6 shows a sample tabulation of user's preferences. Using equation (4), the following are the numerical values for user preferences: (i) if Priority= 1 (High), then User Satisfaction= 1,(ii) if Priority= 2 (Medium), then User Satisfaction= 2/3, and (iii) if Priority= 3 (Low), then User Satisfaction= 1/3.

Consider a case wherein the user's preferred audio/video player supplier – the Windows Media Player – is absent as it is not available in the user's laptop. The method by which the system finds the feasible supplier configuration is shown below:

Case 1: (MSWord, Internet Explorer, Windows Media Player) → not possible,
Case 2: (MSWord, Internet Explorer, Real One Player) → alternative 1
Case 3: (MSWord, Internet Explorer, JetAudio) → alternative 2

then the feasible selection is based on user satisfaction score:

User Satisfaction: Case 2 = (1 + 1 + 2/3)/3 = 8/9 = 0.89, and Case 3 = (1 + 1 + 1/3)/3 = 7/9 = 0.78

Hence, Case 2 is the preferred alternative. Formally, if **$\mathbf{f_2}$: Application → (Supplier, Priority)** where Priority: $\mathbb{N}_1$, then the chosen supplier is given by: $\exists$ x: Application, $\forall$ y: Supplier, $\exists$ p1: Priority, $\forall$ p2: Priority | y • x→(y, p1) $\in$ $\mathbf{f_2}$ $\wedge$ (p1 < p2).

Application	Supplier & Priority		QoS & Priority	
Text Editor	MSWord	1	40 Characters per line	1
	Wordpad	2	60 Characters per line	2
	Notepad	3	80 Characters per line	3
Web Browser	Internet Explorer	1	Medium page loading	1
	Netscape	2	High page loading	2
	BrailleSurf	3	Low page loading	3
Audio Player	Windows Media Player	1	Medium volume	1
	Real One Player	2	High volume	2
	JetAudio	3	Low volume	3

Fig. 6. Tabulation of user's preferences (Supplier and QoS) and their priority rankings

4.2 Optimizing User's Task Configuration

Consider a scenario where all suppliers for an application are available. For example, for a Text Editor application, the amount of user satisfaction with different suppliers would be like:

$c_{MSWord} = 1.0, c_{Wordpad} = 2/3, c_{Notepad} = 1/3$

This indicates that the user is most happy with the top-ranked supplier (MSWord) and least happy with the bottom-ranked supplier (Notepad). In an MSWord set-up, if an equation editor, for example, is not installed, the user's satisfaction decreases, as given by the relationship $c_{MSWord} * f_{MSWord} = (1.0)(0.75) = 0.75$.

Now, consider a case of a dynamic reconfiguration wherein the default supplier is to be replaced by another. Not taking f_s into account yet (assumption: $f_s = 1$), if the current supplier is WordPad, then the user's satisfaction is $c_{Wordpad} = 2/3 = 0.67$. What would happen if it will be replaced by another text editing supplier through dynamic reconfiguration ($x_{supplier} = 1.0$)? Using the relationship $h_{supplier} = (c_{supplier} + c_{replacement}) / 2* c_{supplier}$ then the results of possible alternative configurations are as follows:

Replacing WordPad (supplier 2):
Case 1: Replacement by MSWord (supplier 1): $(0.67)(1) * [(0.67 + 1)/2*(0.67)]^1 = 0.835$
Case 2: Replacement by itself (supplier 2): $(0.67)(1) * [(0.67 + 0.67)/2*(0.67)]^1 = 0.67$
Case 3: Replacement by Notepad (supplier 3): $(0.67)(1) * [(0.67 + 0.33)/2*(0.67)]^1 = 0.50$

Hence, if the reconfiguration aims at satisfying the user, then the second-ranked supplier should be replaced by the top-ranked supplier.

In a similar fashion, the QoS dimensions are given the same scores for their priority ranking. With characters per line as QoS parameter in a text editor application, then

$c_{40\ characters\ per\ line} = 1.0, c_{60\ characters\ per\ line} = 0.67, c_{80\ characters\ per\ line} = 0.33$

Indeed, the feasible configuration for a text editor application is given by:

$$\arg\max_{Text\ Editor} = (f_{MSWord} c_{MSWord})(f_{40\ characters\ per\ line}) = 1.0$$

4.3 Specification for Detecting Suitability of Modality

Petri Net [13] is a formal, graphical, executable technique for the specification and analysis of a concurrent, discrete-event dynamic system. Petri nets are used in deterministic and in probabilistic variants; they are a good means to model concurrent or collaborating systems. They also allow for different qualitative or quantitative analysis that can be useful in safety validation. In the specifications in this paper, only a snapshot of one of the many outcomes is presented due to space constraints. We use HPSim [14] in simulating Petri Net.

In Fig. 7, a Petri Net specification is shown with user's task, modalities, computing device, and the workplace's noise level as inputs to user's condition. As shown, many of these combinations render the modality possible. There is, however, a condition that makes modality and therefore computing for the blind user fail, and that is when the user's computing device is either a PDA or a cellular phone and his workplace is noisy. This is given in equation (10) and is traceable in the Petri Net diagram.

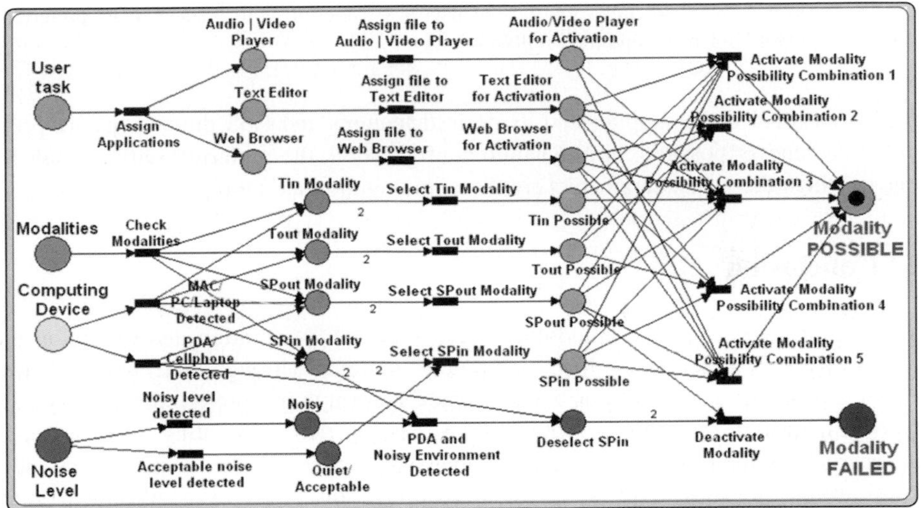

Fig. 7. Petri Net diagram showing the possibility or failure of modality based on the environment's noise level, the computing device and user's task

4.4 Experimental Results

Using user's preferences, we have simulated the variations in user's satisfaction as these preferences are modified through dynamic configuration. The results are presented through various graphs in Fig. 8. The first two graphs deal with application supplier, and the variation of user's satisfaction as additional parameters are taken into account, supplier features and alternative replacements being the parameters. The last one deals with QoS dimensions and their variations.

Graph (a) shows that user's satisfaction does not only rely on a supplier's ranking but also on its features. For example, supplier 2 of no missing feature satisfies the user better than supplier 1 that has 2 missing features. In addition, the result in graph (b) illustrates such satisfaction as a function of current supplier and its features and its alternative supplier replacement. Similarly, the QoS dimension is not only a function of priority but also of its alternative replacements, as shown in graph (c). In general,

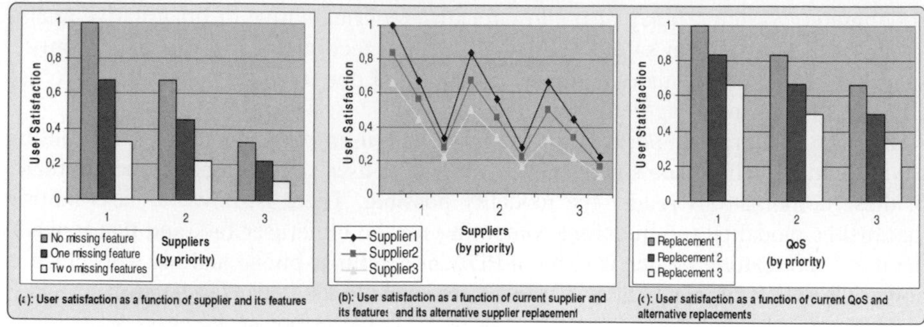

(a): User satisfaction as a function of supplier and its features

(b): User satisfaction as a function of current supplier and its features and its alternative supplier replacement

(c): User satisfaction as a function of current QoS and alternative replacements

Fig. 8. Various graphs showing variations of user's satisfaction with respect to its preferred supplier and QoS dimension and their replacements

user is satisfied if the supplier and its desired features and QoS dimensions are provided. Whenever possible, in a dynamic configuration, the preferred setting result is one in which the set-up parameters are those among the user's top preferences.

5 Conclusion

This paper presented the methodology for a successful migration and execution of user's task in a pervasive MM computing system. Through ML training, we illustrated the acquisition of positive examples to form user's preferred suppliers and QoS dimensions for selected applications. In a rich computing environment, alternative configuration spaces are possible which give the user some choices for configuring the set-ups of some of his applications. We have illustrated that configuration could be dynamic or user-invoked, and the consequences, with respect to user's satisfaction, of these possible configurations. Optimization is achieved if the system is able to configure set-up based on user's preferences.

In this work, we have listed various modalities that are available to a blind user. A modality is possible if there is at least one mode for data input and also at least one mode for data output. Given sets of applications, modalities, computing devices, and environment's noise level, we formulated the conditions where modality would succeed and fail. Similarly, we illustrated the scenario wherein even if a specific modality is already deemed possible, still it is conceivable that modality would fail if there are not sufficient media devices that would support it or the environment restriction imposes the non-use of the needed media devices. We validated all these affirmations through various scenario simulations and formal specifications.

Future works include performance details of user task configurations as simulated on various types of processors and software platforms. This would include evaluation of dynamic configuration performance as the system searches alternative application supplier and QoS dimensions.

References

[1] M. Satyanarayanan, "*Pervasive Computing: Vision and Challenges*", *IEEE Personal Communications*, vol. 8, pp. 10-17, 2001.

[2] A. Awdé, et al, "A Paradigm of a Pervasive Multimodal Multimedia Computing System for the Visually-Impaired Users", GPC 2006, 1st International Conference on Grid and Pervasive Computing, Tunghai University, Taichung, Taiwan, 2006.

[3] H. Ferreira, D. Freitas, "Enhancing the Accessibility of Mathematics for Blind People: The AudioMath Project", ICCHP, 2004, pp. 678-685.

[4] V. Moco, D. Archambault, "Automatic Conversions of Mathematical Braille: A Survey of Main Difficulties in Different Languages", ICCHP *Conference*. Paris, France, 2004.

[5] A. Solon, et al, "Mobile multimodal presentation", New York, NY, USA, 2004.

[6] A. Lécuyer, et al, "HOMERE: a Multimodal System for Visually Impaired People to Explore Virtual Environments", Proc. IEEE Virtual Reality, Washington, USA, 2003.

[7] C. Rousseau, et al, "A Framework for the Intelligent Multimodal Presentation of Information", *Signal Processing Journal*, vol. 86, pp. 3696 - 3713, 2006.

[8] A. Demeure, et al, "Le Modèle d'Evolution en Plasticité des Interfaces: Apport des Graphes Conceptuels", 15ème Conf. francophone sur l'Interaction Homme-Machine (IHM 2003), Caen, France, 2006.

[9] V. Poladian, et al. "Task-based Adaptation for Ubiquitous Computing", *IEEE Transactions on Systems, Man and Cybernetics*, vol. 36, pp. 328 - 340, 2006.

[10] C. Jacquet, et al, "A Context-Aware Locomotion Assistance Device for the Blind", ICCHP 2004, 9th Intl. Conf. on Comp. Helping People with Special Needs, Paris, France.

[11] D. A. Ross, et al, "Talking Braille: A Wireless Ubiquitous Computing Network for Orientation and Wayfinding", 7th Intl. ACM SIGACCESS Conf. on Comp., MD, USA 2005.

[12] M. D. Hina, et al, "Design of an Incremental Learning Component of a Ubiquitous Multimodal Multimedia Computing System", WiMob 2006, 2nd IEEE Intl. Conf. on Wireless and Mobile Computing, Networking and Communications, Montreal, Canada, 2006.

[13] "Petri Net", http://www.winpesim.de/petrinet/

[14] "HPSim", http://www.winpesim.de/

Minimalist Object Oriented Service Discovery Protocol for Wireless Sensor Networks

D. Villa, F.J. Villanueva, F. Moya, F. Rincón, J. Barba, and J.C. López

Dept. of Technology and Information Systems
University of Castilla-La Mancha
School of Computer Science. 13071 - Ciudad Real. Spain
{David.Villa, FelixJesus.Villanueva, Francisco.Moya, Fernando.Rincon, Jesus.Barba, JuanCarlos.Lopez}@uclm.es

Abstract. This paper presents a new Service Discovery Protocol (SDP) suitable for Wireless Sensor Networks (WSN). The restrictions that are imposed by ultra low-cost sensor and actuators devices (basic components of a WSN) are taken into account to reach a minimal footprint solution.

The WSN communication model we use is based on the `picoObject` approach [1] which implements a lightweight middleware for WSN on top of standard object oriented middlewares using a small set of interfaces. The proposed SDP uses also this set, so it supposes the minimal overhead for devices and communication protocols, allowing, at the same time, the deployment of a valuable set of services.[1]

1 Introduction

Wireless Sensor Networks (WSNs) are called to be a key component in any pervasive environment, supporting the interaction (monitoring and driving) with the physical world. A WSN is composed of low-cost nodes which contain three types of elements: a sensor or an actuator, a generic microcontroller and a network interface. Sensors and actuators are oriented either to monitorize a physic magnitude (e.g temperature, humidity, smoke, etc.) or to modify the state of an element which drives such a physical magnitude (e.g a valve). The microcontroller basically adapts raw data and provides communication facilities for applications. At last, the network interface offers wireless network connectivity.

Flexibility and quickly deployment (due mainly to their wireless interface) are the characteristic that make WSNs to become a good solution for multiple applications such medical [4] or meteorology [5] applications, habitat monitoring [6], etc. In general, we can envision a pervasive environment plenty of heterogeneous

[1] This research is partly supported by FEDER and the Spanish Government (under grant TIN2005-08719) and by FEDER and the Regional Government of Castilla-La Mancha (under grants PBC-05-0009-1 and PBI-05-0049).

C. Cérin and K.-C. Li (Eds.): GPC 2007, LNCS 4459, pp. 472–483, 2007.

WSN nodes offering different services, from the most basic (supported by individual nodes or the whole network) to the most complex (ambient intelligent services resident in the environment).

However, the flexibility in the deployment of WSN (avoiding wiring) has not found its counterpart when developing software for such a type of networks. We believe that a real deployment of a WSN has to minimize also the configuration requirements of the application that take advantage of the services supported by every WSN node. With the service discovery protocol (SDP) described in this paper, a WSN node has the capacity to announce its services and offer the possibility to use them without any previous configuration procedure.

The proposed SDP: a) Allows very low-cost nodes to be deployed in an easy and incremental way (following a *Place & Play* philosophy). b) Allows applications to discover and use the services offered along a WSN (such property is really desirable in mobile applications). c) Is designed for heterogeneous WSNs where different nodes have different functionalities and even are implemented in different technologies.

The SDP described in this paper is based on our previous work called `picoObject` [1]. As we report in that reference, this approach allows a very high degree of interoperability with standard distributed object oriented middlewares, and provides also the capability to view and to use the WSN nodes as conventional distributed software objects without any intermediate device. The strong footprint limitations determine the design of a `picoObject`, as well as the design of our SDP (as we will show in the next sections).

The SDP prototype is based on ICE [17] (Internet Communication Engine), a high quality distributed object framework developed by ZeroC, Inc. built upon the experience of CORBA but free of legacy or bureaucracy constraints.

The rest of this paper is organized as follows. Section 2 explains some previous works on SDPs. In section 3 the `picoObject` approach is briefly summarized. Section 4 is devoted to explain our SDP in detail. In section 5 the prototype we have used to validate our proposal is briefly described. Finally we draw some conclusions and outline some future work.

2 Related Work

In the last years, several SDPs have been designed with the aim of automatizing the service discovery and minimizing the configuration procedures required to integrate a service in any networking environment.

Broadly used currently, some SDPs like UPnP [8], JINI lookup service [16], Bluetooth SDP [10] or SLP [9] are considered as the de facto standards. The evolution of fields like ambient intelligent, pervasive computing, or ubiquitous computing has made it possible the development of an important amount of services that use a variety of heterogeneous technologies and that need to interoperate. This growth of services inherently implies complex configuration procedures for integration with other networks services. Consequently, serious efforts have to be made in order to simplify such configuration procedures and to make it possible to support mobile services and service interoperability.

However, the current SDPs are not suitable for WSNs due to the serious footprint restrictions the WSN nodes impose. Such restrictions have to do with power supply, memory limitations, processing capacity, etc., parameters that have not been taken into account in the design of current SDPs. For example, due to footprint limitations, neither an XML parser (like UPnP requires) nor a Java Virtual Machine (needed by the JINI lookup service) could be implemented in a WSN node. Even lightweight protocols oriented to mobile devices like Bluetooth SDP or PDP [13] do not assume such constraints in their design.

Recent works have proposed SDPs for new technologies like mobile ad-hoc networks [12] and [11]. In these highly dynamic environments, in which services are registered in a directory (in a similar way to yellow pages), the directory-based structures cannot be deployed due to the lack of a fixed infrastructure. This has been the problem usually addressed, but, once again, the minimal footprint requeriments of WSN nodes have not been taken into consideration.

On the other hand, current platforms oriented to support WSN (good surveys can be found in [15] and [14]) are working prototypes in which the nodes will have to be reduced in cost (therefore probably in resources) for a eventual massive introduction in the market.

In [7] a resource discovery protocol (called DRD) specially designed for WSN is described. In DRD each node sends a binary XML description to another node that has been selected as the cluster head (CH) (this node assumes the representation of all the nodes under its range) which responds to any possible query (in SQL) in place of its cluster sensors. The CH is selected between all the nodes depending on their remaining energy. Thus it is necessary to give all the nodes the capacity of being a CH. This means that all nodes need SQLlite database, libxml2 and a binary XML parser to implement the CH functionality. Our approach, as we will describe in section 4, provides a way to incrementally add functionality to the nodes, so ultra low-cost sensor nodes can be easily integrated in a first step and, then, according to its capacity, acquire new functionality. It is necessary to clarify that when we are talking about wireless sensor nodes we are thinking on a minimal footprint device, even more limited than current prototype platforms like MICA, MicaZ, RockWell WINS, etc.

Finally, in [3] an homogeneous sensor network (all the nodes have the same functionality) resource discovery protocol is proposed, centering in the optimization of the flooding process by taking advantage of historical queries [7]. Our work supposes that a WSN is formed by heterogeneous nodes implementing different services that do not need to be considered in an homogeneous way (managed by a simple table).

In general, we observe that previous works have not faced the design of SDPs in such a way that: a) they turn out to be suitable for heterogeneous WSN, taking into account the footprint requeriments of small devices, and, 2) they support the use of node services by client applications without the need of a configuration procedure. Therefore, we will focus on these issues.

3 picoObjects

Our SDP has been designed to give support to WSN based on `picoObjects`, although it is perfectly applicable (without any change) to more powerful devices or even to WSN based on other approaches (including, for example, some widely used devices such as the MICA Motes).

The `picoObjects` are implemented as message matching automatons. From a textual description (that includes the object interface description), the `picoObject` compiler can generate these automatons in several programming languages and for several platforms.

This approach allows the `picoObjects` to be embedded either into the smallest microcontroller in the market, into the tiniest embedded Java virtual machine, or even in a low-end FPGA. For a deep description of the `picoObject` approach, please refer to [1]. A `picoObject` implementation example can be found in our webpage [18].

4 Abstract Service Discovery Framework

We have defined an ultra lightweight service discovery protocol, called ASDF (*Abstract Service Discovery Framework*), which, using the object oriented paradigm, provides several valuable features such as: a) An easy way for device announcement. b) Extensibility and scalability. c) Legacy SDP interaction. d) Seamless integration with standard middlewares. e) Auto-configuration for devices (in order to get a *place & play* behavior).

The ASDF is designed keeping in mind minimal footprint devices. For example, the protocol allows the nodes to announce themselves to the network using simple, but completely middleware compliant, messages. In spite of this, the protocol is very scalable and can perfectly be applied to more powerful devices.

4.1 Event Channels

Our protocol uses extensively the middleware standard *event* service. This makes it possible to easily decouple all involved elements. The event channel is a direct implementation of the *observer* [2] design pattern (also known as *publish-subscribe*).

The IceStorm (the ZeroC ICE *event channel* service) is able to employ several transport protocols at same time (at least TCP, SSL, UDP and multicast UDP) in a transparent way for objects and even over the same channel. Each publisher or subscriber can even choose the protocol to use individually.

However, it is not convenient to connect too many nodes to the same event channel due to scalability reasons. Therefore, several event channels (*topics* in ICE parlance) are used. Event channels have minimal resource cost and they can be interconnected by means of "links" to propagate events to each other. These links have some parameters that allow to establish limits or priorities to the event propagation.

Event channel *federation* is another technique to group some nodes (their corresponding event channels) together according to different criteria (functionality, location, class of service...) in the same logic channel, but keeping the ability to propagate certain events to other channels.

4.2 Place and Play Environment

Node deployment is a key issue for sensor networks. It is very convenient that nodes can configure themselves in an autonomous way. When an actor (an actor is a node/device that can expose its functionality by means of an object interface) is connected o returns from a sleep state, the node sends an announcement message (`adv()`) to a specific event channel (called *ASD.announce*). Optionally, these announcements can also be sent periodically. The `adv()` member function is part of the `iListener` interface. Because of this, all the applications or actors that are interested in announcing their services, must implement the aforementioned interface. The description of this interface is as follows:

```
module ASD  {
  interface iListener {
    idempotent void adv(Object* prx, iProperties* prop);
  };
};
```

The argument `prx` is a proxy to contact the object that sends the event. The argument `prop` is an object that serves to access the node properties (see 4.3). The next listing exposes the content of an `adv()` message:

```
Magic Number: 'I','c','e','P'
    Protocol: 1,0 - Encoding: 1,0
    Message Type: Request (0)
    Compression Status: Uncompressed (0)
    Message Size: 54,  Request Message Body
        Request Identifier: 0
        Object Identity Name: publish
        Object Identity Content: asdf
        Operation Name: adv - Ice::OperationMode: normal (0)
        Input Parameters Size: 16
        Input Parameters Encoding: 1,0 - Encapsulated parameters (10 bytes)
```

Sometimes, the `adv()` message arguments are fully static. In these cases, since the total message size is about 80 bytes, these arguments can be stored in the device ROM.

The clients and services interested in the potential announcements that may occur must subscribe to the event channel *ASD.announce*. When a subscriber receives an `adv()` event, it gets the object proxy of the announced actor and uses the introspection mechanisms to interrogate the actor. The subscriber can also list and request the actor properties by means of the argument `prop`.

Although this announcement procedure has a high abstraction level, it can be implemented on very simple devices with an identical behaviour respect to a conventional "object".

4.3 Properties

As mentioned before, the parameter `prop` in the `adv()` message is an object proxy for a "property server". The property server allows the clients to access the actor properties. There are several alternatives:

- The argument `prop` can be a null proxy when it is not necessary or there is not a property server for the actor.
- The proxy `prop` can point to a remote object in a different localization. This allows to implements corrective property servers for many actors whose properties are stored out of the actor, even in a big database. A single servant can dispatch many objects using a "default servant" strategy.
- If the device has enough computing resources, the property server can be implemented in the own device. In this case, both `adv()` arguments, `prx` and `prop`, point to the same object.

The property servers implement the `iProperties` interface:

```
module ASD  {
  interface iProperties {
    Ice::ByteSeq propget(string key);
    void propset(string key, Ice::ByteSeq value);
    Ice::StringSeq proplist(void);
  };
};
```

The properties are specified by means of a string key. The property value is a byte sequence and thereby it can store strings, configuration files, binary drivers, images, maps, Java applets, etc

In any case, the actor properties are considered optional -not required- information. This information is useful for administration, configuration and monitoring tools but it doesn't affect the system basic functionality. The system services never depend on property values or their availability.

4.4 Basic Interface for Actors

All actors (sensors or actuators) implement a very simple interface to expose their state value. The sensor state is the measured value of the physical magnitude. There are different interfaces that depends on the type of data they manage. Some of them are shown next:

```
module iBool {
  interface W { void set(bool v); };
  interface R { nonmutating bool get(); };
};

module iByte {
  interface W { void set(byte v); };
  interface R { nonmutating byte get(); };
};
...
```

4.5 Interaction Model for Actors

Depending on the application interacts with actors, there are four basic types of actor behaviors: **Passive**) To get the state value of a passive sensor, the client needs to invoke explicitly the actor's `get()` method and then will receive the reply in a synchronous way. **Active**) The active actor is able to send a `set()` message in a pre-programmed way to another object (usually an event channel). That message indicates the current state of the actor. **Proactive**) It's also an active sensor but it sends the `set()` event when a change occurs in its state. **Reactive**) A reactive sensor is an active sensor that sends `set()` events only if a client invokes its standard `ice_ping()` method. The `ice_ping()` standard functionality has been extended so when this method is invoked, the actor, besides the conventional `ice_ping()` behaviour, sends an event to the pre-defined event channel to publish its state.

Therefore, when we talk about active actors (or active sensors), we refer to both, reactive and proactive ones. All active objects implement the interface `iActive` that is shown below:

```
module ASD  {
  interface iActive { idempotent void topic(Object* prx); };
};
```

The passive actors requires a two-way communication model while the active ones could use a one-way communication model.

Using the `topic()` method, an specialized service can instruct the actor about the remote object (event channel) where the actor must send its events.

4.6 Actor Set-Up

The active sensors need an event channel to send their state updates. When an actor announces itself, a "channel monitor" service does the following tasks (figure 1):

1) Using the middleware introspection features, it asserts that the new actor is actually an active actor (it implements the `iActive` interface). 2) It creates an event channel using the object identity as the channel name. If that event channel already exists (it has been created before) then no further actions are needed and the process finishes. 3) After creating the corresponding event channel, the monitor invokes the actor's `topic()` member function with the proxy for the new event channel as the argument.

This process is designed keeping in mind that actors are implemented as `picoObjects`: this means that they are not able to create event channels by themselves and need of the existence of the channel monitor. For a more powerful device, capable of running a standard middleware, the monitor makes no sense, since its functionality is performed by the standard middleware procedures.

Since every actor creates its own specialized event channel to send its events, this approach allows to take under control the message flow, improving at the same time the system scalability.

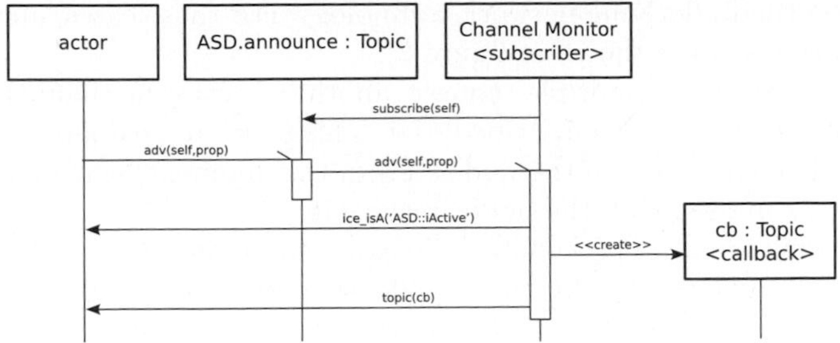

Fig. 1. Sequence diagram for Channel Monitor Service

4.7 Multi-requests

In WSNs, it is usual that a service requires to query to a certain set of sensors: for example, the service may need to compute the temperature average in a big room with many installed sensors. As a way to simplify this operation, we use reactive actors (see section 4.5).

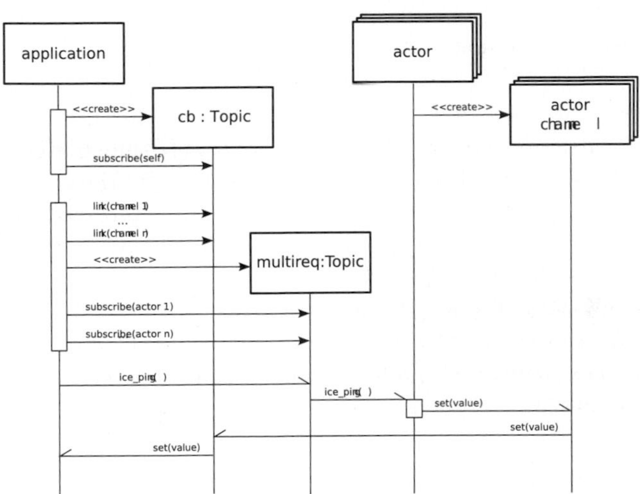

Fig. 2. Sequence diagram for multi-requests

If a client is interested in the value of a set of sensors, it can create a new event channel. All involved sensors event channels are linked to the new one (if it is known that several nodes share some kind of functional or structural relation the new event channel may be created by default). The clients that are interested in the state of this set of sensors may subscribe to the new channel.

The most efficient way to send the `ice_ping()` to a set of actors is that they hold an additional multicast endpoint. But this is not always possible because it depends on the underlying network technology. For these cases, an alternative solution is proposed (as shown in figure 2).

To make it possible a multiple request, another new event channel is created. All the involved sensors are subscribed to it. This task can be done by an external application, transparently to the nodes. From this moment, when a client sends an `ice_ping()` message, all the nodes receive it.

With the multi-request procedure and thanks to the ICE Storm channels event federation mechanism any external application can configurate its particular *vision of the world* attending to different aspects like functionality, position, security, etc.

4.8 Service Lookup

When an application needs to find a object that provides certain service, the application creates an event channel to be used as "callback" and subscribes to it. Then, the application invokes the `lookup()` method over the *ASD.search* event channel indicating the property values it wants and the callback event channel proxy. The `lookup()` method belongs to the `ASD::iSearch` interface. The application is responsible for the event channel dispose.

```
interface iSearch {
  dictionary<string, ByteSeq> PropDict;
  void lookup(Object* prx, PropDict query);
};
```

The actors (subscribed to the *ASD.search* channel) that match the criterion send an `adv()` message to the channel proxy specified by the application in the `lookup()` message. If other applications or services are interested in the potential replies, they can subscribe to the published channel proxy. A sequence diagram of this procedure is shown in figure 3.

To ensure that actor replies are not sent before others can subscribe to the callback channel, the actor waits for a fixed time before the announcement event is sent. Also, other additional random timeout can be implemented to improve the system scalability.

4.9 Legacy SDP Integration

In large heterogeneous pervasive environments where different networks are deployed (multimedia network, personal body networks, control networks, etc.) it is not likely than only one SDP covers all the different networks. It is also unrealistic to assume that all devices implement just the same SDP. Devices and services from different manufacturers will probably implement several SDPs. Again, a real deployment will require interoperability of several SDPs, at least, for a basic interaction.

We are working on the design and implementation of new procedures that allow a complete interoperability with other SDPs. Looking at the current de facto standard protocols (UPnP, Bluetooth SDP and JINI are being considered)

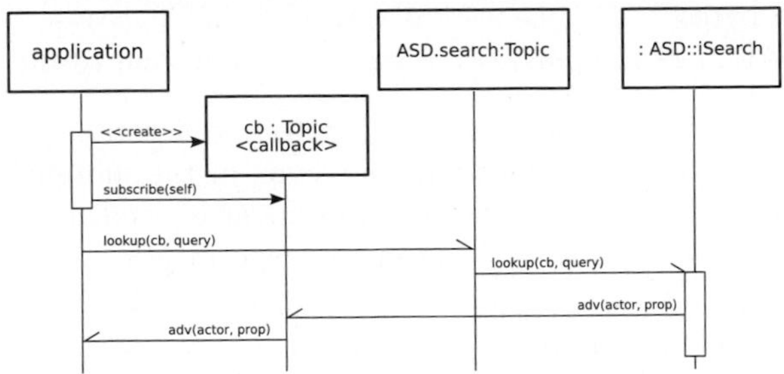

Fig. 3. Sequence diagram for service lookup

Table 1. Size of messages employed in ASDF

Name of the ASDF Message	Size of Message (in bytes)
Ice::Object::ice_ping	46
IceStorm::TopicManager::create	71
IceStorm::Topic::subscribe	97
IceStorm::Topic::link	91
ASD::iListener::adv	96 (+46 if prop. server)
ASD::iActive::topic	88
ASD::iSearch::lookup	>92 (depends on query)
iByte::W::set	42

a set of common primitives will be derived so as to make it easy the development of bridges between the ASDF and other SDPs.

Our target is to provide the ASDF with a basic interoperability to, for example, localize and execute services that are offered by a specific WSN node from an UPnP service and without any modification of such a service. To achieve this, we are working on matching the UPnP primitives with the events that can be directly interpreted by the `ppicoObjects` that are installed in the WSN nodes.

The choice of the primitives to be implemented and the granularity of the implementation have to be carefully selected and will strongly depend on the SDPs to be integrated.

5 Experimental Results

The table 1 shows the size of the messages used in the ASDF protocol, assuming that it has been implemented in ICE. Some of them are standard ICE messages. In the tests, the object identity was 8 bytes long and it used IPv4 endpoints.

In the current prototypes, we are using a 8-bit micro-controller although it is underutilized. Its characteristics are:

- **Model:** Microchip PIC 16LF876A, 10MHz
- **Program memory:** 8 KiB

- **RAM:** 368 bytes
- **I/O:** 1 USART, 22 i/o pins, two 8-bit timers and one 16-bit timer.

The table 2 shows the size of several prototype actors. The indicated size includes the complete implementation that runs in the aforementioned micro-controller. No other library or software component is needed. The `picoObject` execution model is composed by a automaton specification (the bytecode) and a small interpreter (a virtual machine, VM) implemented in assembly language. All of them are about two orders of magnitude smaller than any other previous implementation of small embedded standard middlewares.

Table 2. Footprint for several `picoObject` nodes (in bytes)

Type of actor	bytecode	VM	total footprint	RAM used
TCP passive (without `adv()`)	350	333	683	36
TCP passive (periodic `adv()`)	455	411	866	36
TCP reactive (periodic `adv()`)	527	411	938	64
UDP reactive (periodic `adv()`)	368	411	779	64

6 Conclusions

In this paper we have presented a SDP (called ASDF) suitable for low-cost nodes in the WSN field. This SDP allows a *place & play* behavior, so nodes and services can be deployed in a easy and flexible way without any configuration procedure.

Based on a previous work (`picoObjects`), the proposed SDP provides the WSN nodes with an advertisement service by means of *events*. Additionally, it allows external applications to lookup services offered by the WSN nodes.

The design of the ASDF allows incremental addition of functionality according to the device capabilities. Moreover, we have implemented an ASDF prototype using an standard distributed middleware whose common services (event channels, replication, persistence, location transparency, security, etc.) have allowed an easy and reliable implementation.

Due to the interfaces shown in this paper, an application does not distinguish between the advertisement generated by a service resident in a conventional PC or by a node in a WSN. This fact represents a great advantage for quickl development of applications which use WSN services making unnecessary either to integrate in such applications complex WSN specific protocols or to use different programming languages.

In a near future, our work is mainly focused on widening the range of platforms supported by the `picoObject` compiler at same time that we integrate third party services using different SDPs (UPnP and Bluetooth SDP bridges are currently under development) making it possible the real deployment of large heterogeneous pervasive environments under a *place & play* philosophy.

References

1. D. Villa, F.J. Villanueva, F. Moya, F. Rincón, J. Barba, J.C. López. *Embedding a general purpose middleware for seamless interoperability of networked hardware and software components* Grid and Pervasive Computing, GPC 2006, Taiwan May 2006. Lecture Notes in Computer Science 3947.
2. E. Gamma, R.H., R. Johnson, J. Vlissides, *Design Patterns, Elements of Object-Oriented Software.* 1995, Addison-Wesley.
3. F. Stann and J. Heidemann. *BARD:Bayesian-assisted resource discovery in sensor networks* in Proceedings of the IEEE Infocom, 2005.
4. Timmons, N.F.; Scanlon, W.G., *Analysis of the performance of IEEE 802.15.4 for medical sensor body area networking*, IEEE SECON 2004, October 2004
5. J. Lundquist, D. Cayan, and M. Dettinger., *Meteorology and Hydrology in Yosemite National Park: A Sensor Network Application*, Information Processing in Sensor Networks (IPSN), April 2003
6. A. Mainwaring, J. Polastre, R. Szewczyk, D. Culler, and J. Anderson, *Wireless Sensor Networks for Habitat Monitoring*, WSNA'02, September 2002
7. S. Tilak, K. Chiu, N.B. Abu-Ghazaleh and T. Fountain, *Dynamic Resource Discovery for Wireless Sensor Networks* IFIP International Symposium on Network-Centric Ubiquitous Systems (NCUS 2005)
8. Microsoft, *UPnP Device Architecture v1.0* Available at http://www.upnp.org/download/UPnPDA10_20000613.htm, June 2000.
9. E. Guttman and C. Perkins and J. Veizades and M. Day, *Service Location Protocol, Version 2*, RFC 2608, 1999.
10. Bluetooth SIG, *Specification of the Bluetooth System v2.0*, available at http://www.bluetooth.org. November, 2004.
11. U.C. Kozat and L. Tassiulas. *Service Discovery in mobile ad-hoc networks: an overall perspectiva on architectural choices and network layer support issues* Journal on Ad-hoc Networks, 2004.
12. F. Sailhan and V. Issarny. *Scalable Service Discovery for MANET* Proceedings of the 3rd IEEE conference on Pervasive Computing and communications, 2005.
13. C. Campo and M. Munoz and J.C. Perea and A. Marin and C. Garcia Rubio, *PDP and GSDL, a new service discovery middleware to support spontaneous interactions in pervasive systems*, Pervasive Computing and Communications Workshop, 2005.
14. M. Kuorilehto, M. Hannikainen and T. Hamalainen, *A Survey of Application Distribution in Wireless Sensor Networks* EURASIP journal on Wireless Communications and Networking 2005:5,pp 774-788.
15. P. Baronti, P. Pillai, V. Chook, S. Chessa, A. Gotta, Y. Fun Hu, *Wireless Sensor Networks: a Survey on the State of the Art and the 802.15.4 and ZigBee Standards* Technical Report ISTI-2006-TR-18, Istituto di Scienza e Tecnologie dell'Informazione del CNR, Pisa, Italy, November 2006, pp.41.
16. Sun Microsystems, *Jini Architecture Specification*, ed. 1.2, available online at `http://www.sun.com/`,
17. ZeroC, Inc., *ICE Home Page*, available online at `http://www.zeroc.com/`,
18. ARCO Group, *PicoObject Web demostration example*, available at {`http://arco.inf-cr.uclm.es/marisa.html.en`}

A Novel Data Grid Coherence Protocol Using Pipeline-Based Aggressive Copy Method

Reen-Cheng Wang, Su-Ling Wu, and Ruay-Shiung Chang

Department of Computer Science and Information Engineering,
National Dong Hwa University, 97401, Hualien, Taiwan, R.O.C.
{rcwang, rschang}@mail.ndhu.edu.tw

Abstract. Grid systems are well-known for its high performance computing or large data storage with inexpensive devices. They can be categorized into two major types: computational grid and data grid. Data grid is used for data intensive applications. In data grids, replication is used to reduce access latency. It can also improve data availability, load balancing and fault tolerance. If there are many replicas, they may have coherence problems while being updated. In this paper, based on the aggressive-copy method, we developed an algorithm using pipeline concept, such that the data transfer tasks can be done simultaneously. This novel Pipeline-based Aggressive Copy method can accelerate the update speed and decrease users' waiting times. We used Globus toolkit for our framework. Compared with the existing schemes and from the preliminary simulation results, our method shows notable improvement in overall completion time.

Keywords: Data Grid, Data Replication, Data Coherence.

1 Introduction

Grid [1] computing is a form of distributed computing that involves coordinating and sharing computing, application, data, storage, or network resources across dynamic and geographically dispersed organizations. Heterogeneous devices are connected together via networks to become a large-scale computing infrastructure. From users' perspective, the grid is liked a single computer. Users can have the processing power or storage capacity they want.

In grid computing, especially data intensive application, data management is a vital issue in high performance computing [2]. The data grid [3][4][5][6] is proposed to solve the problems of these applications. The infrastructure is to integrate the data storage devices and data management service into the grid environment. In the context of data grid technology, replication is mostly used to reduce access latency and bandwidth consumption. With replication mechanisms, data can be replicate to more than one place. This is useful to prevent the single site failure problem if the site is in charge of critical data storage. Also, if a data is very popular in the system, users can access the data from each replicated place. This can not only reduce the heavy load of the original site but also achieve load balance in the network system.

C. Cérin and K.-C. Li (Eds.): GPC 2007, LNCS 4459, pp. 484–495, 2007.

While replication mechanisms are processed, there will have coherence problems. Some of the sites may have the newest data while others still hold old ones. This may cause unpredictable errors in the system. Many mechanisms are proposed to reduce the side effects of the coherence problem. In this paper, we propose a novel Pipeline-based Aggressive Copy (PAC) method based on the aggressive copy mechanism to reduce the effect. It can accelerate the update speed and decrease users' waiting time.

The rest of this paper is organized as follows. Section 2 presents an overview of the previous works about coherence problem. Section 3 introduces our method. Experimental results are shown in section 4. And finally, the paper is concluded in section 5.

2 Related Works

One of the common data coherence problem is the dirty read. This happens when an user is updating a replica and another user wants to access the same data from another replica. Traditionally, the problem can be solved by locking mechanism. In [7], two kinds of locking method are described: standard locking and optimistic locking. Standard locking obtains a file write lock before performing the file access and release the lock after processing. Optimistic locking is used in case of a very low probability of lock contention on the file. One could alternatively access without getting a lock and test the modification date of the file after the process. In case the file was updated, one then gets a lock and retries. The tradeoff between these two methods is locking and retransmission overhead.

An improvement of locking methods is the master-slave replication model. The Home-Based Lazy Release Consistency (HLRC) [8] belongs to this model. Every data has its designated home (master) to manage its state. When an update is propagated, differences of each modified data are sent to its home at the end of an interval. This will make the home up-to-date at any time but ignore the other sites (slave). At the time of data acquisition, acquiring process receives write notices from releasing process and invalidates pages indicated by them. When an actual access happens on an invalidated file, faulting process update its stale copy by fetching the fresh copy from the home location. The method was improved in [9]. The new lock protocol for HLRC updates data that is expected to be accessed inside a critical section. The operations have three phases: lock request, lock grant, and data fault handling. The advantage of their proposed protocol reduces page fault handling time and lock-waiting time. [7] also addresses a "snapshot" method, which keeps an old version of the file until the access process is finished, but allow writers to update simultaneously. This is also a master-slave model that does the mechanism in single machine.

EU Data Grid project [5] has implemented a master-slave replica model named *Reptor* described in [10]. [11] improves the model by additional rules. A master copy can only be modified by end users. In opposition to the master replica, a slave replica is read-only. A slave replica is forced to renew according to the last contents of the master replica as a it is altered. The replica catalogue should be in conformity with the master replicas in order to keep track of the up-to-date file information.

Besides of solving dirty read problems, many researches are focused on data replication frameworks. Data replication copies a dataset from one site to another. But replicating a high volume dataset from a single server has significant drawbacks of single server dependency, unequal network load, poor performance, etc. Thus, the practice of transferring datasets from multiple servers in parallel is rising. Most of data replication frameworks can be categorized into the following three types: client-server, peer-to-peer file sharing, and BitTorrent liked file sharing.

Client-Server mode is the simplest method for data replication. The dataset owner will become a server, while the demander acts as a client. The transfer is handled by a protocol, such as FTP or HTTP. The transfer speed is affected by the amount of traffic on the server and the number of other computers that are replicating the file. If the file is large and popular, the demands on the server are more, and the download will be slower. Two protocols, which are named lazy-copy and aggressive-copy, were introduced in [12]. Replicas are only updated from the server as needed if someone accesses it in the lazy-copy based protocol. It can save network bandwidth resources without transferring up-to-date replicas every time when some modifications are made. However, lazy-copy protocol has to pay the penalties for access delay when inter-site updating is required. For the aggressive-copy protocol, replicas are always updated immediately when the original file is modified. In our experiments, we reference the aggressive-copy protocol as "1 to 1" and "1 to All" methods, which correspond to linear and star topologies in the network architecture.

In peer-to-peer file sharing framework, the file-transfer load is distributed between the computers exchanging files. When a site finished its downloading, it then becomes a dataset provider. With suitable search or pre-arranged mechanism, multiple sites can replicate data at the same time. Fast Parallel File Replication (FPFR) [13] is this kind of point-to-multipoint transfer in peer-to-peer file sharing manner. It starts from creating multiple distribution trees and replicates data to multiple sites simultaneously by pipelining point-to-point transfer. It can reduce the total time of replication procedure. We reference the FPFR as "N to N" model in our experiments.

In BitTorrent [14][15] liked file sharing protocols, files are split up into pieces. The demanders of a file barter for pieces of it by uploading and downloading them in a tit-for-tat-like manner to prevent parasitic behavior. Each peer is responsible for maximizing its own download speed by contacting suitable peers, and peers with high upload speeds will with high probability also be able to download with high speeds. When a peer has finished downloading a file, it may become a seed and share the file for others. But it cannot directly be implemented in the grid environment due to its limitations such as, data security, requirement of separate software, lack of flexibility with centralized tracking and the lack of partial usage. For these reasons, we didn't compare this type of protocol in our simulation.

Concluding active methods, such as aggressive-copy or FPFR, full consistency for replica is guaranteed. This can reduce the access delay time while access data in high performance computing. With sufficient bandwidth, it is better than passive methods, such as HLRC or lazy-copy, which suffer from long update time during each replica access. For this reason, in the following section, based on the aggressive copy mechanism, we propose a novel pipeline-based method to enhance the update speed in data grid.

3 The Pipeline-Based Aggressive Copy

3.1 Network Architecture

As shown in Fig. 1, the network architecture is composed of several regions. All regions are connected with broadband network. Each region has many sites inside. We assume that replicas are already existed in our system. In each region, there is a home node which is used to manage the information of other replicas.

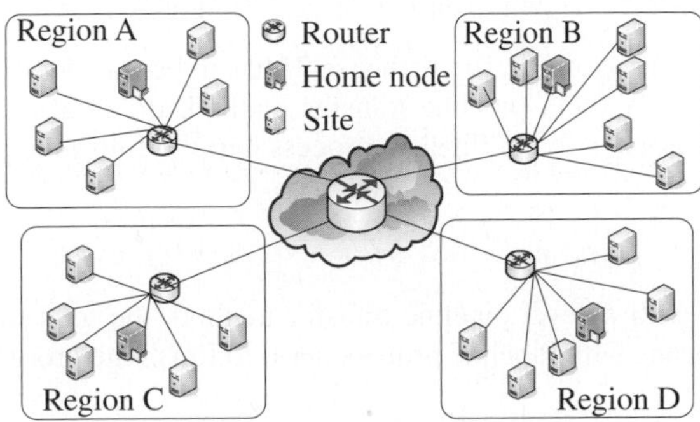

Fig. 1. The network architecture

3.2 Integration with Pipeline Transfer Method

The method adopts the pipeline concept to improve the update speed. We name it Pipeline-based Aggressive Copy (PAC in brief). Most of the networks today are running in full-duplex mode, which means each site can download and upload data simultaneously. If each of them can act as a proxy node for other waiting sites after being updated, the overall performance will increase. To go into details, when a site is receiving data, it can send out the previous data which it already received to another site that does not have this part yet. The inbound and outbound traffic will not conflict with each other due to the full-duplex communication. With suitable arrangements, all the sites can be sorted as a chain and the data may transfer one after another. This pipeline method is shown in Fig. 2(a).

In most cases of data coherent in data grid, only one file is processed in a site. To apply the pipeline transfer with a single file, we cut the file into several blocks. Therefore, the transfer can be seen as many small files pipelined. For example, in Fig. 2(a), the file is divided into five blocks. Assume the transfer time of each block is 2 secs. In the first step, the first node transfers block 1 to the second node and it needs 2 secs. Next, the second node received block 2 from node 1 and transfers block 1 to the third node at the same time, and so on. Therefore, after eight steps, the transmission will finish. Compared with Fig. 2(b) which doesn't use pipeline method, the completion time can be reduced from 10*4=40 secs to (10/5)*8 =16 secs.

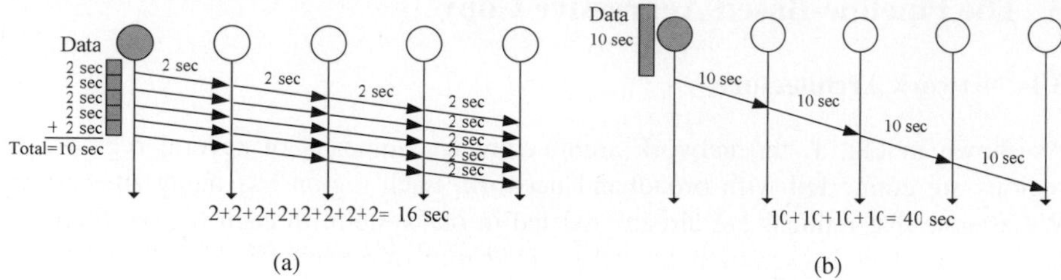

Fig. 2. (a) Pipeline method; (b) Without pipeline method

In a perfect system, assume a file with size M has to be transfer to N nodes, and the network speed is S. Without pipeline transfer method, the total time T_{np} (the lower index word "np" means with No-Pipeline process here) to finish the process will be:

$$T_{np} = \frac{M}{S} * N \tag{1}$$

And for those with P-level pipeline transfer method, the total time T_p (the lower index word "p" means with Pipeline process here) to finish the process will be:

$$T_p = \frac{M}{S * P} * (N + P - 1) \tag{2}$$

Theoretically, the more pieces we cut the better performance it will show. But it is also true that the more pieces we cut the more overhead it will bring. Processing each block will take some extra overhead. Assume the environment is homogenous and for each block processing the overhead is δ. We must modify (1) to (3) and (2) to (4).

$$T_{np}^{\#} = \left(\frac{M}{S} + \delta\right) * N \tag{3}$$

$$T_p^{\#} = \left(\frac{M}{S * P} + \delta\right) * (N + P - 1) \tag{4}$$

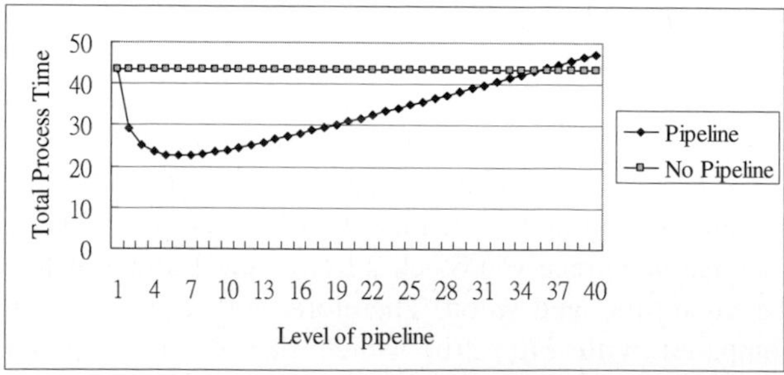

Fig. 3. Block-time relation chart (big dataset)

From Fig. 2, assume a scenario with a large dataset M=100MB, S=10Mbps, and N=4. If δ =850ms, we can plot a block-time relation chart as Fig. 3. From the figure, we can find that the minimum $T_p^{\#}$ occurred when P=7. It can also be calculated from first order differential equation from (4).

If M is quite small, because the δ overhead will become significant than the pipeline acceleration, the relationship between blocks and time will like Fig. 4. In this case, we assume M=1MB. In small file replication, the pipeline method can not be better then the one without pipeline. But the two curve will cross at P=1. Thus, we can categorize this situation into 1-level pipeline category in our PAC.

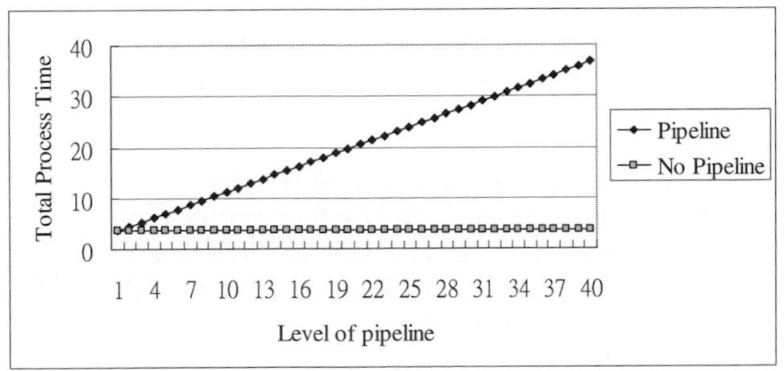

Fig. 4. Block-time relation chart (small dataset)

Furthermore, if the grid is constructed in a heterogonous environment with different network speed and process overhead at each site. Assume each site i is attached to a speed S_i network and its processing overhead is δ_i . The bottleneck site b which causes the longest propagation delay in the environment is found from (5).

$$\exists site(b) \quad which\ makes \left(\frac{M}{S_b * P} + \delta_b \right) = \left(\max\left(\frac{M}{S_i * P} + \delta_i \right) \middle| \forall i \in N \right) \tag{5}$$

The (3) and (4) will be:

$$T_{np}^* = \left(\frac{M}{S_1} + \delta_1 \right) + \left(\frac{M}{S_2} + \delta_2 \right) + \cdots + \left(\frac{M}{S_N} + \delta_N \right) = \sum_{i=1}^{N} \left(\frac{M}{S_i} + \delta_i \right) \tag{6}$$

$$\begin{aligned} T_p^* &= \left(\frac{M}{S_1 * P} + \delta_1 \right) + \left(\frac{M}{S_2 * P} + \delta_2 \right) + \cdots + \left(\frac{M}{S_N * P} + \delta_N \right) + \left(\frac{M}{S_b * P} + \delta_b \right) * (P-1) \\ &= \sum_{i=1}^{N} \left(\frac{M}{S_i * P} + \delta_i \right) + \left(\frac{M}{S_b * P} + \delta_b \right) * (P-1) \end{aligned} \tag{7}$$

This becomes a discrete problem and we are unable to solve P by using differential equation.

Based on the concept of pipeline which truly shows benefit in the previous analysis, we proposes our novel data grid coherence algorithm, PAC, in the following.

3.3 Algorithm and Example of PAC

We use the pipeline method to improve the previous aggressive copy coherence protocol. Assume the home node of each region has the information of other regions and sites in its region. The pipeline method is used to construct a new three step fast file transfer structure.

```
Algorithm PAC:

Predefine: <initialization>
   1. define number of blocks to be cut for each file
   2. define pre-ordered home node sequence circle
   3. define pre-ordered local site sequence
Step 1: <update site>
   1. Inform corresponding home node
   2. Cut the file into pre-defined pieces
   3. Starts to transfer block by block
   4. When corresponding home node received first
      block, it goes to Step 2.
Step 2: <home node replication>
   1. Corresponding home node breaks its incoming path
      from pre-ordered home node sequence circle
   2. Inform next home node
   3. After each block received, pipeline it to next
      home node
   4. If there is no blocks to be transferred, go to
      Step 3
Step 3: <local sites replication>
   1. If it is the corresponding home node of updated
      site, delete the updated site from pre-ordered
      local site sequence
   2. Home node begins to transmit blocks to next site
      in pre-ordered local site sequence
   3. After each block received, pipeline it to next
      local site
Until all processes finish
```

Take Fig. 5 for example. Site *D.3* updates a file. The pre-ordered home node sequence circle is *A->C->D->B->A*. The pre-ordered local site sequence is sorted by site ID in ascending order, such as *D.1->D.2->D.3->D.4->D.5* The pre-defined number of blocks is 3 in the grid. In Step 1.1, *Home Node D* will be informed the dataset is being modified. In Step 1.2, *D.3* will split the file into 3 blocks: block1, block2, and block3. In Step 1.3, *D.3* starts to transfer block1 followed by block2 and block3 to *Home Node D*. In Step 1.4, when *Home Node D* received block1, it goes to Step2.

In Step 2.1, *Home Node D* breaks its incoming path from the pre-ordered home node sequence circle, which makes the circle become a simple sequence *D->B->A->C* without loop. In Step 2.2 and Step 2.3, PAC is performed in *Home Node D -> Home Node B -> Home Node A-> Home Node C*. When *Home Node D* finished replication process with *Home Node B*, it goes to Step3. So for the other Home Nodes, except the last *Home Node C*. Because there is no next home node for *Home Node C*, it will goes to Step 3 immediately after it received block1.

In Step 3.1, *Home Node D* will delete site *D.3* from the pre-ordered local site sequence. Thus, the local site sequence in region D becomes *D.1->D.2->D.4->D.5*. This sequence is used in Step 3.2 and Step 3.3 to do local PAC. *Home Node B*, *Home Node A*, and *Home Node C* will do their local PAC based on their pre-ordered local site sequence, too. The whole process will be finished in Step 3.4.

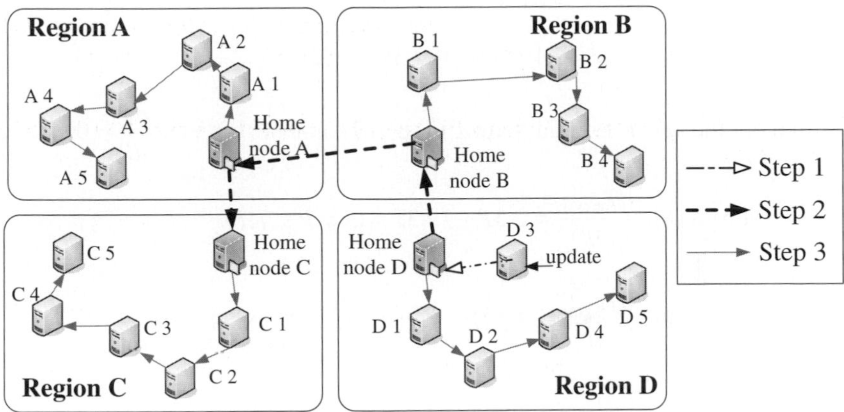

Fig. 5. The transmission in the entire network

4 Experimental Results and Analysis

We implement our PAC algorithm using Globus Toolkit version 4.0 [16][17] and run it on our grid environment named Taiwan UniGrid [18]. The experiments were doing on the scenario with two regions. In region 1, there are five servers which are named from uniblade01 to uniblade05. The sites are located in National Tsing Hua University, Taiwan. The region 2 contains six servers which are named from grid1 to grid6, which are placed in National Dong Hwa University, Taiwan. The uniblade01 and grid1 were assigned to be the home node in each region. Two regions are far away and connected via Internet.

4.1 Suitable Number of Blocks

According to section 3.2, we know that the pipeline will increase the transfer speed. We need to cut a file into pieces to perform our PAC algorithm. It is not hard to calculate the best *P* value of minimum $T_p^{\#}$ from (4) with first order differential. But in real environments, even in a homogeneous scenario, the exact δ is hard to be measured. And also the condition may be complicated as (7) for heterogeneous devices and networks. So we do some experiments in region 2 with different updated file size to observe the block-time relation curve.

From Fig. 3, it is straightforward that block-time relation will be a U-type curve. Thus, after multiple measurements, we average the data and use quadratic regression analysis to find out the fitting polynomial curve for each dataset, as shown in Fig. 6. For different file replication size: 200M, 500M and 1000M, we have the following polynomial curves equations:

$$T_{200M} = 1.25 * P^2 - 19.37P + 125.34 \tag{8}$$

$$T_{500M} = 2.66 * P^2 - 43.80P + 317.75 \tag{9}$$

$$T_{1000M} = 5.10 * P^2 - 82.38P + 626.53 \tag{10}$$

To find out the best P for minimum T in (8), (9), and (10), we let $\frac{dT}{dP} = 0$.

$$\text{From (8), } \frac{dT_{200M}}{dP} = 2.5P - 19.37 = 0 \Rightarrow P \cong 7.75 \tag{11}$$

$$\text{From (9), } \frac{dT_{500M}}{dP} = 5.32P - 43.80 = 0 \Rightarrow P \cong 8.23 \tag{12}$$

$$\text{From (10), } \frac{dT_{1000M}}{dP} = 10.2P - 82.38 = 0 \Rightarrow P \cong 8.07 \tag{13}$$

Because P must be an integer, to round to the nearest, $P=8$ in all (11), (12), and (13). The three polynomial curves show the finish time will reach the minimum value when the number of blocks is eight in our environment. Thus, in the following experiments, we cut each file into eight blocks.

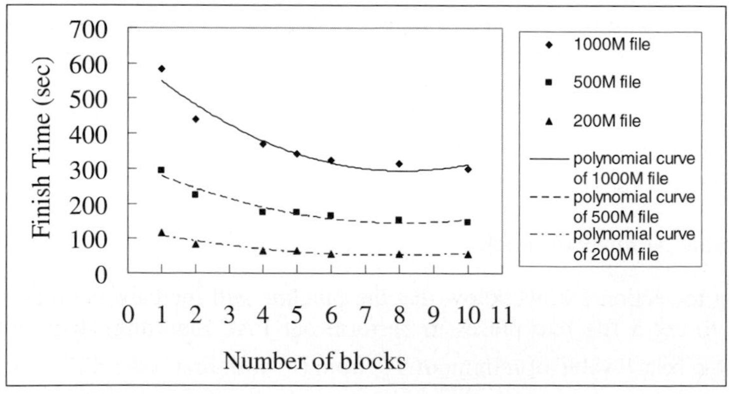

Fig. 6. The blocks-time relation in region 2

4.2 Comparing the Transmission Speed

In this section, we compare our PAC method with three different methods: 1 to 1, 1 to All, and N to N. 1 to 1 means the file is transferred one site after another sequentially until all relevant sites are updated. It is also the traditional aggressive copy protocol with linear topology. 1 to All means all sites request the file from one site. It performs traditional aggressive copy protocol with star topology. N to N means sites will construct a hierarchical structure, and transfer in FPFR manner.

At the first experiment, we test in region 2 only for a local data grid environment. Then, we use all the sites in two regions to test a cross regions situation.

Local Data Grid Test. For more accurate results, we test the update time of each file for 50 times and average the values. In this test, the grid2 is acted as the first updated server. A pre-defined update sequence is grid1(Home node)-> grid2 -> grid3 -> grid4 -> grid5 -> grid6. The 1 to 1 method transfers the file with same sequence but without pipelining. The 1 to All method transfers in six steps: grid2 -> grid1(Home Node); grid2 -> grid3; grid2 -> grid4; grid2 -> grid5; grid2 -> grid6. The N to N method transfers in three steps: grid2 -> grid1(Home Node); grid2 -> grid3 and grid1 -> grid4; grid2 -> grid5 and grid1 -> grid6.

Fig. 7 shows the average results of our tests in a local data grid. The 1 to 1 method is the worst and followed by the 1 to All method. The N to N method improves a lot but our PAC method does better. In the biggest file we test, our PAC method can reduce 48% finish time in compare with "1 to 1" method, 35% finish time in compare with "1 to All" method, and 17% finish time in compare with "N to N" method.

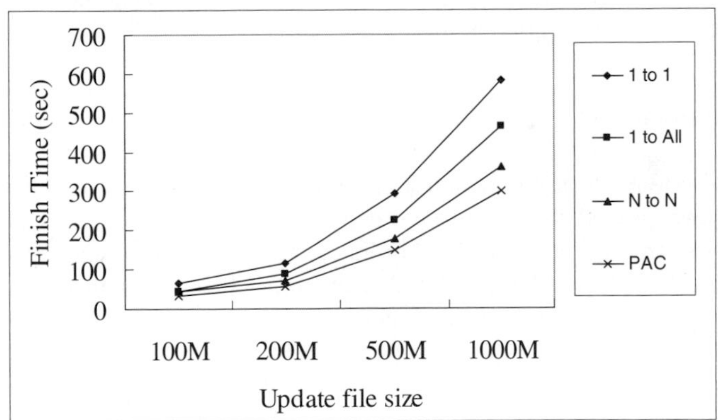

Fig. 7. The finish time in local grid

Cross Region Data Grid Test. Fig. 8 shows the experimental results in cross regions data grid. Because the number of sites is increased and the two regions are far away, the update time increases a lot. We also do 50 tests. The methods used are the same. In the test, because the 1 to All method will transmit file to 5 or 6 cross region sites (based on the randomly picked up first updated server), it performs worth than 1 to 1 method which only has one cross regions file transfer here. In the biggest file we test, our PAC method can reduce 52% finish time in compare with "1 to 1" method, 57% finish time in compare with "1 to All" method, and 44% finish time in compare with "N to N" method.

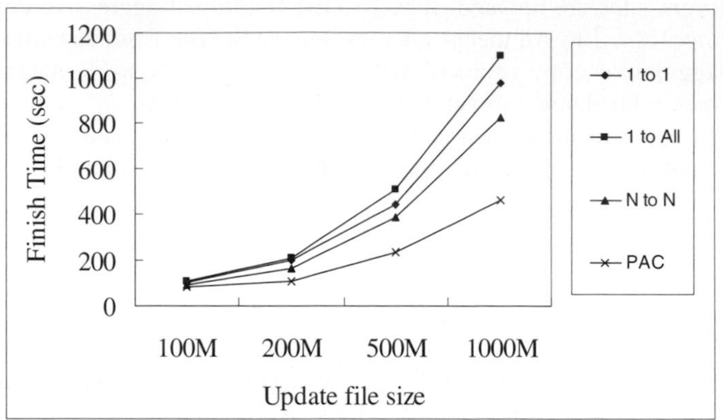

Fig. 8. The update time in cross region grid

The PAC is an event driven protocol. When a dataset has to be cohered, the process will pipeline each subset of data one by one. The datasets those have only a read pattern of access will remain unchanged after their first synchronization. Their corresponding home node will take care of their status. From the experimental results above, the better performance is shown in compared with other protocols no matter in local or cross regions data grid environments.

5 Conclusions

In data grid systems, data replication is necessary in many kinds of situations. Many researches have proved that aggressive copy is a good solution to reduce the data coherence problem in grid computing. In this paper, we contribute another aggressive copy method based on the pipelined concept, which is named Pipeline-based Aggressive Copy (PAC). In theoretical analysis, we prove that the PAC can accelerate the replication process with suitable pipeline level choice. In the worst case, if replication dataset is small, the PAC will act as 1-level pipeline which is the same as no pipeline method to reduce the significant overhead in cutting small dataset into smaller pieces.

In the experiments, we first find out the best pipeline level in our environment by test and analysis. Then we apply this value in local and cross regions experiments, to compare our PAC method with other "1 to 1", "1 to All", and "N to N" methods. Comparing with other methods for the total finish time, the results show that our method is over 17% better in local grid tests and over 44% better in cross region grid tests. These definitely support our method that the pipeline concept in PAC outweighs the overhead it brings.

Acknowledgements

This research is supported in part by ROC NSC under contract numbers NSC95-2422-H-259-001 and NSC94-2213-E-259-005.

References

1. Foster, I., and Kessekman, C.: The Grid: Blueprint for a New Computing Infrastructure. Morgan-Kaufmann, San Francisco, USA (1999)
2. Allcock, B., Bester, J., Bresnahan, J., Chervenak, A., Foster, I., Kesselman, C., Meder, S., Nefedova, V., Quesnel, D., and Tuecke, S.: Data Management and Transfer in High Performance Computational Grid Environments. Parallel Computing Vol. 28(5). (2002) 749-771
3. A. Chervenak, I. Foster, C. Kesselman, C. Salisbury, S. Tuecke: The Data Grid: Towards an Architecture for the Distributed Management and Analysis of Large Scientific Datasets. J. of Network and Computer Applications. Vol. 23(3). (2000) 187-200
4. W. Hoschek, J. Jaen-Martinez, A. Samar, H. Stockinger, K.Stockinger: Data Management in an International Data Grid Project. Proc. The 1st IEEE/ACM Int. Workshop on Grid Computing (2000) 77-90
5. The EU Data Grid Project: http://www.eu-datagrid.org/.
6. GridPhyN project: http://www.griphyn.org
7. D. Dullmann, W. Hoschek, J. Jaen-Martinez, and B. Segal: Models for replica Synchronization and Consistency in a Data Grid. Proc. The 10th IEEE Int. High Performance Distributed Computing Symposium (2001) 67-75
8. Y. Zhou, L. Iftode, and K. Li: Performance Evaluation of Two Home-Based Lazy Release Consistency Protocols for Shared Virtual Memory Systems. ACM SIGOPS Operating Systems Review. Vol. 30. (1996) 75-88
9. H. Yun, S. Lee, J. Lee, and S. Maeng: An Efficient Lock Protocol for Home-based Lazy Release Consistency. Proc. The First IEEE/ACM Int. Cluster Computing and the Grid Symposium (2001) 527-532
10. L. Guy, P. Kunszt, E. Laure, H. Stockinger and K. Stockinger: Replica Management in Data Grids. Technical report. Edinburgh, Scotland (2002)
11. Ruay-Shiung Chang, Jin-Sheng Chang: Adaptable Replica Consistency Service in Data Grid. Proc. The Third Int. Conf. on Information Technology: New Generations (2006) 646-651
12. Y. Sun, and Z. Xu: Grid Replication Coherence Protocol. Proc. The 18th Int. Parallel and Distributed Processing Symposium (2004) 232
13. R. Izmailov, S. Ganguly, and N. Tu: Fast Parallel File Replication in Data Grid. Future of Grid Data Environments workshop, GGF - 10, Berlin (2004)
14. Bit Torrent: http://www.bittorent.com/
15. B. Cohen: Incentives Build Robustness in Bittorrent. In Workshop on Economics of Peer-to-Peer Systems, Berkeley, USA (2003)
16. The Globus Toolkit: http://www-unix.globus.org/toolkit/docs/4.0/
17. I. Foster: Globus Toolkit Version 4: Software for Service-Oriented Systems. IFIP Int. Conf. on Network and Parallel Computing (2005) 2-13
18. Taiwan UniGrid Project Portal Site, 2003, http://unigrid.nchc.org.tw/

A Design of Cooperation Management System to Improve Reliability in Resource Sharing Computing Environment

Ji Su Park, Kwang Sik Chung*, and Jin Gon Shon

Dept. of Computer Science, Korea National Open University
169, Dongsung-dong, Jongro-ku, Seoul, Korea
{bluejs77, kchung0825, jgshon}@knou.ac.kr

Abstract. Resource sharing computing is a project that realizes high performance computing by utilizing the resources of peers that are connected to the Internet. Resource sharing computing provides a dynamic internet environment where peers can freely participate, but it raises questions on the reliability of operation processing. Existing resource sharing computing stores intermediate operation results in peers' local disks. Thus, when faults happen on peers' side, some peers need to wait for processing to reconnect with possibility of considerable delay. In case there is no reconnection, the intermediate operation results cannot be used. In addition, it is difficult to support cooperation due to incompatible modes of operation processing among heterogeneous systems. This thesis is to propose a cooperation management system, and define cooperation and cooperation groups necessary to improve the reliability in the resource sharing computing environment. Cooperation is a series of tasks that involve sorting tasks, processing tasks sequentially, and producing results. Cooperation group is a gathering of peers that can cooperate. Groups are created among different types of systems to enable cooperation among peers within the same group. Also, middle DB Server is proposed in a hierarchical structure to shorten delay and increase the reusability of intermediate operation results. As the intermediate operation results are stored in the middle DB Server in case there occurs a fault on peers' side, waiting time for reconnection is reduced through cooperation, and the reusability of intermediate operation result is improved. In this paper, we propose a structure that can store intermediate operation result in middle DB Server to improve reliability in resource sharing computing environment, and suggest a design for cooperation group service, discovery service, and task management service of cooperation management system.

Keywords: Resource Sharing Computing, Cooperation System. Reliability.

1 Introduction

The advancement of the Internet has accelerated information sharing and distribution, and the existing client-server computing environment has turned into distributed

* Kwang Sik Chung is the corresponding author.

C. Cérin and K.-C. Li (Eds.): GPC 2007, LNCS 4459, pp. 496–506, 2007.

multi-server environment. Furthermore, the source of information has extended from World Wide Web, Database and to personal computers. Due to such changes, users have begun to look for the other alternatives due to limitations in information search, the inaccuracy of search results, and various information search formats. As a result, P2P(Peer-to-Peer) computing where users themselves share computer resource and service via direct exchange has emerged[1,2].

Napster[3] and Soribada[4] that are examples of P2P systems are services to share MP3 music files. These services are gaining popularity in that they do not have files in the center server but just provide location information for personal computers to share files[1]. As P2P systems gained notice, P2P computing began to require more than just sharing files and thus distributed systems that utilize P2P technology were introduced. This is known as resource sharing computing. So far, studies on distributed systems focused on data processing by servers. However, SETI@HOME[5], through SETI@HOME project, has used the computing power of clients in order to gain huge computing power needed to analyze external radio signals, instead of composing distributed computing systems that required expensive servers. Similar movements are found in Korea. KOREA@HOME[6] project has started and some of its projects such as New Drug Candidate, Protein Folding analysis, Global Disk Management, etc. have been completed or are still under way. @HOME projects such as SETI@HOME, KOREA@HOME, etc. ensure that servers request clients to process data and the clients, in return, process data, which is opposite to how distributed systems process data. Since Internet-based distributed system allows individual peers to freely participate in operation or give up in the middle of operation, techniques to improve reliability in existing distributed computing cannot be directly applied to resource sharing computing [8].

In this paper, we attempt to design a cooperation management system that acts in the dynamic internet environment, in order to improve reliability in resource sharing computing environment. Cooperation enables one to carry on implementing halted operation after receiving the intermediate operation result from peers experiencing faults. Cooperation management system is composed of cooperation group service that creates and deletes groups among heterogeneous systems, of discovery service that analyzes peer information, searches for faulted peers, and explores peers available for cooperation from cooperation groups, and of task management service that distributes tasks to peers available for cooperation and requests intermediate operation results from faulted peers. Cooperation management system transmits or receives messages by XML for communication between these services.

2 Related Works

2.1 P2P System

P2P systems can be classified by system structures and objects for sharing. System structures include Hybrid P2P structure that puts a server in the middle for efficient communication and information flow among peers, Pure P2P structure that is consisted of only peers without central server, and Hierarchical P2P structure that utilizes the advantages of Hybrid P2P structure and Pure P2P structure by putting a middle server between servers and peers. In terms of objects for sharing, information sharing systems equals to data-oriented system that shares files and data, or exchanges messages, while resource sharing systems equals to distributed systems that borrowed P2P technology in order to share computer resources such as CPU, memory etc. Resource sharing system divides a big task - that cannot be processed by a single system - into small bits for distributed processing, and finally transmits operation results to a central server for combination. SETI@HOME, KOREA@HOME etc. are a few examples of @HOME project related to such systems.

SETI@HOME is a project led by Berkeley University, and it analyzes data sent by Arecibo - world's largest radio signal astronomical telescope - to find intelligent extraterrestrial life. SETI@HOME project involves installing Screen Saver on personal computers, and analyzing data when the computers are not in use.

KOREA@HOME is a project to analyze huge of information such as New Drug Candidate, Protein Folding analysis, Global Disk Management, etc. KOREA@HOME system is composed of platform server, agent, and client, and it was developed with focus on detailed functions. Functions of platform server include resource-volunteers PC management, implementation and management of task management DB, Homepage operation and management, etc. Agent has basic functions of P2P, interacts with platform server, and carries out tasks. Client creates and submits application tasks, and implements distributed application programs, etc. [15].

2.2 Reliability Problem

Reliability issues remain with both SETI@HOME and KOREA@HOME. Though solutions have been presented, the reliability issues are still to be tackled. To solve reliability problems, SETI@HOME uses techniques to register intermediate operation result every 10 minutes just in case peers fault. It stores intermediate operation result in peers' local disks and runs operation continuously once peer fault is solved. But, if peer fault is not solved, one needs to wait indefinitely until the peer restarts. This causes operation delay. Since intermediate operation result is stored in local disks, the result cannot be reused unless the peer restarts.

There are no operation reliability techniques proposed by KOREA@HOME. It uses a method that reassigns the same operation to a new peer by canceling the operation in case peer fault happens. Projects such as Avaki, FightAIDS@HOME, and Distributed.net etc. also have the reliability issues like SETI@HOME and KOREA@HOME.

3 The Design for Cooperation Management System

3.1 Definition of Cooperation and Cooperation Group

Cooperation is a method that enables several peers to process a task through collaboration, just like many labors collaborate in production process. Cooperation can be classified by either synchronous or asynchronous cooperation. Synchronous cooperation means producing result by dividing a task for simultaneous processing, while asynchronous cooperation means tasks that involve sorting tasks, data processing tasks sequentially, and producing results [17].

In this paper, cooperation means asynchronous cooperation. That is, in case a peer cannot carry on a task allocated by a server due to faults, another peer that can solve these faults can take over the intermediate operation results and continue the remaining operation. Cooperation group is a peer set that can cooperate. In the existing resource sharing computing, peers from heterogeneous systems take part in operation. However, it is difficult to support cooperation among heterogeneous systems due to incompatible modes of processing. Thus, the solution is to create groups among heterogeneous systems so that peers within the same groups can cooperate.

3.2 Environment and Structure of Cooperation Management System

Cooperation management system has a hierarchical structure that is compose of a central server, a high-capacity central DB server, a middle server, a middle DB server, and task nodes of peers. The hierarchical structure of cooperation management system can reduce the bottleneck by balancing the load that is normally centralized on a server in a centralized structure of resource sharing computing, and it ensures the network scalability. However, it is difficult to select a middle server and a middle DB server in a hierarchical structure.

In this paper, we assume an environment where a central server, a high-capacity central DB server, a middle server and a middle DB server are already established, and we do not consider selecting a middle server and a middle DB server. A central server assigns tasks to a middle server, manages the middle server status (such as fault information, CPU, memory etc.) and peer status information, and processes the results received from the middle servers. A middle server observes the peer status, receives tasks from a central server, and allocates them to peers. It also receives operation results from peers, and transmits the result value to the central server after processing them. When a peer fails, the peer's intermediate operation results are stored not in a local disk but in the middle DB server, making it unnecessary to wait for the peer to restart the operation. Peers available for cooperation pick up the intermediate results from the middle DB server and continue the operation, which shortens the delay time and ensures the reusability of intermediate operation results. Peers process the tasks allocated from the middle server and transmit their status information and the processed results.

Figure 1 shows the relationship between a central server and a middle server, between a middle server and a peer, cooperation relationship among peers, and the flow of message transmission and reception in a resource sharing computing structure. The hierarchical system structure, even if the central server fails, enables independent operation on intermediate results that are stored in the middle server. When the middle server stops and fails, another middle server can pick up the task and continue the operation as long as the intermediate results are stored in a high-capacity central DB server.

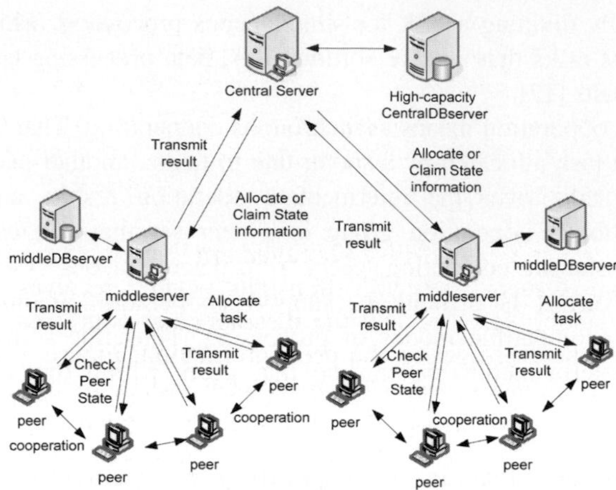

Fig. 1. Structure of System

3.3 System Design

3.3.1 Service Structure

Cooperation management system is composed of a cooperation group service, a discovery service, and a task management service. Figure 2 shows the service structure of cooperation management system. Application is a program that is applied to areas such as new drug candidate search, protein variation analysis, etc. in resource sharing computing, and its core layer represents a protocol for operating a task.

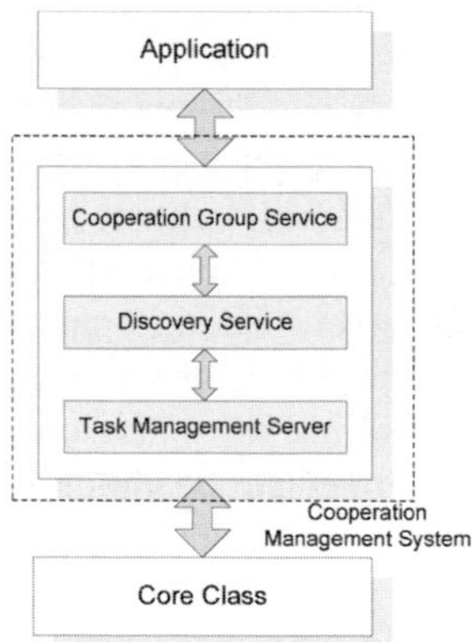

Fig. 2. Service structure of cooperation management system

Cooperation group service is a service that creates and deletes groups that have the same CPU, OS etc. among heterogeneous systems. Cooperation group service mainly creates a cooperation group for peers available for cooperation, adds peers to the group, and deletes faulted peers and groups. Discovery service is a service that searches for peer information to find failing peers, and discovers peers available for cooperation in a cooperation group. Discovery service mainly observes the peer status by constantly examining the peer information received from a cooperation group. And, according to the peer status, it sends the peer information to a task management service and a cooperation group service so that they can carry out tasks, respectively. Task management service mainly allocates tasks to new peers, assigns tasks to peers available for cooperation, and returns the intermediate operation results produced by faulted peers.

3.3.2 Message Flow in Cooperation Management System

Cooperation management system transmits and receives messages for communications among services, and the messages are expressed in XML. In this paper, we refer to the messages as the peer information. Figure 3 shows a message flow in cooperation management system. A peer, when registering, transmits its information to a cooperation group service, while the cooperation group transmits the peer group information to a discovery service. A discovery service grasps the peer status and transmits the information to a task management service and a cooperation group service. The peer information includes the information on the peer, the peer group, and the peer status. A peer, when registering in the cooperation group service, records its basic information such as CPU, OS, memory capacity, hard disk capacity, location, IP address, etc. The cooperation group service receives the peer information, creates a group, and adds the group information to the peer information with the group name. It also transmits the peer information to the discovery service. The discovery service receives the peer information and records the peer status information after analyzing the status of new peers and the exiting peers in the cooperation group. The peer status information is transmitted to the task management service and the cooperation group service.

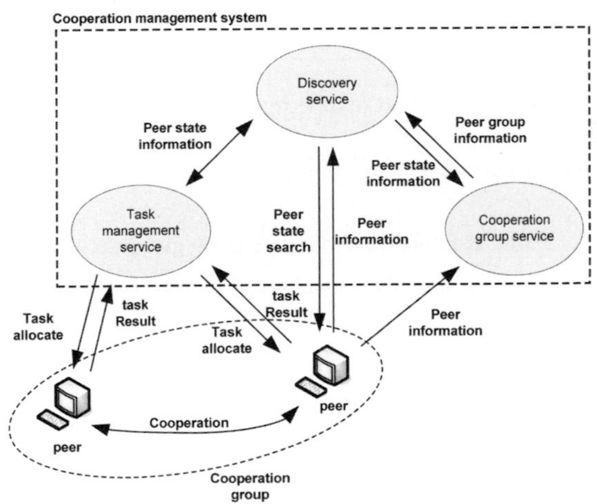

Fig. 3. Message flow in cooperation management system

3.3.3 Cooperation Management Service

The main job of the cooperation group service is to create and delete cooperation groups.

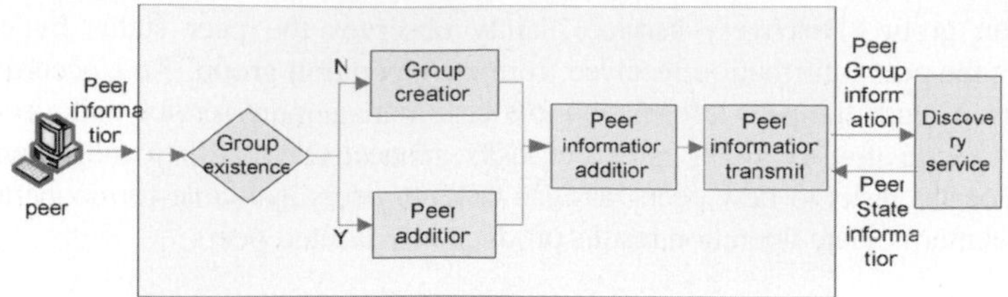

Fig. 4. Flowchart of creating a cooperation group

Figure 4 shows the flow of creating a cooperation group. When registration is requested from a peer, the cooperation group service receives and analyzes the peer information. After analyzing the peer information, it checks whether there is any group that corresponds to the peer's system, and adds the peer to an existing group or to a new group. Once the peer is added to either a new group or an existing one, the cooperation service group transmits the peer information to the discovery service after adding or modifying the group name information to the peer information.

Figure 5 shows the flow of deleting a cooperation group. When receiving information from the discovery service about a peer that failed, it searches for the group the peer belongs to, and deletes the peer. If the deleted peer is the last one in the group, the service deletes the whole group.

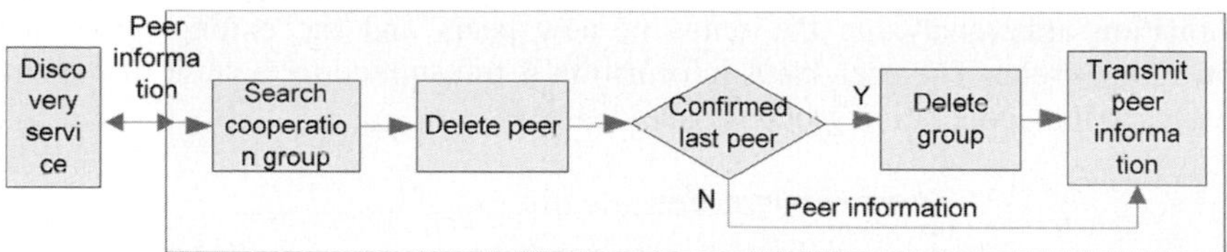

Fig. 5. Flowchart of deleting a cooperation group

Table 1 shows the functions of a cooperation group service.

Table 1. Function of a cooperation group service

Method	Function
addPeerInfo()	add Peer information
isExistGroup()	confirms exist group
genGroup()	create group
delGroup()	delete group
addPeerGroup()	add peer of group
delPeerGroup()	delete peer from group
searchGroupPeer()	search peer from group
sendGroupMsg()	transmit peer group information

3.3.4 Discovery Service

Discovery service receives, from the cooperation group service, the peer information to which group information is added, analyzes whether the peer is available for a task or for cooperation, and then transmits the peer information to the task management service. It continues broadcasting the peer information to see if there is any changes in the peer status, and when the status changes, it sends the peer information to the task management service and cooperation group service. It also analyzes the peer information periodically, and makes sure that the intermediate operation results are saved. Updated peer information is stored in the middle DB server and high-capacity DB server so that the latest information is kept.

Figure 6 shows the flow of a discovery service.

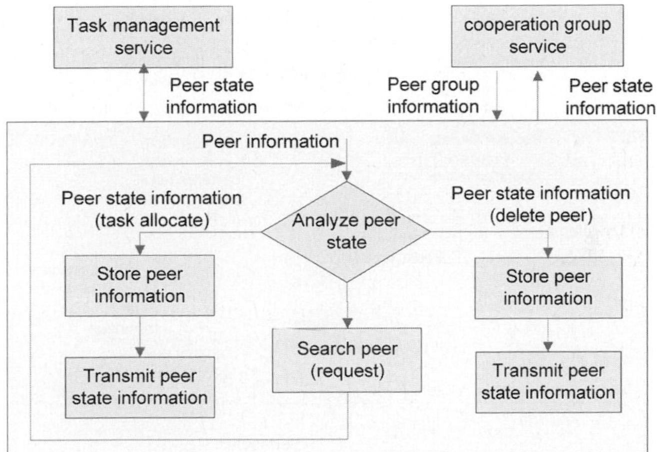

Fig. 6. Flowchart of discovery service

Table 2 shows the functions of a discovery service.

Table 2. Function of a discovery service

Method	Function
acceptPeerInfo()	receive peer information
sendPeerInfo()	transmit peer information
queryPeerInfo()	request peer information
isPeerState()	analyze peer state
broadDiscovery()	continue search and request
savePeerInfo()	store peer information

3.3.5 Task Management Service

A task management service receives the peer status information from a discovery service. If the peer status indicates that the peer is available for a task, the discovery service requests the intermediate operation results and if there is any, it allocates the results to the peer. If there is nothing, it assigns a new task to the peer. If the peer is unable to carry out a task, it requests the interim result to be stored. But, the results cannot be stored if there is no connection due to a peer fault. So, it modifies the peer information, transmits the peer information to a discovery service and continues analyzing the peer status. Figure 7 shows the flow of a task management service.

Table 3 shows the function of a task management service.

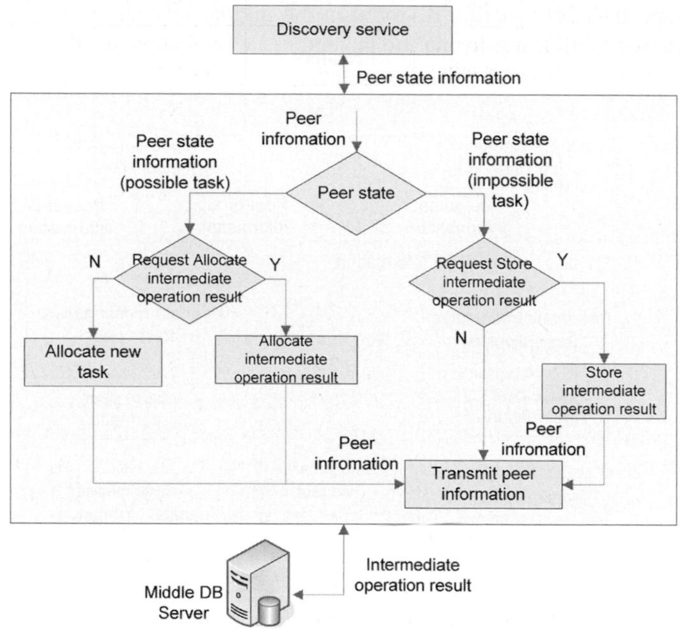

Fig. 7. Flowchart of a task management service

Table 3. Function of a task management service

Method	Function
assignWork()	allocate task
saveWork()	store task
sendPeerStateInfo()	transmit peer state information
acceptPeerStateInfo()	receive peer state information
workCooperation()	task cooperation
isPeerState()	analyze peer state

3.4 Comparison with Other System

The most well-known resource sharing computing systems are SETI@HOME in the U.S. and KOREA@HOME in Korea. As mentioned in 2.2, SETI@HOME and

KOREA@HOME do not ensure operation reliability. Table 4 shows the comparison with other systems.

Table 4. Other system and comparison

System trait	SETI @HOME	KOREA @HOME	FightAIDS @HOME	Proposed system
intermediate operation results Store a place	Local disk	No store	Local disk	middle DB server
intermediate operation results reusability	Limitation to peer self	Restart	Limitation to peer self	Peer in cooperation group
Support of cooperation	No	No	No	Yes
Group service	no	Yes	no	Support of cooperation group
structure	server /client	server /client	server /client	Hierarchical

Since SETI@HOME and FightAIDS@HOME store the intermediate operation results in a local disk, the reuse of the operation results is limited to the peer itself. In addition, there is no cooperation between peers and message transmission and reception is conducted only between a server and a peer with no group supporting it. KOREA@HOME does not use the intermediate results, but restarts a task from the beginning when defects happen. But, it assigns several tasks within the same group so that other peers can pick up the task in case one peer fails and is unable to perform the task. The cooperation management system we proposed has a middle DB server so that the interim results are stored in the middle DB server. As it searches a peer from a cooperation group that is available for cooperation, it has higher reusability of the interim results than other systems, and reduces time spent on waiting for the defected peer to reconnect. Though its hierarchical structure makes it difficult to selection the middle server, network bottleneck is less seen compared with a server/client structure, and its scalability improves the reliability of resource sharing computing.

4 Conclusion

In this paper, we have designed a cooperation management system that supports cooperation to improve the reliability in resource sharing computing environment. The system we have designed is composed of a cooperation group service, a discovery service, and a task management service. For communications between services, the cooperation management system transmits or receives messages which we defined as peer information expressed in XML. A cooperation group service is a service that creates and deletes groups among heterogeneous systems. A discovery service searches for peer information, discovers faulted peers, and look for peers available for cooperation from cooperation groups. A task management service assigns tasks to new peers, allocates tasks to peers available for cooperation, and returns the intermediate operation results of faulted peers. Due to incompatible modes of processing, cooperation is hard to attain among heterogeneous systems. In order to solve the issue, one can create a cooperation group and let peers within the same group cooperate. A hierarchical structure and a middle DB server are suggested for the cooperation management system so that the interim operation results are stored to the middle DB server. Therefore, the reusability of intermediate operation results is improved and the delay time to wait for a peer to reconnect is reduced. It is suggested that further researches be conducted on how to select a middle server and how to search peers in a cooperation group.

References

1. Andy Oram, "Peer-To-Peer", O'reilly, March 2001
2. D. Barkai, "An Introduction to Peer-to-Peer Computing", Intel Developer update magazine, February 2001
3. http://www.napster.com
4. http://www.soribada.com
5. http://setiathome.ssl.berkeley.edu
6. http://www.koreaathome.org
7. http://www.gnutella.com
8. MaengSoon Baik, SungJin Choi, JunWon Yoon, HongSu Kim, ChongSun Hwang and HyunChang Yoo, "Study on Improvement of Reliability for Distributed Computing in P2P Architecture", korea university, December, 2003.
9. JaeGyu Lee, "Force of keyword P2P of network new generation", Micro software, October, 2000.
10. HeeKwan Koo, "Design and Implementation of a Cooperation System Based on JXTA Platform in P2P File sharing Environment", kwangwoon university, thesis of M.S., 2003
11. GiChul Yoon, "P2P model hierarchical for CPU public sharing", Proceedings of Korea Information Science Society Conference, 2001
12. K. Aberer, M. Punceva, M. Hauswirth, R. Schmidt, "Improving Data Access in P2P Systems" IEEE Internet Computing, 6(1):58-67, January-February, 2002
13. "Peer-to-Peer-Enabled Distributed Computering", Intel White Paper
14. "JXTA 2001", www.jxta.org
15. A. Paul, "DNS and BIND", O'Reilly, May 2001
16. JangHo Lee, "A Software Architecture for Supporting Dynamic Cooperation Environment on the Internet", Journal of Korea Information Science Societ, vol. 2, no. 9, April, 2003
17. InGu Kang, "A Structural Comparison of Cooperative Learning and Collaborative Learning", Journal of The Institute for Educational Research, Vol. 18, pp. 183-197, 2003
18. HyunJin Jo, GuSu Kim, Young Ik Eom "Design of Mobile Agent Based Cooperation Group Management Scheme for Dynamic Scalability", Proceedings of Korea Information Science Society Conference, May 2004.
19. Ji Su Park, KwangSik Chung, JinGon Shon, "A Design of Cooperation Management System for Improving Reliability in Resource Sharing on Base Internet, Proceedings of Korea Information Science Society Conference, Vol. 12, No. 2, pp. 937-940, May 2005

A Peer-to-Peer Indexing Service for Data Grids

Henrik Thostrup Jensen[1,2] and Josva Kleist[1,3]

[1] Department of Computer Science, Aalborg University
htj@cs.aau.dk, kleist@cs.aau.dk
[2] Danish Center for Grid Computing
[3] Nordic Data Grid Facility

Abstract. We present an index system for locating files or other data objects in a grid environment. The system is constructed using a distributed hash table, and is scalable, fault-tolerant, and self-organizing. The index is dynamically updated to reflect the state of the storage elements, and can hence deal with nomadic data. The system provides extra services to ease integration with other systems: A registrant service integrates existing storage elements into the system, and a query proxy provides an easy way to query the system. A security model, which builds on the existing grid security model is also provided. An implementation has been created and its performance measured. The system is shown to scale as more nodes are added to the system.

1 Introduction

Managing data is one of the fundamental challenges in grid, and is becoming increasingly important as the amount of data in grids grow. As more data is stored, the number of components increase, making failures and system changes more common. Failures are usually solved by adding redundancy, e.g., file replication. Replication however creates a new task: Managing the locations of replicas. A data indexing system must provide a mapping from an identifier to the locations of the data.

A replica may be unavailable due to a site crash or deletion, or even be nomadic, i.e., move. While the problem with unavailable objects is reduced by replication, nomadic objects are more problematic. In such cases, data is available, but cannot be used as its location is no longer known. To handle nomadic data the index system needs to reflect the actual state of the storage system, not just the state when data was entered into the system.

One event that can cause data movement is change of a hostname. In NorduGrid [1], which has around 50 sites, this event has occurred at least twice. Such changes are relatively rare, but requires manual intervention to get the systems updated. Another case is when a storage element is taken offline. If the data could be migrated to another storage element transparently, much trouble could be spared.

The previous illustrates the requirement for an indexing system which reflect the actual state of the storage system. Not only would such a system handle

C. Cérin and K.-C. Li (Eds.): GPC 2007, LNCS 4459, pp. 507–518, 2007.

nomadic data, it would also become easier to react on changes in the system, e.g., create a new replica if the number replicas falls below a certain threshold.

An index service should be fault-tolerant as other parts of a grid are highly dependant on it. If data cannot be located, a grid can essentially come to a halt. To support a growing storage infrastructure, an index system should be able to scale up by adding more resources.

This article presents a data index system based on a distributed hash table. Together with cooperating storage elements, it provides a dynamically updated index system. The index system can scale by adding more resources, is resilient to faults, and self-organizing. Furthermore the system integrates with existing systems, by adding two services for registering data, and querying. Additionally a security model for the system is presented.

Related work is presented in Section 2. Hereafter Section 3 provides an overview of the system, followed by an in-depth architectural description in Section 4. A prototype implementation is described in Section 5, which Section 6 presents a performance evaluation of. Future work is listed in Section 7, and Section 8 concludes.

2 Related Work

Several data indexing systems has been constructed. One is Globus RLS, based on the Giggle architecture [2]. RLS servers send updates to each other using Bloom Filters, and provide fault tolerance by replicating these to other servers. While a group of RLS servers can act as a fault-tolerant index service, it does not provide a structured way to scale up using more machines. Furthermore an RLS system is very static, and requires manual intervention when adding more servers.

P-RLS [3] is a replica location service based on RLS and the Chord DHT algorithm. The system inherits scalability, load-balancing and fault-tolerance from the Chord protocol. It is shown that latency is logarithmic bounded as the size of the network increases. P-RLS does not deal with integration of existing systems, security, or clashes in identifiers.

Boundary Chord [4] extends Chord with locality awareness, and is used in ChinaGrid [5] for replica location. Due to its locality awareness, many lookups can be performed with low latency. As P-RLS, Boundary Chord does not deal with integration or security.

The EDG Replica system [6] is a distributed index, which maps from global unique identifiers to data locations. The system is based on RLS, and hence inherits the properties of that system.

OceanStore[7] is an infrastructure for storing data. The infrastructure is designed to be highly scalable and fault-tolerant. It is assumed that infrastructure cannot be trusted, and they rely on cryptography and replication to ensure data integrity. Data is nomadic, and is allowed to flow and be cached freely, to provide better availability and locality.

3 System Overview

The purpose of the index system is to map from identifiers to locations. This is achieved using a distributed hash table (DHT), which provide a distributed, scalable, self-organizing, fault-tolerant mechanism for storing and querying key-value mappings. Identifiers are the keys, and locations the values.

Figure 1 illustrates how we envisage the index system: As a layer between storage and a higher layer which handles collections, metadata, or similar. The upper layer refers to data identifiers, and the index system is used to locate data, which is its only purpose. Identifiers are not meant as being the top level entry to find a file, nor are they considered to have any semantic interpretation.

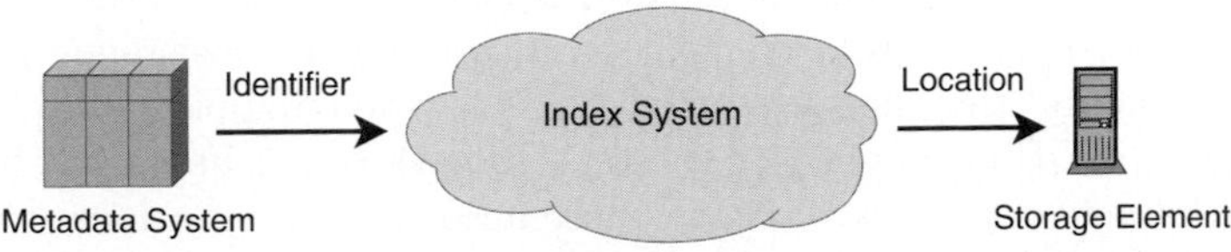

Fig. 1. The index system acts as a layer between storage and higher level services

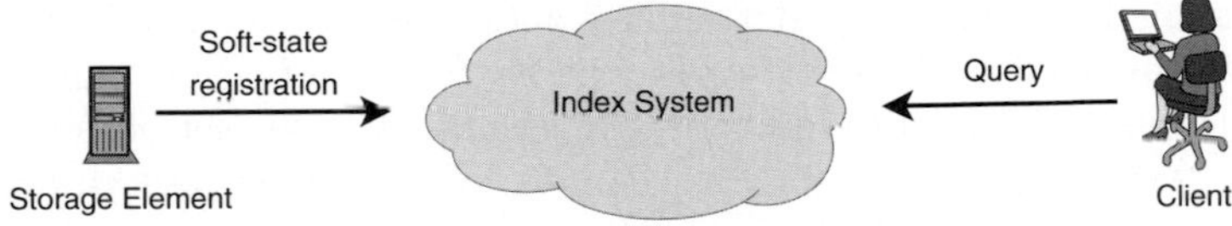

Fig. 2. Storage Element register their data, and clients query for the location

Figure 2 illustrates interactions with the index system: Storage elements populate the system by registering mappings, and clients query the system to locate data. The registration is soft-state, so storage elements must periodically register their data, or the mappings will disappear from the system.

Neither storage elements or clients are considered members of the DHT. Clients are too volatile and short-lived to make it meaningful for them to enter the DHT. There is nothing preventing storage elements to act as index nodes, however we choose to model it as two isolated services.

For integration with existing systems, two services are introduced: Registrants and query proxies. Registrants register mappings on behalf of storage elements that cannot register mappings. Query proxies provides clients a single entry to query the network. This removes the need for clients to support the DHT protocol.

The group of index nodes is dynamic, however a valid certificate is necessary in order to join the network. Furthermore only storage elements with a valid certificate may register identifier-location mappings. This protects the system from being poisoned. The mappings are considered public, so no authorization is necessary to query the system.

4 Architecture

This section describes an index architecture that is scalable, self-organizing and fault tolerant. It meets these goals, by employing a distributed hash table, for the underlying architecture. The reminder of this section describe the architecture of the system.

4.1 Distributed Hash Tables

A distributed hash table (DHT) [8,9,10,11,12] provides a scalable and fault-tolerant lookup mechanism. This is achieved by creating a structured overlay network in which the nodes and data share the same address space. Data is replicated to the nodes which has the address closest to the address of the data. DHTs are self-organizing and resilient to faults. Their consistency guarantees are quite weak, and they are primarily suited towards mapping flat data.

Lookups in a DHT takes $\mathcal{O}(\log n)$ steps to perform, n being the number of nodes in the network. In a worst case scenario, a user may have to perform several high latency lookups to locate a data object on a machine down the hall. This problem can be marginalized, by carefully selecting the size of the routing tables and using parallel lookups. A recent study[13] has shown that a very dynamic DHT with almost a million nodes can provide good performance. By using a parallelism degree of three, the average lookup hop count was 3.08, and the latency around three seconds. We assume that the set of index nodes is relatively stable, and will also be much smaller; hence better performance should be expected.

As the set of index nodes is considered stable, it may be questioned if DHTs is a suitable solution for an index network. We believe that they are, as they provide a structured address space combined with fault-tolerance and scalability.

Any distributed hash table algorithm can be used as a base for our index system. As the DHT is populated and queried by hosts which are not members of the DHT, the implementation must be able to distinguish between these. The construction and searching of the DHT is performed as it would regularly be done in the DHT architecture.

The next section describes the registration process, i.e., how the DHT is populated.

4.2 Mapping Registration

To populate the system, storage elements register identifier-location mappings to the index nodes. This registration is performed with certain intervals to ensure that entries do not disappear from the system. Mappings which are not re-registered after a certain time interval are purged from the system. This ensures that mappings to dead or moved data will disappear from the system.

When a data object has been uploaded, the storage element will register it to the index system. This registration will be kept at the index nodes for a certain amount of time, e.g., four hours. Storage elements keep track of when mappings was last registered, and at regular intervals re-registers those which are about to expire. The process when a storage element start up, is similar to the continuous re-registration, with the exception that all data objects are registered.

As there are a low number of hosts which each register a high amount of entries, the registration process has been modified to suit this. All registrations are performed in batches. Before registration the identifiers are sorted and put into a work queue. This causes the insertion process to walk the overlay network in order, keeping the node cache "warm". From the work queue a number of concurrent registrations is dispatched, i.e., the queue has multiple consumers.

The purpose of this is twofold. It spreads the load over time, and hence avoid bringing the system to its knees when performing registration of many mappings (e.g., at start up). Additionally concurrent registrations prevents slow or crashed index nodes from slowing the registration process significantly.

4.3 Integration

To ease integration, two additional services are added: Third party registrants and query proxies. The purpose of these systems is to integrate with the indexing system on behalf of services or clients which cannot communicate directly with the indexing system. Registrants register mappings on behalf of storage elements, and query proxies provides a single point of entry to query the index system.

Figure 3, illustrates how a user registers a location to the registrant after uploading a file to a storage element. Hereafter the registrant registers the mapping to the index system, in the same manner that a storage element would. A mapping can be registered to several registrants to provide redundancy.

No communication between registrant and service containing the data object is assumed. Therefore the mapping must manually be removed from the registrants when the object is deleted. The system can hence become inconsistent in case the registered file disappears, but its registration is not removed.

Instead of having a mechanism to track where mappings are registered, the registrants report which mappings they register. This is done by creating a hash of the original object location prefixed with a registrant name space. This hash is then registered to the indexing system, the location pointing to the registrant. This makes it possible for a client to see which registrants registers a mapping, making it possible to find and remove the mapping.

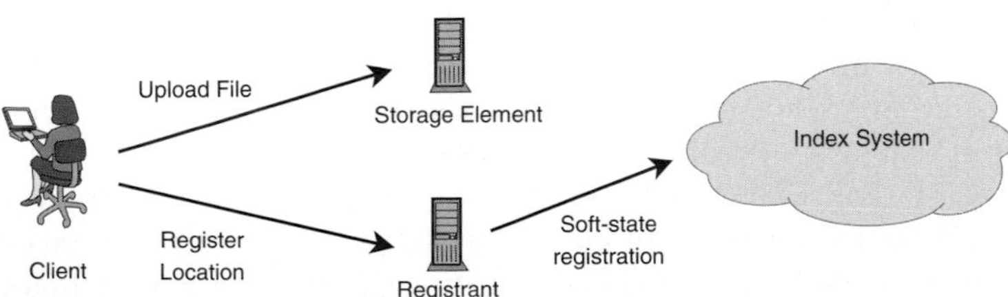

Fig. 3. A user registers a location to the registrant, which register a mapping to the index system

Instead of having a client querying the DHT directly, which requires that it supports the native DHT protocol, the client can use a query proxy. As illustrated on Figure 4, the client issues a query to a query proxy, which then queries the index network, and returns the result to the client. This interface is supplied through a standard protocol, e.g., a web service.

To speed up queries the query proxy employs a large node cache, and a short lived cache of lookup results. As a query proxy is essentially stateless, the service is trivial to replicate - the service merely has to be deployed and started.

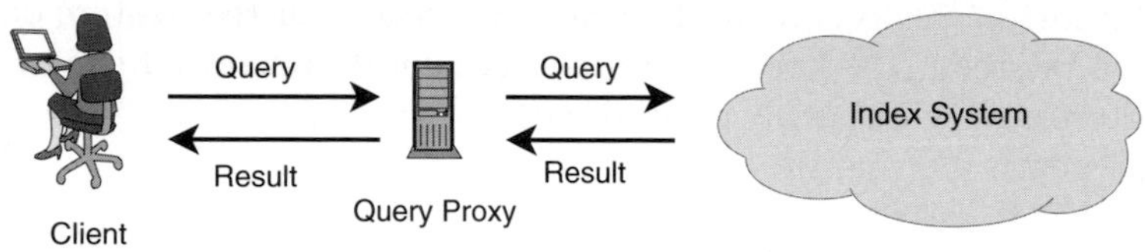

Fig. 4. The client queries the query proxy, which again queries the index network. The result is relayed back to the client.

4.4 Security Model

Typically DHTs has provided no or little security, as their size and dynamics makes conventional security models impractical. Furthermore there is often a relation between the key and data content, e.g, the key being a hash of the data. This, combined with the large number of nodes, makes it difficult for a single attacker to disrupt the network, although attacks are possible e.g., the Sybil attack [14]. The main security requirement for the index system, is that the system should not be poisoned. Furthermore it should not be possible to remove mappings from the system.

There are no restrictions on who can query the index system, as identifier-locations mappings are considered public. The identifier has no meaning as it is hash of a value, and locations are not considered useful by themselves. If needed, client authorization could be added by propagating ACLs from the storage elements to the index nodes. This however would add greatly to the cost of updating and querying the system.

It is assumed that authorized hosts are well behaving, e.g., they do not register mappings they do not have. Identifiers are generated by storage elements and registrants. They are created by creating a secure hash, e.g., SHA224 [15], of random and host unique data. This ensures that identifiers do not clash accidentally. By using this scheme, instead of having the users selecting the identifiers, it is ensured that users cannot cause identifier collision.

The security model used, is the common grid model, where a resource has a certificate signed by a certificate authority. To protect the system against poisoning, only resources with a valid certificate is allowed to register mappings to the index nodes. A valid certificate in this context would be a storage element or index node (due to inter-node-replication) certificate. As there is no confidential data send, data only has to be signed, but not encrypted.

As it would be expensive performing TLS handshake for each RPC, we suggest using DTLS[16], which provide secure datagram communication. Alternatively persistent TLS connections could be used, although this might limit scalability, due to high number of connections in large systems.

To ensure that a node can only have one network identity, the hash of its public key is used as its address. This prevents Sybil attacks, as a node cannot insert itself into the DHT with more than one address.

A potential risk is that a storage elements can register an identifier to a data object, which has been altered or constructed, in such a way that the user will be deceived. However as storage elements are already trusted to store data, they can most likely be trusted to register identifier-location pairs. If needed, a hash of the data should be saved at a third party.

5 Implementation

We have implemented the architecture described in Section 4. As a special query/registration scheme and insertion algorithm was needed, an implementation was created from scratch. The implementation is written in Python, using the Twisted framework, and is around 1800 lines, excluding tests and benchmarks. It uses a UDP protocol, which utilizes XML-RPC [17] for serialization. Currently no security infrastructure has been implemented.

The DHT algorithm used is Kademlia [12]. Kademlia uses an XOR metric, which means that the address space is non-euclidean. This means that there is no successor function, even though the address space is one-dimensional and discrete. No global ordering exists between nodes. Given an address, ordering between nodes exists, but only relative to the address in question.

Each Kademlia node has a routing table, in which addresses to other nodes are stored. The routing table contains many addresses for nodes close to itself, and fewer further away. There is no neighbour set, but the routing table is constructed such that the $2k - 1$ closest nodes will never be evicted, k being the bucket size of the routing table.

The Kademlia routing algorithm works by continuously looking up the closest known node compared to an address. Once a node with a matching address or no closer nodes has been found, the lookup has completed. As the routing algorithm is the core of both the query and insertion algorithm, it is important that it is efficient. Therefore the core walking function dispatches several concurrent lookups. In the the case of hitting slow (e.g., high latency response time) or unavailable nodes, this dramatically reduces lookup time [13].

6 Performance Measurement

This section presents performance measurements of the implemented system. Three kinds of tests are performed: Single node, multi node throughput, and multi node scalability. The single node performance test is done in order to establish a point of reference for multi node systems. All tests where run 16 times, with their minimum, average and maximum score reported.

A cluster with 36 homogeneous nodes where used in the tests. Each node is a Pentium 4 2.8 GHz CPU with 2 Gigabytes of RAM. The nodes are connected with 1 Gbps Ethernet duplex over a single switch.

6.1 Single Node Performance

In this test a single node is set up, and a single client performs queries and insertions to a node at varying concurrency levels. This is used to establish the throughput performance of a single node and which degree of concurrency should be used in the following tests. As index node operations are more heavyweight than client operations, the client should be able to fully saturate the node. The test results can be seen on Figure 5.

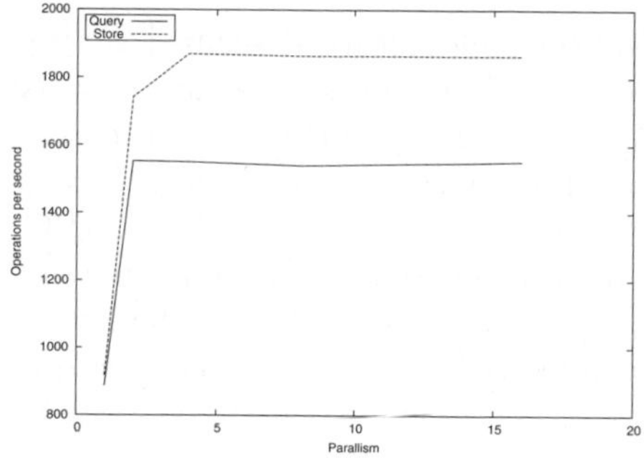

Fig. 5. Query and store performance of a single index node

Without any concurrency the node the system performed 880 queries, or 910 inserts per second. Increasing the degree of concurrency raises the number of queries per second to 1550 and 1860 inserts per second. The higher number of inserts is due to store being a very simple operation which only has to store the incoming data, whereas querying needs to check for data existence and possibly search the routing table.

These number where stable through several runs and to a concurrency degree of sixteen. At higher concurrency levels, timeouts started to occur, supporting the claim that server side operations are more expensive than client side operations. The graph illustrate that a relative low number of concurrent connections, i.e., around four is enough to keep an index nodes busy, given the latency our network infrastructure.

6.2 System Performance

A network of nodes should deliver higher performance than a single node, due to aggregated performance. However a system composed of several nodes, must spend messages coordinating the system. These are intra-node replication and routing table updates. Due to this, linear scale up cannot be expected. Furthermore store operations will produce low numbers as data is replicated to several nodes. A crucial point about the network is not how it initially performs, but that it can scale as nodes are added to the system. In turn, this is what will make the system viable.

Intra-node re-replication and routing table updates was disabled during the runs in order to have more consistent results. In a production environment the functionality should of course be enabled. The addresses of the nodes where configured in order to balance the network, again to obtain consistent results. The replication factor used in the store operation is four, and lookup was performed with a parallelism degree of one, i.e., sequential lookup. The bucket size of the routing tables was eighth.

To measure system throughput, the number of nodes in the system is kept constant, and the number of clients increased until the aggregated system performance stabilizes. The test results are shown on Figure 6.

Store performance is lower than query performance, due to the store operation consisting of more RPC calls. Whereas the query operation only needs to perform a walk to find the node closest to a given address, the store operation must first perform the walk, where after it stores the key-value pair in the k closest nodes (k is set to four in the tests).

Query performance maxes out around 18.600 operations per second. Store performance is around 3.700 operations per second. Both of these suggest linear rise in throughput. It must be remembered that the test system has a low number of nodes, so there is little overhead.

Scalability is measured the reverse way of throughput: The number of clients is held constant, and the number of nodes is increased. This shows how the system perform as more nodes are added. The performance should rise as nodes added to the system. The results are illustrated on Figure 7.

As with the throughput test, store operations score lower due to being more expensive. The graph shows that throughput of the system rises as nodes are added to the system, verifying the scalability of the system. After adding

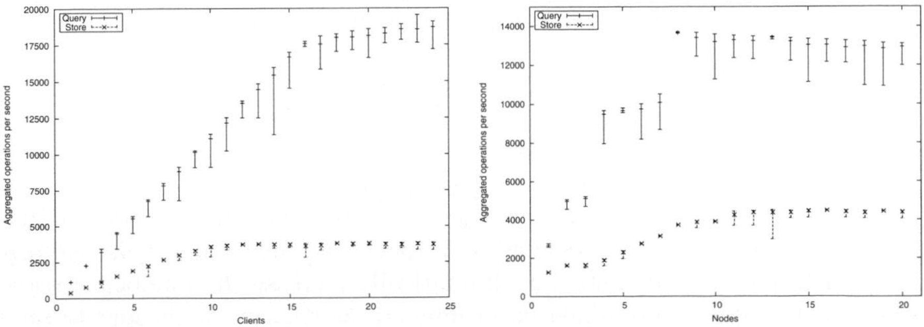

Fig. 6. Throughput test for eighth nodes **Fig. 7.** Scalability test using twelve clients

sufficient nodes, the clients cannot keep the system busy, and performance flattens. The slight decline in performance is probably because clients spending more time in the routing table logic due to a higher number of nodes.

As it can be seen, query performance rises in steps, which was not expected. The jumps where consistent throughout several runs. The reason could not be found, but we believe that it is either due to the addressing scheme in Kademlia, or a bug in our code.

Tests with random node addresses where also performed. These tests fluctuated highly, with performance dropping as much as 50%, and on average around 25%, compared to the balanced network. Small systems are vulnerable to address imbalances as there might be large ranges of the address space in which no nodes exists. This puts a high load of the nodes around the unpopulated area. Large systems will be less prone to this.

Average lookup jump count was not measured. In a system with 36 nodes, a bucket size of 8, and a uniformly network with perfect routing tables, random-to-random node average hop count would be 1.31, and maximum hop count 2. By doubling the size of the bucket for nodes furthest away, as done in Kad [13], the average hop count is lowered to 1.09. In a real world scenario with a random distribution, and imperfect routing tables, the average hop count would be larger. If a client is performing the lookup, one hop should be added. However if the client knows more than one node, which is likely, the number again lowers. Furthermore the replication factor lowers the lookup count, as the node closest to the address does not have to be found, only one close enough.

Although the system tested was relatively small, we found the results encouraging. The throughput test showed little overhead as the system grow. Aggregated system performance was also shown to rise, as more nodes are added to the system. This means that the system can be grown as needed, enabling long term survival of the system.

7 Future Work

Although a security model has been presented in Section 4.4, it has yet not been implemented. The implementation and a following evaluation of feasibility, e.g., performance overhead, is required before the system can be used in production.

The current de- and serialization scheme using XML-RPC uses a lot of CPU time. For instance the 160 bit node identifiers are encoded as strings, which is inefficient in both time and space. We believe that by using a specialized serialization scheme node performance can be further increased.

As a further optimization it might be possible to reduce the number of RPCs necessary to insert data, by batching them together. This would make the registration scheme more complex, but dramatically increase the number of registrations that could be performed in an interval, as it is much cheaper to send one packet containing many mappings, instead of many packets each with one mapping.

8 Conclusion

This article has presented an indexing architecture for objects in data grids. The indexing architecture is constructed using a distributed hash table, and is hence scalable, self-organizing, and fault-tolerant.

Along with cooperating storage elements, which register identifier-location mappings, the index is continually updated to reflect the state of the storage elements. Due to this scheme the system supports nomadic data, i.e., data which move. To provide a stable set of nodes running the index, clients and storage elements are not part of the index. To reduce system load, an efficient registration scheme is used by the storage elements to register mappings.

Registrant and query proxy services are provided for integration with existing systems. The registrant makes it possible to index data, even though the storage element on which the data resides cannot communicate with the index system. The query proxy provides a single point of entry to query the system; hence the client does not need to support the DHTs protocol in order to use the system. A security model utilizing DTLS was presented.

A prototype implementation based on the architecture has been constructed. The implementation is based on the Kademlia DHT algorithm. Performance measurements of the implementation has shown that aggregated system performance rises, as nodes are added to the system, verifying the scalability of the system. The system also showed little overhead when scaling to several nodes.

Given the results, we believe that DHTs are a viable solution for indexing in data grids, as they can provide a system which is scalable, fault-tolerant, and self-organization. Furthermore they can provide a dynamically updated system, which reflect the state of storage elements. Finally the system can scale by adding more nodes, making it possible for a system to grow as needed, ensuring long term feasibility.

References

1. Ellert, M., Grønager, M., Konstantinov, A., Kónya, B., Lindemann, J., Livenson, I., Nielsen, J., Niinimäki, M., Smirnova, O., Wäänänen, A.: Advanced resource connector middleware for lightweight computational grids. Future Generation Computer Systems (2006)
2. Chervenak, A., Deelman, E., Foster, I., Guy, L., Hoschek, W., Iamnitchi, A., Kesselman, C., Kunszt, P., Ripeanu, M., Schwartzkopf, B., Stockinger, H., Stockinger, K., Tierney, B.: Giggle: a framework for constructing scalable replica location services. In: Supercomputing '02: Proceedings of the 2002 ACM/IEEE conference on Supercomputing, Los Alamitos, CA, USA, IEEE Computer Society Press (2002) 1–17
3. Cai, M., Chervenak, A., Frank, M.: A peer-to-peer replica location service based on a distributed hash table. In: SC '04: Proceedings of the 2004 ACM/IEEE conference on Supercomputing, Washington, DC, USA, IEEE Computer Society (2004) 56

4. Jin, H., Wang, C., Chen, H.: Boundary chord: A novel peer-to-peer algorithm for replica location mechanism in grid environment. In: ISPAN '05: Proceedings of the 8th International Symposium on Parallel Architectures,Algorithms and Networks, Washington, DC, USA, IEEE Computer Society (2005) 262–267
5. Jin, H.: Chinagrid: Making grid computing a reality. In: ICADL. (2004) 13–24
6. Cameron, D., et. al.: Replica management in the european datagrid project. Journal of Grid Computing **2**(4) (December 2004) 341–351
7. Kubiatowicz, J., Bindel, D., Chen, Y., Czerwinski, S., Eaton, P., Geels, D., Gummadi, R., Rhea, S., Weatherspoon, H., Wells, C., Zhao, B.: Oceanstore: an architecture for global-scale persistent storage. SIGOPS Oper. Syst. Rev. **34**(5) (2000) 190–201
8. Stoica, I., Morris, R., Karger, D., Kaashoek, M.F., Balakrishnan, H.: Chord: A scalable peer-to-peer lookup service for internet applications. In: SIGCOMM '01: Proceedings of the 2001 conference on Applications, technologies, architectures, and protocols for computer communications, New York, NY, USA, ACM Press (2001) 149–160
9. Rowstron, A., Druschel, P.: Pastry: Scalable, distributed object location and routing for large-scale peer-to-peer systems. In: IFIP/ACM International Conference on Distributed Systems Platforms (Middleware. (November 2001) 329–350
10. Zhao, B.Y., Kubiatowicz, J.D., Joseph, A.D.: Tapestry: An infrastructure for fault-tolerant wide-area location and routing. Technical Report UCB/CSD-01-1141, UC Berkeley (April 2001)
11. Ratnasamy, S., Francis, P., Handley, M., Karp, R., Schenker, S.: A scalable content-addressable network. In: SIGCOMM '01: Proceedings of the 2001 conference on Applications, technologies, architectures, and protocols for computer communications, New York, NY, USA, ACM Press (2001) 161–172
12. Maymounkov, P., Mazières, D.: Kademlia: A peer-to-peer information system based on the xor metric. In: IPTPS '01: Revised Papers from the First International Workshop on Peer-to-Peer Systems, London, UK, Springer-Verlag (2002) 53–65
13. Stutzbach, D., Rejaie, R.: Improving lookup performance over a widely-deployed dht. In: Proceedings of IEEE INFOCOM, Barcelona, Spain. (2006)
14. Douceur, J.R.: The sybil attack. In: IPTPS '01: Revised Papers from the First International Workshop on Peer-to-Peer Systems, London, UK, Springer-Verlag (2002) 251–260
15. Housley, R.: A 224-bit one-way hash function: Sha-224 (2004)
16. Rescorla, E.: Datagram transport layer security (2006)
17. Winer, D.: Xml-rpc specification (1999)

A Novel Recovery Approach for Cluster Federations

Bidyut Gupta, Shahram Rahimi, Raheel Ahmad, and Raja Chirra

Department of Computer Science, Southern Illinois University,
Carbondale IL 62901, USA
{bidyut, rahimi, rahmad, rchirra}@cs.siu.edu

Abstract. In this paper, we have addressed the complex problem of determining a recovery line for cluster federation and have proposed a fast recovery algorithm to handle failures in cluster federations. The main feature of the proposed algorithm is that it can be executed simultaneously by all clusters in the cluster federation. Besides, the number of trips to the stable storage necessary for executing the algorithm is much less compared to the same in some existing works. Also the proposed algorithm does not suffer from any message storm unlike some noted work in this area.

1 Introduction

Cluster federation is a union of clusters, where each cluster contains a certain number of processes. A Cluster may be defined as an independent computer combined into a unified system through software and networking. Clusters are usually deployed to improve speed over that provided by a single computer, while typically being much more cost-effective than single computers of comparable speed or reliability. Cluster computing environments have provided a cost-effective solution to many distributed computing problems by investing inexpensive hardware [1], [2], [9].

With the growing importance of cluster computing, its fault-tolerant aspect deserves significant attention. It is known that checkpointing and rollback recovery are widely used techniques that allows a system to progress inspite of a failure [4]. It may be noted that a distributed system / cluster federation is said to be consistent, if there is no message which is recorded in the state of its receiver but not recorded in the state of its sender [1], [2], [4], [5]. In cluster computing, considering the characteristics of cluster federation architecture, different checkpointing mechanisms should be used within and between clusters. For example, a cluster may employ either coordinated checkpointing scheme or independent (asynchronous) checkpointing scheme for its processes to take their local checkpoints. We term this checkpointing as the primary level of checkpointing. Note that in cluster computing failure of a cluster means failure of its one or more processes. It is also the responsibility of each cluster to determine its consistent local checkpoint set that consists of one checkpoint from each process

C. Cérin and K.-C. Li (Eds.): GPC 2007, LNCS 4459, pp. 519–530, 2007.

present in it. But this consistent local checkpoint set (also known as cluster level checkpoint of the cluster) may not be consistent with the other clusters consistent local checkpoint sets, because clusters interact through messages which result in dependencies between the clusters. Therefore, a collection of consistent local checkpoint sets, one from each cluster in the federation, does not necessarily produce a consistent federation level checkpoint (also known as federation level recovery line). Consequently, rollback of one failed cluster may force some other clusters to rollback in order to maintain consistency of operation by the cluster federation.

Problem Formulation. Very few works have been reported so far for handling the complex problems of recovery in cluster federation computing [1], [2]. In this work, we address this complex problem of determining a recovery line for cluster federations. Our objective is to develop a fast recovery algorithm for cluster federations to determine a consistent federation level checkpoint with very less number of trips to the stable storage in its each iteration. As in [1] and [2], we also assume single cluster failure at a time and the failure model is fail-stop.

2 Relevant Data Structures

Before we state the relevant data structures and their use in our proposed algorithm we need to define the following. A cluster level checkpoint (CLC) of a cluster is defined as a set of local checkpoints, one from each process belonging to the cluster, such that these checkpoints are mutually consistent. In other words a CLC represents a recovery line for the cluster; however this CLC may not be consistent with CLCs of other clusters. As in [1] and [2], we assume that inside a cluster processes take these local checkpoints periodically in a coordinated way. A CLC taken in this way is termed in this paper as regular cluster level checkpoints. Besides, in our approach a cluster also takes a cluster level checkpoint in a coordinated way if it receives an inter cluster application message from another cluster. We call it a forced cluster level checkpoint. Therefore, a forced CLC may be considered as a communication-induced one [6]. As in [2], we assume that the two events of receiving an inter cluster application message and taking a forced CLC occur together atomically. A consistent federation level checkpoint (i.e. a federation level recovery line) is a set of the CLCs, one from each cluster, such that these CLCs are mutually consistent; that is, there is no orphan message in the system with respect to this set of the CLCs.

Let the cluster federation under consideration consist of N clusters, where each cluster consists of a number of processes. The jth process of the ith cluster is denoted as p_j^i and i^{th} cluster as C^i. For cluster C^i consisting of r processes, its mth cluster level checkpoint is represented as $CLC_m^i = \{cp_1^m, cp_2^m, \ldots, cp_{r-1}^m, cp_r^m\}$, where cp_j^m is the mth local checkpoint taken by process p_j of cluster C^i. Note that all these m^{th} local checkpoints are taken following the coordinated checkpointing approach and so are mutually consistent. That is, CLC_m^i represents a recovery line for cluster C^i. In this context, note that by the statement, a process p_j^i in

C^i stores the corresponding CLC_m^i in the stable storage, we mean that process p_j^i stores its local m^{th} checkpoint cp_j^m that belongs to CLC_m^i. Also in cluster computing environment, communication between two clusters means communication between two processes belonging to these two clusters respectively and failure of a cluster means failure of its one or more processes.

Corresponding to every cluster level checkpoint, for example say CLC_m^i, every process p_j^i in cluster C^i maintains the following three vectors at its mth local checkpoint, which are same for all processes in the cluster at their respective m^{th} local checkpoints. Since CLC_m^i is the set of these m^{th} local checkpoints of the processes in C^i and these vectors are same for all processes in C^i, hence for simplicity we will assume that as if cluster C^i maintains these three vectors at CLC_m^i. These three vectors are initialized with 0s at the initial state (starting state) of a cluster (i.e. at the starting states of the processes in it). These vectors are stated below.

1. $V^i_{m(sent)} = [v_m^{i,0}, v_m^{i,1}, \ldots, v_m^{i,N-1}]$, where $\left|V^i_{m(sent)}\right| = N =$ Number of clusters in the cluster federation and $v_m^{i,j}$ represents the number of inter cluster application messages sent from cluster C^i to any cluster C^j. Initially $v_m^{i,j} = 0$, for $0 \le j \le N-1$.
2. $V^i_{m(recv)} = [r_m^{i,0}, r_m^{i,1}, \ldots, r_m^{i,N-1}]$, where $\left|V^i_{m(recv)}\right| = N =$ Number of clusters in the cluster federation and $r_m^{i,j}$ represents the number of inter cluster application messages received by cluster C^i from cluster C^j . Initially $r_{i,j}^{m} = 0$, for $0 \le j \le N-1$.
3. $CIC_m^i = [c_0^{i,0}, c_1^{i,1}, \ldots, c_{m-1}^{i,m-1}]$, and $\left|CIC_m^i\right| = m =$ Number of CLCs taken by C^i, where:

$$CIC_m^i(m) = \begin{cases} CIC_m^i(m-1)+1 & \text{if the } CLC_m^i(m) \text{ is a forced checkpoint} \\ CIC_m^i(m-1) & \text{if the } CLC_m^i(m) \text{ is a regular checkpoint} \end{cases}$$

For example, at the initial checkpoint CLC_0^i, the vector $CIC_0^i = [c_0^{i,0}] = [0]$. And at the second checkpoint CLC_1^i, the corresponding vector $CIC_1^i = [c_0^{i,0}, c_1^{i,1}] = [0, c_1^{i,1}]$, where $c_1^{i,1} = c_0^{i,0} + 1 = 1$, if the checkpoint CLC_1^i is a forced cluster level checkpoint; and $c_1^{i,1} = 0$ if the checkpoint CLC_1^i is a regular cluster level checkpoint. In a similar way all other entries in the vector CIC_m^i are updated. In this work, note that when we do not need to specify a particular checkpoint number, we will simply use the notations $V^i_{(sent)}$, $V^i(recv)$, and CIC^i to represent the three vectors. Each process in a cluster maintains a Boolean flag. The use of this flag has been stated in the following section.

Observation 1. At any cluster level checkpoint CLC_r^i in cluster C^i , the value of the last element of the CIC_r^i vector denotes the total number of forced checkpoints taken by cluster C^i till its checkpoint CLC_r^i.

Observation 2. At any cluster level checkpoint CLC_r^i in cluster C^i , the length of the CIC_r^i vector (i.e. the number of elements in it) denotes the total number of cluster level checkpoints, including both regular and forced ones taken by the cluster C^i till its checkpoint CLC_r^i.

3 Working Principle

In this section we first present how different vectors are updated. We then briefly outline how the proposed recovery mechanism works, followed by an illustration. The updating of the vectors will become clear from the following example. Consider the two cluster system as shown in Fig.1. Two application messages, m1 and m2, are sent from C^i to C^j . Initially, the two clusters take their respective initial cluster level checkpoints CLC_0^i and CLC_0^j. The CIC vectors at the two clusters are given in Table 1.

Fig. 1. An example to explain the updating of vectors

Table 1. Table of the values of vectors at different checkpoints

Check	Checkpoint	$V_{(sent)}$	$V_{(recv)}$	CIC
C^i	CLC_0^i	[0 0]	[0 0]	[0]
	CLC_1^i	[0 2]	[0 0]	[0 0]
C^j	CLC_0^j	[0 0]	[0 0]	[0 0]
	CLC_1^j	[0 0]	[1 0]	[0 1]
	CLC_2^j	[0 0]	[2 0]	[0 1 2]
	CLC_3^j	[0 0]	[2 0]	[0 1 2 2]

In Table 1 consider CIC^j at the cluster level checkpoint CLC_3^j . It is [0 1 2 2]. In this vector, total number of elements (= 4) represents the total number of CLCs (including both regular or forced ones) taken by cluster C^j and the value of the last element (=2) in the vector represents the total number of forced CLCs taken. For a clear understanding of our approach, through out this paper we will use the following interpretations needed to design the proposed recovery algorithm: (1) by the statement a cluster C^k rolls back to its rth cluster level checkpoint CLC_r^k we mean that all processes in cluster C^k rollback to their respective local checkpoints which form together the cluster level checkpoint CLC_r^k; (2) by initiator cluster we mean the cluster that contains the initiator process. In fact, in our work a failed process inside the initiator cluster actually initiates the recovery mechanism after this process recovers from the failure; (3) by the statement a cluster C^k receives a request from the initiator cluster C^i and sends its vector and its Boolean flag to it, we mean that the process

($\in C^k$) receiving the request from the initiator process ($\in Ci$) sends its vector and its flag to the initiator; (4) by the statement the initiator cluster sends / receives a message it means that the initiator process in this cluster actually sends / receives the message; (5) if any of the processes in a cluster rolls back, the respective Boolean flags of all processes in that cluster are set at 1; otherwise these flags are set at 0 each; (6) finally by a computation done or an action taken by the initiator cluster associated with the recovery scheme it means that it is actually performed by the initiator process belonging to this cluster. Similarly, by a computation done or an action taken by any other cluster associated with the recovery scheme it means that it is performed by a process of this cluster.

Recovery mechanism. Unless otherwise needed, we will simply use the notations $V^i_{(sent)}$, $V^i_{(recv)}$, and CIC^i to represent the three vectors. A failed process p^i_j inside a cluster C^i initiates the recovery mechanism after it recovers from the failure. Therefore, cluster C^i acts as the initiator cluster. To start with, this initiator cluster first rolls back to its latest cluster level checkpoint and then sends a request message to each cluster C^k, for $0 \leq k \leq N-1, k \neq i$ asking it to send its $V^k_{(sent)}$ vector corresponding to its latest cluster level checkpoint. After receiving the vector $V^k_{(sent)}$ from all clusters the initiator cluster C^i forms a two dimensional array V^N.

$$V^N = \begin{vmatrix} V^{0,0} & V^{0,1} & \dots & V^{0,N-1} \\ V^{1,0} & V^{1,1} & \dots & V^{1,N-1} \\ & - & \dots & - \\ V^{k,0} & V^{k,1} & \dots & V^{k,N-1} \\ - & - & \dots & - \\ V^{N-1,0} & V^{N-1,1} & \dots & V^{N-1,N-1} \end{vmatrix} = 0$$

where the kth row represents $V^k_{(sent)}$ corresponding to cluster C^k, for $0 \leq k \leq N-1$. The initiator cluster then computes the column sums to create the following vector.

$$V^C = \left| v^0_c, v^1_c, v^2_c, \dots, v^k_c, \dots, v^{N-1}_c \right| = 0$$

where v^k_c = column sum of the entries of the kth column of V^N and is given by $v^k_c = \Sigma V^N(l,k)$, for l = 1 to N. Therefore, v^k_c represents the total number of inter cluster messages sent to cluster C^k from all other clusters. The initiator cluster then unicasts $v^k_c (= V^c(k))$ to each corresponding cluster C^k, for $0 \leq k \leq N-1, k \neq i$. After receiving v^k_c from the initiator, each cluster C^k adds the elements of its $V^k_{(recv)}$ vector (actually as mentioned earlier this computation is performed by the process p^k_x ($\in C^k$) which has received the unicast information v^k_c). Let the sum be v^k_r. Therefore, v^k_r represents the total number of inter cluster messages received by the processes in cluster C^k from all other clusters.

Cluster C^k (i.e. Process p^k_x) now computes $D^k = v^k_r - v^k_c$. The difference D^k (if > 0) between v^k_r and v^k_c gives the exact number of inter cluster orphan messages received by a cluster C^k from all other clusters. Process p^k_x now checks the last element (let it be X) present in CIC^k vector at its latest checkpoint;

this element is the number of forced CLCs taken so far by cluster C^k. Process p_x^k rolls back to its latest checkpoint (say, it is the lth checkpoint) where the last element in its corresponding CIC^k vector is equal to $X - D^k$. It also unicasts a message to all other processes in its cluster to rollback to their respective l^{th} checkpoints. Observe that all these l^{th} checkpoints of the processes of cluster C^k form the cluster level checkpoint CLC_l^k. Thus, effectively it can be said that the cluster C^k rolls back to its cluster level checkpoint CLC_l^k. Observe that all these l^{th} checkpoints of the processes of cluster C^k are assumed to have been taken during the lth execution of the coordinate checkpointing protocol.

We have already mentioned that if any of the processes in a cluster C^k rolls back (i.e. D^k ¿ 0), the Boolean flags of all processes in C_k are set at 1. The effect of this rollback is that the corresponding cluster C^k (i.e. actually process p_x^k) sends this flag value (=1) along with its V^k(sent) corresponding to the checkpoint to which it has rolled back. If the cluster does not roll back (i.e. D^k 0), then it will send only a flag value of 0. The algorithm will terminate when for each cluster C^i, its corresponding flag value is equal to zero. That is, none of the clusters rolls back. Otherwise, the algorithm starts its next iteration. In this case, for any cluster that sent a flag of 0, its sent vector used in the previous iteration is used again in the current iteration.

An Illustration. Fig. 2 gives an illustration of how cluster level checkpoints are taken in our approach as well as how a federation level recovery line is determined. Each horizontal line represents a parallel execution on a cluster. Each cluster C^i (i.e. each process in this cluster) maintains three vectors $V^i_{(sent)}$,$V^i_{(recv)}$, and CIC^i.

Initially all these vectors are initialized with zeros at the initial checkpoints. Cluster C^1 takes a forced cluster level checkpoint CLC_1^1 as soon as it receives the application message m_2 and updates CIC_1^1 from [0] to [01] (we take the last value in the vector at prior checkpoint, increment it by 1 and append it to the vector so that the last element of the new vector gives us the total number of forced checkpoints taken so far) and $V^1_{1(recv)}$ from [000] to [001] because it has received an inter cluster application message from cluster C^2. It also updates $V^1_{1(sent)}$ from [000] to [100] because it has sent an inter cluster application message m^3 to cluster C^0 after the checkpoint CLC_0^1 was taken.

Consider the cluster level checkpoint CLC_2^1 in cluster C^1. As this checkpoint is a regular CLC taken within the cluster, the CIC_2^1 is updated from [01] to [011], $V^1_{2(sent)}$ remains same as [100]. $V^1_{2(recv)}$ also remains same because it has not received any inter cluster application message after the checkpoint CLC_1^1. Similarly all checkpoints for all other clusters are taken and their vectors updated.

Suppose at time t, a failure f occurs in cluster C^1. After recovering from the failure, cluster C^1 first rolls back to the checkpoint CLC_2^1. The algorithm is now initiated by cluster C^1. To start with, initiator cluster C^1 broadcasts a request asking the clusters C^0 and C^2 to send their sent vectors corresponding to their latest checkpoints. In this example cluster C^0 sends the vector [001] and cluster

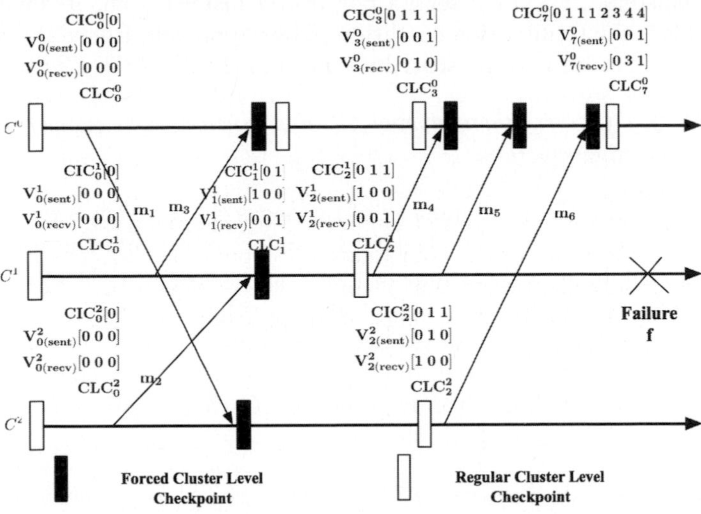

Fig. 2. Federation level Consistent checkpoints $CLC_3^0, CLC_2^1, CLC_2^2$

C^2 sends [010]. After receiving the vectors the initiator creates a two dimensional array and performs the column sum and calculates V^3 in the following way:

$$\begin{vmatrix} 0\,0\,1 \\ 1\,0\,0 \\ 0\,1\,0 \end{vmatrix}$$

$$V^3 = \text{column sum} = 1\ 1\ 1$$

Now, cluster C^1 unicasts v_c^k to each cluster C^k, for k = 0, 2. In this example, at the respective latest checkpoints of the three clusters we get the following: D^0 equal to 3 for cluster C^0, D^1 equal to 0 for cluster C^1, and D^2 equal to 0 for cluster C^2. This implies that cluster C^0 has received three orphan messages with respect to its latest checkpoint CLC_7^0; in fact the orphan messages are m_4, m_5, and m_6. Observe that cluster C^1 and cluster C^2 have received no orphan messages. Now cluster C^0 checks the last element ($= X$) of CIC_7^0. In this example it is 4. Then it calculates the difference d ($=X - D^0$); in this example d is 1 (= 4-3). C^0 will now skip to a latest checkpoint where the last element of CIC^0 vector is equal to 1. This checkpoint is CLC_3^0. Now cluster C^0 rolls back by 4 checkpoints i.e. to CLC_3^0 and sends a flag of 1 along with its $V^0_{3(sent)}$ to the initiator cluster. Cluster C^2 sends only a flag of 0 because it has not rolled back.Since the flag of cluster C^0 is equal to 1 so the algorithm executes its next iteration. After this second iteration, we get D^0 equal to 0 for the checkpoint CLC_3^0 of cluster C^0; D^1 equal to 0 for cluster C^1 for its checkpoint CLC_2^1 and D^2 equal to 0 for cluster C^2 for its checkpoint CLC_2^2. This implies that there is no orphan message in the cluster federation with respect to these three checkpoints.

Now both clusters C^0 and C^2 send a flag of 0. Cluster C^1 has its own flag also set at 0. This is the termination condition of our approach. Hence the federation level recovery line can be represented as the set $CLC_3^0, CLC_2^1, CLC_2^2$.

Lemma 1. *If* $Di > 0$*, then cluster* C^i *has received* D^i *number of orphan messages from other clusters.*

Proof. v_r^i represents the total number of messages cluster C^i has received so far and these are recorded in C^is latest CLC, and v_c^i represents the total number of messages sent by all other clusters to C^i as recorded in their latest CLCs. Therefore $D^i(= v_r^i - v_c^i) > 0$ means that at least some cluster $C^k(k \neq i)$ has sent some message(s) to cluster C^i after taking its latest checkpoint. Since all such D^i messages have been received and recorded in C^is latest CLC, but remain unrecorded by the sending clusters, therefore C^i has received D^i number of orphan messages from rest of the clusters.

Lemma 2. *If* $D^i \leq 0$*, then cluster* C^i *has not received any orphan message.*

Proof. $D^i = 0$ means that the number of messages received by cluster C^i is equal to the number of messages sent to cluster C^i and so the sending events of these messages are already recorded by the sending clusters in their latest checkpoints. Hence, the received messages cannot be orphan. Also, $D^i < 0$ means that the number of the received messages by cluster C^i is less than the number of messages sent to it. It means that all the messages received by cluster C^i have already been recorded by the senders. Hence none of such received messages can be an orphan.

Theorem 1. *Let* $D^i > 0$ *at the* r^{th} *checkpoint* CLC_r^i *of cluster* C^i *and the last element of the* CIC_r^i *vector at this checkpoint be* X*. Let* CLC_m^i *be the latest checkpoint prior to* CLC_r^i *such that the last element of* CIC_m^i *is equal to* XD^i*. Then none of the checkpoints* CLC_r^i, $CLC_r^i - 1$, $CLC_r^i - 2$, $\ldots$, CLC_{m+1}^i *can belong to any federation level recovery line.*

Proof. According to Lemma 1, C^i has received exactly D^i number of orphan messages from all other clusters till its latest checkpoint CLC_r^i. Given that the last element of the CIC_r^i vector at the checkpoint CLC^r is X, this implies that the cluster C^i has taken X forced checkpoints so far according to Observation 1. But a cluster takes a forced CLC whenever it receives an inter cluster application message. Thus, in this case cluster C^i has recorded the events of receiving X inter cluster application messages at the checkpoint CLC_r^i. With respect to the checkpoint CLC_r^i it is clear that D^i is the number of orphan messages received by cluster C^i from all other clusters. So out of these X messages, only XD^i messages are such that their sent events are recorded by some other clusters. Thus cluster C^i has to rollback to a latest checkpoint which has recorded the receiving event of the $(XD^i)^{th}$ inter cluster application message, skipping all the checkpoints which have recorded the events of receiving the orphan inter cluster application messages, received after the $(XD^i)^{th}$ inter cluster application messages.

We also have assumed that the CLC^i_m is the latest checkpoint prior to CLC^i_r such that the last element of CIC^i_m is equal to XD^i, thus CLC^i_m is the latest checkpoint that has recorded the receiving event of the $(XD^i)^{th}$ inter cluster application message. Thus, the application messages which have caused the creation of the checkpoints $CLC^i_r, CLC^i_{r-1}, CLC^i_{r-2}, \ldots, CLC^i_{m+1}$ are orphan and hence these checkpoints can not belong to any federation level recovery line.

Theorem 2. *If $D^i \leq 0$ at the latest checkpoint of each cluster C^i, for $0 \leq i \leq N-1$ (i.e. flag of each C^i is 0), then the recovery algorithm terminates and all such latest checkpoints form a consistent federation level checkpoint of the cluster federation.*

Proof. According to Lemma 2, $D^i \leq 0$ at the latest checkpoint of each cluster C^i means that none of the clusters in the cluster federation has received any orphan message till its latest checkpoint. Thus the set of all such checkpoints, one from each cluster are mutually consistent and hence they form a consistent federation level checkpoint of the cluster federation.

4 Algorithm Recovery

Input : Given the latest N cluster level checkpoints, one for each cluster $C^j, 0 \leq j \leq N-1$, for an N cluster system and the corresponding vectors $V^j_{(sent)}, V^j_{(recv)}$, CIC^j at these checkpoints. *Output*: A federation level recovery line which is also a maximum consistent state. *Assumption*: The algorithm will be restarted if any cluster including the initiator one fails.

The responsibilities of each cluster C^i and the initiator cluster C^k are stated below.

Initiator cluster C^k:

Step 1: it asks each cluster C^i for $0 \leq i \leq N-1$, $i \neq k$, to send its $V^i_{(sent)}$ at its latest checkpoint CLC^i_r ;
Step 2: it receives all $V^i_{(sent)}$ for $0 \leq i \leq N-1$;
Step 3: it computes $V^c = v^0_c, v^1_c, v^2_c, \ldots, v^k_c, \ldots, v^{N-1}_c$;
Step 4: it unicasts $v^i_c(=V^c(i))$ to each cluster C^i, for $0 \leq i \leq N-1$;
Step 5: it receives either a flag or (flag and $V^i_{(sent)}$) from each cluster
if flag $= 0$ for each cluster C^i, for $0 \leq i \leq N-1$
cluster C^k asks every cluster C^i for $0 \leq i \leq N-1$, $i \neq k$ to restart the application program from its last checkpoint corresponding to which $D^i \leq 0$ and cluster C^k does the same for itself; the algorithm terminates;
/* *a federation level recovery line is determined* */
else
control flows to step 3; /* *for any cluster which has sent a flag of 0, its sent vector received in the previous iteration is used again* */

Cluster C^i:

Step 1: cluster C^i receives request from cluster C^k ;
if C^k has requested to restart
processes in C^i restart from their respective local checkpoints corresponding to the CLC^i where $D^i \leq 0$;
else
it sends $V^i_{(sent)}$ at its latest cluster level checkpoint to the initiator cluster C^k;
Step 2: it receives v^i_c from initiator cluster C^k;
Step 3: it computes D^i;
Step 4: if $D^i > 0$ /* C^i needs to rollback */
it caluculates $(X - D^i)$; /* X is the last element in CIC^i_r */
it sends a flag of 1 and $V^i_{(sent)}$ corresponding to its checkpoint CLC^i_m; (i.e. CLC^i_r is replaced by CLC^i_m)
/* C^i rolls back to CLC^i_m and CLC^i_m is the latest checkpoint prior to CLC^i_r so the last element of CIC^i_m is equal to $X - D^i$; that is, the checkpoints CLC^i_r, CLC^i_{r-1}, CLC^i_{r-2}, ..., CLC^i_{m+1} can not belong to any federation level recovery line*/
else
it sends a flag of 0 to cluster C^k.

Correctness Proof. Each Cluster C^i repeats its steps 1, 2, 3 and 4 to arrive at a checkpoint that has not recorded the receipt of any orphan message from the other clusters (using the observations of Lemmas 1 and 2). In other words, it identifies the checkpoints that can not belong to the federation level recovery line and skips them (using the logic of Theorem 1). This decision is made based on the value of D^i.

However, the initiator cluster C^k decides when to terminate the algorithm, i.e., when the cluster level checkpoints can become mutually consistent. Cluster C^k checks to see if $D^i \leq 0$ for each cluster C^i. If so, the algorithm terminates according to Theorem 2. Note that the condition $D^i \leq 0$ must always occur during the execution of the algorithm. It may be observed that in the worst case, because of some typical communication pattern, the domino effect may force processes in all clusters to restart from their initial states where for each cluster C^i we always have $D^i = 0$. Besides, since the algorithm starts with the latest checkpoints, the number of events (states) rolled back at each cluster is a minimum. This is true because, in its Step 4 each cluster C^i skips only the checkpoints that can not belong to a federation level recovery line. Thus, the algorithm determines a federation level recovery line which is the maximum consistent state of the federation as well.

Message Complexity. Suppose the termination of the algorithm requires the construction of the vector V^N by the initiator cluster C^k to occur k times (i.e. k number of iterations). During each such time every cluster in the N-cluster system exchanges a couple of messages with initiator cluster C^k. Thus, $O(N)$ messages are sufficient for each time. Thus, considering k times, the message complexity of the algorithm is $O(kN)$.

5 Comparison

Comparison with the work in [1]. In the architecture considered in [1] multiple coordinated checkpointing subsystems are connected with a single independent checkpointing subsystem, such that the multiple coordinated subsystems can communicate with each other only via the independent subsystem. The assumed restricted architecture is the main short coming of this work. Our proposed approach is independent of any particular architecture.

Comparison with the work in [2]. The main drawback of the algorithm in [2] is that if we consider a particular message pattern where all the clusters have to roll back except the failed cluster, then all these clusters have to send alert messages to every other cluster before the start of the next iteration. This results in a message storm. But in our approach when a cluster fails, only the initiator cluster broadcasts just one control message. Thus, our proposed algorithm does not suffer from any such message storm. Also, in [2] a cluster may have to make much larger number of trips to the stable storage compared to our approach, in order to determine which checkpoint(s) need to be skipped. To compare this number of trips for the two approaches, let us assume the following approximate analysis: after a failure occurs and the system recovers from it, in both our approach and in [2] each cluster will skip on an average r checkpoints per iteration. We also assume that the algorithms will determine the federation level recovery line in k number of iterations. In [2] the number of trips to the stable storage is (k+kr) compared to just k in our approach. Table 2 summarizes the comparisons.

Table 2. Comparison with the work in [2]

Criteria	**Our Algorithm**	**Algorithm [2]**
Message Storm	No	Yes
Simultaneous execution by clusters	Yes	Yes
Architecture dependent	No	No
Number of trips to stable storage	k	k + kr
Message complexity	$O(kN)$	$O(kN^2)$

6 Conclusion

In this paper, we have presented a fast and efficient recovery algorithm for cluster computing environment. The main feature of the recovery algorithm is that it is executed simultaneously by all participating clusters while determining a federation level recovery line. It offers fast execution. It is also independent of the architecture of the cluster federation unlike [1]. Besides, we have shown that the algorithm in its each iteration does not need to compare all vectors at all checkpoints of the clusters: it identifies and skips those that can not belong to the federation level recovery line. It reduces computational overhead to a good extent and as a result its execution becomes even faster. We have also shown that our algorithm offers much smaller number of trips to the stable storage compared to the same in [2]. It does not also suffer from any message storm unlike in [2].

References

1. J. Cao, Y.Chen, K. Zhang and Y. He: Checkpointing in Hybrid Distributed Systems. Proc. of the 7th International Symposium on Parallel Architectures, Algorithms and Networks (ISPAN04), Hong Kong, China, (2004) 136–141
2. S. Monnet, C. Morin, and R. Badrinath: Hybrid Checkpointing for Parallel Applications in cluster Federations. 4th IEEE/ACM International Symposium on Cluster Computing and the Grid, Chicago, IL, USA, (2004) 773–782
3. B. Gupta, S. Rahimi, R. A. Rias, and G. Bangalore: A Low-Overhead Non-Blocking Checkpointing Algorithm for Mobile Computing Environment. Springer Verlag Lecture Notes in Computer Science, vol 3947, 2006, 597–608
4. R. Koo and S. Toueg: Checkpointing and Rollback-Recovery for Distributed Systems. IEEE trans. Software Engineering, vol. SE-13, no. 1, pp.23-31, Jan 1987
5. Y. Wang: Consistent Global Checkpoints that contain a Given Set of Local Checkpoints. IEEE trans. Computers, vol. 46, no. 4, pp. 456-468, April 1997
6. J. Tsai, S.-Y. Kuo, and Y.-M.Wang: Theoretical Analysis for Communication-Induced Checkpointing Protocols with Rollback Dependency Trackability. IEEE Trans. Parallel and Distributed Systems, vol. 9,no. 10,pp 963-971, Oct 1998
7. B. Gupta, S.K. Banerjee and B. Liu: Design of new roll-forward recovery approach for distributed systems. IEEE Proc. Computers and Digital Techniques, vol. 149, issue 3, pp. 105-112, May 2002
8. D. Manivannan, and M. Singhal: Asynchronous recovery without using vector timestamps. Journal of Parallel and Distributed Computing, vol. 62, 1695-1728, 2002
9. Xin Qi , G. Parmer , R. West: An efficient end-host architecture for cluster communication. Proc. 2004 IEEE Intl. Conf. on Cluster Computing, San Diego, California, pp.83-92, September 20-23, 2004

SONMAS: A Structured Overlay Network for Multidimensional Attribute Space

Hsiu-Chin Chen and Chung-Ta King

Department of Computer Science, National Tsing Hua University, Hsinchu, Taiwan

Abstract. In many distributed applications, each participating node can be characterized by one single set of attributes. The problem is to support complex queries, such as range and k-nearest-neighbor (KNN) queries, on this set of multidimensional attributes. Traditional peer-to-peer (P2P) systems either adopt an unstructured interconnection and use flooding to search for matching nodes, or implement a distributed hash table (DHT) to serve as a directory for indexing the attributes. The former suffers from excessive flooding traffic, while the latter has the overhead of updating and maintaining the directory. This paper introduces an attribute-based P2P interconnection strategy that uses the attributes to interconnect the peers instead of hash keys. Under the condition that each node is characterized by one set of attributes, the attribute-based networks can support range and KNN queries, guarantee lookup efficiency, and eliminate the need to maintain a directory.

Keywords: Distributed system, information lookup, interconnection network, multidimensional attribute space, peer-to-peer overlay network.

1 Introduction

Consider a system in which there are N nodes. Each node is characterized by a set of attributes. The attributes represent characteristics of the nodes such as interests, resources, states, readings, etc. The problem is to answer complex queries on these multidimensional attributes such as *range* and *k-nearest-neighbor* (KNN) queries. To solve the problem in a fully distributed manner, traditional P2P systems either adopt an unstructured [4][12][13] interconnection and use flooding to search for matching nodes, or implement a *distributed hash table* (DHT) [8][10][11] to serve as a directory for indexing the attributes. Unfortunately, the former suffers from excessive flooding traffic, while the latter has difficulty of supporting range and KNN queries.

In this paper, we propose an *attributed-based* approach. Since in our target applications every node is characterized by exactly one set of multidimensional attributes, the characterizing attributes can be used to interconnect the nodes. The attribute-based approach is different from unstructured P2P networks such as Gnutella in that the nodes are interconnected into a certain structure based on the multidimensional attributes. This gives theoretical upper bounds for looking up peer nodes. The attribute-based approach is also different from structured P2P systems using hash-based DHT. In DHT-based P2P systems, each node will manage a portion

C. Cérin and K.-C. Li (Eds.): GPC 2007, LNCS 4459, pp. 531 – 542, 2007.

of a distributed hash table, which serves as a directory for information indexing. Information in the system should be published to the distributed hash table. In attribute-based approach, the information to be looked up, i.e. the attributes, is the means by which the peers are interconnected. The advantages are the followings. (1) There is no need to publish the information to some unrelated peers. (2) It can support complex queries such range and KNN queries. (3) There will be no overhead for maintaining a directory and keeping the indices up-to-date.

As an example of the attribute-based approach, we will introduce in this paper one such system, the Structured Overlay Network for Multidimensional Attribute Space (SONMAS). SONMAS is capable of handling range and KNN queries for multidimensional attributes, while still keeping a log(N) routing efficiency. Although a number of previous works have addressed the issue of complex queries in DHT-based P2P systems [15] [16], they still require the indexing information be published to a directory, i.e. the distributed hash table. The most closely related work to SONMAS is *skip graph* [3]. A skip graph can be decomposed into levels of sorted link-lists. There is only one level-0 list and it contains N sorted nodes. There are 2 level-1 lists, and each contains N/2 nodes. All nodes in level-0 list goes to either of the level-1 list with equal probability. The splitting process continues until the lists become singletons. The membership is probabilistic and determined by the membership vectors. Skip graphs have a routing efficiency of O(logN). In skip graphs, all that matters are the ordering of attributes instead of the exact attribute values of nodes. Skip quad-tree [5] is realized by adding skip pointers to a quad-tree. A skip quad-tree is defined for a two-dimensional space. This idea can be generalized to spaces of different dimensions [1] [5]. The Skip web [2] is an example of a P2P network based on the idea of skip quad-tree. However, the reliability issues that are critical for real world P2P scenarios are yet to be addressed. In addition, interest collision problems are not addressed in the current works.

2 System Design

Assume that each node in the system is characterized by exactly one multidimensional attribute. The basic idea of SONMAS is to divide the n-dimensional attribute space into a hierarchy of cubes, upon which an efficient interconnection among the nodes can be built. The cube structure reflects the proximity of nodes in the attribute space. To handle attribute collision, we add an extra dimension, node id, to the attribute space to eliminate any collision.

2.1 Attribute-ID-Hybrid Space

To resolve collision problems in attribute space, we transform the attribute space to an attribute-ID-hybrid space where collisions are not possible. In the attribute-ID-hybrid space, a node's position is determined by appending a unique node ID after its multidimensional attribute:

< attribute-ID-hybrid key > = <attribute key | multi-D node ID>

The node ID can be obtained, say by a uniform hash function. Each attribute-ID-hybrid coordinate is an h-digit number of base b. The leading m digits of an attribute-ID-hybrid coordinate specify a node's attribute, and the rest *s* digits specify a node's ID, where $m + s = h$. The value *m* is a system parameter and should be large enough to cover the size of the attribute space, and the value *s* should be large enough to cover the network size.

Since the length of an attribute-ID-hybrid-key is *h*, the attribute-ID-hybrid space is bounded in each dimension. The base *b* of the hybrid key is related to the degree of a node and the routing efficiency consequently. As we will see later, the average link degree of a node is proportional to $b^d/d\ ln(b)$, where *d* is the space dimension. Therefore, we may trade off routing efficiency by reducing *b* to the minimum value, 2, in exchange for a reduction in the number of states to maintain.

2.2 Space Division and Interconnection Rules

SONMAS interconnections are based on the sub-cell hierarchy of the attribute-ID-hybrid space. The *d*-dimensional attribute-ID-hybrid space is divided into b^d hyper-cubic cells and every cell is sub-divided into b^d sub-cells, where *b* is the base of the hybrid keys. The sub-cells are to be further subdivided until *h* levels of sub-cells are formed, where *h* is the length of the hybrid keys. Notice that when different bases are used in each dimension, the number of sub-cells of a cell will be $b_1 \bullet b_2 \bullet \ldots b_d$, where b_i is the base used in the i-th dimension of the hybrid key. For simplicity, in the following discussions we will assume a common base in every dimension.

In SONMAS, we classify cells or sub-cells by levels. The entire attribute-ID-hybrid space, called the *universe*, is a level-0 cell. The level-*h* cells are the smallest cells and are called the *atom cells*. An atom cell occupies unity volume and contains at most one node. A level-*m* cell, where *m* is the length of the attribute part of an attribute-ID-hybrid coordinate, resolves the attributes to the finest resolution and contains all nodes of identical attributes.

When the sub-cell hierarchy is established, we only need one rule to govern the SONMAS interconnection: a node needs to maintain one-way connections to all its non-empty child cells. When we say a node has a one-way connection to a cell, we mean the node has a one-way connection to an arbitrary member in that cell. Note that a node is a member of $h+1$ cells simultaneously and needs to maintain *h* sets of interconnections, one set of interconnections for each level except for level-*h*. Each set of interconnections has at most b^d links to the b^d sub-cells respectively. Note also that there will be altogether *h* sets of child cells for a node to maintain connections. We record these *h* sets of connections in the *h* levels of sub-tables of routing table respectively.

The *h* levels of sub-tables of a node's routing table are defined as follows. The level-*i* sub-table of a node's routing table records the contact information of the child cells of the level-*i* cell which a node belongs to. Each level-*i* sub-table of a node's routing table records at most b^d entries, and these entries correspond to cells that are siblings to each other. Note that there is usually more than one member in a cell, and each one of them can serve as an access point to the cell. Different nodes are allowed to choose different members as their access to the same cell. Note also that the attribute-ID-hybrid space will be very sparse.

2.3 Basic Operations

This section introduces some basic operations of SONMAS. Due to space limitation, operations such as handling attribute changes, network maintenance, and system optimizations will not be discussed here.

Routing

The basic idea of the SONMAS routing algorithm is to forward the messages through the cell hierarchy by narrowing down the intermediate locations of the messages level by level. Eventually the correct atom cell is reached and so is the destination node. The SONMAS routing algorithm is shown in Figure 1. The *matching level* is defined as the level of the smallest cell that simultaneously includes both the message holder and the message destination. In terms of the numerical representation of attribute-ID-hybrid key, matching level is equivalent to the length of the common prefixes between the key of message holder and the key of message destination.

```
Procedure routing
Upon receiving a message, check matching level between current node and message destination.
m ← matching level
if ( m equals h )
   {The current node is the message destination}
else
   {Check level-m routing sub-table, and select the level-(m+1) sub-cell that contains the destination node}
   if (Selected entry is null)
      {Announce routing failed}
   else
      {Forward the message to the selected entry}
   }
End
```

Fig. 1. The SONMAS routing algorithm

Join/quit

By connecting to well-known portals, or any existing on-line peers, a node can send its join request to the network. The join request is addressed to the joining node itself and will be forwarded in the network according to the routing rule. We define the level that the join request terminates as the stopping level, the cell as the stopping cell, and the node as the stopping node. The responsibility of the stopping node is to process the join request by providing its routing table and sending the join success message to the new node, and sending the join notification message to all members within the stopping cell. In addition, the stopping node as well as those that receive the join notification message need to add the new node in their routing table. The join process is shown in Figure 2. When a node departs, the quitting node is supposed to send its quit notification to all nodes by multicasting through the cell hierarchy.

```
Procedure handling join request
Upon receiving a join request, try to forward this message according to the routing rule.
if (forward fail)
   {Announce the current node being the stopping node, and the matching level being the
   stopping level.
   Provide level-0 through level-(stopping level) of routing table to the new node.
   Send join success message to the new node.
   if (Stopping cell contains more than one member)
      {Notify all members in the stopping cell of the arrival of the new node by multicasting
      through the cell hierarchy.}
   else
      {Notify all members in the level-(stopping level – 1) cell of the arrival of the new node
      by multicast through the cell hierarchy.}
   Put the new node into the routing table and the new-node-list.
   }
End
```

Fig. 2. The join operations

Query

In SONMAS, a special form of range queries, *by-cell-range-searches*, can be supported easily by dividing the query into b^d subtasks and rendering the sub-tasks to the b^d child cells of the target cell. Each sub-task is then subdivided and rendered in a recursive manner. The query results are then collected in a reverse manner. The algorithm is shown in Figure 3. It has an O(logN) time complexity if the attributes are randomly distributed.

```
Procedure handling range queries
Upon receiving a query, check the matching level with the msg.target_ interest.
if ( matching_level < msg.rang_ level )
   {Forward the message according to the routing rule. }
else
   {Check task_level and resolution_level of the query.
   current_task_level ← msg.task_level
   current_task_owner ← msg.task_owner
   if (current task_level = msg.resolution_level)
      {Report the current node's attribute-ID-hybrid key to the current_task_owner.}
   else
      {Divide the task into sub-tasks by: msg.task level ← msg.task_level + 1
      msg.task_owner ← current node
      Send the modified query to all non-empty entries in level-(current_task_level).
      Start timer and wait for reports.
      if (all sub-tasks results are reported or time is up)
         {Report all available results to current_task_owner}
      }
   }
End
```

Fig. 3. Handling by-cell-range-searches

In Figure 3, *range level* is the level of the target cell that specifies the size of the target range. The range level is an integer between 0 and *m*, where *m* is the length of the attribute key as defined in Section 2.1. *Resolution level* is the level when tasks can no longer be subdivided, and the reporting process should begin. The resolution level is an integer ranging from 0 to *h*, where *h* is the length of attribute-ID-hybrid key.

True range queries in which the size and position of the target is not limited by the cell hierarchy can be implemented by a high-level manipulation of by-cell-range-searches. The reason is that an arbitrary range can be decomposed into various target cells of various levels.

3 Evaluation

SONMAS is evaluated by simulations on time efficiency, traffic overhead, system reliability under dynamic environment, as well as query performance. The simulator is written in Java and run on JVM version 1.4.2_01-b06. Throughout all the simulations, uniform end-to-end delay is assumed, and node computation delay is neglected. TCP is assumed for the transportation layer protocol; however, the three-way synchronization time is neglected.

The network size simulated ranges from 10 to 5000 nodes. Three version of SONMAS are evaluated: the full function version equipped with all reliability-related designs including HSA, routing table exchange, and one level introduction; the baseline version in which the above functions are excluded; the intro-off version which contains all reliability-related designs but one level introduction. The metrics used to evaluate our system include average hop count, packet count, and connectivity score. Because of the uniform latency assumption, it is sufficient to represent routing time efficiency with average hop count. The connectivity is measured by querying the universe from a number of randomly selected peers. The connectivity score is defined as the average query score of all these queries. The full score of connectivity is 100.

3.1 Time Efficiency and Traffic Overhead

In the following experiments, the network size ranges from 10 to 5000 nodes, in 1 to 6-dimensional attribute space with choices of bases ranging from 2 to 32. The experiments are conducted as follows. We bring up the network to the size of our choice at constant rate. After a short period of stabilization time, events are started as required by each experiment. For the measurement of routing efficiency, a number of arbitrary packets are sent, and the cumulated path length and packet success rate are recorded. As with the join overhead, a series of join and quit events are arranged after stabilization, and the total number of join operation related packets are recorded as well as cumulated message size in bytes.

The dependence of path length as a function of network size is shown on Figure 4. Each data point is obtained by averaging the result of 100 random tests. Three sets of data, each of different choices of base and dimension, all showed straight lines on the log-scale plot. These results demonstrate that SONMAS has an O(logN) routing efficiency. The effects of path length are shown on Figure 5. Figure 5(a) shows that the routing hop count decreases as the dimensionality increase, while Figure 5(b) shows that the routing hop count decreases as the base increase.

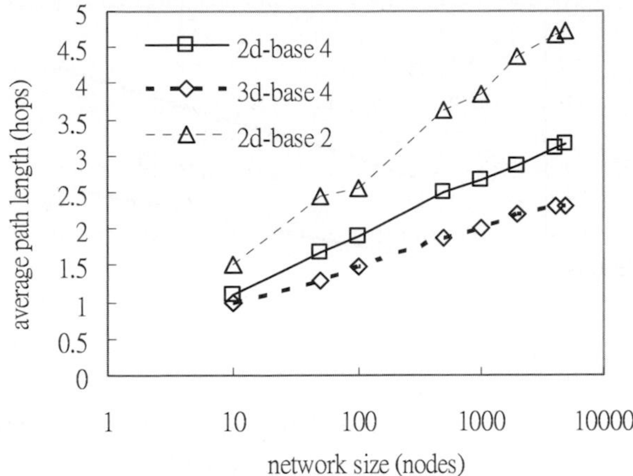

Fig. 4. Path length as a function of network size

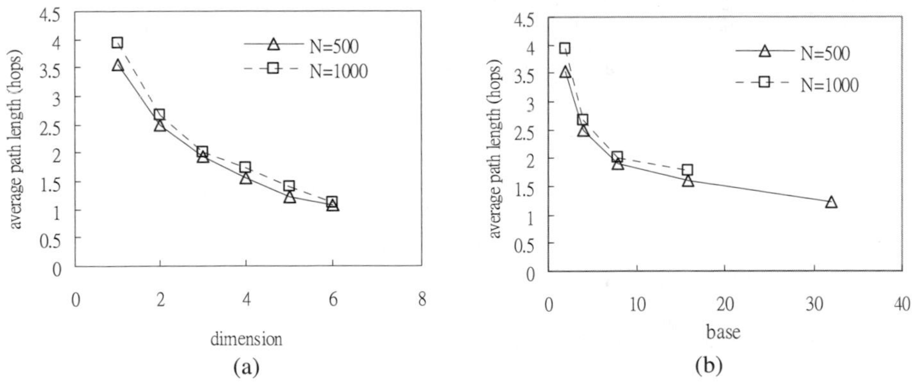

Fig. 5. Effects of overlay structure: (a) path length as a function of dimensionality (base 4), and (b) path length as a function of base (2-D)

The message overhead of the join operation is shown in Figure 6, where the number of packets transmitted per join event versus N is plotted on a log scale. Straight lines are shown on the plot. In other words, the average packet counts for each join event is of O(logN).

The maintenance traffic overhead is shown in Figure 7 in terms of number of packets. Two curves are shown on each plot, one corresponding to the baseline version of SONMAS, and the other corresponding to the full function of SONMAS. In terms of number of packets, the baseline version shows O(logN) and the full function version is a little worse than that.

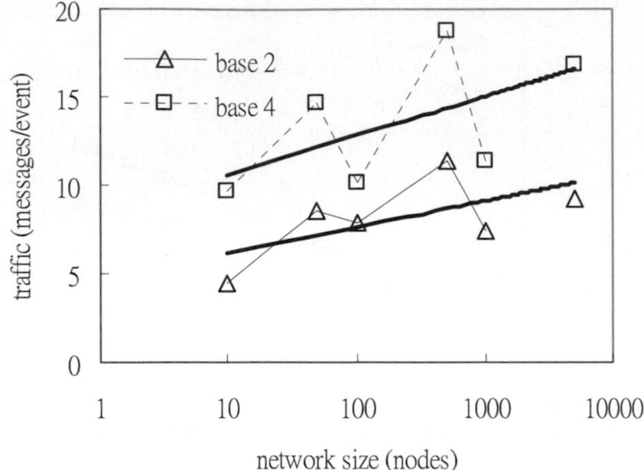

Fig. 6. Join traffic overhead measured as the message count as a function of network size in log scale

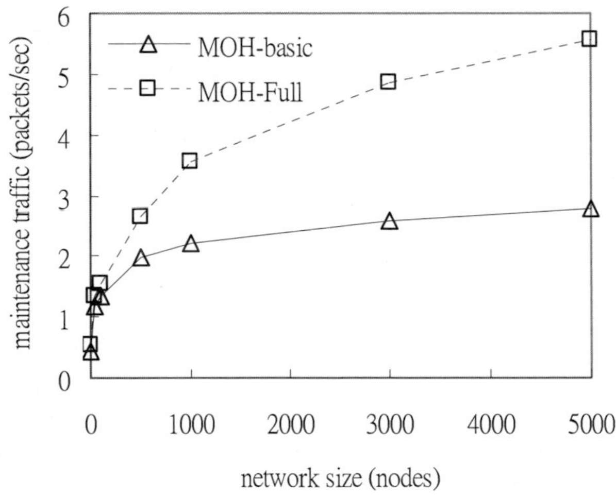

Fig. 7. Maintenance traffic overhead measured as the message count as a function of network size

3.2 Query Performance

The following experiments demonstrate the performance of by-cell-range-searches. The network size varies from 100 to 5000. For the query performance, we ran a number of random queries for each range level of choice ranging from 0 to m, i.e. the length of the attribute part of the hybrid key. The resultant score and the time consumed for each query are recorded. On the other hand, to demonstrate the effect of resolution level, we issue a number of queries initiated from random nodes that argeted on the universe at various resolution levels. The node count of each query result is recorded.

As shown in Figure 8, SONMAS demonstrates a time efficiency of O(logN) for by-cell-range-searches, initiated by arbitrary nodes and centered on arbitrary values with range sizes of arbitrary levels. Figure 9 shows query latency as a function of range level for networks of 100 and 1000 nodes. From the plots, we can see the time consumption decreases linearly as the range level increases, where larger range levels correspond to smaller ranges. However, the curve stops decreasing and becomes a flat line as the range level exceeds. On the other hand, the resolution level also shows expected behavior: the smaller the resolution level is, the fewer the number of nodes found, as shown in Figure 10.

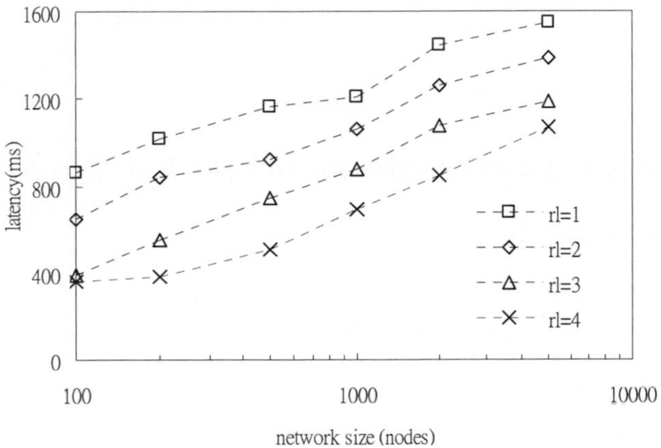

Fig. 8. Query latency as a function of network size with range level from 1 to 4 for dimension 2 and base 2

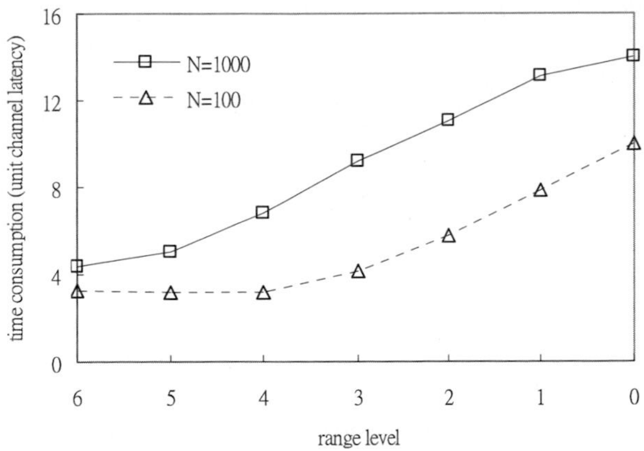

Fig. 9. Latency as a function of range level for dimension 2 and base 2

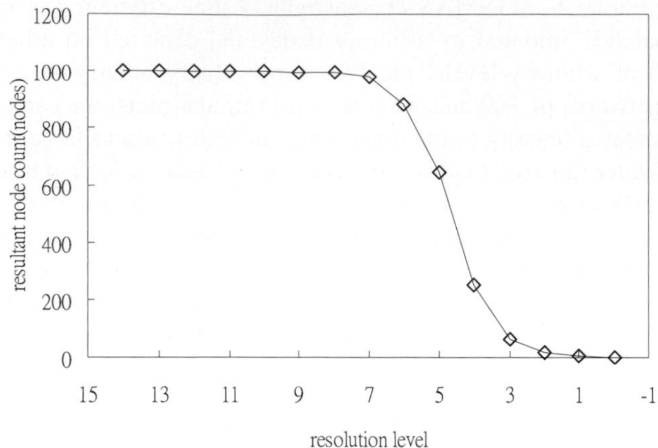

Fig. 10. Node count as a function of resolution level with range level = 0 for dimension 2 and base 2

3.3 Summary

Here, we summarize the major results of the simulations bellow:

- **Routing efficiency**: The $\log_{b^b} N$ routing efficiency of SONMAS is verified.
- **Join overhead**: The join operation takes O(log*N*) messages per event. The traffic mainly comes from the "join success" packet, in which the routing table of the stopping node is attached as the payload. Clearly, if a size limit is put onto the backup lists, the traffic overhead would be reduced to O(logN) bytes per event.
- **Maintenance overhead**: While each node needs to maintain O($\log_{b^b} N$) states, the maintenance overhead seen by a node is O($\log^2$N) bytes per second. It is not hard to imagine that if a size limit is put onto the backup lists, the overhead would be reduced to O(logN) bytes per second.
- **Query**: The O($\log_{b^b} N$) query efficiency of SONMAS is verified. The query efficiency is also a logarithm function of target cell size.

4 Conclusions

SONMAS is an attribute-based P2P system for supporting complex queries on multidimensional attribute space. It targets at applications in which peers characterized by exactly one set of multidimensional attributes are queried to satisfy given range queries. SONMAS interconnects the peers according to the attributes. To deal with possible attribute collisions, SONMAS introduces the attribute-ID-hybrid space to map each node to a unique point in a multidimensional space. Simulation results of SONMAS show scalable routing efficiency and low traffic overhead.

However, there are some remaining issues need to be addressed. The first issue is the non-scalable dimensionality. Since the states a node needs to maintain is $b^d \cdot \log_{b^d} N$, the maintenance overhead is not scalable with dimensionality. For this reason, SONMAS is limited to low-dimensional applications. To accommodate more dimensions, we can trade off the routing efficiency by reducing the base to the minimal value 2. The limitation will depend on peers' computation powers and the Internet capacity.

Another issue is that, although SONMAS provides interconnections between proximal nodes in the attribute space, it is not true for nodes sitting near the boundaries of large cells. Sometimes, a pair of adjacent nodes may fall into two completely different search trees. This is an intrinsic problem of SONMAS due to its cell hierarchy. Some ideas can be applied to improve the performance near cell edges. For example, we can add extra shortcuts between neighbors across the edge of large cells. We may also perform proximal neighbor selection in attribute space instead of in physical space, especially for those sitting near the edge of large cells. Further research is needed to study the effectiveness of these ideas.

Acknowledgments. This work was supported in part by the National Science Council, R.O.C., under Grant NSC 95-2752-E-007-004-PAE, by the MOEA Research Project under Grant No. 95-EC-17-A-04-S1-044, by the Advanced Mobile Context Aware Application & Service Technology Development Project of the Institute for Information Industry, and by the ICL of ITRI.

References

1. Ittai Abraham, James Aspnes, and Jian Yuan, "Skip B-Trees", Proc. Ninth International Conference on Principals of Distributed Systems, (2005) 284-295
2. Lars Arge, David Eppstein, and Michael T. Goodrich, "SkipWebs: Efficient Distributed Data Structures for MultiDimensional Data Sets", Proc. of the Twenty-fourth Annual ACM SIGACT-SIGOPS Symposium on Principles of Distributed Computing (PODC) (2005)
3. James Aspnes and Gauri Shah, "Skip Graphs", Proc. Fourteenth Annual ACM-SIAM Symposium on Discrete Algorithms, (2002) 384-393
4. I. Clarke, O. Sandberg, B. Wiley, and T. W. Hong, "Freenet: A Distributed Anonymous Information Storage and Retrieval System", Proc. Workshop on Design Issues in Anonymity and Unobservability, (2000) 311–320
5. D. Eppstein, M. T. Goodrich, and J. Z. Sun, "The Skip Quadtree: A Simple Dynamic Data Structure for Multidimensional Data", Proc. 21st ACM Symp. On Computational Geometry (SCG) (2005)
6. Prasanna Ganesan, Beverly Yang, and Hector GarciaMolina, "One Torus to Rule Them All: Multidimensional Queries in P2P Systems", Proc. of the Seventh International Workshop on the Web and Databases (WebDB) (2004)
7. Nicholas J. A. Harvey, Michael B. Jones, Stefan Saroiu, Marvin Theimer, and Alec Wolman, "SkipNet: A Scalable Overlay Network with Practical Locality Properties", Proc. of the Fourth USENIX Symposium on Internet Technologies and Systems (USITS), (2003)
8. Sylvia Ratnasamy, Paul Francis, Mark Handley, Richard Karp, and Scott Shenker, "A Scalable Content-Addressable Network", Proc. ACM Symposium on Communications Architectures and Protocols (SIGCOMM) (2001) 161–172

9. Sean Rhea, Dennis Geels, Timothy Roscoe, and John Kubiatowicz, "Handling Churn in a DHT", Proc. 2004 USENIX Technical Conference (2004)
10. A. Rowstron and P. Druschel, "Pastry: Scalable, Decentralized Object Location and Routing for Large-scale Peer-to-peer Systems", Lecture Notes in Computer Science (2001) 161-172
11. I. Stoica, R. Morris, D. Karger, M. F. Kaashoek, and H. Balakrishnan, "Chord: A Scalable Peer-to-Peer Lookup Service for Internet Applications", Proc. of the International Conference on Applications, Technologies, Architectures, and Protocols for Computer Communications (2001) 149-160
12. Napster. http://www.napster.com/
13. Gnutella. http://www.gnutella.com/
14. Chunqiang Tang, Zhichen Xu, Mallik Mahalingam, "pSearch: Information Retrieval in Structured Overlays", ACM SIGCOMM Computer Communication Review (2003) 89 – 94
15. A. R. Bharambe, Mukesh Agrawal, and S. Seshan. "Mercury: Supporting Scalable Multi-Attribute Range Queries," Proc. ACM Symposium on Communications Architectures and Protocols (SIGCOMM) (2004)
16. C. Schmidt, M. Parashar. "Flexible Information Discovery in Decentralized Distributed Systems," Proc. HPDC (2003)

Formal Specification and Implementation of an Environment for Automatic Distribution

Saeed Parsa and Omid Bushehrian

Faculty of Computer Engineering, Iran University of Science and Technology
{parsa,bushehrian}@iust.ac.ir

Abstract. It is desirable to replace supercomputers with low cost networks of computers to run computationally intensive programs. To alleviate the burden of writing distributed programs, automatic translation of sequential to distributed programs is highly recommended. In this paper a new architecture to support automatic translation of sequential to distributed programs is offered. A formal specification of the structure and behavior of the architecture components is presented. The applicability of the specified architecture is demonstrated by presenting its implementation details and evaluating the performance of the resultant distributed program.

1 Introduction

The aim has been to provide an environment to automatically distribute the execution load of computationally intensive programs over a dedicated network of computational nodes. Automatic distribution of sequential programs is of great concern in applying networks of low cost computers to run computationally intensive code.

There have been thorough investigations on automatic distribution of sequential code. However, most of the current approaches put some limitations on the program to be distributed or the distribution policy. Some researches have restricted the problem to cover only multithreaded programs [5][8]. Some others partition the sequential code in order to use remote resources across the network but have failed to achieve a faster distributed program [3][4][6][7]. In the approach presented in [2] only those objects whose accessible objects form disjoint sets can be converted to remote objects. We have developed a framework for automatic translation of a legacy sequential object-oriented program into a corresponding distributed one in order to achieve maximum concurrency in the execution of the program. A major difficulty has been to prove the correctness of the translation process. To resolve the difficulty, we developed a formal abstraction of the translation scheme and formally proved its correctness [11]. To demonstrate the feasibility and realizability of the specified translation scheme, a detailed description of its implementation and evaluation is presented in this paper.

The remaining parts of this paper are organized as follows: An overall description of the building blocks of our proposed architecture for the final distributed program is presented in Section 2. In Section 3, a formal specification of the structure and

C. Cérin and K.-C. Li (Eds.): GPC 2007, LNCS 4459, pp. 543–554, 2007.

behavior of the architecture building blocks is presented. Implementation details are presented in Section 4. An evaluation of the performance of the resulting distributed program is presented in Section 5.

2 Architecture

The aim has been to translate sequential object oriented programs into corresponding distributed ones. To achieve this, in the first stage of the translation, the class dependency graph of the sequential code is extracted. Each edge of the graph is then labeled with the amount of concurrency achieved by assigning the classes at the two ends of the edge to different components of the ultimate distributed architecture. The aim has been to speedup the program execution by replacing ordinary method calls with remote asynchronous calls. Here, as shown in Figure 1, the objective is to achieve the maximum concurrency between the caller and the callee by means of asynchronous calls.

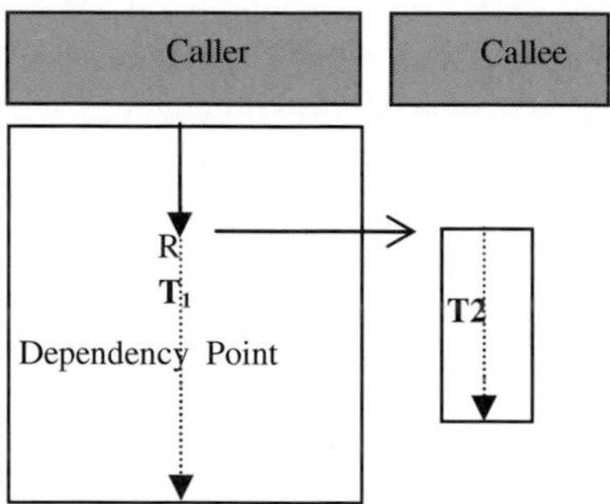

Fig. 1. The amount of concurrency obtained in this asynchronous call is $\min(T_1,T_2)$

As shown in Figure 1, the caller may continue with its execution in parallel with the callee as far as the return value and any other values affected by the callee are not required. In order to locate the very first positions where the results and the return value of an asynchronous call are required a data dependency analysis algorithm among method calls has been used [1]. This data dependency checking, obviously, ensures preservation of the semantics of the sequential code. The proof is presented in [11]. The labeled class dependency graph is then clustered and the program code is partitioned into clusters with maximum concurrency in their executions. Each cluster is assumed to be executed on a different station. As shown in Figure 2, in order to translate ordinary sequential calls into remote asynchronous inter-cluster calls four components, *Port*, *Distributor, Connector* and *Synchronizer* are augmented to each cluster. These components and the resulting architecture are formally described in section 3. A *Port* component is created for each cluster to facilitate its incoming communications with the other clusters. The *Distributor* component performs outgoing inter-cluster invocations. The *Synchronizer* component makes it possible for a caller to receive the value of the call parameters and the results of remote method calls. The *Synchronizer* keeps a record of each remote method call in a table. The record is updated with the values of reference parameters and the return value. A wait statement is inserted at the very first positions where one of the reference parameters or the return value is required. To locate these positions a data dependency analysis approach has been used [1]. The *Connector* component is the middleware aware part of the suggested architecture. All the inter-cluster communications are carried out through this component. A formal description of the above mentioned components is presented in the subsequent sections.

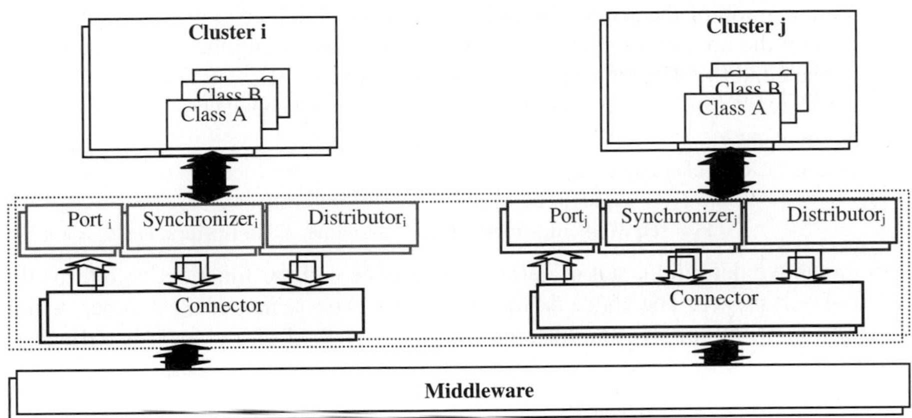

Fig. 2. Proposed distributed architecture

3 Formal Specification

In this section a formal description, which follows the VDM language conventions, of the structure and behavior of the distributed code is presented. Each unit of the distribution is a cluster of highly related classes. A formal specification of the cluster structure and its associated distributing components is presented in section 3.1. The runtime behavior of the distributing mechanism is described in section 3.2.

3.1 Distributed Program Structure

As described above, each component of the resulting distributed program architecture contains a cluster of the original sequential source code and four other components, shown in Figure 2. In this Section a formal description of the structure of the distributed program, called *PartitinedCode,* is presented.

$$PartitinedCode = \textbf{set of } \text{cluster},$$
$$\forall\, Cluster_i \in PartitinedCode : \; Cluster_i = (CT_i , P_i , D_i , G_i , R_i)$$

Where, CT_i addresses a table containing a description of all classes belonging to the $Cluster_i$. The element P_i, is the cluster port, providing possibility of asynchronous remote access to the methods of CT_i classes from within the classes of CT_j where $i \neq j$. The element D_i is the cluster distributor, which provides transparent remote access to the methods of classes in other clusters connected to Cluster_i. The element G_i is a map which relates a method in port P_i to a method in one of the classes of CT_i. R_i is another map which relates one method in D_i to a method of a remote port P_k where $k \neq i$. Before specifying these elements formally, some auxiliary definitions are required:

Types	Set of all language types including primitive types and classes
statements	Set of all language statements
identifiers	Set of all valid language identifiers

3.1.1 Classes and Methods

As described above, the class table of ith cluster, CT_i, is defined as a set of classes:

$$CT_i = \textbf{set of } \text{class}$$
$$\forall s_k \in CT_i : s_k = (\text{classname}_k, T_k, F_k, M_k)$$
$$\text{where } T_k = \textbf{seq of } t,\ t \in \textbf{types},$$
$$F_k = \textbf{seq of } \text{id},\ \text{id} \in \textbf{identifiers},\ \text{classname}_k \in \textbf{identifiers},\ \text{len } T_k = \text{len } F_k$$

In the above definition, **seq of** defines a sequence and the function len returns the length of a sequence. The above definition defines class s_k named classname_k, which has fields F_k with types T_k and methods M_k. Each method of a class s_k is defined as follows:

$$\forall m_j \in M_k : m_j = (\text{methodname}_j, T_j, A_j, r_j, E_j),$$
$$\text{where } T_j = \textbf{seq of } t,\ t \in \textbf{types},\ A_j = \textbf{seq of } \text{id},\ \text{id} \in \textbf{identifiers},\ \text{methodname}_j \in \textbf{identifiers},$$
$$r_j \in \textbf{types},\ E_j = \textbf{seq of } e,\ e \in \textbf{statements},\ \text{len } T_j = \text{len } A_j$$

The above definition defines method m_j of the class s_k. m_j addresses the method methodname_j of the class classname_k with formal parameters A_j of the types T_j and return type r_j and the body of the method includes statements E_j.

In a distributed program, there are two sets of call statements, *intra-calls* and *inter-calls,* to define intra-cluster and asynchronous inter-cluster method calls respectively. In cluster Cluster_r:

$$\forall st \in \textit{intra-calls} : st = (s_n, m_i, V)$$
$$\text{Where: } s_n \in CT_r,\ m_i \in M_n \text{ and V is a vector of the call statement parameters}$$
$$\forall st \in \textit{inter-calls} : st = (m_k, V)$$
$$\text{Where: } m_k \in D_r \text{ (defined below)}$$

3.1.2 Port and Distributor

Each cluster Cluster_i, is associated with two components, port P_i and distributor D_i, to define methods provided and required by the cluster, respectively. Each cluster, Cluster_i, has a single port, P_i, to communicate with the other clusters. The port is defined as a set of methods, which can be accessed from the other clusters by the asynchronous inter-cluster call statements. Each method, m_k, within P_i invokes a method, $G_i(m_k)$, of a class defined within the class table CT_i of the cluster Cluster_i.

$$P_i = \textbf{set} \text{ of method},\ \forall m_k \in P_i : m_k = (\text{methodname}_k, T_k, A_k, r_k, E_k)$$

Map G_i of Cluster_i is defined as follows:

$$G_i = \textbf{map } P_i \textbf{ to } M_i^*,\ M_i^* = \cup M_n \text{ where, } s_n \in CT_i,\ s_n = (\text{classname}_n, T_n, F_n, M_n)$$

G_i maps each method m_k of the port P_i to a method m_t belonging to a class like s_n of $Cluster_i$:

$G_i(m_k) \in M_n$, $G_i(m_k)$ = ($methodname_t$,T_t , A_t , r_t , E_t)

The called method, $G_i(m_k)$, has the same name as the method m_k and belongs to one of the classes, s_n, in the cluster $Cluster_i$. The parameter list, A_k, of the method m_k includes the name of the object "objectRef" which references an instance of the class $classname_n$ and the parameters of method m_t :

T_k = [$classname_n$].T_t A_k = ["objectRef"].A_t $r_t = r_k$

In the above definition the concatenation of two sequences are denoted by symbol '.' . Sequence T_k has one more element, $classname_n$, than T_t. Each cluster, $Cluster_i$, has a single distributor D_i as well. D_i delegates the asynchronous inter-cluster calls of $Cluster_i$ to a remote port P_r. In the following definition, R_i maps each method m_k of D_i to a method $R_i(m_k)$ of remote port P_r.

D_i = **set of** method , R_i= **map** D_i **to** $\bigcup P_r$ for all $r \neq i$
$\forall\, m_k \in D_i$: m_k = ($methodname_k$,T_k ,A_k , r_k ,E_k) ,
$\exists\, P_r$: $R_i(m_k) \in P_r$, $R_i(m_k)$ = ($methodname_t$, T_t, A_t, r_t, E_t), $T_k = T_t$, $A_k = A_t$, $r_t = r_k$

Finally the following property can be stated for each distributed program *PartitinedCode*:

$\forall$ $Cluster_i$, $Cluster_j \in$ *PartitinedCode*,$i \neq j$: $CT_i \cap CT_j = \phi$, $P_i \cap P_j = \phi$

3.2 Runtime Elements

In this section, the behavior of the final distributed program code is described as a set of runtime configurations. In order to perform a remote method call a new configuration is created for the called method at runtime by the caller. Each configuration represents the behavior of the thread created to perform the remote method. The configuration is removed after the termination of the called method, when the caller receives the return value. A configuration g is defined as tuple (σ_g, S_g, P^i_g, m^j_g, N_g , $State_g$) where,

σ_g : Memory space of the configuration g.
S_g : Stack of synchronizers of the configuration g.
P^i_g : the target port of configuration g which belongs to $Cluster_i$
m^j_g: j^{th} method of port P^i which is executed by configuration g
N_g : Physical network node of configuration g
$State_g$: running state of g, $State_g \in$ {"Suspended","Running","Terminated"}

In the above definitions each element of configuration g is subscripted by the configuration name, g. The configuration port P^i_g is the cluster port which provides access, through one of its methods: m^j_g, to the method which should be executed by g. In the following subsections the elements of the configuration tuple are further described.

3.2.1 Memory Spaces

A new configuration g is created in a workstation N_g whenever an inter-cluster call is delegated asynchronously, through a local distributor D, to a method m^j_g of a remote port, P^i_g. The memory space element of g retains the parameter's value of the method

m^j_g, before and after its completion. The memory space element also retains the return value of the method m^j_g. The memory space σ_g of the configuration g consists of a mapping from variable names to values, written ($x \rightarrow v$), or from object identifiers to the existing objects, written (obj $\rightarrow$ ($classname_k$, F_k, V_k)) indicating that identifier obj maps to an object of class $classname_k$. F_k and V_k are two sequences of the field names and their values of the class s_k=($classname_k$,T_k ,F_k , M_k) , $s_k \in CT_i$. For instance consider the following memory space:

$$\sigma = \{(a \rightarrow (A , f_1{:}b, f_2{:}3)),(b \rightarrow (B,f_1{:}c)),(c \rightarrow (C))\}$$

This map shows a memory space containing three identifiers pointing to the objects of types A,B and C, respectively. The set $\{a,b,c\}$ is called the domain of this map and is denoted by **dom** σ. Here, the object pointed to by the identifier, *a,* has two attributes f_1 and f_2. f_1 points to *b* which is an object identifier in its turn. The attribute f_2 holds an integer value. There are two functions called *og* and *serialized* which operate on the memory spaces. The function $og(\sigma,v)$ returns a subset of the memory space, σ, as an object graph containing the object identifier, v, and any object within σ which is accessible via v:

$$og : 2^\sigma \times \mathbf{dom}\ \sigma \rightarrow 2^\sigma ,$$

Below, is a recursive definition of the function, *og*:

$$og(\sigma,v) = \begin{cases} \phi, & \text{if } v \notin \mathbf{dom}\ \sigma \\ (v \rightarrow \sigma(v)) \cup og(\sigma_i,o_i),\ o_i \in fields(v),\ \sigma_1=\sigma-\{v\},\ \sigma_{i+1}= \sigma_i - \mathbf{dom}\ og(\sigma_i ,o_i) \end{cases}$$

The function *og*, traverses the memory space σ and forms a subset of the memory containing the node v and all the nodes accessible via v. The function *fields(v)*, in the above definition of og, returns all the objects, $o_i \in \sigma_i$, immediately accessible via the object σ(v). The *serialized* function returns the value of an object graph *w* in memory space of configuration g:

$$serialized(g, w) =\{(a, \sigma_g(a)) \mid a \in \mathbf{dom}\ w \}\quad w \in 2^\sigma$$

3.2.2 Stack of Synchronizers

The synchronizer element, **Sg**, of a configuration g keeps a record of the names of all reference parameters, return value and a handle identifying the thread created to execute a remote method, m^j_t, invoked via a method, m, within g, in a table. A new configuration t is created for each remotely invoked method within an existing configuration, g. The set D_r and the mapping R_r in the following definition are already defined in section 3.1.2.

Sg = map (**dom** σ_g) to **Threads$_g$**
Threads$_g$ = $\{t \mid t$ is defined as $(\sigma_t, S_t, P^i_t, m^j_t, N_t , State_t) \}$
Where g is defined as: $(\sigma_g, S_g, P^r_g, m^s_g, N_g , State_g)$
$\forall\ t \in Threads_g\ \exists\ m \in D_r,\ R_r(m)= m^j_t\ ,\ m^j_t \in P^i_t$

The synchronizer table is looked up for the names of reference parameters and the return value at the very first positions where one of the reference parameters or the return value is required within g. A *SYNC* statement is inserted at each of these positions. The *SYNC(v)* statement looks up the name *v* in the synchronizer table to find the handle of the corresponding invoked method. The handle is checked to determine the termination of the invoked method. A synchronizer table is created and pushed into the synchronizer stack, S_g, when entering a new method within g, at runtime.

S_g= **seq of Sg**

The *SYNC* method and another method called *REG* operate on S_g. *SYNC(v)* is called whenever a variable, v, affected by a remote method call is required within the caller. To get the value of v, the configuration t = $hd(S_g)(v)$ is accessed through the synchronizer stack, S_g. The function $hd(S_g)$ returns the first synchronizer on the top of the stack.

SYNC(v)
pre: $v \in \text{dom } \sigma_g \wedge t = hd(S_g)(v)$
post: $State_t$="Terminated" $\wedge$
$\sigma_g = \hat{}\sigma_g \dagger (\text{serialized}(t, \cup og(\hat{}\sigma_g, v_i)) \cup (\cup og(\sigma_t, v_i)))$, where $\forall\ v_i : hd(S_g)\ (v_i) = t$

In the above definition of *SYNC*, $\hat{}\sigma_g$ indicates the memory space of the caller configuration, g, before the invocation of *SYNC*; † indicates overriding of $\hat{}\sigma$ with the memory space of the called method. After the invocation of *SYNC*, the caller is suspended until the state, $State_t$ of the target configuration t, becomes "*Terminated*". The *SYNC* operation uses the memory space of the configuration t, to update the memory space σ_g of the caller configuration, g. The updates are accessed via the *serialized* function, described in section 3.2.1. The *REG(v,t)* operation records a parameter v passed as a reference parameter in a remote call, together with the called method configuration, t, in the synchronizer table of the caller configuration.

REG(v, t)
pre: $v \in \text{dom } \sigma_g$
$t \in Threads_g$
post:
$hd(S_g)= hd(\hat{}S_g)\ \dagger\ (v \rightarrow t)$

4 Implementation Model and Results

In this Section considering the architecture design and structural and operational specification of the components applied to distribute a sequential code, the implementation details of these components and the required modifications to the sequential code to generate the desired distributed code is described.

The parameter passing mechanism in asynchronous remote method calls is explained in section 4.1. The required modifications to convert ordinary method calls to corresponding asynchronous remote calls are presented in section 4.2.

4.1 Parameter Passing

There are two approaches for passing reference parameters in asynchronous remote method calls, namely *system-wide object references* [9] and *copy-restore*. In the *system-wide* approach a unique identifier is assigned to each object to be accessed remotely. This identifier includes the network address of the computational node where the object resides on and an indication of the object. All the method calls on this object should be carried out on the computational node where the object is initially created. In contrast, the *copy/restore* approach makes it possible to run methods of an object on different computational nodes by copying the object state to the computational node, and restoring the object state back to the caller after the completion of the call. Applying the *copy/restore* approach for transferring call parameters in an inter-cluster asynchronous call, the callee may reside on any computational node with minimum load within the distributed environment. Therefore, in this approach an object may be accessed on different nodes during its life time and a specific predefined location is not required. As a result, the *copy/restore* approach provides a better load balancing of the distributed program code across the computational nodes.

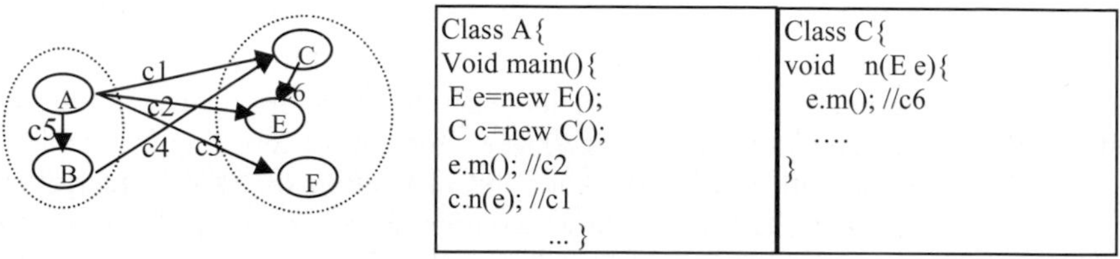

Fig. 3. A sample clustering of the classes

For instance, in Figure 3 the program code is partitioned into two clusters. Here the clustering algorithm is only applied to determine which method calls deserve to be converted to remote asynchronous calls in the sense that they yield speedup in overall program execution. Considering the clustering in Figure 3, the invocations c1, c2, c3 and c4 should be converted into remote asynchronous invocations whereas c5 and c6 should remain intact. The method calls c6 and c2 are applied to a same instance, e, of class E. Applying a *system wide reference* approach, e is created as a local object in cluster 2 and is accessed as remote object in A and C. However, since E and C are in the same cluster, c6 should apply a local instance of E, rather than the remote object e. This problem can be resolved by applying the *copy/restore* approach in expense of incurred overhead of coping object states when performing remote calls.

4.2 Implementation

In order to translate an ordinary method call $a.m(p_1,p_2,\ldots,p_n)$, in a cluster, $Cluster_i$, into a corresponding asynchronous remote method call, the call statement is replaced with $D_i.m(this, p_1, p_2,\ldots, p_n)$ where, D_i is a static distributor class, specified in section 3.1.2, assigned to the cluster, $Cluster_i$, and the parameter *this* refers to the object a. As specified in section 3.1.2, each *Distributor* component has a number of methods to delegate outgoing calls. For each method:

$$\texttt{returnType}\ \ \texttt{m}(\texttt{T}_1\ \texttt{p}_1,\texttt{T}_2\ \texttt{p}_2,\ldots,\texttt{T}_n\ \texttt{p}_n)\{\ \ldots\ \}$$

Within a cluster, $Cluster_j$, which is invoked from within another cluster, $Cluster_i$, a delegator method which is also named m is augmented to the distributor component, D_i, of the cluster, $Cluster_i$, as follows:

Sample method in Distributor D_i	Semantics
ResultHandle m(A this,T_1 p_1,T_2 p_2,...,T_n p_n)	
{ Object[] parlist={this,p1,p2,...,pn} ;	
String portname= Ports.lookup("A");	Map R_i is used to locate the target of call
ResultHandle h= *Connector.connect(portname,"m",parlist);* *return h; }*	Configuration t is created and call parameters are transferred to the memory space of t: $\sigma_t = \bigcup og(\sigma_g, v_i)$, $v_i \in V$

Fig. 4. A sample method in Distributor D_i and its corresponding operational semantics

In the above code, the name of the class, *A*, is looked up in the tables, addressed as CT_i in the above formal specification, to find the cluster, $Cluster_i$, to which *A* belongs. Then, the remote method call is performed by passing the port name of $Cluster_i$, method name, *m*, and the parameters of *m* to the *connect* method of the *Connector* object. The *Connector* object then returns a handle, *h*, which includes a unique reference to the invoked method activation. This handle is then used by the caller to receive the values returned by the remote method, *m*. This is achieved by calling a method called *Add*(), of the Synchronizer component. This method inserts the handle object in an object table, which is an instance of a class called *SyncTable*. A new *syncTable* is created when entering a new scope. The table is pushed into a stack by calling of the *pushSyncTable()* method of the Synchronizer component. When exiting a scope, its *syncTable* is popped off the stack by calling the *popSynchtable()* method. Below, in Figure 5 the definition of the Synchronizer methods and their corresponding specification elements from section 3 are shown.

Method	Specification
void Add(String varname,int seq,Object h){}	*Operation*: REG
void restoreObject(String varname,Restorable v){}	*Operation*: SYNC
Object restoreResult(String varname){}	*Operation*: SYNC
void pushSynchTable(){}	*Element* : S_g
void popSynchTable(){}	*Element* : S_g

Fig. 5. The Synchronizer methods

The method *add()* implements operation *REG* specified in section 3.2.2. Two methods *restoreObject()* and *restoreResult()* implement the operation *SYNC*. The former method is used to restore the values of all reference parameters transferred via the remote method call and the latter is used by the caller to receive the return value.

To wait for the value of an object, o, affected by a remote call, m, the *retoreObject*() method is invoked. This method looks up the object name "o", kept in the parameter *varname*, in the *syncTable* to obtain its handle and waits for the callee to return its value. The returned value is then stored in the object parameter v by calling its *restore*() method. To invoke *restore*(), the class of the object o implements the interface Restoreable described below:

```
interface Restorable {void restore(Object remoteObject);}
```

The method *restoreResult()* acts the same as *restoreObject*() except that it returns the return value of the call statement. Each cluster, Cluster_i, includes a port component, P_i, to receive incoming method calls. For each method $m(T_1\ p_1, T_2\ p_2, \ldots, T_n\ p_n)$ within Cluster_i, which can be invoked remotely, there is a method $m(A\ this, T_1\ p_1, T_2\ p_2, \ldots, T_n\ p_n)$ within the port component where, A is the name of the class to which m belongs.

5 Evaluations

Our proposed distributing environment is implemented in Java. *JavaSymphony* middleware [10] is accessed via the *Connector* component to handle remote calls. The performance of the system is evaluated on a dedicated network of five Pentium 2.4GH PC's. In this section the performance of the distributing environment using two benchmarks is reported. In order to prepare each benchmark for distributed execution, ordinary method calls are replaced with calls to the Distributor class, described in section 4.1. To determine method calls to be converted to remote synchronous calls, the amount of concurrency in the execution of the caller and the callee is considered. A clustering algorithm which is not presented here, determines the method calls to be converted into remote asynchronous calls. The clustering is aimed at the highest concurrency in execution of inter-cluster method calls.

5.1 *ReadTest* Benchmark

ReadTest [1] is a synthetic benchmark which is used to measure how the variations of completion time of asynchronous method calls affect the total speedup achieved by distributing a program code across a dedicated network. *ReadTest(m,n)* is a program which creates m parallel asynchronous calls each with execution time of n milliseconds. Figure 6 presents the results of running *ReadTest(50,n)* with different values for n on four computational nodes.

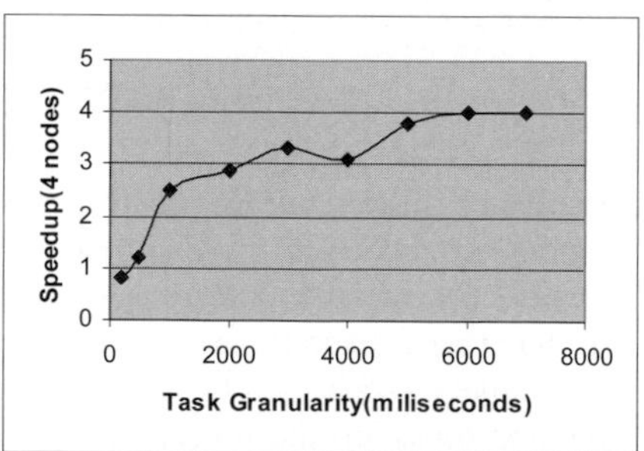

Fig. 6. Effect of remote call execution time on the speedup

This benchmark is a good indicator of the overhead of distributing a program using our distributing environment. As shown in Figure 6, the performance is relatively poor when the execution times of the asynchronous calls are relatively small. Apparently, when the execution time is too small the cost of serializing object states to the remote node and creating, running and synchronizing asynchronous calls, outweigh the benefit gained from the distribution. As shown in Figure 6, the highest amount of speedup is achieved when the execution time of each remote call is greater than 5000 milliseconds.

5.2 *Warshall* Algorithm

We have applied a *copy/restore* mechanism to transfer parameters in remote calls because this mechanism makes it possible to retain an object state within the caller after the completion of the remote method. Thereby, applying a *copy/restore* approach it is possible to invoke different methods of an object on different computational nodes. However, this mechanism suffers from the overhead of passing the value of call parameters. In this section it is shown that despite the relatively long parameter passing time, *copy/restore* mechanism is beneficial to code distribution. This is demonstrated by applying *Warshall* algorithm to compute the connectivity matrix for a 1000×1000 matrix over a network of 1 to 5 dedicated computing nodes within the proposed distributing environment. This algorithm entails many matrix multiplications and for a given digraph determines whether or not there exists a path between each pair of the nodes.

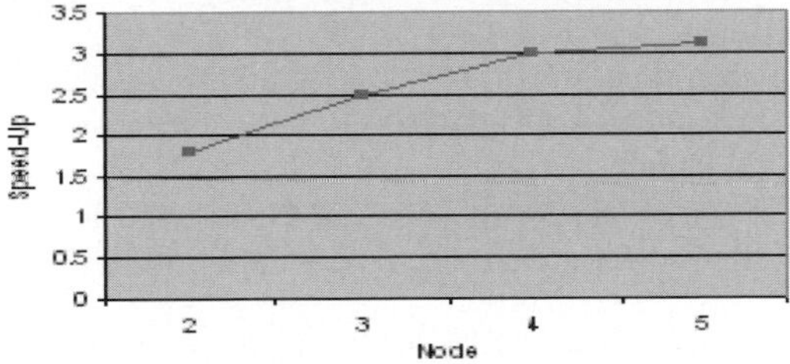

Fig. 7. Speedups achieved by distributing the Java code for the *Warshall* algorithm

The implemented code subdivides the matrix multiplication process among n methods. For instance for n = 2, 1000 multiplications required for computing the connectivity matrix is subdivided in to two 500 multiplications each performed on a separate computational node. In Figure 7, the speed ups achieved for values 2 to 5 for n is presented. It is observed that there is a relatively little growth in the speedups when the number of computational nodes is increased from 4 to 5. Apparently, the communication cost outweighs the benefit gained from the distribution when the number of computational nodes is increased.

6 Conclusions

In this paper the formal specification and implementation of a set of components to translate a legacy object oriented sequential program into a corresponding distributed program is presented. To distribute efficiently, the program is partitioned into clusters in order to achieve concurrency in the execution of the inter-cluster asynchronous calls. A major difficulty with remote method calls is to transfer and receive the value of reference parameters. Formal specification of the structure of distributed program makes it possible to define the distributing components and their application precisely. Applicability of the formal specification is shown by presenting implementation details for the specified structure and behavior of the distributing components. It is shown both in theory and practice that a copy/ restore approach is beneficial for transferring reference parameters in a distributed environment.

References

1. Brayan Chan, Tarek S. Abdelrahman, "Run-Time Support for the Automatic Parallelization of Java Programs" , The Journal of Supercomputing, pp 91–117, 2004
2. Isabelle Attali, Denis Caromel, Romain Guider, "A Step Toward Automatic Distribution of Java Programs", 4th International Conference on Formal Methods for Open Object-Based Distributed Systems (FMOODS 2000), Stanford, California, USA, 2000
3. Roxana E. Diaconescu, Lei Wang, Michael Franz, "Automatic Distribution of Java ByteCode Based on Dependence Analysis", Technical Report No. 03-18, School of Information and Computer Science, University of California, Irvine, 2003
4. Roxana Diaconescu, Lei Wang, Zachary Mouri, Matt Chu, "A Compiler and Runtime Infrastructure for Automatic Program Distribution". 19th International Parallel and Distributed Processing Symposium (IPDPS 2005), IEEE ,2005
5. Mohammad M. Fuad, Michael J. Oudshoorn, "AdJava-Automatic Distribution of Java Applications", 25th Australasian Computer Science Conference (ACSC2002), Monash University, Melbourne, 2002
6. Michiaki Tatsubori, Toshiyuki Sasaki, Shigeru Chiba1, and Kozo Itano, "A Bytecode Translator for Distributed Execution of Legacy Java Software", LNCS 2072, pp. 236–255, 2001
7. Eli Tilevich, Yannis Smaragdakis, "J-Orchestra: Automatic Java Application Partitioning". 16th European Conference on Object Oriented Programming, LNCS 2374, 2002
8. Andre Spiegel, "Pangaea: An Automatic Distribution Front-End for Java", 4th IEEE Workshop on High-Level Parallel Programming Models and Supportive Environments (HIPS '99), San Juan, Puerto Rico, April 1999
9. Andrew S. TanenBaum, Maarten Van Steen, Distributed Systems Principles and Paradigms, PRENTICE HALL, 2002
10. Thomas Fahringer Alexandru Jugravu, "JavaSymphony: New Directives to Control and Synchronize Locality, Parallelism, and Load Balancing for Cluster and GRID-Computing" in Proceedings of Joint ACM Java Grande - ISCOPE 2002 Conference, Seattle, Washington, Nov. 2002
11. Omid Bushehrian, Saeed Parsa, "Formal Description of a Runtime Infrastructure for Automatic Distribution of Programs", The 21th International Symposium on Computer and Information Sciences, LNCS 4263, pp 793-802, 2006

Dynamic Distribution for Data Storage in a P2P Network*

Olivier Soyez[1], Cyril Randriamaro[2], Gil Utard[2], and Francis Wlazinski[3]

[1] INRIA-Futurs, LIFL, Université des Sciences et Technologies de Lille, Bâtiment E, 59655 Villeneuve d'ascq, France
Olivier.Soyez@inria.fr

[2] UbiStorage, Pôle Jules Verne, rue des Indes Noires, 80440 Boves
{Cyril.Randriamaro, Gil.Utard}@ubistorage.com

[3] LaRIA, 5 rue du moulin neuf, 80000 Amiens, France
Francis.Wlazinski@laria.u-picardie.fr

Abstract. This article presents a dynamic data distribution method for data storage in a P2P network. In our system named Us (Ubiquitous storage), peers are arranged in groups called Metapeers to deal with account failure correlation. To minimize end user traffic according to the reconstruction process, distribution must take into account a new measure: the maximum disturbance cost of a peer. In a previous work, we defined a static distribution scheme which minimizes this reconstruction cost derivated from affine plan theory. In this paper we extend this distribution scheme to deal with the dynamic behaviour of peer to peer systems.

1 Introduction

Peer to Peer systems are widely used mechanisms to share resources on Internet. Very popular systems were designed to share CPU (XtremWeb [1], Entropia) or to publish files (Napster, Kazaa, Gnutella). In the same time, systems were designed to share disk space (OceanStore [2,3], Intermemory [4], PAST [5], Farsite [6]). The primary goal of such systems is to provide a transparent distributed storage service. These systems share common issues with CPU or files sharing systems: resource discovery, dynamic point to point network infrastructure, localization mechanisms... But, for sharing disk systems, data lifetime is the primary concern. P2P CPU or file publishing systems can deal with node failures: the computation can be restarted anywhere or the published files resubmitted to the system. For disk sharing systems, node failure is a critical event: the stored data are definitively lost. So data redundancy and data recovery mechanisms are crucial.

In this paper, we focus on the category of peer to peer systems devoted to storage. After a short presentation of the peer to peer storage system named Us (Ubiquitous storage) [7], we introduce some definitions and we present the problem formulation based on a new measure cost: the user's disturbance in a P2P network. We define the theoretical cost of distribution according to the number of peers, number of blocks, and fragmentation factor. We present static distributions based on prime number theory.

* Thanks to Grand-Large INRIA-Futurs team for their contributions and thanks to Ubistorage company (www.ubistorage.com) for their contributions.

C. Cérin and K.-C. Li (Eds.): GPC 2007, LNCS 4459, pp. 555–566, 2007.

Then we compare it with simulations to the most used distribution: the random distribution. Next we describe how to apply it in a dynamic environment over Metapeers, taking into account the failure correlation. Experimental results show the benefit of such distribution versus the random distribution.

2 Us System

For scalability reasons, data are distributed on thin peers using the well known Rabin dispersal technique [8]. Contrarily to other systems like OceanStore [2], where data are distributed on server peers, in Us, data are distributed on end user peers: each Us peer is both storage space consumer and storage space provider. The main goal of Us is to provide a virtual storage device to each user which insures data durability.

Us shares common features with the OceanStore project are data disseminated with data redundancy mechanism. The advantage of such method is scalability. The drawback is that we have to face a higher failure rate of peer because the number of peers is a several order of magnitude greater than the number of peers in OceanStore. Moreovers, peers are less robust than OceanStore servers.

The main mechanism used to insure data durability is redundancy based on erasure code. Such code is the mechanism used by OceanStore and Us to maintain data-survival. To insure data durability Us use usual redundancy mechanism based on erasure code techniques: peers (physical computers) send data blocks to be stored on other peers. Each block is split into f fragments including redundancy information. For durability reasons, each fragment is stored on a different peer.

When a peer fails, all fragments it stored must be rebuilt and redistributed to other peers. To rebuild each fragment, $f - 1$ fragments must be grabbed from some other peers. We take this hypothesis to consider the death of only one peer and then the reconstruction of its fragments set. Thanks to this hypothesis, we can take into account the peers availability, i.e. to be able to always receive the needed fragments for the reconstruction process. For example, if the error correction code ReedSolomon is used, we consider that it is always possible to receive the s fragments (needed to rebuild the data block) between the $f - 1$ fragments. Because it is not reasonable to believe that the s peers storing the s fragments will be all available at the same time for the reconstruction.

For a fragment reconstruction, we consider that a peer is responsible to grab the $f-1$ fragments. Then it regenerates the original bloc and the lost fragment is identified and regenerated.

2.1 Failure Correlation and Metapeers

Depending on geography, a peer failure may be correlated with other peers failures, like electrical damage, flooding. Another kinf of failure due to geographical proximity, would be, if the peers belong to the same physical network and if the network goes down, so will the peers. The notion of failure correlation, introduced in [9], is an important factor for fault tolerance technique. Peers selected for dissemination of fragments of a data block must avoid correlated failures, otherwise correlated failures may catch the redundancy mechanism out.

In Us, peers are arranged in groups called *Metapeer* according to their correlated failure. Each peer belongs to exactly one Metapeer. A couple of peers which exhibits a high probability of correlated failure belong to the same Metapeer. So, a couple of peers coming from two different Metapeers must exhibit low probability of correlation failure. When a block of data is disseminated in Us, peers chosen to store fragments are selected from different *Metapeers*. Two fragments of the same block cannot be stored on peers of the same Metapeer. Due to the data redundancy information, all of the peers of the same Metapeer can be down without data losses. In the current version of Us, the number of Metapeers is fixed. How the Metapeers are constructed is not the topic of this paper, interested reader can consult the Weatherspoon et al paper [9] which presents a framework for online discovery of such Metapeers.

3 Definitions

Let us define some notions and definitions used in this paper. We describe what is a data distribution and costs induced by the reconstruction process.

3.1 Notations

p is a peer, b is a block: a set of f peers, N the total number of peers, f the fragments number of a block, $f \leq N$, NB the number of blocks, α_i the number of fragments stored by peer i, P the set of peers, B the set of stored blocks, B_p the set of blocks p stores a fragment of, i.e. the set of the blocks to rebuild for peer p failure. C_{max} is the reconstruction cost.

3.2 Data Distribution

A data distribution maps fragments from blocks over the peers. For durability reasons, a distribution is restricted by the condition that the f fragments of one block are stored on f distinct peers. Thus we assume that $f \leq N$.

Each block b can be represented by the list of those f peers. The fragments of a peer p belong to distinct blocks. A data distribution D can be defined by:

$$\begin{gathered} D : B \mapsto P^f \\ \forall b \in B, p_1, p_2, ..., p_f \in P, p_1 \neq p_2 \neq ... \neq p_f, \\ b \mapsto \{p_1, p_2, ..., p_f\} \end{gathered}$$

For any data distribution, and for any number of stored blocks, we have

$$NB = \frac{1}{f} * \sum_{i=1}^{N} \alpha_i \tag{1}$$

Now let us introduce the notion of communication cost for peers during the reconstruction process.

3.3 Local Communication Cost of a Peer

The local communication cost $C_{loc(p,q)}$ is the number of fragments that a peer p sends to rebuild fragments of a failed peer q:

$$\forall p, q \in P, C_{loc(p,q)} = |B_p \bigcap B_q|$$

And the total number of fragments needed by the reconstruction is equal to the sum of all local cost peers, except the dead peer q. So we have :

$$\forall q \in P, \alpha_q * (f-1) = \sum_{p=1, p \neq q}^{N} C_{loc(p,q)} \tag{2}$$

3.4 Global Communication Cost of a Peer

For each failed peer q, we determine the most disturbed peer by the reconstruction process. Given that two peers can send packets simultaneously, the global communication cost is defined by the most sending peer, i.e. the global communication cost is the maximum of all local communication costs. Let $C_{glob(q)}$ be the global cost to rebuild peer q fragments:

$$\forall q \in P, C_{glob(q)} = max_{p \in P, p \neq q} C_{loc(p,q)}$$

3.5 Maximal Communication Cost

We consider the worst disturbance which may appear in our reconstruction process. Considering a fragment distribution peers, the maximal communication cost is the maximum of the global communication costs, considering that any peer can fail:

$$C_{max} = \max_{q \in P} C_{glob(q)} = max_{q \in P} max_{p \in P, p \neq q} C_{loc(p,q)}$$

3.6 Problem Formulation

First, we define our objectives, i.e an optimal distribution. Then, we present the definition and property of an ideal distribution, a kind of optimal one.

Definition 1. *Let f be the number of fragments, N be the number of peers, NB be the number of blocks, an* **optimal distribution** *D_{opt} is a data distribution that minimizes the maximal communication cost C_{max} with the given number of stored blocks NB, so let D be an another data distribution:*

$$C_{max}(D_{opt}) \leq C_{max}(D)$$

Let N and f be fixed parameters. Our goal is to provide an optimal distribution for a given value of NB. By definition, this is equivalent to providing an optimal distribution for a given value of C_{max}.

4 Distributions

In this section, we present some distributions. First, in 4.1, we present the random distribution that is usually used in data distribution. This distribution is a reference for our work. In 4.2 and 4.2, we will see an optimal data distributions coming from mathematical theory: finite affine plane distribution for $N = f^2$ and finite projective plane distribution for $N = f^2 - f + 1$. But these distributions are too restrictive for our problem. In 4.2, we give a new method of distribution which respects all of the conditions of our problem : a General Case distribution for any value of N.

4.1 Random Distribution

The random distribution stores the f fragments of each data block on f distinct peers chosen randomly among all the peers. Due to statistics, this distribution must be efficient for a large number of peers. Indeed the probability to obtain equal lists of f peers or with a big number of common peers is weak. Nevertheless, this distribution needs a global knowledge of the full network, which is difficult to implement in a peer to peer network. The storage system PAST [5] is an example of such a distribution use: each peer and all resources have an unique identifier, associated with a dynamic routing system depending on these identifiers. A file is stored on the peer the identifier is the closest to the identifier file. The peer volatility implies that a new peer with a closer identifier can appear after the storage. Then, additional communications must be generated to find the file. Random data distribution is usually a good non optimal data distribution to minimize the reconstruction cost such defined. But unfortunately this distribution does not permit to exploit the physical network topology to avoid failure correlation. To do so, structured distribution strategies must be applied.

4.2 Asymptotically Optimal Data Distribution

We defined distribution schemes which minimizes the reconstruction cost using a mathematical tool : the projective geometry. Distributions are : finite affine plane distribution, finite projective plane and the General Case.

Finite affine plane distribution. Let take an optimal distribution based on the construction of finite affine planes of order f, when this construction is possible. The order of an affine plane is the number n, $n \geq 2$, such that the total number of points is n^2 and the total number of lines is $n(n+1)$, all the lines share n points and all points share $n+1$ lines and the intersection of two lines is no more that one.

So, the analogy with our problem is the order n corresponds to the number f of peers in a block, the points of the finite affine plane of order n are peers, so $N = f^2$, the lines of the finite affine plane of order n are blocks, so $NB = f^2 + f$ and the intersection of two blocks is no more that one, this imply a $C_{max} = 1$.

We have proved in [10], that this distribution is an optimal one. This distribution requires N to be equal to f^2, it is a high restriction. In addition, for some values of f, finding a construction of an affine plane of order f is still an open problem. But this distribution gives a good network structure.

Finite projective plane distribution. In this case, a distribution can be defined by the construction of finite projective planes of order $(f - 1)$, when this construction is possible. The order of the projective plane is n, such that the number of points is $n^2 + n + 1$ and the number of lines is $n^2 + n + 1$, all the lines share $n + 1$ points and all points share $n + 1$ lines. The intersection of two lines is one.

The analogy with our problem is that the order n may correspond to the number $f - 1$ where f is the number of peers in a block and the points of the finite projective plane of order n may correspond to the peers. It follows that the total number of peers is $N = f^2 - f + 1$. The lines of the finite projective plane of order n are blocks. So, we get $NB = f^2 - f + 1$ and the intersection of two blocks is 1.

Like the distribution based on finite affine plane: this distribution is optimal, but requires N to be equal to $f^2 - f + 1$. For some values of f, finding a construction of a projective plane of order $f - 1$ is still an open problem. But this distribution gives a good network structure.

General Case distribution (GC distribution). The GC distribution is designed for f a prime number and any value of N, such that $f^2 \leq N$. First, we construct M_i matrices that are used to build the distribution.

For more information about the GC distribution, please refere to this paper [10]. The GC distribution was proved in [10] to be asymptotically optimal. The main disadvantage is that this distribution is not flexible with N. When N moves, it is not reasonable to redistribute always all of the data. This is the reason why we study now dynamic distributions : distribution that allow N not to be a constant.

5 Data Distribution in a Dynamic P2P System

In this section, we present how the previously defined distributions can be used in a dynamic P2P storage system. A first idea is to distribute data with the GC distribution on all peers. However, when a peer fails, the rebuilt fragments must be stored on other peers. On the one hand, several peers can store the new fragments. Then the structure is blown. On the other hand, new fragments can be stored on the same new peer to guaranty that the damaged structure is rebuilt. Then, the sending parallelization is avoid by the reception.

Satisfying both conditions can be performed by the use of a peer group instead of a single peer for each structure node. Such groups are called Metapeers, used in our peer to peer storage system Us. Now we present the Metapeer distribution.

5.1 Metapeer Distribution

In such a distribution, the set of peers is partitioned in groups called Metapeers and the set of Metapeers is structured by a optimal distribution . Recall that Metapeer stuctura-tion of peers is well suited to tackle the problem of failure correlation. Due to failure correlation, our goal is to have a distribution adapted to the Metapeer structure, and that allows variable values of N.

Let us define a dynamic Metapeer distribution, we use a particular distribution (like GC distribution) and replace peers by Metapeer : node i from the distribution is replaced by Metapeer i. A fragment stored in node i will be stored in one of the peers of Metapeer i.

In the next part, we explain how the routing can be made into the Metapeers and we explain the reconstrution process.

With this structured distribution, we are able to define a mechanism for the management of the dynamic behaviour of peer to peer storage systems. For instance, when a new peer arrives, it first selects the Metapeer it will integrate. To improve data lifetime, the Metapeer is selected in such a way that the new peer is geographically far from peers of other Metapeers (w.r.t. some balancing criterions). The new peer also selects peers of other Metapeers which have good communication bandwidth with it. Then, when a reconstruction must be achieved, it sends fragments to those peers.

Fragments of a block are distributed over Metapeers of the structure. For each selected Metapeer, a specific function selects the storing peer. In order to balance the storage, this function is modified to tend to select the peer that stores the less. Afterwards, the selecting function will take into account the network topology.

For the reconstruction process, if a peer fails in a Metapeer, fragments are rebuilt on peers of the same Metapeer. The chosen peer set should optimise the reception process, i.e. maximize the number of receiving peers. So, an optimal reception happens when the Metapeer size is bigger than the number of sent fragments.

5.2 Over Metapeer Distribution

In the Metapeer distribution, node i from the General Case distribution is replaced by Metapeer i in the dynamic one. A fragment stored in node i will be stored in one of the peers of Metapeer i. The goal is to define which node must be selected in the Metapeer to optimise the dynamic distribution. Now we present a new strategy based on the General Case distribution.

Let us consider the following notations : MP is the number of Metapeer, MP_{Size} is the Metapeer size (i.e. the number of peers inside a Metapeer), MP_i is the ith Metapeer, P_{MP_i} is the set of peers of MP_i, and p^i_j is the jth peer of MP_i, with $1 \leq j \leq MP$ and $1 \leq j \leq MP_{Size}$.

Such matrices are called Metapeer matrices. Each row represents one block storage in the General Case distribution applied on peers.

In a practical way, a function is used to select the storing peer for each Metapeer indicated by the Metapeer matrices. This function can be based on the GC distribution algorithm, when the Metapeer size is sufficient to apply it.

In this case, for each Metapeer matrices row, several blocks can be stored without increasing the reconstruction cost. For example ,with the first row (MP_1, MP_4, MP_7), the f fragments of the first block are stored on peers (p^1_1, p^4_1, p^7_1). Then, the next block fragments that are stored on the same row are stored on peers (p^1_2, p^4_2, p^7_2), and so on, up to the last block that is stored on peers $(p^1_{MP_{Size}}, p^4_{MP_{Size}}, p^7_{MP_{Size}})$.

First we calculate the maximum number of block that can be stored on only one row of the Metapeer matrices, without increasing the reconstruction cost.

Lemma 1. *Let N be the total number of peers grouped in Metapeers, E a set of f Metapeers and MP_{Size} the size of each Metapeer, the Metapeers have the same size. Let NB be the theoretical maximum number of blocks NB stored over E, one fragment per Metapeer with a reconstruction cost of* 1*. Then $NB = MP_{Size}^2$.*

Proof: Let p be equal to MP_{Size} and $E_1, E_2, ..E_f$ the f sets of E , where each set has p elements. We want to create a family D of maximum cardinality of p-uples $(x_1, x_2, ..., x_f)$ that verify $x_i \in E_i$ and for each distinct couple of p-uples $(a_1, a_2, ...,$ $a_f)$ and $(b_1, b_2, ..., b_f)$ of D. The number of indices i such that $a_i = b_i$ must be at most equals to 1.

Imagine that we have this family D. Necessarily, if we take two sets in $E_1, E_2, ..E_f$, all elements couple in these two sets must have only one element in D. So, the maximum number of elements of D is the maximum couples number: $p \times p$.

Let us note that the maximum number can be obtained if p is a prime number and $p \geq f$. ■

Our goal is to find a distribution inside each Metapeer which allows a number of blocks close to that theoretical bound. To do so, we use the same strategy as General Case distribution applied on the peers inside Metapeers. For each row of the distribution matrices, matrices are defined like First Matrices in section 4.2.

Let $E_1, E_2, ..E_f$ be a row of the First Matrices. Let $p = MP_{Size}$ and $p_z^{E_i}$ be a peer such that $0 \leq i \leq f - 1$. We consider the p matrices MM_1, MM_2, ..., MM_p with p rows and f columns defined by $MM_k = \left(a_{ij}^k\right)_{1 \leq i \leq p; 1 \leq j \leq f}$ where $a_{i1}^k = p_k^{E_1}$ and $a_{ij}^k = p_z^{E_j}$ where $z = 1 + ([i - 1 + (k - 1) \times (j - 2)] \text{mod} p)$ $\forall 1 \leq i \leq p$ and $\forall 2 \leq j \leq f$.

Let us remark that: for any couple of integers $1 \leq z, t \leq MP_{Size}$, the peers $p_z^{E_j}$ with j in the interval $[1 + p \times i; p \times (i + 1)]$ only appear in the $(i + 1)^{\text{th}}$ column of the matrices MM_1, ..., MM_k. And two different rows of the matrices MM_1, ..., MM_p have at most one common element.

As in General Case distribution, the number of blocks is optimal if MP_{Size} is a prime number. So a Metapeer distribution implementation very close to GC distribution exists, but the MP_{Size} must respect a fixed condition. So in a dynamic way, it is not possible to always use this implementation. It is the reason why we use an hybrid Metapeer distribution. This Metapeer distribution choose the selecting peer function inside Metapeer depending on the value of the MP_{Size}. If MP_{Size} is not a prime number, then the selecting peer function is the random function, else it is the GC distribution algorithm.

5.3 Intrinsic Cost of Metapeer Distribution

In this part we compare the distribution cost for random distribution and GC distribution with different Metapeer size. For our experimentations, we use a simulator that computes the C_{max} depending on the value N, f, and a given distribution.

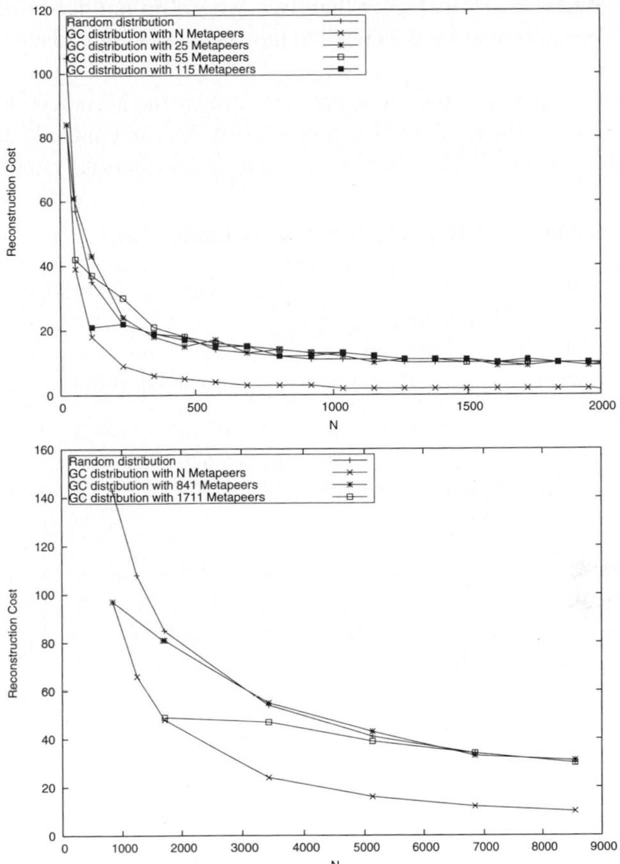

Fig. 1. Reconstruction cost depending on N for $f = 5$ (top) and $f = 29$ (bottom), for random distribution and different Metapeer size

Figure 1 show the impact on the reconstruction cost depending on N. For these simulations, each peer stores around 100 blocks, i.e. each peer can put and store 100 blocks, because the system is a peer to peer system.

The parameters of figure 1 are $f = 5$, $N = 0$ to 2000, $NB = 0$ to 200000. The parameters of figure 1 are $f = 29$, $N = 0$ to 9000, $NB = 0$ to 900000.

We always consider that the Metapeer size is the same for all of the Metapeers. Consequently, Figure 1 and 1 show the reconstruction cost for different Metapeer sizes, depending on N. For example, the first point given by a Metapeer distribution is obtained with a Metapeer size of one, i.e one peer per Metapeer, and consequently with a value of N equals to the total number of Metapeers.

Figure 1 shows that for small values of the Metapeer size, the random distribution cost is worth than the Metapeer one. It confirms the advantage to compute the GC distribution versus a random distribution. Another observation, see Figure 1, is about the Metapeer sizes: the Metapeer distribution cost is close to the random distribution cost, when the Metapeer size is bigger than two. So we do not need to choose a great number of Metapeers. Hence we dont need to have a big structure to manage the failure correlation.

Figure 1 shows that even if the Metapeer sizes grows, the Metapeer distribution cost is always very close to the random distribution cost. We can conclude, that the cost to manage the failure correlation and to have a dynamic distribution is not so high.

5.4 Analysis of Metapeer Distribution in a Dynamic Way

In this part, we observe the evolution of the communication reconstruction cost (C_{max}) during the life of the P2P system. To do so, we simulated distributions on a set of peers, then peer failures are simulated: each time a peer fails, the fragments it stored are redistributed over other peers, then a new peer appears in order to maintain the total number of peers.

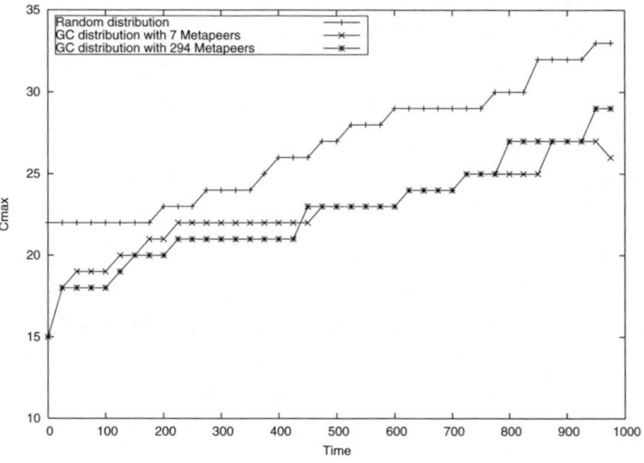

Fig. 2. GC distribution with different Metapeer size

Figure 2 shows the evolution of C_{max} in function to the arrivals and departures of peers in time, called churn [11]. The number of failures is 1000, C_{max} is measured every 25 failures. Each peer saves 100 blocks. Distributions are:

- **Random distribution:** distribution over any distinct peer for the same block, as explained in section 4.1. The reconstructions are performed using a random choice between peers that did not failed, and that are not already used for the current block storage.
- **Number of Metapeers = 7:** our distribution, presented in section 5.2, with $f = 7$, and over $MP = 7$ Metapeers of size 285 and 286. The number of Metapeers is a multiple of f to have good results with the GC distribution. The reconstruction is performed using a random choice between the remaining peers in the Metapeer of the failed peer.
- **Number of Metapeers = 294:** same distribution over $MP = 294$ Metapeers of size 7 and 8.

More Metapeers would have generate Metapeer sizes less than one.
Metapeers size other than this two extremes are less efficient.

At the beginning, our distribution cost is slightly lower than the random one. During the first step, up to 250 failures, GC distribution cost grows faster than the random one and almost reaches it. Then it definitively grows more slowly, increasing the gap between the two costs. Hence, our distribution has a better behaviour with failures. As a future work, simulations will be generated after churn analysis.

6 Conclusion

In peer to peer storage system we have to face a continuous stream of peer failures. So to insure data durability data are usualy disseminated using a dispersal redundant scheme and a dynamic data reconstruction process is used to rebuild lost data. There is a important communication traffic to maintain data integrity. So, it is important to reduce the impact of this reconstruction process on peer.

In this paper, we analysed the influence of data distribution on the cost of the reconstruction process. A good distribution of data is a distribution which minimizes the maximum data set sent by each peer to rebuild data lost by a peer failure. We showed that random distribution of data is usually a good strategy to minimize the reconstruction cost such defined, but unfortunately this random strategy does not permit to exploit the physical network topology to reduce communication time. Moreover, a static optimal distribution is too strict and is not well adapted to the dynamic behaviour of peer to peer systems. So, we propose a distribution which mixes static optimal distribution with a random one. In this distribution, the set of peers are partitioned in groups called Metapeers and the set of Metapeers are structured by the static optimal distribution. The number of Metapeers are selected in such a way we are able to achieve an optimal distribution. Our simulation showed that this distribution is able to achieve better performance than the random distribution.

References

1. Fedak, G., Germain, C., Nri, V., Cappello, F.: Xtremweb : A generic global computing system. In: CCGRID2001, workshop on Global Computing on Personal Devices. (2001)
2. Kubiatowicz, J., Bindel, D., Chen, Y., Eaton, P., Geels, D., Gummadi, R., Rhea, S., Weatherspoon, H., Weimer, W., Wells, C., Zhao, B.: Oceanstore: An architecture for global-scale persistent storage. In: Proceedings of ACM ASPLOS, ACM (2000)
3. Wells, C.: The oceanstore archive: Goals, structures, and self-repair. Master's thesis, University of California, Berkeley (2001)
4. Chen, Y., Edler, J., Goldberg, A., Gottlieb, A., Sobti, S., Yianilos, P.: A prototype implementation of archival intermemory. In: Proceedings of the Fourth ACM International Conference on Digital Libraries. (1999)
5. Druschel, P., Rowstron, A.: PAST: A large-scale, persistent peer-to-peer storage utility. In: Procedings of HOTOS. (2001) 75–80
6. Adya, A., Bolosky, W., Castro, M., Chaiken, R., Cermak, G., Douceur, J., Howell, J., Lorch, J., Theimer, M., Wattenhofer, R.: Farsite: Federated, available, and reliable storage for an incompletely trusted environment (2002)

7. Soyez, O.: Us : Prototype de stockage pair pair. In: RENPAR 2003, la Colle sur Loup, France. (2003) 214–218
8. Rabin, M.O.: Efficient dispersal of information for security, load balancing, and fault tolerance. Journal of ACM **38** (1989) 335–348
9. Weatherspoon, H., Moscovitz, T., Kubiatowicz, J.: Introspective failure analysis: Avoiding correlated failures in peer-to-peer systems. In: Proceedings of International Workshop on Reliable Peer-to-Peer Distributed Systems. (2002)
10. Randriamaro, C., Soyez, O., Utard, G., Wlazinski, F.: Data distribution in a peer to peer storage system. In: GP2PC05 2005, UK, Cardiff. (2005)
11. Li, J., Stribling, J., Gil, T., Morris, R., Kaashoek, F.: Comparing the performance of distributed hash tables under churn (2004)

GRAVY: Towards Virtual File System for the Grid

Thi-Mai-Huong Nguyen[1], Frédéric Magoulès[1], and Cédric Révillon[2]

[1] Applied Mathematics and Systems Laboratory, Ecole Centrale Paris
Grande Voie des Vignes, 92295 Châtenay-Malabry Cedex, France
mai-huong.nguyen@ecp.fr, frederic.magoules@hotmail.com

[2] United Devices (Europe), 6/8 Rue Jean Jaurès, 92807 Puteaux Cedex, France
cedric.revillon@free.fr

Abstract. Today large-scale applications require access to data stored in heterogeneous storage systems located at geographically distributed virtual organizations. In such applications, users are forced to deal with different administrative policies and structures at each site, and various data access mechanisms on each storage system. This implies a lot of human interventions in order to develop dedicated programs and scripts for data transfer between theses systems. This paper presents *GRid-enAbled Virtual file sYstem (GRAVY)* architecture which enables the automation of data transfers between distributed file systems irrespective of their heterogeneity. This feature enables high-level schedulers integrated with GRAVY to control data placements like computational jobs. GRAVY supports multiple data access protocols and provides an easy-to-use interface for novice Grid users.

Keywords: Virtual File System, Grid-computing, Data Management, Interoperability, Middleware.

1 Introduction

The Grid is rapidly emerging as the dominant paradigm for wide-area distributed computing [1]. Its goal is to provide an environment for coordinated resource sharing and problem solving in dynamic, multi-institutional virtual organizations [2]. Most of the current Grid deployments have focused on data-intensive applications where significant processing was done on very large amounts of data [3]. The data required by such applications is largely distributed in various storage systems. The need to access the remote data with "near-local" performance is crucial for scheduling and managing of application execution.

One of the Grid's purposes is to provide users the ability to share and to use data stored on heterogeneous storage systems as easily as if they were located on a single computer. Unfortunately, this vision is still far from being achieved due to the difficulty to deploy, use and maintain such environments. One of the fundamental problems is the existence of many different administrative domains, different storage systems, different data transfer middleware and protocols in Grid environments. This heterogeneity presents an important barrier for data

C. Cérin and K.-C. Li (Eds.): GPC 2007, LNCS 4459, pp. 567–578, 2007.

sharing in the Grid. Novice Grid users, principally scientists who need the power of the Grid to solve problems in their own fields, have difficulties in browsing and transferring data. They may find it difficult and cumbersome to write scripts or programs to perform the data transfer between different systems. Data management appears to be a big challenge, time consuming activity and requires the help of experts with significant expertise in data access related issues.

In this paper, we describe a novel architecture *GRid-enAbled Virtual file sYstem* (GRAVY) which facilitates the collaborative sharing of data in the Grid. GRAVY has the following features:

- *Location transparency*: GRAVY allows users to access data, which is geographically distributed in multiple domains in the Grid without the users having any idea where the data is located.
- *Protocol transparency*: GRAVY provides a generic data transfer architecture that shields users from the complexity of the underlying infrastructures including system's internal organization and data transfer protocols. As a result, data in heterogeneous file systems can be accessed in a uniform way.
- *Extensibility*: GRAVY allows new protocols to be added as the Grid evolves through a set of wrapper interfaces.

The next section of the paper describes data access problems in Grid environments in section 2, which lead to the motivation of our work. Then, we present an overview of related work in section 3. Following this, we describe in section 4 the GRAVY's design and in section 5 the architectural issues of the prototype that we have implemented in Java. This prototype allows users to have the view of a unified location-transparent file system of the Grid and to access to this system without being familiar with protocol's technical details. Next, in section 6 we show the experimental results. Finally, section 7 concludes the paper.

2 Data Access Problems in the Grid

Grid Is a Heterogeneous Environment. A frequent obstacle to the creation of applications that operate effectively in Grid environments is access to remote data. This problem is challenging because the Grid is a heterogeneous environment. Data at each site is accessed through different mechanism including how the data is organized, which transfer protocols are supported, and how the authentication is carried out. Users are forced to deal with such aspect whenever they want to access data at different storage system and it is difficult to efficiently share data between these systems.

Grid Job Needs Distributed Data to Run. In order to run grid data-intensive jobs, the input data need to be transferred to the appropriate location at the time the computation needs it. This task is commonly referred to as file *stage-ins*. The output data is moved back to its home storage systems as the computation is completed. This task is commonly referred to as file *stage-outs*.

In the Grid, and on the Internet, files are accessible through a variety of different protocols supported by storage systems, such as HTTP [4], FTP [5],

SCP/SSH [6], and GridFTP [3], each has its own data interaction styles. The diversity of data interaction styles (e.g., GUI, command-line, APIs) forces users to switch from one interaction style to another for file staging between heterogeneous systems. Hence, it prevents the automation of data transfers. Some interaction styles, such as GUI and command-line are only intended for manual use or simple scripts. Others, such as APIs or Web-Services, allow file staging to be performed in programs. Due to this diversity, users are obliged to manually transfer files between heterogeneous systems by using different tools supported or writing scripts and programs to perform file staging. Manual file staging is not suitable for applications in Grid environments as it supposes users to know in advance which files will be needed during the computation. Generally, users don't have the knowledge of the server that will be chosen for the computations. The choice of computational server is done by job scheduler. So, it is important for job scheduler to have a mediating system that is able to control the placement of data needed for the computation.

3 Related Work

A number of initiatives to address data management in grid environments have been initiated in recent years. We describe below some of these initiatives.

Based on the basic Globus services [7], the DataGrid [8] is a large and complex project that defines a layered architecture of service components for transferring large datasets in heterogeneous environment. This architecture is similar to ours in the sense that both try to separate the physical location of data from its logical view, which is called metadata.

GT4 [9] provides a number of components for data management. These components fall into two basic categories: data movement, which is composed of GridFTP tools and Reliable File Transfer (RFT) service, and data replication, which consists of Replica Location Service (RLS). An important related component, OGSA-DAI [10], provides data access and integration capabilities to data resources, such as databases, within a WebService-based framework.

LegionFS [11] proposes a virtual file system based on NFS protocol. The core of LegionFS functionality is based on an object based system that employs a basic object providing access methods similar to UNIX system calls (e.g., read, write, seek). NFS requests from client will be interpreted to appropriate methods of this basic object.

Within the EGEE project [12], the data management system (DMS) [13] is composed of several components. The first is storage elements (SEs) which are the real element doing the storage of files. In the framework of the DMS, files are available through two namespaces: logical (Logical File Name - LFN) and physical (Storage File Name - SFN). The DMS is responsible for mapping an LFN to one or more SFNs. Other components of DMS are data catalogs that offer access to file replicas using LFN and data scheduler, which assures the availability of data at the chosen site for computation.

A standardization effort of the Global Grid Forum Grid File System working group (GFS-WG) [14] is to provide a service oriented architecture for a Grid File System (GFS) [15] that provides standard interfaces to facilitate the federation and sharing of virtualised data. It should be noted that GFS is a specification, not an implementation.

Adapting peer-to-peer data transfer methods, [16] and [17] propose to use BitTorrent as a protocol for large file transfers in the context of desktop Grids. It is shown that BitTorrent is efficient, scalable when the number of nodes increase, but suffers from a high overhead when transmitting small files. The papers investigate the approachs to overcome these limitations.

Comparing with GRAVY, these solutions are designed to work primarily with their own self-contained middleware, (e.g., LegionFS in Legion middleware, DMS in gLite, RFT in GT4) or suppose to use a principal protocol for data transfers in the Grid (e.g., BitTorrent). On the contrary, GRAVY is designed to integrate into any global scheduling systems and an important feature of GRAVY is that it supports multiple protocols at both server side and remote side.

4 GRAVY: Solution for Data Access Problems in the Grid

In order to mask the heterogeneity of storage systems, our approach is to build a virtual file system GRAVY on top of underlying file systems. This virtual file system allows data to be transferred on-demand between heterogeneous file systems in a uniform fashion irrespective of its access protocol. Fig. 1 shows the conceptual overview of GRAVY. The dashed rectangle is the core services of GRAVY including virtual layer and core layer which consist of four major components: *virtual interfaces*, *transfer manager*, *access manager* and *wrapper interfaces*. Their role is to provide the user layer with uniform and seamless access and management of data transfers between remote file systems on physical layer.

The *virtual interfaces*, which consist of *GridFileSystem* and *GridFile* are designed to simplify and unify the way in which users handle data from heterogeneous data sources. The user layer is able to remotely interact with the virtual interfaces through variety of supported access protocols, including HTTP, FTP, and Web-Services. Local access to virtual interfaces is possible through a set of APIs that allow applications or job schedulers to control data placement.

The core layer is composed of four components: the *FileActionQueue*, the *transfer manager*, the *access manager* and the *wrapper interfaces*. User requests received from the virtual interface are queued in *FileActionQueue*, which examines each request in order to route each correctly to the *transfer manager* or the *access manager*.

We classify the user requests in two categories: transfer requests and access requests. Transfer requests need to be treated differently from access requests, since transfer requests generally have long execution time and they can fail for a variety of reasons at anytime during the execution. They need to be monitored and rescheduled for restart in case of failure. Hence, the *transfer manager*

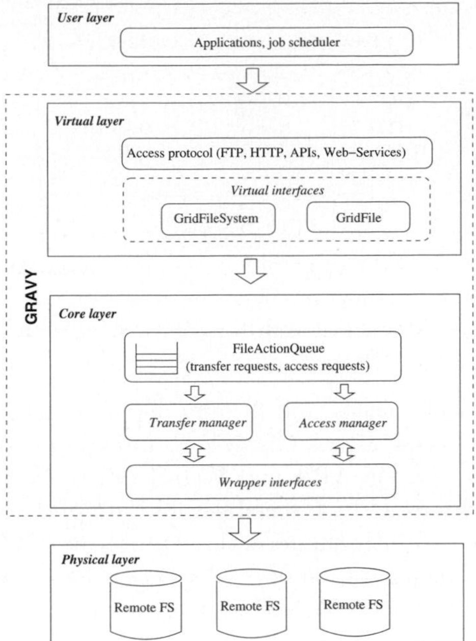

Fig. 1. Conceptual design of GRAVY

is designed to execute transfer requests asynchronously. The *transfer manager* performs the movement of files from one remote file system to the other. In case of transfer failure due to dropped connections, machine reboots or temporary network outages, the *transfer manager* will restart the transfers at another time in order to assure the successful completion of transfers. In contrast, the access requests (e.g., directory creation, file rename) have a short execution time, so the *access manager* is designed to execute access requests synchronously. It performs access operations on the remote file systems and returns immediately to users the result of execution. The *transfer manager* and the *access manager* interact with the remote file systems through *wrapper interfaces*. These interfaces are implemented by the file-system-provider in an appropriate protocol that is specific for each file system.

5 Architectural Issues

5.1 Protocol Resolution

GRAVY supports multiple access protocol in both server side and remote side (Fig. 2). This is a crucial requirement of a virtual file system used in a heterogeneous Grid environment.

Server Side. At the server side, supporting multiple protocols not only allows users to use their preferred file transfer protocol to interact with GRAVY but

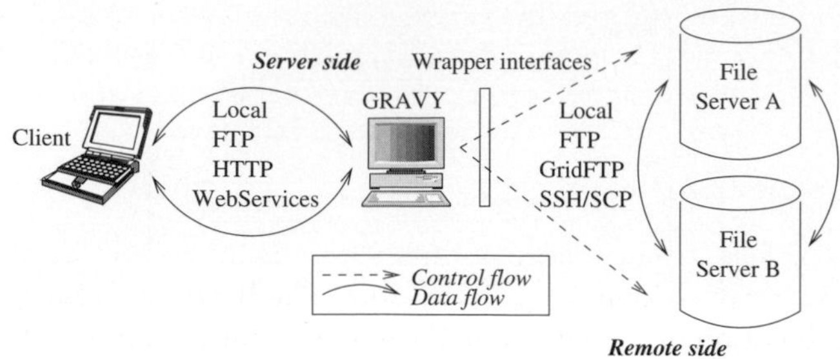

Fig. 2. Multiple access protocol in both server side and remote side

also allows GRAVY to be easily and flexibly deployed according to user needs. For example, HTTP access allows GRAVY to integrate easily into web portals of the Grid. Local access via APIs and Web-Services access allow GRAVY to integrate into applications and job scheduler for data placement control. Besides local access, GRAVY currently supports three protocols: FTP [5], HTTP [4], and Web-Services. The implementation of FTP access is based on [18]. The protocol Web-Services is deployed using WSRF framework implemented in GT4 [9].

Remote Side. At the remote side, supporting a variety of access protocols allows GRAVY to support a large number of existing file systems. Although GridFTP has been promoted as the standard protocol for data movement in the Grid, there is a large number of existing file systems supporting other protocols.

From file-system-provider's point of view, remote file system is simply a storage system abstracted into directories and files and supported by an access protocol (e.g., FTP, GridFTP, HTTP) or a file server in other words. In order to make a file system interoperable with others, he/she needs to develop connectors between protocols supported by this system to all existent protocols in the Grid. This practice is not suitable for the continually evolutional Grid architecture as it requires adding a new protocol connector if a file system supported new protocol is integrated to the Grid. In GRAVY, this task is simplified by the *wrapper interfaces* that are in charge of creation and management of connection between GRAVY and remote file systems. *Wrapper interfaces* play the role of a bridge between GRAVY and remote file systems. They make GRAVY completely modular, it is easy to add support to GRAVY for a new protocol.

Besides the implementation of wrapper interfaces for local file system, we have used client-side libraries provided in GT4 [9] to implement *wrapper interfaces* for FTP and GridFTP protocol, and JSch[19] for SSH protocol. It is the role of file-system-provider to implement the wrapper interfaces in order to integrate a new protocol in GRAVY.

Authentication. Since each protocol has its own authentication mechanism, it enforces its own access control policy. This results the difficulty to establish the confidence across different protocols. Our solution is to adopt the Grid Security

Infrastructure (GSI) provided by Globus [20] because it avoids a centrally-managed security system and supports *single sign-on* for users of the Grid. For other protocols, authentication is performed through anonymous access.

5.2 Naming Management

In grid environment, management of data across multiple virtual organizations presents challenging problems for data naming. The Resource Namespace Service (RNS), a specification of the Grid File System working group of the Global Grid Forum [21], is proposed to provide a naming mechanism to link existing data sources. RNS proposes a three-tier naming architecture that consists of human interface names, logical reference names, and end-point references. Mapping from a human readable name to an actual data location can be realized in two levels of indirection. The first level is mapping human interface names directly to end-point references. The second level is realized by mapping human interface names to logical reference names (that may not be very readable by humans), which in turn map to end-point references.

In GRAVY, we applied the first level of indirection for the naming management. The `GridFileSystem` interface is responsible for decoupling logical view of the data from its physical location. This interface represents the virtual global file system with hierarchical organization of virtual directories where leaves in this tree correspond to physical data locations on remote file system. Users can create their own logical view of grid data where a logical directory may not necessarily correspond to the physical directory. Different users have a different logical view if they have different rights on data resources. The `GridFileSystem` instance is specified using a configuration file written in XML and is initialized at the runtime.

5.3 File Access and File Transfer

GridFile - Virtual File Interface. The fundamental requirement for virtual file systems used in the Grid is that all these file operations in different protocols must be made completely transparent to users. Accessing local file system for listing files, changing directories, etc. should be no different to accessing any remote file system with any access protocol. Transfer operations (e.g., `copy`, `move`) must be as applicable to local files as they are to data hosted on remote file systems. With these concerns in mind, we design the `GridFile` as virtual file object that provides the protocol-independent interface for file access and file transfer in virtual file system. This uniform interface, which provides a set of generic file operations should keep user shielded from protocol peculiarities.

Access Manager. The *access manager* is responsible for carrying out the access requests and returns the result to the virtual layer. The *access manager* translates these requests into specific protocol supported by the remote file system and accomplishes it by interacting with the *wrapper interfaces*.

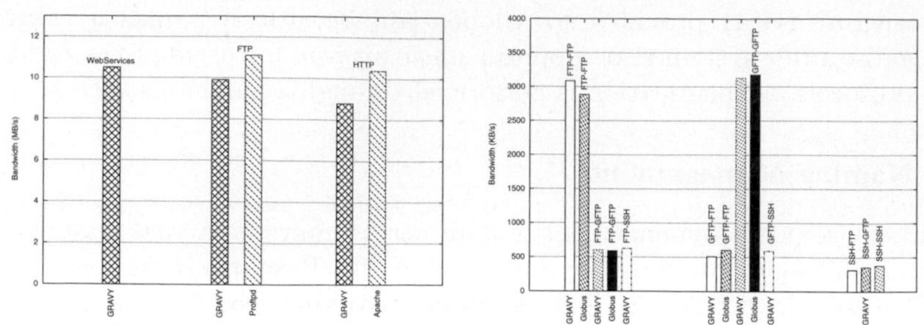

Fig. 3. Server side results (left), Remote side results (right)

Transfer Manager. The *transfer manager* takes care of transferring files between remote file systems. Transfer requests forwarded from *FileActionQueue* contain the information required for performing file transfers (e.g., protocol name, source and destination address, file name). The *transfer manager* uses *"the first-come, first-served"* strategy to execute these requests. It initiates a third-party transfers between remote file systems that use the same protocol. In another case, it opens two connections, one from the source and one to the destination file system for file transfers.

6 Experimental Results

GRAVY's latest version runs on any platform that supports the Java VM 5.0. Firstly, we perform a series of data transfers to test the GRAVY's feature of supporting multiple protocols. Secondly, in order to evaluate the processing efficiency and performance of our prototype, we perform a set of concurrent file transfers and use the modified Andrew benchmark [22] that is the well-known benchmark to test the performance of a distributed file system. The benchmark consists of five phases: (i) create directories, (ii) copy files into the directories, (iii) list file attributes, (iv) scan the files and (v) compile the files.

The experiments are performed on four Pentium 4 3.2 GHz machines with 512 MB of RAM, each running Linux with kernel 2.4.x. They are directly connected to 100 Mbps network adapter.

6.1 Support for Multiple Protocols

We perform file transfers at both server side and remote side in different protocols. The experimental set up is shown in Fig. 2. "Server side" means that the transfers are occurred between client and GRAVY. "Remote side" means that the transfers are launched by GRAVY to move data between remote file systems. At the server side, we compare the bandwidth delivered to client by GRAVY to that delivered by native implementation of each protocococol. At the remote side, we observe the bandwidth obtained for each change of protocol at remote file systems.

Server Side. In the first sets of experiments, our goal is to illustrate that the bandwidth delivered by GRAVY at the server side is very similar to that of the native server. The client asks GRAVY for transferring a file of 50MB in FTP, HTTP and Web-Services respectively. Then we repeat the above transfer using native protocol server (i.e., ProFTP for FTP and Apache for HTTP) to evaluate the bandwidth delivered by GRAVY. The results in Fig. 3(a) show that the bandwidth delivered by GRAVY is just a little lower than the one of the native servers.

Remote Side. We perform file transfers of of 10MBs from file server A to file server B (Fig. 2) using different protocols. The transfers in GridFTP and FTP are repeated with `globus-url-copy` command-line utility supplied with Globus Toolkit to compare with the bandwidth delivered by GRAVY. The results in Fig. 3(b) are averaged of 10 file transfers. We observe that the bandwidth varies a lot across each change of protocol at the remote file system. We get better bandwidths for the transfers using the same protocol. The only exception is the transfers in SSH protocol, the reason is that this protocol doesn't support third-party transfers like FTP or GridFTP. We note that the bandwidth of GRAVY for transfers in FTP and GridFTP is very similar to that of the `globus-url-copy` tool.

6.2 Performance

Many Concurrent File Transfers. In order to test the stability and processing efficiency of GRAVY, we write a client program using GRAVY to launch several concurrent processes reading a remote file into a buffer and writing the data out to a local file. The tests were done with files of 10MB. The result as the transferred KB per second depending on the number of concurrently connecting clients is shown in Fig. 4. Each value is an average of 5 tests. It shows that GRAVY has a problem with many concurrent requests. It is predictable that GRAVY achieves high performance for low numbers of connecting clients. For increasing number of concurrent clients, its performance decreases smoothly but it remains relatively stable.

Andrew Benchmark Results. We use the modified Andrew benchmark to compare GRAVY's performance to the one of Linux 2.4.x local file system and NFS v3. For the NFS measurements, we run the benchmark on a NFS client accessing a single NFS server. For the GRAVY measurements, we implemented a Java program that performs a pattern of file system accesses equivalent to the one of the Andrew benchmark because the current prototype implementation of GRAVY only provides Java interfaces to the file system. We repeat the execution of our Andrew-like Java program on GRAVY with three different configurations. Concretely, the directory on which we run the benchmark is mounted to a different remote file system for each execution. The remote file system is accessible in GridFTP, FTP and SSH protocol respectively. Files used during compilation phase are stored locally for the remote accesses on these remote file systems. The directory that we use as input to the benchmark contains 15 directories and 96 C sources and headers files for a total size of 511KBs. Table 1 shows the results of running the Andrew benchmark on Linux 2.4.x local file system, NFS and GRAVY.

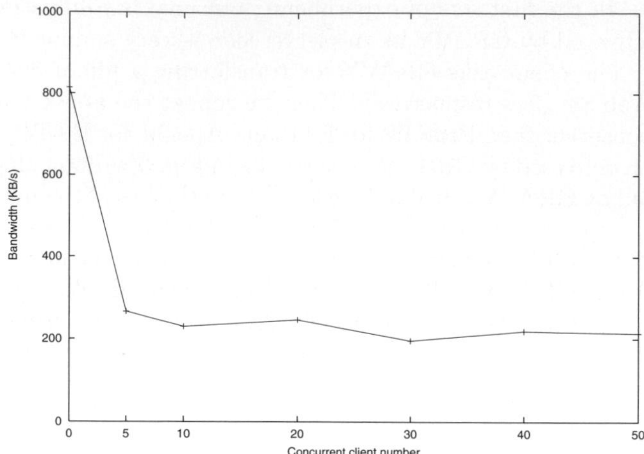

Fig. 4. Processing performance of GRAVY depending on the number of clients concurrently transferring files

Table 1. The Andrew benchmark results on Linux 2.4.x local file system, NFS and GRAVY. Each table entry is an average elapsed time in milliseconds of five runs of the benchmark. The rightmost column shows the average elapsed time of the benchmark runs on GRAVY with three different configurations.

			GRAVY			
Phase	**Local**	**NFS**	**GridFTP**	**FTP**	**SSH**	**Average**
Create directories	8.04	361.66	96128.00	4172.20	17277.60	39192.60
Copy files	93.32	3293.31	194150.60	18635.40	100861.80	104549.27
List files	237.48	2856.21	50848.00	4397.00	39008.20	31417.73
Scan files	298.43	3466.46	17142428.80	15837.40	165160.80	117475.67
Compile	3773.75	4552.05	4015.20	3985.60	4038.60	4013.13
Total	4411.03	14529.68	516570.60	47027.60	326347.00	296648.40

As expected, the local file system has the best performance on all five phases because it performs no network communication. The benchmark results on GRAVY have a high variance for each configuration. We achieve better performance with FTP configuration, followed by SSH and GridFTP configuration respectively. In the compilation phase, all file systems achieve a very similar performance because the performance of this phase is primarily limited by the speed of the CPU. For the other phases, GRAVY is slower than NFS due to the time needed for the authentication and the resolution between logical names and physical data locations.

7 Conclusion

In this paper, we have introduced GRAVY, a grid-enabled virtual file system, which enables the interoperability between heterogeneous file systems in the

Grid. We have pointed out the current challenges for the data access in the Grid and how GRAVY can provide solutions to them. GRAVY integrates underlying heterogeneous file systems into a unified location-transparent file system of the Grid. This virtual file system provides to applications and users a uniform global view and a uniform access through standards APIs and interfaces.

Our approach is validated by a prototype implemented in Java. This prototype shows that the way users access data is simplified and that data transfers between heterogeneous file systems can be automated. This feature allows GRAVY to integrate with high-level scheduler for handling data transfer jobs.

In the future, GRAVY will be enhanced and evolved. We will investigate Peer-To-Peer approach to decentralize GRAVY network in order to improve processing efficiency while ensuring the interoperability between file systems.

Acknowledgments. The authors would like to acknowledge United Devices (Europe) for their support in funding this research as part of the ANVAR project and Hélène Huard, Lei Yu of Ecole Centrale Paris for the precious discussions and their highly valuable comments.

References

1. Cappello, F., Djilali, S., Fedak, G., Hérault, T., Magniette, F., Néri, V., Lodygensky, O.: Computing on large-scale distributed systems: Xtremweb architecture, programming models, security, tests and convergence with grid. Future Generation Computer System **21**(3) (2005) 417–437
2. Foster, I., Kesselman, C., Tuecke, S.: The Anatomy of the Grid: Enabling Scalable Virtual Organizations. The International Journal of High Performance Computing Applications **15**(3) (2001) 200–222
3. Allcock, B., Bester, J., Bresnahan, J., Chervenak, A.L., Foster, I., Kesselman, C., Meder, S., Nefedova, V., Quesnel, D., Tuecke, S.: Data Management and Transfer in High Performance Computational Grid Environments. Parallel Computing Journal **28**(5) (May 2002) 749–771
4. Fielding, R., Irvine, U., Gettys, J., Mogul, J., Frystyk, H., Berners-Lee, T.: RFC-2068: Hypertext Transfer Protocol - HTTP/1.1 (1997) `http://www.w3.org/Protocols/rfc2068/rfc2068.`
5. Postel, J., Reynolds, J.: RFC-959: File Transfer Protocol `http://www.w3.org/Protocols/rfc959/.`
6. Ylonen, T., Lonvick, C.: RFC-4251: The Secure Shell (SSH) Protocol `http://www.ietf.org/ rfc/rfc4251.txt.`
7. Globus Project: `http://www.globus.org.`
8. Chervenak, A., Foster, I., Kesselman, C., Salisbury, C., Tuecke, S.: The Data Grid: Towards an Architecture for the Distributed Management and Analysis of Large Scientific Datasets. Journal of Network and Computer Applications **23** (1999) 187–200
9. Foster, I.: Globus Toolkit Version 4: Software for Service-Oriented Systems. In: IFIP International Conference on Network and Parallel Computing. Volume 3779 of Lecture Notes in Computer Science., Springer-Verlag (2005) 2–13

10. Antonioletti, M., Atkinson, M., Baxter, R., Borley, A., Hong, N.P.C., Collins, B., Hardman, N., Hume, A., Knox, A., Jackson, M., Krause, A., Laws, S., Magowan, J., Paton, N.W., Pearson, D., Sugden, T., Watson, P., Westhead, M.: The Design and Implementation of Grid Database Services in OGSA-DAI. Concurrency and Computation: Practice and Experience **17**(2-4) (February 2005) 357–376
11. White, B.S., Walker, M., Humphrey, M., Grimshaw, A.: LegionFS: A Secure and Scalable File System Supporting Cross-Domain High-Performance Applications. In: Proceedings of the IEEE/ACM Supercomputing Conference (SC2001), Denver, Colorado, USA (November 2001) 59–59
12. Fielding, R., Gettys, J., Mogul, J., Frystyk, H., Berners-Lee, T.: Enabling Grids for E-sciencE (EGEE) (2006) `http://www.eu-egee.org`.
13. Kunszt, P., Badino, P.: EGEE gLite User's Guide - Overview of gLite Data Management. Technical report egee-tech-570643-v1.0, CERN, Geneva, Switzerland (2005)
14. GGF Grid File System working group (gfs-wg): `https://forge.gridforum.org/projects/gfs-wg`.
15. GGF Grid File System working group (gfs-wg): The GGF Grid File System architecture workbook (January 2006) `http://www.ggf.org/documents/GFD.61.pdf`.
16. Wei, B., Fedak, G., Cappello, F.: Collaborative Data Distribution with BitTorrent for Computational Desktop Grids. In: ISPDC '05: Proceedings of the The 4th International Symposium on Parallel and Distributed Computing (ISPDC'05), Washington, DC, USA, IEEE Computer Society (2005) 250–257
17. Wei, B., Fedak, G., Cappello, F.: Scheduling Independent Tasks Sharing Large Data Distributed with BitTorrent. In: Proceedings of Grid Computing, 2005. The 6th IEEE/ACM International Workshop on. (2005)
18. Bhattacharyya, R.: Java FTP server `http://www.myjavaserver.com/~ranab/ftp`.
19. JSCH - Java Secure Channel: `http://www.jcraft.com/jsch`.
20. Foster, I., Kesselman, C., Tsudik, G., Tuecke, S.: A Security Architecture for Computational Grids. In: Proceedings of the 5th ACM Conference on Computer and Communications Security, San Francisco, California, USA, ACM Press (November 2-5 1998) 83–92
21. Pereira, M., Tatebe, O., Luan, L., Anderson, T.: Resource Namespace Service specification (May 2006) `http://www.ggf.org/GGF17/materials/272/Resource_Namespace_Service_Refactored.pdf`.
22. Howard, J., Kazar, M., Menees, S., Nichols, D., Satyanarayanan, M., Sidebotham, R., West, M.: Scale and Performance in a Distributed File System. ACM Transactions on Computer Systems **6**(1) (February 1998) 51–81

A Framework for Dynamic Deployment of Scientific Applications Based on WSRF

Lei Yu and Frédéric Magoulès

Applied Mathematics and Systems Laboratory, Ecole Centrale Paris
Grande Voie des Vignes, 92295 Châtenay-Malabry Cedex, France
lei.yu@ecp.fr, frederic.magoules@hotmail.com

Abstract. One of the challenges of Grid computing is the integration of legacy scientific applications. The Web Services Architecture (WSA) is an ideal technology to integrate legacy applications into the grid environment. Web Services Resource Framework (WSRF) extends Web Services and makes them stateful. Based on WSRF, we implement a framework which utilizes WSRF resource to submit applications and to monitor execution status. We deploy only one Factory Service to create the resources and one Grid Service as the uniform interface for all the applications in each computing resource. We can dynamically deploy some legacy applications in the Grid or remove these applications without stopping the execution of entire system. Moreover, we present an implementation of one meta-scheduler which integrates Grid resources in complex Grid environment.

Keywords: WSRF, Dynamic Deployment, Application Integration,Web services, Meta-Scheduler.

1 Introduction

A Grid is an Internet-connected computing environment where computing and data resources are geographically distributed in different administrative domains, often with separate policies for security and resource use. Because of the role played by Grid technologies in large scale scientific collaborations, grid architectures have grown significantly in recent years. Consequently, many scientific communities are feeling a growing need to integrate their legacy applications into grid environment [1]. Web services are the next stage of evolution for Grid Computing. In a few words Web services are services that can be dynamically discovered and orchestrated, using messaging on the network. The Web Services Architecture (WSA) is an ideal technology to integrate legacy applications into the grid environment [2]. Web Services Resource Framework (WSRF) extends Web Services and makes Web services stateful [3].

The primary goal of our research is to implement a framework for dynamic deployment of scientific applications where the end-users can:

C. Cérin and K.-C. Li (Eds.): GPC 2007, LNCS 4459, pp. 579–589, 2007.

– Apply any legacy code as WSRF-compliant service when they create Grid applications.
– Deploy dynamically any scientific application into the Grid environment.
– Utilize a uniform interface to interact with any deployed application.

In our framework, the scientific applications are described as job description files in XML format [4]. We utilize the WSRF resource [3] to contact a local job manager through Globus [5] to submit the legacy computational job. The factory service manages all these job descriptions and creates the resource according to the client request. The instance service supplies a uniform interface for all applications. This interface is used to submit and to monitor the applications. Our framework has four primary components:

– A *Factory service* that manages all the application descriptions and returns a list of applications to the client interested. It also has a mechanism to monitor the creation, deletion, and modification of the application description. Thus we can dynamically put some applications available or unavailable on the Grid. According to the selected application by the client, the *Factory service* creates a resource and returns an endpoint reference composed of the *Grid service* and the recently created resource to the client;
– A *Grid service* that provides a uniform interface for the Client to invoke the applications in the computing resource and to monitor the status of application executions;
– An *AdminTool* which can interact with *Factory service* in a secure way. The *AdminTool* has a graphic interface and can be used to add, delete and modify the application descriptions by the local administrator;
– A *Grid Scheduler* is a meta-scheduler in our framework. The *Grid Scheduler* manages and monitors all available computing resources in a VO [6]. According to the request of the client, it interacts with *Factory service* in each computing resource to get the applications list, collects the dynamic and static information of computing resources to make a scheduling decision, invokes the *Factory service* in the computing resource to create a WSRF resource for the user, submits applications and monitors the execution status.

In each available computing resource, only one *Factory service* and one *Grid service* run persistently. No other instance service is created. So the creation and the management of application instance are standard and simple.

In this paper, our primary focus is the implementation of *Grid service*, *Factory service* and *Grid Scheduler*. The rest of this paper is as follows. In Section 2 we discuss related work. In Section 3 the model architecture and the implementation are described. In Section 4 the evaluation of the implementation is presented. In Section 5 we conclude with a brief discussion of the future research.

2 Related Work

There are several research efforts aiming at automating the transformation of legacy code into a Grid service. Most of these solutions are based on the general framework to transform legacy applications into Web services outlined in [2], and use Java wrapping in order to generate stubs automatically. One example could be found in [7], where the authors describe a semi-automatic conversion of legacy C code into Java using JNI (Java Native Interface) [8].

Compared to Java wrapping, some solutions [1],[8],[9] are based on a different principle. They offer a front-end Grid service layer that communicates with the client in order to pass input and output parameters, and contacts a local job manager to submit the legacy computational job. The Grid service is defined by OGSA [10] which supports, via standard interfaces and conventions, the creation, termination, management, and invocation of stateful and transient services as named and managed entities with dynamic and managed lifetime. To deploy a legacy application as a Grid service there is no need for the source code. The user only has to describe the legacy parameters in a pre-defined file (description) and to transfer that file to a Factory service. But, the interface by which we can interact with the deployed applications is not uniform. Because the Factory needs a description of the service to create an instance of application. The different description providers could define various service port-types in the descriptions. Therefore the interface of application instance varies according to different service port-types. The other problem is the quantity of service instances. The application is created and deployed as service instance. In this case, if we deploy a large quantity of needed applications in a computing resource, there will be too many service instances to be created. The management of these instances is truly a delicate job.

The GridLAB [11] project aims to provide application tools and middleware for Grid environments. It uses the Grid Application Toolkit (GAT) [12] which is a set of APIs that Grid application programmers can use for uniformly accessing numerous Grid Services and middleware. However, GAT does not address the problem of wrapping existing applications as Web Services [1].

3 Model Design and Implementation

The Globus Toolkit (GT) has been developed since the late 1990s to support the development of service-oriented distributed computing applications and infrastructures. The Web services-based GT4 is the latest release of GT, which provides significant improvements over previous releases in terms of robustness, performance, usability, documentation, standards compliance, and functionality [13]. The implementation of the framework is based on GT4, so before discussing the framework, we will introduce some basic concepts:

The resource approach. Giving Web services the ability to keep state information while still keeping them stateless seems to be a complex problem. Fortunately, GT4 has found a very simple solution: simply keep the Web service and the state information completely separate. Instead of putting the state in the Web service (thus making it stateful, which is generally regarded as a bad thing) we will keep it in a separate entity called a resource, which will store all the state information. Each resource will have a unique key, so whenever we want a stateful interaction with a Web service we simply have to instruct the Web service to use a particular resource [3].

GRAM. The GT4 Grid Resource Allocation and Management (GRAM) service addresses the issues of running a task on a computer, providing a Web services interface for initiating, monitoring, and managing the execution of arbitrary computations on remote computers [13].

MDS. The Globus Toolkits Monitoring and Discovery System (MDS) defines and implements mechanisms for service and resource discovery and monitoring in distributed environments [14].

3.1 The Model Architecture

Fig. 1(a) illustrates the architecture of the model. A *Grid Resource* is a computing resource on which GT4 has been installed and on which the *Factory service* and *Grid service* have been run persistently. We have one *Grid Scheduler* running as meta-scheduler of the VO. The meta-scheduler is the Grid portal for clients and it manages all the *Grid Resources* in the VO. It interacts with the *Factory service* and *Grid service* to create resources, submit computational jobs and monitor the jobs status for clients.

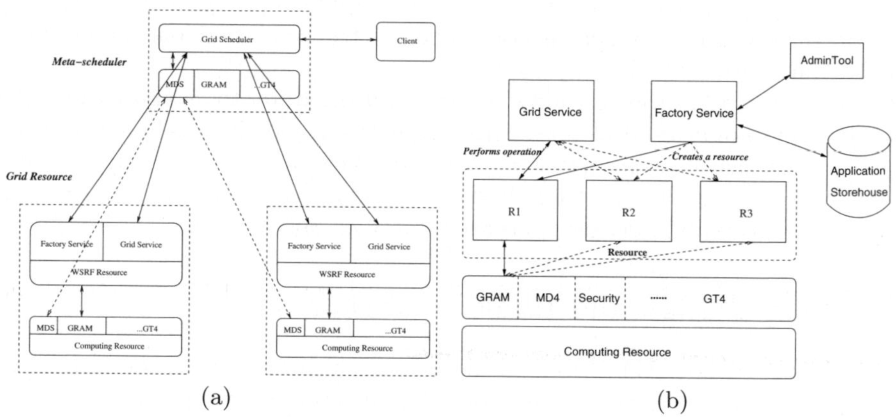

Fig. 1. (a) The Architecture of our Model; (b) The Architecture of Grid Resource

MDS can be configured in a hierarchical fashion with upper levels of the hierarchy aggregating information from the lower-level MDS (Index Services). The upper levels are identified as upstream resources in the hierarchy, and the lower levels are identified as downstream resources [15]. Thus from the local MDS, the *Grid Scheduler* can gather the dynamic and static information from each *Grid Resource* in the VO.

The architecture of *Grid Resource* is shown in Fig. 1(b). An application storehouse stores the application descriptions which support the Job Description Schema [16]. An *AdminTool* interacts with the *Factory service* to add, delete and modify application descriptions. According to the request of *Grid Scheduler*, the *Factory service* can create a resource and submit a computational job for the user. The resources use GRAM to really submit a job to the Computing Resource and subscribe to the Notification of job status [17] to monitor the job execution [3]. The information of application execution is stored inside the resource and, more specifically, in resource properties.

But how can the user set the arguments and stage files of the application? In the Job Description Schema, we have three elements : *argument*, *fileStageIn* and *fileStageOut*[16]. After a *Grid Resource* has been selected by the *Grid Scheduler*, the user specifies all the input parameter values (include *argument*, *fileStageIn* and *fileStageOut*) and sends a submission request to the *Grid Scheduler*. Then the *Grid Scheduler* sets these elements in the Job Description and invokes the operation *createResource* of *Factory service* with the Job Description as the parameter. The Factory service uses the Job Description to initialize the resource.

3.2 Service Implementation

Based on the GT4 and WSRF, we realize our *Grid Scheduler*, *Factory service* and *Grid service*. The PortType [18] of each Service is illustrated in Table 1.

Fig. 2 illustrates the sequence of an user job submission.

1. The user invokes the *openSession* operation of the *Grid Scheduler* to get a client number.
2. The user invokes the *findApplication* operation with client number and the requested application as parameters.
3. The *Grid Scheduler* searches in all the application lists. If it finds the requested application, a Boolean "true" is returned to the user.
4. The user gets "true", so it can invoke the *scheduler* operation in order to submit the application.
5. The *Grid Scheduler* invokes *createResource* of the *Factory Service* to create a resource for the user.
6. After having created the resource, the *Grid Scheduler* submits the job to *Grid Service*
7. The user uses *getJobStatus* to query the job status.
8. If the execution of application is finished, the user invokes *closeSession* to destroy the session.

In the *Grid Scheduler* and *Factory Service*, a mechanism is integrated to detect the modification of application descriptions. When the local administrator uses the *AdminTool* to add, delete and modify the application descriptions, the operations (*addApplication*, *modifyApplication* and *deleteApplication*) of the *Factory Service* are invoked. The *Factory Service* then updates the application list and modifies the job description files in the application storehouse. It sets also a signal to notify the *Grid Scheduler* the modification of the application list. The *Grid Scheduler* monitors the signal status. When it detects the change of signal status, it updates its application lists within a reasonable delay.

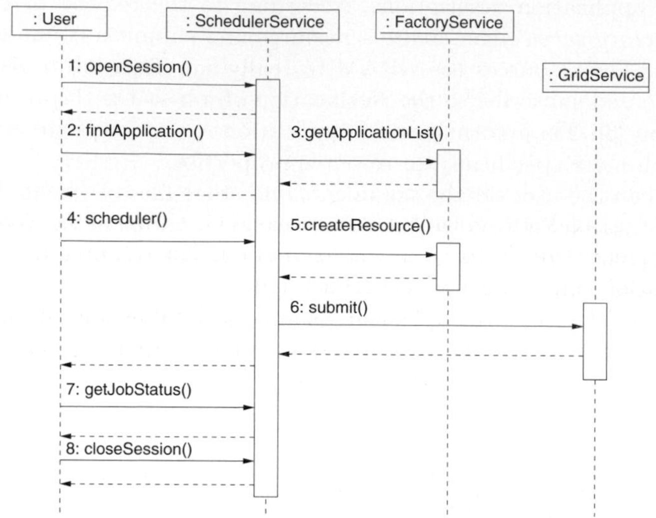

Fig. 2. The Sequence diagram for an user job submission

Table 1. The PortType of Services

The PortType of Grid Scheduler		
	PortType	Description
1	openSession	open a session for user
2	closeSession	close the user session
3	findApplication	search the application in the *Grid Resource*. If there are more than one available *Grid Resource*, we use MDS information to select the best resource for user
4	scheduler	submit the application to *Grid Factory*
5	getJobStatus	return the job execution status

The PortType of Factory Service		
	PortType	Description
1	getApplicationList	return a list to client
2	createResource	create resource for client
3	addApplication	add Job Description
4	modifyApplication	modify Job Description
5	deleteApplication	delete Job Description

The PortType of Grid Service		
	PortType	Description
1	submit	invoke operation *submit* of resource to submit the job to GRAM
2	stop	stop the job execution
3	getJobStatus	get job status from resource

3.3 MDS and Scheduling

As mentioned, we know that the Globus Monitoring and Discovery System (MDS) is a collection of Web services to monitor and discover the resources and services available in a grid. MDS gathers information about resources. This information includes : static information, such as the number of CPUs, clock speed, amount of physical memory, virtual memory, and available disk space, and dynamic information, such as the number of CPUs available, the number of jobs in the queue waiting to be executed, and current resource utilization [15]. The information can be queried via XPath [19].

In the *Grid Scheduler*, we implement a simple scheduling algorithm. When the *Grid Scheduler* finds that there are more than one available *Grid Resource* for the user, it compares the number of available CPUs of each *Grid Resource*. The *Grid Scheduler* selects the resource which has the most available CPUs. If the number of available CPUs is similar, the *Grid Scheduler* calculates the value of $Waitingjobs/TotalCPUs$ for each *Grid Resource*. $Waitingjobs$ is the number of jobs waiting in the local job queue, and $TotalCPUs$ is the number of CPUs on each *Grid Resource*. The resource which has the smallest value is selected. The scheduling algorithm more complex will be considered in the future.

3.4 Security

In any networked environment, security is a paramount concern. GSI is the GT4 component that addresses all security requirements and allows privacy, integrity, and replay protection for grid communication [20]. GT4 provides command-line tools to generate certificate requests that can be mailed out to the CA for verification and signing. Once signed, the CA returns the signed document to identify the entity for which the request was generated. Up to this point, the certificates for the Client and the Web Service container (host certificate) are obtained. As for how to associate Client certificate DNs to local user accounts, Grid map files are to serve, and Globus tools perform the mapping of DNs to user accounts by using the grid map file. Once the Client is authenticated by Web Service container, it can send request to these services.

4 Evaluation

The most important aspect for the job submission is the turn-around time. Turn-around time is the time from a job being accepted by the *Grid Scheduler* or *Factory Service* till the completion (i.e. the job has reached the done state). The turn-around time is measured in 2 cases:

- An application is added dynamically in a *Grid Resource*
- The *Factory Service* and *Grid Service* are used directly to submit a job without the *Grid Scheduler*

4.1 Dynamic Deployment Experiments

As discussed in Section 3, the application can be added dynamically in the system. Thus at first the performance of dynamic deployment is measured. The experimental setup is as follows. The *Factory Service* and *Grid Service* are deployed and tested at two Condor clusters: a cluster named $C1$ with three servers, an other cluster named $C2$ with two servers. Each server has 2 Pentium 4 3.20GHz with 1 GB RAM. The *Grid Scheduler* is installed in a PC powered by Pentium 4 3.00GHz with 512 MB RAM. All the machines are connected by 100 Mb Ethernet. GT 4 is installed in the central manager of Condor pool, and Scheduler Adapters are configured to support the job submission into the Condor pool.

From a laptop, the user submits 30 jobs to the *Grid Scheduler* and the interval of submission is 30 seconds. In the user's opinion, a job is a sequence of *openSession*, *findApplication*, *scheduler*, *getJobStatus* and *closeSession*. At the beginning, the application which the user needs is deployed on $C1$. The application is a simple C program. It waits 5 minutes and then returns. In order to execute the application in the standard universe, *condor_compile* must be used to relink the application with the Condor libraries [21]. After the user has submitted 8 jobs, the local administrator of $C2$ runs *AdminTool* to add the application in $C2$. For comparisons, the user submits 30 jobs once again. The difference with the first time is there is not a dynamic deployment.

Fig. 3(a) shows that the turn-around time of followed jobs dropped down when the application is added in $C2$ (after eighth job). Because the *Grid Scheduler* detects the modification of applications list in $C2$ and it can submit the user job to $C2$. Thus the ninth job does not wait to be submitted to $C1$, instead it is submitted to $C2$ and is executed immediately. Since the system MDS takes time to gather resource information, the *Grid Scheduler* uses the information a little delayed to schedule the jobs. When the fifteenth job is submitted, the *Grid Scheduler* submits continually the job to $C2$, because the *Grid Scheduler* thinks that there are still some free CPUs in $C2$. This is the reason why the turn-around time of the fifteenth job is a little longer. After the submission of the fifteenth job, the turn-around time of followed jobs in the case of dynamic deployment is much more dropped than in the case of the absence of dynamic deployment because of the distribution of job on two clusters.

4.2 Grid Resource Experiments

The *Grid Resource* is the Computing Resource where the *Factory Service* and *Grid Service*, called *User Service*, are deployed. Globus provides a standard interface for communicating with Condor using a standard message format. Similarly the *User Service* is deployed on Globus to provide a uniform interface for the job submission. Jobs are submitted separately to the *User Service* and Globus in order to evaluate the performance of the *User Service*.

In these experiments, the application used is a simple MPI program (in C). It calculates parallel the value of Pi using numerical integration in two machines. In order to execute the application in the MPI universe in Condor, the program to be submitted for execution under Condor will be compiled using *mpicc* [22].

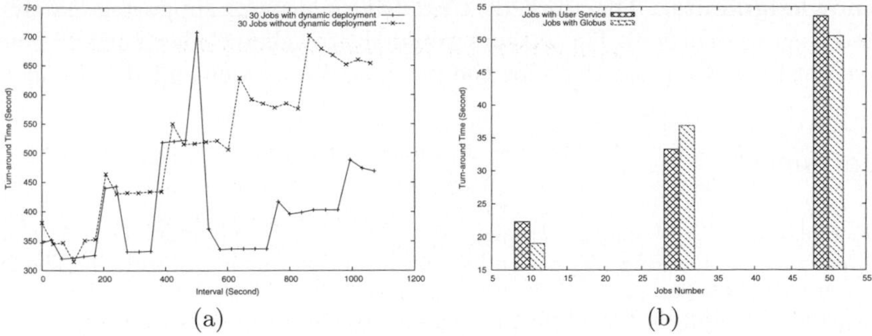

Fig. 3. (a) The performance of submission with meta-scheduler; (b) The comparison of submission among the User Service (Factory Service and Grid Service) and Globus

All the experiments are done on $C2$. In order to execute parallel applications, MPICH (version 1.2.4) [23] is installed on each server of $C2$. From a laptop, a program submits separately 10, 30 and 50 jobs to local *User Service* with interval of submission of 5 seconds. Then the Globus command "$globusrun-ws$" is used to submit jobs. The command submits also 10, 30 and 50 jobs with the same interval.

Fig. 3(b) shows the result. It is shown that the average turn-around time of User Service is a little longer than the time of "$globusrun-ws$", except the case of 30 jobs. The performances of the two infrastructures are very close.

5 Conclusion and Future Work

The framework for dynamic deployment of scientific applications into grid environment has been described. The framework addresses dynamic applications deployment. The local administrator can dynamically put some applications available or unavailable on the *Grid Resource* without stopping the execution of the Globus Toolkit Java Web Services container. A *Grid Scheduler* has been integrated in the framework, which can realize simple job scheduling, select the best *Grid Resource* to submit jobs for the users. The performance of the framework has been evaluated by some experiments. All the components in the framework are realized in the standard of Web Service, so the other meta-schedulers or clients can interact with the components in a standard way.

We plan to complete the *Grid Scheduler* to realize more complex scheduling algorithm and to integrate the workflow. The *Grid Scheduler* is a Web Service. The interaction between the *Grid Scheduler* or between a *Grid Scheduler* and the other meta-scheduler can be realized in the standard of Web service. So we would like to create a hierarchy of meta-scheduler to realize a distributed scheduling.

The rescheduling mechanism in the *Grid Scheduler* should be implemented in the future work. The mechanism ensures the execution of jobs, even if requested applications in some containers are removed dynamically or a container in the Grid breaks down.

Acknowledgments. The work of *Grid Scheduler* was supported partly by United Devices (Europe). The authors would like to acknowledge Thi-Mai-Huong Nguyen of Ecole Centrale Paris for the precious discussions and the comments.

References

1. Kandaswamy, G., Fang, L., Huang, Y., Shirasuna, S., Gannon, D.: A generic framework for building services and scientific workflows for the grid. In: The 2005 ACM/IEEE Conference on SuperComputing. (2005)
2. Kuebler, D., Eibach, W.: Adapting legacy applications as web services. IBM DeveloperWorks (2002) `http://www-128.ibm.com/developerworks/library/ws-legacy/`.
3. Sotomayor, B.: The globus toolkit 4 programmer's tutorial
4. Silva, V.: Quick start to a gt4 remote execution client (2006) `http://www-128.ibm.com/developerworks/grid/library/gr-wsgram/`.
5. Globus Team: Globus toolkit `http://www.globus.org`.
6. Foster, I., Kesselman, C., Tuecke, S.: The anatomy of the grid: Enabling scalable virtual organizations. International Journal of High Performance Computing Applications **15**(3) (2001) 200–222
7. Huang, Y., Taylor, I., Walker, D., Davies, R.: Wrapping legacy codes for grid-based applications. In: Parallel and Distributed Processing Symposium, 2003. Proceedings. International. (22-26 April)
8. Kacsuk, P., Goyeneche, A., Delaitre, T., Kiss, T., Farkas, Z., Boczko, T.: High-level grid application environment to use legacy codes as ogsa grid services. In: Grid Computing, 2004. Proceedings. Fifth IEEE/ACM International Workshop. 428–435
9. Gannon, D., Ananthakrishnan, R., Krishnan, S., Govindaraju, M., Ramakrishnan, L., Slominski, A.: Grid web services and application factories. Computing: Making the Global Infrastructure a Reality. Fox, Berman and Hey, eds.Wiley (2003)
10. Foster, I., Kesselman, C., Nick, J., Tuecke, S.: The physiology of the grid: An open grid services architecture for distributed systems integration (2002)
11. Gridlab: Gridlab products and technologies (2005) `http://www.gridlab.org/about.html`.
12. Gridlab: Grid(lab) grid application toolkit (2004) `http://www.gridlab.org/WorkPackages/wp-1`.
13. Foster, I.: Globus toolkit version 4: Software for service-oriented systems. In: International Conference on Network and Parallel Computing (IFIP). Volume 3779., LNCS Springer-Verlag (2005) 2–13
14. Schopf, J.M., D'Arcy, M., Miller, N., Pearlman, L., Foster, I., Kesselman, C.: Monitoring and discovery in a web services framework:functionality and performance of the globus toolkit's mds4. Technical report, Preprint ANL/MCS-P1248-0405, Argonne National Laboratory, Argonne, IL (2005)
15. Mausolf, J.: Grid in action: Monitor and discover grid services in an soa/web services environment (2005) `http://www-128.ibm.com/developerworks/grid/library/gr-gt4mds/index.html`.
16. Globus Team: Gt 4.0 ws gram: Job description schema doc, `http://www.globus.org/toolkit/docs/4.0/execution/wsgram/schemas/gram_job_description.html`.

17. Globus Team: Submitting a job in java using ws gram http://www.globus.org/toolkit/docs/4.0/execution/wsgram/WS_GRAM_Java_Scenarios.html.
18. W3C: Web services description language (wsdl) 1.1 http://www.w3.org/TR/wsdlTR/wsdl.
19. W3C: Xml path language (xpath) version 1.0 (1999) http://www.w3.org/TR/xpath.
20. Sundaram, B.: Introducing gt4 security (2005) http://www-128.ibm.com/developerworks/grid/library/gr-gsi4intro/.
21. Condor Team: Condor user's manual http://www.cs.wisc.edu/condor/manual/v6.8/2_4Road_map_Running.html.
22. Condor Team: Parallel Applications (Including MPI Applications) http://www.cs.wisc.edu/condor/manual/v6.8/2_10Parallel_Applications.html.
23. Argonne National Laboratory: Getting the MPICH implementation http://www-unix.mcs.anl.gov/mpi/mpich1/download.html.

Group-Based Self-organization Grid Architecture

Jaime Lloret[1], Miguel Garcia[2], Fernando Boronat[3], and Jesus Tomas[4]

Communications Department, Polytechnic University of Valencia
Camino Vera s/n, 46022 Valencia, Spain
{jlloret,fboronat,jtomas}@dcom.upv.es, migarpi@teleco.upv.es

Abstract. Many grid architectures have been developed since the first proto-grid systems in the early 70's, but there are not so many based on groups using an efficient node neighbor selection. This paper proposes a grid architecture based on groups. The architecture organizes logical connections between nodes from different groups of nodes allowing sharing resources, data or computing time between groups. Connections are used to find and share available resources from other groups and they are established based on node's available capacity. Suitable nodes have higher roles in the architecture and their function is to organize connections based on a node selection process. Nodes' logical connections topology changes depending on some dynamic parameters. The architecture is scalable and fault-tolerant. We describe the protocol, its management and real measurements. It could be used as an intergrid protocol.

Keywords: Grid architecture, group-based logical network, neighbor selection, peer-to-peer network, intergrid protocol.

1 Introduction

Grid computing provides always-online computer services to users. It reduces significantly computation time on complex problems. A grid is a system that is concerned with the integration, virtualization and management of services and resources in a distributed and heterogeneous environment. It supports collections of users and resources across traditional administrative and organizational domains that are able to manage and run some processes to carry out an objective [1]. It enables the integrated and collaborative use of high-end computers, networks, databases and scientific instruments, owned and managed by multiple organizations, giving coordinated resource-sharing and problem-solving capabilities to its users.

There are many projects around the world working on developing grids for different purposes at different scales from the academic research communities, from the industry and from government-sponsored infrastructure projects. Grid computing was primarily used to support scientific research into large problems concerning weather, astronomy, and medicine, but the number of potential applications seems to grow every year, because of the increasing corporate interest in turning the technology into business. New applications are based on protocols developed for specific purposes such as the parallel filesystem [2], data storage systems [3], data replication and retrieval systems [4] and data processing systems [5].

The paper is structured as follows. Section 2 examines some Grids architectures, works related with our proposal such as neighbor selection, hierarchical architectures

C. Cérin and K.-C. Li (Eds.): GPC 2007, LNCS 4459, pp. 590 – 602, 2007.

and architectures based on groups, and explains our motivation. There is a description of our architecture proposal in section 3. Analytical model for some types of topologies of nodes used in our architecture and our analysis is explained in section 4. The protocol operation, recovery algorithms and designed messages are shown in section 5. Section 6 shows the performance operation when the architecture is running. Finally, section 7 gives our conclusions and future works.

2 Previous Works and Motivation

In this section we will relate several known grids architectures, we will describe several strategies to establish connections between nodes and, finally, we will explain several works where nodes are divided into groups. It will give the lecturer the state of the art related with our architecture, because it establishes connections between the more suitable nodes from different groups.

Condor Project was born to take advantage of the idle time of the computers in the network. It is a high-throughput distributed batch computing system. Condor is based on a centralized architecture where users submit their jobs, and it chooses when and where to run them based upon a policy, monitors their progress, and finally informs the user upon completion. The NorduGrid project's primary goal is to meet the requirements of production tasks of LHC (Large Hydron Collider) experiments. The NorduGrid topology is decentralized, avoiding a single point of failure. It is a lightweight, non-invasive and dynamic one, while robust and scalable, capable of meeting most challenging tasks of High Energy Physics. These infrastructures use a software platform to organize and run the jobs. Although Globus Toolkit™ is one of the most used, there are others such as Netsolve, Nimrod and AliEn. These production environments implement virtual topologies in distributed ways were nodes establish connections, to become neighbors, as needed to coordinate resources and services.

Throughout the years different types of strategies for neighbors' selection have been developed. Simon et al., in [6], proposed a genetic-algorithm-based neighbor-selection strategy for hybrid peer-to-peer networks, which enhances the decision process performed at the tracker for transfer coordination increasing content availability to the clients from their immediate neighbors. There are proposals where nodes' connections are based on the underlying network, such as Plethora [7] or on their geographic location such as the one described by K. Liu et al. in [8]. Others systems, such as the one presented by X. Zhichen in [9], locate nodes in the topology taking into account that are possibly close to a given node, and then perform RTT measurements to identify the actual closest node.

There are several works in the literature where nodes are divided into groups and connections are established between nodes from different groups, but all of them are developed to solve specific issues. To the extent of our knowledge, there is not any previous interconnection system to structure connections between groups of nodes like the one that will be presented in this paper. A. Wierzbicki et al. presented Rhubarb [10]. It organizes nodes in a virtual network, allowing connections across firewalls/NAT, and efficient broadcasting. The system uses a proxy coordinator. When a node from outside the network wishes to communicate with a node that is inside, it sends a connection request to the proxy coordinator, who forwards the request to the node inside the network. Rhubarb uses a three-level hierarchy of groups, may be sufficient to support a million nodes, but when there are several millions of nodes in the network it could not be enough, so it suffers from scalability problems. On the other hand, all nodes need to know the IP of the proxy coordinator nodes to establish connections with nodes from other virtual networks. Z. Xiang et al. presented a Peer-to-Peer Based Multimedia Distribution Service [11]. It proposes a topology-aware overlay in which nearby peers self-organize into application groups. End hosts within the same group have similar network conditions and can easily collaborate with each other to achieve QoS awareness. When a node in this architecture wants to communicate with a node from other group, the information is routed through several groups until it arrives to the destination. There are some hierarchical architectures were nodes are structured hierarchically and parts of the tree are grouped into groups such as the one presented by Liu Hongjun et al. in [12]. The information has to be routed through the hierarchy to achieve nodes from other groups, so all layers of the hierarchy could be overloaded in case of having many data to be transferred. On the other hand, in case of many groups, the hierarchical structure could become unstructured because there could be many connections establishments between nodes from different groups placed on different layers of the hierarchy.

Grids architectures could be deployed different according to the necessities of the final purpose. Let's suppose we need to organize the grid into groups in order to process parts of an application in parallel, but in certain moments, nodes from a group need some resources, data or computation time from other groups. All architectures previously shown don't solve that problem efficiently, because in the case of centralized architectures, such as Condor project, the server will have many logical connections at the same time to distribute jobs, so it will need many resources. On the other hand, there is a central point of failure and a bottleneck. In the case of fully distributed architectures, the control system use to be very difficult to be implemented and it needs much time to process tasks because of the time needed to reach far nodes. It decreases the performance of the whole system. To address this problem, we propose an architecture based on groups where nodes work in their group as in a regular grid, but they can reach all other groups, if needed, in one hop, diminishing the time to reach resources, data or computing from other groups enhancing the performance of the whole system.

3 Architecture Outline

We propose to split the grid network in groups of nodes. Nodes can reach all nodes in their group to coordinate and sharing resources and services and some of them will have logical connections (from now we will call just connections) with nodes from other groups based on some parameters defined later. A node will collaborate with nodes from its group as a small network and when a node (or the group of nodes) needs data, resources or computing time from another group, one of them requests it to the other group. The reply is sent to the requesting node, and in case of data, it can share it acting as a cache for its group.

Nodes in the proposed architecture could be a regular node or could have one or several of the following roles (a node could run all them simultaneously, depending on its functionality in the group): (i) Distribution role node (DN): A DN will have a connection with one node (becoming adjacent) from each other groups as a hub-and-spoke. The number of connections to other groups can be limited by several parameters described later. Connections are used to send searches for resources, data or computing time between groups. (ii) Area controller role node (AC): ACs organize DNs in zones to have an scalable architecture. They are able to reach a GC in its group and to choose the best DN in their area. (iii) Group controller role node (GC): It could be one or several in each group, depending on the number of DNs in the group. GCs have connections with GCs from other groups. A GC has AC functionalities too, so it has connections with ACs from its group. Both ACs and GCs have DN functionalities. GC organizes nodes in its group and adjacencies between DNs from different groups. From now, we will not consider regular nodes because the proposed architecture works without these leaf nodes, but regular nodes will know how to reach a DN in its grid (it could be announced as a service in the grid protocol).

Figure 1 show a topology example. The network topology of each group could be different, but all nodes in the topology run the same application layer protocol.

When a node joins a group it acquires a unique node identifier (*nodeID*). The first node in a group will have *nodeID*=0x01, and it will assign *nodeIDs* sequentially to new ones. All nodes in a group have the same *groupID*. We define δ as the node promotion parameter. It depends on node's bandwidth and its *nodeID*. It is used to know which node is the best one to have higher role. Nodes with higher bandwidth and older (lower *nodeID*) are preferred to promote. Every β DNs, the DN with higher δ in the group will start AC role and it will create a new area. Every α ACs, the AC with higher δ will start GC role. α and β values depend on the number of nodes in the group and the network topology of the group and they will be discussed in the analytical model section (next section). We define λ as the node capacity. It determines the best node to have an adjacency with. It depends on node's bandwidth, its number of available connections, its maximum number of connections and its % of available load.

We have chosen Short Path First (SPF) algorithm to route information between GCs and between ACs using a two-level SPF-Based System such as the one described by some authors of this paper in [13]. It is fast and allows sending fast searches to find DN adjacencies, but it can be changed by other routing protocol depending on the networks' features. GCs route information using *groupID* parameter and ACs route information using *nodeID* parameter. Link cost (*C*) between nodes is based on node's capacity. The more the node's capacity is, the lower its cost is. Every GC or AC runs SPF algorithm locally and selects the best path to a destination node based on a metric. The metric is based on the number of hops to a destination and the link cost of those nodes involved in the path. Experiments given in [14] show that a database having 10^4 external updates from other GCs will consume 640 Kbytes of memory. Table 1 summarizes all parameters described. Expressions proposed in table 1 for δ, λ, *C* and Metric are based on proves and simulations used for Multimedia Networks [15]. We estimate they fit our architecture proposal requirements.

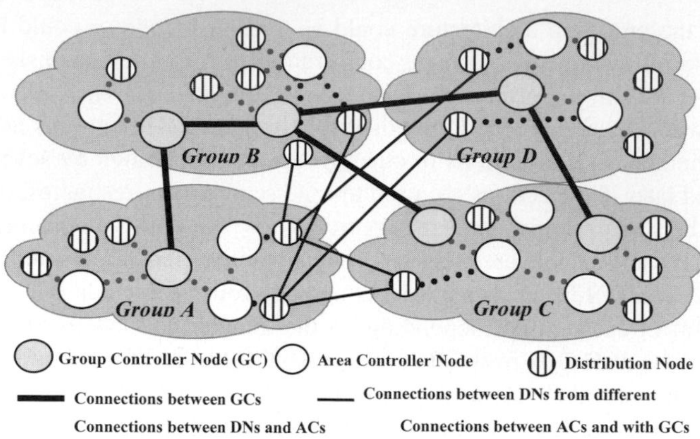

Fig. 1. Architecture organization

Table 1. Parameters summary

Description	Symbol	Expression
Node identifier	*nodeID*	-
Group identifier	*groupID*	-
Parameter to promote a new AC	β	-
Parameter to promote a new GC	α	-
Maximum number of Connections	*Max_Con*	-
Available number of Connections	*Available_Con*	-
Constants used to adjust the weigh of some parameters in the expressions	K_1, K_2, K_3, K_4	-
Node promotion parameter	δ	$\delta = (BW_{up} + BW_{down}) \cdot K_1 + (32 - \log_2(nodeID)) \cdot K_2$
Node capacity	λ	$\lambda = \frac{\text{int}\left[\frac{(BW_{up} + BW_{down})}{256} + 1\right] \cdot Available\_Con \cdot (100 - load) + K_3}{Max\_Con}$
Link cost	*C*	$C = \frac{K_4}{\lambda}$
Metric for node *j*	*Metric (j)*	$Metric(j) = \sum_{i=1}^{n} C_i$

4 Analytical Model and Analysis

In this section we are going to describe the architecture analytically in terms of group of nodes and we will suppose several types of logical topologies for all groups. It allows us to know how many connections will be in our proposal using each one of the logical topologies implemented to validate our model.

Given $G = (V, \lambda, E)$ a network of nodes, where V is a set of DNs (ACs and GCs are DNs too), λ is a set of capacities ($\lambda(i)$ is the i-DN capacity and $\lambda(i) \neq 0$ $\forall$ i-DN) and E is a set of connections between DNs. Let k be a finite number of disjoint subsets of V. V_k is the subset k and $V = \cup (V_k)$. Given a DN_{ki} (i-th DN from the k subset), it will not have any connection with DNs from the same subset ($e_{ki\text{-}kj}=0$ $\forall$ V_k). Every DNv_{ki} has a connection with one DN_{ri} from other subset ($r \neq k$). Let's suppose $n=|V|$ and k the number of subsets of V, then we obtain equation 1.

$$n = \sum_{i=1}^{k} | V_k | \tag{1}$$

Every V_k has regular nodes and DNs (GCs and ACs are DNs too). So, nodes of every group are the sum of all of them. Now we can describe the whole network as a sum of regular nodes and DNs by expression 2.

$$n = \sum_{i=1}^{k} | (n_{regular} + n_{DN})_k | = \sum_{i=1}^{k} (|n_{regular}|)_k + \sum_{i=1}^{k} (|n_{DN}|)_k \tag{2}$$

Regular nodes will be the interior nodes of the topology and DNs will be edge nodes. There are several known laws where the number of interior nodes is related to the edge nodes.

M. Faloutsos et al. show in [16] that many networks could be modelled following several mathematical models. It also shows that the power law fit the real data in correlation coefficients of 96% in Internet. Based on power law we can find Zipf's law, which states that few nodes have many connections while there are many nodes with few connections. B. A. Huberman and L. A. Adamic in [17] proposed the Zipf's law for Internet and Z. Ge et al. proposed Zipf's law for Gnutella and Napster networks in [18]. The mathematical expression for power law that relates edge nodes with interior nodes, and adapted to our case, is given in expression 3.

$$n_{DN} = \frac{1}{2(R+1)}(1 - \frac{1}{n_{regular}^{R+1}})n_{regular} \tag{3}$$

Where n_{DN} is the number of edge nodes, $n_{regular}$ is the number of interior nodes and R varies as a function of the network where it is applied. In the case of Internet it has been varying along the years having -0.81, -0.82 and -0.74 values.

György Hermann introduced another mathematical model in [19]. It proposes, using D. J. Watts and H. S. Strogatz networks model [20], where network connections are established based on efficiency, stability and safety properties. Expression 4 gives their proposed relationship.

$$c \cdot n_{regular} \leq n_{DN} \leq c \cdot n_{regular} \cdot \ln(n_{regular}) \tag{4}$$

Where n_{DN} is the number of edge nodes, $n_{regular}$ is the number of interior nodes and c is a constant which value depends on the network model

In [13], the same authors of this paper propose different relationship between regular nodes and distribution nodes for partially centralized P2P networks. If we are talking about an hybrid P2P network, the number of edge nodes could be equal to the number of regular nodes, but in case of a superpeer P2P network, it is needed a distribution node every 96 regular nodes. Expression 5 summarized these values.

$$n_{DN} = \begin{cases} n_{regular} & \text{in case of a hybrid P2P network} \\ \frac{n_{regular}}{96} & \text{in case of a superpeer P2P network} \end{cases} \tag{5}$$

Figure 2 shows the number of nodes in a group as a function of the number of regular nodes in a group of the proposed architecture. The hybrid P2P network is the same case of minimum value of the Hermann model (Hermann_min).

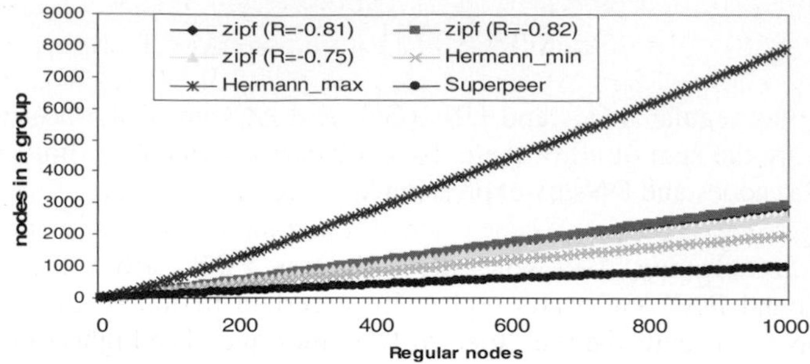

Fig. 2. Number of nodes in a group as a function of the regular nodes

Using Herman maximum value (Hermann_max), we need many nodes in the group, so there will be many DNs. On the other hand, the one that will need less DNs in the group will be topologies such as the superpeer P2P network

5 Protocol Operation

First node in the network starts with *groupID*=0x01 and *nodeID*=0x01 and has all roles in its group. Next new nodes in that group enter as DNs and will acquire roles as a function of their δ. In order to join new groups to the architecture, the GC of the new group must to send a "GG discovery" message, with its *groupID*, to GCs from other groups known in advance or by bootstrapping [21] (a *groupID* value of 0xFF indicates the architecture must assign next available *groupID* value, and if the new GC has a *groupID* value that is used, it will be invited to change the *groupID* indicating next *groupID* available). If there is not any reply in a certain period of time, it will begin the process again. GCs from other groups reply this message with their *networkID* and their λ parameter in the "GC discovery ACK" message. It chooses GCs with higher λ and sends them a "GC connect" message. Then, they reply with a "GC welcome" message indicating that it has joined the architecture. After that, it sends them its neighbor list using "GCDB" message. Its neighbors add this entry to their topological database and recalculate routes using SPF algorithm. When they finish, they will send their database to the new GC to build its database. Next database messages will be updates only. Finally, it will send them "keepalive GC" messages periodically to indicate that it is still alive. If a GC does not receive a "GC keepalive" message from a neighbor for a holdtime, it will erase this entry from its database.

New joining nodes in a group will be DNs. A DN sends a "D discovery" message to ACs previously known or by bootstrapping. Only ACs of its group will reply using "D discovery ACK" messages with their *groupID* and λ. DN will choose the AC with higher λ and it will send it a "D connect" message. AC will reply a "Welcome D" message with assigned *nodeID*. Then, it will add DN's entry to its access table (the owner is the AC of an area and it is formed by all DNs in that area). Finally, DN will send it "Keepalive D" messages periodically. If the AC does not receive a "Keepalive D" message from a DN for a holdtime, it will erase this entry from its table. Next, DN has to establish an adjacency with DNs from other groups, so it will send a "DDB request" message to the AC in its zone. This message contains sender's *groupID*, sender's *nodeID* and its network layer address and the destination groupID (0x00 in case of "all groups"). Then, AC routes it to the GC in its group. GC will send this request to all GCs from other groups in its distribution table (GCs' distribution table is formed by all GCs the owner can reach). When a GC receives this message from other group, it will send a "Find DN" message to ACs in its group in order to find the DN with highest λ in the group. Every request has a unique sequence number to avoid route loops in the group. ACs will reply with their 2 DNs with highest λ using the message "Found DN". GC waits replies for a certain period of time. It chooses 2 highest λ DNs and sends them a "Elected DN" message. The highest one will be the preferred; the second one will act as a backup. This message contains the *nodeID* and the requesting DN's network layer address. When these DNs receive that message, they will send a "DD connect" message to connect with the DN from the other group. Next, they send a "D elected ACK" message to the GC in its group to indicate a connection has established with other group DN. If GC does not receive this message for a hold time, it will send a new message to the next DN with highest λ. This process will be repeated until GC receives both confirmations. When the requesting DN from other group receives these connection messages, it will add DN with highest λ as its first neighbor and the second one as the backup. Then, it replies these connection messages to acknowledge the connection using the "DD welcome" message. If the requesting DN does not receive any connection from other DN for a holdtime, it will send a requesting message again. Finally, both DN will send "keepalive DD" messages periodically. If a DN does not receive a "keepalive DD" message from the other DN for a holdtime, it will erase this entry from its DN's distribution table (it is formed by all neighbor DNs from other groups).

When a GC receives a new groupID in a "GC connect" or in a "GCDB" message, it will send a "New group" message to all ACs in its group with a sequence number to avoid route loops. Then, ACs will forward this message to all DNs in their zone. Subsequently, DNs will begin the process to request DNs from the new group.

When a GC sees there are β more ACs in its group, it will send a "GC conversion" message to the AC with highest δ in its AC distribution table (ACs' distribution table is formed by all ACs in the group). Highest δ AC will send a "change level" to its neighbors to inform them it has changed its level and it will begin the process of authenticating with other GCs.

When the oldest GC sees there are β more DNs in its group, it will send an "AC request" message to all ACs to request a new AC. All ACs will reply an "AC reply" message with the *nodeIDs* of the first and the second DNs with highest δ in its group. GC will process all replies and will choose 2 DNs with highest δ from the whole group. Then, it will send an "AC conversion" message to the first DN with highest δ. This message will be routed to the chosen DN. This DN will become an AC and will send an "AC disconnection" message to its AC. If GC does not receive changes in ACs' distribution table for a hold time, it will send a new "AC request" message to the second DN with highest δ. If this time it fails again, it will begin the process, but avoiding those DNs. New ACs must authenticate with ACs in their group. It can establish its first connections with any AC known in advance or by bootstrapping [21]. First, it sends an "AC discovery" message with its *groupID*. Only ACs with the same *groupID* will reply with their λ. New AC will wait for a hold time and will choose

ACs with highest λ. If there is no reply, new AC will send an "AC discovery" message again. Then, new AC will send an "AC connect" message to the chosen ACs. They will reply with a "Welcome AC" message indicating it is connected to the architecture and they will become its neighbors. New AC will send its neighbor list using "AC neighbors" message to all of them to update their AC distribution database and all of them will recalculate new routes using SPF algorithm and the metric aforementioned. Then, they send their database to the new AC using "ACDB" in order to build its ACs' distribution database. Next times it will only receive updates. New AC will send "AC keepalive" messages to its neighbors periodically. If it is not received from a neighbor for a holdtime, it will erase this entry from its database.

5.1 Recovery Algorithms

Every GC sends its backup information to the highest δ AC in the group periodically. When a GC leaves the architecture voluntarily, it will send a "Failed GC" message to the highest δ AC announcing it. The highest δ AC becomes a GC and acknowledges with a "Failed GC ACK" message. Then, GC leaves the architecture sending a "GC disconnect" message to its neighbors. If that GC does not receive the acknowledgement, it will begin the process with the second highest δ AC. Next, new GC sends a "Change level" message to its neighbors to advertise it has changed its level. It will try to have the same neighbors as the old one using the backup data. Then, it will begin its functionalities as a new GC. When a GC fails, it will be detected by its AC neighbors because the lack of "AC keepalive" messages for a holdtime. First AC detects this failure, updates its ACs' database and propagates it through the group using "ACDB" messages. When the highest δ AC receives this update, it will use the backup information and it will become GC.

Every AC has a table with all DNs in its area and information related with its AC neighbor closest to the GC. They will use this table to know their δ and λ. DN with highest δ will be the AC backup DN and it will receive AC backup data from its AC by incremental updates using "Backup AC" messages. This information is used in case of AC failure. AC sends "AC keepalive" messages to the backup DN periodically. When an AC leaves the architecture, it will send a "Failed AC" message to its closest GC with information about its backup DN. The GC will reply it with the "Failed O1 ACK" message, and then, AC will send an "AC disconnect" message to its neighbors and it will leave the architecture. Next, GC, using the received backup data, chooses the highest δ DN in the group (as it has been explained before) and sends it an "AC conversion" message. New AC will send a "DN disconnection" message to its AC, and then, it will connect with the backup DN to have the backup data and become an AC. Then, new AC sends a "Keepalive D" message to all DNs in its zone. If the GC does not receive changes for a hold time, it will send a new request message to the second DN with highest δ. If the backup DN does not receive this message for a hold time, it will become the new AC. When an AC fails, backup DN can check it because the lack of "keepalive D" messages for a holdtime. If it happens, backup DN sends a "Failed AC" message to the failed AC neighbor. It will be the helper AC to help the failed AC substitution. Helper AC will forward the "Failed AC" message to its closest GC to request a new AC. Then, the process will begin as it has been explained before.

When a DN leaves the architecture voluntarily, it will send a "DN disconnect" message to the AC in its zone and to all its adjacent DNs from other groups. They will delete this entry from its DN's distribution database and adjacent DNs will substitute it with a new DN for that group as explained before. When a DN fails down, AC and adjacent DNs will check it because they do not receive a "keepalive D" message for a hold time. Then, AC will delete this entry from its access table and adjacent DNs will delete this entry from its DNs' distribution database and they will request a new DN.

5.2 Protocol Messages

We have designed and developed 46 messages for the architecture operation. We have considered that *networkID*, *nodeID*, λ and δ parameters use 32 bits, so we can classify them in 40 fixed size messages and 6 messages which size depends on the number of neighbors, the size of the topological database or the backup information. Longer messages are the ones that contain the topological database and the backup information. First time, both messages send the whole information, next times only updates are sent.

6 Performance Evaluation

To evaluate the performance of our proposal under real constraints, we have developed a desktop application using Java programming to run and test the proposed architecture and its protocol. It allows the node to run DN, AC and GC roles, as it is described previously, to work the architecture properly. The application let us choose the group connected to and we can vary some parameters such as k_1, k_2, k_3, Max_Con, upstream and downstream bandwidth, keepalive time, timers and so on.

6.1 Testbed

We have used 42 computers (AMD Athlon™ XP 1700+, 1.47 GHz, 480 MB RAM) with Windows XP Professional Operative System. They were connected to several Cisco Catalyst 2950T-24 Switches over 100BaseT links. The implemented scenario has 3 groups interconnected. All these groups have only one GC (which is also an AC). First group has 12 DNs, second group has 13 DNs and the third group has 17 DNs. In order to take measurements from the scenario, we have connected every group to a switch and all Switches were connected to a switch as a star topology. GCs are connected physically to the central switch, although they pertain to their group. One port of the central switch was configured in a monitor mode (receives the same frames as all other ports), to be able to capture data using a sniffer application. We began to take measurements before we started the GC from the first group, 10 seconds later we started the GC from the second group, 10 seconds later we started the GC from the third group, 10 seconds later we began to start all DNs from the first group, 10 seconds later, we started all DNSs from the second group and finally, 10 seconds later, all DNs from the third group.

6.2 Measurement Results

We have used the testbed in 2 cases with different values for keepalive time (20 vs 30 sec.) and timer (4 vs 10 sec.) to evaluate the performance of the system.

Figure 7 a) shows the bandwidth consumed in the testbed for the first case. The number of Bps (Bytes per sec.) oscillates from 4,000 to 8,000 Bps when the network has converged. Peaks because of keepalive messages are not so significant in this case. Figure 7 b) shows the number of messages per sec. in the network when the architecture is running using values of the first case. There are peaks every 20 sec. starting from a 70 sec. approximately because discovery messages and keepalive messages (every 20 sec.), between DNs and the GC, are added. Figure 7 c) shows the number of broadcasts per sec. in the scenario for first case parameter values. The highest peak appears around 70 sec. (when DNs from the third group were started).

Figure 8 a) shows the bandwidth consumed in the network when the architecture is running using values of the second case. The number of Bps oscillates from 2,000 to 8,000 Bps when the network has converged (the number of octets minimum is lower than the first case). Figure 8 b) shows the number of messages per sec. in the scenario for first case parameter values. There are fewer messages per sec. than in the first case and the minimum peaks are lower. Figure 8 c) shows the number of broadcasts per sec. in the testbed for the second case. When the network has converged, there is an average between 2 a 4 of broadcasts per sec. (less than in the first case).

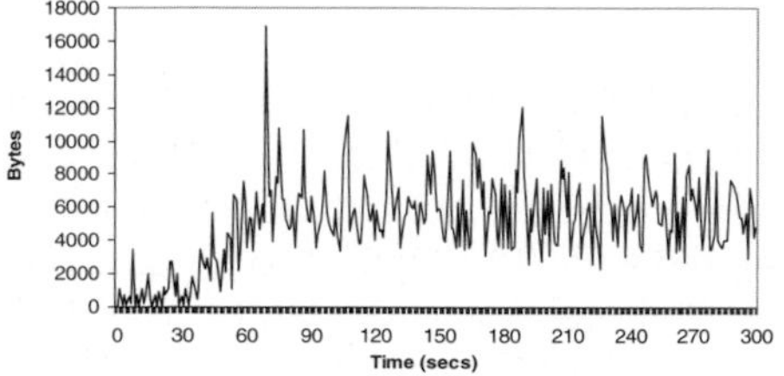

Fig. 7 a). 1st prove bandwidth utilization

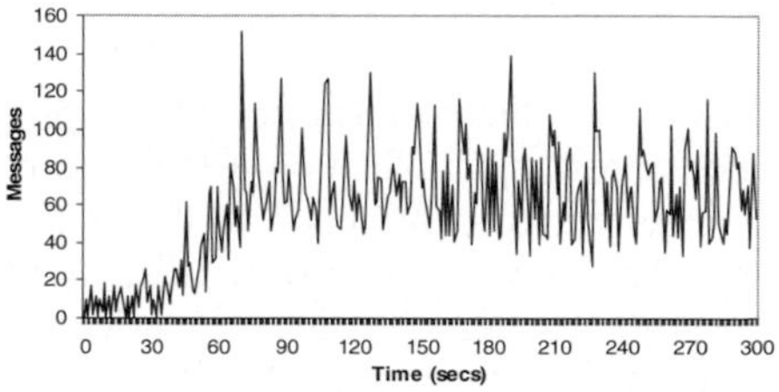

Fig. 7 b). 1st prove number of messages

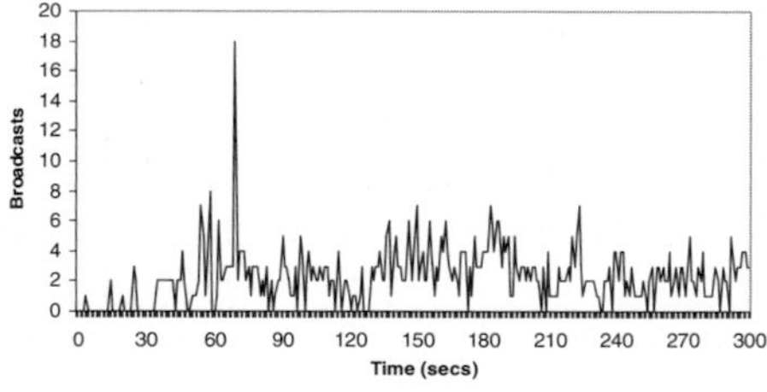

Fig. 7 c). 1st prove number of broadcasts

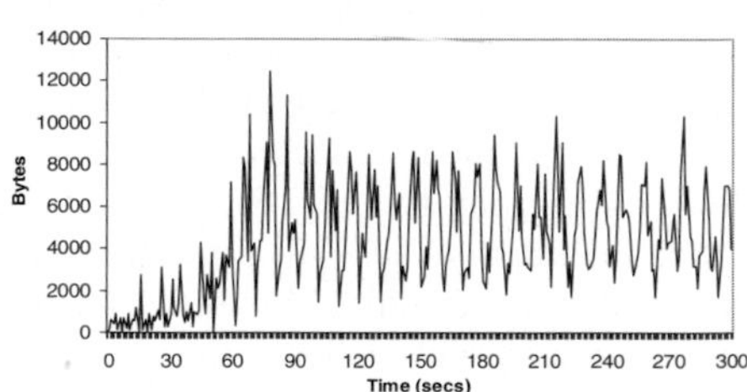

Fig. 8 a). 2nd prove bandwidth utilization

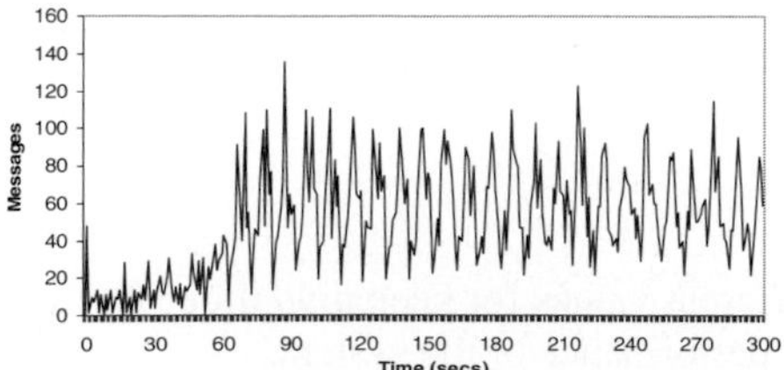

Fig. 8 b). 2nd prove number of messages

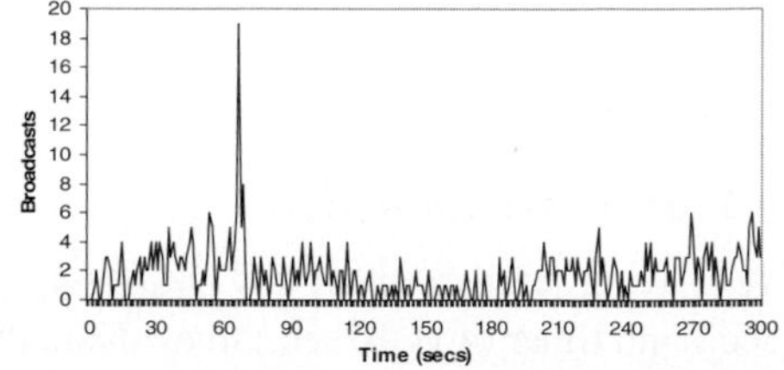

Fig. 8 c). 2nd prove number of broadcasts

When we increase the keepalive time, peaks values are lower and there are less bits per second and messages inside the network, but the time to check a node failure increases. We have observed that when we increase the number of groups in the network, but maintaining the number of nodes constant, the number of broadcast messages is almost the same. Although the number of nodes in the architecture is increased, there is not any proportion with the number of messages sent. If we cause to fail a DN with many connections with DNs from other groups, we can observe that the number of messages increased is not so significant to be seen in the graphs having a quick look. It is needed many DNs to have higher impact in the graphs.

7 Conclusions

We have presented a Grid architecture based on groups that is able to self-organize connections between nodes from different groups based on their available capacity. It is based on three types of roles for nodes of the architecture and their role is based on a promotion parameter. ACs organize DNs in zones to have a scalable architecture and help to establish DN connections routing DN information inside the group and choosing DNs with highest capacity. DNs have connections with DNs from other groups to share resources, data or computing time between groups. GCs have connections with GCs from other groups allowing groups interconnection and helping to organize DN connections. This design allows changing nodes' connections based on the available adjacencies and load from other ASs or DNs. Once the connections are established, to share resources, data or computing time between groups could be done without using ACs and GCs because they are used only for organization purposes. We have chosen SPF algorithm to reduce the latency to request new DNs when there are DN failures or leavings.

We have presented the analytical model and show the number of DNs in the network related with the number of regular nodes for several types of topologies. We have described the protocol operation and the recovery algorithm when any type of node leaves the architecture or fails down. The protocol does not consume so much bandwidth. We have shown that messages with more bandwidth are the backup messages and the one which sends the topological database, so, they are maintained by incremental updates. Real measurements demonstrate it is a feasible architecture because of the bandwidth consumption to manage the system is low and it can be used as an intergrid protocol or to replicate data from a group to other groups.

As future work, we will do some experimental results to adjust δ and λ parameters. On the other hand, we will test very short keepalive time and holdtime in order to reduce convergence times and to have a fast recovery algorithm for critical systems.

References

1. Foster, I., Kesselman, C., and Tuecke, S. The Anatomy of the Grid: Enabling Scalable Virtual Organizations. International Journal of High Performance Computing Applications, 15(3):200 - 222, 2001.
2. García-Carballeira, F., Carretero, J., Calderón, A., García, J. D., Sanchez, L. A global and parallel file system for grids. Future Generation Computer Systems 23 (2007). Pp. 116–122.

3. J.G. Jensen, T. Shah, O. Synge, J. Gordon, G. Johnson, R. Tam, Enabling Grid Access to Mass Storage: Architecture and Design of the EDG Storage Element. Journal of Grid Computing 3 (1–2) (2005) 101–112.
4. Ruay-Shiung, C. and Po-Hung, C. Complete and fragmented replica selection and retrieval in Data Grids, Future Generation Computer Systems. In Press.
5. Ping, L., Kevin, L., Zhongzhi, S. and Qing, H., Distributed data mining in grid computing environments, Future Generation Computer Systems, Vol. 23, Issue 1. Jan 2007. Pp. 84-91
6. Koo, S. G. M., Kannan, K., Lee, C.S.G., A genetic-algorithm-based neighbor-selection strategy for hybrid peer-to-peer networks, Proc. of the 13th IEEE International Conference on Computer Communications and Networks, Chicago, IL, October 2004, pp. 469–474.
7. Ferreira, R. A., Jagannathan, S., Grama, A. Locality in structured peer-to-peer networks, Journal of Parallel and Distributed Computing, Vol. 66, Issue 2. Feb. 2006. Pp. 257-273.
8. Bose, P., Morin, P., Stojmenovic, I., Urrutia, J. Routing with guaranteed delivery in ad hoc wireless networks, Wireless Networking 7 (6) (2001). Pp. 609–616.
9. Xu, Z., Tang, C., Zhang, Z. Building topology-aware overlays using global soft-state. Proc. of the 23rd International Conference on Distributed Computing Systems, 2003. May 2003.
10. Wierzbicki, A., Strzelecki, R., Swierczewski, D. and Znojek, M. Rhubarb: a Tool for Developing Scalable and Secure Peer-to-Peer Applications, in: Second IEEE International Conference on Peer-to-Peer Computing (P2P2002), Linöping, Sweden, 2002.
11. Xiang, Z., Zhang, Q., Zhu, W., Zhang, Z. and Zhang, Y. Peer-to-Peer Based Multimedia Distribution Service, IEEE Transactions on Multimedia 6 (2) (2004).
12. Hongjun, L., Luo, L. P. and Zhifeng, Z. A structured hierarchical P2P model based on a rigorous binary tree code algorithm, Future Generation Computer Systems 23 (2). 2007. Pp. 201-208.
13. Lloret, J., Boronat, F., Palau, C., Esteve, M.: Two Levels SPF-Based System to Interconnect Partially Decentralized P2P File Sharing Networks, International Conference on Autonomic and Autonomous Systems International Conference on Networking and Services Joint ICAS'05 and ICNS'05, (2005).
14. Moy, J.: RFC 1245 - OSPF Protocol Analysis (1991). Available at http://www.faqs.org/rfcs/rfc1245.html
15. Lloret, J., Diaz, J. R., Jimenez, J. M., Boronat, F.: An Architecture to Connect Disjoint Multimedia Networks Based on node's Capacity, Lecture Notes in Computer Science, Vol. 4261. Springer-Verlag, Berlin Heidelberg New York (2006). Pp. 890-899.
16. Siganos, G., Faloutsos, M., Faloutsos, P. and Faloutsos, C. Power Laws and the AS-Level Internet Topology. IEEE/ACM Transactions on Networking, Vol. 11, Issue 4. August 2003.
17. Huberman, B.A. and Adamic, L.A. Growth dynamics of the World-Wide Web, Nature, vol. 40, (1999). pp. 450-457.
18. Ge, Z., Figueiredo, D. R., Jaiswal, S., Kurose, J., Towsley, D. Modeling Peer-Peer File Sharing Systems, Proceedings IEEE INFOCOM 2003, San Francisco, March-April 2003.
19. Hermann, G. Mathematical investigations in network properties. - Proceedings of the IEEE International Conference on Intelligent Engineering Systems. Pp 79-82. September 2005.
20. D. J. Watts and H. S. Strogatz, Nature 393, 440 (1998).
21. Cramer, C., Kutzner, K. and Fuhrmann T. Bootstrapping Locality-Aware P2P Networks. The IEEE International Conference on Networks, Vol. 1. (2004). Pp. 357-361.

UR-Tree: An Efficient Index for Uncertain Data in Ubiquitous Sensor Networks

Dong-Oh Kim, Dong-Suk Hong, Hong-Koo Kang, and Ki-Joon Han

School of Computer Science & Engineering, Konkuk University,
1, Hwayang-Dong, Gwangjin-Gu, Seoul 143-701, Korea
{dokim, dshong, hkkang, kjhan}@db.konkuk.ac.kr

Abstract. With the rapid development of technologies related to Ubiquitous Sensor Network (USN), sensors are being utilized in various application areas. In general, a sensor has a low computing capacity and power and keeps sending data to the central server. In this environment, uncertain data can be stored in the central server due to delayed transmission or other reasons and make query processing produce wrong results. Thus, this paper examines how to process uncertain data in ubiquitous sensor networks and suggests an efficient index, called UR-tree, for uncertain data. The index reduces the cost of update by delaying update in uncertainty areas. In addition, it solves the problem of low accuracy in search resulting from update delay by delaying update only for specific update areas. Lastly, we analyze the performance of UR-tree and prove the superiority of its performance by comparing its performance with that of R-Tree and PTI using various datasets.

Keywords: Ubiquitous Sensor Network (USN), Uncertain Data, Index, May/Must Query, Uncertainty.

1 Introduction

With the recent development of various sensor technologies including temperature sensor, RFID (Radio Frequency IDentification) and GPS (Global Positioning System) and wireless communication technologies such as CDMA, WiFi and WiBro, there are increasing interest and research in technologies related to Ubiquitous Sensor Network (USN) such as environment monitoring and car theft detection [1]. In particular, research is being made actively for efficient query processing in devices with low computing capacity and power like sensor nodes composing USN [2,4].

In general, data sensed by each sensor node on USN are stored into the central server (or an external server) for efficient search. For this, data have to be transmitted from a sensor node to the central server at a high cost. The cost of data update can be saved by reducing the number of times of data update through delaying update. Because of random errors caused by inadequacy in measuring methods such as update delay and systematic errors in data, data sensed by a sensor node may have uncertainty. In addition, due to the uncertainty of sensed data, query processing may produce wrong results [1,10].

Thus, this paper examines how to process uncertain data in USN. Moreover, we propose Uncertainty R-tree (UR-tree), which is an index for uncertain data that can

C. Cérin and K.-C. Li (Eds.): GPC 2007, LNCS 4459, pp. 603–613, 2007.

reduce the cost of update in consideration of the uncertainty on sensed data. UR-tree can index data sensed by each sensor node using uncertainty areas.

An *uncertainty area* is an area(i.e., rectangle around sensed data) where uncertainty is likely to exist. Figure 1 shows sensed data and uncertainty areas used in UR-tree. Figure 1(a) shows data, called $N_1,\ldots,N_5$, sensed by humidity and temperature sensors and query window q. Figure 1(b) shows the uncertainty areas which are represented by shaded rectangles around the sensed data and query window q.

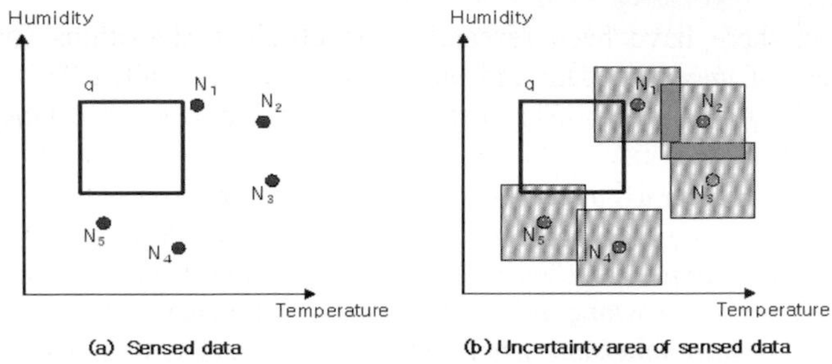

Fig. 1. Sensed data and uncertainty areas

UR-tree can reduce the cost of update by delaying update in uncertainty areas. However, if update is delayed in uncertainty areas, the accuracy of search may go down. That is, there can be case that should not be included in search as in Figure 1(a) but is included when uncertainty areas are considered as in Figure 1(b). To solve this problem, UR-tree delays update only for specific domains, preventing the low accuracy of search.

This paper is organized as follows. Chapter 2 explains how to process uncertain data based on related researches. Chapter 3 presents the index structure of UR-tree and relevant algorithms. Chapter 4 analyzes the performance of UR-tree and proves the superiority of its performance. Lastly, Chapter 5 draws conclusions.

2 Related Works

Research on data processing in consideration of uncertainty began from the area of data modeling for expressing the location of moving objects. In addition, there have been researches for improving the efficiency of query processing algorithms on the location of moving objects and minimizing data transmission to the central server to reflect frequent location changes [6,10]. Particularly for objects moving within a limited space like cars running on the road, the uncertainty of the location of moving objects can be minimized and the cost of update also can be reduced by using road data [3].

With the development of USN, data are being sensed by various sensors including those for reporting the location of moving objects. Therefore, research has been made on data models, query types and query processing methods for uncertain data and on query processing strategies for each query type in order to deal with the uncertainty of data sensed by various types of sensors. Queries on uncertain data are largely divided into probabilistic queries and may/must queries [1].

A probabilistic query specifies the range and probability of specific data as query conditions. For example, "What are the IDs of sensors in which the probability for the current temperature to be over 30℃ is 50% ?" A may/must query specifies the range of specific data and a keyword out of may/must. For example, "What are the IDs of sensors in which the current temperature must (or may) be over 30□ ?"In this paper, we used may/must queries, which are faster than probabilistic queries, for uncertain data.

In addition, there have been researches on efficient algorithms for the nearest neighbor query of uncertain data and on efficient indexes, called PTI, for search by probabilistic threshold query [2]. There were also indexes for efficient search of uncertain data in which each data value has its probability [4] and probabilistically constrained regions for efficient processing of polygon-shaped uncertainty areas in data search [9]. Although these algorithms and indexes improved search performance for uncertain data, however, they did not consider update performance, which should be taken into account in ubiquitous sensor networks with limited resources.

In order to improve update performance in the area of moving objects, the suggested index uses a secondary index for direct access to the IDs of moving objects, or extends MBR and delays update within the extended MBR [7]. Moreover, using the fact that data sensed by each sensor node in USN are very changeable but the variation of the value is very small for a long time, an index was suggested that updates only when a new value deviates from the range of average deviation [11]. However, these indexes were focused on update performance without considering uncertainty.

Lastly, there was a research to process sensed data by expressing them as specific ranges because the cost of update is high if sensed data is directly stored into a cache for efficient search in USN, and another research was made to minimize update within uncertainty areas in aggregate queries [8]. Such a research improved update performance by considering uncertainty elements such as errors in sensed data but lacked consideration of indexes for improving search performance.

3 UR-Tree

UR-tree is an efficient index for sensor data with uncertainty, which can improve update performance in consideration of the uncertainty of data. This chapter describes the index structure of UR-tree and its search, insert and update algorithms.

3.1 Index Structure

USN is composed of sensor nodes. In this paper, we assume that each sensor node N has a unique ID and sensor R and O in charge of sensing. A sensor node with sensor ID_i is called N_i. Data sensed by sensor R and O of sensor node N_i is (N_i.r, N_i.o), and the uncertainty areas of sensor R and O are (-Ur, Ur) and (-Uo, Uo), respectively. Here, the index entry for sensor node N_i is (N_i, (N_i.r -Ur, N_i.o -Uo), (N_i.r +Ur, N_i.o +Uo)). That is, sensed data is expressed as a two-dimensional point (N_i.r, N_i.o), and the uncertainty area of the corresponding data is expressed as a two-dimensional rectangle ((N_i.r -Ur, N_i.o -Uo), (N_i.r +Ur, N_i.o +Uo)). At this point, the uncertainty area of sensed data is called *Uncertainty Bounding Box* (UBB).

The index structure of UR-tree is similar to R-tree [5], but is distinguished in that it uses the uncertainty area in search and uses the update area in update to delay update. In UR-tree, a request for update is composed of ID of a sensor node and newly sensed data. A *secondary index* is used for fast access to the leaf node that has the corresponding ID. Each node in the secondary index has ID and a leaf node pointer. The secondary index can be implemented with a hash table or B-tree. Figure 2 shows examples of UR-tree and secondary index.

Figure 2(a) shows relationships between U_i's, which is UBB of sensor node N_i, and M_j's, which is MBR of tree nodes. As shown in Figure 2(a), U_1 is UBB of sensor node N_1. M_3 which contains U_1 and U_2 is MBR of a tree node of UR-tree. Figure 2(b) shows UR-tree and a secondary index for Figure 2(a). UR-tree is in the form of a tree structure like R-tree. In this case, the maximum number of entries that will fit in one node is three. The leaf node in UR-tree is composed of UBB of each sensor node. The secondary index of Figure 2(b) is pointing the leaf node that has the corresponding sensor node's ID for fast update, delete, and select operations.

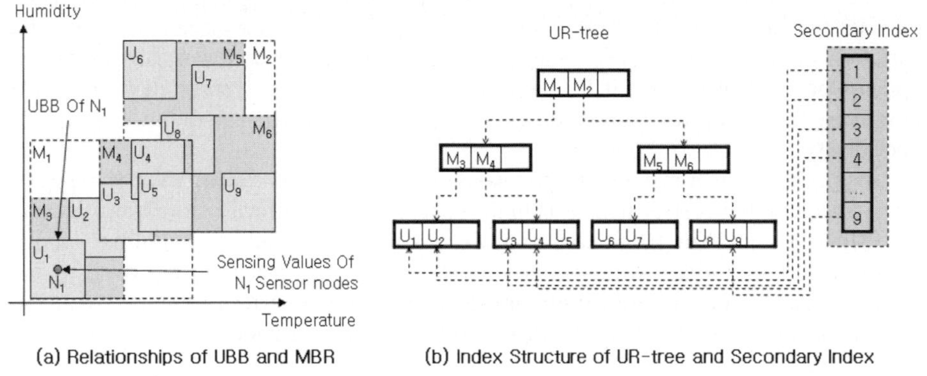

Fig. 2. Examples of UR-tree and secondary index

Figure 3 shows when and how to update data in UR-tree and reason why the update area is necessary to update data in UR-tree. According to Figure 3(a), if update is delayed in UBB, query window q1 overlaps with UBB due to the update delay although UBB should not be retrieved, and query window q2 does not overlap with UBB although UBB should be retrieved. For this reason, update delay can lower the accuracy of search.

Accordingly, in order to enhance the accuracy of search, UBB has the update area to restrict update delay. The update area exists inside UBB and is defined to prevent data update. In UR-tree, if sensed data does not deviate from the update area, the index is not updated, and if the sensed data deviates from the update area, UBB is restructured. In addition, if UBB deviates from the MBR of the index node, the index is restructured. In Figure 3(b) where an update area is defined, UBB is restructured and, as a result, query

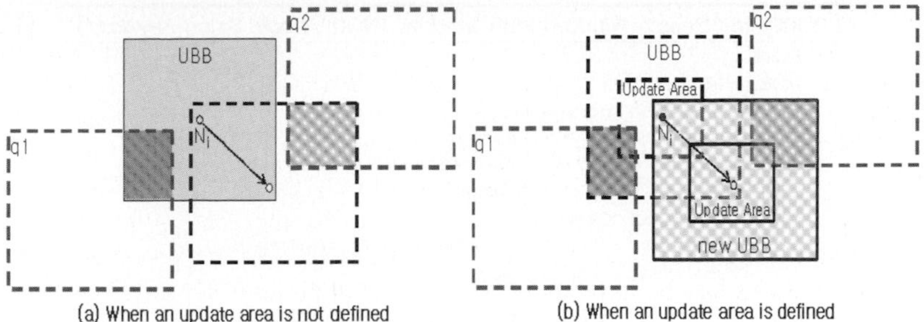

Fig. 3. Data update in UR-tree

window q1 does not overlap with UBB and query window q2 overlaps with UBB. The update area results in tradeoff between update performance affected by update delay in uncertainty areas and search accuracy affected by frequent updates.

3.2 Search Algorithm

UR-tree supports ID-based search and window-based search. Window-based search can use the may/must keyword. Figure 4 shows the ID-based search algorithm of UR-tree.

```
ALGORITHM : Search( ID id)
  BEGIN
    SINODE sinode ← search SECONDARY INDEX to find a SINODE with id
    IF( sinode is NULL )
      RETRUN NULL
    ELSE
      UBB ubb ← sinode.objpt
      RETURN ubb.nodept
    END IF
  END
```

Fig. 4. ID-based search algorithm

In Figure 4, the ID-based search algorithm finds the corresponding node with *id* directly using the secondary index. If *sinode* isn't NULL, the node that contains *ubb*, which is *sinode.objpt*, is returned. In this way, the use of the secondary index enables fast access to a node of specific ID, so it improves performance in ID-based search or update but raises overhead in insert because of the secondary index.

Figure 5 shows the window-based search algorithm of UR-tree. In Figure 5, the window-based search algorithm checks if the corresponding node is contained in or overlaps with the window area. In case it is contained in the window area, the objects of all child nodes of the corresponding node are added to the search results. In case it overlaps with the window area, if it is not a leaf node Search_Window() is executed recursively, and if it is a leaf node the algorithm is processed differently according to *keyword*. If *keyword* is "MAY" and its child nodes are overlapped with the window area, the child nodes are added to the search results. If *keyword* is "MUST" and its child nodes are contained in the window area, the child nodes are added to the search results. Lastly, the search results are returned.

```
ALGORITHM : Search_Window( MBR window, TNODE node, String Keyword)
  BEGIN
    result ← Ø
    IF( window contain node.mbr )
      add object of all leaf node in node to result
    ELSE IF( window overlap node.mbr ) // Search Subtrees
      FOR EACH child node child of node
        IF( child is leaf node )
          IF(( keyword is "MAY") AND ( window contain child.mbr ))
            add object in child to result
          END IF
          IF(( keyword is "MUST") AND ( window overlap child.mbr ))
            add object in child to result
          END IF
        ELSE
          Search_Window( window, child, keyword )
        END IF
      END FOR
    END IF
    RETURN result
  END
```

Fig. 5. Window-based search algorithm

3.3 Insert Algorithm

In UR-tree, the insert algorithm is executed when a value sensed by the sensor node of the corresponding ID is inserted for the first time. Figure 6 shows the insert algorithm of UR-tree. In Figure 6, the insert algorithm checks if the corresponding ID is in the secondary index or a new one. Then, it creates structure *ubb* using MakeUBB() to store the uncertainty area with the ID and the sensed data. In addition, it finds a node to insert *ubb* using Findleaf(). Lastly, if the degree of the corresponding node is the same as the number of child nodes, the algorithm splits the corresponding node, or inserts *ubb* into the corresponding node.

Figure 7 is function Findleaf() used in the insert algorithm. In Figure 7, Findleaf() assigns the child node that contains *ubb* among the child nodes of *node* to *tnode*. If *tnode* is NULL, among the child nodes of *node*, the child node with the smallest MBR

```
ALGORITHM : Insert( ID id, DOUBLE x, DOUBLE y)
  BEGIN
    IF( SECONDARY INDEX have a NODE with id )
      RETURN ERROR
    END IF
    UBB ubb ← MakeUBB(id, x, y)
    NODE cnode ← Findeaf( node, ubb )
    IF( cnode.count is NODEORDER )
      split cnode with ubb
    ELSE
      insert ubb in cnode
    END IF
  END
```

Fig. 6. Insert algorithm

```
ALGORITHM : Findleaf( NODE node, UBB ubb )
BEGIN
  NODE node ← root node of UBR-tree
  WHILE ( node isn't leaf node )
    NODE tnode ← find child node which contain ubb, in node
    IF ( tnode is NULL )
      FOR EACH child node child of node
        MBR newmbr ← add ubb to child.mbr
        IF( newmbr is minimum )
          tnode ← child
        END IF
      END FOR
    END IF
    IF( tnode is leaf node )
      RETURN tnode
    END IF
    node ← tnode
  END WHILE
END
```

Fig. 7. Findleaf() function

containing *ubb* is assigned to *tnode*. Finally if *tnode* is a leaf node, *tnode* is returned, or *tnode* is assigned to *node* and the loop is executed again.

3.4 Update Algorithm

In UR-tree, the update algorithm does not make the index updated if sensed data does not deviate from the update area. However, if the sensed data deviates from the update area, UBB is restructured and, if UBB deviates from the MBR of the index node, the index is restructured. Figure 8 shows the update algorithm of UR-tree.

```
ALGORITHM : Update( ID id, DOUBLE x, DOUBLE y)
BEGIN
  NODE leaf ← Search( ID id )
  IF( leaf.updatearea contain x and y )
    RETURN  // update is not need
  ELSE
    UBB ubb ← MakeUBB( id, x, y )
    MBR newmbr ← add ubb to leaf.mbr
    IF( leaf.parent.mbr contain leaf.mbr and newmbr )
      leaf.mbr ← newmbr
    ELSE
      Delete( id )
      Insert( id, x, y )
    END IF
  END IF
END
```

Fig. 8. Update algorithm

In Figure 8, the update algorithm finds the node of the corresponding ID using Search(). Then, if the sensed data is contained in the update area of the corresponding node, update is finished. If not, uncertainty area *ubb* is created by MakeUBB() using the ID and sensed data. Besides, after update, it is checked whether the MBR of the node changes or not, and if the MBR does not change only *ubb* is updated and if it does the corresponding node is deleted and inserted again.

4 Performance Evaluation

This chapter compares search time, update time, omission error and commission error of UR-tree, R-tree and PTI according to the update area, the uncertainty area, and the window size. A performance evaluation was conducted using a PC with Intel Pentium4 2.53GHz CPU and 1GB memory. Data used in the performance evaluation is presented in Table 1.

Table 1. Performance evaluation data

Name	No. of sensor nodes	Distribution function	Range of starting data	Average range of movement	Min/max range of movement	Total data range	No. of sensors
DataSet1	500	Gaussian	10, 20	0.2	-0.5, 0.5	10, 20	2
DataSet2	500	Gaussian	15, 20	0.2	-0.5, 0.5	10, 20	2

For the performance evaluation, we constructed an index using data corresponding to time T_i as uncertain data, assuming that data uncertainty is caused by the delay of update, and compared it with data corresponding to T_{i+1}, which was assumed to be certain real data. If R_i is the number of results retrieved from T_i data, R_{i+1} that from T_{i+1} data, and R_e the number of results contained in both T_i data and T_{i+1} data, the two factors below are to measure the error of search results.

$$\text{Omission error} = (R_{i+1} - R_e) / R_{i+1} \quad (1)$$

$$\text{Commission error} = (R_i - R_e) / R_i \quad (2)$$

Omission error is the rate of appearing in the result of actual search but not in the result of index search. If this rate is low, it means high accuracy. ***Commission error*** is the rate of appearing in the result of index search but not in the result of actual search. If this rate is low, it means high accuracy.

For example, if the result (IDs) of search using query window q at time T_5, namely, the result of index search is {3,5,8,9,11,15}, and that at T_6, namely, the result of search at each sensor node is {5,8,12}, then R_5, R_6 and R_e are 6, 3 and 2, respectively. Accordingly, omission error is (3-2)/3 = 0.33 and commission error is (6-2)/6 = 0.67. Omission error is 0.33, which means that IDs to be included are not searched, and Commission error is 0.67, which means IDs not to be included are searched. This shows that the accuracy of search has decreased.

Figure 9 shows search time, update time, omission error, and commission error measured with changing the update area from 0.1 to 0.5 when the uncertainty area is 0.1, 0.3 and 0.5 in UR-tree.

As in Figure 9(a), the larger the uncertainty area is, the longer search time is. As in Figure 9(b), the larger the uncertainty area and the update area are, the shorter update time is. In Figure 9(c), if the uncertainty area is too small, the accuracy of search goes down because data to be included in the result are not searched. In addition, as in Figure 9(d), the accuracy of search goes down with the increase of the uncertainty area regardless of the update area because data not to be included in the result are searched.

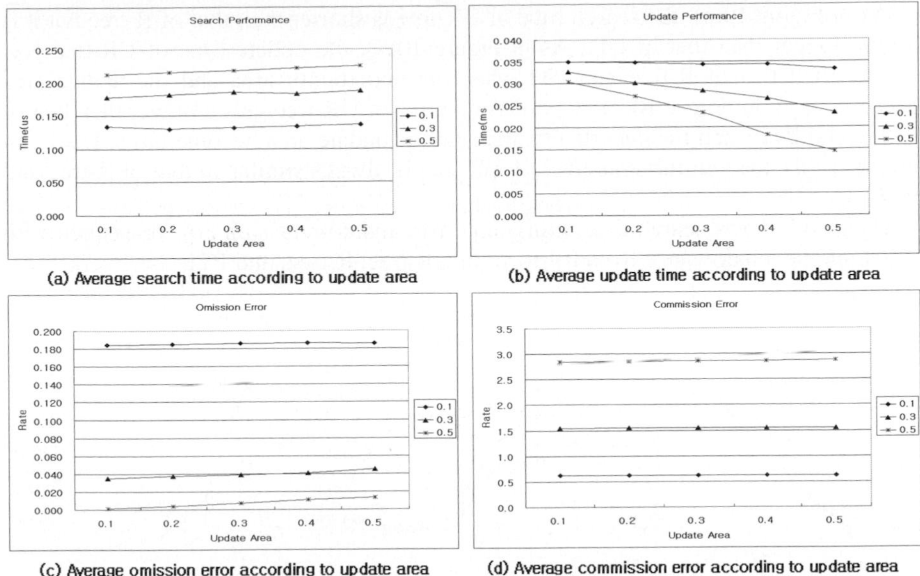

(a) Average search time according to update area

(b) Average update time according to update area

(c) Average omission error according to update area

(d) Average commission error according to update area

Fig. 9. Comparison of performance with update area

Figure 10 shows search time, update time, omission error, and commission error measured with changing the uncertainty area from 0.1 to 0.5 in UR-tree, R-tree, and PTI. Let UR-tree<p> is UR-tree with the update area of p from now on.

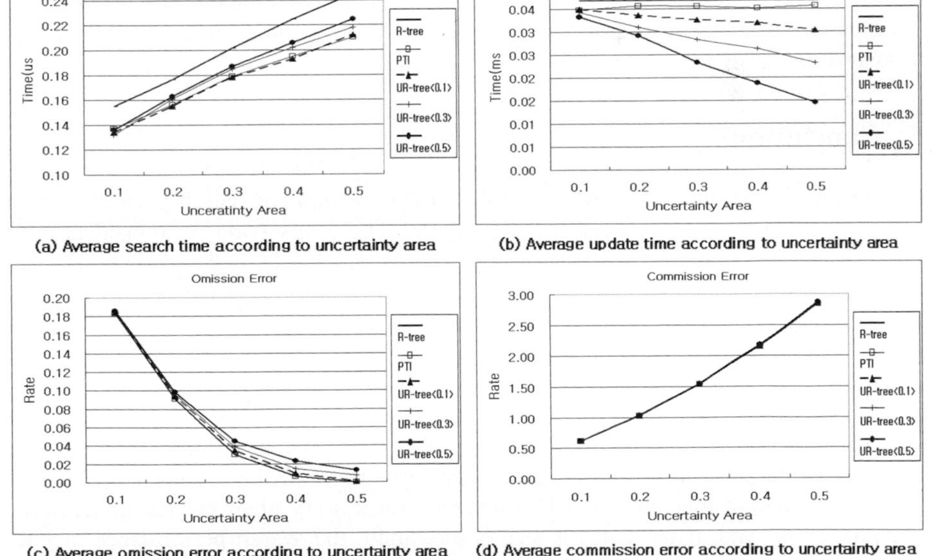

(a) Average search time according to uncertainty area

(b) Average update time according to uncertainty area

(c) Average omission error according to uncertainty area

(d) Average commission error according to uncertainty area

Fig. 10. Comparison of performance with uncertainty area

As in Figure 10(a), the search time of UR-tree is shorter than that of R-tree but it is a little longer than that of PTI. As in Figure 10(b), the update time of UR-tree gets shorter than that of R-tree and PTI when the uncertainty area and the update area become large. In Figure 10(c), the omission error of UR-tree gets a bigger than that of R-tree and PTI when the uncertainty area and the update area become large. Lastly, in Figure 10(d), the commission error of UR-tree is always similar to that of R-tree and PTI.

Figure 11 shows search time, omission error, and commission error measured with changing the window size from 0.1 to 10 in UR-tree, R-tree, and PTI.

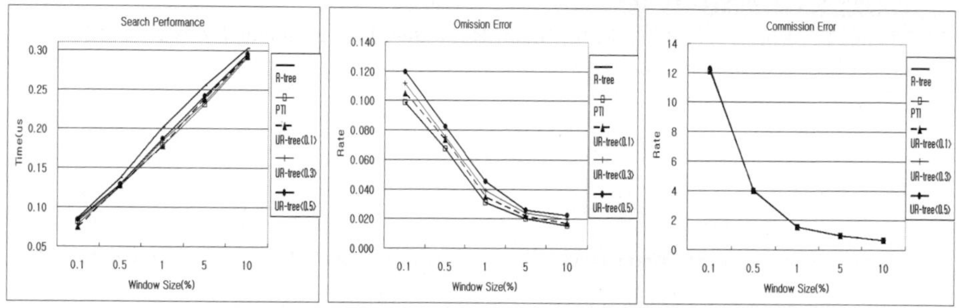

(a) Average search time according to window size (b) Average omission error according to window size (c) Average commission error according to window size

Fig. 11. Comparison of performance with window size

As in Figure 11(a), the search time of UR-tree gets shorter than that of R-tree but it gets a little longer than that of PTI when the window size is large. In Figure 11(b), the omission error of UR-tree gets a little bigger than that of R-tree and PTI when the window size is small. In addition, in Figure 11(c), the commission error of UR-tree is similar to that of R-tree and PTI.

5 Conclusions

If data are stored into the central server in order to improve search performance in USN, update performance becomes a problem. Thus, this paper examined how to process uncertain data in USN and proposed UR-tree, an index for uncertain data that can reduce the update cost of sensed data. UR-tree improved the performance of index update in consideration of uncertainty of data sensed by various sensors. In addition, it minimized the decrease in the accuracy of search caused by update delay by defining an update area.

According to the result of the performance evaluation, the update performance of UR-tree gets better than that of R-tree and PTI when the uncertainty area and the update area become large, but the search performance and the accuracy of UR-tree gets a little worse than that of PTI when the uncertainty area and the update area become large. And, if the window size is too small, the search performance of UR-tree is better than that of R-tree, but the accuracy of UR-tree is a little worse than that of R-tree and PTI.

Acknowledgements

This research was supported by the MIC(Ministry of Information and Communication), Korea, under the ITRC(Information Technology Research Center) support program supervised by the IITA(Institute of Information Technology Assessment).

References

1. Cheng, R., Prabhakar, S.: Managing Uncertainty in Sensor Databases. SIGMOD Record, Vol. 32. No. 4. (2003) 41-46.
2. Cheng, R., Xia, Y., Prabhakar, S., Shah, R., Vitter, J.S.: Efficient Indexing Methods for Probabilistic Threshold Queries over Uncertain Data. Proceedings of the 30th Intl. Conf. on Very Large Databases(VLDB) (2004) 876-887.
3. Civilis, A., Jensen, C.S., Pakalnis, S.: Techniques for Efficient Road-Network-Based Tracking of Moving Objects. IEEE Transactions on Knowledge and Data Engineering, Vol. 17. No. 5. (2005) 698-712.
4. Dai, X., Yiu, M.L., Mamoulis, N., Tao, Y., Vaitis, M.: Probabilistic Spatial Queries on Existentially Uncertain Data. Proceedings of the 9th Intl. Symp. on Spatial and Temporal Databases(SSTD) (2005) 400-417.
5. Guttman, A.: R-trees: A Dynamic Index Structure for Spatial Searching. Proceedings of the ACM SIGMOD Intl. Conf. on Management of Data (1984) 47-57.
6. Hosbond, J.H., Saltenis, S., Ørtoft, R.: Indexing Uncertainty of Continuously Moving Objects. Proceedings of DEXA Workshops (2003) 911-915.
7. Kwon, D.S., Lee, S.J., Lee, S.H.: Indexing the Current Positions of Moving Objects Using the Lazy Update R-tree. Proceedings of the Intl. Conf. on Mobile Data Management(2002) 113-120.
8. Olston, C., Loo, B.T., Widom, J.: Adaptive Precision Setting for Cached Approximate Values. Proceedings of the ACM SIGMOD Intl. Conf. on Management of Data (2001) 355-366.
9. Tao, Y., Cheng, R., Xiao, X., Ngai, W.K., Kao, B., Prabhakar, S.: Indexing Multi-Dimensional Uncertain Data with Arbitrary Probability Density Functions. Proceedings of the 30th Intl. Conf. on Very Large Databases(VLDB) (2005) 922-933.
10. Trajcevski, G., Wolfson, O., Hinrichs, K., Chamberlain, S.: Managing Uncertainty in Moving Objects Databases. ACM Transactions on Database Systems(TODS), Vol. 29. No. 3. (2004) 463-507.
11. Yuni, X., Sunil, P., Shan, L., Reynold, C., Rahul, S.: Indexing Continuously Changing Data with Mean-Variance Tree. Proceedings of the ACM Symposium on Applied Computing (2005) 1125-1132.

ZebraX: A Model for Service Composition with Multiple QoS Constraints*

Xingzhi Feng, Quanyuan Wu, Huaimin Wang, Yi Ren, and Changguo Guo

School of Computer, National University of Defense Technology,
410073 Changsha, China
billytree@gmail.com, {feng_x_z, whm_w}@163.com,
renxiaoyi@21cn.com, cgguo@163.net

Abstract. With the development of theory and technology of Web Service, Web Service Composition (WSC) has become the core Service-Oriented Computing technology. It is important for business process to select the best component services with multi-dimensional QoS assurances to construct a complex one. But there exist some problems, such as evaluation for QoS properties of a service is not full-scale and the criteria is not clear, the weight for each QoS metric doesn't consider both subjective sensations and objective facts. In this paper we propose a WSC model to provide multi-dimensional QoS supports in service selection and replacement. We consider SLA and recovery mechanism for the service failure during its execution. A utility function is defined as the evaluation standard, which aggregates all QoS metrics after normalizing their values. Then we use Subjective-Objective Weight Mode (SOWM) to set the weight of each QoS metric. Finally we introduce our prototype and evaluations, test the availability of the decision mode and the results prove it is predominant compared with other decision modes.

1 Introduction

With the development of theory and technology of Web Service, a single service often can't satisfy the functional need in practical application. Web Service Composition (WSC) has become the core Service-Oriented Computing (SOC) technology. Dynamic resource aggregation and flexible application integration make service composition in a more natural way. Service composition can realize value-added service by the service reuse. It constructs big granularity service function through the communication and collaboration between many small granularity services. It may be used to solve more complex problem to realize value-added service by efficiently collaborating some simple services different in function. Service composition shows a desirable flexibility in system integration and automatic interaction.

However, the composition flexibility comes at the cost of the increasing system engineering complexity. A complex composite service may have a great deal of component services to select; have the different composition possibility, and various

* This work was supported by the National High-Tech Research and Development Plan of China under Grant Nos. 2003AA115210, 2003AA115410, 2005AA112030 ; the National Grand Fundamental Research 973 of China under Grant Nos.2005CB321800; the National Natural Science Foundation of China under Grant Nos. 60603063, 90412011.

C. Cérin and K.-C. Li (Eds.): GPC 2007, LNCS 4459, pp. 614 – 626, 2007.

performance requirements especially in QoS issues such as delay, service time, service cost and availability. Service composition thus brings a series of QoS problems. Component services often need offer different service levels so as to meet the needs of different customer groups. Many of them have same or similar functionality but with different nonfunctional properties such as service time and availability. The QoS problem of Web Service may be defined and offered by different Service Level Agreements (SLAs) between service providers and users. Currently research work in the QoS problems of WSC mainly includes: 1) build up the QoS-based service composition model; 2) component service selection with QoS assurance; 3) dynamic adaptation and failure recovery mechanism.

In this paper we propose a WSC model called ZebraX to provide multi-dimensional QoS supports in service selection and replacement. Wc also consider the SLA issue and the recovery mechanism for the service failure during its execution. A utility function is defined as the evaluation standard, which aggregates all QoS metrics after normalizing their values. Then we discuss the decision modes and use the Subjective-Objective Weight Mode (SOWM) to set the weight of each QoS metric.

The rest of this paper is organized as follows. Section 2 reviews some related work. Section 3 proposes a model for service composition and the utility function definition with QoS assurance, and discusses the decision modes to set the weight for each QoS parameter. Section 4 presents the implementation of our prototype. Section 5 shows the validation of the composition model, evaluation and comparison of the different decision modes. The paper is concluded in Section 6.

2 Related Work

Web service composition has attracted more attention for supporting enterprise application integration. Many industry standards have been in use, such as BPEL4WS (Business Process Execution Language for Web Services) [1] and BPML (Business Process Modeling Language) [2].

Many projects have studied the problem of Web Service composition. The SWORD project [3] gives a simple and efficient mechanism for offline Web Service composition. It uses a rule-based expert system to check whether a composite service can be realized by existing services and generate the execution plan. SWORD is more focused on the service interoperability and no QoS issue has been addressed. The eFlow project [4] provides a dynamic and adaptive service composition mechanism for e-business process management. In eFlow, each service node contains a search recipe, which defines the service selection rules to select a specific service for this node. But the selection rules are based on local criteria and not address the overall QoS assurance problem of the business process. SELF-SERV [5][6] proposes the concept of Service Community that used to classify the services which can be substituted for each other in functionality but has different nonfunctional properties (i.e. QoS value). The authors propose a quality driven approach to select component services during the execution of a composite service in consideration of multiple QoS metrics such as price, duration, reliability and global constraints. They also describe two selection approaches, one based on local (task-level) selection of services and the other based on global allocation of tasks to services using integer programming.

METEOR-S [7][8] proposes a framework for semi-automatically marking up Web Service descriptions with the ontology. They identify four categories of semantics in the full web process lifecycle as Data Semantics, Functional Semantics, Execution Semantics and QoS Semantics, and annotate WSDL files with relevant ontologies. The system selects best component services based on the semantic annotation during the service selection. METEOR-S [7] and SELF-SERV [5] have studied a similar approach. Both of them use the integer linear programming method to solve the service selection problem, which is too complex for runtime decisions. The SLA framework [9] proposes the differentiated levels of Web Services using automated management and service level agreements (SLA). The service levels are differentiated based on many variables such as responsiveness, availability and performance. Although it included several SLA monitoring services to ensure a maximum level of objectivity, but no end-to-end QoS management capability was implemented.

Tao Yu *et al.* [10] design the service selection algorithms to meet the multiple QoS constraints. Their works are not focused on the trustworthiness of QoS criteria of the service. Although the global quality constraints can be satisfied, service selection may not be locally optimized. Therefore, good component service often fails to exert its potential and embody its personality. Our method can raise the efficiency and utility of Web Services reservation by sorting them. In addition, it can help to improve both the total QoS of composite service and that of single Web Service based on users' preference and objective impact. Rainer *et al.* [11] design and implement a proxy architecture WSQoSX. They present a heuristic that uses a backtracking algorithm on the results computed by a relaxed integer program. But they have not well considered the dynamic runtime failures, and the object function isn't normalized. Our utility function is well for evaluation and we also discuss the weight mode problem.

3 QoS-Based Service Composition Model

During the process of Web Service composition, we should consider not only the functionality and behavior of services but also the nonfunctional properties, especially the QoS metrics, which normally include response time, service time, availability, reliability, service cost and loss probability, etc. It is important to the service selection issue to choose right service candidates with multiple QoS metrics to construct a complex one and fulfill the business process. While meet the user's QoS requirements and optimize the performance of the composite service (i.e. maximize the total utility of the composite service). Here we propose a composition model with multiple QoS assurance. We define the utility function which aggregates all QoS metrics of a service, and use this function value as the criteria of nonfunctional properties. The utility function is the sum of each QoS metric value with different weight. We consider many factors to set the weight of each QoS metric.

3.1 Definition of the Concepts

In this paper we use *service class* as a collection of the component services with the common functionality but with different nonfunctional properties, denoted as S. The *service* is each component service in the *service class*, denoted as s. A class interface parameter set (S_{in}, S_{out}) is defined for each service class. We also assume each *service* in the service class can provide a service according to the class interface. The *candidate* is the service level of the *service s*, denoted as *sl*. Each *candidate* associates with a QoS vector $q= [q^1,...,q^m]$. Fig. 1 shows the relation between the *service class*, *service* and *candidate*.

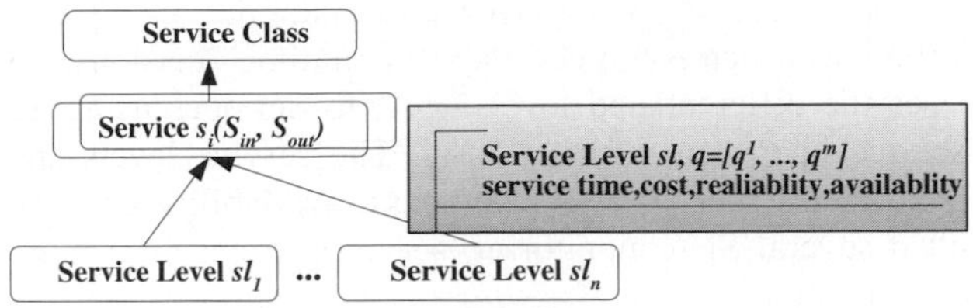

Fig. 1. The relation between the *service class*, *service* and *candidate*

The famous *Travel Planning Service* [12] is used here as an example in Fig. 2. The full business process has a staged graph structure.

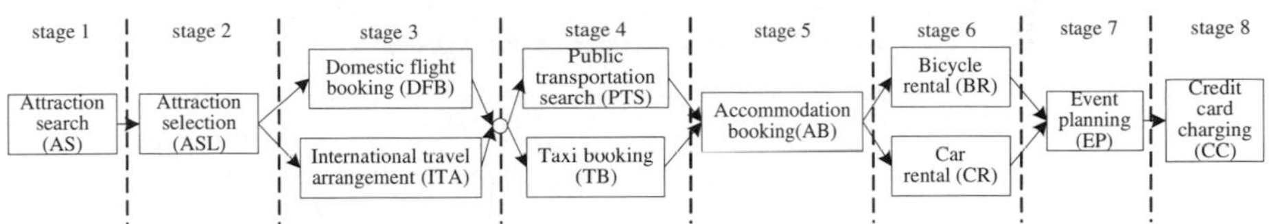

Fig. 2. Travel Planning Service Example

3.2 Definition of the Composition Model

Here we introduce our Web Service composition model called ZebraX with the multiple QoS constraints in the Fig. 3. Our model mainly includes:

1) Process Engine (PE): Maintains the business process plan information in the Repository. It includes Composition Planner, Composition Matcher, Execution Engine (WfMC [13]), Composite Service Manager (CSM) and Service Monitoring (SM). PE selects the best service candidates to construct a complex one to meet the service request. CSM manage the composite services after the aggregation. SM watches business process during its execution. When some component services fail, notify Failure Diagnosis (FD). At execution time the QoS parameters defined by the SLA are monitored by SM. SM analyses the data collected in execution process and compares them to the guaranteed metrics defined in the SLA. In case of deviations between SLA and measured data Failure Diagnosis (FD) is notified.

2) Repository: It includes service candidates catalog and process plan (service execution path) information as showed in Table 1 and Table 2. Service class catalog, rules and QoS metadata also are included. A process plan is defined by a set of service classes and the connection relationships among them.

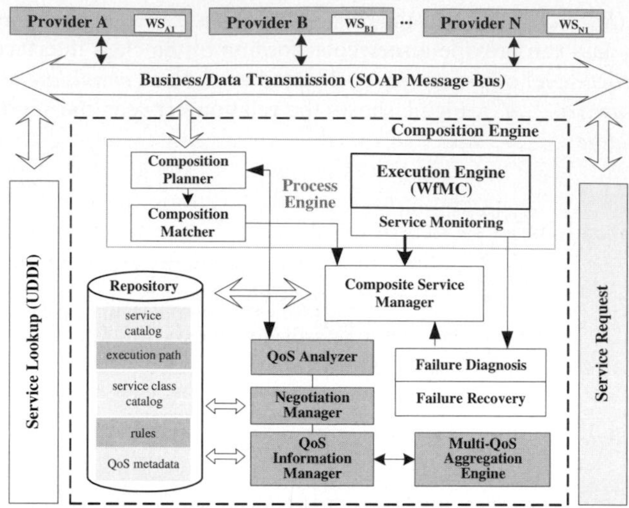

Fig. 3. The Web Service Composition Model with multiple QoS constraints

Table 1. Service Execution Path (Plan)

Exec. Path ID	Service classes in path
EP_1	$S_{AS}, S_{ASL}, S_{DFB}, S_{PTS}, S_{AB}, S_{BR}, S_{EP}, S_{CC}$
...	...

Table 2. Service Candidates Information

ID	Service Name	endpoint	Opera.	service level	QoS ID	service class
1	*s1*	*http://www.*	*op1*	sl_{11}	q_{11}	S_{AS}
2				sl_{12}	q_{12}	
3			*op2*	sl_{13}	q_{13}	
4	...					...

3) QoS Aggregation Group: QoS Analyzer (QA) handles the user's QoS requirements and gets the each QoS metric information by QoS Information Manager (QIM) from QoS metadata in Repository. The information in QoS metadata as showed in Table 3 and Table 4. QIM maintains QoS metric information (such as response time, service cost and availability and so on) and the QoS information of service candidates. Multiple-QoS Aggregation Engine (MQAE) takes into account each QoS metric and computes the utility of each service candidates. It excludes some service candidates by using rules-library $R=\{R_1,R_2,\ldots,R_m\}$ as showed in Table 5. In practice we transform the problem of service selection with multiple QoS constraints into MMKP (Multi-dimension Multi-choice 0-1 Knapsack Problem)[14] and MCOP (Multi-Constraint Optimal Path) problem.

4) Failure Diagnosis (FD)/Failure Recovery (FR): When some component services fail and the process is interrupted, FD checks the problem and FR deals with the

failure by the path replacement. A failure recovery mechanism is designed to ensure that the running process is not interrupted and the failed service can be replaced quickly and efficiently. Bad-performing services can be automatically substituted by other services with the same functionality sending a message to CSM. Guaranteed delivery and Store and forward mechanism also are considered. Furthermore we use Clustering Web services. Clustered service improves the probability of Web service completion by allowing similar Web services to form a cluster (i.e., service class) upon their registration. In case of failure, ZebraX can dynamically route requests to an equivalent backup service from the cluster by adjusting the execution path.

Table 3. QoS Metric Information in QoS metadata

QoS Metric	denotation	property	evaluation for single metric
Service time	*ST*	*Cost Property*	$ST = \sum_{i=1}^{n} ST_{s_i}$
Availability	*AP*	*Benefit Property*	$ln\ AP = \sum_{i=1}^{n} ln\ AP_{s_i}$
Loss probability	*LP*	*Cost Property*	$ln(1-LP) = \sum_{i=1}^{n} ln(1-LP_{s_i})$
…		…	…

Table 4. QoS Information for SLA in QoS metadata

QoS ID	$q_{cost}(s_i)$	$q_{time}(s_i)$	$q_{rel}(s_i)$	$q_{av}(s_i)$	…
q_{11}	0.14	175	0.90	0.92	…
q_{12}	0.20	150	0.95	0.98	…
q_{13}	0.10	158	0.92	0.91	…
…	…	…	…	…	…

Table 5. Rules-library for Multiple-QoS Aggregation Engine

Rules Name	description
R_1	*If two items a and b in the same class* S_i, *QoS metrics satisfy* $q_{ia} \leq q_{ib}$ *and the utility values satisfy* $\mathcal{F}_{ia} \geq \mathcal{F}_{ib}$, $i=1,2,\ldots,m$. *then an optimal solution to MMKP with* $x_{ib}=0$ *exists. Item b can be deleted.*
R_2	*For single QoS metric* q_v, *satisfy:* $\sum_{i=1}^{n} q_{iv} \leq C_{q_v}$.
…	…

3.3 Definition of the Utility Function

The computation of the utility function considers each QoS metric of the candidates in order to reflect the non-functionality of the service candidates deeply and thoroughly.

For there exist some differentiations such as metrology unit and metric type between each QoS metric. In order to rank the Web Services fairly we do some mathematics operations to normalize the metric values. Subsequently we can get a uniform measurement of service qualities independent of units.

Definition 1 (Utility Function). *Suppose there are α QoS metric values to be maximized and β QoS metric values to be minimized. The utility function for candidate k in a service class is defined as follows:*

$$\mathcal{F}(k)=\sum_{i=1}^{\alpha} w_i *(\frac{q_{ai}(k)-q_{ai_{\min}}}{\partial_i})+\sum_{j=1}^{\beta} w_j *(\frac{q_{bj_{max}}-q_{bj}(k)}{\partial_j}) \tag{1}$$

$$\partial_i = q_{ai_{max}} - q_{ai_{\min}},\ if\ q_{ai_{max}} - q_{ai_{\min}} \neq 0,\ else\ (q_{ai}(k)-q_{ai_{\min}})/\partial_i = 1,$$

$$\partial_j = q_{bj_{max}} - q_{bj_{\min}},\ if\ q_{bj_{max}} - q_{bj_{\min}} \neq 0,\ else\ (q_{bj_{max}} - q_{bj}(k))/\partial_j = 1.$$

Where w is the weight for each QoS metric set by user and application requirements ($0 < w_i, w_j < 1$; $\sum_{i=1}^{\alpha} w_i + \sum_{j=1}^{\beta} w_j = 1,\ \alpha+\beta=m$). ∂_i, ∂_j are the difference between maximum and minimize value in the same column. The concrete QoS metrics are defined in the matrix QoS= $[q_{i,j}]_{n\times m}$. $q_{ai\ max}$ ($q_{bj\ max}$) is the maximum value among all values on column i (j) in submatrix $[q_{a\ k,i}]_{n\times\alpha}$ ($[q_{b\ i,j}]_{n\times\beta}$) and $q_{ai\ min}$ ($q_{bj\ min}$)is the minimum value among all values on column i (j) in submatrix $[q_{a\ k,i}]_{n\times\alpha}$ ($[q_{b\ i,j}]_{n\times\beta}$).

Each row in QoS matrix represents a Web Service candidate sl_i ($1\leq i\leq n$, and *n* represents the total number of candidates) while each column represents one of the QoS metrics q_v ($1\leq v\leq m$, and *m* represents total number of QoS metrics).

3.4 Weight Computation

We need make mode decision to select component services according to disproportional QoS attributes of the candidates, which can be formalized into multi-attributes decision problem. The focus is that how to set the weight for each QoS metric. The weight should embody the attention emphasis of the users; the relative importance among different QoS metrics; and reliability of each service candidate. In a word, the weight should consider not only subjective sensations but also objective facts.

Definition 2 (Weak Order). *The set of the candidates S_c satisfies weak order, namely satisfies: 1) connectivity: $\forall s_i, s_j \in S$, then $s_i \rhd s_j$, or $s_j \rhd s_i$, or both;*

2) transitivity: $\forall s_i, s_j, s_k \in S$, if $s_i \rhd s_j$ and $s_j \rhd s_k$, then $s_i \rhd s_k$;

3) equivalence: $s_i \cong s_k$ if and only if $s_i \rhd s_j$ and $s_j \rhd s_i$.

Theorem 1. *Assumed the relation "$\rhd$" denotes weak order in S_c, $S_c = \{ s_1, s_2,\ldots, s_m \}$, then there exists value function of ordinal number with real number value, denoted as v, $\forall s_i, s_j \in S$, then*

$$v(s_i) \geq v(s_j) \Leftrightarrow s_i \rhd s_j$$

The proof of the theorem in detail can be found in [15]. The number of QoS metrics is not limited in this theorem. The value function v is not exclusive, and the function that can be acquired by any monotonously non-decreasing transformation about v is still the value function. The series about this theorem in detail can be found in [16].

There are four modes to set the weights in general: (1) Subjective Weight Mode; (2) Single Weight Mode; (3) Objective Weight Mode; (4) Subjective-Objective Weight Mode. And (2) is a special instance in (1). Taking into account both subjective sensations and objective facts, we use Subjective-Objective Weight Mode to set the weights [17][18].

Definition 3 (Subjective-Objective Weight Mode). *Assumed w_j is the weight of the QoS metric q_j, $w_j^* \in w = (w_1, w_2, \ldots, w_n)'$, $\sum_{j=1}^{n} w_j = 1$, $w_j \geq 0$, $j=1,2,\ldots,n$ can be determined by (2), then $\forall\, s_i, s_j \in S_c$, $s_i \triangleright s_j$ if and only if $B_i w^* \geq B_j w^*$, $i,j = 1,2,\ldots,m$, B is the normalized decision matrix, $B=(b_{ij})_{m\times n}$, $b_j^* = \max\{b_{1j}, b_{2j}, \ldots, b_{mj}\}$. $D = [d_{kj}]_{n\times n}$ is the comparison matrix on the QoS metrics and the elements of matrix D satisfy $d_{kj}>0$, $d_{jk}=1/d_{kj}$, $d_{kk}=1$, $d_{kj} \approx w_k/w_j$, $k,j=1,\ldots,n$, where d_{kj} denotes the relative weight of metric q_k with respect to metric q_j.*

$$\begin{cases} \min f_1 = \sum_{k=1}^{n}\sum_{j=1}^{n} (d_{kj} w_j - w_k)^2 \\ \min f_2 = \sum_{i=1}^{m}\sum_{j=1}^{n} (b_j^* - b_{ij})^2 w_j^2 \quad \text{subject to } \sum_{j=1}^{n} w_j = 1,\ w_j \geq 0,\ j=1,2,\ldots,n \end{cases} \tag{2}$$

4 Implementation

The prototype of our Web Service architecture is implemented in Java preliminarily. We use Apache Tomcat 5.0 as application server. Apache Axis 1.1 is employed as SOAP engine. We adopt Systinet's WASP UDDI Standard 3.1 as our UDDI toolkit and Cloudscape 4.0 database is used as a UDDI registry. Our model provides an environment for rapid composition of Web Services. The processes of integrating multiple component services are: When a service request comes, PE decomposes the user's request as fundamental functions at first, which can be fulfilled by a simple Web Service. QA handles the user's QoS requirements and gets the each QoS metric information by QIM from QoS metadata. Then PE constructs the process plan and finds the service candidates from Service Lookup (e.g. UDDI). By the help of MQAE that takes into account all QoS metrics and computes the utility of each service candidate, PE selects the best service candidates to construct a complex one to meet the service request. SM watches business process during its execution. When some component services fail and the process is interrupted, FD checks the problem and FR deals with the failure by the path replacement.

First of all, the Web Service providers have to register their services at the portal according to pre-defined service classes (e.g. flight booking) (showed in Fig. 4). A corresponding SLA has to be referenced as well.

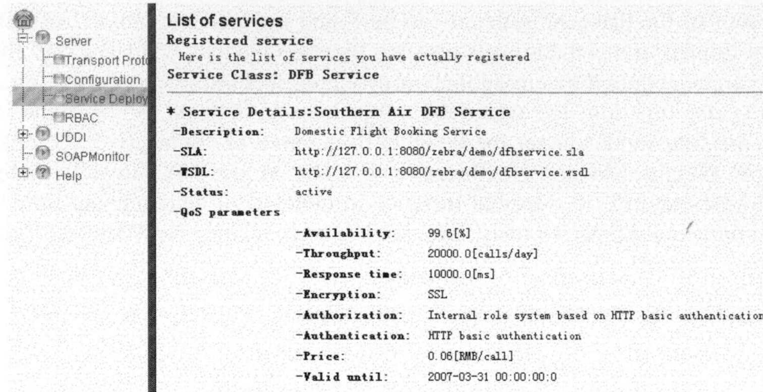

Fig. 4. List of registered Web Services and Service Classes

Fig. 5 shows an excerpt of a SLA for a *DFBService*. Within this SLA an availability of 99.6% and average response time of 0.5ms are assured and the validity of the Web Service is defined as well.

```
<ServiceDefinition name="DFBService">
 <ServiceLevelObjective name="SLO_For_Availablility">
  <Obliged>SouthernAirProvider</Obliged>
  <Validity>
    <Start>2007-02-28T14:00:00.000-05:00</Start>
    <End>2007-03-31T14:00:00.000-05:00</End>
  </Validity>
  <Expression>
    <Implies>
     <Expression>
      <Predicate xsi:type="Greater">
       <SLAParamter>Availability</SLAParameter>
       <Value>99.6</Value>
      </Predicate>
     </Expression>
     <Expression>
      <Predicate xsi:type="Less">
       <SLAParamter>AverageResponseTime</SLAParameter>
       <Value>0.5</Value>
      </Predicate>
     </Expression>
    </Implies>
  </Expression>
  <EvaluationEvent>NewValue</EvaluationEvent>
 </ServiceLevelObjective>
</ServiceDefinition>
```

Fig. 5. Excerpt of a SLA for *DFBService*

The Web Service composition is realized in BPEL4WS. We use ActiveBPEL [19] as the engine for the execution of the BPEL4WS process. Fig. 6 illustrates an excerpt of the invocation of a *Travel Planning Service* modeled by BPEL4WS.

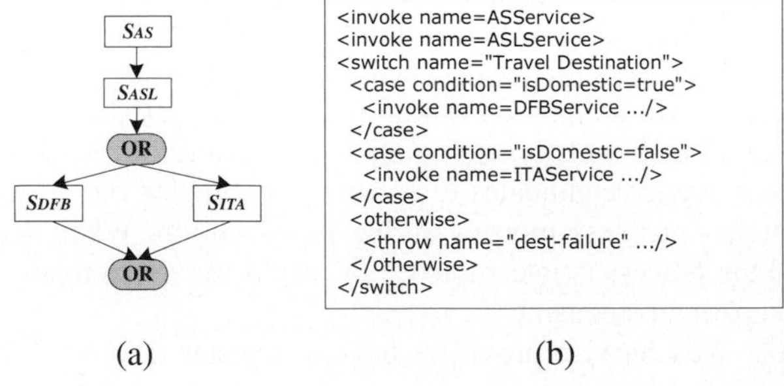


```
<invoke name=ASService>
<invoke name=ASLService>
<switch name="Travel Destination">
  <case condition="isDomestic=true">
    <invoke name=DFBService .../>
  </case>
  <case condition="isDomestic=false">
    <invoke name=ITAService .../>
  </case>
  <otherwise>
    <throw name="dest-failure" .../>
  </otherwise>
</switch>
```

Fig. 6. Excerpt of a Travel Planning Service by the BPEL4WS process

5 Validation of the Model

5.1 Validation of the Composition Model

We use the *composition success ratio* as the evaluation standard that is calculated by *SuccessNumber/RequestNumber*. A QoS-aware service composition is said to be successful, if and only if the composite service satisfies the function requirements and the user's QoS requirements (e.g., delay, execution time, loss probability) [20][21]. To evaluate the performance of dynamic service composition for failure recovery, we define the metric *recovery success ratio* that is calculated by *SuccessNumber/ FailureNumber*. Higher recovery success ratio represents higher failure resilience in the composed service provisioning. For comparison, we also implement two other common approaches: random and static algorithms. The random algorithm randomly selects a functionally qualified component service for each service class in the composition graph. The static algorithm uses pre-defined component service for each service class in the composition graph. Both random and static algorithms don't consider the user's QoS requirements.

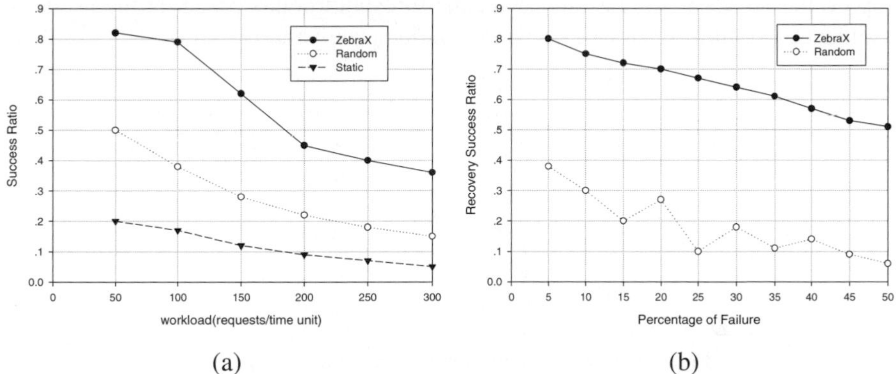

Fig. 7. (a) Composition success ratio comparison among different approaches; (b) Failure recovery success ratio comparison among different approaches

Second, we evaluate the efficiency of our failure recovery mechanism. We consider a dynamic service overlay network where a certain percentage of overlay nodes randomly fail during each time unit. The business processes that include those failed nodes will be affected to experience failures. We measure how many affected processes can be recovered by our recovery mechanism. We use the degree-based Internet topology generator *nem* (network manipulator) [22], a software that can do several tasks related to network analysis and modeling for power law topology model. The graph size we have chosen to study is 4000 nodes and about 12,800 edges (average degree is 3.2). We randomly select 500 nodes as the service candidate nodes in a business process. Fig.7 (b) shows the measured recovery success ratio on this power law overlay network. The request rate is 150 requests per minute. Each recovery success ratio value is averaged over the whole 1000 minute simulation duration. The results show that the failure recovery can achieve high failure recovery success ratio on a moderately changing overlay network by our dynamic recovery mechanism. The recovery success rate degrades as the percentage of node failures increases. However, the failure recovery algorithm can still recover more than 50% failures even on a highly dynamic service overlay network where 50% peers randomly fail. Moreover, our failure recovery approach can achieve higher recovery success rate when higher maintenance overhead is allowed.

5.2 Validation of the Decision Model

In this section, we present the experiments in the testbed to evaluate the proposed Web Service Composition Decision Model of QoS criteria (**WSCDMQ**). We will give the experiment scenario and then some tests are done. We choose the Attraction Selection (ASL) Service S_{ASL} of the above *Travel Planning Service* in Fig. 8 as a sample to do the simulation experiments. Suppose there are 10 Web Services similar in functionality to S_{ASL}, and service providers have provided QoS information namely *execution cost* ($q_{cost}(s_i)$), *execution time* ($q_{time}(s_i)$), *reliability* ($q_{rel}(s_i)$), *availability* ($q_{av}(s_i)$), and an additional criterion *fidelity* ($q_{fid}(s_i)$) which is given by monitor broker. Suppose the 10 Web Services all satisfy the threshold points based on the users' requirements. QoS information of decision criteria is shown in Fig. 9(a).

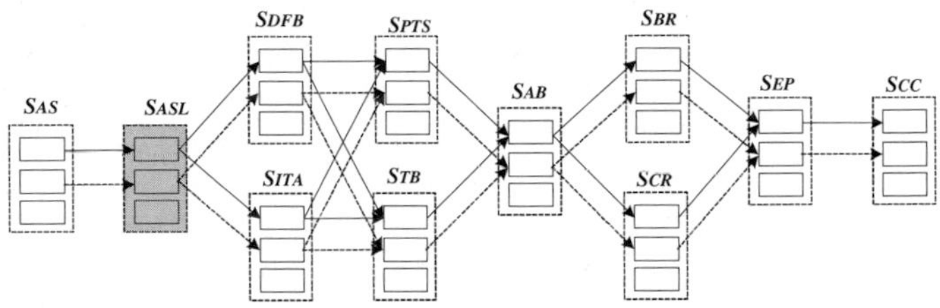

Fig. 8. Service Selection for S_{ASL} in the Service Graph

	$q_{cost}(s_i)$	$q_{time}(s_i)$	$q_{rel}(s_i)$	$q_{av}(s_i)$	q_{fid}
s_1	0.14	175	0.90	0.92	(0.99,0.94,0.90,0.95)
s_2	0.20	150	0.95	0.98	(0.95,0.89,0.93,0.92)
s_3	0.10	158	0.92	0.91	(0.95,0.85,0.90,0.91)
s_4	0.15	152	0.85	0.95	(0.88,0.90,0.90,0.88)
s_5	0.18	165	0.92	0.98	(0.85,0.90,0.95,0.95)
s_6	0.20	175	0.90	0.88	(0.99,0.94,0.92,0.90)
s_7	0.15	190	0.94	0.92	(0.95,0.95,0.92,0.95)
s_8	0.16	155	0.88	0.96	(0.95,0.88,0.95,0.90)
s_9	0.18	150	0.92	0.92	(0.92,0.92,0.90,0.95)
s_{10}	0.15	145	0.92	0.88	(0.92,0.90,0.92,0.90)

(a)

	$q_{cost}(s_i)$	$q_{time}(s_i)$	$q_{rel}(s_i)$	$q_{av}(s_i)$	SWM	OWM	SOWM
s_1	0.59	0.31	0.45	0.38	0.3819	0.4105	0.3388
s_2	0	0.79	0.93	0.92	0.7869	0.7400	0.7766
s_3	0.95	0.60	0.63	0.27	0.5719	0.6012	0.4908
s_4	0.44	0.76	0	0.62	0.5232	0.4490	0.4530
s_5	0.17	0.50	0.67	0.95	0.6032	0.5872	0.5908
s_6	0	0.31	0.46	0	0.2608	0.2523	0.2558
s_7	0.48	0	0.83	0.38	0.3127	0.4001	0.3081
s_8	0.38	0.68	0.29	0.72	0.5713	0.5217	0.5194
s_9	0.18	0.82	0.63	0.38	0.6345	0.5813	0.5952
s_{10}	0.46	0.90	0.64	0	0.6234	0.5836	0.5565

(b)

Fig. 9. (a) Values of 10 Similar Web Services; (b) Utilities for 10 Similar Web Services

In *Subjective-objective weight* mode (SOWM), we set α=0.3 and β=0.7 to reflect the relative importance of the *subjective weight* mode and *objective weight* mode respectively, the comparison matrix *D= [1, 1/3, 1/4, 1/4; 3, 1, 2, 3; 4, 1/2, 1, 4/5; 4,*

1/3, 5/4, 1]. We can obtain the weights w^{*}= (0.10,0.42,0.27,0.21)', and Web Services are sorted, i.e., $s_2 \triangleright s_9 \triangleright s_5 \triangleright s_{10} \triangleright s_8 \triangleright s_3 \triangleright s_4 \triangleright s_1 \triangleright s_7 \triangleright s_6$. We also use the *subjective weight* mode (SWM) and *objective weight* mode (OWM) as a reference.In subjective weight mode (SWM), we can obtain the weights w^{*}= (0.08,0.48,0.24,0.2)' according to matrix D, while in objective weight mode (OWM), weights w^{*} =(0.15, 0.35, 0.31, 0.19)', the result is independent of comparison matrix.

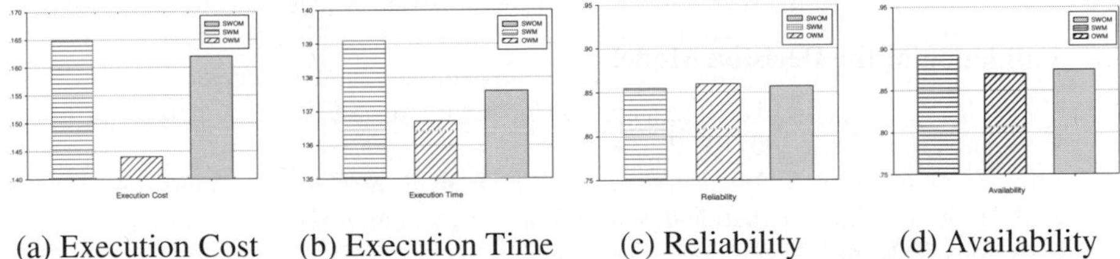

(a) Execution Cost (b) Execution Time (c) Reliability (d) Availability

Fig. 10. Criteria Comparisons among Web Services Selected Under Different Decision Modes

Based on these testing results above, we can conclude that **WSCDMQ** model strike a better balance and is more efficient compared with the other two. *Subjective weight* model and *objective weight* mode are simple to use but with some limitations in applications, while *subjective-objective weight* mode is flexible and reasonable for its applications, as it combines both subjective preference and objective impact.

6 Conclusion and Future Work

In this paper, we study the problem of complex service composition with multiple QoS constraints. We present a QoS-based service composition model and propose the utility function as the evaluating standard as a whole considering all QoS parameters of each component service. Also we discuss the decision modes to set the weights. It can help to select component services based on users' preference and objective impact. It lays down a sound theoretical basis for our further research of dynamic Web service composition. In the end we test the performance of our model and the availability of the decision mode and the results prove it to be viable.

Issues not covered in this paper that are planned as future enhancements are: (1) Add heuristic algorithm to find service candidates with multiple QoS constraints; (2) Consider dynamic adaptation problems during the execution of the business process.

References

1. Curbera, F., Goland, Y., Klein, J., *et al.*: Business Process Execution Language for Web Services,Version 1.1. http://www-106.ibm.com/developerworks/webservices/library/ws-bpel, May 2003.
2. BPMI.org.: Business Process Modeling Language (BPML), Version 1.0, http://www.bpmi.org/bpml.esp, November 2002.

3. Ponnekanti, S.R., Fox, A.: Sword: A developer toolkit for Web service composition. 11th World Wide Web Conference (Engineering Track), Honolulu, Hawaii, May 2002.
4. Casati, F., Ilnicki, S., Jin, L., *et al.*: Adaptive and Dynamic Service Composition in eFlow. Proc. of the 12th International Conference on Advanced Information Systems Engineering(CAiSE 2000), Stockholm, Sweden, June, 2000, pp.13-31.
5. Zeng, L., Benatallah, B., Dumas, M., *et al.*: Quality Driven Web Service Composition. Proc. of 12th International World Wide Web Conference (WWW03), Budapest, Hungary, May 2003.
6. Zeng, L., Benatallah, B., H.H.Ngu, A., *et al.*: QoS-Aware Middleware for Web Services Composition. IEEE Transactions on Software Engineering, vol. 30, no. 5, 2004, pp.311-327.
7. Aggarwal, R., Verma, K., Miller, J., *et al.*: Constraint driven Web service composition in METEOR-S. Proc. of IEEE International Conference on Service Computing (SCC'04), Shanghai, China, Sept. 2004, pp.23-30.
8. Patil, A., Oundhakar, S., Sheth, A., *et al.*: METEOR-S Web service Annotation Framework. Proc. of 13th international World Wide Web conference(WWW04), New York, USA, May 2004, pp.533-562.
9. Dan, A., Davis, D., Kearney, R., *et al.*: Web services on demand: WSLA-driven automated management. IBM Systems Journal, vol. 43, no. 1, 2004, pp.136-158.
10. Yu, T., Lin, K.-J.: Service Selection Algorithms for Composing Complex Services with Multiple QoS Constraints. ICSOC2005, pp.130-143.
11. Berbner, R., Spahn, M., Repp, N., *et al.*: Heuristics for QoS-aware Web Service Composition. Proc. of IEEE International Conference on Web Services (ICWS'06), pp.72-82.
12. Benatallah, B., Sheng, Q.Z., Dumas, M.: The Self-Serv Environment for Web Services Composition. IEEE INTERNET COMPUTING, JANUARY-FEBRUARY 2003, pp.40-48.
13. WfMC, http://www.wfmc.org.
14. Khan, S., Li, K.F., Manning, E.G., *et al.*: Solving the knapsack problem for adaptive multimedia systems. Studia Informatica Universalis, vol. 2, no. 1, Sept. 2002, pp.157-178.
15. Yue, C.: Theory and Methods. the Science Press, China, ISBN 7-03-01081607, Mar. 2003.
16. Hu, J., Guo, C., Wang, H., *et al.*: Quality Driven Web Services Selection. Proc. of IEEE International Conference on e-Business Engineering (ICEBE 2005), Beijing, China, Oct. 2005, pp.681-688.
17. Fan, Z.P.: A New Method for Multiple Attribute Decision Making. Journal of System Engineering, vol. 12, no. 1, 1994, pp.15-17.
18. Ma, J., Fan, Z., Huang, L.: A Subjective and Objective Integrated Approach to Determine Attribute Weights. European Journal of Operational Research, 112(2), 1999, pp.397-404.
19. ActiveBPEL project, http://www.active-endpoints.com/active-bpel-engine-overview.htm.
20. Gu, X., Nahrstedt, K.: Dynamic QoS-aware multimedia service configuration in ubiquitous computing environments. Proc. of IEEE 22nd International Conference on Distributed Computing Systems, Vienna, Austria, July 2002, pp.311-318.
21. Gu, X., Nahrstedt, K.: A scalable QoS-aware service aggregation model for peer-to-peer computing grids. Proc. of the 11th IEEE International Symposium on High Performance Distributed Computing (HPDC-11), Edinburgh, Scotland, July 2002, pp.73-82.
22. Magoni, D., Pansiot, J.-J.: Internet Topology Modeler Based on Map Sampling. Proc. of the Seventh International Symposium on Computers and Communications (ISCC'02). IEEE Computer Society, Taormina, July 2002, pp.1021-1027.

Middleware Support for Java Applications on Globus-Based Grids

Yudith Cardinale, Carlos Figueira, Emilio Hernández,
Eduardo Blanco, and Jesús De Oliveira

Universidad Simón Bolívar,
Departamento de Computación y Tecnología de la Información,
Apartado 89000, Caracas 1080-A, Venezuela
{yudith,figueira,emilio,eduardo}@ldc.usb.ve,
jesus@bsc.co.ve

Abstract. In this paper we describe the execution model supported by SUMA/G, a middleware built on top of Globus for execution of Java applications on the grid. This execution model allows a user to launch Java applications that will run on a grid from her machine without requiring this machine to be part of the grid (e.g. a gLite *User Interface*). Additionally, it allows grid users to regard *local* file systems, i.e. file systems accessible from their local workstations, as part of the set of file systems accessible within the grid. This eliminates the necessity of performing previous uploads of classes and data files, which helps to meet the grid goal of achieving seamless access to distributed resources. We describe how to implement the services offered by this execution model on Globus-based grids. We compare the use of this execution model with the standard mechanisms for submission of Java jobs in LCG/gLite, a flavor of Globus Toolkit 2. We present experiments showing that this execution model can improve performance for running Java applications on Globus-based grids.

1 Introduction

Distributed platforms for compute-intensive processing and resource sharing, known as *grids* [1], provide basic technologies for integrating multi-institutional sets of computational resources. A grid middleware is deployed for achieving the integration goal. Globus [2] is the most widely used grid middleware, available in several versions; it is distributed as *toolkits* that include basic services and libraries for resource monitoring and management, security, file management, job submission, and communication.

Grid users are typically grouped into *Virtual Organizations (VO)* [3]. Each VO is granted the access to a subset of the resources available in the grid. We call *VO Working Space* (VOWS) the set of computing resources accessible by members of a particular VO. A VOWS is mainly composed of the computing platforms that can be used by the VO and the file systems accessible by that VO. For instance, in LCG [4, 5] and gLite [6], there are *Storage Elements* which can store the data files

C. Cérin and K.-C. Li (Eds.): GPC 2007, LNCS 4459, pp. 627–641, 2007.

to be processed. These files were probably uploaded directly by a data provider, or by users from a *User Interface (UI)*. In this case, the set of file systems in a VOWS is composed of the file systems directly accessed from UIs and working nodes, plus the Storage Elements accessible by that VO, typically through gridFTP.

When a user wants to process some data files stored in her local workstations, she must upload those files into her VOWS (e.g. into a file system accessible from a UI) before the data can be processed within a grid. In addition, the data files should be transferred from the UI into the file systems accessible by the working elements before the execution starts. Storage Elements can always be used as intermediate data containers in the grid.

Using the grid could be easier for most users if the file systems accessible from the local workstation were part of the VOWS. For example, the files contained in their laptops could be part of their VOWS. In this case, file prestaging is necessary for the execution of applications on the remote node, and the prestage could be partial (e.g. only a part of a file) or complete (the whole file). Notice that such a feature is not provided by current Globus implementations, because local machines are not part of the grid and the users must login to a UI before accessing other grid components. Moreover, if such a feature is provided, it is desirable that applications are not aware of the prestage phase. Ideally, applications should only call standard I/O functions, instead of using location or grid dependent remote access functions, such as secure RFIO (a GSI enhanced RFIO [7]) or based on GFAL [8], a library for file access provided in LCG/gLite.

In this article we present an execution model for grids that incorporates local file systems into a VOWS, eliminating the necessity of explicitly uploading the data files and programs to a UI or of specifying location dependent file accesses into the application. This execution model has been implemented in SUMA/G [9], a grid middleware specifically targeted at executing Java bytecode on top of Globus grids. This model includes a mechanism for dynamically loading data files and Java classes directly from the local machine on demand, in a transparent way, which means that programs designed for local file system access do not have to be modified for grid execution. We describe how to implement the services offered by this execution model on Globus-based grids. We compare our execution model with a standard Globus-based interface for job execution.

SUMA/G has been partially implemented on top of the Java CoG Kit [10]. More recently, similar platforms to SUMA/G have appeared, such as ProActive [11]. In their current status, SUMA/G and ProActive differ mainly in two aspects. First, SUMA/G is conceived as a middleware to be executed within a Globus environment, while ProActive defines interoperability interfaces with Globus and other grids. Secondly, current version of SUMA/G is more oriented to data service deployment, that is, it provides a meta-service for service installation [12].

The rest of this paper is organized as follows. Section 2 explains the execution model of programs in Globus-based grids and section 3 explains the SUMA/G execution model. Section 4 describes a scheme for providing SUMA/G services as part of a Globus grid. Section 5 shows experiments comparing Java programs performance under LCG/gLite and SUMA/G. Section 6 offers our conclusions and future work.

2 Execution Model in Globus-Based Grids

The Globus Toolkit offers building blocks (as services) that conform the grid infrastructure. These services include resource monitoring and management, security, file management, job submission, and communication. A security infrastructure provides for the control of resources usage. Grid computing resources are typically operated under the control of a scheduler which implements allocation and prioritization policies while optimizing the execution of all submitted jobs for efficiency and performance.

Job submission can be done by using the bare services included in the toolkit. They allow for interactive and off line remote applications execution. A user who is granted access to a remote resource (often chosen by a scheduler) send her/his application (i.e., executable files and libraries) to that resource, together with the input data the application needs. Jobs and the resources required to run them (e.g., parameters, resource usage, I/O files) can be specified through specialized languages, such a the Globus Resource Specification Language (RSL). Globus also supports uploading a program and its input data files; later, the user can request for execution of the previously uploaded programs, and finally download the output.

Our case study is a lightweight grid middleware called gLite [6], which is based on a previous version called LCG (*LHC Computing Grid*) [4, 5], which in turn is a grid middleware implemented on top of Globus services. As these two middlewares share so many features (architecture, execution model, etc.) we will refer to them as LCG/gLite.

2.1 LCG/gLite Architecture

Components of LCG/gLite are currently implemented with Globus Toolkit version 2 (GT2). It also uses CondorG [13] for workload management. The basic architecture is composed of the following modules, among others.

Security: The LCG/gLite security platform is based on Globus Security Infrastructure (GSI) and Virtual Organizations (VO). The GSI enables secure authentication and communication over an open network. GSI uses public key encryption, X.509 certificates, and the SSL communication protocol. Extensions on these standards have been added for single sign-on and delegation. The user authorization can be done: *i)* for the specific grid resource, by matching the user certificate to a local account; or *ii)* through the VO Membership Service, which allows for more detailed definition of the user privileges.

User Interface (UI): The access point to the LCG/gLite grid is the UI. This is a machine where LCG/gLite users have a personal account and where the user certificate is installed. Users submit jobs and access other LCG/gLite services from UI. One or more UIs are available to all VOs.

Computing Element (CE) and Storage Element (SE): A CE receives jobs for execution on its associated computing nodes (*Worker Nodes*, WN).

It is defined as a grid batch queue. Besides the WN, it is based on Local Resource Management System (LRMS), such as PBS and a node acting as a Gatekeeper, which plays the role of front-end to the rest of the grid. Storage Elements provide uniform access to storage resources; a number of data access protocols and interfaces are supported (e.g., GSI-secure file transfer protocol, GSIFTP).

Information Service (IS): The Information Service (IS) provides information about the grid resources and their status. This information is used by other grid components, such as UIs and CEs. The data published in the IS conforms to the GLUE (Grid Laboratory for a Uniform Environment) Schema. Currently, LCG/gLite uses Globus' Monitoring and Discovery Service (MDS), using LDAP as main provider of the Information Service. CEs publish their resources information using a Grid Resource Information Server (GRIS); a site's resources information is compiled at a Grid Index Information Server (GIIS) or, alternatively, a Berkeley DB Information Service (BDII). Another component gathers information from several GIIS/BDII, acting as a cache, storing information about grid resources status.

Job Management: The services of the Workload Management System (WMS) are responsible for the acceptance of submitted jobs and for sending those jobs to the appropriate CE (depending on the job requirements and the available resources). For that purpose, the WMS must retrieve information from the IS and the File Catalog. The Resource Broker (RB) is the machine where the WMS services run.

2.2 LCG/gLite Job Submission

We summarize the main steps for executing a job in LCG/gLite.

1. Before using the services, a user must obtain a digital certificate, register with a VO and obtain an account on an UI. The user logs to the UI machine and creates a proxy certificate.
2. He/she submits the job from the UI to the Resource Broker node, providing a job description file (in Job Description Language, JDL) specifying, for instance, one or more files (Input Sandbox) to be copied from the UI to the RB node.
3. The WMS looks for the best available CE to execute the job through MDS.
4. The WMS prepares the job for submission creating a wrapper script that will be passed, together with other parameters, to the selected CE.
5. The CE receives the request and sends the job for execution to the local LRMS.
6. The LRMS handles the job execution on the available local WN.
7. User files are copied from the RB to the WN where the job is executed. While the job runs, SE files can be accessed through a number of protocols, such as secure RFIO.
8. The job can produce new output data that can be uploaded to the grid (SE) and made available for other grid users to use.

9. If the job reaches the end without errors, the output (not large data files, but just small output files specified by the user in the so called Output Sandbox) is transferred back to the RB node.
10. At this point, the user can retrieve the output of his job from the UI using the WMS Command Level Interface (CLI) or API.

3 Execution Model in SUMA/G

SUMA/G[1] (Scientific Ubiquitous Metacomputing Architecture/Globus) [9] is a grid middleware that transparently executes Java bytecode on remote machines. SUMA/G supports both sequential and parallel applications using MPIJAVA. SUMA/G security and resource management are based on Globus components [14]. In SUMA/G, Java classes and files are loaded on demand from the user's machines, which means that it is not necessary neither previous installation of the user's Java code on the worker node nor packing all classes for submission. Instead, only the reference to the main class is submitted; all Java class files, as well as data files, are loaded on demand with prefetching and buffering support in order to reduce communication overheads [15]. Bytecode and data files servers may be located on machines belonging to the grid, or in user controlled external servers. Compared to Globus job execution model, SUMA/G on demand loading of classes and data provides a higher level of transparency, because there is no need for job description scripts, which are commonly used in Globus platforms.

SUMA/G was originally built on top of commodity software and communication technologies, including Java and CORBA [16]. It has been gradually incorporating Globus general services by using the Java CoG Kit [10]. While it might be possible to implement most of SUMA/G services directly on the Java CoG Kit, some SUMA/G components are still needed since a number of services already provided by SUMA/G are not available in the Java CoG Kit. Some of these services are on-line execution, off-line execution, and classes and data loading on demand. The SUMA/G services are accessible through local clients as command line and graphic interfaces. As an alternative to these standard clients, SUMA/G includes a portal that provides a single web interface to the grid resources.

The Java CoG Kit offers a suitable abstraction of Globus services, and allows for leveraging on Globus technology evolution. Thus, SUMA/G grids can be connected to deployed Globus based grids. The SUMA/G architecture is depicted in Figure 1; the components are described below.

3.1 SUMA/G Components

SUMA/G components, and their role in the execution of applications, are shown below.

Proxy: Receives an object from `Client Stub`, containing application data such as the name of the main class, scheduling constraints (optional) and data

[1] http://suma.ldc.usb.ve

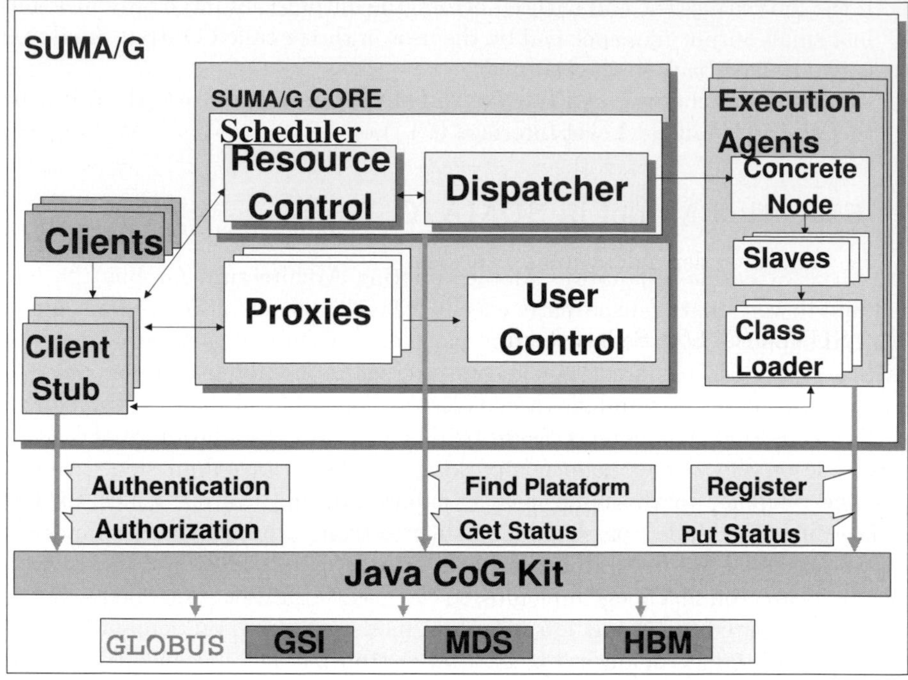

Fig. 1. SUMA/G Architecture

structures to reduce the number of communications (optional); these are called *pre-loaded data*. After checking user permissions, the `Proxy` asks the `Scheduler` for a suitable execution platform, then sends the application object to the selected one. In case of submitting off-line jobs, the `Proxy` keeps results until the user requests them.

Scheduler: Responds to `Proxy` requests based on the application requirements and status information obtained from the grid platform. Using the Globus MDS service, the `Scheduler` learns about grid resources, obtaining information about available execution platforms (including memory size, available libraries and average load), data sets hosted at specific locations, and so on. With this information, the `Scheduler` selects a suitable resource satisfying the application requirements, while looking for load balance in the grid.

User Control: It is in charge of user registration and authentication. The GSI is used for user authentication and authorization in SUMA/G, as well as a mechanism for including all SUMA/G components in the grid security space.

Client Stub: It creates the application object, retrieves results and performance data, and serves `Execution Agent` requests (callbacks) to load classes and data dynamically. It is executed on the user machine or on a SUMA/G entry server. In any case, the user must have a valid certificate installed on that machine.

Execution Agent: On starting, it registers itself at the `Scheduler` as a new available resource. During operation, it receives the application object from the `Proxy` and launches execution, loading classes and files dynamically from the client or from a remote file system through the SUMA/G class loader and the SUMA/G I/O subsystem. Once the application has finished, the `Execution Agent` sends the results back to the client. In a parallel platform, it plays the role of the front-end. Only the front-end of a parallel platform is registered on SUMA/G either as an MPIJAVA enabled platform or as a farm, for multiple independent job executions.

3.2 SUMA/G I/O Subsystem

SUMA/G implements a number of mechanisms to handle remote access to data and classes. All data files and classes requests issued by applications are redirected to the client, which in turn connects to local file systems (i.e., at the client machine) or remote file systems specified by the user (e.g., at machines in which the user has an account) to serve the requests. An alternative mechanism that bypasses the client, directly connecting applications to data repositories (only for data files), is also being implemented [17]. Figure 2 shows current SUMA/G I/O subsystem.

The remote data and classes access mechanisms are:

1. Dynamic class loading. Each application instantiates its own SUMA/G `Class Loader`, which handles the dynamic class loading from the client up to the `Execution Agent` at run time.
2. Standard input, output and error redirection. For interactive applications, the execution environment is modified such that the standard input, output and error are connected to the client issuing the execution request, thus behaving as if it were a local execution.
3. `java.io` redirection. A new package, `suma.io` redefines the basic classes in `java.io`. Thus, through *callbacks* to the client, the data files can be accessed by applications.
4. Buffering. Remote file accesses use buffering to improve performance, by reading or writing blocks, hence reducing the number of *callbacks* to data sources. The kind of buffering support provided in SUMA/G is different from the buffering support provided by buffer cache components commonly found in file system implementations. It rather resembles file prestaging, in the sense that it consists of a single block, which actually could be the whole file. At execution time a block size is specified (or an indicator for prestaging the whole remote file) and the data transfer is performed on demand, when the application executes a read on the file. The data block transferred from the remote file system starts at the first byte accessed by the application. If the application tries to access a byte not contained in the transferred data block, another data block is transferred, overwriting the previous block.

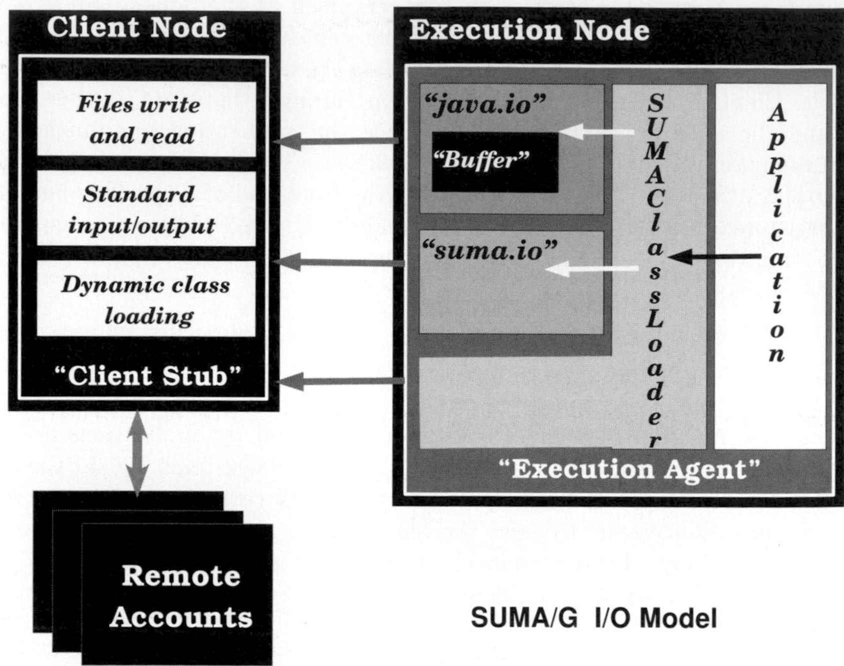

Fig. 2. SUMA/G I/O Subsystem

3.3 SUMA/G Portal

The SUMA/G Portal supports the SUMA/G remote file access mechanisms. The main benefit of the portal is that a single grid user name provides access not only to the resources allowed for the VO the user belongs to, but also to the file systems accessible from the local workstation. In this case the local workstation does not run a SUMA/G client, but a standard web browser. A modified SUMA/G Client Stub runs in the web server side. The access to the local file systems is made by this SUMA/G Client Stub, through a file server, such as *sshd* or *apache*, which must be locally installed. Not only the local file systems can be accessed from the grid side, but also other file systems available in different machines that are not part of the grid. The user grants the access to his/her accounts, after the connection from the web browser to the web portal is conceded. Figure 3 depicts the access scheme provided by the SUMA/G Portal. File access is done through the portal on demand, relieving the user of uploading data and classes into the grid.

The SUMA/G portal is based on GridSphere [18] and uses MyProxy [19] as the credential manager.

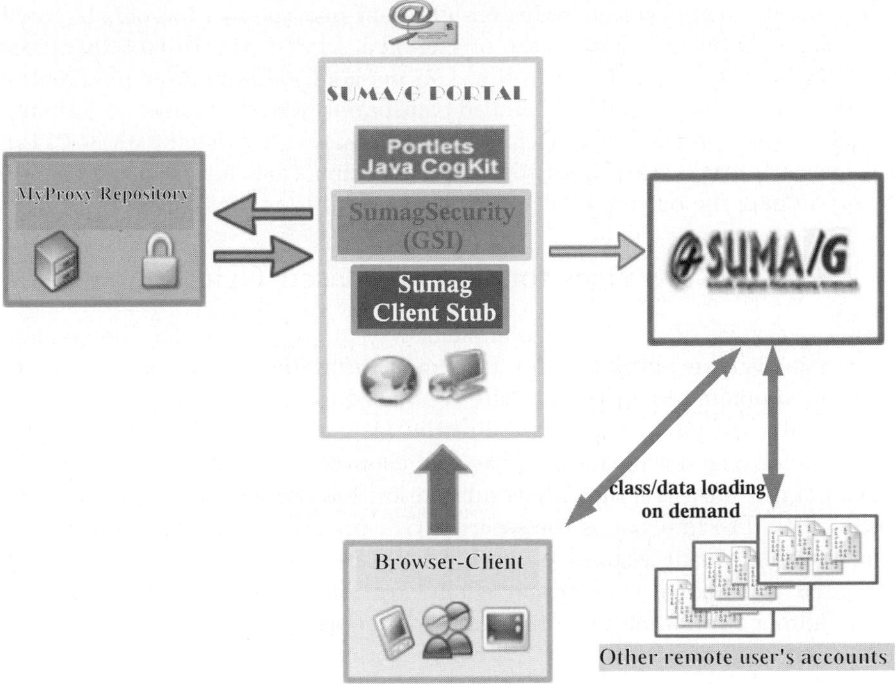

Fig. 3. SUMA/G Portal Access Scheme

3.4 SUMA/G Job Submission

The basics of executing Java programs in SUMA/G are simple. Users can start the execution of programs either through a shell running on the client machine or through the SUMA/G portal. They can invoke either `Execute`, corresponding to the on-line execution mode, or `Submit`, which allows for off-line execution (batch jobs). At this time a proxy credential is generated (by using GSI) that allows processes created on behalf of the user to acquire resources, without additional user intervention. Once the SUMA/G `CORE` receives the request from the client machine, it authenticates the user (through GSI), transparently finds a platform for execution (by querying the MDS), and sends a request message to that platform. An `Execution Agent` at the designated platform receives an object representing the application and starts, in an independent JVM, an `Execution Agent Slave`, which actually executes the application. The SUMA/G Class Loader is started in that new JVM, whose function is to load classes and data during execution. Supported classes and input files sources, and output destinations, include: a) the machine (client) where the application execution command is run and, b) a remote file server on which the user has an account. A pluggable interface allows for implementing several protocols to manage remote files access. Currently, implementations for CORBA and `sftp` are available; support for gridFTP and others will also be provided.

To execute an application, either on-line or off-line, the user has only to specify the main class name. In the case of `Execute` service, the rest of the classes and data files are loaded at run-time, on demand, without user intervention. Standard input and output are handled transparently, as if the user were running the application on the local machine. For the `Submit` service, SUMA/G `Client` transparently packs all classes together with input files and delivers them to SUMA/G `CORE`; the output is kept in SUMA/G until the user requests it.

4 SUMA/G Services for Globus Based Grids

In this section we describe how to implement SUMA/G services for Globus-based grids. The main benefit offered for Java applications on Globus-based grids concerns the usability: for instance, there is no need for previous `ssh` login to a UI. Additionally, the jobs are launched directly, without the need for job description files or uploading/downloading of files and classes.

A SUMA/G infrastructure needs adaptation for Globus-based grids on some basic issues. The first one is the security. GSI provides a suitable security platform for the grid; it is used by both LCG/gLite and SUMA/G. Another issue is related to resource control and administration. There must be a common, global administration and control entity for the aggregated set of resources. In this sense, integrating SUMA/G in a Globus-based grid, namely LCG/gLite grid, implies a number of considerations, including:

- Handling cooperation between SUMA/G `CORE` and LCG/gLite components to service requests
- Adding
  - SUMA/G commands to LCG/gLite User Interface, for execution of Java applications
  - SUMA/G `Execution Agents` to LCG/gLite Computing Elements
  - SUMA/G `Execution Agent Slaves` to LCG/gLite Worker Nodes.

The job flow and components interaction are depicted in figure 4. Next sections give details on handling the security, resource control and administration, and a description of the execution of Java applications using a SUMA/G middleware integrated in a LCG/gLite grid.

4.1 Security

SUMA/G uses the Globus Security Infrastructure (through the Java CoG Kit) for user authentication, authorization, and delegation. SUMA/G users must have a valid certificate installed on their machines, instead of having the certificate installed in the UI. Certificates in both SUMA/G and the LCG/gLite grid have to be signed by a common Certification Authority. Before SUMA/G users can use LCG/gLite grid resources, they must register with the LCG/gLite Registration Service, providing the Virtual Organization (VO) they belong to. VOs are specially important for users authorization. One or more VOs for SUMA/G users should be registered with LCG/gLite. As for privacy, all SUMA/G components communicate through encrypted channels using SSL.

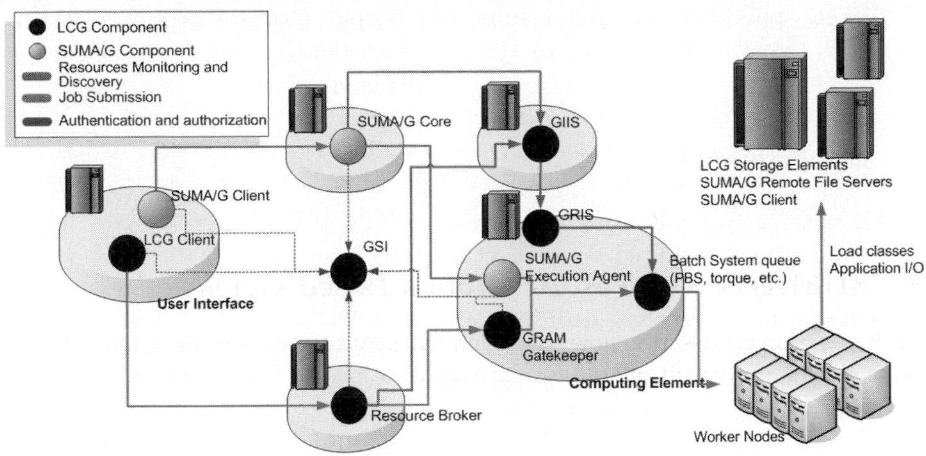

Fig. 4. SUMA/G middleware in a LCG/gLite grid: component interaction during a job submission

4.2 Resource Control and Administration

A simple implementation consists of delegating SUMA/G `Resource Control` functions on LCG/gLite's GIIS. Every Computing Element having a SUMA/G `Execution Agent` is registered (labeled as a SUMA/G service) on its local GRIS, which is periodically consulted by GIIS to keep a global knowledge of the grid resources status. Hence, all resources status and control are handled by a common entity, the LCG/gLite grid GIIS.

4.3 Execution of a Java Application

The steps for executing a Java application on a LCG/gLite grid using the added SUMA/G service are:

1. The user executes a SUMA/G command to submit her/his job at the UI. The command instantiates a SUMA/G `Client Stub`.
2. The `Client` sends the job request, together with a proxy certificate, to the SUMA/G `CORE`.
3. Once SUMA/G `CORE` accomplishes user authentication, it consults LCG/gLite's GIIS to obtain a list of suitable Computing Elements with SUMA/G `Execution Agent`; it then chooses one Computing Element.
4. SUMA/G enqueues the job at the selected Computing Element for execution.
5. When ready to execute, the `Execution Agent` at the Computing Element launches an `Execution Agent Slave` on a Worker Node to execute the application (or in several worker nodes if it is a parallel program).
6. During execution, applications transparently load classes and files, and write output to files, from possible different sites, such as a Storage Element, the UI, a user's remote directory, etc.

7. When application finishes, results and output files are kept in SUMA/G CORE; they can be retrieved by the user from the UI using command `sumag GetResults`.

5 Experiments

We chose three applications to test the execution models described above. These applications were executed on both LCG/gLite (using gLite 3.0) and SUMA/G grids. The grids were deployed in a laboratory environment, over the same execution platform, namely a dedicated cluster of PC's running Scientific Linux 3.0.6 CERN. These PC's have the following characteristics: double processor 800 MHz Pentium III, 512 MBytes of memory, connected with 100 Mbps Ethernet. Applications, execution contexts and results are explained below.

5.1 Applications

MolDyn: is a Java application included in the JavaGrande benchmark suite [20]. It is an N-body code modeling particles interacting under a Lennard-Jones potential in a cubic spatial volume with periodic boundary conditions. The number of particles is given by N. In these experiments, we use the "Size B" version, where N is 8788. The application is composed by five classes, plus a package of five more classes (1003 total code lines); it does not have I/O.

PIC: is a Particle-in-Cell simulation code [21] in Java [2]. It needs three command line parameters: (*tend*, *dt*), and the output file name (about 64 KB). It consists of four java classes. In these experiments, the parameters are fixed to 100 (tend) and 0.2 (dt).

TSPmpi: is a Java application that solves the Traveling Salesman Problem using a parallel genetic algorithm. The goal is to find the shortest path visiting N cities exactly once, starting and ending in the same city. The implementation is a master-slave message passing program, where the master sends the best solution so far to the slaves, which in turn compute a new solution using a genetic algorithm and send it to the master. The number of iterations is introduced as a command line parameter (10, for these experiments). The slaves write to file the best solution they have found every while. The program has 17 classes. In these experiments, the applications reads a 386 KBytes cities specification input file (`usa13509.tsp`), indicated in the command line, and writes out 212 KBytes (the itinerary) both to file and standard output.

5.2 Execution

5.2.1 LCG/gLite

The general steps followed for executing the applications in the LCG/gLite grid are: 1) Identify all classes and input files used by application; pack them all in a

[2] This code was kindly provided by Dr. Vladimir Getov.

"tar.gz" file. 2) Adapt script[3] that guides execution at the CE to each application. The script includes the execution command and command line execution parameters. 3) Create a (simple) *Job Description Language* (JDL) file, basically specifying the script file, and input and output files (*sandbox*). 4) Run commands at the UI to submit the job (providing the JDL file) and get its status and results.

The commands run at the UI are:

1. Submission: `glite-job-submit --vo usb -o job-id_file jdl_file`
2. Status: `glite-job-status -i job-id_file`
3. Get results: `glite-job-get-output -i job-id_file`

We created JDL and script files for every one of the three applications.

5.2.2 SUMA/G

Applications are run through a single (submit) command executed at the UI. Results are fetched using command "`sumag GetResults job_id`".

For *MolDyn*, the main class is called "JGFMolDynBenchSizeB". The command is very simple since there are no command line parameters and since it's a sequential (default) application:

"`sumag Submit JGFMolDynBenchSizeB`"

For *PIC*, the main class is called "es2d". It needs three command line parameters:

"`sumag Submit es2d 100 0.2 output_file`"

TSPmpi is a parallel application, so we must specify the number of processors (`-n 4`). The main class is called COGMpi; it needs two command line parameters:

"`sumag Submit COGAMpi usa13509.tsp 10 -n 4`"

Input files, standard input, and classes are dynamically loaded from the UI to the WN; output files, and standard output and error are stored in SUMA/G `CORE`.

5.3 Results

The average wall clock time results are summarized in Table 1. The results shown consist of elapsed time from job submission until execution completion, including time spent saving results on temporary storage. Both SUMA/G and LCG/gLite store results of off-line executions on a grid component, so the user can get them later. Table 1 also shows the improvement (speed up) obtained using SUMA/G with respect to using LCG/gLite.

Wall clock times in SUMA/G are shorter than in LCG/gLite (between 10% and 43%), even though the back end platform is the same. LCG/gLite jobs spend

[3] LCG/gLite distributions include template scripts for Java, MPI, etc.

Table 1. Average wall clock time in LCG/gLite and SUMA/G grids

Application	LCG/gLite	SUMA/G	*Speed Up*
MolDyn	696 sec.	399 sec.	42.67%
PIC	3054 sec.	2741 sec.	10.25%
TSPmpi	2781 sec.	2037 sec.	26.75%

considerable time (about 300 seconds) queuing in several middleware components (using transfer protocols such as gridFTP). Additionally, for parallel MPI programs, a full home directory is copied in every WN, which, for TSPmpi execution, accounts for the extra (approx.) 400 seconds. We expect that these differences will decrease in percent terms as applications take longer; hence, we conclude that the SUMA/G execution model does not introduce a significant performance overhead. When running on a multisite grid context, execution time overhead for remote classes and file loading will be partially hidden by SUMA/G buffering and prefetching mechanisms [15].

6 Conclusions

SUMA/G middleware offers an execution model for Java applications that is potentially very attractive to users, since the grid is used in the same fashion a local Java Virtual Machine is used. Grid users do not have to log into a User Interface, nor transfer the files (programs or data) as a previous step for the computation phase. Moreover, if the data files were accessed directly by the applications from the file system where they reside, it would not be necessary to rewrite the applications for doing gridFTP transfers previous to the execution. It meets Java users expectations, facilitating applications porting to the grid: applications can be run first on local machines, then executed on the grid without any change to classes. This enhanced interaction meets the grid goal of achieving seamless access to complex, distributed resources to users, in a simple way.

We described how to implement these services, offered by the SUMA/G execution model, on Globus-based grids. We showed that this execution model can improve performance, besides enhancing usability for running Java applications. Our experiments indicated improvements from 10 to 46 % in a local environment.

We are currently working on the integration of SUMA/G with Globus toolkits based on Web services.

References

[1] Foster, I., Kesselman, C.: Computational Grids. In: The Grid: Blueprint for a New Computing Infrastructure. Morgan Kaufmann Publishers, Inc. (1999) 15–51

[2] Foster, I., Kesselman, C.: Globus: A Metacomputing Infrastructure Toolkit. The International Journal of Supercomputer Applications and High Performance Computing **11**(2) (1997) 115–128

[3] Foster, I., Kesselman, C., Tuecke, S.: The Anatomy of the Grid: Enabling Scalable Virtual Organizations. International Journal of High Performance Computing Applications **15**(3) (2001)
[4] LCG Team: LCG: Worldwide LHC Computing Grid. http://lcg.web.cern.ch/lcg/ (2006)
[5] Evans, L.R.: The Large Hadron Collider Project. In: European School of High-Energy Physics, Carry-le-Rouet, France (1996) 275–286 CERN 97-03.
[6] gLite: Lightweight Middleware for Grid Computing (2006) http://glite.web.cern.ch/glite/.
[7] IN2P3: Remote File Input Output (2006) http://doc.in2p3.fr/doc/public/products/rfio/rfio.html.
[8] GFAL: Gfal (2003) http://grid-deployment.web.cern.ch/grid-deployment/gis/GFAL/gfal.3.html.
[9] Cardinale, Y., Hernández, E.: Parallel Checkpointing on a Grid-enabled Java Platform. Lecture Notes in Computer Science **3470**(EGC2005) (2005) 741 – 750
[10] von Laszewski, G., Foster, I., Gawor, J., Smith, W., Tuecke, S.: CoG Kits: A Bridge between Commodity Distributed Computing and High-Performance Grids. In: ACM Java Grande 2000 Conference, San Francisco, CA (2000) 97–106
[11] Baduel, L., Baude, F., Caromel, D., Contes, A., Huet, F., Morel, M., Quilici, R.: Programming, Deploying, Composing, for the Grid. In: Grid Computing: Software Environments and Tools. Springer-Verlag (2006)
[12] Blanco, E., Cardinale, Y., Figueira, C., Hernández, E., Rivas, R., Rukoz, M.: Remote Data Service Installation on a Grid-enabled Java Platform. In: Proceedings of the 17th International Symposium on Computer Architecture and High Performance Computing, Rio de Janeiro, Brasil (2005)
[13] Frey, J., Tannenbaum, T., Livny, M., Foster, I., Tuecke, S.: Condor-G: A Computation Management Agent for Multi-Institutional Grids. In: Tenth International Symposium on High Performance Distributed Computing (HPDC-10), IEEE Press (2001)
[14] The Globus Alliance: The Globus Toolkit (2006) http://www.globus.org/.
[15] Cardinale, Y., De Oliveira, J., Figueira, C.: Remote class prefetching: Improving performance of java applications on grid platforms. In: The Fourth International Symposium on Parallel and Distributed Processing and Applications (ISPA'2006). (2006)
[16] Cardinale, Y., Curiel, M., Figueira, C., García, P., Hernández, E.: Implementation of a CORBA-based metacomputing system. Lecture Notes in Computer Science **2110** (2001) Workshop on Java in High Performance Computing.
[17] Cardinale, Y., Figueira, C., Hernández, E.: Acceso Seguro a Datos Confidenciales en Grids. In: Actas de la XXXII Conferencia Latinoamericana de Informática CLEI 2006 (CD-ROM), Santiago de Chile, Chile (2006)
[18] Project, G.: http://www.gridsphere.org (2006)
[19] J. Novotny, S. Tuecke, V.W.: An online credential repository for the grid: Myproxy. In: Proceedings of of the 10th IEEE International Symposium on High Performance Distributed Computing. (2001)
[20] EPCC: The Java Grande Forum Benchmark Suite. http://www.epcc.ed.ac.uk/-javagrande (2006)
[21] Lu, Q., Getov, V.: Mixed-language high-performance computing for plasma simulations . Scientific Programming **11**(1) (2003) 57–66

Component Assignment for Large Distributed Embedded Software Development

Zhigang Gao and Zhaohui Wu

College of Computer Science, Zhejiang University,
Hangzhou, Zhejiang, P.R. China, 310027
{gaozhigang, wzh}@zju.edu.cn

Abstract. With the increasingly complexity of ubiquitous computing environment, large and distributed embedded software are used more and more widely. After a design model has been completed, assigning components in the design model while meeting multiple runtime constraints is a critical problem in model-based large distributed embedded software development. In this paper, we propose a new method of component assignment. This method uses backtracking algorithm to search the assignment space, and a balance distance function to decide the feasible assignment scheme. Unlike other methods that view computation, communication, and memory resources as independent resources, this method analyzes their holistic influence on component assignment with the goal of keeping the balance between computation resource consumption and memory resource consumption, and the balance of execution density among different processors. Experimental evaluation shows the component assignment method has high success ratios, low time overheads, and good scalability.

Keywords: Ubiquitous computing, embedded software, model-based development, component assignment, backtracking algorithm.

1 Introduction

Ubiquitous computing, as a new computing paradigm, is increasingly permeating into the production and daily lives. Ubiquitous computing environment is an environment that integrates people, environment, and devices into a whole seamlessly and naturally. Embedded devices play an important role in a ubiquitous computing environment. With the increasingly complexity of ubiquitous computing environment, large and distributed embedded systems are used more and more widely, which makes the development of embedded software becomes more and more difficult. In order to improve reliability, reusability, maintainability, and reduce development costs, model-based methodology is presented, and has proved to be effective [1, 2] in embedded software development. In model-based development, design models are used to implement platform-independent functions, and implementation models represent software implementation on a specific platform. For model-based large distributed embedded software development, the transformation from a design model to an implement model is usually divided into two steps: first, assign the components of a design mode to an execution platform; second, generate runtime tasks and assign their timing and scheduling properties, such as deadlines, priorities. In the process of the

C. Cérin and K.-C. Li (Eds.): GPC 2007, LNCS 4459, pp. 642–654, 2007.

model transformation, assigning components in the design model while meeting multiple runtime constraints is a critical problem because component assignment need not only meet the resource constraints of the platform, but also helps to generate real-time embedded software in next step of model transformation, which makes it more difficult to deal with.

Currently, there are many research efforts on task and resource assignment problem in distributed environments [3, 4, 5, 6]. However, these research efforts either consider only one kind of resource, or deal with multiple resources one by one. Onishi et al. [12] proposed a method for component assignment. However, they focus on the problem of improving system reliability. Wang et al. [7] proposed a method for component assignment with multiple resource constraints. Wu et al. [13] proposed an adaptive method for component assignment with multiple constraints. However, they view computation, communication, and memory resources as independent resources, and consider components to be independent entities. In fact, communication resource together with computation resource influences timing characteristic of components; both the memory resource of the processor and the computation resource of the processor are influenced when a component is assigned to a processor; and there exists precedent relationship among components, which influences the runtime computation resource overheads of components.

In this paper, we propose a new method of component assignment. This method analyzes the holistic influence of computation, memory, and communication resource consumption of components on component assignment, and uses backtracking algorithm to explore the assignment space. It considers the balance between computation capability and memory capacity, the balance of execution density among different processors, and the precedent relationship among components.

The rest of this paper is organized as follows. Section 2 presents the design model, platform model, and deployment graph. Section 3 describes the process of component assignment. Some experimental evaluation is given in section 4. Finally, the paper concludes with section 5.

2 Software Model

In this section, we present the design model, platform model, and deployment graph used in this paper. They are extensions of the software models presented by Wang et al. [7].

2.1 Design Model

The design model used in this paper is M_d=(TrS), where TrS is a set of transactions composed of orderly interconnected components. We first give the definition of a component, and then give the definition of a transaction.

Definition 1. A component M_c=(IP, OP, AM, MC) is a software entity, where IP is a set of input ports; OP is a set of output ports; AM is a set of actions (when receiving a message, a component carries out a specific computation, which is called an action.); MC is the memory resource consumption of a component. It is defined as the maximum runtime memory overheads of a component.

A component sequence that is triggered by an external event in order to complete a specific function is called a transaction. It is defined as follows.

Definition 2. A transaction is defined as M_{Tr}=(CS, Msg, T, D, RC), where CS is a set of components in this transaction; Msg is a set of messages passing from the output port of a component to the input port of next component; T and D are the transaction's period and deadline respectively; RC is the set of resource consumption functions. Resource consumption functions include the computation resource consumption function CRC and the communication resource consumption function MLEN.

CRC is a function that maps actions into positive rational numbers. In distributed systems, computation capability of different processors may be different. When an action a_i is executed on different processors, its worst-case execution time (WCET) EXE(a_i) will be different. In order to uniformly measure the action's execution time among different processors, we use the method reported in [8], that is, use its WCET on a reference platform RF as EXE(a_i). We use CRC(a_i) = EXE(a_i)/T_i to denote the computation resource consumption of an action a_i, where T_i is the period of the transaction to which a_i belongs. When a component is included in multiple transactions, its computation resource consumption is the sum of the computation resource consumption in all the transactions in which it involves.

MLEN is a function that maps messages in transactions into non-negative rational numbers. We use the maximum length of a message $Msg_{(i)}$, denoted as MLEN($Msg_{(i)}$), to represent the communication resource consumption of $Msg_{(i)}$.

In this paper, we use EXE(C_i) to denote EXE(a_i) when no confusion will be caused. When multiple transactions cut through the same component, we assume they trigger the same action in the component. We also assume transactions' deadlines are no more than their periods.

In this paper, we assume once a design model is given, the components, the transactions, the transactions' timing constraints (periods and end-to-end deadlines), and the resource consumption of the components are all known.

2.2 Platform Model

Definition 3. A platform model M_{pt}=(PS, N) represents a runtime environment for embedded software, where PS is a set of processors (with different computation capability and memory capacity); N is a shared network connecting all the processors. A processor P_i can provide the computation resource CR(P_i) and the memory resource MR(P_i).

It should be noted that we assume the computation resource of the reference platform RP is 1. The computation resource of P_i, CR(P_i), is a relative value corresponding to that of RP. We use BW(N) to denote the bandwidth of the network N.

2.3 Deployment Graph

Definition 4. A deployment graph is defined as M_{dg}=(PS, CSD, TL, CM), where PS is the set of processors; CSD is the set of components in M_d; TL is the set of message links among processors; CM is the function that maps CSD to PS.

We assume the communication resource consumption between internal messages (the messages passing within a processor) is zero, and the messages passing among tasks have their maximum length.

The problem of component assignment can be stated as following: given the design model, and the platform model, the problem of component assignment is to find a deployment graph such that the computation, memory, and communication resource constraints (in our component assignment method, we use execution density to evaluate computation and communication resource consumption) are all met.

3 Component Assignment

Due to precedent relationship among components, a component of a transaction can only be in an active state (be ready to run) in a specific time scope in order to meet the timing constraint of this transaction. We call the maximum time scope of a component being in an active state its *active period*. The active periods of components and the priorities of messages are needed in the process of component assignment. In this section, we first propose the assignment method of active periods and priorities of messages, and then detail the process of component assignment.

3.1 Assignment of Active Periods of Components

Wang et.al [10] present the notions of Earliest Start Time (EST) and Latest Completion Time (LCT) of components. But there is a difference between design models in this paper and structure models in their paper: when more than one input events trigger the same output of a component, their paper uses the "*and*" relationship, that is to say, in order to trigger the component's action, all input events must arrive. In design models of this paper, we use the "*or*" relationship among these input events, that is to say, either of the input events can trigger a component's action. Because of the above difference, we make a corresponding modification to the calculation method of EST and LCT.

In the following part of section 3.1, we assume C_i is a component in transaction Tr_k, and Tr_k is triggered at time 0.

The EST of C_i is defined as follows:

$$EST(C_i, Tr_k) = \sum_{C_j \in PC(C_i, Tr_k)} EXE(C_j) \tag{1}$$

Where $PC(C_i,Tr_k)$ is the set of precedent components of C_j in transaction Tr_k.

The LCT of C_i is defined as follows:

$$LCT(C_i, Tr_k) = D(Tr_k) - \sum_{C_j \in SC(C_i, Tr_k)} EXE(C_j) \tag{2}$$

Where $D(Tr_k)$ is the deadline of Tr_k; $SC(C_i,Tr_k)$ is the set of subsequent components of C_i in transaction Tr_k.

The active period of C_i in transaction Tr_j is defined as $AP(C_i,Tr_k)=[\, EST(C_i,Tr_k), LCT(C_i,Tr_k)]$.

We can know from the above definitions that the active period of C_i in transaction Tr_k is its largest feasible active time scope when Tr_k is triggered. Of course, not all components in a transaction can be active in their active periods. When a component is included in multiple transactions, it will have multiple active periods.

3.2 Priority Assignment of Messages

For priority assignment of messages, we adopt the deadline monotonic method. The earlier the deadline of a transaction is, the higher the priority of its messages is. If one message is involved in multiple transactions, we use the highest priority as its priority. In Fig. 1, two external events, E1 and E2, trigger three transactions, Tr_1, Tr_2, and Tr_3. Tr_1 consists of C_1, C_2, and C_3; Tr_2 consists of C_1, C_2, and C_4; Tr_3 consists of C_5, C_6, and C_7. When receiving the message $Msg_{(1)}$, C_2 outputs messages $Msg_{(2)}$ and $Msg_{(3)}$. Assuming $D(Tr_1)<D(Tr_2)<D(Tr_3)$, the order of the priorities of messages is $Pr(Msg_{(1)}) = Pr(Msg_{(2)}) > Pr(Msg_{(3)}) > Pr(Msg_{(4)}) = Pr(Msg_{(5)})$.

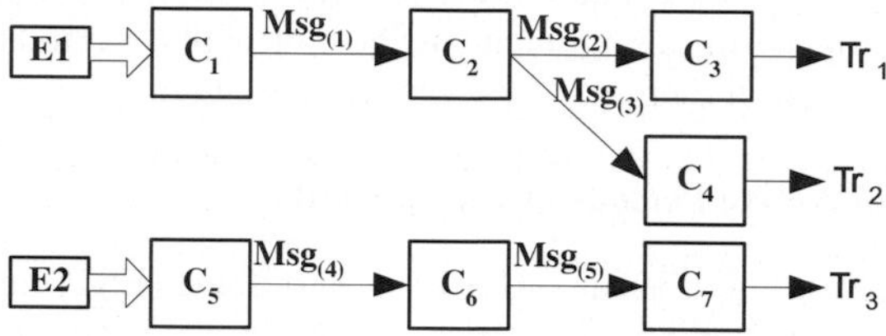

Fig. 1. A design model with three transactions

3.3 Component Assignment Algorithm

If there are m components in a design model and n processors in the corresponding platform model, there will be n^m kinds of deployment graph (of course, some of them are feasible, and the others are infeasible). We call every deployment graph a *component assignment scheme*. For complex software for large distributed embedded system, n and m maybe be very large, and it is too time-consuming to search all component assignment schemes for the optimal one. In this paper, we use backtracking algorithm to find a feasible scheme for the component assignment problem.

The component assignment algorithm is shown in **Algorithm CA**.

Algorithm CA(M_d, M_{pt})

```
/* CSD represents the set of all components in Md. bFalg denotes the return value of algorithm CA*/
Sort all components in CSD in ascending order of the disorder degree DF.
bFalg=BK(CSD);
return bFalg;
```

The input of **Algorithm CA** is a design model M_d and a platform model M_{pt}. The output of this algorithm is a deploy graph. If all components in CSD are assigned to processors, the process of the component assignment succeeds. Otherwise, it fails.

The component assignment algorithm consists of two steps: component sort and backtracking assignment.

First, component sort. The assignment order of components has important influence on finding a component assignment scheme as fast as possible [11]. When a component C_i is assigned to a processor P_i, it will consume some computation resources and some memory resources, and C_i's input and output messages will consume some communication resources. During component assignment, keeping the balance between computation resource consumption and memory resource consumption is important for making full use of a processor. In a transaction, the input message of a component is exact the output message of its direct precedent component. Therefore, when computing a component's communication resource consumption, we need only computation the communication resource consumption of either the input or output messages of the component. In this paper, we use the computation resource consumption of a component's input messages as its communication resource consumption. For the first component of a transaction, its communication resource consumption is believed to be zero. If a component not only has littler communication resource consumption but also has suitable consumption and memory resource consumption (i.e. helps to keep the balance between computation resource consumption and memory resource consumption of processors), its assignment has advantageous influence on the later component assignment.

We use a disorder degree function DF to evaluate a component assignment's influence on systems. DF is defined as follows:

$$DF(C_i) = k_1 \bullet \sqrt{\sum_{P_j \in PS} \left(\frac{CRC(C_i)}{CR(P_j)} - \frac{MC(C_i)}{MR(P_j)}\right)^2} + k_2 \bullet \frac{\sum_{Msg_{(k)} \in IN(C_i)} MLEN(Msg_{(k)})}{\sum_{Tr_n \in TrS} \underset{Msg_{(m)} \in MS(Tr_n)}{MAX} (Msg_{(m)})} \quad (3)$$

In equation (3), $IN(C_i)$ is the set of input messages of C_i; $MS(Tr_n)$ is the set of the messages in transaction Tr_n; MAX is the function that calculates the maximum value. The first item with coefficient k_1 denotes the difference between the computation and memory resource consumption of C_i and the computation and memory resource provided by processors in PS. The second item with coefficient k_2 denotes the ratio of the communication resource consumption of C_j to the maximum communication resource consumption. Because we assume transactions' deadlines are no more than their periods, there is at most one message of a transaction in the network N at a time. Therefore, only the maximum message of each transaction is calculated in the denominator of the second item. Using different k_1 and k_2 can adjust the weight of the two factors. For example, for a platform model composed by processors that have a large difference between computation and memory resources and a high-speed network, we can use a large k_1 and a small k_2.

Second, backtracking assignment. In this step, the backtracking algorithm is used to search the possible assignment of each component one by one in order to find a feasible component assignment scheme. We use a component assignment table (CAT) to store all assignment of a component. One item in a component assignment table is called an *assignment point*. An assignment point is a 3-tuple, denoted as (C_i, P_j, BF(C_i, P_j)), where BF(C_i, P_j) is the balance distance function that is used to evaluate the effect when C_i is assigned to the processor P_j. The littler a BF is, the better it is. The BF is defined as follows:

$$BF(C_i, P_i) = \gamma_1 \bullet \left| \sum_{C_j \in CS_{(P_i)}} \frac{CRC(C_j)}{CR(P_i)} - \sum_{C_j \in CS_{(P_i)}} \frac{MC(C_j)}{MR(P_i)} \right| + \gamma_2 \bullet \left| ED(P_i) - \frac{\sum_{P_j \in PS} ED(P_j)}{n} \right| \quad (4)$$

In the right of equation (4), there are two items with the coefficient γ_1 and γ_2. The first item is an index that reflects the utilization difference between the computation resource consumption on P_i and the memory resource consumption on P_i when C_i is assigned to P_i. The second item denotes the execution density (ED) difference between all components on P_i and the average execution density on all processors. Like k_1 and k_2 in equation (3), γ_1 and γ_2 are the weight of the two factors, and can be set according to the platform model. The items in the CAT of each component are sorted in ascending order of BF.

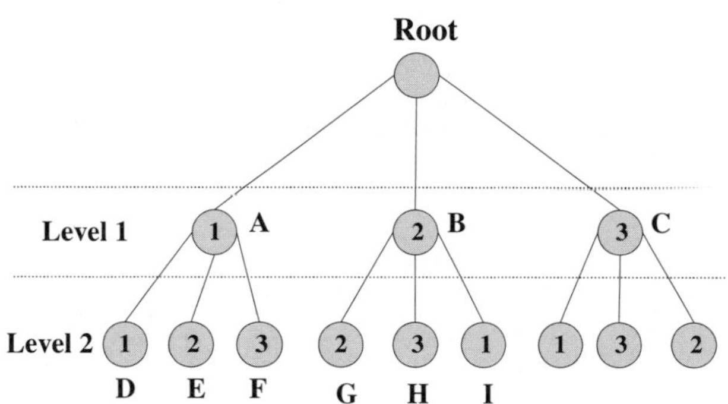

Fig. 2. The process of component assignment

Fig. 2 is an example of component assignment. It shows all assignment schemes when two components, C_1 and C_2, are assigned to three processors, P_1, P_2, and P_3. Level 1 denotes the component assignment of the component C_1 who has the least DF. Node A, node B, and node C are corresponding to C_1's assignment points: (C_1, P_1, BF(C_1, P_1)), (C_1, P_2, BF(C_1, P_2)), and (C_1, P_3, BF(C_1, P_3)) respectively. Similarly, the second level denotes the component assignment of the component C_2 who has the second least DF. It should be noted that the order of the assignment points of C_2 depends on that of C_1. For this reason, the order of the assignment points under node A is D=(C_2, P_1, BF(C_2, P_1)), E=(C_2, P_2, BF(C_2, P_2)), and F=(C_2, P_3, BF(C_2, P_3)), different from those under node B: G=(C_2, P_2, BF(C_2, P_2)), H=(C_2, P_3, BF(C_2, P_3)), and I=(C_2, P_1, BF(C_2, P_1)). In the same level, the node in the leftmost has the least BF, and the node in the rightmost has the largest BF. The backtracking algorithm searches a feasible component assignment scheme in the order of left-order-first. In Fig. 2, if component assignment fails in D, E, and F, then the algorithm backtracks to the next assignment point of C_1—Node B, and then initializes the CAT of C_2 and search a feasible component assignment of C_2. This process is recursive until a feasible component assignment scheme is found. The backtracking algorithm is shown in **Algorithm BK**.

Algorithm BK(CSD)

```
/* t is the path depth of backtracking algorithm. n is
the number of processors. The nodes other than the root
node are corresponding to the assignment points of compo-
nents. The path from the root node to a leaf node denotes
an assignment order of components*/
  if (t > n+1) return true;
  for (i = The first child node of current node; i <= The
     last child node of current node; i++ ) {
     Pj = The processor used in i;
     ED(Pj);
     if (Constraint(Pj) and Bound(Pj)) {
        Initialize next component's component assignment
      table, and sort assignment points of each component
      in ascending order of the balance distance BF.
      BK(t+1);
      }
   }
  if (t is less than n and no unprocessed child node)
    return false;
  }
```

In **Algorithm BK**, $ED(P_i)$ is the execution density of all components assigned to processor P_i.

When calculating $ED(P_i)$, we cannot simply add up all the EDs of the components assigned to P_i for the following reasons: in the same transaction, discontinuous components assigned to one processor is impossible to run continuously. Adding up all the EDs of the components will obtain a pessimistic result.

In section 3.1, we introduce the notion of active period. It is the biggest time span for a component's running. In distributed environment, the components of a transaction can be assigned to more than one processor. We call the components that can execute continuously a *component segment* (CSE). The execution density of a CSE is defined as follows:

$$ED(p,Tr_i) = \frac{\sum_{C_i \in CS(p)} EXE(C_i)}{LCT(C_l,Tr_i) - EST(C_f,Tr_i) - CT(Msg_{(p)})} \quad (5)$$

In equation (5), p is a CSE; CS(p) is the set of components in p; C_f is the first component in p, C_l is the last component in p;. Execution density reflects the influence of computation resource consumption and communication resource consumption on the runtime of components. Using the ED to evaluate the runtime influence of components is an optimistic method. We can obtain an optimization component assignment scheme because one goal of component assignment is to keep the balance of EDs among processors. Furthermore, it has larger searching space when assigning components. When a component assignment scheme is proved failed when tasks are generated, we can search for other feasible component assignment schemes. From the definition of active period, it is obvious that the ED of a CSE is lager than the ED of any component in CSE, i.e. it is the run-time worst cast of a CSE. So we use the ED of a CSE to denote the ED of continuous components in a transaction.

The ED(P_i) is defined as follows:

$$ED(P_i) = \sum_{Tr_j \in TrS(P_i)} \underset{p \in CSS(Tr_j)}{MAX} (ED(p, Tr_j)) \tag{6}$$

In equation (6), p is a CSE in Tr_j; CSS(Tr_j) is the set of CSE in Tr_j; TrS(P_i) is the set of transaction in P_i.

CT($Msg_{(p)}$) is the worst-case transmission time (WCTT) of the input message of CSE(p). In the right of equation (5), the denominator means the active period of p should minus the time overheads of $Msg_{(p)}$.

In real-time scheduling, networks are usually regarded as processors, and network messages are regarded as tasks in order to perform response time analysis of network messages. If there are m transactions in M_d, there are at most m messages in the network N at a time. When $Msg_{(p)}$ and the longest messages of other m-1 transactions are sent to N simultaneously, $Msg_{(p)}$ will get its WCTT. For a message $Msg_{(p)}$, its WCTT can be calculated using equation (5) by iterative method.

$$t = C_{(p)} + \sum_{j \in H(Msg_{(p)})} \frac{t}{T_j} \bullet C_{(j)} + \underset{k \in L(Msg_{(p)})}{MAX} (C_{(k)}) \tag{7}$$

Where $C_{(p)}$ is the maximum transmission time of $Msg_{(p)}$, denoted as MLEN($Msg_{(p)}$)/BW(N); H($Msg_{(p)}$) is the set of messages whose priorities are higher than that of $Msg_{(p)}$; L($Msg_{(p)}$) is the set of messages whose priorities are lower than that of $Msg_{(p)}$. The last item in equation (7) denotes the blocking time suffered by $Msg_{(p)}$ due to blocking effects coming from being transmitted network messages with lower priority.

Two functions, *Bound* and a *Constraint*, are defined to decide whether prune a node or not in backtracking algorithm.

The *Bound* function of a node with assignment point (C_i, P_j, BF(C_i, P_j)) is defined as follows:

$$Bound(P_j) = (MR(P_j) \geq \sum_{C_i \in CS(P_j)} MC(C_i)) and (\sum_{C_k \in CS_{(P_j)}} \frac{CRC(C_k)}{CR(P_j)} < 1) \tag{8}$$

In the right of equation (8), CS(P_j) is the set of components in P_j; $MR(P_j) \geq \sum_{C_i \in CS(P_j)} MC(C_i)$ means if the available memory resource of P_j is no less than the gross runtime memory consumption of CS(P_j), the memory requirements of CS(P_j) could be met. $\sum_{C_k \in CS_{(P_j)}} \frac{CRC(C_k)}{CR(P_j)} < 1$ means the total utilization of computation resource in P_i should be less than 1.

The *constraint* function of a node is defined as follows:

$$Constraint(P_j) = ED(P_j) \leq TD \tag{9}$$

Where TD is the threshold of ED in P_j. It is a value less than 1 and can be set by user.

If both equation (8) and equation (9) are *true* for current node, next path will be searched. If **Algorithm BK** returns *true*, a feasible component assignment scheme has been found and vice versa.

4 Experiments Evaluation

As mentioned in section 1, there are few research efforts on component assignment problem that combined multiple resource consumption in embedded software development domain. We call the method presented in this paper BK+BF. In order to compare, we construct another algorithm named BK+CR, which views computation resources, memory resources, and communication resources as independent resources, and does not consider the balance of execution density.

In the following, if we do not give extra explanations, the "ratio" or "utilization" refers to a relative value comparing to the total computation, memory, or communication resources of all processors and the network.

The design model used in this paper is generated randomly. A component has the number of input messages: 1-5, the number of output messages: 1-3. The ratio of computation (or memory) resource consumption to all computation (or memory) resources provided by PS is less than 90 per cent. Because communication resource overheads have been considered into ED, there is no threshold of communication resource consumption in BK+BF. In BK+CR, the ratio of maximum communication resource consumption to all communication resources provided by PS is less than 90 per cent. The TD in equation (9) is set to 0.9. The coefficients in (3) and (4) are set to 1.

We first evaluate the computation time under the condition of different utilization of computation, memory, and communication resource consumption. Of course, in BK+BF, we ignore the utilization of communication resource consumption. Under a specific utilization, the design model has 100 components. We use the number of the visited nodes in backtracking algorithm to represent time overheads. The platform model has 15 processors, and a network with 1Mb/s. The Fig. 3 shows the results under different utilization. Note that in horizon axis, utilization denotes the value of the utilization of computation, memory, and communication resource consumption. For example, 10% denotes the utilization of computation, memory, and communication resources is all 10%. The vertical axis denotes the number of the visited nodes in backtracking algorithm. We can see the number of the visited nodes increases in the BK+BF and the BK+CR with the increment of utilization. In little utilization, the visited nodes in BK+CR are less than that in BK+BF because BK+CR do not consider

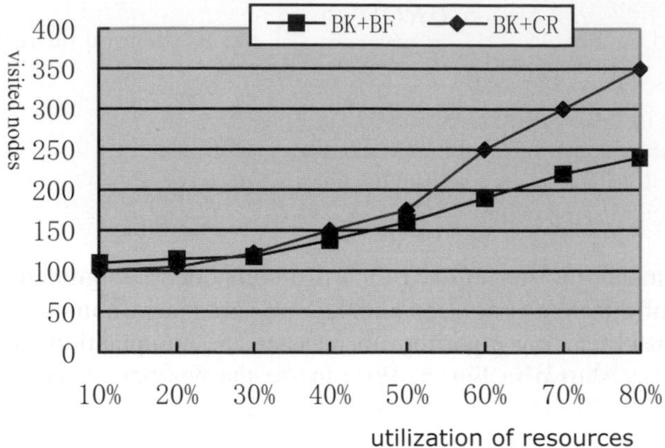

Fig. 3. The visited nodes vs different utilization of resources

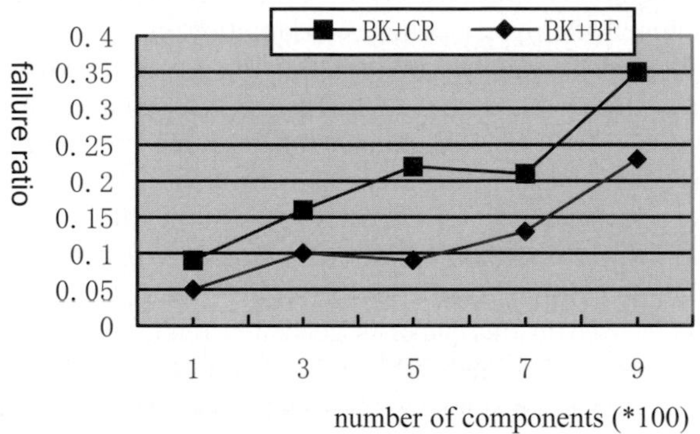

Fig. 4. The failure ratios with different number of components

the balance between computation resources and communication resources in component sort and backtracking assignment, and can easily find a feasible component assignment scheme. However, in big utilization, the visited nodes in BK+CR are more than that in BK+BF due to the same reason.

In the second experiment, we evaluate the failure ratios with different component number. This test is performed on 20 processors connected with a network with the speed of 1Mbits/s. The computation resource of processors ranges from 1 to 10, and memory capacity ranges from 100B (bytes) to 30000B. For a class of design model with the given components, we randomly generate 50 design models and use the average value of their failure rations (the computation resource consumption and memory resource consumption decrease with the increase of the number of components). For each design model, we use the BK+BF and BK+CR to find a component assignment scheme, and then generate tasks using the algorithm in [9]. If a component assignment scheme can be generated a schedulable tasks set (each transaction's WCRT is less than its deadline), we believe it is successful. The experimental results are shown in Fig. 4. We can see the BK+BF has lower failure ratios than that of BK+CR. It is because BK+BF not only considers the balance between computation resource consumption and memory resource consumption, but also the balance of execution density on processors. However, BK+CR only considers the utilization of computation, memory, and communication resources, and does not consider the precedent relationship among components, and the runtime influence of components' execution, so leads to higher failure ratios when embedded software is generated from design models.

We also compare the scalability of the two component assignment methods under the condition of different processor number and component number. We use the visited nodes in backtracking algorithm to measure the computation time. The experimental results are shown in Fig. 5. We can see the number of the visited nodes increases in the BK+BF and the BK+CR with the increment of the number of processors and components. The visited nodes in BK+BF increase smoothly with the increment of the number of processors and components. The BK+BF visits fewer nodes than BK+CR because it considers the balance between computation resource consumption and memory resource consumption, and the balance of execution density among different processors, and is more likely to find better component assignment schemes with less computation costs. It shows the BK+BF algorithm has a good scalability, and suitable to large distributed systems.

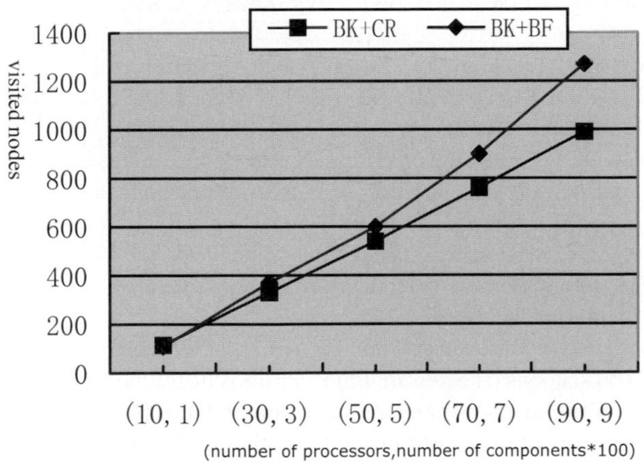

Fig. 5. The visited nodes vs different number of processors and components

5 Conclusions and Future Work

With the increasingly complexity of ubiquitous computing environment, large and distributed embedded systems are used more and more widely. This paper proposes a new method of component assignment for large distributed embedded systems. This method analyzes the holistic influence of computation, memory, and communication resource consumption of components during component assignment. This method uses backtracking algorithm to explore assignment spaces. During component assignment, it considers the balance between computation resource consumption and memory resource consumption on processors, and the balance of execution density among different processors in order to find an optimization assignment scheme.

References

1. Wang, S., Shin, K.G.: An Architecture for Embedded Software Integration Using Reusable Components. CASES. (2000) 110-118
2. Gao, Z., Wu, Z., Ye, R., Yue, L.: A Model-Based Development Method for SmartOSEK OS. The 5th International Conference on Computer and Information Technology. (2005) 781-787
3. Tindell, K.W., Burns, A., Wellings, A.J.: Allocating Real-Time Tasks: An NP-Hard Problem Made Easy. Real-Time Systems Journal. Vol. 4, no. 2. (1992)
4. Gai, P., Lipari, G., Natale, M.D.: Minimizing memory utilization of real-time task sets in single and multi-processor systems-on-chip. In Proceedings of the 22nd Real-Time Systems Symposium (RTSS 2001). (2001) 73–83
5. Hou, C.J., Shin, K.G.: Allocation of periodic Task Modules with Precedence and Deadline Constraints in Distributed Real-Time Systems. IEEE Transactions on Computers. Vol. 46, no. 12. (1997)
6. Ramamoorthi, R., Rifkin, A., Dimitrov, B., Chandy K.M.: A general resource reservation framework for scientific computing. In Proceedings of the 1st International Scientific Computing in Object-Oriented Parallel Environments Conference (ISCOPE), vol. 1343. (1997) 283–290
7. Wang, S., Merrick, J.R., Shin, K.G.: Component Allocation with Multiple Resource Constraints for Large Embedded Real-Time Software Design. IEEE Real-Time and Embedded Technology and Applications Symposium. (2004) 219-226
8. Wang, S., Shin, K.G.: Early-stage performance modeling and its application for integrated embedded control software design. In ACM Workshop on Software Performance (WOSP). (2004) 110-114
9. Gao, Z., Wu, Z., Li, H.: A Task Generation Method for the Development of Embedded Software. The International Conference on Computational Science 2006 (ICCS 2006). LNCS, vol. 3994. (2006) 918-921
10. Wang, S., Shin, K.G.: Task construction for model-based design of embedded control software. IEEE Transactions on Software Engineering. Vol. 32, no. 4. (2006) 254-264
11. Kumar, V.: Algorithms for constraint satisfaction problems: a survey. A.I. Magazine. Vol. 13, no. 1. (1992) 32–44
12. Onishi, J., Kimura, S., James, R.J.W., Nakagawa, Y.: Solving the Redundancy Allocation Problem With a Mix of Components Using the Improved Surrogate Constraint Method. IEEE Transactions on Reliability : Accepted for future publication. (2006)
13. Wu, Q., Wu, Z.: Adaptive component allocation in ScudWare middleware for ubiquitous computing. The 2005 IFIP International Conference on Embedded and Ubiquitous Computing. Lecture Notes in Computer Science, vol. 3824, (2005) 1155–1164

LDFSA: A Learning-Based Dynamic Framed Slotted ALOHA for Collision Arbitration in Active RFID Systems*

Hyuntae Cho, Woonghyun Lee, and Yunju Baek**

Department of Computer Science and Engineering,
Pusan National University, Busan,
Republic of Korea
{marine,yunju}@pnu.edu

Abstract. In recent large scale deployment of active RFID systems has been introduced by many applications, but a variety of critical issues remain unresolved. Especially, the impact of collision is the most essential problem. In this paper, we propose a Learning-based Dynamic Framed Slotted ALOHA algorithm (LDFSA) which mitigates collision from the active RFID tags and complies with international standard, ISO/IEC 18000-7. In addition, this paper includes the performance evaluations of the proposed LDFSA algorithm with the conventional algorithms. According to the result, the proposed LDFSA algorithm shows better performance than other conventional algorithms.

Keywords: LDFSA, slotted ALOHA, active RFID, anti-collision, collision arbitration.

1 Introduction

Identification of multiple objects is especially challenging if many objects are distributed in a field. Several technologies are available for identification. Bar code is the most pervasive technology, but reading them requires a line of sight between the reader device and the object, manual, and close-ranging scanning. But a Radio Frequency Identification (RFID) system provides remote, non-line-of-sight, and automatic reading. The RFID system identifies the unique tags' ID or detailed information saved in them attached to objects. There are two types in the RFID tag: the active type which generates power from internal resources such as a battery and the passive type which gets energy from the transceiver by radio frequency [1].

The RFID system conceptually consists of a reader and a number of tags. The reader in the RFID system broadcasts the request message to tags. Upon

** Corresponding Author.

* "This work was supported by the Korea Research Foundation Grant funded by the Korean Government(MOEHRD)" (The Regional Research Universities Program/Research Center for Logistics Information Technology).

C. Cérin and K.-C. Li (Eds.): GPC 2007, LNCS 4459, pp. 655–665, 2007.

receiving the message, all tags send the response back to the reader. If only one tag responds, the reader successfully collects information of the tag. But if there are two or more responses from tags, their responses will collide on the common communication channel, and thus cannot be read by the reader. The ability to identify multiple tags simultaneously is regarded as a critical issue for more advanced applications such as to check out numerous items at the supermarket. It might take a lot of time to check out them one by one, which requires an efficient identification method checking a large number of goods at one time without any delay. To overcome the collision problem, much research [2,3,4,5] has been introduced in passive RFID applications. Nevertheless, anti-collision mechanism in the active RFID field has been absent. Collision arbitration for the active RFID should be differed from previous solutions because their requirements, such as computing power, the capacity of memory, power efficiency, and so on, do not agree with that for the passive type. So, distinct approaches for the active RFID system should be needed and designed.

In addition, the RFID tags attached to objects at a site can be read in other sites. For instance, an RFID tag attached to an item in Korea can be read by the readers in the store of L.A., the U.S.A. In this new system, because each site can have a unique RFID reader system, RFID tags can not read at their destinations. In order for these heterogeneous systems to be compatible, conformance with international standards is important. ISO/IEC 18000-7[6] was enacted as an international standard for container identification in port environments. Active RFID systems should be designed and developed according to this standard. ISO/IEC 18000-7 for the active RFID system describes the dynamic framed slotted ALOHA technique to reduce tag collision. So, this paper will concentrate on collision arbitration without any deviation from international standard. This paper proposes a Learning-based Dynamic Framed Slotted ALOHA algorithms (LDFSA) to enhance the efficiency of tag identification and compares the performance of the LDFSA algorithm with those of the conventional Basic Framed Slotted ALOHA (BFSA) and Dynamic Framed Slotted ALOHA (DFSA) algorithms.

The organization of the paper is as follows. We present traditional approaches for collision arbitration in the next section. Then, we describe our algorithm, the learning-based dynamic framed slotted ALOHA. Finally, we conclude this paper in section 5 after describing the performance evaluation of the LDFSA in section 4.

2 Related Work for Anti-collision

Slotted ALOHA algorithm[4,5] suggested by ISO/IEC 18000-7, is the collision arbitration method where each tag transmits its identification to the reader in a slot of a frame and the reader identifies the tag when it receives information of the tag without collision. A time slot is a time interval where tags respond their messages. The reader can identify the tag when only one tag access a time slot. The current RFID system uses a kind of slotted ALOHA known by framed slotted ALOHA algorithm. A frame is a time epoch between requests of a reader and includes a set of slots. A collection round, referred to as a read cycle, is a tag identifying process that consists of a frame. This section briefly describes existing framed slotted ALOHA anti-collision algorithms.

2.1 Basic Framed Slotted ALOHA Algorithm

Basic Framed Slotted ALOHA (BFSA)[1] algorithm uses a fixed frame size and does not change the size during the process of tag identification. In BFSA, the reader offers information to the tags about the frame size and the random number which is used to select a slot in the frame. Each tag selects a slot number for access using the random number and responds to the slot number in the frame. Since the frame size of BFSA algorithm is fixed, its implementation is simple. However, it has a limitation that drops efficiency of tag identification.

2.2 Dynamic Framed Slotted ALOHA Algorithm

Dynamic Framed Slotted ALOHA (DFSA) algorithm, which is used in ISO/IEC 18000-7, changes the frame size for efficient tag identification. To determine the frame size, it uses information such as the number of slots used to identify the tag and the number of the slots collided. So DFSA algorithm can solve partially the problem of BFSA that use a fixed frame size and identify the tag efficiently because the reader regulates the frame size according to the number of tags. But, the frame size change alone can not reduce sufficiently the tag collision when there are a number of tags because it can not increase the frame size indefinitely.

3 The Proposed Learning-Based Dynamic Framed Slotted ALOHA (LDFSA) Algorithm

The prior dynamic framed slotted ALOHA algorithm changes the frame size to increase the efficiency of the tag identification. However, DFSA do not consider active RFID properties such as power efficiency, computing power and so on. Furthermore, because DFSA do not maintain any collision information, tag collision increases in a next collection command round. In this section, we propose a Learning-based Dynamic Framed Slotted ALOHA algorithm which solves this problem.

Since the active RFID tag gets energy from internal resources such as batteries, tag's energy can affect a total RFID system. To enhance the lifetime of the system, the active RFID tag should sleep as long as possible. Thus, the reader sends a wake-up signal before getting tags' information within interrogation zone. And then, the reader interrogates tags using the collection command which includes the frame size that can be varied dynamically. Initial round for collecting tags' information is composed of a wake-up signal, a collection command broadcasting, a frame, and a sleep period as shown in Figure 1. Basically, the reader broadcasts a wake-up signal to all tags within interrogation zone before sending a collection command. After that, when the reader sends the collection command, it includes initial frame size from which the number of total tags in the

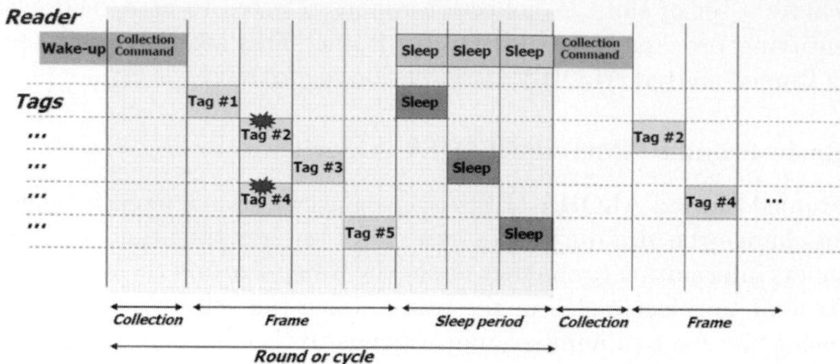

Fig. 1. Basic architecture of a Learning-based Dynamic Framed Slotted ALOHA

interrogation zone can be estimated. The estimated number of tags is used for determining a next frame size. Initial frame size can vary system performance. We evaluated the performance by varying the number of initial frame size. The result will be dealt with in section 4. For the detail demonstration of our algorithm, we will mention the algorithm by separating into two parts: a point of view of the reader, and a point of view of the tag. Followings demonstrate pseudo codes of the LDFSA for anti-collision.

- *RFID reader operation*

```
Object implementation of RFID reader;
sucessList : tags list read by the reader;
frameSize : estimated by the number of tags;

Operation antiCollision()
broadCast(initTagLearning());
broadCast(wakeupCommand);

settingInitialNumberOfSlots(frameSize);
for i in threeEmptyRound do
     broadCast(collectionCommand, frameSize);
     for i in oneRound do
          sucessList = getTagInfo();
     od
     for i in  i == sucessList.len do
          uniCast(successList.tagID, sleepCommand);
     od
     if (this round == empty round)
          totalEmpty++;
     fi
     frameSize = calFrameSize(estimateNumberOfTag());
od
```

- *RFID tag operation*

```
Object implementation of RFID tag;
Operation run( )

while(listen(wakupCommand));
for i in Tag.status == wakeup do
     while(listen(ReaderCommand));
     switch ReaderCommand:
          case : SLEEP
               correctPrediction(success);
               setTagstatus(Sleep);
          case : P2P
               Reply(data);
          case : BROADCAST
               correctPrediction(fail);
               selectSlot(frameSize);
               Reply(data, selectedslot);
od
```

First, the reader action is separated into five parts: sending a wake-up message, broadcasting a collection command, estimating the number of tags, determining the frame size, and transmitting sleep command. The most important things between them are to estimate the number of tags and to determine the frame size. They are closely correlated each other. To determine the frame size, we have to use information such as the number of slots used to identify the tag and the number of the slots collided. Cha[4] described how to estimate the number of tags as follows. A system reaches maximum throughput when p is equal to *1/n*. we can get optimal collision rate *Crate* for maximum throughput.

$$C_{rate} = \lim_{n\to\infty} \frac{P_{coll}}{1 - P_{succ}} = 0.418 \tag{1}$$

The number of the collided tags, *Ctags* in a slot is calculated by

$$C_{tags} = \frac{1}{C_{rate}} = 2.3922 \tag{2}$$

Let *Mcoll* be the number of collided slots in a frame after a round. Then the number of estimated tags is calculated by

$$NumberofEstimatedTags = 2.3922 \times M_{coll} \tag{3}$$

We use above equations to estimate the number of tags. And then we have to determine the frame size for the next collection round. If we can estimate the number of unread tags, we can determine the frame size that will maximize the system efficiency or the tag collision probability. Lee[5] introduced how to determine the frame size. When the number of tags is n, the optimal frame size can be derived as follows.

$$N = \frac{1}{1 - e^{-\frac{1}{n}}} = \frac{e^{\frac{1}{n}}}{e^{\frac{1}{n}} - 1} \tag{4}$$

When n is large, it can be simplified as follow.

$$N \simeq \frac{1 + \frac{1}{n}}{1 + \frac{1}{n} - 1} = n + 1, n \gg 1 \tag{5}$$

The above equation tells us that when the number of tags and the frame size are approximately the same, the system efficiency becomes the maximum.

Second, the tag's behavior includes selecting their slot, responding to the reader and a learning phase for the next collection command from the reader. Each tag that receives a collection command from the reader selects a slot number to access the common communication channel by using the random number and responds to the slot number in the frame with its ID and other information. Tags use learning mechanism to get their slot for accessing communication channel. The tag stores it's current slot number to the internal memory such as EEPROM. After that, if the tag receives a sleep command from the reader, it determines that its response is successful and increases the probability that use for the next collection command round by using prediction method. Otherwise the tag determines that it is collided and decreased the probability that can reduce collision for the next round.

Figure 2 shows an example of slot selection using learning mechanism. When a tag selects their slot for responding, the each slot of the tag extracts the random number. Each slot of the tag has their probability that used for selecting the number of a slot. Initial probability for all tags is set to the same value. And then each slot performs modulo operation using its probability and the random number. Initially, because every slot has the same probability, the slot with the maximum random value will be chosen. The tag will transmit the response message by using that slot. After that, if the tag receives a sleep command from the reader, it determines that its response is successful and increases the probability that use for the next collection round using learning mechanism. Otherwise the tag determines that it is collided and decreased the probability that can reduce collision for the next round.

For example, let the slot size of the tag be five, and initial probability be one hundred. Each slot generates their random number as Table 1. The second slot generated a random number as 90 and has highest the result of modulation operation (90 mod 100 = 90). As according to the grade of results, the second slot is selected for responding a message to the reader. After that, if the response is successful, learning mechanism will provide compensation that increases the probability. If the response is failed, the selector will decrease probability. The LDFSA will accumulate data used to select their slot according to progressing the cycle or round and thus mitigate collision problem in the reader. The LDFSA is in need of a large of memories for maintaining information which used to select the slot of the tag. Active RFID tags have sufficient capacity for realistic applications.

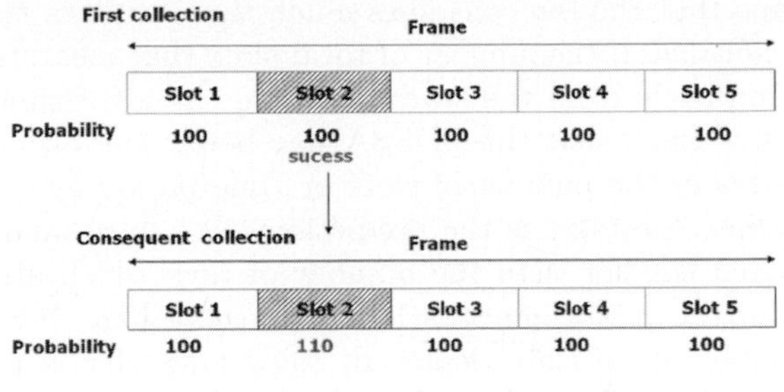

(a) Only one tag responds (success)

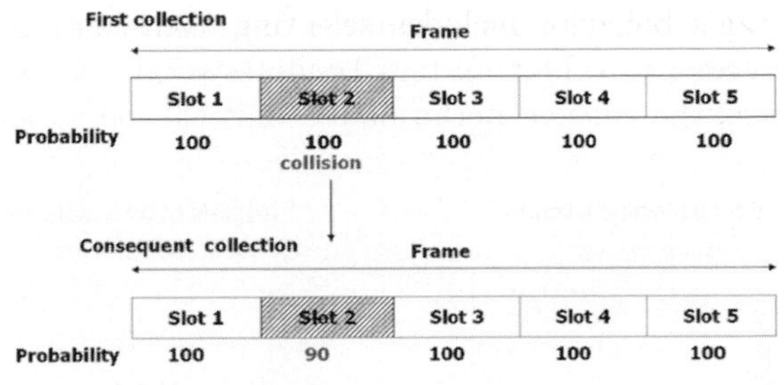

(b) Two or more tags respond (collision)

Fig. 2. LDFSA compensates according to whether it collids

Table 1. Process of learning operation of LDFSA

Number of slot	1	2	3	4	5
Random number	270	90	65	130	85
Result of modulo	70	90	65	30	85

4 Performance Evaluation of LDFSA

In this section, we compare the performance of the LDFSA algorithm with the conventional Basic Framed Slotted ALOHA (BFSA) and Dynamic Framed Slotted ALOHA (DFSA). In order to evaluate the performance, we have assumption that the reader repeats collection rounds until it collects all tags and the number of iteration for a consequent collection operation performed by the reader is basically set to one hundred times. Every experiment was repeated ten times and then averaged.

4.1 Simulation

First of all we describe a result of how the LDFSA affect the active RFID system according to whether the response is successful or not. Our simulation is separated into two models. In Figure 3, what the number of average round is higher than others means that the tag consumes much time for data transmission and thus reduces its lifetime. If the number of total slots that mean time period during total collection cycle from the reader is high, the algorithm requires much time. Figure 3 illustrates that the LDFSA has better performance than other algorithms in terms of the number of slots or time period needed to collect all tags. In detail, when the tag has the prediction mechanism and the number of initial slots is much smaller than the number of tags which are distributed in active RFID field, the performance is less 4 percent than DFSA. However, in case a large number of tags are deployed, tag's longevity is prolonged up to 19.7% that is the mean of all of experiment, and collection time that gets all tags' information is diminished down to 14.7%. In figure for average round for collecting all tags, as according to the number of initial slots is high, the number of total rounds needed to collect all tags becomes small. As earlier mentioned, the LDFSA showed the efficient performance that can be applied to a realistic

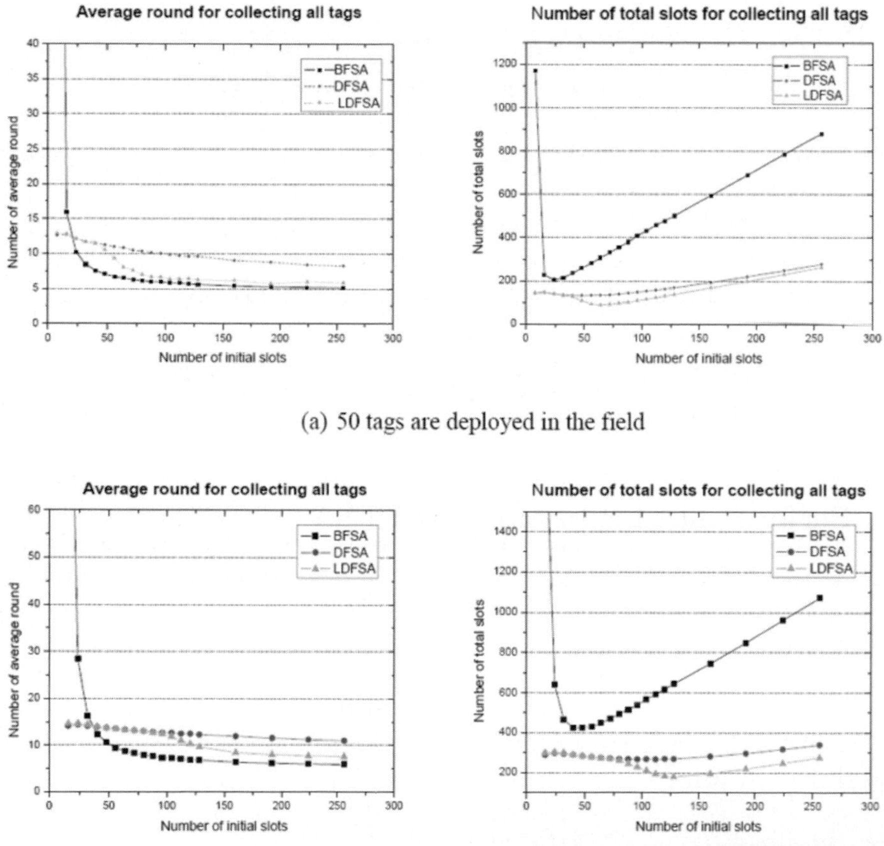

(a) 50 tags are deployed in the field

(b) 100 tags are deployed in the field

Fig. 3. The effect of LDFSA

application. In addition, we performed the evaluation to measure how the LDFSA affect performance according to the number of tags. The number of tags varied from 10 to 100 and the number of initial slots is 80. As a result shown in Figure 4, the average number of rounds of the LDFSA is more than BFSA. However, the average number of slots that affect the system is remarkably reduced.

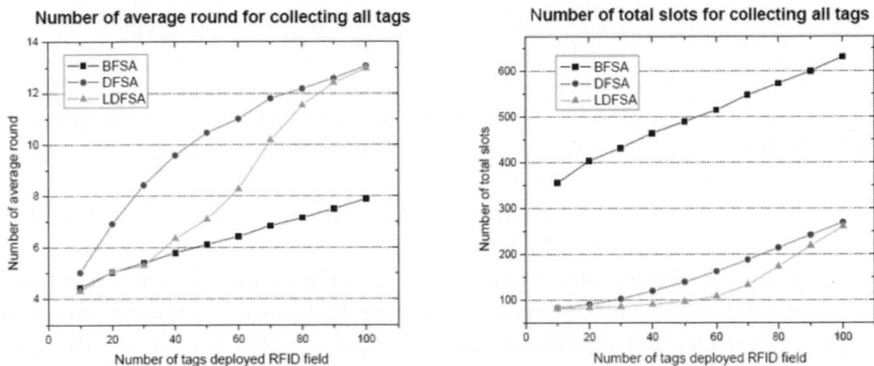

Fig. 4. The efficiency of the LDFSA according to the number of tags : (a) The average number of rounds (b) the average number of slots

Table 2. Impact of moving tags in LDFSA

	Average number of frames	Average number of slots
No movement	8.098	108.056
50% movement	8.298	112.145

Realistic applications, such as the port environment that get the containers in and out of the ports, require tag's movement like processing items into and out of a store or a RFID field. Therefore, collision arbitration should consider this requirement to enhance the efficiency of the realistic application so that we can mitigate an accumulation of goods. Table 2 shows a result of impact of tags' movement. For evaluation, environments were set to 50 tags are deployed and the number of initial slots is also 80. We inspected the impact of tags' movement in case a half of total tags replaced new tags in the active RFID field. The result shows that tags' movement does not dramatically affect the active RFID system.

4.2 Experiment and Verification

As earlier mentioned, tags in heterogeneous RFID systems, which have different RFID system, can not read at their destinations. So, conformance with international standard, ISO/IEC 18000-7, is most important. LITeTag [7] was designed

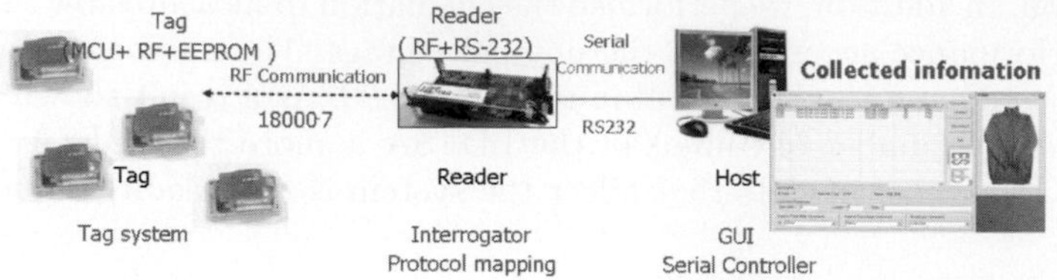

Fig. 5. Active RFID system which complies ISO/IEC 18000-7

for the active RFID system which strictly complies with the international standard, ISO/IEC 18000-7. LITeTag use DFSA algorithm, which was defined by the standard, to arbitrate collision.

Figure 5 shows the active RFID system, LITeTag system, which consists RFID tags, a reader, and a host. In LITeTag, Atmel's ATmega128L was chosen as the processing unit of the hardware platform. It is able to operate at a maximum frequency of 8MHz, providing reasonable processing power to explore a wide variety of applications and provides sufficient memory resources for a wide range of experiments. The on-chip memory includes 4KB of RAM, 4KB of EEPROM, and 128KB of flash memory. 53 general purpose I/O pins and serial ports, such as RS-232 and SPI, are provided by the CPU. The communication subsystem of LITeTag is based on either the XEMICS's XE1203F, named version 1.0, or Chipcon's CC1100, referred to as version 2.0. They are connected to the processor through an SPI interface and data bus. We choose the version 2.0 of LITeTag, which equips with CC1100 RF, to experiment the proposed LDFSA. And then, We ported the proposed LDFSA to the LITeTag and evaluated our the algorithm. As a result, the LDFSA did not deviate from international standard and completely operated on the LITeTag platform.

5 Conclusion and Future Works

In this paper, we proposed the Learning-based Dynamic Framed Slotted ALOHA algorithm which can reduce collision from active RFID tags. We described the conventional slot allocation algorithm, which is the method to allocate the frame size by the number of tags. We also compared the performance of the proposed LDFSA with two conventional framed slotted ALOHA algorithms and built RFID systems to deploy in realistic application. The proposed LDFSA algorithm shows better performance than conventional algorithms. If the proposed LDFSA algorithm is used in the active RFID system where the ability to simultaneously identify muliple tags is crucial for many applications, it will contributed to improved the performance of the active RFID system. Our future work includes advanced research for the secure, energy efficient and more realistic applications.

References

1. Klaus Finkenzeller: RFID Handbook: fundamentals and applications in contactless smart cards and identification, Wiley press, 2003
2. Bogdan Carbunar, Murali Krishna Ramanathan, Mehmet Koyuturk, Christoph Hoffmann, and Ananth Grama: Redundant reader elimination in RFID systems, Proceeding of Second Annual IEEE Communications Society Conference on Sensor and Ad Hoc Communications and Networks, 2005
3. Jia Zhai, Gi-Nam Wang: An Anti-collision Algorithm Using Two-Functioned Estimation for RFID Tags, Lecture Notes in Computer Science, vol. 3483, pp. 702-711, 2005
4. Jae-Ryong Cha, Jae-Hyun Kim: Dynamic framed slotted ALOHA algorithms using fast tag estimation method for RFID system, Proceeding of IEEE Consumer Communications and Networking Conference, 2006
5. Su-Ryun Lee. Sung-Dong Joo, Chae-Woo Lee: An Enhanced Dynamic Framed Slotted ALOHA Algorithm for RFID Tag Identification, Proceeding of the 2nd Annual International Conference on Mobile and Ubiquitous Systems: Networks and Services, 2005
6. ISO/IEC 18000-7: Information technology - radio frequency identification for item management - Part 7: parameters for active air interface communications at 433 MHz, ISO/IEC 2004
7. Hyuntae Cho, Hoon Choi, Woonghyun Lee, Yeonsu Jung, and Yunju Baek: LITeTag: Design and Implementation of an RFID System for IT-based Port Logistics , Journal of Communications (JCM), vol. 1, Issue 4 (ISSN 1796-2021), July 2006., pp. 48-57

Implementation of OSD Security Framework and Credential Cache*,**

Gu Su Kim, Kwang Sun Ko, Ungmo Kim, and Young Ik Eom

School of Info. and Comm. Eng., Sungkyunkwan Univ.,
300 Cheoncheon-dong, Jangan-gu, Suwon, Kyeonggi-do, 440-746, Korea
{gusukim, rilla91, umkim, yieom}@ece.skku.ac.kr

Abstract. The concept of Object-based Storage Devices (OSD), which is standardized by the ANSI T10 technical committee, is an emerging storage paradigm that replaces storages of traditional fixed-size block abstraction with those of variable-size objects that virtualizes the underlying physical storage. In this paper, we describe our substantial implementation of the OSD security framework in OASIS, which is an OSD system developed at ETRI (Electronics and Telecommunications Research Institute) in Korea. We also describe our credential caching subsystem, called Lcache, which is implemented in the client side of our OSD security framework in order to improve the performance of issuing credentials.

1 Introduction

Recently, data storage has become a vital, fast-growing part of the enterprise IT environment, as new business initiatives drive companies to accumulate vast amounts of information. The traditional model for storage, known as Direct Attached Storage (DAS), involves a hard disk drive and a disk array or a RAID system attached directly to a server or desktop machine. Because DAS model disperses data widely among many servers, it is inefficient and poorly-suited for managing mass storage in network environments. Storage Area Network (SAN) [1][2] place the storage servers on the client network and enable direct access to the storage servers. This design aims at improving I/O performance and system scalability of distributed file system as it removes the file-server from the critical data path. However, SAN security is essentially weak and the only partial solutions use methods provided by the physical level in Fiber Channel SANs [3]. Network Attached Storage (NAS) [4] is system-independent shareable storage that is connected directly to the network and is accessible to heterogeneous servers and client computers. However, because the storage system of NAS shares

* This research was supported by MIC, Korea under ITRC IITA-2006-(C1090-0603-0046).

** This research was supported by the Ubiquitous Computing and Network (UCN) Project, the MIC 21st Century Frontier R&D Program in Korea.

C. Cérin and K.-C. Li (Eds.): GPC 2007, LNCS 4459, pp. 666–671, 2007.

the same network with clients and application servers, heavy data traffic can have undesirable effects, such as bottlenecks and reduced network performance.

Object-based Storage Devices(OSD) [5] is a new storage paradigm (in particular for network accessible storage), in which the abstraction of array of blocks is replaced with the abstraction of collection of objects [6]. OSD paradigm was first proposed in CMU as an academic research project [7][8], outstandingly actualized and implemented by IBM Haifa Lab., and it still is an active area of research in academic and commercial worlds. In this paper, we describe our implementation of the OSD security framework in OASIS based on the OSD standard [9] and its credential caching subsystem, called Lcache, implemented in OASIS security framework. The proposed security framework for the OSD system is implemented on Linux systems, as a kernel module.

2 OSD Security Framework

In OSD systems, a client accesses data just by specifying object ID and offset, and the system is responsible for mapping the object ID and the offset to the actual location on the physical storage. From the security perspective, one major goal of the system is to work well not only on top of secure network infrastructures, but also in the environments with no such infrastructure. This requirement has led OSD designers to introduce a new concept of access control; the main difference of the OSD systems from existing block storage systems is that every command in OSD systems is accompanied by a cryptographically secure capability. The security model presented by the OSD standard [5] introduces the credential-based access control and is composed of four active entities: client, object store, security manager, and policy/storage manager.

First of all, a client requests a credential to the security manager, with which it later accesses the object store. The security manager, when it receives the request for credential, requests the capability of the client to the policy/storage manager. The capability, which is produced by the policy/storage manager, says whether the client's access are authorized or not. The security manager creates a credential that includes the capability and the capability key which is a cryptographically hashed value of the capability by using secure hash algorithms, such as HMAC-SHA1. The client, when it receives the credential issued by the security manager, composes a CDB(Command Descriptor Block) that includes storage commands, credential, and so on, and sends it to the object store. The object store, on receiving the CDB, checks the validity of the CDB by using secret keys which are hierarchically structured and shared with the security manager. Finally, the object store admits or denies the client's access as a result of the validity check.

In the OSD model, whenever the clients want to access to object stores, it is always necessary to get credential from the security manager and the only clients in possession of credentials can get service by the object stores. This may incur high network traffic and computation overhead in operational systems, and so, the OSD security framework needs some mechanisms to reduce the frequency of the clients' requests for credentials to the security manager.

3 OASIS Security Framework and Lcache

In this Section, we describe the architecture of the security framework based on the OSD standard and Lcache.

3.1 Implementation of OASIS Security Framework

OASIS system, implemented based on the OSD standard, consists of three subjects: clients, metadata servers, and OSD servers. Each subject also has several sub-blocks as necessary; the number and the constitution of these sub-blocks depend on the methods of implementation. Figure 1 shows the subjects and architecture of OASIS system in terms of security.

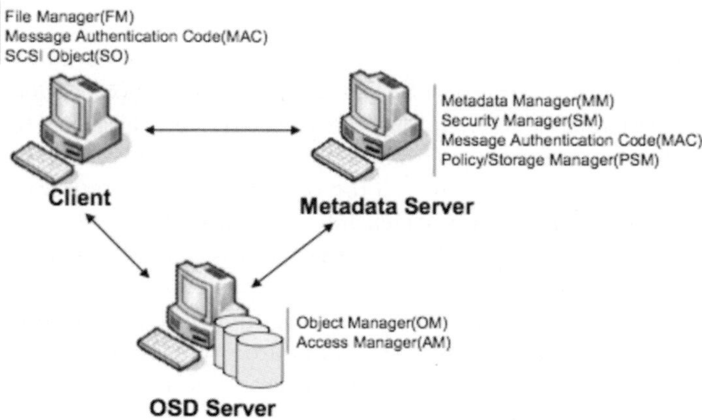

Fig. 1. The subjects and architecture of OASIS system in terms of security

As can be seen, in the Client, FM component presents the file system of OSD server to users and MAC requests the credential to the Metadata Server and verifies the response integrity check value in the return value of the command to the OSD server. SCSI Objects supports SCSI commands for FM component. In the Metadata Server, MM component handles the requests from the users or administrators and SM issues the credential for the command related to a specific object. MAC component is similar to the client's MAC component. PM component manages user's access policy to the OSD server. Lastly, in the OSD server, OM component performs the command from the client and AM component verifies the integrity check value in the command from the client. In our proposed framework, all subjects operate on Linux systems, connected each other via an IP-based open network. It uses the Internet Small Computer Systems Interface (iSCSI) mechanism [10][11] and all the components are implemented as kernel modules.

The proposed security framework, identical to the OSD standard [5], uses seven hierarchical keys: master keys , root keys, partition keys, and a working key.

Each authentication key is used for generating an *integrity check value*, and each generation key is used for generating lower-level hierarchical keys. Furthermore, the OSD server and the metadata server share the hierarchical keys; hierarchical keys, managed by each individual OSD server, are also managed in the metadata server. The implementation may be divided into six major sub-functionalities. These functionalities are as follows: *the creation of a request integrity check value, the validation of request integrity check value, the creation of a capability key, the creation of response integrity check value*, and *the validation of response integrity check value*. Detail descriptions of these functionalities can be presented in [12].

3.2 LCache

In OASIS, the credential cache mechanism is adopted for minimizing the cost of issuing a credential for the same object repeatedly, while there is no credential cache mechanism in the OSD specification. Our credential cache, called Lcache, is implemented on the client side by using kernel module programming. Lcache uses the LRU(Least Recently Used) algorithm because the client's reference to the object has the locality property. Figure 2 shows the Lcache structure.

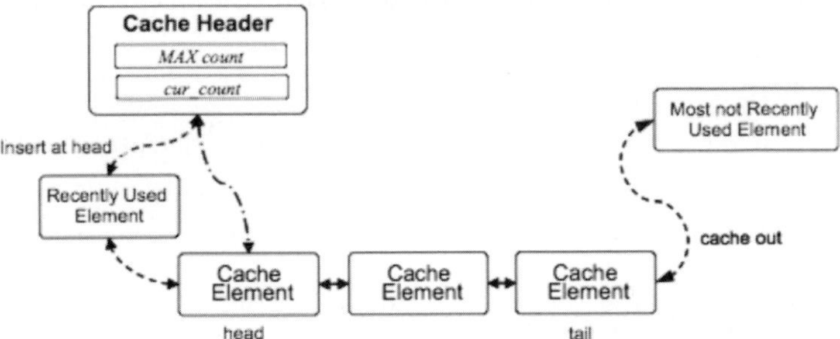

Fig. 2. Lcache structure

The Lcache in the OASIS is implemented with the doubly linked list, composed of cache elements and sorted by most recently used category. Cache header contains *curr_count* and *MAX_count*. The *cur_count* means the number of elements that can exist in the credential cache and *MAX_count* means the maximum number of elements in the credential cache. If the *cur_count* gets greater than *MAX_count*, the last element at the rear of the list is cached out. When client tries to retrieve a credential in the credential cache and cache hit happens, the retrieved credential is located at the front of the list. LRU sequence of the credentials in the Lcache is maintained through this mechanisem.

Our credential cache is implemented with the *slab* cache, which is a low level cache supported by Linux system, in order to improve the memory allocation speed. The *slab* cache operates garbage collector for the memory object and reduces the cost for the memory allocation and revocation.

The cost that it takes for the client to complete a transaction with the Lcache support is as follows:

$$T_c = P_r \cdot C_h \cdot n + (1 - P_r) \cdot (C_m + C_r) \cdot n + C_o n \quad (1)$$

In formula (1), T_c is the average cost that it takes for the client to complete one transaction. In the formula, P_r is the hit ratio of the credential in Lcache, $(1 - P_r)$ is the miss ratio of the credential in Lache, C_h is the cost that it takes for the client to handle the Lcache in the case of cache hit, and C_m is the cache management cost in the case of cache miss. Also, C_r is the cost that it takes for the client to get the credential from the metadata server, C_o is the cost that it takes for the client to get response from the metadata server per client's request, and n is the number of operations executed in one transaction.

In formula (1), the term $P_r \cdot C_h \cdot n$ shows the average cost that it takes for the client to handle the Lcache in the case of cache hit and the term $(1 - P_r) \cdot (C_m + C_r) \cdot n$ shows the average cost that it takes for the client to manage the Lcache and for the metadata server to issue a credential to the client in the case of cache miss. The term $C_o \cdot n$ is the cost that it takes for the client to receive response from the metadata server for one transaction. The cost that it takes for the client to complete one transaction without the credential cache is defined as $T_c' = C_r \cdot n + C_o \cdot n$. So, the performance gain with Lcache can be computed as follows:

$$\begin{aligned} G &= T_c' - T_c \\ &= (C_r \cdot n + C_o \cdot n) - \{P_r \cdot C_h \cdot n + (1 - P_r) \cdot (C_m + C_r) \cdot n + C_o n\} \\ &\simeq C_r \cdot n - (1 - P_r) \cdot C_r \cdot n \quad (\textit{because } C_h \simeq 0 \textit{ and } C_m \simeq 0) \\ &= P_r \cdot C_r \cdot n \end{aligned} \quad (2)$$

In formula (2), because the values of C_h and C_m, which are the cache management cost, are very low in comparison of other parameters, the cache management cost can be ignored, and the performance gain that can be obtained by using the Lcache becomes the additional credential creation cost. So, by using Lcache, the cost for one transaction can be approximated to the first credential creation cost.

4 Conclusion

In this paper, the implementation of a security framework, based on the OSD standard, is presented. For the security framework in the OASIS system, we developed the MAC component in the client side, the SM and MAC components in the server side, and the AM component in the OSD server side. These components in the security framework were implemented on the Linux system using kernel module programming. These components have six major-functionalities: *the creation of a request integrity check value, the creation of a credential the creation of a capability key, the validation of request integrity check value, the creation of response integrity check value*, and *the validation of response integrity check value.*

In order to improve the performance of OASIS security framework, furthermore, we developed the credential cache, called Lcache, on the MAC component in the client side. Lcache is implemented with the Linux *slab* cache in kernel module to improve the memory allocation speed. With our Lcache scheme, it is possible to reduce the total credential creation cost and eventually to improve the performance of OASIS security framework.

References

1. G. Gibson, et. al., "A Cost-Effective, High-Bandwidth Storage Architecture," Proc. of International Conference on Architectural Support for Programming Languages and Operating Systems (ASPLOS), 1998.
2. G. Gibson, et. al., "File Server Scaling with Network-Attached Secure Disks," Proc. of the ACM International Conference on Measurement and Modelling of Computer System, Seattle, WA, Jun. 1997.
3. A. Azagury, et. al., "A Two-layered Approach for Securing an Object Store Network," Proc. of IEEE International Security In Storage Workshop, Dec. 2002.
4. Trend Micro, Inc., Securing Data in Network Attached Storage (NAS) Environments: ServerProtect for NAS, White paper, Jul. 2001.
5. SNIA - Storage Networking Industry Association, OSD: Object Based Storage Devices, OSD Technical Work Group.
6. M. Factor, D. Nagle, D. Naor, E. Riedel, and J. Satran, "The OSD Security Protocol," Proc. of the 3rd International IEEE Security in Storage Workshop (SISW05), Dec. 2005.
7. G. Gibson, et. al., "File Server Scaling with Network-attached Secure Disks," Proc. of the ACM International Conference on Measurement and Modelling of Computer System, Seattle, WA, Jun. 1996.
8. G. Gibson, et. al., Filesystems for Network-attached Secure Disks, Technical Report. CS.97.112, CMU, 1997.
9. American National Standard for Information Technology, SCSI Object-Based Storage Device Commands (OSD), INCITS 400-2004, 2004.
10. J. Satran, K. Meth, C. Sapuntzakis, M. Chadalapaka, and E. Zeidner, RFC 3720: Internet Small Computer Systems Interface (iSCSI), Apr. 2004.
11. Linux-iSCSI Project, http://linux-iscsi.sourceforge.net/.
12. Kwangsun Ko, Gu Su Kim, June Kim, JungHyun Han, Ungmo Kim, and Young Ik Eom, "Design and Implementation of a Security Framework based on the Object-based Storage Device Standard," Lecture Notes in Computer Science 3980, Springer-Verlag, May 2006.

SEMU: A Framework of Simulation Environment for Wireless Sensor Networks with Co-simulation Model

Shih-Hsiang Lo, Jiun-Hung Ding, Sheng-Je Hung, Jin-Wei Tang, Wei-Lun Tsai, and Yeh-Ching Chung

Department of Computer Science, National Tsing Hua University, Taiwan
{albert, adjunhon, claboy, garnet, welentsai}@sslab.cs.nthu.edu.tw, ychung@cs.nthu.edu.tw

Abstract. This paper presents a framework of simulation environment (SEMU) which allows developers to understand the behavior of applications or protocols for a wireless sensor network (WSN) before deploying real nodes in a physical environment. For eliminating the gap between simulation and real deployment, SEMU has supported fast real code emulation by dynamic binary translation technique. SEMU also models the controlled environment as virtual operating system (Virtual OS) to coordinate the interactions of large number of nodes. In addition, we have proposed a co-simulation model to enhance the accuracy of pure software simulation. Then a further synchronization problem will be addressed and resolved by the co-simulation model. The evaluation results show SEMU is really a fast scalable WSN simulator with real code emulation.

Index Terms: Simulator, wireless sensor networks, dynamic binary translation, hardware and software co-simulation.

1 Introduction

A wireless sensor network (WSN) is a network composed of a large number of sensor nodes, which are deployed in the environment. Recently, with the rapid development of WSNs, providing development tools such as simulation environment before deploying real nodes in physical environments is getting more important. A well simulation environment can help developers build their prototype models to know the interactions and the behavior of each node. In addition, most of WSN applications will deploy a large number of nodes in a simulation environment. However, the simulation speed depends on the simulation fidelity and scale. Therefore how to build up a fast scalable WSN simulation environment with the fine-grained information is the main research problem in this paper.

In this paper, a framework of simulation environment (SEMU) is presented. SEMU has a first version implementation and an extension model for hardware and software co-simulation. In order to extract the real behavior of each node, SEMU supports real applications to run on the virtual nodes. And, the new development trend shows us the powerful nodes [2], [4], [9] are also applied to WSNs. Consequently, our first implementation version of SEMU supports the virtual nodes to directly run the real Linux applications on the Linux platform.

For the extension of SEMU, co-simulation model, this paper has addressed two problems when SEMU uses pure software simulation models. One problem is that

C. Cérin and K.-C. Li (Eds.): GPC 2007, LNCS 4459, pp. 672 – 677, 2007.

software sensing channel models are difficult to be built the same as real sensing channels, and furthermore they fail to interact with physical environments. The other problem shows that the pure software simulation needs a considerable amount of effort to model the behavior of real communication devices and real communication protocol. By the co-simulation model, SEMU can further satisfy the requirement of WSN development, and collect more realistic profiling information and physical environment conditions during simulation.

This rest of paper is organized as follows. In the next Section, we state the related work to compare different approaches of real code emulation and co-simulation model. Section 3 clearly illustrates the overall design of the simulation framework. Then Section 4 introduces the hardware and software co-simulation model based on SEMU. In Section 5 provides our evaluation results. Finally, Section 6 concludes this paper.

2 Related Works

In the literature, several WSN simulators have been proposed to support real applications targeted on different platforms. These approaches can be divided into two categories. One is static translation which maps the real code into the simulation platform before run time. The other is dynamic translation which interprets the real code during simulation. Besides, related works about co-simulation in WSN simulators are also described here.

TOSSIM [7] is a notable example to represent the static translation technique. TOSSIM is a discrete event simulator which can directly run a TinyOS [6] application through compilation support. This method is an excellent way to reduce the runtime overhead for code translation with advanced compiler supports. Nevertheless, the supported languages highly depend on the modified compiler.

There are some simulators using the dynamic translation technique [1], [3], [5]. Atemu [3] is a fine grained sensor node emulator for AVR processor based systems. Although the low-level emulation of the sensor node hardware can acquire the high-fidelity results, the run time interpretation overhead makes the emulation speed much slower than other approaches.

EmStar [5] is an environment for developing wireless embedded systems software in Linux-based software framework. EmStar provides a pure simulation, a true distributed deployment, and two hybrid modes. The software stack of Emstar is composed of several components, and each of them presents a Linux process with its own address space. However, it can not emulate the real binary codes which run on the real platform.

Embra runs as part of the SimOS simulation system [1]. To achieve high simulation speed, Embra uses dynamic binary translation (DBT) technique to generate code sequences which simulate the workload.

For co-simulation, SensorSim [10] use a gateway node and a simulated protocol stack to connect the real nodes. Since the real nodes and simulated nodes are not time synchronized, real node can not interact with simulated node on the correct time. EmStar [5] has proposed three kinds of hybrid modes for WSN simulation including data replay, ceiling array and portable array. Our co-simulation model is similar to the three hybrid modes of EmStar. However our co-simulation model can provide run time profiling to help SEMU to resolve synchronization problem. Hence our co-simulation model can improve SEMU for developing WSN applications with more accurate model.

3 The Framework of SEMU

When we design SEMU, we take following design issues into account: fast real code emulation for Linux application, a simulation engine for harmony and environment model. According to these design issues, we have proposed a framework for SEMU as Fig. 1. It consists of five layers, VM layer, Communication layer, Virtual OS layer, Module layer, and Native OS layer. The framework has become as a backbone for our future extensions.

The top layer, Virtual Machine (VM) layer, achieves fast real code emulation on Linux platforms. In VM layer, a virtual node represents as an emulation of a real node. A virtual node can consist of several virtual machines. Through communication links between VM and Communication layer, virtual nodes can interact with the simulation environment. We use a modified QEMU as our VM layer [10].

Communication layer is partitioned into three parts including Communicator, Gateway and Connector. Communicator enables VM layer to communicate with Virtual OS layer. Gateway is used for hybrid simulation, as hardware and software co-simulation. As to Connector, it lets the Distributed GUI and the simulation engine can be run on different machines and work together.

The Virtual Operating System (Virtual OS) layer stands for the control center to harmonize the simulation. As general operating system, SEMU provides BootLoader to initialize the whole system and to boot Virtual OS. The BLR Shell provides a command interface of BootLoader for simulation users. SIM Kernel is also a service provider which helps virtual nodes to forward their service requests to Module layer and Native OS layer. Through OS Shell, run time simulation system can be operated by users.

In the Module layer, all of the components enhance the functionalities of the simulation framework. In the current work, the Module layer has supplied seven components. SIMState maintains all simulation status and references of the simulation objects in a centralized way. SIMState is configured with initial states by Configer before starting the SIM Kernel. In order to arrange the chaotic messages, Logger will analyze log information with classification. For simulating parallel execution of multiple nodes in a sequential computer, an adequate Scheduler needs to be applied. Time Manager is to resolve synchronization problems. Node Model supplies device configurations for developers to form a node element. Users can integrate their protocol algorithms into the Protocol Stack. Environment will provide several models to reflect real conditions in physical environment.

The bottom layer of SEMU is Native Operating System (Native OS) layer. For system emulation, SEMU takes native operating system as the foundation of framework.

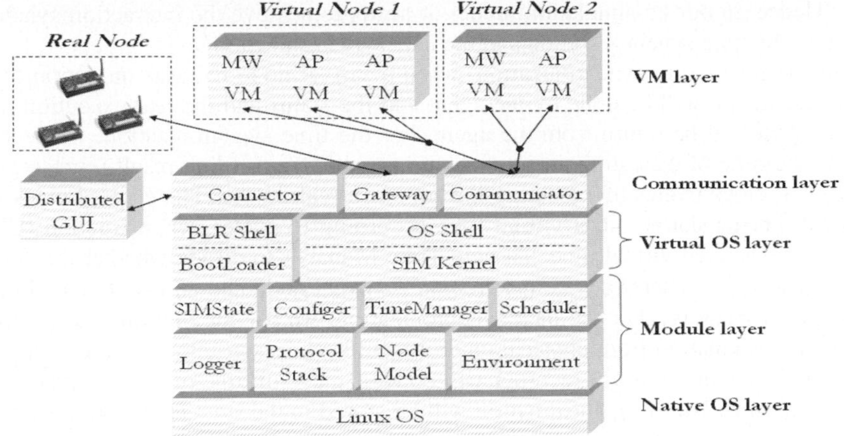

Fig. 1. The architecture of SEMU

4 Co-simulation Model

In this section, we discuss the extension model of SEMU, co-simulation model, and address the synchronization problem when hardware and software run together.

The co-simulation model supports the real communication and sensing channel by cooperating with real node devices. The co-simulation model consists of three components including Communication Agent, Sensing Agent and Environment Recorder. Communication Agent helps SEMU make use of real communication device and real communication protocol to gather more realistic communication latency and to support more accurate model than pure software simulation. Then Sensing Agent can provide real sensing channels for collecting raw data from physical environment. By Environment Recorder, packets and sensing information with timestamp can be recorded in the buffer, which is similar to Digital Video Recorder. SEMU can use Environment Recorder to track the real time events and make the events re-present.

We propose a WSN co-simulation model to extend the SEMU design. In our co-simulation model, SIM Kernel serves all virtual nodes to request actions, such as sending, receiving and sensing. SIM Kernel will choose an agent which can represent the realistic behavior of the node. When an agent is chosen for the request, it will do the corresponding action and provide the run time profiling information. After finishing the action, it will notify the SIM Kernel of results including the execution time and the status for the action. Then SIM Kernel will request Time Manager whether the action can be completed. If Time Manager grants the request, the SIM Kernel will return the real data such as the packet or sensing data from environment recorder to the virtual node. Otherwise, SIM Kernel will block the virtual node until the request is granted by Time Manager.

From our co-simulation model, we must make sure that virtual nodes and the agents will cooperate with each other, virtual nodes will take the execution time of the agents into account, and virtual nodes will access the data according to their virtual time. Hence, in our co-simulation model, it needs to achieve the interaction synchronization, the time synchronization and the data synchronization.

For the interaction synchronization, when a virtual node requests an action to an agent, the action will be done by the agent and the status and the real execution time of the agent will be return from the agent. For the time synchronization, we need to profile the time of executing an action in an agent. The profiling result represents as number of clock cycles of executing the action in real device. The elapsed clock cycles will be translated into a virtual time according to cycles per instruction (CPI). Then the generated virtual time can help Time Manager to decide whether the action is granted or not. Therefore, we ensure that a virtual node and an agent can work in time synchronization. For the data synchronization, we use an environment recorder to collect information from physical environment such as sensing data and packets in wall time. The environment recorder will convert the wall time of the information to the virtual time. All of the information will be stored in the storage. The frequency of sensing or receiving depends on the requirement of a WSN application.

5 Evaluation Results

In our experiment, virtual nodes are deployed as grid and will cooperate to broadcast an event to whole network. The event will be sent by a specific virtual node deployed on the corner. Then this event will be relayed by a flooding protocol until all of the virtual nodes receiving it. We want to know how fast SEMU can complete the simulation as the number of virtual nodes increasing. We performed the experiment on a Celeron 3.0ghz machine with 1.5 GB of RAM running Linux 2.6.11. SEMU can run fast below 1250 virtual nodes. When the number of nodes is over 1250, the execution time of simulation increases quickly under the machine with 1.5 GB of physical RAM. Because if we create more virtual nodes, the simulation will use swap space, in which the simulation runs slowly. Hence, the scalability of SEMU highly relates to the resource management of Linux OS.

6 Conclusion

In this paper, we have presented a framework of SEMU to develop a WSN simulator. The framework allows developers to understand the behaviors of a WSN applications or protocols before real deployment. Due to the trend of complex software platforms used in the WSN, such as Linux, the implementation of SEMU supports a real Linux application to run directly on the SEMU by fast real code emulation. We also have proposed a co-simulation model to enhance the accuracy of pure software simulation. The synchronization problem between virtual nodes and real nodes is addressed and resolved by the co-simulation model. Finally, the evaluation results show that SEMU can support fast real code emulation. Consequently, the framework of WSN simulation environment, SEMU, really assists developers in the development of WSN applications.

Acknowledgments. The work of this paper is partially supported by National Science Council and Ministry of Economic Affairs under NSC 95-2221-E-007-018 and MOEA 95-EC-17-A-04-S1-044.

References

1. E. Witchel , and M. Rosenblum, "Embra: fast and flexible machine simulation", Proceedings of the 1996 ACM SIGMETRICS international conference on Measurement and modeling of computer systems, p.68-79, May 23-26, 1996, Philadelphia, Pennsylvania, United States.
2. I. Downes, Leili B. Rad*, and H. Aghajan, "Development of a Mote for Wireless Image Sensor Networks" In Proc. of Cognitive Systems and Interactive Sensors (COGIS), March 2006.
3. J. Polley, D. Blazakis, J. McGee, D. Rusk, J. S. Baras, and M. Karir, "ATEMU: A fine-grained sensor network simulator," in Proceedings of SECON'04, First IEEE Communications Society Conference on Sensor and Ad Hoc Comunications and Networks, 2004.
4. L. Nachman, R. Kling, R. Adler, J. Huang, and V. Hummel, "The intel mote platform: a bluetooth-based sensor network for industrial monitoring." in IPSN 2005, pp. 437–442, Apr. 2005.
5. L. Girod, J. Elson, A. Cerpa, T. Stathopoulos, N. Ramanathan, and D. Estrin, "Emstar: a software environment for developing and deploying wireless sensor networks," in Proceedings of the USENIX Technical Conference, 2004.
6. P. Levis, S. Madden, J. Polastre, R. Szewczyk, K. Whitehouse, A. Woo, D. Gay, J. Hill, M. Welsh, E. Brewer, and D. Culler, "TinyOS: An operating system for wireless sensor networks" In Ambient Intelligence. Springer-Verlag, 2004.
7. P. Levis, N. Lee, M. Welsh, and D. Culler, "TOSSIM: accurate and scalable simulation of entire tinyOS applications", Proceedings of the 1st international conference on Embedded networked sensor systems, November 05-07, 2003, Los Angeles, California, USA.
8. QEMU project. http://fabrice.bellard.free.fr/qemu/.
9. Stargate: a platform X project. http://platformx.sourceforge.net/.
10. Sung Park, Andreas Savvides, and Mani B. Srivastava, "SensorSim: a simulation framework for sensor networks", Proceedings of the 3rd ACM international workshop on Modeling, analysis and simulation of wireless and mobile systems, p.104-111, August 20-20, 2000, Boston, Massachusetts, United States.

Combining Software Agents and Grid Middleware

Richard Olejnik[1], Bernard Toursel[1], Maria Ganzha[2], and Marcin Paprzycki[2]

[1] Laboratoire d'Informatique Fondamentale, de Lille (LIFL UMR CNRS 8022)
Universite des Sciences et Technologies de Lille, USTL - Lille, France
{olejnik, toursel}@lifl.fr

[2] Systems Research Institute Polish Academy of Sciences, Warsaw, Poland
{maria.ganzha, marcin.paprzycki}@ibspan.waw.pl

Abstract. Recently, the *Desktop-Grid ADaptive Application in Java* (*DG-ADAJ*) project has been unveiled. Its goal is to provide an environment which facilitates adaptive control of distributed applications written in Java for the Grid or the Desktop Grid. However, in its current state it can be used only in closed environments (e.g. within a single laboratory), as it lacks features that would make it ready for an "open Grid." The aim of this paper is to show how the *DG-ADAJ* can be augmented by usage of software agents and ontologies to make it more robust.

1 Introduction

The starting point for this research was development of Grid-enabled data mining software suite taking place within the *Distributed Data Mining* (*DisDaMin*) project (for details see [4,5]). In conjunction, the *Desktop-Grid Adaptive Application in Java* (*DG-ADAJ*) project develops middleware platform for the Grid that, among others, could be used as a base for deployment of *DisDaMin* algorithms. It is the *DG-ADAJ* middleware that is of our particular interest in this paper. Specifically, we discuss how some of its natural shortcomings can be overcome by adding software agents as resource brokers and high level managers.

To achieve this goal we, first, present the *DG-ADAJ* project and discuss its most important features. We follow with a discussion of its shortcomings within an "open Grid." In the next section we describe an agent team based broker system and show how the two can be combined to create a robust Grid middleware.

2 *DG-ADAJ* Platform

Desktop Grid – Adaptive Distributed Application in Java (*DG-ADAJ*) is a middleware platform for Grid computing. It aims at facilitating a Single System Image (SSI) and enabling efficient execution of heterogeneous applications with irregular and unpredictable execution control. In Figure 1 we present the general overview of the *DG-ADAJ* architecture.

C. Cérin and K.-C. Li (Eds.): GPC 2007, LNCS 4459, pp. 678–685, 2007.

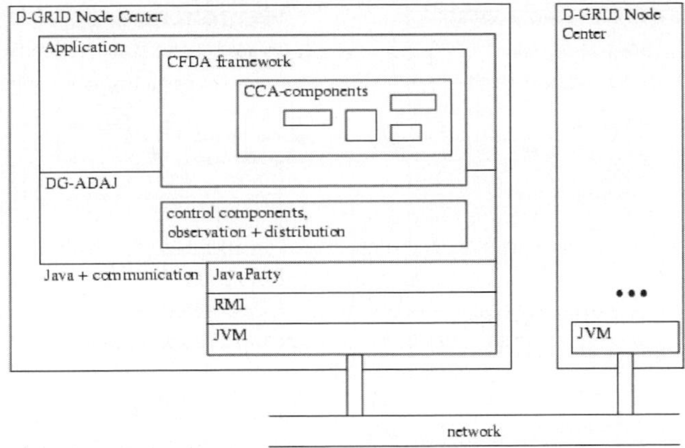

Fig. 1. DG-ADAJ Architecture

DG-ADAJ is an execution environment that is designed and implemented above the JavaParty and Java/RMI platforms according to a multi-layer structure, using several APIs (see Figures 1 and 2). One of its important features are mechanisms based on control components (for more details of the *Common Component Architecture* (CCA), see [1]) for controlling granularity of computations and distribution of applications on the Desktop Grid platform. Note that use of components allows *DG-ADAJ* to be an environment for Java applications.

In addition to standard components, Super-Components have been developed to allow assembling together several components (they become *inner components* of a Super-Component). Super-Components implement framework services to manage their inner components. Specifically, connections between inner-components are achieved the same way as connection between standard components, while connections between inner-components and outer-components (components outside of the Super-Component) are achieved through a special mechanism of delegation between inner and outer ports (see Figure 3). Finally, the remote component is a special type of Super-Component which is implemented using the JavaParty notion of Remote class (defined using the JavaParty keyword *remote*).

DG-ADAJ runtime optimizes dynamic and static placement of the application objects within Java Virtual Machines of the Desktop Grid or the Grid [7]. Furthermore, *DG-ADAJ* provides special mechanisms, at the middleware level, which assure dynamic and automatic adaptation to variations of computation methods and execution platforms. This dynamic, on–line load balancing is based on object monitoring and relation graph optimization algorithms. Specifically, application observation mechanism in *DG-ADAJ* provides knowledge of behavior of the application during its execution. This knowledge is obtained by observation of object activity. A *DG-ADAJ* application comprises two types of objects: global and local. Global objects are observable, remote access and migratable. Local objects are traditional Java objects which are linked to a global object.

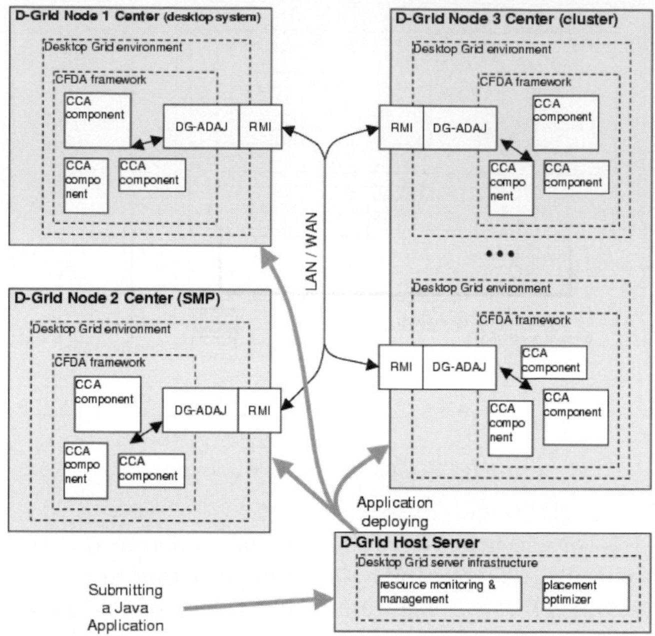

Fig. 2. The layered structure of the DG-ADAJ Environment

Observation of a global object corresponds to monitoring its communication with other objects (global or local). Specifically, three components are used for the observation mechanism: (1) the *object graph*, which is built using relations between application objects, (2) the *relation tracer*, which stores information concerning these relations, and (3) the *observer*, which is responsible for the observation information update [8]). Observation of relationships between objects allows also computation of object activity (local and remote) representing their load. Overall, based on observations of object activity and on their relations, objects can be selected and moved from or to a computing node.

These mechanisms were experimented with in an earlier, built for cluster computing, version of *DG-ADAJ* (see, [6]). In the new version of *DG-ADAJ* load balancing takes into account also local load of each node, allowing computing nodes to be shared between several applications.

3 Agent Brokers Augmenting *DG-ADAJ*

Let us now assume that a *DisDamin* application is going to utilize the *DJ-ADAJ* environment to run within an "open Grid;" understood as a computational infrastructure consisting of nodes spread across the Internet. These nodes have different owners (including individuals who offer their home PC) that offer services and expect to be remunerated for their usage. In this case the Grid is

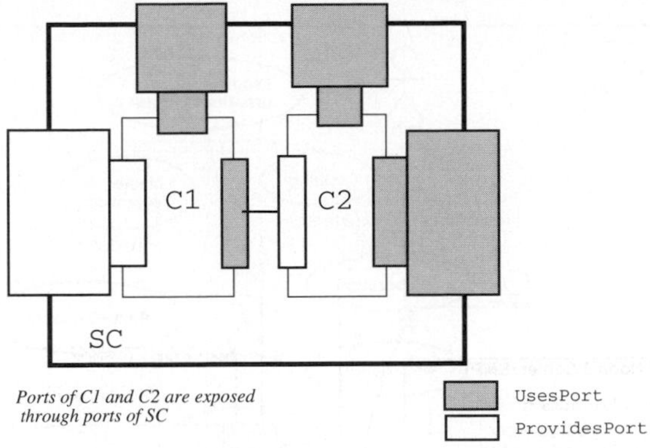

Fig. 3. Super-component

a highly dynamic structure. There are two levels of dynamicity that can be observed. First, a given node suddenly becomes overloaded — when its owner starts using it. Second, a given node disappears without a trace when the PC goes down due to a current spike. Interestingly, while the *DG-ADAJ* monitors performance of individual nodes and can deal with the first scenario, currently it cannot deal naturally with disappearing nodes. Observe that this is not a big problem in the case of a "closed Grid" e.g. in a laboratory, where all nodes are under some form of control of a system administrator.

Furthermore, *DG-ADAJ* does not include methods for resource brokering (which includes both resource description and matchmaking). While in a laboratory it is possible to know in advance, which machines will constitute the Grid, this is no the case in the "open Grid." Here, before any computational job is executed, nodes which will run it have to be found / selected first.

Finally, let us stress that resource brokering should involve an economic model, where resource providers are paid for rendered services. In return, quality of service (QOS) assurances have to be provided in a form of a service level agreement (SLA) "singed" by service-users and service-providers. These features are currently out of scope of the *DG-ADAJ* project.

In response to these "shortcomings" we propose to augment the *DG-ADAJ* with software agent "components." We follow here the proposal described in [2,3], where more details of the agent-broker system can be found. Let us start with the use case diagram and a brief discussion of functionalities depicted there.

The main idea of the proposed system is utilization of agent teams consisting of a number of *worker agents* and a leader, the *LMaster agent*. It is the *LMaster* with whom *user agents* negotiate terms of task execution, and who decides whether to accept a new *worker agent* to the team. The *LMaster* agent has its mirror (*LMirror* agent). Its role is to be able to immediately take over — become the new *LMaster* — if the original *LMaster* goes down. In the case of *LMirror*'s disappearance, the *LMaster* immediately promotes one of *worker agents* to the role of *LMirror*. Note that an agent team may assure an SLA, as in the case when

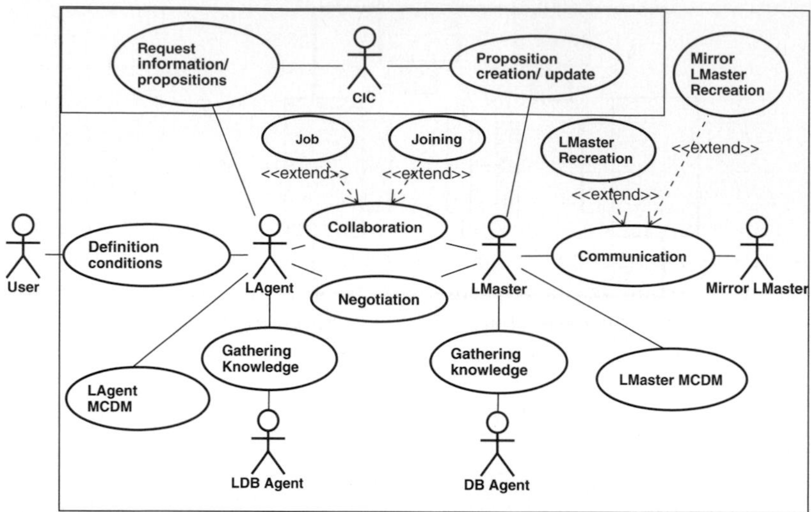

Fig. 4. Use Case diagram of the proposed system

one machine/worker goes down, the *LMaster* is able to recognize the situation and redirect the job to another machine (and complete it almost on time).

For a team to be visible to potential users or team members, it must "post" its *team advertisement* for others to see. In our system (following results presented in [9]) we utilize a *yellow page* type approach and *LMaster* agents post their team advertisements within the *Client Information Center* (*CIC*). Such an advertisement contains information about offered resources (e.g. hardware capabilities, available software, price etc.) and / or "team metadata" (e.g. terms of joining, provisioning, specialization etc.). In this way *yellow pages* may be used: (1) by *user agents* looking for resources satisfying requirements of their task, and (2) by *worker agents* searching for a team to join. For example, *worker agent* representing computational resource with installed *DisDamin* software, may want to join a team specializing in solving problems utilizing *DisDamin* software.

Let us observe that in the case of a "closed Grid," this agent structure can be unchanged, though it also could be simplified. Here, instead of an evolutionary formation of agent teams (where workers and managers pick teams/agents of their linking), a team can be predefined by the administrator of the system. In this case also the *LMaster* and the *LMirror* agents can be selected to run on most stable (though not necessarily most powerful) machines. Overall, regardless of the scenario, the proposed approach adds a level of fault tolerance to the system and allows it to utilize Service Level Agreements and economic basis of functioning.

In the system, user initiates the execution of the job by providing its *user agent* with specific requirements such as: *resource requirements*—specification of resources needed to execute the task, and *execution constraints*—time, budget etc.

From there on, the *user agent* acts autonomously. First, it queries the *CIC* for resources matching requirements and obtains a list of query-matching teams. Then it negotiates with *LMasters* representing selected teams, taking into account specified *execution constraints* to find the best team for the job. In the case of a closed environment it is possible to enforce that the (only existing/predefined by the administrator) agent team will execute the job.

Similarly, user can request that its agent joins a team, and specify conditions for joining (e.g. frequency of guaranteed jobs or share of generated revenue). In this case the *user agent* queries the *CIC* and obtains list of teams of interest; negotiates with them, decides which team to join and starts working for it. As stated above, in the case of a closed environment, the agent team(s) can be predefined. Observe that in both cases the economic model is taken into consideration.

To describe Grid resources we have decided to utilize ontologies. Unfortunately, there is no all-agreed ontology of the Grid and therefore we utilize an extremely simplified, RDF based, one [2]. What follows is an instance of that ontology describing worker *PC1541*, which has 16 Intel processors running at 3.0 GHz, 1 Gbyte of memory per processor, and 5 Gbytes of disk space available as a "Grid service:"

```
:LMaster3
  :hasContactAID
  ''monster@e-plant:1099/JADE'';
  :hasWorker  :PC1541.

:PC2929
  :a  :Computer;
  :hasCPU
  [
   a  :CPU;
   :hasCPUType  :Intel;
   :hasCPUFrequency  "3.0";
   :hasCPUnumber  "16";
 ] ;
  :hasUserDiskQuota  "5000";
  :hasMemory  "1024".
```

Note that this simplistic ontology can be relatively easily replaced by a more realistic one as soon as such (all agreed by the Grid community) ontology becomes available. However, for the application like the *DisDamin* this ontology is quite sufficient as it specifies all the information necessary to perform initial distribution of data into computing nodes.

4 Combining Agent-Brokers and DG-ADAJ

Since agent-brokers and the DG-ADAJ are implemented in Java (recall that *DG-ADAJ* has been designed to facilitate programming of Java applications), combining them should be relatively easy. This is especially so that we have clearly delineated responsibilities. Agent-brokers act as "top level management" and are responsible for resource brokering, setting the job to be executed and monitoring its successful completion. Components of *DG-ADAJ* are responsible for actually running the job. More specifically, in Figure 5 we depict how JADE agent platform ([10]) can be incorporated into the *DG-ADAJ* environment. Specifically, we propose that both the *DG-ADAJ* and JADE share the Java Virtual Machine and the RMI. In this way the RMI becomes the communication mechanism between the two environments.

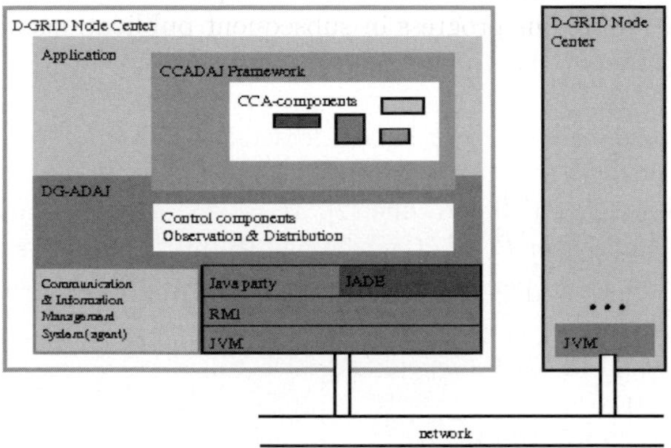

Fig. 5. Introducing JADE agents into DG-ADAJ

Taking this into account, we envision the following scenario taking place (in an open Grid system). User specifies the requirements for the data mining task. The *LAgents* communicates with the *CIC* and obtains list of agent teams that are capable of executing this job. Then—using contract net protocol—the *LAgent* negotiates conditions of job execution (including the SLA) and picks one of them. Obviously, we assume that the selected team will run *DG-ADAJ* and the required application software. Information about the job is then transferred to the selected team. This information includes, among others, information where data sources are located. The *LMaster* communicates with selected *LAgents* in its team (utilizing information about available machines—including information about workload obtained from the workload monitoring component of the *DG-ADAJ*), and decides which machines will be used to execute the job. Job information is send to *DG-ADAJ* components on selected machines and the job is left with them to execute. Upon completion of the job/task, the *DG-ADAJ* communicates with the *LAgents* involved in the process. These agents confirm to the *LMaster* that the process is complete (and send to it the final result-set). The *LMaster*, in turn, communicates with the *LAgent* representing the user and completes all processes involved in finalizing the task (e.g. payment, results transfer etc.).

5 Concluding Remarks

In this paper we have presented the *DG-ADAJ* project that provides middleware platform for the Desktop Grid and Grid. Our analysis indicated that, due to its underlying assumptions, the current state of the *DG-ADAJ* is lacking certain features to make it robust enough for the "open Grid." We have proposed to augment the *DG-ADAJ* with agent-brokers that will take care of high-level management functions, and with Grid resource ontology. We have also discussed how the two can be joined in a unified system. We are currently studying the specific way in which agent brokers can be implemented into the *DG-ADAJ* system and will report our progress in subsequent publications.

References

1. I.Alshabani, R. Olejnik and B. Toursel. Parallel Tools for a Distributed Component Framework *1st International Conference on Information & Communication Technologies: from Theory to Applications (ICTTA04)*. Damascus, Syria, April 2004.
2. M. Dominiak, W. Kuranowski, M. Gawinecki, M. Ganzha, M. Paprzycki, Utilizing agent teams in grid resource management — preliminary considerations, *Proceedings of the J. V. Atanasov Conference*, IEEE CS Press, Los Alamitos, CA, 2006, 46-51
3. M. Dominiak, W. Kuranowski, M. Gawinecki, M. Ganzha, M. Paprzycki, Efficient Matchmaking in an Agent-based Grid Resource Brokering System, *Proceedings of the International Multiconference on Computer Science and Information Technology*, PTI Press, 2006, 327-335
4. V. Fiolet and B. Toursel, *Distributed Data Mining*, In Scalable Computing: Practice and Experiences, Vol. 6, Number 1, March 2005, pp. 99-109.
5. V. Fiolet and B. Toursel, *Progressive Clustering for Database Distribution on a Grid*, In Proc. of ISPDC 2005, IEEE Computer Society, july 2005, pp. 282-289.
6. R. Olejnik, A. Bouchi, B. Toursel. Object observation for a java adaptative distributed application platform. *Intl. Conference on Parallel Computing in Electrical Engineering PARELEC 2002*, pp. 171-176., Warsaw, Poland, September 2002.
7. E. Laskowski, M. Tudruj, R. Olejnik, B. Toursel. *Bytecode Scheduling of Java Programs with Branches for Desktop Grid. to appear in the Future Generation Computer Systems*, Springer Verlag.
8. A. Bouchi, R. Olejnik and B.Toursel. *A new estimation method for distributed Java object activity.* 16th International Parallel and Distributed Processing Symposium, Marriott Marina, Fort Lauderdale, Florida, April 2002.
9. Trastour, D., Bartolini, C., Preist, C.: Semantic Web Support for the Business-to-Business E-Commerce Lifecycle. In: *Proceedings of the WWW'02: International World Wide Web Conference*, Hawaii, USA. ACM Press, New York, USA, pp.89-98, 2002.
10. JADE: Java Agent Development Framework. See `http://jade.cselt.it`

A Web Service-Based Brokering Service for e-Procurement in Supply Chains

Giner Alor-Hernandez[1], Ruben Posada-Gomez[1], Juan Miguel Gomez-Berbis[2], and Ma. Antonieta Abud-Figueroa[1]

[1] Division of Research and Postgraduate Studies
Instituto Tecnologico de Orizaba.
Av. Instituto Tecnologico 852, Col Emiliano Zapata. 09340 Orizaba, Veracruz, México
[2] Departamento de Informática
Escuela Politécnica Superior, Universidad Calos III de Madrid
{galor, rposada, mabud}@itorizaba.edu.mx,
juanmiguel.gomez@uc3m.es

Abstract. Service-Oriented Architecture (SOA) development paradigm has emerged to improve the critical issues of creating, modifying and extending solutions for business processes integration incorporating process automation and automated exchange of information between organizations. Web services technology follows the SOA's principles for developing and deploying applications. Besides, Web services are considered as the platform for SOA, for both intra- and inter-enterprise communication. However, an SOA does not incorporate information about occurring events into business processes that are the main features of supply chain management. These events and information delivery are addressed in an Event-Driven Architecture (EDA). Having this into account, we propose a Web service-based system named BPIMS-WS that offers a brokering service for the procurement of products in supply chain management scenarios. As salient contributions, our system provides a hybrid architecture combining features both SOA and EDA and a set of mechanisms for business processes pattern management, monitoring based on UML sequence diagrams, Web services-based management, event publish/subscription and reliable messaging service.

Keywords: Event-Driven Architecture, Service-Oriented Architecture, Web Services

1 Introduction

Service-Oriented Architecture (SOA) is an architectural paradigm for creating and managing "business services" that can access these functions, assets, and pieces of information with a common interface regardless of the location or technical makeup of the function or piece of data [1]. With an SOA infrastructure, we can represent software functionality as discoverable Web Services on the network. A Web service is a software component that is accessible by means of messages sent using standard web protocols, notations and naming conventions, including the XML protocol [2]. The notorious success that the application of the Web service technology has achieved in B2B e-Commerce has also lead to consider it as a promising technology

C. Cérin and K.-C. Li (Eds.): GPC 2007, LNCS 4459, pp. 686–693, 2007.

for designing and building effective business collaboration in supply chains. Deploying Web services reduces the integration costs and brings in the required infrastructure for business automation, obtaining a quality of service that could not be achieved otherwise [3, 4].

However, an SOA infrastructure does not address all the capabilities needed in a typical supply chain management scenario. It does not have the ability to monitor, filter, analyze, correlate, and respond in real time to events. These limitations are addressed with an Event-Driven Architecture (EDA). An EDA combined with SOA, provides that ability to create a SCM architecture that enables business. An EDA is an architectural paradigm based on using events that initiate the immediate delivery of a message that informs to numerous recipients about the event so they can take appropriate action. Based on this understanding, in this paper we propose a Web service-based system that offers a brokering service to facilitate the business processes integration in supply chains. Our brokering service is part of a complex system named BPIMS-WS [5,6] (BPIMS-WS stands for Business Processes Integration and Monitoring System based on Web Services) which provides a virtual marketplace where people, agents and trading partners can collaborate by using current Web services technology in a flexible and automated manner.

2 BPIMS-WS Architecture

The BPIMS-WS architecture has a layered design. Furthermore, BPIMS-WS presents a component-based and a hybrid architecture borrowing features from SOA and EDA. In a SOA context, BPIMS-WS acts as a Business Process Management (BPM) platform based on the SOA paradigm facilitating the creation and execution of highly transparent and modular process-oriented applications and enterprise workflows. In this sense, BPIMS-WS provides a set of Web services that comprise publication, search and invocation operations which are explained below:

- **Publication** comprises Web services which carry out operations intended to store information in a service registry about: (i) potential businesses partners, (ii) products, and (iii) services.
- **Search and Meta-Information** comprise Web services that provide operations deemed to search the access points where the product technical information can be found. The Meta-Information operations are intended to retrieve both services information and BPIMS-WS meta-information.
- **Invocation** comprises Web services that invoke the business processes related for the procurement of a product.

In an EDA context, BPIMS-WS provides a software infrastructure designed to support a more real-time method of integrating event-driven application processes which occur throughout existing applications and are largely defined by their meaning to the business and their granularity. Regardless of the event's granularity, BPIMS-WS focuses on ensuring that interested parties, usually other applications, are notified immediately when an event happens. In this context, BPIMS-WS provides a set of Web services which carry out subscription and notification services. These kinds of services are explained below:

- **Subscription** comprises a service where multiple interested parties can publish their events to automatically and immediately incorporate information into business processes and decisions.
- **Notification** introduces asynchronous communications in which information is sent without the expectation of an immediate response or the requirement to maintain a live connection between the two systems while waiting for a response.

These operations are performed by our brokering service proposed. Its general architecture is shown in Fig. 1. Each component has a defined function explained as follows:

SOAP Message Analyzer determines the structure and content of the documents exchanged in business processes involved in SCM collaborations. Since BPIMS-WS is based on Web services as information technology, this component determines the information involved of the incoming SOAP messages by means of XML parsers and tools. A DOM API is used to generate the tree structure of the SOAP messages, whereas SAX is used to determine the application logic for every node in the SOAP messages. A set of Java classes based on JAX-P were developed to build the XML parser.

Service Registry is the mechanism for registering and publishing information about business processes, products and services among supply chain partners and to update and adapt to SCM scenarios. In this sense, we used a UDDI node for describing services, discovering businesses, and integrating business services. In our UDDI node, commercial enterprises, services and products both are classified and registered. For the classification of business processes, products and services in the registry, we used broadly accepted ontologies like NAICS, UNSPSC and RosettaNet. NAICS is a standard classification system for North American Industry; UNSPSC provides an open, global multi-sector standard for efficient, accurate classification of products and services and; RosettaNet defines the technical and business dictionaries.

Subscription Registry is the mechanism for registering interactions in which systems publish information about an event to the network so that other systems, which have subscribed and authorized to receive such messages, can receive that information and act on it accordingly. According to the cause at the time that an event occurs, knowledge often referred to as event causality, in this work we have considered both vertical and horizontal causality which means that the event's source and cause reside both on different and on the same conceptual layers in an architectural stack, respectively.

Discovery Service is a component used to discover business processes implementations. This component discovers Web services like authentication, payments, and shipping at run time from a SCM scenario. These Web services can be obtained from suitable service providers and can be combined into innovative and attractive product offerings to customers. When there is more than one service provider of the same function, it can be used to choose one service based on the client's requirements. Inside the discovery service, there is a query formulator which builds queries based on the domain ontology that will be sent to the registry service. This module retrieves a set of suitable services selected from the previous step and creates feasible/compatible sets of services ready for binding. The discovery service uses sophisticated techniques to dynamically discover web services and to formulate queries to UDDI nodes.

Dynamic Binding Service is a component that binds compatible business processes described as Web services. In this sense, the module acts as an API wrapper that maps the interface source or target business process to a common interface supported by BPIMS-WS.

Dynamic Invoker transforms data from one format to another. This component can be seen as a data transfer object which contains the data flowing between the requester to the provider applications of Web services. We used Web Services Invocation Framework (WSIF) that is a simple Java API for invoking Web services, no matter how or where the services are provided.

WSDL Document Analyzer validates WSDL documents that describe business processes by their interfaces which are provided and used by supply chain partners. WSDL documents employ XML Schema for the specification of information items either product technical information or business processes operations. In this context, this component reports the business processes operations, input and output parameters, and their data types in a XML DOM tree. We used WSDL4J to convert the XML DOM nodes in Java objects.

WS-RM-based Messaging Service is the communication mechanism for the collaboration among the parties involved along the whole chain. BPIMS-WS uses the Web Services Reliable Messaging (WS-RM) which is a protocol that provides a standard, interoperable way to guarantee message delivery to applications or Web services. In this sense, BPIMS-WS provides a guaranteed delivery and processing that allows in a reliable way, how to deliver messages between distributed applications in the presence of software components, systems, or network failures through WS-RM.

Response Formulator receives the responses from the suppliers about a requested product. This module retrieves useful information from the responses and builds a XML document with information coming from the service registry and the invocations' responses. This XML document is presented in HTML format using the Extensible Stylesheet Language (XSL).

Workflow Engine coordinates Web services by using a BPEL4WS-based business process language. It consists of building at design time a fully instantiated workflow description where business partners are dynamically defined at execution time. In supply chain management, workflows can not be determined since business partners are not known before hand and because they are continuously changing their client-provider roles through collaboration. For this reason, we have designed and implemented a repository of generic BPEL4WS workflow definitions which describe increasingly complex forms of recurring situations abstracted from the various stages from SCM. This repository contains workflow patterns of interactions involved in e-procurement scenarios. These workflows patterns describe the types of interactions behind each business process, and the types of messages that are exchanged in each interaction. The design of this repository is presented in [7].

The BPIMS-WS hybrid architecture has a layered design following four principles: (1) Integration, (2) Composition, (3) Monitoring and (4) Management which are described next.

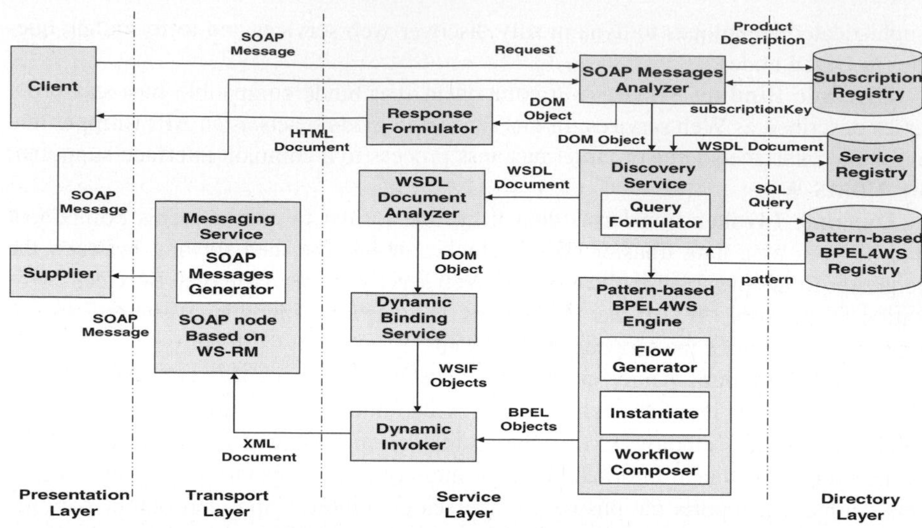

Fig. 1. General architecture of the Web services-based brokering service

3 Web Services Discovery, Composition, Monitoring and Management in BPIMS-WS

BPIMS-WS provides basic services for publishing and querying Web services. These services represent the basic operations in BPIMS-WS. The structure and behavior of the Web services discovery in BPIMS-WS can be understood with the following example. Assume that a client has a production line which can not be stopped. At certain moment, she detects her stock levels have diminished and therefore she needs to find what providers are available related to her product. By doing this, the client must select the type of the product she wants from a range of options offered through an Internet portal [5]. Then, BPIMS-WS obtains the request and formulates a query to the service registry. The result to the query is a list of all the suppliers that includes the requested product in their stocks. Next BPIMS-WS extracts the required information and builds a XML document. This document XML is presented in HTML using a stylesheet. The answer contains information concerning to the provider and product. By means of basic Web services, a client can know what registered enterprises in the service registry can offer a certain product.

Orchestration is currently presented as a way to coordinate Web services in order to define business processes. In BPIMS-WS, a composite Web service is obtained by the orchestration of several simple Web services. Composite Web services can be created in both design and execution time. In BPIMS-WS, for the execution of a composite Web service is firstly necessary to locate a suitable template from the BPEL4WS repository that describes the intended commercial activities. In this schema, the templates are completely determined since commercial partners are known before hand.

The need to conduct business in real-time is among the most daunting yet strategic challenges facing today's enterprise. BPIMS-WS offers capabilities for business activities monitoring. For the monitoring process, it is necessary to listen to the request/response SOAP messaging of Web service-based business collaboration. The SOAP messaging identifies the participants and their communications during the long-running interactions of the participants in the collaboration. For this end, BPIMS-WS intercepts all SOAP messages to generate a UML sequence diagram from the information about the participants and the order in which the messages are exchanged. For the monitoring of activities, a set of Java classes has been developed to represent a UML diagram in a SVG (Scalable Vector Graphics) representation that can be visualized in an SVG enabled Internet browser. The exchange of SOAP messages during some kinds of business collaboration may be developed very quickly. Therefore, to avoid reducing the performance of the Web services execution, the dynamic generation of UML diagrams uses a buffered mechanism to deal with a fast pacing production of SOAP messages.

As Web services become pervasive and critical to business operations, the task of managing Web services and implementations of our brokering service architecture is imperative to the success of business operations involved in SCM. In this sense, we developed a basic web services manager with capabilities for discovering the availability, performance, and usage, as well as the control and configuration of Web services provided by BPIMS-WS. The underlying technology used to the implementation is JMX (Java Management eXtension). The JMX architecture consists of three levels: instrumentation, agent, and distributed services. JMX provides interfaces and services adequate to monitoring and managing systems requirements. The main component for web services management is a JMX Bridge, which acts as a bridge between the world of resources managed by JMX and Web services. In BPIMS-WS, Web services interfaces to JMX are available. Rather than provide a JMX specific Web service interface, BPIMS-WS provides a Web service interface to a manageable resource. Under our approach, the resources can be implemented on different technologies because only it is necessary to define a Web service interface for a resource.

4 Related Works and Discussion

Chung-Nin [8] developed a system named eXFlow for business processes integration on EAI and B2B e-commerce. However, eXFlow provides only support for Web services discovery, invocation, orchestration and monitoring. Web services management is not considered and since eXFlow is based on an SOA architecture, asynchronous messaging is not provided. Lakhal [9] proposes another system named THROWS, an architecture for highly available distributed execution of Web services compositions. In THROWS architecture, the execution control is hierarchically delegated among dynamically discovered engines. However, THROWS is in the design phase so that is being developed. Arpinar [10] provides an architecture for semi-automatic Web services composition combining both centralized model and peer-to-peer approaches. This proposal has only support for Web services discovery, invocation, orchestration and monitoring. Web services management is not considered and the architecture is being developed. Turner [11] developed a system which acts as an

Integration Broker for Heterogeneous Information Sources (IBHIS). IBHIS is already implemented but process activity monitoring is not included. Radetzki [12] proposes a system named IRIS (Interoperability and Reusability of Internet Services) for Web services composition through a set of graphic interfaces. In IRIS, Web services discovery and orchestration are provided by an ontology-based registry approach. However, IRIS is addressed to the simulation of Web services composition therefore Web services execution is not included. Howard [13] proposes a framework named KDSWS (Knowledge-based Dynamic Semantic Web Services) which addresses in an integrated end-to-end manner, the life-cycle of activities involved in brokering and managing of Semantic Web Services. However, agent monitoring is not considered and the architecture is subjected to ongoing work. Srinivasan [14] provides an architecture for Web services discovery under a goal-oriented approach. Web services discovery is carried out by means of services chains satisfying certain constraints. This architecture provides only support for Web services management and monitoring and is in design phase. Yu [15] proposes a framework for Dynamic Web Service Invocation. This framework is based on an SOA architecture. Publication/subscription and notification mechanisms are used in Web services discovery in UDDI nodes. However, an experimental prototype is provided which does not consider Web services orchestration, monitoring and management. Finally, Aggarwal [16] developed a system named METEOR-S (Managing End-To-End OpeRations for Semantic Web services) which is a constraint driven Web Service composition tool. In METEOR-S architecture, web services management is not considered. Nevertheless, METEOR-S has been implemented and working well.

5 Conclusions

In this paper, we have described BPIMS-WS, a hybrid architecture we have developed so far that provides a comprehensive framework for developing business integration, collaboration and monitoring in SCM scenarios. Among the applications we envisioned for BPIMS-WS, the orchestration of long-term supply chains involving operation research methods to minimize costs, reduce delivery times and maximize quality of service along with artificial intelligence methods to provide semantic matching and to define business partners profile management is now under consideration.

References

1. Mike P. Papazoglou. Service-Oriented Computing: Concepts, Characteristics and Directions. In Proc. of the Fourth International Conference on Web Information Systems Engineering (WISE'03).
2. Steve Vinoski. Integration with Web Services. IEEE Internet Computing. November-December 2003 pp 75-77.
3. Adams, H., Dan Gisolfi, James Snell, Raghu Varadan. "Custom Extended Enterprise Exposed Business Services Application Pattern Scenario," http://www-106.ibm.com/developerworks /webservices/library/ws-best5/, Jan. 1, 2003
4. Samtani, G. and D. Sadhwani, "Enterprise Application Integration and Web Services," in Web Services Business Strategies and Architectures, P. Fletcher and M. Waterhouse, Eds. Birmingham, UK: Expert Press, LTD, pp. 39-54, 2002a.

5. Giner Alor Hernández, César Sandoval Hernández, José Oscar Olmedo Aguirre. "BPIMS-WS: Brokering Architecture for Business Processes Integration for B2B E-commerce". In Proc. of the International Conference on Electronics, Communications, and Computers. (CONIELECOMP 2005). IEEE Press. pp 160-165
6. Juan Miguel Gómez, Giner Alor Hernandez, José Oscar Olmedo, Christoph Bussler. "A B2B conversational Architecture for Semantic Web Services based on BPIM-WS". In Proc. of the 10th IEEE International Conference on Engineering of Complex Computer Systems. (IEEE ICECCS 2005). IEEE Press. pp 252-259.
7. César Sandoval Hernández, Giner Alor Hernández, José Oscar Olmedo Aguirre. "Dinamic Generation of Organizational BPEL4WS workflows". In Proc. of I International Conference on Electrical and Electronics Engineering and X Conference on Electrical Engineering (ICEEE-CIE 2004). IEEE Press. ISBN: 0-7803-8532-2.
8. Nathan Chung-Nin Chung,Wen-Shih Huang,Tse-Ming Tsai and Seng-cho T.Chou. eX-Flow:A Web Services-Compliant System to Support B2B Process Integration. In Proc. of the 37th Hawaii International Conference on System Sciences 2004.
9. Neila Ben Lakhal, Takashi Kobayashi and Haruo Yokota. THROWS: An Architecture for Highly Available Distributed Execution of Web Services Compositions. In Proc. of the 14th International Workshop on Research Issues on Data Engineering: Web Services for E-Commerce and E-Government Applications (RIDE'04).
10. I.Budak Arpinar, Boanerges Aleman-Meza, Ruoyan Zhang and Angela Maduko. Ontology-Driven Web Services Composition Platform. In Proc. of the IEEE International Conference on E-Commerce Technology.
11. Mark Turner, Fujun Zhu, Ioannis Kotsiopoulos, Michelle Russell, David Budgen, Keith Bennett, Pearl Brereton, John Keane, Paul Layzell and Michael Rigby. Using Web Service Technologies to create an Information Broker: An Experience Report. In Proc. of the 26th International Conference on Software Engineering (ICSE'04).
12. Uwe Radetzki and Armin B.Cremers. IRIS: A Framework for Mediator-Based Composition of Service-Oriented Software. In Proc. of the IEEE International Conference on Web Services (ICWS'04).
13. Randy Howard and Larry Kerschberg. A Knowledge-based Framework for Dynamic Semantic Web Services Brokering and Management. In Proc. of the 15th International Workshop on Database and Expert Systems Applications (DEXA'04).
14. Ananth Srinivasan and David Sundaram. Web Services for Enterprise Collaboration: A Framework and a Prototype. In Proc. of the 30th EUROMICRO Conference (EUROMICRO'04).
15. JianJun Yu and Gang Zhou. Dynamic Web Service Invocation Based on UDDI. In Proc. of the IEEE International Conference on E-Commerce Technology for Dynamic E-Business (CEC-East'04).
16. Rohit Aggarwal, Kunal Verma, John Miller and William Milnor. Constraint Driven Web Service Composition in METEOR-S. In Proc. of the 2004 IEEE International Conference on Services Computing (SCC'04).

A Thin Client Approach to Supporting Adaptive Session Mobility

Dan MacCormac, Mark Deegan, Fred Mtenzi, and Brendan O'Shea

School of Computing, Dublin Institute of Technology,
Kevin St, Dublin 8, Ireland
{dan.maccormac, mark.deegan, fred.mtenzi, brendan.oshea}@comp.dit.ie

Abstract. Recent growth in computing devices from the smartphone to the desktop computer has led to users interacting with multiple computing devices throughout the course of the day. Modern computing sessions are a graphically rich, multi-tasking experience, representing a considerable amount of state. There is seldom the ability to automatically move a session from one device to another; instead users must manually restore applications to their previous state. Without session mobility, the problems of unsynchronised information and communication barriers become apparent. We present a thin client approach to supporting session mobility across a broad range of devices. We use an adaptive approach, thereby supporting a fine granularity of devices. Furthermore, our approach enables rich diverse sessions composed of applications specific to a range of platforms, reducing constraints imposed by mobile devices, and boosting productivity by allowing access to a wider range of applications from a single device.

1 Introduction

Growth in the use of both mobile and stationary computing devices, in addition to increased bandwidth being offered by 3G providers, has led to users interacting with a wider range of devices in day to day life. The task of manually re-instating a computing session when moving from one device to another can be frustrating, time consuming, and sometimes impossible depending on the correlation between the current and previous device. This task is common, for example in academic, medical and corporate environments, where people may work at several terminals at different times throughout the day. Consequently there is a growing demand among users for continuity in interaction when moving between devices. Providing a method of moving a session from one device to another which is called *session mobility*, helps to significantly increase productivity while eliminating the cumbersome task of attempting to manually restore session state.

Consider Alice who benefits from session mobility. In the morning, Alice reads her e-mail on her PDA while travelling to work on the train. When she arrives at the office, her session is transferred to her desktop computer without interrupting the message she is currently composing. Before lunch, Bob in Alaska

C. Cérin and K.-C. Li (Eds.): GPC 2007, LNCS 4459, pp. 694–701, 2007.

initiates an instant messaging session with Alice. Rather than being confined to her desktop computer, she decides to continue the conversation on her smartphone as she leaves for lunch. Later that afternoon, Alice is scheduled to give a brief presentation to her colleagues. As she enters the conference room, her session is seamlessly transferred to a public terminal, allowing effortless delivery of her presentation. On her way home she books tickets for a concert on the same instance of the web browser she opened that morning. Achieving the level of mobility outlined in Alice's scenario becomes possible when we consider merging appropriate technologies, and adding additional elements such as a knowledge management component to take advantage of user and domain information. Deployment of such a system in a Pervasive computing framework can facilitate inter-device communication and enable seamless hand-off of sessions from one device to another.

The remainder of this paper is structured as follows. In section 2 we discuss related work in the area of session mobility. From the problems outlined above, we have identified several key requirements of our system, which we outline in Section 3 as well as presenting the corresponding architecture of the system. In Section 4 we outline the implementation of the system, and in Section 5 we evaluate and discuss the performance and relevance of our approach. Finally, in Section 6 we present our concluding remarks and discuss potential future work.

2 Related Work in the Area

The work outlined in this paper focuses on enabling mobility of legacy applications across heterogeneous devices. We aim to provide *seamless* integration of the interface of the mobility enabled application into the users current environment, allowing both mobile and stationary applications to work side by side. Moreover, our approach takes into consideration the diverse range and capabilities of various target platforms, providing adaptive methods of session mobility. This reduces footprint when moving sessions to mobile devices with constrained capabilities. We use a thin client approach to providing session mobility. Existing thin client solutions which display an entire desktop environment confine users to particular Operating Systems. This prevents users from merging the power of applications which are specific to a variety of platforms.

The problem of providing web interface mobility has been discussed in [1]. The system supports applications built using a multi-modal approach, and is capable of choosing the most appropriate mode for the current device. However, to take full advantage of the capabilities of the system, applications must be built using a specialised toolkit. Similarly, in [2], the authors present a "multi-browsing" system which allows the movement of web interfaces across multiple displays. This work supports the movement of existing web applications, broadening its usage scope. Both of the above approaches focus specifically on mobility of web applications. As the interaction with mobile devices becomes more complex in response to their growing capabilities, the need to support mobility of a wider range of applications becomes apparent. ROAM, a system to support the movement of Java based applications between heterogeneous devices is presented in [3]. This work also requires developers to build applications using a specific approach thereby limiting the applicability of this work. In [4], the authors present TAPAS (Telecommunication Architecture for Plug And Play Systems), an approach to supporting user and session mobility. This approach allows for a broad range of applications and allows access to personalised applications within foreign domains. However, as with the previous examples, this work requires applications to be built using a specialised toolkit. Guyot et al. [5] investigate smart card performance as a token for session mobility between Windows and Linux. This work supports mobility of a wide range of applications, and is also capable of remotely fetching and installing necessary applications which were available on the previous terminal but not on the present terminal. The approach taken in this work involves the restoration of a session based on a session state file. Our approach involves the dynamic movement of an application from one device to another. Furthermore, this work does not address the use of mobile devices, which is central to our work.

3 Design Goals and System Architecture

In this section we outline the design goals of our approach and present the system architecture. A brief discussion on the relationship between the design goals and the resulting system architecture follows.

3.1 Design Goals

When designing our approach to session mobility we established the following objectives.

- Enable the mobility of legacy applications
- Avoid modification to existing applications and Operating Systems
- Support heterogeneous client platforms
- Support seamless integration of mobility enabled applications where possible
- Enable sharing of workspaces with multiple users for presentations and collaborative work
- Support efficient management of network resources

3.2 System Architecture

We present the system using a multi-layered architecture, as illustrated in Fig. 1. At the lowest level – the Protocol layer – sits the chosen protocols which are X11 as used by the X Window System and RFB which is used by VNC. VNC is suitable for displaying sessions on mobile devices with limited resources, while the X Window system is better suited to traditional computers such as laptops and desktops. On top of the Protocol layer, we have added an Extension layer to support the mobility of legacy applications, as well as the multiplexing of applications for collaborative work. The VNC system inherently supports mobility of application interfaces. Supporting application mobility at the X Window level is possible through the use of an X11 pseudo-server [6] which enables dynamic movement of X11 clients. On top of the Protocol and Extension layers, is the Management layer. The Management layer is the nucleus of our approach, controlling the lower layers and enabling efficient management of resources. It is composed of two core modules – the Service and Database modules. The Service module facilitates communication between the higher and lower layers of the system. The Database modules complement the Service modules by storing and managing network resource information such as network status, available terminals and device information. Finally, at the highest level is the Application layer. This layer provides an interface to the lower layers of the system, enabling people and devices to interact with the system using a uniform interface. Application layer I/O is achieved using TCP clients and a central server. Protocol messages are encapsulated in an XML based communication language which was created specifically for this system and other pervasive computing applications which are under active development such as Location Based Services.

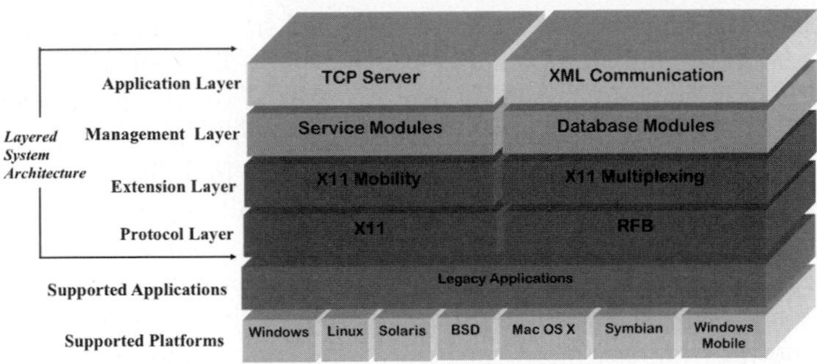

Fig. 1. Layered system architecture showing supported platforms and applications

Extending existing thin client technologies has allowed us to meet our objective of enabling the mobility of legacy applications in a seamless manner. By using more than one thin client protocol, we enable adaptive session mobility and hence support of heterogeneous devices. By combining Database and Service modules we have added a knowledge management component to our approach, enabling efficient management of network resources.

4 Implementing an Adaptive Approach to Session Mobility

The session mobility server was implemented in a Linux environment. Additionally, we created light-weight client applications for several test systems such as Windows, Linux and BSD. Using these client side applications, requests can be sent to the application server to move a session from one device to another, specifying either an IP address or *Zone* name as a destination. Zones represents groups of computing devices which are managed by the Database modules. If a zone name is specified, the system will choose an appropriate vacant device in the given zone. This is useful in environments composed of a large number of public workstations such as University laboratories where users simply want to use the closest vacant device.

The Application Layer was implemented using a C based TCP server and and a custom built request parser driven by Expat, an open source XML parser. At the Management layer, both the Service and Database modules were implemented using shell scripting, as well as employing a variety of open source Linux tools. In the first prototype of the system the databases are structured using XML based entries, allowing for an extremely light-weight database architecture. The Extension layer, which enables session mobility and multiplexing is driven by three open-source tools; xmove [6], VNC [7], and xtv [8]. X11 mobility is supported by xmove, a pseudo-server for X11 client movement. The pseudo-server is an intermediary, which is positioned between the client and server, allowing interception of X protocol messages. This intercepted information can then be used as a basis for window movement. It acts in a similar manner to a standard X server, and as a result legacy applications do not distinguish between a real or pseudo server. Therefore any application started on the pseudo-server will be capable of having its output redirected to another X server; real or pseudo. As we mentioned, VNC inherently provides session mobility. Moving sessions to light-weight device can be achieved by attaching all applications to a virtual VNC desktop on the server which is then accessible from any terminal device using appropriate client software. Multiplexing is achieved via xtv which allows remote users to view the contents of an X session within a client window. xtv clients cannot provide any input, instead a view-only session is provided. VNC can be used to provide a collaborative shared workspaces. All tools run at the application level, requiring no change to the underlying windowing system, which was one of our initial design objectives.

5 Evaluating the Performance of Our Approach

To evaluate the performance of the system, we set up a small testbed consisting of a Linux server running our session mobility software and several client machines representing user workstations. We performed a series of tests to establish the time taken to move a session for one device to another using our approach. Our test sessions consisted of five common applications, including a text editor, web browser, and a terminal window, each running on machines with equivalent specifications. Tests demonstrated that the average time taken to move a session from one device to another using the X11 pseudo-server approach was just over 4 seconds. In the case of mobile devices, we must also leverage the capabilities of VNC which increases session mobility cost. Test results showed that VNC takes an average of 3 seconds to display a session, increasing mobility cost by

75% in the case of our test session. However, we can eliminate this overhead by executing both tasks concurrently, hence mobility cost can be attributed to the last task to complete – most likely X11 movement. We present our results in comparison to other common approaches to session mobility, as shown in Fig. 2.

The first method, which we have observed students in Computer Science courses to use, involves storing a virtual machine on a portable flash drive, and carrying it from one machine to the next. The time taken to suspend and resume this virtual machine is significant and depends largely on the level of state change within the virtual machine. Furthermore, allocating larger memory to the virtual machine and running more applications simultaneously increases suspend/resume time experienced. The second approach to providing session mobility which we have compared our implementation to is that of Microsoft's Terminal Services. Suspending a Terminal Services session merely involves closing the client window and thus there is virtually no time associated with suspending the session. Restoring a Terminal Services session takes approx 2 - 3 seconds, which is very close to the time taken by our system. Moreover, the resume time indicated by our approach is identical to the time required for direct movement of a session from one client to another, since a resume operation is achieved in the same manner as moving a session. As a result, the difference between time taken by Terminal Services and our implementation is marginal: just over 1 second; at least in case of relatively light sessions.

We also considered the overhead added by interposing a pseudo-server between X client and server. In [6], tcpdump (a tool which captures network packets and assigns a time-stamp) is used to establish the latency added by xmove as opposed to using a standard X server. Test results showed that xmove is virtually unnoticeable when communication between client and server is asynchronous; for

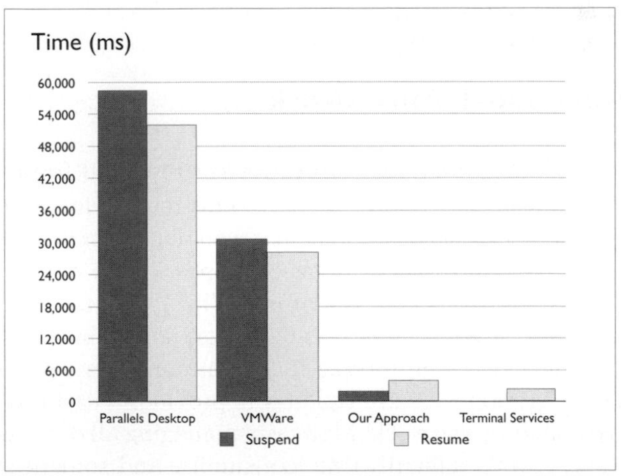

Fig. 2. Comparison of test results

example in the case of a colour page redraw, a delay time of 4% is added. In a scenario where communication is synchronous, meaning the client must wait for acknowledgement from the server between each message, the overhead becomes noticeable. The tests showed that for communication which involved a series of synchronous messages sent between client and server, xmove added an overhead of approx. 2 ms, bringing the roundtrip time from 3 ms to over 5 ms. This is significant, since it accumulates overtime. However, clients do not regularly communicate in this fashion; when they do it is often during start-up procedures or at other times when the user is expecting a delay, rather than time critical periods.

Finally, we evaluated the overhead added by the Management and Application layers of the system. Test results showed that these layers add an average overhead of 1.8 ms which we feel is negligible. We also observed that the mobility cost grows in parallel with the number of active applications in a users session. This is due to the processing performed by the pseudo-server at the Extension layer, whereas the adjacent layers exhibit similar time patterns despite the number of applications within the session. In addition to this, all applications do not move immediately, but rather sequentially. The results are based on the time elapsed between the initial request and the time at which the final application moves, meaning other applications may move substantially faster.

Aside from the competitive session movement times demonstrated, our implementation offers the advantage of a rich heterogeneous environment in comparison to the alternative methods outlined. While users can run individual systems in parallel using VMWare's tabbed environment, these parallel environments lack consolidation and the task of switching between tabs quickly becomes cumbersome. The approach of running several entire operating systems uses considerable system resources, and furthermore resuming a virtual machine on a processor architecture which differs from the previous architecture is known to be problematic.

6 Conclusion and Future Work

There is seldom the ability for users to move their session from one device to another. Existing implementations of such systems tend to focus on one Operating System. By merging existing thin client technologies and adding Extension, Management and Application layers, it becomes possible to move sessions across a broad range of devices in a seamless manner. This alleviates the need for users to manually re-instate sessions, which can take several minutes; the aggregate cost of which is significant when interacting with numerous devices. The ability to share this mobile session with multiple users provides a useful tool for presentations as well as collaborative work. Manually managing all of these technologies to provide such services is difficult, time consuming and sometimes impossible. In the past, such barriers have been a deterrent to the use of these technologies.

There are several areas of this work which have yet to be explored in further detail. The need for load balancing between multiple servers is a fundamental issue; master and slave servers supporting non-residual process migration is one possible approach. There are also several security enhancements which could be added to our work, for example mandatory use of SSH tunnelling for all sessions. Other challenges include preventing dropped sessions due to broken network connections and adding support for local resource redirection such as printers and USB devices. In addition to addressing limitations of the current system, the next phase of research involves the exploration of the use of sensory identification tokens such as Bluetooth and RFID tagged objects as a trigger for the movement of sessions. Sensory tokens could also be used to store session state information, adding a further level of flexibility to system. As we enhance our work to date, in addition to evaluating other Ubiquitous computing concepts, the unification of these individual approaches into a single diverse infrastructure will help to validate our vision of an intelligent pervasive computing environment.

Acknowledgements. Dan MacCormac gratefully acknowledges the contribution of the Irish Research Council for Science, Engineering and Technology: funded by the National Development Plan. The authors also wish to thank to Dr. Kudakwashe Dube for his discussion of this work.

References

1. Bandelloni, R., Paterno, F.: Flexible interface migration. In: IUI '04: Proceedings of the 9th international conference on Intelligent user interfaces, New York, NY, USA, ACM Press (2004) 148–155
2. Johanson, B.: Multibrowsing: Moving web content across multiple displays. In: UBICOMP 2001. LNCS 2201, Springer Verlag (2001) 346–353
3. Chu, H., Song, H., Wong, C., Kurakake, S., Katagiri, M.: Roam, a seamless application framework. Systems and Software **69** (2004) 209–226
4. Shiaa, M.M., Liljeback, L.E.: User and session mobility in a plug-and-play network architecture. IFIP WG6.7 Workshop and EUNICE Summer School, Trondheim, Norway, (2002)
5. Guyot, V., Boukhatem, N., Pujolle, G.: Smart card performances to handle session mobility. Internet, 2005.The First IEEE and IFIP International Conference in Central Asia on **1** (2005) 5
6. Solomita, E., Kempf, J., Duchamp, D.: XMOVE: A pseudoserver for X window movement. The X Resource **11** (1994) 143–170
7. Richardson, T., Stafford-Fraser, Q., Wood, K., Hopper, A.: Virtual network computing. Internet Computing, IEEE **2** (1998) 33 – 38
8. Adbel-Wahab, H.M., Feit., M.A.: Xtv: A framework for sharing x window clients in remote synchronous collaboration. In: In Proceedings, IEEE Tricomm '91: Communications for Distributed Applications and Systems. (1991)

Automatic Execution of Tasks in MiPeG

Antonio Coronato, Giuseppe De Pietro, and Luigi Gallo

ICAR-CNR, Via Castellino 111, 80131 Napoli, Italy
{coronato.a, depietro.g, gallo.l}@na.icar.cnr.it

Abstract. *Grid computing* and *pervasive computing* have rapidly emerged and affirmed respectively as the paradigm for high performance computing and the paradigm for user-friendly computing. The conjunction of such paradigms are now generating a new one, the *Pervasive Grid Computing*, which aims at extending classic grids with characteristics of pervasive computing like spontaneous and transparent integration of mobile devices, context-awareness, proactivity, and so on. In this paper, we present mechanisms and a software infrastructure for executing tasks in a pervasive grid. In particular, the proposed solution, which provides an implementation of the *Utility Computing* model, enables users to submit tasks and to pick up results without concerning on requiring and handling hardware resources.

1 Introduction

During the last decade, new computing models have emerged and rapidly affirmed. In particular, terms like *Grid Computing*, *Pervasive Computing*, and *Utility Computing* have become of common use not only in the scientific and academic world, but also in business fields.

The *Grid computing* model has demonstrated to be an effective way to deal with very complex problems. The term "The Grid" is now adopted to denote the virtualization of distributed computing and data resources such as processing, network bandwidth and storage capacity to create a single system image, granting users and applications seamless access to vast IT capabilities [1]. As a result, Grids are geographically distributed environments, equipped with shared heterogeneous services and resources accessible by users and applications to solve complex computational problems and to access to big storage spaces.

The goal for *Pervasive computing* is the development of environments where highly heterogeneous hardware and software components can seamlessly and spontaneously interoperate, in order to provide a variety of services to users independently of the specific characteristics of the environment and of the client devices [2]. Therefore, mobile devices should come into the environment in a natural way, as their owner moves, and transparently. The owner will not have to carry out manual configuration operations for being able to approach the services and the resources, and the environment has to be able to self-adapt and self-configure in order to host incoming mobile devices.

On the other hand, *Utility Computing* aims at providing users with computational power in a transparent manner, similarly to the way in which electrical utilities supply power to their customers. In this scenario, computing services are seen as "utilities"

C. Cérin and K.-C. Li (Eds.): GPC 2007, LNCS 4459, pp. 702–709, 2007.

that users pay to access to, just as is in the case of electricity, gas, telecommunications and water [3].

Current grid applications, although they offer services and resources to their users, are neither pervasive nor able to implement the *Utility Computing* vision. As a matter of fact, whenever a user wants to execute an own application, has to i) ask the grid for resources; ii) allocate tasks; iii) launch and control executions; iv) get results; and v) release resources. This practice has several limitations:

1. User-environment interactions are very little transparent;
2. Users have direct control of allocated resources – The user requires (and sometimes locks) resources of the grid;
3. Resources are handled in an insecure and inefficient way – A malicious user could require a larger amount of resources with respect the ones really needed or an inexperienced user could underestimate the resources really needed.

This work presents a software infrastructure that extends classic grids by enabling users to directly submit tasks for executions. After having been submitted, tasks are completely handled by the environment. In particular, they are encapsulated in mobile agents, which are allocated and executed by the environment. It is worth noting that such mobile agents can also be allocated and executed on mobile devices, which become active resources for the grid, in a completely transparent way. In addition a certain degree of dependability has been conferred to the service in handling mobile tasks.

The rest of the paper is organized as follows. Section 2 discusses some motivations, related work and contribution. Section 3 describes the proposed solution. Finally, section 4 concludes the paper.

2 Motivations and Contributions

2.1 Motivations

Mobile and wireless devices have not been considered, for a long time, as useful resources by traditional Grid environments. As a matter of fact, only recently they have been adopted as interface tools for accessing Grid services and resources. However, Considering the Metcalfe's law, which claims that usefulness of a network-based system proportionally grows with the square of the number of active nodes, and also considering that mobile devices capabilities have substantially be improved over the time, it can justifiably be stated that mobile and wireless devices are now of interest for the Grid community, not only as access devices, but also as active resources [4].

However, integration of mobile devices is not costless [7]. This is mainly due to the consideration that current Grid middleware infrastructures don't support mobile devices for three main reasons: 1) they are still too heavy with respect to mobile and wearable equipments; 2) they are not network-centric; i.e. they assume fixed TCP/IP connections and do not deal with wireless networks and other mobile technologies; and, 3) they typically support only one interaction paradigm, that is SOAP messaging, whereas the Pervasive model requires a variety of mechanisms [10].

Over the last years, some valuable efforts have been made in order to make Grid infrastructures able to support wireless technologies and mobile devices. In particular, the paradigm of Wireless Grid has been proposed [5-8]. More recently, this paradigm has evolved in the Pervasive Grid model [9-10], which again aims at making Grid environments able to integrate mobile devices, but in a pervasive way, that is seamlessly and transparently. In addition, services should be context-aware and somehow pro-active.

This effort has officially been formalized in 2003 when a Global Grid Forum Research Group, called Ubicomp-RG, was established in order to explore the possibilities of synergy between Pervasive and Grid communities.

Other related work is reported in the following.

In [5] mobile devices are considered as active resources for the Grid. In particular, authors developed a software infrastructure for deploying Grid services on mobile nodes. This solution relies on a lightweight version of the .NET framework, namely the .NET Compact Framework, which enables to deploy on mobile devices simple Grid Services that require limited amount of resources. It is important to note that such a solution applies only to mobile devices equipped with the Microsoft Pocket PC operating system and requires several manual operations for installation and configuration.

In [10] authors propose a framework for self-optimizing the execution of tasks in GAIA [11]. In that scenario, a task is meant as a sequence of high-level actions (say for an example, "print N copies of this document and then show it as a presentation"). The user indicates the sequence of actions and then the environment choose the resources (and services) needed. On the contrary, in our scenario a task is just a software program.

2.2 Our Contribution

Our contribution consists in a model and a software infrastructure that enable grid users to distribute and execute tasks on a changing group of mobile and fixed devices.

Such a software infrastructure relies on MiPeG, a *Mi*ddleware for *Pe*rvasive *G*rids that provides several facilities for integrating and handling mobile devices and users in grid applications. MiPeG consists of a set of basic services exposed as Grid Services; i.e., they are compliant with the OGSA specifications [12]. It integrates with the Globus Toolkit [13], which is the de-facto standard platform for Grid applications, in order to extend its functionalities and to provide mechanisms for augmenting classic grid environments with pervasive characteristics. It also partly relies on the JADE framework [14] to implement some mobile agent based components.

The proposed environment distinguishes from classic and wireless grids for the following main characteristics:

a. **Transparent integration of mobile devices as active resources** – This feature requires the installation of lightweight software plug-in, which consists in an agent container, onboard the mobile device. After that, whenever the mobile device enters the environment, it becomes an active resource for the grid; in other words, the environment can allocate and execute tasks on it, in a completely transparent way for its owner.
b. **Self-execution of applications** – Users submit their own code and some execution parameters. On the contrary, in classic grids users requires resources and

then are fully in charge of launching execution, controlling it, picking up results and releasing resources. Obviously, the possibility of submitting just the code, not only ease the task for users, but also protect the environment from malicious and inexpert users.

c. **Reliable execution of tasks** – Tasks are encapsulated in mobile agents that can be allocated by the environment both on fixed and mobile devices. Thanks to a cloning mechanism, the environment is able to recover from several kinds of failures.

3 Utility Framework

3.1 Service Architecture

The *UtilityService* is an application service able to dynamically distribute and execute user's tasks on a grid of either fixed or mobile resources. Users willing of executing their applications directly submit their code without caring of choosing and allocating resources of the grid.

In current grids, whenever a user wants to execute an own application, has to i) ask the grid for resources; ii) allocate tasks; iii) launch and control executions; iv) get results; and v) release resources.

As already pointed out in the introductory section, this practice has several limitations. To overcome such limitations, the *UtilityService* extends classic grids by enabling users to directly submit tasks for executions. After having been submitted, tasks are completely handled by the environment, which gathers the results and sends them back to the user.

To achieve this objective, user tasks are encapsulated in mobile agents and then allocated in a distributed platform that controls execution.

As shown in figure 1, the *UtilityService* consists of the following components:

- *Container* – This is the run-time software environment that provides the basic functionalities for executing and coordinating mobile agents;
- *Platform* – This is the set of hardware nodes equipped with a *Container* and able to execute tasks;
- *TaskHandler* – This is the hardware element that hosts the coordinating components. It is also the user entry point to the service;
- *Subordinate* – This is an hardware node that hosts mobile agents for execution. It can be either a fixed or a mobile resource;
- *Initiator* – This is the hardware element used by the user to submit source code for execution;
- *TaskAllocation* – This is the *Container* that handles the mobile agents hosting user tasks;
- *TaskRecovery* – This is the *Container* that stores cloned mobile agents. It is required to activate clones in case of failure of the cloned agent;
- *Worker* – This agent encapsulates the user's task for execution and sends execution results to the *Collector*. More *Workers* can be hosted by the same *Subordinate*;

- *DeviceManager* – This agent interacts with the *ContexService* to receive the list and the state of available resources in the grid. In addition to this, it receives heartbeats from every *Subordinate*;
- *Telltale* – This is a software element that monitors some *Subordinate*'s parameters and communicates them to the *DeviceManager*;
- *WorkerManager* – This agent coordinates *Workers* allocation and migration within the environment accordingly with a scheduling algorithm;
- *Collector* – This agent receives the results from every active *Worker* and collects them in the *Results* archive;
- *Results* – This is the archive that stores execution results until they are sent back to the user.

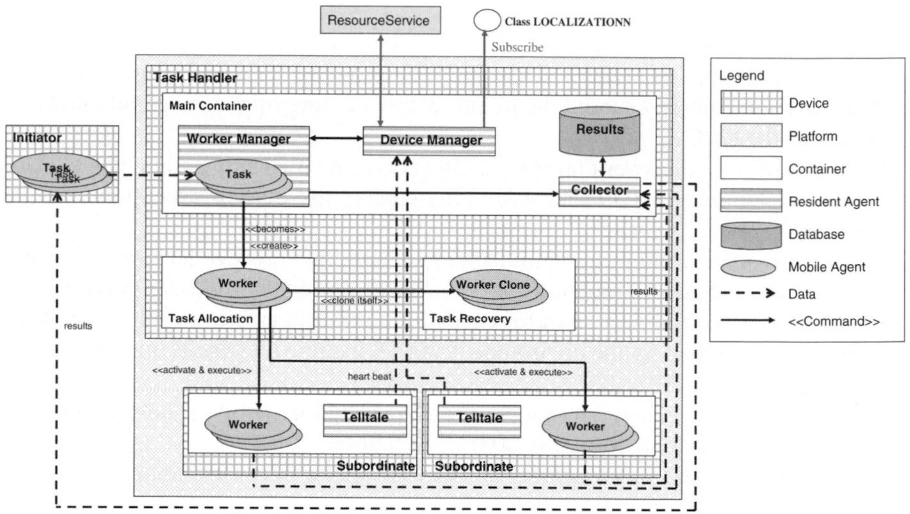

Fig. 1. Interfaces and Architecture of the *UtilityService*

Whenever a user wants execute a task, has to contact the *Initiator* and to submit the code. After that, the *Initiator* embeds such a code in a mobile agent, namely a *Worker*, into the *TaskAllocation* container ready to be executed. Before distribution and execution, the task is forced to clone itself and the clone is inserted in the *TaskRecovery* container. This is performed in order to confer a certain degree of dependability to the service. Next, the task is allocated in one or more *Subordinates*, which will execute them and produce results. Allocation is driven by the *DeviceManager* depending on the current state of active resources of the grid. From now on, two main possibilities are in order. The *Worker* completes its execution by sending results to the *Collector* that, in turn, stores them in the *Results* archive; or, the *Worker* fails. In the latter case, failure is detected by the *DeviceManager* that doesn't receive heartbeats from the *Telltale* anymore. As a consequence, the *DeviceManager* activates the *Worker*'s clone and requires its execution on a new *Subordinate*.

The software framework exhibits some autonomic behaviors. In particular, it self-manage allocation and execution of tasks and self-recover from nodes failures.

3.2 Scheduling Algorithms

We have defined a specific scheduling algorithm, namely DDT (*D*ynamic *D*istribution of *T*asks), which aims at minimizing the time of execution for user tasks. The objective is, in the case of multiple submission of tasks, to distribute such tasks in the platform taking care of resources state in order to achieve better performance.

Since resource conditions rapidly change in time (especially for mobile resources), the *Telltale* periodically executes a benchmark algorithm (identical for all the devices) and sends the benchmark result (B_i, benchmark value for the resource *i*) to the *DeviceManager*. Then, the *DeviceManager* calculates the mobile average of the last five values received for each active resource and orders such devices according to these values (the slower device is the last in the list). Next, it calculates the *relative speed-up* ($RS_{i,i+1}$) for each device, which is the ratio between the benchmark execution times of the device *i* and the next device in the list ($RS_{i,i+1} = B_{i+1} / B_i$).The *relative speed-up* for the slowest device is set to 1.

Relative speed-ups are used by the *DeviceManager* to choose the device on which to send a task. The basic idea is: if a device executes the benchmark in a time that is the half of the time of another device, probably it will execute even the task in the half of the time.

Accordingly to this idea, *Workers* are sent on the devices as the beads in an abacus; that is, *Workers* are allocated on the device with the highest *relative speed-up* till the number of *Workers* allocated (say N) is equal to the *relative speed-up* of the device itself. Next *Worker* is sent to the second device (which is the fastest of the relative list), then another group of N *Workers* is sent to the previous device, in turn, this allocation is repeated until the number of *Workers* on the second device becomes equal to its *relative speed-up*. As the number of *Workers* gets equal to the *relative speed-up*, the next *Worker* to allocate is sent to the third device.

Figure 2 shows an example of allocation of tasks. In particular, we considered the case of eleven *Workers* to allocate in a grid of four devices. Since the *relative speed-up* between devices D1 and D2 is 3.20, the algorithm allocates three *Workers* on the device D1 per every *Worker* allocated on the device D2. Differently, being the *relative speed-up* between devices D2 and D3 equal to 2.19, only after having allocated two *Workers* on the device D2, a new *Worker* will be allocated on the device D3.

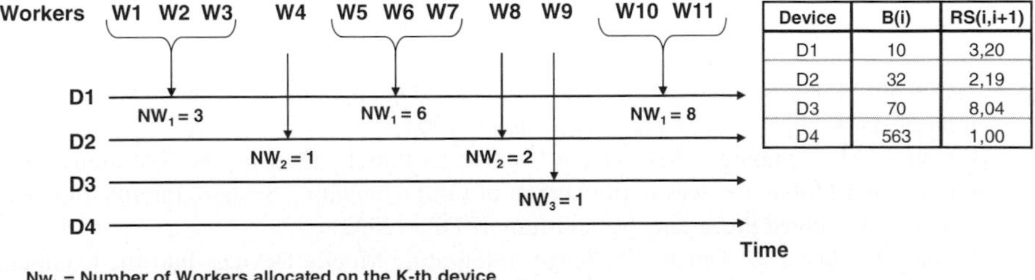

Device	B(i)	RS(i,i+1)
D1	10	3,20
D2	32	2,19
D3	70	8,04
D4	563	1,00

Fig. 2. Example of distribution of tasks

If there are still *Workers* that cannot be allocated in the first turn (that is, after having allocated *Workers* on all devices), they will wait until a new device enters the environment or at least one *Worker* completes its execution.

Finally, it must be noted that the list of ordered devices is reconstructed (and the benchmark executed) whenever one of the following events occurs:

- a new device enters in the environment;
- a device leaves the environment;
- a *Worker* finishes its execution.

This is a preliminary scheduling algorithm that enables to take care of events related to the high dynamicity of a pervasive environment, in which mobile devices chaotically enters and exits. However, alternative schemes are in order to be defined and tested.

4 Conclusions and Future Work

This paper proposes a model and an application service able to dynamically distribute and execute user-submitted tasks on a grid of mobile and fixed devices in a pervasive way. Following the *Utility Computing* paradigm, the computational power is given in a completely transparent way.

Currently, the proposed approach is applicable whenever the application to execute consists in a single task that has to be executed many times (even with different input values) or in many different tasks that don't need to cooperate each other.

Future works will aim at developing new coordinating models that take care of possible inter-task cooperation; i.e. multithreaded/multiprocess applications. As well, the scheduling algorithm should be improved.

In addition, other dependability and security issues are in order.

References

1. I. Foster, C. Kesselman: The Grid: Blueprint for a New Computing Infrastructure. Morgan Kaufmann (1999)
2. D. Saha, A. Murkrjee: Pervasive Computing: A Paradigm for the 21st Century. IEEE Computer (2003)
3. J. W. Ross, G. Westerman: Preparing for utility computing: The role of IT architecture and relationship management. IBM System Journal, Vol. 43, NO 1 (2004)
4. L. W. McKnight, J. Howinson, S. Bradner: Wireless Grids. IEEE Internet Computing (2004)
5. D. C. Chu, M. Humphrey: Mobile OGSI.NET: Grid Computing on Mobile Devices. International Workshop on Grid Computing, GRID (2004)
6. B. Clarke, M. Humphrey: Beyond the 'Device as Portal': Meeting the Requirements of Wireless and Mobile Devices in the Legion of Grid Computing System. International Parallel and Distributed Processing Symposium, IPDPS (2002)
7. T. Phan, L. Huang, C. Dulan: Challenge: Integrating Mobile Devices Into the Computational Grid. International Conference on Mobile Computing and Networking, MobiCom (2002)

8. N. Daves, A. Friday, O. Storz: Exploring the Grid's Potential for Ubiquitous Computing. IEEE Pervasive Computing (2004)
9. V. Hingne, A. Joshi, T. Finin, H. Kargupta, E. Houstis: Towards a Pervasive Grid. International Parallel and Distributed Processing Symposium, IPDPS (2003)
10. G. Coulson, P. Grace, G. Blair, D. Duce, C. Cooper, M. Sagar: A Middleware Approach for Pervasive Grid Environments. Workshop on Ubiquitous Computing and e-ResearchNational eScience Centre, Edinburgh, UK (2005)
11. M. Román, C. K. Hess, R. Cerqueira, A. Ranganathan, R. H. Campbell, K. Nahrstedt: Gaia: A Middleware Infrastructure to Enable Active Spaces. IEEE Pervasive Computing (2002) 74-83
12. H. Kishimoto, J. Treadwell: Defining the Grid: A Roadmap for OGSA Standards. http://www.gridforum.org/documents/GFD.53.pdf
13. I. Foster: Globus Toolkit Version 4: Software for Service-Oriented Systems. IFIP International Conference on Network and Parallel Computing, Springer-Verlag LNCS 3779 (2005) 2-13
14. M. Ciampi, A. Coronato, G. De Pietro: Middleware Services for Pervasive Grids, in the proc. of the International Symposium on Parallel and Distributed Processing and Application, ISPA (2006)
15. F. Bellifemmine, A. Poggi, G. Rimassa: Jade Programmers Guide, http://sharon.cselt.it/projects/jade/doc/programmersguide.pdf
16. F. Bellifemmine, A. Poggi, G. Rimassa: JADE – FIPA Compliant Agent Framework. PAAM (1999)

Providing Service-Oriented Abstractions for the Wireless Sensor Grid

Edgardo Avilés-López and J. Antonio García-Macías

Computer Science Department
CICESE Research Center
Km. 107 Carretera Tijuana-Ensenada
Ensenada, Baja California, Mexico
{avilesl,jagm}@cicese.mx

Abstract. The computing grid no longer encompasses only traditional computers to perform coordinated tasks, as also low-end devices are now considered active members of the envisioned pervasive grid. Wireless sensor networks play an important role in this vision, since they provide the means for gathering vast amounts of data from physical phenomena. However, the current integration of wireless sensor networks and the grid is still primitive; one important aspect in this integration is providing higher-level abstractions for the development of applications, since accessing the data from wireless sensor networks currently implies dealing with very low-level constructs. We propose TinySOA, a service-oriented architecture that allows programmers to access wireless sensor networks from their applications by using a simple service-oriented API via the language of their choice. We show an implementation of TinySOA and some sample applications developed with it that exemplify how easy grid applications can integrate sensor networks.

1 Introduction

Initial grid computing developments focused on the computational capabilities of distributed systems for processing large amounts of data and for conveniently sharing resources; as such, grid computing has also been referred to as utility computing, computing on tap, or on-demand computing. Recent initiatives such as the OGSA [1] have expanded this early focus to comprise a more data-centric approach, as well as distributed services. Increasingly, the data for these distributed services comes from small devices capable of sensing physical phenomena, performing computing tasks, and communicating their results to other devices [2]; these intelligent sensing devices form what is known as wireless sensor networks (WSN).

Integrating the grid with wireless sensor networks (forming what is often called the wireless sensor grid) is a goal that is getting considerable attention from researchers and practitioners. Researchers at Harvard and other institutions [3] are working on the development of a robust and scalable data collection network called Hourglass; the goal of Hourglass is to integrate sensor data into

C. Cérin and K.-C. Li (Eds.): GPC 2007, LNCS 4459, pp. 710–715, 2007.

grid applications, using a publish-subscribe model for such purpose. Lim et al. [4] identify the issues and challenges for the design of sensor grids, and propose an architecture called the scalable proxy-based architecture for sensor grids (SPRING). Both Hourglass and SPRING are currently works in progress, as are other efforts, and setting a standard by consensus within the community will certainly require continued efforts.

From the many issues and challenges being addressed for integrating wireless sensor networks and the grid, we consider an important one here: providing programmers with adequate abstractions and tools for developing applications that can incorporate access to the resources provided by WSN. A notable example of work in this direction is TAG [5] where the WSN is abstracted as a database and data can be obtained by issuing SQL queries. The service-oriented approach has been explored as an alternative [6], where an external entity is charged with processing requests for services; however, in the cited paper no details are given as to how components are conformed, how interactions are made, and what protocols are used. More recently [7, 8], a reflective service-oriented middleware has been proposed, but it has not been tested with an actual WSN, as it is only simulated with Java components.

We believe that the service-oriented approach provides adequate abstractions for application developers, and that it is a good way to integrate the grid with WSN. Currently, if an application programmer wants to develop a system for monitoring certain phenomena using a WSN, she may need to learn a new language (e.g., NesC), a new programming paradigm (e.g., component-based programming), a new embedded operating system (e.g., TinyOS), and probably even some details about the underlying hardware platform; this situation is of course far from optimal, as an application programmer should only concentrate on application-level issues and ideally use the programming languages and tools that she is accustomed to. With this in mind we propose TinySOA, an architecture based on the well-known service oriented paradigm.

In the next section we give details regarding the different elements of the architecture, their roles and interactions; in Sect. 3 we present TinyVisor, a system that implements the conceptual framework of TinySOA and that acts as proof of concept for the development of applications with a real WSN. Then, in Sect. 4 we give some concluding remarks and outline future work.

2 TinySOA: Service-Oriented Architecture for WSN

Providing better abstractions to application programmers has been a long-time motivation in software engineering. Therefore, we have witnessed advances in programming methodologies and paradigms ranging from sequential programming, modular programming, object-oriented programming, component-based programming, and more recently service-oriented programming. This recent approach arises in response to modern needs and complexities such as distributed software, application integration, as well as heterogeneity in platforms, protocols and devices, including Internet integration. Given its compliance to modern software development and the wide positive reception it has gained in academic and industrial environments, we believe that a service-oriented architecture is well suited for the integration of wireless sensor networks to the worldwide grid.

The architecture we propose, named TinySOA, can be well understood in terms of an execution scenario, where all the operations take place in three well-defined sections:

- Capture. The area where the WSN resides. Using the publish/subscribe model the WSN communicates its sensor readings and also management information to "outside" entities via a gateway (typically a sink node), which also can be used to pass requests to the network.
- Concentration. This area is where most of the processing takes place. All sensor data, and any other type of information, received from the capture area is compiled and classified for further use. Access to data and network control is provided by a server enabled with web services.
- Application. Here can be found the monitoring, visualization, and other applications created using the services provided by the concentration area.

Two types of services, internal and external, are provided by the architecture. This is achieved with the intervention of four components: node, gateway, registry and server, as shown in Fig. 1 and described below.

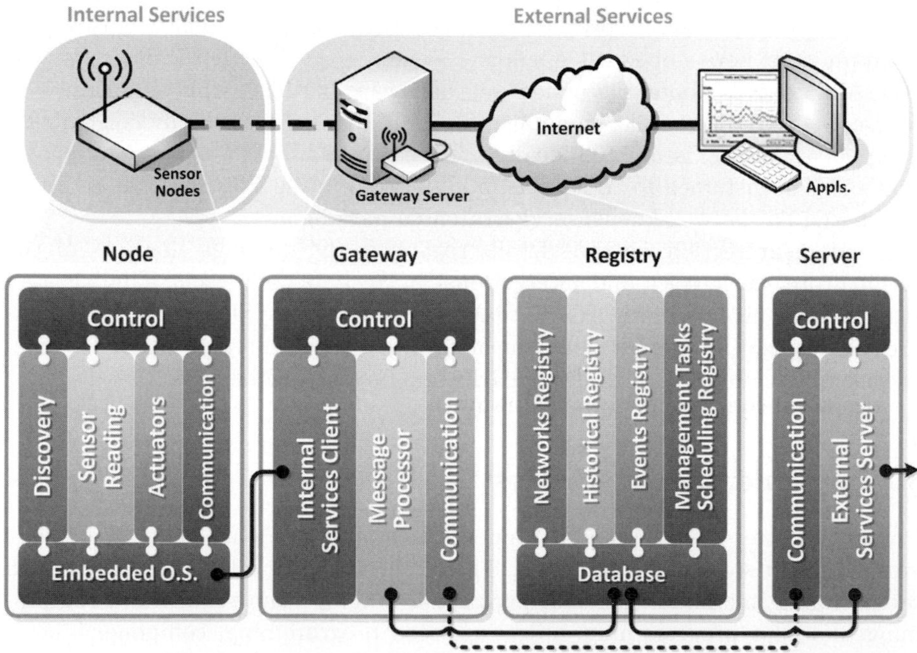

Fig. 1. The main components of the TinySOA architecture

- Node. This component encapsulates all the functionality of a sensing node, and resides in all sensing nodes in the network. Nodes provide internal services. They have several subcomponents for different purposes, such as service discovery, reading sensors data, controlling actuators, and communicating data and requests via a gateway from and to the network. Also, the embedded operating system is an important subcomponent that abstracts low levels details such as communication with the hardware platform, topology control, etc.
- Gateway. This component is typically located in a specialized node or in a computer, and acts as a bridge between a WSN and the outside world (e.g., the grid). It is worth noting that there can be several WSNs, as long as each one of them has their own gateway. Several subcomponents provide the gateway functionality: a control subcomponent is in charge of initializing all gateway activities, and also manages all other subcomponents; another one deals with all the interaction with internal services provided by the nodes; a message processor handles registration and sensor reading messages, but also interacts with the registry component. There is also an optional communication subcomponent, whose purpose is to handle immediate requests that need urgent attention without going through the task management registry subcomponent first.
- Registry. All the information about the infrastructure is stored in this component. Several subcomponents, in the form of registries, contain information about currently available (or past) sensor networks, historical records of sensor readings and control information, events indicated by the users of external services, as well as task management scheduling information (e.g., changing the sensors sampling rate). All these subcomponents rely on a database management subcomponent.
- Server. The main functionality here is to act as a provider of web services, abstracting each available WSN as a separate web service. These provide an interface to consult the services offered by the network, check the registry, consult and register events and maintenance tasks. The control subcomponent is in charge of initializing the server, and an optional communication subcomponent allows to immediately send commands to the network, without going through the task management registry (interacting with its analogous subcomponent in the gateway).

3 Implementation and Tests

One of the intended purposes of TinySOA is to be used as a basis for the construction of middleware systems that provide appropriate abstractions for the development of applications using WSN. Therefore, in order to test the feasibility of using TinySOA for such purposes, we implemented a middleware system that integrates all the elements in the architecture. Also, we developed several applications with varying complexity running on top of this middleware system; this allowed us to verify the advantages in development time and ease of use that programmers would find using our proposed architecture.

The hardware platform for our prototype includes MicaZ motes with MTS-310CA sensing boards, and MIB510 programming boards, all manufactured by Crossbow Technology, Inc.[1] This platform uses the TinyOS [9] embedded operating system. As implemented in our prototype, the Node component is located in the MicaZ motes, and the Gateway, Registry and Server components are located in a single computer (although they could be located in different computers or specialized devices). If more than one WSN is connected to the system, each one should be associated with a different instance of the Gateway component.

When a node starts working, it discovers what services it can offer (i.e., what types of sensors it has) and then publishes them, so they can be available for other entities to use them; of course, also the available sensor networks are registered. This way, any program can just issue queries to the registry to find out what networks are available, what services they offer, etc., through a simple service-oriented that provides functions to obtain information about the network(s), including network ID, name and description, as well as a listing of nodes, sensing parameters, times, and actuators; there are also functions to manage events, readings, and tasks.

Using the API, we constructed several applications that were later integrated into a system called TinyVisor (we omit the figures showing the screen captures for lack of space in this article). At startup, the URL of a server can be provided and then an automatic discovery process locates the web services registry and related repositories, but also all available WSNs. An interactive dialog shows the information related to the discovered WSNs including the name, description, and web service URL; from there it is possible to select the network that is going to be used for monitoring and visualization. Once the network is selected, the information regarding its nodes and the sensed data can be visualized either in data mode graph mode, or topology mode. This implementation of TinyVisor was developed using the Java programming language, but any other language could have been used, provided that it has the capabilities for accessing web services; in fact, we have developed several other simple applications using languages such as PHP and C#, for proofs of concepts.

4 Conclusions

The conventional wired grid is continuously being extended to integrate more and richer computing and data sources; wireless sensor networks play an important role in this trend and some have suggested that they will constitute the "eyes" and "ears" of the computational grid. However, the integration of wireless sensor networks and the grid is still largely work in progress; we consider that an important part in this integration is allowing grid application developers to access the resources provided by sensor networks without having to delve into low-level aspects of these networks, as it is currently required. With this in mind, we propose TinySOA, a service-oriented architecture that allows programmers to access wireless sensor networks from their applications by using a simple

[1] More information about this company and their products at `http://www.xbow.com`

service-oriented API via the language of their choice. We show an implementation of TinySOA, called TinyVisor, to exemplify how easy grid applications can integrate sensor networks.

We are currently designing an in-depth evaluation methodology to further evaluate the degree to which TinySOA can help application developers; this includes measuring the acceptance of the architecture, e.g., via the technology acceptance model [10], and presenting a test population of programmers with a development and integration problem and giving them the tools provided by TinySOA to develop some applications with the language of their choice; this could help elucidate and measure the benefits provided by TinySOA.

Acknowledgements

Financial support for this project was provided by the Mexican Council for Science and Technology (CONACyT).

References

[1] Foster, I., Kishimoto, H., Savva, A., Berry, D., Djaoui, A., Grimshaw, A., Horn, B., Maciel, F., Siebenlist, F., Subramaniam, R., Treadwell, J., Reich, J.V.: The open grid services architecture, version 1.5. Open Grid Forum. July 24, 2006

[2] Akyildiz, I., Su, W., Sankarasubramaniam, Y., Cayirci, E.: A survey on wireless sensor networks. IEEE Communications Magazine **40**(8) (2002) 102–114

[3] Gaynor, M., Welsh, M., Moulton, S., Rowan, A., LaCombe, E., Wynne, J.: Integrating wireless sensor networks with the grid. IEEE Internet Computing (2004)

[4] Lim, H., Teo, Y., Mukherjee, P., Lam, V., Wong, W., See, S.: Sensor grid: Integration of wireless sensor networks and the grid. Proceedings IEEE Local Computer Network (LCN) Conference. Sydney, Australia. November 2005

[5] Madden, S., Franklin, M., Hellerstein, J., Hong, W.: Tag: A tiny aggregation service for ad-hoc sensor networks. Proc. ACM Symposium on Operating Systems Design and Implementation (OSDI). Boston, MA, USA. December 2002

[6] Golatowski, F., Blumenthal, J., Handy, M., Haase, M.: Service-oriented software architecture for sensor networks. Intl. Workshop on Mobile Computing (IMC 2003). Rockstock, Germany. June 2003 93–98

[7] Delicato, F., Pires, P., Pirmez, L., da Costa Carmo, L.: A flexible web service based architecture for sensor networks. IEEE Workshop on Mobile and Wireless Networks (MWN 2003). Rhode Island, NY, USA. May 2003

[8] Delicato, F., Pires, P., Rust, L., Pirmez, L., de Rezende, J.: Reflective middleware for wireless sensor networks. 20th Annual ACM Symposium on Applied Computing (ACM SAC'2005). Santa Fe, USA. March 2005 730–735

[9] Hill, J., Szewczyk, R., Woo, A., Hollar, S., Culler, D., Pister, K.: System architecture directions for networked sensors. 9th. International Conference on Architectural Support for Programming Languages and Operating SYstems. Cambridge, MA, USA. November 2000

[10] Venkatesh, V., Davis, F.: A model of the antecedents of perceived ease of use: Development and test. Journal of Decision Sciences **27**(3) (1996) 451–482

Bio-inspired Grid Information System with Epidemic Tuning

Agostino Forestiero, Carlo Mastroianni, Fausto Pupo, and Giandomenico Spezzano

Institute of High Performance Computing and Networking ICAR-CNR
Via P. Bucci 41C, 87036 Rende (CS), Italy
{forestiero, mastroianni, pupo, spezzano}@icar.cnr.it

Abstract. This paper proposes a bio-inspired approach for the construction of a Grid information system in which metadata documents that describe Grid resources are disseminated and logically reorganized on the Grid. A number of ant-like agents travel the Grid through P2P interconnections and use probability functions to replicate resource descriptors and collect those related to resources with similar characteristics in nearby Grid hosts. Resource reorganization results from the collective activity of a large number of agents, which perform simple operations at the local level, but together engender an advanced form of "swarm intelligence" at the global level. An adaptive tuning mechanism based on the epidemic paradigm is used to regulate the dissemination of resources according to users' needs. Simulation analysis shows that the epidemic mechanism can be used to balance the two main functionalities of the proposed approach: entropy reduction and resource replication.

1 Introduction

To support the design and execution of complex applications, modern distributed systems must provide enhanced services such as the retrieval and access to content, the creation and management of content, and the placement of content at appropriate locations. In a Grid, these services are offered by a pillar component of Grid frameworks, the *information system*. This paper discusses a novel approach for the construction of a Grid information system which allows for an efficient management and discovery of resources. The approach, proposed in [5] in its basic version, exploits the features of (i) epidemic mechanisms tailored to the dissemination of information in distributed systems [6] and (ii) self organizing systems in which "swarm intelligence" emerges from the behavior of a large number of agents which interact with the environment [1, 3].

The proposed ARMAP protocol (*Ant-based Replication and MApping Protocol*) disseminates Grid resource descriptors (i.e., metadata documents) in a controlled way, by spatially sorting (or *mapping*) such descriptors according to their semantic classification, so to achieve a logical reorganization of resources. For the sake of simplicity, in the following an information document describing a Grid resource will be simply referred to as a *resource*.

Each ARMAP agent travels the Grid through P2P interconnections among Grid hosts, and uses simple probability functions to decide whether or not to *pick* resources from or *drop* resources into the current Grid host. Resource reorganization results

C. Cérin and K.-C. Li (Eds.): GPC 2007, LNCS 4459, pp. 716–723, 2007.

from pick and drop operations performed by a large number of agents, and is inspired by the activity of some species of ants and termites that cluster and map items within their environment [1]. A self-organization approach based on ants' pheromone [7] enables each agent to regulate its activity, i.e. its *operation mode*, only on the basis of local information. Indeed, each agent initially works in the *copy* mode: it can generate new resource replicas and disseminate them on the Grid. However, when it realizes from its own past activity that a sufficient number of replicas have been generated, it switches to the *move* mode: it only moves resources from one host to another without generating new replicas. This switch is performed when the level of a pheromone variable, which depends on agent's activity, exceeds a given threshold.

The ARMAP protocol can effectively be used to build a Grid information system in which (i) resources are properly replicated and (ii) the overall entropy is reduced. A balance between these two features can be achieved by regulating the pheromone threshold, i.e. by shortening or extending the time interval in which agents operate under the *copy* mode. Tuning of the pheromone mechanism can be *static* or *adaptive*. In the first case, the threshold is set before ARMAP protocol is started, whereas, in the case of adaptive tuning, the threshold can be tuned by a supervisor agent while ARMAP is running, depending on users' needs. This introduces a twofold control mechanism: each agent uses local information to self-regulate its activity, whereas a supervisor agent dynamically sets a global system parameter, i.e., the pheromone threshold, and propagates the value of this parameter via an epidemic mechanism.

The remainder of the paper is organized as follows. Section 2 describes the ARMAP protocol. Section 3 analyzes the performance of the ARMAP protocol, both with static tuning and adaptive tuning and Section 4 concludes the paper.

2 Ant-Inspired Reorganization of Grid Resources

The aim of the ARMAP protocol [5] is to achieve a logical organization of Grid resources by spatially sorting them on the Grid according to their semantic classification. It is assumed that the resources have been previously classified into a number of classes *Nc*, according to their semantics and functionalities (see [2]).

The ARMAP protocol has been analyzed in a P2P Grid in which hosts are arranged in a 2-dimension toroidal space, and each host is connected to at most 8 neighbor peers. The Grid has a dynamic nature, and hosts can disconnect and rejoin the network. When connecting to the Grid, a host generates a number of agents given by a discrete Gamma stochastic function, with average *Ngen*, and sets the life time of these agents to *PlifeTime*, which is the average connection time of the host, calculated on the basis of the host's past activity. This mechanism allows for controlling the number of agents that operate on the Grid: indeed, the number of agents is maintained to a value which is about *Ngen* times the number of hosts.

Periodically each ARMAP agent sets off from the current host and performs a number of hops through the P2P links that interconnect the Grid hosts. Then the agent uses appropriate *pick* and *drop* functions in order to replicate and move resources from one peer to another. More specifically, at each host an agent must decide whether or not to *pick* the resources of a given class, and then carry them in its successive movements, or to *drop* resources that it has previously picked from another host. Pick and drop probability functions are discussed in the following.

Pick operation. Whenever an ARMAP agent hops to a Grid host, it must decide, for each resource class, whether or not to *pick* the resources of that class which are managed by the current host. In order to achieve replication and mapping functionalities, a *pick* random function is defined with the intention that the probability of picking the resources of a given class decreases as the local region of the Grid accumulates such resources and vice versa. This assures that as soon as the equilibrium condition is broken (i.e., resources of different classes are accumulated in different regions), the reorganization of resources is more and more pushed.

The *Ppick* random function, defined in formula (1), is the product of two factors, which take into account, respectively, the relative accumulation of resources of a given class (with respect to other classes), and their absolute accumulation (with respect to the initial number of resources of that class). In particular, the *fr* fraction is computed as the number of resources of the class of interest, accumulated within the *visibility region*, divided by the overall number of resources that are accumulated in the same region. The visibility region includes the peers that are reachable from the current peer with a given number of hops, i.e. within the *visibility radius*. The visibility radius is set to 1, so that the visibility region is composed of at most 9 hosts (if all the neighbor peers are active), the current one included. The *fa* fraction is computed as the number of resources *owned* by the hosts located in the visibility region out of the overall number of resources that are *maintained* by such hosts, including the resources deposited by agents. The inverse of *fa* gives an estimation of the extent to which such hosts have accumulated resources of the class of interest. k1 and k2 are non-negative constants which are both set to 0.1 [1].

$$\mathrm{Ppick} = \left(\frac{\mathrm{k1}}{\mathrm{k1}+\mathrm{fr}}\right)^2 \cdot \left(\frac{(\mathrm{fa})^2}{\mathrm{k2}+(\mathrm{fa})^2}\right)^2 \qquad (1)$$

The pick operation can be performed with two different modes. If the *copy* mode is used, the agent, when executing a pick operation, leaves the resources on the current host, generates a replica of each of them, and carries such replicas until it will drop them in another host. Conversely, with the *move* mode, as an agent picks the resources, it removes them from the current host (except those *owned* by this host), thus preventing an excessive proliferation of replicas.

Drop operation. As well as the pick function, the drop function is first used to break the initial equilibrium and then to strengthen the mapping of resources of different classes in different Grid regions. Whenever an agent gets to a new Grid host, it must decide, if it is carrying some resources of a given class, whether or not to *drop* such resources in the current host. As opposed to the pick operation, the drop probability function *Pdrop*, shown in formula (2), is proportional to the relative accumulation of resources of the class of interest in the visibility region. In (2) the threshold constant k3 is set to 0.3 [1].

$$\mathrm{Pdrop} = \left(\frac{\mathrm{fr}}{\mathrm{k3}+\mathrm{fr}}\right)^2 \qquad (2)$$

2.1 System Entropy and Pheromone Mechanism

A spatial entropy function, based on the well known Shannon's formula for the calculation of information content, is defined to evaluate the effectiveness of the ARMAP protocol. For each peer *p*, the local entropy *Ep* gives an estimation of the extent to which the resources have already been mapped within the visibility region centered in *p*. *Ep* has been normalized, so that its value is comprised between 0 and 1. As shown in formula (3), the overall entropy *E* is defined as the average of the entropy values *Ep* computed at all the Grid hosts. In (3), *fr(i)* is the fraction of resources of class *Ci* that are located in the visibility region with respect to the overall number of resources located in the same region.

$$Ep = \frac{\sum_{i=1..Nc} fr(i) \cdot \log_2 \frac{1}{fr(i)}}{\log_2 Nc}, \quad E = \frac{\sum_{p \varepsilon Grid} Ep}{Np} \qquad (3)$$

In [5] it was shown that the overall spatial entropy can be minimized if each agent exploits both the ARMAP modes, i.e. *copy* and *move*. In the first phase, the agent *copies* the resources that it picks from a Grid host, but when it realizes from its own activeness that the mapping process is at an advanced stage, it begins simply to *move* resources from one host to another, without creating new replicas.

In fact, the *copy* mode cannot be maintained for a long time, since eventually every host would have a very large number of resources of all classes, thus weakening the efficacy of resource mapping. The protocol is effective only if agents, after replicating a number of resources, switch from *copy* to *move*. A self-organization approach based on ants' pheromone mechanism enables each agent to perform this mode switch only on the basis of local information. This approach is inspired by the observation that agents perform more operations when the system entropy is high, but operation frequency gradually decreases as resources are properly reorganized. In particular, at given time intervals, i.e. every 2,000 seconds, each agent counts up the number of times that it has evaluated the pick and drop probability functions, and the number of times that it has actually performed *pick* and *drop* operations. At the end of each time interval, the agent makes a deposit into its pheromone base, by adding a pheromone amount equal to the ratio between the number of "unsuccessful" operations and the total number of operation attempts. An evaporation mechanism is used to give a higher weigh to recent behavior of the agent. Specifically, at the end of the i-th time interval, the pheromone level Φi is computed with formula (4).

$$\Phi i = Ev \cdot \Phi i - 1 + \varphi i \qquad (4)$$

The evaporation rate *Ev* is set to 0.9, and φi is the fraction of unsuccessful operations performed in the last time interval. With such settings, the value of Φi is always comprised between 0 and 10. As soon as the pheromone level exceeds *Tf*, the agent realizes that the frequency of *pick* and *drop* operations has remarkably reduced, so it switches its protocol mode from *copy* to *move*. The value of *Tf* can be used to tune the number of agents that work in *copy* mode and are therefore able to create new resource replicas, as discussed in the next section.

3 Adaptive Tuning and Epidemic Control

The performance of the ARMAP protocol has been evaluated with an event-based simulator written in Java. Simulation runs have been performed with the following setting of network and protocol parameters The number of peers *Np*, or Grid size, is set to 2500, corresponding to a 50x50 toroidal grid of peers. The average connection time of a specific peer, *Plifetime*, is generated according to a Gamma distribution function, with an average value set to 100,000 seconds. The use of the Gamma function assures that the Grid contains very dynamic hosts, that frequently disconnect and rejoin the network, as well as much more stable hosts. Every time a peer disconnects from the Grid, it loses all the resource descriptors previously deposited by agents, thus contributing to the removal of obsolete information. The average number of Grid resources owned and published by a single peer is set to 15. Grid resources are classified in a number of classes *Nc*, which is set to 5. The mean number of agents that travel the Grid is set to *Np*/2: this is accomplished, as explained in Section 2, by setting the mean number of agents generated by a peer, *Ngen*, to 0.5. The average time *Tmov* between two successive agent movements (i.e. between two successive evaluations of *pick* and *drop* functions) is set to 60 s. The maximum number of P2P hops that are performed within a single agent movement, *Hmax*, is set to 3. The visibility radius *Rv*, defined in Section 2 and used for the evaluation of pick and drop functions, is set to 1. Finally, the pheromone threshold *Tf*, defined in Section 2.1, ranges from 3 to 10.

The following performance indices are used. The overall entropy *E*, defined in Section 2.1, is used to estimate the effectiveness of the ARMAP protocol in the reorganization of resources. The *Nrpr* index is defined as the mean number of replicas that are generated for each resource. Since new replicas are only generated by ARMAP agents that work in the *copy* mode, the number of such agents, *Ncopy*, is another interesting performance index.

A first set of simulation runs have been performed to evaluate the performance of the ARMAP protocol and investigate the effect of *static* tuning. Static tuning is obtained by setting the pheromone threshold *Tf* before the ARMAP protocol is set off, but it does not allow to change the threshold value dynamically. Figure 1 reports the number of agents that work in *copy* mode (also called *copy* agents in the following) versus time, for different values of the pheromone threshold *Tf*. When ARMAP is initiated, all the agents (about 1250, half the number of peers) are generated in the *copy* mode, but subsequently several agents switch to *move*, as soon as their pheromone value exceeds the threshold *Tf*. This corresponds to the sudden drop of curves that can be observed in Figure 1. This drop does not occur if *Tf* is equal to 10 because this value can never be reached by the pheromone (see formula (4)); hence with *Tf*=10 all agents remain in *copy* along all their lives. After the first phase of the ARMAP process, an equilibrium is reached because the number of new agents which are generated by hosts (such agents always set off in *copy* mode) and the number of agents that switch from *copy* to *move* get balanced. Moreover, if the pheromone threshold *Tf* is increased, the average interval of time in which an agent works in *copy* becomes longer, and therefore the average number of *copy* agents, after the transition phase, becomes larger.

A proper tuning of the pheromone threshold is a very efficient method to enforce or reduce the generation of new replicas and the intensity of resource dissemination. However, a more intense dissemination is not always associated to a better resource reorganization, i.e. to a more effective spatial separation of resources belonging to different classes. Figure 2(a) shows that lower values of the overall entropy are achieved with lower values of the pheromone threshold. Notice that virtually no entropy decrease is observed if all the agents operate in *copy* (*Tf*=10), which confirms that the mode switch is strictly necessary to perform an effective resource reorganization. Figure 2(b) shows the mean number of replicas generated per resource and confirms that resource dissemination is more intense if the pheromone threshold is increased, because a larger number of *copy* agents operate on the network. It can be concluded that *copy* agents are useful to replicate and disseminate resources but it is the *move* agents that perform the resource reorganization and are able to reduce the overall entropy by creating Grid regions specialized in specific classes of resources.

A balance between the two main functionalities of ARMAP (resource replication and spatial reorganization) can be performed by adaptively tuning the pheromone threshold. The value of *Tf* should be increased if more replicas are needed, while it should be reduced if a better spatial mapping of resources must be obtained. Adaptive tuning can be achieved by a few *supervisor agents* that, according to the needs and the level of satisfaction of users, communicate to ARMAP agents a new value of the pheromone threshold, and so enforce or reduce the activity of agents. Information is transmitted to agents through an *epidemic mechanism*, which mimics [4] the spread of a contagious disease in which infected entities contaminate other "healthy" entities.

ARMAP adaptive tuning works as follows. When a supervisor agent decides to change the pheromone threshold, it initially communicates the new threshold value to the peer in which such agent resides: infection will then spread from this peer. Each agent which visits this infected peer will be contaminated and its own pheromone threshold will be changed. In turn, whenever an infected agent visits a non-infected peer, the latter will be contaminated and will subsequently infect other agents. So, in a short time, most agents will be "*infected*" with the new threshold value.

Figure 3 shows the trend of *E* and *Nrpr* in the case of adaptive tuning. In this figure, dotted curves depict the values obtained, under static tuning, with *Tf*=5, *Tf*=7 and *Tf*=9. Continuous curves report the performances achieved with a threshold initially set to 7 and then switched by a supervisor peer first to 9 (at time=200,000 s) and then to 5 (at time=500,000 s). The continuous lines labeled with circles correspond to an ideal scenario in which a *global control* mechanism immediately communicates the new pheromone threshold to all agents. On the other hand, the continuous lines labeled with stars are achieved by exploiting the above described *epidemic* mechanism, which is initiated by the mentioned supervisor agent. It can be noticed that with both mechanisms, after a threshold change, the trends of *E* and *Nrpr* undergo a transition phase, and then converge to the curves obtained with static tuning, so confirming the effectiveness and consistency of adaptive tuning. Before converging, however, the *Nrpr* curves related to adaptive tuning show an *overshoot* (more noticeable in the upward switch than in the downward one), which is a distinguishing feature of the step response of a second order system. We are currently investigating the rational of this macroscopic behavior and how it is generated by microscopic operations.

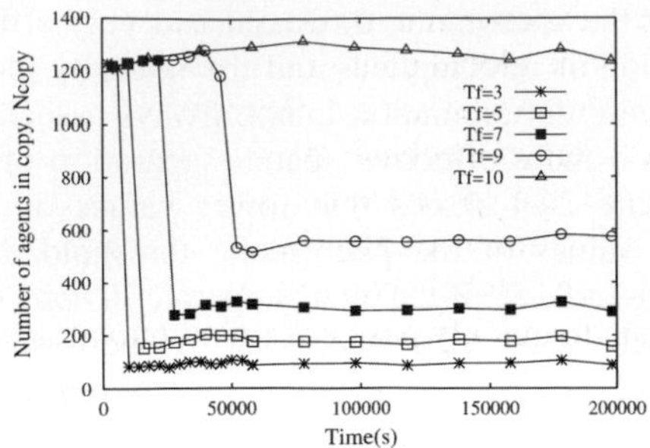

Fig. 1. Static tuning. Mean number of agents in *copy* mode, for different values of the pheromone threshold *Tf*

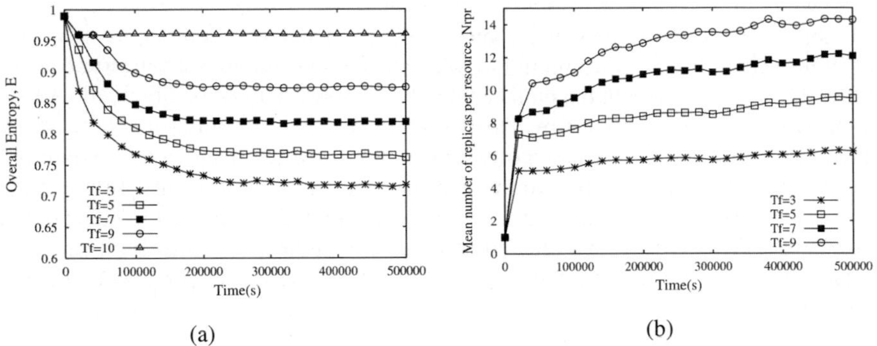

Fig. 2. Static tuning. Overall system entropy *E* (a) and mean number of replicas per resource *Nrpr* (b), for different values of the pheromone threshold *Tf*

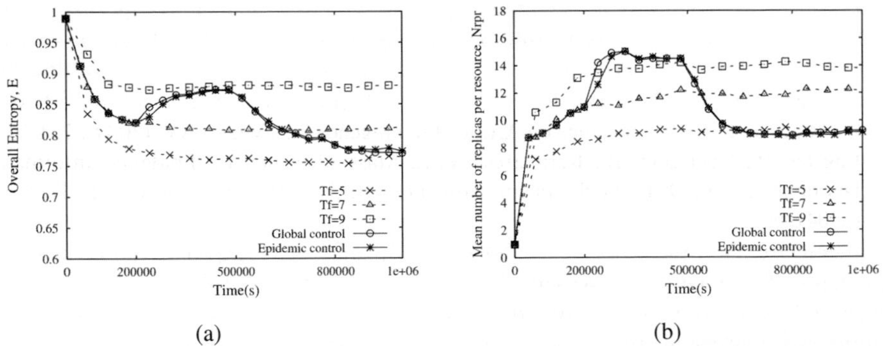

Fig. 3. Adaptive tuning. Overall system entropy *E* (a) and mean number of replicas *Nrpr* (b), when the pheromone threshold *Tf* is changed from 7 to 9 (after 200,000 s) and then to 5 (after 500,000 s). Comparison between global (ideal) and epidemic control is shown.

The transition phases experienced with the epidemic control are slightly slower than those measured with the global control due to the time necessary to propagate the infection to a significant number of agents. However, the additional delay experienced when exploiting the epidemic mechanism is definitely tolerable, especially in the downward switch. Overall, the epidemic mechanism is efficient and requires no extra message load, since information is carried at no cost by ARMAP agents which travel the Grid. Conversely, the global control would require an onerous and well synchronized mechanism to quickly pass information to all agents.

4 Conclusions

This paper proposes an approach for the construction of a Grid information system which manages and reorganizes Grid resources according to their characteristics. The ant-inspired ARMAP protocol is executed by a number of ant-like agents that travel the Grid through P2P interconnections among hosts. Agents disseminate metadata documents on the Grid, and aggregate information related to similar resources in neighbor Grid nodes, so contributing to decrease the overall system entropy. Resource replication and reorganization can be tuned by appropriately setting a pheromone threshold in order to foster or reduce the activeness of ARMAP agents. This paper introduces an epidemic mechanism to achieve adaptive tuning, i.e., to progressively inform agents about any change in the pheromone threshold. Simulation results show that the ARMAP protocol is able to achieve the mentioned objectives, and is inherently scalable, as agents' operations are driven by self-organization and fully decentralized mechanisms, and no information is required about the global state of the system.

References

1. Bonabeau, E., Dorigo, M., Theraulaz, G.: Swarm Intelligence: From Natural to Artificial Systems, Oxford University Press, Santa Fe Institute Studies in the Sciences of Complexity (1999)
2. Crespo, A., Garcia-Molina, H.: Routing indices for peer-to-peer systems. In: 22 nd International Conference on Distributed Computing Systems ICDCS'02, Vienna, Austria (2002), 23-33
3. Dasgupta, P.: Intelligent Agent Enabled P2P Search Using Ant Algorithms, Proceedings of the 8th International Conference on Artificial Intelligence, Las Vegas, NV, (2004), 751-757.
4. Eugster, P., Guerraoui, R., Kermarres, A.M., Massoulieacute, L.: Epidemic Information Dissemination in Distributed System, Computer, IEEE Computer Society, vol. 37, No. 5 (2004), 60-67
5. Forestiero, A., Mastroianni, C., Spezzano, G.: A Multi Agent Approach for the Construction of a Peer-to-Peer Information System in Grids, Proc. of the 2005 International Conference on Self-Organization and Adaptation of Multi-agent and Grid Systems SOAS, Glasgow, Scotland (2005)
6. Petersen, K., Spreitzer, M., Terry, D., Theimer, M., Demers, A.: Flexible Update Propagation for Weakly Consistent Replication, Proc. of the 16th Symposium on Operating System Principles, ACM (1997), 288-301
7. Van Dyke Parunak, H., Brueckner, S. A., Matthews, R., Sauter, J.: Pheromone Learning for Self-Organizing Agents, IEEE Transactions on Systems, Man, and Cybernetics, Part A: Systems and Humans, vol. 35, no. 3 (2005)

Credibility Assignment in Knowledge Grid Environment

Saeed Parsa and Fereshteh-Azadi Parand

Faculty of computer engineering,
Iran University of Science and Technology, Narmak, Tehran, Iran
{parsa, parand}@iust.ac.ir

Abstract. Credibility of knowledge grid members who act as a cooperative decision making community, affects the degree of accuracy of the decisions made. Apparently, decisions made by a decision maker should be affected by the degree of the decision maker's credibility. The problem is how to estimate decision makers' credibility within a knowledge grid environment, specially, those environments in which the number of decision makers is altered dynamically. In this article, a new approach to estimate the credibility of decision makers based upon the opinion of the other members of decision makers' community within a dynamic knowledge grid environment is proposed.

1 Introduction

Knowledge grid is an intelligent interconnection environment, built on top of computational grid, to facilitate creation of virtual organizations.

Fusion of information is of basic concern in all kinds of knowledge-based systems such as decision-making. A major consideration in information fusion is the inclusion of source credibility information in the fusion process [12].

In this paper, a new approach to estimate the credibility of decision makers in knowledge grid environment is proposed. Apparently, the credibility of each decision maker affects the impact of its decision on the consensus decision.

Source credibility is a user generated or sanctioned knowledge base [12]. According to Foster [6], openness, flexibility, and dynamics are major attributes of grid environments. Therefore, in a grid environment addition and removal of decision makers should be performed dynamically. In addition, the openness property of the grid environment should be considered. Since in an open environment there is no general perspective of decision makers and knowledge resources, the sanction determination of source credibility is not possible.

Assessment of source credibility could be performed either objectively or subjectively [8]. In [17], a fuzzy collaborative assessment approach combining the objective and subjective assessment strategies is suggested. All criteria used for website and knowledge organization assessment are considered as objective strategies. Subjective assessment strategies assess the quality of knowledge service through the cooperation between experts and agents. The overall subjective assesment for a criterion is calculated as a weighted average of acceptable assesments made by the individual experts. However, no method is suggested to estimate the weight, assigned to each decision-maker assesment, reflecting the reliability of the decision-maker (expert, agent).

C. Cérin and K.-C. Li (Eds.): GPC 2007, LNCS 4459, pp. 724 – 729, 2007.

Since there are few objective criteria for the assessment of decision makers, applicable in all decision-making problems, it is more suitable and feasible to apply subjective criteria for assessment of decision-makers. Another problem concerning knowledge grid environments is the need for transitive property of credibility such that if 'A' is known as a credible decision maker verifying the answer set of another decision maker, 'B', then 'B' will be considered as a credible decision maker. In the other words, propagation of credibility confirmation is a desired property. In order to determine the source credibility, many approaches such as probability theory [11], Bayesian theory [2, 3] and possibility theory [5, 7] can be used. Considering the nature of vagueness in knowledge grid environments, mainly caused by the lack of knowledge, not randomized functionality of the system, the use of possibility theory for modeling of these systems seems to be more appropriate than probability theory.

Based upon the above considerations, in Section 2.1 a new user generated approach for propagation and determination of source credibility is proposed. In this approach, applying fuzzy markov chain, source credibility is determined subjectively and changes gradually. The proposed approach has some advantages such as compatibility with reality, extendibility, and robustness in comparison with the methods which are based upon the probability theory.

Nomencluture

DM_i	Decision maker i^{th}
DP_N	Decision Problem N^{th}
DM	Decision makers set
D_k	Decision k^{th}
$AssCrePoss_i$	Credibility possibility distribution which is assigned by the ith decision-maker to the decision makers community
$crePoss_{ij}(subject_m)$	Credibility possibility which is assigned by the ith decision maker to jth decision maker for subject m
$\overline{R_i}(DP_N)$	Fuzzy response of ith decision-maker for DP_N
$\mu_{\overline{R_i}(DP_N)}(D_k)$	Membership degree of decision k to the decision set which is generated by ith decision maker for decision problem Nth, DP_N.
$Sim(R_i(DP_N, D_k) \wedge R_j(DP_N, D_k))$	Similarity between membership degree of D_k to the decision set of ith and j^{th} decision makers for DP_N
$AssCreM$	Assigned Credibility Matrix
$crePoss_i$	Aggregate value of credibility possibility which is assigned to the ith decision maker by decision makers-community.

2 Credibility Assignment to Decision Makers

Knowledge grid is an infrastructure that enables collaborative decision-making Decision makers may have different degrees of credibility. In this section, a new approach to determine the value of the decision maker's credibility based upon the other decision makers' opinion is proposed.

2.1 Formal Definition

Suppose there is a group of N decision makers in knowledge grid environment, indexed by the set $DM = \{DM_1, DM_2, DM_{,} . . , DM_N\}$. Each of these decision makers collects information from its accessible knowledge resources and has special capability of decision-making. With considering its knowledge about the other decision makers, each of these decision makers such as DM_i defines an assigned credibility possibility distribution for each subject.

$$AsscrePoss_i = \cup\, crePoss_{ij} \tag{1}$$

where $crePoss_{ij}$ is the degree of credibility possibility, assigned by the ith decision maker to the jth one and

$$0 \le crePoss_{i1} \cup crePoss_{i2} \cup .... \cup crePoss_{in} \le 1 \qquad \forall DM_i \in DM \tag{2}$$

The degree of credibility possibility of the jth decision-maker from the point of view of the ith decision-maker, $crePoss_{ij}{}^{t}$, for any subject when a new query is received could be calculated as follows

$$\begin{aligned} &crePoss_{ij}^{t}(Subject_m) = f(crePoss_{ij}^{t-1}(Subject_m), crePoss_{ii}^{t}(Subject_{m)}) \\ &\wedge sim(R_i(DP_N, D_K), R_j(DP_N, D_K))) \\ &D_K \in \overline{(R_j(DP_N)} \cap \overline{R}_i(DP_N))\ DP_N \in Subject_m \end{aligned} \tag{3}$$

From the above relation it can be deduced that the crePoss value assigned to a decision maker changes gradually as the knowledge of the others about the decision maker increases.

The $crePoss_{ij}$ values for each subject are kept in a matrix called the assigned credibility possibility matrix, AssCreM, as shown in Figure 1.

$$\begin{bmatrix} crePoss_{11}(Subject_m) & crePoss_{12}(Subject_m) & ... & crePoss_{iN}(Subject_m) \\ crePoss_{21}(Subject_m) & crePoss_{22}(Subject_m) & ... & crePoss_{2N}(Subject_m) \\ & & & \\ crePoss_{N1}(Subject_m) & & & crePoss_{NN}(Subject_m) \end{bmatrix}$$

Fig. 1. Assigned credibility possibility matrix, AssCreM

After the matrix AssCreM is built, each decision maker opinion, $crePos_{ij}$ is influenced by the opinions of the other decision maker N times, where N is the number of decision makers. Credibility assignment to each decision maker can be defined with a fuzzy relation implemented as a max-min composition. At each stage, n+1, the max-min composition influences the opinion of each decision maker, $crePoss_{ij}^{n+1}$, by the others' opinions as follows:

$$crePoss_{ij}^{n+1} = \max\left\{crePoss_{ik} \wedge crePoss_{kj}^{n}\right\} \; k = 1,...,N \quad ,crePoss_{ij}^{1} = crePoss_{ij} \quad (4)$$

Our goal is to gain a possibility distribution for the credibility of the decision makers, using a distributed model. In our distributed model, the credibility of decision maker DM_i, $crePoss_i$, is a function of $crePoss_{ki}$ $k = 1,..,N$, the credibility assigned by DM_k to DM_i, considering $crePoss_k$, the credibility of the decision maker DM_k:

$$crePoss_i = \overline{F}(crePoss_{ki}{}^{N}, crePoss_k), k = 1..N \quad (5)$$

In the above relation $\overline{F}$ indicates the max-min function. To apply the max-min function, a set of equations , $\overrightarrow{crePoss} = AssCreM^{N} \; o \; \overrightarrow{crePoss}$, is obtained where, the vector $\overrightarrow{crePoss} = \langle crePoss_1, crePoss_2, ..., crePoss_N \rangle$ indicates the credibility possibility distribution for the decision makers community; o is the max-min operator and $AssCreM$ is a matrix whose components are the degree of credibility of each decision maker from the point of view of the other decision makers.

Theorem 1: If the decision maker DM_i, increases $crePoss_{ik}$, then from the point of view of DM_i the DM_k's determination capability in determining the credibility of the other decision makers will not be reduced.

Proof: Let the credibility value of the kth decision maker from the point of view of the ith decision maker, $crePoss_{ik}$, changes from α to β such that $\beta \succ \alpha$. In this case, $\alpha \wedge crePoss_{kj}^{t} \leq \beta \wedge crePoss_{kj}^{t}$, where j represents any decision maker in the grid environment. As a result $crePoss_{ik} \wedge crePoss_{kj}^{t}$ will not decrease and the possibility that $\beta \wedge crePoss_{kj}^{t}$ be the maximum value of $\left\{crePoss_{ip} \wedge crePoss_{pj}^{t}\right\}$ $P = 1,....,N$ will increase. Since $crePoss_{kj}^{t}$ indicates the credibility degree of DM_j in judgment of DM_k at the time t, the role of DM_k in determination of the credibility of DM_j will not decrease.

Theorem 2: If $crePoss \; o \; AssCreM = crePoss$ then $crePoss \; o \; AssCreM^{N} = crePoss$ [1].

Considering theorem 2, to work out the value of the credibility vector, $crePoss$, instead of using the relation, $crePoss \; o \; AssCreM^{N} = crePoss$, the relation $crePoss \; o \; AssCreM = crePoss$ can be used to obtain a distribution, $crePoss$. Such a distribution is called stationary distribution.

Example 1: Suppose there are three decision makers $DM = \{DM_1, DM_2, DM_3\}$, a max function, f, and a min function, g. It is desirable to calculate the credibility possibility of the second decision maker such that the condition of the function F, defined above in relation (5), is satisfied.

Using theorem 2 and equation 5, the possibility measure of the second decision maker's credibility computes as follows:

$$crePoss_2 = f(g(crePoss_1, crePoss_{12}), g(crePoss_2, crePoss_{22}), g(crePoss_3, crePoss_{32}))$$

Where $crePoss_1$, $crePoss_2$ and $crePoss_3$ represent the aggregate credibility of the first, second and third decision makers, respectively and $crePoss_{12}$, $crePoss_{22}$, $crePoss_{32}$ is the assigned credibility to the second decision maker by the first, second and third decision makers respectively .

2.2 Solution of the Equation Set

In order to solve the equation set $crePoss\ o\ AssCreM = crePoss$, the fuzzy markov chain model [11] is used. Since $AssCreM$ is a fuzzy transitive matrix, $crePoss$ should be an eigen fuzzy set. Also, since $crePoss$ is a possibility distribution, it is appropriate to obtain the greatest eigen fuzzy set satisfying the equation set $crePoss\ o\ AssCreM = crePoss$.

3 Comparison

In this section, three known criteria for the evaluation of credibility assignment systems are applied to compare our proposed approach with a typical approach which is based upon probability concepts.

1. Ease of extendibility: The total value of credibility probability value assigned to individual decision makers should be one whereas credibility possibility values assigned to decision makers are independent. Therefore, it is more difficult to alter the number of decision makers in a probabilistic based environment.
2. Robustness: Within a probabilistic environment, a small change in weights assigned to decision makers causes a high variation in final credibility values aassigned to decision makers. Suppose $crePoss(\varepsilon) = \begin{bmatrix} 1-\varepsilon & \varepsilon \\ \varepsilon & 1-\varepsilon \end{bmatrix}$ for $(0 \le \varepsilon \prec 1)$. If $\varepsilon = 0$ then $crePoss^*(o) \underline{\underline{\Delta}} \lim_{t\to\infty} CrePoss^t(o) = \begin{bmatrix} 1 & 0 \\ 0 & 1 \end{bmatrix}$ but if ε is small but greater than zero then $crePoss^*(o) \underline{\underline{\Delta}} \lim_{t\to\infty} crePoss^t(\varepsilon) = \begin{bmatrix} 0/5 & 0/5 \\ 0/5 & 0/5 \end{bmatrix} \Rightarrow crePoss^*(o)$ if $\varepsilon \to o$.
   However, applying a possibility approach a small variation in the assigned credibilies causes a minor variation in the final credibility values.

$$crePoss^2(\varepsilon) = crePoss(\varepsilon) o crePoss(\varepsilon) = \begin{bmatrix} \max\{(1-\varepsilon),\varepsilon\} & \max\{\varepsilon,\varepsilon\} \\ \max\{\varepsilon,\varepsilon\} & \max\{\varepsilon,(1-\varepsilon)\} \end{bmatrix}$$

$$= \begin{bmatrix} 1-\varepsilon & \varepsilon \\ \varepsilon & 1-\varepsilon \end{bmatrix} = crePoss(\varepsilon)$$

$$crPoss^*(\in) = \begin{bmatrix} 1-\varepsilon & \varepsilon \\ \varepsilon & 1-\varepsilon \end{bmatrix} \to \begin{bmatrix} 1 & 0 \\ 0 & 1 \end{bmatrix} = crePoss^*(o)$$

3. The order of stationary distribution calculation algorithm in both probabilistic and possibilistic approaches are n^2. Nevertheless, in probabilistic approach, the operators applied to compute stationary distributions are plus and multiplication while, in possibilistic approaches fuzzy 'or' and 'and' operators are applied. Therefore, calculations in possibilistic appraches are faster and cheaper compared with probabilistic approache.

4 Conclusion

In knowledge grid environment there is no centralized credibility determination agent so each decision maker's credibility can be estimated by collecting the others opinion. In this paper, it is suggested to measure the opinions by a possibility value rather than the probability of the credibility when the number of decision makers is variant. In addition, it is proved that the possibility of credibility can tolerate uncertainty more than the probability.

References

[1] K.E. Avrachenkov, E. Sanchez, Fuzzy Markov Chains and Decision-Making, Fuzzy Optimization and decision-making, 1(2) (2002) 143-159.

[2] R.K. Chauhan, Bayesian analysis of reliability and hazard rate function of a mixture model. Microelectronics Reliability. 37 (6) (1997) 935-941.

[3] H. Chung, Fuzzy reliability estimation using Bayesian approach Computers& Industrial Engineering. 46 (2004) 467-493.

[4] F. Delmotte, P. Borne,: Modeling of reliability with possibility theory. IEEE - Transactions on Systems, Man, and Cybernetics. Part A 28 (1) (1998) 78-88.

[5] I. Foster, C. Kesselman, S. Tuecke, The anatomy of the grid: enabling scalable virtual organizations,Intl. J. Supercomputer Appl. 15 (3) (2001) 6-13.

[6] P. Guo, H. Tanaka, M. Inuiguchi, Self-organizing fuzzy aggregation models to rank the objects with multiple attributes. IEEE Transactions on Systems, Man, and Cybernetics, Part A 30 (5) (2000) 573-580.

[7] L. Pipino, Y.W. Lee, R. Y. Wang, Data quality assessment. ACM Communication. 45(4)(2002) 211-218.

[8] A.G. Vassakis, Safety assessment, reliability, and the probability-operation diagram : IEEE Transactions on Reliability, 45 (1) (1996) 90-94

[9] R. Yager, A framework for multi-source data fusion. Inf. Sci. 163(1-3) (2004) 175-200

[10] H. Zhuge, H.Liu, A fuzzy collaborative assessment approach for Knowledge Grid. Future Generation Comp. Syst. 20 (1) (2004) 101-111.

Image Streaming and Recognition for Vehicle Location Tracking Using Mobile Devices

Jin-Suk Kang[1], Taikyeong T. Jeong[2], Sang Hyun Oh[3], and Mee Young Sung[1]

[1] Dept. of Computer Science and Engneering, University of Incheon,
177 Dohwa-dong, Nam-gu, Incheon, 402-749, Korea
{jskang01, mysung}@incheon.ac.kr

[2] Dept. Of Communications Eng, Myongji University,
San 38-2 Namdong, Chuin-ku, Yoingin City, Kyonggi-do, 449-728, Korea
ttjeong@mju.ac.kr

[3] Dept. Of Computer Science Engineering, Yonsei University,
134 Sinchon-Dong, Seodaemun-Gu, Seoul 120-749, Korea
osh@database.yonsei.ac.kr

Abstract. The image of a license plate is scanned by the camera attached to a mobile PDA device and the numbers on the plate are detected by the image processing parts in the proposed Mobile system. Then the numbers and the location of a mobile PDA device are encoded and transmitted along with the location information to a remote server through a wireless communication network. Finally, the server decodes the transmitted data as a text format and transmits it to the destination user. Consequently, this paper contributes a case study on the embedded system for designing of intelligent interface between a moving vehicle and a mobile PDA device, using a spatial relative distance scheme. The experimental results show that detection and tracking of a location of moving vehicle can be conducted efficiently with a mobile PDA device in real-time through wireless communication system and Internet.

Keywords: Image recognition, Mobile device, Vehicle Tracking.

1 Introduction

The progress of computer science and information technology, including the Internet, has rapidly accelerated the spread of the personal computer, and some mobile devices such as handheld PCs (HPCs), PDA's (Personal Digital Assistants) have become widespread aspect of a continuous growth of the Internet Technology business [1]. This allows people to use various services without limits of time and space. Machines like mobile phones and PDAs with electronic control systems work by using small-sized OS (Windows CE, Embedded Linux, pSOS, etc) in ROM, not like a hard disc of normal PC, RAM, etc. are called embedded systems [1, 2].

In this paper, we demonstrate the system for automatically detecting vehicle registration numbers through a device with a digital camera and PDA in an embedded system. First, the system retrieves an area of vehicle registration numbers, detects letters and numbers on the vehicle license plate, and sends it in text format. This is a break from the subjective method of detecting registration numbers after watching vehicles, and lends objectivity to detection of vehicle registration numbers through an

C. Cérin and K.-C. Li (Eds.): GPC 2007, LNCS 4459, pp. 730 – 737, 2007.

image processing algorithm [3]. By processing with digitized images of vehicle registration numbers which it is sometime different to discern with the naked eye, it detects a vehicle registration number accurately. This can be applied to various areas such as prevention of car robberies, security, and in pursuing location because through this, it is possible to refer to information of vehicles and chase locations [4, 5,6].

2 System Platform and Spatial Relative Distance

2.1 Spatial Relative Distance

To provide PDA's movement and locations, an operating server with a location code DB which includes the corresponding location codes to each destinations should be equipped. This server provides terminal clients with vehicle's number related to destination and location code produced from a location code DB through on/off-line. The terminal client transmits the location code referred to the destination including the location code, the destination information and the required contents to an operating server [9]. In addition, global positioning system (GPS) technology is a method of finding out a location by receiving a broadcasted GPS signal from a satellite moving around the Earth. This is used most often to find out general locations. The method of measuring the user's location in real time is to receive the error revised value from various base stations. The information on clock and the orbit of satellite from satellite provide the information on location.[8] Then, correlative distance is calculated after the revised error is calculated. After performing Kalman filtering, the information is provided through the process of measuring the user's location (See Figure 1.) [3].

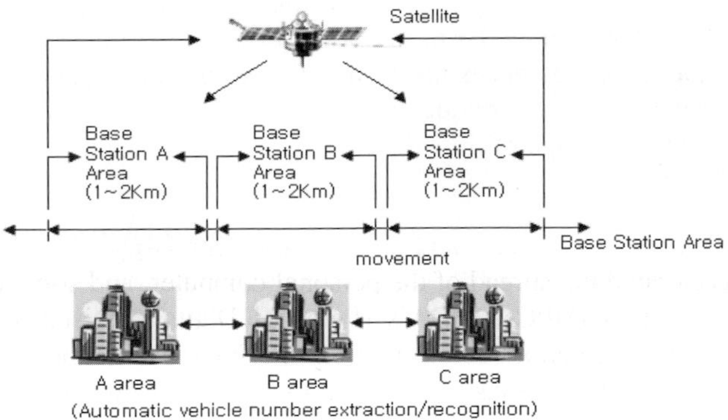

Fig. 1. Base Station Area Location

In Figure 2, the operation server holds member DB, location code DB and geographical positioning DB. All save related information. Here, the location code DB related to the destination is saved. The location code data is organized through a combination of codes set by the service provider, such as information on the longitude and latitude of destination and number requested by user, etc. In geographical positioning DB, various geographical information and location data in relations to the destination are saved. If required, location code DB and geographical positioning DB are not separated, but can be used as in a single combination DB [9, 10].

For the real-time user location measuring method, values with correction for error are received from multiple base stations. Then, clock and satellite orbit information etc. are received from an information satellite. Afterwards, the revised errors are calculated and the correlated distance is estimated. As the next step, Kalman filtering is carried out and user location is measured to provide information [6, 11, 12].

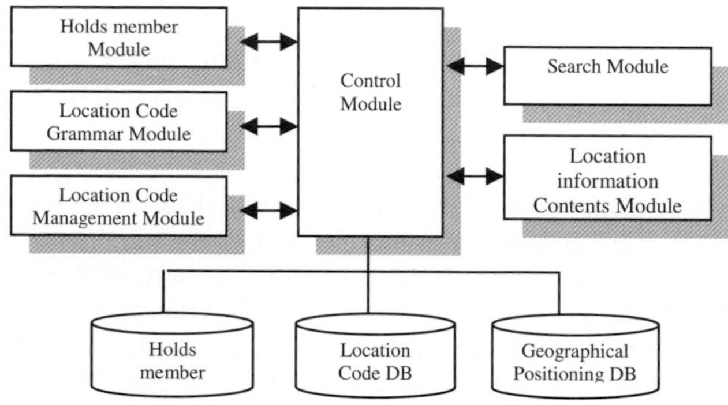

Fig. 2. A Block Diagram of Location Database Structure

2.2 Minimization of Spatial for Information on Location

Figure 3 shows a method to calculate a real time spatial relative distance using a data window, and to position a user of a multi-reference station position information system. When there are three base stations by j, a satellite which provides the information of location, it is necessary to add value through the processes which all the satellites provide, then to divide by the number of satellites, and to perform dispersed processes in a range of time [8].

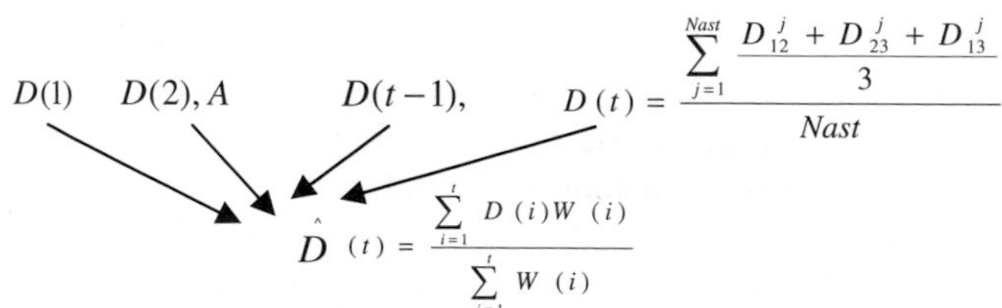

$D(1)$ $D(2), A$ $D(t-1),$
$D(t) = \frac{\sum_{j=1}^{Nast} \frac{D_{12}^{j} + D_{23}^{j} + D_{13}^{j}}{3}}{Nast}$
$\hat{D}(t) = \frac{\sum_{i=1}^{t} D(i)W(i)}{\sum_{i=1}^{t} W(i)}$

Fig. 3. Spatial for Information on Location Relative Distance

Figure 4 shows modeling of the Kalman filter. The Kalman filter receives error compensating values, x_1, x_2 and x_3, from the reference station, and then calculates the error compensating value Vector X [x_1, x_2, x_3] presumed with Raw Data including clock information and satellite orbit information. Here, $X_1, X_2, X_3, \hat{X}, D, \hat{D}, d_{i,j}, \delta$ and R refer to the error compensating value of the user, the error compensating value of reference station, the error compensating value of reference station, presumed X Vector, that is $[X_1, X_2, X_3]$, relative distance. Relative distance in a window, distance between station and j, error variance, and finally noise from measuring process of position information receiver respectively are reviewed [3, 6].

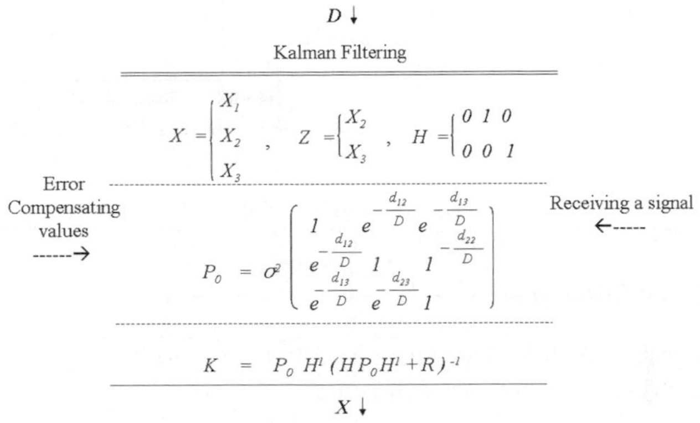

Fig. 4. Modeling of Spatial Relative Distance on Kalman filter

3 Extraction and Recognition of License Plate Image

3.1 Image Expression and PDA

A PDA's memory space is more limited than a general PC's. Therefore, it often has problems in processing the spatial data used in a PC. In general, spatial data is large, and many calculation processes are required to conduct query process among data. In this respect, sequential record memory structure is needed in order to express spatial data in a PDA with extremely limited memory space. Since sequential record structure memorizes data in a certain order, making search query time longer, it may be more efficient to express spatial data by putting index space on image from the PDA camera. [7]. In this case, if you process inputted images and store the data in memory space as a sequential structure, the search time will be longer since a search for domain query is sequentially conducted. In this respect, we express spatial data that went through image process as an index structure. Figure 5 shows that data space is divided into certain size and expressed as an index file in PDA. Here, one record is composed of the index number (Next), MBR domain of spatial object (MBR) and real spatial object data (OBJ). In other words, one record has one object, and the object is stored in the form of a connect list by a record index of the other object in the same cell. Each cell has a structure as an object in a cell pointing to the first node of memorized connect list.

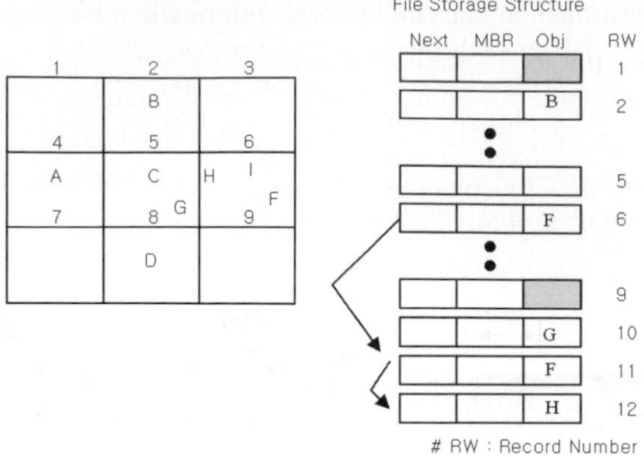

Fig. 5. Mobile PDA Indexed Sequential File Structure

3.2 Image Recognition Stage

The important part of a still image taken by a PDA camera is the algorithm to detect the license plate domain. There are two general methods in use: one to detect license plates using brightness information, and the other to identify characteristics by edge detection and Hough transformation. The first one, however, is overly sensitive to the environment, with a lower recognition rate when there are noises around. The second uses vertical and horizontal components in the license plate domain, with lowered recognition rate and longer processing time in case of damage or noise in plate edge, which is not proper for real time processing. In this paper, we improved the quality of the image through a high-frequency emphasis filter, and extracted the license plate domain through a partial image match using vertical brightness value distribution change and license plate model. During this process, data expression of the transformed image is not memorized in mobile PDA memory space as a sequential structure, but memorized as an index structure in order to provide a more efficient and fat search, extracting characteristics of license plate domain.

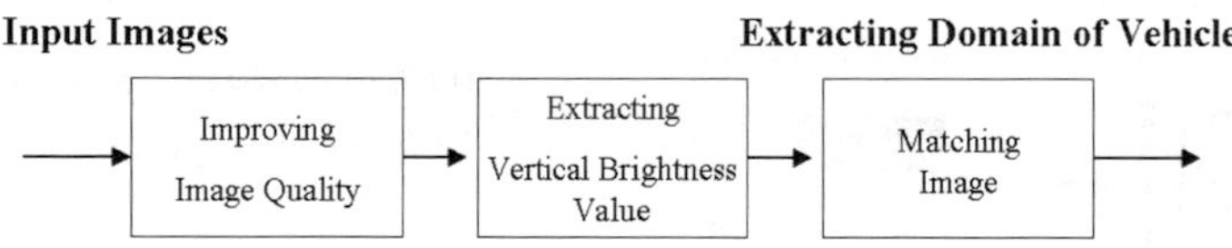

Fig. 6. A Block Diagram of Preprocess Stage

3.2.1 Matching Image with License Plate Model

More than two objects are needed to image match. Here, we match it with the vertical domain extracted before, by using characteristics of the license plate, and make it a binarized license plate model. In this case, we use the following characteristics of the license plate. First, the ratio of the license plate is 2:1 in width and height respectively. Second, letters on the license plate and inside have the contrast brightness value relative to each other. Third, the ratio of the upper part and lower part of license plate is 1:2. Figure 7 shows a relative ratio, which is an original characteristic of license plate. We extract the vertical outline from vertical domain of the vehicle in order to shorten license plate domain extraction time through image match. We then extract by matching license plate model to vehicle candidate domain resulting from studying brightness value distribution. [5].

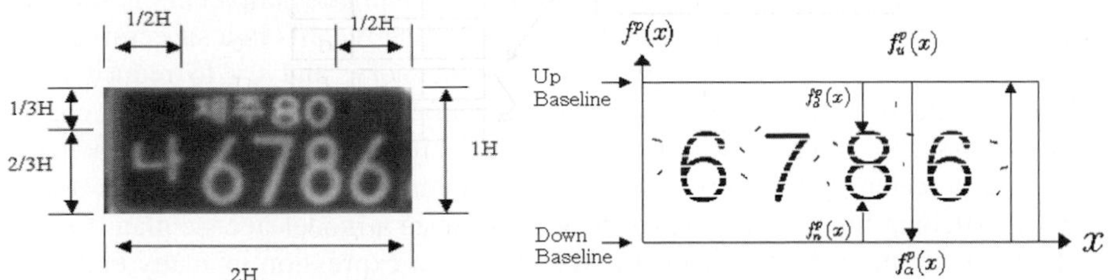

Fig. 7. Relative Ratio of License Plate Domain and Edge Value Extraction

The upper left and bottom right coordinates of a minimum adjacent quadrangle of a connecting factor, are (X_1, Y_2) and (X_2, Y_2) respectively, and we retrieve $f^P(x)$ using the first edge component which is detected in the vertical direction from the upper and bottom standard lines, like Figure 7 with its images formed as edge value.

That is, we calculate a distance $f_u^P(x)$ until the first edge component appears when searching towards the vertical upper direction from the bottom standard line and the distance $f_d^P(x)$ towards the vertical bottom direction from the upper standard line, and send them to a Gaussian filter expressing sign $f_u^P(x)$ and $f_d^P(x)$ added signal $f^P(x) = f_u^P(x) + f_d^P(x)$ to mark them as less sensitive to noise. It is used to detect the local maximum value among values processed through Gaussian filtering. The maximum value is used as the base to process image splitting.

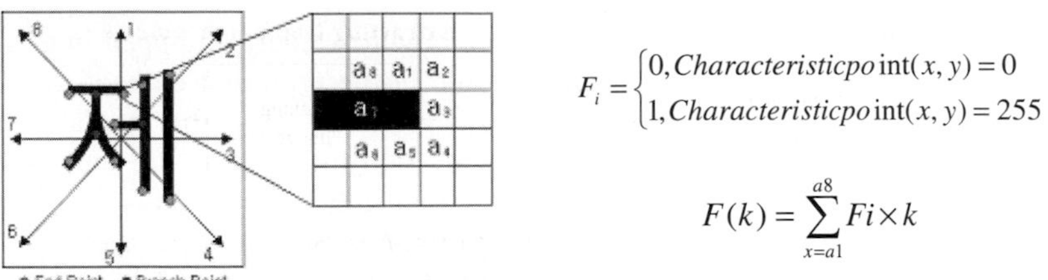

Fig. 8. Improvement of Field Effect Method(FEM)

We apply field effect method (FEM) for efficient recognition, to judge whether there are letters/numbers in the direction of 8 is shown in Figure 8, and to recognize a similarity with a standard pattern. Also, we recognize letters by finding the direction of a characteristic point to learn the location point, [12], and to decide direction by grasping the condition of pixels in Figure 8.

4 Concluding Remarks

This paper discusses an experiment with a gray image of size of 320 × 240 pixels, taken by a PDA camera of HP iPaq 3630model, which has Windows CE operating system and 32MB memory. The extracted result's of numbers and letters is shown in Figure 9. In particular, we reduce search time by sorting records in a successive index structure in an embedded system with limit of memory, and try to reduce to the utmost the rate of error in information on location of a vehicle through chasing location of spatial relative distance. We prove that it is possible to actualize processing procedures of pattern recognition for numbers and letters. This is used in PDA by matching images of stopped image data from a model license plate from an inputted vehicle through PDA camera. We expect an expression of many embedded systems, based on the progress of related applications.

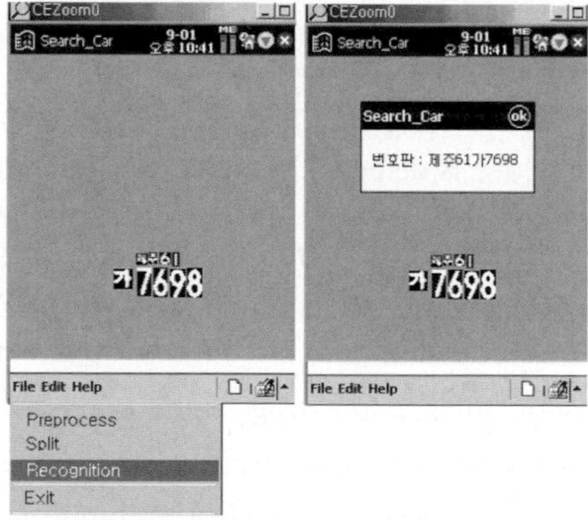

Fig. 9. Extracted Result s of Numbers and Letters

The still image of the license plate is captured by the camera equipped in a mobile PDA device. Then the image processing module in the proposed embedded system extracts the number information from the image data, using the spatial relative distance scheme. After this, the number and location information are encoded and transmitted to a remote sever. At the server, the digitized information is decoded and converted to a text format. Finally, it is sent to the end user by the server through a communication network. In order to handle the space data acquired from a mobile PDA device efficiently, we design an internal storage structure where the location and number information of a vehicle is stored in the unit of variable length record with the successive index to reduce the search time of stored data in an embedded system with the memory limits. In addition, to minimize the error rate of the location information of a vehicle, we propose a method for tracking the location information based on spatial relative distance. With the experimental results, we show that it is adequate to trace the location and to recognize the numbers on the license plate of a vehicle with a small camera attached to a mobile PDA. We have proposed an image processing method and spatial relative distance scheme for use in the wireless communication network and Internet.

Acknowledgement

This work was supported by the 2 Stage Brain Korea 21 Project in 2007 and by grant No. RTI05-03-01 from the Regional Technology Innovation Program of the Ministry of Commerce, Industry and Energy (MOCIE) Republic of Korea.

References

1. J. Feldman, S. Czukerberg, "Notebook System", *US Patent* No. 5553959, 1996.
2. A. John, et. al. Open eBook Publication Structure 1.0.1: Recommended Specification. Technical report, *Open eBook Forum*, http://www.openebook.org/, 2001
3. R. C. Gonzalez and R. E. Woods "Digital Image Processing", *Addison Wesley*, pp. 447~455.
4. A. Antonacopoulos, D. Karatzas and J. Ortiz Lopez, "Accessing textual information embedded in internet images," *Proc. of SPIE*, vol. 4311, pp.198-205, Feb. 2001
5. M. G. He, A. L. Harvey and T. Vinary, "Vehicle number plate location for character recognition", *ACCV'95 2nd Asian Conference on Computer Vision*, pp. 1425~1428, December 5-8, Singapore,
6. Fuhui Long, Hongjiang Zhang and David Dagan Feng, " Fundamentals of Content-Based Image Retrieval", *IEEE Trans. On Image Processing*, Vol.10, No.1, Jan. 2001
7. J. Heiner, S. Hudson, and K. Tanaka, "Linking and Messaging from Real Paper in the Paper PDA", *CHI Letters (Proc. of the ACM Symposium on User Interface Software and Technology)*, vol. 1, no. 1, pp. 179-186, November, 1999.
8. J. S. Kang, C. H. Park, J. H. Kim and Y. S. Choi, "Implementation of Embedded System Vehicle Tracking and License Plates Recognition using Spatial Relative Distance," *Proc. of 26th International Conference on Information Technology Interface,* pp. 167-172, June, 2004
9. J. Hansson and C. Norstrom, "Embedded Database for Embedded Real-Time Systems: A Component-Based Approach", *Technical Report, Linkoping University and Malardalen University*, Sweden, 2002.
10. Mckoi, http://mckoi.com/database/, 2000
11. J. R. Parker, "Algorithms for image processing and computer vision," *John Wiley & Sons, New York*, 1997
12. J. Zhou and D. Lopresti, "Extracting Text form WWW Images", *Proc. of the 4th International Conference on Document Analysis and Recognition (ICDAR'97)*, Ulm, Germany, August 1997
13. R. C. Gonzalez and R. E. Woods, "Digital Image Processing," *Addison Wesley*, pp. 447-455
14. J. Miura, T. Kanda, and Y. Shiral, "An active vision system for real-time traffic sign recognition," In Proc. IEEE International Conference on Intelligent Transportation Systems. Dearborn, MI, USA, 2000.

Research on Planning and Deployment Platform for Wireless Sensor Networks

Yuebin Bai[1], Jinghao Li[1], Qingmian Han[2], Yujun Chen[1], and Depei Qian[1]

[1] School of Computer Science and Engineering, Beihang University, Beijing, China
[2] School of Telecommunications Engineering, Xidian University, Xi'an, China
yuebinb@163.com

Abstract. With the actual applications of the wireless sensor networks growing, the challenges of the actual deployment get more and more. To improve deployment efficiency, reduce the deployment cost and evaluate the deployment risk, a planning and deployment platform for wireless sensor networks has been built. In this paper, the workflow of the planning and deployment platform for wireless sensor networks and its implementation framework are emphasized. The implementation framework, which is based on J-Sim simulator, provides the implementation details of the platform. An integrated workflow for the platform is illuminated to comprehend the framework clearly.

Keywords: Wireless Sensor Networks, Planning, Network Simulation, Performance Evaluation and Optimization, Software Platform.

1 Introduction

Impeded by the bottleneck of the information collection in the information chain, researchers are more and more interested in the development of wireless sensor networks (WSNs). Currently, WSNs have been widely used in fields like habitat monitoring, health-care, smart home, industries, and military [1, 2]. There are various challenges to deploy the above mentioned WSN applications into an actual environment; thereby we propose the planning and deployment platform for WSNs.

WSN has a lot of special characteristics. First, it depends on the actual application itself. Based on different application deployment scenarios, the implementation technique and deployment environment are usually different. Second, there are hundreds of sensor nodes in a WSN. Finally, because of the bandwidth, energy and process capability etc limitations, various errors always occur in the WSN. From above mentioned restrictions, manual deployment of WSN is impossible. So, research work on the methods of WSN planning and a planning and deployment software platform is very important.

To study how to plan a WSN, the WSN should be seen as a whole. Planning and deployment for WSNs focuses on the WSNs collective performance, and the WSNs macroscopically behavior. This study contains several WSNs specific terms, e.g. connectivity, coverage, protocols, and simulation etc.

C. Cérin and K.-C. Li (Eds.): GPC 2007, LNCS 4459, pp. 738–743, 2007.

There are limited literature on planning and deployment for WSNs, but a lot on the WSN simulator. In this paper, a planning and deployment platform for wireless sensor networks is proposed. More specifically, the implementation framework of the platform is introduced to validate the feasibility of the architecture, The framework is based on the open-source J-Sim [3] simulator. In sum, the goal of the platform is to build a planning software platform for wireless sensor network, and it can:

- support WSNs deployment solution
- reduce the deployment cost and improve the efficiency of deployment
- afford the whole network performance evaluation
- test new routing protocols and MAC protocols
- accelerate the WSNs practicality

The paper is organized as the following. Section 2 introduces the workflow. Section 3 presents implementation framework of the platform. Section 4 concludes this paper and presents the future work..

2 The Workflow Analysis of the Platform

In this section, an integrated workflow of the platform is proposed, just like what's shown in figure 1. It helps us to understand the platform clearly and to form an implementation framework of the platform.

The main steps of building a workflow can be described as follows:

Step 1: manually or stochastically place some nodes into the virtual environment, and draw an integrated network topology graph. Initialize some WSN parameters.

Step 2: Validate coverage and determine whether the WSN satisfies the density requirement and whether the sensor nodes are enough. If not, then go back to Step 1 to add some new sensor nodes.

Step 3: Validate connectivity and determine whether the WSN is connective. If not, then go back to Step 1 to modify some nodes' positions. Go through Step1, 2 and d3 until all requirements are satisfied.

Step 4: Choose MAC protocol and routing protocol.

Step 5: Run the simulator.

Step 6: Show the simulation result in terms of visual plots according to the above mentioned performance metrics. Now, users can perform optimization based on the performance results. If the MAC protocol or routing protocol is not suited for the particular WSN application, go back to Step 4 as the dotted line shows Provided that some key nodes' positions are not correct/ideal?,, go back to Step 1 following the dotted line. Once everything is well planed, we can get an optimal WSN deployment solution.

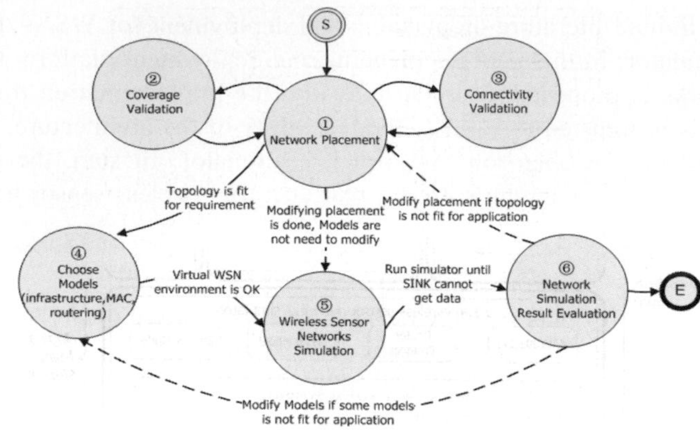

Fig. 1. The Workflow of the Platform

3 The Implementation Framework Design

This section describes the conceptual framework design of the platform. It provides a scalable, highly configurable and practical solution to plan and deploy a real WSN. One of the key features of this architecture is the ability to simulate the actual environment using the J-Sim simulator, thereby ensuring reliable deployment solution. The framework of the platform, shown in Figure 2, implements an integrated process to plan and deploy a real WSN. In the following subsections, these components in details will be given.

3.1 Network Deployment

The network deployment aims to find an optimal placement solution. It contains three main modules, pre-placement, coverage validation and connectivity validation. The pre-placement finishes the placement of the sensor nodes. Users can manually place each node; of course, stochastic placement is needed. Now, quite a lot literature has studies it; in [4], the author proposes three typical types of stochastic sensor placement. Moreover, it has a drag-and-draw graphics user interface (GUI) to help user to operate the network topology.

Except this, the network topology structure should also guarantee the requirement of the coverage and connectivity. Coverage validation helps users to determine whether the number of the nodes is enough, and whether the nodes density and coverage are satisfied. Connectivity validation is to determine the network topology graph connectivity. There is much literature to refer in [5], it shows that each node asymptotically connects with other nodes within a circle area.

3.2 Simulation

To support WSN deployment solution for a real application, it is needed to simulate the WSN and carry out the quantitative analysis of the WSN. So simulation is the fundamental component of the architecture.

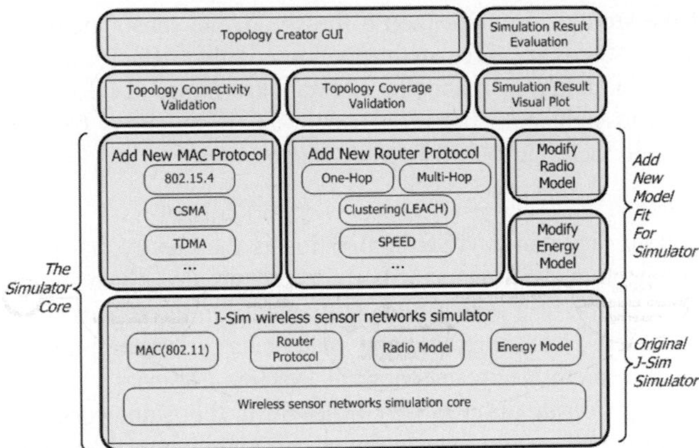

Fig. 2. The Implementation Framework of the Platform

J-Sim is chosen as the simulator for the platform. J-Sim is an open-source, component-based compositional network simulation environment that is developed entirely in Java. J-Sim was chosen due to its loosely-coupled, component-based programming model, as well as its completed Sensor Network packets [6, 7]. The target of simulation is to reproduce the actual WSN in the virtual environment. Therefore, J-Sim divides a WSN into three main types of nodes and two main types of wireless channels: sensor node, target node, and SINK node; sense channel and communication channel [6]. Target node is the stimulation generator of the phenomenon. Sensor node acts as the actual sensor which senses and sends data back to the base station. SINK node acts as the base station. Sensor nodes capture signals generated by target nodes through a sensor channel, and send reports to the SINK nodes or to the next hop sensor node by the communication channel.

J-Sim also includes several kinds of WSN models, such as radio models, energy models, MAC protocol models, and routing protocol models. But just like MAC 802.11 protocol, J-Sim is only a wireless protocol. Not all models are suited for special WSN simulation. To improve the accuracy of simulation, the platform should add some new special WSN models, which is the main work of the platform. The extensions are shown as follows.

A. Protocol models

Just as figure 2 show, the platform adds new MAC protocols; they are 802.15.4, TDMA, CSMA, etc. The platform also adds some new special WSN routing protocols according to different network characteristics. They are One-Hop, Multi-Hop, and Hierarchical (LEACH) [8]. Other well known routing protocols, for example SPEED [9], may be added later.

B. Radio models

All the previous preparation work does not help the platform support environment factor (i.e. assume that there are no obstructions in the environment), so the radio propagation model is needed to ensure the accuracy of simulations. Radio propagation models attempt to predict the received signal strength at a given distance from the transmitter. If the strength is more than a threshold, the sensor begins to receive the packet. In addition, there are three main phenomena that affect wireless communication which should be taken into account. A standard model used to simulate a clear, unobstructed line-to-sight path between two nodes is the Friss free-space equation. More accurate radio model also will be added later.

C. Energy models

The most important factor in a WSN application is the energy, as well as the energy model in the architecture. J-Sim energy model is too simple, which should be extended. The energy consumption of a sensor node is divided into three parts: CPU energy consumption, sense energy consumption, and radio energy consumption. Thanks to the development of the micro-electro-mechanical systems, the sense energy consumption and the CPU energy consumption is very little. So in the framework, the CPU energy consumption and the radio energy consumption are mainly considered. A sensor's CPU can be in one of the following four states: active, idle, sleep and off. Similarly, a sensor's radio also has four states: transmit, receive, idle, and sleep. There are two methods to calculate the energy consumption. The first method is to assign every state a constant value. When there is transferring into a different state, relevant value will be subtracted from the sensor remnant energy.. The second method is to calculate energy according to some equations. For example, in the radio transmit state, energy consumption is in association with the distant between the two nodes. The longer the distant, the more the energy consumption is. This is much flexible than the first one.

4 Conclusions

The platform is a software environment to plan the deployment of the WSN applications. Its target is to identify the application specific requirements, simulate the whole WSN, and then get an optimal deployment solution, including the number of nodes, the type of the node, the placement method, and protocols etc.

In this paper, the two important aspects of planning and deployment platform for WSN are emphasized. The platform is based on simulation technology, and contains a lot of models By extending and modifying the J-Sim, The platform supports many numerical insights by the combination of various protocols. It offers an integrated process for planning an actual deployment. According to the framework, a prototype of the platform has been built. It shows that the platform is reliable and useful. In future work, performance evaluation and optimization of planning and deployment for WSN will be reinforced further. More new protocols and models need be investigated, such as route protocols, environment models, obstacle models, and new radio models etc.

Acknowledgements

This research work is supported by the National Natural Science Foundation of China (granted Nos. 90612004, 90412011, 60673180 and 90104022), and the Co-Funding Project of Beijing Municipal Commission of Education under granted No.SYS100060412. The authors would thank great support.

References

1. Deborah Estrin, Ramesh Govindan, John Heidemann, and Satish Kumar.: Next century challenges: scalable coordination in sensor networks. ACM/IEEE International Conference on Mobile Computing and Networking archive, ACM Press, Seattle, Washington, United States, (1999), pp. 263-270.
2. Sameer Tilak, Nael Abu-Ghazaleh, and Wendi heizelman.: A taxonomy of wireless micro-sensor network models. Mobile Computing and Communications Review, (2002), pp. 28-36.
3. J-Sim Homepage. http://www.j-sim.org. (2005).
4. Ishizuka. M, Aida. M.: Performance study of node placement in sensor networks. Proc. IEEE ICDCSW'04, (2004), pp. 598-603.
5. P. Gupta and P. R. Kumar.: Critical power for asymptotic connectivity. Proceedings of the 37th IEEE Conference on Decision and Control, (1998), pp. 1106-1110.
6. Ahmed Sobeih, Wei-Peng Chen, Jennifer C.Hou, Lu-Chuan Kung, Ning Li, Hyuk Lim, Hung-Ying Yyan, and honghai Zhang.: J-Sim: A simulation and emulation environment for wireless sensor networks. http://www.j-sim.org/v1.3/sensor/JSim.pdf, (2005).
7. Sung Park, Andreas Savvides, and Mani B. Srivastava.: SensorSim: A Simulation Framework for Sensor Networks. Proceeding of the 3rd ACM international workshop on Modeling, analysis and simulation of wireless and mobile systems, Boston, MA, (2000).
8. W. B. Heinzelman, A. P. Chandrakasan, and H. Balakrishnan.: An Application-Specific Protocol Architecture for Wireless Microsensor Networks. IEEE Trans. Wireless Communications, Oct. (2002), pp 660-670.
9. He T, Stankovic J A, Lu C, Abdelzaher T F.: SPEED: A stateless protocol for real-time communication in sensor networks. In Proc 23rd Int'l Conf on Distributed Computing Systems, Providence, Rhode Island. (2003).

Server-Side Parallel Data Reduction and Analysis

Daniel L. Wang, Charles S. Zender, and Stephen F. Jenks

University of California, Irvine, Irvine, CA 92697
{wangd,zender,sjenks}@uci.edu

Abstract. Geoscience analysis is currently limited by cumbersome access and manipulation of large datasets from remote sources. Due to their data-heavy and compute-light nature, these analysis workloads represent a class of applications unsuited to a computational grid optimized for compute-intensive applications. We present the Script Workflow Analysis for MultiProcessing (SWAMP) system, which relocates data-intensive workflows from scientists' workstations to the hosting datacenters in order to reduce data transfer and exploit locality. Our colocation of computation and data leverages the typically reductive characteristics of these workflows, allowing SWAMP to complete workflows in a fraction of the time and with much less data transfer. We describe SWAMP's implementation and interface, which is designed to leverage scientists' existing script-based workflows. Tests with a production geoscience workflow show drastic improvements not only in overall execution time, but in computation time as well. SWAMP's workflow analysis capability allows it to detect dependencies, optimize I/O, and dynamically parallelize execution. Benchmarks quantify the drastic reduction in transfer time, computation time, and end-to-end execution time.

1 Introduction

Despite the frenetic pace of technology advancement towards faster, better, and cheaper hardware, terascale data reduction and analysis remain elusive for most. Disk technology advances now enable scientists to store such data volumes locally, but long-haul network bandwidth considerations all but prohibit frequent terascale transfers. Bell et al. have noted that downloading data for computation is worthwhile only if the analysis involves more than 100,000 CPU cycles per byte of data, meaning that a 1GB dataset is only worth downloading if analysis requires 100 teracycles, or nearly 14 hours on a 2GHz CPU [1]. A typical case of evaluating global temperature change in 10 years requires averaging 8GB down to 330KB, and takes just 11 minutes to compute on a modern workstation, after spending over half an hour to download the input data over a speedy 30Mbits/s link. In data-intensive scientific analysis, data volume rather than CPU speed drives throughput, pointing to a need for a system that colocates computation with data.

Our Script Workflow Analysis for Multi-Processing (SWAMP) system provides a facility for colocating comput ation with data sources, leveraging shell

C. Cérin and K.-C. Li (Eds.): GPC 2007, LNCS 4459, pp. 744–750, 2007.

script-based analysis methods to specify details through an interface piggy-backed over the Data Access Protocol (DAP) protocol [2]. Scripts of netCDF Operator (NCO) [3] commands are sent through an interface extended from DAP's subsetting facility and processed by a server-side execution engine. Resultant datasets may be retrieved in the same DAP request or deferred for later retrieval. The SWAMP execution engine additionally parses scripts for data-dependencies and exploits parallelism opportunities from the extracted workflow. By melding a computation service with a data hosting service, SWAMP eliminates data movement inefficiencies that are not addressed in current frameworks, which treat high data volume and high computational intensity as separate problems.

2 Background

The Grid computing field continues to grow rapidly in both hardware and software infrastructure. Computational grids offer highly parallel and distributed heterogeneous computing resources bound together by open standards, implemented by middleware such as the Globus Toolkit [4]. These grids are able to flexibly allocate resources and appropriately schedule generic applications, but are targeted towards large, compute-limited applications, such as grand challenges [5,6] where input data locality is not a primary scheduling concern. The Globus toolkit for grid systems allows users to define input and output files to be staged to and from compute nodes [7], but, as a generic system, does not detect when data movement costs exceed computational costs.

The Pegasus framework [8,9,10] leverages grid technology for complex data-dependent scientific workflows. Scientists use tools to specify workflows as directed acyclic task graphs containing data dependencies. Pegasus implements advanced resource allocation and locality-aware scheduling, but does not integrate with data services or apply automatic dependence extraction. Its locality-aware scheduling makes it worth considering for SWAMP backend processing.

Data grids focus on providing legible accessibility to terascale and petascale datasets with computational service limited to simple subsetting, if available. The Open-source Project for a Network Data Access Protocol (OPeNDAP) server serves a significant fraction of available geoscience data [2], and is the data service with which SWAMP integrates. The Earth System Grid II (ESG) project provides data via a later version of OPeNDAP (Hyrax), and is in the process of exploring the implementation of filtering servers that permit data to be processed and reduced closer to its point of residence [11]. We are exploring integration of SWAMP with ESG II data services. Other systems such as [12] [13] [14] exist to process or serve data in the geosciences data, but SWAMP differs from these projects in its shell-script interface and its focus on a class of application workflows that are data-intensive and compute-light.

3 Overview of SWAMP

The goal of the SWAMP system is to bring casual terascale computing to the average scientist. "Casual" implies that the system's interface must encourage everyday usage, while "terascale" implies that the system's design must support terabyte data volumes. SWAMP is designed to support scientists' everyday shell scripts and supports high data volumes by shifting computation to data sources, trading expensive long-haul WAN bandwidth for relatively cheap LAN bandwidth. Computation efficiency is further enhanced by detecting and exploiting operator parallelization and I/O optimization opportunities in the scripted workflows. SWAMP differs from existing systems in its focus on a shell-script-based interface, aiming to derive data dependencies automatically with as little help from the scientist as possible. SWAMP also differs in its focus on data-intensive, compute-light workflows, targeting a class of data-heavy workflows where I/O, rather than CPU considerations dominate the decision to distribute computation.

3.1 Shell-Script Interface

The netCDF Operators (NCO) [15] are popular in the geoscience community for their ability to process gridded data at the granularity of files or sets of files, rather than single variables. This coarse granularity is crucial for practical analysis of the high volumes of data commonly resulting from satellite/surface measurements or Earth simulation runs. Because of their efficiency and ease at this scale, scientists commonly use compositions of these *operators* to describe their data analysis in shell scripts. SWAMP is unique in its ability to automatically parallelize shell-script execution through a custom parser that understands NCO command-line options and parameters. Special tags to flag intermediate (temporary) and output filenames are the only modifications needed. The resulting syntax, a subset of Bourne shell syntax, becomes a domain-specific language whose primitives are application binaries operating on files in a filesystem instead of variables in memory.

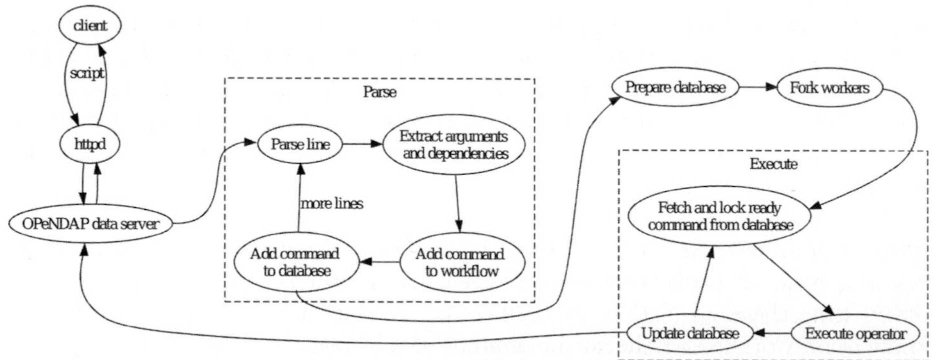

Fig. 1. SWAMP operation

3.2 Parallel Execution Engine

SWAMP scripts are processed on an execution engine implemented as an OPeNDAP data handler. This execution engine parses the user script for basic correctness and dataflow information, and manages execution of the script commands, optionally detecting and exploiting parallelism where available. Filenames are remapped to server-configured paths, and commands involving remote files are split into fetch and execute commands, allowing download to be overlapped with execution. Figure 1 summarizes parsing and execution in SWAMP.

Experience has shown that real scientific workflow scripts exhibit significant script-line-level parallelism. To exploit this, SWAMP builds a dependency tree at parse time. Initially, the only commands ready to execute are the tree roots, but as commands finish, dependent commands which have no unfinished parents become ready as well. After parsing, SWAMP forks off worker processes to begin parallel script execution. Workers cooperate in a peer model, communicating and preventing duplicate work by updating execution state in a shared relational database, currently SQLite. Thus, we can satisfy n-wide execution as long as n commands are ready to execute. SWAMP's SQLite database is stored in a standard Linux tmpfs RAM-based filesystem. Originally, the database was stored on standard disk, but performance suffered greatly due to I/O contention in concurrent execution modes.

4 Results

4.1 Test Setup

We tested our system with a script that resamples Community Atmospheric Model simulation data into time-steps that can be better compared against observed NASA Quick Scatterometer (QuikSCAT) data [16]. In this script, ten years of data at 20-minute timesteps are masked for their surface wind speed values at 6:00AM and 6:00PM, the local times from the QuikSCAT satellite passes. The script contains over 14,000 NCO command-lines for masking, averaging, concatenating, and editing, which produce 228MB of resultant data from 8230MB of input data, and generate 26GB of temporary intermediate files in the process.

We tested our system on a dual Opteron 270 with 16GB of memory with dual 500GB SATA drives in RAID 1, running CentOS 4.3 Linux. Figure 2 summarizes the test results. Transfer times listed are estimated assuming 3MBytes/s ($3*2^{20}$) bandwidth, based on NPAD *pathdiag* [17] measurement of 30Mbits/s bandwidth between UCI and the National Center for Atmospheric Research(NCAR). In our example, a scientist can avoid downloading nearly 8GB, obtaining just 228MB of output rather than the entire input dataset and saving 46 minutes of transfer time. Our baseline case shows the execution time of the original shell script and the time to download the input data, and takes 99 minutes overall.

4.2 Performance Gain

Test results are summarized in Figure 2. Figure 2(b) shows that SWAMP's overhead over baseline is slight, with parse and script analysis increasing computational time by 14% (1 worker case, no opt), but more than compensated when I/O optimization is enabled. Figure 2(a) shows the domination of transfer time savings, along with the parallezation benefit that is only through SWAMP's unique script dependency extraction. Parallelization easily saturates the test system's four CPU cores, bringing overall time from 99 minutes without SWAMP to 16 minutes with SWAMP configured for four workers, giving a 6x performance gain.

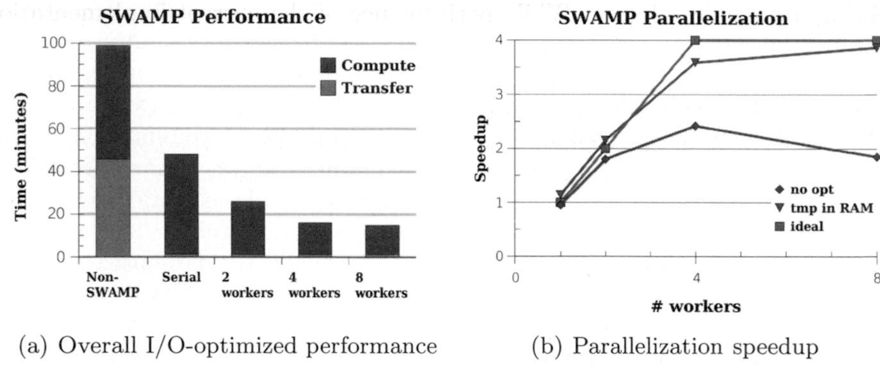

(a) Overall I/O-optimized performance (b) Parallelization speedup

Fig. 2. SWAMP performance

4.3 I/O Optimization

In Figure 2(b), we compare the performance of SWAMP with varying numbers of worker processes and toggling intermediate file optimization. Heavy I/O contention was obvious in early testing, leading to our development of a mechanism for explicitly storing intermediate files in a tmpfs (ramdisk-backed) filesystem rather than a disk-backed filesystem. Referring to Figure 2(b), we see that the performance degradation with a disk-backed filesystem at 8 workers is significant ($\approx$24% relative to 4 workers), but eliminated by our I/O optimization. With this simple optimization, we see SWAMP's performance closely tracking an ideal speedup curve.

4.4 Summary

Our system targets scientists with compute capacity or network connectivity less than what a data center offers, which we believe should include most scientists. Data centers should benefit as well from reduced external network usage, which is often more costly than computational capacity. Our tests quantify the significant savings in bandwidth usage and the corresponding transfer time due to the relocation of computation off the desktop. Our tests also show the potential performance increase which is enabled by simple analysis of scripts.

5 Conclusion

A server-side data reduction and analysis system saves scientists time and bandwidth, enabling them to exploit potentially greater computing resources with minimal additional effort. We have leveraged existing script-based methods of analysis and the widely used DAP protocol to provide simple distributed computing to non-computer-scientists. Combining computation with data services has drastically reduced network transfer, and exploiting script-level parallelism has yielded linear speedup with CPU count, thus yielding a 6 times performance improvement in our test. Our tests have also shown the importance of I/O issues in data intensive workflows, quantifying the performance degradation and offering a possible solution. While performance of the current implementation already provides a significant speedup, future implementations will further exploit clustering and parallelism available at the data center, further enhancing performance. Systems such as ours that colocate computation with data will be well poised to meet the demands of more comprehensive, more detailed, and more frequent analyses, and will facilitate data-intensive science.

Acknowledgments

The authors would like to thank Scott Capps, whose research makes use of the above workflow. This research is supported by the National Science Foundation under Grants ATM-0231380 and IIS-0431203.

References

1. Bell, G., Gray, J., Szalay, A.: Petascale computational systems. IEEE Computer **39**(1) (2006) 110–112
2. Cornillon, P.: OPeNDAP: Accessing data in a distributed, heterogeneous environment. Data Science Journal **2** (2003) 164–174
3. Zender, C.S.: netCDF Operators (NCO) for analysis of self-describing gridded geoscience data. Submitted to Environ. Modell. Softw. (2006) Available from `http://dust.ess.uci.edu/ppr/ppr_Zen07.pdf`.
4. Foster, I., Kesselman, C.: The Grid: Blueprint for a New Computing Infrastructure. Morgan Kaufmann, San Francisco, CA (1998)
5. Feigenbaum, E.A.: Some challenges and grand challenges for computational intelligence. J.ACM **50**(1) (2003) 32–40
6. Gray, J.: What next?: A dozen information-technology research goals. J.ACM **50**(1) (2003) 41–57
7. Foster, I., Kesselman, C.: Globus: A Metacomputing Infrastructure Toolkit. International Journal of Supercomputer Applications **11**(2) (1997) 115–128
8. Maechling, P., Chalupsky, H., Dougherty, M., Deelman, E., Gil, Y., Gullapalli, S., Gupta, V., Kesselman, C., Kim, J., Mehta, G., Mendenhall, B., Russ, T., Singh, G., Spraragen, M., Staples, G., Vahi, K.: Simplifying construction of complex workflows for non-expert users of the southern california earthquake center community modeling environment. SIGMOD Rec. **34**(3) (2005) 24–30

9. Singh, G., Deelman, E., Mehta, G., Vahi, K., Su, M.H., Berriman, G.B., Good, J., Jacob, J.C., Katz, D.S., Lazzarini, A., Blackburn, K., Koranda, S.: The pegasus portal: web based grid computing. In: SAC '05: Proceedings of the 2005 ACM symposium on Applied computing, New York, NY, USA, ACM Press (2005) 680–686
10. Deelman, E., Singh, G., Su, M.H., Blythe, J., Gil, Y., Kesselman, C., Mehta, G., Vahi, K., Berriman, G.B., Good, J., Laity, A., Jacob, J.C., Katz, D.S.: Pegasus: A framework for mapping complex scientific workflows onto distributed systems. Scientific Programming **13**(3) (2005) 219–238
11. Bernholdt, D., Bharathi, S., Brown, D., Chanchio, K., Chen, M., Chervenak, A., Cinquini, L., Drach, B., Foster, I., Fox, P., Garcia, J., Kesselman, C., Markel, R., Middleton, D., Nefedova, V., Pouchard, L., Shoshani, A., Sim, A., Strand, G., Williams, D.: The earth system grid: Supporting the next generation of climate modeling research. Proceedings of the IEEE **93**(3) (2005) 485–495
12. Abramson, D., Kommineni, J., McGregor, J.L., Katzfey, J.: An atmospheric sciences workflow and its implementation with web services. Future Gener. Comput. Syst. **21**(1) (2005) 69–78
13. Woolf, A., Haines, K., Liu, C.: A Web Service Model for Climate Data Access on the Grid. International Journal of High Performance Computing Applications **17**(3) (2003) 281–295
14. Chen, L., Agrawal, G.: Resource allocation in a middleware for streaming data. In: Proceedings of the 2nd workshop on Middleware for grid computing, New York, NY, USA, ACM Press (2004) 5–10
15. Zender, C.S.: NCO User's Guide, version 3.1.4. http://nco.sf.net/nco.pdf (2006)
16. Tsai, W.Y., Spencer, M., Wu, C., Winn, C., Kellogg, K.: SeaWinds on QuikSCAT: Sensor Description and Mission Overview. In: Proceedings of the IEEE International Geoscience and Remote Sensing Symposium. Volume 3., Honolulu, HI (2000) 1021–1023
17. Mathis, M., Heffner, J., Reddy, R.: Web100: extended tcp instrumentation for research, education and diagnosis. SIGCOMM Comput. Commun. Rev. **33**(3) (2003) 69–79

Parallel Edge Detection on a Virtual Hexagonal Structure

Xiangjian He, Wenjing Jia, Qiang Wu, and Tom Hintz

Computer Vision and Visualization Research Group
University of Technology, Sydney
Australia
{sean, wejia, wuq, hintz}@it.uts.edu.au

Abstract. This paper presents an edge detection method based on bilateral filtering taking into account both spatial closeness and intensity similarity of pixels in order to preserve important visual cues provided by edges and reduce the sharpness of transitions in intensity values as well. In addition, the edge detection method proposed in this paper is achieved on sampled images represented on a newly developed virtual hexagonal structure. Due to the compact and circular nature of the hexagonal lattice, a better quality edge map is obtained. We also present a parallel implementation for edge detection on the virtual hexagonal structure that significantly increases the computation speed.

Keywords: Edge detection, parallel processing, image analysis, Gaussian filtering, hexagonal image structure.

1 Introduction

In 1986, Canny [1] developed an optimal edge detection scheme using linear filtering with a Gaussian kernel to suppress noise and reduce the sharpness of transition in intensity values. In order to recover missing weak edge points and eliminate false edge points, two edge strength thresholds are set to examine all the candidate edge points. Those below the lower threshold are marked as non-edge. Those which are above the lower threshold and can be connected to points whose edge strengths are above the higher threshold through a chain of edge points are marked as edge points [2]. However, the performance of Canny edge detection relies on Gaussian filtering. Gaussian filtering not only removes image noise and suppresses image details but also weakens the edge information [2]. In this paper, an additional filter called range filter [3] is combined with the conventional Gaussian filter to get a bilateral filter in order to reduce the blur effect using the Gaussian filter only. Moreover, the success of Canny edge detection is often limited when it comes to curved features. In this paper, a new edge detection algorithm is implemented on a virtual hexagonal structure, which was only introduced recently in [4]. Hexagonal lattice promises better efficiency and less aliasing [5].

In the past years, we have seen an ever-growing flood of data, particularly visual data. This causes an increasing need to process large data sets quickly. In particular, for real-time image processing, the useful information always feeds into the system instantly and is required to be processed in real-time too. One solution for high-performance image processing is through a parallel or distributed implementation. In this paper, we introduce parallel edge detection on a hexagonal image structure.

C. Cérin and K.-C. Li (Eds.): GPC 2007, LNCS 4459, pp. 751 – 756, 2007.

2 A Virtual Hexagonal Structure

Hexagonal grids have higher degrees of symmetry than the square grids. This symmetry results in a considerable saving of both storage and computation time [5, 6]. Sheridan [7] proposed a one-dimensional addressing scheme for a hexagonal structure, called Spiral Architecture, as shown in Fig. 1 and Fig. 2.

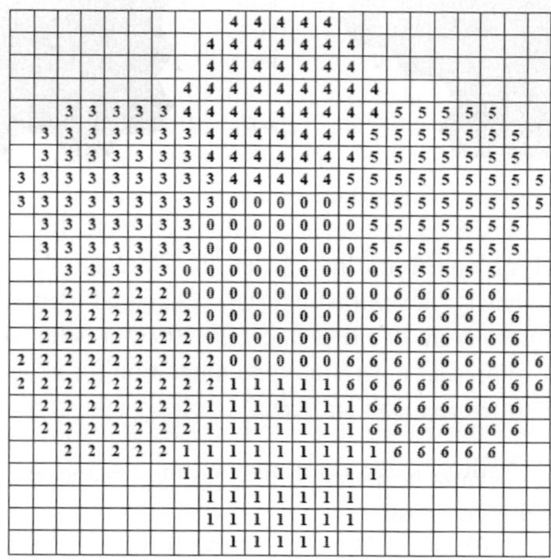

Fig. 1. A cluster of seven hexagonal pixels [9]

In this section, we introduce a software approach to the construction of a hexagonal structure [4]. To construct hexagonal pixels, each square pixel is first separated into 7×7 small pixels, called *sub-pixels*. The light intensity for each of these sub-pixels is set to be the same as that of the pixel from which the sub-pixels are separated. Each virtual hexagonal pixel is formed by 56 sub-pixels as shown in Fig. 1. The light intensity of each constructed hexagonal pixel is computed as the average of the intensities of the 56 sub-pixels forming the hexagonal pixel. Fig. 1 shows a collection of seven hexagonal pixels constructed with spiral addresses from 0 to 6.

In order to arrange hexagonal pixels also in rows and columns as seen in square structure, we review the definitions of rows and columns [8] below. Let R and C represent the number of rows and number of columns needed to move from the central hexagonal pixel to the hexagonal pixel containing the given sub-pixel taking into account the moving direction corresponding to the signs of R and C. Here, pixels on the same column are on the same vertical line. The row with R = 0 consists of the pixels on the horizontal line passing the central pixel and on the columns with even C values, and the pixels on the horizontal line passing the pixel with address 3 and on the columns with odd C values. Other rows are formed in the same way. Fig. 2 shows columns and rows in a hexagonal structure consisting of 49 hexagons.

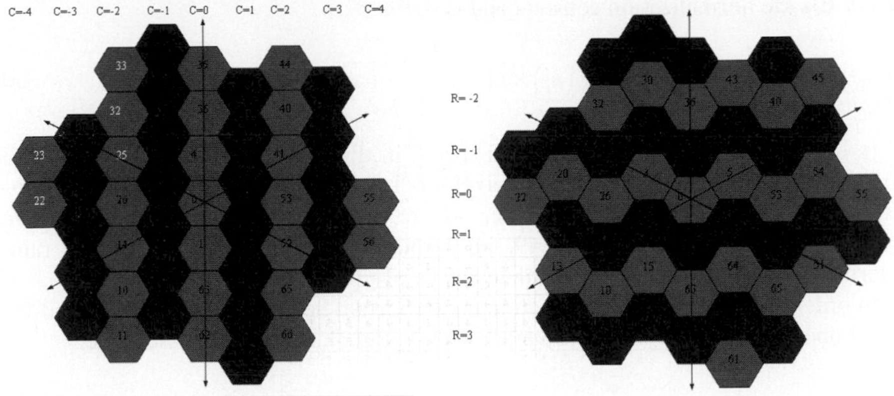

Fig. 2. Columns and rows on a hexagonal structure

3 Edge Detection

In this section, the performance of edge detection will go through three steps: noise filtering using a bilateral filter, edge detection using Sobel operator and edge refining using thresholds.

Before the edge map of an image is found, it is common that image noise is removed (or suppressed) by applying a filter that blurs or smoothes the image. One commonly used filter is implemented by convolution of the original image function with a Gaussian kernel as defined in Equation (2) below. In order to achieve a more desirable level of smoothing in applications, a bilateral filter has recently been introduced as shown in [2]. In this form of filtering, a *range filter* is combined with a *domain filter*. We explain how a bilateral filter works using mathematical terms as follows [2]. Let $f:\Re^2 \rightarrow \Re$ be the original brightness function of an image which maps the coordinates of a pixel, (x, y) to a value in light intensity. Let a_0 be the reference pixel. Then, for any given pixel a at location (x, y), the coefficient assigned to intensity value $f(a)$ at a for the range filter is $r(a)$ computed by the similarity function s as:

$$r(a)=s\left(f(a),f(a_0)\right)=e^{-\frac{(f(a)-f(a_0))^2}{2\sigma_1^2}} \tag{1}$$

Similarly, the coefficient assigned for the domain filter is $g(a)$ computed by the closeness function c as:

$$g(a)=c(a,a_0)=e^{-\frac{(a-a_0)^2}{2\sigma_2^2}} \tag{2}$$

Therefore, for the reference pixel a_0, its new intensity value, denoted by $h(a_0)$, is

$$h(a_0)=k^{-1}\sum_{i=0}^{n-1} f(a_i)\times g(a_i)\times r(a_i) \tag{3}$$

where k is the normalization constant and is defined as

$$k = \sum_{i=0}^{n-1} g(a_i) \times r(a_i) \tag{4}$$

In order to increase the computation speed, in this paper, σ_2 is set to be 1 and the convolution window is set to be a 49 pixel block (assuming the distance between two adjacent square pixels is 1) on either square or hexagonal structure. Hence, for formula (3) and (4) above, $n = 49$. Furthermore, σ_1, the parameter for the range filtering, is computed as the standard deviation of grey values in input image.

In order to implement edge detection on the virtual hexagonal structure, a modified Sobel operator, as presented in [2] and shown in Fig. 3, is applied in this paper.

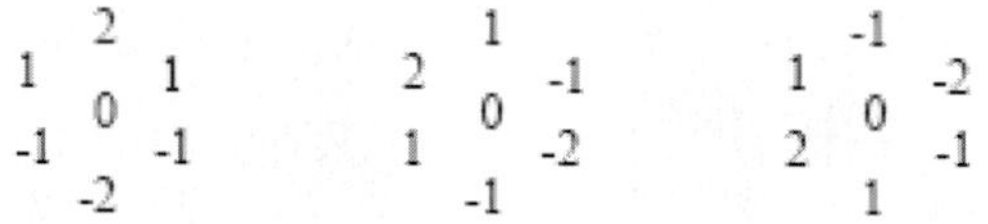

2 1 -1
1 1 2 -1 1 -2
0 0 0
-1 -1 1 -2 2 -1
-2 -1 1

Fig. 3. Modified Sobel operator

After the edge detection step shown in Subsection 3.2, all sub-pixels have been assigned new intensity values that show the edge sub-pixels and their strengths. An edge map on the original square structure can hence be obtained by simply computing the intensity value of every square pixel as the average of the intensities of the sub-pixels constituting thc square pixel. This edge map shows the square edge pixels and their strengths. We can then follow the remaining steps of Canny's method to obtain the final edge map by using one lower threshold and one higher threshold.

For parallel computation, a completed object image was partitioned into 56 parts dependent on location of sub-pixel in each virtual hexagonal pixel (See Fig. 1). A parallel algorithm for edge detection can then be implemented using Master-Slave model and presented as follows.

1) Master node imports the original image from the file and converts it into the virtual hexagonal structure;
2) Master node partitions the image on the virtual hexagonal structure into 56 sub-images with the similar sub-image size;
3) Seven child processes in the master node deliver every 8 sub-images to a specific slave node individually;
4) Each slave node processes the assigned 8 sub-images using bi-lateral filtering as shown in Section 3 to smooth sub-images, and the Sobel operator defined in Section 3 to compute the edge intensities and strengths of all sub-pixels on the sub-images;
5) Master node collects the smoothed results with edge intensities and strengths from slave nodes and makes up the final edge detection results through the edge refining step shown in Section 3.

4 Experimental Results

A 8-bit grey level Lena image of size 256×256 is chosen as our sample image to be processed (see Fig. 4(a)). Three different edge maps are produced in order to demonstrate the performance both in accuracy and speed improved by new edge detection method. The first edge map is obtained after the bilateral filtering but based on square structure using sequential approach. The second and the third edge maps are obtained after the bilateral filtering based on the virtual hexagonal structure. The second edge map is created using sequential approach as shown in [9], and the third edge map is produced using parallel approach as sown in Section 4. It is found that σ_1 is close to 65 for all three cases. The higher threshold used is 0.125 and the lower threshold is 0.05.

(a) Original Lena image

(b) Edge map after bilateral on square

(c) Edge map after bilateral filtering on hex

(d) Edge map after parallel bilateral filtering on hex

Fig. 4. Edge maps of the filtered images

Fig. 4(c) demonstrates a better performance than Fig. 4(b) for detecting edges in diagonal directions. This can be seen from the lip edges in Fig. 4(c) that are closer to real lip boundaries. Fig. 4(d) shows an improved edge map with clearer edges and less dotted edge points compared with the map in Fig. 4(c). This is mainly because different (though similar) σ_1 values are computed and used for different sub-images when using parallel algorithm introduced in this paper.

The processing time for edge detection is also decreased from about 10 seconds using a single PC (Pentium 1.1GHz CPU with 760MB RAM) down to 5 seconds under parallel (or distributed) processing using 8 PCs with similar specifications.

5 Conclusions

In this paper, a parallel edge detection method is presented. The use of bilateral filtering combined with the advantages of hexagonal image architecture has achieved encouraging edge detection performance under the similar experimental conditions. We take the advantages of higher degree of symmetry and equality of distances to neighbouring pixels that are special to hexagonal structure for better performance of image filtering and more accurate computation of gradients including edges and their strength. Compared with the sequential processing, distributed (and parallel) processing really improves the edge performance.

References

1. J. F. Canny, "A Computational Approach to Edge Detection", *IEEE Trans. On Pattern Analysis and Machine Intelligence*, vol. PAMI-8, pp. 679-698, Nov. 1986.
2. Qiang Wu, Xiangjian He and Tom Hintz, "Bilateral Filtering Based Edge Detection on Hexagonal Architecture", *Proc. 2005 IEEE International Conference on Acoustics, Speech, and Signal Processing*, Philadelphia, PA, USA, Volume II, 2005, pp.713-716.
3. D. Barash, "Fundamental relationship between bilateral filtering, adaptive smoothing, and the nonlinear diffusion equation", *IEEE Transactions on Pattern Analysis and Machine Intelligence*, vol. 24, pp. 844-847, 2002.
4. Xiangjian He, Tom Hintz, Qiang Wu, Huaqing Wang and Wenjing Jia "A New Simulation of Spiral Architecture", *International Conference on Image Processing, Computer Vision and Pattern Recognition*, June, 2006, pp. 570-575.
5. R. M. Mersereau, "The Processing of Hexagonally Sampled Two-Dimensional Signals", *Proc. the IEEE*, Vol. 67, pp. 930-949, 1979.
6. I. Her, "Geometric Transformations on the Hexagonal Grid", *IEEE Trans. on Image Processing*, vol. 4, 1995.
7. P. Sheridan, T. Hintz, and D. Alexander, "Pseudo-invariant Image Transformations on a Hexagonal Lattice", *Image and Vision Computing*, vol. 18, pp. 907-917, 2000.
8. Xiangjian He, Huaqing Wang, Namho Hur, Wenjing Jia, Qiang Wu, Jinwoong Kim, and Tom Hintz, "Uniformly Partitioning Images on Virtual Hexagonal Structure", *9th International Conference on Control, Automation, Robotics and Vision*, ICARCV 2006, Singapore, December 2006, pp.891-896.
9. Xiangjian He, Wenjing Jia, Namho Hur, Qiang Wu, Jinwoong Kim and Tom Hintz, "Bilateral Edge Detection on a Virtual Hexagonal Structure", *Lecture Notes in Computer Science* (ISVC2006), LCNS, Springer, 2006, Vol.4292, pp.1092-1101.

Author Index

Printing: Mercedes-Druck, Berlin
Binding: Stein + Lehmann, Berlin

Lecture Notes in Computer Science

For information about Vols. 1–4361

please contact your bookseller or Springer

Vol. 4483: C. Baral, G. Brewka, J. Schlipf (Eds.), Logic Programming and Nonmonotonic Reasoning. IX, 327 pages. 2007. (Sublibrary LNAI).

Vol. 4480: A. LaMarca, M. Langheinrich, K.N. Truong (Eds.), Pervasive Computing. XIII, 369 pages. 2007.

Vol. 4464: E. Dawson, D.S. Wong (Eds.), Information Security Practice and Experience. XIII, 361 pages. 2007.

Vol. 4463: I. Măndoiu, A. Zelikovsky (Eds.), Bioinformatics Research and Applications. XV, 653 pages. 2007. (Sublibrary LNBI).

Vol. 4462: D. Sauveron, K. Markantonakis, A. Bilas, J.-J. Quisquater (Eds.), Information Security Theory and Practices. XII, 255 pages. 2007.

Vol. 4459: C. Cérin, K.-C. Li (Eds.), Advances in Grid and Pervasive Computing. XVI, 759 pages. 2007.

Vol. 4453: T. Speed, H. Huang (Eds.), Research in Computational Molecular Biology. XVI, 550 pages. 2007. (Sublibrary LNBI).

Vol. 4450: T. Okamoto, X. Wang (Eds.), Public Key Cryptography – PKC 2007. XIII, 491 pages. 2007.

Vol. 4448: M. Giacobini et al. (Ed.), Applications of Evolutionary Computing. XXIII, 755 pages. 2007.

Vol. 4447: E. Marchiori, J.H. Moore, J.C. Rajapakse (Eds.), Evolutionary Computation,Machine Learning and Data Mining in Bioinformatics. XI, 302 pages. 2007.

Vol. 4446: C. Cotta, J. van Hemert (Eds.), Evolutionary Computation in Combinatorial Optimization. XII, 241 pages. 2007.

Vol. 4445: M. Ebner, M. O'Neill, A. Ekárt, L. Vanneschi, A.I. Esparcia-Alcázar (Eds.), Genetic Programming. XI, 382 pages. 2007.

Vol. 4444: T. Reps, M. Sagiv, J. Bauer (Eds.), Program Analysis and Compilation, Theory and Practice. X, 361 pages. 2007.

Vol. 4443: R. Kotagiri, P.R. Krishna, M. Mohania, E. Nantajeewarawat (Eds.), Advances in Databases: Concepts, Systems and Applications. XXI, 1126 pages. 2007.

Vol. 4440: B. Liblit, Cooperative Bug Isolation. XV, 101 pages. 2007.

Vol. 4439: W. Abramowicz (Ed.), Business Information Systems. XV, 654 pages. 2007.

Vol. 4438: L. Maicher, A. Sigel, L.M. Garshol (Eds.), Leveraging the Semantics of Topic Maps. X, 257 pages. 2007. (Sublibrary LNAI).

Vol. 4433: E. Şahin, W.M. Spears, A.F.T. Winfield (Eds.), Swarm Robotics. XII, 221 pages. 2007.

Vol. 4432: B. Beliczynski, A. Dzielinski, M. Iwanowski, B. Ribeiro (Eds.), Adaptive and Natural Computing Algorithms, Part II. XXVI, 761 pages. 2007.

Vol. 4431: B. Beliczynski, A. Dzielinski, M. Iwanowski, B. Ribeiro (Eds.), Adaptive and Natural Computing Algorithms, Part I. XXV, 851 pages. 2007.

Vol. 4430: C.C. Yang, D. Zeng, M. Chau, K. Chang, Q. Yang, X. Cheng, J. Wang, F.-Y. Wang, H. Chen (Eds.), Intelligence and Security Informatics. XII, 330 pages. 2007.

Vol. 4429: R. Lu, J.H. Siekmann, C. Ullrich (Eds.), Cognitive Systems. X, 161 pages. 2007. (Sublibrary LNAI).

Vol. 4427: S. Uhlig, K. Papagiannaki, O. Bonaventure (Eds.), Passive and Active Network Measurement. XI, 274 pages. 2007.

Vol. 4426: Z.-H. Zhou, H. Li, Q. Yang (Eds.), Advances in Knowledge Discovery and Data Mining. XXV, 1161 pages. 2007. (Sublibrary LNAI).

Vol. 4425: G. Amati, C. Carpineto, G. Romano (Eds.), Advances in Information Retrieval. XIX, 759 pages. 2007.

Vol. 4424: O. Grumberg, M. Huth (Eds.), Tools and Algorithms for the Construction and Analysis of Systems. XX, 738 pages. 2007.

Vol. 4423: H. Seidl (Ed.), Foundations of Software Science and Computational Structures. XVI, 379 pages. 2007.

Vol. 4422: M.B. Dwyer, A. Lopes (Eds.), Fundamental Approaches to Software Engineering. XV, 440 pages. 2007.

Vol. 4421: R. De Nicola (Ed.), Programming Languages and Systems. XVII, 538 pages. 2007.

Vol. 4420: S. Krishnamurthi, M. Odersky (Eds.), Compiler Construction. XIV, 233 pages. 2007.

Vol. 4419: P.C. Diniz, E. Marques, K. Bertels, M.M. Fernandes, J.M.P. Cardoso (Eds.), Reconfigurable Computing: Architectures, Tools and Applications. XIV, 391 pages. 2007.

Vol. 4418: A. Gagalowicz, W. Philips (Eds.), Computer Vision/Computer Graphics Collaboration Techniques. XV, 620 pages. 2007.

Vol. 4416: A. Bemporad, A. Bicchi, G. Buttazzo (Eds.), Hybrid Systems: Computation and Control. XVII, 797 pages. 2007.

Vol. 4415: P. Lukowicz, L. Thiele, G. Tröster (Eds.), Architecture of Computing Systems - ARCS 2007. X, 297 pages. 2007.

Vol. 4414: S. Hochreiter, R. Wagner (Eds.), Bioinformatics Research and Development. XVI, 482 pages. 2007. (Sublibrary LNBI).

Vol. 4412: F. Stajano, H.J. Kim, J.-S. Chae, S.-D. Kim (Eds.), Ubiquitous Convergence Technology. XI, 302 pages. 2007.

Vol. 4411: R.H. Bordini, M. Dastani, J. Dix, A.E.F. Seghrouchni (Eds.), Programming Multi-Agent Systems. XIV, 249 pages. 2007. (Sublibrary LNAI).

Vol. 4410: A. Branco (Ed.), Anaphora: Analysis, Algorithms and Applications. X, 191 pages. 2007. (Sublibrary LNAI).

Vol. 4409: J.L. Fiadeiro, P.-Y. Schobbens (Eds.), Recent Trends in Algebraic Development Techniques. VII, 171 pages. 2007.

Vol. 4407: G. Puebla (Ed.), Logic-Based Program Synthesis and Transformation. VIII, 237 pages. 2007.

Vol. 4406: W. De Meuter (Ed.), Advances in Smalltalk. VII, 157 pages. 2007.

Vol. 4405: L. Padgham, F. Zambonelli (Eds.), Agent-Oriented Software Engineering VII. XII, 225 pages. 2007.

Vol. 4403: S. Obayashi, K. Deb, C. Poloni, T. Hiroyasu, T. Murata (Eds.), Evolutionary Multi-Criterion Optimization. XIX, 954 pages. 2007.

Vol. 4401: N. Guelfi, D. Buchs (Eds.), Rapid Integration of Software Engineering Techniques. IX, 177 pages. 2007.

Vol. 4400: J.F. Peters, A. Skowron, V.W. Marek, E. Orłowska, R. Słowiński, W. Ziarko (Eds.), Transactions on Rough Sets VII, Part II. X, 381 pages. 2007.

Vol. 4399: T. Kovacs, X. Llorà, K. Takadama, P.L. Lanzi, W. Stolzmann, S.W. Wilson (Eds.), Learning Classifier Systems. XII, 345 pages. 2007. (Sublibrary LNAI).

Vol. 4398: S. Marchand-Maillet, E. Bruno, A. Nürnberger, M. Detyniecki (Eds.), Adaptive Multimedia Retrieval: User, Context, and Feedback. XI, 269 pages. 2007.

Vol. 4397: C. Stephanidis, M. Pieper (Eds.), Universal Access in Ambient Intelligence Environments. XV, 467 pages. 2007.

Vol. 4396: J. García-Vidal, L. Cerdà-Alabern (Eds.), Wireless Systems and Mobility in Next Generation Internet. IX, 271 pages. 2007.

Vol. 4395: M. Daydé, J.M.L.M. Palma, Á.L.G.A. Coutinho, E. Pacitti, J.C. Lopes (Eds.), High Performance Computing for Computational Science - VECPAR 2006. XXIV, 721 pages. 2007.

Vol. 4394: A. Gelbukh (Ed.), Computational Linguistics and Intelligent Text Processing. XVI, 648 pages. 2007.

Vol. 4393: W. Thomas, P. Weil (Eds.), STACS 2007. XVIII, 708 pages. 2007.

Vol. 4392: S.P. Vadhan (Ed.), Theory of Cryptography. XI, 595 pages. 2007.

Vol. 4391: Y. Stylianou, M. Faundez-Zanuy, A. Esposito (Eds.), Progress in Nonlinear Speech Processing. XII, 269 pages. 2007.

Vol. 4390: S.O. Kuznetsov, S. Schmidt (Eds.), Formal Concept Analysis. X, 329 pages. 2007. (Sublibrary LNAI).

Vol. 4389: D. Weyns, H.V.D. Parunak, F. Michel (Eds.), Environments for Multi-Agent Systems III. X, 273 pages. 2007. (Sublibrary LNAI).

Vol. 4385: K. Coninx, K. Luyten, K.A. Schneider (Eds.), Task Models and Diagrams for Users Interface Design. XI, 355 pages. 2007.

Vol. 4384: T. Washio, K. Satoh, H. Takeda, A. Inokuchi (Eds.), New Frontiers in Artificial Intelligence. IX, 401 pages. 2007. (Sublibrary LNAI).

Vol. 4383: E. Bin, A. Ziv, S. Ur (Eds.), Hardware and Software, Verification and Testing. XII, 235 pages. 2007.

Vol. 4381: J. Akiyama, W.Y.C. Chen, M. Kano, X. Li, Q. Yu (Eds.), Discrete Geometry, Combinatorics and Graph Theory. XI, 289 pages. 2007.

Vol. 4380: S. Spaccapietra, P. Atzeni, F. Fages, M.-S. Hacid, M. Kifer, J. Mylopoulos, B. Pernici, P. Shvaiko, J. Trujillo, I. Zaihrayeu (Eds.), Journal on Data Semantics VIII. XV, 219 pages. 2007.

Vol. 4379: M. Südholt, C. Consel (Eds.), Object-Oriented Technology. VIII, 157 pages. 2007.

Vol. 4378: I. Virbitskaite, A. Voronkov (Eds.), Perspectives of Systems Informatics. XIV, 496 pages. 2007.

Vol. 4377: M. Abe (Ed.), Topics in Cryptology – CT-RSA 2007. XI, 403 pages. 2006.

Vol. 4376: E. Frachtenberg, U. Schwiegelshohn (Eds.), Job Scheduling Strategies for Parallel Processing. VII, 257 pages. 2007.

Vol. 4374: J.F. Peters, A. Skowron, I. Düntsch, J. Grzymała-Busse, E. Orłowska, L. Polkowski (Eds.), Transactions on Rough Sets VI, Part I. XII, 499 pages. 2007.

Vol. 4373: K. Langendoen, T. Voigt (Eds.), Wireless Sensor Networks. XIII, 358 pages. 2007.

Vol. 4372: M. Kaufmann, D. Wagner (Eds.), Graph Drawing. XIV, 454 pages. 2007.

Vol. 4371: K. Inoue, K. Satoh, F. Toni (Eds.), Computational Logic in Multi-Agent Systems. X, 315 pages. 2007. (Sublibrary LNAI).

Vol. 4370: P.P Lévy, B. Le Grand, F. Poulet, M. Soto, L. Darago, L. Toubiana, J.-F. Vibert (Eds.), Pixelization Paradigm. XV, 279 pages. 2007.

Vol. 4369: M. Umeda, A. Wolf, O. Bartenstein, U. Geske, D. Seipel, O. Takata (Eds.), Declarative Programming for Knowledge Management. X, 229 pages. 2006. (Sublibrary LNAI).

Vol. 4368: T. Erlebach, C. Kaklamanis (Eds.), Approximation and Online Algorithms. X, 345 pages. 2007.

Vol. 4367: K. De Bosschere, D. Kaeli, P. Stenström, D. Whalley, T. Ungerer (Eds.), High Performance Embedded Architectures and Compilers. XI, 307 pages. 2007.

Vol. 4366: K. Tuyls, R. Westra, Y. Saeys, A. Nowé (Eds.), Knowledge Discovery and Emergent Complexity in Bioinformatics. IX, 183 pages. 2007. (Sublibrary LNBI).

Vol. 4364: T. Kühne (Ed.), Models in Software Engineering. XI, 332 pages. 2007.

Vol. 4362: J. van Leeuwen, G.F. Italiano, W. van der Hoek, C. Meinel, H. Sack, F. Plášil (Eds.), SOFSEM 2007: Theory and Practice of Computer Science. XXI, 937 pages. 2007.